THE ESSENTIAL PROSE

by Dorothy Van Ghent
and Willard Maas

THE BOBBS-MERRILL COMPANY, INC.

A Subsidiary of Howard W. Sams & Co., Inc., Publishers

INDIANAPOLIS   NEW YORK   KANSAS CITY

Copyright © 1965 by The Bobbs-Merrill Company, Inc.
Printed in the United States of America

Library of Congress Catalog Card Number: 62-10527
FIRST PRINTING

◞§ *To Marie Menken*

Foreword

THE ESSENTIAL PROSE *has two general aims: to provide materials for the teaching of discursive writing, and at the same time to give the student a fairly broad and various acquaintance with his cultural heritage. It has seemed to us that the second objective is a natural corollary of the first, for the best and most stimulating models of English prose are inevitably those that have established themselves as classics—both ancient and modern—of our literature.*

To carry out these purposes as effectively as possible, we have followed each of the ninety-three selections with a generous set of analytical questions that explore both the substance of the piece and its rhetorical strategies. The questions suggest central problems for discussion in class and for written exercises to be done either in or outside the classroom. These exercises vary in length and purpose from the précis composed as a single sentence or single paragraph to the essay-length project suggested in relation to each selection.

Our second objective—to give the student, while he is learning to write effective prose, an exciting experience of his cultural birthright— has led us to include a number of pieces in translation. In each case the translation used is of the first order of English prose. Chaucer, Shakespeare, Milton, and a host of other classical English authors furnished their minds and learned their craftsmanship from works in other languages or works translated from other languages. Modern students should have the same privilege.

The contents of the book are ordered according to those themes and subjects that mark out the most significant areas of our lives: first, the individual experience *of adolescence, of the relationship between father and son, of men and women in love, of the stress of the extreme situation where character is tested, of the inevitability and the challenge of death; next the* collective experience *of our social nature and condition, what history has to tell us about that nature and condition, and what we have dreamed collectively as social ideals toward which the human race ventures; and finally, some of the* orders of knowledge *by which we strive to understand ourselves, the order of the external natural world about us, the order of our own minds, the order of that part of the psyche which we call "soul" or "spirit," the order of creativity in art, and, at the end, a few insights into the process of learning itself.*

A second table of contents shows the selections arranged by rhetorical forms and elements. Here there is some overlapping of types, inasmuch as effective prose achieves its ends by various discursive means used all at once. To distinguish ends and means and to calculate their worth and effectiveness are problems put to the student.

The individual teacher will be able to reorganize the readings and the ideas suggested by them in his own most fertile order, while the student—no matter in what order he reads—will find himself submerged in and excited by that best of all intellectual experiences, the experience of the charm of great writers.

DOROTHY VAN GHENT
WILLARD MAAS

New York
May 1965

Acknowledgments

The editors wish to express their gratitude for the help and advice of Paul Cavanaugh, Adele Menken, Irving Miller, Henry and Anne Paolucci, Marion Reese, Nathan Resnick, and Roger Van Ghent.

CONTENTS

One ❧ The Individual Experience

Two ⁓§ *The Collective Experience*   361

Contents

. . . . .

arranged by rhetorical forms and elements

✍§ NOTE: *The rhetorical categories used below are, for the most part, traditional ones. Effective prose exposition uses a number of methods all at once. Some of the pieces, therefore, are listed under several different headings, according to the main rhetorical types they exemplify and according to other types they may illustrate.* ও

Methods of Exposition

Argument and Persuasion

Description and Narration

Informal Discourse (Letter, Journal, Diary)

Diction and Style

Research

Suggestions for short research papers are made in
connection with the following:

"... a perception, not only of the pastness of the past ...

Moses by Michelangelo

. . . but of its presence."   T. S. ELIOT

Draped Reclining Woman by Henry Moore

ONE ⋙ THE INDIVIDUAL EXPERIENCE

Private Lives

THE FOUR *pieces in this section are autobiographical and all concern
extreme youth. The writing in each is vividly individual, but what
is most remarkable and moving in them is not their individualizing
differences but the common pulse of a universal experience that one
feels in each of them.*

*The experience could be defined as initiation into the primal
verities. In the chapter from Gorky's* MY CHILDHOOD, *the old grandmother, with her nose like a sponge and her "wondrous" words that
lodge like everlasting flowers in the child's mind, has a role like that
of a prehistoric priestess in a primitive* rite de passage. *In Yeats's
account of his fifteenth year, the boy invents certain age-old rituals
of isolation and austerity to carry him through the dark mysteries of
adolescence. In the selection from Emlyn Williams'* GEORGE: AN EARLY
AUTOBIOGRAPHY, *the frantically exotic plots of second-rate movies
provide the sacral substitute for initiation rites. And in Anne Frank's
diary we watch a fourteen-year-old entering the initiatory experiences
of adolescence, with gay heart, under the shadow of death.*

All four of these selections can teach the student very specific and vigorous approaches to the problems of writing, approaches which the questions at the end of each selection attempt to point out. Writing assignments of a quite personal character are suggested, to encourage a sense of the value of concreteness and of personal experience.

Maxim Gorky ⋖§ An End and a Beginning

⋖§ Russian novelist, short-story writer, and playwright (1868-1936). Gorky left home at twelve to become a vagabond. The squalor to which he was witness is reflected in the novel *Mother*, the internationally famous play *The Lower Depths*, and the autobiographical accounts, *My Childhood*, from which the present selection is taken, and *My Universities.* §⋗

I N a narrow, darkened room, my father, dressed in a white and unusually long garment, lay on the floor under the window. The toes of his bare feet were curiously extended, and the fingers of the still hands, which rested peacefully upon his breast, were curved; his merry eyes were tightly closed by the black disks of two copper coins; the light had gone out of his still face, and I was frightened by the ugly way he showed his teeth.

My mother, only half clad in a red petticoat, knelt and combed my father's long, soft hair, from his brow to the nape of his neck, with the same black comb which I loved to use to tear the rind of watermelons; she talked unceasingly in her low, husky voice, and it seemed as if her swollen eyes must be washed away by the incessant flow of tears.

From *My Childhood* by Maxim Gorky (Garden City: Garden City Publishing Co., 1926). Reprinted with the permission of Appleton-Century.

Holding me by the hand was my grandmother, who had a big, round head, large eyes, and a nose like a sponge — a dark, tender, wonderfully interesting person. She also was weeping, and her grief formed a fitting accompaniment to my mother's, as, shuddering the while, she pushed me towards my father; but I, terrified and uneasy, obstinately tried to hide myself against her. I had never seen grown-up people cry before, and I did not understand the words which my grandmother uttered again and again:

"Say good-by to daddy. You will never see him any more. He is dead — before his time."

I had been very ill, had only just left my bed in fact, and I remember perfectly well that at the beginning of my illness my father used to merrily bustle about me. Then he suddenly disappeared and his place was taken by my grandmother, a stranger to me.

"Where did you come from?" I asked her.

"From up there, from Nijni," she answered; "but I did not walk here, I came by boat. One does not walk on water, you little imp."

This was ludicrous, incomprehensible, and untrue; upstairs there lived a bearded, gaudy Persian, and in the cellar an old, yellow Kalmuck[1] who sold sheepskins. One could get downstairs by riding on the banisters, or if one fell that way, one could roll. I knew this by experience. But where was there room for water? It was all untrue and delightfully muddled.

"And why am I a little imp?"

"Why? Because you are so noisy," she said, laughing.

She spoke sweetly, merrily, melodiously, and from the very first day I made friends with her; all I wanted now was for her to make haste and take me out of that room.

My mother pressed me to her; her tears and groans created in me a strange feeling of disquietude. It was the first time I had seen her like this. She had always appeared a stern woman of few words; neat, glossy, and strongly built like a horse, with a body of almost savage strength, and terribly strong arms. But now she was swollen and palpitating, and utterly desolate. Her hair, which was always coiled so neatly about her head, with her large, gaily trimmed cap, was tumbled about her bare shoulders, fell over her face, and part of it which remained plaited,

[1] Mongolian of southeastern Russia.

trailed across my father's sleeping face. Although I had been in the
room a long time she had not once looked at me; she could do nothing
but dress my father's hair, sobbing and choking with tears the while.

Presently some swarthy gravediggers and a soldier peeped in at
the door.

The latter shouted angrily:

"Clear out now! Hurry up!"

The window was curtained by a dark shawl, which the wind in-
flated like a sail. I knew this because one day my father had taken me
out in a sailing-boat, and without warning there had come a peal of
thunder. He laughed, and holding me against his knees, cried, "It is
nothing. Don't be frightened, Luke!"

Suddenly my mother threw herself heavily on the floor, but almost
at once turned over on her back, dragging her hair in the dust; her impassive, white face had become livid, and showing her teeth like my
father, she said in a terrible voice, "Close the door! . . . Alexis . . . go
away!"

Thrusting me on one side, grandmother rushed to the door crying:

"Friends! Don't be frightened; don't interfere, but go away, for the
love of Christ. This is not cholera but childbirth. . . . I beg of you to go,
good people!"

I hid myself in a dark corner behind a box, and thence I saw how
my mother writhed upon the floor, panting and gnashing her teeth; and
grandmother, kneeling beside her, talked lovingly and hopefully.

"In the name of the Father and of the Son . . . ! Be patient, Varusha!
Holy Mother of God! . . . Our Defense . . . !"

I was terrified. They crept about on the floor close to my father,
touching him, groaning and shrieking, and he remained unmoved and
actually smiling. This creeping about on the floor lasted a long time;
several times my mother stood up, only to fall down again, and grandmother rolled in and out of the room like a large, black, soft ball. All
of a sudden a child cried.

"Thank God!" said grandmother. "It is a boy!" And she lighted a
candle.

I must have fallen asleep in the corner, for I remember nothing
more.

The next impression which my memory retains is a deserted corner
in a cemetery on a rainy day. I am standing by a slippery mound of

sticky earth and looking into the pit wherein they have thrown the coffin of my father. At the bottom there is a quantity of water, and there are also frogs, two of which have even jumped on to the yellow lid of the coffin.

At the graveside were myself, grandmother, a drenched sexton, and two cross gravediggers with shovels.

We were all soaked with the warm rain which fell in fine drops like glass beads.

"Fill in the grave," commanded the sexton, moving away.

Grandmother began to cry, covering her face with a corner of the shawl which she wore for a head-covering. The gravediggers, bending nearly double, began to fling the lumps of earth on the coffin rapidly, striking the frogs, which were leaping against the sides of the pit, down to the bottom.

"Come along, Lenia," said grandmother, taking hold of my shoulder; but having no desire to depart, I wriggled out of her hands.

"What next, O Lord?" grumbled grandmother, partly to me, and partly to God, and she remained for some time silent, with her head drooping dejectedly.

The grave was filled in, yet still she stood there, till the gravediggers threw their shovels to the ground with a resounding clangor, and a breeze suddenly arose and died away, scattering the raindrops; then she took me by the hand and led me to a church some distance away, by a path which lay between a number of dark crosses.

"Why don't you cry?" she asked, as we came away from the burial-ground. "You ought to cry."

"I don't want to," was my reply.

"Well, if you don't want to, you need not," she said gently.

This greatly surprised me, because I seldom cried, and when I did it was more from anger than sorrow; moreover, my father used to laugh at my tears, while my mother would exclaim, "Don't you dare to cry!"

After this we rode in a droshky through a broad but squalid street, between rows of houses which were painted dark red.

As we went along, I asked grandmother, "Will those frogs ever be able to get out?"

"Never!" she answered. "God bless them!"

I reflected that my father and my mother never spoke so often or so familiarly of God.

.   .   .   .

A few days later my mother and grandmother took me aboard a steamboat, where we had a tiny cabin.

My little brother Maxim was dead, and lay on a table in the corner, wrapped in white and wound about with red tape. Climbing on to the bundles and trunks I looked out of the porthole, which seemed to me exactly like the eye of a horse. Muddy, frothy water streamed unceasingly down the pane. Once it dashed against the glass with such violence that it splashed me, and I involuntarily jumped back to the floor.

"Don't be afraid," said grandmother, and lifting me lightly in her kind arms, restored me to my place on the bundles.

A gray, moist fog brooded over the water; from time to time a shadowy land was visible in the distance, only to be obscured again by the fog and the foam. Everything about us seemed to vibrate, except my mother who, with her hands folded behind her head, leaned against the wall fixed and still, with a face that was grim and hard as iron, and as expressionless. Standing thus, mute, with closed eyes, she appeared to me as an absolute stranger. Her very frock was unfamiliar to me.

More than once grandmother said to her softly, "Varia, won't you have something to eat?"

My mother neither broke the silence nor stirred from her position.

Grandmother spoke to me in whispers, but to my mother she spoke aloud, and at the same time cautiously and timidly, and very seldom. I thought she was afraid of her, which was quite intelligible, and seemed to draw us closer together.

"Saratov!" loudly and fiercely exclaimed my mother with startling suddenness. "Where is the sailor?"

Strange, new words to me! Saratov? Sailor?

A broad-shouldered, gray-headed individual dressed in blue now entered, carrying a small box which grandmother took from him, and in which she proceeded to place the body of my brother. Having done this she bore the box and its burden to the door on her out-stretched hands; but, alas! being so stout she could only get through the narrow doorway of the cabin sideways, and now halted before it in ludicrous uncertainty.

"Really, Mama!" exclaimed my mother impatiently, taking the tiny coffin from her. Then they both disappeared, while I stayed behind in the cabin regarding the man in blue.

"Well, mate, so the little brother has gone?" he said, bending down to me.

"Who are you?"

"I am a sailor."

"And who is Saratov?"

"Saratov is a town. Look out of the window. There it is!"

Observed from the window, the land seemed to oscillate; and revealing itself obscurely and in a fragmentary fashion, as it lay steaming in the fog, it reminded me of a large piece of bread just cut off a hot loaf.

"Where has grandmother gone to?"

"To bury her little grandson."

"Are they going to bury him in the ground?"

"Yes, of course they are."

I then told the sailor about the live frogs that had been buried with my father.

He lifted me up, and hugging and kissing me, cried, "Oh, my poor little fellow, you don't understand. It is not the frogs who are to be pitied, but your mother. Think how she is bowed down by her sorrow."

Then came a resounding howl overhead. Having already learned that it was the steamer which made this noise, I was not afraid; but the sailor hastily set me down on the floor and darted away, exclaiming, "I must run!"

The desire to escape seized me. I ventured out of the door. The dark, narrow space outside was empty, and not far away shone the brass on the steps of the staircase. Glancing upwards, I saw people with wallets and bundles in their hands, evidently going off the boat. This meant that I must go off too.

But when I appeared in front of the gangway, amidst the crowd of peasants, they all began to yell at me.

"Who does he belong to? Who do you belong to?"

No one knew.

For a long time they jostled and shook and poked me about, until the gray-haired sailor appeared and seized me, with the explanation:

"It is the Astrakhan[2] boy from the cabin."

And he ran off with me to the cabin, deposited me on the bundles and went away, shaking his finger at me, as he threatened, "I'll give you something!"

---

[2] Southeastern Russian.

The noise overhead became less and less. The boat had ceased to vibrate, or to be agitated by the motion of the water. This window of the cabin was shut in by damp walls; within it was dark, and the air was stifling. It seemed to me that the very bundles grew larger and began to press upon me; it was all horrible, and I began to wonder if I was going to be left alone forever in that empty boat.

I went to the door, but it would not open; the brass handle refused to turn, so I took a bottle of milk and with all my force struck at it. The only result was that the bottle broke and the milk spilled over my legs, and trickled into my boots. Crushed by this failure, I threw myself on the bundles crying softly, and so fell asleep.

When I awoke the boat was again in motion, and the window of the cabin shone like the sun.

Grandmother, sitting near me, was combing her hair and muttering something with knitted brow. She had an extraordinary amount of hair which fell over her shoulders and breast to her knees, and even touched the floor. It was blue-black. Lifting it up from the floor with one hand and holding it with difficulty, she introduced an almost toothless wooden comb into its thick strands. Her lips were twisted, her dark eyes sparkled fiercely, while her face, encircled in that mass of hair, looked comically small. Her expression was almost malignant, but when I asked her why she had such long hair she answered in her usual mellow, tender voice:

"Surely God gave it to me as a punishment. . . . Even when it is combed, just look at it! . . . When I was young I was proud of my mane, but now I am old I curse it. But you go to sleep. It is quite early. The sun has only just risen."

"But I don't want to go to sleep again."

"Very well, then don't go to sleep," she agreed at once, plaiting her hair and glancing at the berth on which my mother lay rigid, with upturned face. "How did you smash that bottle last evening? Tell me about it quietly."

So she always talked, using such peculiarly harmonious words that they took root in my memory like fragrant, bright, everlasting flowers. When she smiled the pupils of her dark, luscious eyes dilated and beamed with an inexpressible charm, and her strong white teeth gleamed cheerfully. Apart from her multitudinous wrinkles and her swarthy complexion, she had a youthful and brilliant appearance. What spoiled her was her bulbous nose, with its distended nostrils, and red lips, caused by her habit of taking pinches of snuff from her black snuff-box mounted with silver, and by her fondness for drink. Everything about her was dark, but within she was luminous with an inextinguishable, joyful and ardent flame, which revealed itself in her eyes. Although she was bent, almost humpbacked, in fact, she moved lightly and softly, for all the world like a huge cat, and was just as gentle as that caressing animal.

Until she came into my life I seemed to have been asleep, and hidden away in obscurity; but when she appeared she woke me and led me to the light of day. Connecting all my impressions by a single thread, she wove them into a pattern of many colors, thus making herself my friend for life, the being nearest my heart, the dearest and best known of all; while her disinterested love for all creation enriched me, and built up the strength needful for a hard life.

.   .   .   .

Forty years ago boats traveled slowly; we were a long time getting to Nijni, and I shall never forget those days almost overladen with beauty.

Good weather had set in. From morning till night I was on the deck with grandmother, under a clear sky, gliding between the autumn-gilded shores of the Volga, without hurry, lazily; and, with many resounding groans, as she rose and fell on the gray-blue water, a barge attached by a long rope was being drawn along by the bright red steamer. The barge was gray, and reminded me of a wood-louse.

Unperceived, the sun floated over the Volga. Every hour we were in the midst of fresh scenes; the green hills rose up like rich folds on earth's sumptuous vesture; on the shore stood towns and villages; the golden autumn leaves floated on the water.

"Look how beautiful it all is!" grandmother exclaimed every minute, going from one side of the boat to the other, with a radiant face, and eyes wide with joy. Very often, gazing at the shore, she would forget me; she would stand on the deck, her hands folded on her breast, smiling and in silence, with her eyes full of tears. I would tug at her skirt of dark, sprigged linen.

"Ah!" she would exclaim, starting. "I must have fallen asleep, and begun to dream."

"But why are you crying?"

"For joy and for old age, my dear," she would reply, smiling. "I am getting old, you know — sixty years have passed over my head."

And taking a pinch of snuff, she would begin to tell me some wonderful stories about kind-hearted brigands, holy people, and all sorts of wild animals and evil spirits.

She would tell me these stories softly, mysteriously, with her face close to mine, fixing me with her dilated eyes, thus actually infusing into me the strength which was growing within me. The longer she spoke, or rather sang, the more melodiously flowed her words. It was inexpressibly pleasant to listen to her.

I would listen and beg for another, and this is what I got:

"In the stove there lives an old goblin; once he got a splinter into his paw, and rocked to and fro whimpering, 'Oh, little mice, it hurts very much; oh, little mice, I can't bear it!' "

Raising her foot, she took it in her hands and wagged it from side to side, wrinkling up her face so funnily, just as if she herself had been hurt.

The sailors who stood round — bearded, good-natured men — listening and laughing, and praising the stories, would say:

"Now, Grandmother, give us another."

Afterwards they would say:

"Come and have supper with us."

At supper they regaled her with vodka, and me with water-melon; this they did secretly, for there went to and fro on the boat a man who forbade the eating of fruit, and used to take it away and throw it in the river. He was dressed like an official, and was always drunk; people kept out of his sight.

On rare occasions my mother came on deck, and stood on the side farthest from us. She was always silent. Her large, well-formed body, her grim face, her heavy crown of plaited, shining hair — all about her was compact and solid, and she appeared to me as if she were enveloped in a fog or a transparent cloud, out of which she looked unamiably with her gray eyes, which were as large as grandmother's.

Once she exclaimed sternly:

"People are laughing at you, Mama!"

"God bless them!" answered grandmother, quite unconcerned. "Let them laugh, and good luck to 'em."

I remember the childish joy grandmother showed at the sight of Nijni. Taking my hand, she dragged me to the side, crying:

"Look! Look how beautiful it is! That's Nijni, that is! There's something heavenly about it. Look at the church too. Doesn't it seem to have wings?" And she turned to my mother, nearly weeping. "Varusha, look, won't you? Come here! You seem to have forgotten all about it. Can't you show a little gladness?"

My mother, with a frown, smiled bitterly.

When the boat arrived outside the beautiful town between two rivers blocked by vessels, and bristling with hundreds of slender masts, a large boat containing many people was drawn alongside it. Catching the boat-hook in the gangway, one after another the passengers came on board. A short, wizened man, dressed in black, with a red-gold beard, a bird-like nose, and green eyes, pushed his way in front of the others.

"Papa!" my mother cried in a hoarse, loud voice, as she threw herself into his arms; but he, taking her face in his little red hands and hastily patting her cheeks, cried:

"Now, silly! What's the matter with you? . . ."

Grandmother embraced and kissed them all at once, turning round and round like a peg-top; she pushed me towards them, saying quickly:

"Now — make haste! This is Uncle Michael, this is Jaakov, this is Aunt Natalia, these are two brothers both called Sascha, and their sister Katerina. This is all our family. Isn't it a large one?"

Grandfather said to her:

"Are you quite well, Mother?" and they kissed each other three times.

He then drew me from the dense mass of people, and laying his hand on my head, asked:

"And who may you be?"

"I am the Astrakhan boy from the cabin."

"What on earth is he talking about?" Grandfather turned to my mother, but without waiting for an answer, shook me and said: "You are a chip of the old block. Get into the boat."

Having landed, the crowd of people wended its way up the hill by a road paved with rough cobblestones between two steep slopes covered with trampled grass.

Grandfather and mother went in front of us all. He was a head shorter than she was, and walked with little hurried steps; while she, looking down on him from her superior height, appeared literally to float beside him. After them walked dark, sleek-haired Uncle Michael,

wizened like grandfather, bright and curly-headed Jaakov, some fat
women in brightly colored dresses, and six children, all older than myself
and all very quiet. I was with grandmother and little Aunt Natalia. Pale,
blue-eyed and stout, she frequently stood still, panting and whispering:

"Oh, I can't go any farther!"

"Why did they trouble you to come?" grumbled grandmother
angrily. "They are a silly lot!"

I did not like either the grown-up people nor the children; I felt
myself to be a stranger in their midst — even grandmother had somehow
become estranged and distant.

Most of all I disliked my uncle; I felt at once that he was my enemy,
and I was conscious of a certain feeling of cautious curiosity towards
him.

We had now arrived at the end of our journey.

At the very top, perched on the right slope, stood the first building
in the street — a squat, one-storied house, decorated with dirty pink
paint, with a narrow overhanging roof and bow-windows. Looked at
from the street it appeared to be a large house, but the interior, with its
gloomy, tiny rooms, was cramped. Everywhere, as on the landing-stage,
angry people strove together, and a vile smell pervaded the whole place.

I went out into the yard. That also was unpleasant. It was strewn
with large, wet cloths and lumbered with tubs, all containing muddy
water, of the same hue, in which other cloths lay soaking. In the corner
of a half-tumbled-down shed the logs burned brightly in a stove, upon
which something was boiling or baking, and an unseen person uttered
these strange words:

"Santaline, fuchsin, vitriol!"[3]

⨾§ FOR DISCUSSION AND WRITING

1. How is interest achieved immediately in the first two paragraphs? Are
   we immediately interested because the father is dead and the mother is
   grieving, or because of the *way* these facts are told, the particular details
   that are highlighted? Which details?

2. Throughout this piece, everything is *seen* with unusual concreteness and

---

[3] The family runs a dye business, and these are materials used in dyeing.

clarity. Pick out, from different parts, a dozen or so examples of keen visualization. Write these down, in order to familiarize yourself closely with the actual way the words perform. Now analyze and compare them, asking yourself how the vividness is achieved. For instance, is it by adjectives? verbs? nouns naming concrete things? a particular kind of diction or a particular kind of phrasing? similes? Pick out a few of the similes; how effective are they? why are they effective?

3. The point of view is that of a child. How do we know that the child is very young? (Be specific in illustrating your answers to all such questions.) Now, as a slight exercise in analyzing that extremely important aspect of any piece of writing, the point of view, try to substitute a different point of view—that of an impersonal (and, of course, adult) author. Copy out a couple of paragraphs or a page, substituting always "he" for "I" (or a name—say, Maxim), and rearranging the rest of the grammar as necessary. Does anything significant seem to be changed by this substitution? Now imagine the whole piece written from the impersonal (authorial) point of view. Write a critical paragraph explaining what would be gained or lost by the change of point of view.

4. Now, instead of tampering with the point of view, let us observe it. It is that of a very young child, but obviously the writing is not that of a child: this all-so-obvious fact needs pointing out in order that we become aware of the *technical* aspect of what we call the "point of view" in a piece of writing (for we use the term somewhat differently in other connections, as when we speak of a person's opinion as his "point of view"). How is it that we are given the impressions of a young child, impressions that do not seem to be adulterated by any adult attitude, and yet the writing is clearly controlled by an adult intelligence? You may think such a question so self-evident that it doesn't deserve an answer; but when we come conscientiously as students to the central problems of writing, we have to become analytical of matters that we have accepted, through habit, as self-evident. How, in this piece, is the point of view of the child maintained while the adult author stays at the controls of the writing? Do we ever feel the definite presence of the adult author behind the child? Or is the technique all a matter of indirection, through style?

5. The experiences recorded here are of death and birth in their primitive crudeness. These subjects lend themselves to treatment in either of two obvious ways: they could be treated with the most brutal "realism" or "naturalism" (words that have rather confused meanings, but we use

them here with their common import), or they could be treated as what Robert Penn Warren has called "soft subjects"—subjects offering the temptation of sentimentality. How does the point of view of the child prevent the subject-matter from suffering the distortion of brutality or the distortion of sentimentality? Carefully pick out certain parts of the piece for illustration, and write a paragraph in answer to the question.

6. Though this piece is only the first chapter of an autobiography of Gorky's childhood, it has its own unity. There are many, perhaps an infinite number of ways of achieving unity; but in the kinds of writing we are encountering here at first—autobiographical accounts of the emotional hazards of extreme youth—unity is usually achieved in some emotional and (or) symbolic way. Looking on the chapter from Gorky in terms of "initiation" (an "initiation" presumes a natural unity, for it implies a fairly profound change of state, as from ignorance to knowledge or from one stage of life to another), write a critical paragraph supporting the view that the piece does have a self-substantial unity or does not. Certain strange words are uttered at the end: "Santaline, fuchsin, vitriol!" Do these mysterious words act symbolically to close, as it were, one phase of life and announce another, equally dark and enigmatic?

7. It's a terribly difficult assignment to write about your own early childhood, for one's childhood is as lost as the experiences of Paleolithic children. But try—in a writing of about 500 words. With Gorky in mind, try to find the concrete detail, the sharp visualization. And, like Gorky, don't try to make transitions between one thing and another with words padding out time: just move immediately from event or impression to event or impression, for that is the way one would experience them. In other words, don't bother to *talk about* your subject: just *give* it, concretely.

William Butler Yeats ⋙ An Irish Boyhood

⋙ Irish poet, the greatest modern poet in the English language (1865-1939). Also a playwright, Yeats restored verse to contemporary drama. He was one of the founders of the famous Abbey Theatre in Dublin, for which Synge and O'Casey wrote some of their great works. As a boy, Yeats went to school in both London and Dublin, and he spent much of his vacation time in Sligo, Ireland, where he became fascinated by Irish legends that were to inspire many of his poems and plays. In later life, he became a member of the Irish Senate, and in 1923 he was awarded the Nobel Prize for literature.

⋙

I WAS now fifteen; and as he did not want to leave his painting my father told me to go to Harcourt Street and put myself to school. I found a bleak eighteenth-century house, a small playing-field full of mud and pebbles, fenced by an iron railing, and opposite a long hoarding[1] and a squalid, ornamental railway station. Here, as I soon found, nobody gave a thought to decorum. We worked in a din of voices. We began the morning with prayers, but when class began the head-master, if he was in the humour, would laugh at Church and Clergy. "Let them say what they like," he would say, "but the earth does go round the sun."[2] On

[1] Board fence or billboard.

[2] Galileo is supposed to have muttered this under his breath (*"eppur si muove"*) after his forced recantation.

the other hand there was no bullying and I had not thought it possible that boys could work so hard. Cricket and football, the collection of moths and butterflies, though not forbidden, were discouraged. They were for idle boys. I did not know, as I used to, the mass of my school-fellows; for we had little life in common outside the class-rooms. I had begun to think of my school work as an interruption of my natural history studies, but even had I never opened a book not in the school course, I could not have learned a quarter of my night's work. I had always done Euclid easily, making the problems out while the other boys were blundering at the blackboard, and it had often carried me from the bottom to the top of my class; but these boys had the same natural gift and instead of being in the fourth or fifth book were in the modern books at the end of the primer; and in place of a dozen lines of Virgil with a dictionary, I was expected to learn with the help of a crib a hundred and fifty lines. The other boys were able to learn the translation off, and to remember what words of Latin and English corresponded with one another, but I, who it may be had tried to find out what happened in the parts we had not read, made ridiculous mistakes; and what could I, who never worked when I was not interested, do with a history lesson that was but a column of seventy dates? I was worst of all at literature, for we read Shakespeare for his grammar exclusively.

One day I had a lucky thought. A great many lessons were run through in the last hour of the day, things we had learnt or should have learnt by heart overnight, and not having known one of them for weeks, I cut off that hour without anybody's leave. I asked the mathematical master to give me a sum to work and nobody said a word. My father often interfered, and always with disaster, to teach me my Latin lesson. "But I have also my geography," I would say. "Geography," he would reply, "should never be taught. It is not a training for the mind. You will pick up all that you need, in your general reading." And if it was a history lesson, he would say just the same, and "Euclid," he would say, "is too easy. It comes naturally to the literary imagination. The old idea, that it is a good training for the mind, was long ago refuted." I would know my Latin lesson so that it was a nine days' wonder, and for weeks after would be told it was scandalous to be so clever and so idle. No one knew that I had learnt it in the terror that alone could check my wandering mind. I must have told on him at some time or other for I remember the head-master saying, "I am going to give you

an imposition[3] because I cannot get at your father to give him one."
Sometimes we had essays to write; and though I never got a prize, for
the essays were judged by handwriting and spelling, I caused a measure
of scandal. I would be called up before some master and asked if I
really believed such things, and that would make me angry for I had
written what I had believed all my life, what my father had told me, or
a memory of the conversation of his friends. I was asked to write an
essay on "Men may rise on stepping-stones of their dead selves to higher
things."[4] My father read the subject to my mother who had no interest
in such matters. "That is the way," he said, "boys are made insincere and
false to themselves. Ideals make the blood thin, and take the human
nature out of people." He walked up and down the room in eloquent
indignation, and told me not to write on such a subject at all, but upon
Shakespeare's lines, "To thine own self be true, and it must follow as
the night the day thou canst not then be false to any man." At another
time, he would denounce the idea of duty; "Imagine," he would say,
"how the right sort of woman would despise a dutiful husband"; and
he would tell us how much my mother would scorn such a thing. Maybe
there were people among whom such ideas were natural, but they
were the people with whom one does not dine. All he said was, I now
believe right, but he should have taken me away from school. He would
have taught me nothing but Greek and Latin, and I would now be a
properly educated man, and would not have to look in useless longings
at books that have been, through the poor mechanism of translation, the
builders of my soul, nor face authority with the timidity born of excuse
and evasion. Evasion and excuse were in the event as wise as the house-
building instinct of the beaver. . . .

Our house for the first year or so was on the top of a cliff, so that
in stormy weather the spray would soak my bed at night, for I had taken
the glass out of the window, sash and all. A literary passion for the open
air was to last me for a few years. Then for another year or two, we had
a house overlooking the harbour where the one great sight was the going
and coming of the fishing fleet. We had one regular servant, a fisherman's
wife, and the occasional help of a big, red-faced girl who ate a whole pot
of jam while my mother was at church and accused me of it. Some such

[3] Disciplinary exercise given to a student as a punishment.
[4] From Tennyson's *In Memoriam*.

arrangement lasted until long after the time I write of, and until my
father going into the kitchen by chance found a girl, engaged during a
passing need, in tears at the thought of leaving our other servant, and
promised that they should never be parted. I have no doubt that we
lived at the harbour for my mother's sake. She had, when we were
children, refused to take us to a seaside place because she heard it
possessed a bathing box,[5] but she loved the activities of a fishing village.
When I think of her, I almost always see her talking over a cup of tea in
the kitchen with our servant, the fisherman's wife, on the only themes
outside our house that seemed of interest — the fishing people of Howth,
or the pilots and fishing people of Rosses Point. She read no books, but
she and the fisherman's wife would tell each other stories that Homer
might have told, pleased with any moment of sudden intensity and
laughing together over any point of satire. There is an essay called
"Village Ghosts" in my *Celtic Twilight* which is but a record of one
such afternoon, and many a fine tale has been lost because it had not
occurred to me soon enough to keep notes. My father was always praising her to my sisters and to me, because she pretended to nothing she
did not feel. She would write him letters, telling of her delight in the
tumbling clouds, but she did not care for pictures, and never went to
an exhibition even to see a picture of his, nor to his studio to see the day's
work, neither now nor when they were first married. I remember all this
very clearly and little after it until her mind had gone in a stroke of
paralysis and she had found, liberated at last from financial worry, perfect happiness feeding the birds at a London window. She had always,
my father would say, intensity, and that was his chief word of praise;
and once he added to the praise, "No spendthrift ever had a poet for a
son, though a miser might."

The great event of a boy's life is the awakening of sex. He will
bathe many times a day, or get up at dawn and having stripped leap
to and fro over a stick laid upon two chairs and hardly know, and never
admit, that he had begun to take pleasure in his own nakedness, nor will
he understand the change until some dream discovers it. He may never
understand at all the greater change in his mind.

It all came upon me when I was close upon seventeen like the bursting of a shell. Somnambulistic country girls, when it is upon them, throw

[5] A box in which one stood (for modesty's sake) while bathing, in Victorian times.

plates about or pull them with long hairs in simulation of the polter-geist, or become mediums for some genuine spirit-mischief, surrendering to their desire of the marvellous. As I look backward, I seem to discover that my passions, my loves and my despairs, instead of being my enemies, a disturbance and an attack, became so beautiful that I had to be constantly alone to give them my whole attention. I notice that now, for the first time, what I saw when alone is more vivid in my memory than what I did or saw in company.

A herd had shown me a cave some hundred and fifty feet below the cliff path and a couple of hundred above the sea, and told me that an evicted tenant called Macrom, dead some fifteen years, had lived there many years, and shown me a rusty nail in the rock which had served perhaps to hold up some wooden protection from wind and weather. Here I stored a tin of cocoa and some biscuits, and instead of going to my bed, would slip out on warm nights and sleep in the cave on the excuse of catching moths. One had to pass over a rocky ledge, safe enough for any one with a fair head, yet seeming, if looked at from above, narrow and sloping; and a remonstrance from a stranger who had seen me climbing along it doubled my delight in the adventure. When, however, upon a bank holiday, I found lovers in my cave, I was not content with it again till I heard that the ghost of Macrom had been seen a little before the dawn, stooping over his fire in the cave-mouth. I had been trying to cook eggs, as I had read in some book, by burying them in the earth under a fire of sticks.

At other times, I would sleep among the rhododendrons and rocks in the wilder part of the grounds of Howth Castle. After a while my father said I must stay indoors half the night, meaning that I should get some sleep in my bed; but I, knowing that I would be too sleepy and comfortable to get up again, used to sit over the kitchen fire till half the night was gone. Exaggerated accounts spread through the school, and sometimes when I did not know a lesson some master would banter me about the way my nights were spent. My interest in science began to fade, and presently I said to myself, "It has all been a misunderstanding." I remembered how soon I tired of my specimens, and how little I knew after all my years of collecting, and I came to believe that I had gone through so much labour because of a text, heard for the first time in St. John's Church in Sligo,[6] and copied Solomon, who had knowledge

[6] Town in northern Ireland where Yeats spent his summers and where he is buried.

of hyssop and of tree that I might be certain of my own wisdom. I still carried my green net but I began to play at being a sage, a magician or a poet. I had many idols, and as I climbed along the narrow ledge I was now Manfred[7] on his glacier, and now Prince Athanase with his solitary lamp, but I soon chose Alastor[8] for my chief of men and longed to share his melancholy, and maybe at last to disappear from everybody's sight as he disappeared drifting in a boat along some slow-moving river between great trees. When I thought of women they were modelled on those in my favourite poets and loved in brief tragedy, or like the girl in *The Revolt of Islam*,[9] accompanied their lovers through all manner of wild places, lawless women without homes and without children. . . .

I began to make blunders when I paid calls or visits, and a woman I had known and liked as a child told me I had changed for the worse. I wanted to be wise and eloquent, an essay on the younger Ampère[10] had helped me to this ambition, and when I was alone I exaggerated my blunders and was miserable. I had begun to write poetry in imitation of Shelley and of Edmund Spenser, play after play — for my father exalted dramatic poetry above all other kinds — and I invented fantastic and incoherent plots. My lines but seldom scanned, for I could not understand the prosody in the books, although there were many lines that taken by themselves had music. I spoke them slowly as I wrote and only discovered when I read them to somebody else that there was no common music, no prosody. There were, however, moments of observations; for, even when I caught moths no longer, I still noticed all that passed; how the little moths came out at sunset, and how after that there were only a few big moths till dawn brought little moths again; and what birds cried out at night as if in their sleep.

At Sligo, where I still went for my holidays, I stayed with my uncle, George Pollexfen, who had come from Ballina to fill the place of my grandfather, who had retired. My grandfather had no longer his big house, his partner William Middleton was dead, and there had been legal trouble. He was no longer the rich man he had been, and his sons and daughters were married and scattered. He had a tall, bare house

[7] Faustian hero of Byron's *Manfred.*
[8] Heroes of Shelley's poems *Prince Athanase* and *Alastor.*
[9] Poem by Shelley.
[10] French essayist and historian (1800-1864), son of the French physicist.

overlooking the harbour, and had nothing to do but work himself into a rage if he saw a mud-lighter[11] mismanaged or judged from the smoke of a steamer that she was burning cheap coal, and to superintend the making of his tomb. There was a Middleton tomb and a long list of Middletons on the wall, and an almost empty place for Pollexfen names, but he had said, because there was a Middleton there he did not like, "I am not going to lie with those old bones"; and already one saw his name in large gilt letters on the stone fence of the new tomb. He ended his walk at St. John's churchyard almost daily, for he liked everything neat and compendious as upon shipboard, and if he had not looked after the tomb himself the builder might have added some useless ornament. He had, however, all his old skill and nerve. I was going to Rosses Point on the little trading steamer and saw him take the wheel from the helmsman and steer her through a gap in the channel wall, and across the sand, an unheard-of course, and at the journey's end bring her alongside her wharf at Rosses without the accustomed zigzagging or pulling on a rope but in a single movement. He took snuff when he had a cold, but had never smoked nor taken alcohol; and when in his eightieth year his doctor advised a stimulant, he replied, "No, no, I am not going to form a bad habit."

My brother had partly taken my place in my grandmother's affections. He had lived permanently in her house for some years now, and went to a Sligo school where he was always bottom of his class. My grandmother did not mind that, for she said, "He is too kindhearted to pass the other boys." He spent his free hours going here and there with crowds of little boys, sons of pilots and sailors, as their well-liked leader, arranging donkey races or driving donkeys tandem, an occupation which requires all one's intellect because of their obstinacy. Besides he had begun to amuse everybody with his drawings; and in half the pictures he paints to-day I recognise faces that I have met at Rosses or the Sligo quays. It is long since he has lived there, but his memory seems as accurate as the sight of the eye.

George Pollexfen was as patient as his father was impetuous, and did all by habit. A well-to-do, elderly man, he lived with no more comfort than when he had set out as a young man. He had a little house and one old general servant and a man to look after his horse, and every year he gave up some activity and found that there was one more food

[11] A dredging barge.

that disagreed with him. A hypochondriac, he passed from winter to summer through a series of woolens that had always to be weighed; for in April or May or, whatever the date was, he had to be sure he carried the exact number of ounces he had carried upon that date since boyhood. He lived in despondency, finding in the most cheerful news reasons of discouragement, and sighing every twenty-second of June over the shortening of the days. Once in later years, when I met him in Dublin sweating in a midsummer noon, I brought him into the hall of the Kildare Street Library, a cool and shady place, without lightening his spirits; for he but said in a melancholy voice, "How very cold this place must be in wintertime." Sometimes when I had pitted my cheerfulness against his gloom over the breakfast table, maintaining that neither his talent nor his memory nor his health were running to the dregs, he would rout me with the sentence, "How very old I shall be in twenty years." Yet this inactive man, in whom the sap of life seemed to be dried away, had a mind full of pictures. Nothing had ever happened to him except a love affair, not I think very passionate, that had gone wrong, and a voyage when a young man. My grandfather had sent him in a schooner to a port in Spain where the shipping agents were two Spaniards called O'Neill, descendants of Hugh O'Neill, Earl of Tyrone, who had fled from Ireland in the reign of James I; and their Irish trade was a last remnant of the Spanish trade that had once made Galway wealthy. For some years he and they had corresponded for they cherished the memory of their origin. In some Connaught burying-ground, he had chanced upon the funeral of a child with but one mourner, a distinguished foreign-looking man. It was an Austrian count burying the last of an Irish family, long nobles of Austria, who were always carried to that half-ruined burying-ground.

My uncle had almost given up hunting and was soon to give it up altogether, and he had once ridden steeplechases and been, his horse-trainer said, the best rider in Connaught. He had certainly great knowledge of horses, for I have been told, several counties away, that at Ballina he cured horses by conjuring. He had, however, merely great skill in diagnosis, for the day was still far off when he was to give his nights to astrology and ceremonial magic. His servant, Mary Battle, who had been with him since he was a young man, had the second sight and that, may be, inclined him to strange studies. One morning she was about to bring him a clean shirt, but stopped saying there was blood on the shirt-

front and that she must bring him another. On his way to his office he
fell, crossing over a little wall, and cut himself and bled on the linen
where she had seen the blood. In the evening, she told him that the shirt
she had thought bloody was quite clean. She could neither read nor
write and her mind, which answered his gloom with its merriment,
was rammed with every sort of old history and strange belief. Much of
my *Celtic Twilight* is but her daily speech.

My uncle had the respect of the common people as few Sligo men
have had it; he would have thought a stronger emotion an intrusion on
his privacy. He gave to all men the respect due to their station or their
worth with an added measure of ceremony, and kept among his work-
men a discipline that had about it something of a regiment or a ship,
knowing nothing of any but personal authority. If a carter, let us say,
was in fault, he would not dismiss him, but send for him and take his
whip away and hang it upon the wall; and having reduced the offender,
as it were, to the ranks for certain months, would restore him to his post
and his whip. This man of diligence and of method, who had no enterprise but in contemplation, and claimed that his wealth, considerable
for Ireland, came from a brother's or partner's talent, was the confidant
of my boyish freaks and reveries. When I said to him, echoing some book
I had read, that one never knew a countryside till one knew it at night
he was pleased (though nothing would have kept him from his bed a
moment beyond the hour); for he loved natural things and had learnt
two cries of the lapwing, one that drew them to where he stood and
one that made them fly away. And he approved, and arranged my
meals conveniently, when I told him I was going to walk round Lough
Gill and sleep in a wood. I did not tell him all my object, for I was
nursing a new ambition. My father had read to me some passage out of
Walden, and I planned to live some day in a cottage on a little island
called Innisfree, and Innisfree was opposite Slish Wood where I meant
to sleep.

I thought that having conquered bodily desire and the inclination of
my mind towards women and love, I should live, as Thoreau lived, seeking wisdom. There was a story in the county history of a tree that had
once grown upon that island guarded by some terrible monster and
borne the food of the gods. A young girl pined for the fruit and told her
lover to kill the monster and carry the fruit away. He did as he had been
told, but tasted the fruit; and when he reached the mainland where she

had waited for him, he was dying of its powerful virtue. And from sorrow and from remorse she too ate of it and died. I do not remember whether I chose the island because of its beauty or for the story's sake, but I was twenty-two or three before I gave up the dream.

I set out from Sligo about six in the evening, walking slowly, for it was an evening of great beauty; but though I was well into Slish Wood by bed-time, I could not sleep, not from the discomfort of the dry rock I had chosen for my bed, but from my fear of the wood-ranger. Somebody had told me, though I do not think it could have been true, that he went his round at some unknown hour. I kept going over what I should say if found and could not think of anything he would believe. However, I could watch my island in the early dawn and notice the order of the cries of the birds.

I came home next day unimaginably tired and sleepy, having walked some thirty miles partly over rough and boggy ground. For months afterwards, if I alluded to my walk, my uncle's general servant (not Mary Battle, who was slowly recovering from an illness and would not have taken the liberty) would go into fits of laughter. She believed I had spent the night in a different fashion and had invented the excuse to deceive my uncle, and would say to my great embarrassment, for I was as prudish as an old maid, "And you had good right to be fatigued."

Once when staying with my uncle at Rosses Point where he went for certain months of the year, I called upon a cousin towards midnight and asked him to get his yacht out, for I wanted to find what sea birds began to stir before dawn. He was indignant and refused; but his elder sister had overheard me and came to the head of the stairs and forbade him to stir, and that so vexed him that he shouted to the kitchen for his sea boots. He came with me in great gloom for he had people's respect, he declared, and nobody so far said that he was mad as they said I was, and we got a very sleepy boy out of his bed in the village and set up sail. We put a trawl out, as he thought it would restore his character if he caught some fish, but the wind fell and we were becalmed. I rolled myself in the mainsail and went to sleep for I could sleep anywhere in those days. I was awakened towards dawn to see my cousin and the boy turning out their pockets for money and had to rummage in my own pockets. A boat was rowing in from Roughley with fish and they wanted to buy some and pretend they had caught it, but all our pockets were empty. I had wanted the birds' cries for the poem that became fifteen years afterwards "The Shadowy Waters," and it had been full of observation had I been able to write it when I first planned it. I had found again the windy light that moved me when a child. I persuaded myself that I had a passion for the dawn, and this passion, though mainly histrionic like a child's play, an ambitious game, had moments of sincerity. Years afterwards when I had finished *The Wanderings of Oisin*, dissatisfied with its yellow and its dull green, with all that overcharged colour inherited from the romantic movement, I deliberately reshaped my style, deliberately sought out an impression as of cold light and tumbling clouds. I cast off traditional metaphors and loosened my rhythm, and recognising that all the criticism of life known to me was alien and English, became as emotional as possible but with an emotion which I described to myself as cold. It is a natural conviction for a painter's son to believe that there may be a landscape that is symbolical of some spiritual condition and awakens a hunger such as cats feel for valerian.[12]

ᴗ᧥ FOR DISCUSSION AND WRITING

1. What notable differences do you find between your own high-school training at the age of fifteen and that of Yeats? Where in the piece do you find implicit criticism of Yeats's schooling? Are there indications of Yeats's difference from his schoolfellows?

2. What are Yeats's father's pedagogical ideas, and what do you think of them? Explain the father's attitude toward the boy's essay assignment on the lines from Tennyson: "Men may rise on stepping-stones of their dead selves to higher things." What do you think of Yeats's statement that his father should have taken him away from school and taught him nothing but Greek and Latin, so that he "would now be a properly educated man"?

3. Adolescence is a period of breaking away from the strong childhood ties of family, a period of searching for one's own identity and emotional independence. Can you suggest, then, any reason why, in this sensitive account of Yeats's own adolescence, the portrayal of the characters of his father, mother, grandfather, and uncle should assume such importance and appear

---

[12] An herb to which cats are attracted.

so vividly? Does this question suggest to you an idea for a theme of your own?

4. From the various indications of what kind of person Yeats's father was, could you make a "thumbnail" sketch of him—say of three lines? Notice that the portrait of the mother takes just half a page; analyze precisely how it is done and what individualizing traits are highlighted.

5. What specific means does Yeats use to characterize the grandfather? The uncle is a more complex character: what chief characteristics does Yeats indicate? What means does he use to indicate them? Notice how often in these character portraits the person is "given" through something he *says* or *does* (instead of by a general descriptive statement).

6. Try writing a short descriptive paper about one or two of the persons closest to you in your family (because these are probably the people you will have observed most carefully), and in your description try to rely mostly on certain real actions and words said—those actions and words which are most characteristic or "symbolic" of the person.

7. What particular emotional urgencies of the adolescent boy does Yeats emphasize? Is the desire to go away by oneself (to the woods, to a secret cave, and so on) representative of this period of youth or not? Can you explain the desire? Do girls feel this need as well as boys?

8. Is the fantasy of becoming a great, lonely, mysterious, powerful, but misunderstood figure—a "sage, a magician or a poet," for instance—common in adolescence or not? Can you explain why such fantasies do occur?

9. Write a short paper on the difficulties, tensions, and aspirations of adolescence, not using abstract textbook information but your own observation. Or write a paper, both descriptive and critical, about the drawbacks of your own elementary or high-school education, or about particular tensions school may have aroused. It will be well to keep the writing quite personal, since that will help you to avoid big generalizations and to visualize your subject in terms of actual, concrete experience.

Emlyn Williams ◄§ Pubertas, Pubertatis

◄§ Welsh actor and playwright, born in 1905. Best known of his plays are *Night Must Fall* and *The Corn is Green*. In the autobiographical piece reprinted here, he himself is the titular "George." Williams spoke only Welsh until he was eight, which may be one reason for the tangy freshness of his prose. *Pubertas* and *pubertatis* are the Latin nominative and genitive forms of the word "puberty" (as a schoolboy might recite such forms). §►

THE WINTER term, my English essays became more elaborate; I knew that from behind her thick glasses gentle Miss Morris was not missing much, and that she might pass on any unusual effort to Miss Cooke. Then one school morning in November, we were heaved out of routine and packed home cheering with excitement borrowed from our elders: the war which had touched me so little was over. We ran down hysterical Holywell High Street, hastily Union-Jacked, but by the time I had reached the Quay my champagne was flat. It seemed wrong to arrive home from H.C.S. before midday dinner; was I the one boy in the country who would sooner have stayed at school on Armistice Day? But what was I to do with myself? I had sevenpence, saved out of the sixpence a week Mam gave me, to cover pencils, sweets or — nearly always — the Hip.[1] An urge which had been forming for months suddenly crystallized. I wanted to tell a story, on paper.

I walked down to Fewster's, bought a wad of foolscap,[2] sat at the kitchen table, and wrote across the top, in flowing scroll, "HEARTS OF YOUTH, a novel by George Williams, aged 13; Chapter One, The Eyes of a Viper." I resisted putting "Episode One." Then, in impeccable copperplate,[3] "The sun sparkled and shimmered, one summer's day in 1602, as a boy and girl walked hand in hand in a beautiful garden outside Paris." With a facility derived from writing essays straight off, I altered not one word. "The boy René was tall and graceful, his blue eyes fathomless: the girl every whit as fair." One well-behaved cliché glided after the other on oiled wheels: "The scent of delphiniums wafted over the well-tended paths." I had never seen a delphinium, but it sounded exotic. "He held her to him and gazed into her liquid eyes." A line later, the reader was to raise an eyebrow at the news that this demonstrative pair were brother and sister: I felt as yet unequipped for a love story, but the romantic convention was so strong that from the start their devotion overstepped the mark. " 'My dearest,' she breathed, with no idea of the turmoil to come. . . ."

Turmoil it was to be. She was kidnapped by a Turk seeking recruits for the Imperial Harem, whereupon her distracted brother followed via dungeons, bandits, shipwrecks and stolen horses racing for leagues until "at long last the shimmering Golden Horn." After bribing his way into the Palace he beheld "a sight ne'er yet vouchsafed to white eyes; the veiled Harem, lying on their divans in various languid attitudes and wearing agates, emeralds, sapphires, garnets, rubies, onyxes, beryls, topazes, turquoises, pearls and diamonds." It is hardly to be wondered at that the girls looked languid, considering the weight they were carrying. René was captured, fastened by the waist from the highest minaret and shot at with red-hot arrows, watched by all affrighted Constantinople (Chapter Seven, The Human Pendulum). Miraculously he escaped, rescued his sister from a fate I knew little of (she apparently knew less, for her only comment was "My jailers were harsh, but from the Sultan I had nothing to fear"), and the last chapter left the pair safe in Paris, with

[1] Probably Hippodrome, the local movie theater.
[2] Cheap writing paper.
[3] Elegant handwriting like that used in copperplate printing.

no cloud except presumably what would happen to either if the other married.

I wrote "The End" on page 68 and after class, hot in the face, casually informed Miss Cooke that I had written a novel. "Heavens, what next . . . well, the handwriting's good — Miss Morris, look at this!" If only I could have handed them a printed book with a picture on the cover: René swinging from the minaret. . . . But I had started to tell a story, gone on telling, and finished it. The script was returned to me a week later, with a good-humored compliment, "You have certainly given your imagination full play." One wet dinner hour, in a forbidden classroom, I showed it to Millie Tyrer and Eira Parry. "An adventure story, you know, just came to me. . . ." They were impressed, "Oo George, what lovely writing," and I was enjoyably reading aloud — "the girl every whit as fair" — when in walked Miss Cooke; after my casualness, it was humiliating. "Back to your cloakroom girls, and Williams, keep to the boys' side. Get along." My parents were impressed by the handwriting and the length, but I did not offer it to them; how could they be interested in the glamour of the East? It did not occur to me that possibly Dic the Mariner knew more about Constantinople than René and the Sultan's harem put together.

Neither Miss Cooke nor Miss Morris had criticized my first work, and it is understandable why. Having in the past fallen under the spell of the second-rate, I had reproduced it perfectly, and it is not possible to pick perfection to pieces. At Christmas the novelist hung his stocking for the last time, orange, apple, pencils and drawing book, but first there was Prize Distribution. It was gratifying that the applause when I advanced for my prize — a first, *Canute the Great*, again unreadable — was not humiliatingly less than Wally's for his Woodwork. I also won *Kim* in soft red leather, a "Special Prize for Hygiene." "Hygiene," said my mother, who on Olympus would have been Goddess of Cleanliness, "what's that?"

After the ceremony, with the unaccustomed fall of school darkness, the spluttering gaslights gave the Central Hall an exotic look; the pupils were special too, in their Sunday best, some boys sporting their first long trousers. Girls took turns at the piano, plucking out languorous waltzes that delighted and disturbed. Dancing was not a school subject, so any attempt at it was holiday fun; couples would link up, mostly girl with girl, but occasionally a blushing boy would venture to be taught by a girl, half in parody. It was a restless hour; one waited, flushed and adrift, teased into an expectation which had to expend itself in laughter, a carefully diffident display of prize books, clowning, and parlour games. Then the train, unfamiliar too by winter night light; between Flint and the Quay, with Totty and Co.'s laughter still in my ears, the blackness flashing past produced a reaction of loneliness.

My standing with my schoolmates continued to be good but I still had no friends. Every advantage has to be paid for: while my obsession with the written word was gradually helping me to pull down one wall — the frontier between me and the cosmopolitan world — it was also building another, the barrier between me and my immediate fellow creatures. The friends I had made on paper, from my *Welsh Singer* trio to David and the Tullivers on the Floss,[4] were such that nobody could live up to them, and the Chum who accompanied me invisibly over Rubbishland had not materialized. Three weeks' holiday, what now?

Walks up the line, into the working-class weather, past the dead-sea, brickyard with the old tins and the cat corpses; from our ashpit, I would look up at the wise bland moon high in the heavens, free of the Quay. Indoors, the Christmas fire and the holly Job[5] and I had gathered up the line; outside, carol singers wooed the night air of the grim little town. I tiptoed round to the alley, looked up between the high ravine into High Street, turned and pressed myself against the right wall; it was the side of the bakehouse attached to the bread shop, and at night it was toast-warm to the touch, a voluptuous private moment. Voices, footsteps — might one of them halt? There would then be the moonlit gleam of eye and smile, strong hand on my shoulder, humorous, stern melting into forgiving, forgiving hardening into stern, "George!" . . . But the steps jaunted by, with raucous laughter nothing to do with me. A last look at the moon, and back into the safe Spartan womb of 314a, back to the book.

These holidays involved an idea of Mr. Boyer's, an essay on "A Visit to a Factory." One dark evening with Dad six-till-ten, I set out over Hawarden Bridge with a notebook and pass, to the envy of ten-year-old Job who already looked forward to working in Summers'; and like a stray insect I scuttled through a vast streetless city of black sheds, intermin-

4 Characters in George Eliot's *The Mill on the Floss.*
5 His brother.

able rumbling walls, swiveling cranes, belching chimneys, wagons snarling along rails. I ought to have been excited by the pervasive all-powerful activity, but apart from pleasure that my father was a part of the machine-metropolis, I was conscious only of ruthlessness. I stumbled upon Dad's shed; though we both knew that I was expected, I was as proud and puzzled to see him as he was to see me. He introduced me to his mate Mr. Hughes from Flint, whose son Ivor was due at H.C.S. in a year's time. "Well," said Dad to him, "this is the boy!" I realized, with a swelling of the heart, why the cuttings were so grimy: privately and in good taste, he was beginning to boast about me.

They were guarding some sort of machine, and feeding it oil, cinders and — for all I knew — sandwiches. But I evinced interest, and wrote as if I were from the Press. Dad showed me round: a pounding nightmare of glutinous pistons entering serpent-like into hissing abdomens of steel, wheels and rods writhing in an inextricable rhythm to the inaudible music of a witches' sabbath: then the shed where, six feet away — he held me back — I watched a gigantic cube of molten steel throbbing along with red-hot sparks pouring from it. It had a malevolent beauty that held my look like love. Then there was a great pit of white bubbling wickedness that only had to be looked at to burn eyes out of a head. "Has anybody ever fallen in?" I whispered in a shout. Dad knew me well enough to give the answer. "Know why they put that rail? Boy slipped, never seen again." I shivered and asked about carbon monoxide; I was gratified to find that he knew more chemistry than I did. I walked out of the money-making cauldron and was glad of the mute estuary night; if that was life, I wanted no part of it. Mr. Boyer found my essay a dull effort.

By the middle of the spring term the film drug was losing its power. I found myself bored by Eddie Polo and Buck Jones and began to antici-pate the vistas of scrub and the masked heroes rearing horses against the sky; there was a lull in magic, enlivened by a class book — the horrific-ally unsuitable study of madness by Maupassant called *Le Horla* — and by the discovery of *Bleak House*.[6] But *Bleak House*, long as it was, came to its end.

Then the Saturday afternoon, a windy day of sun-chasing clouds that felt like the beginning of something, when outside the Hip, yet another

[6] Novel by Dickens.

W. S. Hart poster was suddenly covered with a slip, "Special Show Sat Mat." I was relieved, but not sanguine. A thin audience of children; as we waited for the pianist to enter and the windows to disappear, a weedy boy whom I did not know whispered to me with a leer, " 'Ere, ever been to bed with yer sister?" It was an unexpected question. "I have no sister," I answered politely, and moved to another seat. The pianist attacked what looked like a sheaf of special music, darkness, then "OWING TO THE NATURE OF THIS PICTURE NO OTHER ITEM WILL BE SHOWN." This dismayed me — no choice? — and when Mr. T. P. O'Connor flashed on I gave a sigh of frustration. He had written one word, and I could only think of sermons. "Intolerance."

"A Film by D. W. Griffith." A preacher? Words faded in, "Out of the Cradle Endlessly Rocking . . ." then a veiled figure, in a shaft of mysterious light, seated at the cradle of the world. I sat forward. A close shot of a book, *Intolerance*; the book slowly opened, onto the words "Love's Struggle through the Ages. . . ." I never sat back.

The film was as bold as the title. Four stories forged ahead like horses drawing a chariot; with the cradle the focus moved mesmerically from one to another, to and fro, till the tempo mounted in four crescendos to a triumphant dénouement. The old hypnosis crept up to my head; the Quay, my family, school, my secret thoughts, everything dissolved away and the only reality was my two eyes fixed on the flickering screen.

Story One was modern, made unforgettable by a last-minute rescue from the electric chair, Story Two about Christ, no less, from manger to cross, suggested by a shadow, a hand, a foot, Story Three the Massacre of Saint Bartholomew, Paris 1572, but Story Four was the one marvelously mine. It was set in Babylon, around the corrupt splendors of the Prince and Princess Beloved, with in the marketplace the Mountain Girl, a tomboyish creature of sixteen, auctioned as a slave. On the very night of the Great Feast —soaring flights of stairs, barbaric pillars, immense stone elephants, with high above, revelers no larger than bees simmering in silhouette against the city flares — commotion, look, on the great wall, something. . . . Subtitle, "The moving finger writes, and having writ . . ." Then the siege, on a staggering scale, battering rams, molten catapulted rocks, ladders shooting up from vast engines, the defenders hurtling to their doom; every battle I had ever read of came to thrilling life. The Mountain Girl, struck by an arrow, sank happy and unwept to her death, day dawned on the horror-stained streets of Paris and the sun went down on Calvary. As the light faded from the three crosses, my heart was wrung by a tragedy which had been harangued past my deaf ears every Sunday since I could walk.

Sinking into my parlor corner, I had no recollection of my walk home; gradually my impressions assembled. Babylon was the real wonder, and even more than the Feast and the Siege, the Mountain Girl had ravished me, the sexless adolescent tossing her short hair at the crones around her and aping the boys by wiping her hand across her wide beautiful mouth as she drove her cart breakneck over the plains to warn the Palace. My love for this androgynous creature was twofold: one moment I worshipped her as an enchanting girl, the next I saw her as a wild dedicated lad, my friend across three thousand years.

This last was quick to flower into another vision, of myself as this boy. Home from school in the parlor, I would pull my hair down into my eyes and strain at the reins, face working and eyes flashing when they were not darting to the mirror, a narcissistic Jehu.[7] The family abed, I would take the two dusty red pompons from the mantelpiece and fix one to each ear; then I put a hand up the kitchen chimney, brushed my lips with the soft soot and stared at myself sideways in the little shaving mirror. "George, how long are you going to be, wasting oil?" The nose was too strong, whether for tomboy or boy, but mark how the teeth flashed joyously below the dusky curve of the mouth: "Coming, just finishing my geography. . . ." Then again, many an evening, a wanderer in Rubbishland might have been astonished to see a schoolboy, a book under his arm, leap to the battlement top of a grass-grown dump. The Chaldean air thick with smoke, out of the blood-red sunset advances the locust army, arrows whistle; just as he aims he is mortally struck, in a close-up. The face twitches, empties of expression, the knees give, the Mountain Boy rolls down the slope to oblivion, scrambles up, brushes himself off, picks up his Algebra and walks home to fish and chips.

It was not long before Geo Wms the film star—Roy King, I would call myself — gave place to the novelist, though there was one week-end, in passing, after which Miss Morris had a glimpse of Geo Wms the dramatist; she had set "a short piece, in dialogue, based on an historical episode." I still had not seen or read a play, not counting *As You Like It,* but the result was *The Blue Band,* a forty-page "drama" set in Paris the

[7] Old Testament king who made a furious chariot attack in battle.

night of the Massacre — not the easiest piece to stage as it had twenty
full-stage scenes lasting half a minute each. But that was a flash in the
pan. The Easter holidays were devoted to Book One — a novel must now
be planned on the scale of *Bleak House* — of *The Tombs of Terror*, a
romance of ancient Thebes. The copperplate flowed as impeccably but
the style was richer, stickier: a mixture of the *Sunday Companion*,
Dickens, Lord Lytton, and Griffith subtitles. For the plot and setting, I
heaped into the stewpot *Out of Egypt* and the suspense from every serial
I had even seen. "The Sun Sets! The great molten mass is sinking o'er the
rim of the deserts. What is that couchant figure so sinister in its sublime
immensity? The Great Sphinx . . ."

The hero, not unexpectedly, was a hermaphroditic street dancer described as "the boy Pearla." "His face was wonderfully fair for so trying
a climate, with an expression almost magnetic. . . . Healthy red lips. . . .
His whole soul was in his dance, a wonderful feeling which can only be
acquired by some people. . . ." The Princess Nemesis saw him dance —
Chapter Six, The Leap to Fame — but there was a secret society of
priests with a green viper whose bite turned the victim to stone. Towards
the end the copperplate got out of hand as it sprawled drunkenly on;
by Page 107, the novelist had lost all proportion and was working up into
a frenzied spiral of suspense which he knew in his heart must taper into
nothing, the victim of its own excess. Chapter Twelve, The Death Knell.
"A minute to live! A mumble, a hiss. . . . In a few minutes Pearla the
Sacred Dancer of Mystery will be a solid statue. . . . Death! Death!!
Death!!! Two seconds to live!" End of Book One, to be continued. It
never was.

With a present from Miss Cooke of *The Irving Shakespeare*, my
clutch of books — penny bargains, prizes, discards — had swollen to
fifteen, and at Dad's suggestion we spent an engrossed Saturday sawing
at two old orange-boxes, a penny each from Ma Williams the Chip
Shop, to make a primitive two-shelf bookcase which just fitted the top of
the cupboard next to my parlor corner. I unearthed an old paintbox and
gave the raw whorled wood a coat of maroon along the edges; with the
books in place, it seemed to me beautiful. My pleasure from now on was
to watch the shelves steadily fill.

In the meantime the disquieting spring flowed towards summer.
One early evening, my parents had taken my brothers to some sort

of Sports, and for the first time ever I found myself alone in our home, in a silence unique and strange. I felt suddenly hungry; with an impulse as irresistible as any in the calendar of sin, I went into the parlor, sat on the floor and opened the little cupboard in the dresser where my mother kept her sacred store of sugar, butter, jam, and raisins. One by one, I opened the little parcels and scooped out a small helping of each; as I ate, vile and gluttonous, I thought I heard a step, and knew that if my parents entered I would never recover. I put everything carefully back and reopened my book, sick and slightly more conscious of wickedness than ever before or since. Was it a strange by-symptom of growing pains? One Saturday, just as I began to dread my darkening upper lip drawing the street call "Beaver!" the end of the kitchen table was cleared and Dad gave me a shaving lesson with his razor. My secret thoughts were pressing forward, and I needed to be talked to. A sensible young master would have been a help, but from my elders and my books there was silence.

Silence too from the Silver Screen; but the pictures moved, and filmmakers did not find the Censor difficult to hoodwink. While I liked some of the girls in class and was at ease with them, my visions were of the grown women I saw on the pictures. Between those two impassive Roman matrons in the Hip, Mr. T. P. O'Connor tended to introduce a shadow-life unsettling to a schoolboy bursting out of his clothes at knee and elbow. Once the heady upheaval of *Intolerance* had settled into something to be lived with, it was the Babylonian orgy that stayed: flower-strewn bodies writhing on stair after stair, luscious odalisques, glimpsed in slow passing where a halt would have broken the spell, their bare breasts moving shamelessly to unheard cymbals. In 314a back bedroom, when I was not leaning in a sheet over the bedstead balustrade of the Palace I would be half-lying, biting at a pomegranate under gold tables where besotted carousers sprawled in a dubious twilight. Children's Mat Sat One Penny.

Temptation drew nearer in the person of Theda Bara, as Salome or Cleopatra: a heavy-lidded heavy-mouthed courtesan writhing slowly on vast couches with a bangle round the ankle of one naked foot. It was the foot, somehow — close enough, from the twopenny-ha'pennies, to handle — that told me the rest was mine. Of that rest, I saw the bosom swelling under its jeweled helmets, the veiled curve of the hips — no, the gym slips in school had nothing to fear. And when the hero, rugged

in white breeches and stripped to the virile waist, sank on tne edge of
the couch, leant at an acute angle and placed his hand on a plump rump
— "The Southern Night, Marvelous One, is made for Love . . ." — the
lights clicking up for the variety turn found me in no mood for terriers
staggering through hoops while their mistress played the xylophone in a
crinoline. When I got to bed on those nights, there would follow me into
it a series of full-bosomed hussies, accompanied on occasion by their
menfolk. By the time I got to sleep, it was a big bed.

Though my books kept a general silence, I received food for thought
from an unexpected source. "Ever read Genesis 39 verse twelve?" Harold
Mears whispered with a leer. Home, I settled into my corner and opened
an English Old Testament. "She caught him by his garment, saying, Lie
with me. . . ." So that was Potiphar's Wife. "Reading the Bible," said
Mam, "good life, what's the matter with you?"

✑ FOR DISCUSSION AND WRITING

1. Explain the strong drive toward imaginative writing that attacks Williams
   at the age of thirteen. Do you think that it was simply a peculiarity of his
   temperament or that it is a more or less typical need for expression in
   adolescence? One must remember that the Welsh country boy had no
   television; do you think that television alters the youthful creative impulse
   or not?

2. A strong sense of comic irony operates in this piece (much more than in
   the Yeats selection, for instance). Point out various places where the
   writer's sense of comic irony comes through clearly. One can imagine the
   adult intellect commenting ironically on the excesses of adolescence; but
   in the places you have pointed out, does the presence of the adult author
   really appear in any material way, usurping that of the boy? Analyze how
   the trick is done, how the dual point of view is maintained—the ironical
   one of the adult author and the naïve one of the boy.

3. The syntax of this piece is notably different from that of the Gorky or
   Yeats. "Syntax" means sentence structure, the grammatical order of words.
   Here the syntax obeys inner psychological and emotional impulses that
   often explode ordinary sentence structure. Find and write down a dozen

examples. Explain what is achieved by such syntactical transgressions. A sense of heartbeat? An acceleration of pace? A closer feeling of responsive nerves?

4. Instead of quoting verbatim from his early writing, Williams could have stated the typical subject matter of the writings and made some generalization about their naïveté and flamboyance. What is gained by quoting specific passages? How do the quotations serve to characterize not only the boy himself but also certain typical tendencies of that period of youth?

5. Where do you find in this piece any indications of the adolescent loneliness found in the selection from Yeats? What very different means did the two boys adopt to encounter that strange and difficult loneliness?

6. Evaluate the influences on Williams' boyhood. He calls them "second-rate," but most of us grow up under similar "second-rate" influences. Write a short essay on the way adolescent beguilements—such as comic books, movies, and television—release fantasy and are *necessary* for the release of fantasy. Why is fantasy at this time a necessary and good thing?

7. Write about high-school graduation as a high divide in life—the final ceremony of an "initiation." With such a subject, it is easy to indulge in sentimental clichés, but try to avoid both generalizations and clichés. Look back at the Williams piece and see how he "gives," rather than "talks about," a transitional phase of life.

8. In one of the last notations, Williams shows the boy stealing and gobbling the locked-up sweets, and then, immediately, becoming engrossed in what Potiphar's wife did. How do these two rather absurd incidents contain all the anomalies of passage from childhood to adolescence?

Anne Frank ◄§ The Secret Annexe

◄§ Born in Amsterdam in 1929, of Jewish parents, Anne died in the Bergen-Belsen death camp when she was sixteen. Her diary was written during the two years her family lived in hiding in the loft of a warehouse. The last entry was made on August 4, 1944, when the German police raided the building. §►

SUNDAY MORNING, JUST BEFORE ELEVEN O'CLOCK,

16 APRIL, 1944

Darlingest Kitty,[1]

Remember yesterday's date, for it is a very important day in my life. Surely it is a great day for every girl when she receives her first kiss? Well, then, it is just as important for me too! Bram's kiss on my right cheek doesn't count any more, likewise the one from Mr. Walker on my right hand.

How did I suddenly come by this kiss? Well, I will tell you.

Yesterday evening at eight o'clock I was sitting with Peter on his divan, it wasn't long before his arm went round me. "Let's move up a bit," I said, "then I don't bump my head against the cupboard." He moved up, almost into the corner, I laid my arm under his and across his

[1] An imaginary friend to whom Anne addressed her diary.

back, and he just about buried me, because his arm was hanging on my shoulder.

Now we've sat like this on other occasions, but never so close together as yesterday. He held me firmly against him, my left shoulder against his chest; already my heart began to beat faster, but we had not finished yet. He didn't rest until my head was on his shoulder and his against it. When I sat upright again after about five minutes, he soon took my head in his hands and laid it against him once more. Oh, it was so lovely, I couldn't talk much, the joy was too great. He stroked my cheek and arm a bit awkwardly, played with my curls and our heads touching most of the time. I can't tell you, Kitty, the feeling that ran through me all the while. I was too happy for words, and I believe he was as well.

We got up at half past eight. Peter put on his gym shoes, so that when he toured the house he wouldn't make a noise, and I stood beside him. How it came about so suddenly, I don't know, but before we went downstairs he kissed me, through my hair, half on my left cheek, half on my ear; I tore downstairs without looking round, and am simply longing for today!

Yours, Anne

MONDAY, 17 APRIL, 1944

Dear Kitty,

Do you think that Daddy and Mummy would approve of my sitting and kissing a boy on a divan — a boy of seventeen and a half and a girl of just under fifteen? I don't really think they would, but I must rely on myself over this. It is so quiet and peaceful to lie in his arms and to dream, it is so thrilling to feel his cheek against mine, it is so lovely to know that there is someone waiting for me. But there is indeed a big "but," because will Peter be content to leave it at this? I haven't forgotten his promise already, but . . . he *is* a boy!

I know myself that I'm starting very soon, not even fifteen, and so independent already! It's certainly hard for other people to understand, I know almost for certain that Margot would never kiss a boy unless there had been some talk of an engagement or marriage, but neither Peter nor I have anything like that in mind. I'm sure too that Mummy never touched a man before Daddy. What would my girl friends say about it if they knew that I lay in Peter's arms, my heart against his chest, my head on his shoulder and with his head against mine!

Oh, Anne, how scandalous! But honestly, I don't think it is; we are shut up here, shut away from the world, in fear and anxiety, especially just lately. Why, then, should we who love each other remain apart? Why should we wait until we've reached a suitable age? Why should we bother?

I have taken it upon myself to look after myself; he would never want to cause me sorrow or pain. Why shouldn't I follow the way my heart leads me, if it makes us both happy? All the same, Kitty, I believe you can sense that I'm in doubt, I think it must be my honesty which rebels against doing anything on the sly! Do you think it's my duty to tell Daddy what I'm doing? Do you think we should share our secret with a third person? A lot of the beauty would be lost, but would my conscience feel happier? I will discuss it with "him."

Oh, yes, there's still so much I want to talk to him about, for I don't see the use of only just cuddling each other. To exchange our thoughts, that shows confidence and faith in each other, we would both be sure to profit by it!

Yours, Anne

FRIDAY, 28 APRIL, 1944

Dear Kitty,

I have never forgotten my dream about Peter Wessel (see beginning of January). If I think of it, I can still feel his cheek against mine now, and recall that lovely feeling that made everything good.

Sometimes I have had the same feeling here with Peter, but never to such an extent, until yesterday, when we were, as usual, sitting on the divan, our arms around each other's waists. Then suddenly the ordinary Anne slipped away and a second Anne took her place, a second Anne who is not reckless and jocular, but one who just wants to love and be gentle.

I sat pressed closely against him and felt a wave of emotion come over me, tears sprang into my eyes, the left one trickled onto his dungarees, the right one ran down my nose and also fell onto his dungarees. Did he notice? He made no move or sign to show that he did. I wonder if he feels the same as I do? He hardly said a word. Does he know that he has two Annes before him? These questions must remain unanswered.

At half past eight I stood up and went to the window, where we always say good-by. I was still trembling, I was still Anne number two.

He came towards me, I flung my arms around his neck and gave him a kiss on his left cheek, and was about to kiss the other cheek, when my lips met his and we pressed them together. In a whirl we were clasped in each other's arms, again and again, never to leave off. Oh, Peter does so need tenderness. For the first time in his life he has discovered a girl, has seen for the first time that even the most irritating girls have another side to them, that they have hearts and can be different when you are alone with them. For the first time in his life he has given of himself and, having never had a boy or girl friend in his life before, shown his real self. Now we have found each other. For that matter, I didn't know him either, like him having never had a trusted friend, and this is what it has come to. . . .

Once more there is a question which gives me no peace: "Is it right? Is it right that I should have yielded so soon, that I am so ardent, just as ardent and eager as Peter himself? May I, a girl, let myself go to this extent?" There is but *one* answer: "I have longed so much and for so long — I am so lonely — and now I have found consolation."

In the mornings we just behave in an ordinary way, in the afternoons more or less so (except just occasionally); but in the evenings the suppressed longings of the whole day, the happiness and the blissful memories of all the previous occasions come to the surface and we only think of each other. Every evening, after the last kiss, I would like to dash away, not to look into his eyes any more — away, away alone in the darkness.

And what do I have to face, when I reach the bottom of the staircase? Bright lights, questions, and laughter; I have to swallow it all and not show a thing. My heart still feels too much; I can't get over a shock such as I received yesterday all at once. The Anne who is gentle shows herself too little anyway and, therefore, will not allow herself to be suddenly driven into the background. Peter has touched my emotions more deeply than anyone has ever done before — except in my dreams. Peter has taken possession of me and turned me inside out; surely it goes without saying that anyone would require a rest and a little while to recover from such an upheaval?

Oh Peter, what have you done to me? What do you want of me? Where will this lead us? Oh, now I understand Elli; now, now that I am going through this myself, now I understand her doubt; if I were older and he should ask me to marry him, what should I answer? Anne, be honest! You would not be able to marry him, but yet, it would be hard to let him go. Peter hasn't enough character yet, not enough will power, too little courage and strength. He is still a child in his heart of hearts, he is no older than I am; he is only searching for tranquillity and happiness.

Am I only fourteen? Am I really still a silly little school-girl? Am I really so inexperienced about everything? I have more experience than most; I have been through things that hardly anyone my age has undergone. I am afraid of myself, I am afraid that in my longing I am giving myself too quickly. How, later on, can it ever go right with other boys? Oh, it is so difficult, always battling with one's heart and reason; in its own time, each will speak, but do I know for certain that I have chosen the right time?

Yours, Anne

TUESDAY, 2 MAY, 1944

Dear Kitty,

On Saturday evening I asked Peter whether he thought that I ought to tell Daddy a bit about us; when we'd discussed it a little, he came to the conclusion that I should. I was glad, for it shows that he's an honest boy. As soon as I got downstairs I went off with Daddy to get some water; and while we were on the stairs I said, "Daddy, I expect you've gathered that when we're together Peter and I don't sit miles apart. Do you think it's wrong?" Daddy didn't reply immediately, then said, "No, I don't think it's wrong, but you must be careful, Anne; you're in such a confined space here." When we went upstairs, he said something else on the same lines. On Sunday morning he called me to him and said, "Anne, I have thought more about what you said." I felt scared already. "It's not really very right — here in this house; I thought that you were just pals. Is Peter in love?"

"Oh, of course not," I replied.

"You know that I understand both of you, but you must be the one to hold back. Don't go upstairs so often, don't encourage him more than you can help. It is the man who is always the active one in these things; the woman can hold him back. It is quite different under normal circumstances, when you are free, you see other boys and girls, you can get away sometimes, play games and do all kinds of other things; but here, if you're together a lot, and you want to get away, you can't; you see each other every hour of the day — in fact, all the time. Be careful, Anne, and don't take it too seriously!"

"I don't, Daddy, but Peter is a decent boy, really a nice boy!"

"Yes, but he is not a strong character; he can be easily influenced, for good, but also for bad; I hope for his sake that his good side will remain uppermost, because, by nature, that is how he is."

We talked on for a bit and agreed that Daddy should talk to him too.

On Sunday morning in the attic he asked, "And have you talked to your father, Anne?"

"Yes," I replied, "I'll tell you about it. Daddy doesn't think it's bad, but he says that here, where we're so close together all the time, clashes easily arise."

"But we agreed, didn't we, never to quarrel; and I'm determined to stick to it!"

"So will I, Peter, but Daddy didn't think that it was like this, he just thought we were pals; do you think that we still can be?"

"I can — what about you?"

"Me too, I told Daddy that I trusted you. I do trust you, Peter, just as much as I trust Daddy, and I believe you to be worthy of it. You are, aren't you, Peter?"

"I hope so." (He was very shy and rather red in the face.)

"I believe in you, Peter," I went on, "I believe that you have good qualities, and that you'll get on in the world."

After that, we talked about other things. Later I said, "If we come out of here, I know quite well that you won't bother about me any more!"

He flared right up. "That's not true, Anne, oh no, I won't let you think that of me!"

Then I was called away.

Daddy has talked to him; he told me about it today. "Your father thought that the friendship might develop into love sooner or later," he said. But I replied that we would keep a check on ourselves.

Daddy doesn't want me to go upstairs so much in the evenings now, but I don't want that. Not only because I like being with Peter; I have told him that I trust him. I do trust him and I want to show him that I do, which can't happen if I stay downstairs through lack of trust.

No, I'm going!

Yours, Anne

Dear Kitty,

First, just the news of the week. We're having a holiday from politics; there is nothing, absolutely nothing to announce. I too am gradually beginning to believe that the invasion will come. After all, they can't let the Russians clear up everything; for that matter, they're not doing anything either at the moment.

Mr. Koophuis comes to the office every morning again now. He's got a new spring for Peter's divan, so Peter will have to do some upholstering, about which, quite understandably, he doesn't feel a bit happy.

Have I told you that Boche has disappeared? Simply vanished — we haven't seen a sign of her since Thursday of last week. I expect she's already in the cats' heaven, while some animal lover is enjoying a succulent meal from her. Perhaps some little girl will be given a fur cap out of her skin. Peter is very sad about it.

Since Saturday we've changed over, and have lunch at half past eleven in the mornings, so we have to last out with one cupful of porridge; this saves us a meal. Vegetables are still very difficult to obtain: we had rotten boiled lettuce this afternoon. Ordinary lettuce, spinach and boiled lettuce, there's nothing else. With these we eat rotten potatoes, so it's a delicious combination!

As you can easily imagine we often ask ourselves here despairingly: "What, oh, what is the use of the war? Why can't people live peacefully together? Why all this destruction?

The question is very understandable, but no one has found a satisfactory answer to it so far. Yes, why do they make still more gigantic planes, still heavier bombs and, at the same time, prefabricated houses for reconstruction? Why should millions be spent daily on the war and yet there's not a penny available for medical services, artists, or for poor people?

Why do some people have to starve, while there are surpluses rotting in other parts of the world? Oh, why are people so crazy?

I don't believe that the big men, the politicians and the capitalists alone, are guilty of the war. Oh no, the little man is just as guilty, otherwise the peoples of the world would have risen in revolt long ago! There's in people simply an urge to destroy, an urge to kill, to murder and rage, and until all mankind, without exception, undergoes a great change, wars will be waged, everything that has been built up, cultivated, and grown will be destroyed and disfigured, after which mankind will have to begin all over again.

I have often been downcast, but never in despair; I regard our hiding as a dangerous adventure, romantic and interesting at the same time. In my diary I treat all the privations as amusing. I have made up my mind now to lead a different life from other girls and, later on, different from ordinary housewives. My start has been so very full of interest, and that is the sole reason why I have to laugh at the humorous side of the most dangerous moments.

I am young and I possess many buried qualities; I am young and strong and am living a great adventure; I am still in the midst of it and can't grumble the whole day long. I have been given a lot, a happy nature, a great deal of cheerfulness and strength. Every day I feel that I am developing inwardly, that the liberation is drawing nearer and how beautiful nature is, how good the people are about me, how interesting this adventure is! Why, then should I be in despair?

Yours, Anne

FRIDAY, 5 MAY, 1944

Dear Kitty,

Daddy is not pleased with me; he thought that after our talk on Sunday I automatically wouldn't go upstairs every evening. He doesn't want any "necking," a word I can't bear. It was bad enough talking about it, why must he make it so unpleasant now? I shall talk to him today. Margot has given me some good advice, so listen; this is roughly what I want to say:

"I believe, Daddy, that you expect a declaration from me, so I will give it you. You are disappointed in me, as you had expected more reserve from me, and I suppose you want me to be just as a fourteen-year-old should be. But that's where you're mistaken!

"Since we've been here, from July 1942 until a few weeks ago, I can assure you that I haven't had any easy time. If you only knew how I cried in the evenings, how unhappy I was, how lonely I felt, then you would understand that I want to go upstairs!

"I have now reached the stage that I can live entirely on my own, without Mummy's support or anyone else's for that matter. But it hasn't just happened in a night; it's been a bitter, hard struggle and I've shed many a tear, before I became as independent as I am now. You can laugh at me and not believe me, but that can't harm me. I know that I'm a separate individual and I don't feel in the least bit responsible to any of you. I am only telling you this because I thought that otherwise you might think that I was underhand, but I don't have to give an account of my deeds to anyone but myself.

"When I was in difficulties you all closed your eyes and stopped up your ears and didn't help me; on the contrary, I received nothing but warnings not to be so boisterous. I was only boisterous so as not to be miserable all the time. I was reckless so as not to hear that persistent voice within me continually. I played a comedy for a year and a half, day in, day out, I never grumbled, never lost my cue, nothing like that — and now, now the battle is over. I have won! I am independent both in mind and body. I don't need a mother any more, for all this conflict has made me strong.

"And now, now that I'm on top of it, now that I know that I've fought the battle, now I want to be able to go on in my own way too, the way that I think is right. You can't and mustn't regard me as fourteen, for all these troubles have made me older; I shall not be sorry for what I have done, but shall act as I think I can. You can't coax me into not going upstairs, *either* you forbid it, *or* you trust me through thick and thin, but then leave me in peace as well!"

Yours, Anne

SATURDAY, 6 MAY, 1944

Dear Kitty,

I put a letter, in which I wrote what I explained to you yesterday, in Daddy's pocket before supper yesterday. After reading it, he was, according to Margot, very upset for the rest of the evening. (I was upstairs doing the dishes.) Poor Pim,[2] I might have known what the effect of such an epistle would be. He is so sensitive! I immediately told Peter not to ask or say anything more. Pim hasn't said any more about it to me. Is that yet in store, I wonder?

Here everything is going on more or less normally again. What they tell us about the prices and the people outside is almost unbelievable, half a pound of tea costs 350 florins,[*] a pound of coffee 80 florins,

---

[2] Anne's father.

[*] A florin is equal to approximately twenty-eight cents.

butter 35 florins per pound, an egg 1.45 florin. People pay 14 florins for an ounce of Bulgarian tobacco! Everyone deals in the black market, every errand boy has something to offer. Our baker's boy got hold of some sewing silk, 0.9 florin for a thin little skein, the milkman manages to get clandestine ration cards, the undertaker delivers the cheese. Burglaries, murders, and theft go on daily. The police and night watchmen join in just as strenuously as the professionals, everyone wants something in their empty stomachs and because wage increases are forbidden the people simply have to swindle. The police are continually on the go, tracing girls of fifteen, sixteen, seventeen and older, who are reported missing every day.

Yours, Anne

SUNDAY MORNING, 7 MAY, 1944

Dear Kitty,

Daddy and I had a long talk yesterday afternoon, I cried terribly and he joined in. Do you know what he said to me, Kitty? "I have received many letters in my life, but this is certainly the most unpleasant! You, Anne, who have received such love from your parents, you, who have parents who are always ready to help you, who have always defended you whatever it might be, can you talk of feeling no responsibility towards us? You feel wronged and deserted; no, Anne, you have done us a great injustice!

"Perhaps you didn't mean it like that, but it is what you wrote; no, Anne, we haven't deserved such a reproach as this!"

Oh, I have failed miserably; this is certainly the worst thing I've ever done in my life. I was only trying to show off with my crying and my tears, just trying to appear big, so that he would respect me. Certainly, I have had a lot of unhappiness, but to accuse the good Pim, who has done and still does do everything for me — no, that was too low for words.

It's right that for once I've been taken down from my inaccessible pedestal, that my pride has been shaken a bit, for I was becoming much too taken up with myself again. What Miss Anne does is by no means always right! Anyone who can cause such unhappiness to someone else, someone he professes to love, and on purpose, too, is low, very low!

And the way Daddy has forgiven me makes me feel more than ever ashamed of myself, he is going to throw the letter in the fire and is so sweet to me now, just as if he had done something wrong. No, Anne, you still have a tremendous lot to learn, begin by doing that first, instead of looking down on others and accusing them!

I have had a lot of sorrow, but who hasn't at my age? I have played the clown a lot too, but I was hardly conscious of it; I felt lonely, but hardly ever in despair! I ought to be deeply ashamed of myself, and indeed I am.

What is done cannot be undone, but one can prevent it happening again. I want to start from the beginning again and it can't be difficult, now that I have Peter. With him to support me, I can and will!

I'm not alone any more; he loves me. I love him, I have my books, my storybook and my diary, I'm not so frightfully ugly, not utterly stupid, have a cheerful temperament and want to have a good character!

Yes, Anne, you've felt deeply that your letter was too hard and that it was untrue. To think that you were even proud of it! I will take Daddy as my example, and I *will* improve.

                                                                Yours, Anne

                                                    THURSDAY, 11 MAY, 1944
Dear Kitty,

I'm frightfully busy at the moment, and although it sounds mad, I haven't time to get through my pile of work. Shall I tell you briefly what I have got to do? Well, then, by tomorrow I must finish reading the first part of *Galileo Galilei*, as it has to be returned to the library. I only started it yesterday, but I shall manage it.

Next week I have got to read *Palestine at the Crossroads* and the second part of *Galilei*. Next I finished reading the first part of the biography of *The Emperor Charles V* yesterday, and it's essential that I work out all the diagrams and family trees that I have collected from it. After that I have three pages of foreign words gathered from various books, which have all got to be recited, written down, and learned. Number four is that my film stars are all mixed up together and are simply gasping to be tidied up; however, as such a clearance would take several days, and since Professor Anne, as she's already said, is choked with work, the chaos will have to remain a chaos.

Next Theseus, Oedipus, Peleus, Orpheus, Jason, and Hercules[3]

---

[3] Greek mythological heroes.

are all awaiting their turn to be arranged, as their different deeds lie crisscross in my mind like fancy threads in a dress; it's also high time Myron and Phidias[4] had some treatment, if they wish to remain at all coherent. Likewise it's the same with the seven and nine years' war; I'm mixing everything up together at this rate. Yes, but what can one do with such a memory! Think how forgetful I shall be when I'm eighty!

Oh, something else, the Bible; how long is it still going to take before I meet the bathing Suzanna? And what do they mean by the guilt of Sodom and Gomorrah? Oh, there is still such a terrible lot to find out and to learn. And in the meantime I've left Lisolette of the Pfalz completely in the lurch.

Kitty, can you see that I'm just about bursting?

Now, about something else: you've known for a long time that my greatest wish is to become a journalist someday and later on a famous writer. Whether these leanings towards greatness (or insanity?) will ever materialize remains to be seen, but I certainly have the subject in my mind. In any case, I want to publish a book entitled *Het Achterhuis*[5] after the war. Whether I shall succeed or not, I cannot say, but my diary will be a great help. I have other ideas as well, besides *Het Achterhuis*. But I will write more fully about them some other time, when they have taken a clearer form in my mind.

Yours, Anne

THURSDAY, 25 MAY, 1944

Dear Kitty,

There's something fresh every day. This morning our vegetable man was picked up for having two Jews in his house. It's a great blow to us, not only that those poor Jews are balancing on the edge of an abyss, but it's terrible for the man himself.

The world has turned topsy-turvy, respectable people are being sent off to concentration camps, prisons, and lonely cells, and the dregs that remain govern young and old, rich and poor. One person walks into the trap through the black market, a second through helping the Jews or other people who've had to go "underground"; anyone who isn't a member of the N.S.B. doesn't know what may happen to him from one day to another.

[4] Ancient Greek sculptors.

[5] The "Secret Annexe" where Anne's family lived in hiding.

This man is a great loss to us too. The girls can't and aren't allowed to haul along our share of potatoes, so the only thing to do is to eat less. I will tell you how we shall do that; it's certainly not going to make things any pleasanter. Mummy says we shall cut out breakfast altogether, have porridge and bread for lunch, and for supper fried potatoes and possibly once or twice per week vegetables or lettuce, nothing more. We're going to be hungry, but anything is better than being discovered.

Yours, Anne

THURSDAY, 15 JUNE, 1944

Dear Kitty,

I wonder if it's because I haven't been able to poke my nose outdoors for so long that I've grown so crazy about everything to do with nature? I can perfectly well remember that there was a time when a deep blue sky, the song of the birds, moonlight and flowers could never have kept me spellbound. That's changed since I've been here.

At Whitsun, for instance, when it was so warm, I stayed awake on purpose until half past eleven one evening in order to have a good look at the moon for once by myself. Alas, the sacrifice was all in vain, as the moon gave far too much light and I didn't dare risk opening a window. Another time, some months ago now, I happened to be upstairs one evening when the window was open. I didn't go downstairs until the window had to be shut. The dark, rainy evening, the gale, the scudding clouds held me entirely in their power; it was the first time in a year and a half that I'd seen the night face to face. After that evening my longing to see it again was greater than my fear of burglars, rats, and raids on the house. I went downstairs all by myself and looked outside through the windows in the kitchen and the private office. A lot of people are fond of nature, many sleep outdoors occasionally, and people in prisons and hospitals long for the day when they will be free to enjoy the beauties of nature, but few are so shut away and isolated from that which can be shared alike by rich and poor. It's not imagination on my part when I say that to look up at the sky, the clouds, the moon, and the stars makes me calm and patient. It's a better medicine than either valerian or bromine; Mother Nature makes me humble and prepared to face every blow courageously.

Alas, it has had to be that I am only able — except on a few rare occasions — to look at nature through dirty net curtains hanging before very dusty windows. And it's no **pleasure** looking through these any longer, because nature is just the one thing that really must be unadulterated.

Yours, Anne

SATURDAY, 15 JULY, 1944

Dear Kitty,

We have had a book from the library with the challenging title of: *What Do You Think of the Modern Young Girl?* I want to talk about this subject today.

The author of this book criticizes "the youth of today" from top to toe, without, however, condemning the whole of the young brigade as "incapable of anything good." On the contrary, she is rather of the opinion that if young people wished, they have it in their hands to make a bigger, more beautiful and better world, but that they occupy themselves with superficial things, without giving a thought to real beauty.

In some passages the writer gave me very much the feeling she was directing her criticisms at me, and that's why I want to lay myself completely bare to you for once and defend myself against this attack.

I have one outstanding trait in my character, which must strike anyone who knows me for any length of time, and that is my knowledge of myself. I can watch myself and my actions, just like an outsider. The Anne of every day I can face entirely without prejudice, without making excuses for her, and watch what's good and what's bad about her. This "self-consciousness" haunts me, and every time I open my mouth I know as soon as I've spoken whether "that ought to have been different" or "that was right as it was." There are so many things about myself that I condemn; I couldn't begin to name them all. I understand more and more how true Daddy's words were when he said: "All children must look after their own upbringing." Parents can only give good advice or put them on the right paths, but the final forming of a person's character lies in their own hands.

In addition to this, I have lots of courage, I always feel so strong and as if I can bear a great deal, I feel so free and so young! I was glad when I first realized it, because I don't think I shall easily bow down before the blows that inevitably come to everyone.

But I've talked about these things so often before. Now I want to come to the chapter of "Daddy and Mommy don't understand me."

Daddy and Mummy have always thoroughly spoiled me, were sweet to me, defended me, and have done all that parents could do. And yet I've felt so terribly lonely for a long time, so left out, neglected, and misunderstood. Daddy tried all he could to check my rebellious spirit, but it was no use, I have cured myself, by seeing for myself what was wrong in my behavior and keeping it before my eyes.

How is it that Daddy was never any support to me in my struggle, why did he completely miss the mark when he wanted to offer me a helping hand? Daddy tried the wrong methods, he always talked to me as a child who was going through difficult phases. It sounds crazy, because Daddy's the only one who has always taken me into his confidence, and no one but Daddy has given me the feeling that I'm sensible. But there's one thing he's omitted: you see, he hasn't realized that for me the fight to get on top was more important than all else. I didn't want to hear about "symptoms of your age," or "other girls," or "it wears off by itself"; I didn't want to be treated as a girl-like-all-others, but as Anne-on-her-own-merits. Pim didn't understand that. For that matter, I can't confide in anyone, unless they tell me a lot about themselves, and as I know very little about Pim, I don't feel that I can tread upon more intimate ground with him. Pim always takes up the older, fatherly attitude, tells me that he too has had similar passing tendencies. But still he's not able to feel with me like a friend, however hard he tries. These things have made me never mention my views on life nor my well-considered theories to anyone but my diary and, occasionally, to Margot. I concealed from Daddy everything that perturbed me; I never shared my ideals with him. I was aware of the fact that I was pushing him away from me.

I couldn't do anything else. I have acted entirely according to my feelings, but I have acted in the way that was best for my peace of mind. Because I should completely lose my repose and self-confidence, which I have built up so shakily, if, at this stage, I were to accept criticisms of my half-completed task. And I can't do that even from Pim, although it sounds very hard, for not only have I not shared my secret thoughts with Pim but I have often pushed him even further from me, by my irritability.

This is a point that I think a lot about: why is it that Pim annoys me? So much so that I can hardly bear him teaching me, that his affectionate ways strike me as being put on, that I want to be left in peace and would really prefer it if he dropped me a bit, until I felt more certain in my attitude towards him? Because I still have a gnawing feeling of guilt over that horrible letter that I dared to write him when I was so wound up. Oh, how hard it is to be really strong and brave in every way!

Yet this was not my greatest disappointment; no, I ponder far more over Peter than Daddy. I know very well that I conquered him instead of he conquering me. I created an image of him in my mind, pictured him as a quiet, sensitive, lovable boy, who needed affection and friendship. I needed a living person to whom I could pour out my heart; I wanted a friend who'd help to put me on the right road. I achieved what I wanted, and, slowly but surely, I drew him towards me. Finally, when I had made him feel friendly, it automatically developed into an intimacy which, on second thought, I don't think I ought to have allowed.

We talked about the most private things, and yet up till now we have never touched on those things that filled, and still fill, my heart and soul. I still don't know quite what to make of Peter, is he superficial, or does he still feel shy, even of me? But dropping that, I committed one error in my desire to make a real friendship: I switched over and tried to get at him by developing it into a more intimate relation, whereas I should have explored all other possibilities. He longs to be loved and I can see that he's beginning to be more and more in love with me. He gets satisfaction out of our meetings, whereas they just have the effect of making me want to try it out with him again. And yet I don't seem able to touch on the subjects that I'm so longing to bring out into the daylight. I drew Peter towards me, far more than he realizes. Now he clings to me, and for the time being, I don't see any way of shaking him off and putting him on his own feet. When I realized that he could not be a friend for my understanding, I thought I would at least try to lift him up out of his narrow-mindedness and make him do something with his youth.

"For in its innermost depths youth is lonelier than old age." I read this saying in some book and I've always remembered it, and found it to be true. Is it true then that grownups have a more difficult time here than we do? No. I know it isn't. Older people have formed their opinions about everything, and don't waver before they act. It's twice as hard for us young ones to hold our ground, and maintain our opinions, in a time when all ideals are being shattered and destroyed, when people are showing their worst side, and do not know whether to believe in truth and right and God.

Anyone who claims that the older ones have a more difficult time here certainly doesn't realize to what extent our problems weigh down on us, problems for which we are probably much too young, but which thrust themselves upon us continually, until, after a long time, we think we've found a solution, but the solution doesn't seem able to resist the facts which reduce it to nothing again. That's the difficulty in these times: ideals, dreams, and cherished hopes rise within us, only to meet the horrible truth and be shattered.

It's really a wonder that I haven't dropped all my ideals, because they seem so absurd and impossible to carry out. Yet I keep them, because in spite of everything I still believe that people are really good at heart. I simply can't build up my hopes on a foundation consisting of confusion, misery, and death. I see the world gradually being turned into a wilderness, I hear the ever approaching thunder, which will destroy us too, I can feel the sufferings of millions and yet, if I look up into the heavens, I think that it will all come right, that this cruelty too will end, and that peace and tranquillity will return again.

In the meantime, I must uphold my ideals, for perhaps the time will come when I shall be able to carry them out.

Yours, Anne

EPILOGUE

Anne's diary ends here. On August 4, 1944, the Grüne Polizei made a raid on the "Secret Annexe." All the occupants, together with Kraler and Koophuis, were arrested and sent to German and Dutch concentration camps.

The "Secret Annexe" was plundered by the Gestapo. Among a pile of old books, magazines, and newspapers which were left lying on the floor, Miep and Elli found Anne's diary. Apart from a very few passages, which are of little interest to the reader, the original text has been printed.

Of all the occupants of the "Secret Annexe," Anne's father alone returned. Kraler and Koophuis, who withstood the hardships of the Dutch camp, were able to go home to their families.

In March, 1945, two months before the liberation of Holland, Anne died in the concentration camp at Bergen-Belsen.

✎§ FOR DISCUSSION AND WRITING

1. For what good psychological reason does Anne address her diary as "Kitty," as if the diary were another girl? How is the illusion of the diary as a person —a confidante—kept up in other ways? Note how she objectifies herself also ("Now, Anne") as if she were two people carrying on a dialogue. Point out occasions when she discusses herself as two people; what are the different characteristics of the two Annes?

2. Does it seem to you that Anne's sense of dual personality is psychologically normal? Or is it unusually accentuated? Does the diary, as "Kitty," act as a projection of one of Anne's selves, or as a neutral "captive audience"? Write a paragraph in which you show that the diary serves a problem-solving function for her. Write another paragraph supporting the idea that Anne is unusually honest and objective about herself and others (Peter and her father, for instance), or that she is highly introverted and self-centered.

3. This diary has become extraordinarily famous, both here and in Europe. Do you feel that its fame is due largely to the tragic circumstances in which it was written? Or do you think the diary has its own intrinsic value as a sensitive and moving portrait of a young girl? Write a paragraph support-ing one of these positions. Or is there a third critical position to take?

4. Anne says that she wants to become a writer. Do you find specific indica-tions that she has a writer's potentialities? Point these out. Does her ten-dency toward self-analysis and analysis of her relations with other people seem to you a "writer's" trait? What kind of writer?

5. Note in her description of the crisis with her father over her relation with Peter that she relates much of the episode in dialogue—the actual conver-sation with her father and afterwards her conversation with Peter. Does this handling of the episode seem to you to indicate a writer's instinct?

Why? Try rewriting these two conversations in *indirect* discourse. Is there a difference in effectiveness? Now try a slight exercise in direct discourse yourself: recall some fairly critical incident between two people and write it in dialogue. Change it into indirect discourse. What is the loss or gain between the two types of handling?

6. Keeping a diary of the kind that Anne kept, one that is not merely a set of humdrum entries but that acts as a kind of forum for one's inner self, one's feelings and problems, can be an enormously fruitful psychological activity—and it can also help materially to develop one's writing ability. Fortunately, it is an activity that becomes more pleasurable and even necessary, the longer and more conscientiously one keeps it up. Write a fairly extensive diary entry for one day, describing and discussing with yourself those things that have real significance for you. Try to write up the entry in such a way that, if you were to reread it six months later, the day would "come alive" again, returning vividly to your memory.

Fathers and Sons

THE IMPRINT *that the parent-child relationship leaves on our minds is
one which, subtly and ineluctably, rules our lives. Nowhere has that
relationship been set forth more powerfully than in the last book of
the* ILIAD,[1] *where the old king comes alone at night into the enemy's
camp to beg for the desecrated body of his son, saying, "Achilles,
fear the gods, and be merciful to me, remembering your own father,
though I am even more entitled to compassion, since I have brought
myself to do a thing that no one else on earth has done—I have raised
to my lips the hand of the man who killed my son." The towers of
Ilium will fall in flame, the princes slain, the princesses led weeping
into slavery; Agamemnon will be poleaxed like a bull in the
slaughterhouse; Orestes will plunge his sword in the breast that nursed
him, then go screaming into exile with the snake-haired Furies
hacking at his brain-roots; Odysseus will be washed up on the Ithacan
rocks, a sodden and filthy piece of wreckage, to be tossed a bone
like a tramp and cursed from his own threshold—all that is yet to come,
the pain, bloodshed, and madness that arose from the inextinguishable
guilt of the war. But first there is this moment of quiet, in the night*

[1] It is perhaps needful to remind students that the *Iliad* is a poem, the greatest poem
of ancient times. The prose translation here does, however, keep Homer's dramatic
vitality. Those who want to read more of the *Iliad* might go to Richmond Latti-
more's recent and noble translation of the poem in verse.

in the tented camp, on the shore where the black ships are beached, when what it means to be a father, what it means to be a son, are rendered with matchless humanity and nobility.

From the ILIAD *to Lord Chesterfield is a leap from a semi-pastoral society, invaded by Bronze-Age warriors, to eighteenth-century security, worldliness, and wit. Instead of the tragic simplicity of Priam's appeal to Achilles, we have the urbanity of the diplomat-father's advice to his son on how to behave in a drawing room and how to polish off one's wild oats with metropolitan distinction. The soundness of the advice is matched by the elegance of the semicolons, balancing clause against clause in a dance-measure like that of Pope's or Dryden's couplets.*

No uncertainties there, about who knows what to do and how it should be done. But shortly thereafter the paternal-filial bond began to show strain and warping. The father, poor fellow, had been carrying on his back the immense burden of a symbolism which racial history had laid on him; he was the porter designated by his genetic and economic role to bear the wisdom of the ages and transfer it to his heirs so that they might live and prosper like their father and his father before him. Between the eighteenth and the nineteenth centuries, when there were revolutions going on all over, a good deal of that baggage, the wisdom of the ages, was shuffled off, and fathers began to cut a poorer figure. In Jane Austen's novels, the father is irresponsible or a wheel-chair invalid or dead (thus no need to think up a useful role for him); in Stendhal he is a peasant brute; in Balzac he is a psychopath; in Dickens an ass or a crook.

In our own century, Sherwood Anderson's "Discovery of a Father" cuts through the father-son clichés on which we are nurtured and tries the father in an equivocal balance; traditionally above judgment, he is judged by a son not yet dry behind the ears and found culpably wanting. All the tremendous inherited symbolism of the father is put in question here. Shockingly and wonderfully, the relationship is reconstituted by a night swim, father and son joined again in wordless trust through the influence of the primal maternal mystery, water. This is a story of baptism and rebirth, strangely moving in its truthfulness and simplicity.

In the selection from Joyce, called here "A Sundering," and in Kafka's "Letter to His Father," one sees the primordial enchanted image of the father undergoing ruinous transformation, creating ruin about it. The image is immortal; we cannot get rid of it; it inhabits the child and the adult through all their generations forever. That is why it is so boundlessly important what kind of imprint the father leaves, as an immortal portion of himself, on the child's mind. Simon Dedalus, dragging his son from pub to pub as he brags and slobbers with his old Cork cronies, and Kafka's father, bloated with paternal rectitude, witlessly unaware that his son is another person and not a mere adjunct of himself, seem, in their obliviousness, to be acting out a blind tragedy in which only the child has eyes to see where the wound is coming from—this infinite wrong that can never be healed. Never, unless by some psychological miracle, the child should learn a rare charity and take on the role of parent to his own father, cherishing him as one would a child. This, possibly, is what happened in Joyce's FINNEGANS WAKE.

In Proust's "Filial Sentiments of a Parricide," the enchantment exercised by the image of the father is so powerful that the son never finds his separateness. We are led back through ancient paths to mad Orestes, who stabbed his mother, and to that great king, Oedipus, who slew his father and usurped his father's place in the bed of the queen, then tore out his own eyes because, seeing, they had been blind. These are sacred, kingly characters, having suffered so terribly the obscure, fateful ways of human inheritance and responsibility.

The students reading these pieces will be able to confront and, it is hoped, to write about this most important of all culture-dramas—the drama of the relationship between parent and child—with a unique freshness, immediacy, and perceptiveness, simply because they are young and are themselves plunged in that drama.

Homer ᦒ Priam and Achilles

ᦒ Almost nothing is known about the greatest poet of ancient Greece. Herodotus says that he lived "400 years before my time," that is, around 850 B.C. His birthplace was somewhere on the coast of Asia Minor or on one of the near islands. The Trojan war, if it is an authentic historical event, probably occurred around 1250 B.C. In Plato's *Ion* the chief interlocutor, for whom the dialogue is named, is one of the minstrel poets, or "rhapsodes," who recited Homer's poems at great public festivals, making them a part of popular culture. ᦒ

[*The previous action in the* Iliad *that is relevant here may be summarized briefly. Agamemnon, commander-in-chief of the Greek armie and Achilles, their greatest warrior and hero, quarrel over the spoils of war, and Achilles feels that Agamemnon has unfairly "pulled his rank" in taking as concubine a girl claimed by Achilles. So Achilles refuses to fight, morosely keeping to his tents during the battles between the Greeks and the Trojans. Eventually, Achilles' closest friend, Patroclus, is killed by Hector, son of the Trojan king, Priam, and the Trojans' chief warrior. Then Achilles comes out to fight, and he kills Hector. But he is not satisfied with that: in his furious vengeance for the death of his friend, he drags Hector's body, tied to his chariot, daily in the dust around the funeral barrow of Patroclus. The narrative below, from the last book of the poem, begins at this point.*]

ZEUS was obeyed by Thetis,[1] goddess of the Silver Feet, who at once sped down from the peak of Olympus[2] to her son's hut. She found him moaning piteously while his comrades bustled round him in busy prepa-

From the *Iliad* by Homer, translated by E. V. Rieu (Harmondsworth: Penguin Books Ltd., 1950), Book XXIV. Reprinted with the permission of the publisher.

[1] Achilles' mother, daughter of an ancient sea-god. She was given by the gods in marriage to a mortal, Peleus, Achilles' father.

[2] Historic mountain in Greece, anciently thought to be the home of the gods.

ration of the morning meal, for which a large woolly sheep was being slaughtered in the hut. Achilles' lady Mother sat down close beside him, stroked him with her hand and spoke to him. 'My child,' she said, 'how much longer are you going to eat your heart out in lamentation and misery, forgetful even of your food and bed? Is there no comfort in a woman's arms — for you, who have so short a time to live and stand already in the shadow of Death and inexorable Destiny? Listen to me now and understand that I come to you from Zeus, who wishes you to know that the gods are displeased with you and that he himself is the angriest of them all, because in your senseless fury you refused to part with Hector's body and have kept it by your beaked ships. Come now, give it back and accept a ransom for the dead.'

'So be it,' said Achilles of the swift feet. 'If the Olympian is in earnest and himself commands me, let them bring the ransom and take away the corpse.'

While the two conversed down there among the ships — and Mother and son had much to say to one another — Zeus despatched Iris[3] to sacred Ilium.[4] 'Off with you, Iris, fast as you can,' he said. 'Leave your Olympian home and take a message to King Priam in Ilium. Tell him to ransom his son by going to the Achaean[5] ships himself with gifts to melt Achilles' heart. He must go alone, without a single Trojan to escort him, except maybe one of the older heralds, who could drive the mule-cart and bring back to Troy the body of the man whom the great Achilles killed. Tell him not to think of death and to have no fears whatever. We will send him the best of escorts, Hermes the Giant-Slayer, who will remain in charge till he has brought him into Achilles' presence. Once inside the hut no one is going to kill him, neither Achilles himself nor anybody else. Achilles will see to that. He is no fool; he knows what he is doing, and he is not a godless man. On the contrary, he will spare his suppliant and show him every courtesy.'

Iris of the Whirlwind Feet flew off on her errand and came to Priam's palace, where sounds of lamentation met her. In the courtyard Priam's sons were sitting round their father, drenching their clothes with tears, and there in the middle sat the old man like a figure cut in stone,

---

[3] Goddess of the rainbow and messenger of Zeus.

[4] Troy.

[5] Greek.

wrapped up in his cloak, with his head and neck defiled by the dung he had gathered in his hands as he grovelled on the ground. His daughters and his sons' wives were wailing through the house, thinking of the many splendid men who had lost their lives at Argive[6] hands and now lay dead.

The Angel of Zeus went up to Priam and addressed him. She spoke in a gentle voice, but his limbs began at once to tremble. 'Courage, Dardanian Priam!'[7] she said. 'Compose yourself and have no fears. I come here not as a herald of evil but on a friendly mission. And I am sent to you by Zeus, who, far off as he is, is much concerned on your behalf and pities you. The Olympian bids you ransom Prince Hector by taking presents to Achilles which will melt his heart. You must go alone, without a single Trojan to escort you, except maybe one of the older heralds, who could drive the mule-cart and bring back to Troy the body of your son whom the great Achilles killed. You are not to think of death, and to have no fears at all, since the best of escorts, Hermes the Giant-Slayer,[8] will accompany you and remain in charge till he has brought you into Achilles' presence. Once inside the hut, no one is going to kill you, neither Achilles himself nor anybody else. Achilles will see to that. He is no fool; he knows what he is doing, and he is not a godless man. No, he will spare his suppliant and show you every courtesy.'

Her message delivered, Fleet-foot Iris disappeared. Priam told his sons at once to get ready a smooth-running mule-cart with a wicker body lashed on top. Then he went to his lofty bedroom, which was built of cedar-wood and was full of precious ornaments. He called to Hecabe, his wife. 'My dear,' he said to her, 'an Olympian Messenger has come to me from Zeus and told me to ransom Hector's body by going to the Achaean ships with gifts to melt Achilles' heart. Tell me, what do you make of that? I myself feel impelled to go down to the ships and pay this visit to the great Achaean camp.'

His wife cried out, 'Alas!' when she heard this. 'Where is the wisdom which people from abroad and your own subjects used to praise in you? How can you think of going by yourself to the Achaean ships,

[6] Greeks of Argos, in the Peloponnesus.

[7] Dardanos, son of Zeus, was supposed to be the ancestor of the Trojan kings.

[8] Hermes charmed the many-eyed giant Argus to sleep and slew him.

into the presence of a man who has killed so many gallant sons of yours? You must have a heart of iron. Once you are in his power, once he sets eyes on you, that beast of prey, that treacherous brute, will show you no mercy at all, nor have any respect for your person. No; all we can do now is to sit at home and bewail our son from here. *This* must be the end that inexorable Destiny spun for him with the first thread of life when I brought him into the world — to glut the nimble dogs, far from his parents, in the clutches of a monster whose very heart I would devour if I could get my teeth in it. That would requite him for what he has done to my son, who after all was not playing the coward when Achilles killed him, but fighting, without any thought of flight or cover, in defense of the sons and deep-bosomed daughters of Troy.'

'I mean to go,' said the venerable godlike Priam. 'Do not keep me back or go about the house yourself like a bird of ill-omen — you will not dissuade me. If any human being, an augur[9] or a priest, had made me this suggestion, I should have doubted his good faith and held aloof. But I heard the goddess' voice myself; I saw her there in front of me. So I am going, and I will not act as though she had never spoken. If I am doomed to die by the ships of the bronze-clad Achaeans, then I choose death. Achilles can kill me out of hand, once I have clasped my son in my arms and wept my fill.'

Going to his coffers, Priam lifted their ornamented lids and took out twelve beautiful robes, twelve single cloaks, as many sheets, as many white mantles and as many tunics to go with them. He also weighed and took ten talents[10] of gold; and he took two shining tripods, four cauldrons and a very lovely cup, which the Thracians had given him when he went to them on an embassy. It was a household treasure that the old man valued highly, but so great was his desire to recover his beloved son that he did not hesitate to part with it also.

There were a number of townsfolk in the portico. Priam gave these the rough side of his tongue and sent them all about their business. 'Away with you,' he cried, 'riffraff and wastrels! Have you no cause for tears in your own homes, that you must come and vex me here? Is it a trifling thing to you that Zeus the Son of Cronos has afflicted me with the loss of my finest son? If so, you will learn better. The Achaeans will

[9] One qualified to read omens.
[10] Certain weights of gold used as money.

find you easier game by far with Hector dead. And as for me, I only
hope I may go down to Hades' Halls before I see the city plundered
and laid waste.'

As he spoke he fell upon them with his staff, and they fled from the
house before the violent old man. Next he fell foul of his sons. He
shouted angrily at Helenus, Paris and the excellent Agathon; at Pam-
mon and Antiphonus and warlike Polites; Deiphobus, Hippothous and
lordly Dius. He trounced all nine of them and then he told them once
more what to do. 'Bestir yourself,' he cried, 'my good-for-nothing and
inglorious sons! I only wish you had all been killed beside the gallant
ships instead of Hector. Ah, how calamity has dogged me! I had the
best sons in the broad realm of Troy. Now all of them are gone, the godlike Mestor, Troilus that happy charioteer, and Hector, who walked
among us like a god and looked more like a god's son than a man's.
The war has taken them and left me these, a despicable crew — yes,
rascals all of you, heroes of the dance, who win your laurels on the
ball-room floor when you are not engaged in robbing your own people
of their sheep and kids. Can't you get busy, sirs? I want the cart prepared
at once and all these things put in it. I am waiting to be off.'

Priam's sons were terrified by his fulminations and quickly fetched
a fine new mule-cart with strong wheels and lashed a wicker body on it.
They took down from its peg a yoke of box-wood for the mules, with
a knob in the middle and the proper guides for the reins; and with the
yoke they brought out a yoke-band nine cubits long. They laid the yoke
carefully on the polished shaft, in the notch at the end of it, slipped
the ring over the pin, carried the yoke-band round the knob with three
turns either way, then wound it closely round the shaft and tucked the
loose end in. This done, they went to the bedroom, fetched the princely
gifts that were to buy back Hector's corpse, and packed them in the
wooden cart. Then they yoked the sturdy mules, who were trained to
work in harness and had been presented to the King with the compliments of the Mysian people. Finally, to Priam's chariot they yoked the
horses that the old man kept for his own use and fed at the polished
manger.

As Priam and the herald stood lost in anxious thought while the
vehicles were prepared for them under the high roof of the palace, they
were approached by Hecabe in great distress, carrying a golden cup

of mellow wine in her right hand for them to make a drink-offering before they left. She came up to the chariot and spoke to Priam himself. 'There,' she said. 'Make a libation to Father Zeus and pray for your safe return from the enemy's hands, since you are set on going to the ships. You go against my will, but if go you must, address your prayer to the Son of Cronos, the Lord of the Black Cloud, the god of Ida,[11] who sees the whole of Troyland spread beneath him. Ask for a bird of omen, a swift ambassador from him. And let it be his favourite prophetic bird, the strongest thing on wings, flying on your right so that you can see it with your own eyes and put your trust in it as you go down to the ships of the horse-loving Danaans.[12] But if all-seeing Zeus refuses to send you his messenger, I should advise you not to go down to the Argive ships, however much you may have set your heart on it.'

'My dear,' said the godlike Priam, 'I will surely do as you suggest. It is a good thing to lift up one's hands to Zeus and ask him for his blessing.' The old man then told his housekeeper to pour clean water on his hands. She brought a jug and basin and attended on him. When he had washed his hands he took the cup from his wife, went to the middle of the forecourt to pray, looked up into the sky as he poured out the wine, and made his petition aloud. 'Father Zeus, you that rule from Ida, most glorious and great; grant that Achilles may receive me with kindness and compassion; and send me a bird of omen, your swift ambassador, the one that you yourself like best, the strongest thing on wings. Let it fly on the right so that I can see it with my own eyes and put my trust in it as I go down to the ships of the horse-loving Danaans.'

Zeus the Thinker heard Priam's prayer and instantly sent out an eagle, the best of prophetic birds. He was one of those dusky hunters whose colour calls to mind the ripening grape, and when his wings were spread they would have stretched across the stout double doors of the lofty bedroom in a rich man's house. They spied him flying on their right across the town, and were overjoyed at the sight. He warmed the hearts of all.

The old man hastily mounted his chariot and drove out by the gateway and its echoing colonnade. He was preceded by the four-wheeled cart, drawn by the mules and driven by the wise Idaeus. Then

[11] Mountain in Asia Minor.
[12] Another name for the Greeks.

came Priam's horses. The old man used his whip and drove them quickly through the town; yet even so a crowd of friends kept up with him, wailing incessantly as though he had been going to his death. But when they had made their way down through the streets and reached the open country, these people, his sons and sons-in-law, turned back into Ilium and went home.

Zeus, with his all-observant eye, saw the two men strike out across the plain. He felt sorry for the old king and turned at once to his Son Hermes. He said: 'Hermes, a task for you. Escorting men is your prerogative and pleasure; and you are amiable with those you like. So off you go now, and conduct King Priam to the Achaeans' hollow ships in such a way that not a single Danaan shall see and recognize him till he reaches Peleus' son.'

Zeus had spoken. The Guide and Giant-Killer at once obeyed him and bound under his feet the lovely sandals of untarnishable gold that carried him with the speed of the wind over the water or the boundless earth; and he picked up the wand which he can use at will to cast a spell on our eyes or wake us from the soundest sleep. With this wand in his hand the mighty Giant-Slayer made his flight and soon reached Troyland and the Hellespont. There he proceeded on foot, looking like a young prince at that most charming age when the beard first starts to grow.

Meanwhile the two men had driven past the great barrow of Ilus and stopped their mules and horses for a drink at the river. Everything was dark by now, and it was not till Hermes was quite close to them that the herald looked up and saw him. He at once turned round to Priam and said: 'Look, your majesty; we must beware. I see a man, and I am afraid we may be butchered. Let us make our escape in the chariot, or if not that, fall at his knees and implore his mercy.'

The old man was dumbfounded and filled with terror; the hairs stood up on his supple limbs; he was rooted to the spot and could not say a word. But the Bringer of Luck did not wait to be accosted. He went straight up to Priam, took him by the hand and began to question him. 'Father,' he said, 'where are you driving to with those horses and mules through the solemn night when everyone else is asleep? Are you not afraid of the fiery Achaeans, those bitter enemies of yours, so close at hand? If one of them saw you coming through the black night with such a tempting load, what could you do? You are not young enough to cope with anyone that might assault you; and your companion is an old man too. However, I certainly do not mean you harm. In fact I am going to see that no one else molests you; for you remind me of my own father.'

'Our plight, dear son,' said the venerable old king, 'is very much as you describe it. But even so some god must have meant to protect me when he let me fall in with a wayfarer like you, who come as a godsend, if I may judge by your distinguished looks and bearing, as well as your good sense, which all betoken gentle birth.'

'Sir,' said the Guide and Slayer of Argus, 'you are very near the mark! But now I ask you to confide in me. Are you sending a hoard of treasure to some place of safety in a foreign land? Or has the time come when you are all deserting sacred Ilium in panic at the loss of your best man, your own son, who never failed to keep the enemy at bay?'

Priam the old king replied with a question: 'Who are you, noble sir, that speak to me so kindly of the fate of my unhappy son? Who are your parents?' To which Hermes replied: 'I suppose you are testing me, my venerable lord, and trying to discover what I know of Prince Hector. Well, I have seen him with my own eyes, and seen him often, in the field of honour. And what is more, I saw him hurl back the Argives on their ships and mow them down with his bronze, while we stood by and marvelled, since Achilles would not let us fight, having quarrelled with King Agamemnon. For I must tell you that I am a squire of Achilles, who came here in the same good ship as he. I am a Myrmidon[13] and my father is Polyctor, a rich man and about as old as yourself. He has seven sons, of whom I am the youngest; and when we drew lots it fell to me to join the expedition here. To-night I left the ships and came onto the plain, because at daybreak the bright-eyed Achaeans are intending to assault the town. They are tired of sitting here, and so eager for a fight that the Achaean chieftains cannot hold them in.'

Priam replied: 'If you really are a squire of Prince Achilles, I implore you to tell me the whole truth. Is my son still by the ships, or has Achilles already thrown him piecemeal to his dogs?'

'So far, my lord, neither the dogs nor the birds of prey have eaten him,' said the Slayer of Argus. 'His body is intact and lies there in the hut beside Achilles' ship. And though he has been there for eleven days, his flesh has not decayed at all, nor has it been attacked by the worms

13 A soldier of Achilles' personal troops.

that devour the bodies of men killed in battle. It is true that every day at the peep of dawn Achilles drags him mercilessly round the barrow[14] of his beloved comrade; but he does no harm to him by that. If you went into the hut yourself, you would be astonished to see him lying there as fresh as dew, the blood all washed away and not a stain upon him. Also, his wounds have closed, every wound he had; and there were many men who struck him with their bronze. Which shows what pains the blessed gods are taking in your son's behalf though he is nothing but a corpse, because they love him dearly.'

The old man rejoiced when he heard this and said: 'My child, what an excellent thing it is, whatever else one does, to give the gods their proper offerings! I am thinking of my son, who, as surely as he lived, never neglected the gods of Olympus in our home. It is for that that they are giving him credit at this moment, though he has met his fate and died. But now I beg you to accept this beautiful cup from me, and under the protecting hand of Heaven, yourself to see me safely to the ships and into my lord Achilles' hut.'

'Sir,' said the Guide and Giant-Killer, 'you are an old man and I am young; yet you tempt me to take a bribe from you behind Achilles' back. No! If I were to defraud my master I should be thoroughly ashamed and terrified of the consequences to myself. However, I am ready to serve you as escort all the way to famous Argos and to be your faithful henchman on board ship or on the land. No one would be tempted to attack you through undervaluing your guard.'

With that, the Bringer of Luck leapt into the horse-chariot, seized the whip and reins, and put fresh heart into the horses and mules. When they came to the trench and the wall round the ships, they found the sentries just beginning to prepare their supper. But the Slayer of Argus put them all to sleep, unfastened the gates, thrust back the bars, and ushered Priam in with his cartload of precious gifts. And they went on, to the lofty hut of Peleus' son.

The Myrmidons had built this hut for their prince with planks of deal cut by themselves, and had roofed it with a downy thatch of rushes gathered in the meadows. It stood in a large enclosure surrounded by a close-set fence, and the gate was fastened by a single pine-wood bar. It used to take three men to drive home this mighty bolt and three to draw it; three ordinary men of course — Achilles could work it by himself.

14 Mound over a grave.

And now Hermes, Bringer of Luck, opened up for the old king, drove in
with the splendid presents destined for the swift Achilles, and said to
Priam as he dismounted from the chariot: 'I would have you know, my
venerable lord, that you have been visited by an immortal god, for I am
Hermes, and my Father sent me to escort you. But I shall leave you now,
as I do not intend to go into Achilles' presence. It would be unbecoming
for a deathless god to accept a mortal's hospitality. But go inside yourself, clasp Achilles' knees, and as you pray to him invoke his father and
his lady Mother and his son, so as to touch his heart.'

With that, Hermes went off to high Olympus. Priam leapt down
from his chariot, and leaving Idaeus there to look after the horses and
mules, walked straight up to the hut where Prince Achilles usually sat.
He found him in. Most of his men were sitting some way off, but two of
them, the lord Automedon and the gallant Alcimus, were waiting on
him busily, as he had just finished eating and drinking and his table had
not yet been moved. Big though Priam was, he came in unobserved,
went up to Achilles, grasped his knees and kissed his hands, the terrible,
man-killing hands that had slaughtered many of his sons. Achilles was
astounded when he saw King Priam, and so were all his men. They
looked at each other in amazement, as people do in a rich noble's hall
when a foreigner who has murdered a man in his own country and is
seeking refuge abroad bursts in on them like one possessed.

But Priam was already praying to Achilles. 'Most worshipful
Achilles,' he said, 'think of your own father, who is the same age as I,
and so has nothing but miserable old age ahead of him. No doubt his
neighbours are oppressing him and there is nobody to save him from
their depredations. Yet he at least has one consolation. While he knows
that you are still alive, he can look forward day by day to seeing his
beloved son come back from Troy; whereas my fortunes are completely
broken. I had the best sons in the whole of this broad realm, and not one,
not one I say, is left. There were fifty when the Achaean expedition
came. Nineteen of them were borne by one mother and the rest by other
ladies in my palace. Most of them have fallen in action, and Hector, the
only one I still could count on, the bulwark of Troy and the Trojans, has
now been killed by you, fighting for his native land. It is to get him
back from you that I have come to the Achaean ships, bringing this
princely ransom with me. Achilles, fear the gods, and be merciful to me,
remembering your own father, though I am even more entitled to com-

passion, since I have brought myself to do a thing that no one else on earth has done — I have raised to my lips the hand of the man who killed my son.'

Priam had set Achilles thinking of his own father and brought him to the verge of tears. Taking the old man's hand, he gently put him from him; and overcome by their memories they both broke down. Priam, crouching at Achilles' feet, wept bitterly for man-slaying Hector, and Achilles wept for his father, and then again for Patroclus. The house was filled with the sounds of their lamentation. But presently, when he had had enough of tears and recovered his composure, the excellent Achilles leapt from his chair, and in compassion for the old man's grey head and grey beard, took him by the arm and raised him. Then he spoke to him from his heart: 'You are indeed a man of sorrows and have suffered much. How could you dare to come by yourself to the Achaean ships into the presence of a man who has killed so many of your gallant sons? You have a heart of iron. But pray be seated now, here on this chair, and let us leave our sorrows, bitter though they are, locked up in our own hearts, for weeping is cold comfort and does little good. We men are wretched things, and the gods, who have no cares themselves, have woven sorrow into the very pattern of our lives. You know that Zeus the Thunderer has two jars standing on the floor of his Palace, in which he keeps his gifts, the evils in one and the blessings in the other. People who receive from him a mixture of the two have varying fortunes, sometimes good and sometimes bad, though when Zeus serves a man from the jar of evil only, he makes him an outcast, who is chased by the gadfly of despair over the face of the earth and goes his way damned by gods and men alike. Look at my father, Peleus. From the moment he was born, Heaven showered its brightest gifts upon him, fortune and wealth unparalleled on earth, the kingship of the Myrmidons, and though he was a man, a goddess for his wife. Yet like the rest of us he knew misfortune too — no children in his palace to carry on the royal line, only a single son doomed to untimely death.[15] And what is more, though he is growing old, he gets no care from me, because I am sitting here in your country, far from my own, making life miserable for you and your children. And you, my lord — I understand there was a time when fortune smiled upon you also. They say that there was no one to compare with

[15] The gods gave Achilles the choice of living a long life in security or dying an early death as a hero, and he chose the latter.

you for wealth and splendid sons in all the lands that are contained by Lesbos in the sea, where Macar reigned, and Upper Phrygia and the boundless Hellespont. But ever since the Heavenly Ones brought me here to be a thorn in your side, there has been nothing but battle and slaughter round your city. You must endure and not be broken-hearted. Lamenting for your son will do no good at all. You will be dead yourself before you bring him back to life.'

'Do not ask me to sit down, your highness,' said venerable Priam, 'while Hector lies neglected in your huts, but give him back to me without delay and let me set my eyes on him. Accept the splendid ransom that I bring. I hope you will enjoy it and get safely home, because you spared me when I first appeared.'

'Old man, do not drive me too hard,' said the swift Achilles, frowning at Priam. 'I have made up my mind without your help to give Hector back to you. My own Mother, the Daughter of the Old Man of the Sea, has brought me word from Zeus. Moreover, I have seen through *you*, Priam. You cannot hide the fact that some god brought you to the Achaean ships. Nobody, not even a young man at his best, would venture by himself into our camp. For one thing he would never pass the sentries unchallenged; and if he did, he would find it hard to shift the bar we keep across our gate. So do not exasperate me now, sir, when I have enough already on my mind, or I may break the laws of Zeus and, suppliant though you are, show you as little consideration as I showed Hector in my huts.'

This frightened the old man, who took the reprimand to heart. Then, like a lion, the son of Peleus dashed out of doors, taking with him two of his squires, the lord Automedon and Alcimus, who were his favourites next to the dead Patroclus. They unyoked the horses and the mules, brought in the herald, old King Priam's crier, and gave him a stool to sit on. Then they took out of the polished waggon the princely ransom that had won back Hector's corpse. But they left a couple of white mantles and a fine tunic, in which Achilles could wrap up the body when he let Priam take it home. The prince then called some women-servants out and told them to wash and anoint the body, but in another part of the house, so that Priam should not see his son. (Achilles was afraid that Priam, if he saw him, might in the bitterness of grief be unable to restrain his wrath, and that he himself might fly into a rage and kill the old man, thereby sinning against Zeus.) When the maidservants had washed and anointed the body with olive-oil, and had wrapped it in a fine mantle and tunic, Achilles lifted it with his own hands onto a bier, and his comrades helped him to put it in the polished waggon. Then he gave a groan and called to his beloved friend by name: 'Patroclus, do not be vexed with me if you learn, down in the Halls of Hades, that I let his father have Prince Hector back. The ransom he paid me was a worthy one, and I will see that you receive your proper share even of that.'

The excellent Achilles went back into the hut, sat down on the inlaid chair he had left — it was on the far side of the room — and said to Priam: 'Your wishes are fulfilled, my venerable lord: your son has been released. He is lying on a bier and at daybreak you will see him for yourself as you take him away. But meanwhile let us turn our thoughts to supper. . . . Later, you can weep once more for your son, when you take him into Ilium. He will indeed be much bewept.'

The swift Achilles now bestirred himself and slaughtered a white sheep, which his men flayed and prepared in the usual manner. They deftly chopped it up, spitted the pieces, roasted them carefully and then withdrew them from the fire. Automedon fetched some bread and set it out on the table in handsome baskets; Achilles divided the meat into portions; and they helped themselves to the good things spread before them.

Their thirst and hunger satisfied, Dardanian Priam let his eyes dwell on Achilles and saw with admiration how big and beautiful he was, the very image of a god. And Achilles noted with equal admiration the noble looks and utterance of Dardanian Priam. It gave them pleasure thus to look each other over. But presently the old king Priam made a move. 'Your highness,' he said, 'I beg leave now to retire for the night. It is time that my companion and I went to bed and enjoyed the boon of sleep. My eyelids have not closed upon my eyes since the moment when my son lost his life at your hands. Ever since then I have been lamenting and brooding over my countless sorrows, grovelling in the dung in my stable-yard. Now at last I have had some food and poured sparkling wine down my throat; but before that I had tasted nothing.'

Thereupon Achilles instructed his men and maidservants to put bedsteads in the portico and to furnish them with fine purple rugs, spread sheets over these and add some thick blankets on top for covering. Torch in hand, the women went out of the living-room and busied themselves at this task. Two beds were soon prepared; and now the great runner Achilles spoke to Priam in a brusquer tone. 'You must sleep out of doors, my friend,' he said, 'in case some Achaean general pays me a visit. They often come here to discuss their plans with me — it is our custom. If one of them were to see you here at dead of night, he would at once tell Agamemnon the Commander-in-Chief, and your recovery of the body would be delayed. Another point. Will you tell me how many days you propose to devote to Prince Hector's funeral, so that I myself may refrain from fighting and keep the army idle for that space of time?'

To this the venerable king replied: 'If you really wish me to give Prince Hector a proper funeral, you will put me under an obligation, Achilles, by doing as you say. You know how we are cooped up in the city; it is a long journey to the mountains to fetch wood, and my people are afraid of making it. As for Hector's obsequies, we should be nine days mourning him in our homes. On the tenth we should bury him and hold the funeral feast, and on the eleventh build him a mound. On the twelfth, if need be, we will fight.'

'My venerable lord,' replied the swift and excellent Achilles, 'everything shall be as you wish. I will hold up the fighting for the time you require.'

With that, he gripped the old man by the wrist of his right hand, to banish all apprehension from his heart. So Priam and the herald settled down for the night there in the forecourt of the building, with much to occupy their busy minds, while Achilles slept in a corner of his well-made wooden hut with the beautiful Briseis[16] at his side.

Everyone else, men under arms and gods, spent the whole night in the soft lap of sleep. But Hermes, god of Luck, kept wondering how he was to bring King Priam away from the ships unchallenged by the trusty watchmen at the gate; and he could not get to sleep. In the end he went to the head of Priam's couch and said to him: 'My lord, it seems that, since Achilles spared you, you have no misgivings left, to judge by the soundness of your slumbers in the enemy camp. Just now he let you have the body of your son — at a great price. Would not the sons that are left you have to pay three times as much for you alive, if King Agamemnon and the whole army came to know that you are here?'

16 The girl who was the cause of the quarrel between Agamemnon and Achilles.

The old man's fears were roused, and he woke up the herald. Hermes then yoked the mules and horses for them and drove them quickly through the camp himself. They passed unrecognized; and as Dawn drew her saffron cloak over the countryside, they reached the ford of eddying Xanthus, the noble River whose Father is immortal Zeus. There Hermes, taking leave of them, set out for high Olympus; and the two men, wailing and weeping, drove the horses on towards the town while the mules came along with the body.

Cassandra,[17] beautiful as Golden Aphrodite, was the first among the men and girdled womenfolk of Troy to recognize them as they came. She had climbed to the top of Pergamus and from that point she saw her father standing in the chariot with the herald, his town-crier. She saw Hector too, lying on a bier in the mule-cart. She gave a scream and cried for all the town to hear: 'Trojans and women of Troy, you used to welcome Hector when he came home safe from battle. He was the darling of every soul in the town. Come out and see him now.'

Cassandra's cries plunged the whole town in grief, and soon there was not a man or woman left in Troy. They met the King with Hector's body at no great distance from the gates. His loving wife and lady mother fell upon the well-built waggon, to be the first to pluck their hair for him[18] and touch his head. They were surrounded by a wailing throng. Indeed the townsfolk would have stayed there by the gates and wept for Hector all day long till sunset, if the old man, who was still in the chariot, had not commanded them to make way for the mules and told them they could mourn for Hector later to their hearts' content, when he had got him home. The people, thus admonished, fell back on either side and made a passage for the cart, leaving the family to bring Hector to the palace.

Once there, they laid him on a wooden bed and brought in musicians to lead in the laments and sing the melancholy dirges while the women wailed in chorus. White-armed Andromache,[19] holding the head of Hector killer of men between her hands, gave them the first lament:

'Husband, you were too young to die and leave me widowed in our home. Your son, the boy that we unhappy parents brought into the world, is but a little baby. And I have no hope that he will grow into a

[17] Priam's daughter, who had the gift of prophecy.
[18] To cut off a lock of one's hair in honor of the dead.
[19] Hector's wife.

man: Troy will come tumbling down before that can ever be. For you, her guardian, have perished, you that watched over her and kept her loyal wives and little babies safe. They will be carried off soon in the hollow ships, and I with them. And you, my child, will go with me to labour somewhere at a menial task under a heartless master's eye; or some Achaean will seize you by the arm and hurl you from the walls to a cruel death, venting his wrath on you because Hector killed a brother of his own, maybe, or else his father or a son. Yes, when he met Hector's hands, many an Achaean bit the dust of this wide world; for your father was by no means kindly in the heat of battle. And that is why the whole of Troy is wailing for him now. Ah, Hector, you have brought utter desolation to your parents. But who will mourn you as I shall? Mine is the bitterest regret of all, because you did not die in bed and stretching out your arms to give me some tender word that I might have treasured in my tears by night and day.'

Such was Andromache's lament; and the women joined her. Next, Hecabe took up for them the impassioned dirge: 'Hector, dearest to me of all my sons, the gods loved you well while you were with me in the world; and now that Destiny has struck you down they have not forgotten you. Swift-foot Achilles took other sons of mine, and sent them over the barren seas for sale in Samos or in Imbros or in smoke-capped Lemnos. And he took your life with his long blade of bronze; but though he dragged you many times round the barrow of the friend you killed (not that he brought Patroclus back to life by that), you have come home to me fresh as the morning dew and are laid out in the palace like one whom Apollo of the Silver Bow has visited and put to death with gentle darts.'

Her words and sobs stirred all the women to unbridled grief. But Helen followed now and led them in a third lament: 'Hector, I loved you far the best of all my Trojan brothers. Prince Paris brought me here and married me (I wish I had perished first), but in all nineteen years since I came away and left my own country, it is from you that I have never heard a single harsh or spiteful word. Others in the house insulted me — your brothers, your sisters, your brothers' wealthy wives, even your mother, though your father could not be more gentle with me if he were my own. But you protested every time and stopped them, out of the kindness of your heart, in your own courteous way. So these tears of sorrow that I shed are both for you and for my miserable self. No one else is left in the wide realm of Troy to treat me gently and befriend me. They shudder at me as I pass.' Thus Helen through her tears; and the countless multitude wailed with her.

And now the old king Priam told his people what to do. 'Trojans,' he said, 'bring firewood to the town, and do not be afraid that the Argives may catch you in an ambuscade. Achilles undertook, when he let me leave the black ships, that they should not attack us till the dawn of the twelfth day from then.'

At Priam's orders, they yoked mules and bullocks to their waggons and assembled speedily outside the town. It took them nine days to gather the huge quantity of wood required. But when the dawn of the tenth day brought light to the world, they carried out the gallant Hector with tears on their cheeks, laid his body on top of the pyre and set fire to the wood.

Dawn came once more, lighting the East with rosy hands, and saw the people flock together at illustrious Hector's pyre. When all had arrived and the gathering was complete, they began by quenching the fire with sparkling wine in all parts of the pyre that the flames had reached. Then Hector's brothers and comrades-in-arms collected his white bones, lamenting as they worked, with many a big tear running down their cheeks. They took the bones, wrapped them in soft purple cloths and put them in a golden chest. This chest they quickly lowered into a hollow grave, which they covered with a layer of large stones closely set together. Then, hastily, they made the barrow, posting sentinels all round, in case the bronze-clad Achaeans should attack before the time agreed. When they had piled up the mound, they went back into Troy, foregathered again, and enjoyed a splendid banquet in the palace of King Priam, nursling of Zeus.

Such were the funeral rites of Hector, tamer of horses.

✎ FOR DISCUSSION AND WRITING

1. In order to bring this ancient story closer to our own climate of thought, let us assume that the "gods" correspond in some degree with those profound psychological functions we call instinct and intuition. Often enough, in our own dreams and fantasies, instinctive or intuitive impulses arise out

of our deepest unconscious and take the visual form of human or godlike beings; sometimes the dream-personage speaks, giving directives and commands in a mysterious language (which usually seems absurd to us, on waking up). Such dreams and fantasies are most likely to occur at a time of emotional crisis. Let us consider Achilles' vision of his goddess-mother, Thetis, and Priam's vision of Iris, the messenger of Zeus, in this way—as, so to speak, thought-processes so compelling and urgent that they enter consciousness with all the concreteness of visual images and of voices sounding in the mind.

Is the emotional condition of Achilles and of Priam such as might encourage such fantasies? (Note that Priam says later that he has not eaten since Hector's death. Fasting itself promotes visions.) Achilles is not naturally brutal; he is a complex, sophisticated character; "he knows what he is doing, and he is not a godless man," as Iris says to Priam. Since he has actually been committing an impious crime in his treatment of Hector's corpse (not allowing it burial), what would you say was the likelihood that he might suddenly wake up to the senselessness of his vengeance and get just such an idea as Thetis puts in his head—to give back Hector's body and accept a ransom? What appropriateness is there in the fact that it is a vision (a visual memory, let us say) of his *mother* that gives him the idea? Incidentally, are dreams or memories of one's mother as a goddess-like person unusual?

2. This whole episode, in the final book of the *Iliad,* is built around the powerful symbolism of the father-son relationship, which has, in Homeric society, much the same strength and significance that it has in the Old Testament (as, for instance, in the story of Abraham and Isaac, of Jacob and his sons, of David and Absalom). Hector is the greatest of Priam's sons, the chief defender of Troy, and the old man is broken up by his death. Attempt a similar explanation—like that given in Question 1— for his getting the sudden idea of making a personal appeal to Achilles for his son's body.

3. What is the reaction of Priam's wife, Hecabe, when she hears his plan? As she rails at him, do you get a genuine characterization of her? How does Priam treat her arguments? When the irritable old man rages down into the courtyard, scolding his sons as good-for-nothings and laying about him with his staff, do you feel that this is a psychologically sound characterization? Why or why not? (Like the patriarchs of the Old Testament, Priam apparently has numerous sons from concubines as well as from Hecabe, for tribal strength and continuity depended on having many

sons.) In what sense could you apply the term "realism" to these scenes, and to the description of the harnessing of the mules and preparation of the mule-cart? (Note that kings' sons have to work like stableboys here.)

4. For the old man to enter the enemy's camp alone and confront his son's killer is an extremely dangerous enterprise; the Greeks could murder him and Troy would undoubtedly fall at once, without its king. But when we follow a desperate "hunch," one that comes from the deepest part of our nature, it often seems that luck is with us—as if our truest impulses turned other things to our benefit; natural occurrences (like the eagle that suddenly flies over Troy) seem good omens and give us a psychological boost; sometimes, in a particularly tight place, strangers suddenly appear as if out of the blue and offer help. Could you interpret the appearance of Hermes (note that he is called "Bringer of Luck") in this way?

5. For sheer narrative skill and "story interest," Homer is unbeatable. Notice that the incident of Hermes' appearance and offer to guide the old man into the camp is treated as a little dramatic "scene," involving doubt and fear, questions, explanations, and reassurances, all handled through dialogue. Whenever possible, Homer contrives little realistic "scenes" of this kind to carry the narrative forward; this is one of the most valuable techniques of the modern storyteller as well. Point out in earlier and later parts of the tale other places where the technique of the "scene" is used.

6. In the great confrontation between Achilles and Priam, where, specifically, does the significance (or "symbolism") of the father-son relationship appear again and again as the dominating psychological element? What part does it play in Achilles' astonished reaction? How does Priam build on it to win Achilles over? Where is it indicated that what moves Achilles most deeply is the old man's courage in entering alone into such danger, only so that he might obtain his son's body for decent burial? Where, in Achilles' responses, do you find signs of a sensitive, complex, but also dangerous personality?

7. To round off this tremendous episode with such simple, homely matters as sharing a camp supper and going to bed seems an incredible piece of artistic daring (but there is more eating and going to bed in Homer than in any other author in history). Explain why this way of concluding the episode seems so "right" and is so moving. Where do you find the Homeric kind of "realism" in the details of the preparation of the supper and making the beds?

8. Priam dreams of Hermes, who advises him to get out of the camp during the night. Since our dream-thoughts do take the form of visual images, sometimes accompanied by words spoken, and since it is natural for dreams to have reference to what has been occupying one's mind—perhaps unconsciously—before sleep, could you explain Hermes' advice to Priam as simply an anxious mind's using its native wit and acting again on a "hunch," rather than as a supernatural visitation?

9. The questions have already touched on various aspects which might suggest either a critical or a descriptive essay; for instance, Homer's narrative technique, his "realism," the gods as representations of psychic attitudes taking visual form, the character of Achilles. Another subject might be a comparison of the significance, or symbolic value, of the son-father relationship as represented by Homer, and its modern significance; or the modern attitude toward old age as contrasted with that shown in this episode from the *Iliad*.

Lord Chesterfield ❧ Letter to His Son

❧ English statesman and diplomat (1694-1773), most famous for his letters to his illegitimate son Philip Stanhope; also gave his name to a style of overcoat and a kind of couch. ❧

BATH, OCTOBER 19, 1748.

Dear Boy,

Having, in my last, pointed out what sort of company you should keep, I will now give you some rules for your conduct in it; rules which my own experience and observation enable me to lay down and communicate to you with some degree of confidence. I have often given you hints of this kind before, but then it has been by snatches; I will now be more regular and methodical. I shall say nothing with regard to your bodily carriage and address, but leave them to the care of your dancing-master, and to your own attention to the best models: remember, however, that they are of consequence.

Talk often, but never long; in that case, if you do not please, at least you are sure not to tire your hearers. Pay your own reckoning, but

From *Letters to His Son* by Philip Dormer Stanhope, 4th Earl of Chesterfield (first published in 1774). The selection used here is reprinted from *Letters to His Son and Others* (London: J. M. Dent & Sons, 1945).

do not treat the whole company; this being one of the very few cases in which people do not care to be treated, every one being fully convinced that he has wherewithal to pay.

Tell stories very seldom, and absolutely never but where they are very apt, and very short. Omit every circumstance that is not material, and beware of digressions. To have frequent recourse to narrative betrays great want of imagination.

Never hold anybody by the button, or the hand, in order to be heard out; for, if people are not willing to hear you, you had much better hold your tongue than them.

Most long talkers single out some one unfortunate man in company (commonly him whom they observe to be the most silent, or their next neighbour) to whisper, or at least, in a half voice, to convey a continuity of words to. This is excessively ill-bred, and, in some degree, a fraud; conversation-stock being a joint and common property. But, on the other hand, if one of these unmerciful talkers lays hold on you, hear him with patience, and at least seeming attention, if he is worth obliging; for nothing will oblige him more than a patient hearing, as nothing would hurt him more than either to leave him in the midst of his discourse, or to discover your impatience under your affliction.

Take, rather than give, the tone of the company you are in. If you have parts,[1] you will show them, more or less, upon every subject; and, if you have not, you had better talk sillily upon a subject of other people's than of your own choosing.

Avoid as much as you can, in mixed companies, argumentative polemical conversations; which, though they should not, yet certainly do, indispose, for a time, the contending parties towards each other; and, if the controversy grows warm and noisy, endeavour to put an end to it by some genteel levity or joke. I quieted such a conversation hub-bub once, by representing to them that, though I was persuaded none there present would repeat, out of company, what passed in it, yet I could not answer for the discretion of the passengers in the street, who must necessarily hear all that was said.

Above all things, and upon all occasions, avoid speaking of yourself, if it be possible. Such is the natural pride and vanity of our hearts, that it perpetually breaks out, even in people of the best parts, in all the various modes and figures of the egotism.

[1] If you are intelligent.

Some abruptly speak advantageously of themselves, without either pretence or provocation. They are impudent. Others proceed more artfully, as they imagine, and forge accusations against themselves, complain of calumnies which they never heard, in order to justify themselves, by exhibiting a catalogue of their many virtues. "They acknowledge it may, indeed, seem odd, that they should talk in that manner of themselves; it is what they do not like, and what they never would have done; no, no torture should ever have forced it from them, if they had not been thus unjustly and monstrously accused. But, in these cases, justice is surely due to one's self, as well as to others; and, when our character is attacked, we may say, in our own justification, what otherwise we never would have said." This thin veil of modesty drawn before vanity, is much too transparent to conceal it, even from very moderate discernment.

Others go more modestly and more slyly still (as they think) to work; but, in my mind, still more ridiculously. They confess themselves (not without some degree of shame and confusion) into all the cardinal virtues; by first degrading them into weaknesses, and then owning their misfortune, in being made up of those weaknesses. "They cannot see people suffer, without sympathizing with, and endeavouring to help them. They cannot see people want, without relieving them; though, truly, their own circumstances cannot very well afford it. They cannot help speaking truth, though they know all the imprudence of it. In short, they know that, with all these weaknesses, they are not fit to live in the world, much less to thrive in it. But they are now too old to change, and must rub on as well as they can." This sounds too ridiculous and *outré*, almost for the stage; and yet, take my word for it, you will frequently meet with it upon the common stage of the world. And here I will observe, by the bye, that you will often meet with characters in nature so extravagant, that a discreet poet would not venture to set them upon the stage in their true and high colouring.

This principle of vanity and pride is so strong in human nature, that it descends even to the lowest objects; and one often sees people angling for praise, where, admitting all they say to be true (which, by the way, it seldom is), no just praise is to be caught. One man affirms that he had rode post[2] an hundred miles in six hours: probably it is a lie; but supposing it to be true, what then? Why, he is a very good post-

2 Rode fast, like a mail (post) carrier.

boy, that is all. Another asserts, and probably not without oaths, that
he has drank six or eight bottles of wine at a sitting; out of charity, I
will believe him a liar; for, if I do not, I must think him a beast.

Such, and a thousand more, are the follies and extravagancies,
which vanity draws people into, and which always defeat their own
purpose, and, as Waller says upon another subject:

> Make the wretch the most despised,
> Where most he wishes to be prized.*

The only sure way of avoiding these evils is never to speak of yourself at all. But when historically you are obliged to mention yourself,
take care not to drop one single word, that can directly or indirectly be
construed as fishing for applause. Be your character what it will, it will
be known; and nobody will take it upon your own word. Never imagine
that anything you can say yourself will varnish your defects, or add
lustre to your perfections; but, on the contrary, it may, and nine times
in ten will, make the former more glaring, and the latter obscure. If you
are silent upon your own subject, neither envy, indignation, nor ridicule
will obstruct or allay the applause which you may really deserve; but
if you publish your own panegyric, upon any occasion, or in any shape
whatsoever, and however artfully dressed or disguised, they will all
conspire against you, and you will be disappointed of the very end you
aim at.

Take care never to seem dark and mysterious; which is not only
a very unamiable character, but a very suspicious one too; if you seem
mysterious with others, they will be really so with you, and you will
know nothing. The height of abilities is, to have *volto sciolto* and *pensieri
stretti*;[3] that is, a frank, open, and ingenuous exterior, with a prudent
and reserved interior; to be upon your own guard, and yet, by a seeming
natural openness, to put people off theirs. Depend upon it, nine in ten
of every company you are in will avail themselves of every indiscreet
and unguarded expression of yours, if they can turn it to their own
advantage. A prudent reserve is therefore as necessary as a seeming
openness is prudent. Always look people in the face when you speak to

---

* These lines are adapted from Waller's *On Love*. The couplet is:
> Postures which render him despised,
> Where he endeavors to be prized.

[3] A candid appearance and reserved thoughts.

them; the not doing it is thought to imply conscious guilt; besides that, you lose the advantage of observing by their countenances what impression your discourse makes upon them. In order to know people's real sentiments, I trust much more to my eyes than to my ears; for they can say whatever they have a mind I should hear; but they can seldom help looking what they have no intention that I should know.

Neither retail nor receive scandal willingly; for though the defamation of others may for the present gratify the malignity of the pride of our hearts, cool reflection will draw very disadvantageous conclusions from such a disposition; and in the case of scandal, as in that of robbery, the receiver is always thought as bad as the thief.

Mimicry, which is the common and favourite amusement of little low minds, is in the utmost contempt with great ones. It is the lowest and most illiberal of all buffoonery. Pray, neither practise it yourself, nor applaud it in others. Besides that, the person mimicked is insulted; and, as I have often observed to you before, an insult is never forgiven.

I need not, I believe, advise you to adapt your conversation to the people you are conversing with; for I suppose you would not, without this caution, have talked upon the same subject and in the same manner to a Minister of state, a Bishop, a philosopher, a Captain, and a woman. A man of the world must, like the chameleon, be able to take every different hue, which is by no means a criminal or abject, but a necessary complaisance, for it relates only to manners, and not to morals.

One word only as to swearing; and that I hope and believe is more than is necessary. You may sometimes hear some people in good company interlard their discourse with oaths, by way of embellishment, as they think; but you must observe, too, that those who do so are never those who contribute in any degree to give that company the denomination of good company. They are always subalterns, or people of low education; for that practice, besides that it has no one temptation to plead, is as silly and as illiberal as it is wicked.

Loud laughter is the mirth of the mob, who are only pleased with silly things; for true wit or good sense never excited a laugh since the creation of the world. A man of parts and fashion is therefore only seen to smile, but never heard to laugh.

But, to conclude this long letter; all the above-mentioned rules, however carefully you may observe them, will lose half their effect if unaccompanied by the Graces. Whatever you say, if you say it with a supercilious, cynical face, or an embarrassed countenance, or a silly, disconcerted grin, will be ill received. If, into the bargain, *you mutter it, or utter it indistinctly and ungracefully,* it will be still worse received. If your air and address are vulgar, awkward, and *gauche,* you may be esteemed indeed if you have great intrinsic merit; but you will never please, and without pleasing you will rise but heavily. Venus, among the ancients, was synonymous with the Graces, who were always supposed to accompany her; and Horace tells us, that even youth, and Mercury, the god of arts and eloquence, would not do without her.

> —*Parum comis* sine te Juventas
> Mercuriusque.[4]

They are not inexorable ladies, and may be had if properly and diligently pursued. Adieu!

✑ FOR DISCUSSION AND WRITING

1. We can probably agree that Lord Chesterfield's advice to his son is, on the whole, eminently sane and practical, even today. Or would you disagree with this opinion? Point out a half-dozen instances where you think the advice has twentieth-century relevance—or a half-dozen instances to the contrary. This is a "worldly" kind of father: where do you find his worldliness best expressed? Is the quality of worldliness, as shown here, a good thing in a father or not? Is there a great difference, or little, between the qualities required for success in the highly competitive modern world and those required in the eighteenth century? How do you know?

2. Analyze the following sentences: 1) the first sentence in the second paragraph; 2) the fourth paragraph; 3) the last sentence in the fifth paragraph; 4) the second sentence in the sixth paragraph. (It is easier to analyze these if you copy them out. The copying gives you an actual "muscular" experience of the style.) What do these sentences have in common in the way in which they are constructed? Describe their syntax. What words apply to this kind of writing: balanced? antithetical? pithy? epigrammatic? Make the sublime effort of putting each of these four sentences in your own words, in a way that avoids the semicolon. Make the more sub-

---

[4] *Odes* I. 30: "Without thee, youth and even Mercury himself have no charm."

lime effort of writing one sentence of advice to yourself, or your brother or sister or mother or father or aunt or uncle, in the style of Lord Chesterfield, *with* a semicolon.

3. Judge Lord Chesterfield's advice, bit by bit, and write a paragraph in summary of your judgment.

4. Guess at the character of the old man from this letter.

5. Are these the counsels of morality, prudence, or expedience? What is the difference among these three?

6. Do you know of, or can you imagine, a father today writing a letter of this kind of detailed advice on manners to his son (a son in college, let us say)? If not, what has happened? Is the difference one of fathers? sons? culture? psychology? economic or "class" status? An essay subject is obviously suggested here.

Sherwood Anderson ✑ Discovery of a Father

✑ American short-story writer and novelist (1876-1941), whose stories in *Winesburg, Ohio* and *Triumph of the Egg* created a new idiom in the American short story. ҙ✑

YOU hear it said that fathers want their sons to be what they feel they cannot themselves be, but I tell you it also works the other way. A boy wants something very special from his father. I know that as a small boy I wanted my father to be a certain thing he was not. I wanted him to be a proud, silent, dignified father. When I was with other boys and he passed along the street, I wanted to feel a flow of pride: "There he is. That is my father."

But he wasn't such a one. He couldn't be. It seemed to me then that he was always showing off. Let's say someone in our town had got up a show. They were always doing it. The druggist would be in it, the shoe-store clerk, the horse doctor, and a lot of women and girls. My

From *Sherwood Anderson's Memoirs* (New York: Harcourt, Brace & World, Inc., 1942); copyright © 1939 by Eleanor Anderson. Reprinted by permission of Harold Ober Associates Incorporated.

father would manage to get the chief comedy part. It was, let's say, a Civil War play and he was a comic Irish soldier. He had to do the most absurd things. They thought he was funny, but I didn't.

I thought he was terrible. I didn't see how mother could stand it. She even laughed with the others. Maybe I would have laughed if it hadn't been my father.

Or there was a parade, the Fourth of July or Decoration Day. He'd be in that, too, right at the front of it, as Grand Marshal or something, on a white horse hired from a livery stable.

He couldn't ride for shucks. He fell off the horse and everyone hooted with laughter, but he didn't care. He even seemed to like it. I remember once when he had done something ridiculous, and right out on Main Street, too. I was with some other boys and they were laughing and shouting at him and he was shouting back and having as good a time as they were. I ran down an alley back of some stores and there in the Presbyterian Church sheds I had a good long cry.

Or I would be in bed at night and father would come home a little lit up and bring some men with him. He was a man who was never alone. Before he went broke, running a harness shop, there were always a lot of men loafing in the shop. He went broke, of course, because he gave too much credit. He couldn't refuse it and I thought he was a fool. I had got to hating him.

There'd be men I didn't think would want to be fooling around with him. There might even be the superintendent of our schools and a quiet man who ran the hardware store. Once I remember there was a white-haired man who was a cashier of the bank. It was a wonder to me they'd want to be seen with such a windbag. That's what I thought he was. I know now what it was that attracted them. It was because life in our town, as in all small towns, was at times pretty dull and he livened it up. He made them laugh. He could tell stories. He'd even get them to singing.

If they didn't come to our house they'd go off, say at night, to where there was a grassy place by a creek. They'd cook food there and drink beer and sit about listening to his stories.

He was always telling stories about himself. He'd say this or that wonderful thing had happened to him. It might be something that made him look like a fool. He didn't care.

If an Irishman came to our house, right away father would say he was Irish. He'd tell what county in Ireland he was born in. He'd tell things that happened there when he was a boy. He'd make it seem so real that, if I hadn't known he was born in southern Ohio, I'd have believed him myself.

If it was a Scotchman the same thing happened. He'd get a burr into his speech. Or he was a German or a Swede. He'd be anything the other man was. I think they all knew he was lying, but they seemed to like him just the same. As a boy that was what I couldn't understand.

And there was mother. How could she stand it? I wanted to ask but never did. She was not the kind you asked such questions.

I'd be upstairs in my bed, in my room above the porch, and father would be telling some of his tales. A lot of father's stories were about the Civil War. To hear him tell it he'd been in about every battle. He'd known Grant, Sherman, Sheridan and I don't know how many others. He'd been particularly intimate with General Grant so that when Grant went East, to take charge of all the armies, he took father along.

"I was an orderly at headquarters and Sim Grant said to me, 'Irve,' he said, 'I'm going to take you along with me.'"

It seems he and Grant used to slip off sometimes and have a quiet drink together. That's what my father said. He'd tell about the day Lee surrendered and how, when the great moment came, they couldn't find Grant.

"You know," my father said, "about General Grant's book, his memoirs. You've read of how he said he had a headache and how, when he got word that Lee was ready to call it quits, he was suddenly and miraculously cured.

"Huh," said father. "He was in the woods with me.

"I was in there with my back against a tree. I was pretty well corned. I had got hold of a bottle of pretty good stuff.

"They were looking for Grant. He had got off his horse and come into the woods. He found me. He was covered with mud.

"I had the bottle in my hand. What'd I care? The war was over. I knew we had them licked."

My father said that he was the one who told Grant about Lee. An orderly riding by had told him, because the orderly knew how thick he was with Grant. Grant was embarrassed.

"But, Irve, look at me. I'm all covered with mud," he said to father. And then, my father said, he and Grant decided to have a drink together. They took a couple of shots and then, because he didn't want Grant to show up potted before the immaculate Lee, he smashed the bottle against the tree.

"Sim Grant's dead now and I wouldn't want it to get out on him," my father said.

That's just one of the kind of things he'd tell. Of course the men knew he was lying, but they seemed to like it just the same. When we got broke, down and out, do you think he ever brought anything home? Not he. If there wasn't anything to eat in the house, he'd go off visiting around at farmhouses. They all wanted him. Sometimes he'd stay away for weeks, mother working to keep us fed, and then home he'd come bringing, let's say, a ham. He'd got it from some farmer friend. He'd slap it on the table in the kitchen. "You bet I'm going to see that my kids have something to eat," he'd say, and mother would just stand smiling at him. She'd never say a word about all the weeks and months he'd been away, not leaving us a cent for food. Once I heard her speaking to a woman in our street. Maybe the woman had dared to sympathize with her. "Oh," she said, "it's all right. He isn't ever dull like most of the men in this street. Life is never dull when my man is about."

But often I was filled with bitterness, and sometimes I wished he wasn't my father. I'd even invent another man as my father. To protect my mother I'd make up stories of a secret marriage that for some strange reason never got known. As though some man, say the president of a railroad company or maybe a Congressman, had married my mother, thinking his wife was dead and then it turned out she wasn't.

So they had to hush it up but I got born just the same. I wasn't really the son of my father. Somewhere in the world there was a very dignified, quite wonderful man who was really my father. I even made myself half believe these fancies.

And then there came a certain night. He'd been off somewhere for two or three weeks. He found me alone in the house, reading by the kitchen table.

It had been raining and he was very wet. He sat and looked at me for a long time, not saying a word. I was startled, for there was on his face the saddest look I had ever seen. He sat for a time, his clothes dripping. Then he got up.

"Come on with me," he said.

I got up and went with him out of the house. I was filled with wonder but I wasn't afraid. We went along a dirt road that led down into a valley, about a mile out of town, where there was a pond. We walked in silence. The man who was always talking had stopped his talking.

I didn't know what was up and had the queer feeling that I was with a stranger. I don't know whether my father intended it so. I don't think he did.

The pond was quite large. It was still raining hard and there were flashes of lightning followed by thunder. We were on a grassy bank at the pond's edge when my father spoke, and in the darkness and rain his voice sounded strange.

"Take off your clothes," he said. Still filled with wonder, I began to undress. There was a flash of lightning and I saw that he was already naked.

Naked, we went into the pond. Taking my hand he pulled me in. It may be that I was too frightened, too full of a feeling of strangeness, to speak. Before that night my father had never seemed to pay any attention to me.

"And what is he up to now?" I kept asking myself. I did not swim very well, but he put my hand on his shoulder and struck out into the darkness.

He was a man with big shoulders, a powerful swimmer. In the darkness I could feel the movement of his muscles. We swam to the far edge of the pond and then back to where we had left our clothes. The rain continued and the wind blew. Sometimes my father swam on his back and when he did he took my hand in his large powerful one and moved it over so that it rested always on his shoulder. Sometimes there would be a flash of lightning and I could see his face quite clearly.

It was as it was earlier, in the kitchen, a face filled with sadness. There would be the momentary glimpse of his face and then again the darkness, the wind and the rain. In me there was a feeling I had never known before.

It was a feeling of closeness. It was something strange. It was as though there were only we two in the world. It was as though I had been jerked suddenly out of myself, out of my world of the schoolboy, out of a world in which I was ashamed of my father.

He had become blood of my blood; he the strong swimmer and I the boy clinging to him in the darkness. We swam in silence and in silence we dressed in our wet clothes, and went home.

There was a lamp lighted in the kitchen and when we came in, the water dripping from us, there was my mother. She smiled at us. I remember that she called us "boys."

"What have you boys been up to?" she asked, but my father did not answer. As he had begun the evening's experience with me in silence, so he ended it. He turned and looked at me. Then he went, I thought, with a new and strange dignity out of the room.

I climbed the stairs to my own room, undressed in the darkness and got into bed. I couldn't sleep and did not want to sleep. For the first time I knew that I was the son of my father. He was a story teller as I was to be. It may be that I even laughed a little softly there in the darkness. If I did, I laughed knowing that I would never again be wanting another father.

FOR DISCUSSION AND WRITING

1. Refer back to the third question on the selection from Gorky, where the technical "point of view" of the writer was discussed. Is the point of view in the present piece that of a young boy (how young?) or that of an older man writing of his young boyhood? Or is it a combination of the two? Consider the diction—choice of words—carefully (you might compare it with the diction in the selection from Yeats, or with that of Joyce in the piece following this one) and the kind of sentences Anderson produces: how would you describe the diction here and the sentence construction? Do they have anything to do with one's feeling that it is a young boy's mind, rather than an older man's, that is represented?

2. Anderson says: "A boy wants something very special from his father." This is a generalization about boys that is assumed to apply to most or all boys. Does it? Does it apply to girls? What about its relevance to mothers? Write a well-considered and unified paragraph on one of these questions.

3. Do you get obliquely (or directly) the full character of the father? Or is something left in mystery? He is obviously not an ideal moral character, but nevertheless Anderson manages to present him sympathetically. Point out several places where his not-so-admirable idiosyncrasies invite sym-

pathy: how is this managed? How are other people's attitudes used to offset or counterbalance the boy's attitude?

4. Imagine the spurious story about Grant told in indirect discourse (or, as an exercise, rewrite it yourself in indirect discourse). What is gained by direct quotation?

5. Anderson says, "I had got to hating him." Is this a natural or typical reaction at some point (or perhaps at many points) in the child-parent relation? Is it an effect of overidealization of the parent and overidealization of the parental function? How can parents prevent such overidealization and the consequent hostility—or even demoralization—of the child when parents show feet of clay? This might be a theme subject.

6. What is the mother's attitude? She has a fairly tough proposition in enjoying a husband who is so remiss in family responsibility. What (on the general grounds of a son's psychology) makes it impossble for the boy to share her attitude?

7. Anderson speaks of his fantasy of having another parentage, of there being some mistake in his birth. This, incidentally, is a common motif in fairy tales, as in those stories in which a king's son or daughter is brought up by peasants. Have you encountered a similar fantasy in yourself or others? This too might be a theme subject—but you would want to analyze the background of such a fantasy and its particular psychology.

8. Explain the final incident in this piece in terms of an "initiation." Initiation into what? In what sense is the incident mysterious? Is the mysteriousness simply obscurity (is one just left muddled as to what it means?), or does it have to do with the essential mystery in human beings?

9. Another theme topic: parents as social guardians and parents as people.

James Joyce ⊷§ A Sundering

⊷§ Irish novelist and short-story writer (1882-1941), one of the towering figures in modern literature, whose innovations in *Ulysses* and *Finnegans Wake* radically changed not only the forms and the very conception of fiction, but also the history of the English language. The selection here is from his earlier novel, *A Portrait of the Artist as a Young Man*. The student who wishes to read further in Joyce should start either with the *Portrait* or with the collection of short stories called *Dubliners*, rather than with the later work, which he might find a bit overwhelming. §⊷

S TEPHEN was once again seated beside his father in the corner of a railway carriage at Kingsbridge. He was travelling with his father by the night mail[1] to Cork. As the train steamed out of the station he recalled his childish wonder of years before and every event of his first day at Clongowes.[2] But he felt no wonder now. He saw the darkening lands slipping away past him, the silent telegraphpoles passing his window swiftly every four seconds, the little glimmering stations, manned by a few silent sentries, flung by the mail behind her and twinkling for a moment in the darkness like fiery grains flung backwards by a runner.

From *A Portrait of the Artist as a Young Man* by James Joyce. Copyright 1916 by BW Huebsch, Inc., 1944 by Nora Joyce. Reprinted by permission of The Viking Press, Inc. This selection is from the Compass Edition.

[1] Train.
[2] His first school.

He listened without sympathy to his father's evocation of Cork and of scenes of his youth — a tale broken by sighs or draughts from his pocket flask whenever the image of some dead friend appeared in it, or whenever the evoker remembered suddenly the purpose of his actual visit. Stephen heard, but could feel no pity. The images of the dead were all strangers to him save that of Uncle Charles, an image which had lately been fading out of memory. He knew, however, that his father's property was going to be sold by auction and in the manner of his own dispossession he felt the world give the lie rudely to his phantasy.

At Maryborough he fell asleep. When he awoke the train had passed out of Mallow and his father was stretched asleep on the other seat. The cold light of the dawn lay over the country, over the unpeopled fields and the closed cottages. The terror of sleep fascinated his mind as he watched the silent country or heard from time to time his father's deep breath or sudden sleepy movement. The neighbourhood of unseen sleepers filled him with strange dread, as though they could harm him, and he prayed that the day might come quickly. His prayer, addressed neither to God nor saint, began with a shiver, as the chilly morning breeze crept through the chink of the carriage door to his feet, and ended in a trail of foolish words which he made to fit the insistent rhythm of the train; and silently, at intervals of four seconds, the telegraphpoles held the galloping notes of the music between punctual bars. This furious music allayed his dread and, leaning against the window ledge, he let his eyelids close again.

They drove in a jingle across Cork while it was still early morning and Stephen finished his sleep in a bedroom of the Victoria Hotel. The bright warm sunlight was streaming through the window and he could hear the din of traffic. His father was standing before the dressingtable, examining his hair and face and moustache with great care, craning his neck across the water jug and drawing it back sideways to see the better. While he did so he sang softly to himself with quaint accent and phrasing:

> " 'Tis youth and folly
> Makes young men marry.
> So here, my love, I'll
> No longer stay.
> What can't be cured, sure

Must be injured,[3] sure.
So I'll go on to Amerikay.

"My love she's handsome,
My love she's bony:
She's like good whisky
When it is new;
But when 'tis old
And growing cold
It fades and dies like
The mountain dew."

The consciousness of the warm sunny city outside his window and the tender tremors with which his father's voice festooned the strange sad happy air, drove off all the mists of the night's ill humour from Stephen's brain. He got up quickly to dress and, when the song had ended, said:

— That's much prettier than any of your other *come-all-yous*.[4]

— Do you think so? asked Mr. Dedalus.

— I like it, said Stephen.

— It's a pretty old air, said Mr. Dedalus, twirling the points of his moustache. Ah, but you should have heard Mick Lacy sing it; Poor Mick Lacy! He had little turns for it, grace notes he used to put in that I haven't got. That was the boy who could sing a *come-all-you*, if you like.

Mr. Dedalus had ordered drisheens[5] for breakfast and during the meal he cross-examined the waiter for local news. For the most part they spoke at cross purposes when a name was mentioned, the waiter having in mind the present holder and Mr. Dedalus his father or perhaps his grandfather.

Well, I hope they haven't moved the Queen's College anyhow, said Mr. Dedalus, for I want to show it to this youngster of mine.

Along the Mardyke the trees were in bloom. They entered the grounds of the college and were led by the garrulous porter across the quadrangle. But their progress across the gravel was brought to a halt after every dozen or so paces by some reply of the porter's —

— Ah, do you tell me so? And is poor Pottlebelly dead?

— Yes, sir. Dead, sir.

[3] "Must be endured" (Irish pronunciation).

[4] Irish folksong.

[5] Sausages.

During these halts Stephen stood awkwardly behind the two men, weary of the subject and waiting restlessly for the slow march to begin again. By the time they had crossed the quadrangle his restlessness had risen to fever. He wondered how his father, whom he knew for a shrewd suspicious man, could be duped by the servile manners of the porter; and the lively southern speech which had entertained him all the morning now irritated his ears.

They passed into the anatomy theatre where Mr. Dedalus, the porter aiding him, searched the desks for his initials. Stephen remained in the background, depressed more than ever by the darkness and silence of the theatre and by the air it wore of jaded and formal study. On the desk he read the word *Foetus* cut several times in the dark stained wood. The sudden legend startled his blood: he seemed to feel the absent students of the college about him and to shrink from their company. A vision of their life, which his father's words had been powerless to evoke. sprang up before him out of the word cut in the desk. A broad shoul-dered student with a moustache was cutting in the letters with a jack knife, seriously. Other students stood or sat near him laughing at his handiwork. One jogged his elbow. The big student turned on him, frowning. He was dressed in loose grey clothes and had tan boots.

Stephen's name was called. He hurried down the steps of the theatre so as to be as far away from the vision as he could be and, peering closely at his father's initials, hid his flushed face.

But the word and the vision capered before his eyes as he walked back across the quadrangle and towards the college gate. It shocked him to find in the outer world a trace of what he had deemed till then a brutish and individual malady of his own mind. His monstrous reveries came thronging into his memory. They too had sprung up before him, suddenly and furiously, out of mere words. He had soon given in to them, and allowed them to sweep across and abase his intellect, wonder-ing always where they came from, from what den of monstrous images, and always weak and humble towards others, restless and sickened of himself when they had swept over him.

— Ay, bedad! And there's the Groceries sure enough! cried Mr. Dedalus. You often heard me speak of the Groceries, didn't you, Stephen. Many's the time we went down there when our names had been marked, a crowd of us, Harry Peard and little Jack Mountain and Bob Dyas and Maurice Moriarty, the Frenchman, and Tom O'Grady and Mick Lacy

that I told you of this morning and Joey Corbet and poor little good
hearted Johnny Keevers of the Tantiles.

The leaves of the trees along the Mardyke were astir and whispering
in the sunlight. A team of cricketeers passed, agile young men in flannels
and blazers, one of them carrying the long green wicket bag. In a quiet
by street a German band of five players in faded uniforms and with
battered brass instruments was playing to an audience of street arabs
and leisurely messenger boys. A maid in a white cap and apron was
watering a box of plants on a sill which shone like a slab of limestone
in the warm glare. From another window open to the air came the
sound of a piano, scale after scale rising into the treble.

Stephen walked on at his father's side, listening to stories he had
heard before, hearing again the names of the scattered and dead revellers
who had been the companions of his father's youth. And a faint sickness
sighed in his heart. He recalled his own equivocal position in Belvedere,[6]
a free boy, a leader afraid of his own authority, proud and sensitive and
suspicious, battling against the squalor of his life and against the riot
of his mind. The letters cut in the stained wood of the desk stared upon
him, mocking his bodily weakness and futile enthusiasms and making
him loathe himself for his own mad and filthy orgies. The spittle in his
throat grew bitter and foul to swallow and the faint sickness climbed to
his brain so that for a moment he closed his eyes and walked on in darkness.

He could still hear his father's voice —

— When you kick out for yourself, Stephen — as I daresay you will
one of these days — remember, whatever you do, to mix with gentlemen.
When I was a young fellow I tell you I enjoyed myself. I mixed with
fine decent fellows. Everyone of us could do something. One fellow had
a good voice, another fellow was a good actor, another could sing a
good comic song, another was a good oarsman or a good racket player,
another could tell a good story and so on. We kept the ball rolling anyhow and enjoyed ourselves and saw a bit of life and we were none the
worse of it either. But we were all gentlemen, Stephen — at least I hope
we were — and bloody good honest Irishmen too. That's the kind of
fellows I want you to associate with, fellows of the right kidney. I'm
talking to you as a friend, Stephen. I don't believe a son should be afraid
of his father. No, I treat you as your grandfather treated me when I was

[6] Belvedere College in Dublin.

a young chap. We were more like brothers than father and son. I'll never forget the first day he caught me smoking. I was standing at the end of the South Terrace one day with some maneens[7] like myself and sure we thought we were grand fellows because we had pipes stuck in the corners of our mouths. Suddenly the governor passed. He didn't say a word, or stop even. But the next day, Sunday, we were out for a walk together and when we were coming home he took out his cigar case and said — By the by, Simon, I didn't know you smoked, or something like that. Of course I tried to carry it off as best as I could — if you want a good smoke, he said, try one of these cigars. An American captain made me a present of them last night in Queenstown.

Stephen heard his father's voice break into a laugh which was almost a sob.

— He was the handsomest man in Cork at that time, by God he was! The women used to stand to look after him in the street.

He heard the sob passing loudly down his father's throat and opened his eyes with a nervous impulse. The sunlight breaking suddenly on his sight turned the sky and clouds into a fantastic world of sombre masses with lakelike spaces of dark rosy light. His very brain was sick and powerless. He could scarcely interpret the letters of the signboards of the shops. By his monstrous way of life he seemed to have put himself beyond the limits of reality. Nothing moved him or spoke to him from the real world unless he heard in it an echo of the infuriated cries within him. He could respond to no earthly or human appeal, dumb and insensible to the call of summer and gladness and companionship, wearied and dejected by his father's voice. He would scarcely recognise as his own thoughts, and repeated slowly to himself:

— I Stephen Dedalus. I am walking beside my father whose name is Simon Dedalus. We are in Cork, in Ireland. Cork is a city. Our room is in the Victoria Hotel. Victoria and Stephen and Simon. Simon and Stephen and Victoria. Names.

The memory of his childhood suddenly grew dim. He tried to call forth some of its vivid moments but could not. He recalled only names. Dante, Parnell, Clane, Clongowes. A little boy had been taught geography by an old woman who kept two brushes in her wardrobe. Then he had been sent away from home to a college, he had made his first

---

[7] Young sprouts (literally, little men).

communion and eaten slim jim[8] out of his cricket cap and watched the firelight leaping and dancing on the wall of a little bedroom in the infirmary and dreamed of being dead, of mass being said for him by the rector in a black and gold cope, of being buried then in the little graveyard of the community off the main avenue of lines. But he had not died then. Parnell had died. There had been no mass for the dead in the chapel, and no procession. He had not died but he had faded out like a film in the sun. He had been lost or had wandered out of existence for he no longer existed. How strange to think of him passing out of existence in such a way, not by death, but by fading out in the sun or by being lost and forgotten somewhere in the universe! It was strange to see his small body appear again for a moment: a little boy in a grey belted suit. His hands were in his side pockets and his trousers were tucked in at the knees by elastic bands.

On the evening of the day on which the property was sold Stephen followed his father meekly about the city from bar to bar. To the sellers in the market, to the barmen and barmaids, to the beggars who importuned him for a lob Mr. Dedalus told the same tale, that he was an old Corkonian, that he had been trying for thirty years to get rid of his Cork accent up in Dublin and that Peter Pickackafax beside him was his eldest son but that he was only a Dublin jackeen.[9]

They had set out early in the morning from Newcombe's coffee-house, where Mr. Dedalus' cup had rattled noisily against its saucer, and Stephen had tried to cover that shameful sign of his father's drinking-bout of the night before by moving his chair and coughing. One humiliation had succeeded another — the false smiles of the market sellers, the curvetings and oglings of the barmaids with whom his father flirted, the compliments and encouraging words of his father's friends. They had told him that he had a great look of his grandfather and Mr. Dedalus had agreed that he was an ugly likeness. They had unearthed traces of a Cork accent in his speech and made him admit that the Lee was a much finer river than the Liffey. One of them, in order to put his Latin to the proof, had made him translate short passages from Dilectus, and asked him whether it was correct to say: *Tempora mutantur nos et mutamur in illis,* or *Tempora mutantur et nos mutamur in illis.*[10] Another, a brisk old man,

[8] A chocolate chew.

[9] Good-for-nothing.

[10] "Times change us and we change with them," or "Times change and we change ourselves to suit the times."

whom Mr. Dedalus called Johnny Cashman, had covered him with confusion by asking him to say which were prettier, the Dublin girls or the Cork girls.

— He's not that way built, said Mr. Dedalus. Leave him alone. He's a levelheaded thinking boy who doesn't bother his head about that kind of nonsense.

— Then he's not his father's son, said the little old man.

— I don't know, I'm sure, said Mr. Dedalus, smiling complacently.

— Your father, said the little old man to Stephen, was the boldest flirt in the city of Cork in his day. Do you know that?

Stephen looked down and studied the tiled floor of the bar into which they had drifted.

— Now don't be putting ideas into his head, said Mr. Dedalus. Leave him to his Maker.

— Yerra, sure I wouldn't put any ideas into his head. I'm old enough to be his grandfather. And I am a grandfather, said the little old man to Stephen. Do you know that?

— Are you? asked Stephen.

— Bedad I am, said the little old man. I have two bouncing grandchildren out at Sunday's Well. Now, then! What age do you think I am! And I remember seeing your grandfather in his red coat riding out to hounds. That was before you were born.

— Ay, or thought of, said Mr. Dedalus.

— Bedad I did, repeated the little old man. And, more than that, I can remember even your greatgrandfather, old John Stephen Dedalus, and a fierce old fire-eater he was. Now, then! There's a memory for you!

— That's three generations — four generations, said another of the company. Why, Johnny Cashman, you must be nearing the century.

— Well, I'll tell you the truth, said the little old man. I'm just twentyseven years of age.

— We're as old as we feel, Johnny, said Mr. Dedalus.

— And just finish what you have there, and we'll have another. Here, Tim or Tom or whatever your name is, give us the same again here. By God, I don't feel more than eighteen myself. There's that son of mine there not half my age and I'm a better man than he is any day of the week.

— Draw it mild now, Dedalus, I think it's time for you to take a back seat, said the gentleman who had spoken before.

— No, by God! asserted Mr. Dedalus. I'll sing a tenor song against him or I'll vault a fire-barred gate against him or I'll run with him after the hounds across the country as I did thirty years ago along with the Kerry Boy and the best man for it.

— But he'll beat you here, said the little old man, tapping his forehead and raising his glass to drain it.

— Well, I hope he'll be as good a man as his father. That's all I can say, said Mr. Dedalus.

— If he is, he'll do, said the little old man.

— And thanks be to God, Johnny, said Mr. Dedalus, that we lived so long and did so little harm.

— But did so much good, Simon, said the little old man gravely. Thanks be to God we lived so long and did so much good.

Stephen watched the three glasses being raised from the counter as his father and his two cronies drank to the memory of their past. An abyss of fortune or of temperament sundered him from them. His mind seemed older than theirs: it shone coldly on their strifes and happiness and regrets like a moon upon a younger earth. No life or youth stirred in him as it had stirred in them. He had known neither the pleasure of companionship with others nor the vigour of rude male health nor filial piety. Nothing stirred within his soul but a cold and cruel and loveless lust. His childhood was dead or lost and with it his soul capable of simple joys and he was drifting amid life like the barren shell of the moon.

> "Art thou pale for weariness
> Of climbing heaven and gazing on the earth,
> Wandering companionless? . . ."

He repeated to himself the lines of Shelley's fragment. Its alternation of sad human ineffectualness with vast inhuman cycles of activity chilled him, and he forgot his own human and ineffectual grieving.

✐ FOR DISCUSSION AND WRITING

1. In the questions on the first piece in this book, the chapter from Gorky's *My Childhood*, we discussed what is meant by the writer's "point of view," in the technical sense of the term. Sherwood Anderson, in "Discovery of a Father," uses a first-person point of view that stays close to

the mentality and the idiom of a young boy. Joyce, on the other hand, uses a third-person point of view. One might think, offhand, that the third-person point of view could never give the sense of *being inside a mind* with such immediacy as the first-person does; but, in actual fact, which of the two pieces gives you the more immediate and intimate sense of "being inside a mind"? As a slight exercise in analysis of point of view, examine Joyce's third-person technique carefully, and then try rewriting the first paragraph of Anderson's "Discovery of a Father," using the third person instead of the first. (You can call the boy Sherwood.) Now try rewriting Joyce's first paragraph from the first-person point of view. What essential differences in effect do you discover?

2. In the Joyce and Anderson pieces, are there any similarities in the characterization of the two fathers? What about the two sons? Do you find much characterization of the son in the Anderson piece? in the Joyce? Again considering "point of view," do you think it would be easy or possible to draw up a vivid characterization of yourself, writing in the first person? In this respect, what advantage does the third-person point of view have?

3. The Joyce piece is a section of his novel *A Portrait of the Artist as a Young Man*. Ordinarily one would not expect a short excerpt from a novel to have independent unity—like the unity of a short story. One reason the parts of Joyce's *Portrait* do have their own unity is that each concerns a certain specific stage of development in a boy's life. Do you feel that this piece has unity? Do you find in it some central idea or attitude to which the various little scenes and Stephen's brooding thoughts are all related and which ties them together? Is that controlling idea or attitude stated anywhere in the piece?

4. Are Mr. Dedalus' personal characteristics and behavior sufficient to explain the boy's acute embarrassment and despair? Obviously father and son are two radical incommensurables here. How would you define the schism between them? Would you say their relationship—or failure of relationship—was a representative one or a special case? If special, is it unique?

5. Mr. Dedalus makes fairly frequent displays of his sense of fatherhood. Point out some occasions of this. Is he actually *aware* of his son as an individual person, or does he use his son merely as an adjunct of his own personality?

6. What irony is there in the circumstance that while Mr. Dedalus is busily looking for his own initials, Stephen finds the word "foetus" carved on a desk? Can you explain the extraordinary effect this word has on Stephen?

7. The pieces from Yeats's and Williams' autobiographies both dealt in indirect ways with sexual awakening in adolescence. The sexual element is much stronger and more explicit here. To what extent does this element seem to you to account for Stephen's sense of "dispossession"—his despairing sense of alienation from his surroundings and from other people? Would you say that what Stephen is suffering is fairly typical of adolescence or not? On what do you base your answer?

8. One can discriminate certain main structural aspects: the *subject matter* (comprised simply of the visit to Cork and to Queen's College and the alcoholic exchanges as Mr. Dedalus makes the rounds of the bars); a controlling *idea, attitude,* or *"theme"* (which you have been asked to define in Question 3); and finally, a *mode of treatment* of subject and theme. The mode of treatment here is that of irony—irony achieved mainly by juxtaposing the boy's despairing, alienated state of mind with the father's fat-headed, complacent sentimentalities. Analyze the way in which this ironic method is used in the section where Stephen discovers the word "foetus" and his father holds forth on the value of "mixing with gentlemen"; also in the later section where Mr. Dedalus and Johnny Cashman alcoholically discuss Stephen and the virtues of the older generation. Glance back over the Anderson piece; was irony used there to any extent?

9. If your reading or your discussions in English courses have ever touched on the subject of dramatic "catharsis" (the "purging" of emotions), could you point out anything in the nature of catharsis at the end? How is it achieved? Does it have anything to do with giving unity to the piece?

10. A natural subject for a short essay arises here: on the relationship (within your experience) of the younger and older generations, either as a relationship failed or a relationship achieved. Try to profit from Joyce's model in using living illustration.

Franz Kafka ✑ Letter to His Father

✑ German-Bohemian novelist and short-story writer (1883-1924), now recognized, decades after his death, as a supremely original artist of the rank of Joyce, Proust, Yeats, Rilke, and Eliot. The "Letter to his Father" is of particular interest to Kafka's readers, inasmuch as one finds in this personal document the seed of what Philip Rahv calls "the typical Kafkan narrative, the obsessive theme, the nuclear fable concerning the victim of an unappeasable power to which he returns again and again, varying and complicating its structure with astonishing resourcefulness, and erecting on so slender a foundation such marvelous superstructures as that of the myth of the Old Commander in *In the Penal Colony*, the myth of the Law in *The Trial* and of the celestial bureaucracy in *The Castle*." ✑

DEAREST FATHER:

You asked me recently why I maintain that I am afraid of you. As usual, I was unable to think of any answer to your question, partly for the very reason that I am afraid of you, and partly because an explanation of the grounds for this fear would mean going into far more details than I could even approximately keep in mind while talking. And if I now try to give you an answer in writing, it will still be very incomplete, because even in writing this fear and its consequences hamper me in relation to you and because [anyway] the magnitude of the subject goes far beyond the scope of my memory and power of reasoning. . . .

Compare the two of us: I, to put it in a very much abbreviated form, a Löwy[1] with a certain basis of Kafka, which, however, is not set in motion by the Kafka will to life, business, and conquest, but by a Löwy-ish spur that urges more secretly, more diffidently, and in another direction, and which often fails to work entirely. You, on the other hand, a true Kafka in strength, health, appetite, loudness of voice, eloquence, self-satisfaction, worldly dominance, endurance, presence of mind, knowledge of human nature, a certain way of doing things on a grand scale, of course also with all the defects and weaknesses that go with all these advantages and into which your temperament and sometimes your hot temper drive you. . . .

However it was, we were so different and in our difference so dangerous to each other that, if anyone had tried to calculate in advance how I, the slowly developing child, and you, the full-grown man, would stand to each other, he could have assumed that you would simply trample me underfoot so that nothing was left of me. Well, that didn't happen. Nothing alive can be calculated. But perhaps something worse happened. And in saying this I would all the time beg of you not to forget that I never, and not even for a single moment, believe any guilt to be on your side. The effect you had on me was the effect you could not help having. But you should stop considering it some particular malice on my part that I succumbed to that effect.

I was a timid child. For all that, I am sure I was also obstinate, as children are. I am sure that Mother spoilt me too, but I cannot believe I was particularly difficult to manage; I cannot believe that a kindly word, a quiet taking of me by the hand, a friendly look, could not have got me to do anything that was wanted of me. Now you are after all at bottom a kindly and softhearted person (what follows will not be in contradiction to this, I am speaking only of the impression you made on the child), but not every child has the endurance and fearlessness to go on searching until it comes to the kindliness that lies beneath the surface. You can only treat a child in the way you yourself are constituted, with vigor, noise, and hot temper, and in this case this seemed to you, into the bargain, extremely suitable, because you wanted to bring me up to be a strong brave boy. . . .

There is only one episode in the early years of which I have a direct memory. You may remember it, too. Once in the night I kept on whimpering for water, not, I am certain, because I was thirsty, but probably

[1] Löwy was the name of Kafka's mother's family.

partly to be annoying, partly to amuse myself. After several vigorous threats had failed to have any effect, you took me out of bed, carried me out onto the *pavlatche*[2] and left me there alone for a while in my nightshirt, outside the shut door. I am not going to say that this was wrong — perhaps at that time there was really no other way of getting peace and quiet that night — but I mention it as typical of your methods of bringing up a child and their effect on me. I dare say I was quite obedient afterwards at that period, but it did me inner harm. What was for me a matter of course, that senseless asking for water, and the extraordinary terror of being carried outside were two things that I, my nature being what it was, could never properly connect with each other. Even years afterwards I suffered from the tormenting fancy that the huge man, my father, the ultimate authority, would come almost for no reason at all and take me out of bed in the night and carry me out onto the *pavlatche*, and that therefore I was such a mere nothing for him.

That then was only a small beginning, but this sense of nothingness that often dominates me (a feeling that is in another respect, admittedly, also a noble and fruitful one) comes largely from your influence. What I would have needed was a little encouragement, a little friendliness, a little keeping open of my road, instead of which you blocked it for me, though of course with the good intention of making me go another road. But I was not fit for that. You encouraged me, for instance, when I saluted and marched smartly, but I was no future soldier, or you encouraged me when I was able to eat heartily or even drink beer with my meals, or when I was able to repeat songs, singing what I had not understood, or prattle to you using your own favorite expressions, imitating you, but nothing of this had anything to do with my future. And it is characteristic that even today you really only encourage me in anything when you yourself are involved in it, when what is at stake is your own sense of self-importance.

At that time, and at that time everywhere, I would have needed encouragement. I was, after all, depressed even by your mere physical presence. I remember, for instance, how we often undressed together in the same bathing hut. There was I, skinny, weakly, slight; you strong, tall, broad. Even inside the hut I felt myself a miserable specimen, and what's more, not only in your eyes but in the eyes of the whole world, for you were for me the measure of all things. But then when we went

2 Balcony.

out of the bathing hut before the people, I with you holding my hand, a little skeleton, unsteady, barefoot on the boards, frightened of the water, incapable of copying your swimming strokes, which you, with the best of intentions, but actually to my profound humiliation, always kept on showing me, then I was frantic with desperation and all my bad experiences in all spheres at such moments fitted magnificently together. . . .

In keeping with that, furthermore, was your intellectual domination. You had worked your way up so far alone, by your own energies, and as a result you had unbounded confidence in your opinion. For me as a child that was not yet so dazzling as later for the boy growing up. From your armchair you ruled the world. Your opinion was correct, every other was mad, wild, *meshugge*,[3] not normal. With all this your self-confidence was so great that you had no need to be consistent at all and yet never ceased to be in the right. It did sometimes happen that you had no opinion whatsoever about a matter and as a result all opinions that were at all possible with respect to the matter were necessarily wrong, without exception. You were capable, for instance, of running down the Czechs, and then the Germans, and then the Jews, and what is more, not only selectively but in every respect, and finally nobody was left except yourself. For me you took on the enigmatic quality that all tyrants have whose rights are based on their person and not on reason. At least so it seemed to me.

Now where I was concerned you were in fact astonishingly often in the right, which was a matter of course in talk, for there was hardly ever any talk between us, but also in reality. Yet this too was nothing particularly incomprehensible; in all my thinking I was, after all, under the heavy pressure of your personality, even in that part of it — and particularly in that — which was not in accord with yours. All these thoughts, seemingly independent of you, were from the beginning loaded with the burden of your harsh and dogmatic judgments; it was almost impossible to endure this, and yet to work out one's thoughts with any measure of completeness and permanence. I am not here speaking of any sublime thoughts, but of every little enterprise in childhood. It was only necesary to be happy about something or other, to be filled with the thought of it, to come home and speak of it, and the answer was an ironical sigh, a shaking of the head, a tapping of the table with one finger: "Is that all you're so worked up about?" or "I wish I had your

[3] Crazy.

worries!" or "The things some people have time to think about!" or
"What can you buy yourself with that?" or "What a song and dance
about nothing!" Of course, you couldn't be expected to be enthusiastic
about every childish triviality, toiling and moiling as you used to. But
that wasn't the point. The point was, rather, that you could not help
always and on principle causing the child such disappointments, by
virtue of your antagonistic nature, and further that this antagonism
was ceaselessly intensified through accumulation of its material, that
it finally became a matter of established habit even when for once you
were of the same opinion as myself, and that finally these disappointments of the child's were not disappointments in ordinary life but,
since what it concerned was your person, which was the measure of all
things, struck to the very core. Courage, resolution, confidence, delight
in this and that, did not endure to the end when you were against whatever it was or even if your opposition was merely to be assumed; and
it was to be assumed in almost everything I did. . . .

You have, I think, a gift for bringing up children; you could, I am
sure, have been of use to a human being of your own kind with your
methods; such a person would have seen the reasonableness of what you
told him, would not have troubled about anything else, and would
quietly have done things the way he was told. But for me a child everything you shouted at me was positively a heavenly commandment, I
never forgot it, it remained for me the most important means of forming
a judgment of the world, above all of forming a judgment of you yourself, and there you failed entirely. Since as a child I was together with
you chiefly at meals, your teaching was to a large extent teaching about
proper behavior at table. What was brought to the table had to be
eaten up, there could be no discussion of the goodness of the food — but
you yourself often found the food uneatable, called it "this swill," said
"that brute" (the cook) had ruined it. Because in accordance with your
strong appetite and your particular habit you ate everything fast, hot and
in big mouthfuls, the child had to hurry, there was a somber silence at
table, interrupted by admonitions: "Eat first, talk afterwards," or "faster,
faster, faster," or "there you are, you see, I finished ages ago." Bones
musn't be cracked with the teeth, but you could. Vinegar must not be
sipped noisily, but you could. The main thing was that the bread should
be cut straight. But it didn't matter that you did it with a knife dripping

with gravy. One had to take care that no scraps fell on the floor. In the end it was under your chair that there were most scraps. At table one wasn't allowed to do anything but eat, but you cleaned and cut your fingernails, sharpened pencils, cleaned your ears with the toothpick. Please, Father, understand me rightly: these would in themselves have been utterly insignificant details, they only became depressing for me because you, the man who was so tremendously the measure of all things for me, yourself did not keep the commandments you imposed on me. Hence the world was for me divided into three parts: into one in which I, the slave, lived under laws that had been invented only for me and which I could, I did not know why, never completely comply with; then into a second world, which was infinitely remote from mine, in which you lived, concerned with government, with the issuing of orders and with annoyance about their not being obeyed; and finally into a third world where everybody else lived happily and free from orders and from having to obey. I was continually in disgrace, either I obeyed your orders, and that was a disgrace, for they applied, after all, only to me, or I was defiant, and that was a disgrace too, for how could I presume to defy you, or I could not obey because, for instance, I had not your strength, your appetite, your skill, in spite of which you expected it of me as a matter of course; this was the greatest disgrace of all. What moved in this way was not the child's reflections, but his feelings. . . .

It was true that Mother was illimitably good to me, but all that was for me in relation to you, that is to say, in no good relation. Mother unconsciously played the part of a beater during a hunt. Even if your method of upbringing might in some unlikely case have set me on my own feet by means of producing defiance, dislike, or even hate in me, Mother canceled that out again by kindness, by talking sensibly (in the maze and chaos of my childhood she was the very pattern of good sense and reasonableness), by pleading for me, and I was again driven back into your orbit, which I might perhaps otherwise have broken out of, to your advantage and to my own. Or it was so that no real reconciliation ever came about, that Mother merely shielded me from you in secret, secretly gave me something, or allowed me to do something, and then where you were concerned I was again the furtive creature, the cheat, the guilty one, who in his worthlessness could only pursue backstairs methods even to get the things he regarded as his right. Of course,

I then became used to taking such courses also in quest of things to which, even in my own view, I had no right. This again meant an increase in the sense of guilt.

It is also true that you hardly ever really gave me a whipping. But the shouting, the way your face got red, the hasty undoing of the braces and the laying of them ready over the back of the chair, all that was almost worse for me. It is like when someone is going to be hanged. If he is really hanged, then he's dead and it's all over. But if he has to go through all the preliminaries to being hanged and only when the noose is dangling before his face is told of his reprieve, then he may suffer from it all his life long. Besides, from so many occasions when I had, as you clearly showed you thought, deserved to be beaten, when you were however gracious enough to let me off at the last moment, here again what accumulated was only a huge sense of guilt. On every side I was to blame, I was in debt to you.

You have always reproached me (and what is more either alone or in front of others, you having no feeling for the humiliation of this latter, your children's affairs always being public affairs) for living in peace and quiet, warmth, and abundance, lacking for nothing, thanks to your hard work. I think here of remarks that must positively have worn grooves in my brain, like: "When I was only seven I had to push the barrow from village to village." "We all had to sleep in one room." "We were glad when we got potatoes." "For years I had open sores on my legs from not having enough clothes to wear in winter." "I was only a little boy when I was sent away to Pisek to go into business." "I got nothing from home, not even when I was in the army, even then I was sending money home." "But for all that, for all that — Father was always Father to me. Ah, nobody knows what that means these days! What do these children know of things? Nobody's been through that! Is there any child that understands such things today?" Under other conditions such stories might have been very educational, they might have been a way of encouraging one and strengthening one to endure similar torments and deprivations to those one's father had undergone. But that wasn't what you wanted at all; the situation had, after all, become quite different as a result of all your efforts, and there was no opportunity to distinguish oneself in the world as you had done. Such an opportunity would first of all have had to be created by violence and revolution, it would have meant breaking away from home (assuming one had had the

resolution and strength to do so and that Mother wouldn't have worked
against it, for her part, with other means). But all that was not what you
wanted at all, that you termed ingratitude, extravagance, disobedience,
treachery, madness. And so, while on the one hand you tempted me to
it by means of example, story, and humiliation, on the other hand you
forbade it with the utmost severity. . . .

(Up to this point there is in this letter relatively little I have intentionally passed over in silence, but now and later I shall have to be silent
on certain matters that it is still too hard for me to confess — to you and
to myself. I say this in order that, if the picture as a whole should be
somewhat blurred here and there, you should not believe that what is
to blame is any lack of evidence; on the contrary, there is evidence
that might well make the picture unbearably stark. It is not easy to strike
a median position.) Here, it is enough to remind you of early days. I
had lost my self-confidence where you were concerned, and in its place
had developed a boundless sense of guilt. (In recollection of this bound-
lessness I once wrote of someone, accurately: "He is afraid the shame
will outlive him, even.") I could not suddenly undergo a transformation
when I came into the company of other people; on the contrary, with
them I came to feel an even deeper sense of guilt, for, as I have already
said, in their case I had to make good the wrongs done them by you in
the business, wrongs in which I too had my share of responsibility. Besides, you always, of course, had some objection to make, frankly or
covertly, to everyone I associated with, and for this too I had to beg his
pardon. The mistrust that you tried to instill into me, at business and at
home, towards most people (tell me of any single person who was of
importance to me in my childhood whom you didn't at least once tear
to shreds with your criticism), this mistrust, which oddly enough was
no particular burden to you (the fact was that you were strong enough
to bear it, and besides, it was in reality perhaps only a token of the auto-
crat), this mistrust, which for me as a little boy was nowhere confirmed
in my own eyes, since I everywhere saw only people excellent beyond
all hope of emulation, in me turned into mistrust of myself and into
perpetual anxiety in relation to everything else. There, then, I was in
general certain of not being able to escape from you. . . .

I found equally little means of escape from you in Judaism. Here
some escape would, in principle, have been thinkable, but more than
that, it would have been thinkable that we might both have found each

other in Judaism or even that we might have begun from there in harmony. But what sort of Judaism was it I got from you? In the course of the years I have taken roughly three different attitudes to it.

As a child I reproached myself, in accord with you, for not going to the synagogue enough, for not fasting, and so on. I thought that in this way I was doing a wrong not to myself but to you, and I was penetrated by a sense of guilt, which was, of course, always ready to hand.

Later, as a boy, I could not understand how, with the insignificant scrap of Judaism you yourself possessed, you could reproach me for not (if for no more than the sake of piety, as you put it) making an effort to cling to a similar insignificant scrap. It was indeed really, so far as I could see, a mere scrap, a joke, not even a joke. On four days in the year you went to the synagogue, where you were, to say the least of it, closer to the indifferent than to those who took it seriously, patiently went through the prayers by way of formality, sometimes amazed me by being able to show me in the prayer book the passage that was being said at the moment, and for the rest, so long (and this was the main thing) as I was there in the synagogue I was allowed to hang about wherever I liked. And so I yawned and dozed through the many hours (I don't think I was ever again so bored, except later at dancing lessons) and did my best to enjoy the few little bits of variety there were, as, for instance, when the Ark of the Covenant was opened, which always reminded me of the shooting galleries where a cupboard door would open in the same way whenever one got a bull's-eye, only with the difference that there something interesting always came out and here it was always just the same old dolls with no heads. Incidentally, it was also very frightening for me there, not only, as goes without saying, because of all the people one came into close contact with, but also because you once mentioned, by the way, that I too might be called up to read the Torah.[4] That was something I went in dread of for years. But otherwise I was not fundamentally disturbed in my state of boredom, unless it was by the *bar mizvah*,[5] but that meant no more than some ridiculous learning by heart, in other words, led to nothing but something like the ridiculous passing of an examination, and then, so far as you were concerned, by little, not very significant incidents, as when you were called up to read

[4] Part of the Hebrew Bible.

[5] Jewish boys' initiation, at the age of thirteen, into the religious community.

the Torah and came well out of the affair, which to my way of feeling
was purely social, or when you stayed on in the synagogue for the
prayers for the dead, and I was sent away, which for a long time, obviously because of being sent away and lacking, as I did, any deeper
interest, aroused in me the more or less unconscious feeling that what
was about to take place was something indecent. — That was how it was
in the synagogue, and at home it was, if possible, even more poverty-
stricken, being confined to the first evening of Passover, which more
and more developed into a farce, with fits of hysterical laughter, admittedly under the influence of the growing children. (Why did you
have to give way to that influence? Because you brought it about in the
first place.) And so there was the religous material that was handed on
to me, to which may be added at most the outstretched hand pointing
to "the sons of the millionaire Fuchs," who were in the synagogue with
their father at the high holidays. How one could do anything better
with this material than get rid of it as fast as possible was something I
could not understand; precisely getting rid of it seemed to me the most
effective act of "piety" one could perform. . . .

I showed no foresight at all with regard to the significance and
possibility of a marriage for me; this up to now the greatest terror of my
life has come upon me almost completely unexpectedly. The child had
developed so slowly, these things were outwardly all too remote from
him; now and then the necessity of thinking of them did arise; but that
here a permanent, decisive and indeed the most grimly bitter ordeal was
imminent was something that could not be recognized. In reality, however, the plans to marry became the most large-scale and hopeful
attempt at escape, and then the failure was on a correspondingly large
scale, too.

I am afraid that, because in this sphere everything I try is a failure,
I shall also fail to make these attempts to marry comprehensible to you.
And yet on this depends the success of this whole letter, for in these
attempts there was, on the one hand, concentrated everything I had at
my disposal in the way of positive forces, and, on the other hand, here
there also accumulated, and with downright fury, all the negative forces
that I have described. . . .

How, now, was I prepared for this? As badly as possible. . . .

I remember going for a walk one evening with you and Mother;

it was on the Josefsplatz near where the Länderbank is today; and I
began talking about these interesting things,[6] in a stupidly boastful,
superior, proud, cool (that was spurious), cold (that was genuine) and
stammering manner, as indeed I usually talked to you, reproaching
the two of you for my having been left uninstructed, for the fact that it
was my schoolmates who first had to take me in hand, that I had been in
the proximity of great dangers (here I was brazenly lying, as was my
way, in order to show myself brave, for as a consequence of my timidity
I had, except for the usual sexual misdemeanors of city children, no very
exact notion of these "great dangers"), but finally hinted that now,
fortunately, I knew everything, no longer needed any advice, and that
everything was all right. I began talking about this, in any case, mainly
because it gave me pleasure at least to talk about it, and then too out of
curiosity, and finally too in order somehow to avenge myself on the two
of you for something or other. In keeping with your nature you took it
quite simply, only saying something to the effect that you could give me
some advice about how I could go in for these things without danger. . . .

It is not easy to judge the answer you gave me then; on the one
hand, there was, after all, something staggeringly frank, in a manner of
speaking, primeval, about it; on the other hand, however, as regards the
instruction itself, it was uninhibited in a very modern way. I don't know
how old I was at the time, certainly not much over sixteen. It was nevertheless a very remarkable answer for such a boy to be given, and the
distance between the two of us is also shown in the fact that this was
actually the first direct instruction bearing on real life that I ever received from you. But its real meaning, which sank into my mind even
then, but only much later came partly to the surface of my consciousness,
was this: what you were advising me to do was, after all, in your opinion
and, still far more, in my opinion at that time, the filthiest thing possible.
The fact that you were prepared to see to it that physically speaking I
should not bring any of the filth home with me was incidental, for in
that way you were only protecting yourself, your own household. The
main thing was, rather, that you remained outside your own advice, a
married man, a pure man, exalted above these things; this was intensified for me at that time probably even more through the fact that marriage too seemed to me to be shameless and hence it was impossible for
me to refer the general information I had picked up about marriage to

[6] Sexual matters.

my parents. In this way you became still more pure, rose still higher. The thought that you might perhaps have given yourself similar advice too before marriage was to me utterly unthinkable. So there was almost no smudge of earthly filth on you at all. And precisely you were pushing me, just as though I were predestined to it, down into this filth, with a few frank words. And so if the world consisted only of me and you, a notion I was much inclined to have, then this purity of the world came to an end with you and, by virtue of your advice, the filth began with me. . . .

A similar clash between us took place in quite different circumstances some twenty years later, as a fact horrible, in itself, however, much less damaging — for where was there anything in me, the thirty-six-year-old, that could still be damaged? I am referring to a little discussion on one of the few agitated days after I had informed you of my last marriage project. What you said to me was more or less as follows: "She probably put on some specially chosen blouse, the thing these Prague Jewesses are good at, and straightaway, of course, you made up your mind to marry her. And, what's more, as fast as possible, in a week, tomorrow, today. I can't make you out, after all, you're a grown man, here you are in town, and you can't think of any way of managing but going straight off and marrying the next best girl. Isn't there anything else you can do? If you're frightened, I'll go along with you myself." You put it in more detail and more plainly, but I can no longer recall the particular points, perhaps too things became a little misty before my eyes, I was almost more interested in Mother, as she, though perfectly in agreement with you, nevertheless took something from the table and left the room with it.

You have, I suppose, scarcely ever humiliated me more deeply with words and have never more clearly shown me your contempt. When you spoke to me in a similar way twenty years earlier, looking at it through your eyes one might even have seen in it some respect for the precocious city boy, who in your opinion could already be initiated into life without more ado. Today this consideration could only intensify the contempt, for the boy who was about to take his first leap into life got stuck halfway and seems to you today to be richer by no experience but only more pitiable by twenty years. My deciding on a girl meant nothing at all to you. You had (unconsciously) always kept down my power of decision and now believed (unconsciously) that you knew what it was worth. Of my attempts at escape in other directions you knew nothing, thus you could not know anything, either, of the thought processes that had led me to this attempt to marry, and had to try to guess at them, and your guess was in keeping with your total judgment of me, a guess at the most abominable, crude, and ridiculous thing possible. And you did not for a moment hesitate to say this to me in just such a manner. The shame you inflicted on me with this was nothing to you in comparison to the shame that I would, in your opinion, inflict on your name by this marriage.

Now, as it happens, with regard to my attempts at marriage there is much you can say in reply, and you have indeed done so: you could not have much respect for my decision since I had twice broken the engagement to F. and twice renewed it again, since I had dragged you and Mother to Berlin to celebrate the engagement, and all for nothing, and the like. All this is true — but how did it come about? . . .

Here, in the attempt to marry, two seemingly antagonistic elements in my relations with you unite more intensely than anywhere else. Marriage is certainly the pledge of the most acute form of self-liberation and independence. I should have a family, the highest thing that one can achieve, in my opinion, and so too the highest thing you have achieved; I should be your equal; all old and everlastingly new shame and tyranny would now be mere history. That would, admittedly, be like a fairy tale, but precisely there does the questionable element lie. It is too much; so much cannot be achieved. . . .

If I want to become independent in the particular unhappy relationship in which I stand to you, I must do something that will have, if possible, no relation to you at all; marrying is, it is true, the greatest thing of all and provides the most honorable independence, but it is also at the same time in the closest relation to you. . . .

I picture this equality that would then arise between us, and which you would be able to understand better than any other form of equality, as so beautiful precisely because I could then be a free, grateful, guiltless, upright son, and you could be an untroubled, untyrannical, sympathetic, contented father. But to this end it would be necessary to make all that has happened be as though it had never happened, which means, we ourselves should have to be cancelled out.

But we being what we are, marrying is barred to me through the fact that it is precisely and peculiarly your most intimate domain. Sometimes I imagine the map of the world spread out flat and you stretched out diagonally across it. And what I feel then is that only those territories come into question for my life that either are not covered by you or are not within your reach. And, in keeping with the conception that I have of your magnitude, these are not many and not very comforting territories, and above all marriage is not among them. . . .

FOR DISCUSSION AND WRITING

1. This extraordinary document is of a kind that many of the rest of us might like to have the courage, the insight and patience, and the dispassionate self-knowledge to compose. Kafka never sent the letter—and that, perhaps, was just as well, for such a letter probably performs its own healing function simply by being written; one cannot imagine that Kafka's father, perusing it, would have been enlightened. An attempt at communication of this kind ordinarily stirs up such confused emotions that it is almost impossible to keep a clear head and fair judgment: point out several parts of the letter where Kafka does exactly that—showing extraordinary clarity of mind and fairness in analyzing the relationship with his father. How much of that impression of clear-headedness and fairness depends on his use of precise illustration—real events and details remembered from the past?

2. Work up, out of the materials of the letter, a rather solid character portrait of the father. Does the picture Kafka draws of the relationship seem to you tc represent a natural and inevitable psychological development from the characters of the father and son, or not? Why?

3. Compare with this letter the selection from Joyce. Though Simon Dedalus is a different kind of person, both he and Kafka's father are what are called "extroverts," while Stephen and Kafka both correspond with the "introverted" type. (This psychological jargon is clumsy, but it gives us a rough means of differentiating temperaments.) How close and valid a comparison can you make between the father-son relationships in Joyce and Kafka?

4. Sherwood Anderson says: "A boy wants something very special from his father." Well, Kakfa certainly got it—all the paternal power and mag-

netism, breadwinner responsibility, economic success, social prestige, and moral authority that make up the heroic "father-image." "You were for me the measure of all things," Kafka says. Analyze what is wrong with this state of affairs, in terms of an adult's assumption of absolute rectitude and absolute power over a child. It is said that "power corrupts, and absolute power corrupts absolutely"; this may be the primal temptation of the parent—the exercise of power, for its own sake, over the child. Could you write an essay on this subject?

5. In view of the psychological magnitude and complexity of the problem Kafka discusses here, do you think the minor details he cites—like his father's eating habits, his cleaning his nails at the table or digging in his ears with a toothpick—are so small and niggling as to be irrelevant? Why are details of behavior so immensely important in this kind of problem?

6. Do you find in Kafka's discussion of his father's conventional, fairly meaningless observances of Judaism, and the boy's confusion about these matters, any parallel with your own experience of parental attitudes toward religion and the confusion these leave in a child's mind?

7. Toward the end of the letter, Kafka describes his clumsy adolescent attempt to obtain sexual knowledge and direction from his father. Is the shock and failure here unusual or is it common at this point in adolescence?

8. Certain obvious theme-subjects fairly clamor to be written up, on the stimulus of this letter. Most clamorous—and most difficult—is a letter to one's own father, or, for that matter, to one's mother—a letter which, like Kafka's, would never actually be sent, but in which one might get a good many things off one's mind. Subjects in the realm of psychological evaluation and criticism suggest themselves galore.

Marcel Proust ✑ Filial Sentiments of a Parricide

✑ French novelist (1871-1922), whose many-volumed masterpiece, *Remembrance of Things Past*, is one of the greatest novels in all literature. (See, page 875, a small but famous section from the "Overture" of that work.) ⧫

WHEN M. van Blarenberghe the elder died several months ago, I remembered that my mother had known his wife very well. Since the death of my parents I am (in a sense which it would be irrelevant to describe here) less myself, more their son. Without giving up my own friends, I turn more readily to theirs. And the letters I write now are for the most part ones I think they would have written, ones they can write no longer, letters of congratulation or condolence to friends of theirs whom I often scarcely know. So when Mme. van Blarenberghe lost her husband, I wished to tell her of the grief my parents would have felt. I recalled that some years earlier I had occasionally dined with her son at the houses of mutual friends. To him I wrote, speaking more for my late parents than for myself. I got in reply the following beautiful

From *Pastiches et Mélanges* by Marcel Proust. Copyright © Editions Gallimard. "Filial Sentiments of a Parricide" first appeared in English in *Partisan Review*, January 1948, translated by Barbara Anderson.

letter, conspicuous for great filial love. I think that this document should
be made public because of the meaning given it by the drama that
followed so shortly, especially the meaning it gives to the drama. Here
is the letter:

LES TIMBRIEUX, PAR JOSSELIN (MORBIHAN)
September 24, 1906

I deeply regret, dear sir, that I was unable to thank you sooner for
the sympathy you showed me in my sorrow. But my grief has been so
great that on the advice of doctors I have been traveling for the past
four months. I am only now, and with painful effort, beginning to take
up my regular life again. Surely you will forgive me.

I wish to tell you, however belatedly, that I was much moved by
your remembering our old and excellent relations and profoundly
touched by the sentiment that inspired you to write me and my mother
in the name of your parents, who left us so prematurely. I did not have
the honor of knowing them well, but I remember how much my father
appreciated your father and what a pleasure it was for my mother to
see Mme. Proust. It was most considerate of you to send us their message from beyond the grave. I will soon return to Paris and if I succeed
at all in overcoming the need for isolation which I have felt since the
death of him who absorbed my every interest and inspired my every
joy, I would be very happy to meet you and talk with you of the past.
Very affectionately,
H. VAN BLARENBERGHE

This letter touched me very much. I pitied one who suffered so, I
pitied him, yet I envied him: he still had his mother. In consoling her he
would console himself. I could not agree to his suggestion of a meeting,
only because I was prevented by practical details. But above all the
letter wrought a favorable change in my memory of him. The good relations to which he alluded were really of the most banal social kind. At
the tables where we sometimes dined, I had scarcely had a chance to
talk with him, but the great intellectual distinction of our hosts on those
occasions remained for me, and still remains, a guaranty that Henri van
Blarenberghe, under his rather conventional exterior — the index, perhaps, of his surroundings rather than of his real personality — hid an
original and lively nature. Besides, among those strange flashes of the

memory which our brain, so small and yet so vast, stores in prodigious
number, if I seek those which represent Henri van Blarenberghe, the
flash which always remains most vivid to me is of a face smiling in a
way that was particularly fine, the lips still parted after having thrown
off some witty remark. Pleasant and rather distinguished, so I "resaw"
him, as one might say. Our eyes have more part than we can believe
in this active exploration of the past which we call memory. If you look
at someone while his mind is intent upon bringing back something from
the past, restoring it to life for an instant, you will see that his eyes go
suddenly blind to the surrounding objects which they reflected an
instant before. "Your eyes are blank, you are somewhere else," we say;
however, we see only the external signs of the phenomenon that takes
place in the mind. At such a moment the most beautiful eyes in the
world no longer touch us with their beauty; they are, to change the
meaning of a phrase of Wells's, no more than "machines to explore
time," the telescopes of the invisible, which become at best measures to
gauge one's advancing age. One feels indeed, when one sees the unsteady gaze of old men, the gaze worn out with endless adaptation to a
time so different, often so distant from their own, blindfold itself in
order to recall the past, one feels indeed that the curve of their gaze,
crossing ''the shadow of the days" they have lived, comes to rest several
feet before them, so it seems, but in reality fifty or sixty years behind. I
remember how the enchanting eyes of Princess Mathilde were transformed when they fixed themselves on images of the great men and
magnificent scenes of the beginning of the century. Such images, emanat-
ing from her memories, she saw and we shall never see. At the moments
when my eyes met hers, I had a sense of the supernatural; her gaze, by
some feat of resurrection, firmly and mysteriously joined the present to
the past.

Pleasant and rather distinguished, I said, and it is thus that, in one
of the more vivid images my memory had stored of him, I resaw Henri
van Blarenberghe. But after receiving this letter, I retouched the image
in the depths of my memory by interpreting, in terms of a profounder
sensibility, a mind less mundane, certain details of his glance and bearing which could, indeed, permit of a more sympathetic and arresting
meaning than I had at first allowed. Then, recently, at the request of a
friend, I asked him for information concerning an employee of the
Chemins de fer de l'Est (M. van Blarenberghe was president of the

Board of Directors). Because he had ignored my change of address, his reply, written on the twelfth of last January, did not reach me until the seventeenth, not fifteen days ago, less than eight days before the drama.

48, RUE DE LA BIENFAISANCE

January 12, 1907

DEAR SIR,

I have asked the Compagnie de l'Est for the whereabouts of X, but they have no record of him. Are you right about the name? — if so, the man has disappeared from the company without a trace; he must have had a very provisional and minor connection.

I am distressed at the news of your health since the sad and untimely death of your parents. If it is any consolation to you, I have suffered many physical and moral ailments in attempting to recover from the shock of my father's death. One must always hope. . . . I do not know what the year 1907 holds for me, but let us pray that it may bring some improvement to us both, and that in several months we shall be able to see each other.

Please accept, I beg you, my deepest sympathy.

H. VAN BLARENBERGHE

Five or six days after getting this letter, I recalled, on waking up in the morning, that I had meant to answer it. The day had brought one of those unexpected cold spells which, like high tides of the air, wash over the dykes raised between ourselves and nature by great towns, and battering our closed windows, reaching into our very rooms, make our chilly shoulders feel, through a quickening touch, the furious return of the elements. Days troubled by brusque barometric changes, by shocks even more grave. No joy, after all, in so much violence. We weep for the snow which is about to fall and, as in the lovely verse of André Rivoire, things have the air of "waiting for the snow." Scarcely does "a depression move towards the Balearics," as the newspapers say, or Jamaica begin to quake, when at the same instant in Paris the sufferers from migraine, rheumatism, asthma, no doubt the insane too, reach their crises; the nerves of so many people are united with the farthest points of the universe by bonds which the victims often wish less tight. If the influence of the stars on at least some of them shall one day be recognized . . . , to whom does the poet's line apply better than to such nervous ones? —

Et de longs fils soyeux l'unissent aux étoiles.[1]

On getting up I prepared to answer Henri van Blarenberghe. But before writing him I wanted to glance at *Figaro*,[2] to proceed to that abominable and voluptuous act called "reading the newspapers," thanks to which all the world's misfortunes and cataclysms of the last twenty-four hours, the battles costing fifty thousand lives, the crimes, the strikes, the bankruptcies, the fires, the poisonings, the suicides, the divorces, the crude emotions of statesman and actor, transmuted for our personal consumption, makes for us, who are not involved, a fine little morning treat, an exciting and tonic accompaniment to the sipping of *café au lait.* The fragile thread of *Figaro*, soon enough broken by an indolent gesture, alone divides us from all the world's misery. From the first sensational news of so many people's grief, news we shall soon enjoy relating to friends who have not yet read the paper, we are brought briskly back to the existence which, at the first moment of waking, we had felt it futile to recapture. And if at moments we melt into tears, it is at a phrase like this one: "An impressive silence gripped all hearts, drums sounded on the field, the troops presented arms, a tremendous cry rose up: 'Three cheers for Fallières!' " For this we weep, as we refuse to weep for misfortunes closer to our hearts. Base hypocrites who weep only for the anguish of Hercules or the travels of a President of the Republic! Nevertheless, that morning I did not enjoy reading *Figaro*. I had just skimmed with delight through the volcanic eruptions, the ministerial crises, the duels of *apaches*,[3] and I was calmly beginning to read a column whose title, "A Drama of Madness," was peculiarly adapted to quicken my morning energies, when suddenly I saw that the victim was Mme. van Blarenberghe; that the murderer, who had presently killed himself, was her son, Henri van Blarenberghe, whose letter lay near me waiting to be answered: *"One must always hope. . . . I do not know what 1907 holds for me, but let us pray it will bring improvement,"* etc. One must always hope! I do not know what 1907 holds for me! Life had not been long in answering him. 1907 had not cast off her first month before she

[1] "And long silken threads unite him to the stars."

[2] French newspaper.

[3] Parisian gang members.

brought him her present: musket, revolver, and dagger, and a veil for his mind such as Athena fitted on that of Ajax so that he would slaughter the shepherds and flocks in the Greek camp without knowing what he did. "I it was who put the false images in his eyes. And he rushed upon them, striking here and there, thinking that with his own hand he killed the Atrides, hurling himself now on the sheep, now on the shepherds. I made him the prey of raging madness; I forced him into the snares. He came back, his head dripping with sweat and his hands red with blood."[4] As long as the mad strike they know nothing; then, the fit having passed, what anguish! Tekmessa, Ajax's wife, described it: "His madness is over, his frenzy has fallen like the breath of Motos. But, having recovered his wits, he is now tormented by a new affliction; for to contemplate his own evil deeds when he alone has caused them bitterly increases his anguish. Once he knows what has happened, he cries out in lamentation, he who used to say that a man was ignoble to weep. He sits immobile, shrieking, plotting, no doubt, some dark design against himself." But when the madness is over for Henri van Blarenberghe, it is not butchered sheep and shepherds he has before him. The anguish does not die at once since he himself is not yet dead when he sees his murdered mother before him; since he himself is not yet dead when he hears his dying mother say to him, like Prince Andrey's wife in Tolstoy: "Henri, what have you done to me! What have you done to me!"[5] "When they reached the landing between the first and second floors," says *Le Matin*,[6] "the servants saw Mme. van Blarenberghe, her face distorted by terror, descend two or three steps, crying: "Henri! Henri! what have you done!' Then the poor woman, covered with blood, threw her arms in the air and fell on her face. . . . The horrified servants went out to get help. A little later, four policemen whom one of them had found forced open the murderer's door. Besides slashing himself with a dagger, he had ripped open the whole left side of his face with a bullet. *His eye lay on the pillow.*" Here I no longer think of Ajax. In that eye "which lay on the pillow" I recognize the eye of the miserable Oedipus, torn out in the most terrible act in the history of human suffering! "Oedipus bursts in with loud cries, goes, comes, demands a sword. . . . With a dread shriek he throws himself against the double doors, pulls

[4] From Sophocles' *Ajax*.
[5] In Tolstoy's *War and Peace*.
[6] French newspaper.

the boards from the hinges, rushes into the room where he sees Jocasta
hanging by the cord which had strangled her. Seeing her thus, the
wretch trembles with horror, looses the cord; his mother's body falls to
the ground. He rips the gold brooches from Jocasta's garments, with
them he tears his wide-open eyes, saying that they shall no longer see
the evil he has suffered and the disaster he had caused, and, shouting
curses, again he strikes his eyes, the lids open, and from his bloody eye-
balls a rain, a hail of black blood flows down his cheeks. He cries that the
parricide must be shown to all the Cadmeans. He wants to be driven
from the land. Ah, their old felicity was a true felicity; but from this day
on they shall know all the evils that have a name. Lamentations, ruin,
death, disgrace."[7] And in thinking of Henri van Blarenberghe's pain
when he saw his dead mother, I think of another mad man, of Lear
clasping the body of his daughter Cordelia. "Oh! she's gone forever!
She's as dead as earth. No, no, no life! Why should a dog, a horse, a rat,
have life, and thou no breath at all? Thou'lt come no more, never, never,
never, never, never! Look on her, look, her lips, look there, look there!"

In spite of his horrible wounds Henri van Blarenberghe did not die
at once. And I cannot help finding very harsh (although perhaps necessary; can one be sure what really constituted the drama? Remember
the brothers Karamazov) the act of the superintendent of police. "The
unfortunate man was not dead. The superintendent took him by the
shoulders and said: 'Do you hear me? Answer.' The murderer opened
his one eye, blinked for an instant and fell back in a coma." To this cruel
superintendent I want to speak the words used by Kent in the scene from
King Lear which I quoted just now to stop Edgar from arousing the
already fainting Lear: "Vex not his ghost: O! let him pass; he hates him
that would upon the rack of this tough world stretch him out longer."

If I have insisted on repeating these great tragic names, especially
those of Ajax and Oedipus, the reader should understand why, and also
why I have published these letters and written this page. I wished to
show in what a pure and religious atmosphere of moral beauty, be-
spattered but not defiled, occurred this explosion of madness and blood.
I wished to open the room of crime to the air of heaven, to show that this
commonplace event was exactly one of those Greek dramas, the presentation of which was almost a religious ceremony and that the poor
parricide was not a criminal brute, a being outside humanity, but a noble

[7] From Sophocles' *Oedipus Rex*.

example of humanity, a man of enlightened soul, a tender and dutiful son whom the most ineluctable fatality — let us say pathological fatality, as the world would say — has thrown, most unfortunate of mortals, into a crime and an expiation worthy of fame.

"I do not easily believe in death," says Michelet[8] in an admirable passage. It is true that he says it of a sea nettle, whose death, so little different from its life, is scarcely notable; and one might also wonder whether Michelet's phrase may not be simply one of those "basic recipes" which great writers soon acquire, thanks to which they are sure of being able to serve up to their clientele at a moment's notice the particular feast which it demands of them. Although I believe without difficulty in the death of a sea nettle, I cannot easily believe in the death of a person, even in the simple eclipse, the simple decay of his reason. Our sense of the soul's continuity is very strong. What! this spirit which, a moment ago, controlled life by its views, controlled death, inspired in us so much respect, there it is, controlled by life, by death, weaker than our own spirit which, however much it may desire, can no longer bow before what has so quickly become little more than a nonentity! It is with madness as with the impairment of faculties in the old, as with death. What? The man who yesterday wrote the letter quoted above, so noble, so intelligent, this man today. . . . ? And also, for the smallest details are important here, the man who was attached so wisely to the small things of life, who answered a letter so elegantly, who met an overture so correctly, who respected the opinion of others, who desired to appear to them, if not influential, at least amiable, who conducted his game on the social exchequer with such finesse and integrity! . . . I say that all this is very important, and if I have quoted the whole first part of the second letter which, to tell the truth, may seem interesting to no one but myself, it is because that practical good sense seems still more remote from what has happened than the beautiful and profound sadness of the last lines. Often, in a ravaged spirit, it is the main branches, the crown, which survive the longest, after disease has already cleared away all the lower branches. Here, the spiritual plant is intact. And just now, as I was copying these letters, I would have liked to be able to communicate the extreme delicacy, and more, the incredible preciseness of the hand which had written so clearly and neatly.

"What have you done to me! What have you done to me!" If we think of it, perhaps there is no truly loving mother who would not be

[8] Nineteenth-century French historian.

able, on her last day and often long before, to reproach her son with these words. At bottom, we make old, we kill all those who love us, by the anxiety we cause them, by that kind of uneasy tenderness we inspire and ceaselessly put in a state of alarm. If we can see in a beloved body the slow work of destruction side by side with the painful fondness which rouses it, see the faded eyes, the hair long rebelliously black at last vanquished like the rest and growing white, the arteries hardened, the kidneys choked up, the heart strained, courage gone before life, the walk slackened and heavy, the spirit knowing it can hope for nothing yet unwearyingly rebounding with invincible hopes, the gaiety even, innate and seemingly immortal, which made such a pleasant companion for sadness, now finally exhausted, perhaps the one who can see this, in that tardy moment of lucidity which even lives most bewitched by idle fancies may have, for even Don Quixote had such a moment, perhaps that one, like Henri van Blarenberghe when he had dispatched his mother with a blow of the dagger, would shrink from the horror of his life and rush for a revolver so that he might die at once. In most men a vision so painful (supposing that they are able to rise to it) blots out immediately the slightest rays of the joy of living. But what joy, what reason for living, what life can withstand this vision? Which, the vision or the joy of living is true, which is "the Truth"?

◁§ FOR DISCUSSION AND WRITING

1. Make a clean-cut distinction between the *subject matter* of this piece and the *central* or *controlling idea*. Is the controlling idea anywhere stated?

2. What specific relevance and significance does the prefatory material (van Blarenberghe's letters and Proust's comments on van Blarenberghe) have?

3. How is Proust's motivation in writing the piece tied up with his own personal circumstances?

4. Reread the passage about *eyes* (just after the first letter), beginning "Our eyes have more part than we can believe in this active exploration of the past which we call memory," and ending with "her gaze, by some feat of resurrection, firmly and mysteriously joined the present to the past." Is this merely a digression, or is it related to the subject matter and the central idea?

5. Consider the comments on the weather (just after the second letter). Are they in any way related to the central idea?

6. What is the function of the passage, immediately following, about newspaper scandals as titbits for breakfast? Analyze the *tone* of the sentence: "I had just skimmed with delight through the volcanic eruptions, the ministerial crises, the duels of *apaches*, and I was calmly beginning to read a column whose title, 'A Drama of Madness,' was peculiarly adapted to quicken my morning energies. . . ."

7. Proust's chief technique of exposition here is that of analogy. He uses three major analogies—with Ajax, Oedipus, and Lear. Each of these is associated with a different state of mind and has a different bearing on Henri van Blarenberghe's tragedy. Analyze carefully the different associations in each (consult a classical dictionary if necessary) and the way in which they relate to van Blarenberghe. Write a closely considered paragraph summing up the function of these analogies in giving dimension, perspective, and human significance to van Blarenberghe's case.

8. Proust might have stated the analogies in his own words, but instead he uses direct quotations from Sophocles' *Ajax* and *Oedipus Rex* and from *King Lear*. What is the gain in effectiveness through the use of the quotations?

9. Copy down the long sentence in the final paragraph, beginning "If we can see in a beloved body the slow work of destruction. . . ." (This work of copying may seem an extravagance, but it is really the best means of discovering for oneself just how a certain writer's "style" operates.) Now analyze the grammar of the sentence. Where is the main clause? How many objects has the verb "see?" Is the grammar actually obscure? Is the sentence unclear, or does it acquire mounting power through its succession of parallelisms? How many concrete *images* are there in the sentence? Rephrase the sentence in your own words without using any concrete imagery. Evaluate the difference of effect.

10. Write a short essay on the theme set by Proust in the statement: "At bottom, we make old, we kill all those who love us. . . ." Or make an examination of the items of scandal in one of the more lurid daily newspapers, and write an essay (using specific illustration) on the psychological attraction in this kind of news.

Men and Women in Love

THE HEADING *of this section may be somewhat misleading at first glance;*
for the phrase "in love" suggests what is commonly known as
"romantic love." Yet one can surely say that St. John of the Cross and
St. Teresa of Avila were "in love" with God, and that Socrates was
"in love" with the good. The preposition "in" seems to proclaim a
heightened state of sensibility and a more complete possession of all
one's faculties by love, than the word "love" alone.

We are greatly impoverished by the loss of almost all our
inherited symbols for the phenomena of love, except for (and one says
this with dubiety) romantic love; even the symbolism of romantic
love is curiously monotonous and almost self-consciously illusionary,
as it is shaped and reshaped in the films, television, women's magazines,
advertisements for glamorous cosmetics and perfumes, and the "you"
and "goo" of popular lyrics. Without symbols we cannot converse
about the subtle varieties and paradoxes of love—cannot even think
them, for we think through symbols. Certainly one wouldn't, without
a grin, reduce those phenomena to "stimulus and response" or
"conditioned reflexes," although that kind of vocabulary, suitable for
rats, is about all we have left for analyzing the experience of human
beings in love. It is impossible, for instance, to imagine a group of people

at a cocktail party (the modern equivalent of Plato's symposium) seriously discussing love. Sex, yes. But love?

It was much easier for the ancient Greeks to communicate with each other, in a creative exchange of ideas, about the nature of love and its various forms because they had an enormously rich vocabulary of symbols: the gods themselves—who were both states of mind and powers abroad in the universe—and all the divine myths and the hero myths. Thus, at that marvelous supper in the SYMPOSIUM, it was entirely natural that the prize-winning tragedian of the day and other young Athenians, students of philosophy, should be asked to discourse on love, while the rest of the guests listened, reclining on benches around the banquet table, as the great wine cup went round—listened, criticized, and praised. And who but Socrates, "master in the mysteries of love," a froglike figure with his potbelly and bowlegs, his snub nose, gargoyle mouth, and bugged-out eyes, should deliver the crowning discourse on the subject?

Like a flight of angels the radiant hierarchy mounts, from love of the beautiful body and other separate things, to the quality that makes them beautiful and beloved, to the institutions of regulative law, to that final vision of the good, whose image had been implanted even in the lowliest loved object. At the end of the party (there was no room to include it here), Socrates, having drunk everybody but Agathon under the table, goes out into the dawn with this companion, arguing now that comedy and tragedy "grow on the same tree." But we lose the rest of that promising discussion as they go on down the street. . . .

There could be nothing like it ever again.

Stendhal (the French do this far better than Anglo-Saxons) analyzes and classifies four kinds of love, in the selection from his charming and witty book ON LOVE: passion-love (as the terms are translated here), sympathy-love, sensual love, and vanity-love. Stendhal's own fantastically attractive hero, Julien Sorel, in THE RED AND THE BLACK, *studied Napoleon's military strategy and tactics in planning his first assault on his beloved's virtue, then came to tragic disaster between passion-love and vanity-love.*

It is probably under the classification of passion-love that what we know as "romantic love" best fits. At any rate, that is where Stendhal puts those deeply sophisticated, God-tormented lovers, Abelard and Heloise, and where it seems likely that he would have put John Keats's tragic passion. From the two letters of the medieval lovers printed here, and from Keats's letters to Fanny Brawne, the student may judge for himself.

Passion-love seems, from those great examples and others—Tristan and Iseult, Dido throwing herself on the burning pyre as Aeneas sails from Carthage, Antony and Cleopatra, Heathcliff and Cathy— to be destructive in its operation; and that perhaps is why it has so often been represented as an enchantment beyond human control (the magic love-potion, the power of Venus, the gypsy spell of the serpent of the Nile, an unregenerate savagery of wind and earth), for what comes from such unknown depths of the unconscious to obsess the whole personality seems otherwise inexplicable. The Spanish philosopher, Ortega y Gasset, does not see eye to eye at all with Stendhal on the subject of passion-love, for he is aware of the obsessive, destructive, death-directed character of such love; passion, he says, is "a pathological state." Ortega concentrates on an analysis of "romantic love," which little resembles the shoddy, artificially hopped-up erotic romanticism we spoke of earlier. This love, as he defines it, is "the most delicate and total act of a soul," it reflects "the state and nature of the soul," and therefore "we can find in love the most decisive symptom of what a person is." Plato would not disagree. (But our poverty of symbols makes trouble again. What does Ortega mean by "soul"?)

It is typical of the great German poet, Rilke, that when a young poet wrote him, sending manuscripts of poems and asking criticism,

Rilke's reply should not be about the young man's poetry but about his life—about loneliness and love, the "difficult work of love"—for where else can the poet find his discipline? For Rilke himself, the great lovers, especially the unrequited ones, together with the great heroes, were the chief symbols by which he thought. "When longing comes over you," he wrote in the first of the DUINO ELEGIES,

> *sing the great lovers: the fame*
> *of all they can feel is far from immortal enough.*
> *Those whom you almost envied, those forsaken, you found*
> *so far beyond the requited in loving. Begin*
> *ever anew their never attainable praise.*[1]

In a particularly obstreperous piece by D. H. Lawrence, which brings in his cow, Wordsworth's primrose by the river's brim, the chickens in the back yard, Lawrence's wife, his horse, and several other matters, the ancient pagan symbol of Eros comes much nearer to us than in any other of the modern pieces here. Lawrence's Eros, like that of Socrates' teacher, Diotima, is "rough and squalid," and at the same time a "great spirit" mediating "between gods and men," working "whether we are awake or asleep" to bring about perpetual rebirth in both bodies and souls.

[1] From the *Duino Elegies* by Rainier Maria Rilke. Translated by J. B. Leishman and Stephen Spender. Copyright 1939, W. W. Norton & Co., Inc.

Plato ⌘ The Wisdom of Diotima

⌘ Athenian philosopher (429-347 B.C.), pupil of Socrates and in turn teacher of Aristotle. His dialogues, cast in the dramatic form of dialectical discussions between Socrates and his students, have had an inexhaustibly profound influence on Western thought. ⌘

I WILL rehearse a tale of love which I heard from Diotima of Mantineia, a woman wise in this and in many other kinds of knowledge, who in the days of old, when the Athenians offered sacrifice before the coming of the plague, delayed the disease ten years. She was my instructress in the art of love, and I shall repeat to you what she said to me. . . . As you, Agathon,[1] suggested. I must speak first of the being and nature of Love, and then of his works. First

The argument was communicated to Socrates by Diotima.

From the *Symposium* by Plato, translated by Benjamin Jowett (New York: Random House, 1937).

[1] Tragic dramatist, whose works do not survive. The "symposium" (anciently meaning a drinking party after a banquet, where a lively interchange of ideas took place) was held in Agathon's honor, to celebrate one of his dramatic successes. Along with several other guests, he had been asked to deliver a discourse on the subject of love, after which Socrates is prevailed upon to speak on the same subject.

I said to her in nearly the same words which he used to me, that Love was a mighty god, and likewise fair; and she proved to me as I proved to him that by my own showing, Love was neither fair nor good. 'What do you mean, Diotima,' I said, 'is Love then evil and foul?' 'Hush,' she cried, 'must that be foul which is not fair?' 'Certainly,' I said. 'And is that which is not wise, ignorant? do you not see that there is a mean between wisdom and ignorance?' 'And what may that be?' I said, 'Right opinion,'[2] she replied; 'which, as you know, being incapable of giving a reason, is not knowledge . . . , but is clearly something which is a mean between ignorance and wisdom.' 'Quite true,' I replied. 'Do not then insist,' she said, 'that what is not fair is of necessity foul, or what is not good evil; or infer that because love is not fair and good he is therefore foul and evil; for he is in a mean between them.' 'Well,' I said, 'Love is surely admitted by all to be a great god.' 'By those who know or by those who do not know?' 'By all.' 'And how, Socrates,' she said with a smile, 'can Love be acknowledged to be a great god by those who say that he is not a god at all?' 'And who are they?' I said. 'You and I are two of them,' she replied. 'How can that be?' I said. 'It is quite intelligible,' she replied; 'for you yourself would acknowledge that the gods are happy and fair — of course you would — would you dare to say that any god was not?' 'Certainly not,' I replied. 'And you mean by the happy, those who are the possessors of things good or fair?' 'Yes.' 'And you admitted that Love, because he was in want,[3] desires those good and fair things of which he is in want?' 'Yes, I did.'

---

[2] The Greeks distinguished between true knowledge (wisdom), which can be demonstrated by reason and is true everywhere and always, and "opinion," which is based on our empirical experience only, rather than on reasoning.

[3] Throughout this discussion, as will be seen, love is conceived of as *desire for* something, and therefore as "in want" of, or lacking, the thing desired.

'But how can he be a god who has no portion in what is either good or fair?' 'Impossible.' 'Then you see that you also deny the divinity of Love.'

'What then is Love?' I asked; 'Is he mortal?' 'No.' 'What then?' 'As in the former instance, he is neither mortal nor immortal, but in a mean between the two.' 'What is he, Diotima?' 'He is a great spirit, *He is a great spirit who mediates between gods and men;* and like all spirits he is intermediate between the divine and the mortal.' 'And what,' I said, 'is his power?' 'He interprets,' she replied, 'between gods and men, conveying and taking across to the gods the prayers and sacrifices of men, and to men the commands and replies of the gods; he is the mediator who spans the chasm which divides them, and therefore in him all is bound together, and through him the arts of the prophet and the priest, their sacrifices and mysteries and charms, and all prophecy and incantation, find their way. For God mingles not with man; but through Love all the intercourse and converse of god with man, whether awake or asleep, is carried on. The wisdom which understands this is spiritual; all other wisdom, such as that of arts and handicrafts, is mean and vulgar. Now these spirits or intermediate powers are many and diverse, and one of them is Love.' 'And who,' I said, 'was his father, and who his mother?' 'The tale,' she said, 'will take time; nevertheless I will *the son of Plenty and Poverty;* tell you. On the birthday of Aphrodite there was a feast of the gods, at which the god Poros or Plenty, who is the son of Metis or Discretion, was one of the guests. When the feast was over, Penia or Poverty, as the manner is on such occasions, came about the doors to beg. Now Plenty, who was the worse for nectar (there was no wine in those days), went into the garden of Zeus and fell into a heavy sleep; and Poverty considering her own straitened circumstances, plotted to have a child by him, and accordingly she lay down at his side and conceived *a shoeless, houseless, ill-favoured vagabond, who is always conspiring against the fair and good;*

Love, who partly because he is naturally a lover of the beautiful, and because Aphrodite is herself beautiful, and also because he was born on her birthday, is her follower and attendant. And as his parentage is, so also are his fortunes. In the first place he is always poor, and anything but tender and fair, as the many imagine him; and he is rough and squalid, and has no shoes, nor a house to dwell in; on the bare earth exposed he lies under the open heaven, in the streets, or at the doors of houses, taking his rest; and like his mother he is always in distress. Like his father too, whom he also partly resembles, he is always plotting against the fair and good; he is bold, enterprising, strong, a mighty hunter, always weaving some intrigue or other, keen in the pursuit of wisdom, fertile in resources; a philosopher at all times, terrible as an enchanter, sorcerer, sophist. He is by nature neither mortal nor immortal, but alive and flourishing at one moment when he is in plenty, and dead at another moment, and again alive by reason of his father's nature. But that which is always flowing in is always flowing out, and so he is never in want and never in wealth; and, further, he is in a mean between ignorance and knowledge. The truth of the matter is this: No god is a philosopher or seeker after wisdom, for he is wise already; nor does any man who is wise seek after wisdom. Neither do the ignorant seek after wisdom. For herein is the evil of ignorance, that he who is neither good nor wise is nevertheless satisfied with himself: he has no desire for that of which he feels no want.' 'But who then, Diotima,' I said, 'are the lovers of wisdom, if they are neither the wise nor the foolish?' 'A child may answer that question,' she replied; 'they are those who are in a mean between the two; Love is one of them. For wisdom is a most beautiful thing, and

Love is of the beautiful;[4] and therefore Love is also a philosopher or lover of wisdom, and being a lover of wisdom is in a mean between the wise and the ignorant. And of this too his birth is the cause; for his father is wealthy and wise, and his mother poor and foolish. Such, my dear Socrates, is the nature of the spirit Love. The error in your conception of him was very natural, and as I imagine from what you say, has arisen out of a confusion of love and the beloved, which made you think that love was all beautiful. For the beloved is the truly beautiful, and delicate, and perfect, and blessed; but the principle of love is of another nature, and is such as I have described.'

not wise, but a lover of wisdom.

I said: 'O thou stranger woman, thou sayest well; but, assuming Love to be such as you say, what is the use of him to men?' 'That, Socrates,' she replied, 'I will attempt to unfold: of his nature and birth I have already spoken; and you acknowledge that love is of the beautiful. But some one will say: Of the beautiful in what, Socrates and Diotima? — or rather let me put the question more clearly, and ask: When a man loves the beautiful, what does he desire?' I answered her 'That the beautiful may be his.' 'Still,' she said, 'the answer suggests a further question: What is given by the possession of beauty?' 'To what you have asked,' I replied, 'I have no answer ready.' 'Then,' she said, 'let me put the word "good" in the place of the beautiful, and repeat the question once more: If he who loves loves the good, what is it then that he loves?' 'The possession of the good,' I said. 'And what does he gain who possesses the good?' 'Happiness,' I replied; 'there is less difficulty in answering that question.' 'Yes,' she said, 'the happy are made happy by the acquisition of good things. Nor is there any need

Love is of the beautiful, but in what?

Of the possession of the beautiful, which is also the possession of the good, which is happiness.

4 Love desires the beautiful.

*Yet love
is not
commonly
used
in this
general
sense.*

to ask why a man desires happiness; the answer is already final.' 'You are right,' I said. 'And is this wish and this desire common to all? and do all men always desire their own good, or only some men? — what say you?' 'All men,' I replied; 'the desire is common to all.' 'Why, then,' she rejoined, 'are not all men, Socrates, said to love, but only some of them? whereas you say that all men are always loving the same things.' 'I myself wonder,' I said, 'why this is.' 'There is nothing to wonder at,' she replied; 'the reason is that one part of love is separated off and receives the name of the whole, but the other parts have other names.' 'Give an illustration,' I said. She answered me as follows: 'There is poetry, which, as you know, is complex and manifold. All creation or passage of non-being into being is poetry or making,[5] and the processes of all art are creative; and the masters of arts are all poets or makers.' 'Very true.' 'Still,' she said, 'you know that they are not called poets, but have other names; only that portion of the art which is separated off from the rest, and is concerned with music and metre, is termed poetry, and they who possess poetry in this sense of the word are called poets.' 'Very true,' I said. 'And the same holds of love. For you may say generally that all desire of good and happiness is only the great and subtle power of love; but they who are drawn towards him by any other path, whether the path of money-making or gymnastics or philosophy, are not called lovers — the name of the whole is appropriated to those whose affection takes one form only — they alone are said to love, or to be lovers.' 'I dare say,' I replied, 'that you are right.' 'Yes,' she added, 'and you hear people say that lovers are seeking for their

[5] The word "poetry" derives from the Greek verb *poiein*, "to make." All processes of creating or "making" may therefore be called poetry. But, Diotima points out, we reserve the word for only certain kinds of creativity.

other half; but I say that they are seeking neither
for the half of themselves, nor for the whole, unless
the half or the whole be also a good. And they will
cut off their own hands and feet and cast them
away, if they are evil; for they love not what is
their own, unless perchance there be some one who
calls what belongs to him the good, and what
belongs to another the evil. For there is nothing
which men love but the good. Is there anything?'
'Certainly, I should say, that there is nothing.'
'Then,' she said, 'the simple truth is, that men love
the good.' 'Yes,' I said. 'To which must be added
that they love the possession of the good?' 'Yes,
that must be added.' 'And not only the possession,
but the everlasting possession of the good?' 'That
must be added too.' 'Then love,' she said, 'may be
described generally as the love of the everlasting
possession of the good?' 'That is most true.'

 "Then if this be the nature of love, can you
tell me further,' she said, 'what is the manner of
the pursuit? what are they doing who show all this
eagerness and heat which is called love? and what
is the object which they have in view? Answer me.'
'Nay, Diotima,' I replied, 'if I had known, I should
not have wondered at your wisdom, neither should
I have come to learn from you about this very
matter.' 'Well,' she said, 'I will teach you: — The
object which they have in view is birth in beauty,
whether of body or soul.' 'I do not understand you,'
I said; 'the oracle requires an explanation.' 'I will
make my meaning clearer,' she replied. 'I mean to
say, that all men are bringing to the birth in their
bodies and in their souls. There is a certain age at
which human nature is desirous of procreation —
procreation which must be in beauty and not in
deformity; and this procreation is the union of man
and woman, and is a divine thing; for conception
and generation are an immortal principle in the

*Love is
birth, is
creation;
is the
divine
power of
conception or
parturition;*

mortal creature, and in the inharmonious they can never be. But the deformed is always inharmonious with the divine, and the beautiful harmonious. Beauty, then, is the destiny or goddess of parturition who presides at birth, and therefore, when approaching beauty, the conceiving power is propitious, and diffusive, and benign, and begets and bears fruit: at the sight of ugliness she frowns and contracts and has a sense of pain, and turns away, and shrivels up, and not without a pang refrains from conception. And this is the reason why, when the hour of conception arrives, and the teeming nature is full, there is such a flutter and ecstasy about beauty whose approach is the alleviation of the pain of travail. For love, Socrates, is not, as you imagine, the love of the beautiful only.' 'What

is not the love of the beautiful only, but of birth in beauty.

then?' 'The love of generation and of birth in beauty.' 'Yes,' I said. 'Yes, indeed,' she replied. 'But why of generation?' 'Because to the mortal creature, generation is a sort of eternity and immortality,' she replied; 'and if, as has been already admitted, love is of the everlasting possession of the good, all men will necessarily desire immortality together with good: Wherefore love is of immortality.'

All this she taught me at various times when she spoke of love. And I remember her once saying

Whence arises the great power of love in men and animals?

to me, 'What is the cause, Socrates, of love, and the attendant desire? See you not how all animals, birds, as well as beasts, in their desire of procreation, are in agony when they take the infection of love, which begins with the desire of union; whereto is added the care of offspring, on whose behalf the weakest are ready to battle against the strongest even to the uttermost, and to die for them, and will let themselves be tormented with hunger or suffer anything in order to maintain their young. Man may be supposed to act thus from reason; but why should animals have these passionate feelings?

Can you tell me why?' Again I replied that I did not know. She said to me: 'And do you expect ever to become a master in the art of love, if you do not know this?' 'But I have told you already, Diotima, that my ignorance is the reason why I come to you; for I am conscious that I want a teacher; tell me then the cause of this and of the other mysteries of love.' 'Marvel not,' she said, 'if you believe that love is of the immortal, as we have several times acknowledged; for here again, and on the same principle too, the mortal nature is seeking as far as is possible to be everlasting and immortal: and this is only to be attained by generation, because generation always leaves behind a new existence in the place of the old. Nay even in the life of the same individual there is succession and not absolute unity: a man is called the same, and yet in the short interval which elapses between youth and age, and in which every animal is said to have life and identity, he is undergoing a perpetual process of loss and reparation — hair, flesh, bones, blood, and the whole body are always changing. Which is true not only of the body, but also of the soul, whose habits, tempers, opinions, desires, pleasures, pains, fears, never remain the same in any one of us, but are always coming and going; and equally true of knowledge, and what is still more surprising to us mortals, not only do the sciences[6] in general spring up and decay, so that in respect of them we are never the same; but each of them individually experiences a like change. For what is implied in the word "recollection," but the departure of knowledge, which is ever being forgotten, and is renewed and preserved by recollection, and appears to be the same although in reality new, according to that law of succession by which all mortal things are preserved, not absolutely the same, but by substitu-

The mortal nature is always changing and generating, body and soul alike;

the sciences come and go, and

are preserved by recollection; and all human things, unlike the divine, are made immortal by a law of succession.

[6] All forms of knowledge.

tion, the old worn-out mortality leaving another new and similar existence behind — unlike the divine, which is always the same and not another? And in this way, Socrates, the mortal body, or mortal anything, partakes of immortality; but the immortal in another way. Marvel not then at the love which all men have of their offspring; for that universal love and interest is for the sake of immortality.'

The struggles and sufferings of human life are all of them animated by the desire of immortality.

I was astonished at her words, and said: 'Is this really true, O thou wise Diotima?' And she answered with all the authority of an accomplished sophist: 'Of that, Socrates, you may be assured — think only of the ambition of men, and you will wonder at the senselessness of their ways, unless you consider how they are stirred by the love of an immortality of fame. They are ready to run all risks greater far than they would have run for their children, and to spend money and undergo any sort of toil, and even to die, for the sake of leaving behind them a name which shall be eternal. Do you imagine that Alcestis[7] would have died to save Admetus, or Achilles to avenge Patroclus, or your own Codrus[8] in order to preserve the kingdom for his sons, if they had not imagined that the memory of their virtues, which still survives among us, would be immortal? Nay,' she said, 'I am persuaded that all men do all things, and the better they are the more they do them, in hope of the glorious fame of immortal virtue; for they desire the immortal.

'Those who are pregnant in the body only, betake themselves to women and beget children — this is the character of their love; their offspring, as

[7] Alcestis is the heroine of a play by Euripides. Her husband, Admetus, king of Thessaly, was mortally sick, but his life was spared when Alcestis offered to die in his stead.

[8] Traditionally, the last king of Athens, about 1050 B.C.

they hope, will preserve their memory and give
them the blessedness and immortality which they
desire in the future. But souls which are pregnant
— for there certainly are men who are more creative
in their souls than in their bodies — conceive that
which is proper for the soul to conceive or contain.
And what are these conceptions? — wisdom and
virtue in general. And such creators are poets and
all artists who are deserving of the name inventor.
But the greatest and fairest sort of wisdom by far is
that which is concerned with the ordering of states
and families, and which is called temperance and
justice. And he who in youth has the seed of these
implanted in him and is himself inspired, when he
comes to maturity desires to beget and generate. He
wanders about seeking beauty that he may beget
offspring — for in deformity he will beget nothing
— and naturally embraces the beautiful rather than
the deformed body; above all when he finds a fair
and noble and well-nurtured soul, he embraces the
two in one person, and to such an one he is full of
speech about virtue and the nature and pursuits of
a good man; and he tries to educate him; and at the
touch of the beautiful which is ever present to his
memory, even when absent, he brings forth that
which he had conceived long before, and in company with him tends that which he brings forth;
and they are married by a far nearer tie and have
a closer friendship than those who beget mortal
children, for the children who are their common
offspring are fairer and more immortal. Who, when
he thinks of Homer and Hesiod and other great
poets, would not rather have their children than
ordinary human ones? Who would not emulate
them in the creation of children such as theirs,
which have preserved their memory and given them
everlasting glory? Or who would not have such

The creations of the soul, — conceptions of wisdom and virtue, the works of poets and legislators, — are fairer far than any mortal children.

children as Lycurgus[9] left behind him to be the
saviours, not only of Lacedaemon, but of Hellas,
as one may say? There is Solon,[10] too, who is the
revered father of Athenian laws; and many others
there are in many other places, both among Hellenes and barbarians, who have given to the world
many noble works, and have been the parents of
virtue of every kind; and many temples have been
raised in their honour for the sake of children such
as theirs; which were never raised in honour of
any one, for the sake of his mortal children.

'These are the lesser mysteries of love, into
which even you, Socrates, may enter; to the greater
and more hidden ones[11] which are the crown of
these, and to which, if you pursue them in a right
spirit, they will lead, I know not whether you will
be able to attain. But I will do my utmost to inform
you, and do you follow if you can. For he who
would proceed aright in this matter should begin
in youth to visit beautiful forms; and first, if he be
guided by his instructor aright, to love one such
form only — out of that he should create fair
thoughts; and soon he will of himself perceive that
the beauty of one form is akin to the beauty of
another; and then if beauty of form in general is
his pursuit, how foolish would he be not to recognize that the beauty in every form is one and the
same! And when he perceives this he will abate his
violent love of the one, which he will despise and
deem a small thing, and will become a lover of all
beautiful forms; in the next stage he will consider
that the beauty of the mind is more honourable
than the beauty of the outward form. So that if a

*He who
would be
truly initiated
should
pass from
the concrete to
the abstract,
from the
individual
to the
universal,
from the
universal
to the
universe
of truth
and
beauty.*

[9] Traditionally thought to have founded the laws and constitution of Sparta (Lacedaemon), presumably in the ninth century B.C.

[10] Athenian sage and lawgiver, ca. 638-559 B.C.

[11] In analogy with the religious rites (mysteries) performed at Eleusis; the Lesser
Mysteries were held in the spring, the Greater Mysteries in the fall.

virtuous soul have but a little comeliness, he will
be content to love and tend him, and will search
out and bring to the birth thoughts which may improve the young, until he is compelled to contemplate and see the beauty of institutions and laws,
and to understand that the beauty of them all is of
one family, and that personal beauty is a trifle; and
after laws and institutions he will go on to the
sciences, that he may see their beauty, being not
like a servant in love with the beauty of one youth
or man or institution, himself a slave mean and
narrow-minded, but drawing towards and contemplating the vast sea of beauty, he will create many
fair and noble thoughts and notions in boundless
love of wisdom; until on that shore he grows and
waxes strong, and at last the vision is revealed to
him of a single science, which is the science of
beauty everywhere. To this I will proceed; please
to give me your very best attention:

'He who has been instructed thus far in the
things of love, and who has learned to see the
beautiful in due order and succession, when he
comes toward the end will suddenly perceive a
nature of wondrous beauty (and this, Socrates, is
the final cause of all our former toils) — a nature
which in the first place is everlasting, not growing
and decaying, or waxing and waning; secondly, not
fair in one point of view and foul in another, or at
one time or in one relation or at one place fair, at
another time or in another relation or at another
place foul, as if fair to some and foul to others, or
in the likeness of a face or hands or any other part
of the bodily frame, or in any form of speech or
knowledge, or existing in any other being, as for
example, in an animal, or in heaven, or in earth,
or in any other place; but beauty absolute, separate,
simple, and everlasting, which without diminution
and without increase, or any change, is imparted

*He should
view
beauty,
not relatively,
but absolutely;
and he
should
pass by
stepping-
stones
from
earth to
heaven.*

to the ever-growing and perishing beauties of all
other things. He who from these ascending under
the influence of true love, begins to perceive that
beauty, is not far from the end. And the true order
of going, or being led by another, to the things of
love, is to begin from the beauties of earth and
mount upwards for the sake of that other beauty,
using these as steps only, and from one going on to
two, and from two to all fair forms, and from fair
forms to fair practices, and from fair practices to
fair notions, until from fair notions he arrives at the
notion of absolute beauty, and at last knows what
the essence of beauty is. This, my dear Socrates,'
said the stranger of Mantineia, 'is that life above
all others which man should live, in the contemplation of beauty absolute; a beauty which if you once
beheld, you would see not to be after the measure
of gold, and garments, and fair boys and youths,
whose presence now entrances you; and you and
many a one would be content to live seeing them
only and conversing with them without meat or
drink, if that were possible — you only want to
look at them and to be with them. But what if man
had eyes to see the true beauty — the divine beauty,
I mean, pure and clear and unalloyed, not clogged
with the pollutions of mortality and all the colours
and vanities of human life — thither looking, and
holding converse with the true beauty simple and
divine? Remember how in that communion only,
beholding beauty with the eye of the mind, he will
be enabled to bring forth, not images of beauty, but
realities (for he has hold not of an image but of a
reality),[12] and bringing forth and nourishing true
virtue to become the friend of God and be immortal,

[12] Plato's usual distinction between the experience of the senses, which gives us
only more or less faulty copies ("images," imitations) of the true forms of things,
and philosophical truth, by which alone their "reality" may be known. See the
Allegory of the Cave for a more complete treatment of this distinction (page 882).

if mortal man may. Would that be an ignoble life?'

Such, Phaedrus — and I speak not only to you, but to all of you — were the words of Diotima; and I am persuaded of their truth. And being persuaded of them, I try to persuade others, that in the attainment of this end human nature will not easily find a helper better than love. And therefore, also, I say that every man ought to honour him as I myself honour him, and walk in his ways, and exhort others to do the same, and praise the power and spirit of love according to the measure of my ability now and ever.

✑ FOR DISCUSSION AND WRITING

1. Diotima says that Love is not a god but a "great spirit," "intermediate between the divine and the mortal," through whom all converse and intercourse of gods with men, "whether awake or asleep," is carried on. The Greek mind in the fourth century B.C. did not function so differently from our own that we cannot find a common ground for understanding such conceptions. Modern psychology speaks of an "Eros function" or "Eros principle" in the psyche, and though different schools of psychology offer differing interpretations of that function, it is from all points of view a creative principle, a principle of psychic health and development, and a principle tending toward integration of the personality and social integration. Furthermore, being a function of the unconscious mind, it works "whether we are awake or asleep." In what way, or ways, can one compare this "Eros principle" with the "great spirit" of whose operations Diotima speaks? Assuming that our "gods" are largely those with which the modern sciences are concerned—"-ologies" of various kinds—can you work out any analogies in which the Eros principle of the psyche serves to mediate between our limited individual minds and the truths and visions of the sciences? For instance, could you say that the Eros principle is operating as mediator when you become excited by some new perception in one of your college courses and when you voluntarily seek for more information about it?

Having read Diotima's argument to the end, do you find a fairly large number of such parallels, suggesting that Plato's understanding of the creative operations of the mind and modern understanding of those operations are not discrepant in essentials? You might use this as topic for a short paper.

2. How would you express the meaning of the fable about the birth of Love? Do you see any reason, or reasons, why the subject of love should require paradoxes for its definition? What are some of the chief paradoxes Plato uses here? Can they be put in nonfigurative language?

3. As a whole, what does this discourse gain by using the technique of dialogue (Diotima putting questions to Socrates that he can't answer, and answering them herself, while Socrates just asks questions or simply agrees)? You might try to imagine it as a straight didactic exposition, certainly only half as long; what essential quality would be lost?

4. Both Diotima and Socrates seem to take it for granted that "men love the good." Does the proposition seem to you somewhat more doubtful? Why?

5. What does Diotima mean by saying that all men are constantly "bringing to the birth in their bodies and in their souls"? (In case you balk at the word "soul" you can supply "psyche" or "mind." "Psyche," incidentally, is the Greek word for "soul," psychology being discourse about the soul.) Try to translate this statement into your own words: "Conception and generation are an immortal principle in the mortal creature."

6. Gather from your friends and family some definitions of love and attempt to compose these opinions either in the form of straight exposition or as a "symposium" (round-table discussion).

Heloise and Abelard ✑§ Two Letters

✑§ Pierre Abelard (1070-1142), brilliant theologian of the University of Paris, canon of the cathedral of Notre Dame, and poet, fell in love at the age of thirty-seven with his pupil Heloise, then nineteen. Her uncle and guardian, Fulbert, who was also a canon of the cathedral, sent thugs to fall upon Abelard in his sleep and emasculate him. In disgrace and despair, Abelard fled from Paris, and Heloise entered a convent. ξ๛

[HELOISE TO ABELARD]

To her Lord, her Father, her Husband, her Brother; his Servant, his Child, his Wife, his Sister, and to express all that is humble, respectful and loving to her Abelard, Heloise writes this.

A CONSOLATORY letter of yours to a friend happened some days since to fall into my hands; my knowledge of the writing and my love of the hand gave me the curiosity to open it. In justification of the liberty I took, I flattered myself I might claim a sovereign privilege over everything which came from you. Nor was I scrupulous to break through the rules of good breeding when I was to hear news of Abelard. But how dear did my curiosity cost me! What disturbance did it occasion, and how surprised I was to find the whole letter filled with a particular and melancholy account of our misfortunes! I met with my name a hundred times; I never saw it without fear — some heavy calamity always followed it. I saw yours too, equally unhappy. . . . What reflections did I not make! I began to consider the whole afresh, and perceived myself

From an anonymous translation published in London in 1722 and by Simon and Schuster, Inc., in *A Treasury of the World's Great Letters*.

pressed with the same weight of grief as when we first began to be miserable. Though length of time ought to have closed up my wounds, yet the seeing them described by your hand was sufficient to make them all open and bleed afresh. . . .

I reproached myself for having been so long without venting my sorrows, when the rage of our unrelenting enemies still burns with the same fury. Since length of time, which disarms the strongest hatred, seems but to aggravate theirs; since it is decreed that your virtue shall be persecuted till it takes refuge in the grave — and even then, perhaps, your ashes will not be allowed to rest in peace! — let me always meditate on your calamities, let me publish them through all the world, if possible, to shame an age that has not known how to value you. . . .

Let me have a faithful account of all that concerns you; I would know everything, be it ever so unfortunate. Perhaps by mingling my sighs with yours I may make your sufferings less, for it is said that all sorrows divided are made lighter.

Tell me not by way of excuse you will spare me tears; the tears of women shut up in a melancholy place and devoted to penitence are not to be spared. . . . Write to me then immediately and wait not for miracles; they are too scarce, and we too much accustomed to misfortunes to expect a happy turn. I shall always have this, if you please, and this will always be agreeable to me, that when I receive any letter from you I shall know you still remember me. . . .

We may write to each other; so innocent a pleasure is not denied us. Let us not lose through negligence the only happiness which is left us, and the only one perhaps which the malice of our enemies can never ravish from us. I shall read that you are my husband and you shall see me sign myself your wife. In spite of all our misfortunes you may be what you please in your letter. Letters were first invented for consoling such solitary wretches as myself. Having lost the substantial pleasures of seeing and possessing you, I shall in some measure compensate this loss by the satisfaction I shall find in your writing. There I shall read your most sacred thoughts; I shall carry them always about with me, I shall kiss them every moment. . . .

You cannot but remember (for lovers cannot forget) with what pleasure I have passed whole days in hearing your discourse. How when you were absent I shut myself from everyone to write to you; how uneasy I was till my letter had come to your hands; what artful management it required to engage messengers. This detail perhaps surprises you, and you are in pain for what may follow. But I am no longer ashamed that my passion had no bounds for you, for I have done more than all this. I have hated myself that I might love you. I came hither to ruin myself in a perpetual imprisonment that I might make you live quietly and at ease.

Nothing but virtue, joined to a love perfectly disengaged from the senses, could have produced such effects. Vice never inspires anything like this: it is too much enslaved to the body. When we love pleasures we love the living and not the dead. We leave off burning with desire for those who can no longer burn for us. This was my cruel uncle's notion; he measured my virtue by the frailty of my sex, and thought it was the man and not the person I loved. But he has been guilty to no purpose. I love you more than ever; and so revenge myself on him. I will still love you with all the tenderness of my soul till the last moment of my life. If, formerly, my affection for you was not so pure, if in those days both mind and body loved you, I often told you even then that I was more pleased with possessing your heart than with any other happiness, and the man was the thing I least valued in you.

You cannot but be entirely persuaded of this by the extreme unwillingness I showed to marry you, though I knew that the name of wife was honorable in the world and holy in religion; yet the name of your mistress had greater charms because it was more free. The bonds of matrimony, however honorable, still bear with them a necessary engagement, and I was very unwilling to be necessitated to love always a man who would perhaps not always love me. I despised the name of wife that I might live happy with that of mistress; and I find by your letter to your friend you have not forgot that delicacy of passion which loved you always with the utmost tenderness — and yet wished to love you more!

But oh! where is that happy time? I now lament my lover, and of all my joys have nothing but the painful memory that they are past. Now learn, all you my rivals who once viewed my happiness with jealous eyes, that he you once envied me can never more be mine. I loved him; my love was his crime and the cause of his punishment. My beauty once charmed him; pleased with each other, we passed our brightest days in tranquillity and happiness. If that were a crime, 'tis a crime I am yet fond of, and I have no other regret save that against my will I must now be innocent.

But what do I say? My misfortune was to have cruel relatives whose malice destroyed the calm we enjoyed; had they been reasonable I had now been happy in the enjoyment of my dear husband. Oh! how cruel were they when their blind fury urged a villain to surprise you in your sleep! Where was I — where was your Heloise then? What joy should I have had in defending my lover; I would have guarded you from violence at the expense of my life. Oh! whither does this excess of passion hurry me? Here love is shocked and modesty deprives me of words.

But tell me whence proceeds your neglect of me since my being professed?[1] You know nothing moved me to it but your disgrace, nor did I give my consent, but yours. Let me hear what is the occasion of your coldness, or give me leave to tell you now my opinion. Was it not the sole thought of pleasure which engaged you to me? And has not my tenderness, by leaving you nothing to wish for, extinguished your desires?

Wretched Heloise! you could please when you wished to avoid it; you merited incense when you could remove to a distance the hand that offered it: but since your heart has been softened and has yielded, since you have devoted and sacrificed yourself, you are deserted and forgotten!

I am convinced by a sad experience that it is natural to avoid those to whom we have been too much obliged, and that uncommon generosity causes neglect rather than gratitude. My heart surrendered too soon to gain the esteem of the conqueror; you took it without difficulty and threw it aside with ease. But ungrateful as you are I am no consenting party to this, and though I ought not to retain a wish of my own, yet I still preserve secretly the desire to be loved by you.

When I pronounced my sad vow I then had about me your last letters in which you protested your whole being wholly mine, and would never live but to love me. It is to you therefore I have offered myself; you had my heart and I had yours; do not demand anything back. You must bear with my passion as a thing which of right belongs to you, and from which you can be no ways disengaged. . . .

Is it so hard for one who loves to write? I ask for none of your letters filled with learning and writ for your reputation; all I desire is such letters as the heart dictates, and which the hand cannot transcribe

[1] Having taken religious vows.

fast enough. How did I deceive myself with hopes that you would be wholly mine when I took the veil, and engaged myself to live forever under your laws? For in being professed I vowed no more than to be yours only, and I forced myself voluntarily to a confinement which you desired for me. Death only then can make me leave the cloister where you have placed me; and then my ashes shall rest here and wait for yours in order to show to the very last my obedience and devotion to you.

Why should I conceal from you the secret of my call? You know it was neither zeal nor devotion that brought me here. Your conscience is too faithful a witness to permit you to disown it. Yet here I am, and here I will remain; to this place an unfortunate love and a cruel relation have condemned me. But if you do not continue your concern for me, if I lose your affection, what have I gained by my imprisonment? What recompense can I hope for? The unhappy consequences of our love and your disgrace have made me put on the habit of chastity, but I am not penitent of the past. Thus I strive and labor in vain. Among those who are wedded to God I am wedded to a man; among the heroic supporters of the Cross I am the slave of a human desire; at the head of a religious community I am devoted to Abelard alone.

What a monster am I! Enlighten me, O Lord, for I know not if my despair of Thy grace draws these words from me! I am, I confess, a sinner, but one who, far from weeping for her sins, weeps only for her lover; far from abhorring her crimes, longs only to add to them; and who, with a weakness unbecoming my state, please myself continually with the remembrance of past delights when it is impossible to renew them.

Good God! What is all this? I reproach myself for my own faults, I accuse you for yours, and to what purpose? Veiled as I am, behold in what a disorder you have plunged me! How difficult it is to fight for duty against inclination. I know what obligations this veil lays upon me, but I feel more strongly what power an old passion has over my heart. . . .

Oh, for pity's sake help a wretch to renounce her desires — her self — and if possible even to renounce you! If you are a lover — a father, help a mistress, comfort a child! These tender names must surely move you; yield either to pity or to love. If you gratify my request I shall continue a religious, and without longer profaning my calling. . . .

I expect this from you as a thing you cannot refuse me. God has a peculiar right over the hearts of great men He has created. When

He pleases to touch them He ravishes them, and lets them not speak nor breathe but for His glory. Till that moment of grace arrives, O think of me — do not forget me — remember my love and fidelity and constancy: love me as your mistress, cherish me as your child, your sister, your wife! Remember I still love you, and yet strive to avoid loving you. What a terrible saying is this! I shake with horror, and my heart revolts against what I say. I shall blot all my paper with tears. I end my long letter wishing you, if you desire it (would to Heaven I could!), forever adieu!

[ABELARD TO HELOISE]

COULD I have imagined that a letter not written to yourself would fall into your hands, I had been more cautious not to have inserted anything in it which might awaken the memory of our past misfortunes. I described with boldness the series of my disgraces to a friend, in order to make him less sensible to a loss he had sustained.

If by this well-meaning device I have disturbed you, I purpose now to dry up those tears which the sad description occasioned you to shed; I intend to mix my grief with yours, and pour out my heart before you: in short, to lay open before your eyes all my trouble, and the secret of my soul, which my vanity has hitherto made me conceal from the rest of the world, and which you now force from me, in spite of my resolutions to the contrary.

It is true, that in a sense of the afflictions which have befallen us, and observing that no change of our condition could be expected; that those prosperous days which had seduced us were now past, and there remained nothing but to erase from our minds, by painful endeavors, all marks and remembrances of them. I had wished to find in philosophy and religion a remedy for my disgrace; I searched out an asylum to secure me from love. I was come to the sad experiment of making vows to harden my heart.

But what have I gained by this? If my passion has been put under a restraint my thoughts yet run free. I promise myself that I will forget you, and yet cannot think of it without loving you. My love is not at all lessened by those reflections I make in order to free myself. The silence

I am surrounded by makes me more sensible to its impressions, and while I am unemployed with any other things, this makes itself the business of my whole vocation. Till after a multitude of useless endeavors I begin to persuade myself that it is a superfluous trouble to strive to free myself; and that it is sufficient wisdom to conceal from all but you how confused and weak I am.

I remove to a distance from your person with an intention of avoiding you as an enemy; and yet I incessantly seek for you in my mind; I recall your image in my memory, and in different disquietudes I betray and contradict myself. I hate you! I love you! Shame presses me on all sides.

Religion commands me to pursue virtue since I have nothing to hope for from love. But love still preserves its dominion over my fancies and entertains itself with past pleasures. Memory supplies the place of a mistress. Piety and duty are not always the fruits of retirement; even in deserts, when the dew of heaven falls not on us, we love what we ought no longer to love.

The passions, stirred up by solitude, fill these regions of death and silence; it is very seldom that what ought to be is truly followed here and that God only is loved and served. Had I known this before I had instructed you better. You call me your master; it is true you were entrusted to my care. I saw you, I was earnest to teach you vain sciences; it cost you your innocence and me my liberty.

Your uncle, who was fond of you, became my enemy and revenged himself on me. If now having lost the power of satisfying my passion I had also lost that of loving you, I should have some consolation. . . . How miserable am I! I find myself much more guilty in my thoughts of you, even amidst my tears, than in possessing you when I was in full liberty. I continually think of you; I continually call to mind your tenderness.

In this condition, O Lord! if I run to prostrate myself before your altar, if I beseech you to pity me, why does not the pure flame of the Spirit consume the sacrifice that is offered? Cannot this habit of penitence which I wear interest Heaven to treat me more favorably? But Heaven is still inexorable, because my passion still lives in me; the fire is only covered over with deceitful ashes, and cannot be extinguished but by extraordinary grace. We deceive men, but nothing is hid from God.

You tell me that it is for me you live under that veil which covers you; why do you profane your vocation with such words? Why provoke a jealous God with a blasphemy? I hoped after our separation you would have changed your sentiments; I hoped too that God would have delivered me from the tumult of my senses. We commonly die to the affections of those we see no more, and they to ours; absence is the tomb of love. But to me absence is an unquiet remembrance of what I once loved which continually torments me. I flattered myself that when I should see you no more you would rest in my memory without troubling my mind; that Brittany and the sea would suggest other thoughts; that my fasts and studies would by degrees delete you from my heart. But in spite of severe fasts and redoubled studies, in spite of the distance of three hundred miles which separates us, your image, as you describe yourself in your veil, appears to me and confounds all my resolutions.

What means have I not used! I have armed my hands against myself; I have exhausted my strength in constant exercises; I comment upon Saint Paul; I contend with Aristotle: in short, I do all I used to do before I loved you, but all in vain; nothing can be successful that opposes you. Oh! do not add to my miseries by your constancy. . . . Why use your eloquence to reproach me for my flight and for my silence? Spare the recital of our assignations and your constant exactness to them; without calling up such disturbing thoughts I have enough to suffer. What great advantages would philosophy give us over other men, if by studying it we could learn to govern our passions? What efforts, what relapses, what agitations do we undergo! And how long are we lost in this confusion, unable to exert our reason, to possess our souls, or to rule our affections? . . .

How can I separate from the person I love the passion I should detest? Will the tears I shed be sufficient to render it odious to me? I know not how it happens, there is always a pleasure in weeping for a beloved object. It is difficult in our sorrow to distinguish penitence from love. The memory of the crime and the memory of the object which has charmed us are too nearly related to be immediately separated. And the love of God in its beginning does not wholly annihilate the love of the creature.

But what excuses could I not find in you if the crime were excusable? Unprofitable honor, troublesome riches, could never tempt me: but those charms, that beauty, that air, which I yet behold at this instant, have occasioned my fall. Your looks were the beginning of my guilt;

your eyes, your discourse, pierced my heart; and in spite of that ambition and glory which tried to make a defense, love was soon the master.

God, in order to punish me, forsook me. You are no longer of the world; you have renounced it: I am a religious devoted to solitude; shall we not take advantage of our condition? Would you destroy my piety in its infant state? Would you have me forsake the abbey into which I am but newly entered? Must I renounce my vows? I have made them in the presence of God; whither shall I fly from His wrath should I violate them? Suffer me to seek ease in my duty. . . .

Regard me no more, I entreat you, as a founder or any great personage; your praises ill agree with my many weaknesses. I am a miserable sinner, prostrate before my Judge, and with my face pressed to the earth I mix my tears with the earth. Can you see me in this posture and solicit me to love you? Come, if you think fit, and in your holy habit thrust yourself between my God and me, and be a wall of separation. Come and force from me those sighs and thoughts and vows I owe to Him alone. Assist the evil spirits and be the instrument of their malice. What cannot you induce a heart to do whose weakness you so perfectly know?

Nay, withdraw yourself and contribute to my salvation. Suffer me to avoid destruction, I entreat you by our former tender affection and by our now common misfortune. It will always be the highest love to show none; I here release you from all your oaths and engagements. Be God's wholly, to whom you are appropriated; I will never oppose so pious a design. How happy shall I be if I thus lose you! Then shall I indeed be a religious and you a perfect example of an abbess. . . .

I will confess to you I have thought myself hitherto an abler master to instill vice than to teach virtue. My false eloquence has only set off false good. My heart, drunk with voluptuousness, could only suggest terms proper and moving to recommend that. The cup of sinners overflows with so enchanting a sweetness, and we are naturally so much inclined to taste it, that it needs only to be offered to us.

On the other hand the chalice of saints is filled with a bitter draught and nature starts from it.[2] And yet you reproach me with cowardice for giving it to you first. I willingly submit to these accusations. I cannot enough admire the readiness you showed to accept the religious habit; bear therefore with courage the Cross you so resolutely took up. Drink

[2] Revolts against it.

of the chalice of saints, even to the bottom, without turning your eyes with uncertainty upon me. . . .

To make it more easy consider why I pressed you to your vow before I took mine; and pardon my sincerity and the design I have of meriting your neglect and hatred if I conceal nothing from you. When I saw myself oppressed by my misfortune I was furiously jealous, and regarded all men as my rivals. Love has more of distrust than assurance. I was apprehensive of many things because of my many defects, and being tormented with fear because of my own example I imagined your heart so accustomed to love that it could not be long without entering on a new engagement. Jealousy can easily believe the most terrible things.

I was desirous to make it impossible for me to doubt you. I was very urgent to persuade you that propriety demanded your withdrawal from the eyes of the world; that modesty and our friendship required it; and that your own safety obliged it. After such a revenge taken on me you could expect to be secure nowhere but in a convent.

I will do you justice, you were very easily persuaded. My jealousy secretly rejoiced in your innocent compliance; and yet, triumphant as I was, I yielded you up to God with an unwilling heart. I still kept my gift as much as was possible, and only parted with it in order to keep it out of the power of other men. I did not persuade you to religion out of any regard to your happiness, but condemned you to it like an enemy who destroys what he cannot carry off. And yet you heard my discourses with kindness, you sometimes interrupted me with tears, and pressed me to acquaint you with those convents I held in the highest esteem. What a comfort I felt in seeing you shut up. I was now at ease and took a satisfaction in considering that you continued no longer in the world after my disgrace, and that you would return to it no more. . . . Till then I thought your youth and beauty would foil my design and force your return to the world. Might not a small temptation have changed you? Is it possible to renounce oneself entirely at the age of two-and-twenty? At an age which claims the utmost liberty could you think the world no longer worth your regard? How much did I wrong you, and what weakness did I impute to you? . . . I watched your eyes, your every movement, your air; I trembled at everything. You may call such self-interested conduct treachery, perfidy, murder. A love so like to hatred should provoke the utmost contempt and anger.

I went every day trembling to exhort you to this sacrifice; I admired without daring to mention it then, a brightness in your beauty which I had never observed before. Whether it was the bloom of a rising virtue, or an anticipation of the great loss I was to suffer, I was not curious in examining the cause, but only hastened your being professed. I engaged your prioress in my guilt by a criminal bribe with which I purchased the right of burying you. The professed of the house were alike bribed and concealed from you, at my directions, all their scruples and disgusts. I omitted nothing, either little or great; and if you had escaped my snares I myself would not have retired; I was resolved to follow you everywhere. The shadow of myself would always have pursued your steps and continually have occasioned either your confusion or your fear, which would have been a sensible gratification to me.

But, thanks to Heaven, you resolved to take the vows. I accompained you to the foot of the altar, and while you stretched out your hand to touch the sacred cloth I heard you distinctly pronounce those fatal words that forever separated you from man. . . .

Necessity and despair were at the root of my proceedings, and thus I offered an insult to Heaven rather than a sacrifice. God rejected my offering and my prayer, and continued my punishment by suffering me to continue my love. Thus I bear alike the guilt of your vows and of the passion that preceded them, and must be tormented all the days of my life.

If God spoke to your heart as to that of a religious whose innocence had first asked Him for favors, I should have matter of comfort; but to see both of us the victims of a guilty love, to see this love insult us in our very habits and spoil our devotions, fills me with horror and trembling. Is this a state of reprobation? Or are these the consequences of a long drunkenness in profane love?

We cannot say love is a poison and a drunkenness till we are illuminated by grace; in the meantime it is an evil we dote on. When we are under such a mistake, the knowledge of our misery is the first step towards amendment. Who does not know that 'tis for the glory of God to find no other reason in man for His mercy than man's very weakness? When He has shown us this weakness and we have bewailed it, He is ready to put forth His omnipotence and assist us. Let us say for our comfort that what we suffer is one of those terrible temptations which have sometimes disturbed the vocations of the most holy.

God can grant His presence to men in order to soften their calamities whenever He shall think fit. It was His pleasure when you took the veil to draw you to Him by His grace. I saw your eyes, when you spoke your last farewell, fixed upon the Cross. It was more than six months before you wrote me a letter, nor during all that time did I receive a message from you. I admired this silence, which I durst not blame, but could not imitate. I wrote to you, and you returned me no answer: your heart was then shut, but this garden of the spouse is now opened; He is withdrawn from it and has left you alone.

By removing from you He has made trial of you; call Him back and strive to regain Him. We must have the assistance of God, that we may break our chains; we are too deeply in love to free ourselves.

Our follies have penetrated into the sacred places; our amours have been a scandal to the whole kingdom. They are read and admired; love which produced them has caused them to be described. We shall be a consolation to the failings of youth forever; those who offend after us will think themselves less guilty. We are criminals whose repentance is late; oh, let it be sincere! Let us repair as far as is possible the evils we have done, and let France, which has been the witness of our crimes, be amazed at our repentance. Let us confound all who would imitate our guilt; let us take the side of God against ourselves, and by so doing prevent His judgment.

Our former lapses require tears, shame, and sorrow to expiate them. Let us offer up these sacrifices from our hearts, let us blush and let us weep. If in these feeble beginnings, O Lord, our hearts are not entirely Thine, let them at least feel that they ought to be so.

Deliver yourself, Heloise, from the shameful remains of a passion which has taken too deep root. Remember that the least thought for any other than God is an adultery. If you could see me here with my meager face and melancholy air, surrounded with numbers of persecuting monks, who are alarmed at my reputation for learning and offended at my lean visage, as if I threatened them with a reformation, what would you say of my base sighs and of those unprofitable tears which deceive these credulous men? Alas! I am humbled under love, and not under the Cross. Pity me and free yourself. If your vocation be, as you say, my work, deprive me not of the merit of it by your continual inquietudes. . . .

I have been indeed your master, but it was only to teach sin. You call me your father; before I had any claim to the title, I deserved that of parricide. I am your brother, but it is the affinity of sin that brings me that distinction. I am called your husband, but it is after a public scandal.

If you have abused the sanctity of so many holy terms in the superscription of your letter to do me honor and flatter your own passion, blot them out and replace them with those of murderer, villain, and enemy, who has conspired against your honor, troubled your quiet, and betrayed your innocence. You would have perished through my means but for an extraordinary act of grace, which, that you might be saved, has thrown me down in the middle of my course.

This is the thought you ought to have of a fugitive who desires to deprive you of the hope of ever seeing him again. But when love has once been sincere how difficult it is to determine to love no more! 'Tis a thousand times more easy to renounce the world than love. I hate this deceitful, faithless world; I think no more of it; but my wandering heart still eternally seeks you, and is filled with anguish at having lost you, in spite of all the powers of my reason. . . .

There are some whom God saves by suffering. Let my salvation be the fruit of your prayers; let me owe it to your tears and your exemplary holiness. Though my heart, Lord, be filled with the love of Thy creature, Thy hand can, when it pleases, empty me of all love save for Thee.

To love Heloise truly is to leave her to that quiet which retirement and virtue afford. I have resolved it: this letter shall be my last fault. Adieu.

If I die here I will give orders that my body be carried to the house of the Paraclete. You shall see me in that condition, not to demand tears from you, for it will be too late; weep rather for me now and extinguish the fire which burns me.

You shall see me in order that your piety may be strengthened by horror of this carcase, and my death be eloquent to tell you what you brave when you love a man. I hope you will be willing, when you have finished this mortal life, to be buried near me. Your cold ashes need then fear nothing, and my tomb shall be the more rich and renowned.

✍ FOR DISCUSSION AND WRITING

1. What is Heloise's attitude toward her religious vows? What reason does she give for making them? How does she explain her unwillingness to marry Abelard?

2. Does her state of mind seem clear and rational, or emotionally disturbed and confused? This is a good translation that reflects the French original without distortion, so that one may speak of Heloise's "style"—her style of thinking as well as of expression. French literature is full of heroes and heroines who analyze their most profound emotions with the subtlety and clarity of inspired psychologists. Where do you find in Heloise's style indications that she belongs within that tradition of elaborate analysis?

3. What does Abelard give as his reasons for persuading her to take vows? Does he seem candid, or does he appear to be using his confession of duplicity in order to change Heloise's idea of his character and thus perhaps sway her mind to greater temperance and contentment?

4. How would you describe Abelard's spiritual condition? What is the particular nature of his inner struggle? Is he more convincing as a lover or as a religious advocate?

5. The story of these two is one of the famous love stories of history. What reason or reasons would you give for its fame? The character of the actors? The extraordinary conditions of the drama itself? The particular spiritual conflict in which they are engaged?

6. What do you think Plato's opinion of these two would be?

7. As a theme assignment, try writing an imaginary love letter.

Stendhal ⪧ The Crystallization of Love

⪧ Pseudonym of Marie Henri Beyle (1783-1842), French novelist whose
The Red and the Black and *The Charterhouse of Parma* are among the wittiest
novels ever written. ⪦

CHAPTER I

On Love

I AM trying to account for that passion all of whose developments are
inherently beautiful.

There are four different kinds of love:

1. Passion-love, that of the Portuguese Nun, of Héloïse for Abélard,
of Captain de Vésel, of the Cento man-at-arms.[1]

2. Sympathy-love, such as was prevalent in Paris in 1760, and is
found in the memoirs and romances of that period, in Crébillon, Lauzun,
Duclos, Marmontel, Chamfort, Madame d'Épinay, etc., etc.

[1] The *Letters of a Portuguese Nun*, unfolding the true story of a woman seduced,
 abandoned, and still passionately in love, went into many French and English editions in the seventeenth and eighteenth centuries. As for the captain and the man-
 at-arms mentioned here, Stendhal, when asked about them, said he had forgotten
 their story.

It is a picture in which everything, even to the shadows, must be rose coloured, and into which nothing unpleasant must intrude under any pretext whatever, at the risk of infringing custom, fashion, refinement, etc. A well-bred man knows in advance everything that he must do and expect in the various stages of this kind of love; as there is nothing passionate or unexpected about it, it is often more refined than real love, for it is always sprightly; it is like a cold and pretty miniature compared with a picture by the Caracci; and, whereas passion-love carries us away against all our interests, sympathy-love always knows how to adjust itself to them. It is true that if you strip this poor form of love of its vanity, very little remains; without its vanity, it is like a feeble convalescent who is scarcely able to drag himself along.

3. Sensual love.

Whilst out shooting, to meet a fresh, pretty country girl who darts away into a wood. Every one knows the love founded on pleasures of this kind; however unromantic and wretched one's character, it is there that one starts at the age of sixteen.

4. Vanity-love.

The great majority of men, especially in France, desire and possess a fashionable woman as they would possess a fine horse, as a necessary luxury for a young man. Their vanity, more or less flattered and more or less stimulated, gives rise to rapture. Sometimes sensual love is present also, but not always; often there is not even sensual pleasure. The Duchesse de Chaulnes used to say that a duchess is never more than thirty years old to a snob; and people who frequented the Court of that upright man, King Louis of Holland, still recall with amusement a pretty woman at the Hague who could never bring herself to think a man anything but charming if he was a Duke or a Prince. But, faithful to the monarchic principle, as soon as a Prince arrived at Court she dropped the Duke. She was a kind of insignia of the Corps Diplomatique.

The most agreeable form of this rather insipid relationship is the one in which sensual pleasure is increased by habit. In that case past memories make it seem something like real love; there is piqued vanity and sadness on being abandoned; and, becoming seized by romantic ideas, you begin to think you are in love and melancholy, for your vanity always aspires to have a great passion to its credit. The one thing certain is that to whatever kind of love one owes one's pleasures, so long as they are accompanied by mental exhilaration, they are very keen and their memory is entrancing; and in this passion, contrary to most others, the memory of what we have lost always seems sweeter than anything that we can hope for in the future.

Sometimes, in vanity-love, habit and the despair of finding anything better produces a kind of friendship, the least agreeable of all its kinds; it prides itself on its *security*, etc.

Sensual pleasure, being part of our nature, is within the grasp of every one, but it only holds a very low place in the eyes of tender and passionate beings. Although they may be ridiculous in drawing-rooms, although worldly people may often make them unhappy by their intrigues, on the other hand they taste pleasures utterly inaccessible to those hearts who only thrill to vanity or to gold.

Some virtuous and affectionate women have almost no idea at all of sensual pleasure; they have only very rarely laid themselves open to it, if I may put it so, and even then the raptures of passion-love have almost made them forget the pleasures of the body.

Some men are the victims and instruments of a satanic pride, a sort of Alfieri pride. These people, who are perhaps cruel because, like Nero, they live in constant fear, judging every one by their own heart, these people, I say, cannot obtain any sensual pleasure unless it is accompanied by circumstances which flatter their pride abnormally, that is to say, unless they can perpetrate some cruelty on the companion of their pleasures. . . . These men cannot feel the emotion of security with anything less.

However, instead of distinguishing four different kinds of love, one could easily adopt eight or ten shades. There are perhaps as many different ways of feeling as of seeing amongst men; but these differences in terms do not affect the reasoning that follows. Every kind of love that one meets here below is born, lives, dies or becomes immortal, according to the same laws.

CHAPTER II

The Birth of Love

THIS is what goes on in the mind:
  1. Admiration.

2. One says to one's self: "How delightful to kiss her, to be kissed in return," etc.

3. Hope.

One studies her perfections. It is at this moment that a woman should surrender herself, to get the greatest possible sensual pleasure. The eyes of even the most modest women light up the moment hope is born; passion is so strong and pleasure is so acute that they betray themselves in the most obvious manner.

4. Love is born.

To love is to derive pleasure from seeing, touching and feeling through all one's senses and as closely as possible, a lovable person who loves us.

5. The first crystallization begins.

We take a joy in attributing a thousand perfections to a woman of whose love we are sure; we analyze all our happiness with intense satisfaction. This reduces itself to giving ourselves an exaggerated idea of a magnificent possession which has just fallen to us from Heaven in some way we do not understand, and the continued possession of which is assured to us.

This is what you will find if you let a lover turn things over in his mind for twenty-four hours.

In the salt mines of Salzburg a bough stripped of its leaves by winter is thrown into the depths of the disused workings; two or three months later it is pulled out again, covered with brilliant crystals: even the tiniest twigs, no bigger than a tomtit's claw, are spangled with a vast number of shimmering, glittering diamonds, so that the original bough is no longer recognizable.

I call crystallization that process of the mind which discovers fresh perfections in its beloved at every turn of events.[2]

For instance, should a traveller speak of the coolness of Genoese orange groves by the seashore on a scorching summer day, you immediately think how delightful it would be to enjoy this coolness in her company!

One of your friends breaks his arm out hunting: how sweet, you think, to be nursed by a woman you love! To be with her always and

---

[2] What Stendhal calls "crystallization" we would probably call "projection." The lover projects upon the beloved qualities which exist only in his imagination and which have little or no relation to the actual person.

to revel in her constant love would almost make your pain blessèd; and you leave your friend's broken arm still more firmly convinced of the angelic sweetness of your mistress. In short, it is sufficient to think of a perfection in order to see it in the person you love.

This phenomenon which I have allowed myself to call *crystallization*, arises from the promptings of Nature which urge us to enjoy ourselves and drive the blood to our brains, from the feeling that our delight increases with the perfections of the beloved, and from the thought: "She is mine." The savage has no time to get beyond the first step. He grasps his pleasures, but his brain is concentrated on following the buck fleeing from him through the forest, and with whose flesh he must repair his own strength as quickly as possible, at the risk of falling beneath the hatchet of his enemy.

At the other extreme of civilization, I have no doubt that a sensitive woman arrives at the point of experiencing no sensual pleasure except with the man she loves. This is in direct opposition to the savage. But, amongst civilized communities woman has plenty of leisure, whilst the savage lives so close to essentials that he is obliged to treat his female as a beast of burden. If the females of many animals have an easier lot, it is only because the subsistence of the males is more assured.

But let us leave the forests and return to Paris. A passionate man sees nothing but perfection in the woman he loves; and yet his affections may still wander, for the spirit wearies of monotony, even in the case of the most perfect happiness.

So what happens to rivet his attention is this:

6. Doubt is born.

When his hopes have first of all been raised and then confirmed by ten or a dozen glances, or a whole series of other actions which may be compressed into a moment or spread over several days, the lover, recovering from his first amazement and growing used to his happiness, or perhaps merely guided by theory which, based always on his most frequent experiences, is really only correct in the case of light women, the lover, I say, demands more positive proofs of love and wants to advance the moment of his happiness.

If he takes too much for granted he will be met with indifference, coldness or even anger: in France there will be a suggestion of irony which seems to say: "You think you have made more progress than you really have." A woman behaves in this way either because she is recovering from a moment of intoxication and obeys the behests of modesty, which she is alarmed at having transgressed, or merely from prudence or coquettishness.

The lover begins to be less sure of the happiness which he has promised himself; he begins to criticize the reasons he gave himself for hoping.

He tries to fall back on the other pleasures of life. *He finds they no longer exist.* He is seized with a dread of appalling misery, and his attention becomes concentrated.

7. Second crystallization.

Now begins the second crystallization, producing as its diamonds various confirmations of the following idea:

"She loves me."

Every quarter of an hour, during the night following the birth of doubt, after a moment of terrible misery, the lover says to himself: "Yes, she loves me"; and crystallization sets to work to discover fresh charms; then gaunt-eyed doubt grips him again and pulls him up with a jerk. His heart misses a beat; he says to himself: "But does she love me?" Through all these harrowing and delicious alternations the poor lover feels acutely: "With her I would experience joys which she alone in the world could give me."

It is the clearness of this truth and the path he treads between an appalling abyss and the most perfect happiness, that make the second crystallization appear to be so very much more important than the first.

The lover hovers incessantly amongst these three ideas:

1. She is perfect in every way.

2. She loves me.

3. How can I get the strongest possible proof of her love for me?

The most heart-rending moment in love that is still young is when it finds that it has been wrong in its chain of reasoning and must destroy a whole agglomeration of crystals.

Even the fact of crystallization itself begins to appear doubtful.

CHAPTER III

. . . The thing that ensures the duration of love is the second crystallization, during which at every moment one realizes that one must either be loved or perish. How, with this conviction ever present in one's mind, and grown into a habit by several months of love, can one bear even the thought of ceasing to love? The more determined a man's character, the less liable is he to be inconstant.

This second crystallization is practically non-existent in love inspired by women who surrender themselves too quickly.

As soon as the crystallizations have taken place, especially the second one, which is much the stronger, indifferent eyes no longer recognize the bough:

For, 1. It is adorned by perfections or diamonds which they do not see;

2. It is adorned by perfections which are not perfections in their sight. . . .

CHAPTER IV

In the mind of a completely unbiased person, that, for instance, of a young girl living in a country house in an isolated part of the country — the most insignificant unexpected event may lead to a little admiration, and if this is followed by the slightest ray of hope, it causes the birth of love and crystallization.

In a case of this kind, the first attraction of love is that it is a distraction.

Surprise and hope are powerfully assisted by the need of love and the melancholy which one has at the age of sixteen. It is fairly clear that the main anxiety of that age is a thirst for love, and it is characteristic of that thirst not to be unreasonably particular about the kind of draught that chance may offer to slake it. . . .

CHAPTER V

Man is not free to refuse to do the thing which gives him more pleasure than any other conceivable action.

Love is like a fever; it comes and goes without the will having any part in the process. That is one of the principal differences between sympathy-love and passion-love, and one can only congratulate one's self on the fine qualities of the person one loves as on a lucky chance.

Love, indeed, belongs to every age: take, for instance, the passion of Madame du Deffand for the unattractive Horace Walpole. . . .

CHAPTER VI

The Salzburg Bough

DURING love, crystallization hardly ever stops. This is its history: so long as you are on a distant footing with the person you love, crystallization takes place from an *imaginary solution*; it is only in your imagination that you are certain of the existence of any particular perfection in the woman you love. After you have arrived at terms of intimacy, constantly renewed fears are calmed by more real solutions. In this way, happiness is never uniform except in its source. Every day has a different flower.

If the loved woman surrenders to the passion she feels and falls into the grievous error of killing fear by the ardour of her transports, crystallization stops for a moment; but, when love loses its ardour, that is to say, its fears, it acquires the charm of complete unconstraint, of boundless confidence, and a sweet familiarity comes to deaden all the sorrows of life and bring fresh interest into one's pleasures.

If you are deserted, crystallization starts again; and the thought of every act of admiration and each delight which she can bestow on you and of which you had ceased to think, ends in this harrowing reflection: "That rapturous joy will *never* be mine again! And it is through my own fault that I have lost it!" If you try to find happiness in emotions of a different kind your heart refuses to react to them. . . .

CHAPTER VII

Differences between the Birth of Love in the Two Sexes

WOMEN attach themselves by their favours. As nineteen-twentieths of their ordinary day-dreams are connected with love, these day-dreams are all concentrated on one person after intimacy; they endeavour to justify such an extraordinary proceeding, so decisive and so contrary to all the habits of modesty. Men have no task of this kind to perform; later, a woman's imagination pictures minutely and at her leisure such moments of delight.

Since love makes one doubt even the most clearly proven things, the woman who before intimacy was so sure that her lover was a man above the common herd, is terrified lest he has only been trying to add another woman to his list of conquests, as soon as she thinks she has nothing more to refuse him.

That is the moment for the appearance of the second crystallization which, because of the fear that accompanies it, is much the stronger.

A woman thinks that from being a queen she has made herself a slave. This state of mind and soul is encouraged by the nervous intoxication which is the result of indulgence in pleasures which are all the more emotional in proportion to the rarity of their occurrence. Again, a woman seated before her embroidery frame, a dull form of work which only occupies her hands, dreams of her lover, whereas he, galloping across the plains with his squadron, is in a position where the slightest miscalculation may lead to his being placed under arrest.

I should imagine, therefore, that the second crystallization is much stronger in the case of women, because they have more to fear, their vanity and honour are at stake, and they have less to distract them from it. . . .

✑ FOR DISCUSSION AND WRITING

1. Do Stendhal's four kinds of love have their parallel types in the twentieth century? What examples of each can you cite either in real life or in fiction or in the movies? On reflection (or by picking other people's brains), put the results of a small survey in essay form, employing Stendhal's categories (though you might feel the need to add others) to diagnose certain conspicuous tendencies in modern love or in modern fantasies of love as shown in the movies, movie magazines, stories in women's magazines, and so on.

2. What distinction does Stendhal make between "passion-love" and "sensual love"? If you have read the letters of Heloise and Abelard just preceding

this piece, in which class would you put their love? One can imagine Heloise, as a nineteen-year-old girl, entranced by Abelard's great intellectual distinction and fame, and flattered by his interest in her. Which of Stendhal's types of love would this be?

3. Understanding "crystallization" as corresponding fairly closely with what we call "projection," appraise the psychological soundness of Stendhal's description of the process of falling in love. Proust's *Remembrance of Things Past* affords an immensely extended analysis of the psychology of crystallization; in sum, Proust shows that the lover is never in love with his presumed love-object but only with his own crystallizations formed around the object. Support such a thesis with examples.

4. How is the curious form of Stendhal's writing here adapted to swift movements of thought not wholly under guard of the conventions that govern "essay writing"?

John Keats ᴥᶳ Letters to Fanny Brawne

ᴥᶳ English poet (1795-1821), some of whose poems are generally acknowledged to be among the great poems in the language. His letters, written to
his brothers and his friends between 1815 and the onset of his fatal illness
early in 1820, are nearly as famous as his poems. He fell in love with Fanny
Brawne in December, 1818, when Fanny was eighteen and Keats twenty-
three. ᶳᴥ

1 July 1819.

My dearest Lady,

I am glad I had not an opportunity of sending off a Letter which I
wrote for you on Tuesday night — 'twas too much like one out of Ro⟨u⟩s-
seau's Heloise.[1] I am more reasonable this morning. The morning is the
only proper time for me to write to a beautiful Girl whom I love so
much: for at night, when the lonely day has closed, and the lonely,
silent, unmusical Chamber is waiting to receive me as into a Sepulchre,
then believe me my passion gets entirely the sway, then I would not
have you see those R⟨h⟩apsodies which I once thought it impossible I
should ever give way to, and which I have often laughed at in another,
for fear you should ⟨think me⟩ either too unhappy or perhaps a little

From the Maurice Buxton Forman edition of *Letters of John Keats* (London: Oxford
University Press, 1935). Reprinted with the permission of the publisher.

[1] *La Nouvelle Héloïse,* a novel by Jean Jacques Rousseau, had set a fashion in romantic sentiment. (The bracketed corrections of Keats's spelling, etc., are those of
M. Buxton Forman.)

mad. I am now at a very pleasant Cottage window, looking onto a beautiful hilly country, with a glimpse of the sea; the morning is very fine. I do not know how elastic my spirit might be, what pleasure I might have in living here and breathing and wandering as free as a stag about this beautiful Coast if the remembrance of you did not weigh so upon me. I have never known any unalloy'd Happiness for many days together: the death or sickness of some one has always spoilt my hours — and now when none such troubles oppress me, it is you must confess very hard that another sort of pain should haunt me. Ask yourself my love whether you are not very cruel to have so entrammelled me, so destroyed my freedom. Will you confess this in the Letter you must write immediately and do all you can to console me in it — make it rich as a draught of poppies to intoxicate me — write the softest words and kiss them that I may at least touch my lips where yours have been. For myself I know not how to express my devotion to so fair a form: I want a brighter word than bright, a fairer word than fair. I almost wish we were butterflies and liv'd but three summer days — three such days with you I could fill with more delight than fifty common years could ever contain. But however selfish I may feel, I am sure I could never act selfishly: as I told you a day or two before I left Hampstead, I will never return to London if my Fate does not turn up Pam[2] or at least a Court-card. Though I could centre my Happiness in you, I cannot expect to engross your heart so entirely — indeed if I thought you felt as much for me as I do for you at this moment I do not think I could restrain myself from seeing you again tomorrow for the delight of one embrace. But no — I must live upon hope and Chance. In case of the worst that can happen, I shall still love you — but what hatred shall I have for another! Some lines I read the other day are continually ringing a peal in my ears:

> To see those eyes I prize above mine own
> Dart favors on another —
> And those sweet lips (yielding immortal nectar)
> Be gently press'd by any but myself —
> Think, think Francesca, what a cursed thing
> It were beyond expression!

Do write immediately. There is no Post from this Place, so you must address Post Office, Newport, Isle of Wight. I know before night I shall

2 The knave of clubs in the game of loo.

curse myself for having sent you so cold a Letter; yet it is better to do it as much in my senses as possible. Be as kind as the distance will permit to your

J. Keats.

8 July 1819.

My sweet Girl,

Your Letter gave me more delight, than any thing in the world but yourself could do; indeed I am almost astonished that any absent one should have that luxurious power over my senses which I feel. Even when I am not thinking of you I receive your influence and a tenderer nature steeling upon me. All my thoughts, my unhappiest days and nights have I find not at all cured me of my love of Beauty, but made it so intense that I am miserable that you are not with me: or rather breathe in that dull sort of patience that cannot be called Life. I never knew before, what such a love as you have made me feel, was; I did not believe in it; my Fancy was affraid of it, lest it should burn me up. But if you will fully love me, though there may be some fire, 'twill not be more than we can bear when moistened and bedewed with Pleasures. You mention 'horrid people' and ask me whether it depend upon them, whether I see you again. Do understand me, my love, in this. I have so much of you in my heart that I must turn Mentor when I see a chance of harm beffaling you. I would never see any thing but Pleasure in your eyes, love on your lips, and Happiness in your steps. I would wish to see you among those amusements suitable to your inclinations and spirits; so that our loves might be a delight in the midst of Pleasures agreeable enough, rather than a resource from vexations and cares. But I doubt much, in case of the worst, whether I shall be philosopher enough to follow my own Lessons: if I saw my resolution give you a pain I could not. Why may I not speak of your Beauty, since without that I could never have lov'd you. I cannot conceive any beginning of such love as I have for you but Beauty. There may be a sort of love for which, without the least sneer at it, I have the highest respect and can admire it in others: but it has not the richness, the bloom, the full form, the enchantment of love after my own heart. So let me speak of you⟨r⟩ Beauty, though to my own endangering; if you could be so cruel to me as to try elsewhere its Power. You say you are affraid I shall think you do not love me — in saying this you make me ache the more to be near

you. I am at the diligent use of my faculties here, I do not pass a day
without sprawling some blank verse or tagging some rhymes; and here
I must confess, that, (since I am on that subject,) I love you the more in
that I believe you have liked me for my own sake and for nothing else.
I have met with women whom I really think would like to be married
to a Poem and to be given away by a Novel. I have seen your Comet,
and only wish it was a sign that poor Rice would get well whose illness
makes him rather a melancholy companion: and the more so as so to
conquer his feelings and hide them from me, with a forc'd Pun. I kiss'd
your writing over in the hope you had indulg'd me by leaving a trace of
honey — What was your dream? Tell it me and I will tell you the
interpretation thereof.

Ever yours, my love!
John Keats.

Do not accuse me of delay — we have not here an opportunity of
sending letters every day. Write speedily.

25 July 1819.

My sweet Girl,
I hope you did not blame me much for not obeying your request of
a Letter on Saturday: we have had four in our small room playing at
cards night and morning leaving me no undisturb'd opportunity to
write. Now Rice and Martin are gone I am at liberty. Brown to my sorrow confirms the account you give of your ill health. You cannot conceive how I ache to be with you: how I would die for one hour —— for
what is in the world? I say you cannot conceive; it is impossible you
should look with such eyes upon me as I have upon you: it cannot be.
Forgive me if I wander a little this evening, for I have been all day
employ'd in a very abstr⟨a⟩ct Poem and I am in deep love with you —
two things which must excuse me. I have, believe me, not been an age
in letting you take possession of me; the very first week I knew you I
wrote myself your vassal; but burnt the Letter as the very next time I
saw you I thought you manifested some dislike to me. If you should ever
feel for Man at the first sight what I did for you, I am lost. Yet I should
not quarrel with you, but hate myself if such a thing were to happen —
only I should burst if the thing were not as fine as a Man as you are as
a Woman. Perhaps I am too vehement, then fancy me on my knees,
especially when I mention a part of your Letter which hurt me; you say

speaking of Mr Severn 'but you must be satisfied in knowing that I admired you much more than your friend'. My dear love, I cannot believe there ever was or ever could be any thing to admire in me especially as far as sight goes — I cannot be admired, I am not a thing to be admired. You are, I love you; all I can bring you is a swooning admiration of your Beauty. I hold that place among Men which snubnos'd brunettes with meeting eyebrows do among women — they are trash to me — unless I should find one among them with a fire in her heart like the one that burns in mine. You absorb me in spite of myself — you alone: for I look not forward with any pleasure to what is call'd being settled in the world; I tremble at domestic cares — yet for you I would meet them, though if it would leave you the happier I would rather die than do so. I have two luxuries to brood over in my walks, your Loveliness and the hour of my death. O that I could have possession of them both in the same minute. I hate the world: it batters too much the wings of my self-will, and would I could take a sweet poison from your lips to send me out of it. From no others would I take it. I am indeed astonish'd to find myself so careless of all cha⟨r⟩ms but yours — rememb⟨e⟩ring as I do the time when even a bit of ribband was a matter of interest with me. What softer words can I find for you after this — what it is I will not read. Nor will I say more here, but in a Postscript answer any thing else you may have mentioned in your Letter in so many words — for I am distracted with a thousand thoughts. I will imagine you Venus to-night and pray, pray, pray to your star like a He⟨a⟩then.

> *Your's ever, fair Star,*
> *John Keats.*

13 Oct. 1819

My dearest Girl,

This moment I have set myself to copy some verses out fair. I cannot proceed with any degree of content. I must write you a line or two and see if that will assist in dismissing you from my Mind for ever so short a time. Upon my Soul I can think of nothing else. The time is passed when I had power to advise and warn you against the unpromising morning of my Life. My love has made me selfish. I cannot exist without you. I am forgetful of every thing but seeing you again — my Life seems to stop there — I see no further. You have absorb'd me. I have a sensation at the present moment as though I was dissolving — I should be exquisitely miserable without the hope of soon seeing you. I should be affraid to separate myself far from you. My sweet Fanny, will your heart never change? My love, will it? I have no limit now to my love — You⟨r⟩ note came in just here — I cannot be happier away from you. 'Tis richer than an Argosy of Pearles. Do not threat me even in jest. I have been astonished that Men could die Martyrs for religion — I have shudder'd at it. I shudder no more — I could be martyr'd for my Religion — Love is my religion — I could die for that. I could die for you. My Creed is Love and you are its only tenet. You have ravish'd me away by a Power I cannot resist; and yet I could resist till I saw you; and even since I have seen you I have endeavoured often 'to reason against the reasons of my Love'. I can do that no more — the pain would be too great. My love is selfish. I cannot breathe without you.

> *Yours for ever*
> *John Keats.*

⟨*May 1820.*⟩

My dearest Girl,

I wrote a Letter for you yesterday expecting to have seen your mother. I shall be selfish enough to send it though I know it may give you a little pain, because I wish you to see how unhappy I am for love of you, and endeavour as much as I can to entice you to give up your whole heart to me whose whole existence hangs upon you. You could not step or move an eyelid but it would shoot to my heart — I am greedy of you. Do not think of any thing but me. Do not live as if I was not existing — Do not forget me — But have I any right to say you forget me? Perhaps you think of me all day. Have I any right to wish you to be unhappy for me? You would forgive me for wishing it, if you knew the extreme passion I have that you should love me — and for you to love me as I do you, you must think of no one but me, much less write that sentence. Yesterday and this morning I have been haunted with a sweet vision — I have seen you the whole time in your shepherdess dress. How my senses have ached at it! How my heart has been devoted to it! How my eyes have been full of Tears at it! I⟨n⟩deed I think a real Love is enough to occupy the widest heart — Your going to town alone, when I heard of it was a shock to me — yet I expected it — *promise me you will not for some time, till I get better.* Promise me this and fill the paper full of the most endearing names. If you cannot do so with good

will, do my Love tell me — say what you think — confess if your heart
is too much fasten'd on the world. Perhaps then I may see you at a
greater distance, I may not be able to appropriate you so closely to
myself. Were you to loose a favorite bird from the cage, how would
your eyes ache after it as long as it was in sight; when out of sight you
would recover a little. Perhaps if you would, if so it is, confess to me
how many things are necessary to you besides me, I might be happier, by
being less tantaliz'd. Well may you exclaim, how selfish, how cruel, not
to let me enjoy my youth! to wish me to be unhappy! You must be so if
you love me — upon my Soul I can be contented with nothing else. If
you could really what is call'd enjoy yourself at a Party—if you can
smile in peoples faces, and wish them to admire you *now*, you never
have nor ever will love me. I see *life* in nothing but the certainty of your
Love — convince me of it my sweetest. If I am not somehow convinc'd I
shall die of agony. If we love we must not live as other men and women
do — I cannot brook the wolfsbane of fashion and foppery and tattle.
You must be mine to die upon the rack if I want you. I do not pretend
to say I have more feeling than my fellows — but I wish you seriously
to look over my letters kind and unkind and consider whether the Person
who wrote them can be able to endure much longer the agonies and
uncertainties which you are so peculiarly made to create — My recovery
of bodily hea⟨l⟩th will be of no benefit to me if you are not all mine
when I am well. For God's sake save me — or tell me my passion is of
too awful a nature for you. Again God bless you

J. K.

No — my sweet Fanny — I am wrong. I do not want you to be unhappy
— and yet I do, I must while there is so sweet a Beauty — my loveliest
my darling! Good bye! I Kiss you — O the torments!

⟨5 July?⟩ 1820.

My dearest Girl,

    I have been a walk this morning with a book in my hand, but as
usual I have been occupied with nothing but you: I wish I could say in
an agreeable manner. I am tormented day and night. They talk of my
going to Italy.[3] 'Tis certain I shall never recover if I am to be so long
separate from you: yet with all this devotion to you I cannot persuade

---

[3] Keats had suffered his first hemorrhage from tuberculosis in February 1820. He left
for Italy in September and died in Rome six months later.

myself into any confidence of you. Past experience connected with the fact of my long separation from you gives me agonies which are scarcely to be talked of. When your mother comes I shall be very sudden and expert in asking her whether you have been to Mrs Dilke's, for she might say no to make me easy. I am literally worn to death, which seems my only recourse. I cannot forget what has pass'd. What? nothing with a man of the world, but to me dreadful. I will get rid of this as much as possible. When you were in the habit of flirting with Brown you would have left off, could your own heart have felt one half of one pang mine did. Brown is a good sort of Man — he did not know he was doing me to death by inches. I feel the effect of every one of those hours in my side now; and for that cause, though he has done me many services, though I know his love and friendship for me, though at this moment I should be without pence were it not for his assistance, I will never see or speak to him until we are both old men, if we are to be. I *will* resent my heart having been made a football. You will call this madness. I have heard you say that it was not unpleasant to wait a few years — you have amusements — your mind is away — you have not brooded over one idea as I have, and how should you? You are to me an object intensely desireable — the air I breathe in a room empty of you is unhealthy. I am not the same to you — no — you can wait — you have a thousand activities — you can be happy without me. Any party, any thing to fill up the day has been enough. How have you pass'd this month? Who have you smil'd with? All this may seem savage in me. You do not feel as I do — you do not know what it is to love — one day you may — your time is not come. Ask yourself how many unhappy hours Keats has caused you in Loneliness. For myself I have been a Martyr the whole time, and for this reason I speak; the confession is forc'd from me by the torture. I appeal to you by the blood of that Christ you believe in: Do not write to me if you have done anything this month which it would have pained me to have seen. You may have altered — if you have not — if you still behave in dancing rooms and other societies as I have seen you — I do not want to live — if you have done so I wish this coming night may be my last. I cannot live without you, and not only you but *chaste you; virtuous you.* The Sun rises and sets, the day passes, and you follow the bent of your inclination to a certain extent — you have no conception of the quantity of miserable feeling that passes through me in a day. — Be serious! Love is not a plaything — and again do not write unless you can do it with a crystal conscience. I would sooner die for want of you than ——

Yours for ever
J. Keats.

◄§ FOR DISCUSSION AND WRITING

1. When Keats's letters to Fanny Brawne were first published, they raised quite a storm of protest from critics and other readers who found them offensive and their publication a breach of taste—the main feeling being that it was unfair to the dead poet to expose his most private emotions so nakedly and distressingly. There are more letters to Fanny than those printed here, but these are representative, showing the increasingly painful character of Keats's love. (One must remember that Keats was already tuberculous before he ever met Fanny, having caught the disease while he was nursing his dying younger brother, Tom.) What do you think of the objection to their publication? Do the letters damage your opinion of Keats? What emotional aspects are the most disturbing?

2. Do you find signs of the *poet* in the letters? Point out specific instances of the poet's sensibility or mentality or temperament as shown in either the content or the expression.

3. Do the intensity and rawness of his feeling seem to you normal or distinctly excessive? Does Keats himself seem conscious of abnormality or excessiveness? Is it in any way natural or to be expected that so finely keyed a person should love like this? On what do you base your answers?

4. It has been suggested in the foreword to this section (see page 137) that, among Stendhal's four classifications of love, that of Keats for Fanny would be of the kind Stendhal calls "passion-love"; it is also suggested there that, judging from famous examples, this kind of love tends to be destructive—even "death-directed"—because it obsesses the whole personality and is entirely uncontrollable, as if one were under some witch's spell. Illustrate this syndrome by two or three passages in the letters.

5. If you know Keats's poetry and like it, discuss in a short paper your impression of him as a poet and your impression of him as a lover.

6. Or here are a couple of concrete suggestions for some experimental literary criticism. One of the letters ends, "Your's ever, fair Star," and just before that Keats has said, "I will imagine you Venus to-night and pray, pray, pray to your star like a Heathen." Keats scholars have always associated these words with the "Bright Star" sonnet, which he may have written at this time. The sonnet is given below. You might try a short paper interpreting the sonnet and showing its relationship with the letters to Fanny. Also given below is the well-known and haunting ballad, "La Belle Dame sans Merci." Having read the love letters, you might write on some correspondences between Keats's emotional relationship with Fanny and that of the knight-at-arms with the fairy lady in the ballad.

Sonnet

Bright star, would I were stedfast as thou art —
    Not in lone splendour hung aloft the night
And watching, with eternal lids apart,
    Like nature's patient, sleepless Eremite,
The moving waters at their priestlike task
    Of pure ablution round earth's human shores,
Or gazing on the new soft-fallen mask
    Of snow upon the mountains and the moors —
No — yet still stedfast, still unchangeable,
    Pillow'd upon my fair love's ripening breast,
To feel for ever its soft fall and swell,
    Awake for ever in a sweet unrest,
Still, still to hear her tender-taken breath,
    And so live ever — or else swoon to death.

La Belle Dame sans Merci

O what can ail thee, Knight-at-arms,
    Alone and palely loitering?
The sedge has wither'd from the lake,
    And no birds sing.

O what can ail thee, Knight-at-arms,
    So haggard, and so woe-begone?
The squirrel's granary is full
    And the harvest's done.

I see a lily on thy brow
    With anguish moist and fever dew;

And on thy cheeks a fading rose
   Fast withereth too.

I met a lady in the meads,
   Full beautiful, a faery's child;
Her hair was long, her foot was light
   And her eyes were wild.

I made a garland for her head,
   And bracelets too, and fragrant zone;
She look'd at me as she did love,
   And made sweet moan.

I set her on my pacing steed,
   And nothing else saw all day long;
For sidelong would she bend, and sing
   A faery's song.

She found me roots of relish sweet,
   And honey wild, and manna dew;
And sure in language strange she said,
   I love thee true.

She took me to her elfin grot,
   And there she wept and sigh'd full sore,
And there I shut her wild wild eyes —
   With kisses four.

And there she lullèd me asleep,
   And there I dream'd, Ah woe betide!
The latest dream I ever dreamt
   On the cold hill side.

I saw pale kings and princes too,
   Pale warriors, death-pale were they all;
Who cried — "La belle Dame sans merci
   Hath thee in thrall!"

I saw their starv'd lips in the gloam
   With horrid warning gapèd wide,
And I awoke, and found me here
   On the cold hill's side.

And this is why I sojourn here
   Alone and palely loitering;
Though the sedge is wither'd from the lake
   And no birds sing.

José Ortega y Gasset ✑ *Toward a Psychology of Love*

✑ Spanish philosopher and essayist (1893-1955), who wrote on many aspects of contemporary life. His best-known work is *The Revolt of the Masses*, of which an excerpt is given in the present volume (see page 421). ﻬ

1

NOTHING is so flattering to a man as to hear women say that he is interesting. But when is a man interesting in the opinion of a woman? This is one of the most subtle and difficult questions to raise. In order to tackle it systematically, an entirely new and heretofore unattempted discipline would have to be developed, one which I have considered and reconsidered for years. I call it *Knowledge of Man* or *Philosophical Anthropology*. This discipline will reveal to us that souls, like bodies, have different forms. With varying degrees of clarity, depending upon individual insight, we all perceive this diversity of personality structure in the people whom we encounter. It is difficult, nevertheless, to transform our surface perceptions into clear concepts, into complete knowledge. We sense others, but we do not know them.

From the book-length essay *On Love* by José Ortega y Gasset, translated by Toby Talbot, Meridian Books, The World Publishing Company, Chapter VII. Copyright © 1957 by The World Publishing Company.

Everyday language has accumulated, however, a wealth of delicate insights which are conveyed by highly suggestive verbal capsules. One speaks, in fact, of hardy souls and gentle souls, of souls which are dour or sweet, profound or superficial, strong or weak, plodding or flighty. One speaks of magnanimous and pusillanimous men, thus recognizing stature in souls as well as bodies. One says of someone that he is a man of action or on the other hand that he is a contemplative man, that he is "cerebral" or sentimental, etc. No one has attempted to analyze methodically the precise meaning of the many different designations under which we classify the marvelous diversity of the human *fauna*. All these expressions merely allude to the structural differences of the inner person, and point toward constructing a psychological anatomy. It is clear that a boy's soul will of necessity have a different structure from an old man's, and an ambitious man a different spiritual make-up from a dreamer. This study, if undertaken somewhat systematically, might result in a new-styled, cogent charactery, which would permit us to describe with hitherto unsuspected refinement the varieties of human inwardness. Among them might appear what, according to women, is the *interesting man*.

To enter upon a thorough analysis of the interesting man fills me with fear, since we face thereupon a maze of problems. The first and most obvious thing to be said about the interesting man is this: the interesting man is the man with whom women fall in love. But this immediately leads us astray, and plunges us into greater perils. We are thrust straight into the jungle of love. And the fact is that no land in human topography is less explored than love. It could in fact be said that everything remains to be said of love; or rather, that everything remains to be thought about it.

A store of crude ideas fixed in people's heads prevents them from seeing the facts with normal clarity. Everything is confused and distorted. There are many reasons for this. In the first place, love, by nature, is part of one's secret life. One cannot tell about one's love; in the telling it vanishes or vaporizes. Everyone has to rely upon his personal experience, almost always meager, for it is not easy to profit from that of one's neighbor. What would have happened, however, to physics if each physicist possessed only his personal observations? In the second place, what happens is that the men who are most capable of thinking about love are the ones who have experienced it the least, whereas those who have experienced it are usually incapable of thinking about it, of subtly analyzing its iridescent and ever-vague plumage. Finally, an experiment on love is a most thankless task. If a doctor talks about digestion, people listen modestly and curiously. But if a psychologist speaks about love, everyone listens to him disparagingly, or they do not listen to him at all; they never even bother to find out what he has to say, because they all believe themselves to be experts on the subject. In few instances does the habitual stupidity of people appear so manifestly. They act as though love were not, after all, as theoretical a subject as others, hermetically sealed away from anyone who approaches it with inadequate intellectual tools!

It is the same as with the subject of Don Juan. Everyone thinks he has the true interpretation of Don Juanism, that most obscure, abstruse, delicate problem of our time. The fact is that, with few exceptions, men can be divided into three classes: those who think they are Don Juan, those who think they have been Don Juan, and those who think they could have been Don Juan but did not want to be. The last are the ones who propose, with worthy intention, to attack Don Juan, and perhaps decree his dismissal.

There exist, then, numerous reasons why the sciences which everyone presumes to understand — love and politics — are the ones which have progressed least. Those who are best qualified to speak about love and politics have kept silent simply to avoid listening to the clichés which ignorant people hasten to utter as soon as either subject is touched upon.

It ought to be made clear, therefore, that neither the Don Juans nor those in love know anything in particular about Don Juan or love. Probably the only person who can speak with precision on both matters is he who lives at a distance from both, but is yet, like the astronomer in regard to the sun, attentive and curious. Knowing things is not being them, nor being them knowing them. In order to see an object it is necessary to be detached from it. Separation converts it from experienced reality into an object of knowledge. Any other view would lead us, for example, to believe that the zoologist, in order to study ostriches, must himself become an ostrich; which is exactly what Don Juan becomes when he speaks about himself.

For my part, I can say that I have not attained sufficient clarity on this important matter, in spite of having thought about it a great deal.

Fortunately, Don Juan is not under discussion now. What should be said, perhaps, is that Don Juan is always an interesting man, contrary to what his enemies wish to make us believe. It is evident, however, that not every interesting man is a Don Juan — and with this comment on him let us eliminate his dangerous profile from these notes. As for love, it will be less easy to avoid its intrusion into our purview. I find myself, therefore, forced to formulate with apparent dogmatism, without development or proof, some of my thoughts about love which differ radically from accepted ideas. The reader ought to take them merely as a necessary clarification of what I have to say about the *interesting man* and not insist, for the moment, on deciding whether or not they are correct.

2

As I suggested before, the first thing which ought to be said about the interesting man is that he is the man with whom women fall in love. But, one may immediately object that all normal men find love in some woman, and, consequently, all must be interesting. To which I must peremptorily give two answers. First: not one woman, but many, fall in love with the interesting man. The "all" and the "nothing," the "many" and the "none" should be understood as oversimplifications which do not aim at exactness. Exactness in dealing with every problem of life would be most inexact, and quantitative judgments are made rather to express typical situations, norms, tendencies.

The belief that love is a dull and banal affair is one of the greatest impediments in the way of understanding the erotic phenomena. This view results from a common confusion: with the single noun *love* we designate the most diverse psychological states. For this reason our concepts and generalizations never concur with reality. What holds true for love in one meaning of the world does not hold for another, and our observation, perhaps valid in the area of eroticism where it was made, turns out to be false when extended to others.

The origin of this confusion is clear. All manner of attractions between man and woman are manifested, broadly speaking, in a limited range of social and private behavior. The man who likes a woman's body; the man who is attracted to her out of vanity; the man who goes out of his mind as a victim of the ignoble effect a woman can produce with a skillful tactic of attraction and disdain; the man who simply sticks to a woman out of tenderness, loyalty, sympathy, "affection"; the man who falls into a state of passion; and finally, the man who is truly in love, behave in a more or less identical manner. If someone observes their actions from afar, he does not notice the subtle qualifications of "more or less." By paying attention only to the broad pattern of behavior he judges that there is nothing different about it, and, therefore, decides that there is nothing distinctive about the sentiment which inspires it either. But all he would have to do is to take a magnifying glass and study them close up to see that only the general pattern of actions is alike, and that there are among them the most diverse variations. It is an enormous error to analyze a love affair by its actions and words. Generally neither the one nor the other reflects love but, rather, they constitute a repertoire of grand gestures, rites, and formulae, created by society, which sentiment finds at its disposal, like a piece of available equipment thrust upon it and which it finds itself obliged to use. It is only the small original gesture, the tone, and the most subtle signs of behavior which allow us to differentiate between the various kinds of love.

I speak now only of true romantic love, which is radically different from sensual ardor, *amour-vanité*, ignoble involvements, "affection," and "passion." Here is a varied amorous *fauna* whose multiform composition could well be categorized.

Romantic love — which is, in my opinion, the prototype and summit of all eroticisms — is characterized by its simultaneously possessing these two ingredients: a feeling of being "enchanted" by another being who produces complete "illusion" in us, and a feeling of being absorbed by him to the core of our being, as if he had torn us from our own vital depths and we were living transplanted, our vital roots within him. Another way of saying this is that a person in love feels himself totally surrendered to the one he loves; so that it does not matter whether bodily or spiritual surrender has actually taken place. It is possible for a person in love to succeed in preventing, by virtue of reflective considerations, — social decorum, difficulties of any nature — the surrender of his will to the one he loves. What is essential is that he *feels* himself, regardless of the decision of his will, surrendered to the other.

There is no contradiction in this, because the fundamental surrender is not carried out on the plane of will, but occurs more deeply within the person. There is no will to surrender: there is an unwilled surrender. And regardless of where our will leads us, we remain unwittingly surrendered to the beloved, even if we are led to the other end of the world to be away from him.

This extreme case of disassociation, of antagonism between will and love, serves to emphasize the peculiarity of the latter, and should be taken into account as a possible complication — *possible*, but certainly quite improbable. Considerations of self-defense against the beloved rarely influence the will of a person genuinely in love. This is true to such a point that if, in practice, one sees that the beloved's will is active, that he "presents considerations," and finds "very respectable" reasons for not loving or for loving less, it is usually the surest sign that, actually, he is not in love. Such a soul feels itself vaguely attracted by the other but has not been uprooted from itself — which is only to say that this man is not in love.

The combination of these two elements, enchantment and surrender, is, then, essential to the love which we are discussing. This combination is no accident. Both do not merely chance to co-exist, but rather one is born out of and takes nourishment from the other. What exists in love is surrender due to enchantment.

A mother surrenders to her child, a friend to his friend, but not because of "illusion" or "enchantment." The mother does so out of a deep-rooted instinct which has almost nothing to do with her spirituality. The friend surrenders by a clear decision of his will. He possesses loyalty, which by its very nature is a reflective virtue. We might say that the friend takes himself in his own hand and offers himself to another. What is true of love, however, is that our soul escapes from our hand and is sucked in by the other. This suction which another personality exercises upon one's life sustains the latter in a state of levitation, uproots it from its own being and transplants it to the beloved, where the original roots seem to take root again, as in new soil. Thanks to this a person in love lives not off himself but off the other, as a child, before birth, lives bodily off its mother, in whose womb it is planted and immersed.

This absorption of the lover by the beloved is simply the effect of enchantment. Another being enchants us, and we feel this enchantment in the form of a continual, gently elastic pull from within. The much overworked word "enchantment" is the one, nevertheless, which best expresses the type of attraction which the beloved exercises upon the lover. Its use ought to be restored by resuscitating the connotation of magic which it originally possessed.

In sexual attraction there is no real attraction. A suggestive body excites one's appetite, one's desire for it. However, our desire does not lead toward the desired object but, on the contrary, our soul pulls away from the desired object toward itself. That is why it is very accurate to say that the object *awakens* a desire, as if to indicate that it does not participate in the process of desiring itself, but rather that its role ends when it stimulates desire, leaving us to do the rest. The psychological phenomenon of desire and that of "being enchanted" produce reverse reactions. In the first, the object tends to be absorbed, while in the second the "I" is absorbed. Appetite, therefore, does not result in surrender of oneself, but, on the contrary, in the capture of the object.[1]

Equally, there is no real surrender in "passion." Lately this inferior form of love has achieved undeserved merit and favor. Some think that the measure of one's love is in proportion to one's proximity to the suicide or murder of Werther or Othello, and the insinuation is that every other form of love is imaginary and "cerebral." I think that, on the contrary, the term "passion" should be restored to its ancient pejorative meaning. Turning a revolver on oneself or on another does not guarantee in the slightest the quality or even the quantity of a sentiment. "Passion" is a pathological state which implies defectiveness of soul. A person vulnerable to the mechanism of obsession, or one possessing a very simple, crude nature will turn every germ of feeling that befalls him into "passion," that is, mania.[2] Let us tear down the romantic trap-

---

[1] This old term "appetite" encompasses an error in psychological description, which, however, is very common. It confuses the psychic phenomenon which it is trying to classify with the consequences incurred. Because I want something, I try to move toward it, in order to *take it.* This "moving toward" — *petere* — is the means which desire finds to satisfy itself, but it is not desire itself. On the other hand, the final act, the capture of the object, the bringing of it toward myself, the embracing of the object within myself, is the original manifestation of desire.

The habit of confusing love with its consequences has also obscured the description of love. The amorous sentiment, the most fertile in the life of the psyche, spawns innumerable acts which accompany it like the followers of a Roman patrician. Thus, desire toward the beloved is always born of love; but these desires are not love. On the contrary, they presuppose love because they arise from it. [Author.]

[2] The man who kills or kills himself because of love would do it equally for any other cause: a dispute, a loss of fortune, etc. [Author.]

pings that have adorned passion. Let us cease believing that the measure of a man's love lies in how stupid he has become or is willing to be.

Far from it: it would be well to establish the following aphorism as a general principle in the psychology of love: *since love is the most delicate and total act of a soul, it will reflect the state and nature of the soul. The characteristics of the person in love must be attributed to love itself.* If the individual is not sensitive, how can his love be sentient? If he is not profound, how can his love be deep? As one is, so is his love. For this reason, *we can find in love the most decisive symptom of what a person is.* All other acts and appearances can deceive us with regard to his true nature, but his love affairs reveal to us the carefully concealed secret of his being. This is especially true in the choice of the beloved. In no other action do we reveal our innermost character as we do in erotic choice.

Frequently we hear that intelligent women fall in love with stupid men, and vice versa, foolish women with clever men. I confess that although I have heard this many times, I have never believed it, and in every case in which I was able to draw closer and apply the psychological magnifying lens, I have found either that those men and women were not actually intelligent or that their chosen ones were not stupid.

Passion is not, therefore, the height of amorous feeling but, on the contrary, its degeneration in inferior souls. In it there is not — or, at least there does not have to be — either enchantment or surrender. Psychiatrists know that the obsessed man struggles against his obsession, that he does not accept it, but yet is dominated by it. Thus there can be great passion with very little love. This will indicate to the reader that my interpretation of the amorous phenomenon is in direct opposition to the false mythology which makes of passion an elemental, primitive force engendered in the obscure bosom of human animality which brutally overpowers the person and ignores any appreciable role of loftier, more subtle portions of the soul.

Ignoring for the present the possible connection between love and certain cosmic instincts latent in our being, I think that love is indeed the complete opposite of an elemental force. I would say — aware though I am of the margin of error — that love, rather than being an elemental force, almost resembles a literary genre. This is a formula which — naturally — will provoke more than one reader before he considers it.

Certainly, if this claimed to be the final word, it would be excessive and unacceptable. All that I wish to suggest, however, is that love is not an instinct but rather a creation, and, in man, no primitive creation at that. The savage has no inkling of it, the Chinese and the Indian are unfamiliar with it, the Greeks of the time of Pericles barely recognized it.[3] Could not both features — that of being a spiritual creation and that of appearing only in certain stages and forms of human culture — serve well as the definition of a literary genre?

Love can be as clearly distinguished from its other pseudomorphs as from sensual ardor and "passion." This includes what I have called "affection." In "affection" — which, at best, is usually the form of matrimonial love — two people feel mutual sympathy, fidelity, adhesion, but there is no enchantment and surrender. Each lives absorbed in himself, without rapture in the other, and each emits from within himself gentle rays of consideration, benevolence, corroboration.

What has been said is sufficient to give some meaning — that is all I am attempting now — to this affirmation: if one wishes to see clearly into the phenomenon of love, it is necessary, above all, to free oneself from the common idea which sees it as a universal sentiment, within the reach of almost everyone's experience, occurring at every minute everywhere, regardless of the society, race, nationality or period in which we live. The features which the preceding pages outline reduce considerably the frequency of love, by removing many things from its sphere which are erroneously included. One final step and we may say without undue exaggeration that *love is an infrequent occurrence, a sentiment which only certain souls can hope to experience: in fact, a specific talent which some individuals possess, ordinarily granted in conjunction with other talents but which may occur alone.* Truly, falling

---

[3] Plato had a perfect awareness of this sentiment and described it wonderfully, but it would never have occurred to him to confuse it with what a Greek of his time felt toward a woman. Love, in Plato, is romantic love in perhaps its first appearance in history. But it is the love of the mature, more cultivated man for the beautiful, discreet young man. Plato, without hesitation, sees in this love a privilege of Greek culture, a spiritual invention, and, in addition, a central institution of the new human life. We are revolted by this Doric way of love and with good reason, but pure truth obliges us to recognize in it one of the historic roots of this admirable Western invention of love for a woman. If the reader thinks for a while he will note that this is more complex and subtle than the common man thinks, and the comparison between love and a literary genre will seem less fantastic. [Author.]

in love is a marvelous talent which some creatures possess, like the gift of composing verses, the spirit of sacrifice, melodic inspiration, personal bravery, like knowing how to take command. Not everyone falls in love, nor do those capable of falling in love fall in love with just anyone. The divine event occurs only when certain rigorous conditions are present both in the subject and in the object. Very few can be lovers, and very few beloved. Love has its *ratio,* its law, its never-changing unitarian essence, which does not exclude from its exergue abundant casuistic distinctions and variability.[4]

3

All one has to do is to enumerate some of the conditions and assumptions of being in love to make its extreme infrequency obvious and plain. Without claiming to be final, we could say that these conditions form three classes, since there are three components of love: *perception,* in order to see the person who is going to be loved; *emotion,* with which we respond sentimentally to the vision of what is beloved; and the *constitution* of our being, the nature of the soul in its totality. Although perception and emotion may function properly, it is impossible for love to uproot, invade, or mold our character if the constitution of our soul is insubstantial and inflexible, dispersed or without vigorous resources.

In order to be enchanted we must be, above all, capable of *seeing* another person — simply opening one's eyes will not do. One needs a peculiar kind of initial curiosity which is much more integral, deep-rooted and broad than mere curiosity about things (like scientific,

---

[4] There exists today a group of men, among whom I am proud to find myself, that opposes the empirical tradition, according to which everything happens by chance and without any unified form, changing from time to time and place to place, making it unnecessary to find any law of events other than the "more or less" of statistical induction. In opposition to such vast anarchy we renew the older and more profound tradition of philosophy which seeks in all things the "essence," the single mode.

Clearly, it would be much more simple and convenient to think that love has infinite forms, that it is different in each case, etc. I hope always to remain aloof from the intellectual abasement which elicits this way of thinking and flatters inert minds so greatly. The ultimate mission of the intellect will always be to search for the "essence," that is to say, the unique mode of being of each reality. [Author.]

technical, or tourist curiosity, or curiosity to "see the world," etc.),
or even about the particular acts of people (for example, gossip). One
must be vitally curious about humanity, and more concretely, about the
individual as a living totality, an individual *modus* of existence. Without this curiosity, the most eminent creatures can pass before us and
make no impression upon us. The ever-lit lamp of the evangelical virgins
is the symbol of this virtue which constitutes, as it were, the threshold
of love.

But note that such curiosity, in truth, presupposes many other
things. It is a vital luxury which only organisms with a high level of
vitality can possess. The weak individual is incapable of disinterested,
initial attention to what occurs outside of himself. He fears the unexpected which life may hold enveloped in the folds of its billowing skirt,
and he becomes hermetic to the extent that he does not immediately
relate to others with total interest. This paradox of "disinterested"
interest permeates love in all its functions and actions like the red mark
which is stamped on all cables from the Royal English Navy.

Simmel — following Nietzsche — has said that the essence of life
consists precisely in longing for more life. Living is to live even more,
a desire to increase one's own palpitations. When it is not this, life is
sick and, in its measure, is not life. The ability to interest oneself in
a thing for what it is in itself and not in view of the profit which it will
render us is the magnificent gift of generosity which flourishes only
at the peaks of the greatest altitudes of vitality. A body weak from a
medical standpoint does not in itself indicate a deficiency in vitality, as,
by contrast, a Herculean physique does not guarantee organic energy
(this is very frequently true of athletes).

Almost all men and women live submerged in the sphere of their
own interests (some, without doubt, beautiful and respectable), and
are incapable of feeling the migratory urge toward what is outside
themselves. Whether treated well or badly by the landscape that surrounds them, they live definitively satisfied with the line of their horizon
and do not miss the vague possibilities which they might realize only
at a cost. This limited range is incompatible with deep-seated curiosity,
which is, finally, an untiring instinct for migration, a wild urge to depart
from oneself to the other.[5]

[5] In every society, race, and period, the possibility of frequent love fails because one
or another condition is deficient. In Spain you need seek no further to explain the

That is why it is so difficult for the *petit bourgeois* and the *petite bourgeoise* to fall in love in an authentic manner; for them, life consists in an insistence on what is known and habitual, an unshakable satisfaction with the same daily routine.

This curiosity, which is simultaneously an eagerness for life, can only be found in porous souls where free air — cosmic air charged with stardust — circulates, unconfined by any limiting wall. But curiosity is not enough to make us "see" the delicate, complex structure of a person. Curiosity predisposes the eye, but the vision must be discerning. And such discernment is indeed the prime talent and extraordinary endowment which acts as a component in love. It serves as a special intuition which permits us to gain an immediate intimate knowledge of other men, the nature of their souls in conjunction with the meaning expressed by their bodies. Thanks to this we can "discriminate" between people, appreciate their quality, their triviality or their excellence; in short, their degree of vital perfection. Do not think by this that I am trying to intellectualize the sentiment of love. Discernment has nothing to do with intelligence, and although its presence is more likely in clear-minded creatures, it can exist in solitude, like poetic talent which so often finds a home in almost imbecilic men. Actually, it is unlikely to be found except in persons endowed with some sharpness of intellect, but the degree of discernment does not depend upon the degree of intelligence. Thus it happens that this intuition is usually found to be relatively more frequent in women than in men, whereas intellectual endowment is to be found more often among men.

Those who imagine love to be a half-magical, half-mechanical effect will oppose my assertion that discernment is one of its essential attributes. According to them, love always blossoms "without reason." It is illogical, anti-rational and, in fact, excludes all discernment. This is one of the central points where I find myself obliged to differ resolutely from accepted ideas. . . .

---

rarity of the erotic event, for the very first assumption is lacking. There are extremely few Spaniards, especially Spanish women, endowed with curiosity, and it is difficult to find someone who feels a yearning to peer out at life, to see what it has to offer. It is curious to attend a "society" gathering in our country: the lack of animation in dialogue and gestures soon reveals that one is among slumbering people (biologists call the winter drowsiness of certain species *vita minima*). No demand is made of the passing hour, and nothing is expected of one another, nor, in general, of existence. From my point of view it is immoral for a being not to make the most intense effort every instant of his life. [Author.]

Love, although there may be nothing intellectual about it, is like reasoning in that it does not spring up out of nowhere and, so to speak, *ex nihilo,* but has its psychic source in the qualities of the beloved. The presence of these engenders and nourishes love, or, to put it another way, no one loves without reason; whoever is in love has, all the while, a conviction that his love is justified. To love is, furthermore, "to believe" (to feel) that that which is loved is, in fact, lovable for itself, just as thinking is believing that things are, in reality, what we think they are. It is possible that in both cases we are mistaken, that neither that which is loved is what we feel it is, nor that which is real is what we think it is; but in any case we keep on loving and thinking as long as we have our conviction. The logical character of thought consists of this quality of feeling oneself justified and living precisely *from* one's justification, relying on it at every instant, corroborating it with the proof of one's reason. Leibniz expresses the same thing by saying that thought is not blind, but that it thinks a thing *because it sees* that it is as it thinks it. Equally, love loves, because it sees that the object is lovable. . . .

Many instances of amorous anomaly can be reduced to confusions in the lover's perception of the beloved; an optical illusion or mirage no less strange or explicable than those which our eyes often commit, without causing us to call ourselves blind. Precisely because love makes mistakes at times — although much less frequently than is believed — we have to restore to it the attribute of vision, for, as Pascal wished: "Poets have no right to picture love as blind: its bandage must be pulled off and henceforth it must be given the use of its eyes."

✍️ FOR DISCUSSION AND WRITING

1. The essay has three numbered parts. Glance through it again and define the main purpose of each section—that is, try to ascertain the principle of organization in the essay.

2. Ortega says, in the central part of the essay, that he speaks only of "romantic love." What does he mean by romantic love? By what principal qualities does he define this kind of love? In what movies or novels about love have you found these qualities? If you know some of the older love stories, Tristan and Iseult, Antony and Cleopatra, *Wuthering Heights, Anna Karenina,* have you found those qualities in them?

3. How does Ortega differentiate the love of a mother or of a friend from the kind he is concerned with? How does he distinguish sexual attraction from the love that produces "enchantment" and "surrender"?

4. How does his use of the word "passion" differ from its common use? If you have read the selection from Stendhal on love, how does Ortega's interpretation of "passion" differ from Stendhal's "passion-love"? Ortega speaks of "passion" as "a pathological state which implies defectiveness of soul"; to indulge in speculation, what do you think he would make of Keats's letters to Fanny Brawne or those of Heloise and Abelard? Later on he says that "there can be great passion with very little love"; can you confirm the statement?

5. A central statement in the essay is this: "since love is the most delicate and total act of a soul, it will reflect the state and nature of the soul," and for this reason, "we can find in love the most decisive symptom of what a person is." Appraise Ortega's psychological perception here. What does he mean by the word "soul"?

6. In saying that love "resembles a literary genre," he sounds a little confusing to our ears; but he is trying to suggest a radical difference between love, which is creative, and the mechanisms of instinct. What kind of creativity do you think he means? Do you agree or disagree with his distinction of love from instinct, and on what grounds?

7. How soundly does the essay support the statement that "love is an infrequent occurrence, a sentiment which only certain souls can hope to experience: in fact, a specific talent which some individuals possess," and what do you think of the statement?

8. Ortega's prose style, in Spanish, has simplicity and elegance, and it preserves those qualities in translation. The essay here may offer some difficulty in thought and require a somewhat stern measure of concentration, but thus the mind is exercised and stretched. Attempt to analyze the structure of three or four of his sentences. Do they offer any complexity? Are they difficult to follow?

9. Since there are abundant opportunities to observe the behavior of people who presumably love each other, gather together a number of observations of their words and behavior, and write a critical commentary on love.

Rainer Maria Rilke ⋅⋅⋅ The Difficult Work of Love

⋅⋅⋅ German poet (1875-1926), born in Prague. Though Rilke is a "difficult" poet, highly individual in sensibility and in his use of language, his *Sonnets to Orpheus* and *Duino Elegies* have had excellent translations in English. ⋅⋅⋅

ROME, MAY 14TH, 1904

My Dear Mr. Kappus,[1]

You see — I have copied your sonnet, because I found that it is lovely and simple and born in the form in which it moves with such quiet propriety. It is the best of those of your poems that you have let me read. And now I give you this copy because I know that it is important and full of new experience to come upon a work of one's own written in a strange hand. Read the lines as though they were unfamiliar to you,

[1] Mr. Kappus, a young poet, had sent Rilke some of his poems for criticism. Rilke's response is characteristic; instead of engaging in literary discussion, he talks about what is most important in the young man's life.

and you will feel deep within you how much they are your own.

It was a pleasure to me to read this sonnet and your letter often; I thank you for both.

And you should not let yourself be bewildered in your solitude by the fact that there is something in you that wants to get out of it. This very wish will help you, if you use it quietly and deliberately and like a tool, to spread out your solitude over wide country. People have (with the help of the conventions) oriented all their solutions towards the easy, and towards the lighter side of what is easy; but it is clear that we must hold to what is difficult, everything alive holds to it, everything in Nature grows and defends itself in its own way and is characteristic out of itself, seeks at all costs to be so and against all opposition. We know little, but that we must hold to what is difficult is a certainty that will not forsake us; it is good to be solitary, for solitude is difficult; that something is hard must be a reason the more for us to do it.

To love is good, too; for loving is difficult. For one human being to love another: that is perhaps the hardest of all our tasks, the ultimate, the last test and proof, the work for which all other work is but preparation. For this reason young people, who are beginners in everything, are not yet *capable* of love: they have to learn it. With their whole being, with all their forces, gathered close about their lonely, timid upward-beating heart, must they learn to love. But learning-time is always a long, secluded time, and so loving, for a long time ahead and far on into life, is — solitude, enhanced and deepened loneness for him who loves. Love is at first not anything that means unfolding, surrendering, and uniting with another (for that would be a union of the unclarified and unfinished, the still subordinate), it is a high inducement to the individual to ripen, to become something in himself, to become world, to become world to himself for another's sake, it is a great, an exorbitant demand upon him, something that chooses him out and calls him to vast things. Only in this sense, as the task of working at themselves ("to hearken and to hammer day and night") should young people be allowed to use the love that is given them. Unfolding and surrender and every form of living their lives together is not for them (who must save and accumulate for a long, long time), is the ultimate, is perhaps that for which human lives as yet scarcely suffice.

But in this young people err so often and so grievously: that they (in whose nature it lies to have no patience) cast themselves upon each other, when love takes possession of them, scatter themselves, just as they are, in all their untidiness, disorder, confusion. . . . And then what? What is life to do with this heap of half-battered existence which they call their common living and which they would gladly call their happiness, if it were possible, and their future? Thus each loses himself for the sake of the other and loses the other and many others, that were yet to come. And loses the expanses and the possibilities, exchanges the approach and flight of gentle, divining things for an unfruitful perplexity out of which nothing can come, nothing save a little disgust, disillusionment and poverty, and salvation in one of the many conventions that have been put up in great number like public refuge stations along this most dangerous road. No realm of human experience is so furnished with conventions as this: life-preservers of most varied invention, boats and swimming-bladders are here; the social attitude has known how to provide shelters of every sort, for, as it was disposed to take love-life as a pastime, it had also to proffer it in an easy form, cheap, safe and sure, as public pastimes are.

It is true that many young people who love wrongly, that is, simply with abandon and unalone (the average will of course always be like that), feel the oppressiveness of a failure and want to make the condition into which they have fallen viable and fruitful in their own personal way — ; for their nature tells them that questions of love can, less even than all else that is important, be solved publicly and by one compromise or another; that they are questions, intimate questions between human beings, which in any case demand a new, special, *only* personal answer — : but how should they, who have already flung themselves together and no longer mark off and distinguish themselves from each other, who therefore no longer possess individuality of their own, be able to find a way out of themselves, out of the depth of their already shattered solitude?

They act in a common helplessness, and then, if, with the best intentions, they try to avoid the convention that threatens them (say, marriage), they land in the prisoning arms of some less obvious, but equally deadly conventional solution; for then everything, far around them is — convention; there where people act out of a union early fused and turbid, *every* move is conventional: every relation to which such entanglement leads, has its convention, be it ever so unusual (that is, immoral in the ordinary sense); why, even separation would here be a conventional step, an impersonal chance decision without strength and without fruit.

Whoever looks seriously at it finds that, as in the case of death, that is difficult, neither has there yet been discovered for difficult love any enlightenment, any solution, any hint of a way, and for these two problems that we carry muffled up and hand on without opening, there will be no general rule based upon common consent to be found out. But in the same measure by which we begin as individuals to try to live, these great things will come nearer to meet the individual us. The demands which the difficult work of love makes upon our development are more than life-size, and we as beginners have not strength to cope with them. But if we nevertheless hold out and take this love upon us as a burden and an apprenticeship, instead of losing ourselves in all the light and frivolous play, behind which people have hidden from the most seriously serious side of their existence — then a little progress and an alleviation will perhaps be perceptible to those who come long after us; that would be much.

We are only just now beginning to look upon the relation of one individual person to a second individual without prejudice and realistically, and our attempts to live such associations have no example before them. And yet in the changing course of time there is already a good deal that wants to help our timorous novitiate.

Girls and women in their new, their own unfolding will but in passing be imitators of masculine vices and virtues and repeaters of masculine professions. After the uncertainty of such transitions it will become apparent that women only went through the whole range and variety of those (often ridiculous) disguises in order to clean their own most characteristic nature of the distorting influences of the other sex. Women, in whom life lingers and dwells more immediately, more fruitfully and more confidently, must naturally have become fundamentally riper people, more human people, than man who is easy-going, by the weight of no fruit of his body pulled down below the surface of life, and who, presumptuous and hasty, undervalues what he thinks he loves. This humanity of woman, carried out in suffering and humiliation, will then, when in the commutations of her external situation she will have stripped off the conventions of being only feminine, come to light, and those men, who do not yet feel it approaching to-day, will be astonished and stunned by it. Some day (and of this, particularly in the northern countries, reliable signs already clearly speak), some day there will be girls and women whose name will no longer signify merely an opposite of the masculine, but something in itself, something that makes one think, not of any complement and limit, but of life and existence: the female human being.

This advance will (at first much against the will of the men who have been outstripped) change the experiencing of love, which is now full of error, will alter it from the ground up, reshape it into a relation that is meant to be of one human being to another, no longer of man to woman. And this more human love (that will fulfill itself, infinitely considerate and gentle, and good and clear in binding and releasing) will resemble that which we are with struggle and endeavor preparing, the love that consists in this, that two solitudes protect and touch and greet each other.

And this further: do not believe that that great love with which you, a boy, were once charged, was lost; can you say whether great and good desires did not ripen in you at the time and resolutions by which you are still living to-day? I believe that that love remains so strong and powerful in your memory because it was your first deep being alone and the first inward work you did on your life. — All good wishes to you, dear Mr. Kappus!

Yours:

Rainer Maria Rilke.

ↄ§ FOR DISCUSSION AND WRITING

1. When one has read this letter, one can return to the beginning with perhaps better understanding of Rilke's meaning when he says that "it is clear
   that we must hold to what is difficult, everything alive holds to it . . . ," and
   that "it is good to be solitary, for solitude is difficult." A psychoanalyst
   would probably not agree, but how are these statements explained by
   what Rilke says later about love?

2. Why does he say that young people "are not yet *capable* of love"? Why,
   in the context of our own cultural habits and expectations, is this actually
   a rather shocking statement? Do you find Rilke's development of this view
   cogent or untenable? American education does not foster the notion that

"learning-time is always a long, secluded time," requiring solitude. What is to be said for Rilke's view?

3. Ortega, in the preceding essay, spoke of love as "surrender and enchantment"; but Rilke says, "Love is at first not anything that means unfolding, surrendering, and uniting with another." They are speaking out of different contexts and perspectives. What is that difference? (You will have to reconsider the place where the statement occurs.) Why, according to Rilke, cannot the young "surrender" and "unite"?

4. What does he mean by the "conventions" that society provides as "life-preservers" for the common disillusionments of love? He says that every confused erotic entanglement "has its convention," even if "immoral in the ordinary sense"; what is his meaning? Find illustrations of such "conventions" within the common experience of young people.

5. Why does he speak of love as a "difficult work"?

6. At the end of the letter Rilke evidently refers to some unhappy experience in love that his young correspondent had told him of. He says, "I believe that that love remains so strong and powerful in your memory because it was your first deep being alone and the first inward work you did on your life." How does the comment reverse the usual attitude toward past love affairs?

7. For a theme, make a fairly detailed comparison of Rilke's views with those which you are most familiar with, either of students or of older people. Or write on the "sexual revolution" that is said to have transformed, or to be in the process of transforming, modern sexual mores; but to give your essay edge and scope, try to bring Rilke's attitudes to bear on the subject also, by way of contrast. Or take up the statement that young people are not capable of love, which should suggest lively discussion.

D. H. Lawrence ⋘ . . . Love Was Once a Little Boy

⋘ English novelist, short-story writer, poet, and essayist (1885-1930). Lawrence's highly original genius changed the conventions of each art that he touched. The student may best approach him through the novels *Sons and Lovers* and *Women in Love,* his brilliant essays on American literature, and his exquisite poems on beasts and flowers. The present selection was apparently written at the Lawrences' ranch in New Mexico. Its title remains mysterious to the editors. ⋙

COLLAPSE, as often as not, is the result of persisting in an old attitude towards some important relationship, which, in the course of time, has changed its nature.

Love itself is a relationship, which changes as all things change, save abstractions. If you want something really more durable than diamonds you must be content with eternal truths like "twice two are four."

Love is a relationship between things that live, holding them together in a sort of unison. There are other vital relationships. But love is this special one.

In every living thing there is the desire, for love, or for the relationship of unison with the rest of things. That a tree should desire to

From *The Later D. H. Lawrence,* edited by William York Tindall (New York: Alfred A. Knopf, Inc., 1952). Reprinted by permission of Laurence Pollinger Limited. Acknowledgment is also made to the Estate of the late Mrs. Frieda Lawrence.

develop itself between the power of the sun, and the opposite pull of the earth's centre, and to balance itself between the four winds of heaven, and to unfold itself between the rain and the shine, to have roots and feelers in blue heaven and innermost earth, both, this is a manifestation of love: a knitting together of the diverse cosmos into a oneness, a tree.

At the same time, the tree must most powerfully exert itself and defend itself, to maintain its own integrity against the rest of things.

So that love, as a desire, is balanced against the opposite desire, to maintain the integrity of the individual self.

Hate is not the opposite of love. The real opposite of love is individuality.

We live in the age of individuality, we call ourselves the servants of love. That is to say, we enact a perpetual paradox.

Take the love of a man and a woman, to-day. As sure as you start with a case of "true love" between them, you end with a terrific struggle and conflict of the two opposing egos or individualities. It is nobody's fault: it is the inevitable result of trying to snatch an intensified individuality out of the mutual flame.

Love, as a relationship of unison, means and must mean *to some extent,* the sinking of the individuality. Woman for centuries was expected to sink her individuality into that of her husband and family. Nowadays the tendency is to insist that a man shall sink his individuality into his job, or his business, primarily, and secondarily into his wife and family.

At the same time, education and the public voice urge man and woman into intenser individualism. The sacrifice takes the old symbolic form of throwing a few grains of incense on the altar. A certain amount of time, labour, money, emotion are sacrificed on the altar of love, by man and woman: especially emotion. But each calculates the sacrifice. And man and woman alike, each saves his individual ego, her individual ego, intact, as far as possible, in the scrimmage of love. Most of our talk about love is cant, and bunk. The treasure of treasures to man and woman to-day is his own, or her own ego. And this ego, each hopes it will flourish like a salamander in the flame of love and passion. Which it well may: but for the fact that there are two salamanders in the same flame, and they fight till the flame goes out. Then they become grey cold lizards of the vulgar ego.

It is much easier, of course, when there *is* no flame. Then there is no serious fight.

You can't worship love and individuality in the same breath. Love is a mutual relationship, like a flame between wax and air. If either wax or air insists on getting its own way, or getting its own back too much, the flame goes out and the unison disappears. At the same time, if one yields itself up to the other entirely, there is a guttering mess. You have to balance love and individuality, and actually sacrifice a portion of each.

You have to have some sort of balance.

The Greeks said equilibrium. But whereas you can quite nicely balance a pound of butter against a pound of cheese, it is quite another matter to balance a rose and a ruby. Still more difficult is it to put male man in one scale and female woman in the other, and equilibrate that little pair of opposites.

Unless, of course, you abstract them. It's easy enough to balance a citizen against a citizeness, a Christian against a Christian, a spirit against a spirit, or a soul against a soul. There's a formula for each case. Liberty, Equality, Fraternity, etc., etc.

But the moment you put young Tom in one scale, and young Kate in the other: why, not God Himself has succeeded as yet in striking a nice level balance. Probably doesn't intend to, ever.

Probably it's one of the things that are most fascinating because they are *nearly* possible, yet absolutely impossible. Still, a miss is better than a mile. You can at least draw blood.

How can I equilibrate myself with my black cow Susan? I call her daily at six o'clock. And sometimes she comes. But sometimes, again, she doesn't, and I have to hunt her away among the timber. Possibly she is lying peacefully in cowy inertia, like a black Hindu statue, among the oak-scrub. Then she rises with a sighing heave. My calling was a mere nothing against the black stillness of her cowy passivity.

Or possible she is away down in the bottom corner, lowing *sotto voce* and blindly to some far-off, inaccessible bull. Then when I call at her, and approach, she screws round her tail and flings her sharp, elastic haunch in the air with a kick and a flick, and plunges off like a buck rabbit, or like a black demon among the pine trees, her udder swinging like a chime of bells. Or possibly the coyotes have been howling in the night along the top fence. And then I call in vain. It's a question of saddling a horse and sifting the bottom timber. And there at last the horse suddenly winces, starts: and with a certain pang of fear I too catch sight of something black and motionless and alive, and terribly silent, among the tree-trunks. It is Susan, her ears apart, standing like some spider suspended motionless by a threat, from the web of the eternal silence. The strange faculty she has, cow-given, of becoming a suspended ghost, hidden in the very crevices of the atmosphere! It is something in her *will*. It is her tarnhelm.[1] And then, she doesn't know me. If I am afoot, she knows my voice, but not the advancing me, in a blue shirt and cord trousers. She waits, suspended by the thread, till I come close. Then she reaches forward her nose, to smell. She smells my hand: gives a little snort, exhaling her breath, with a kind of contempt, turns, and ambles up towards the homestead, perfectly assured. If I am on horseback, although she knows the grey horse perfectly well, at the same time she *doesn't* know what it is. She waits till the wicked Azul, who is a born cow-punching pony, advances mischievously at her. Then round she swings, as if on the blast of some sudden wind, and with her ears back, her head rather down, her black back curved, up she goes, through the timber, with surprising, swimming swiftness. And the Azul, snorting with jolly mischief, dashes after her. And when she is safely in her milking-place, still she watches with her great black eyes as I dismount. And she has to smell my hand before the cowy peace of being milked enters her blood. Till then, there is something *roaring* in the chaos of her universe. When her cowy peace comes, then her universe is silent, and like the sea with an even tide, without sail or smoke: nothing.

That is Susan, my black cow.

And how am I going to equilibrate myself with her? Or even, if you prefer the word, to get in harmony with her?

Equilibrium? Harmony? with that black blossom! Try it!

She doesn't even know me. If I put on a pair of white trousers, she wheels away as if the devil was on her back. I have to go behind her, talk to her, stroke her, and let her smell my hand; and smell the white trousers. She doesn't know they are trousers. She doesn't know that I am a gentleman on two feet. Not she. Something mysterious happens in her blood and her being, when she smells me and my nice white trousers.

Yet she knows me, too. She likes to linger, while one talks to her.

[1] In the *Ring of the Nibelung*, a helmet rendering its wearer invisible.

She knows quite well she makes me mad when she swings her tail in my face. So sometimes she swings it, just on purpose: and looks at me out of the black corner of her great, pure-black eye, when I yell at her. And when I find her, away down the timber, when she is a ghost, and lost to the world, like a spider dangling in the void of chaos, then she is relieved. She comes to, out of a sort of trance, and is relieved, trotting up home with a queer, jerky cowy gladness. But she is never *really* glad, as the horses are. There is always a certain untouched chaos in her.

Where she is when she's *in* the trance, heaven only knows.

That's Susan! I have a certain relation to her. But that she and I are in equilibrium, or in harmony, I would never guarantee while the world stands. As for her individuality being in balance with mine, one can only feel the great blank of the gulf.

Yet a relationship there is. She knows my touch and she goes very still and peaceful, being milked. I, too, I know her smell and her warmth and her feel. And I share some of her cowy silence, when I milk her. There *is* a sort of relation between us. And this relation is part of the mystery of love: the individuality on each side, mine and Susan's, suspended in the relationship.

> Cow Susan by the forest's rim
> A black-eyed Susan was to him
> And nothing more —[2]

One understands Wordsworth and the primrose and the yokel. The yokel had no relation at all — or next to none — with the primrose. Wordsworth gathered it into his own bosom and made it part of his own nature. "I, William, am also a yellow primrose blossoming on a bank." This, we must assert, is an impertinence on William's part. He ousts the primrose from its own individuality. He doesn't allow it to call its soul its own. It must be identical with *his* soul. Because, of course, by begging the question, there is but One Soul in the universe.

This is bunk. A primrose has its own peculiar primrosy identity, and all the oversouling in the world won't melt it into a Williamish oneness. Neither will the yokel's remarking: "Nay, boy, that's nothing. It's only a primrose!" — turn the primrose into nothing. The primrose will

[2] A parody of Wordsworth's

> A primrose by the river's brim
> A yellow primrose was to him,
> And nothing more.

neither be assimilated nor annihilated, and Boundless Love breaks on
the rock of one more flower. It has its own individuality, which it opens
with lovely naïveté to sky and wind and William and yokel, bee and
beetle alike. It *is* itself. But its very floweriness is a kind of communion
with all things: the love unison.

In this lies the eternal absurdity of Wordsworth's lines. His own
behaviour, primrosely, was as foolish as the yokel's.

> "A primrose by the river's brim
> A yellow primrose was to him
> And nothing more — "

> A primrose by the river's brim
> A yellow primrose was to him
> And a great deal more —

> A primrose by the river's brim
> Lit up its pallid yellow glim
> Upon the floor —

> And watched old Father William trim
> His course beside the river's brim
> And trembled sore —

> The yokel, going for a swim
> Had very nearly trod on him
> An hour before.

> And now the poet's fingers slim
> Were reaching out to pluck at him
> And hurt him more.

> Oh gentlemen, hark to my hymn!
> To be a primrose is my whim
> Upon the floor,
> And nothing more.

> The sky is with me, and the dim
> Earth clasps my roots. Your shadows skim
> My face once more. . . .
> Leave me therefore
> Upon the floor;
> Say *au revoir*. . . .

Ah William! The "something more" that the primrose was to you, was yourself in the mirror. And if the yokel actually got as far as beholding a "yellow primrose," he got far enough.

You see it is not easy even for a poet to equilibrate himself even with a mere primrose. He didn't leave it with a soul of its own. It had to have his soul. And nature had to be sweet and pure, Williamish. Sweet-Williamish at that! Anthropomorphized! Anthropomorphism, that allows nothing to call its soul its own, save anthropos: and only a special brand, even of him!

Poetry can tell alluring lies, when we let our feelings, or our ego, run away with us.

And we must always beware of romance: of people who love nature, or flowers, or dogs, or babies, or pure adventure. It means they are getting into a love-swing where everything is easy and nothing opposes their own egoism. Nature, babies, dogs are *so* lovable, because they can't answer back. The primrose, alas! couldn't pipe up and say: "Hey! Bill! get off the barrow!"

That's the best of men and women. There's bound to be a lot of back chat. You can *Lucy Gray*[3] your woman as hard as you like, one day she's bound to come back at you: "Who are *you* when you're at home?"

A man isn't going to spread his own ego over a woman, as he has done over nature and primroses, and dogs, or horses, or babies, or "the people," or the proletariat or the poor-and-needy. The old hen takes the cock by the beard, and says: *"That's me, mind you!"*

Man is an individual, and woman is an individual. Which sounds easy.

But it's not as easy as it seems. These two individuals are as different as chalk and cheese. True, a pound of chalk weighs as much as a pound of cheese. But the proof of the pudding is in the eating, not the scales.

That is to say, you can announce that men and women should be equal and *are* equal. All right. Put them in the scales.

Alas! my wife is about twenty pounds heavier than I am.

Nothing to do but to abstract. *L'homme est né libre:*[4] with a napkin round his little tail.

[3] Wordsworth has several poems about Lucy Gray, but the one Lawrence probably has in mind here is the one in which Lucy is called "A violet by a mossy stone." Here also he would be on the side of the "yokels," to whom Lucy would be Lucy and "nothing more."

[4] "Man is born free."

Nevertheless, I am a citizen, my wife is a citizeness: I can vote, she can vote, I can be sent to prison, she can be sent to prison, I can have a passport, she can have a passport, I can be an author, she can be an authoress. Ooray! OO-bloomin' ray!

You see, we are both British subjects. Everybody bow!

Subjects! Subjects! Subjects!

Madame is already shaking herself like a wet hen.

But yes, my dear! we are both subjects. And as subjects, we enjoy a lovely equality, liberty, my dear! Equality! Fraternity or Sorority! my dear!

Aren't you pleased?

But it's no use talking to a wet hen. That "subject" was a cold douche.

As subjects, men and women may be equal.

But as objects, it's another pair of shoes. Where, I ask you, is the equality between an arrow and a horseshoe? or a serpent and a squash blossom? Find me the equation that equates the cock and the hen.

You can't.

As inhabitants of my back yard, as loyal subjects of my *rancho*, they, the cock and the hen, are equal. When he gets wheat, she gets wheat. When sour milk is put out, it is as much for him as for her. She is just as free to go where she likes, as he is. And if she likes to crow at sunrise, she may. There is no law against it. And he can lay an egg, if the fit takes him. Absolutely nothing forbids.

Isn't that equality? If it isn't, what is?

Even then, they're two very different objects.

As equals, they are just a couple of barnyard fowls, clucking! generalized!

But dear me, when he comes prancing up with his red beard shaking, and his eye gleaming, and she comes slowly pottering after, with her nose to the ground, they're two very different objects. You never think of equality: or of inequality, for that matter. They're a cock and a hen, and you accept them as such.

You don't think of them as equals, or as unequals. But you think of them *together*.

Wherein, then, lies the togetherness?

Would you call it love?

I wouldn't.

Their two egos are absolutely separate. He's a cock, she's a hen. He never thinks of her for a moment as if she were a cock like himself; and she never thinks for a moment that he is a hen like herself. I never hear anything in her squawk which would seem to say: *"Aren't I a fowl as much as you are, you brute!"* Whereas I always hear women shrieking at their men: "Aren't I a human being as much as you are?"

It seems beside the point.

I always answer my spouse, with sweet reasonableness: "My dear, we are both British Subjects. What can I say more, on the score of equality? You are a British Subject as much as I am."

Curiously, she hates to have it put that way. She wants to be a human being as much as I am. But absolutely and honestly, I don't know what a human being is. Whereas I do know what a British Subject is. It can be defined.

And I can see how a *Civis Romanum*, or a British Subject, can be free, whether it's he or she. The he-ness or the she-ness doesn't matter. But how a *man* can consider himself free, I don't know. Any more than a cock-robin or a dandelion.

Imagine a dandelion suddenly hissing: *"I am free and I will be free!"* Then wriggling on his root like a snake with his tail pegged down! . . .

There's a cock and there's the hen, and their two egos or individualities seem to stay apart without friction. They never coo at one another, nor hold each other's hand. I never see her sitting on his lap and being petted. True, sometimes he calls for her to come eat a tidbit. And sometimes he dashes at her and walks over her for a moment. She doesn't seem to mind. I never hear her squawking: *"Don't you think you can walk over me!"*

Yet she's by no means downtrodden. She's just herself, and seems to have a good time: and she doesn't like it if he is missing.

So there is this peculiar togetherness about them. You can't call it love. It would be too ridiculous.

What then?

As far as I can see, it is desire. And the desire has a fluctuating intensity, but it is always there. His desire is always towards her, even when he has absolutely forgotten her. And by the way she puts her feet down, I can see she always walks in her plumes of desirableness, even when she's going broody.

The mystery about her, is her strange undying desirableness. You can see it in every step she takes. She is desirable. And this is the breath of her life.

It is the same with Susan. The queer cowy mystery of her is her changeless cowy desirableness. She is far, alas, from any bull. She never even remotely dreams of a bull, save at rare and brief periods. Yet her whole being and motion is that of being desirable: or else fractious. It seems to unite her with the very air, and the plants and trees. Even to the sky and the trees and the grass and the running stream, she is subtly, delicately and *purely* desirable, in cowy desirability. It is her cowy mystery. Then her fractiousness is the fireworks of her desirableness.

To me she is fractious, tiresome, and a faggot. Yet the subtle desirableness is in her, for me. As it is in a brown hen, or even a sow. It is like a peculiar charm: the creature's femaleness, her desirableness. It is her sex, no doubt: but so subtle as to have nothing to do with function. It is a mystery, like a delicate flame. It would be false to call it love, because love complicates the ego. The ego is always concerned in love. But in the frail, subtle desirousness of the true male, towards everything female, and the equally frail, indescribable desirability of every female for every male, lies the real clue to the equating, or the *relating*, of things which otherwise are incommensurable.

And this, this desire, is the reality which is inside love. The ego itself plays a false part in it. The individual is like a deep pool, or tarn, in the mountains, fed from beneath by unseen springs, and having no obvious inlet or outlet. The springs which feed the individual at the depths are sources of power, power from the unknown. But it is not until the stream of desire overflows and goes running downhill into the open world, that the individual has his further, secondary existence.

Now we have imagined love to be something absolute and personal. It is neither. In its essence, love is no more than the stream of clear and unmuddied, subtle desire which flows from person to person, creature to creature, thing to thing. The moment this stream of delicate but potent desire dries up, the love has dried up, and the joy of life has dried up. It's no good trying to turn on the tap. Desire is either flowing, or gone, and the love with it, and the life too.

This subtle streaming of desire is beyond the control of the ego. The ego says: "This is *my* love, to do as I like with! This is *my* desire, given me for my own pleasure."

But the ego deceives itself. The individual cannot possess the love which he himself feels. Neither should he be entirely possessed by it. Neither man nor woman should sacrifice individuality to love, nor love to individuality.

If we lose desire out of our life, we become empty vessels. But if we break our own integrity, we become a squalid mess, like a jar of honey dropped and smashed.

The individual has nothing, really, to do with love. That is, his individuality hasn't. Out of the deep silence of his individuality runs the stream of desire, into the open squash blossom of the world. And the stream of desire may meet and mingle with the stream from a woman. But it is never *himself* that meets and mingles with *herself:* any more than two lakes, whose waters meet to make one river, in the distance, meet in themselves.

The two individuals stay apart, forever and ever. But the two streams of desire, like the Blue Nile and the White Nile, from the mountains one and from the low hot lake the other, meet and at length mix their strange and alien waters, to make a Nilus Flux.

See then the childish mistake we have made, about love. We have *insisted* that the two individualities should "fit." We have insisted that the "love" between man and woman must be "perfect." What on earth that means, is a mystery. What would a perfect Nilus Flux be? — one that never overflowed its banks? or one that always overflowed its banks? or one that had exactly the same overflow every year, to a hair's-breadth?

My dear, it is absurd. Perfect love is an absurdity. As for casting out fear, you'd better be careful. For fear, like curses and chickens, will also come home to roost.

Perfect love, I suppose, means that a married man and woman never contradict one another, and that they both of them always feel the same thing at the same moment, and kiss one another on the strength of it. What blarney! It means, I suppose, that they are absolutely intimate: this precious intimacy that lovers insist on. They tell each other *everything:* and if she puts on chiffon knickers, he ties the strings for her: and if he blows his nose, she holds the hanky.

Pfui! Is anything so loathsome as intimacy, especially the married sort, or the sort that "lovers" indulge in!

It's a mistake and ends in disaster. Why? Because the individualities of men and women are incommensurable, and they will no more meet than the Mountains of Abyssinia will meet with Lake Victoria Nyanza. It is far more important to keep them distinct, than to join them. If they are to join, they will join in the third land where the two streams of desire meet.

Of course, as citizen and citizeness, as two persons, even as two spirits, man and woman can be equal and intimate. But this is their outer, more general or common selves. The individual man himself, and the individual woman herself, this is another pair of shoes.

It is a pity that we have insisted on putting all our eggs in one basket: calling love the basket, and ourselves the eggs. It is a pity we have insisted on being individuals only in the communistic, semi-abstract or generalized sense: as voters, money-owners, "free" men and women: free in so far as we are all alike, and individuals in so far as we are commensurable integers.

By turning ourselves into integers: every man to himself and every woman to herself a Number One; an infinite number of Number Ones; we have destroyed ourselves as desirous or desirable individuals, and broken the inward sources of our power, and flooded all mankind into one dreary marsh where the rivers of desire lie dead with everything else, except a stagnant unity.

It is a pity of pities women have learned to think like men. Any husband will say: *"they haven't."* But they have: they've all learned to think like some other beastly man, who is not their husband. Our education goes on and on, on and on, making the sexes alike, destroying the original individuality of the blood, to substitute for it this dreary in-dividuality of the ego, the Number One. Out of the ego streams neither Blue Nile nor White Nile. The infinite number of little human egos makes a mosquito marsh, where nothing happens except buzzing and biting, ooze and degeneration.

And they call this marsh, with its poisonous will-o-the-wisps, and its clouds of mosquitoes, *democracy*, and the reign of love!!

You can have it.

I am a man, and the Mountains of Abyssinia, and my Blue Nile flows towards the desert. There should be a woman somewhere far south, like a great lake, sending forth her White Nile towards the desert, too: and the rivers will meet among the Slopes of the World, somewhere.

But alas, every woman I've ever met spends her time saying she's as good as any man, if not better, and she can beat him at his own game.

So Lake Victoria Nyanza gets up on end, and declares it's the Mountains of Abyssinia, and the Mountains of Abyssinia fall flat and cry: *"You're all that, and more, my dear!"* — and between them, you're bogged.

I give it up.

But at any rate it's nice to know *what's* wrong, since wrong it is.

If we were men, if we were women, our individualities would be lone and a bit mysterious, like tarns, and fed with power, male power, female power, from underneath, invisibly. And from us the streams of desire would flow out in the eternal glimmering adventure, to meet in some unknown desert.

Mais nous avons changé tout cela.[5]

I'll bet the yokel, even then, was more himself, and the stream of his desire was stronger and more gurgling, than William Wordsworth's. For a long time the yokel retains his own integrity, and his own real stream of desire flows from him. Once you break this, and turn him, who was a yokel, into still another Number One, an assertive newspaper-parcel of an ego, you've done it!

But don't, dear, darling reader, when I say "desire," immediately conclude that I mean a jungleful of rampaging Don Juans. . . . When I say that a woman should be eternally desirable, *don't* say that I mean every man should want to sleep with her, the instant he sets eyes on her.

On the contrary. Don Juan was only Don Juan because he *had* no real desire. He had broken his own integrity, and was a mess to start with. No stream of desire, with a course of its own, flowed from him. He was a marsh in himself. He mashed and trampled everything up, and desired no woman, so he ran after every one of them, with an itch instead of a steady flame. And tortured by his own itch, he inflamed his itch more and more. That's Don Juan, the man who *couldn't* desire a woman. He shouldn't have tried. He should have gone into a monastery at fifteen.

As for the yokel, his little stream may have flowed out of commonplace little hills, and been ready to mingle with the streams of any easy, puddly little yokeless. But what does it matter! And men are far less promiscuous, even then, than we like to pretend. It's Don Juanery, sex-in-the-head, no real desire, which leads to profligacy or squalid promiscuity. The yokel usually met desire with desire: which is all right: and sufficiently rare to ensure the moral balance.

Desire is a living stream. If we gave free rein, or a free course, to our

[5] "But we have changed all that."

living flow of desire, we shouldn't go far wrong. It's quite different from giving a free rein to an itching, prurient imagination. That is our vileness.

The living stream of sexual desire itself does not often, in any man, find its object, its confluent, the stream of desire in a woman into which it can flow. The two streams flow together, spontaneously, not often, in the life of any man or woman. Mostly, men and women alike rush into a sort of prostitution, because our idiotic civilization has never learned to hold in reverence the true desire-stream. We force our desire from our ego: and this is deadly.

Desire itself is a pure thing, like sunshine, or fire, or rain. It is desire that makes the whole world living to me, keeps me in the flow connected. It is my flow of desire that makes me move as the birds and animals move through the sunshine and the night, in a kind of accomplished innocence, not shut outside of the natural paradise. For life is a kind of Paradise, even to my horse Azul, though he doesn't get his own way in it, by any means, and is sometimes in a real temper about it. Sometimes he even gets a bellyache, with wet alfalfa. But even the bellyache is part of the natural paradise. Not like human ennui.

So a man can go forth in desire, even to the primroses. But let him refrain from falling all over the poor blossom, as William did. Or trying to incorporate it in his own ego, which is a sort of lust. Nasty anthropomorphic lust.

Everything that exists, even a stone, has two sides to its nature. It fiercely maintains its own individuality, its own solidity. And it reaches forth from itself in the subtlest flow of desire.

It fiercely resists all inroads. At the same time it sinks down in the curious weight, or flow, of that desire which we call gravitation. And imperceptibly, through the course of ages, it flows into delicate combination with the air and sun and rain.

At one time, men worshipped stones: symbolically, no doubt, because of their mysterious durability, their power of hardness, resistance, their strength of remaining unchanged. Yet even then, worshipping man did not rest till he had erected the stone into a pillar, a menhir, symbol of the eternal desire, as the phallus itself is but a symbol.

And we, men and women, are the same as stones: the powerful resistance and cohesiveness of our individuality is countered by the mysterious flow of desire, from us and towards us.

It is the same with the worlds, the stars, the suns. All is alive, in its own degree. And the centripetal force of spinning earth is the force of earth's individuality: and the centrifugal force is the force of desire. Earth's immense centripetal energy, almost passion, balanced against her furious centrifugal force, holds her suspended between her moon and her sun, in a dynamic equilibrium.

So instead of the Greek: *Know thyself!* we shall have to say to every man: *"Be Thyself! Be Desirous!"* — and to every woman: *"Be Thyself! Be Desirable!"*

Be Thyself! does not mean: *Assert thy ego!* It means, be true to your own integrity, as man, as woman: let your heart stay open, to receive the mysterious inflow of power from the unknown: know that the power comes to you from beyond, it is not generated by your own will: therefore all the time, be watchful, and reverential towards the mysterious coming of power into you. . . .

The powers that enter me fluctuate and ebb. And the desire that goes forth from me waxes and wanes. Sometimes it is weak, and I am almost isolated. Sometimes it is strong, and I am almost carried away.

But supposing the cult of Individualism, Liberty, Freedom, and so forth, has landed me in the state of egoism, the state so prettily and nauseously described by Henley in his *Invictus*: which, after all, is but the yelp of a house-dog, a domesticated creature with an inferiority complex!

> "It matters not how strait the gate,
>   How charged with punishments the scroll,
>   I am the master of my fate;
>   I am the captain of my soul."

Are you, old boy? Then why hippety-hop?

He was a cripple at that!

As a matter of fact, it is the slave's bravado! The modern slave is he who does not receive his powers from the unseen, and give reverence, but who thinks he is his own little boss. Only a slave would take the trouble to shout: *"I am free!"* That is to say, to shout it in the face of the open heavens. In the face of men, and their institutions and prisons. Yes-yes! But in the face of the open heavens I would be ashamed to talk about freedom. I have no life, no real power, unless it will come to me. And I accomplish nothing, not even my own fulfilled existence, unless I go forth, delicately, desirous, and find the mating of my desire; even if it be only the sky itself, and trees, and the cow Susan, and the inexpressible consolation of a statue of an Egyptian Pharaoh, or the *Old Testament*, or even three rubies. These answer my desire with fulfilment. What bunk then to talk about being master of my fate! when my fate depends upon these things: — not to mention the unseen reality that sends strength, or life into me, without which I am a gourd rattle.

The ego, the little conscious ego that I am, that doll-like entity, that mannikin made in ridiculous likeness of the Adam which I am: am I going to allow that that is *all of me?* And shout about it?

Of course, if I am nothing but an ego, and woman is nothing but another ego, then there is really no vital difference between us. Two little dolls of conscious entities, squeaking when you squeeze them. And with a tiny bit of an extraneous appendage to mark which is which.

"Woman is just the same as man," loudly said the political speaker, "Save for a very little difference."

"Three cheers for the very little difference!" says a vulgar voice from the crowd.

But that's a chestnut.

"Quick! Sharp! On the alert!
Let every gentleman put on his shirt!
And be *quick* if you please!
Let every lady put on her chemise!"

Though nowadays, a lady's chemise won't save her face.

In or out her chemise, however, doesn't make much difference to the modern woman. She's a finished-off ego, an assertive conscious entity, cut off like a doll from any mystery. And her nudity is about as interesting as a doll's. If you can *be* interested in the nudity of a doll, then jazz on, jazz on!

The same with the men. No matter how they pull their shirts off they never arrive at their own nakedness. They have none. They can only be undressed. Naked they cannot be. Without their clothes on, they are like a dismantled street-car without its advertisements: sort of public article that doesn't refer to anything.

The Ego! Anthropomorphism! Love! What it works out to in the end is that even anthropos disappears, and leaves a sawdust mannikin wondrously jazzing.

"My little sisters, the birds!" says Francis of Assisi.

"*Whew!*" goes the blackbird.

"Listen to me, my little sisters, you birds!"

"*Whew!*" goes the blackbird. "I'm a cock, mister!"

Love! What's the good of woman who isn't desirable, even though she's as pretty as paint, and the waves in her hair are as permanent as the pyramids!

He buried his face in her permanent wave, and cried: "Help! Get me out!" . . .

&§ FOR DISCUSSION AND WRITING

1. In ancient Greek thought, Love (Eros) was a cosmic force that brought about the conception and development of all things. What similar extension of the meaning of the word "love" does Lawrence make in the first few paragraphs?

2. He opposes love to individuality. How cogent is this opposition? As you see by the rest of the essay, he is a fervent individualist: how does this attitude affect his conception of love? What does he think of the equality of the sexes?

3. How does Susan, the cow, elucidate Lawrence's argument? Given his extension of the meaning of "love" at the beginning, is he justified in using Susan as illustration? One of Lawrence's great gifts is his ability to describe animals, preserving the mysteriousness of their animal nature but with extraordinary accuracy of observation. In what details of the description of Susan do you find this kind of insight?

4. Recalling Ortega's concern with "perception" as a necessary component of love (the disinterested ability really to "see" another person as a distinct individual), do you find any basis of similarity between Ortega's and Lawrence's views?

5. How soon do you begin to find in Lawrence signs of a characteristically personal style of writing? Cite specific instances where the personal character of the style shows in vocabulary, in sentence structure, in imagery and metaphor, in variety of rhythm (the best way to make this analysis

is to write down the examples). "Tone" is the most elusive of prose qualities to define and describe, though we perceive a person's tone instantly when he speaks. Distinguish any difference of tone when Lawrence talks of Susan and when he talks of Wordsworth; when he talks of "British subjects" and when he talks of the cock and the hen in his back yard.

6. What relation does Wordsworth's primrose have to Lawrence's argument? How does the very *way* he describes the cock and the hen—"he comes prancing up with his red beard shaking, and his eye gleaming, and she comes slowly pottering after, with her nose to the ground"—support his argument?

7. By "desire" and "desirableness" does he mean sexual desire? In this context, what relation have "desire" and "desirableness" to love? what relation to the ego? to individuality?

8. Why does Lawrence substitute "Be Thyself" for the Delphic "Know Thyself"? What is there in Lawrence's sense of life and living creatures that would make it impossible to "know" oneself? Why does he object to Henley's "I am the master of my fate," etc.?

9. Is this essay "unified and coherent," as we are always told that essays should be? Or is Lawrence capriciously devious, wayward, and unsteady in the development of his thought? You need a strong argument either way, and it might be worthwhile to build a firmly unified paragraph in support of your view.

10. It is to be hoped that Lawrence's unique capacity to irritate, to rouse hackles and explode tempers, will already have suggested a number of essay subjects, as for instance "What Lawrence Didn't Know about Love" or "Does Love Prohibit Individualism?" or "A Defense of Equality in Marriage" or "Lawrence's Cowy Mystique." But at this time it might be an excellent critical project to make a thoughtful, analytical comparison of two or three of the pieces in this section—probably Rilke, Ortega, and Lawrence make the best combination—showing what seems to be central and perhaps common in their thought.

The Extreme Situation

HERACLITUS *said, 2,500 years ago, that "destiny is character." This conception of destiny or fate is different from the still more ancient but also more persistent notion of fate as an occult kind of predetermination in external events, having little or nothing to do with personal character. Few of us think of ourselves as having a destiny, though we fairly often feel and speak as if there were an impersonal fatality in the nature of things: "That's the way the ball bounces." Yet sometimes at moments of extreme urgency—of love or danger or anger or grief or despair—hidden potentialities of character are revealed with all the finality and irrevocability of destiny.*

On this principle of the "moment of truth" dramatists and story writers in every age have pivoted their plots. The most obvious instance of the kind is the murder mystery, where it may be the murderer himself in whom destiny is revealed as character ("He knew then that he would have to kill her"), or the Private Eye or C.I.D. agent who shows his inner resources by getting himself sandbagged, concussed, kicked to a pulp, and manfully coming back for more. Some of the earlier pieces in the present volume—for instance, the selection from the ILIAD, *Proust's "Filial Sentiments of a Parricide," and even, in its homely but subtle way, Sherwood Anderson's "Discovery of a Father"— focus on such moments of revelation.*

The five pieces that follow all concern situations in which character is sharply revealed, in an extremity; but because these are no ordinary tests, the human quality that is brought into view has something mysterious about it—coming from more profound depths than those qualities informing the personality that is visible by everyday light, and carrying something of that sense of the mystery of the human being that the great tragic dramatists evoke.

All are from life. In Joan's answers to her examiners, even after months of prison, a character of extraordinary consistency is seen finding its way infallibly, at every turn of the maze of inquisition, to its destiny. Clearly, the events of the trial do not simply befall her—she shapes them. In the last pages of Scott's diary, the mounting power and intensity of the simple, factual notations are an effect not so much of the hardships suffered as of the way the man deliberately designs his actions, his personal and purely human destiny (as distinct from the fatality of frostbite, blizzard, and starvation)—in a word, how he gives significant form to death. The chapter from T. E. Lawrence's great book illuminates the improbable possibilities of character— enchantingly in the encounter with the little Turk, and at the end, with the death of Farraj, by too fearfully paradoxical a demand on loyalty and compassion for any moral preparation or imaginative foreseeing. Hanson Baldwin's "R.M.S. Titanic" shows the destiny that is character in a quite different way: there is the dim, monstrous fatality of the iceberg gliding past out of the night, and there are the 2,201 persons on the ship, the great, the powerful, the wealthy, and those 706 "immigrants to the land of promise" (the cliché has its right to be here)—each thrown with full force on his personal fatality of cowardice, shame, brutality of egoism, the imperative of selflessness, the grace of courage, the patience of heroism. And in Isak Dinesen's "Shooting Accident," an incident from her life in Africa, a child of seven is astonished into the strange gesture of that destiny which comes from within, the mysterious personal signature which no one could invent—here so simple as laying a coin on the table to pay his one small debt before walking into a darkness savage and imponderable, but chosen.

Joan of Arc ⮜⧅ "I Have Nothing More to Say"

⮜⧅ The following pages are taken from the records of Joan's trial. Her early life is given in her own words; her interviews with Robert de Baudricourt and the Dauphin, and her activities in battle are as reported at the trial either by herself or by witnesses; and the questions of her examiners and Joan's answers are from the court records.

The general background of Joan's career is that of the Hundred Years' War, which lasted from 1337 to 1453, and through which England lost virtually all her possessions in France, and France—till then disunited in independent principalities—became a united nation under Charles VII. Joan was born in 1412 in the village of Domremy, (part of the Burgundian domain, as distinct, at that time, from "France"). Her parents were well-to-do peasants. When she was thirteen she heard her first angelic "voices," and when she was seventeen she went at their bidding to the French commander at Vaucouleurs and obtained from him escort to the Dauphin. Charles gave her armor and troops to march on Orléans, which was held by the English. Under her leadership the French won notable victories, and she was able to carry out the mission her "voices" had given her—to lead Charles to Reims and see him crowned there as King of France.

Thereafter she followed the advice of her captains and attempted to push on to Paris, but at the siege of Compiègne she became isolated from her troops and was captured by the Burgundians, who had made common cause with the British. She was taken to Rouen and tried in ecclesiastical court for sorcery by the Bishop of Beauvais, assisted by members of the faculty of the University of Paris, which was under English control. On May 30th, 1431, she was burned at the stake. She was then nineteen.

The eventual expulsion of the English and the unification of France were largely the result of the impetus Joan gave to national feeling. In 1450 Charles held a revision of her trial, and in 1555 there was another revision which formally pronounced her innocent of the charge under which she was condemned. She was beatified in 1909 and canonized in 1920. ⧅⮞

AMONG my own people, I was called Jehanette; since my coming into France, I am called Jehanne.

From the translation by Willard Trask in *Joan of Arc, A Self Portrait* (Stackpole Sons, 1936). Reprinted by permission of Willard Trask.

I was born in the village of Domremy. My father's name is Jacques d'Arc, my mother's Isabelle.

As long as I lived at home, I worked at common tasks about the house, going but seldom afield with our sheep and other cattle. I learned to sew and spin: I fear no woman in Rouen at sewing and spinning.

As to my schooling, I learned my faith, and was rightly and duly taught to do as a good child should.

From my mother I learned "Our Father," "Hail Mary," and "I believe." And my teaching in my faith I had from her and from no one else.

Once a year I confessed my sins to our parish-priest, or, when he was unable, to another with his permission. And I received the sacrament of the Eucharist at Easter time.

Not far from Domremy there is a tree called the Ladies' Tree, and others call it the Fairies' Tree,[1] and near it there is a fountain. And I have heard that those who are sick with fever drink at the fountain or fetch water from it, to be made well. Indeed, I have seen them do so, but I do not know whether it makes them well or not. I have heard, too, that the sick, when they can get up, go walking under the tree. It is a great tree, a beech, and from it our fair May-branches come; and it was in the lands of Monseigneur Pierre de Bourlemont. Sometimes I went walking there with the other girls, and I have made garlands under the tree for the statue of the Blessed Virgin of Domremy.

I have often heard it said by old people (they were not of my own elders) that the fairies met there. My godmother even told me that she had seen fairies there, but I do not know whether it was true or not. I never saw any fairies under the tree to my knowledge. I have seen girls hang wreaths on the branches; I have sometimes hung my own with the others, and sometimes we took them away with us and sometimes we left them behind.

---

[1] Throughout the trial, Joan's examiners were trying to get her to confess to witch-craft. Here, evidently, they have laid a trap for her by asking whether, as a child, she shared the common peasant belief that certain trees, springs, wells, and so on, were sacred to the "fairies"—that is, to ancient pagan gods who had, in the course of time, become reduced to "fairies." Dancing round the Maypole and the giving of May baskets are—like the May branches and May dancing Joan speaks of— residua of such beliefs.

I do not know whether, after I reached years of discretion, I ever danced at the foot of the tree; I may have danced there sometimes with the children; but I sang there more than I danced. . . .

When I was thirteen, I had a voice from God to help me to govern myself. The first time, I was terrified. The voice came to me about noon: it was summer, and I was in my father's garden. I had not fasted the day before. I heard the voice on my right hand, towards the church. There was a great light all about.

I vowed then to keep my virginity for as long as it should please God.

I saw it many times before I knew that it was Saint Michael. Afterwards he taught me and showed me such things that I knew that it was he.

He was not alone, but duly attended by heavenly angels. I saw them with the eyes of my body as well as I see you. And when they left me, I wept, and I wished that they might have taken me with them. And I kissed the ground where they had stood, to do them reverence.

Above all, Saint Michael told me that I must be a good child, and that God would help me. He taught me to behave rightly and to go often to church. He said that I would have to go into France.

He told me that Saint Catherine and Saint Margaret would come to me, and that I must follow their counsel; that they were appointed to guide and counsel me in what I had to do, and that I must believe what they would tell me, for it was at our Lord's command.

He told me the pitiful state of the Kingdom of France.

And he told me that I must go to succour the King of France.

Saint Catherine and Saint Margaret had rich crowns upon their heads. They spoke well and fairly, and their voices are beautiful — sweet and soft.

The name by which they often named me was *Jehanne the Maid, child of God.*

They told me that my King would be restored to his Kingdom, despite his enemies. They promised to lead me to Paradise, for that was what I asked of them.

Twice and thrice a week the voice told me that I must depart and go into France.

And the voice said that I would raise the siege before Orléans. And it told me to go to Vaucouleurs, to Robert de Baudricourt, captain of the town, who would give me men to go with me.

And I answered the voice that I was a poor girl who knew nothing of riding and warfare. . . .

My mother had told me that my father often dreamed that I would run away with a band of soldiers. That was more than two years after I first heard the voices. She told me that he had said to my brothers, "If I believed that the thing I have dreamed about her would come to pass, I would want you to drown her; and if you would not, I would drown her myself." On account of these dreams, my father and mother watched me closely and kept me in great subjection. And I was obedient in everything.

But since God had commanded me to go, I must do it. And since God had commanded it, had I had a hundred fathers and a hundred mothers, and had I been a king's daughter, I would have gone.

It pleased God thus to act through a simple maid in order to turn back the King's enemies.

I went to my uncle and told him that I would visit him for a time. I was in his house for about a week; then I told him that I must go to Vaucouleurs. And my uncle took me there.

When I came to Vaucouleurs I knew Robert de Baudricourt, though I had never seen him before. The voice told me that it was he.

And I told him that I must go into France.

HER WORDS TO ROBERT DE BAUDRICOURT

The Kingdom of France is not the Dauphin's but my Lord's. But my Lord wills that the Dauphin shall be made King and have the Kingdom in custody. The Dauphin shall be King despite his enemies, and I shall lead him to his anointing.

Twice he refused and rejected me.

AT HER LODGING TO JEAN DE METZ

I am come to this town, which is the King's, to ask Robert de Baudricourt to take me or send me to the King. And he heeds neither me nor my words. Nevertheless, I must be with the King before mid-Lent, though I wear my legs to the knees on the road. For there is none in this world — neither kings, nor dukes, nor the King of Scotland's daughter, nor any other — who can restore the Kingdom of France. Nor is there any succour for it but from me.

Far rather would I sit and sew beside my poor mother, for this thing is not of my condition. But I must go, and I must do this thing, because my Lord will have it so.

Rather now than tomorrow, and tomorrow than the day after!

And the third time he received me and gave me men. The voice had told me that so it would come to pass. . . .

I set out from Vaucouleurs in men's clothing. I carried a sword that Robert de Baudricourt had given me, but no other arms. With me there were a knight, a squire, and four serving-men.

Robert de Baudricourt made those who went with me swear that they would guide me well and safely. To me at parting he said: "Go, and, whatever may come of it, let it come!" . . .

I came to Chinon about noon and put up at an inn, and, after dinner, I went to the King in his castle. And when I entered the King's chamber, I knew him among the rest, for the voice counselled me and revealed it to me. And I told the King that I would go to make war on the English.

HER WORDS TO CHARLES

I bring you news from God, that our Lord will give you back your kingdom, bringing you to be crowned at Reims, and driving out your enemies. In this I am God's messenger. Do you set me bravely to work, and I will raise the siege of Orléans.

For three weeks I was examined by learned men in Chinon and Poitiers, and the King received a sign concerning what I had done before he would believe in me. . . .

HER ANSWERS TO HER EXAMINERS

I do not know A from B.[2]

I am come from the King of Heaven to raise the siege of Orléans and to lead the Dauphin to Reims to be crowned and anointed. . . .

HER WORDS TO CHARLES

I shall last a year, and but little longer: we must think to do good work in that year. Four things are laid upon me: to drive out the English; to bring you to be crowned and anointed at Reims; to rescue the Duke of Orléans from the hands of the English; and to raise the siege of Orléans.

And the King set me to work, giving me ten or twelve thousand men, and I went to Orléans.

LETTER, MARCH 22, 1429

† *JHESUS MARIA* †

King of England, and you, Duke of Bedford, who call yourself Regent of the Kingdom of France; you, William de la Pole, Earl of Suffolk; John, Lord Talbot; and you, Thomas, Lord Scales, who call yourselves lieutenants of the said Duke of Bedford: Do justice to the King of Heaven; surrender to the Maid, who is sent here from God, King of Heaven, the keys of all the good towns you have taken and violated in France. She is come from God to uphold the blood royal. She is ready to make peace if you will do justice, relinquishing France and paying for what you have withheld.

As to you, you archers and men-at-arms, gentle[3] and others, who are before the town of Orléans, go hence into your own country in God's name; and if you do not so, expect to hear news of the Maid, who will shortly come to see you, to your very great damage.

King of England, if you do not so, I am a commander, and in whatever place in France I come upon your men, I will make them leave it, will they or nill they; and if they will not yield obedience, I will have them

---

[2] Joan could not read or write. The letter to the King of England that follows was dictated.

[3] Noble, of high birth.

all slain. I am sent here from God, King of Heaven, to put you, hand to hand, out of all France. Yet if they will yield obedience, I will grant them mercy.

And think not otherwise: for you shall not hold the Kingdom of France from God, King of Heaven, Saint Mary's son, but King Charles shall hold it, the true heir. For so God, King of Heaven, wills it; and so it has been revealed to him by the Maid, and he shall enter Paris with a fair company.

If you will not believe this news from God and the Maid, wherever we find you, there we shall strike; and we shall raise such a battle-cry as there has not been in France in a thousand years, if you will not do justice. And know surely that the King of Heaven will send more strength to the Maid than you can bring against her and her good soldiers in any assault. And when the blows begin, it shall be seen whose right is the better before the God of Heaven.

You, Duke of Bedford: The Maid prays and beseeches you not to bring on your own destruction. If you will do her justice, you may yet come in her company there where the French shall do the fairest deed that ever was done for Christendom. So answer if you will make peace in the city of Orléans. And if you do not so, consider your great danger speedily.

Written this Tuesday in Holy Week.

ORLÉANS: CAPTURE OF THE ENGLISH FORTRESS OF SAINT-LOUP, MAY 4

To her page
Ha! wretched boy! you did not tell me that French blood was flowing! Where are those who should arm me?
To horse! To horse!

ORLÉANS: CAPTURE OF THE BRIDGE, MAY 7

I was the first to set a ladder against the fortress on the bridge, and, as I raised it, I was wounded in the throat by a cross-bow bolt. But Saint Catherine comforted me greatly. And I did not cease to ride and do my work.

To her soldiers
Courage! Do not fall back: in a little the place will be yours. Watch!

when you see the wind blow my banner against your bulwark, you shall take it!

In, in, the place is yours!

To the English captain
Glasdale, Glasdale, yield, yield to the King of Heaven. You have called me "whore": I pity your soul and the souls of your men.

To those who offered to charm her wound
I would rather die than do what I know to be sin.

ORLÉANS: THE ENGLISH RAISE THE SIEGE, MAY 8

To her soldiers
In God's name! they go. Let them depart. And go we to give thanks to God. We shall not follow them farther, for it is Sunday. Seek not to harm them. It suffices me that they go.

MELUN, WEEK OF APRIL 16

Last Easter week, — I was standing near the moat at Melun, — my voices told me that I would be taken prisoner before Saint John's Day, and that it must be so, and that I must not be frightened but accept it willingly, and God would help me.

And I begged of my voices that, when I should be taken, I might die straightway, without long travail in prison.

NEAR CRÉPY-EN-VALOIS, AUGUST 10 OR 11

To the Archbishop of Reims
This is a good people. I have seen no other people so joyful at the coming of our most noble King. And would that I might be so happy, when I shall end my days, as to be buried in the earth of this place!

(He answers, "O Jehanne, where do you expect to die?" Then Jehanne:)

Wherever it may please God, for I am no more sure of the hour or the season or the place than you. And would that it were pleasing to God my maker that I might now turn back, laying off my arms, and go to serve my father and my mother, keeping their sheep with my sister and my brothers; they would be very glad to see me!

COMPIÈGNE, MAY 23

I came to Compiègne at a secret hour in the morning, and entered the town, I think, without our enemies knowing it. And the same day, towards evening, I made the sally in which I was taken.

I had a sword which had been taken from a Burgundian. I got it at Lagny, and I carried it from Lagny to Compiègne because it was a good war-sword, good to give good buffets and good thrusts. I was riding a half-courser.

I did not know that I would be taken that day.

I crossed the bridge and the bulwark, and went with a company of our soldiers against Monseigneur de Luxembourg's men. I drove them back twice, as far as the Burgundian camp, and a third time half-way. Then the English who were there cut us off, both me and my men, coming between me and the bulwark. And so my men fell back. And as I fell back flankwise into the fields towards Picardie, near the bulwark, I was taken.

HER FIRST APPEARANCE BEFORE HER JUDGES IN THE CHAPEL ROYAL, ROUEN CASTLE, WEDNESDAY, FEBRUARY 21

Concerning my father and mother and what I have done since I took the road to France I will willingly swear to tell the truth. But the revelations which have come to me from God I have never told or revealed to anyone, except to Charles, my King. Nor would I reveal them if I were to be beheaded. A week from today I shall have learned whether I may reveal them. . . .

I protest against being kept in chains and irons.

It is true that I have wished, and that I still wish, what is permissible for any captive: to escape!

TUESDAY, FEBRUARY 27

"How have you fared since Saturday?"[4]
You can see very well how I have fared. I have fared as well as I could.

---

[4] The italicized questions are those put to her at the trial.

"Have you heard the voice that comes to you, since Saturday?"
Yes indeed. I have heard it many times.

"Did you hear it in this room on Saturday?"
That has nothing to do with your trial! I did hear it here.

I did not understand it well. I did not understand anything that I could repeat to you until I had returned to my room.

It told me to answer you bravely.

I asked the voice for counsel on the things about which I was questioned. On some points I have had counsel. Concerning others that I may be asked to answer I will not answer without leave. If I were to answer without leave, perhaps I should not have the voices for protection. But when I shall have leave from our Lord I shall not be afraid to speak, for then I shall have good protection.

The voice is Saint Catherine's voice and Saint Margaret's. And their heads are crowned with a fair crown, most richly and most preciously. Concerning that, I have leave from our Lord. And if you doubt it, send to Poitiers where I was questioned before.
I know very well that it is they, and I can very well tell them apart!

"Which of them appeared to you first?"
I did not recognize them as soon as that. I knew once, but I have forgotten. If I can have leave, I will tell you willingly; it is set down in the register at Poitiers. And I had comfort from Saint Michael.

"Is it long since you first had the voice of Saint Michael?"
I am not saying "the voice of Saint Michael"; I am telling you of great comfort.

I have told you often enough that they are Saint Catherine and Saint Margaret. Believe me if you like!

"Are you forbidden to tell what sign you have that they are Saint Catherine and Saint Margaret?"
I have not yet clearly understood whether that is forbidden me or not.

"Did God command you to put on men's clothing?"[5]
My clothing is a small matter, one of the least. But I did not put on men's

[5] That Joan dressed like a soldier seems to have bothered her examiners greatly. Clearly, living and fighting with men, she had to.

clothing by the counsel of any man on earth. I did not put on this clothing, nor do anything else, except at the bidding of God and the angels.

All that I have done is by our Lord's bidding. And if he had bid me put on other clothing I should have put it on because it was at his bidding.

All that I have done at our Lord's bidding I believe that I have done rightly. And I expect good protection for it and good succour.

"When you saw the voice coming to you, was there any light?"
There was light all about, and so there should be! All light does not come to you.

"Was there an angel over your King's head when you saw him for the first time?"
By Blessed Mary! If there was, I know nothing about it. I did not see one.

"Was there any light?"
There were more than three hundred knights and fifty torches — without counting the spiritual light!

"How did it happen that your King had faith in what you said?"
He had good tokens; and because of his learned men.

"What revelations did your King have?"
You shall not get that from me yet, nor this year!

"Did you ever offer prayers to the end that your sword should be more fortunate?"
It is a good thing to know that I would want my arms to be fortunate.

THURSDAY, MARCH 1

About what I know which concerns this trial I will freely tell the truth, and I will tell you just as much as I should tell if I were before the Pope of Rome.

"What have you to say as to our lord the Pope, and as to whom you believe is the true Pope?"
Are there two?

"Have you talked with Saint Catherine and Saint Margaret since Tuesday?"
Yes, but I do not know the hour.

"What day was it?"
Yesterday and today. There is no day that I do not hear them.

"Do you always see them in the same dress?"
I always see them in the same form. I know nothing of their garments.

"What form do you see?"
I see the face.

"Have the saints who appear to you hair?"
It is a good thing to know!

"Was their hair long and hanging?"
I do not know. And I do not know if there was any semblance of arms
or of other members. They spoke well and fairly, and I understood them
well.

"How do they speak if they do not have members?"
I leave that to God. They speak the French tongue.

"Does not Saint Margaret speak English?"
Why should she speak English when she is not of the English party?

"In what form was Saint Michael when he appeared to you?"
I saw no crown upon him. I know nothing of his garments.

"Was he naked?"
Do you think that God has not wherewith to clothe him?

"Had he hair?"
Why should it have been cut off? I have not seen Blessed Michael since
I left the castle of Crotoy; I do not see him very often.

MONDAY, MARCH 12

*"Was the angel who brought the sign the angel who first appeared to
you, or was it another?"*
It is always one and the same. And he has never failed me.

*"Has not the angel failed you in worldly things in allowing you to be
taken prisoner?"*
I believe, since it pleases our Lord, that it is best that I am a prisoner.

"Has he not failed you in the things of grace?"[6]

---

[6] Divine favor and mercy, spiritual well-being.

How can he have failed me, when he comforts me every day? I mean by the comfort from Saint Catherine and Saint Margaret.

"Do you call them, or do they come without your calling?"
They often come without my calling. And sometimes, if they did not come quickly, I prayed our Lord to send them.

"Did you ever call them, and they did not come?"
I have never had need of them and not had them.

"When you promised our Lord to keep your virginity, was it to him that you spoke?"
It ought to be enough to promise it to those who were sent by him, that is, Saint Catherine and Saint Margaret.

"When you saw Saint Michael and the angels, did you show them reverence?"
Yes.

"Were they with you long?"
They often come among Christian people and are not seen. I have seen them many times among Christians.

SATURDAY, MARCH 17

"Will you submit yourself to the determination of our mother, holy Church, in respect to all your words and deeds, whether good or evil?"
As for the Church, I love it and I would wish to support it with all my might for the sake of our Christian faith: it is not I who should be prevented from going to church and hearing mass![7] As for the good work I have done and my first coming, I must needs leave that with the King of Heaven, who sent me to Charles, son of Charles King of France, who shall be King. And you shall see that the French will very soon achieve a great task which God will send to the French, and such that almost the whole Kingdom of France will tremble. And I say it, so that when it comes to pass it will be remembered that I said it.

"Answer whether you will refer yourself to the determination of the Church?"
I refer myself to our Lord who sent me, to Our Lady, and to all the

---

[7] In prison she was not allowed to hear mass or take the sacraments—one form of the pressure that was put upon her to confess witchcraft.

blessed saints in Paradise. It seems to me that our Lord and the Church are one and the same, and that no one should make difficulties about that. Why do you make difficulties about it not being one and the same?

In the Room Off the Hall of State, Tuesday, March 27

First, for your admonishing me for my good and in our faith, I thank you and all this company. As for the counsellor that you offer me, I thank you too: but I do not intend to forsake the counsel of our Lord.

I believe that our holy father the Pope of Rome and the bishops and other churchmen are there to guard the Christian faith and to punish those who are faulty. But as for me I will not submit myself in respect to my deeds, save to the church in Heaven alone — that is, to God, the Virgin Mary and the saints in Paradise. And I firmly believe that I have not been faulty in our Christian faith. Nor would I wish to be.

I do not do wrong to serve God!

If the judges refuse to let me hear mass, it certainly lies in our Lord to let me hear it, when he shall please to, without them.

At Arras and at Beaurevoir I was many times admonished to wear women's clothing: I refused, and I still refuse. As to other womanly duties, there are enough other women to perform them.

As to the Duke of Burgundy, I begged him, by letters and through his ambassadors, that there might be peace. As to the English, the peace that is needed with them is that they should go back to their homes in England.

There was neither sorcery nor any other evil art in anything that I have done.

If the English had believed my letter they would have done wisely. And before seven years are ended, they shall be well aware of the things that I wrote to them.

I did not send it out of pride or presumption, but at the bidding of our Lord.

First I asked them to make peace. And in case they would not make peace, I was all ready to fight.

Wednesday, March 28

. . . It lies with our Lord to make revelations to whom he pleases.

As for signs, if those who ask for one are not worthy of it, I am not accountable for that!

I believe, as firmly as I believe that our Lord Jesus Christ suffered death to redeem us from the pains of Hell, that they are Saint Michael and Saint Gabriel and Saint Catherine and Saint Margaret, whom our Lord sends to comfort and counsel me.

I shall call them to help me as long as I live.

I ask in this manner:
"Most sweet God, in honor of your holy passion I beg you, if you love me, to reveal to me what I am to answer to these churchmen. As to this clothing I well know by what commandment I began to wear it. But I do not know the manner in which I am to quit it. Therefore, may it please you to teach me."
And immediately they come.

That Jesus has failed me I deny.

As to the Church militant,[8] I wish to show it all the honor and reverence that I can. As for referring my deeds to the Church militant, I must needs refer them to our Lord, who caused me to do what I have done.

I am a good Christian.

The offenses that you bring against me I have not committed: as for the rest, I refer it to our Lord.

SHE IS THREATENED WITH TORTURE IN THE PRESENCE OF THE INSTRUMENTS[9]

Donjon of the Castle, Wednesday, May 9

Truly, if you were to have me torn limb from limb and send my soul out of my body, I would say nothing else. And if I did say anything, afterwards I should always say that you had made me say it by force.

I have asked my voices to counsel me whether I should submit to the

[8] The Church on earth, thought of as in warfare against evil — as distinguished from "the Church triumphant."

[9] The instruments of torture.

Church, because the churchmen were pressing me to submit to the Church. And my voices have told me that, if I want our Lord to help me, I must lay all my deeds before him.

LAST SESSION: SHE IS AGAIN ADMONISHED

Wednesday, May 23

If I were at the place of execution, and I saw the fire lighted, and the faggots catching and the executioner ready to build up the fire, and if I were in the fire, even so I would say nothing else, and I would maintain what I have said at this trial until death.

I have nothing more to say.

FOR DISCUSSION AND WRITING

1. We are inclined to shrug off phenomena like Joan's visions and voices as "purely psychological" (whatever that may mean). But even a mystical interpretation of those phenomena must, if it is intelligent, find for them a basis in Joan's character and the circumstances that formed her character; it must be just as "psychological" as any other interpretation, for mystical experiences occur only in human psyches. Joan was illiterate (she tells her examiners she does not know A from B); her childhood seems to have been serene; she learned simple household tasks; she helped her sister and brothers tend sheep; she was thirteen—just entering puberty—when she first heard the "voices." What probable grounds for her visionary experiences do these circumstances suggest? What if she had been taught to read and had been an avid reader of comic books at thirteen, had had television in the home and phonograph recordings of the Beatles, and had been going steady with a boy friend? These are ridiculous questions in the medieval context, but what do they suggest, by contrast, as to the way in which we must approach the "psychology" of Joan's visions?

2. She was in prison for many months and was examined and re-examined endlessly by her inquisitors. Remembering that she was only nineteen, what would you say about the consistency of her character as revealed by the way she handles the questions put to her? Would you call her a tough type (and in what sense of "tough")? "earthy"? shrewd? impertinent? intellectual? a person of strong common sense? intuitive? a "mystical" type? On what do you base your answers?

3. Examine some of her answers specifically. What does her frame of mind seem to be, or what effort does she seem to be making in specific instances? For example, when she is asked if she saw a light with her voices, and again, if there was a light when she first saw the king; when she is asked if she ever offered prayers that her sword should be more fortunate (evidently a trap to get her to admit some sort of superstitious belief); and when she is asked who she believes is the true Pope.

4. Examine similarly her answers to the questions about whether the saints who appear to her have hair, what language they speak, whether Saint Michael was naked and if he has hair. Does she seem merely vague about these things? Does she seem evasive? If evasive, is it the evasiveness of mental confusion, or of someone trying to wriggle out of a falsehood, or of an intelligence that sees behind the motives of her examiners and maintains its integrity by reserve? Is she contemptuous of her examiners? Are some of the questions such as might well arouse contempt?

5. If humor is a quality that can and does appear even in tragic circumstances, do you find in Joan a sense of humor? Explain.

6. You may wish to write on some aspect suggested by the questions here, but the subject is an excellent one for a short research paper—for Joan's case has held inexhaustible fascination for writers, and the research ought to afford a pleasant relief from ordinary assignments and an exciting reading-excursion. Below are a few references. For a short paper, you might follow up just one, and for a longer paper two or three.

    George Bernard Shaw: *Saint Joan.*
    Jean Anouilh: *The Lark.*
    Mark Twain: *Personal Recollections of Joan of Arc.*
    C. W. Lightbody: *The Judgments of Joan.*
    P. B. Barret: *The Retrial of Joan of Arc.*
And there are biographies by the following:
    Anatole France
    Jules Michelet
    Andrew Lang
    V. Sackville-West

Robert Falcon Scott ⁓§ The Last March

⁓§ English explorer of the Antarctic continent (1868-1912). Captain Scott commanded two expeditions into Antarctica. The first, begun in 1901, penetrated into the interior of the continent, accomplishing several scientific objectives, and was completed in 1904. The second expedition started in 1910, with the main objective of discovering the South Pole. Scott and his team made the great march to the pole, to find, with cruel disappointment, that the Norwegians had beaten them to it; the Norwegian flag was already planted there. The last stages of the return trip are recorded here from Scott's diary, found when the frozen bodies of Scott and two of his men were discovered eight months later. §⤳

WEDNESDAY, *February* 29. — Lunch. Cold night. Minimum Temp. −37.5°; −30° with north-west wind, force 4, when we got up. Frightfully cold starting; luckily Bowers and Oates in their last new finnesko;[1] keeping my old ones for present. Expected awful march and for first hour got it. Then things improved and we camped after 5½ hours marching close to lunch camp. Next camp is our depôt and it is exactly 13 miles. It ought not to take more than 1½ days; we pray for another fine one. The oil will just about spin out in that event, and we arrive 3 clear days' food in hand. The increase of ration has had an enormously beneficial result. Mountains now looking small. Wind still very light from west — cannot understand this wind.

Reprinted by permission of Dodd, Mead & Company from *Scott's Last Expedition.* Copyright 1913 by Dodd, Mead & Company.

[1] Boots made of tanned reindeer skin with the fur outside.

Thursday, March 1. — Lunch. Very cold last night — minimum −41.5°. Cold start to march, too, as usual now. Got away at 8 and have marched within sight of depôt; flag something under 3 miles away. We did 11½ yesterday and marched 6 this morning. Heavy dragging yesterday and *very* heavy this morning. Apart from sledging considerations the weather is wonderful. Cloudless days and nights and the wind trifling. Worse luck, the light airs come from the north and keep us horribly cold. For this lunch hour the exception has come. There is a bright and comparatively warm sun. All our gear is out drying.

Friday, March 2. — Lunch. Misfortunes rarely come singly. We marched to the (Middle Barrier) depôt fairly easily yesterday afternoon, and since that have suffered three distinct blows which have placed us in a bad position. First we found a shortage of oil; with most rigid economy it can scarce carry us to the next depôt on this surface (71 miles away). Second, Titus Oates disclosed his feet, the toes showing very bad indeed, evidently bitten by the late temperatures. The third blow came in the night, when the wind, which we had hailed with some joy, brought dark overcast weather. It fell below −40° in the night, and this morning it took 1½ hours to get our foot gear on, but we got away before eight. We lost cairn² and tracks together and made as steady as we could N. by W., but have seen nothing. Worse was to come — the surface is simply awful. In spite of strong wind and full sail³ we have only done 5½ miles. We are in a *very* queer street since there is no doubt we cannot do the extra marches and feel the cold horribly.

Saturday, March 3. — Lunch. We picked up the track again yesterday, finding ourselves to the eastward. Did close on 10 miles and things looked a trifle better; but this morning the outlook is blacker than ever. Started well and with good breeze; for an hour made good headway; then the surface grew awful beyond words. The wind drew forward; every circumstance was against us. After 4½ hours things so bad that we camped, having covered 4½ miles. One cannot consider this a fault of our own — certainly we were pulling hard this morning — it was more than three parts surface which held us back — the wind at strongest, powerless to move the sledge. When the light is good it is

² Mound left to mark trail.
³ On sledge, to help in dragging it.

easy to see the reason. The surface, lately a very good hard one, is coated with a thin layer of woolly crystals, formed by radiation no doubt. These are too firmly fixed to be removed by the wind and cause impossible friction on the runners. God help us, we can't keep up this pulling, that is certain. Amongst ourselves we are unendingly cheerful, but what each man feels in his heart I can only guess. Pulling on foot gear in the morning is getting slower and slower, therefore every day more dangerous.

Sunday, March 4. — Lunch. Things looking *very* black indeed. As usual we forgot our trouble last night, got into our bags, slept splendidly on good hoosh,[4] woke and had another, and started marching. Sun shining brightly, tracks clear, but surface covered with sandy frostrime. All the morning we had to pull with all our strength, and in 4½ hours we covered 3½ miles. Last night it was overcast and thick, surface bad; this morning sun shining and surface as bad as ever. One has little to hope for except perhaps strong dry wind — an unlikely contingency at this time of year. Under the immediate surface crystals is a hard sastrugi[5] surface, which must have been excellent for pulling a week or two ago. We are about 42 miles from the next depôt and have a week's food, but only about 3 to 4 days' fuel — we are as economical of the latter as one can possibly be, and we cannot afford to save food and pull as we are pulling. We are in a very tight place indeed, but none of us despondent *yet,* or at least we preserve every semblance of good cheer, but one's heart sinks as the sledge stops dead at some sastrugi behind which the surface sand lies thickly heaped. For the moment the temperature is on the $-20°$ — an improvement which makes us much more comfortable, but a colder snap is bound to come again soon. I fear Oates at least will weather such an event very poorly. Providence to our aid! We can expect little from man now except the possibility of extra food at the next depôt. It will be real bad if we get there and find the same shortage of oil. Shall we get there? Such a short distance it would have appeared to us on the summit! I don't know what I should do if Wilson and Bowers weren't so determinedly cheerful over things.

Monday, March 5. — Lunch. Regret to say going from bad to worse. We got a slant of wind yesterday afternoon, and going on 5 hours we

---

[4] Thick soup made of pemmican (dried beef, suet, raisins, and sugar) and biscuit.
[5] Hard ridges of snow formed by wind and shaped like waves.

converted our wretched morning run of 3½ miles into something over
9. We went to bed on a cup of cocoa and pemmican solid with the chill
off. The result is telling on all, but mainly on Oates, whose feet are in a
wretched condition. One swelled up tremendously last night and he is
very lame this morning. We started march on tea and pemmican as
last night — we pretend to prefer the pemmican this way. Marched for
5 hours this morning over a slightly better surface covered with high
moundy sastrugi. Sledge capsized twice; we pulled on foot, covering
about 5½ miles. We are two pony marches and 4 miles about from our
depôt. Our fuel dreadfully low and the poor Soldier[6] nearly done. It
is pathetic enough because we can do nothing for him; more hot food
might do a little, but only a little, I fear. We none of us expected these
terribly low temperatures, and of the rest of us Wilson is feeling them
most; mainly, I fear, from his self-sacrificing devotion in doctoring
Oates' feet. We cannot help each other, each has enough to do to take
care of himself. We get cold on the march when the trudging is heavy,
and the wind pierces our warm garments. The others, all of them, are
unendingly cheerful when in the tent. We mean to see the game through
with a proper spirit, but it's tough work to be pulling harder than we
ever pulled in our lives for long hours, and to feel that the progress is
so slow. One can only say 'God help us!' and plod on our weary way,
cold and very miserable, though outwardly cheerful. We talk of all sorts
of subjects in the tent, not much of food now, since we decided to take
the risk of running a full ration. We simply couldn't go hungry at this
time.

Tuesday, March 6. — Lunch. We did a little better with help of wind
yesterday afternoon, finishing 9½ miles for the day, and 27 miles from
depôt. But this morning things have been awful. It was warm in the
night and for the first time during the journey I overslept myself by more
than an hour; then we were slow with foot gear; then, pulling with all
our might (for our lives) we could scarcely advance at rate of a mile
an hour; then it grew thick and three times we had to get out of harness
to search for tracks. The result is something less than 3½ miles for the
forenoon. The sun is shining now and the wind gone. Poor Oates is
unable to pull, sits on the sledge when we are track-searching — he is

[6] Oates.

wonderfully plucky, as his feet must be giving him great pain. He makes no complaint, but his spirits only come up in spurts now, and he grows more silent in the tent. We are making a spirit lamp to try and replace the primus[7] when our oil is exhausted. It will be a very poor substitute and we've not got much spirit. If we could have kept up our 9-mile days we might have got within reasonable distance of the depôt before running out, but nothing but a strong wind and good surface can help us now, and though we had quite a good breeze this morning, the sledge came as heavy as lead. If we were all fit I should have hopes of getting through, but the poor Soldier has become a terrible hindrance, though he does his utmost and suffers much I fear.

Wednesday, March 7. — A little worse I fear. One of Oates' feet *very* bad this morning; he is wonderfully brave. We still talk of what we will do together at home.

We only made 6½ miles yesterday. This morning in 4½ hours we did just over 4 miles. We are 16 from our depôt. If we only find the correct proportion of food there and this surface continues, we may get to the next depôt [Mt. Hooper, 72 miles farther] but not to One Ton Camp. We hope against hope that the dogs[8] have been to Mt. Hooper; then we might pull through. If there is a shortage of oil again we can have little hope. One feels that for poor Oates the crisis is near, but none of us are improving, though we are wonderfully fit considering the really excessive work we are doing. We are only kept going by good food. No wind this morning till a chill northerly air came ahead. Sun bright and cairns showing up well. I should like to keep the track to the end.

Thursday, March 8. — Lunch. Worse and worse in morning; poor Oates' left foot can never last out, and time over foot gear something awful. Have to wait in night foot gear for nearly an hour before I start changing, and then am generally first to be ready. Wilson's feet giving trouble now, but this mainly because he gives so much help to others. We did 4½ miles this morning and are now 8½ miles from the depôt — a ridiculously small distance to feel in difficulties, yet on this surface we know we cannot equal half our old marches, and that for that effort

---

[7] Oil-burning cooking stove. "Spirit" is alcohol.

[8] Scott hoped that a supporting party, drawn by dogs, had delivered supplies. The party had been turned back by a blizzard.

we expend nearly double the energy. The great question is, What shall
we find at the depôt? If the dogs have visited it we may get along a good
distance, but if there is another short allowance of fuel, God help us
indeed. We are in a very bad way, I fear, in any case.

Saturday, March 10. — Things steadily downhill. Oates' foot worse. He
has rare pluck and must know that he can never get through. He asked
Wilson if he had a chance this morning, and of course Bill had to say
he didn't know. In point of fact he has none. Apart from him, if he went
under now, I doubt whether we could get through. With great care we
might have a dog's chance, but no more. The weather conditions are
awful, and our gear gets steadily more icy and difficult to manage. At
the same time of course poor Titus is the greatest handicap. He keeps
us waiting in the morning until we have partly lost the warming effect
of our good breakfast, when the only wise policy is to be up and away
at once; again at lunch. Poor chap! it is too pathetic to watch him; one
cannot but try to cheer him up.

Yesterday we marched up the depôt, Mt. Hooper. Cold comfort.
Shortage on our allowance all round. I don't know that anyone is to
blame. The dogs which would have been our salvation have evidently
failed. . . .

This morning it was calm when we breakfasted, but the wind came
from W.N.W. as we broke camp. It rapidly grew in strength. After
travelling for half an hour I saw that none of us could go on facing such
conditions. We were forced to camp and are spending the rest of the
day in a comfortless blizzard camp, wind quite foul.

Sunday, March 11. — Titus Oates is very near the end, one feels. What
we or he will do, God only knows. We discussed the matter after breakfast; he is a brave fine fellow and understands the situation, but he
practically asked for advice. Nothing could be said but to urge him to
march as long as he could. One satisfactory result to the discussion; I
practically ordered Wilson to hand over the means of ending our
troubles to us, so that anyone of us may know how to do so. Wilson had
no choice between doing so and our ransacking the medicine case. We
have 30 opium tabloids apiece and he is left with a tube of morphine.
So far the tragical side of our story.

The sky completely overcast when we started this morning. We
could see nothing, lost the tracks, and doubtless have been swaying a

good deal since — 3.1 miles for the forenoon — terribly heavy dragging
— expected it. Know that 6 miles is about the limit of our endurance
now, if we get no help from wind or surfaces. We have 7 days' food and
should be about 55 miles from One Ton Camp to-night, $6 \times 7 = 42$,
leaving us 13 miles short of our distance, even if things get no worse.
Meanwhile the season rapidly advances.

Monday, March 12. — We did 6.9 miles yesterday, under our necessary
average. Things are left much the same, Oates not pulling much, and
now with hands as well as feet pretty well useless. We did 4 miles this
morning in 4 hours 20 min. — we may hope for 3 this afternoon,
$7 \times 6 = 42$. We shall be 47 miles from the depôt. I doubt if we can
possibly do it. The surface remains awful, the cold intense, and our
physical condition running down. God help us! Not a breath of favourable wind for more than a week, and apparently liable to head winds at
any moment.

Wednesday, March 14. — No doubt about the going downhill, but
everything going wrong for us. Yesterday we woke to a strong northerly
wind with temp. $-37°$. Could n't face it, so remained up camp till 2,
then did 5¼ miles. Wanted to march later, but party feeling the cold
badly as the breeze (N.) never took off entirely, and as the sun sank
the temp. fell. Long time getting supper in dark.

This morning started with southerly breeze, set sail and passed
another cairn at good speed; half-way, however, the wind shifted to
W. by S. or W.S.W., blew through our wind clothes and into our mits.
Poor Wilson horribly cold, could not get off ski for some time. Bowers
and I practically made camp, and when we got into the tent at last we
were all deadly cold. Then temp. now midday down $-43°$ and the
wind strong. We *must* go on, but now the making of every camp must
be more difficult and dangerous. It must be near the end, but a pretty
merciful end. Poor Oates got it again in the foot. I shudder to think
what it will be like to-morrow. It is only with greatest pains rest of us
keep off frostbites. No idea there could be temperatures like this at
this time of year with such winds. Truly awful outside the tent. Must
fight it out to the last biscuit, but can't reduce rations.

Friday, March 16 or Saturday 17. — Lost track of dates, but think the
last correct. Tragedy all along the line. At lunch, the day before yes-

terday, poor Titus Oates said he could n't go on; he proposed we should leave him in his sleeping-bag. That we could not do, and induced him to come on, on the afternoon march. In spite of its awful nature for him he struggled on and we made a few miles. At night he was worse and we knew the end had come.

Should this be found I want these facts recorded. Oates' last thoughts were of his Mother, but immediately before he took pride in thinking that his regiment would be pleased with the bold way in which he met his death. We can testify to his bravery. He has borne intense suffering for weeks without complaint, and to the very last was able and willing to discuss outside subjects. He did not — would not — give up hope to the very end. He was a brave soul. This was the end. He slept through the night before last, hoping not to wake; but he woke in the morning — yesterday. It was blowing a blizzard. He said, 'I am just going outside and may be some time.' He went out into the blizzard and we have not seen him since.

I take this opportunity of saying that we have stuck to our sick companions to the last. In case of Edgar Evans,[9] when absolutely out of food and he lay insensible, the safety of the remainder seemed to demand his abandonment, but Providence mercifully removed him at this critical moment. He died a natural death, and we did not leave him till two hours after his death. We knew that poor Oates was walking to his death, but though we tried to dissuade him, we knew it was the act of a brave man and an English gentleman. We all hope to meet the end with a similar spirit, and assuredly the end is not far.

I can only write at lunch and then only occasionally. The cold is intense, —40° at midday. My companions are unendingly cheerful, but we are all on the verge of serious frostbites, and though we constantly talk of fetching through I don't think anyone of us believes it in his heart.

We are cold on the march now, and at all times except meals. Yesterday we had to lay up for a blizzard and to-day we move dreadfully slowly. We are at No. 14 pony camp, only two pony marches from One Ton Depôt. We leave here our theodolite,[10] a camera, and Oates' sleeping-bags. Diaries, &c., and geological specimens carried at Wilson's special request, will be found with us or on our sledge.

[9] Evans had died of concussion of the brain from an accident.
[10] Surveying instrument.

Sunday, March 18. — To-day, lunch, we are 21 miles from the depôt. Ill fortune presses, but better may come. We have had more wind and drift from ahead yesterday; had to stop marching; wind N.W., force 4, temp. —35°. No human being could face it, and we are worn out *nearly*.

My right foot has gone, nearly all the toes — two days ago I was proud possessor of best feet. These are the steps of my downfall. Like an ass I mixed a small spoonful of curry powder with my melted pemmican — it gave me violent indigestion. I lay awake and in pain all night; woke and felt done on the march; foot went and I didn't know it. A very small measure of neglect and have a foot which is not pleasant to contemplate. Bowers takes first place in condition, but there is not much to choose after all. The others are still confident of getting through — or pretend to be — I don't know! We have the last *half* fill of oil in our primus and a very small quantity of spirit — this alone between us and thirst. The wind is fair for the moment, and that is perhaps a fact to help. The mileage would have seemed ridiculously small on our outward journey.

Monday, March 19. — Lunch. We camped with difficulty last night, and were dreadfully cold till after our supper of cold pemmican and biscuit and a half a pannikin of cocoa cooked over the spirit. Then, contrary to expectation, we got warm and all slept well. To-day we started in the usual dragging manner. Sledge dreadfully heavy. We are 15½ miles from the depôt and ought to get there in three days. What progress! We have two days' food but barely a day's fuel. All our feet are getting bad — Wilson's best, my right foot worst, left all right. There is no chance to nurse one's feet till we can get hot food into us. Amputation is the least I can hope for now, but will the trouble spread? That is the serious question. The weather doesn't give us a chance — the wind from N. to N.W. and —40° temp. to-day.

Wednesday, March 21. — Got within 11 miles of depôt Monday night; had to lay up all yesterday in severe blizzard. To-day forlorn hope, Wilson and Bowers going to depôt for fuel.

Thursday, March 22 and 23. — Blizzard bad as ever — Wilson and Bowers unable to start — to-morrow last chance — no fuel and only one or two of food left — must be near the end. Have decided it shall be natural — we shall march for the depôt with or without our effects and die in our tracks.

Thursday, March 29. — Since the 21st we have had a continuous gale from W.S.W. and S.W. We had fuel to make two cups of tea apiece and bare food for two days on the 20th. Every day we have been ready to start for our depôt 11 *miles* away, but outside the door of the tent it remains a scene of whirling drift. I do not think we can hope for any better things now. We shall stick it out to the end, but we are getting weaker, of course, and the end cannot be far.

It seems a pity, but I do not think I can write more.

R. Scott.

For God's sake look after our people.

Wilson and Bowers were found in the attitude of sleep, their sleeping-bags closed over their heads as they would naturally close them.

Scott died later. He had thrown back the flaps of his sleeping-bag and opened his coat. The little wallet containing the three notebooks was under his shoulders and his arm flung across Wilson. So they were found eight months later.

With the diaries in the tent were found the following letters:

TO MRS. E. A. WILSON

My Dear Mrs. Wilson,

If this letter reaches you Bill and I will have gone out together. We are very near it now and I should like you to know how splendid he was at the end — everlastingly cheerful and ready to sacrifice himself for others, never a word of blame to me for leading him into this mess. He is not suffering, luckily, at least only minor discomforts.

His eyes have a comfortable blue look of hope and his mind is peaceful with the satisfaction of his faith in regarding himself as part of the great scheme of the Almighty. I can do no more to comfort you than to tell you that he died as he lived, a brave, true man — the best of comrades and staunchest of friends.

My whole heart goes out to you in pity,

Yours,

R. Scott

TO MRS. BOWERS

My Dear Mrs. Bowers,

I am afraid this will reach you after one of the heaviest blows of your life.

I write when we are very near the end of our journey, and I am finishing it in company with two gallant, noble gentlemen. One of these is your son. He had come to be one of my closest and soundest friends, and I appreciate his wonderful upright nature, his ability and energy. As the troubles have thickened his dauntless spirit ever shone brighter and he has remained cheerful, hopeful, and indomitable to the end.

The ways of Providence are inscrutable, but there must be some reason why such a young, vigorous and promising life is taken.

My whole heart goes out in pity for you,

Yours,

R. Scott

To the end he has talked of you and his sisters. One sees what a happy home he must have had and perhaps it is well to look back on nothing but happiness.

He remains unselfish, self-reliant and splendidly hopeful to the end, believing in God's mercy to you.

TO SIR J. M. BARRIE

My Dear Barrie,

We are pegging out in a very comfortless spot. Hoping this letter may be found and sent to you, I write a word of farewell. . . . More practically I want you to help my widow and my boy — your godson. We are showing that Englishmen can still die with a bold spirit, fighting it out to the end. It will be known that we have accomplished our object in reaching the Pole, and that we have done everything possible, even to sacrificing ourselves in order to save sick companions. I think this makes an example for Englishmen of the future, and that the country ought to help those who are left behind to mourn us. I leave my poor girl and your godson, Wilson leaves a widow, and Edgar Evans also a widow in humble circumstances. Do what you can to get their claims recognised. Goodbye. I am not at all afraid of the end, but sad to miss many a humble pleasure which I had planned for the future on our long marches. I may not have proved a great explorer, but we have done the greatest march ever made and come very near to great success. Goodbye, my dear friend,

Yours ever,

R. Scott

We are in a desperate state, feet frozen, &c. No fuel and a long way from food, but it would do your heart good to be in our tent, to hear our songs and the cheery conversation as to what we will do when we get to Hut Point.

Later. — We are very near the end, but have not and will not lose our good cheer. We have four days of storm in our tent and nowhere's food or fuel. We did intend to finish ourselves when things proved like this, but we have decided to die naturally in the track.

As a dying man, my dear friend, be good to my wife and child. Give the boy a chance in life if the State won't do it. He ought to have good stuff in him. . . . I never met a man in my life whom I admired and loved more than you, but I never could show you how much your friendship meant to me, for you had much to give and I nothing.

MESSAGE TO THE PUBLIC

The causes of the disaster are not due to faulty organisation, but to misfortune in all risks which had to be undertaken.

1. The loss of pony transport in March 1911 obliged me to start later than I had intended, and obliged the limits of stuff transported to be narrowed.

2. The weather throughout the outward journey, and especially the long gale in 83° S., stopped us.

3. The soft snow in lower reaches of glacier again reduced pace.

We fought these untoward events with a will and conquered, but it cut into our provision reserve.

Every detail of our food supplies, clothing and depôts made on the interior ice-sheet and over that long stretch of 700 miles to the Pole and back, worked out to perfection. The advance party would have returned to the glacier in fine form and with surplus of food, but for the astonishing failure of the man whom we had least expected to fail. Edgar Evans was thought the strongest man of the party.

The Beardmore Glacier is not difficult in fine weather, but on our return we did not get a single completely fine day; this with a sick companion enormously increased our anxieties.

As I have said elsewhere we got into frightfully rough ice and Edgar Evans received a concussion of the brain — he died a natural death, but left us a shaken party with the season unduly advanced.

But all the facts above enumerated were as nothing to the surprise which awaited us on the Barrier. I maintain that our arrangements for returning were quite adequate, and that no one in the world would have expected the temperatures and surfaces which we encountered at this time of the year. On the summit in lat. 85° 86° we had —20°, —30°. On the Barrier in lat. 82°, 10,000 feet lower, we had —30° in the day, —47° at night pretty regularly, with continuous head wind during our day marches. It is clear that these circumstances come on very suddenly, and our wreck is certainly due to this sudden advent of severe weather, which does not seem to have any satisfactory cause. I do not think human beings ever came through such a month as we have come through, and we should have got through in spite of the weather but for the sickening of a second companion, Captain Oates, and a shortage of fuel in our depôts for which I cannot account, and finally, but for the storm which has fallen on us within 11 miles of the depôt at which we hoped to secure our final supplies. Surely misfortune could scarcely have exceeded this last blow. We arrived within 11 miles of our old One Ton Camp with fuel for one last meal and food for two days. For four days we have been unable to leave the tent — the gale howling about us. We are weak, writing is difficult, but for my own sake I do not regret this journey, which has shown that Englishmen can endure hardships, help one another, and meet death with as great a fortitude as ever in the past. We took risks, we knew we took them; things have come out against us, and therefore we have no cause for complaint, but bow to the will of Providence, determined still to do our best to the last. But if we have been willing to give our lives to this enterprise, which is for the honour of our country, I appeal to our countrymen to see that those who depend on us are properly cared for.

Had we lived, I should have had a tale to tell of the hardihood, endurance, and courage of my companions which would have stirred the heart of every Englishman. These rough notes and our dead bodies must tell the tale, but surely, surely, a great rich country like ours will see that those who are dependent on us are properly provided for.

R. Scott

⌐§ FOR DISCUSSION AND WRITING

1. We hear a great deal about "leadership" and the qualities that go to make it up—whether the qualities that a President of the United States has, should have, or does not have, or the nefarious qualities of a malignant magnetism and "power complex" that make a Hitler, a Mussolini, or a Stalin, or what we have heard in commencement addresses and had dinned into us from kindergarten by educators relentlessly bent on making "leaders." In these pages of Scott's diary, you find reflected certain specific qualities of "leadership." Point out the places in the diary where these appear. The entries are extremely simple and factual, the tone even and unexclamatory; is there anything in the *way* he speaks that reflects an aspect of "leadership"?

2. Would you say that Scott was an imaginative man? a sensitive man? Are there certain kinds of sensitivity and imagination which a man with his responsibility, in these circumstances, would be better off without? Is he insensitive? callous or ruthless (for instance toward Oates)? Is he a man of sympathy? Is sympathy a form of imagination?

3. Do you find any signs of defeatism? For instance, is this one?—"I don't know what I should do if Wilson and Bowers weren't so determinedly cheerful over things." Where are the first signs of losing hope? What would you say keeps such a person going when the situation has become patently hopeless?

4. What gives to Oates's "I am just going outside and may be some time" its tragic poignancy?

5. The keeping of the diary itself became toward the end terribly difficult, not only because of freezing hands, but also, one imagines, because of the immense moral effort it required under the certainty of death in that glacial wasteland. Can you define whatever attitude or quality it is that would make Scott keep up the diary entries to the last moment? Is it a matter of "pride"? what kind of pride? a sense of responsibility? to whom, himself or others? or to some ideal? What is there in the fact of the diary itself that answers some of these questions, since the diary was meant as communication, and communication implies a relationship with others even though one may be freezing to death in the Antarctic with no certainty that the diary will ever be found?

6. How would you define "courage"? "heroism"? a "hero"? Was Titus Oates a "hero"?

7. You may have found possible theme subjects in the questions, but again a small exercise in research is suggested for those who like to read about the adventures of explorers and the records of the great explorations. Below are a few suggestions for this kind of research-reading. A short paper might be based on one of these or a longer paper on two or more.

On the Antarctic:

R. F. Scott: *The Voyage of the "Discovery."* (The *Discovery* was the ship with which he set out on his first expedition.)

Roald Amundsen: *The South Pole.*

E. H. Shackleton: *The Heart of Antarctica.*

Richard E. Byrd: *Little America.*

On the Arctic:

Roald Amundsen: *Amundsen's Northwest Passage.*

Vilhjalmar Stefansson: *My Life with the Eskimo* and *The Friendly Arctic.*

And there is a recent book by Lawrence Kirwan called *A History of Polar Exploration.*

T. E. Lawrence ❧ Desert Spring

❧ English archaeologist and leader of the Arab revolt in the first World War (1888-1935). As an officer under Allenby in the Middle Eastern campaign, but acting largely on independent initiative, he organized Arabian guerrilla activity against the Turks, by insistent raids eventually cutting off their northward retreat, and finally, in 1918, leading the Arab forces into Damascus. The fabulous narrative of these experiences is told in *Seven Pillars of Wisdom*, a book of extraordinary beauty. The film "Lawrence of Arabia" that was made from the book distorts it egregiously, both by sheer clumsiness and by following a version of Lawrence's character set forth by Richard Aldington in a biography—a version that has the merit only of sensationalism and for which there is not a shred of evidence. ❧

The names of the Arab tribesmen, the place names, and the references to British tactics and military movements can be stumbling-blocks in the reading of this piece, but one is advised to take them nonchalantly, as one learns to take the multiple and unidentifiable names of characters in Russian novels. If one keeps one's head, they work by osmosis.

AFTER Joyce and Dawnay had gone, I rode off from Aba el Lissan, with Mirzuk.[1] Our starting day promised to crown the spring-freshness of this lofty tableland. A week before there had been a furious blizzard, and some of the whiteness of the snow seemed to have passed into the light. The ground was vivid with new grass; and the sunlight, which slanted across us, pale like straw, mellowed the fluttering wind.

With us journeyed two thousand Sirhan camels, carrying our ammunition and food. For the convoy's sake we marched easily, to reach the railway after dark. A few of us rode forward, to search the line by

From *Seven Pillars of Wisdom* by T. E. Lawrence (New York: Doubleday & Company, Inc.) Reprinted with the permission of the publisher.

[1] Joyce and Dawnay were British officers on the staff of General Allenby, commander-in-chief in the Middle Eastern campaign. Aba el Lissan was an Arab camp. Mirzuk was one of the Arab tribal leaders.

daylight, and be sure of peace during the hours these scattered numbers would consume in crossing.

My bodyguard was with me, and Mirzuk had his Ageyl,[2] with two famous racing camels. The gaiety of the air and season caught them. Soon they were challenging to races, threatening one another, or skirmishing. My imperfect camel-riding (and my mood) forbade me to thrust among the lads, who swung more to the north, while I worked on, ridding my mind of the lees of camp-clamour and intrigue. The abstraction of the desert landscape cleansed me, and rendered my mind vacant with its superfluous greatness: a greatness achieved not by the addition of thought to its emptiness, but by its subtraction. In the weakness of earth's life was mirrored the strength of heaven, so vast, so beautiful, so strong.

Near sunset the line became visible, curving spaciously across the disclosed land, among low tufts of grass and bushes. Seeing everything was peaceful I pushed on, meaning to halt beyond and watch the others over. There was always a little thrill in touching the rails which were the target of so many of our efforts.[3]

As I rode up the bank my camel's feet scrambled in the loose ballast, and out of the long shadow of a culvert to my left, where, no doubt, he had slept all day, rose a Turkish soldier. He glanced wildly at me and at the pistol in my hand, and then with sadness at his rifle against the abutment, yards beyond. He was a young man; stout, but sulky-looking. I stared at him, and said, softly, 'God is merciful'. He knew the sound and sense of the Arabic phrase, and raised his eyes like a flash to mine, while his heavy sleep-ridden face began slowly to change into incredulous joy.

However, he said not a word. I pressed my camel's hairy shoulder with my foot, she picked her delicate stride across the metals and down the further slope, and the little Turk was man enough not to shoot me in the back, as I rode away, feeling warm towards him, as ever towards a life one has saved. At a safe distance I glanced back. He put thumb to nose, and twinkled his fingers at me.

We lit a coffee-fire as beacon for the rest, and waited till their dark lines passed by. Next day we marched to Wadi el Jinz; to flood-

[2] Name of Arab tribe.

[3] A good deal of Lawrence's guerrilla work at this time was in demolition of the Turkish-held railway.

pools, shallow eyes of water set in wrinkles of the clay, their rims lashed about with scrubby stems of brushwood. The water was grey, like the marly valley bed, but sweet. There we rested for the night, since the Zaagi[4] had shot a bustard, and Xenophon[5] did rightly call its white meat good. While we feasted the camels feasted. By the bounty of spring they were knee-deep in succulent greenstuff.

A fourth easy march took us to the Atara, our goal, where our allies, Mifleh, Fahad and Adhub,[6] were camped. Fahad was still stricken, but Mifleh, with honeyed words, came out to welcome us, his face eaten up by greed, and his voice wheezy with it.

Our plan, thanks to Allenby's lion-share,[7] promised simply. We would, when ready, cross the line to Themed, the main Beni Sakhr watering. Thence under cover of a screen of their cavalry we would move to Madeba, and fit it as our headquarters, while Allenby put the Jericho-Salt road in condition. We ought to link up with the British comfortably without firing a shot.

Meanwhile we had only to wait in the Atatir, which to our joy were really green, with every hollow a standing pool, and the valley beds of tall grass prinked with flowers. The chalky ridges, sterile with salt, framed the water-channels delightfully. From their tallest point we could look north and south, and see how the rain, running down, had painted the valleys across the white in broad stripes of green, sharp and firm like brush-strokes. Everything was growing, and daily the picture was fuller and brighter till the desert became like a rank water-meadow. Playful packs of winds came crossing and tumbling over one another, their wide, brief gusts surging through the grass, to lay it momentarily in swathes of dark and light satin, like young corn after the roller. On the hill we sat and shivered before these sweeping shadows, expecting a heavy blast — and there would come into our faces a warm and perfumed breath, very gentle, which passed away behind us as a silver-grey light down the plain of green. Our fastidious camels grazed an hour or so, and then lay down to digest, bringing up stomach-load after stomach-load of butter-smelling green cud, and chewing weightily.

---

[4] An Arab tribesman.

[5] Athenian historian and general, contemporary of Plato.

[6] Tribal leaders.

[7] Allenby's forces were to move on Damascus from Jerusalem while the Arabs cut off the Turkish retreat northward.

At last news came that the English had taken Amman. In half an hour we were making for Themed, across the deserted line. Later messages told us that the English were falling back, and though we had forewarned the Arabs of it, yet they were troubled. A further messenger reported how the English had just fled from Salt. This was plainly contrary to Allenby's intention, and I swore straight out that it was not true. A man galloped in to say that the English had broken only a few rails south of Amman, after two days of vain assaults against the town. I grew seriously disturbed in the conflict of rumour, and sent Adhub, who might be trusted not to lose his head, to Salt with a letter for Chetwode or Shea, asking for a note on the real situation. For the intervening hours we tramped restlessly over the fields of young barley, our minds working out plan after plan with feverish activity.

Very late at night Adhub's racing horse-hooves echoed across the valley and he came in to tell us that Jemal Pasha[8] was now in Salt, victorious, hanging those local Arabs who had welcomed the English. The Turks were still chasing Allenby far down the Jordan Valley. It was thought that Jerusalem would be recovered. I knew enough of my countrymen to reject that possibility; but clearly things were very wrong. We slipped off, bemused, to the Atatir again.

This reverse, being unawares, hurt me the more. Allenby's plan had seemed modest, and that we should so fall down before the Arabs was deplorable. They had never trusted us to do the great things which I foretold; and now their independent thoughts set out to enjoy the springtide here. They were abetted by some gipsy families from the north with the materials of their tinkering trade on donkeys. The Zebn tribesmen greeted them with a humour I little understood — till I saw that, beside their legitimate profits of handicraft, the women were open to other advances.

Particularly they were easy to the Ageyl; and for a while they prospered exceedingly, since our men were eager and very generous. I also made use of them. It seemed a pity to be at a loose end so near to Amman, and not bother to look at it. So Farraj[9] and I hired three of the merry little women, wrapped ourselves up like them, and strolled through the village. The visit was successful, though my final determination was that the place should be left alone. We had one evil moment,

[8] Turkish commander.

[9] Young Arab boy on Lawrence's bodyguard who is killed in this expedition.

by the bridge, when we were returning. Some Turkish soldiers crossed our party, and taking us all five for what we looked, grew much too friendly. We showed a coyness, and good turn of speed for gipsy women, and escaped intact. For the future I decided to resume my habit of wearing ordinary British soldiers' rig in enemy camps. It was too brazen to be suspect.

After this I determined to order the Indians from Azrak back to Feisal,[10] and to return myself. We started on one of those clean dawns which woke up the senses with the sun, while the intellect, tired after the thinking of the night, was yet abed. For an hour or two on such a morning the sounds, scents and colours of the world struck man individually and directly, not filtered through or made typical by thought; they seemed to exist sufficiently by themselves, and the lack of design and of carefulness in creation no longer irritated.

We marched southward along the railway, expecting to cross the slower-moving Indians from Azrak; our little party on prize camels swooping from one point of vantage to another, on the look-out. The still day encouraged us to speed over all the flint-strewn ridges, ignoring the multitude of desert paths which led only to the abandoned camps of last year, or of the last thousand or ten thousand years: for a road, once trodden into such flint and limestone, marked the face of the desert for so long as the desert lasted.

By Faraifra we saw a little patrol of eight Turks marching up the line. My men, fresh after the holiday in the Atatir, begged me to ride on them. I thought it too trifling, but when they chafed, agreed. The younger ones instantly rushed forward at a gallop. I ordered the rest across the line, to drive the enemy away from their shelter behind a culvert. The Zaagi, a hundred yards to my right, seeing what was wanted, swerved aside at once. Mohsin[11] followed him a moment later, with his section; whilst Abdulla and I pushed forward steadily on our side, to take the enemy on both flanks together.

Farraj, riding in front of everyone, would not listen to our cries nor notice the warning shots fired past his head. He looked round at our manoeuvre, but himself continued to canter madly towards the bridge, which he reached before the Zaagi and his party had crossed the line.

[10] Indian troops had been sent by Allenby to work with Lawrence's Arabs. Feisal was prince of the reigning family in Mecca and commander of the Arab forces.

[11] An Arab tribesman.

The Turks held their fire, and we supposed them gone down the further side of the embankment into safety; but as Farraj drew rein beneath the archway, there was a shot, and he seemed to fall or leap out of the saddle, and disappeared. A while after, the Zaagi got into position on the bank and his party fired twenty or thirty ragged shots, as though the enemy was still there.

I was very anxious about Farraj. His camel stood unharmed by the bridge, alone. He might be hit, or might be following the enemy. I could not believe that he had deliberately ridden up to them in the open and halted; yet it looked like it. I sent Feheyd to the Zaagi and told him to rush along the far side as soon as possible, whilst we went at a fast trot straight in to the bridge.

We reached it together, and found there one dead Turk, and Farraj terribly wounded through the body, lying by the arch just as he had fallen from his camel. He looked unconscious; but, when we dismounted, greeted us, and then fell silent, sunken in that loneliness which came to hurt men who believed death near. We tore his clothes away and looked uselessly at the wound. The bullet had smashed right through him, and his spine seemed injured. The Arabs said at once that he had only a few hours to live.

We tried to move him, for he was helpless, though he showed no pain. We tried to stop the wide, slow bleeding, which made poppy-splashes in the grass; but it seemed impossible, and after a while he told us to let him alone, as he was dying, and happy to die, since he had no care of life. Indeed, for long he had been so,[12] and men very tired and sorry often fell in love with death, with that triumphal weakness coming home after strength has been vanquished in a last battle.

While we fussed about him Abd el Latif shouted an alarm. He could see about fifty Turks working up the line towards us, and soon after a motor trolley was heard coming from the north. We were only sixteen men, and had an impossible position. I said we must retire at once, carrying Farraj with us. They tried to lift him, first in his cloak, afterwards in a blanket; but consciousness was coming back, and he screamed so pitifully that we had not the heart to hurt him more.

We could not leave him where he was, to the Turks, because we had

---

[12] Farraj had lost his taste for life since the death of his friend Daud. These two lively youngsters had been the first to attach themselves to Lawrence as a personal body-guard.

seen them burn alive our hapless wounded. For this reason we were all agreed, before action, to finish off one another, if badly hurt: but I had never realized that it might fall to me to kill Farraj.

I knelt down beside him, holding my pistol near the ground by his head, so that he should not see my purpose; but he must have guessed it, for he opened his eyes, and clutched me with his harsh, scaly hand, the tiny hand of these unripe Nejd[13] fellows. I waited a moment, and he said, 'Daud[14] will be angry with you', the old smile coming back so strangely to this grey shrinking face. I replied, 'salute him from me'. He returned the formal answer, 'God will give you peace', and at last wearily closed his eyes.

The Turkish trolley was now very close, swaying down the line towards us like a dung-beetle: and its machine-gun bullets stung the air about our heads as we fled back into the ridges. Mohsin led Farraj's camel, on which were his sheepskin and trappings, still with the shape of his body in them, just as he had fallen by the ridge. Near dark we halted; and the Zaagi came whispering to me that all were wrangling as to who should ride the splendid animal next day. He wanted her for himself; but I was bitter that these perfected dead had again robbed my poverty: and to cheapen the great loss with a little one I shot the poor beast with my second bullet.

Then the sun set on us. Through the breathless noon in the valleys of Kerak the prisoned air had brooded stagnantly without relief, while the heat sucked the perfume from the flowers. With darkness the world moved once more, and a breath from the west crept out over the desert. We were miles from the grass and flowers, but suddenly we felt them all about us, as waves of this scented air drew past us with a sticky sweetness. However, quickly it faded, and the night-wind, damp and wholesome, followed. Abdulla brought me supper, rice and camel-meat (Farraj's camel). Afterwards we slept.

✌ FOR DISCUSSION AND WRITING

1. This is a mind, a sensibility, a character of very great complexity (one has only to think, in contrast, of Scott's grave, forthright simplicity). That

---

[13] Desert Bedouin.
[14] See note 12.

complexity of personality is felt here in the manifold relationships that are set up and sustained even in so short a piece—relationships of man and men, men and beasts, men and landscape, the particular occasion in the desert and high military strategies being planned in Cairo or Jerusalem, the acute personal feeling of the day or hour or moment with its individual textures, and the vast abstraction of desert spaces or of ten thousand years of time trodden into the limestone of a desert path. Point out some of the places where such relationships are interwoven. What others do you find? Is it accurate to say that this kind of perception of intertwined relationships reflect character? Do the "style" of the writing, the diction itself, the movement of the phrasing, the imagery used to evoke things seen, reflect that complexity of relationships—and character? Explain your answer and illustrate it.

2. The desert spring holds all of this together, from the first paragraph to the last. How frequently is there reference to the spring weather and what it brings forth? The movements of Lawrence and the tribesmen are necessarily directed by the ruthless motives of war, and therefore always closely related to the infliction of death or the suffering of it. Define the relation between the desert spring that brings delight even to camels ("they were knee-deep in succulent greenstuff"), and the fatality of death with which these men must constantly consort.

3. In the encounter with the young Turkish soldier at the railway culvert, how are the potentiality of death and the feeling induced by the spring weather implicitly shown in relationship?

4. How is "seeing" managed? That is, how does Lawrence contrive to make the reader see as he sees? This is not an easy thing to do, though it seems easy when you find it done well. Point out five or six phrases or sentences where Lawrence makes you see something very clearly. How is it done?

5. When Lawrence's men make the attack on the Turkish patrol, is there any indication in Farraj's actions of a deliberate rush toward death? (The incident is particularly moving in the context of the earlier part of the book, where the boy is delightfully gay and mischievous.) In the description of the wounded boy—in the paragraph beginning "We tried to move him" —what image brings death and the springtime together in one unit?

6. In the handling of the shooting (beginning "I knelt down beside him"), is any emotion expressly stated? By what specific means does this "understated" incident acquire its intensity of implication?

7. Why does Lawrence shoot Farraj's camel?

8. By what means does the final paragraph complete the piece as a unity? What is the effect of the parenthesis: "(Farraj's camel)"?

9. Subject for a short paper: the responsibilities of leadership as shown by Lawrence and Scott; or the ambiguity of heroism—a phrase which one might consider as applying to Lawrence.

Hanson W. Baldwin ✑§ R. M. S. Titanic

✑§ The author was born in 1903. He is at present military editor for the *New York Times.* ॐ

THE White Star liner *Titanic*, largest ship the world had ever known, sailed from Southampton on her maiden voyage to New York on April 10, 1912. The paint on her strakes was fair and bright; she was fresh from Harland and Wolff's Belfast yards, strong in the strength of her forty-six thousand tons of steel, bent, hammered, shaped and riveted through the three years of her slow birth.

There was little fuss and fanfare at her sailing; her sister ship, the *Olympic* — slightly smaller than the *Titanic* — had been in service for some months and to her had gone the thunder of the cheers.

But the *Titanic* needed no whistling steamers or shouting crowds to call attention to her superlative qualities. Her bulk dwarfed the ships near her as longshoremen singled up her mooring lines and cast off the

From "R.M.S. Titanic" by Hanson W. Baldwin, first published in *Harper's Magazine* for January 1934. Reprinted by permission of Willis Kingsley Wing. Copyright © 1933, by Harper & Row, Publishers, Incorporated; renewed 1961.

turns of heavy rope from the dock bollards. She was not only the largest ship afloat, but was believed to be the safest. Carlisle, her builder, had given her double bottoms and had divided her hull into sixteen water-tight compartments, which made her, men thought, unsinkable. She had been built to be and had been described as a gigantic lifeboat. Her designers' dreams of a triple-screw giant, a luxurious, floating hotel, which could speed to New York at twenty-three knots, had been care-fully translated from blue prints and mold-loft lines at the Belfast yards into a living reality.

The *Titanic's* sailing from Southampton, though quiet, was not wholly uneventful. As the liner moved slowly toward the end of her dock that April day, the surge of her passing sucked away from the quay the steamer *New York*, moored just to seaward of the *Titanic's* berth. There were sharp cracks as the manila mooring lines of the *New York* parted under the strain. The frayed ropes writhed and whistled through the air and snapped down among the waving crowd on the pier; the *New York* swung toward the *Titanic's* bow, was checked and dragged back to the dock barely in time to avert a collision. Seamen muttered, thought it an ominous start.

Past Spithead and the Isle of Wight the *Titanic* steamed. She called at Cherbourg at dusk and then laid her course for Queenstown. At 1:30 P.M. on Thursday, April 11, she stood out of Queenstown harbor, screaming gulls soaring in her wake, with 2,201 persons — men, women, and children — aboard.

Occupying the Empire bedrooms and Georgian suites of the first-class accommodations were many well-known men and women — Col-onel John Jacob Astor and his young bride; Major Archibald Butt, mili-tary aide to President Taft, and his friend, Frank D. Millet, the painter; John B. Thayer, vice-president of the Pennsylvania Railroad, and Charles M. Hays, president of the Grand Trunk Railway of Canada; W. T. Stead, the English journalist; Jacques Futrelle, French novelist; H. B. Harris, theatrical manager, and Mrs. Harris; Mr. and Mrs. Isidor Straus; and J. Bruce Ismay, chairman and managing director of the White Star line.

Down in the plain wooden cabins of the steerage class were 706 immigrants to the land of promise, and trimly stowed in the great holds was a cargo valued at $420,000: oak beams, sponges, wine, calabashes, and an odd miscellany of the common and the rare.

The *Titanic* took her departure on Fastnet Light and, heading into the night, laid her course for New York. She was due at Quarantine the following Wednesday morning.

Sunday dawned fair and clear. The *Titanic* steamed smoothly toward the west, faint streamers of brownish smoke trailing from her funnels. The purser held services in the saloon in the morning; on the steerage deck aft the immigrants were playing games and a Scotsman was puffing "The Campbells Are Coming" on his bagpipes in the midst of the uproar.

At 9 A.M. a message from the steamer *Caronia* sputtered into the wireless shack:

> CAPTAIN, TITANIC — WESTBOUND STEAMERS REPORT BERGS
> GROWLERS AND FIELD ICE IN 42 DEGREES N. FROM 49 DEGREES
> TO 51 DEGREES W. 12TH APRIL.
>
> > COMPLIMENTS —
> >
> > > BARR.

It was cold in the afternoon; the sun was brilliant, but the *Titanic*, her screws turning over at 75 revolutions per minute, was approaching the Banks.

In the Marconi cabin Second Operator Harold Bride, earphones clamped on his head, was figuring accounts; he did not stop to answer when he heard MWL, Continental Morse for the nearby Leyland liner, *Californian*, calling the *Titanic*. The *Californian* had some message about three icebergs; he didn't bother then to take it down. About 1:42 P.M. the rasping spark of those days spoke again across the water. It was the *Baltic*, calling the *Titanic*, warning her of ice on the steamer track. Bride took the message down and sent it up to the bridge. The officer-of-the-deck glanced at it; sent it to the bearded master of the *Titanic*, Captain E. C. Smith, a veteran of the White Star service. It was lunch time then; the Captain, walking along the promenade deck, saw Mr. Ismay, stopped, and handed him the message without comment. Ismay read it, stuffed it in his pocket, told two ladies about the icebergs, and resumed his walk. Later, about 7:15 P.M., the Captain requested the return of the message in order to post it in the chart room for the information of officers.

Dinner that night in the Jacobean dining room was gay. It was bitter on deck, but the night was calm and fine; the sky was moonless but studded with stars twinkling coldly in the clear air.

After dinner some of the second-class passengers gathered in the saloon, where the Reverend Mr. Carter conducted a "hymn singsong." It was almost ten o'clock and the stewards were waiting with biscuits and coffee as the group sang:

> O, hear us when we cry to Thee
> For those in peril on the sea.

On the bridge Second Officer Lightoller — short, stocky, efficient — was relieved at ten o'clock by First Officer Murdock. Lightoller had talked with other officers about the proximity of ice; at least five wireless ice warnings had reached the ship; lookouts had been cautioned to be alert; captains and officers expected to reach the field at any time after 9:30 P.M. At twenty-two knots, its speed unslackened, the *Titanic* plowed on through the night.

Lightoller left the darkened bridge to his relief and turned in. Captain Smith went to his cabin. The steerage was long since quiet; in the first and second cabins lights were going out; voices were growing still, people were asleep. Murdock paced back and forth on the bridge, peering out over the dark water, glancing now and then at the compass in front of Quatermaster Hichens at the wheel.

In the crow's nest, Lookout Frederick Fleet and his partner, Leigh, gazed down at the water, still and unruffled in the dim, starlit darkness. Behind and below them the ship, a white shadow with here and there a last winking light; ahead of them a dark and silent and cold ocean.

There was a sudden clang. "Dong-dong. Dong-dong. Dong-dong. Dong!" The metal clapper of the great ship's bell struck out 11:30. Mindful of the warnings, Fleet strained his eyes, searching the darkness for the dreaded ice. But there were only the stars and the sea.

In the wireless room, where Phillips, first operator, had relieved Bride, the buzz of the *Californian's* set again crackled into the earphones:

Californian: "Say, old man, we are stuck here, surrounded by ice."
Titanic: "Shut up, shut up; keep out. I am talking to Cape Race; you are jamming my signals."

Then, a few minutes later — about 11:40 . . .

Out of the dark she came, a vast, dim, white, monstrous shape, directly in the *Titanic's* path. For a moment Fleet doubted his eyes. But she was a deadly reality, this ghastly *thing*. Frantically, Fleet struck three bells — *something dead ahead*. He snatched the telephone and called the bridge:

"Iceberg! Right ahead!"

The First Officer heard but did not stop to acknowledge the message.

"Hard astarboard!"

Hichens strained at the wheel; the bow swung slowly to port. The monster was almost upon them now.

Murdock leaped to the engine-room telegraph. Bells clanged. Far below in the engine room those bells struck the first warning. Danger! The indicators on the dial faces swung round to "Stop!" Then "Full speed astern!" Frantically the engineers turned great valve wheels; answered the bridge bells. . . .

There was a slight shock, a brief scraping, a small list to port. Shell ice — slabs and chunks of it — fell on the foredeck. Slowly the *Titanic* stopped.

Captain Smith hurried out of his cabin.

"What has the ship struck?"

Murdock answered, "An iceberg, sir. I hard-astarboarded and reversed the engines, and I was going to hard-aport around it, but she was too close. I could not do any more. I have closed the watertight doors."

Fourth Officer Boxhall, other officers, the carpenter, came to the bridge. The Captain sent Boxhall and the carpenter below to ascertain the damage.

A few lights switched on in the first and second cabins; sleepy passengers peered through porthole glass; some casually asked the stewards:

"Why have we stopped?"

"I don't know, sir, but I don't suppose it is anything much."

In the smoking room a quorum of gamblers and their prey were still sitting round a poker table; the usual crowd of kibitzers looked on. They had felt the slight jar of the collision and had seen an eighty-foot ice mountain glide by the smoking-room windows, but the night was calm and clear, the *Titanic* was "unsinkable"; they hadn't bothered to go on deck.

But far below, in the warren of passages on the starboard side forward, in the forward holds and boiler rooms, men could see that the *Titanic*'s hurt was mortal. In No. 6 boiler room, where the red glow from the furnaces lighted up the naked, sweaty chests of coal-blackened firemen, water was pouring through a great gash about two feet above the floor plates. This was no slow leak; the ship was open to the sea; in ten minutes there were eight feet of water in No. 6. Long before then the stokers had raked the flaming fires out of the furnaces and had scrambled through the watertight doors into No. 5 or had climbed up the long steel ladders to safety. When Boxhall looked at the mail room in No. 3 hold, twenty-four feet above the keel, the mailbags were already floating about in the slushing water. In No. 5 boiler room a stream of water spurted into an empty bunker. All six compartments forward of No. 4 were open to the sea; in ten seconds the iceberg's jagged claw had ripped a three-hundred-foot slash in the bottom of the great *Titanic*.

Reports came to the bridge; Ismay in dressing gown ran out on deck in the cold, still, starlit night, climbed up the bridge ladder.

"What has happened?"

Captain Smith: "We have struck ice."

"Do you think she is seriously damaged?"

Captain: "I'm afraid she is."

Ismay went below and passed Chief Engineer William Bell fresh from an inspection of the damaged compartments. Bell corroborated the Captain's statement; hurried back down the glistening steel ladders to his duty. Man after man followed him — Thomas Andrews, one of the ship's designers, Archie Frost, the builder's chief engineer, and his twenty assistants — men who had no posts of duty in the engine room but whose traditions called them there.

On deck, in corridor and stateroom, life flowed again. Men, women, and children awoke and questioned; orders were given to uncover the lifeboats; water rose into the firemen's quarters; half-dressed stokers streamed up on deck. But the passengers — most of them — did not know that the *Titanic* was sinking. The shock of the collision had been so slight that some were not awakened by it; the *Titanic* was so huge that she must be unsinkable; the night was too calm, too beautiful, to think of death at sea.

Captain Smith half ran to the door of the radio shack. Bride, partly dressed, eyes dulled with sleep, was standing behind Phillips, waiting.

"Send the call for assistance."

The blue spark danced: "CQD — CQD — CQD — CQ — "

Miles away Marconi men heard. Cape Race heard it, and the steamships *La Provence* and *Mt. Temple.*

The sea was surging into the *Titanic's* hold. At 12:20 the water burst into the seamen's quarters through a collapsed fore-and-aft wooden bulkhead. Pumps strained in the engine rooms — men and machinery making a futile fight against the sea. Steadily the water rose.

The boats were swung out — slowly; for the deckhands were late in reaching their stations, there had been no boat drill, and many of the crew did not know to what boats they were assigned. Orders were shouted; the safety valves had lifted, and steam was blowing off in a great rushing roar. In the chart house Fourth Officer Boxhall bent above a chart, working rapidly with pencil and dividers.

12:15 A.M. Boxhall's position is sent out to a fleet of vessels: "Come at once; we have struck a berg."

To the Cunarder *Carpathia* (Arthur Henry Rostron, Master, New York to Liverpool, fifty-eight miles away): "It's a CQD, old man. Position 41-46 N.; 50-14 W."

The blue spark dancing: "Sinking; cannot hear for noise of steam."

12:30 A.M. The word is passed: "Women and children in the boats." Stewards finish waking their passengers below; life preservers are tied on; some men smile at the precaution. "The *Titanic* is unsinkable." The *Mt. Temple* starts for the *Titanic;* the *Carpathia,* with a double watch in her stokeholds, radios, "Coming hard." The CQD changes the course of many ships — but not of one; the operator of the *Californian,* near by, has just put down his earphones and turned in.

The CQD flashes over land and sea from Cape Race to New York; newspaper city rooms leap to life and presses whir.

On the *Titanic,* water creeps over the bulkhead between Nos. 5 and 6 firerooms. She is going down by the head; the engineers — fighting a losing battle — are forced back foot by foot by the rising water. Down the promenade deck, Happy Jock Hume, the bandsman, runs with his instrument.

12:45 A.M. Murdock, in charge on the starboard side, eyes tragic, but calm and cool, orders boat No. 7 lowered. The women hang back; they want no boat ride on an ice-strewn sea; the *Titanic* is unsinkable. The men encourage them, explain that this is just a precautionary measure: "We'll see you again at breakfast." There is little confusion;

passengers stream slowly to the boat deck. In the steerage the immigrants chatter excitedly,

A sudden sharp hiss — a streaked flare against the night; Boxhall
sends a rocket toward the sky. It explodes, and a parachute of white stars
lights up the icy sea. "God! Rockets!" The band plays ragtime.

No. 8 is lowered, and No. 5. Ismay, still in dressing gown, calls for
women and children, handles lines, stumbles in the way of an officer,
is told to "get the hell out of here." Third Officer Pitman takes charge
of No. 5; as he swings into the boat Murdock grasps his hand. "Good-by
and good luck, old man."

No. 6 goes over the side. There are only twenty-eight people in a
lifeboat with a capacity of sixty-five.

A light stabs from the bridge; Boxhall is calling in Morse flashes,
again and again, to a strange ship stopped in the ice jam five to ten
miles away. Another rocket drops its shower of sparks above the ice-
strewn sea and the dying ship.

1:00 A.M.   Slowly the water creeps higher; the fore ports of the
Titanic are dipping into the sea. Rope squeaks through blocks; lifeboats
drop jerkily seaward. Through the shouting on the decks comes the
sound of the band playing ragtime.

The "Millionaires' Special" leaves the ship — boat No. 1, with a
capacity of forty people, carries only Sir Cosmo and Lady Duff Gordon
and ten others. Aft, the frightened immigrants mill and jostle and rush
for a boat. An officer's fist flies out; three shots are fired into the air,
and the panic is quelled. . . . Four Chinese sneak unseen into a boat and
hide in its bottom.

1:20 A.M.   Water is coming into No. 4 boiler room. Stokers slice
and shovel as water laps about their ankles — steam for the dynamos,
steam for the dancing spark! As the water rises, great ash hoes rake
the flaming coals from the furnaces. Safety valves pop; the stokers retreat aft, and the watertight doors clang shut behind them.

The rockets fling their splendor toward the stars. The boats are more
heavily loaded now, for the passengers know the *Titanic* is sinking.
Women cling and sob. The great screws aft are rising clear of the sea.
Half-filled boats are ordered to come alongside the cargo ports and
take on more passengers, but the ports are never opened — and the boats
are never filled. Others pull for the steamer's light miles away but never
reach it; the light disappears, the unknown ship steams off.

The water rises and the band plays ragtime.

1:30 A.M.   Lightoller is getting the port boats off; Murdock the starboard. As one boat is lowered into the sea a boat officer fires his gun along the ship's side to stop a rush from the lower decks. A woman tries to take her great Dane into a boat with her; she is refused and steps out of the boat to die with her dog. Millet's "little smile which played on his lips all through the voyage" plays no more; his lips are grim, but he waves good-by and brings wraps for the women.

Benjamin Guggenheim, in evening clothes, smiles and says, "We've dressed up in our best and are prepared to go down like gentlemen."

1:40 A.M.   Boat 14 is clear, and then 13, 16, 15, and C. The lights still shine, but the *Baltic* hears the blue spark say, "Engine room getting flooded."

The *Olympic* signals, "Am lighting up all possible boilers as fast as can."

Major Butt helps women into the last boats and waves good-by to them. Mrs. Straus puts her foot on the gunwale of a lifeboat, then she draws back and goes to her husband: "We have been together many years; where you go I will go." Colonel John Jacob Astor puts his young wife in a lifeboat, steps back, taps cigarette on fingernail: "Good-by, dearie; I'll join you later."

1:45 A.M.   The foredeck is under water, the fo'c'sle head almost awash; the great stern is lifted high toward the bright stars; and still the band plays. Mr. and Mrs. Harris approach a lifeboat arm in arm.

Officer: "Ladies first, please."

Harris bows, smiles, steps back: "Of course, certainly; ladies first."

Boxhall fires the last rocket, then leaves in charge of boat No. 2.

2:00 A.M.   She is dying now; her bow goes deeper, her stern higher. But there must be steam. Below in the stokeholds the sweaty firemen keep steam up for the flaring lights and the dancing spark. The glowing coals slide and tumble over the slanted grate bars; the sea pounds behind that yielding bulkhead. But the spark dances on.

The *Asian* hears Phillips try the new signal — SOS.

Boat No. 4 has left now; boat D leaves ten minutes later. Jacques Futrelle clasps his wife: "For God's sake, go! It's your last chance; go!" Madame Futrelle is half forced into the boat. It clears the side.

There are about 660 people in the boats, and 1,500 still on the sinking *Titanic*.

On top of the officers' quarters men work frantically to get the two collapsibles stowed there over the side. Water is over the forward part of A deck now; it surges up the companionways toward the boat deck. In the radio shack, Bride has slipped a coat and lifejacket about Phillips as the first operator sits hunched over his key, sending — still sending — "41-46 N.; 50-14 W. CQD — CQD — SOS — SOS — "

The Captain's tired white face appears at the radio-room door: "Men, you have done your full duty. You can do no more. Now, it's every man for himself." The Captain disappears — back to his sinking bridge, where Painter, his personal steward, stands quietly waiting for orders. The spark dances on. Bride turns his back and goes into the inner cabin. As he does so, a stoker, grimed with coal, mad with fear, steals into the shack and reaches for the lifejacket on Phillips' back. Bride wheels about and brains him with a wrench.

2:10 A.M.   Below decks the steam is still holding, though the pressure is falling — rapidly. In the gymnasium on the boat deck the athletic instructor watches quietly as two gentlemen ride the bicycles and another swings casually at the punching bag. Mail clerks stagger up the boat-deck stairways, dragging soaked mail sacks. The spark still dances. The band still plays — but not ragtime:

> Nearer my God to Thee,
> Nearer to Thee . . .

A few men take up the refrain; others kneel on the slanting decks to pray. Many run and scramble aft, where hundreds are clinging above the silent screws on the great uptilted stern. The spark still dances and the lights still flare; the engineers are on the job. The hymn comes to its close. Bandmaster Hartley, Yorkshireman violinist, taps his bow against a bulkhead, calls for "Autumn" as the water curls about his feet, and the eight musicians brace themselves against the ship's slant. People are leaping from the decks into the nearby water — the icy water. A woman cries, "Oh, save me, save me!" A man answers, "Good lady, save yourself. Only God can save you now." The band plays "Autumn":

> God of Mercy and Compassion!
> Look with pity on my pain . . .

The water creeps over the bridge where the *Titanic*'s master stands; heavily he steps out to meet it.

2:17 A.M. "CQ —" The *Virginian* hears a ragged, blurred CQ, then an abrupt stop. The blue spark dances no more. The lights flicker out; the engineers have lost their battle.

2:18 A.M. Men run about blackened decks; leap into the night; are swept into the sea by the curling wave which licks up the *Titanic's* length. Lightoller does not leave the ship; the ship leaves him; there are hundreds like him, but only a few who live to tell of it. The funnels still swim above the water, but the ship is climbing to the perpendicular; the bridge is under and most of the foremast; the great stern rises like a squat leviathan. Men swim away from the sinking ship; others drop from the stern.

The band plays in the darkness, the water lapping upwards:

> Hold me up in mighty waters,
> Keep my eyes on things above,
> Righteousness, divine atonement,
> Peace and everlas . . .

The forward funnel snaps and crashes into the sea; its steel tons hammer out of existence swimmers struggling in the freezing water. Streams of sparks, of smoke and steam, burst from the after funnels. The ship upends to fifty—to sixty degrees.

Down in the black abyss of the stokeholds, of the engine rooms, where the dynamos have whirred at long last to a stop, the stokers and the engineers are reeling against hot metal, the rising water clutching at their knees. The boilers, the engine cylinders, rip from their bed plates; crash through bulkheads; rumble — steel against steel.

The *Titanic* stands on end, poised briefly for the plunge. Slowly she slides to her grave —slowly at first, and then more quickly — quickly — quickly.

2:20 A.M. The greatest ship in the world has sunk. From the calm, dark waters, where the floating lifeboats move, there goes up, in the white wake of her passing, "one long continuous moan."

The boats that the *Titanic* had launched pulled safely away from the slight suction of the sinking ship, pulled away from the screams that came from the lips of the freezing men and women in the water. The boats were poorly manned and badly equipped, and they had been unevenly loaded. Some carried so few seamen that women bent to the oars. Mrs. Astor tugged at an oar handle; the Countess of Rothes took a tiller. Shivering stokers in sweaty, coal-blackened singlets and light trousers steered in some boats; stewards in white coats rowed in others. Ismay was in the last boat that left the ship from the starboard side; with Mr. Carter of Philadelphia and two seamen he tugged at the oars. In one of the lifeboats an Italian with a broken wrist — disguised in a woman's shawl and hat — huddled on the floor boards, ashamed now that fear had left him. In another rode the only baggage saved from the *Titanic* — the carry-all of Samuel L. Goldenberg, one of the rescued passengers.

There were only a few boats that were heavily loaded; most of those that were half empty made but perfunctory efforts to pick up the moaning swimmers, their officers and crew fearing that they would endanger the living if they pulled back into the midst of the dying. Some boats beat off the freezing victims; fear-crazed men and women struck with oars at the heads of swimmers. One woman drove her fist into the face of a half-dead man as he tried feebly to climb over the gunwale. Two other women helped him in and stanched the flow of blood from the ring cuts on his face.

One of the collapsible boats, which had floated off the top of the officers' quarters when the *Titanic* sank, was an icy haven for thirty or forty men. The boat had capsized as the ship sank; men swam to it, clung to it, climbed upon its slippery bottom, stood knee-deep in water in the freezing air. Chunks of ice swirled about their legs; their soaked clothing clutched their bodies in icy folds. Colonel Archibald Gracie was cast up there, Gracie who had leaped from the stern as the *Titanic* sank; young Thayer who had seen his father die; Lightoller who had twice been sucked down with the ship and twice blown to the surface by a belch of air; Bride, the second operator, and Phillips, the first. There were many stokers, half-naked; it was a shivering company. They stood there in the icy sea, under the far stars, and sang and prayed — the Lord's Prayer. After a while a lifeboat came and picked them off, but Phillips was dead then or died soon afterward in the boat.

Only a few of the boats had lights; only one — No. 2 — had a light that was of any use to the *Carpathia*, twisting through the ice field to the rescue. Other ships were "coming hard" too; one, the *Californian*, was still dead to opportunity.

The blue sparks still danced, but not the *Titanic*'s. *Le Provence* to *Celtic:* "Nobody has heard the *Titanic* for about two hours."

It was 2:40 when the *Carpathia* first sighted the green light from No. 2 boat; it was 4:10 when she picked up the first boat and learned that the *Titanic* had foundered. The last of the moaning cries had just died away then.

Captain Rostron took the survivors aboard, boatload by boatload. He was ready for them, but only a small minority of them required much medical attention. Bride's feet were twisted and frozen; others were suffering from exposure; one died, and seven were dead when taken from the boats, and were buried at sea.

It was then that the fleet of racing ships learned they were too late; the *Parisian* heard the weak signals of MPA, the *Carpathia*, report the death of the *Titanic*. It was then — or soon afterward, when her radio operator put on his earphones — that the *Californian*, the ship that had been within sight as the *Titanic* was sinking, first learned of the disaster.

And it was then, in all its white-green majesty, that the *Titanic*'s survivors saw the iceberg, tinted with the sunrise, floating idly, pack ice jammed about its base, other bergs heaving slowly near by on the blue breast of the sea.

◢§ FOR DISCUSSION AND WRITING

1. Simple but expertly handled ironies run through this piece. What major irony is there in the total situation—the meeting of iceberg and *Titanic?* What irony is implicit in the gigantism of the name itself and the description of the ship ("the greatest ship in the world")? In the myths and tragic dramas of ancient Greece, the great heroes often suffered a kind of blindness through their own greatness, and thus brought upon themselves their tragic fall. Is there any relationship between such stories and the catastrophe of the *Titanic?*

2. The author maintains through much of the piece a technique of simple factuality almost like that of a recorder of statistical data—the hours of the clock, the names of the passengers, the revolutions per minute of the ship's screws, the number of degrees north, the number of degrees west, and so on: a manner of telling that could not be pursued indefinitely without boredom—but that has specific ironic effect under the circumstances.

What, as you would define it, is that effect? Irony is often, perhaps always, a matter of contrast through inference; with what aspect of circumstances is the dead-pan technique set in implicit contrast?

3. In the handling of the radio message from the *Caronia* (the radio operator "did not stop to answer") and from the *Californian* ("he didn't bother then to take it down") and from the *Baltic* (various persons take it, glance at it, send it on—"it was lunch time then"—hand it to someone else who stuffs it in his pocket), what ironies are involved? Is the irony implicit or explicit?

4. What facets of character appear in these notations: "Benjamin Guggenheim, in evening clothes, smiles and says, 'We've dressed up in our best and are prepared to go down like gentlemen.'" Colonel John Jacob Astor "taps cigarette on fingernail" after putting his young wife in a lifeboat and stepping back: "'Good-by, dearie; I'll join you later.'" Is this *simply* the well-bred upper lip? "In the gymnasium on the boat deck the athletic instructor watches quietly as two gentlemen ride the bicycles and another swings casually at the punching bag." What other notations are particularly revelatory of varieties of character?

5. Could you say that the whole piece is organized by irony? Substantiate your answer. What particularly grim irony is there in the next to the last paragraph, with "It was then—or soon afterward, when her radio operator put on his earphones . . ."? What special aspect of the final paragraph closes with ironic precision the fatal spectacle?

6. Write a short, well-considered paper on the superiority of modern technology over nature—or the other way around; or a paper on the astronaut as a new kind of hero. Write on your own contemporary heroes and why they are heroes (one might have a hero who is a horse or a dancer or a prize fighter). Write on some situation in your own experience that was a test of character.

Isak Dinesen ✑ Shooting Accident on an African Farm

✑ Baroness Karen Blixen, Danish writer of tales and memoirs (1885-1962). She wrote in English as well as in Danish; the episode here—from *Out of Africa*—was written in English. Her father had distinction as a writer, and lived for several years as a trapper with the Pawnee Indians in Minnesota. She went with her husband, in 1914, to British East Africa and established a coffee plantation, which, after her divorce in 1921, she continued to manage for another ten years. Her *Seven Gothic Tales*, *Winter's Tales*, and *Last Tales* are the work of a great storyteller, a master of the art. ଛ

ON the evening of the nineteenth of December, I walked out of my house before going to bed, to see if there was any rain coming. Many farmers in the highlands were, I believe, doing the same thing at that hour. Sometimes, in a lucky year, we would get a few heavy showers just round Christmas, and it was a great thing for the young coffee, which has set on the trees after the flowering in the short rains of October. This night there was no sign of rain. The sky was serene and silently triumphant, resplendent with stars.

The Stellar Heaven of the Equator is richer than that of the North, and you see it more because you are out more at night. In Northern Europe, winter nights are too cold to allow one much pleasure in the contemplation of the stars, and in summer one hardly distinguishes them within the clear night sky, that is as pale as a dog-violet.

The tropical night has the companionability of a Roman Catholic Cathedral compared to the Protestant Churches of the North, which let you in on business only. Here in the great room everybody comes and goes, this is the place where things are going on. To Arabia and Africa, where the sun of the midday kills you, night is the time for travelling and enterprise. The stars have been named here, they have been guides to human beings for many centuries, drawing them in long lines across the desert-sands and the Sea, one towards the East, and another to the West, or the North and South. Cars run well at night, and it is pleasant to motor under the stars, you get into the habit of fixing visits to friends up-country by the time of the next full moon. You start Safaris by the new moon, to have the benefit of the whole row of moonlight nights. It is then strange, when back on a visit to Europe, to find your friends of the towns living out of touch with the moves of the moon and almost in ignorance of them. The young moon was the sign of action to Khadija's camel man,[1] whose Caravan was to start off when she appeared in the sky. With his face towards her he was one of the "Philosophers who spin out of moonlight systems of the Universe". He must have looked at her much, that he made her his sign in which to conquer.

I had got a name amongst the Natives, because a number of times I had happened to be, on the farm, the first to see the new moon, like a thin silver bow in the sunset; particularly because, two or three years running, I had been the first to catch sight of the new moon of the month of Ramadan, the Mohammedan's holy Month.

The farmer slowly turns his eyes all round the Horizon. First to the East, for from the East, if it comes, comes the rain, and there stands clear Spica in the Virgin.[2] Then South, to greet the Southern Cross, doorkeeper of the great world, faithful to travellers and beloved by them, and higher up, under the luminous streak of the Milky Way, Alpha and Beta in the Centaur. To the South West sparkles Sirius, great in heaven, and the thoughtful Canopus, and to the West above the faint

[1] Mohammed. Khadija was an elderly widow, whom he married. The crescent moon appears on the Islamic flag.

[2] Spica is a first-magnitude star in the constellation Virgo. Alpha and Beta are the two brightest stars in the constellation Centaurus. Sirius (the "Dog Star") is the brightest star in the sky, Canopus the next brightest. Rigel, Betelgeuze, and Bellatrix are giant stars in Orion.

outline of the Ngong Hills, now nearly unbroken, the radiant diamond ornament, Rigel, Betelgeuze and Bellatrix. He turns to the North last, for to the North we go back in the end, and there he runs upon the Great Bear himself, only he is now calmly standing on his head on account of the heavenly perspective, and that has all the air of a bearish joke, that cheers the heart of the Nordic emigrant.

People who dream when they sleep at night, know of a special kind of happiness which the world of the day holds not, a placid ecstasy, and ease of heart, that are like honey on the tongue. They also know that the real glory of dreams lies in their atmosphere of unlimited freedom. It is not the freedom of the dictator, who enforces his own will on the world, but the freedom of the artist, who has no will, who is free of will. The pleasure of the true dreamer does not lie in the substance of the dream, but in this: that there things happen without any interference from his side, and altogether outside his control. Great landscapes create themselves, long splendid views, rich and delicate colours, roads, houses, which he has never seen or heard of. Strangers appear and are friends or enemies, although the person who dreams has never done anything about them. The ideas of flight and pursuit are recurrent in dreams and are equally enrapturing. Excellent witty things are said by everybody. It is true that if remembered in the daytime they will fade and lose their sense, because they belong to a different plane, but as soon as the one who dreams lies down at night, the current is again closed and he remembers their excellency. All the time the feeling of immense freedom is surrounding him and running through him like air and light, an unearthly bliss. He is a privileged person, the one who has got nothing to do, but for whose enrichment and pleasure all things are brought together; the Kings of Tarshish[3] shall bring gifts. He takes part in a great battle or ball, and wonders the while that he should be, in the midst of those events, so far privileged as to be lying down. It is when one begins to lose the consciousness of freedom, and when the idea of necessity enters the world at all, when there is any hurry or strain anywhere, a letter to be written or a train to catch, when you have got to work, to make the horses of the dream gallop, or to make the rifles go off, that the dream is declining, and turning into the nightmare, which belongs to the poorest and most vulgar class of dreams.

[3] Ancient trading city of legendary wealth mentioned in the Bible; its location is uncertain.

The thing which in the waking world comes nearest to a dream is night in a big town, where nobody knows one, or the African night. There too is infinite freedom: it is there that things are going on, destinies are made round you, there is activity to all sides, and it is none of your concern.

Here now, as soon as the sun was down the air was full of bats, cruising as noiselessly as cars upon asphalt, the night-hawk swept past too: the bird that sits on the road and in the eyes of which the lights of your car gleam red a moment before he flutters up vertically in front of your wheels. The little spring-hares were out on the roads, moving in their own way, sitting down suddenly and jumping along to a rhythm, like miniature Kangaroos. The Cicada sing an endless song in the long grass, smells run along the earth and falling stars run over the sky, like tears over a cheek. You are the privileged person to whom everything is taken. The Kings of Tarshish shall bring gifts.

A few miles out, in the Masai Reserve, the Zebra are now changing their pasture, the flocks wander over the grey plain like lighter stripes upon it, the Buffalo are out grazing on the long slopes of the Hills. My young men of the farm would come by, two or three together, walking one after the other like narrow dark shadows on the lawn, they were afoot and aiming straight at their own object, they were not working for me, and it was none of my concern. They themselves accentuated the position by just slackening their pace as they caught sight of my burning cigarette-end outside the house, and saluting without stopping.

"*Jambo* Msabu."

"*Jambo* Morani" — young warriors, — "where are you going?"

"We are going to Kathegu's manyatta. Kathegu has a big Ngoma on to-night. Good-bye Msabu."

If they walk together in bigger parties they will bring their own drum to the dance, and you hear it a long way away, like the throbbing of a small pulse in the finger of the night. And suddenly, to the ear that has not been listening for it, comes what is not so much a sound as a deep vibration of the air, the distant short roar of the lion. He is afoot, he is hunting, things are going on, out there where he is. It is not repeated, but it has widened the horizon; the long dungas and the water-hole are brought to you.

As I was standing before my house a shot fell, not far off. One shot.

Then again the stillness of the night closed on all sides. After a while, as if they had been pausing to listen and were now taking it up once more, I heard the Cicada chiming their monotonous little song in the grass.

There is something strangely determinate and fatal about a single shot in the night. It is as if someone had cried a message to you in one word, and would not repeat it. I stood for some time wondering what it had meant. Nobody could aim at anything at this hour, and, to scare away something, a person would fire two shots or more.

It might have been my old Indian carpenter Pooran Singh down at the mill, firing at a couple of Hyena that had slunk into the millyard and were eating the straps of oxhide hung up there, with stones as weights to them, to be made into reins for our waggons. Pooran Singh was no hero, but he might have put the door of his hut ajar for the sake of his reins and blown off his old shotgun. Still he would have let off both barrels, and would probably have loaded and shot again, once he had tasted the sweetness of heroism. But one shot, — and then silence?

I waited for some time for the second shot; nothing came, and as I looked again at the sky there was no rain coming either. So I went to bed, taking a book with me, and leaving the lamp to burn. In Africa, when you pick up a book worth reading, out of the deadly consignments which good ships are being made to carry out all the way from Europe, you read it as an author would like his book to be read, praying to God that he may have it in him to go on as beautifully as he has begun. Your mind runs, transported, upon a fresh deep green track.

Two minutes later a motorcycle rounded the drive at a terrific speed and stopped in front of the house, and someone knocked hard upon the long window of my sitting room. I put on a skirt and a coat and a pair of shoes, took the lamp and went out. Outside was my mill-manager, wild-eyed and sweating in the lamplight. His name was Belknap, he was an American and an exceptionally capable, inspired mechanic, but of an uneven mind. With him things were either nearing the Millennium, or dark without a glimpse of hope. When he first came into my employ he had upset me by his varying views of life, and of prospects and conditions of the farm, as if he had had me up in an enormous mental swing; later I had got used to them. These ups and downs were no more than a kind of emotional daily gymnastics to a lively temperament, much in need of exercise, and to which too little was happening; it is a common phenomenon with energetic young white men in Africa, particularly with those who have spent their early life in towns. But here he came out of the hands of a tragedy, and was as yet undecided as to whether he should satiate his hungry soul by making the most of it, or escape from its grimness by making as little of it as possible, and in this dilemma he looked like a very young boy running for his life to announce a catastrophe; he stuttered as he spoke. In the end he made very little of it, for it held no part in it for him to play, and fate had let him down once more.

By this time, Farah[4] had come from his house, and listened to his narrative with me.

Belknap told me how peacefully and pleasantly the tragedy had started. His Cook had had a day off, and in his absence a party had been given in the kitchen by the seven years old kitchen Toto,[5] Kabero, a son of my old Squatter and nearest neighbour on the farm, the old fox Kaninu. As, late in the evening, the company became very gay, Kabero had brought in his master's gun and, to his wild friends of the plains and shambas,[6] had acted the part of a white man. Belknap was a keen poultry farmer, he made capons and poulardes and bought up pure-bred chicken at the Nairobi sales, and he kept a shotgun on his verandah to frighten away hawks and cerval-cats. When later we talked the case over, Belknap held that the gun had not been loaded, but that the children had looked up the cartridges and loaded it themselves, but here I think that his memory failed him, they could hardly have done it if they had wanted to, and it was more likely that the gun had for once been left loaded on the verandah. However it got there, the cartridge was in the barrel when Kabero, in the greatness of youth and popularity, aimed straight in amongst his guests and pulled the trigger. The shot had boomed through the house. Three of the children had been slightly wounded, and had fled from the kitchen in terror. Two were there now, badly hurt or dead. Belknap finished his tale by a long anathema of the continent of Africa and of the things that happen there.

While he talked, my houseboys had come out, very silent; they went in again, and brought out a hurricane-lamp. We got out dressing and disinfectant. It would be a waste of time to try to start the car, and

[4] Overseer of the plantation.

[5] Kitchen boy.

[6] Plots of cultivated ground.

we ran as quick as we could through the forest down to Belknap's house. The swinging hurricane-lamp threw our shadows from the one side of the narrow road to the other. As we ran on, we were met by a succession of short raw cracked shrieks, — death squeals of a child.

The kitchen door was flung back, as if Death, after having rushed in, had rushed out again, and left the place in dire devastation, a chicken-house that the badger has been in. There was a kitchen lamp burning on the table and smoking sky-high, and in the small room the smell of gunpowder still hung. The gun was on the table beside the lamp. There was blood all over the kitchen, I slipped in it on the floor. Hurricane-lamps are difficult to direct on to any particular spot, but they give a very striking illumination of a whole room or situation; I remember the things I have seen by the light of a hurricane-lamp better than others.

I knew the children who had been shot, from the plains of the farm, where they had herded their fathers' sheep. Wamai, Jogona's son, a lively little boy who had for some time been a pupil at the school, was lying on the floor between the door and the table. He was not dead, but not far from death, and unconscious even, though he groaned a little. We lifted him aside, to be able to move. The child that shrieked was Wanyangerri, who had been the youngest of the party in the kitchen. He was sitting up, leaning forwards, towards the lamp; the blood spouted, like water from a pump, from his face, — if one could still say that, for he must have stood straight in front of the barrel when it was fired and it had taken his lower jaw clean off. He held his arms out from his sides and moved them up and down like pump-spears, as the wings of a chicken go, after it has had its head cut off.

When you are brought suddenly within the presence of such disaster, there seems to be but one advice, it is the remedy of the shooting-field and the farmyard: that you should kill quickly and at any cost. And yet you know that you cannot kill, and your brain turns with fear. I put my hands to the child's head and pressed it in my despair, and, as if I had really killed him, he at the same moment stopped screaming, and sat erect with his arms hanging down, as if he was made of wood. So now I know what it feels like to heal by imposition of hands.

It is a difficult thing to bandage a patient whose face is half shot off, in your endeavour to stop the bleeding you may choke him. I had to lift the little boy on to Farah's knee, and make Farah hold his head in position for me, for if it fell forward I could not get the dressing fastened, and if it fell back the blood ran down and filled his throat. In the end, while he sat so still, I got the bandages placed.

We lifted Wamai on to the table and held the lamp up to look at him. He had received the full charge of the gun into his throat and chest, he did not bleed much, only a thin trail of blood ran down from the corner of his mouth. It was surprising to see this Native child, who had been as full of life as a fawn, so quiet now. While we looked at him his own face changed and took on an expression of deep surprise. I sent Farah to the house to fetch the car, for we had no time to waste in bringing the children into hospital.

While we waited I inquired after Kabero, the boy who had fired the gun and shed all this blood. Belknap then told me a queer story about him. A couple of days earlier Kabero had bought an old pair of shorts from his master, and was to pay him with a rupee from his wages. When the shot fell, and Belknap ran out to the kitchen, Kabero was standing in the middle of the room with the smoking gun in his hand. He stared at Belknap for a second, and then dived into the pocket of the very shorts that he had so newly bought and had put on for the party, drew up a rupee and laid it on the table with his left hand, while with his right he threw the gun also on the table. And in that final settlement with the world he was gone; he actually, although we did not know of it at the moment, in this great gesture, disappeared from the face of the earth. It was an unusual behaviour in a Native, for they generally manage to keep a debt, and in particular a debt to a white man, within the outskirts of their mind. Perhaps the moment to Kabero had looked so much like the day of judgment, that he felt he had got to play up to it; perhaps he was trying, in the hour of need, to secure a friend. Or the shock, the boom, and the death of his friends round him, had knocked in the whole of the boy's small sphere of ideas, so that bits of the periphery had been flung into the very centre of his consciousness.

At that time I had an old Overland car. I shall never write anything against her, for she served me well through many years. But it was rare that she could be induced to run on more than two cylinders. Her lights were out of order too, so that I used to drive in to dances at the Muthaiga Club with a hurricane-lamp swaddled in a red silk handkerchief, for a back light. She had to be pushed into starting, and upon this night it took a long time.

Visitors to my house had been complaining of the state of my road, and during the death-drive of that night I realized that they had been right. I first let Farah drive, but I thought that he was deliberately going into all the deep holes and waggon-tracks of the road, and I took the steering-wheel myself. For this I had to get off by the pond to wash my hands in the dark water. The distance to Nairobi seemed infinitely long, I thought that I might have driven home to Denmark in the time that it took us.

The Native Hospital of Nairobi lies on the hill just before you drive down into the cup of the town. It was dark now, and seemed peaceful. We had much trouble to wake it up; in the end we got hold of an old Goan doctor or doctor's assistant, who appeared in a queer sort of negligée. He was a big fat man of a very placid manner, and had a strange way of making the same gesture first with one hand and then with the other. As I helped to lift Wamai out of the car I thought that he stirred and stretched himself a little, but when we brought him into the brightly lighted room in the hospital, he was dead. The old Goan kept waving his hand at him, saying: "He is dead." And then again at Wanyangerri, saying: "He is alive." I never saw this old man again, for I never came back to the hospital at night, which was probably his hour there. At the time, I thought his manner very annoying, but afterwards I felt as if Fate itself in a number of big white cloaks, the one on the top of the other, had met us at the threshold of the house, dealing out Life and Death impartially.

Wanyangerri woke up from his trance when we took him into the Hospital, and at once got into a terrible panic; he would not be left but clung to me and to anybody near him and cried and wept in the greatest anguish. The old Goan in the end calmed him by some injection, looked at me over his spectacles and said: "He is alive." I left the children there, the dead and the live, upon two stretchers, for their different fates.

Belknap, who had come in with us on his motor-bicycle, mostly so as to help us to push the car into starting should she stop on the road, now thought that we ought to report the accident to the Police. So we drove down into town to the River Road Police Station, and thereby ran straight into the night-life of Nairobi. There was no white Police Officer present when we came, and while they sent for him we waited outside in the car. The street had an avenue of tall Eucalyptus trees, the tree of all pioneer-towns of the highlands; at night their very long narrow leaves give out a queer pleasant smell, and look strange in the light of the street-lamps. A big buxom young Swaheli woman was carried into the Police Station by a group of Native Policemen, she resisted with all her might, scratched their faces, and screamed like a pig. A party of brawlers were brought in, still eager, upon the steps of the Station, to go for one another; and a thief, I believe, who had just been caught, came down the street with a whole tail of night-revellers after him, who were taking his part, or the part of the Police, and were loudly debating the case. In the end a young Police Officer arrived, straight, I believe, from a gay party. He was a disappointment to Belknap, for he began to take down his report with the keenest interest and at a terrific speed, but then fell into deep thoughts, dragged his pencil slowly over the page and finally gave up writing and put his pencil back into his pocket. I was cold in the night air. At last we could drive home.

While I was still in bed the next morning, I felt, by the concentrated stillness outside the house, that there were many people about it. I knew who they were: the old men of the farm, squatting upon the stones, munching, sniffing their tobacco, spitting, and whispering. I also knew what they wanted: they had come to inform me that they wished to set a Kyama on the case of the shot of last night, and of the death of the children.

A Kyama is an assembly of the Elders of a farm, which is authorized by the Government to settle the local differences amongst the Squatters. The members of the Kyama gather round a crime, or an accident, and will sit over it for many weeks, battening upon mutton, talk, and disaster. I knew that now the old men would want to talk the whole matter over with me, and also that they would, if they could, in the end make me come into their court to give the final judgment in the case. I did not want to take up an endless discussion of the tragedy of the night, at this moment, and sent for my horse to get out and away from them.

As I came out from the house I found, as I expected, the whole circle of the Ancients to the left of it, near the boys' huts. For the sake of their own dignity as an assembly they pretended not to see me, until they realized that I was going away. They then stumbled on to their old legs in great haste, and began to flap their arms at me. I waved my hand to them in return, and rode off.

I rode into the Masai Reserve. I had to cross the river to get there;

riding on, I got into the Game Reserve in a quarter of an hour. It had
taken me some time, while I had lived on the farm, to find a place where
I could get over the river on horseback: the descent was stony, and the
slope up the other side very steep, but "once in, — how the delighted
spirit pants for joy".

Here lay before you a hundred miles' gallop over grass and open
undulating land; there was not a fence nor a ditch, and no road. There
was no human habitation except the Masai villages, and those were
deserted half the year, when the great wanderers took themselves and
their herds off to other pastures. There were low thorn trees regularly
spread over the plain, and long deep valleys with dry river-beds of big
flat stones, where you had to find a deer-path here and there to take you
across. After a little while you became aware of how still it was out
here. Now, looking back on my life in Africa, I feel that it might
altogether be described as the existence of a person who had come
from a rushed and noisy world, into a still country.

A little before the rains, the Masai burn off the old dry grass, and
while the plains are thus lying black and waste they are unpleasant to
travel on: you will get the black charred dust, which the hoofs of your
horse raise, all over you and into your eyes, and the burnt grass-stalks
are sharp as glass; your dogs get their feet cut on them. But when the
rains come, and the young green grass is fresh on the plains, you feel
as if riding upon springs, and the horse gets a little mad with the
pleasantness. The various kinds of gazelles come to the green places
to graze, and there look like toy animals stood upon a billiard table.
You may ride into a herd of Eland; the mighty peaceful beasts will
let you get close to them before they start trotting off, their long horns
streaming backwards over their raised necks, the large loose flaps of
breastskin, that make them look square, swaying as they jog. They
seem to have come out of an old Egyptian epitaph, but there they have
been ploughing the fields, which gives them a familiar and domesticated
air. The Giraffe keep farther away in the Reserve.

At times, in the first month of the rains, a sort of wild white fragrant
Pink flowers so richly all over the Reserve that at a distance the plains
look patched with snow.

I turned to the animal world from the world of men; my heart
was heavy with the tragedy of the night. . . .

As I was riding back to the farm, on crossing the river and actually in the water, I met a party of Kaninu's sons, three young men and a boy. They carried spears and came along quickly. When I stopped them and asked for news of their brother Kabero they stood, the water half way to their knees, with still set faces and downcast eyes; they spoke lowly. Kabero, they said, had not come back, and nothing had been heard of him since he had run away last night. They were now certain that he was dead. He would either have killed himself in his despair — since the idea of suicide comes very natural to all Natives, and even to Native children, — or he had been lost in the bush and the wild animals had eaten him. His brothers had been round looking for him in all directions, they were now on their way out into the Reserve to try to find him there.

When I came up the river-bank on my own land, I turned and looked out over the plain; my land was higher up than the land of the Reserve. There was no sign of life anywhere on the plain, except that a long way out the Zebra were grazing and galloping about. As the party of searchers emerged from the bush on the other side of the river, they went on quickly, walking one by one; their small group looked like a short caterpillar rapidly winding its way along on the grass. At times the sun glinted on their weapons. They seemed fairly confident of their direction, but what would it be? In their search for the lost child, their only guide would be the vultures that are always hanging in the sky above a dead body on the plain, and will give you the exact spot of a lion-kill.

But this would be only a very small body, not much of a feast for the gluttons of the air, there would not be many of them to spot it, nor would they be staying on for a very long time.

All this was sad to think of. I rode home.

꘏ FOR DISCUSSION AND WRITING

1. Does the rather long passage on the night and the stars at the beginning seem to you to have a function in relation to the central episode of the piece? If you look on this narrative, as it was suggested that you look on the one by T. E. Lawrence, as being formed by the perception or intuition of relationships among many things, the function of the opening paragraphs may become clearer. "The sky was serene and silently triumphant,

resplendent with stars": Where else in the piece do you get the sense of vast impersonality? of the radical and mysterious "otherness" of nature from the human? How are such perceptions related to the horror that strikes the children? Is the relationship single and static, or does its aspect change as one looks at it from a different direction? What is the effect of naming the great star names, prefatory to a shocking, senseless, and useless tragedy?

2. What does Dinesen mean by comparing the freedom of those who have dreams to "the freedom of the artist, who has no will, who is free of will"? Why does she follow the part on night and the stars with this part on dreams? Is it a merely random succession or is this part also indirectly related to the central incident? Notice that she likens both dreams and night in a big town to the African night because in all of these "things are going on, destinies are made round you, there is activity to all sides, and it is none of your concern"—then turns to the "destinies" being made by bats, night-hawks, hares, zebra, buffalo. How is it proper to use the word "destinies" for these creatures? Why is it important that all of this is "none of your concern"? Does the incident of the shooting accident, which is to come, in some sense *require* that the mind turn to stars, night, dreams, the mysterious activities of animals, to find perspective in things that, blessedly, do not involve human will or judgment or anguish—that are "none of your concern"? So also the young men of the farm going to their dance, and finally the lion's roar. Then a long breath, a space, and: "As I was standing before my house a shot fell, not far off. One shot." Does the long preface prepare a greater dramatic impact and tension for this new beginning, than if the narrative started here? Explain.

3. What is Kabero's "great gesture," and why is it "great"? Compare it, for instance, with Othello's last "gesture" (a speech):

> Set you down this;
> And say besides, that in Aleppo once,
> Where a malignant and a turban'd Turk
> Beat a Venetian and traduc'd the state,
> I took by th' throat the circumcised dog,
> And smote him, thus.   (*Stabs himself.*)

Can one say that Kabero's gesture is, in its own way, as "great" as Othello's?

4. When, in the next section, she tells of her ride into the Masai Reserve, and says, "I turned to the animal world from the world of men," what

motivation do you find in this action? What is the relationship with the intuitions with which the piece started? How does that relationship form a unifying structure for the narrative?

5. What, in the perspective established at the beginning, is the effect of the paragraph at the end: "But this would be only a very small body . . . nor would they be staying on for a very long time"? It seems little enough to say: "All this was sad to think of. I rode home." But is it best to let the landscape carry the implication?

6. There are evidently, even for young children, spontaneous situations like unpremeditated "tests" from which character emerges with strange clarity and finality. Probably no one escapes such tests, and they occur again and again. Can you adapt the idea of the "extreme situation" to some minor experience, of apparent ordinariness, and write a short paper showing how character was unexpectedly revealed?

Attitudes Toward Death

IN A STORY *by Lionel Trilling, a student sitting in the back of a classroom thinks, in a luminous cataleptic moment as the professor drones on: "Poor old guy, he's going to die pretty soon. But I will never die." This charming intimation of immortality we all knew once, though not perhaps with such candor. Jessica Mitford's* THE AMERICAN WAY OF DEATH *(from which the piece "Mortuary Solaces" is drawn) reveals the early illusion become in maturity a deceit practiced on death; though we may admit that we owe a death to nature, we have developed an elaborate machinery for taking the deathiness part out of it. To keep up with the Joneses in this affair is alarmingly expensive. Miss Mitford documents the material expense. But the costliness to instinct is incalculable. We are probably unique among civilizations in having robbed ourselves of our mysteries.*

The attitudes toward death shown in the other pieces in this section put in a more natural perspective that instinctive concern with our mortality which, despite morticians' cosmetics, occupies—with birth and love—our profoundest dreams and the greatest art and poetry we inherit. On his last afternoon spent with his students, before drinking the hemlock, Socrates again exercises his invincible charm, but this time the dialectic is for keeps. Sir Thomas Browne's URN BURIAL is one of the splendors of seventeenth-century English prose; if the student has a robust digestion for polysyllables, he is initiated into a ceremonious world of antique marvels where "the dead eat asphodels." Reflecting in Westminster Abbey, Joseph Addison improves with gentle irony on all our epitaphs, including that modest one of two terminal dates with only a hyphen between. The burning fountain that consumed Shelley is described by Trelawny, while Byron's behavior has the compulsive character of the primitive archimime, the clown within, who betrays us into buffoonery on our most solemn occasions. He used to wear a beak and a tail to certify him as an authentic member of the cast, and performed his atrocious antics between the strides of Death's tall black aristocratic legs. G. B. Shaw writes Mrs. Campbell how his mother would have enjoyed seeing her own pentecostal "garnet coloured lovely flame," and how, shaking with laughter when the cooks sieved and shook out her residua into a heap of dust and a heap of bone scraps, she wondered in his ear, "Which of the two heaps is me?" André Gide's journal-notes on the death of Charles-Louis Philippe are written with a loving fidelity that evokes, in the obscure mourning of a peasant village, all human loss and grief. These, too, are indispensable.

Plato ᴥᴈ The Death of Socrates

ᴥᴈ See note on Plato, page 139. Socrates, Plato's teacher, lived from 469 to 399 B.C. He did not leave any writings of his own but is immortalized through Plato's Socratic dialogues. (One has some first-hand information about him also through the *Memorabilia* of Xenophon, who was another of Socrates' pupils.) Evidently Plato's whole conception of philosophical communication and of what a teacher can do for a student derives from Socrates' performance; for Socrates' influence was entirely one of personal contact, and Plato, in an epistle, suggests that there is no really effective teaching except through the personality of the teacher. This would seem to have determined the form of Plato's own writings, that great invention of the dialogue for philosophical discourse; for, through this form, one has the experience of meeting the teacher directly, as a person.

The accusations brought against Socrates at his trial were that he corrupted the youth of the city and taught such abominations as that the moon was a stone instead of a goddess. These were merely transparent rationalizations of the city fathers to get rid of a man who endeavored to help young people to think—for thinking is always dangerous to the apathy and mental lethargy of the accepted status quo, and most dangerous to the power-group manipulating the status quo. Ꮆᴥ

ECHECRATES Were you yourself, Phaedo, in the prison with Socrates on the day when he drank the poison?

PHAEDO Yes, Echecrates, I was.

ECH I wish that you would tell me about his death. What did he say in his last hours? We were informed that he died by taking poison, but no one knew anything more. . . .

PHAED Did you not hear of the proceedings at the trial?

ECH Yes; some one told us about the trial, and we could not understand why, having been condemned, he was put to death, as [it] appeared, not at the time, but long afterwards. What was the reason of this?

PHAED An accident, Echecrates. The reason was that the stern of

From the *Phaedo* by Plato, translated by Benjamin Jowett (New York: Random House, 1937).

the ship which the Athenians send to Delos happened to have been crowned on the day before he was tried.

ECH   What is this ship?

PHAED   This is the ship in which, as the Athenians say, Theseus went to Crete when he took with him the fourteen youths,[1] and was the savior of them and of himself. And they were said to have vowed to Apollo at the time, that if they were saved they would make an annual pilgrimage to Delos. Now this custom still continues, and the whole period of the voyage to and from Delos, beginning when the priest of Apollo crowns the stern of the ship, is a holy season, during which the city is not allowed to be polluted by public executions; and often, when the vessel is detained by adverse winds, there may be a very considerable delay. As I was saying, the ship was crowned on the day before the trial, and this was the reason why Socrates lay in prison and was not put to death until long after he was condemned.

ECH   What was the manner of his death, Phaedo? What was said or done? And which of his friends had he with him? Or were they not allowed by the authorities to be present? And did he die alone?

PHAED   No; there were several of his friends with him.

ECH   If you have nothing to do, I wish that you would tell me what passed, as exactly as you can.

PHAED   I have nothing to do, and will try to gratify your wish. For to me too there is no greater pleasure than to have Socrates brought to my recollection; whether I speak myself or hear another speak of him.

ECH   You will have listeners who are of the same mind with you, and I hope that you will be as exact as you can.

PHAED   I remember the strange feeling which came over me at being with him. For I could hardly believe that I was present at the death of a friend, and therefore I did not pity him, Echecrates; his mien and his language were so noble and fearless in the hour of death that to me he appeared blessed. I thought that in going to the other world

---

[1] Apparently Athens had been, historically, under tribute to the Minoan dynasty of Crete. Theseus, the legendary hero of Athens, was said to have accompanied the ship bearing the annual tribute of youths and maidens to Crete — destined to fight in the bull ring, or, as the myth has it, to be sacrificed to the Minotaur (a creature half man, half bull). The reference that Plato makes is to the traditional ceremony commemorating Theseus' killing of the Minotaur and releasing Athens from paying tribute. A memorial ship was sent annually to Delos, where Apollo had an oracle. The "crowning" of the ship apparently refers to placing wreaths upon it.

he could not be without a divine call, and that he would be happy, if any man ever was, when he arrived there; and therefore I did not pity him as might seem natural at such a time. But neither could I feel the pleasure which I usually felt in philosophical discourse (for philosophy was the theme of which we spoke). I was pleased and I was also pained, because I knew that he was soon to die, and this strange mixture of feeling was shared by us all; we were laughing and weeping by turns. . . .

ECH   And what was the discourse of which you spoke?

PHAED   I will begin at the beginning, and endeavor to repeat the entire conversation. . . .

[Phaedo tells of the gathering of Socrates' friends and favorite pupils in the cell on the last day. Those brought into the dialogue are Crito, Simmias, Cebes, and Apollodorus (Plato was not there — he is said to have been ill). Socrates leads them into a discussion of the nature of the soul and of why the philosopher does not fear death. But first Crito brings him a message from the jail attendant.]

You must first let me hear what Crito wants; he was going to say something to me.

Only this, Socrates, replied Crito: — the attendant who is to give you the poison has been telling me that you are not to talk much, and he wants me to let you know this; for that by talking, heat is increased, and this interferes with the action of the poison; those who excite themselves are sometimes obliged to drink the poison two or three times.

Then, said Socrates, let him mind his business and be prepared to give the poison two or three times, if necessary; that is all.

I was almost certain that you would say that, replied Crito; but I was obliged to satisfy him.

Never mind him, he said.

And now I will make answer to you, O my judges, and show that he who has lived as a true philosopher has reason to be of good cheer when he is about to die, and that after death he may hope to receive the greatest good in the other world. And how this may be, Simmias and Cebes, I will endeavor to explain. For I deem that the true disciple of philosophy is likely to be misunderstood by other men; they do not perceive that he is ever pursuing death and dying; and if this is true, why, having had the desire of death all his life long, should he repine at the arrival of that which he has been always pursuing and desiring?

Simmias laughed and said: Though not in a laughing humor, I swear that I can not help laughing, when I think what the wicked world will say when they hear this. They will say that this is very true, and our people at home will agree with them in saying that the life which philosophers desire is truly death, and that they have found them out to be deserving of the death which they desire.

And they are right, Simmias, in saying this, with the exception of the words "they have found them out;" for they have not found out what is the nature of this death which the true philosopher desires, or how he deserves or desires death. But let us leave them and have a word with ourselves: Do we believe that there is such a thing as death?

To be sure, replied Simmias.

And is this anything but the separation of soul and body? And being dead is the attainment of this separation when the soul exists in herself, and is parted from the body and the body is parted from the soul — that is death?

Exactly: that and nothing else, he replied.

And what do you say of another question, my friend, about which I should like to have your opinion, and the answer to which will probably throw light on our present inquiry: Do you think that the philosopher ought to care about the pleasures — if they are to be called pleasures — of eating and drinking?

Certainly not, answered Simmias.

And what do you say of the pleasures of love — should he care about them?

By no means.

And will he think much of the other ways of indulging the body, for example, the acquisition of costly raiment, or sandals or other adornments of the body? Instead of caring about them, does he not rather despise anything more than nature needs? What do you say?

I should say that the true philosopher would despise them.

Would you not say that he is entirely concerned with the soul and not with the body? He would like, as far as he can, to be quit of the body and turn to the soul.

That is true.

In matters of this sort philosophers, above all other men, may be observed in every sort of way to dissever the soul from the body.

That is true.

Whereas, Simmias, the rest of the world are of opinion that a life which has no bodily pleasures and no part in them is not worth having; but that he who thinks nothing of bodily pleasures is almost as though he were dead.

That is quite true.

What again shall we say of the actual acquirement of knowledge? — is the body, if invited to share in the inquiry, a hinderer or a helper? I mean to say, have sight and hearing any truth in them? Are they not, as the poets are always telling us, inaccurate witnesses? and yet, if even they are inaccurate and indistinct, what is to be said of the other senses? — for you will allow that they are the best of them?

Certainly, he replied.

Then when does the soul attain truth? — for in attempting to consider anything in company with the body she is obviously deceived.

Yes, that is true.

Then must not existence be revealed to her in thought, if at all?

Yes.

And thought is best when the mind is gathered into herself and none of these things trouble her — neither sounds nor sights nor pain nor any pleasure, — when she has as little as possible to do with the body, and has no bodily sense or feeling, but is aspiring after being?

That is true.

And in this the philosopher dishonors the body; his soul runs away from the body and desires to be alone and by herself?

That is true.

Well, but there is another thing, Simmias: Is there or is there not an absolute justice?

Assuredly there is.

And an absolute beauty and absolute good?

Of course.

But did you ever behold any of them with your eyes?

Certainly not.

Or did you ever reach them with any other bodily sense? (and I speak not of these alone, but of absolute greatness, and health, and strength, and of the essence or true nature of everything). Has the reality of them ever been perceived by you through the bodily organs? or rather, is not the nearest approach to the knowledge of their several natures made by him who so orders his intellectual vision as to have the most exact conception of the essence of that which he considers?

Certainly.

And he attains to the knowledge of them in their highest purity who goes to each of them with the mind alone, not allowing when in the act of thought the intrusion or introduction of sight or any other sense in the company of reason, but with the very light of the mind in her clearness penetrates into the very light of truth in each; he has got rid, as far as he can, of eyes and ears and of the whole body, which he conceives of only as a disturbing element, hindering the soul from the acquisition of knowledge when in company with her — is not this the sort of man who, if ever man did, is likely to attain the knowledge of existence?

There is admirable truth in that, Socrates, replied Simmias.

And when they consider all this, must not true philosophers make a reflection, of which they will speak to one another in such words as these: We have found, they will say, a path of speculation which seems to bring us and the argument to the conclusion, that while we are in the body, and while the soul is mingled with this mass of evil, our desire will not be satisfied, and our desire is of the truth. For the body is a source of endless trouble to us by reason of the mere requirement of food; and also is liable to diseases which overtake and impede us in the search after truth: and by filling us as full of loves, and lusts, and fears, and fancies, and idols, and every sort of folly, prevents our ever having, as people say, so much as a thought. For whence come wars, and fightings, and factions? whence but from the body and the lusts of the body? For wars are occasioned by the love of money, and money has to be acquired for the sake and in the service of the body; and in consequence of all these things the time which ought to be given to philosophy is lost. Moreover, if there is time and an inclination towards philosophy, yet the body introduces a turmoil and confusion and fear into the course of speculation, and hinders us from seeing the truth; and all experience shows that if we would have pure knowledge of anything we must be quit of the body, and the soul in herself must behold all things in themselves: then, I suppose, that we shall attain that which we desire, and of which we say that we are lovers, and that is wisdom; not while we live, but after death, as the argument shows; for if while in company with the body, the soul can not have pure knowledge, one of two things seems to follow — either knowledge is not be to attained at all, or, if at all, after death. For then, and not till then, the soul will be in herself alone and without the body. In this present life, I reckon that we make the nearest approach to knowledge when we have the least possible concern or interest in the body, and are not saturated with the bodily nature, but remain pure until the hour when God himself is pleased to release us. And then the foolishness of the body will be cleared away and we shall be pure and hold converse with other pure souls, and know of ourselves the clear light everywhere; and this is surely the light of truth. For no impure thing is allowed to approach the pure. These are the sort of words, Simmias, which the true lovers of wisdom can not help saying to one another, and thinking. You will agree with me in that?

Certainly, Socrates.

But if this is true, O my friend, then there is great hope that, going whither I go, I shall there be satisfied with that which has been the chief concern of you and me in our past lives. And now that the hour of departure is appointed to me, this is the hope with which I depart, and not I only, but every man who believes that he has his mind purified.

Certainly, replied Simmias.

And what is purification but the separation of the soul from the body, as I was saying before; the habit of the soul gathering and collecting herself into herself, out of all the courses of the body; the dwelling in her own place alone, as in another life, so also in this, as far as she can; — the release of the soul from the chains of the body?

Very true, he said.

And what is that which is termed death, but this very separation and release of the soul from the body?

To be sure, he said.

And the true philosophers, and they only, study and are eager to release the soul. Is not the separation and release of the soul from the body their especial study?

That is true.

And, as I was saying at first, there would be a ridiculous contradiction in men studying to live as nearly as they can in a state of death, and yet repining when death comes.

Certainly.

Then Simmias, as the true philosophers are ever studying death, to them, of all men, death is the least terrible. . . . Wherefore, I say, let a man be of good cheer about his soul, who has cast away the pleasures and ornaments of the body as alien to him, and rather hurtful in their effects, and has followed after the pleasures of knowledge in this life; who has adorned the soul in her own proper jewels, which are temperance, and justice, and courage, and nobility, and truth — in these arrayed she is ready to go on her journey to the world below,[2] when her time comes. You, Simmias and Cebes, and all other men, will depart at some time or other. Me already, as the tragic poet would say, the voice of fate calls. Soon I must drink the poison; and I think that I had better repair to the bath first, in order that the women may not have the trouble of washing my body after I am dead.

When he had done speaking, Crito said: And have you any commands for us, Socrates — anything to say about your children, or any other matter in which we can serve you?

Nothing particular, he said: only, as I have always told you, I would have you look to yourselves; that is a service which you may always be doing to me and mine as well as to yourselves. And you need not make professions;[3] for if you take no thought for yourselves, and walk not according to the precepts which I have given you, not now for the first time, the warmth of your professions will be of no avail.

We will do our best, said Crito. But in what way would you have us bury you?

In any way that you like; only you must get hold of me, and take care that I do not walk away from you. Then he turned to us, and added with a smile: — I can not make Crito believe that I am the same Socrates who has been talking and conducting the argument; he fancies that I am the other Socrates whom he will soon see, a dead body — and he asks, How shall he bury me? And though I have spoken many words in the endeavor to show that when I have drunk the poison I shall leave you and go to the joys of the blessed, — these words of mine, with which I comforted you and myself, have had, as I perceive, no effect upon Crito. And therefore I want you to be surety for me now, as he was surety for me at the trial: but let the promise be of another sort; for he was my surety to the judges that I would remain, but you must be my surety to him that I shall not remain, but go away and

[2] Hades, the abode of the dead.
[3] Assert any beliefs.

depart; and then he will suffer less at my death, and not be grieved when he sees my body being burned or buried. I would not have him sorrow at my hard lot, or say at the burial, Thus we lay out Socrates, or, Thus we follow him to the grave or bury him; for false words are not only evil in themselves, but they infect the soul with evil. Be of good cheer, then, my dear Crito, and say that you are burying my body only, and do with that as is usual, and as you think best.

When he had spoken these words, he arose and went into the bath-chamber with Crito, who bid us wait; and we waited, talking and thinking of the subject of discourse, and also of the greatness of our sorrow; he was like a father of whom we were being bereaved, and we were about to pass the rest of our lives as orphans. When he had taken the bath his children were brought to him — (he had two young sons and an elder one); and the women of his family also came, and he talked to them and gave them a few directions in the presence of Crito; and he then dismissed them and returned to us.

Now the hour of sunset was near, for a good deal of time had passed while he was within. When he came out, he sat down with us again after his bath, but not much was said. Soon the jailer, who was the servant of the eleven,[4] entered and stood by him, saying: — To you, Socrates, whom I know to be the noblest and gentlest and best of all who ever came to this place, I will not impute the angry feelings of other men, who rage and swear at me, when, in obedience to the authorities, I bid them drink the poison — indeed, I am sure that you will not be angry with me; for others, as you are aware, and not I, are the guilty cause. And so fare you well, and try to bear lightly what must needs be; you know my errand. Then bursting into tears he turned away and went out.

Socrates looked at him and said: I return your good wishes, and will do as you bid. Then turning to us, he said, How charming the man is: since I have been in prison he has always been coming to see me, and at times he would talk to me, and was as good as could be to me, and now see how generously he sorrows for me. But we must do as he says, Crito; let the cup be brought, if the poison is prepared: if not, let the attendant prepare some.

Yet, said Crito, the sun is still upon the hill-tops, and many a one has taken the draught late, and after the announcement has been made

[4] Civic penal officers.

to him, he has eaten and drunk, and indulged in sensual delights; do not hasten then, there is still time.

Socrates said: Yes, Crito, and they of whom you speak are right in doing thus, for they think that they will gain by the delay; but I am right in not doing thus, for I do not think that I should gain anything by drinking the poison a little later; I should be sparing and saving a life which is already gone; I could only laugh at myself for this. Please then to do as I say, and not to refuse me.

Crito, when he heard this, made a sign to the servant; and the servant went in, and remained for some time, and then returned with the jailer carrying the cup of poison. Socrates said: You, my good friend, who are experienced in these matters, shall give me directions how I am to proceed. The man answered: You have only to walk about until your legs are heavy, and then to lie down, and the poison will act. At the same time he handed the cup to Socrates, who in the easiest and gentlest manner, without the least fear or change of color or feature, looking at the man with all his eyes, Echecrates, as his manner was, took the cup and said: What do you say about making a libation out of this cup to any god? May I, or not? The man answered: We only prepare, Socrates, just so much as we deem enough. I understand, he said: yet I may and must pray to the gods to prosper my journey from this to that other world — may this then, which is my prayer, be granted to me. Then holding the cup to his lips, quite readily and cheerfully he drank off the poison. And hitherto most of us had been able to control our sorrow; but now when we saw him drinking, and saw too that he had finished the draught, we could no longer forbear, and in spite of myself my own tears were flowing fast; so that I covered my face and wept over myself, for certainly I was not weeping over him, but at the thought of my own calamity in having lost such a companion. Nor was I the first, for Crito, when he found himself unable to restrain his tears, had got up and moved away, and I followed; and at that moment, Apollodorus, who had been weeping all the time, broke out into a loud cry which made cowards of us all. Socrates alone retained his calmness: What is this strange outcry? he said. I sent away the women mainly in order that they might not offend in this way, for I have heard that a man should die in peace. Be quiet then, and have patience. When we heard that, we were ashamed, and refrained our tears; and he walked about until, as he said, his legs began to fail, and then he lay on his back, according to the directions, and the man who gave him the poison now and then looked at his feet and legs; and after a while he pressed his foot hard, and asked him if he could feel; and he said, No; and then his leg, and so upwards and upwards, and showed us that he was cold and stiff. And he felt then himself and said: When the poison reaches the heart, that will be the end. He was beginning to grow cold about the groin, when he uncovered his face, for he had covered himself up, and said (they were his last words) — he said: Crito, I owe a cock to Asclepius;[5] will you remember to pay the debt? The debt shall be paid, said Crito; is there anything else? There was no answer to this question; but in a minute or two a movement was heard, and the attendants uncovered him; his eyes were set, and Crito closed his eyes and mouth.

Such was the end, Echecrates, of our friend, whom I may truly call the wisest, and justest, and best of all men whom I have ever known.

⋟ FOR DISCUSSION AND WRITING

1. We considered the narrative "point of view" a number of times in the first section of this book. In some of the Socratic dialogues, Plato contrives a fairly intricate handling of the "point of view." Note how he switches here from the straight dramatic dialogue between Phaedo and Echecrates ("dramatic" in the sense that this is the method of drama) to the "point of view" of Phaedo as narrator of what happened in Socrates' cell, although Phaedo's narration remains close to the method of dramatic dialogue. Thus, while we are given the illusion of overhearing what went on, everything is actually filtered through or reflected by the attitudes of those who knew and loved Socrates. Why, considering the subject matter, is this fairly complicated contrivance of "point of view" useful and valuable here?

2. Look up the following words in a large Webster's or Oxford dictionary (the smaller, collegiate dictionaries do not amplify the definitions adequately): "dialectic"—making sure you get Plato's use of the word;

---

[5] Socrates has evidently just remembered that he had promised the offering of a cock to the god of medicine and healing, Asclepius, who had a shrine on the Acropolis of Athens.

"maieutic," as applied to a method of teaching; and "Socratic," also as applied to a method of discussion and teaching. If you aren't sure of the word "deduction," look that up too. Now apply each of these words to the central discussion that takes place in this piece, making ready a specific statement as to each application (best done by writing the statement down). That is, how does the discussion exhibit dialectic? and so on, with each of the given terms.

3. Recapitulate in a sentence outline the main steps of the discussion (since the steps are few, this will be a short outline). Now make a note in the margin of your outline as to what is the major premise of the argument (if you aren't sure what a "premise" is, look that up too). Make another marginal note indicating what is the final deduction. Is the argument logically sound? What criticism would you make of the major premise?

4. (In the following questions, avoid the unthinking confusion of projecting upon Socrates some sort of religious attitude vaguely associated with Christianity, since he died 400 years before the birth of Christ.) Why does Socrates say that the "true disciple of philosophy" is "ever pursuing death and dying"? How does he define death? What does he mean by "soul"? Where do you find him making a radical distinction between "soul" and "body"? What has modern psychology done to that distinction? and modern medicine?

5. Why does he say that the body is a hindrance to philosophical study? What does he mean by "truth"? by the "knowledge of existence"? by "the essence or true nature of everything"? by "reality"? by "absolute justice," "absolute beauty," etc.? (Obviously you can't deal with these questions as a scholar of Plato would, but only on the basis of the present dialogue—although the selection from the *Symposium*, given earlier, would be a help. On the other hand, you may think such questions a frivolous waste of time, irrelevant to the practical matters in life, such as, for instance, how to earn a living when you graduate. But the huge problems in ideology, politics, civil rights issues, that we confront today should be adequate witness to the importance of understanding what we *mean* by the general terms that we constantly use—an importance quite as vital now as Socrates felt it to be in the Athens of his time.)

6. Consider the use of the terms "soul," "thought," "mind," "intellectual vision," and "knowledge," in the following quotations: 1) "Then when does the soul attain truth?" 2) "And thought is best when the mind is gathered

into herself. . . ." 3) ". . . him who so orders his intellectual vision as to have the most exact conception of the essence of that which he considers." 4) "And he attains to the knowledge of them in their highest purity who goes to each of them with the mind alone. . . ." Find the context of each of the quotations so that the references are clear. Which of the terms seem to mean the same thing?

7. Turning from the argument to the quality of the whole piece, what makes this picture of Socrates' last day so moving? How would you describe the character and personality of Socrates as shown here? The last words of famous people are always of interest in one way or another. What odd little sidelight on Socrates do you find in his last words?

8. Since college is a place for argument, the next time you find yourself in an informal argumentative session, watch its procedure, especially the kind of use that is made of general terms and the confusions and cross-purposes that arise therefrom; try to reproduce the discussion, as accurately as you can remember it, on paper as a theme assignment. Or set up a situation in which you yourself use the maieutic method, and reproduce on paper what happens. Or you might write a short paper—it might well be a humorous one—on the troubles the student's body makes for the student's mind.

Jessica Mitford ✑ Mortuary Solaces

✑ The author was born in England in 1918 and is a sister of the satirical novelist, Nancy Mitford. She is married to an American lawyer and lives in Oakland, California. Her autobiography appeared in 1960, entitled *Daughters and Rebels*. ⮞

EMBALMING is indeed a most extraordinary procedure, and one must wonder at the docility of Americans who each year pay hundreds of millions of dollars for its perpetuation, blissfully ignorant of what it is all about, what is done, how it is done. Not one in ten thousand has any idea of what actually takes place. Books on the subject are extremely hard to come by. They are not to be found in most libraries or bookshops.

In an era when huge television audiences watch surgical operations in the comfort of their living rooms, when, thanks to the animated cartoon, the geography of the digestive system has become familiar territory even to the nursery school set, in a land where the satisfaction of curiosity about almost all matters is a national pastime, the secrecy surrounding embalming can, surely, hardly be attributed to the inherent

gruesomeness of the subject. Custom in this regard has within this
century suffered a complete reversal. In the early days of American
embalming, when it was performed in the home of the deceased, it was
almost mandatory for some relative to stay by the embalmer's side and
witness the procedure. Today, family members who might wish to be
in attendance would certainly be dissuaded by the funeral director.
All others, except apprentices, are excluded by law from the preparation
room.

A close look at what does actually take place may explain in large
measure the undertaker's intractable reticence concerning a procedure
that has become his major *raison d'être*. Is it possible he fears that public
information about embalming might lead patrons to wonder if they
really want this service? If the funeral men are loath to discuss the
subject outside the trade, the reader may, understandably, be equally
loath to go on reading at this point. For those who have the stomach
for it, let us part the formaldehyde curtain. . . .

The body is first laid out in the undertaker's morgue — or rather,
Mr. Jones is reposing in the preparation room — to be readied to bid
the world farewell.

The preparation room in any of the better funeral establishments
has the tiled and sterile look of a surgery, and indeed the embalmer-
restorative artist who does his chores there is beginning to adopt the
term "dermasurgeon" (appropriately corrupted by some mortician-
writers as "demisurgeon") to describe his calling. His equipment, consisting of scalpels, scissors, augurs, forceps, clamps, needles, pumps,
tubes, bowls and basins, is crudely imitative of the surgeon's as is his
technique, acquired in a nine- or twelve-month post-high-school course
in an embalming school. He is supplied by an advanced chemical
industry with a bewildering array of fluids, sprays, pastes, oils, powders,
creams, to fix or soften tissue, shrink or distend it as needed, dry it here,
restore the moisture there. There are cosmetics, waxes and paints to
fill and cover features, even plaster of Paris to replace entire limbs.
There are ingenious aids to prop and stabilize the cadaver: a Vari-Pose
Head Rest, the Edwards Arm and Hand Positioner, the Repose Block
(to support the shoulders during the embalming), and the Throop
Foot Positioner, which resembles an old-fashioned stocks.

Mr. John H. Eckels, president of the Eckels College of Mortuary
Science, thus describes the first part of the embalming procedure: "In

the hands of a skilled practitioner, this work may be done in a comparatively short time and without mutilating the body other than by slight incision — so slight that it scarcely would cause serious inconvenience if made upon a living person. It is necessary to remove the blood, and doing this not only helps in the disinfecting, but removes the principal cause of disfigurements due to discoloration."

Another textbook discusses the all-important time element: "The earlier this is done, the better, for every hour that elapses between death and embalming will add to the problems and complications encountered. . . ." Just how soon should one get going on the embalming? The author tells us, "On the basis of such scanty information made available to this profession through its rudimentary and haphazard system of technical research, we must conclude that the best results are to be obtained if the subject is embalmed before life is completely extinct — that is, before cellular death has occurred. In the average case, this would mean within an hour after somatic death." For those who feel that there is something a little rudimentary, not to say haphazard, about this advice, a comforting thought is offered by another writer. Speaking of fears entertained in early days of premature burial, he points out, "One of the effects of embalming by chemical injection, however, has been to dispel fears of live burial." How true; once the blood is removed, chances of live burial are indeed remote.

To return to Mr. Jones, the blood is drained out through the veins and replaced by embalming fluid pumped in through the arteries. As noted in *The Principles and Practices of Embalming*, "every operator has a favorite injection and drainage point — a fact which becomes a handicap only if he fails or refuses to forsake his favorites when conditions demand it." Typical favorites are the carotid artery, femoral artery, jugular vein, subclavian vein. There are various choices of embalming fluid. If Flextone is used, it will produce a "mild, flexible rigidity. The skin retains a velvety softness, the tissues are rubbery and pliable. Ideal for women and children." It may be blended with B. and G. Products Company's Lyf-Lyk tint, which is guaranteed to reproduce "nature's own skin texture . . . the velvety appearance of living tissue." Suntone comes in three separate tints: Suntan; Special Cosmetic Tint, a pink shade "especially indicated for young female subjects"; and Regular Cosmetic Tint, moderately pink.

About three to six gallons of a dyed and perfumed solution of formaldehyde, glycerin, borax, phenol, alcohol and water is soon circulating through Mr. Jones, whose mouth has been sewn together with a "needle directed upward between the upper lip and gum and brought out through the left nostril," with the corners raised slightly "for a more pleasant expression." If he should be bucktoothed, his teeth are cleaned with Bon Ami and coated with colorless nail polish. His eyes, meanwhile, are closed with flesh-tinted eye caps and eye cement.

The next step is to have at Mr. Jones with a thing called a trocar. This is a long, hollow needle attached to a tube. It is jabbed into the abdomen, poked around the entrails and chest cavity, the contents of which are pumped out and replaced with "cavity fluid." This done, and the hole in the abdomen sewn up, Mr. Jones's face is heavily creamed (to protect the skin from burns which may be caused by leakage of the chemicals), and he is covered with a sheet and left unmolested for a while. But not for long — there is more, much more, in store for him. He has been embalmed, but not yet restored, and the best time to start the restorative work is eight to ten hours after embalming, when the tissues have become firm and dry.

The object of all this attention to the corpse, it must be remembered, is to make it presentable for viewing in an attitude of healthy repose. "Our customs require the presentation of our dead in the semblance of normality . . . unmarred by the ravages of illness, disease or mutilation," says Mr. J. Sheridan Mayer in his *Restorative Art*. This is rather a large order since few people die in the full bloom of health, unravaged by illness and unmarked by some disfigurement. The funeral industry is equal to the challenge: "In some cases the gruesome appearance of a mutilated or disease-ridden subject may be quite discouraging. The task of restoration may seem impossible and shake the confidence of the embalmer. This is the time for intestinal fortitude and determination. Once the formative work is begun and affected tissues are cleaned or removed, all doubts of success vanish. It is surprising and gratifying to discover the results which may be obtained."

The embalmer, having allowed an appropriate interval to elapse, returns to the attack, but now he brings into play the skill and equipment of sculptor and cosmetician. Is a hand missing? Casting one in plaster of Paris is a simple matter. "For replacement purposes, only a cast of the back of the hand is necessary; this is within the ability of the average operator and is quite adequate." If a lip or two, a nose or an ear should be missing, the embalmer has at hand a variety of restorative waxes with which to model replacements. Pores and skin texture are simulated by stippling with a little brush, and over this cosmetics are laid on. Head off? Decapitation cases are rather routinely handled. Ragged edges are trimmed, and head joined to torso with a series of splints, wires and sutures. It is a good idea to have a little something at the neck — a scarf or high collar — when time for viewing comes. Swollen mouth? Cut out tissue as needed from inside the lips. If too much is removed, the surface contour can easily be restored by padding with cotton. Swollen necks and cheeks are reduced by removing tissue through vertical incisions made down each side of the neck. "When the deceased is casketed, the pillow will hide the suture incisions . . . as an extra precaution against leakage, the suture may be painted with liquid sealer."

The opposite condition is more likely to present itself — that of emaciation. His hypodermic syringe now loaded with massage cream, the embalmer seeks out and fills the hollowed and sunken areas by injection. In this procedure the backs of the hands and fingers and the under-chin area should not be neglected.

Positioning the lips is a problem that recurrently challenges the ingenuity of the embalmer. Closed too tightly, they tend to give a stern, even disapproving expression. Ideally, embalmers feel, the lips should give the impression of being ever so slightly parted, the upper lip protruding slightly for a more youthful appearance. This takes some engineering, however, as the lips tend to drift apart. Lip drift can sometimes be remedied by pushing one or two straight pins through the inner margin of the lower lip and then inserting them between the two front upper teeth. If Mr. Jones happens to have no teeth, the pins can just as easily be anchored in his Armstrong Face Former and Denture Replacer. Another method to maintain lip closure is to dislocate the lower jaw, which is then held in its new position by a wire run through holes which have been drilled through the upper and lower jaws at the midline. As the French are fond of saying, *il faut souffrir pour être belle.*[1]

If Mr. Jones has died of jaundice, the embalming fluid will very likely turn him green. Does this deter the embalmer? Not if he has intestinal fortitude. Masking pastes and cosmetics are heavily laid on,

[1] You have to suffer if you want to be beautiful.

burial garments and casket interiors are color-correlated with particular care, and Jones is displayed beneath rose-colored lights. Friends will say, "How *well* he looks." Death by carbon monoxide, on the other hand, can be rather a good thing from the embalmer's viewpoint: "One advantage is the fact that this type of discoloration is an exaggerated form of a natural pink coloration." This is nice because the healthy glow is already present and needs but little attention.

The patching and filling completed, Mr. Jones is now shaved, washed and dressed. Cream-based cosmetic, available in pink, flesh, suntan, brunette and blond, is applied to his hands and face, his hair is shampooed and combed (and, in the case of Mrs. Jones, set), his hands manicured. For the horny-handed son of toil special care must be taken; cream should be applied to remove ingrained grime, and the nails cleaned. "If he were not in the habit of having them manicured in life, trimming and shaping is advised for better appearance — never questioned by kin."

Jones is now ready for casketing (this is the present participle of the verb "to casket"). In this operation his right shoulder should be depressed slightly "to turn the body a bit to the right and soften the appearance of lying flat on the back." Positioning the hands is a matter of importance, and special rubber positioning blocks may be used. The hands should be cupped slightly for a more lifelike, relaxed appearance. Proper placement of the body requires a delicate sense of balance. It should lie as high as possible in the casket, yet not so high that the lid, when lowered, will hit the nose. On the other hand, we are cautioned, placing the body too low "creates the impression that the body is in a box."

Jones is next wheeled into the appointed slumber room where a few last touches may be added — his favorite pipe placed in his hand or, if he was a great reader, a book propped into position. (In the case of little Master Jones a Teddy bear may be clutched.) Here he will hold open house for a few days, visiting hours 10 A.M. to 9 P.M.

✎ҙ FOR DISCUSSION AND WRITING

1. The ancient Egyptian practice of embalming was directly tied up with Egyptian religious belief in immortality. The dead person needed his body intact in the other world, where he had first to encounter many dangers

—the forces of darkness and corruption, the danger of having his mouth crammed full of dirt (an easily imaginable supposition), of losing his way in the labyrinth of the grave, of being devoured by worms and snakes —before meeting with his divine judges, having his heart weighed in a balance, and being accepted by the immortals as a newly risen "Osiris" (for he then became like the god). For all these events he had to have mobile limbs, be able to breathe and speak and eat and think. (The rituals he had to learn by heart, to use in the other world, are found in the Egyptian *Book of the Dead*; a good copy has also interesting illustrations of these matters, taken from ancient papyri and tomb engravings. You might like to see what Herodotus has to say about Egyptian embalming, page 486 of this book.) Does American embalming have a religious purpose? What is its purpose?

2. More clearly than any other of the readings so far, the Mitford piece has a distinct and easily definable *tone:* how would you characterize the tone? By what specific elements of the writing is that tone conveyed?

3. Mitford uses a great many direct quotations from undertakers' manuals, and these, of course, give the piece a sound research base and carry the conviction of validity. But is simple information the main purpose and effect of the quotations? What conspicuous effect do they have on our critical judgment of the proceedings described?

4. Compare some of Mitford's own phrases—such as "Just how soon should one get going . . ." and "The next step is to have at Mr. Jones . . ."—with the kind of writing used in the manuals. What, specifically, is the contrast? and what is its effect? How, in general, would you characterize the writing in the manuals? as "dignified"? as "specious"? as "euphemistic"? as "jargon"? Give examples. Try to define the purpose of that kind of writing— for it certainly has a definite psychological purpose.

5. Analyze the effect of the following: 1) ". . . . we must conclude that the best results are to be obtained if the subject is embalmed before life is completely extinct. . . ." 2) "One of the effects of embalming by chemical injection, however, has been to dispel fears of live burial." And Mitford's comment: "How true . . ." 3) ". . . Lyf-Lyk tint, which is guaranteed to reproduce 'nature's own skin texture . . .' " (with Suntan, among other tints, in case you haven't been able to get a good sun tan before dying). 4) "About three to six gallons of . . . formaldehyde, glycerin, borax, phenol, alcohol and water is soon circulating through Mr. Jones, whose mouth has been

sewn together with a 'needle directed upward between the upper lip and
gum and brought out through the left nostril,' with the corners raised
slightly 'for a more pleasant expression.' If he should be bucktoothed, his
teeth are cleaned with Bon Ami and coated with colorless nail polish."
5) " 'This is the time for intestinal fortitude. . . .' " 6) "Head off? Decapitation cases are rather routinely handled." 7) "Death by carbon monoxide, on the other hand, can be rather a good thing from the embalmer's
viewpoint: 'One advantage is. . . .' "

6. We have the expression "gallows humor"; do you find something of the
   sort in the preceding examples? Irony, of course, is rampant throughout
   the piece. By what specific technique is the ironic effect produced?

7. Here is a final quotation: regarding the placement of the body in the
   casket, "On the other hand, we are cautioned, placing the body too low
   'creates the impression that the body is in a box.' " This seems to contain
   in a nutshell the whole ghastly irony and idiocy of the procedure. Why?

8. In a short paper, describe from your own experience certain funeral procedures as you may have witnessed them. Or obtain descriptions from
   other people; for instance, from people of a different religious denomination, or from older members of your family who may have known a
   different tradition with regard to death and burial. Or if you have a friend
   who is a "mortician," get him to read the Mitford piece and write up his
   reactions. Or write your own considered appreciation or criticism of
   American conventions in this immensely significant area of behavior, showing, if you can, their relationship with other aspects of our culture.

Sir Thomas Browne *The Dead Eat Asphodels

*English physician and scholar in many fields (1605-1682). As a doctor, he practiced in London for the greater part of his life. He was learned in philosophy, astronomy, and ornithology, and was master of six languages. The writing of the *Urn Burial*, from which the present selection is taken, was occasioned by the discovery in Norwich of a number of Roman funerary urns. His other famous work is the *Religio Medici*.*

BEFORE Plato could speak, the soul had wings in Homer, which fell not, but flew out of the body into the mansions of the dead; who also observed that handsome distinction of Demas and Soma, for the body conjoined to the soul, and body separated from it. Lucian spoke much truth in jest, when he said that part of Hercules which proceeded from Alcmena perished, that from Jupiter remained immortal.[1] Thus Socrates was content that his friends should bury his body, so they would not think they buried Socrates; and, regarding only his immortal part, was indifferent to be burnt or buried. From such considerations, Diogenes[2] might contemn sepulture, and, being satisfied that the soul

From *Hydriotaphia, or Urn Burial* by Sir Thomas Browne (first published in 1658).

[1] Lucian was a Greek prose satirist of the second century B.C. Alcmena, Hercules' mother, was mortal.

[2] Greek cynic philosopher of the fifth century B.C.

could not perish, grow careless of corporal interment. The Stoicks, who thought the souls of wise men had their habitation about the moon, might make slight account of subterraneous deposition; whereas the Pythagoreans and transcorporating philosophers, who were to be often buried, held great care of their interment. And the Platonicks rejected not a due care of the grave, though they put their ashes to unreasonable expectations, in their tedious term of return and long set revolution. . . .[3]

That, in strewing their tombs, the Romans affected the rose; the Greeks amaranthus and myrtle: that the funeral pyre consisted of sweet fuel, cypress, fir, larix, yew, and trees perpetually verdant, lay silent expressions of their surviving hopes. Wherein Christians, who deck their coffins with bays, have found a more elegant emblem; for that it, seeming dead, will restore itself from the root, and its dry and exsuccous leaves resume their verdure again; which, if we mistake not, we have also observed in furze. Whether the planting of yew in churchyards hold not its original from ancient funeral rites, or as an emblem of resurrection, from its perpetual verdure, may also admit conjecture. . . .

They[4] burnt not children before their teeth appeared, as apprehending their bodies too tender a morsel for fire, and that their gristly bones would scarce leave separable relicks after the pyral combustion. That they kindled not fire in their houses for some days after was a strict memorial of the late afflicting fire. And mourning without hope, they had an happy fraud against excessive lamentation, by a common opinion that deep sorrows disturb their ghosts.

That they buried their dead on their backs, or in a supine position, seems agreeable unto profound sleep, and common posture of dying; contrary to the most natural way of birth; nor unlike our pendulous posture, in the doubtful state of the womb. Diogenes was singular, who preferred a prone situation in the grave; and some Christians like neither, who decline the figure of rest, and make choice of an erect posture.

That they carried them out of the world with their feet forward, not inconsonant unto reason, as contrary unto the native posture of

---

[3] The Stoics were a school of philosophy founded by Zeno around 308 B.C. The Pythagoreans were followers of Pythagoras, sixth-century philosopher, who believed in the transmigration of souls. "The Platonicks" is evidently a reference to a neo-Platonic conception of a 2,000-year cycle when all things began again.

[4] The ancients.

man, and his production first into it; and also agreeable unto their opinions, while they bid adieu unto the world, not to look again upon it; whereas Mahometans, who think to return to a delightful life again, are carried forth with their heads forward, and looking toward their houses. . . .

That they sucked in the last breath of their expiring friends, was surely a practice of no medical institution, but a loose opinion that the soul passed out that way, and a fondness of affection, from some Pythagorical foundation, that the spirit of one body passed into another, which they wished might be their own.

That they poured oil upon the pyre, was a tolerable practice, while the intention rested in facilitating the accension. But to place good omens in the quick and speedy burning, to sacrifice unto the winds for a dispatch in this office, was a low form of superstition.

The archimime, or jester, attending the funeral train, and imitating the speeches, gesture, and manners of the deceased, was too light for such solemnities, contradicting their funeral orations and doleful rites of the grave.

That they buried a piece of money with them as a fee of the Elysian ferryman,[5] was a practice full of folly. But the ancient custom of placing coins in considerable urns, and the present practice of burying medals in the noble foundations of Europe, are laudable ways of historical discoveries, in actions, persons, chronologies; and posterity will applaud them.

Nor were only many customs questionable in order to their obsequies, but also sundry practices, fictions, and conceptions, discordant or obscure, of their state and future beings. Whether unto eight or ten bodies of men to add one of a woman, as being more inflammable, and unctuously constituted for the better pyral combustion, were any rational practice; or whether the complaint of Periander's[6] wife be tolerable, that wanting her funeral burning, she suffered intolerable cold in hell, according to the constitution of the infernal house of Pluto, wherein cold makes a great part of their tortures; it cannot pass without some question.

Why the female ghosts appear unto Ulysses, before the heroes and masculine spirits, — why the Psyche or soul of Tiresias is of the mascu-

[5] Charon, who ferried the souls of the dead over the river Styx.

[6] Seventh-century tyrant of Corinth.

line gender,[7] who, being blind on earth, sees more than all the rest in hell; why the funeral suppers consisted of eggs, beans, smallage, and lettuce, since the dead are made to eat asphodels about the Elysian meadows, — why, since there is no sacrifice acceptable, nor any propitiation for the covenant of the grave, men set up the deity of Morta,[8] and fruitlessly adored divinities without ears, it cannot escape some doubt.

The dead seem all alive in the human Hades of Homer, yet cannot well speak, prophesy, or know the living except they drink blood, wherein is the life of man. And therefore the souls of Penelope's paramours, conducted by Mercury,[9] chirped like bats, and those which followed Hercules, made a noise but like a flock of birds.

The departed spirits know things past and to come; yet are ignorant of things present. Agamemnon foretells what should happen unto Ulysses; yet ignorantly enquires what is become of his own son. The ghosts are afraid of swords in Homer; yet Sibylla[10] tells Aeneas in Virgil, the thin habit of spirits was beyond the force of weapons. The spirits put off their malice with their bodies, and Caesar and Pompey accord in Latin hell; yet Ajax, in Homer, endures not a conference with Ulysses: and Deiphobus[11] appears all mangled in Virgil's ghosts, yet we meet with perfect shadows among the wounded ghosts of Homer. . . .

The particulars of future beings must needs be dark unto ancient theories, which Christian philosophy yet determines but in a cloud of opinions. A dialogue between two infants in the womb concerning the state of this world, might handsomely illustrate our ignorance of the next, whereof methinks we yet discourse in Plato's den,[12] and are but embryo philosophers. . . .

[7] Theban prophet, blind, and legendarily of both sexes. The soul (the "Psyche") has always the feminine gender (as also the Latin word for soul, *anima*).

[8] Goddess of death.

[9] Mercury, among his many other functions, conducted souls to Hades.

[10] The Sibyl of Cumae, prophetess in Virgil's *Aeneid.*

[11] Son of Priam, slain by Menelaus in the Trojan War.

[12] See "The Allegory of the Cave," page 882.

ᴥᔕ FOR DISCUSSION AND WRITING

1. Sir Thomas was a physician. What suggestion of interests a physician might have do you find in the piece? Can you imagine the likely tenor of a conversation between him and any physician of your acquaintance? On which side would the chief difficulties lie? If you have a turn for parody or imaginary dialogues, you might compose such a conversation as a theme assignment.

2. If you find yourself seduced by this antique charmer, could you say what integral part in the personality of his writing is played by such portentous polysyllables as "subterraneous deposition," "facilitating the accension," "transcorporating philosophers," "unctuously constituted for the better pyral combustion"? But his richest rhythms and sonorities are often composed of quite simple words in brief phrases. Point out some.

3. Analyze the syntax of the paragraph (a single sentence) beginning "Why the female ghosts appear unto Ulysses . . ." and ending "it cannot escape some doubt." What is the main clause? How many parallel "why"— clauses are there? What structure have they in common? How is the rhythm of each varied?

4. What major syntactical parallelisms do you find between whole paragraphs? One thing that these parallelisms conspicuously do is to tie up each new progression of thought with those that come before. Alerting your ear to your own syntactical habits, experiment with parallelisms; if they feel clumsy and elephantine—no matter; the perception itself widens your scope.

5. Explain the meaning of the final sentence—which is one of those that haunt the memory like a musical movement.

Joseph Addison ❧ Reflections in Westminster Abbey

❧ English essayist and journalist (1672-1719). Addison is best known for his collaboration with Richard Steele on the periodicals *The Tatler* and *The Spectator.* ❧

Wᴴᴱᴺ I am in a serious humour, I very often walk by myself in Westminster-abbey;[1] where the gloominess of the place, and the use to which it is applied, with the solemnity of the building, and the condition of the people who lie in it, are apt to fill the mind with a kind of melancholy, or rather thoughtfulness, that is not disagreeable. I yesterday passed a whole afternoon in the churchyard, the cloisters, and the church, amusing myself with the tomb-stones and inscriptions that I met with in those several regions of the dead. Most of them recorded nothing else of the buried person, but that he was born upon one day, and died upon another; the whole history of his life being comprehended in those

From *The Spectator*, Number 26, dated Friday, March 30, 1711. The present selection is reprinted from *The British Essayists*, Vol. V, ed. A. Chalmers (Boston: Little Brown and Company, 1866).

[1] Gothic cathedral in London where all English monarchs have been crowned since William I; burial place of kings, statesmen, poets, and others of distinction, including Addison himself.

two circumstances that are common to all mankind. I could not but look upon these registers of existence, whether of brass or marble, as a kind of satire upon the departed persons; who had left no other memorial of them, but that they were born, and that they died. They put me in mind of several persons mentioned in the battles of heroic poems, who have sounding names given them, for no other reason but that they may be killed, and are celebrated for nothing but being knocked on the head. . . .

The life of these men is finely described in holy writ by 'the path of an arrow,' which is immediately closed up and lost.

Upon my going into the church, I entertained myself with the digging of a grave; and saw in every shovel-full of it that was thrown up, the fragment of a bone or skull intermixed with a kind of fresh mouldering earth that some time or other had a place in the composition of a human body. Upon this I began to consider with myself, what innumerable multitudes of people lay confused together under the pavement of that ancient cathedral; how men and women, friends and enemies, priests and soldiers, monks and prebendaries, were crumbled amongst one another, and blended together in the same common mass; how beauty, strength, and youth, with old age, weakness, and deformity, lay undistinguished, in the same promiscuous heap of matter.

After having thus surveyed this great magazine of mortality, as it were in the lump, I examined it more particularly by the accounts which I found on several of the monuments which are raised in every quarter of that ancient fabric. Some of them were covered with such extravagant epitaphs, that if it were possible for the dead person to be acquainted with them, he would blush at the praises which his friends have bestowed upon him. There are others so excessively modest, that they deliver the character of the person departed in Greek or Hebrew, and by that means are not understood once in a twelvemonth. In the poetical quarter, I found there were poets who had no monuments, and monuments which had no poets. I observed, indeed, that the present war had filled the church with many of these uninhabited monuments, which had been erected to the memory of persons whose bodies were perhaps buried in the plains of Blenheim,[2] or in the bosom of the ocean.

I could not but be very much delighted with several modern

2, In Bavaria, where the Duke of Marlborough, in 1704, defeated the French, in the War of the Spanish Succession.

epitaphs, which are written with great elegance of expression and just-
ness of thought, and therefore do honour to the living as well as the
dead. As a foreigner is very apt to conceive an idea of the ignorance
or politeness of a nation from the turn of their public monuments and
inscriptions, they should be submitted to the perusal of men of learning and genius before they are put in execution. Sir Cloudesley Shovel's
monument has very often given me great offence. Instead of the brave
rough English admiral, which was the distinguishing character of that
plain gallant man, he is represented on his tomb by the figure of a beau,
dressed in a long periwig, and reposing himself upon velvet cushions,
under a canopy of state. The inscription is answerable to the monument;
for instead of celebrating the many remarkable actions he had performed in the service of his country, it acquaints us only with the manner
of his death, in which it was impossible for him to reap any honour. The
Dutch, whom we are apt to despise for want of genius, show an infinitely
greater taste of antiquity and politeness in their buildings and works of
this nature, than what we meet with in those of our own country. The
monuments of their admirals, which have been erected at the public
expense, represent them like themselves, and are adorned with rostral
crowns and naval ornaments, with beautiful festoons of sea-weed,
shells, and coral.

But to return to our subject. I have left the repository of our English kings for the contemplation of another day, when I shall find my
mind disposed for so serious an amusement. I know that entertainments
of this nature are apt to raise dark and dismal thoughts in timorous
minds, and gloomy imaginations; but for my own part, though I am
always serious, I do not know what it is to be melancholy; and can therefore take a view of nature, in her deep and solemn scenes, with the same
pleasure as in her most gay and delightful ones. By this means I can
improve myself with those objects, which others consider with terror.
When I look upon the tombs of the great, every emotion of envy dies in
me; when I read the epitaphs of the beautiful, every inordinate desire
goes out; when I meet with the grief of parents upon a tombstone, my
heart melts with compassion; when I see the tomb of the parents themselves, I consider the vanity of grieving for those whom we must quickly
follow. When I see kings lying by those who deposed them, when I
consider rival wits placed side by side, or the holy men that divided the
world with their contests and disputes, I reflect with sorrow and aston-

ishment on the little competitions, factions, and debates of mankind. When I read the several dates of the tombs, of some that died yesterday, and some six hundred years ago, I consider that great day when we shall all of us be contemporaries, and make our appearance together.

ℰ∮ FOR DISCUSSION AND WRITING

1. Roughly three generations (sixty-seven years) separate Sir Thomas Browne and Joseph Addison. What seems to have happened to English prose in the meantime? Make an attempt to describe the difference succinctly.

2. Addison speaks of "amusing myself with the tomb-stones" and being "entertained . . . with the digging of a grave." Do these seem to you reasonable pleasures or the perversity of a morbid temperament? Consider the whole paragraph beginning "Upon my going into the church. . . ." Make a comparison between the type of observations found here and the animated cartoons where Bugs Bunny, Sylvester the Cat, Popeye, and their entourage continuously experience explosions in their anatomies that smash them to a geyser of sparks or to some acute disorganization of their humble similitude to the human, like the shape of a disemboweled accordion. Is the comparison a fair one? Do the animated cartoons illuminate more civilized propensities than Addison's "great magazine of mortality"?

3. Where does Addison find humor in death? Is there propriety in such an attitude? Or is humor in this area discreditable?

4. Analyze the syntax of the second sentence in the third paragraph. What is the main clause? How many objects has "consider"? What are the structural parallelisms in the "how"-clauses? Is there a definable relationship between the way the sentence mounts its parts, one upon the other, and the *subject matter* of the sentence?

5. Visit some of the public monuments in your town and write your "Reflections" upon them (sometimes the worst stimulate more reflection than the best).

Edward Trelawny ⋘ Shelley's Funeral

⋘ English adventurer (1792-1881) who met Shelley and Byron in Italy and wrote of them in his *Recollections*. ⋙

On Monday, July 8, 1822, I went with Shelley to his bankers, and then to a store. It was past one P.M. when we went on board our respective boats, — Shelley and Williams[1] to return to their home in the Gulf of Spezzia; I in the 'Bolivar' to accompany them into the offing. When we were under weigh, the guard-boat boarded us to overhaul our papers. I had not got my port clearance, the captain of the port having refused to give it to the mate, as I had often gone out without. The officer of the Health Office consequently threatened me with forty days' quarantine. It was hopeless to think of detaining my friends. Williams had been for days fretting and fuming to be off; they had no time to spare, it was past two o'clock, and there was very little wind.

From *Recollections* by Edward Trelawny, as edited by J. E. Morpurgo for the Philosophical Library, 1952.

[1] Edward Williams and his wife were living with the Shelleys at the time.

Sullenly and reluctantly I re-anchored, furled my sails, and with a ship's glass watched the progress of my friends' boat. My Genoese mate observed, — 'They should have sailed this morning at three or four A.M., instead of three P.M. They are standing too much in shore; the current will set them there.'

I said, 'They will soon have the land-breeze.'

'May-be,' continued the mate, 'she will soon have too much breeze; that gaff top-sail is foolish in a boat with no deck and no sailor on board.' Then pointing to the S.W., 'Look at those black lines and the dirty rags hanging on them out of the sky — they are a warning; look at the smoke on the water; the devil is brewing mischief.'

There was a sea-fog, in which Shelley's boat was soon after enveloped, and we saw nothing more of her.

Although the sun was obscured by mists, it was oppressively sultry. There was not a breath of air in the harbour. The heaviness of the atmosphere and an unwonted stillness benumbed my senses. I went down into the cabin and sank into a slumber. I was roused up by a noise overhead and went on deck. The men were getting up a chain cable to let go another anchor. There was a general stir amongst the shipping; shifting berths, getting down yards and masts, veering out cables, hauling in of hawsers, letting go anchors, hailing from the ships and quays, boats sculling rapidly to and fro. It was almost dark, although only half-past six o'clock. The sea was of the colour, and looked as solid and smooth as a sheet of lead, and covered with an oily scum. Gusts of wind swept over without ruffling it, and big drops of rain fell on its surface, rebounding, as if they could not penetrate it. There was a commotion in the air, made up of many threatening sounds, coming upon us from the sea. Fishing-craft and coasting-vessels under bare poles rushed by us in shoals, running foul of the ships in the harbour. As yet the din and hubbub was that made by men, but their shrill pipings were suddenly silenced by the crashing voice of a thunder squall that burst right over our heads. For some time no other sounds were to be heard than the thunder, wind, and rain. When the fury of the storm, which did not last for more than twenty minutes, had abated, and the horizon was in some degree cleared, I looked to seaward anxiously, in the hope of descrying Shelley's boat, amongst the many small craft scattered about. I watched every speck that loomed on the horizon, thinking that they

would have borne up on their return to the port, as all the other boats
that had gone out in the same direction had done.

I sent our Genoese mate on board some of the returning craft to
make inquiries, but they all professed not to have seen the English boat.
So remorselessly are the quarantine laws enforced in Italy, that, when
at sea, if you render assistance to a vessel in distress, or rescue a drowning stranger, on returning to port you are condemned to a long and
rigorous quarantine of fourteen or more days. The consequence is,
should one vessel see another in peril, or even run it down by accident,
she hastens on her course, and by general accord, not a word is said or
reported on the subject. But to resume my tale. I did not leave the
'Bolivar' until dark. During the night it was gusty and showery, and the
lightning flashed along the coast: at daylight I returned on board, and
resumed my examinations of the crews of the various boats which had
returned to the port during the night. They either knew nothing, or
would say nothing. My Genoese, with the quick eye of a sailor, pointed
out, on board a fishing-boat, an English-made oar, that he thought he
had seen in Shelley's boat, but the entire crew swore by all the saints
in the calendar that this was not so. Another day was passed in horrid
suspense. On the morning of the third day I rode to Pisa. Byron had
returned to the Lanfranchi Palace. I hoped to find a letter from the
Villa Magni: there was none. I told my fears to Hunt, and then went
upstairs to Byron. When I told him, his lip quivered, and his voice fal-
tered as he questioned me. I sent a courier to Leghorn to despatch the
'Bolivar', to cruise along the coast, whilst I mounted my horse and rode
in the same direction. I also despatched a courier along the coast to go
as far as Nice. On my arrival at Via Reggio I heard that a punt, a water-
keg, and some bottles had been found on the beach. These things I
recognised as having been in Shelley's boat when he left Leghorn.
Nothing more was found for seven or eight days, during which time of
painful suspense I patrolled the coast with the coast-guard, stimulating
them to keep a good look-out by the promise of a reward. It was not
until many days after this that my worst fears were confirmed. Two
bodies were found on the shore, — one near Via Reggio, which I went
and examined. The face and hands, and parts of the body not protected
by the dress, were fleshless. The tall slight figure, the jacket, the volume
of Sophocles in one pocket, and Keats's poems in the other, doubled

back, as if the reader, in the act of reading, had hastily thrust it away, were all too familiar to me to leave a doubt on my mind that this multi-lated corpse was any other than Shelley's. The other body was washed on shore three miles distant from Shelley's, near the tower of Migliarino, at the Bocca Lericcio. I went there at once. This corpse was much more mutilated; it had no other covering than, — the shreds of a shirt, and that partly drawn over the head, as if the wearer had been in the act of taking it off, — a black silk handkerchief, tied sailor-fashion round the neck, — socks, — and one boot, indicating also that he had at-tempted to strip. The flesh, sinews, and muscles hung about in rags, like the shirt, exposing the ribs and bones. I had brought with me from Shelley's house a boot of Williams's, and this exactly matched the one the corpse had on. That, and the handkerchief, satisfied me that it was the body of Shelley's comrade. Williams was the only one of the three who could swim, and it is probable he was the last survivor. It is like-wise possible, as he had a watch and money, and was better dressed than the others, that his body might have been plundered when found. . . .

Shelley always declared that in case of wreck he would vanish in-stantly, and not imperil valuable lives by permitting others to aid in saving his, which he looked upon as valueless. It was not until three weeks after the wreck of the boat that a third body was found — four miles from the other two. This I concluded to be that of the sailor boy, Charles Vivian, although it was a mere skeleton, and impossible to be identified. It was buried in the sand, above the reach of the waves. I mounted my horse, and rode to the Gulf of Spezzia, put up my horse, and walked until I caught sight of the lone house on the sea-shore in which Shelley and Williams had dwelt, and where their widows still lived. Hitherto in my frequent visits — in the absence of direct evidence to the contrary — I had buoyed up their spirits by maintaining that it was not impossible but that the friends still lived; now I had to extinguish the last hope of these forlorn women. I had ridden fast, to prevent any ruder messenger from bursting in upon them. As I stood on the threshold of their house, the bearer, or rather confirmer, of news which would rack every fibre of their quivering frames to the utmost, I paused, and, look-ing at the sea, my memory reverted to our joyous parting only a few days before.

The two families, then, had all been in the verandah, overhanging a sea so clear and calm that every star was reflected on the water, as if it had been a mirror; the young mothers singing some merry tune, with the accompaniment of a guitar. Shelley's shrill laugh — I heard it still — rang in my ears, with Williams's friendly hail, the general *buona notte*[2] of all the joyous party, and the earnest entreaty to me to return as soon as possible, and not to forget the commissions they had severally given me. I was in a small boat beneath them, slowly rowing myself on board the 'Bolivar', at anchor in the bay, loath to part from what I verily believed to have been at that time the most united, and happiest, set of human beings in the whole world. And now by the blow of an idle puff of wind the scene was changed. Such is human happiness.

My reverie was broken by a shriek from the nurse Caterina, as, crossing the hall, she saw me in the doorway. After asking her a few questions, I went up the stairs, and, unannounced, entered the room. I neither spoke, nor did they question me. Mrs. Shelley's large grey eyes were fixed on my face. I turned away. Unable to bear this horrid silence, with a convulsive effort she exclaimed:

'Is there no hope?'

I did not answer, but left the room, and sent the servant with the children to them.

The following is Mary Shelley's[3] account of the fatal voyage: 'The heats set in, in the middle of June; the days became excessively hot, but the sea breeze cooled the air at noon, and extreme heat always put Shelley in spirits: a long drought had preceded the heat, and prayers for rain were being put up in the churches, and processions of relics for the same effect took place in every town. At this time we received letters announcing the arrival of Leigh Hunt[4] at Pisa. Shelley was very eager to see him. I was confined to my room by severe illness, and could not move; it was agreed that Shelley and Williams should go to Leghorn in the boat. Strange that no fear of danger crossed our minds! Living on the sea-shore, the ocean became as a plaything: as a child may sport with a lighted stick, till a spark inflames a forest and spreads destruction over all, so did we fearlessly and blindly tamper with danger, and make a game of the terrors of the ocean. Our Italian neighbours even trusted themselves as far as Massa in the skiff; and the running down the line of coast to Leghorn, gave no more notion of peril than a fair-weather island navigation would have done to those who had never seen the sea. Once, some months

2 Good night.

3 Mary Shelley, daughter of the English philosopher William Godwin, wrote the thriller-novel *Frankenstein*.

4 English essayist, journalist, and poet.

before, Trelawny had raised a warning voice as to the difference of our calm bay, and the open sea beyond; but Shelley and his friend, with their one sailor boy, thought themselves a match for the storms of the Mediterranean, in a boat which they looked upon as equal to all it was put to do.

'On the 1st of July they left us. If ever shadow of future ill darkened the present hour, such was over my mind when they went. During the whole of our stay at Lerici, an intense presentiment of coming evil brooded over my mind, and covered this beautiful place, and genial summer, with the shadow of coming misery — I had vainly struggled with these emotions — they seemed accounted for by my illness, but at this hour of separation they recurred with renewed violence. I did not anticipate danger for them, but a vague expectation of evil shook me to agony, and I could scarcely bring myself to let them go. The day was calm and clear, and a fine breeze rising at twelve they weighed for Leghorn; they made the run of about fifty miles in seven hours and a half: the "Bolivar" was in port, and the regulations of the health-office not permitting them to go on shore after sunset, they borrowed cushions from the larger vessel, and slept on board their boat.

'They spent a week at Pisa and Leghorn. The want of rain was severely felt in the country. The weather continued sultry and fine. I have heard that Shelley all this time was in brilliant spirits. Not long before, talking of presentiment, he had said the only one that he ever found infallible, was the certain advent of some evil fortune when he felt peculiarly joyous. Yet if ever fate whispered of coming disaster, such inaudible, but not unfelt, prognostics hovered around us. The beauty of the place seemed unearthly in its excess: the distance we were at from all signs of civilisation, the sea at our feet, its murmurs or its roaring for ever in our ears, — all these things led the mind to brood over strange thoughts, and, lifting it from everyday life, caused it to be familiar with the unreal. A sort of spell surrounded us, and each day, as the voyagers did not return, we grew restless and disquieted, and yet, strange to say, we were not fearful of the most apparent danger.

'The spell snapped, it was all over; an interval of agonising doubt — of days passed in miserable journeys to gain tidings, of hopes that took firmer root, even as they were more baseless — were changed to the certainty of the death that eclipsed all happiness for the survivors for evermore.'

The next day I prevailed on them to return with me to Pisa. The misery of that night and the journey of the next day, and of many days and nights that followed, I can neither describe nor forget. It was ultimately determined by those most interested, that Shelley's remains should be removed from where they lay, and conveyed to Rome, to be interred near the bodies of his child, and of his friend Keats, with a suitable monument, and that Williams's remains should be taken to England. To do this, in their then far advanced state of decomposition, and to obviate the obstacles offered by the quarantine laws, the ancient custom of burning and reducing the body to ashes was suggested. I wrote to our minister at Florence, Dawkins, on the subject, and solicited his friendly intercession with the Lucchese and Florentine governments, that I might be furnished with authority to accomplish our purpose. . . .

I got a furnace made at Leghorn, of iron-bars and strong sheet-iron, supported on a stand, and laid in a stock of fuel, and such things as were said to be used by Shelley's much loved Hellenes on their funeral pyres.

On August 13, 1822, I went on board the 'Bolivar', with an English acquaintance, having written to Byron and Hunt to say I would send them word when everything was ready, as they wished to be present. I had previously engaged two large feluccas, with drags and tackling, to go before, and endeavour to find the place where Shelley's boat had foundered; the captain of one of the feluccas having asserted that he was out in the fatal squall, and had seen Shelley's boat go down off Via Reggio, with all sail set. With light and fitful breezes we were eleven hours reaching our destination. . . .

A rude hut, built of young pine-tree stems, and wattled with their branches, to keep the sun and rain out, and thatched with reeds, stood on the beach to shelter the look-out man on duty. A few yards from this was the grave, which we commenced opening — the Gulf of Spezzia and Leghorn at equal distances of twenty-two miles from us. As to fuel I might have saved myself the trouble of bringing any, for there was an ample supply of broken spars and planks cast on the shore from wrecks, besides the fallen and decaying timber in a stunted pine forest close at hand. The soldiers collected fuel whilst I erected the furnace, and then the men of the Health Office set to work, shovelling away the sand which covered the body, while we gathered round, watching anxiously. The first indication of their having found the body, was the appearance of the end of a black silk handkerchief — I grubbed this out with a stick, for we were not allowed to touch anything with our hands — then some shreds of linen were met with, and a boot with the bone of the leg and the foot in it. On the removal of a layer of brush-wood, all that now remained of my lost friend was exposed — a shapeless mass of bones and flesh. The limbs separated from the trunk on being touched.

'Is that a human body?' exclaimed Byron; 'why it's more like the carcase of a sheep, or any other animal, than a man: this is a satire on our pride and folly.'

I pointed to the letters E. E. W. on the black silk handkerchief.

Byron looking on, muttered, 'The entrails of a worm hold together longer than the potter's clay, of which man is made. Hold! let me see the jaw,' he added, as they were removing the skull, 'I can recognise any one by the teeth, with whom I have talked. I always watch the lips and mouth: they tell what the tongue and eyes try to conceal.'

I had a boot of Williams's with me; it exactly corresponded with the one found in the grave. The remains were removed piecemeal into the furnace.

'Don't repeat this with me,' said Byron; 'let my carcase rot where it falls.'

The funereal pyre was now ready; I applied the fire, and the materials being dry and resinous the pine-wood burnt furiously, and drove us back. It was hot enough before, there was no breath of air, and the loose sand scorched our feet. As soon as the flames became clear, and allowed us to approach, we threw frankincense and salt into the furnace, and poured a flask of wine and oil over the body. The Greek oration was omitted, for we had lost our Hellenic bard. It was now so insufferably hot that the officers and soldiers were all seeking shade.

'Let us try the strength of these waters that drowned our friends,' said Byron, with his usual audacity. 'How far out do you think they were when their boat sank?'

'If you don't wish to be put into the furnace, you had better not try; you are not in condition.'

He stripped, and went into the water, and so did I and my companion. Before we got a mile out, Byron was sick, and persuaded to return to the shore. My companion, too, was seized with cramp, and reached the land by my aid. At four o'clock the funereal pyre burnt low, and when we uncovered the furnace, nothing remained in it but dark-coloured ashes, with fragments of the larger bones. Poles were now put under the red-hot furnace, and it was gradually cooled in the sea. I gathered together the human ashes, and placed them in a small oak-box, bearing an inscription on a brass plate, screwed it down, and placed it in Byron's carriage. He returned with Hunt to Pisa, promising to be with us on the following day at Via Reggio. I returned with my party in the same way we came, and supped and slept at the inn. On the following morning we went on board the same boats, with the same things and party, and rowed down the little river near Via Reggio to the sea, pulled along the coast towards Massa, then landed, and began our preparations as before.

Three white wands had been stuck in the sand to mark the Poet's grave, but as they were at some distance from each other, we had to cut a trench thirty yards in length, in the line of the sticks, to ascertain the exact spot, and it was nearly an hour before we came upon the grave.

In the mean time Byron and Leigh Hunt arrived in the carriage, attended by soldiers, and the Health Officer, as before. The lonely and grand scenery that surrounded us so exactly harmonised with Shelley's genius, that I could imagine his spirit soaring over us. The sea, with the islands of Gorgona, Capraji, and Elba, was before us; old battlemented watch-towers stretched along the coast, backed by the marble-crested Apennines glistening in the sun, picturesque from their diversified outlines, and not a human dwelling was in sight. As I thought of the delight Shelley felt in such scenes of loneliness and grandeur whilst living, I felt we were no better than a herd of wolves or a pack of wild dogs, in tearing out his battered and naked body from the pure yellow sand that lay so lightly over it, to drag him back to the light of day; but the dead have no voice, nor had I power to check the sacrilege — the work went on silently in the deep and unresisting sand, not a word was spoken, for the Italians have a touch of sentiment, and their feelings are easily excited into sympathy. Even Byron was silent and thoughtful. We were startled and drawn together by a dull hollow sound that followed the blow of a mattock; the iron had struck a skull, and the body was soon uncovered. Lime had been strewn on it; this, or decomposition, had the effect of staining it of a dark and ghastly indigo colour. Byron asked me to preserve the skull for him; but remembering that he had formerly used one as a drinking-cup, I was determined Shelley's should not be so profaned. The limbs did not separate from the trunk, as in the case of Williams's body, so that the corpse was removed entire into the furnace. I had taken the precaution of having more and larger pieces of timber, in consequence of my experience of the day before of the difficulty of consuming a corpse in the open air with our apparatus. After the fire was well kindled we repeated the ceremony of the previous day; and more wine was poured over Shelley's dead body than he had consumed during his life. This with the oil and salt made the yellow flames glisten and quiver. The heat from the sun and fire was so intense that the atmosphere was tremulous and wavy. The corpse fell open and the heart was laid bare. The frontal bone of the skull, where it had been struck with the mattock, fell off; and, as the back of the head rested on the red-hot bottom bars of the furnace, the brains literally seethed, bubbled, and boiled as in a cauldron, for a very long time.

Byron could not face this scene, he withdrew to the beach and swam off to the 'Bolivar'. Leigh Hunt remained in the carriage. The fire was so fierce as to produce a white heat on the iron, and to reduce its contents to grey ashes. The only portions that were not consumed were some fragments of bones, the jaw, and the skull, but what surprised us all, was that the heart remained entire. In snatching this relic from the fiery furnace, my hand was severely burnt; and had any one seen me do the act I should have been put into quarantine.

After cooling the iron machine in the sea, I collected the human ashes and placed them in a box, which I took on board the 'Bolivar'. Byron and Hunt retraced their steps to their home, and the officers and soldiers returned to their quarters. I liberally rewarded the men for the admirable manner in which they behaved during the two days they had been with us.

As I undertook and executed this novel ceremony, I have been thus tediously minute in describing it.

Byron's idle talk during the exhumation of Williams's remains, did not proceed from want of feeling, but from his anxiety to conceal what he felt from others. When confined to his bed and racked by spasms, which threatened his life, I have heard him talk in a much more unorthodox fashion, the instant he could muster breath to banter. He had been taught during his town-life, that any exhibition of sympathy or feeling was maudlin and unmanly, and that the appearance of daring and indifference, denoted blood and high breeding.

In his *Autobiography* Hunt described the scene thus:

'The ceremony of the burning was alike beautiful and distressing. Trelawny, who had been the chief person concerned in ascertaining the fate of his friends, completed his kindness by taking the most active part on this last mournful occasion. He and his friend Captain Shenley were first upon the ground, attended by proper assistants. Lord Byron and myself arrived shortly afterwards. His lordship got out of his carriage, but wandered away from the spectacle, and did not see it. I remained inside the carriage, now looking on, now drawing back with feelings that were not to be witnessed.

'None of the mourners, however, refused themselves the little comfort of supposing, that lovers of books and antiquity, like Shelley and his companion, Shelley in particular with his Greek enthusiasm, would not have been sorry to foresee this part of their fate. The mortal part of him, too, was saved from corruption; not the least extraordinary part of his history. Among the materials for burning, as many of the gracefuller and more classical articles as could be procured — frankincense, wine, etc. — were not forgotten; and to these Keats's volume was added. The beauty of the flame arising from the funeral pile was extraordinary. The weather was beautifully fine. The Mediterranean, now soft and lucid, kissed the shore as if to make peace with it. The yellow sand and blue sky were intensely contrasted with one another: marble mountains touched the air with coolness; and the flame of the fire bore away towards heaven in vigorous amplitude, waving and quivering with a brightness of inconceivable beauty. It seemed as though it contained the glassy essence of vitality. You might have expected a seraphic countenance to look out of it, turning once more before it departed, to thank the friends that had done their duty.

'Yet, see how extremes can appear to meet even on occasions the most overwhelming; nay, even by reason of them; for as cold can perform the effect of fire, and burn us, so can despair put on the monstrous aspect of mirth. On returning from one of our visits to the seashore, we dined and drank; I mean, Lord Byron and myself; dined little, and drank too much. Lord Byron had not shone that day, even in his cups, which usually brought out his best qualities. As to myself, I had bordered upon emotions which I have never suffered myself to indulge, and which, foolishly as well as impatiently, render calamity, as somebody termed it, "an affront, and not a misfortune". The barouche drove rapidly through the forest of Pisa. We sang, we laughed, we shouted. I even felt a gaiety the more shocking, because it was real and a relief. What the coachman thought of us, God knows; but he helped to make up a ghastly trio. He was a good-tempered fellow, and an affectionate husband and father; yet he had the reputation of having offered his master to kill a man. I wish to have no such waking dream again. It was worthy of a German ballad.'

When I arrived at Leghorn, as I could not immediately go on to Rome, I consigned Shelley's ashes to our Consul at Rome, Mr. Freeborn, requesting him to keep them in his custody until my arrival. When I reached Rome, Freeborn told me that to quiet the authorities there, he had been obliged to inter the ashes with the usual ceremonies in the Protestant burying-place. When I came to examine the ground with the man who had the custody of it, I found Shelley's grave amidst a cluster of others. The old Roman wall partly inclosed the place, and there was a niche in the wall formed by two buttresses — immediately under an ancient pyramid, said to be the tomb of Caius Cestius. There were no graves near it at that time. This suited my taste, so I purchased the recess, and sufficient space for planting a row of the Italian upright cypresses. As the souls of heretics are foredoomed by the Roman priests, they do not affect to trouble themselves about their bodies. There was no 'faculty' to apply for, nor bishop's licence to exhume the body. The custode or guardian who dwelt within the inclosure and had the key of the gate, seemed to have uncontrolled power within his domain, and scudi[5] impressed with the image of Saint Peter with the two keys, ruled him. Without more ado, masons were hired, and two tombs built in the recess. In one of these, when completed, I deposited the box, with Shelley's ashes, and covered it in with solid stone, inscribed with a Latin epitaph, written by Leigh Hunt. . . . To which I added two lines from Shelley's favourite play *The Tempest*.

> Nothing of him that doth fade,
> But doth suffer a sea change into something
> Rich and strange.

FOR DISCUSSION AND WRITING

1. Where do you find in the different reports of Trelawny, Mary Shelley, and Leigh Hunt anything that you could call, at a guess, an index of the personality of the writer? (Such indices might lie in dozens of different inflections of mind or voice: a fondness for certain kinds of adjectives, a weakness for clichés of sentiment, a suspicious tendency toward inflation of language—the subject obviously being of a kind that might encourage such a tendency; the detail of an operation or equipment, simplicity or dignity of feeling, an observation or image that opens a horizon or discloses an intuition.)

2. Do Byron's quoted comments suggest any index of a similar kind? (Trelawny's reporting is not considered entirely reliable, but Byron's remarks seem Byronic enough.)

---

[5] Italian coins.

3. The idea of the funeral pyre was as practical—in view of the quarantine laws—as it was poetic. What makes it "poetic" (if we take that word to mean simply "like poetry")? Like what poetry? or what quality or element in poetry? Or you may have a sound basis for feeling that the exhumation of the decomposed fish-eaten bodies for combustion on a funeral pyre was anything but poetic—an ugly indulgence in an effete and grotesque gesture: what basis?

4. What is the suitability of the lines from *The Tempest?*

5. If you know and like some of Shelley's poems, you might reread them to see if water and fire have any prominence in them, then write a short paper on what you find that seems to bear a relationship to the manner of Shelley's death and funeral.

George Bernard Shaw ⇒⅋ She Would Have Enjoyed It

⇒⅋ British dramatist (1856-1950). Shaw's fame is so alive that one need say little about him. At the moment, the student will probably be best acquainted with him through the musical *My Fair Lady*, the book of which was made from Shaw's *Pygmalion*. The letter here is from Shaw's correspondence with Mrs. Patrick Campbell, an actress, for whom Shaw wrote several plays (she played the part of Liza in *Pygmalion*) and for whom he had a romantic attachment. ⅋⇒

The Mitre, Oxford.
22nd February 1913

WHAT a day! I must write to you about it, because there is no one else who didnt hate her mother, and even who doesnt hate her children. Whether you are an Italian peasant or a Superwoman I cannot yet find out; but anyhow your mother was not the Enemy.

Why does a funeral always sharpen one's sense of humor and rouse one's spirits? This one was a complete success. No burial horrors. No mourners in black, snivelling and wallowing in induced grief. Nobody knew except myself, Barker and the undertaker. Since I could not have a splendid procession with lovely colors and flashing life and triumphant music, it was best with us three. I particularly mention the undertaker because the humor of the occasion began with him. I went down in the tube to Golders Green with Barker, and walked to the

From *The Shaw-Campbell Letters* (New York: Alfred A. Knopf, Inc.; London: Gollancz). Reprinted by permission of Curtis Brown Ltd.

Crematorium; and there came also the undertaker presently with his hearse, which had walked (the horse did) conscientiously at a funeral pace through the cold; though my mother would have preferred an invigorating trot. The undertaker approached me in the character of a man shattered with grief; and I, hard as nails and in loyally high spirits (rejoicing irrepressibly in my mother's memory), tried to convey to him that this professional chicanery, as I took it to be, was quite unnecessary. And lo! it wasn't professional chicanery at all. He had done all sorts of work for her for years, and was actually and really in a state about losing her, not merely as a customer, but as a person he liked and was accustomed to. And the coffin was covered with violet cloth — not black.

I must rewrite that burial service; for there are things in it that are deader than anyone it has ever been read over; but I had it read not only because the parson must live by his fees, but because with all its drawbacks it is the most beautiful thing that can be read as yet. And the parson did not gabble and hurry in the horrible manner common on such occasions. With Barker and myself for his congregation (and Mamma) he did it with his utmost feeling and sincerity. We could have made him perfect technically in two rehearsals; but he was excellent as it was; and I shook his hand with unaffected gratitude in my best manner.

At the passage "earth to earth, ashes to ashes, dust to dust" there was a little alteration of the words to suit the process. A door opened in the wall; and the violet coffin mysteriously passed out through it and vanished as it closed. People think that door the door of the furnace; but it isn't. I went behind the scenes at the end of the service and saw the real thing. People are afraid to see it; but it is wonderful. I found there the violet coffin opposite another door, a real unmistakable furnace door. When it lifted there was a plain little chamber of cement and firebrick. No heat. No noise. No roaring draught. No flame. No fuel. It looked cool, clean, sunny, though no sun could get there. You would have walked in or put your hand in without misgiving. Then the violet coffin moved again and went in feet first. And behold! The feet burst miraculously into streaming ribbons of garnet coloured lovely flame, smokeless and eager, like pentecostal tongues, and as the whole coffin passed in it sprang into flame all over; and my mother became that beautiful fire.

The door fell; and they said that if we wanted to see it all through, we should come back in an hour and a half. I remembered the wasted little figure with the wonderful face, and said "Too long" to myself; but we went off and looked at the Hampstead Garden Suburb (in which I have shares), and telephoned messages to the theatre, and bought books, and enjoyed ourselves generally.

By the way I forgot one incident. Hayden Coffin[1] suddenly appeared in the chapel. *His* mother also. The end was wildly funny, she would have enjoyed it enormously. When we returned we looked down through an opening in the floor to a lower floor close below. There we saw a roomy kitchen, with a big cement table and two cooks busy at it. They had little tongs in their hands, and they were deftly and busily picking nails and scraps of coffin handles out of Mamma's dainty little heap of ashes and samples of bone. Mamma herself being at that moment leaning over beside me, shaking with laughter. Then they swept her up into a sieve, and shook her out; so that there was a heap of dust and a heap of calcined bone scraps. And Mamma said in my ear, "Which of the two heaps is me, I wonder!"

And that merry episode was the end, except for making dust of the bone scraps and scattering them on a flower bed.

O grave, where is thy victory?

In the afternoon I drove down to Oxford, where I write this. The car was in a merry mood, and in Notting Hill Gate accomplished a most amazing skid, swivelling right round across the road one way and then back the other, but fortunately not hitting anything.

The Philanderer, which I came down to see (Mona Limerick as Julia) went with a roar from beginning to end. Tomorrow I drive to Reading and thence across Surrey into Kent to the Barkers. The deferred lunch at the German Embassy will take place on Monday. Unless I find at Adelphi Terrace before 1.15 a telegram forbidding me ever to see you again, I *know* I shall go straight from the Embassy to your bedside. I must see you again after all these years.

Barrie is in bed ill (caught cold in Oxford a week ago) and ought to be petted by somebody.

I have many other things of extreme importance to say, but must leave them until Monday. By the way you first said you were leaving Hinde St on the 23rd; but you said last time to Lady Jekyll "Another ten days". If you are gone when I call I shall hurl myself into the area and perish.

[1] Comedian and light-opera singer.

And so goodnight, friend who understands about one's mother, and other things.

G.B.S.

~&ঽ FOR DISCUSSION AND WRITING

1. The first paragraph of this letter rather violently explodes certain conventions of feeling. It should suggest to you a theme topic. If the essay form seems inhibitively formal for the occasion, you might write a letter to a friend, real or imaginary, "who understands about one's mother, and other things."

2. Can you explain Shaw's high spirits at the funeral? Does his attitude seem to you scandalous, or otherwise? His attitude seems to depend at least as much on the character of the deceased as on that of the writer: could you characterize Shaw's mother from what is implied about her here? Does Shaw's attitude seem to be affected by any religious belief?

3. Is Shaw's curiosity about the backstage machinery of the cremation a "morbid curiosity"? a healthy curiosity? usual in the circumstances? unusual? Would you say that writers might be expected to have this kind of curiosity more than other people? and if so, why?

4. Pick out two or three sentences or phrases which seem to you vividly descriptive. Why are they?

André Gide ⤪ The Death of Charles-Louis Philippe

⤪ French novelist, playwright, and man of letters (1869-1951). Gide was a constant experimentalist in his writing and thought; his influence on contemporary literature and his symbolic stature as a person and as a critic of mores are very great. Those books of his in which the student might well be interested and which have good English translations are *The Immoralist, The Counterfeiters*, and *Lafcadio's Adventures*. Charles-Louis Philippe was a French novelist; he died in 1909. ⤫

AT the end of the corridor in the Velpeau hospital a room door remains open. Philippe is there. Ah, what does it matter now that the long windows of that room open directly into a big bright garden! It would have been good for his convalescence; but already he has lost consciousness; he is still struggling, but has already left us.

I approach the bed where he is dying; here are his mother, a friend whom I don't know, and Mme Audoux, who recognizes and welcomes me. I lead her out to the parlor for a minute.

Philippe has been here a week. At first the typhoid fever seemed very mild and, in the beginning, of so ill-defined a character that it was treated as a mere grippe. Then, for several days, Philippe was treated

Reprinted by permission of Alfred A. Knopf, Inc. from *Journals of André Gide*, translated by Justin O'Brien. Copyright 1947 by Alfred A. Knopf, Inc. The selection here is from Volume I.

as typhoid cases are treated today; but the regime of cold baths was very impractical in his little lodging on the Quai Bourbon. Tuesday evening he was carried to the Velpeau hospital; nothing alarming until Sunday; then suddenly meningitis sets in; his heart beats wildly; he is lost. Dr. Élie Faure, his friend, who, against all hope, carries on and will continue to surround him with care, from time to time risks an injection of spartein or of camphorated oil; but already the organism has ceased to react.

We return to the bedside. Yet how many struggles still and with what difficulty this poor suffering body resigns itself to dying! He is breathing very fast and very hard — very badly, like someone who has forgotten how.

The muscles of his neck and of the lower part of his face tremble; one eye is half open, the other closed. I rush to the post office to send some telegrams; almost none of Philippe's friends is informed.

At the Velpeau hospital again. Dr. Élie Faure takes the invalid's pulse. The poor mother queries: "How is the fever developing?" Through her suffering she is careful to speak correctly; she is a mere peasant, but she knews who her son is. And during these lugubrious days, instead of tears, she sheds floods of words; they flow evenly, monotonously, without accent or melody, in a somewhat hoarse tone, which at first surprises as if it didn't properly interpret her suffering; and her face remains dry.

After lunch I come back again; I cannot realize this loss. I find Philippe only slightly weaker, his face convulsed, shaken; struggling with slightly less energy against death.

Wednesday morning

Chanvin was waiting for me in the parlor. We are led, on the right side of the courtyard, to a little secret room, with an entrance on an angle — hiding as if ashamed. The rest of the establishment does not know of its existence, for we are in a *house of health*,[1] which you enter only to be cured, and this is the chamber of the dead. The new guest is led into this room at night, when the rest of the house is asleep; on the wall a notice specifies: "not before 9 P.M. or after 7 A.M." And the guest will leave here only by way of that low door, the bolted door I see over there at the end of the room, opening directly on the other street. . . .

There he is: very small on a large shroud; wearing a brownish suit;

[1] *Maison de santé*, hospital.

very erect, very rigid, as if at attention for the roll call. Hardly changed, moreover; his nostrils, somewhat pinched; his little fists very white; his feet lost in big white socks rising up like cotton nightcaps.

A few friends are in the room, weeping silently. The mother comes toward us, unable to weep, but moaning. Each time another person comes in she begins a new complaint like a professional mourner of antiquity. She is not speaking to us but to her son. She calls him; she leans over him, kisses him: "Good little boy!" she says to him. . . . "I knew all your little habits. . . . Ah, close you in now! close you in forever. . . ."

At first this sorrow surprises one, so eloquent it is; no expression in the intonation, but an extraordinary invention in the terms of endearment . . . then, turning toward a friend, without changing her tone, she gives an exact indication as to the funeral charges or the time of departure. She wants to take her son away as quickly as possible, take him away from everybody, have him to herself, down in their country: "I'll go and see you every day, every day." She caresses his forehead. Then turning toward us again: "Pity me, gentlemen! . . ."

Marguerite Audoux tells us that the last half-hour was horrible. Several times everyone thought all was over; the frightful breathing stopped; the mother would then throw herself onto the bed: "Stay with us a bit more, my dear! Breathe a bit more; once more! just once more!" And as if "the good little boy" heard her, in an enormous effort all his muscles could be seen to tighten, his chest to rise very high, very hard, and then fall back. . . . And Dr. Élie Faure, seized with despair, would exclaim sobbing: "But I did everything I could. . . ."

He died at nine P.M. . . .

The mother wants to take the body away this very night; at eight o'clock a brief ceremony will gather together a few friends, either at the hospital or at the station. I shall not go, but want to see Philippe once more. We go back there. Léautaud accompanies us.

Here we are again in the mortuary room. Bourdelle has come to take the death-mask; the floor is littered with splashes of plaster. Yes indeed, we shall be happy to have this exact testimony; but those who know him only through it will never imagine the full expression of this strapping little fellow, whose whole body had such a special significance. Yes, Toulouse-Lautrec was just as short as he, but deformed; Philippe was upright; he had small hands, small feet, short legs; his forehead well formed. Beside him, after a short time, one became ashamed of being too tall.

In the courtyard a group of friends. In the room, the mother, Marguerite Audoux (oh, how beautiful the quality of her grief seems to me!), Fargue; Léautaud, very pale against his very black beard, is swallowing his emotion. The mother is still moaning; Fargue and Werth are examining a time-table; it is agreed that we shall meet tomorrow morning at the Quai d'Orsay station for the eight-fifteen train.

Thursday, 8 o'clock

Quai d'Orsay station, where Chanvin and I arrive, fortunately well ahead of time, for there we discover that the eight-fifteen train leaves from the Gare de Lyon. Alas, how many friends, ill informed as we were, will not have time to get to the other station as we do at once! We don't see one in the train. Yet several had promised to come.

All night long it rained and there was a strong wind; now the air, somewhat calmed, is warm; the countryside is drenched; the sky is uniformly desolate.

We have taken tickets to Moulins. From the time-table that I buy in Nevers, I discover that to reach Cérilly it still takes three or four hours from Moulins in a little dawdling train, plus a long ride in the stage-coach; and that the little train will have left when we arrive. Can we make that leg of the trip in a carriage?

In Moulins we get refusals from three hacksters; the distance is too great: we shall need an automobile. And here it is! We light out into the country. The air is not cold; the hour is beautiful. In a moment the wind wipes away our fatigue, even our melancholy, and speaking of Philippe, we say: if you are watching us from some part of heaven, how amused you must be to see us racing after you along the road!

Beautiful country ravaged by winter and the storm; on the lavender edge of the sky how delicate are the greens of the pastures!

Bourbon-l'Archambault. This is where your twin sister and your brother-in-law, the pastry-cook, live. Ah! here is the hearse coming back from Cérilly. . . . Evening is falling. We enter the little village just before nightfall. The auto is put in the coach-house of the hotel where we have left our bags. Here we are on the village square. We are moving about in one of Philippe's books. We are told the way to his house. It is there on the road halfway up the hill, past the church, almost opposite the house of *Père Perdix*.[2] On the ground floor the shutters of the only window are closed like the eyelids of someone plunged in meditation; but the door is ajar. Yes, this is the right place: someone opens the door as he leaves, and in the narrow room opposite the entrance, between lighted candles, we see the coffin draped with black cloth and covered with wreaths. The mother rushes toward us, is amazed to see us; was her child so much loved! She introduces us to some village people who are there: friends come from Paris on purpose; she is proud of it. A woman is sobbing in a corner; it is his sister. Oh, how she resembles him! Her face explains our friend's, which was slightly deformed by a scar on the left side of the jaw which the beard did not quite hide. The brother-in-law cordially comes up to us and asks if we don't want to see Charles-Louis's room before more people come.

The whole house is built on his scale; because it was very small he came out of it very small. Beside the bed-sitting-room, which is the one you enter, the bright empty room where the maker of sabots,[3] his father, used to work; it gets its light from a little court, as does Philippe's room on the second floor. Small, unornamented room; on the right of the window, a little table for writing; above the table, some shelves with a few books and the high pile of all his school notebooks. The view one might have from the window is cut short by two or three firs that have grown right against the wall of the courtyard. That is all; and that was enough. Philippe was comfortable here. The mother does the honors of the place:

"Look carefully, gentlemen; this is all important if you are going to talk about him."

In the front of the house, the best parlor, in which is collected the little luxury of this humble dwelling: decorated mantel, framed portraits, draperies; this is the room that is never used.

"Even though we are poor people, you see that we are not in dire poverty."

She intends that at the hotel where we are staying we should consider ourselves as her guests as long as we remain in Cérilly.

"Do you want to see Papa Partridge's house?" asks the brother-in-law; "it should interest you."

[2] *Papa Partridge*, novel by Philippe.
[3] Wooden shoes.

And we go with him to the last house in the village; but the room in which we are received has been redone. As we are leaving, the brother-in-law leans toward us:

"The man you see over there is Jean Morantin; you know, the *lord of the village*. When Louis spoke of him in his book, people wanted to get him worked up. He said: no, no, I know little Philippe! He's a good boy; he certainly didn't intend to say anything bad about me."

We return to the hotel, where we find Valery Larbaud, just arrived from Vichy, and we spend the evening with him.

The funeral takes place Friday morning at ten o'clock. No other friend has come; yes, Guillaumin, the author of *La Vie d'un simple;*[*] he lives on a farm thirteen kilometers from here. We still "hope" for a quarter of an hour more; Cérilly lies between several railroad lines and can be reached from several different directions. Finally the short procession starts moving.

Small gray and brown romanesque church, filled with shadow and sound counsel. The deacon comes toward us where we remain grouped around the coffin:

"This way, gentlemen! Come this way, where we have a big fire."

And we approach a brazier near the apse. Twice during the ceremony the brother-in-law comes toward us; the first time to tell us that Marcel Ray has just arrived from Montpellier with his wife; then, the second time, leaning toward us:

"You should visit the Chapel of the Saints; my brother-in-law spoke of that too in his books."

The ceremony ends; we walk toward the cemetery. The sky is overcast. Occasionally a low moving cloud befogs the distant landscape. Here is the open grave. On the other side of the grave, opposite me, I watch the sobbing sister, who is being supported. Is it really Philippe that we are burying? What lugubrious comedy are we playing here? A village friend, decorated with lavender ribbon,[**] a shopkeeper or functionary of Cérilly, steps forward with some manuscript pages in his hand and begins his speech. He speaks of Philippe's shortness, of his

[*] *The Life of a Simple Man.*
[**] A badge of honor awarded by the state.

unimpressive appearance, which prevented him from attaining honors, of his successive failures in the posts he would have liked to hold: "You were perhaps not a great writer," he concludes, "but . . ." Nothing could be more stirring that this naïve reflection of the modesty Philippe always showed in speaking of himself, by which this excellent man was doubtless taken in. But some of us feel our hearts wrung; I hear someone whisper near me: "He's making a failure out of him!" And I hesitate a moment to step up before the grave and say that only Cérilly could speak so humbly of Philippe; that, seen from Paris, Philippe's stature seems to us very great. . . . But, alas, wouldn't Philippe suffer from the distance thus established between him and those of his little village, from which his heart never wandered?

Moreover, Guillaumin follows the other speaker; his speech is brief, full of measure and tact, very moving. He speaks of another child of Cérilly who went away like Philippe and died at thirty-five like him, just a century ago: the naturalist Perron. A little monument on the square immortalizes him. I shall copy the pious and touching inscription:

PERRON

DRIED UP LIKE

A YOUNG TREE

THAT SUCCUMBS

UNDER THE WEIGHT

OF ITS OWN FRUIT

Another side of the monument bears a bronze relief showing François Perron seated under a mangrove dotted with cockatoos in an Australian landscape peopled with familiar kangaroos.

An automobile stops at the gate of the cemetery; it is Fargue arriving just as the speeches are ending.

I am happy to see him here; his grief is very great, like that of all who are here; but it seems, besides, that Fargue represents a whole group of absent friends among the very best and that he comes bearing their homage.

We return to the hotel, where Mme Philippe invites us to dinner; her son-in-law, M. Tournayre, represents her. I am seated beside him; he tells me certain details of his brother-in-law's early childhood:

"Already at the age of five or six little Louis used to play 'going to school'; he had made up little notebooks, which he would put under his arm and then say: 'Good-by, Mamma; I am going to school.'

"Then he would sit down in a corner of the other room, on a stool, turning his back to everything.... Finally, a quarter of an hour later, the class being over, he *would come home*: 'Mamma, school is over.'

"But one fine day, without saying a word to anyone, slipping out, he really went to school; he was only six; the teacher sent him home. Little Louis came back again. Then the teacher asked: 'What have you come here for?' 'Why — to learn.'

"He is sent home again; he is too young. The child insists so much that he gets a dispensation. And thus he begins his patient education."

O "good little boy," I understand now what made you like so much, later on, *Jude the Obscure*. Even more than your gifts as a writer, than your sensitivity, than your intelligence, how much I admire that wondering application which was but one form of your love!

╼§ FOR DISCUSSION AND WRITING

1. Save for some notable exceptions, diaries and journals, like letters, do not belong to the category of "literature," their function being personal. What qualities of the present excerpt from Gide's *Journals* put it distinctly in the category of "literature"?

2. Note Gide's consistent use of the present tense. This is a tense difficult to use at long stretches—largely because the act of writing about events normally presupposes that one is writing about them *after* they have happened. Obviously here, too, Gide's narration is of events already past. Do you see any good reason for his putting them in the present tense? What is the specific effect of his writing in the present tense?

3. Set down a number of examples, from a half dozen to a dozen, of his close, attentive observation of details (about people or places or actions) that give to the piece a quality of immediacy, high visibility, and concreteness, as if the reader had Gide's own intimate post of observation.

4. Just because these are notes in a daybook or journal, they might naturally ramble at random, having no need for general coherence and unity. What *is* the principle of coherence and unity here?

5. Actually, the kind of immediacy and spontaneity of both impression and expression that a private journal might have are just those characteristics that give the piece its fine vividness, precision, and individuality, as well as its emotional conviction. Point out two or three places where this is evident.

6. Write down a "thumbnail," one-or-two-sentence characterization of Philippe himself, as seen both by Gide and by Philippe's family and the villagers. (Notice that we come to know Philippe only indirectly, through the way others thought of him.) Write one-sentence "thumbnails" of Philippe's mother and of any one other person who appears in the piece.

7. What is the specific contrast between the way the villagers think of Philippe and the way Gide (and, by implication, the literary sophisticates of Paris) think of him? How does Gide use this contrast to give broader significance to the whole episode?

8. One of the chief horrors clinging to the idea of death is that it is meaningless and makes human life meaningless (this attitude toward death—constituting the real "problem" of death—is as old as the Book of Job and is a major motif in the contemporary philosophical movement called Existentialism). Look back over the pieces in this section and write a short paper comparing the attitudes toward death shown in them, with the central idea in mind: how, in each, is death presented, not as meaningless, but as meaningful?

TWO ❧ THE COLLECTIVE EXPERIENCE

The Human Condition

SIR JULIAN HUXLEY *speaks of the delight with which Pere Teilhard
de Chardin caught up and repeated a phrase which Huxley had used
in conversation: Huxley had said that in the modern period
"evolution had at last become conscious of itself." The phrase might
describe the thematic center around which the pieces in this section
group themselves. Certainly one can describe thus Teilhard's own
luminous vision of the evolutionary process in its modern phase:
"We hold it in our hands," he says, "responsible for its past to its
future." A basic assumption of that classic of anthropology, Ruth
Benedict's* PATTERNS OF CULTURE, *is that a comparative study of cultures
opens the mind to those fertile confluences and exchanges by which
man has ever (to use a thought-provoking word of Teilhard's) become
more "hominised," more and more "man," through the creative
realization of his human potentiality. The account given here of Zūni
life is of a culture that is itself static; but to become aware of the
communal organization of Zūni, the hardihood in survival of this
culture which is so much more ancient than our own North American
civilization, and its extraordinary peacefulness and serenity, is to
fertilize in the mind possibilities which make our social anxieties,
violence, and cold-war consciousness look grotesquely primitive.
There are, in short, other ways for human life to develop than that of
compulsive destructiveness and the wasted energy of anxiety.*

Malthus and Swift were doubtless quite unaware of what a Julian Huxley or a Teilhard, let alone a Darwin, would call "evolution"; but nevertheless, in Swift's MODEST PROPOSAL *and in Malthus'* ESSAY ON THE PRINCIPLE OF POPULATION, *there is a consciousness that the collective human problems of poverty and "population explosion" can have solutions of a controlled evolutionary nature. The very fact that the "Malthusian problem" can be presented for intelligent analysis, and that solutions (even unfeasible ones) can be rationally considered, presumes an ability in man to take in hand certain aspects of his own evolution. Swift's* PROPOSAL *is placed, unchronologically, after Malthus'* ESSAY *here, for the Malthusian problem was not invented by Malthus but was horrifyingly rampant in Swift's Ireland and motivated the fantastic solution suggested in the* PROPOSAL. *Ortega y Gasset's* COMING OF THE MASSES *looks in a quite different way upon the social phenomena brought about by the eruption of sheer multitude—the problem now is to "find room" for oneself; but implicit in this chapter from a famous book is, again, the consciousness of something to be done, an imperative of attitude and action, by which modern man can—if he wishes—create the necessary room for that "minority" who prefer to "make great demands on themselves" (the minority that has always spearheaded human evolution), in a culture established by "masses" who prefer to make no demands on themselves but to be "just like everybody."*

Laurens van der Post's lecture on the "dark eye" in Africa and James Baldwin's letter to his nephew take up an aspect of the modern collective experience—the conflict of races—that is probably of far greater import for human destiny than cold war or atomic bomb. Van der Post's concern, as an Afrikaner, is with that institution of his country, apartheid, which stands with rigid and frightening obstinacy in the way of those natural confluences and exchanges between men that make human evolution possible. And Baldwin's letter, a document of love, proposes a motive for attitude and action that is one of the oldest consciously evolutionary motives man has known.

Pierre Teilhard de Chardin ✑ The Homo Sapiens Complex

✑ French geologist, paleontologist, and Jesuit priest (1881-1955). The selection here is taken from Teilhard's brilliant work on evolution, *The Phenomenon of Man*. In Sir Julian Huxley's introduction to that book, the student will find an illuminating account of Teilhard's life and thought. His work as scientific adviser to the Geological Survey of China, at Tientsin and later at Peking, took him on many expeditions, including that which unearthed the skull of Peking man. The war isolated him in China for six painful years, during which, nevertheless, he was able to bring the results of a lifetime's research and reflection to full elaboration. On his return to France he was awarded signal scientific honors, but, ironically, found his higher academic appointment blocked by the superiors of his order and even permission to publish refused in Rome. It was not until after his death that his work, left in manuscript with a friend, could be published.

"A great man of science and a great soul," Arnold J. Toynbee says of him. "His work gives our generation the comprehensive view it sorely needs." And Sir Julian Huxley: "The force and purity of Père Teilhard's thought and expression, in fruitful combination with his capacity for loving comprehension of all values, has given the world a picture not only of rare clarity but pregnant with compelling conclusions." ৯৯

O NE of the great surprises of botany is to see at the beginning of the Cretaceous period the world of cycads and conifers abruptly submerged and replaced by a forest of angiosperms, plane trees, oaks, etc., the bulk of our modern forms bursting ready-made on the Jurassic flora of some unknown region of the globe. No less is the anthropologist bewildered when he discovers, superimposed upon each other, hardly separated in the caves by a floor of stalagmites, Mousterian man and Cromagnon man

From *The Phenomenon of Man*, by Pierre Teilhard de Chardin. English translation by Bernard Wall and Introduction by Julian Huxley. Copyright © 1959 by Wm. Collins Sons & Co., Ltd., London, and Harper & Brothers, New York. Reprinted by permission of Harper & Row, Publishers, Incorporated.

or Aurignacian man. Here there is hardly any geological hiatus at all, yet none the less we find a fundamental rejuvenation of mankind. We find the sudden invasion of *Homo sapiens*, driven by climate or the restlessness of his soul, sweeping over the Neanderthaloids.

Where did he come from, this new man? Some anthropologists would like to see in him the culmination of certain lines of development already pin-pointed in earlier epochs — a direct descendant, for example, of *Sinanthropus*. For definite technical reasons, however, and still more because of overall analogies, it is better to view things in another way. Without doubt, somewhere or other and *in his own way*, Upper Palaeolithic man must have passed through a pre-hominid[1] phase and then through a Neanderthaloid one. . . .

Assuming one can trust bones to give us an idea of flesh and blood, what were in fact those first representatives, in the age of the reindeer, of a new human verticil[2] freshly opening? Nothing more or less than what we see living today in approximately the same regions of the earth. Negroes, white men and yellow men (or at the most pre-negro, pre-white and pre-yellow), and those various groups already for the most part settled to north, to south, to east, to west, in their present geographical zones. That is what we find all over the ancient world from Europe to China at the end of the last Ice Age. Accordingly when we study Upper Palaeolithic man, not only in the essential features of his anatomy but also in the main lines of his ethnography, it is really ourselves and our own infancy that we are finding, not only the skeleton of modern man already there, but the framework of modern humanity. We see the same general bodily form; the same fundamental distribution of races; the same tendency (at least in outline) for the ethnic groups to join up together in a coherent system, over-riding all divergence. And (how could it fail to follow?) the same essential aspirations in the depths of their soul.

Among the Neanderthaloids, as we have seen, a psychic advance was manifest, shown amongst other signs by the presence in the caves of the first graves. Even to the more brutal Neanderthals, everyone is prepared to grant the flame of a genuine intelligence. Most of it, however, seems to have been used up in the sheer effort to survive and repro-

[1] Protohuman.

[2] Adaptation of a botanical term referring to a whorl of flowers or leaves fanning out about the same point on a stalk.

duce. If there was any left over, we see no signs of it or fail to recognise them. What went on in the minds of those distant cousins of ours? We have no idea. But in the age of the reindeer, with *homo sapiens,* it is a definitely liberated thought which explodes, still warm, on to the walls of the caves. Within them, these new-comers brought art, an art still naturalistic but prodigiously accomplished. And thanks to the language of art, we can for the first time enter right into the consciousness of these vanished beings whose bones we put together. There is a strange spiritual nearness, even in detail. Those rites expressed in red and black on the walls of caves in Spain, in the Pyrenees and Périgord, are after all still practised under our eyes in Africa, in Oceania, and even in America. What difference is there, for example, between the sorcerer of the Trois-Frères Cave dressed up in his deerskin, and some oceanic god? But that's not the most important point. We could make mistakes in interpreting in modern terms the prints of hands, the bewitched bisons, and the fertility symbols which give expression to the preoccupation and religion of an Aurignacian or a Magdalenian man. Where we could not be mistaken is in perceiving in the artists of those distant ages a power of observation, a love of fantasy, and a joy in creation (manifest as much in the perfection of movement and outline as in the spontaneous play of chiselled ornament — these flowers of a consciousness not merely reflecting upon itself, but rejoicing in so doing. So the examination of skeletons and skulls has not led us astray. In the Upper Quaternary period it is indeed and in the fullest sense present-day man at whom we are looking, not yet adult, admittedly, but having nevertheless reached the 'age of reason.' And when we compare him to ourselves, his brain is already perfect, so perfect that since that time there seems to have been no measurable variation or increased perfection in the organic instrument of our thought.

Are we to say, then, that the evolution in man ceased with the end of the Quaternary era?

Not at all. But, without prejudice to what may still be developing slowly and secretly in the depths of the nervous system, evolution has since that date overtly overflowed its anatomical modalities to spread, or perhaps even at heart to transplant itself, into the zones of psychic spontaneity both individual and collective.

Henceforward it is in that form almost exclusively that we shall be recognising it and following its course.

THE NEOLITHIC METAMORPHOSIS

Throughout living phyla,[3] at all events among the higher animals where we can follow the process more easily, social development is a progress that comes relatively late. It is an achievement of maturity. In man, for reasons closely connected with his power of reflection, this transformation is accelerated. As far back as we can meet them, our great-great-ancestors are to be found *in groups* and gathered round the fire.

Definite as may be the signs of association at those remote periods, the whole phenomenon is far from being clearly outlined. Even in the Upper Palaeolithic era, the peoples we meet with seem to have constituted no more than loosely bound groups of wandering hunters. It was only in the Neolithic age that the great cementing of human elements began which was never thenceforward to stop. The Neolithic age, disdained by pre-historians because it is too young, neglected by historians because its phases cannot be exactly dated, was nevertheless a critical age and one of solemn importance among all the epochs of the past, for in it Civilisation was born.

Under what conditions did that birth take place? Once again, and always in conformity with the laws regulating our vision of time in retrospect, we do not know. . . . What is certain is that, after a gap geologically negligible, but long enough nevertheless for the selection and domestication of all the animals and plants on which we are still living today, we find sedentary and socially organised men in place of the nomadic hunters of the horse and the reindeer. In a matter of ten or twenty thousand years man divided up the earth and struck his roots in it.

In this decisive period of socialisation, as previously at the instant of reflection, a cluster of partially independent factors seems to have mysteriously converged to favour and even to force the pace of hominisation.[4] Let us try to sort them out.

First of all come the incessant advances of multiplication. With the rapidly growing number of individuals the available land diminished.

---

[3] Plural of *phylum,* a primary subdivision or "branch" whose members have a common descent.

[4] The process by which the protohuman stock became human, and by which man continues to realize more and more of his potentialities, that is, to become *more* human. The word is one of Teilhard's original and arresting coinages.

The groups pressed against one another. As a result migrations were on a smaller scale. The problem now was how to get the most out of ever more diminishing land, and we can well imagine that under pressure of this necessity the idea was born of conserving and reproducing on the spot what had hitherto been sought for and pursued far and wide. Agriculture and stock-breeding, the husbandman and the herdsman, replaced mere gathering and hunting.

From that fundamental change all the rest followed. In the growing agglomerations the complex of rights and duties began to appear, leading to the invention of all sorts of communal and juridical structures whose vestiges we can still see today in the shadow of the great civilisations among the least progressive populations of the world. In regard to property, morals and marriage, every possible social form seems to have been tried.

Simultaneously, in the more stable and more densely populated environment created by the first farms, the need and the taste for research were stimulated and became more methodical. It was a marvellous period of investigation and invention when, in the unequalled freshness of a new beginning, the eternal groping of life burst out in conscious reflection. Everything possible seems to have been attempted in this extraordinary period: the selection and empirical improvement of fruits, cereals, live-stock; the science of pottery; and weaving. Very soon followed the first elements of ideographic writing, and soon the first beginnings of metallurgy. . . .

At the end of this metamorphosis (whose existence, once again, we can only just infer from the results) the world was practically covered with a population whose remains — polished stone implements, mill stones and shards, found under recent humus or sand deposits — litter the old earth of the continents.

Mankind was of course still very much split up. To get an idea of it, we must think of what the first white men found in America or Africa — a veritable mosaic of groups, profoundly different both ethnically and socially.

But mankind was already outlined and linked up. Since the age of the reindeer the peoples had been little by little finding their definitive place, even in matters of details. Between them exchanges increased in the commerce of objects and the transmission of ideas. Traditions became organised and a collective memory was developed. Slender and granular as this first membrane might be, the noosphere[5] there and then began to close in upon itself — and to encircle the earth. . . .

THE PROLONGATIONS OF THE NEOLITHIC AGE
AND THE RISE OF THE WEST

There is no need for me to emphasise the reality, diversity and continual germination of human collective units, at any rate potentially divergent; such as the birth, multiplication and evolution of nations, states and civilisations. We see the spectacle on every hand, its vicissitudes fill the annals of the peoples. But there is one thing that must not be forgotten if we want to enter into and appreciate the drama. However hominised[6] the events, the history of mankind in this rationalised form really does prolong — though in its own way and degree — the organic movements of life. It is *still* natural history through the phenomena of social ramification that it relates.

Much more subtle and fraught with biological potentialities are the phenomena of confluence. Let us try to follow them in their mechanism and their consequences.

Between animal branches or phyla of low 'physical' endowment, reactions are limited to competition and eventually to elimination. The stronger supplants the weaker and ends by stifling it. The only slight exceptions to this brutal, almost mechanical law of substitution are those (mostly functional) associations of 'symbiosis' in inferior organisms — or with the most socialized insects, the enslavement of one group by another.

With man (at all events with Post-Neolithic man) simple elimination tends to become exceptional, or at all events secondary. However brutal the conquest, the suppression is always accompanied by some degree of assimilation. Even when partially absorbed, the vanquished still reacts on the victor so as to transform him. We might well borrow a geological word from the process — endomorphosis[7] — and it is the

---

[5] The "thinking layer of the earth," superposed on the layer of organic life, the biosphere, which in turn is superposed on the layer of inorganic material, the lithosphere. The whole environment of human thought, or, in Huxley's words, of "psycho-social evolution."

[6] See Note 4.

[7] The change in chemical composition produced in a rock by the invasion and assimilation of rock of a different kind.

more appropriate of course in the case of a peaceful cultural invasion, and yet still more if it is a question of populations, equally resistant and active, which interpenetrate slowly under prolonged tension. What happens then is mutual permeation of the psychisms[8] combined with a remarkable and significant interfecundity. Under this two-fold influence, veritable biological combinations are established and fixed which associate and blend ethnic traditions at the same time as cerebral genes. Formerly, on the tree of life we had a mere tangle of stems; now over the whole domain of *Homo sapiens* we have synthesis.

But of course we do not find this everywhere to the same extent.

Because of the haphazard configuration of continents on the earth, some regions are more favourable than others for the concourse and mixing of races — extended archipelagoes, junctions of valleys, vast cultivable plains, particularly when irrigated by a great river. In such privileged places there had been a natural tendency ever since the installation of settled life for the human mass to concentrate, to fuse, and for its temperature to rise. Whence the no doubt 'congenital' appearance on the Neolithic layer of certain foci of attraction and organisation, the prelude and presage of some new and superior state for the noosphere. Five of these foci, of varying remoteness in the past, can easily be picked out — Central America, with its Maya civilisation; the South Seas, with Polynesian civilisation; the basin of the Yellow River, with Chinese civilisation; the valleys of the Ganges and the Indus, with Indian civilisation; and lastly the Nile Valley and Mesopotamia with Egyptian and Sumerian civilisation. The last three foci may have first appeared almost at the same period, the first two were much later. But they were all largely independent of one another, each struggling blindly to spread and ramify, as though it were alone destined to absorb and transform the earth.

Basically can we not say that the essential thing in history consists in the conflict and finally the gradual harmonisation of these great psycho-somatic currents?

In fact this struggle for influence was quickly localised. The Maya centre which was too isolated in the New World, and the Polynesian centre which was too dispersed on the monotonous dust of its distant islands, soon met their respective fates, one being completely extinguished and the other radiating in a vacuum. So finally the contest for

[8] Different kinds of mentality or psychic nature.

the future of the world was fought out by the agricultural plain dwellers of Asia and North Africa. One or two thousand years before our era the odds between them may have seemed fairly equal. But we today, in the light of events, can see that even at that stage there were the seeds of weakness in two of the contestants in the East.

Either by its own genius or as an effect of immensity, China (and I mean the *old* China, of course) lacked both the inclination and the impetus for deep renovation. A singular spectacle is presented by this gigantic country which only yesterday represented — still living under our eyes — a scarcely changed fragment of the world as it could have been ten thousand years ago. The population was not only fundamentally agricultural but essentially organised according to the hierarchy of territorial possessions — the emperor being nothing more than the biggest proprietor. It was a population ultra-specialised in brick work, pottery and bronze, a population carrying to the lengths of superstition the study of pictograms and the science of the constellations; an incredibly refined civilisation, admittedly, but unchanged as to method since its beginning, like the writing which betrays the fact so ingenuously. Well into the nineteenth century it was still Neolithic, not rejuvenated, as elsewhere, but simply interminably complicated in on itself, not merely continuing on the same lines, but remaining on the same level, as though unable to lift itself above the soil where it was formed.

And while China, already encrusted in its soil, multiplied its gropings and discoveries without ever taking the trouble to build up a science of physics, India allowed itself to be drawn into metaphysics, only to become lost there. India — the region *par excellence* of high philosophic and religious pressures: we can never make too much of our indebtedness to the mystic influences which have come down to each and all of us in the past from this 'anticyclone.' But however efficacious these currents for ventilating and illuminating the atmosphere of mankind, we have to recognise that, with their excessive passivity and detachment, they were incapable of building the world. The primitive soul of India arose in its hour like a great wind but, like a great wind also, again in its hour, it passed away. How indeed could it have been otherwise? Phenomena regarded as an illusion (Maya) and their connections as a chain (Karma), what was left in these doctrines to animate and direct human evolution? . . .

Then step by step we are driven nearer to the more western zones of the world — to the Euphrates, the Nile, the Mediterranean — where an exceptional concurrence of places and peoples was, in the course of a few thousand years, to produce that happy blend, thanks to which reason could be harnessed to facts and religion to action. And this without losing any of their upward thrust — in fact quite the contrary. Mesopotamia, Egypt, Greece — with Rome soon to be added — and above all the mysterious Judaeo-Christian ferment which gave Europe its spiritual form. . . .

It is easy for the pessimist to discount this period, so extraordinary among the civilisations which have fallen into ruins one after the other. Is it not far more scientific to recognise, yet once again, beneath these successive oscillations, the great spiral of life: thrusting up, irreversibly, in relays, following the master-line of its evolution? Susa, Memphis, and Athens can crumble. An ever more highly organised consciousness of the universe is passed from hand to hand, and glows steadily brighter. . . .

At this point of our investigation, we would be allowing sentiment to falsify the facts if we failed to recognise that during historic time the principal axis of anthropogenesis has passed through the West. It is in this ardent zone of growth and universal recasting that all that goes to make man today has been discovered, or at any rate *must have been rediscovered*. For even that which had been known elsewhere only took on its definitive human value in becoming incorporated in the system of European ideas and activities. It is not in any way naïve to hail as a great event the discovery by Columbus of America.

In truth, a neo-humanity has been germinating round the Mediterranean during the last six thousand years, and precisely at this moment it has finished absorbing the last vestiges of the Neolithic mosaic with the budding of another layer on the noosphere, and the densest of all.

The proof of this lies in the fact that from one end of the world to the other, all the peoples, to remain human or to become more so, are inexorably led to formulate the hopes and problems of the modern earth in the very same terms in which the west has formulated them.

A CHANGE OF AGE

In every epoch man has thought himself at a 'turning-point of history.' And to a certain extent, if he be thought to be on a mountain spiral, he has not been wrong. But there are moments when this impression of transformation becomes accentuated and is thus particularly justified.

And we are certainly not exaggerating the importance of our contemporary existences in estimating that, pivoted upon them, a turn of profound importance is taking place in the world which may even crush them.

When did this turn begin? It is naturally impossible to say exactly. Like a great ship, the human mass only changes its course gradually, so much so that we can put far back — at least as far as the Renaissance — the first vibrations which indicate the change of route. It is clear, at any rate, that at the end of the eighteenth century the course had been changed in the West. Since then, in spite of our occasional obstinacy in pretending that we are the same, we have in fact entered a different world.

Firstly, economic changes. Advanced as it was in many ways two centuries ago, our civilisation was still based fundamentally on the soil and its partition. The type of 'real' property, the nucleus of the family, the prototype of the state (and even the universe) was still, as in the earliest days of society, the arable field, the territorial basis. Then, little by little, as a result of the 'dynamisation' of money, property has evaporated into something fluid and impersonal, so mobile that already the wealth of nations themselves has almost nothing in common with their frontiers.

Secondly, industrial changes. Up to the eighteenth century, in spite of the many improvements made, there was still only one known source of chemical energy — fire. And there was only one sort of mechanical energy employed—muscle, human or animal, multiplied by the machine.

Lastly, social changes and the awakening of the masses.

Merely from looking at these external signs we can hardly fail to suspect that the great unrest which has pervaded our life in the West ever since the storm of the French Revolution springs from a nobler and deeper cause than the difficulties of a world seeking to recover some ancient equilibrium that it has lost. There is no question of shipwreck. What we are up against is the heavy swell of an unknown sea which we are just entering from behind the cape that protected us. What is troubling us intellectually, politically and even spiritually is something quite simple. With his customary acute intuition, Henri Breuil[9] said to me one day: 'We have only just cast off the last moorings which held us to the

---

[9] French archaeologist who first directed Teilhard's interests into the study of human evolution where his life's work was to center.

Neolithic age.' The formula is paradoxical but illuminating. In fact the more I have thought over these words, the more inclined I have been to think that Breuil was right.

We are, at this very moment, passing through an age of *transition*.

The age of industry; the age of oil, electricity and the atom; the age of the machine, of huge collectivities and of science — the future will decide what is the best name to describe the era we are entering. The word matters little. What does matter is that we should be told that, at the cost of what we are enduring, life is taking a step, and a decisive step, in us and in our environment. After the long maturation that has been steadily going on during the apparent immobility of the agricultural centuries, the hour has come at last, characterised by the birth pangs inevitable in another change of state. There were the first men — those who witnessed our origin. There are others who will witness the great scenes of the end. To us, in our brief span of life, falls the honour and good fortune of coinciding with a critical change of the noosphere.

In these confused and restless zones in which present blends with future in a world of upheaval, we stand face to face with all the grandeur, the unprecedented grandeur, of the phenomenon of man. Here if anywhere, now if ever, have we, more legitimately than any of our predecessors, the right to think that we can measure the importance and detect the direction of the process of hominisation. Let us look carefully and try to understand. And to do so let us probe beneath the surface and try to decipher the particular form of mind which is coming to birth in the womb of the earth today.

Our earth of factory chimneys and offices, seething with work and business, our earth with a hundred new radiations — this great organism lives, in final analysis, because of and for the sake of, a new soul. Beneath a change of age lies a change of thought. Where are we to look for it, where are we to situate this renovating and subtle alteration which, without appreciably changing our bodies, has made new creatures of us? In one place and one only — in a new intuition involving a total change in the physiognomy of the universe in which we move — in other words, in an awakening.

What has made us in four or five generations so different from our forebears (in spite of all that may be said), so ambitious too, and so worried, is not merely that we have discovered and mastered other forces of nature. In final analysis it is, if I am not mistaken, that we have become conscious of the movement which is carrying us along, and have thereby realised the formidable problems set us by this reflective exercise of the human effort. . . .

UNITY OF STRUCTURE. 'VERTICILS' AND 'FANNINGS OUT.'

On every scale, this is the pattern[10] we see on the tree of life. We found it again at the origins of mankind and of the principal human waves. We have seen it with our own eyes today in the complex ramifications of nations and races. And now, with an eye rendered more sensitive by training, we shall be able to discern the same pattern again in forms which are more and more immaterial and near.

Our habit is to divide up our human world into compartments of different sorts of 'realities': natural and artificial, physical and moral, organic and juridical, for instance.

In a space-time, legitimately and perforce extended to include the movements of the mind within us, the frontiers between these pairs of opposites tend to vanish. Is there after all such a great difference from the point of view of the expansion of life between a vertebrate either spreading its limbs like a bat or equipping them with feathers, and an aviator soaring on wings with which he has had the ingenuity to provide himself? In what way is the ineluctable play of the energies of the heart less physically real than the principle of universal attraction? And, conventional and impermanent as they may seem on the surface, what are the intricacies of our social forms, if not an effort to isolate little by little what are one day to become the structural laws of the noosphere? In their essence, and provided they keep their vital connection with the current that wells up from the depths of the past, are not the artificial, the moral and the juridical simply the hominised versions of the natural, the physical and the organic?

From this point of view, which is that of the future natural history of the world, distinctions we cling to form habit (at the risk of over-partitioning the world) lose their value. And thenceforward the ramifications of evolution reappear and go on close to us in a thousand social phenomena which we should never have imagined to be so closely linked with biology; in the formation and dissemination of languages, in the development and specialisation of new industries, in the formulation and propagation of philosophic and religious doctrines. . . .

[10] That is, a unified organization taking the form of "verticils" and "fannings out."

Mutation reappears undeniably at the origin of the ramifications of institutions and ideas which interlace to form human society. Everywhere around us it is constantly cropping up, and precisely under the two forms that biology has divined and between which it hesitates: on the one hand we have mutations narrowly limited round a single focus or home; on the other 'mass mutations' in which whole blocks of mankind are swept along as by a flood. Here, however, because the phenomenon takes place in ourselves with its procedure in full view, we cannot be mistaken: we can see that in interpreting the progressive leaps of life in an active and finalist way we are not in error. For if our 'artificial' constructions are really nothing but the legitimate sequel to our phylogenesis,[11] *invention* also — this revolutionary act from which the creations of our thought emerge one after the other — can legitimately be regarded as an extension in reflective form of the obscure mechanism whereby each new form has always germinated on the trunk of life.

This is no metaphor, but an analogy founded in nature. We find the same thing in both — only it is easier to define in the hominised state.

And, here again, we find that light reflected on itself, glancing off and in a flash descending to the lowest frontiers of the past. But this time what its beam illuminates in us at our lowest stages is no longer an endless play of tangled verticils, but a long sequence of discoveries. In the same beam of light the instinctive gropings of the first cell link up with the learned gropings of our laboratories. So let us bow our heads with respect for the anxieties and joys of 'trying all and discovering all.' The passing wave that we can feel was not formed in ourselves. It comes to us from far away; it set out at the same time as the light from the first stars. It reaches us after creating everything on the way. The spirit of research and conquest is the permanent soul of evolution. And hence, throughout all time, *unity of movement.* 'The rise and expansion of consciousness.'

Man is not the centre of the universe as once we thought in our simplicity, but something much more wonderful — the arrow pointing the way to the final unification of the world in terms of life. Man alone constitutes the last-born, the freshest, the most complicated, the most subtle of all the successive layers of life.

This is nothing else than the fundamental vision and I shall leave it at that.

---

11 The biological evolution of the race, as distinguished from *ontogenesis*, the development of an individual organism.

But this vision, mind you, only acquires its full value — is indeed only defensible — through the simultaneous illumination within ourselves of the laws and conditions of heredity.

As I have already had occasion to say, we do not yet know how characters are formed, accumulated and transmitted in the secret recesses of the germ cells. Or rather, so long as it is talking of plants and animals, biology has not yet found a way of reconciling in phylogenesis the spontaneous activity of individuals with the blind determinism of the genes. In its inability to do so it is inclined to make the living being the passive and powerless witness of the transformations he undergoes — without being able to influence them and without being responsible for them.

But then (and this is the moment to settle the question once and for all), in the phylogenesis of mankind, what becomes of the part, obvious enough, played by the power of invention?

What evolution perceives of itself in man by reflecting itself in him is enough to dispel or at least to correct these paradoxical appearances.

Certainly in our innermost being we all feel the weight, the stock of obscure powers, good or bad, a sort of definite and unalterable 'quantum' handed down to us once and for all from the past. But with no less clarity we see that the further advance of the vital wave beyond us depends on how industriously we use those powers. How could we doubt them when we see them directly before us, through all the channels of 'tradition,' stored up irreversibly in the highest form of life accessible to our experience — I mean the collective memory and intelligence of the human biota? Still under the influence of our tendency to disparage the 'artificial,' we are apt to regard these social functions — tradition, education and upbringing — as pale images, almost parodies, of what takes place in the natural formation of species. If the noosphere is not an illusion, is it not much more exact to recognise in these communications and exchanges of ideas the higher form, in which they conclude by becoming fixed in us, of the less supple modes of biological enrichments by *additivity*?

In short, the further the living being emerges from the anonymous masses by the radiation of his own consciousness, the greater becomes the part of his activity which can be stored up and transmitted by means of education and imitation. From this point of view man only represents an extreme case of transformation. Transplanted by man into the thinking layer of the earth, heredity, without ceasing to be germinal (or chromosomatic) in the individual, finds itself, by its very life-centre, settled in a reflecting organism, collective and permanent, in which phylogenesis merges with ontogenesis. . . .

Passive as it may have been before reflection, heredity now springs to life, supremely active, in its noospheric form — that is to say by becoming hominised.

Hence we were not saying enough when we said that evolution, by becoming conscious of itself in the depths of ourselves, only needs to look at itself in the mirror to perceive itself in all its depths and to decipher itself. In addition it becomes free to dispose of itself — it can give itself or refuse itself. Not only do we read in our slightest acts the secret of its proceedings; but for an elementary part *we hold it in our hands,* responsible for its past to its future.

Is this grandeur or servitude? Therein lies the whole problem of action.

⤳ FOR DISCUSSION AND WRITING

1. The student who does not much like to have to put in hardheaded work over his reading assignments should stay away from this piece, for it requires muscular attentiveness, frequent use of the dictionary, and willingness to have one's mind stretched by new and difficult concepts. This is not the canned or packaged textbook variety of evolutionary fact and theory, to be stocked away in a cupboard of useful information about the past history of plants and animals. On the contrary, it is an imperative of action, *something to do* and that one is engaged in doing, for good or ill, whether one wants to or not. To leap to the end of the piece, what horizon of action does Teilhard's vision of human evolution open out to the individual?

2. Despite the acknowledged difficulty of his thought (and being the concentrate of a lifetime's profound research and reflection, how could it be other than difficult?), Teilhard has a brilliant gift for visualization, analogy, and metaphor, by which he is able to condense vast perspectives of knowledge in luminous phrases that make his thought as clear as the

houses across the street. This is the kind of gift of communication that is not blurred or distorted by translation, for it conveys thought like a perception of the senses. Point out five instances of the kind.

3. What demarcates *homo sapiens* from the Neanderthals, according to this account, letting us in to the reflective consciousness of the earliest men who were like ourselves? Explain the meaning of the sentence next to the last in the first section, beginning "But, without prejudice. . . ."

4. What development is meant by "the neolithic metamorphosis" (first subheading)? What is meant (toward the end of the second section) by "a collective memory"? Consider the last sentence in this section: "Slender and granular as this first membrane might be, the noosphere there and then began to close in upon itself—and to encircle the earth." In what way does the statement show that gift of visualization of thought spoken of in the second question? Do you find in it any suggestion of Teilhard's background in geology?

5. Explain the two last sentences in the first paragraph of the next section. He goes on to speak of "phenomena of confluence"; reread the third and fourth paragraphs in this section and put in your own words (best done in writing) what is meant.

6. In each case, what prevented four of the five foci of civilization he mentions from animating and directing the course of human evolution in the modern period? What factors in the civilization originating in Mesopotamia and around the Mediterranean gave it the evolutionary fertility that we have inherited? "Falling towers," T. S. Eliot says in *The Waste Land,* "Jerusalem Athens Alexandria Vienna London—unreal." What quite different understanding does Teilhard have of the fact that "Susa, Memphis, and Athens can crumble"? Why does he say that "it is not in any way naïve to hail as a great event the discovery by Columbus of America"?

7. What "critical change of the noosphere" does he describe in the third section? Our age, lived in the threatening atmosphere of the atomic bomb and suffering from other more pervasive and profound instabilities, is frequently referred to as an "age of anxiety"; where and how does Teilhard speak of modern anxiety?

8. Explain the whole paragraph in the last section beginning "In a spacetime, legitimately and perforce extended . . ." and ending "In their essence

. . . are not the artificial, the moral and the juridical simply the hominised versions of the natural, the physical and the organic?"

9. How does Teilhard relate human invention to biological evolution? Explain, in the perspective of the whole discussion, the statement at the end that we hold evolution in our hands and are "responsible for its past to its future."

10. Take as the subject for an essay the idea of "hominisation" as you yourself have experienced it in growing up, its difficulties and its sudden "mutations." Or write a paper on those psychological or social factors which seem to you to invalidate Teilhard's vision of further evolution in the "noosphere."

Ruth Benedict ·§ The Pueblos of New Mexico

·§ American anthropologist (1887-1948) who made extensive studies among the Pueblo, Apache, and Blackfoot Indians. Her *Patterns of Culture* is a classic in the comparative study of cultures. ঌ

THE Pueblo Indians of the Southwest are one of the most widely known primitive peoples in Western civilization. They live in the midst of America, within easy reach of any transcontinental traveller. And they are living after the old native fashion. Their culture has not disintegrated like that of all the Indian communities outside of Arizona and New Mexico. Month by month and year by year, the old dances of the gods are danced in their stone villages, life follows essentially the old routines, and what they have taken from our civilization they have remodelled and subordinated to their own attitudes.

They have a romantic history. All through that part of America which they still inhabit are found the homes of their cultural ancestors, the cliff-dwellings and great planned valley cities of the golden age of

"The Pueblos of New Mexico," from *Patterns of Culture* by Ruth Benedict (Boston: Houghton Mifflin Company, 1961), pp. 57-129. Reprinted by permission of the publisher.

the Pueblos. Their unbelievably numerous cities were built in the twelfth and thirteenth centuries, but we can follow their history much further back to its simple beginnings in one-room stone houses to each of which an underground ceremonial chamber was attached. These early Pueblo people, however, were not the first who had taken this Southwest desert for their home. An earlier people, the Basketmakers, had lived there so long before that we cannot calculate the period of their occupancy, and they were supplanted, and perhaps largely exterminated, by the early Pueblo people.

The Pueblo culture flourished greatly after it had settled upon its arid plateau. It had brought with it the bow and arrow, a knowledge of stone architecture, and a diversified agriculture. Why it chose for the site of its greatest development the inhospitable, almost waterless valley of the San Juan, which flows into the Colorado River from the north, no one ventures to explain. It seems one of the most forbidding regions in the whole of what is now the United States, yet it was here that there grew up the greatest Indian cities north of Mexico. These were of two kinds, and they seem to have been built by the same civilization at the same period: the cliff-dwellings, and the semicircular valley citadels. The cliff-dwellings dug into the sheer face of the precipice, or built on a ledge hundreds of feet from the valley floor, are some of the most romantic habitations of mankind. We cannot guess what the circumstances were that led to the construction of these homes, far from the cornfields and far from any water-supply, which must have been serious if they were planned as fortifications, but some of the ruins enduringly challenge our admiration of ingenuity and beauty. One thing is never omitted in them, no matter how solid the rock ledge upon which the pueblo is built: the underground ceremonial chamber, the kiva, is hewed out to accommodate a man upright, and is large enough to serve as a gathering-room. It is entered by a ladder through a hatchway.

The other type of dwelling was a prototype of the modern planned city: a semicircular sweep of wall that rose three stories at the fortified exterior and was terraced inward as it approached the underground kivas that clustered in the embrace of the great masonry arms. Some of these great valley cities of this type have not only the small kivas, but one great additional temple similarly sunk into the earth and of the most finished and perfect masonry.

The peak of Pueblo civilization had been reached and passed before the Spanish adventurers came searching for cities of gold. It seems likely that the Navajo-Apache tribes from the north cut off the supplies of water from the cities of these ancient peoples and overcame them. When the Spanish came, they had already abandoned their cliff-dwellings and great semicircular cities and had settled along the Rio Grande in villages they still occupy. Toward the west there were also Acoma, Zuñi, and Hopi, the great western Pueblos.

Pueblo culture, therefore, has a long homogeneous history behind it, and we have special need of this knowledge of it because the cultural life of these peoples is so at variance with that of the rest of North America. Unfortunately archaeology cannot go further and tell us how it came about that here in this small region of America a culture gradually differentiated itself from all those that surrounded it and came always more and more drastically to express a consistent and particular attitude toward existence. . . .

The Zuñi are a ceremonious people, a people who value sobriety and inoffensiveness above all other virtues. Their interest is centered upon their rich and complex ceremonial life. Their cults of the masked gods, of healing, of the sun, of the sacred fetishes, of war, of the dead, are formal and established bodies of ritual with priestly officials and calendric observances. No field of activity competes with ritual for foremost place in their attention. Probably most grown men among the western Pueblos give to it the greater part of their waking life. It requires the memorizing of an amount of word-perfect ritual that our less trained minds find staggering, and the performance of neatly dovetailed ceremonies that are charted by the calendar and complexly interlock all the different cults and the governing body in endless formal procedure.

The ceremonial life not only demands their time; it preoccupies their attention. Not only those who are responsible for the ritual and those who take part in it, but all the people of the Pueblo, women and families who 'have nothing,' that is, that have no ritual possessions, centre their daily conversation about it. While it is in progress, they stand all day as spectators. If a priest is ill, or if no rain comes during his retreat, village gossip runs over and over his ceremonial missteps and the implications of his failure. Did the priest of the masked gods give offence to some supernatural being? Did he break his retreat by going home to his wife before the days were up? These are the subjects of talk in the village for a fortnight. If an impersonator wears a new feather on his mask, it eclipses all talk of sheep or gardens or marriage or divorce. . . .

If they are asked the purpose of any religious observance, they have a ready answer. It is for rain. This is of course a more or less conventional answer. But it reflects a deep-seated Zuñi attitude. Fertility is above all else the blessing within the bestowal of the gods, and in the desert country of the Zuñi plateau, rain is the prime requisite for the growth of crops. The retreats of the priests, the dances of the masked gods, even many of the activities of the medicine societies are judged by whether or not there has been rain. To 'bless with water' is the synonym of all blessing. Thus, in the prayers, the fixed epithet the gods apply in blessing to the rooms in Zuñi to which they come, is 'water-filled,' their ladders are 'water-ladders,' and the scalp taken in warfare is 'the water-filled covering.' The dead, too, come back in the rain clouds, bringing the universal blessing. People say to the children when the summer afternoon rain clouds come up the sky, 'Your grandfathers are coming,' and the reference is not to individual dead relatives, but applies impersonally to all forbears. The masked gods also are the rain and when they dance they constrain their own being — rain — to descend upon the people. The priests, again, in their retreat before their altars sit motionless and withdrawn for eight days, summoning the rain.

> From wherever you abide permanently
> You will make your roads come forth.
> Your little wind blown clouds,
> Your thin wisp of clouds
> Replete with living waters,
> You will send forth to stay with us.
> Your fine rain caressing the earth,
> Here at Itiwana,*
> The abiding place of our fathers,
> Our mothers,
> The ones who first had being,
> With your great pile of waters
> You will come together.

Rain, however, is only one of the aspects of fertility for which prayers are constantly made in Zuñi. Increase in the gardens and in-

* 'The Middle,' the ceremonial name of Zuñi, the centre of the world. [Author's note.]

crease in the tribe are thought of together. They desire to be blessed with
happy women:

> Even those who are with child,
> Carrying one child on the back,
> Holding another on a cradle board,
> Leading one by the hand,
> With yet another going before. . . .

Like all the Pueblos, and perhaps in greater degree than the rest,
Zuñi is rich. It has gardens and peach orchards and sheep and silver and
turquoise. These are important to a man when they make it possible for
him to have a mask made for himself, or to pay for the learning of ritual,
or to entertain the tribal masked gods at the Shalako. For this last he
must build a new house for the gods to bless at housewarming. All that
year he must feed the cult members who build for him, he must provide
the great beams for the rafters, he must entertain the whole tribe at the
final ceremony. There are endless responsibilities he must assume. For
this purpose he will plant heavily the year before and increase his herd.
He will receive help from his clan group, all of which he must return in
kind. Riches used in this way are of course indispensable to a man of
prestige, but neither he nor anyone else is concerned with the reckoning
of possessions, but with the ceremonial rôle which he has taken. A
'valuable' family, in native parlance, is always a family which owns permanent fetishes, and a man of importance is one who has undertaken
many ceremonial rôles.

All the traditional arrangements tend to make wealth play as small
a part as possible in the performance of ritual prerogatives. Ceremonial
objects, even though they are recognized personal property and attained
by the expenditure of money and effort, are free to the use of anyone who
can employ them. There are many sacred things too dangerous to be
handled except by those who have qualified, but the tabus are not property tabus. Hunting fetishes are owned in the hunters' society, but anyone who is going hunting may take them for his use. He will have to assume the usual responsibilities for using holy things; he will have to plant
prayer-sticks and be continent and benevolent for four days. But he
pays nothing, and those who possess the fetishes as private property have
no monopoly of their supernatural powers. Similarly a man who has no

mask borrows one freely and is not thought of as a beggar or a suppliant. . . .

The basic contrast between the Pueblos and the other cultures of North America is the contrast that is named and described by Nietzsche in his studies of Greek tragedy. He discusses two diametrically opposed ways of arriving at the values of existence. The Dionysian pursues them through 'the annihilation of the ordinary bounds and limits of existence'; he seeks to attain in his most valued moments escape from the boundaries imposed upon him by his five senses, to break through into another order of experience. The desire of the Dionysian, in personal experience or in ritual, is to press through it toward a certain psychological state, to achieve excess. The closest analogy to the emotions he seeks is drunkenness, and he values the illuminations of frenzy. With Blake, he believes 'the path of excess leads to the palace of wisdom.' The Apollonian distrusts all this, and has often little idea of the nature of such experiences. He finds means to outlaw them from his conscious life. He 'knows but one law, measure in the Hellenic sense.' He keeps the middle of the road, stays within the known map, does not meddle with disruptive psychological states. In Nietzsche's fine phrase, even in the exaltation of the dance he 'remains what he is, and retains his civic name.' . . .

The American Indians as a whole, and including those of Mexico, were passionately Dionysian. They valued all violent experience, all means by which human beings may break through the usual sensory routine, and to all such experiences they attributed the highest value.

The Indians of North America outside the Pueblos have, of course, anything but a uniform culture. They contrast violently at almost every point, and there are eight of them that it is convenient to differentiate as separate culture areas. But throughout them all, in one or another guise, there run certain fundamental Dionysian practices. The most conspicuous of these is probably their practice of obtaining supernatural power in a dream or vision. . . . On the western plains men sought these visions with hideous tortures. They cut strips from the skin of their arms, they struck off fingers, they swung themselves from tall poles by straps inserted under the muscles of their shoulders. They went without food and water for extreme periods. They sought in every way to achieve an order of experience set apart from daily living. . . .

On the western plains they believed that when the vision came it determined their life and the success they might expect. If no vision came, they were doomed to failure. 'I was going to be poor; that is why I had no vision.' If the experience was of curing, one had curing powers, if of warfare, one had warrior's powers. If one encountered Double Woman, one was a transvestite and took woman's occupations and habits. If one was blessed by the mythical Water Serpent, one had supernatural power for evil and sacrificed the lives of one's wife and children in payment for becoming a sorcerer. Any man who desired general strengthening or success in particular ventures sought visions often. They were necessary for warpaths and for curings and for all kinds of miscellaneous occasions: calling the buffalo, naming children, mourning, revenge, finding lost articles. . . .

It might be from a dream that the supernatural power came to them. Some of the accounts of visions are unmistakable dream experiences, whether they occurred in sleep or under less normal conditions. Some tribes valued the dreams of sleep more highly than any other experiences. Lewis and Clark complained when they crossed the western plains in the early days that no night was fit for sleeping; some old man was always rousing to beat on his drum and ceremonially rehearse the dream he had just had. It was a valuable source of power.

In any case the criterion of whether or not the experience had power was necessarily a matter for the individual to decide. It was recognized as subjective, no matter what other social curbs were imposed upon its subsequent practice. Some experiences had power and some had not, and they distinguished by the flash of significance that singled out those that were valuable. . . .

This belief in the power of a vision experience on the western plains is a cultural mechanism which gives a theoretically unlimited freedom to the individual. He might go out and get this supremely coveted power, no matter to what family he belonged. Besides this, he might claim his vision as authority for any innovation, any personal advantage which he might imagine, and this authority he invoked was an experience in solitude which in the nature of the case could not be judged by another person. It was, moreover, probably the experience of greatest instability that he could achieve. It gave individual initiative a scope which is not easily equalled. . . .

Everywhere among the North American Indians, therefore, except in the Southwest Pueblos, we encounter this Dionysian dogma and practice of the vision-dream from which comes supernatural power. The Southwest is surrounded by peoples who seek the vision by fasting, by torture, by drugs and alcohol. But the Pueblos do not accept disruptive experiences and they do not derive supernatural power from them. If a Zuñi Indian has by chance a visual or auditory hallucination it is regarded as a sign of death. It is an experience to avoid, not one to seek by fasting. . . . The Pueblos are close to the Mexican plateau where the peyote button is obtained, and the Apache and the tribes of the plains with which they came most in contact were peyote-eaters. But the practice gained no foothold in the pueblos. A small anti-government group in Taos, the most atypical and Plains-like of the Pueblos, has recently taken it up. But elsewhere it has never been accepted. In their strict Apollonian *ethos*, the Pueblos distrust and reject those experiences which take the individual in any way out of bounds and forfeit his sobriety.

This repugnance is so strong that it has even been sufficient to keep American alcohol from becoming an administrative problem. Everywhere else on Indian reservations in the United States alcohol is an inescapable issue. There are no government regulations that can cope with the Indian's passion for whiskey. But in the pueblos the problem has never been important. They did not brew any native intoxicant in the old days, nor do they now. Nor is it a matter of course, as it is for instance with the near-by Apaches, that every trip to town, for old men or young, is a debauch. It is not that the Pueblos have a religious tabu against drinking. It is deeper than that. Drunkenness is repulsive to them. In Zuñi after the early introduction of liquor, the old men voluntarily outlawed it, and the rule was congenial enough to be honoured.

Torture was even more consistently rejected. The Pueblos, especially the eastern Pueblos, were in contact with two very different cultures in which self-torture was of the greatest importance, the Plains Indians and the Mexican Penitentes. Pueblo culture also shares many traits with the now extinct torture-using civilization of ancient Mexico, where on all occasions one drew blood from parts of one's own body, especially from the tongue, as an offering to the gods. On the plains, self-torture was specialized as a technique for obtaining states of self-oblivion during which one obtained a vision. . . .

The Pueblos do not understand self-torture. Every man's hand has its five fingers, and unless they have been tortured to secure a sorcery confession they are unscarred. There are no cicatrices upon their backs, no marks where strips of skin have been taken off. They have no rites in which they sacrifice their own blood, or use it for fertility. They used to hurt themselves to a certain extent in a few initiations at the moments of greatest excitement, but in such cases the whole matter was almost an affair of collegiate exuberance. In the Cactus Society, a warrior cult, they dashed about striking themselves and each other with cactus-blade whips; in the Fire Society they tossed fire about like confetti. Neither psychic danger nor abnormal experience is sought in either case. Certainly in the observed fire tricks of the Pueblos — as also in the fire tricks of the Plains — it is not self-torture that is sought. In the Fire Walk, whatever the means employed, feet are not burned, and when the fire is taken into the mouth the tongue is not blistered. . . .

If ecstasy is not sought by fasting, by torture, or by drugs or alcohol, or under the guise of the vision, neither is it induced in the dance. Perhaps no people in North America spend more time in the dance than the Southwest Pueblos. But their object in it never is to attain self-oblivion. It is by the frenzy of the dance that the Greek cult of Dionysus was best known, and it recurs over and over in North America. The Ghost Dance of the Indians that swept the country in the 1870's was a round dance danced monotonously till the dancers, one after the other, fell rigid, prostrate on the ground. During their seizure they had visions of deliverance from the whites, and meanwhile the dance continued and others fell. It was the custom in most of the dozens of tribes to which it penetrated to hold the dance every Sunday. There were other and older dances also that were thoroughly Dionysian. The tribes of northern Mexico danced, frothing at the mouth, upon the altar. The shamans' dances of California required a cataleptic seizure. . . .

Of all this there is no suggestion in all the dance occasions of Zuñi. The dance, like their ritual poetry, is a monotonous compulsion of natural forces by reiteration. The tireless pounding of their feet draws together the mist in the sky and heaps it into the piled rain clouds. It forces out the rain upon the earth. They are bent not at all upon an ecstatic experience, but upon so thorough-going an identification with nature that the forces of nature will swing to their purposes. This intent dictates the form and spirit of Pueblo dances. There is nothing wild about them. It is the cumulative force of the rhythm, the perfection of forty men moving as one, that makes them effective.

No one has conveyed this quality of Pueblo dancing more precisely than D. H. Lawrence. 'All the men sing in unison, as they move with the soft, yet heavy bird tread which is the whole of the dance, with bodies bent a little forward, shoulders and heads loose and heavy, feet powerful but soft, the men tread the rhythm into the centre of the earth. The drums keep up the pulsating heart beat and for hours, hours, it goes on.' Sometimes they are dancing the sprouting corn up out of the earth,[1] sometimes they are calling the game animals by the tramp of their feet, sometimes they are constraining the white cumulus clouds that are slowly piling up the sky on a desert afternoon. Even the presence of these in the sky, whether or not they vouchsafe rain, is a blessing from the supernaturals upon the dance, a sign that their rite is accepted. If rain comes, that is the sign and seal of the power of their dance. It is the answer. They dance on through the swift Southwest downpour, their feathers wet and heavy, their embroidered kilts and mantles drenched. But they have been favoured by the gods. The clowns make merry in the deep adobe mud, sliding at full length in the puddles and paddling in the half-liquid earth. It is their recognition that their feet in the dance have the compulsion of natural forces upon the storm clouds and have been powerful to bring the rain. . . .

Without initiative and the ability to act alone, an Indian of the plains was not recognized in his society. The testimony of early explorers, the rise of outstanding individuals in their conflicts with the whites, the contrast with the Pueblos, all go to show how their institutions fostered personality, almost in the Nietzschean sense of the superman. They saw life as the drama of the individual progressing upward through grades of men's societies, through acquisition of supernatural power, through feasts and victories. The initiative rested always with him. His deeds of prowess were counted for him personally, and it was his prerogative to boast of them on ritual occasions, and to use them in every way to further his personal ambitions.

The ideal man of the Pueblos is another order of being. Personal authority is perhaps the most vigorously disparaged trait in Zuñi. 'A man who thirsts for power or knowledge, who wishes to be as they scornfully phrase it "a leader of his people," receives nothing but censure and will very likely be persecuted for sorcery,' and he often has been. Native authority of manner is a liability in Zuñi, and witchcraft is the ready

[1] Compare D. H. Lawrence's "Dance of the Sprouting Corn," page 1007.

charge against a person who possesses it. He is hung by the thumbs until he 'confesses.' It is all Zuñi can do with a man of strong personality. The ideal man in Zuñi is a person of dignity and affability who has never tried to lead, and who has never called forth comment from his neighbours. Any conflict, even though all right is on his side, is held against him. Even in contests of skill like their foot-races, if a man wins habitually he is debarred from running. They are interested in a game that a number can play with even chances, and an outstanding runner spoils the game: they will have none of him.

A good man has, in Dr. Bunzel's words, 'a pleasing address, a yielding disposition, and a generous heart.' The highest praise, describing an impeccable townsman, runs: 'He is a nice polite man. No one ever hears anything from him. He never gets into trouble. He's Badger clan and Muhekwe kiva, and he always dances in the summer dances.' He should 'talk lots,' as they say — that is, he should always set people at their ease — and he should without fail co-operate easily with others either in the field or in ritual, never betraying a suspicion of arrogance or a strong emotion.

He avoids office. He may have it thrust upon him, but he does not seek it. When the kiva offices must be filled, the hatchway of the kiva is fastened and all the men are imprisoned until someone's excuses have been battered down. The folktales always relate of good men their unwillingness to take office — though they always take it. A man must avoid the appearance of leadership. When the chosen person has been prevailed upon and has been initiated in the office, he has not been given authority in our sense. His post carries with it no sanction for important action. The council of Zuñi is made up of the highest priests, and priests have no jurisdiction in cases of conflict or violence. They are holy men and must not have a quarrel put before them. Only the war chiefs have some measure of executive authority, not in war so much as in peace-time policing powers. They make proclamation of a coming rabbit hunt, or coming dances, they summon priests and co-operate with the medicine societies. The crime that they traditionally have to deal with is witchcraft. Another crime, that of betraying to the uninitiated boys the secret of the kachinas, is punished by the masked gods themselves, summoned by the head of the kachina cult. There are no other crimes. Theft rarely occurs and is a private matter. Adultery is no crime and the strain that arises from such an act is easily taken care of under their marriage arrangements. Homicide, in the one case that is remembered, was settled quickly by payments between the two families. . . .

This same lack of personal exercise of authority is as characteristic of domestic situations as it is of religious. The matrilineal and matrilocal household of course makes necessary a different allocation of authority from that with which we are familiar. But matrilineal societies do not usually dispense with a male person of authority in the household even though the father does not qualify. The mother's brother as the male head of the matrilineal household is arbiter and responsible head. But Zuñi does not recognize any authority as vested in the mother's brother, and certainly not in the father. Neither of them disciplines the children of his household. Babies are much fondled by the men folk. They carry them when they are ailing and hold them in their laps evenings. But they do not discipline them. The virtue of co-operation holds domestic life true to form just as it holds religious life, and no situations arise that need to be drastically handled. What would they be? Marriage is in other cultures the almost universal occasion where some authority is exercised. But among the Pueblos it is arranged with little formality. Marriage elsewhere in the world involves property rights and economic exchange, and on all such occasions the elders have prerogatives. But in Zuñi marriage there are no stakes in which the elders are interested. The slight emphasis upon possessions among the Pueblos makes a casual affair not only of the elsewhere difficult situation of marriage but of a dozen others, all those which according to other cultural forms involve investment of group property for the young man. Zuñi simply eliminates the occasions.

Every arrangement militates against the possibility of the child's suffering from an Oedipus complex. Malinowski[2] has pointed out for the Trobriands that the structure of society gives to the uncle authority that is associated in our culture with the father. In Zuñi, not even the uncles exercise authority. Occasions are not tolerated which would demand its exercise. The child grows up without either the resentments or the compensatory day-dreams of ambition that have their roots in this familiar situation. When the child himself becomes an adult, he has not the motivations that lead him to imagine situations in which authority will be relevant. . . .

---

[2] Bronislaw Malinowski, distinguished Polish-born anthropologist whose work lay chiefly among the Trobriand Islanders.

Just as according to the Zuñi ideal a man sinks his activities in those of the group and claims no personal authority, so also he is never violent. Their Apollonian commitment to the mean in the Greek sense is never clearer than in their cultural handling of the emotions. Whether it is anger or love or jealousy or grief, moderation is the first virtue. The fundamental tabu upon their holy men during their periods of office is against any suspicion of anger. Controversies, whether they are ceremonial or economic or domestic, are carried out with an unparalleled lack of vehemence.

Every day in Zuñi there are fresh instances of their mildness. One summer a family I knew well had given me a house to live in, and because of some complicated circumstances another family claimed the right to dispose of the dwelling. When feeling was at its height, Quatsia, the owner of the house, and her husband were with me in the living-room when a man I did not know began cutting down the flowering weeds that had not yet been hoed out of the yard. Keeping the yard free of growth is a chief prerogative of a house-owner, and therefore the man who claimed the right to dispose of the house was taking this occasion to put his claim publicly upon record. He did not enter the house or challenge Quatsia and Leo, who were inside, but he hacked slowly at the weeds. Inside, Leo sat immobile on his heels against the wall, peaceably chewing a leaf. Quatsia, however, allowed herself to flush. 'It is an insult,' she said to me. 'The man out there knows that Leo is serving as priest this year and he can't be angry. He shames us before the whole village by taking care of our yard.' The interloper finally raked up his wilted weeds, looked proudly at the neat yard, and went home. No words were ever spoken between them. For Zuñi it was an insult of sorts, and by his morning's work on the yard the rival claimant sufficiently expressed his protest. He pressed the matter no further.

Marital jealousy is similarly soft-pedalled. They do not meet adultery with violence. A usual response on the plains to the wife's adultery was to cut off the fleshy part of her nose. This was done even in the Southwest by non-Pueblo tribes like the Apache. But in Zuñi the unfaithfulness of the wife is no excuse for violence. The husband does not regard it as a violation of his rights. If she is unfaithful, it is normally a first step in changing husbands, and their institutions make this sufficiently easy so that it is a really tolerable procedure. They do not contemplate violence.

Wives are often equally moderate when their husbands are known to be unfaithful. As long as the situation is not unpleasant enough for relations to be broken off, it is ignored. The season before one of Dr. Bunzel's visits in Zuñi one of the young husbands of the household in which she lived had been carrying on an extra-marital affair that became bruited about all over the pueblo. The family ignored the matter completely. At last the white trader, a guardian of morals, expostulated with the wife. The couple had been married a dozen years and had three children; the wife belonged to an important family. The trader set forth with great earnestness the need of making a show of authority and putting an end to her husband's outrageous conduct. 'So,' his wife said, 'I didn't wash his clothes. Then he knew that I knew that everybody knew, and he stopped going with that girl.' It was effective, but not a word was passed. There were no outbursts, no recriminations, not even an open recognition of the crisis.

Wives, however, are allowed another course of action which is not sanctioned in the case of deserted husbands. A wife may fall upon her rival and beat her up publicly. They call each other names and give each other a black eye. It never settles anything, and even in the rare cases when it occurs, it dies down as quickly as it has flared. It is the only recognized fist-fight in Zuñi. If on the other hand a woman remains peacefully with her husband while he conducts amour after amour, her family are angry and bring pressure to bear upon her to separate from him. 'Everybody says she must love him,' they say, and all her relatives are ashamed. She is disobeying the rules that are laid down for her.

For the traditional course is that of divorce. If a man finds his wife's female relatives uncongenial, he is free to return to his mother's household. It provides a means of avoiding domestic intimacy with individuals he dislikes, and he merely dissolves the relationships which he has found difficult to handle amicably. . . .

The attitude toward sex in Zuñi parallels certain standards we know in our civilization as Puritanical, but the contrasts are quite as striking as the parallels. The Puritan attitude toward sex flows from its identification as sin, and the Zuñi have no sense of sin. Sin is unfamiliar to them, not only in sex but in any experience. They do not suffer from guilt complexes, and they do not consider sex as a series of temptations to be resisted with painful efforts of the will. Chastity as a way of life is regarded with great disfavour, and no one in their folktales is criticized more

harshly than the proud girls who resist marriage in their youth. They
stay in and work, ignoring the occasions when they should legitimately
be admired by the young men. But the gods do not take the steps they
were supposed to take in Puritan ethics. They come down and contrive
in spite of obstacles to sleep with them, and teach them delight and
humility. By these 'amiable disciplinary means' they bring it about that
the girl shall embrace in marriage the proper happiness of mortals.

Pleasant relations between the sexes are merely one aspect of
pleasant relations with human beings. Where we make a fundamental
distinction, their phrase of commendation is, 'Everybody likes him. He
is always having affairs with women.' Or, 'Nobody likes him. He never
has trouble over women.' Sex is an incident in the happy life.

Their cosmological ideas are another form in which they have given
expression to their extraordinarily consistent spirit. The same lack of
intensity, of conflict, and of danger which they have institutionalized
in this world, they project also upon the other world. The supernaturals,
as Dr. Bunzel says, 'have no animus against man. Inasmuch as they may
withhold their gifts, their assistance must be secured by offerings,
prayers and magical practices.' But it is no placation of evil forces. The
idea is foreign to them. They reckon, rather, that the supernaturals like
what men like, and if men like dancing so will the supernaturals. Therefore they bring the supernaturals back to dance in Zuñi by donning their
masks, they take out the medicine bundles and 'dance' them. It gives
them pleasure. Even the corn in the storeroom must be danced. 'During
the winter solstice, when all ritual groups are holding their ceremonies,
the heads of households take six perfect ears of corn and hold them in a
basket while they sing to them. This is called "dancing the corn" and is
performed that the corn may not feel neglected during the ceremonial
season.' So too the great Dance of the Corn, now no longer performed,
culminated in this enjoyment they had the means of sharing with the
corn ears. . . .

It is difficult for us to lay aside our picture of the universe as a
struggle between good and evil and see it as the Pueblos see it. They do
not see the seasons, nor man's life, as a race run by life and death. Life is
always present, death is always present. Death is no denial of life. The
seasons unroll themselves before us, and man's life also. Their attitude
involves 'no resignation, no subordination of desire to a stronger force,

but the sense of man's oneness with the universe.' When they pray they say to their gods,

> We shall be one person.

They exchange intimate relationship terms with them:

> Holding your country,
> Holding your people,
> You will sit down quietly for us.
> As children to one another
> We shall always remain.
> My child,
> My mother,
> According to my words
> Even so may it be.

They speak of exchanging breath with their gods:

> . . . Do not despise the breath of your fathers,
> But draw it into your body. . . .
> That we may finish our roads together.
> May my father bless you with life;
> May your road be fulfilled.

The breath of the gods is their breath, and by their common sharing all things are accomplished.

✒ FOR DISCUSSION AND WRITING

1. Miss Benedict's subject is one that naturally lends itself to exposition by the use of examples and by comparison and contrast. What specific illustrations does she give of the "ceremonious" character of Zuñi culture?

2. Does our own culture have anything comparable to the ceremonies and ritual observances of the Zuñi? If you can think of some examples, do any of them have as wide a public range and inclusiveness as those of the Zuñi?

3. What is the main purpose of the Zuñi rituals? Do we have any "calendric observances"? If so, are they religious or secular? Do they have any purpose however distantly related to the purpose of the major Zuñi rites?

4. What is the Zuñi attitude toward property? (You might find it interesting, at this time or later, to compare Zuñi attitudes in this and other matters with the customs practiced in an Israeli kibbutz, as described in the article beginning on page 686.)

5. To make a major distinction, Miss Benedict borrows from Nietzsche the terms "Dionysian" and "Apollonian": explain the distinction as made here. How does she use it for purposes of comparison and contrast? Point out a half-dozen specific instances she gives of the contrast between "Dionysian" and "Apollonian" ways of life.

6. Does our own culture seem to fall into either of these classifications? Do you know of any specific customs or characteristic attitudes in our own culture that might be described either way?

7. She speaks of the Plains Indians as holding individualism in high regard: what illustrations does she give of the fact? How does our culture generally regard individualism? In what specific ways is our attitude toward individualism shown? Is that attitude consistent or are there contradictions in it? What is the Zuñi attitude toward individualism?

8. One of the contrasts Miss Benedict makes between the Plains Indians and the Zuñi is their typical use of the dance: what is the contrast? Do you know of any occasions in our society—say, in the teen-age group —when the dance has a "Dionysian" purpose?

9. What is the Zuñi attitude toward the personal use of power or exercise of authority? What is the "ideal personality" among the Zuñi? Do we have any "ideal" types in our own culture? (Consider, for instance, various United States presidents.)

10. How does the role of the father among the Zuñi contrast with his role in our society? Do the Zuñi have any principle of discipline or control over children? If you have read Kafka's "Letter to His Father" in this book, what would you say about the likelihood of a similar situation among the Zuñi? What would they think of Kafka's father?

11. What is the Zuñi attitude toward sex? What contrast does Miss Benedict draw with general attitudes toward sex in our own culture? She says the Zuñi have "no sense of sin"; is this, from your own point of view, to be applauded or deplored?

12. Deliberately using a technique like Miss Benedict's of example, comparison, and contrast, write a short paper on one of the following subjects: our use of ceremony and ritual (you might start, for instance, with college life); or individualism in our society; or a personal appraisement of the advantages or disadvantages of an "Apollonian" culture like that of the Zuñi.

Thomas Robert Malthus ✑ The Principle of Population

✑ English writer on political economy (1766-1834), who fathered what is known as the "Malthusian principle." The immediate polemical targets of his famous *An Essay on the Principle of Population*, published in 1798, were the "Godwin perfectibilists," those who, like William Godwin, believed in the perfectibility of society. (Godwin was Mary Shelley's father, and Shelley's own social thinking was greatly influenced by him.) Malthus' *Essay* aroused a storm of controversy. It is still pertinent in our own time, with the "population explosion" that is one of today's most critical problems. Malthus is represented here by the first chapter of the 1798 *Essay* and the last chapter of the 1803 revision. ⟩

THE great and unlooked for discoveries that have taken place of late years in natural philosophy, the increasing diffusion of general knowledge from the extension of the art of printing, the ardent and unshackled spirit of inquiry that prevails throughout the lettered and even unlettered world, the new and extraordinary lights that have been thrown on political subjects which dazzle and astonish the understanding, and particularly that tremendous phenomenon in the political horizon, the French revolution, which, like a blazing comet, seems destined either to inspire with fresh life and vigour, or to scorch up and destroy the shrinking inhabitants of the earth, have all concurred to lead able men into the opinion that we were touching on a period big with the most important changes, changes that would in some measure be decisive of the future fate of mankind.

It has been said that the great question is now at issue, whether man shall henceforth start forwards with accelerated velocity towards illimitable, and hitherto unconceived improvement, or be condemned to a perpetual oscillation between happiness and misery, and after every effort remain still at an immeasurable distance from the wished-for goal.
. . .

I have read some of the speculations on the perfectibility of man and society with great pleasure. I have been warmed and delighted with the enchanting picture which they hold forth. I ardently wish for such happy improvements. But I see great, and, to my understanding, unconquerable difficulties in the way to them. These difficulties it is my present purpose to state, declaring, at the same time, that so far from exulting in them, as a cause of triumph over the friends of innovation, nothing would give me greater pleasure than to see them completely removed.

The most important argument that I shall adduce is certainly not new. The principles on which it depends have been explained in part by Hume, and more at large by Dr. Adam Smith. It has been advanced and applied to the present subject, though not with its proper weight, or in the most forcible point of view, by Mr. Wallace, and it may probably have been stated by many writers that I have never met with. I should certainly therefore not think of advancing it again, though I mean to place it in a point of view in some degree different from any that I have hitherto seen, if it had ever been fairly and satisfactorily answered.

The cause of this neglect on the part of the advocates for the perfectibility of mankind is not easily accounted for. I cannot doubt the talents of such men as Godwin and Condorcet. I am unwilling to doubt their candour. To my understanding, and probably to that of most others, the difficulty appears insurmountable. Yet these men of acknowledged ability and penetration, scarcely deign to notice it, and hold on their course in such speculations, with unabated ardour and undiminished confidence. I have certainly no right to say that they purposely shut their eyes to such arguments. I ought rather to doubt the validity of them, when neglected by such men, however forcibly their truth may strike my own mind. Yet in this respect it must be acknowledged that we are all of us too prone to err. If I saw a glass of wine repeatedly presented to a man, and he took no notice of it, I should be apt to think that he was blind or uncivil. A juster philosophy might teach me rather to think that my eyes deceived me and that the offer was not really what I conceived it to be.

In entering upon the argument I must premise that I put out of the question, at present, all mere conjectures, that is, all suppositions, the probable realization of which cannot be inferred upon any just philosophical grounds. A writer may tell me that he thinks man will ultimately become an ostrich. I cannot properly contradict him. But before he can expect to bring any reasonable person over to his opinion, he ought to shew, that the necks of mankind have been gradually elongating, that the lips have grown harder and more prominent, that the legs and feet are daily altering their shape, and that the hair is beginning to change into stubs of feathers. And till the probability of so wonderful a conversion can be shewn, it is surely lost time and lost eloquence to expatiate on the happiness of man in such a state; to describe his powers, both of running and flying, to paint him in a condition where all narrow luxuries would be contemned, where he would be employed only in collecting the necessaries of life, and where, consequently, each man's share of labour would be light, and his portion of leisure ample.

I think I may fairly make two postulata.

First, That food is necessary to the existence of man.

Secondly, That the passion between the sexes is necessary and will remain nearly in its present state.

These two laws, ever since we have had any knowledge of mankind, appear to have been fixed laws of our nature, and, as we have not hitherto seen any alteration in them, we have no right to conclude that they will ever cease to be what they now are, without an immediate act of power in that Being who first arranged the system of the universe, and for the advantage of his creatures, still executes, according to fixed laws, all its various operations.

I do not know that any writer has supposed that on this earth man will ultimately be able to live without food. But Mr. Godwin has conjectured that the passion between the sexes may in time be extinguished. As, however, he calls this part of his work a deviation into the land of conjecture, I will not dwell longer upon it at present than to say that the best arguments for the perfectibility of man are drawn from a contemplation of the great progress that [man] has already made from the savage state and the difficulty of saying where he is to stop. But towards the extinction of the passion between the sexes, no progress whatever has hitherto been made. It appears to exist in as much force at present as it did two thousand or four thousand years ago. There are individual exceptions now as there always have been. But, as these exceptions do not appear to increase in number, it would surely be a very unphilosophical mode of arguing, to infer merely from the existence of an exception, that the exception would, in time, become the rule, and the rule the exception.

Assuming then, my postulata as granted, I say, that the power of population is indefinitely greater than the power in the earth to produce subsistence for man.

Population, when unchecked, increases in a geometrical ratio. Subsistence increases only in an arithmetical ratio. A slight acquaintance with numbers will shew the immensity of the first power in comparison of the second.

By that law of our nature which makes food necessary to the life of man, the effects of these two unequal powers must be kept equal.

This implies a strong and constantly operating check on population from the difficulty of subsistence. This difficulty must fall some where and must necessarily be severely felt by a large portion of mankind.

Through the animal and vegetable kingdoms, nature has scattered the seeds of life abroad with the most profuse and liberal hand. She has comparatively sparing in the room and the nourishment necessary to rear them. The germs of existence contained in this spot of earth, with ample food, and ample room to expand in, would fill millions of worlds in the course of a few thousand years. Necessity, that imperious all pervading law of nature, restrains them within the prescribed bounds. The race of plants, and the race of animals shrink under this great restrictive law. And the race of man cannot, by any efforts of reason, escape from it. Among plants and animals its effects are waste of seed, sickness, and premature death. Among mankind, misery and vice. The former, misery, is an absolutely necessary consequence of it. Vice is a highly probable consequence, and we therefore see it abundantly prevail, but it ought not, perhaps, to be called an absolutely necessary consequence. The ordeal of virtue is to resist all temptation to evil.

This natural inequality of the two powers of population and of production in the earth and that great law of our nature which must constantly keep their effects equal form the great difficulty that to me appears insurmountable in the way to the perfectibility of society. All other arguments are of slight and subordinate consideration in comparison of this. I see no way by which man can escape from the weight of this law which pervades all animated nature. No fancied equality, no agrarian regulations in their utmost extent, could remove the pressure of it even for a single century. And it appears, therefore, to be decisive against the possible existence of a society, all the members of which should live in ease, happiness, and comparative leisure; and feel no anxiety about providing the means of subsistence for themselves and families.

Consequently, if the premises are just, the argument is conclusive against the perfectibility of the mass of mankind. . . .

OF OUR RATIONAL EXPECTATIONS RESPECTING THE FUTURE IMPROVEMENT OF SOCIETY

. . . In every old state, it is observed that a considerable number of grown-up people remain for a time unmarried. The duty of practising the common and acknowledged rules of morality during this period has never been controverted in theory, however it may have been opposed in practice. This branch of the duty of moral restraint has scarcely been touched by the reasonings of this work. It rests on the same foundation as before, neither stronger nor weaker. And knowing how incompletely this duty has hitherto been fulfilled, it would certainly be visionary to expect that in future it would be completely fulfilled.

The part which has been affected by the reasonings of this work is not therefore that which relates to our conduct during the period of celibacy, but to the duty of extending this period till we have a prospect of being able to maintain our children. And it is by no means visionary to indulge a hope of some favourable change in this respect; because it is found by experience that the prevalence of this kind of prudential restraint is extremely different in different countries, and in the same countries at different periods.

It cannot be doubted that throughout Europe in general, and most particularly in the northern states, a decided change has taken place in the operation of prudential restraint, since the prevalence of those war-like and enterprising habits which destroyed so many people. In later times the gradual diminution and almost total extinction of the plagues which so frequently visited Europe in the seventeenth and beginning of the eighteenth centuries, produced a change of the same kind. And in this country, it is not to be doubted that the proportion of marriages has become smaller since the improvement of our towns, the less frequent returns of epidemics, and the adoption of habits of greater cleanliness. During the late scarcities[1] it appears that the number of marriages diminished; and the same motives which prevented many people from marrying during such a period, would operate precisely in the same way if, in future, the additional number of children reared to manhood from the introduction of the cow-pox were to be such as to crowd all employments, lower the price of labour, and make it more difficult to support a family.

Universally, the practice of mankind on the subject of marriage has been much superior to their theories; and however frequent may have been the declamations on the duty of entering into this state, and the advantage of early unions to prevent vice, each individual has practically found it necessary to consider of the means of supporting a family before he ventured to take so important a step. That great *vis medicatrix reipublicae*,[2] the desire of bettering our condition, and the fear of making it worse, has been constantly in action, and has been constantly directing people into the right road, in spite of all the declamations which tended to lead them aside. Owing to this powerful spring of health in every state, which is nothing more than an inference from the general course of the laws of nature, irresistibly forced on each man's attention, the prudential check to marriage has increased in Europe; and it cannot be unreasonable to conclude that it will make further advances. If this take place without any marked and decided increase of a vicious intercourse with the sex, the happiness of society will evidently be promoted by it; and with regard to the danger of such increase, it is consolatory to remark that those countries in Europe where marriages are the latest or least frequent, are by no means particularly distinguished by vices of this kind. It has appeared that Norway, Switzerland, England, and Scotland are above all the rest in the prevalence of the preventive check; and though I do not mean to insist particularly on the virtuous habits of these countries, yet I think that no person would select them as the countries most marked for profligacy of manners. Indeed, from the little that I know of the continent, I should have been inclined to select them as most distinguished for contrary habits, and as rather above than below their neighbours in the chastity of their women, and consequently in the

[1] 1800-1801.
[2] Force of social welfare.

virtuous habits of their men. Experience therefore seems to teach us that it is possible for moral and physical causes to counteract the effects that might at first be expected from an increase of the check to marriage; but allowing all the weight to these effects which is in any degree probable, it may be safely asserted, that the diminution of the vices arising from indigence would fully counterbalance them; and that all the advantages of diminished mortality and superior comforts, which would certainly result from an increase of the preventive check, may be placed entirely on the side of the gains to the cause of happiness and virtue.

It is less the object of the present work to propose new plans of improving society than to inculcate the necessity of resting contented with that mode of improvement which already has in part been acted upon as dictated by the course of nature, and of not obstructing the advances which would otherwise be made in this way.

It would be undoubtedly highly advantageous that all our positive institutions, and the whole tenour of our conduct to the poor, should be such as actively to co-operate with that lesson of prudence inculcated by the common course of human events; and if we take upon ourselves sometimes to mitigate the natural punishments of imprudence, that we could balance it by increasing the rewards of an opposite conduct. But much would be done if merely the institutions which directly tend to encourage marriage were gradually changed, and we ceased to circulate opinions and inculcate doctrines which positively counteract the lessons of nature. . . .

If the principles which I have endeavored to establish be false, I most sincerely hope to see them completely refuted; but if they be true, the subject is so important, and interests the question of human happiness so nearly, that it is impossible they should not in time be more fully known and more generally circulated, whether any particular efforts be made for the purpose or not.

Among the higher and middle classes of society, the effect of this knowledge will, I hope, be to direct without relaxing their efforts in bettering the condition of the poor; to show them what they can and what they cannot do; and that, although much may be done by advice and instruction, by encouraging habits of prudence and cleanliness, by discriminate charity, and by any mode of bettering the present condition of the poor which is followed by an increase of the preventive check; yet that, without this last effect, all the former efforts would be futile;

and that, in any old and well-peopled state, to assist the poor in such a manner as to enable them to marry as early as they please, and rear up large families, is a physical impossibility. This knowledge, by tending to prevent the rich from destroying the good effects of their own exertions, and wasting their efforts in a direction where success is unattainable, would confine their attention to the proper objects, and thus enable them to do more good.

Among the poor themselves, its effects would be still more important. That the principal and most permanent cause of poverty has little or no *direct* relation to forms of government, or the unequal division of property; and that, as the rich do not in reality possess the *power* of finding employment and maintenance for the poor, the poor cannot, in the nature of things, possess the *right* to demand them; are important truths flowing from the principle of population, which, when properly explained, would by no means be above the most ordinary comprehensions. And it is evident that every man in the lower classes of society who became acquainted with these truths, would be disposed to bear the distresses in which he might be involved with more patience; would feel less discontent and irritation at the government and the higher classes of society, on account of his poverty; would be on all occasions less disposed to insubordination and turbulence; and if he received assistance, either from any public institution or from the hand of private charity, he would receive it with more thankfulness, and more justly appreciate its value.

If these truths were by degrees more generally known (which in the course of time does not seem to be improbable from the natural effects of the mutual interchange of opinions), the lower classes of people, as a body, would become more peaceable and orderly, would be less inclined to tumultuous proceedings in seasons of scarcity, and would at all times be less influenced by inflammatory and seditious publications, from knowing how little the price of labour and the means of supporting a family depend upon a revolution. The mere knowledge of these truths, even if they did not operate sufficiently to produce any marked change in the prudential habits of the poor with regard to marriage, would still have a most beneficial effect on their conduct in a political light; and undoubtedly, one of the most valuable of these effects would be the power that would result to the higher and middle classes of society, of gradually improving their governments, without the apprehension of those revolutionary excesses, the fear of which, at present, threatens to deprive Europe even of that degree of liberty which she had before experienced to be practicable, and the salutary effects of which she had long enjoyed.

On the whole, therefore, though our future prospects respecting the mitigation of the evils arising from the principle of population may not be so bright as we could wish, yet they are far from being entirely disheartening, and by no means preclude that gradual and progressive improvement in human society which, before the late wild speculations on this subject, was the object of rational expectation. To the laws of property and marriage, and to the apparent narrow principle of self-interest which prompts each individual to exert himself in bettering his condition, we are indebted for all the noblest exertions of human genius, for everything that distinguishes the civilised from the savage state. A strict inquiry into the principle of population obliges us to conclude that we shall never be able to throw down the ladder by which we have risen to this eminence; but it by no means proves that we may not rise higher by the same means. The structure of society, in its great features, will probably always remain unchanged. We have every reason to believe that it will always consist of a class of proprietors and a class of labourers; but the condition of each, and the proportion which they bear to each other, may be so altered as greatly to improve the harmony and beauty of the whole. It would indeed be a melancholy reflection that, while the views of physical science are daily enlarging, so as scarcely to be bounded by the most distant horizon, the science of moral and political philosophy should be confined within such narrow limits, or at best be so feeble in its influence, as to be unable to counteract the obstacles to human happiness arising from a single cause. But however formidable these obstacles may have appeared in some parts of this work, it is hoped that the general result of the inquiry is such as not to make us give up the improvement of human society in despair. The partial good which seems to be attainable is worthy of all our exertions; is sufficient to direct our efforts, and animate our prospects. And although we cannot expect that the virtue and happiness of mankind will keep pace with the brilliant career of physical discovery; yet, if we are not wanting to ourselves, we may confidently indulge the hope that, to no unimportant extent, they will be influenced by its progress and will partake in its success.

꿏 FOR DISCUSSION AND WRITING

1. Examine the syntactical structure of the first sentence. Where is the main clause? How many parallel subordinate clauses are there? This is a long sentence, filling up a whole paragraph; do its length and complexity lead to confusion, or is the sentence quite clear? As a written exercise, break the whole paragraph up into short sentences. Compare your paragraph with the original one; what is the comparative effectiveness of the original as against your version?

2. Now consider the third paragraph, which begins with several short sentences. Do you find a type of parallelism between these? Does the parallelism account for the relative effectiveness of the series of short sentences here?

3. Where does Malthus first state the main concern of the essay? What are his means of persuasion in the first few paragraphs by which he attempts to win over his readers to an assenting attitude? Where does he state the position of his opponents? Does he make any use of humor? What is the point of the paragraph about the ostrich? The analogy is rather grotesque; is it effective?

4. What are his postulates? What *is* a postulate? Where does he make his first statement of the "principle of population" that is his objective?

5. Restate in your own words his argument in the three paragraphs beginning "Through the animal and vegetable kingdoms . . ." and ending "Consequently, if the premises are just, the argument is conclusive. . . ." What is his conclusion about the perfectibility of society?

6. In the second part of the essay given here ("Of Our Rational Expectations . . ."), what does he say is the "prudential check to marriage"? He says that this check is a "law of nature": do marriage customs in our own society suggest such a law of nature? What modern program or programs have been put forward to provide the "check" that Malthus recommends?

7. What is Malthus' attitude toward the cause of poverty and the "rights" (if any) of the poor? Consider the statement: "And it is evident that every man in the lower classes of society who became acquainted with these truths, would be disposed to bear the distresses in which he might be in-

volved with more patience; would feel less discontent. . . ." What is your opinion of his position here? Has time justified it or discredited it?

8. Note the statement in the middle of the final paragraph, "The structure of society, in its great features, will probably always remain unchanged." Has time justified the statement, or the reverse?

9. Write a short paper answering Malthus' argument, attempting to adopt something of his suavity and agreeableness of manner, and using at least once the rhetorical device we noted in the first two questions. Or write a paper setting forth your own opinions on the perfectibility of society.

Jonathan Swift ⇜ A Modest Proposal

For Preventing the Children of Poor People from Being a Burthen to Their Parents or the Country and for Making Them Beneficial to the Public

⇜ English satirist (1667-1745). Swift was born in Ireland and returned there as Dean of Saint Patrick's Cathedral in Dublin. There he wrote his magnificently imaginative *Gulliver's Travels*, as well as the *Drapier's Letters* and the *Modest Proposal*. The latter made him virtually an Irish national hero. He left his Deanship to go back to England, but under great discouragement returned to Ireland to take minor church posts and to live out an old age threatened with madness. He was buried in Saint Patrick's. ⇝

IT is a melancholy object to those who walk through this great town, or travel in the country, when they see the streets, the roads, and cabin doors crowded with beggars of the female sex followed by three, four, or six children, all in rags and importuning every passenger for an alms. These mothers, instead of being able to work for their honest livelihood, are forced to employ all their time in strolling, to beg sustenance for their helpless infants, who, as they grow up, either turn thieves for want of work or leave their dear native country to fight for the Pretender in Spain or sell themselves to the Barbadoes.

I think it is agreed by all parties that this prodigious number of children, in the arms or on the backs or at the heels of their mothers and frequently of their fathers, is in the present deplorable state of the kingdom a very great additional grievance, and therefore whoever

From *A Modest Proposal* by Jonathan Swift (first published in 1729).

could find out a fair, cheap, and easy method of making these children sound and useful members of the commonwealth would deserve so well of the public as to have his statue set up for a preserver of the nation.

But my intention is very far from being confined to provide only for the children of professed beggars; it is of a much greater extent, and shall take in the whole number of infants at a certain age who are born of parents in effect as little able to support them as those who demand our charity in the streets.

As to my own part, having turned my thoughts for many years upon this important subject and maturely weighed the several schemes of other projectors, I have always found them grossly mistaken in their computation. It is true, a child just dropped from its dam may be supported by her milk for a solar year, with little other nourishment, at the most not above the value of two shillings, which the mother may certainly get, or the value in scraps, by her lawful occupation of begging; and it is exactly at one year old that I propose to provide for them in such a manner as, instead of being a charge upon their parents or the parish or wanting food and raiment for the rest of their lives, they shall on the contrary contribute to the feeding, and partly to the clothing, of many thousands.

There is likewise another great advantage in my scheme, that it will prevent those voluntary abortions and that horrid practice of women murdering their bastard children, alas! too frequent among us, sacrificing the poor innocent babes, I doubt more to avoid the expense than the shame, which would move tears and pity in the most savage and inhuman breast.

The number of souls in this kingdom being usually reckoned one million and a half, of these I calculate there may be about two hundred thousand couple whose wives are breeders, from which number I subtract thirty thousand couple who are able to maintain their own children (although I apprehend there cannot be so many, under the present distresses of the kingdom); but this being granted, there will remain a hundred and seventy thousand breeders. I again subtract fifty thousand for those women who miscarry or whose children die by accident or disease within the year. There only remain a hundred and twenty thousand children of poor parents annually born. The question therefore is how this number shall be reared and provided for, which, as I have already said, under the present situation of affairs is utterly impossible by all the methods hitherto proposed. For we can neither employ them in handicraft or agriculture; we neither build houses (I mean in the country) nor cultivate land; they can very seldom pick up a livelihood by stealing, till they arrive at six years old, except where they are of towardly parts, although I confess they learn the rudiments much earlier, during which time they can, however, be properly looked upon only as *probationers;* as I have been informed by a principal gentleman in the County of Cavan who protested to me that he never knew above one or two instances under the age of six, even in a part of the kingdom so renowned for the quickest proficiency in that art.

I am assured by our merchants that a boy or a girl before twelve years old is no saleable commodity, and even when they come to this age they will not yield above three pounds or three pounds and half a crown at most on the exchange, which cannot turn to account either to the parents or the kingdom, the charge of nutriment and rags having been at least four times that value.

I shall now, therefore, humbly propose my own thoughts, which I hope will not be liable to the least objection.

I have been assured by a very knowing American of my acquaintance in London that a young, healthy child well nursed is, at a year old, a most delicious, nourishing, and wholesome food, whether stewed, roasted, baked, or boiled; and I make no doubt that it will equally serve in a fricassee or a ragout.

I do therefore humbly offer it to public consideration that of the hundred and twenty thousand children already computed, twenty thousand may be reserved for breed, whereof only one fourth part to be males, which is more than we allow to sheep, black cattle, or swine; and my reason is that these children are seldom the fruits of marriage, a circumstance not much regarded by our savages; therefore one male will be sufficient to serve four females. That the remaining hundred thousand may, at a year old, be offered in sale to the persons of quality and fortune through the kingdom, always advising the mother to let them suck plentifully in the last month, so as to render them plump and fat for a good table. A child will make two dishes at an entertainment for friends; and when the family dines alone, the fore- or hindquarter will make a reasonable dish, and seasoned with a little pepper or salt, will be very good boiled on the fourth day, especially in winter. I have reckoned, upon a medium, that a child just born will weigh twelve pounds, and in a solar year, if tolerably nursed, will increase to twenty-eight pounds.

I grant this food will be somewhat dear, and therefore very proper for the landlords, who, as they have already devoured most of the parents, seem to have the best title to the children.

Infant's flesh will be in season throughout the year, but more plentifully in March and a little before and after; for we are told by a grave author, an eminent French physician, that fish being a prolific diet, there are more children born in Roman Catholic countries about nine months after Lent than at any other season; therefore, reckoning a year after Lent, the markets will be more glutted than usual, because the number of Popish infants is at least three to one in this kingdom; and therefore it will have one other collateral advantage, by lessening the number of Papists among us. I have already computed the charge of nursing a beggar's child (in which list I reckon all cottagers, laborers, and four fifths of the farmers) to be about two shillings per annum, rags included; and I believe no gentleman would repine to give ten shillings for the carcass of a good fat child, which, as I have said, will make four dishes of excellent nutritive meat, when he has only some particular friend or his own family to dine with him. Thus the squire will learn to be a good landlord and grow popular among his tenants; the mother will have eight shillings net profit and be fit for work till she produces another child.

Those who are more thrifty (as I must confess the times require) may flay the carcass, the skin of which, artificially dressed, will make admirable gloves for ladies and summer boots for fine gentlemen.

As to our city of Dublin, shambles[1] may be appointed for this purpose in the most convenient parts of it; and butchers, we may be assured, will not be wanting, although I rather recommend buying the children alive than dressing them hot from the knife as we do roasting pigs.

A very worthy person, a true lover of his country, and whose virtues I highly esteem, was lately pleased in discoursing on this matter to offer a refinement upon my scheme. He said that many gentlemen of this kingdom having of late destroyed their deer, he conceived that the want of venison might be well supplied by the bodies of young lads and maidens, not exceeding fourteen years of age nor under twelve, so great a number of both sexes in every country being now ready to starve for want of work and service; and these to be disposed of by their parents if

[1] Slaughterhouses.

alive, or otherwise by their nearest relations. But with due deference to so excellent a friend and so deserving a patriot, I cannot be altogether in his sentiments; for as to the males, my American acquaintance assured me, from frequent experience, that their flesh was generally tough and lean, like that of our school-boys, by continual exercise, and their taste disagreeable; and to fatten them would not answer the charge. Then as to the females, it would, I think, with humble submission, be a loss to the public, because they would soon become breeders themselves: and besides, it is not improbable that some scrupulous people might be apt to censure such a practice (although indeed very unjustly) as a little bordering upon cruelty, which, I confess, has always been with me the strongest objection against any project, however so well intended.

But in order to justify my friend, he confessed that this expedient was put into his head by the famous Psalmanazar, a native of the island Formosa, who came from thence to London above twenty years ago and in conversation told my friend that in his country, when any young person happened to be put to death, the executioner sold the carcass to persons of quality as a prime dainty and that in his time the body of a plump girl of fifteen, who was crucified for an attempt to poison the emperor, was sold to his imperial Majesty's prime minister of state and other great mandarins of the court in joints from the gibbet at four hundred crowns. Neither, indeed, can I deny that if the same use were made of several plump young girls in this town who, without one single groat to their fortunes, cannot stir abroad without a chair, and appear at playhouse and assemblies in foreign fineries which they never will pay for, the kingdom would not be the worse.

Some persons of a desponding spirit are in great concern about that vast number of poor people who are aged, diseased, or maimed, and I have been desired to employ my thoughts what course may be taken to ease the nation of so grievous an encumbrance. But I am not in the least pain upon the matter, because it is very well known that they are every day dying and rotting by cold, and famine, and filth, and vermin, as fast as can be reasonably expected. And as to the young laborers, they are now in almost as hopeful a condition; they cannot get work and consequently pine away for want of nourishment to a degree that if at any time they are accidentally hired to common labor, they have not strength to perform it; and thus the country and themselves are happily delivered from the evils to come.

I have too long digressed and therefore shall return to my subject. I think the advantages by the proposal which I have made are obvious and many, as well as of the highest importance.

For first, as I have already observed, it would greatly lessen the number of Papists, with whom we are yearly overrun, being the principal breeders of the nation as well as our most dangerous enemies, and who stay at home on purpose to deliver the kingdom to the Pretender,[2] hoping to take their advantage by the absence of so many good Protestants, who have chosen rather to leave their country than stay at home and pay tithes, against their conscience, to an Episcopal curate.

Secondly, the poorer tenants will have something valuable of their own which by law may be made liable to distress and help to pay their landlord's rent, their corn and cattle being already seized and money a thing unknown.

Thirdly, whereas the maintenance of a hundred thousand children from two years old and upward cannot be computed at less than ten shillings apiece per annum, the nation's stock will thereby be increased fifty thousand pounds per annum, beside the profit of a new dish introduced to the tables of all gentlemen of fortune in the kingdom who have any refinement in taste. And the money will circulate among ourselves, the goods being entirely of our own growth and manufacture.

Fourthly, the constant breeders, beside the gain of eight shillings sterling per annum by the sale of their children, will be rid of the charge of maintaining them after the first year.

Fifthly, this food would likewise bring great custom to taverns, where the vintners will certainly be so prudent as to procure the best receipts for dressing it to perfection and consequently have their houses frequented by all the fine gentlemen who justly value themselves upon their knowledge in good eating; and a skillful cook who understands how to oblige his guests will contrive to make it as expensive as they please.

Sixthly, this would be a great inducement to marriage, which all wise nations have either encouraged by rewards or enforced by laws and penalties. It would increase the care and tenderness of mothers toward their children when they were sure of a settlement for life to the poor babes, provided in some sort by the public, to their annual profit or expense. We should see an honest emulation among the mar-

2 Son of James II.

ried women, which of them could bring the fattest child to the market. Men would become as fond of their wives during the time of their pregnancy as they are now of their mares in foal, their cows in calf, or sows when they are ready to farrow, nor offer to beat or kick them (as is too frequent a practice) for fear of a miscarriage.

Many other advantages might be enumerated. For instance, the addition of some thousand carcasses in our exportation of barreled beef; the propagation of swine's flesh and improvement in the art of making good bacon, so much wanted among us by the great destruction of pigs, too frequent at our table, which are no way comparable in taste or magnificence to a well-grown, fat yearling child, which, roasted whole, will make a considerable figure at a lord mayor's feast or any other public entertainment. But this and many others I omit, being studious of brevity.

Supposing that one thousand families in this city would be constant customers for infant's flesh, beside others who might have it at merry-meetings, particularly at weddings and christenings, I compute that Dublin would take off annually about twenty thousand carcasses and the rest of the kingdom (where probably they will be sold somewhat cheaper) the remaining eighty thousand.

I can think of no one objection that will possibly be raised against this proposal unless it should be urged that the number of people will be thereby much lessened in the kingdom. This I freely own, and it was indeed one principal design in offering it to the world. I desire the reader will observe that I calculate my remedy for this one individual kingdom of Ireland and for no other that ever was, is, or I think ever can be, upon earth. Therefore let no man talk to me of other expedients: of taxing our absentees at five shillings a pound; of using neither clothes nor household furniture except what is of our own growth and manufacture; of utterly rejecting the materials and instruments that promote foreign luxury; of curing the expensiveness of pride, vanity, idleness, and gaming in our women; of introducing a vein of parsimony, prudence, and temperance; of learning to love our country, in the want of which we differ even from Laplanders and the inhabitants of Tupinamba; of quitting our animosities and factions, nor acting any longer like the Jews, who were murdering one another at the very moment their city was taken; of being a little cautious not to sell our country and conscience for nothing; of teaching landlords to have at least one degree of mercy toward their tenants; lastly, of putting a spirit of honesty, industry, and skill into our shop-keepers, who, if a resolution could now be taken to buy only our native goods, would immediately unite to cheat and exact upon us in the price, the measure, and the goodness, nor could ever yet be brought to make one fair proposal of just dealing, though often and earnestly invited to it.

Therefore, I repeat, let no man talk to me of these and the like expedients till he has at least some glimpse of hope that there will be ever some hearty and sincere attempt to put them in practice.

But as to myself, having been wearied out for many years with offering vain, idle, visionary thoughts and at length utterly despairing of success, I fortunately fell upon this proposal, which, as it is wholly new, so it has something solid and real, of no expense and little trouble, full in our own power, and whereby we can incur no danger in disobliging England. For this kind of commodity will not bear exportation, the flesh being of too tender a consistence to admit a long continuance in salt, although perhaps I could name a country which would be glad to eat up our whole nation without it.

After all, I am not so violently bent upon my own opinion as to reject any offer proposed by wise men which shall be found equally innocent, cheap, easy, and effectual. But before something of that kind shall be advanced in contradiction to my scheme and offering a better, I desire the author or authors will be pleased maturely to consider two points: first, as things now stand, how they will be able to find food and raiment for a hundred thousand useless mouths and backs; and secondly, there being a round million of creatures in human figure throughout this kingdom whose whole subsistence, put into a common stock, would leave them in debt two millions of pounds sterling, adding those who are beggars by profession to the bulk of farmers, cottagers, and laborers, with the wives and children who are beggars in effect, I desire those politicians who dislike my overture, and may perhaps be so bold as to attempt an answer, that they will first ask the parents of these mortals whether they would not at this day think it a great happiness to have been sold for food at a year old in the manner I prescribe, and thereby have avoided such a perpetual scene of misfortunes as they have since gone through by the oppression of landlords, the impossibility of paying rent without money or trade, the want of common sustenance, with neither house nor clothes to cover them from the inclemencies of the weather, and the most inevitable prospect of entailing the like or greater miseries upon their breed forever.

I profess in the sincerity of my heart that I have not the least personal interest in endeavoring to promote this necessary work, having no other motive than the public good of my country, by advancing our trade, providing for infants, relieving the poor, and giving some pleasure to the rich. I have no children by which I can propose to get a single penny, the youngest being nine years old and my wife past childbearing.

✍️ FOR DISCUSSION AND WRITING

1. What is the force of the word "modest" in the title of the piece? Swift's *A Modest Proposal* came out in 1729, Malthus' *Essay on Population* in 1798; but the problem with which Malthus was concerned greatly antedated, of course, his writing about it; in what sense does Swift's proposal bear on the same problem? Malthus, in the latter part of his essay, writes at some length on our *"rational* expectations" of solving the problem, and especially of how the poor may be taught *rational* attitudes and habits in this respect; toward the end of his proposal, Swift also refers to what could be considered rational measures, but what does he think of men's capability for rational action?

2. What are the usual distinctions between satire and irony? (If you aren't familiar with them, the dictionary will help.) What have these two modes in common? How would you classify Swift's *Proposal?* Or is an absolute classification as either one or the other possible or useful? In general, how does the *Proposal* show these two qualities: intensification of incongruities, and a kind of "double-talking" discrepancy between the literal meaning and the implied meaning?

3. Point out the specific place in the piece where Swift first lets slip the mask of solemn, honest straightforwardness and drops a clue as to the monstrosity of what he is suggesting. Consider the diction of the following phrases: "a child just dropped from its dam"; the mother's "lawful occupation of begging"; "I calculate there may be about two hundred thousand couple whose wives are breeders." Which words are incongruous? A most important aspect of effective satire is that it uses actuality or truth as the basis of its distortions. In those incongruous words you have just pointed out,

what is the actuality or truth (at least by inference) that gives them their sting?

4. Swift starts to use statistics here: subtracting "thirty thousand couple," there will remain "a hundred and seventy thousand breeders"; he subtracts again "fifty thousand" for miscarriages and child mortality by accident or disease; and he goes on to speak of the age at which children may (hopefully) acquire proficiency in stealing (at least those of "towardly parts"); and begins to reckon up how much a child may bring in pounds as a "saleable commodity." What, specifically, is the incongruity of the statistical method in the context of the particular subject? If there were not some inferential base of truth and actuality in this ironical procedure, it would be pointless and ineffectual. You may not be able to speak for early eighteenth-century habits of thought, but the statistical method applied to human phenomena has immense and ever greater importance in our own time. Can you think of one of its modern applications that reduces human beings to so many mathematical units for exploitation on the market?

5. In what particular element (it may be a single word) lies the ironic pinch of the following: "therefore one male will be sufficient to serve four females"; "the remaining hundred thousand may, at a year old, be offered in sale to the persons of quality and fortune through the kingdom"; the detail of the menus suggested; "this food will be . . . very proper for the landlords"; "those who are more thrifty (as I must confess the times require) may flay the carcass . . ."; the proposal "would increase the care and tenderness of mothers"?

6. A satirical paper is suggested. Some students will have a genuine turn for this kind of writing, while others will not; so the length of the paper could be extremely short or as long as your impulse may last. Reflect for a little while and think up some proposal, as monstrous as Swift's, for solving one of the more pressing modern social problems, such as integration, unemployment, poverty, medical care, care of the old, the cold war, the atomic threat, or others. Remember the necessity (for effectiveness in this genre) of keeping a solid inferential basis of fact, and that the proverb "Truth is stranger than fiction" has had striking illustration in our time, so that whatever grotesque proposals you suggest may have a measure of possibility (as German scientific practice in the death camps under Hitler out-Swifted even Swift's imagination).

José Ortega y Gasset ﺤᔥ The Coming of the Masses

ᔥ See note on page 191. The selection here is the first chapter of Ortega's famous work *The Revolt of the Masses.* ᔥ

THERE is one fact which, whether for good or ill, is of utmost importance in the public life of Europe at the present moment. This fact is the accession of the masses to complete social power. As the masses, by definition, neither should nor can direct their own personal existence, and still less rule society in general, this fact means that actually Europe is suffering from the greatest crisis that can afflict people, nations, and civilisation. Such a crisis has occurred more than once in history. Its characteristics and its consequences are well known. So also is its name. It is called the rebellion of the masses. In order to understand this formidable fact, it is important from the start to avoid giving to the words "rebellion," "masses," and "social power" a meaning exclusively or primarily

political. Public life is not solely political, but equally, and even primarily, intellectual, moral, economic, religious; it comprises all our collective
habits, including our fashions both of dress and of amusement.

Perhaps the best line of approach to this historical phenomenon
may be found by turning our attention to a visual experience, stressing
one aspect of our epoch which is plain to our very eyes. This fact is quite
simple to enunciate, though not so to analyse. I shall call it the fact of agglomeration, of "plenitude." Towns are full of people, houses full of
tenants, hotels full of guests, trains full of travellers, cafés full of customers, parks full of promenaders, consulting-rooms of famous doctors
full of patients, theatres full of spectators, and beaches full of bathers.
What previously was, in general, no problem, now begins to be an
everyday one, namely, to find room.

That is all. Can there be any fact simpler, more patent, more constant in actual life? Let us now pierce the plain surface of this observation and we shall be surprised to see how there wells forth an unexpected
spring in which the white light of day, of our actual day, is broken up
into its rich chromatic content. What is it that we see, and the sight of
which causes us so much surprise? We see the multitude, as such, in possession of the places and the instruments created by civilisation. The
slightest reflection will then make us surprised at our own surprise. What
about it? Is this not the ideal state of things? The theatre has seats to
be occupied — in other words, so that the house may be full — and now
they are overflowing; people anxious to use them are left standing outside. Though the fact be quite logical and natural, we cannot but recognise that this did not happen before and that now it does; consequently,
there has been a change, an innovation, which justifies, at least foɪ ʰhe
first moment, our surprise.

To be surprised, to wonder, is to begin to understand. This is the
sport, the luxury, special to the intellectual man. The gesture characteristic of his tribe consists in looking at the world with eyes wide open in
wonder. Everything in the world is strange and marvellous to well-open
eyes. This faculty of wonder is the delight refused to your football "fan,"
and, on the other hand, is the one which leads the intellectual man
through life in the perpetual ecstasy of the visionary. His special attribute is the wonder of the eyes. Hence it was that the ancients gave
Minerva her owl, the bird with ever-dazzled eyes.

Agglomeration, fullness, was not frequent before. Why then is it now? The components of the multitudes around us have not sprung from nothing. Approximately the same number of people existed fifteen years ago. Indeed, after the war[1] it might seem natural that their number should be less. Nevertheless, it is here we come up against the first important point. The individuals who made up these multitudes existed, but not *qua* multitude. Scattered about the world in small groups, or solitary, they lived a life, to all appearances, divergent, dissociate, apart. Each individual or small group occupied a place, its own, in country, village, town, or quarter of the great city. Now, suddenly, they appear as an agglomeration, and looking in any direction our eyes meet with the multitudes. Not only in any direction, but precisely in the best places, the relatively refined creation of human culture, previously reserved to lesser groups, in a word, to minorities. The multitude has suddenly become visible, installing itself in the preferential positions in society. Before, if it existed, it passed unnoticed, occupying the background of the social stage; now it has advanced to the footlights and is the principal character. There are no longer protagonists; there is only the chorus.

The concept of the multitude is quantitative and visual. Without changing its nature, let us translate it into terms of sociology. We then meet with the notion of the "social mass." Society is always a dynamic unity of two component factors: minorities and masses. The minorities are individuals or groups of individuals which are specially qualified. The mass is the assemblage of persons not specially qualified. By masses, then, is not to be understood, solely or mainly, "the working masses." The mass is the average man. In this way what was mere quantity — the multitude — is converted into a qualitative determination: it becomes the common social quality, man as undifferentiated from other men, but as repeating in himself a generic type. What have we gained by this conversion of quantity into quality? Simply this: by means of the latter we understand the genesis of the former. It is evident to the verge of platitude that the normal formation of a multitude implies the coincidence of desires, ideas, ways of life, in the individuals who constitute it. It will be objected that this is just what happens with every social group, however select it may strive to be. This is true; but there is an essential difference. In those groups which are characterised by not being multitude and mass, the effective coincidence of its members is based on some desire, idea, or ideal, which of itself excludes the great number. To form a

[1] The First World War.

minority, of whatever kind, it is necessary beforehand that each member separate himself from the multitude for *special,* relatively personal, reasons. Their coincidence with the others who form the minority is, then, secondary, posterior to their having each adopted an attitude of singularity, and is consequently, to a large extent, a coincidence in not coinciding. There are cases in which this singularising character of the group appears in the light of day: those English groups, which style themselves "nonconformists," where we have the grouping together of those who agree only in their disagreement in regard to the limitless multitude. This coming together of the minority precisely in order to separate themselves from the majority is a necessary ingredient in the formation of every minority. Speaking of the limited public which listened to a musician of refinement, Mallarmé[2] wittily says that this public by its presence in small numbers stressed the absence of the multitude.

Strictly speaking, the mass, as a psychological fact, can be defined without waiting for individuals to appear in mass formation. In the presence of one individual we can decide whether he is "mass" or not. The mass is all that which sets no value on itself — good or ill — based on specific grounds, but which feels itself "just like everybody," and nevertheless is not concerned about it; is, in fact, quite happy to feel itself as one with everybody else. Imagine a humble-minded man who, having tried to estimate his own worth on specific grounds — asking himself if he has any talent for this or that, if he excels in any direction — realises that he possesses no quality of excellence. Such a man will feel that he is mediocre and commonplace, ill-gifted, but will not feel himself "mass."

When one speaks of "select minorities" it is usual for the evil-minded to twist the sense of this expression, pretending to be unaware that the select man is not the petulant person who thinks himself superior to the rest, but the man who demands more of himself than the rest, even though he may not fulfil in his person those higher exigencies. For there is no doubt that the most radical division that it is possible to make of humanity is that which splits it into two classes of creatures: those who make great demands on themselves, piling up difficulties and duties; and those who demand nothing special of themselves, but for whom to live is to be every moment what they already are, without imposing on them-

2 Nineteenth-century French Symbolist poet.

selves any effort towards perfection; mere buoys that float on the waves. This reminds me that orthodox Buddhism is composed of two distinct religions: one, more rigorous and difficult, the other easier and more trivial: the Mahayana — "great vehicle" or "great path" — and the Hinayana — "lesser vehicle" or "lesser path." The decisive matter is whether we attach our life to one or the other vehicle, to a maximum or a minimum of demands upon ourselves.

The division of society into masses and select minorities is, then, not a division into social classes, but into classes of men, and cannot coincide with the hierarchic separation of "upper" and "lower" classes. It is, of course, plain that in these "upper" classes, when and as long as they really are so, there is much more likelihood of finding men who adopt the "great vehicle," whereas the "lower" classes normally comprise individuals of minus quality. But, strictly speaking, within both these social classes, there are to be found mass and genuine minority. As we shall see, a characteristic of our times is the predominance, even in groups traditionally selective, of the mass and the vulgar. Thus, in the intellectual life, which of its essence requires and presupposes qualification, one can note the progressive triumph of the pseudo-intellectual, unqualified, unqualifiable, and, by their very mental texture, disqualified. Similarly, in the surviving groups of the "nobility," male and female. On the other hand, it is not rare to find to-day amongst working men, who before might be taken as the best example of what we are calling "mass," nobly disciplined minds.

There exist, then, in society, operations, activities, and functions of the most diverse order, which are of their very nature special, and which consequently cannot be properly carried out without special gifts. For example: certain pleasures of an artistic and refined character, or again the functions of government and of political judgment in public affairs. Previously these special activities were exercised by qualified minorities, or at least by those who claimed such qualification. The mass asserted no right to intervene in them; they realised that if they wished to intervene they would necessarily have to acquire those special qualities and cease being mere mass. They recognised their place in a healthy dynamic social system.

If we now revert to the facts indicated at the start, they will appear clearly as the heralds of a changed attitude in the mass. They all indicate that the mass has decided to advance to the foreground of social life, to occupy the places, to use the instruments and to enjoy the pleasures hitherto reserved to the few. It is evident, for example, that the places were never intended for the multitude, for their dimensions are too limited, and the crowd is continuously overflowing; thus manifesting to our eyes and in the clearest manner the new phenomenon: the mass, without ceasing to be mass, is supplanting the minorities.

No one, I believe, will regret that people are to-day enjoying themselves in greater measure and numbers than before, since they have now both the desire and the means of satisfying it. The evil lies in the fact that this decision taken by the masses to assume the activities proper to the minorities is not, and cannot be, manifested solely in the domain of pleasure, but that it is a general feature,of our time. Thus — to anticipate what we shall see later — I believe that the political innovations of recent times signify nothing less than the political domination of the masses. The old democracy was tempered by a generous dose of liberalism and of enthusiasm for law. By serving these principles the individual bound himself to maintain a severe discipline over himself. Under the shelter of liberal principles and the rule of law, minorities could live and act. Democracy and law — life in common under the law — were synonymous. To-day we are witnessing the triumphs of a hyperdemocracy in which the mass acts directly, outside the law, imposing its aspirations and its desires by means of material pressure. It is a false interpretation of the new situation to say that the mass has grown tired of politics and handed over the exercise of it to specialised persons. Quite the contrary. That was what happened previously; that was democracy. The mass took it for granted that after all, in spite of their defects and weaknesses, the minorities understood a little more of public problems than it did itself. Now, on the other hand, the mass believes that it has the right to impose and to give force of law to notions born in the café. I doubt whether there have been other periods of history in which the multitude has come to govern more directly than in our own. That is why I speak of hyperdemocracy.

The same thing is happening in other orders, particularly in the intellectual. I may be mistaken, but the present-day writer, when he takes his pen in hand to treat a subject which he has studied deeply, has to bear in mind that the average reader, who has never concerned himself with this subject, if he reads does so with the view, not of learning something from the writer, but rather, of pronouncing judgment on him when he is not in agreement with the commonplaces that the said reader carries in his head. If the individuals who make up the mass believed themselves specially qualified, it would be a case merely of personal error, not a sociological subversion. *The characteristic of the hour is that the commonplace mind, knowing itself to be commonplace, has the assurance to proclaim the rights of the commonplace and to impose them wherever it will.* As they say in the United States: "to be different is to be indecent." The mass crushes beneath it everything that is different, everything that is excellent, individual, qualified and select. Anybody who is not like everybody, who does not think like everybody, runs the risk of being eliminated. And it is clear, of course, that this "everybody" is not "everybody." "Everybody" was normally the complex unity of the mass and the divergent, specialised minorities. Nowadays, "everybody" is the mass alone. Here we have the formidable fact of our times, described without any concealment of the brutality of its features.

ᴇᢏ FOR DISCUSSION AND WRITING

1. It is highly possible that your first reaction to this piece will be antagonistic —that is, before you have read it clear through and understood its general basis. If you find your hackles rising, what would you say is the cause of your feeling of hostility toward Ortega's presentation of his position? We are confronted, in the greater part of our experience, with attitudes directly opposing what Ortega seems to be saying in the earlier part of the piece; but we must, in all conscience, agree that it is a good thing to have to consider the grounds for an attitude differing from those with which we are habitually familiar. Here is a European, and a special kind of European, a Spaniard; we should have the intellectual concern (the "wonder," as he puts it) to lay aside our customary "stock responses" and listen. What does he mean by the "masses"? What is your reaction to the third sentence in the piece, beginning "As the masses, by definition, neither should nor can direct their own personal existence, and still less rule society in general . . ."? Why does he say "by definition"? Where does he support this statement by a definition?

2. Note his use of visualization in the second paragraph. At first glance, this exercise in visualization seems to simplify the problem almost childishly

(why should it seem a "problem" at all, worth exercising the mind about, that theaters, cafés, beaches, and so on, are crowded?). But later, when he says that "the concept of the multitude is quantitative and visual," what is the inferred contrast with those human values that are *not* to be perceived by quantitative or visual impact? At the end of the second paragraph he puts the problem with extreme simplicity: "to find room." Does the question of "finding room" apply to more in modern life than finding a room in a hotel or a table in a café? In your own experience, does it apply to "finding room" for your mind and your responses in a classroom? If you live in a large city, does it apply to "finding room" for yourself not only on a crowded subway but in the impersonal, and often brutally impersonal, atmosphere of a city? Does it apply also to the difficulty of being an individual person, one's self, under the conventions of small-town life? or of other kinds of conventional group life?

3. In the third paragraph, Ortega asks, "Is this not the ideal state of things?" Well, is it or isn't it? How do our idealistic social theories and our personal inclinations conflict in the problem thus set up?

4. How does he define a "minority" as against the "mass"? We are used to thinking of "minorities" in sociological terms (racial minorities, etc.); how does Ortega's use of the term differ? When a writer defines his own terms, we must accept his definition for the conduct of the argument, so that we are thinking with him and not at cross purposes. Given Ortega's definitions of "minority" and "mass," how would you appraise both the definitions and the relative values he implies by them?

5. Write a paper on the "mass" type of person you have found in your experience, or on "mass culture" as promulgated in various media.

Laurens van der Post ⋅⋅§ Africa Is Old

⋅⋅§ Born in South Africa in 1906 of Dutch parents, Colonel van der Post served for ten years during World War II with the Allied forces in Ethiopia, North Africa, Syria, and the Dutch East Indies, conducting guerrilla operations. He spent three of those years as a prisoner of the Japanese, in solitary confinement for a large part of the time and under daily threat of execution. After the war he led several British expeditions into little-known parts of Africa, one of them into the Kalahari Desert in search of traces of the original Bushmen—an experience described in a book of extraordinary beauty, *The Lost World of the Kalahari*. He has also written novels and other books about Africa that are distinguished by profound spiritual insight and extraordinarily evocative descriptive writing.

The selection here is abridged from a lecture that he gave in a number of European cities on the subject of apartheid in South Africa, which was published, together with representative questions asked by the audiences and his answers, in *The Dark Eye in Africa*. §⋅⋅

AFRICA is old in the longest measure of time on earth. It is old in a way which makes the lovely white mountains in Switzerland not solid immovable matter but waves curling and breaking in the storm of time, wherein even Everest is but the ghostly spume of spray torn by an angry gust from curling breakers. Long before vegetable, organic or biological matter were in being, the rocks and earth of Africa as we know them today were already formed. Indeed, those of us who are born in Africa are born with a sense of this old oldness deep within us. For Africa was once part of a vast land-continent to which geologists, with a touch of whimsicality unusual to their sober and austere kind, have given the name of Gondwana-land, a name which has an odd gone-with-the-wind nostalgia implicit in its sound. So vast was this continent that it included part of Brazil, the Deccan, Madagascar and Australia. When I first went to Australia, although at the time I did not know this geological fact, my senses told me at once that here, beyond rational explanation, was a land physically akin to Africa. You have only to look at the great waters which separate Africa today from the other fragments of Gondwana-land and, remembering how slowly and patiently water nibbles away at rock, you can get an idea of how incredibly old Africa really is. In those far, remote days Africa was separated from Europe by the great sea of Tethys, but as this sea shrank and life appeared on the newly formed coasts, as the sea-boards gradually linked up into the pattern of earth that we know today and created everywhere opportunities of vast interchanges of life and emerging cultures, Africa was enabled by a miraculous design of nature to be an exception to the general. Her coastline, no matter how the sea nibbled at it, kept its defences intact and, when it gave way, retreated in good Macedonian order.[1] To this day the coastline of Africa not only offers no convenient natural harbours but most of it, together with the interior, is raised above the water level and the rivers come tumbling out of it in swift, churning, angry torrents that make navigation up these streams impossible. Where the earth was not so raised this ancient land threw up vast seas of desert which could be crossed only by a few initiates at their peril. Also, as if to make quite sure that her defences completely sealed Africa off from the outer world, nature developed the most redoubtable champions in the mosquito and tsetse fly and other minute parasites, all able to strike down any invader with a wonderful selection of deadly diseases, from sleeping sickness, malaria, dysentery and typhoid, to leprosy and bubonic plague. One day I hope to persuade my fellow-Africans to put up a monument to the despised mosquito and tsetse fly for discharging so well this task of defending Africa against invasion. Just another example, one might think, of the way in which destiny so often selects its most significant instruments from the humble, drab and inconspicuous, no matter whether they be merely tsetse flies and mosquitoes, or peasant girls and house-painters!

So in this way Africa was enabled, undisturbed, to develop its own forms of life and its own nature on an infinitely richer and more varied scale than any other continent. I wish I could show you this miracle of

[1] Referring to the disciplined tactics of the phalanx, developed by Philip of Macedon.

Africa, instead of merely talking about it, for even today there are large
sections of it which are as they have always been, immense tracts whose
people still observe their traditional ways in another and more ancient
dimension of time. There are still primeval territories, scenes of unex-
ploited mountain and lake, river, plain and forest, and patterns of animal life that you see nowhere else in the world. For instance, there are
more than one hundred and thirty kinds of lively, bounding antelope in
Africa which are unknown anywhere else in the world. No country ever
had such varieties of life, from the most minute viruses and microbes,
insects, reptiles and animals to its human beings. Wherever the invader
tried to attack Africa he found it filled to the brim with a vivid, flame-
flickering, dancing life of its own, ranging in size from the mosquito to
the elephant. When three hundred years ago my ancestors landed at the
southern extremity of Africa, there were not merely prancing bushmen
and slant-eyed Hottentots to greet them but also hippopotamuses with
the same portly shape and air as those Lord Mayors who carry the gold
chains of office on their stomachs, kingly lions, royal leopards, rhinoc-
eros as irritable as peppery generals whose livers have been ruined by
whiskey and curry in the tropics, and wise old elephants, patient as elder
statesmen, wading into the breakers to look the new arrivals over! I have
often stayed in one of the oldest houses in Cape Town, which stands on
the seashore and still bears the name "Leeuwenhof," the Court of Lions,
so-called because when it was built the lions were prowling nightly in
what has since become a lovely civilized garden.

Nor was this fullness, richness and variety of life confined merely to
the animals. Inside the defences of this redoubtable African fortress of
original life, man lived and developed an extraordinary varied and vivid
being of his own. There was the pygmy bushman, the little yellow man
with his Mongolian eye and enlarged posterior, who neither husbands
animals nor cultivates the land but trusts himself to nature and the
rhythm of the seasons like fish to the sea, and who feels far more secure
in this natural environment than ever he does in the one that "superior"
man presumed to give him. There was the Hottentot, taller and possessing a secret eye, who was more "advanced" in our understanding of
the word in that he owned dogs and hump-backed cattle and walked
slowly behind his fat nomadic herds, his skin shining like newly strung
telephone wires in the sun. Then in the east there was the Bantu with
his heavy slow-stepping grace, and in the west the Negro with his

baroque sense of fate, and numbers of other sub-divisions and colourful Nilotic and Hamitic variants. Contrast those with Australia's one aboriginal race, and do you wonder that I call this development miraculous?

So for thousands and thousands of years this rich life was truly contained and nourished by Africa on African soil and uniquely in the African way. I know of no other life which has possessed for so long this seclusion and continuity, this privileged isolation from foreign influence and greed. It seems to me that Africa gives the most dramatic example of life developing from an invisible point in time where, as Euclid might have put it, history has as yet no size or magnitude but only position, right on into our own age, always following a development which was not according to man's idea of life so much as according to life's own plan for itself. For in this African development there was the minimum amount of conscious interference in life's processes; the minimum amount of direction from the producer in the desperate pantomime of our time.

In the last century, of course, the scene has changed brusquely. This picture which I have given you is vanishing fast, though it is still valid in large tracts of the great continent. The bushman is still living in the Kalahari Desert, just as he did in the beginning of time. I have recently been there and I have seen him in his natural and innocent society, still using his love-making ritual, the cupid's bow, which hitherto for me had been little more than an image on a Greek vase. I have also been in sleeping-sickness country just below the great escarpments of Abyssinia and seen black people of superb physique, garlands of wild flowers round their necks, marching towards me unexpectedly out of the singing grass and playing on pipes exactly like the Pipes of Pan which, too, I had only known from Greek vases. I assure you there is enough of this life still left in Africa to show us what it was like before we came on the scene. Indeed, it is odd when one considers the efficiency with which we dig up old ruins all over the world in order to get some idea of what ancient man and his world was like, and then remembers that here in Africa we have ancient man still alive, his ancient spirit burning bright within him, and yet we leave his mind despised, ignored and utterly neglected. Allow me to give you one example of how automatic this under-valuation can be. Some years ago when I was organizing an expedition to the great Kalahari Desert of Southern Africa, two scientists of international repute arrived with letters of introduction at my advanced base. They asked if they could accompany the expedition because they were doing research work on the bushman of Africa. When I asked what kind of research, they explained that they were making a comparative study of the head-measurements of primitive peoples all over the world. They described at length the methods they used and showed me an impressive catalogue of detail already observed. After a long while of this I asked, "What about the inside of their heads? Are you not interested in what goes on inside them?"

"That," they said with conclusive professional superiority, "is a different branch of science." Yet they were very upset because I saw no point in taking them with me. Over and over again I have been humbled by what goes on in the minds and hearts of these and other primitive peoples. When, as I have done, one takes part in this "life for life's sake," when one moves through its daily scene for a round of seasons, one no longer sees oneself as someone apart from nature and above and in command of life, but rather as someone small and helpless, yet immersed in a rich scheme of being for sheer being's sake. One realizes that it is not we who are filled with spirit or soul, but rather the dark and despised people about us. They have so much of it that it overflows into the trees, rocks, rivers, lakes, birds, snakes and animals that surround them. The bushman makes gods out of all the animals around him; the Hottentots kneel to an insect, the praying mantis; the Bantu listens to the spirits of his ancestors in the noise of his cattle stirring in their kraals of thorn at night, made restive by the roar of the lion and the hyena's werewolf wailing; the Negro appeases and invokes the gods in endless fetishes and images of wood and clay. But one and all they are humble parts of life and at one with it, knowing that, in order to get through their tiny, trembling day, they are in constant need of support from a power greater than themselves. They all have their own ways of evoking this support — elaborate rituals, strict codes of behaviour, colorful ceremonial evolved out of their experience of life — and their own social ethics in terms of which they are initiated into life and ushered out from it. They are poorer in almost every way than we and no more successful, perhaps, in these matters than we are. But in one great respect they are richer. Whatever happens to them, their lives are never lonely for lack of spirit nor do they find life wanting in meaning. To this day you have only to hear the bushman, Bantu, Hottentot or Negro laugh, to realize how true that still is.

Then suddenly we, European man, burst in upon this scene. As I have said, my own ancestors were among the first successfully to land at the southern cape of Africa three centuries ago, but the natural defences of greater Africa did not seriously begin to give way to outside invasion until about a hundred years ago, and only finally crumbled during the nineties of the last century. When that happened the white man could not have been less prepared for what he was about to find. A long period of pure reason, which had begun with the Reformation and been stimulated by the French Revolution, was deep at work in his spirit, setting him at variance with his intuitions and instincts. The materialism of the Industrial Revolution already dominated his values and motives; his mastery of the physical means of life and his increasing annihilation of distance together with the conquest of what he understood to be time, had already brought man far down the broad way to exceeding his humanity and setting himself up as a controller of destiny. Walking into Africa in that mood he was, by and large, quite incapable of understanding Africa, let alone of appreciating the raw material of mind and spirit with which this granary of fate, this ancient treasure house of the lost original way of life, was so richly filled. He had, it is true, an insatiable eye for the riches in the rocks, for diamonds and gold. But for the diamonds and gold of an ancient lost world sparkling in the many dark eyes raised in wonder and bewilderment to him, for the precious metal ringing true in the deep-toned laughter of the indigenous peoples round him, he had no interest. To this day if I want information about the stones and mineral deposits of Africa I am embarrassed by the richness of the material instantly placed at my disposal. Yet if I want information about the plants and grasses, as I recently did, I am staggered by the decline in the quality and quantity of the material offered to me. And when I want information that goes below the superficial mechanism of their society, about the peoples of Africa themselves, their spirits, languages and minds, about the things they find funny and the things they believe wonderful, I am dismayed and saddened by the terrible lack of material and interest generally displayed. I am certain all this is because European man arrived in Africa already despising Africa and African beings. He arrived there, not for Africa's sake, but for what he could get out of Africa on his own behalf. He arrived as a superior person ready to impose himself and his way of living on Africa, not doubting for a second that his was the better way and that it was all for

Africa's good. The same thing which made him despise the African made him despise the African's social organization, his goods and chattels, his agriculture, the way he tended his crops as well as his cattle. Chiefs, tribal organizations, witch doctors and ancient rituals were abolished swiftly by the administrator with his pen. And the settler and agricultural expert followed fast to impose their European cattle, their European seed and way of farming, upon Africa. The missionary, either in the van or close behind, came to abolish the black man's spirits, give him a new sense of sin, do away with his practice of religion as base superstition, and win him over to a new and superior white god. The rejection of Africa in all dimensions was as complete as it could possibly be. In the beginning there was some slight fighting resistance from the African, but looking back on it all now the wonder to me is that there was so little. I can only put it down to the fact that at first the African took the European at his own estimation of himself. The enormous power the European had over physical things, which you must remember were never merely physical things to the African but containers of all-powerful spirits, convinced him that the European was more than human.

I am old enough to remember the enormous hush that fell over Africa in the wake of the coming of European man. In the African heart there was a calm and tense air of expectation of growing wonders to come, and as a result there was also the most moving and wonderful readiness of the African to serve, to imitate and to follow the European, and finally an unqualified preparedness to love and be loved. My childhood memories of the light of that preparedness in African eyes and its absence in the same eyes today often keeps me awake at night. If you doubt me, remember the small forces that the white man had to use in his first barbarous conflicts. That was due not merely to the superiority of the white men's weapons in battle. Today we have even bigger and better weapons than we had then, yet the African has started to fight back against the white man in Kenya, for instance, as never before. No, I think the initial readiness of the black man to serve the white man was perhaps because, unconsciously, he had long waited for someone like the white man to come and bring him something which only the white man could provide. So, when he did come, it was as if it was in answer to some dream far back in the African mind and in response to some deep submerged hope that Africa had of the future. The white

man's coming seemed to imply the fulfilment of a promise which had
been made to the African far back by life in its first beginnings. If this
were not so, I think the African would quickly have lost heart and died
out of sheer discouragement as many an Indian tribe and nation died in
the Americas, or as many Papuans and other South Sea islanders died at
the coming of the white man in the Pacific. Yet the black man in Africa
has not only multiplied but has gone on serving the white man in a way
that is almost too good to be true. "Too good to be true." May I ask you
to remember that phrase?

This period of the hush, of suspended indigenous development in
Africa, was a moment of immense potentiality and hope in the contact
between black and white. It contained great opportunity and possibilities for good, which the European at the time had not the power to
understand. Often have I seen this period of innocence in the personal
relationships between human beings. I have seen it once or twice, too,
in the histories of people. I saw it in Indonesia after the last Japanese
war. There was a moment then when the relief at the defeat of Japan
left the whole of occupied Indonesia in a mood out of which something
true, good and lasting might have instantly sprung. I saw the moment
vanish and a distorted and twisted element come out of it with a mind
and a will and a direction of its own, a form of distorted actuality which
now has to live out its alloted span and die before anything else can take
its place. In Africa, too, I see this moment of innocence and opportunity
rapidly vanishing. I think it began to disappear after the First World
War. I noticed then that the spell we had over the black man was broken,
and I was so perturbed with this first intimation that later I wrote a book
about it.* Still, at that time, the situation was not too bad. But when I
came back from this last war, wherever I went I was horrified by the
change. Events that were rarities in my childhood days were commonplace: ritual murder, flesh eating, secret societies raised against
authority, lightning eruptions of violence and murder, and often apparently inexplicable outbreaks in areas that had known no unrest for a
long time. These things were everywhere on the increase as were also
the other classic signs of great inner unrest: a gathering drift of displaced persons into towns, the growing numbers of frustrated unemployed and unemployable intellectuals at street corners, the increase of

* *In a Province* (Hogarth Press, 1935) which today seems to have an odd prophetic
ring about it. [Author's note.]

political agitation and social confusion, the apparently senseless smashing of shop windows and inexplicable riots in civilized streets.

Before the war with Germany I wrote, "The windows of the individual mind are shattered long before stones are thrown in the street and the police put to flight by the mob. There is a riot in the human heart and the forces of law and order in the spirit are first overthrown by a nightmare horde. Already deep down in the human soul the individual is melting into the crowd."** In Africa the same sort of development could mean only one thing for me. The black African's sense of security and of oneness with life, had been shaken in a most profound way, his access to life's inmost meaning rudely barred. The spell of the European over him was not only breaking but his confidence in the European way of life was so shaken that, in a desperate effort to avert the disaster and annihilation which now seemed to threaten him from within, he turned back to the angry power of his disregarded, discredited and neglected spirits. Only appeasement of these spirits, as he sees it, can prevent him from losing his hurt aboriginal soul forever. For no matter how vicious are the forms wherein it expresses itself, or how effective the economic and materialistic trappings wherein it disguises itself, the conflict in Africa is, at heart, a battle about being and nonbeing, about having a soul of one's own or not having a soul at all.

We have a striking illustration of what I mean in the Mau-Mau activities in Kenya, for what has happened to the Kikuyu in Kenya is what has happened to so many other races in Africa. The white man has first discredited the African way of living and dealing with the forces of nature about and within, and then obliged him increasingly to live in a way which rejects the institutions, customs, initiation rites and rituals by which, for centuries, he has struck a balance with those overwhelming aspects of nature which are incomprehensible to reason and quite beyond conscious control and rational articulation. I do not want to imply that it was necessarily bad that this African way of living was discarded. It was inevitable in the nature of things that sooner or later it would either have to die of itself or else be rejected by the Africans themselves before they could move on to something more complete. But what is deplorable is that having discredited this ancient way of living we have not put an honourable alternative in its place. No human being or society, however self-sufficient and rational it may appear, can live

** Written in 1935. [Author's note.]

without institutions that deal with those aspects of life which cannot be explained rationally. No community can be left indefinitely outside in the night of the human spirit, in the beast-infested jungle which lies beyond the conscious fortifications which civilized culture raises for *us* in life. If a community cannot get within the protection of those fortifications by fair means, then it will do so by foul. If civilized reason and conscious strength will not aid it, then animal cunning and brute force will. Having then destroyed the cultural defences of the Kikuyu people, it was imperative that we should give them the protection of our way of life and free access to our own institutions. It was all the more imperative in the case of the Kikuyu because they are one of the most intelligent African peoples. But having destroyed their natural defences, we then denied them our own. Having taken away their way of life, we then made it impossible for them to acquire any other. Having supplanted their law by ours, we then gave them no right to live as our law demanded but rather forced them to drift suspended in dark acceptance of a state of non-being. That is something that no human race can do and survive. What most terrifies the primitive man is not physical danger but the fear that he may lose his soul. This is implicit in all his ritual, religion and daily behaviour. I believe Mau-Mau is a desperate attempt on the part of the Kikuyu to prevent such a loss of national soul. What is going on out there at the moment is, in a deep primitive sense, a war of religion. It may be a struggle for a form of religion so crude and base that it must revolt all civilized senses and one which the European is forced to reject with all his power. But it is a war of religion for all that. It is a fight of the Kikuyu for their old Kikuyu gods. It is a battle, as the Romans would have said, for the "ashes of their fathers and the temples of their gods."

I could give you many illustrations of similar processes and point out to you that, as a consequence of unenlightened white policy, somewhere in Africa's hidden being is piling up a sinister power of accumulated energy sufficient to shatter the world that is taking away its soul. Africa is being charged like one of the electronic piles used to split the atom. For Africa, from earth and beast up to the most intelligent of its indigenous children, is not letting this loss of soul take place without a terrible struggle. . . .

Again one asks, if this is so, why is the European behaving as he is?

Why cannot he see what he is doing to Africa and correct his ways in time? But all these questions bring me to what I consider to be the most sinister element of all. I myself believe that the European's own eye is so darkened that he can no longer see himself or the things round about him in their full reality. The inner light, "the natural fire within the dark wood of life," as Dante put it, by which man once lived, is being put out and darkness is welling up like a sea both within and without him. I think the European is blindly and ignorantly provoking all these events in Africa because, in his deepest nature, he is provoking them in himself.

Ever since the Reformation, European man has been increasingly at war with himself, and certain aspects of his nature which he has found particularly useful and rewarding for producing his own type of civilization and culture have been developed excessively at the expense of others, thus doing violence to a very deep and real part of himself. This is not necessarily a bad thing. Up to a point it is the way in which all civilizations have come about. It is, if you like, the Promethean sin[2] which all communities commit in order to enable their culture to evolve. But even such a noble sin, if it is not to lead to disaster, must keep within its own classic proportions. Even virtue owes homage to proportion. If it cannot learn the discipline of proportion freely from within, it has to learn it from disaster without, for whatever goes too far begets a violent reaction in order that it may be brought back into position. Unfortunately it appears to be the rule of life that societies find it almost impossible, without disaster in the physical world, to reverse an outworn evolutionary process. Except for that wonderful creative moment in our history when the two extremities of human nature — the natural instinctive pagan element and the rational, conscious, forward-moving Christian awareness — came close enough to produce that flash of lightning which still dazzles our imagination and which we call the Renaissance, except for that moment of rebirth and awakening of modern man, we have swung to an extreme wherein the natural man within us not only has had very little honour but also his rich intuitive and instinctive

[2] Prometheus was one of the Titans, "earthborn" nature powers; he stole some of the planetary fire and gave it to man, along with the arts which the control of fire makes possible; he was thus the mythical founder of civilization. Zeus, jealous of the power man acquired by this gift, punished Prometheus as a criminal, chaining him to Mount Caucasus, where an eagle tore at his liver.

promptings have been thrown summarily out of the courts of our reason, just as the aborigines of our time have been despised and rejected by Western man.

In a profound sense every man has two halves to his being: he is not one person so much as two persons trying to act in unison. I believe that in the heart of each human being there is something which I can only describe as a "child of darkness" who is equal and complementary to the more obvious "child of light." Whether we know it or not we all have within us a natural instinctive man, a dark brother, to whom we are irrevocably joined as to our own shadow. However much our conscious reason may reject him, he is there for good or ill, clamouring for recognition and awareness and a fair share of life just as the less conscious black man of Africa is struggling and clamouring for life, light and honour in our societies. I need not emphasize how the rational, calculating, acutely reasoning and determined human being that Western man has made of himself has increasingly considered this side of himself not as a brother but as an enemy, capable, with his upsurges of rich emotion and colourful impulses, of wrecking conscious man's carefully planned and closely reasoned way of existence.

I find some confirmation of this in the violence of our present-day colour prejudice. Hitherto this violence had not existed in Europe. When my forefathers landed more than three hundred years ago in the Cape of Good Hope, the colour prejudice was much less marked, and today we have the million "coloured" people of the Cape colony[3] as proof of it. In the traditional ritual of the Christian churches, too, one of the three wise men of the East was a black man and his presence among the three sages who attended Christ in his crib at Bethlehem seemed necessary to make the symbolism of the event complete in European imagination. But in recent generations this colour prejudice among Europeans has become so powerful and destructive that it threatens to break out in increasing bloodshed in Africa. Significantly, too, everywhere in the world it has become more powerful and explosive according to the extent to which the distance has widened between overrational, specialized modern man and his natural roots. This separation of the white man with his bright morning face from his own dark rejected brother within, increases with frightening acceleration. So prejudice against the black skin of the

[3] One of the rigid classifications of apartheid, "coloured" designates those of mixed European and Bantu blood.

natural African has deepened and made it a dangerous symbol, for now the white man in Africa sees reflected in the natural dark man round him that dark aspect of himself which he has rejected. Consequently he confuses the reflection without with the dark reality within, and without hesitation engages in fruitless and mutually disastrous battle with it.

We have talked all through this century of the white man's burden in Africa, yet what fatal irony there is in the phrase. Would it not be more accurate at the moment to talk of the black man's burden? I refer of course to this burden of terrible unconscious projection which modern European man thrusts upon the natural African who, by reason of his primitive instinctual life and "participation almost mystical" in his natural environment, is such a suitable container for it. Yet it is this very projection, outcome of the insidious civil war raging in the innermost being of modern man, which prevents the white man from ever seeing the black man as he really is. The white man can see in the black man only those aspects which confirm and justify his own projection and enable it to pass itself off as an outward and genuinely objective condition — which it is not. The results for both parties, of course, are deplorable. Since the European possesses physical power, this dreadful confusion compels him to create a form of society wherein the black man is condemned to play only that part which the increasingly exacting projection of the white man demands of him. The black man is thereby prevented from being himself and from living out his own unique being. He is like Adam in the Garden after he had tasted the forbidden fruit of the tree of knowledge, standing among the leaves still trembling with the magnetic nearness of the Old Testament God of Judgment and Justice. A power greater than himself banishes the African from the garden of his archaic state forever. The white man and his determined, unrecognizable projection stand in the way, refusing him the forward thrust of life, denying him the right to be his changing self. Behind him an archangel with a flaming sword seals the ancient gate forever; before him a thin-lipped white sentry with a machine-gun bars the way. The black man, too, therefore, has an unlived aspect of himself, a darker brother within, which constant denial daily makes great with the spirit of revenge and powerful with unused energies, and which is fast growing into an angry giant about to burst his bonds and use his strength like a colossus.

Meanwhile, the same processes have gone on developing in the white man. His unlived aspect, too, the despised and rejected dark brother of his own being, has grown greater and daily more terrible. Up to now these things in life have ended only in one way. The unlived aspects in the two opposites overwhelm their oppressors, the conscious restraints that have imprisoned them for so long break loose and they interlock in fatal battle. After the catastrophic demonstrations that this century has given us of the lengths to which the European social animal will go in projecting into the world round him this quarrel within himself, we have no longer any excuse for not recognizing this technique in the lives of nations. Let us revert again to terms of energy, for thereby we can use an impersonal idiom native to the problem. In physics one cannot introduce a negative charge of electricity in a given field without instantly inducing an equal and opposite charge of positive electricity. No matter how great may be your one-sided charge, an equal and opposite keeps pace and parallel with it until finally both become so powerful that they leap the space which separates one from the other and make the zig-zag spark we call electricity. A negative individual and racial projection behaves in exactly the same way. We can give it any name we please according to the level of life on which our energies are engaged. If we are Socialists we can see it as a class war; if Marxists, as a struggle between capital and labour; if vitalists and mechanists, as a battle between idealism and materialism; if philosophers and artists we see it as the unresolved battle between the Apollonian and Dionysian, or the classic and romantic urges; if priests, as Christianity versus paganism; and if we are a South African statesman we see it as the struggle of black versus white. But basically I believe it is this hypothesis of the unlived aspect of self in man and his communities resorting to expression by foul means because it has been denied the fair means, which explains the confusion and explosive prejudices of our time. Above all, only this explains life's strange need of the terrible arbitration of war and disaster in living creative issues. The rational, cultured, scientific, progressive Germany of 1914 gives admirable illustration of this. As Germany grew steadily from an obscure electorate of the Holy Roman Empire and expanded into the great German Reich, as she grew more successful and powerful in the demonstrable world without, so she became charged with a sinister negative energy within. This sinister fever mounted in the German spirit in proportion to her success in the material world throughout the whole nineteenth century. As tension between darkness and light in the German soul mounted it was violently projected onto Germany's neighbours, quickly inducing among them an opposite concentration which expressed itself politically in a rapidly expanding system of defensive alliances. When this moment arrives in the spirit of either an individual or a nation, the fruits of that spirit, its vision and its thinking, cease to be contemporary. The human spirit then falls back on one discarded and discredited bastion after the other until in the end, a hungry mythology takes over and, alas, the mythology which took over in the German heart and mind was a particularly frightening one. So far as I know, German mythology is the only mythology in which the forces of evil are finally triumphant. For in *Götterdämmerung*[4] the cosmic scene closes, you may remember, with the forces of darkness streaming over the rainbow bridge to defeat the gods of light and their companionate order. Could there be a more accurate description of what has happened twice to the German spirit in this century?

In Africa the process has not yet reached that point, but the spirit of the white man has built up a terrible negative charge. The white man's "no" to the black man is daily more uncompromising and automatically induces an equal and opposite charge in the spirit of the black man. On both sides the eye has darkened and still is darkening.[5] Anatole France said that human beings frequently kill one another over the words they use, whereas if only they had understood the meaning the words were trying to convey they would have embraced. There is a higher level to that truth. I wonder if you remember the legend of the white and the black knight in the saga of the Round Table? Two knights, one in black armour and one in white, were riding through a dark and dangerous wood in search of a chivalrous errand when they met. Visors down because of probable danger they challenged one another and, without further explanation, fought. They fought until they were both wounded to death and finally lay stretched out on the grass beside each other. Then, in dying, they uncovered their heads — and saw that they were brothers.

---

[4] "Twilight of the gods"—the fourth and last part of Wagner's tetralogy, *The Ring of the Nibelung*.

[5] The title of the book in which this lecture appears, *The Dark Eye in Africa,* is explained by van der Post as coming from a Malay phrase, *Mata Kelap,* or "dark eye," referring to a kind of murderous insanity that may suddenly attack an habitually gentle person, sending him out, knife in hand, to kill all those he most loves. It is said of him then that "his eye has darkened within him."

Perhaps this implication that the black man and the white man could be brothers sounds too fanciful in view of what is happening in Africa today. Yet there are the proverbs of many nations which suggest that hatred is akin to love. I suggest to you, therefore, that the struggle in Africa is so deadly and tragic just because, secretly, the black natural man in Africa attracts the European no matter how much he consciously rejects him. I say this with confidence because, after all, I was born in Africa and have not only lived with the prejudices of which I am speaking but have also shared them. Then one day I realized that far back in my childhood there was a moment when none of these prejudices had existed in me. I discovered in looking back that the real kings, queens and princes, the witches and the wizards and magicians and all the vivid fairy-tale personalities who gave my childhood a richer meaning were not the virtuous, disapproving Europeans but our black, yellow and copper-coloured servants, almost all of whom have long since vanished, though their names still make music in me. It was they who played a part in my imagination which no European could ever usurp. I suspect that at a deep level the same thing is true of my countrymen in South Africa. And, I suspect that if the European in Africa could only rediscover and honour in his imagination this natural moment at the beginning of his own life, then this unnatural tension would begin to disappear. At the present, of course, there is no outward sign that this will happen.

Anyway, it is not part of my talk tonight to tell you how I think such a rediscovery of this, our lost and legitimate natural self, can come about. My main object has been merely to describe to you what I consider to be the inner origins of this unrest in Africa. But may I add this. I seem to remember that Dr. Jung says somewhere that the aspect of themselves which human beings sacrifice in the attainment of a given object in their lives is reborn *alive* and comes back after many years, knife in hand, demanding to sacrifice that which sacrificed it. I think in this we have a picture of the dilemma, not only of Africa, but of the whole modern world. The whole problem of modern culture expresses the need for some transcendent factor or purpose wherein neither white nor black, neither natural nor thinking man, will have to be sacrificed to one another but both joined and made complete in one transcending purpose. After all, the two opposites of electricity need no longer be expressed through the bright and dangerous medium of lightning but can now be transformed and resolved together into a source of creative energy. . . .

I travel about the world a great deal and everywhere I am impressed by the interest taken in the conflict in Africa. In countries that have no cultural or historical associations with Africa I find this intense, extraordinary interest in what is happening there. Even I who was born in Africa have experienced again and again a need which made no rational sense to me to return and explore Africa. Then one night, sitting alone in the bush in Africa with nothing but my black bearers around me, suddenly I realized the meaning of my own compulsion, and perhaps, too, the explanation of the world's extraordinary interest in Africa. I realized in a flash that I walked Africa in this manner because only thus was I able to walk among the mysteries and uncomprehended complexities of my own heart and mind. I discovered that I travelled in Africa in this way because it brought me to unknown places in my own uncomprehended spirit which I could not have reached in any other manner. Perhaps therein reside the miracle and the meaning of Africa for all of us. Modern man with his grievous and crippling realization of having lost the sense of his own beginnings, with his agonizing feeling of great and growing estrangement from nature, finds that life holds up Africa like a magic mirror miraculously preserved before his darkening eyes. In this great glass of time the inmost reflection of his ancient, timeless spirit stares out at him, and he can, could he but realize it, rediscover there his despised and rejected natural self, recognizing before it is too late the full horror of his stubborn rejection of it.

✍ FOR DISCUSSION AND WRITING

1. Define the relationship between van der Post's central concern in this piece and the description of Africa at the beginning—the continent's immense age, its natural barriers against invasion, and the rich variety of its forms of life. What importance does van der Post give to the fact that African life had for so long a time the "minimum amount of conscious interference"? What is the significance of the episode about the two scientists who wanted to accompany him to the Kalahari to collect the head-measurements of the natives? What does he mean by "life for life's sake" as lived in Africa? Is it, or is it not, the habit of Western man to live "life for life's sake"?

2. Explain the following: "One realizes that it is not we who are filled with spirit or soul, but rather the dark and despised people about us. They have so much of it that it overflows into the trees, rocks, rivers, lakes, birds, snakes and animals that surround them." Our usual attitude toward such primitive beliefs as van der Post describes is that they are benighted superstitions, false in their assumptions about nature, childish, unwholesome, and deplorable: how does van der Post's attitude differ? What does he mean by saying that the Africans who hold to their ancient beliefs, though "they are poorer in almost every way than we," in one respect are richer, for "their lives are never lonely for lack of spirit nor do they find life wanting in meaning"? The inference here is that modern Western people do suffer from loneliness in the universe and from want of meaning in life; how can this inference be supported?

3. What reason does van der Post give for the relative lack of resistance of the African in the first stages of European invasion? What does he give as the deeper cause of the violence of African resistance when it did at last set in, in recent years? What does he mean by saying that "the conflict in Africa is, at heart, a battle about being and non-being, about having a soul of one's own or not having a soul at all"? How valid do you consider this statement: "No human being or society, however self-sufficient and rational it may appear, can live without institutions that deal with those aspects of life which cannot be explained rationally"? What aspects of life are meant? Cannot all aspects of life "be explained rationally"?

4. What is van der Post's explanation of the behavior of the European toward the African? (One should be aware of the fact that he speaks from experience of the South African institution of apartheid, the most rigid and monstrous expression of what he is talking about.) What does he mean by "the two extremities of human nature," one of which European man, in his rational development, has tried to deny within himself? Explain what he says about our "projection" of this denied part of ourselves upon the African. (It is perhaps not entirely clear here that the "dark" and "light" parts of the individual psyche—or the "natural" and the "rational," the "instinctive" and the "conscious"—are descriptive of both the dark races and the white, both being thought of as integral to the whole human being, whether African or European. This point was brought out in the questions from the audience after van der Post's lecture.)

5. What illustration does van der Post cite, from the period of the Second World War, of the monstrous revenge taken by the instinctive part of man's

nature when it is denied? How, in general, does he tie up a great social issue (the African conflict) with a "civil war" that takes place within the individual himself? Why does he say that "our lost and legitimate natural self" must be rediscovered before the modern racial conflict can be solved?

6. Write a paper critically appraising van der Post's convictions. Or a paper extending his views to the American issue of integration. For instance, can you show by examples of racial prejudice that the hidden core of the trouble lies in that kind of "projection" van der Post speaks of—projection of a part of oneself, which one has denied life, upon the Negro, so that one's racial hostility is really hostility to one's own rejected, instinctive self?

James Baldwin ⊸§ Letter to My Nephew

⊸§ American novelist, essayist, and playwright, born in Harlem in 1924, the son of a minister, Baldwin wrote of his early life in his first novel, *Go Tell It on the Mountain*. He appeared as an eloquent spokesman for his race in *The Fire Next Time*. §⊸

Dear James:

I have begun this letter five times and torn it up five times. I keep seeing your face, which is also the face of your father and my brother. Like him, you are tough, dark, vulnerable, moody — with a very definite tendency to sound truculent because you want no one to think you are soft. You may be like your grandfather in this, I don't know, but certainly both you and your father resemble him very much physically. Well, he is dead, he never saw you, and he had a terrible life; he was defeated long before he died because, at the bottom of his heart, he really believed what white people said about him. This is one of the reasons that he became so holy. I am sure that your father has told you something about all that. Neither you nor your father exhibit any tendency towards holiness: you really *are* of another era, part of what happened when the Negro left the land and came into what the late E. Franklin Frazier called "the cities of destruction." You can only be destroyed by believing that you really are what the white world calls a *nigger*. I tell you this because I love you, and please don't you ever forget it.

I have known both of you all your lives, have carried your Daddy in my arms and on my shoulders, kissed and spanked him and watched him learn to walk. I don't know if you've known anybody from that far back; if you've loved anybody that long, first as an infant, then as a child, then as a man, you gain a strange perspective on time and human pain and effort. Other people cannot see what I see whenever I look into your father's face as it is today are all those other faces which were his. Let him laugh and I see a cellar your father does not remember and a house he does not remember and I hear in his present laughter his laughter as a child. Let him curse and I remember him falling down the cellar steps, and howling, and I remember, with pain, his tears, which my hand or your grandmother's so easily wiped away. But no one's hand can wipe away those tears he sheds invisibly today, which one hears in his laughter and in his speech and in his songs. I know what the world has done to my brother and how narrowly he has survived it. And I know, which is much worse, and this is the crime of which I accuse my country and my countrymen, and for which neither I nor time nor history will ever forgive them, that they have destroyed and are destroying hundreds of thousands of lives and do not know it and do not want to know it. One can be, indeed one must strive to become, tough and philosophical concerning destruction and death, for this is what most of mankind has been best at since we have heard of man. (But remember: *most* of mankind is not *all* of mankind.) But it is not permissible that the authors of devastation should also be innocent. It is the innocence which constitutes the crime.

Now, my dear namesake, these innocent and well-meaning people, your countrymen, have caused you to be born under conditions not very far removed from those described for us by Charles Dickens in the London of more than a hundred years ago. (I hear the chorus of the innocents screaming, "No! This is not true! How *bitter* you are" — but I am writing this letter to *you*, to try to tell you something about how to handle *them*, for most of them do not yet really know that you exist. I *know* the conditions under which you were born, for I was there. Your countrymen were *not* there, and haven't made it yet. Your grandmother was also there, and no one has ever accused her of being bitter. I suggest that the innocents check with her. She isn't hard to find. Your countrymen don't know that *she* exists, either, though she has been working for them all their lives.)

Well, you were born, here you came, something like fifteen years ago; and though your father and mother and grandmother, looking about the streets through which they were carrying you, staring at the walls into which they brought you, had every reason to be heavyhearted, yet they were not. For here you were, Big James, named for me — you were a big baby, I was not — here you were: to be loved. To be loved, baby, hard, at once, and forever, to strengthen you against the loveless world. Remember that: I know how black it looks today, for you. It looked bad that day, too, yes, we were trembling. We have not stopped trembling yet, but if we had not loved each other none of us would have survived. And now you must survive because we love you, and for the sake of your children and your children's children.

This innocent country set you down in a ghetto in which, in fact, it intended that you should perish. Let me spell out precisely what I mean by that, for the heart of the matter is here, and the root of my dispute with my country. You were born where you were born and faced the future that you faced because you were black and *for no other reason*. The limits of your ambition were, thus, expected to be set forever. You were born into a society which spelled out with brutal clarity, and in as many ways as possible, that you were a worthless human being. You were not expected to aspire to excellence: you were expected to make peace with mediocrity. Wherever you have turned, James, in your short time on this earth, you have been told where you could go and what you could do (and *how* you could do it) and where you could live and whom you could marry. I know your countrymen do not agree with me about this, and I hear them saying, "You exaggerate." They do not know Harlem, and I do. So do you. Take no one's word for anything, including mine — but trust your experience. Know whence you came. If you know whence you came, there is really no limit to where you can go. The details and symbols of your life have been deliberately constructed to make you believe what white people say about you. Please try to remember that what they believe, as well as what they do and cause you to endure, does not testify to your inferiority but to their inhumanity and fear. Please try to be clear, dear James, through the storm which rages about your youthful head today, about the reality which lies behind the words *acceptance* and *integration*. There is no reason for you to try to become like white people and there is no basis whatever for their impertinent assumption that *they* must accept *you*. The really terrible thing, old buddy, is that *you* must accept *them*. And I mean that very seriously. You must accept them and accept them with love. For these innocent people have no other hope. They are, in effect, still trapped in a history which they do not understand; and until they understand it, they cannot be released from it. They have had to believe for many years, and for innumerable reasons, that black men are inferior to white men. Many of them, indeed, know better, but, as you will discover, people find it very difficult to act on what they know. To act is to be committed, and to be committed is to be in danger. In this case, the danger, in the minds of most white Americans, is the loss of their identity. Try to imagine how you would feel if you woke up one morning to find the sun shining and all the stars aflame. You would be frightened because it is out of the order of nature. Any upheaval in the universe is terrifying because it so profoundly attacks one's sense of one's own reality. Well, the black man has functioned in the white man's world as a fixed star, as an immovable pillar: and as he moves out of his place, heaven and earth are shaken to their foundations. You, don't be afraid. I said that it was intended that you should perish in the ghetto, perish by never being allowed to go behind the white man's definitions, by never being allowed to spell your proper name. You have, and many of us have, defeated this intention; and, by a terrible law, a terrible paradox, those innocents who believed that your imprisonment made them safe are losing their grasp of reality. But these men are your brothers — your lost, younger brothers. And if the word *integration* means anything, this is what it means: that we, with love, shall force our brothers to see themselves as they are, to cease fleeing from reality and begin to change it. For this is your home, my friend, do not be driven from it; great men have done great things here, and will again, and we can make America what America must become. It will be hard, James, but you come from sturdy, peasant stock, men who picked cotton and dammed rivers and built railroads, and, in the teeth of the most terrifying odds, achieved an unassailable and monumental dignity. You come from a long line of great poets, some of the greatest poets since Homer. One of them said, *The very time I thought I was lost, My dungeon shook and my chains fell off.*

You know, and I know, that the country is celebrating one hundred years of freedom one hundred years too soon. We cannot be free until they are free. God bless you, James, and Godspeed.

Your uncle,

James

✒ FOR DISCUSSION AND WRITING

1. What specific qualities can you point out in Baldwin's writing here (qualities of the mode of expression itself, the diction, the way the sentences are formed, the imagery) that are due to the letter form and particularly to the fact that the letter is written to a child? They are qualities of literary distinction: why?

2. Explain the implication in what is said of the boy's grandfather (Baldwin's father, a minister): ". . . he had a terrible life; he was defeated long before he died because, at the bottom of his heart, he really believed what white people said about him. This is one of the reasons that he became so holy."

3. What is meant by "the cities of destruction"? What kind of perception and what quality of character is Baldwin trying to teach the boy? Love is evident in the letter, but how, implicitly or explicitly, does the letter show love as a force more than personal, transcending the relationship of uncle and nephew, and acting as a force in the larger social problem?

4. What is the meaning of the statement that "it is the innocence which constitutes the crime"?

5. Consider the following statements: "You must accept them [white people] and accept them with love. For these innocent people have no other hope. They are, in effect, still trapped in a history which they do not understand; and until they understand it, they cannot be released from it." And this: ". . . These men are your brothers—your lost, younger brothers." What relationship do you find here with Laurens van der Post's thesis in the preceding piece?

6. As a writing assignment, you might use the letter form (which has the advantage of setting up a live situation of communication, a motive of speaking directly *to someone*—even though the someone may be an imagined person) to write your own reactions to and thoughts about the civil rights revolution that is going on in this country. Try to center your writing about some controlling feeling or idea, and keep it simple—away from abstractions, close to experience. Or, getting away from racial issues entirely, you might use this form to write to a person younger than yourself (real or imaginary) about those things you feel it is most important the younger person should know (for all of us carry in us the child we once were, whom we see in other children, and have the impulse to tell that child what we have learned that would help him).

The Historical Dimension

"THE HISTORICAL *sense*," *T. S. Eliot said,*[1] "*involves a perception, not only of the pastness of the past, but of its presence." Time, in America, has not set down its spatial and spiritual dimension in the comfortably hollowed steps of ancestral temples at familiar turnings of the street, where the young and the very poor may find, for a moment of sun on intimate stones, the universe centered and oriented; nor in tombs of heroes and gods whose marvels speak through the reverence of great art; nor even in ancient trees or wells or roads where the past is human and sentient, a living virtue of leaves and water, of the path under one's feet. Over great stretches of our minds, tumbleweeds blow in an empty wind between pallid horizons giving no information, or else we have tunneled ourselves into subways noisy with urgency, to wrench an abstract future out of a mechanical, unborn present. One of the first problems posed in the following section is "What is history for?" In his* THE IDEA OF HISTORY, *R. G. Collingwood says that it is for "human self-knowledge." The definition echoes the ancient Delphic inscription "Know thyself." Knowing oneself, Collingwood says, "means knowing, first, what it is to be a man; secondly, knowing what it is to be the kind of man you are." And the only clue to that*

[1] In "Tradition and the Individual Talent," the next to last essay in this book.

knowledge is history, which "teaches us what man has done and thus what man is." It is a wide program for history—to teach self-knowledge, to become "present" in ourselves as a function of consciousness, evaluative and directive. It goes far outside of textbooks.

The pieces in this section do not pretend to historical survey; they involve only the pleasures and dangers of history as literature. We are led to the past by masters and spellbinders. Toynbee presents that tremendous image (so often haunting one's dreams) of the cliff-climbers and the ledge-hangers, the Yang and the Yin of our ethnic destiny, in which he gives us the company of Job and Faust, and—consolingly—of Adam and Eve. Herodotus chats about Egypt like an uncle. Alexander the Great, in Plutarch's biography of him, becomes amazingly young and near, bringing the whole ancient world with him to the doorstep of the United Nations on the East River, in New York City. One hears the Bach-like polyphony of Gibbon's DECLINE AND FALL OF THE ROMAN EMPIRE in the centuries of Nero and Hadrian, then comes close to Hadrian himself in Eleanor Clark's evocation of that time when "the oracles had gone dumb" and history halted, stupendous and miserable, between epochs.

To go from Hadrian to Parkman's account of the death of Pontiac —commander-in-chief of one of the great lost rebellions of the American Indians—is like going to an undiscovered continent in the abysm of our own minds, our ancestral earth, with whose natives we have never made our peace, though they haunt us with their ceremonial peace pipes and gear of war. In Edmund Wilson's TO THE FINLAND STATION, the sound and reverberation of that war in the human spirit come closer.

> Murmur of maternal lamentation . . .
> hordes swarming
> Over endless plains, stumbling in cracked earth
> Ringed by the flat horizon only

What is the city over the mountains
Cracks and reforms and bursts in the violet air . . . [1]

The city of which T. S. Eliot speaks in The Waste Land *might have been Hiroshima in that "noiseless flash" of the first atomic bomb that John Hersey describes—history created in America, creating another haunted vacuum. Eugene Kinkead's study of American prisoners of war in Korea is appropriately entitled "The Study of Something New in History," for it witnesses the way people act in a vacuum of self-knowledge, that infinitely valuable knowledge by which the past informs us "what it is to be a man."*

[1] From "The Waste Land," by T. S. Eliot, *Collected Poems 1909-1962* (Harcourt, Brace & World, Inc.), lines 367-72.

R. G. Collingwood ❦ What Is History?

❦ Professor of Philosophy at Oxford and practicing historian (1889-1943). A many-sided scholar himself, Collingwood sought a rapprochement between philosophy and history. His work inevitably stirred up controversy and resentment among specialists in these fields, for it demanded that philosophical concepts be studied in the perspective of historical conditions (philosophers could thus no longer be ignorant of history), and that history be studied in the context of the philosophical beliefs of a period (historians could thus no longer remain ignorant of philosophy). These aspects of his thought, as well as its pungency, and the ease and grace of his wide learning are evident in the selection taken from the introductory chapter of *The Idea of History*. ❧

WHAT history is, what it is about, how it proceeds, and what it is for, are questions which to some extent different people would answer in different ways. But in spite of differences there is a large measure of agreement between the answers. And this agreement becomes closer if the answers are subjected to scrutiny with a view to discarding those which proceed from unqualified witnesses. History, like theology or natural science, is a special form of thought. If that is so, questions about the nature, object, method, and value of this form of thought must be answered by persons having two qualifications.

First, they must have experience of that form of thought. They must be historians. In a sense we are all historians nowadays. All educated persons have gone through a process of education which has in-

From *The Idea of History* by R. G. Collingwood. Oxford University Press, 1957. Reprinted by permission of the publisher.

cluded a certain amount of historical thinking. But this does not qualify them to give an opinion about the nature, object, method, and value of historical thinking. For in the first place, the experience of historical thinking which they have thus acquired is probably very superficial; and the opinions based on it are therefore no better grounded than a man's opinion of the French people based on a single week-end visit to Paris. In the second place, experience of anything whatever gained through the ordinary educational channels, as well as being superficial, is invariably out of date. Experience of historical thinking, so gained, is modelled on text-books, and text-books always describe not what is now being thought by real live historians, but what was thought by real live historians at some time in the past when the raw material was being created out of which the text-book has been put together. And it is not only the results of historical thought which are out of date by the time they get into the text-book. It is also the principles of historical thought: that is, the ideas as to the nature, object, method, and value of historical thinking. In the third place, and connected with this, there is a peculiar illusion incidental to all knowledge acquired in the way of education: the illusion of finality. When a student is *in statu pupillari*[1] with respect to any subject whatever, he has to believe that things are settled because the text-books and his teachers regard them as settled. When he emerges from that state and goes on studying the subject for himself he finds that nothing is settled. The dogmatism which is an invariable mark of immaturity drops away from him. He looks at so-called facts with a new eye. He says to himself: 'My teacher and text-books told me that such and such was true; but is it true? What reasons had they for thinking it true, and were these reasons adequate?' On the other hand, if he emerges from the status of pupil without continuing to pursue the subject he never rids himself of this dogmatic attitude. And this makes him a person peculiarly unfitted to answer the questions I have mentioned. No one, for example, is likely to answer them worse than an Oxford philosopher who, having read Greats[2] in his youth, was once a student of history and thinks that this youthful experience of historical thinking entitles him to say what history is, what it is about, how it proceeds, and what it is for.

---

[1] Having pupil's status; under instruction.
[2] Having done the reading for the final examination for the bachelor's degree in classics at Oxford.

The second qualification for answering these questions is that a man should not only have experience of historical thinking but should also have reflected upon that experience. He must be not only an historian but a philosopher; and in particular his philosophical thought must have included special attention to the problems of historical thought. Now it is possible to be a quite good historian (though not an historian of the highest order) without thus reflecting upon one's own historical thinking. It is even easier to be a quite good teacher of history (though not the very best kind of teacher) without such reflection. At the same time, it is important to remember that experience comes first, and reflection on that experience second. Even the least reflective historian has the first qualification. He possesses the experience on which to reflect; and when he is asked to reflect on it his reflections have a good chance of being to the point. An historian who has never worked much at philosophy will probably answer our four questions in a more intelligent and valuable way than a philosopher who has never worked much at history.

I shall therefore propound answers to my four questions such as I think any present-day historian would accept. Here they will be rough and ready answers, but they will serve for a provisional definition of our subject-matter and they will be defended and elaborated as the argument proceeds.

(*a*) *The definition of history*. Every historian would agree, I think, that history is a kind of research or inquiry. What kind of inquiry it is I do not yet ask. The point is that generically it belongs to what we call the sciences: that is, the forms of thought whereby we ask questions and try to answer them. Science in general, it is important to realize, does not consist in collecting what we already know and arranging it in this or that kind of pattern. It consists in fastening upon something we do not know, and trying to discover it. Playing patience with things we already know may be a useful means towards this end, but it is not the end itself. It is at best only the means. It is scientifically valuable only in so far as the new arrangement gives us the answer to a question we have already decided to ask. That is why all science begins from the knowledge of our own ignorance: not our ignorance of everything, but our ignorance of some definite thing — the origin of parliament, the cause of cancer, the chemical composition of the sun, the way to make a pump work without muscular exertion on the part of a man or a horse or some other docile animal. Science is finding things out: and in that sense history is a science.

(b) *The object of history.* One science differs from another in that it finds out things of a different kind. What kind of things does history find out? I answer, *res gestae:*[3] actions of human beings that have been done in the past. Although this answer raises all kinds of further questions many of which are controversial, still, however they may be answered, the answers do not discredit the proposition that history is the science of *res gestae*, the attempt to answer questions about human actions done in the past.

(c) *How does history proceed?* History proceeds by the interpretation of evidence: where evidence is a collective name for things which singly are called documents, and a document is a thing existing here and now, of such a kind that the historian, by thinking about it, can get answers to the questions he asks about past events. Here again there are plenty of difficult questions to ask as to what the characteristics of evidence are and how it is interpreted. But there is no need for us to raise them at this stage. However they are answered, historians will agree that historical procedure, or method, consists essentially of interpreting evidence.

(d) Lastly, *what is history for?* This is perhaps a harder question than the others; a man who answers it will have to reflect rather more widely than a man who answers the three we have answered already. He must reflect not only on historical thinking but on other things as well, because to say that something is 'for' something implies a distinction between A and B, where A is good for something and B is that for which something is good. But I will suggest an answer, and express the opinion that no historian would reject it, although the further questions to which it gives rise are numerous and difficult.

My answer is that history is 'for' human self-knowledge. It is generally thought to be of importance to man that he should know himself: where knowing himself means knowing not his merely personal peculiarities, the things that distinguish him from other men, but his nature as man. Knowing yourself means knowing, first, what it is to be a man; secondly, knowing what it is to be the kind of man you are; and thirdly, knowing what it is to be the man *you* are and nobody else is. Knowing yourself means knowing what you can do; and since nobody knows what

[3] Literally, things done.

he can do until he tries, the only clue to what man can do is what man has done. The value of history, then, is that it teaches us what man has done and thus what man is. . . .

The Creation of Scientific History by Herodotus

. . . The Greeks quite clearly and consciously recognized both that history is, or can be, a science, and that it has to do with human actions. Greek history is not legend, it is research; it is an attempt to get answers to definite questions about matters of which one recognizes oneself as ignorant. It is not theocratic,[4] it is humanistic. . . . Moreover, it is not mythical. The events inquired into are not events in a dateless past, at the beginning of things: they are events in a dated past, a certain number of years ago.

This is not to say that legend, either in the form of theocratic history or in the form of myth, was a thing foreign to the Greek mind. The work of Homer is not research, it is legend; and to a great extent it is theocratic legend. The gods appear in Homer as intervening in human affairs in a way not very different from the way in which they appear in the theocratic histories of the Near East. Similarly, Hesiod[5] has given us an example of myth. Nor is it to say that these legendary elements, theocratic or mythical as the case may be, are entirely absent even from the classical works of the fifth-century historians. F. M. Cornford in his *Thucydides Mythistoricus* (London, 1907) drew attention to the existence of such elements even in the hard-headed and scientific Thucydides.[6] He was of course perfectly right; and similar legendary elements are notoriously frequent in Herodotus. But what is remarkable about the Greeks was not the fact that their historical thought contained a certain residue of elements which we should call non-historical, but the fact that, side by side with these, it contained elements of what we call history.

The four characteristics of history which I enumerated in the Introduction were (*a*) that it is scientific, or begins by asking questions, whereas the writer of legends begins by knowing something and tells what he knows; (*b*) that it is humanistic, or asks questions about things done by men at determinate times in the past; (*c*) that it is rational, or

---

[4] Does not interpret the past as determined by acts of God.

[5] Greek poet of the eighth century B.C., who wrote in his *Theogony* of the origin of the universe and the dynasties of the gods.

[6] Fifth-century B.C. historian of the Peloponnesian War.

bases the answers which it gives to its questions on grounds, namely appeal to evidence; (*d*) that it is self-revelatory, or exists in order to tell man what man is by telling him what man has done. Now the first, second, and fourth of these characteristics clearly appear in Herodotus: (i) The fact that history as a science was a Greek invention is recorded to this day by its very name. History is a Greek word, meaning simply an investigation or inquiry. Herodotus, who uses it in the title of his work, thereby 'marks a literary revolution' (as Croiset, an historian of Greek literature, says). Previous writers had been . . . writers-down of current stories: 'the historian', say How and Wells,[7] 'sets out to "find" the truth.' It is the use of this word, and its implications, that make Herodotus the father of history. The conversion of legend-writing into the science of history was not native to the Greek mind, it was a fifth-century invention, and Herodotus was the man who invented it. (ii) It is equally clear that history for Herodotus is humanistic as distinct from either mythical or theocratic. As he says in his preface, his purpose is to describe the deeds of men. (iii) His end, as he describes it himself, is that these deeds shall not be forgotten by posterity. Here we have my fourth characteristic of history, namely that it ministers to man's knowledge of man. In particular, Herodotus points out, it reveals man as a rational agent: that is, its function is partly to discover what men have done and partly to discover why they have done it. . . . Herodotus does not confine his attention to bare events; he considers these events in a thoroughly humanistic manner as actions of human beings who had reasons for acting as they did: and the historian is concerned with these reasons.

These three points reappear in the preface of Thucydides, which was obviously written with an eye on that of Herodotus. . . . To make it clear that he is no logographer but a scientific student, asking questions instead of repeating legends, he defends his choice of subject by saying that events earlier than those of the Peloponnesian War cannot be accurately ascertained. . . . He emphasizes the humanistic purpose and the self-revelatory function of history, in words modelled on those of his predecessor. And in one way he improves on Herodotus, for Herodotus makes no mention of evidence (the third of the characteristics mentioned above), and one is left to gather from the body of his work what his idea of evidence was; but Thucydides does say explicitly that historical inquiry rests on evidence. . . .

[7] Authors of a commentary on Herodotus.

Anti-Historical Tendency of Greek Thought

In the meantime, I should like to point out how remarkable a thing is this creation of scientific history by Herodotus, for he was an ancient Greek, and ancient Greek thought as a whole has a very definite prevailing tendency not only uncongenial to the growth of historical thought but actually based, one might say, on a rigorously anti-historical metaphysics. History is a science of human action: what the historian puts before himself is things that men have done in the past, and these belong to a world of change, a world where things come to be and cease to be. Such things, according to the prevalent Greek metaphysical view, ought not to be knowable, and therefore history ought to be impossible.

For the Greeks, the same difficulty arose with the world of nature since it too was a world of this kind. If everything in the world changes, they asked, what is there in such a world for the mind to grasp? They were quite sure that anything which can be an object of genuine knowledge must be permanent; for it must have some definite character of its own, and therefore cannot contain in itself the seeds of its own destruction. If it is to be knowable it must be determinate; if it is determinate, it must be so completely and exclusively what it is that no internal change and no external force can ever set about making it into something else. Greek thought achieved its first triumph when it discovered in the objects of mathematical knowledge something that satisfied these conditions. A straight bar of iron may be bent into a curve, a flat surface of water may be broken into waves, but the straight line and the plane surface, as the mathematician thinks of them, are eternal objects that cannot change their characteristics.

Following the line of argument thus opened up, Greek thought worked out a distinction between two types of thought, knowledge proper . . . and what we translate by 'opinion.' . . .[8] Opinion is the empirical semi-knowledge we have of matters of fact, which are always changing. It is our fleeting acquaintance with the fleeting actualities of the world; it thus only holds good for its own proper duration, for the here and now; and it is immediate, ungrounded in reasons, incapable of demonstration. True knowledge, on the contrary, holds good not only here and now but everywhere and always, and it is based on demonstrative reasoning and thus capable of meeting and overthrowing error by the weapon of dialectical criticism.

Thus, for the Greeks, process could be known only so far as it was

[8] See Plato's *Symposium*, page 140, where this distinction is made.

perceived, and the knowledge of it could never be demonstrative. An exaggerated statement of this view, as we get it in the Eleatics,[9] would misuse the weapon of dialectic, which is really valid only against error in the sphere of knowledge strictly so called, to prove that change does not exist and that the 'opinions' we have about the changing are really not even opinions but sheer illusions. Plato rejects that doctrine and sees in the world of change something not indeed intelligible but real to the extent of being perceptible, something intermediate between the nullity with which the Eleatics had identified it and the complete reality and intelligibility of the eternal. On such a theory, history ought to be impossible. For history must have these two characteristics: first it must be about what is transitory, and secondly it must be scientific or demonstrative. But on this theory what is transitory cannot be demonstratively known; it cannot be the object of science; it can only be a matter of . . . perception, whereby human sensibility catches the fleeting moment as it flies. And it is essential to the Greek point of view that this momentary sensuous perception of momentary changing things cannot be a science or the basis of a science.

Greek Conception of History's Nature and Value

The ardour with which the Greeks pursued the ideal of an unchanging and eternal object of knowledge might easily mislead us as to their historical interests. It might, if we read them carelessly, make us think them uninterested in history, somewhat as Plato's attack on the poets[10] might make an unintelligent reader fancy that Plato cared little for poetry. In order to interpret such things correctly we must remember that no competent thinker or writer wastes his time attacking a man of straw. An intense polemic against a certain doctrine is an infallible sign that the doctrine in question figures largely in the writer's environment and even has a strong attraction for himself. The Greek pursuit of the eternal

[9] Followers of Parmenides of Elea (5th century B.C.), who taught that true being is one and indivisible, that it cannot not-be, and therefore that change (coming into being or ceasing to be) is unreal.

[10] In the *Republic* it is argued that poets should not be allowed in the ideal commonwealth because they deal in fictions, composing "images" or "copies" of things at a third remove from true (eternal) "reality," and because their stories—like those of Homer and the tragic dramatists—show men in the blind excitement of passions. But elsewhere, as in the *Phaedrus*, Plato spoke very differently of poets.

was as eager as it was, precisely because the Greeks themselves had an unusually vivid sense of the temporal. They lived in a time when history was moving with extraordinary rapidity, and in a country where earthquake and erosion change the face of the land with a violence hardly to be seen elsewhere. They saw all nature as a spectacle of incessant change, and human life as changing more violently than anything else. Unlike the Chinese, or the medieval civilization of Europe, whose conception of human society was anchored in the hope of retaining the chief features of its structure unchanged, they made it their first aim to face and reconcile themselves to the fact that such permanence is impossible. This recognition of the necessity of change in human affairs gave to the Greeks a peculiar sensitiveness to history.

Knowing that nothing in life can persist unchanged, they came habitually to ask themselves what exactly the changes had been which, they knew, must have come about in order to bring the present into existence. Their historical consciousness was thus not a consciousness of agelong tradition moulding the life of one generation after another into a uniform pattern; it was a consciousness of violent . . . catastrophic changes from one state of things to its opposite, from smallness to greatness, from pride to abasement, from happiness to misery. This was how they interpreted the general character of human life in their dramas, and this was how they narrated the particular parts of it in their history. The only thing that a shrewd and critical Greek like Herodotus would say about the divine power that ordains the course of history is that . . . it rejoices in upsetting and disturbing things. He was only repeating . . . what every Greek knew: that the power of Zeus is manifested in the thunderbolt, that of Poseidon in the earthquake, that of Apollo in the pestilence, and that of Aphrodite in the passion that destroyed at once the pride of Phaedra and the chastity of Hippolytus.[11]

It is true that these catastrophic changes in the condition of human

---

[11] In the powers attributed to the great gods of the Greek pantheon there resides a profound wisdom of the opposing forces of creation and destruction that surge throughout all nature and life. It is the destructive attributes of the gods that are mentioned here: Zeus, the supreme god of the heavens, with his lightning; Poseidon, god of the sea, as the "earth-shaker"; Apollo, god of the sun, of prophecy, poetry, and music, as also the bringer of the plague; and Aphrodite, goddess of love, in her opposite aspect as destroyer. Euripides' *Hippolytus* tells of the lust of Phaedra, wife of Theseus, for her stepson Hippolytus, and of the horrible destruction sent upon them.

life, which to the Greeks were the proper theme of history, were unintelligible. There could be . . . of them no demonstrative scientific knowledge.[12] But all the same history had for the Greeks a definite value. Plato himself laid it down that right opinion (which is the sort of pseudo-knowledge that perception gives us of what changes) was no less useful for the conduct of life than scientific knowledge, and the poets maintained their traditional place in Greek life as the teachers of sound principles by showing that in the general pattern of these changes certain antecedents normally led to certain consequents. Notably, an excess in any one direction led to a violent change into its own opposite. Why this was so they could not tell; but they thought it a matter of observation that it was so; that people who became extremely rich or extremely powerful were thereby brought into special danger of being reduced to a condition of extreme poverty or weakness. There is here no theory of causation; the thought does not resemble that of seventeenth-century inductive science with its metaphysical basis in the axiom of cause and effect; the riches of Croesus[13] are not the cause of his downfall, they are merely a symptom, to the intelligent observer, that something is happening in the rhythm of his life which is likely to lead to a downfall. Still less is the downfall a punishment for anything that, in an intelligible moral sense, could be called wrongdoing. When Amasis in Herodotus . . . broke off his alliance with Polycrates,[14] he did it simply on the ground that Polycrates was too prosperous: the pendulum had swung too far one way and was likely to swing as far in the other. Such examples have their value to the person who can make use of them; for he can use his own will to arrest these rhythms in his life before they reach the danger-point, and check the thirst for power and wealth instead of allowing it to drive him to excess. Thus history has a value; its teachings are useful for human life; simply because the rhythm of its changes is likely to repeat itself, similar antecedents leading to similar consequents; the history of notable events is worth remembering in order to serve as a basis for prognostic judgements, not demonstrable but probable, laying down not what will happen but what is likely to happen, indicating the points of danger in rhythms now going on.

[12] See the distinction between "knowledge" and "opinion" in the preceding section of the essay, page 465.

[13] Immensely wealthy 6th-century B.C. king of Lydia in Asia Minor.

[14] Amasis was king of Egypt and Polycrates tyrant of Samos in the 6th century B.C.

This conception of history was the very opposite of deterministic, because the Greeks regarded the course of history as flexible and open to salutary modification by the well-instructed human will. Nothing that happens is inevitable. The person who is about to be involved in a tragedy is actually overwhelmed by it only because he is too blind to see his danger. If he saw it, he could guard against it. Thus the Greeks had a lively and indeed a naïve sense of the power of man to control his own destiny, and thought of this power as limited only by the limitations of his knowledge. The fate that broods over human life is, from this Greek point of view, a destructive power only because man is blind to its workings. Granted that he cannot understand these workings, he can yet have right opinions about them, and in so far as he acquires such opinions he becomes able to put himself in a position where the blows of fate will miss him.

On the other hand, valuable as the teachings of history are, their value is limited by the unintelligibility of its subject-matter; and that is why Aristotle said that poetry is more scientific than history, for history is a mere collection of empirical facts, whereas poetry extracts from such facts a universal judgement.[15] History tells us that Croesus fell and that Polycrates fell; poetry, according to Aristotle's idea of it, makes not these singular judgements but the universal judgement that very rich men, as such, fall. Even this is, in Aristotle's view, only a partially scientific judgement, for no one can see why rich men should fall; the universal cannot be syllogistically demonstrated; but it approaches the status of a true universal because we can use it as the major premiss for a new syllogism applying this generalization to fresh cases. Thus poetry is for Aristotle the distilled essence of the teaching of history. In poetry the lessons of history do not become any more intelligible and they remain undemonstrated and therefore merely probable, but they become more compendious and therefore more useful.

Such was the way in which the Greeks conceived the nature and value of history. They could not, consistently with their general philosophical attitude, regard it as scientific. They had to consider it as, at bottom, not a science but a mere aggregate of perceptions. What, then,

[15] See Aristotle's *Poetics*, page 1027. The usual translation of the statement is that poetry is more philosophic than history, whereas Collingwood uses the word "scientific." "Poetry," as Aristotle speaks of it, has its ancient inclusive meaning, referring to all the arts that use rhythmical language, including drama.

was their conception of historical evidence? The answer is that, conformably with this view, they identified historical evidence with the reports of facts given by eyewitnesses of those facts. Evidence consists of eyewitnesses' narratives, and historical method consists of eliciting these.

Greek Historical Method and Its Limitations

Quite clearly, it was in this way that Herodotus conceived of evidence and method. This does not mean that he uncritically believed whatever eyewitnesses told him. On the contrary, he is in practice highly critical of their narratives. And here again he is typically Greek. The Greeks as a whole were skilled in the practice of the law courts, and a Greek would find no difficulty in applying to historical testimony the same kind of criticism which he was accustomed to direct upon witnesses in court. The work of Herodotus or Thucydides depends in the main on the testimony of eyewitnesses with whom the historian had personal contact. And his skill as a researcher consisted in the fact that he must have crossquestioned an eyewitness of past events until he had called up in the informant's own mind an historical picture of those events far fuller and more coherent than any he could have volunteered for himself. The result of this process was to create in the informant's mind for the first time a genuine knowledge of the past events which he had perceived. . . .

This conception of the way in which a Greek historian collected his material makes it a very different thing from the way in which a modern historian may use printed memoirs. Instead of the easy-going belief on the informant's part that his prima facie[16] recollection was adequate to the facts, there could grow up in his mind a chastened and criticized recollection which had stood the fire of such questions as 'Are you quite sure that you remember it just like that? Have you not now contradicted what you were saying yesterday? How do you reconcile your account of that event with the very different account given by so-and-so?' This method of using the testimony of eyewitnesses is undoubtedly the method which underlies the extraordinary solidity and consistency of the narratives which Herodotus and Thucydides finally wrote about fifth-century Greece.

[16] On first view; unexamined.

No other method deserving the name scientific was available to the fifth-century historians, but it had [certain] limitations:

First, it inevitably imposed on its users a shortness of historical perspective. The modern historian knows that if only he had the capacity he could become the interpreter of the whole past of mankind; but whatever Greek historians might have thought of Plato's description of the philosopher as the spectator of all time, they would never have ventured to claim Plato's words as a description of themselves. Their method tied them on a tether whose length was the length of living memory: the only source they could criticize was an eyewitness with whom they could converse face to face. It is true that they relate events from a remoter past, but as soon as Greek historical writing tries to go beyond its tether, it becomes a far weaker and more precarious thing. . . .

Nevertheless, this contrast in Herodotus and Thucydides between the unreliability of everything farther back than living memory and the critical precision of what comes within living memory is a mark not of the failure of fifth-century historiography but of its success. The point about Herodotus and Thucydides is not that the remote past is for them still outside the scope of scientific history but that the recent past is within that scope. Scientific history has been invented. Its field is still narrow; but within that field it is secure. Moreover, this narrowness of field did not matter much to the Greeks, because the extreme rapidity with which their own civilization was developing and changing afforded plenty of first-class historical material within the confines set by their method, and for the same reason they could produce first-rate historical work without developing what in fact they never did develop, any lively curiosity concerning the remote past.

Secondly, the Greek historian's method precludes him from choosing his subject. He cannot, like Gibbon, begin by wishing to write a great historical work and go on to ask himself what he shall write about. The only thing he can write about is the events which have happened within living memory to people with whom he can have personal contact. Instead of the historian choosing the subject, the subject chooses the historian; I mean that history is written only because memorable things have happened which call for a chronicler among the contemporaries of the people who have seen them. One might almost say that in ancient Greece there were no historians in the sense in which there

were artists and philosophers; there were no people who devoted their
lives to the study of history; the historian was only the autobiographer
of his generation and autobiography is not a profession. . . .

The greatness of Herodotus stands out in the sharpest relief when,
as the father of history, he is set against a background consisting of the
general tendencies of Greek thought. The most dominant of these was
anti-historical, as I have argued, because it involved the position that
only what is unchanging can be known. Therefore history is a forlorn
hope, an attempt to know what, being transitory, is unknowable.
But we have already seen that, by skilful questioning, Herodotus was
able . . . to attain knowledge in a field where Greeks had thought it
impossible.

His success must remind us of one of his contemporaries, a man
who was not afraid, either in war or in philosophy, to embark on forlorn hopes. Socrates brought philosophy down from heaven to earth by
insisting that he himself knew nothing, and inventing a technique
whereby, through skilful questioning, knowledge could be generated in
the minds of others as ignorant as himself. Knowledge of what? Knowledge of human affairs: in particular, of the moral ideas that guide human
conduct.

The parallel between the work of the two men is so striking that I
put Herodotus side by side with Socrates as one of the great innovating
geniuses of the fifth century.

&5 FOR DISCUSSION AND WRITING

1. In common use the meaning of the word "history" is taken pretty much
   for granted, and few people would think that it required definition. Before reading this piece, how would you have defined history? Before
   entering on his own definition, Collingwood gives certain qualifications a
   person should have in order to give a responsible definition of history:
   what are the qualifications? What does he think of opinions derived
   through "ordinary educational channels"? What is wrong with them?
   What does he mean by the "illusion of finality" propagated in this way?

2. Note that his definition is actually a cluster of four definitions, each
   applying to an aspect of history: its generic nature as a science, its

particular object, its procedure or method, and its use or value. How does he define each of these aspects? How does he expand the idea of the value of history as "self-knowledge"? A little later, in the second section of the piece, he uses the words "scientific," "humanistic," and "rational" for the first three aspects, respectively; explain the application of the term in each case. How would you appraise (in terms of clarity and suitability to the subject, for instance) Collingwood's technique of exposition so far?

3. Beginning with the second section, his method changes from that of *definition* to that of *analysis*. Though these expository methods would probably never be found "pure" in any fairly thoughtful and complex piece of prose exposition, why does Collingwood's subject in this and the following sections require the analytical method? What characteristics of history, as defined, are found in the work of Herodotus and Thucydides?

4. In the third section, what aspect of ancient Greek thought does he say stands opposed to the historical attitude? If you have read one or both of the selections from Plato given earlier in this book, what can you cite from one or the other of them in illustration of the point here? What contrast do you find with the modern scientific attitude toward change or "process"? Do we have any "eternal objects"?

5. Explain the sentence: "The Greek pursuit of the eternal was as eager as as it was, precisely because the Greeks themselves had an unusually vivid sense of the temporal." What happenings do you know of, in the "classical" period of Greece, that illustrate the statement that "history was moving with extraordinary rapidity"? (If you don't know anything about the period, now is certainly a good time to look it up.) If you have read the selection from Teilhard de Chardin in this book, what relationship do you see here with what Teilhard says about Chinese civilization in contrast with the civilization originating in the Near East and Mediterranean area?

6. Collingwood speaks of Greek drama as illustrating the Greek sense of change; do you know any of the ancient dramas that illustrate this? (Actually, the simplest definition of tragedy, and one that Aristotle uses in the *Poetics*, is a fall from high place to low. See page 1029.) Collingwood also refers to the conception of the gods as an illustration in point; how do his particular references serve here? Although ancient Greek thought did not consider the history of changing events a mode of "true knowl-

edge," in the metaphysical sense, how nevertheless did it find history valuable for self-knowledge?

7. How does Collingwood explain Aristotle's view of poetry as more "scientific" (or "philosophic"—see note 15) than history? What was the conception of historical "evidence" in the ancient historians? (If you read the selection from Herodotus that follows, you might keep this point in mind and watch for indications of how Herodotus got his evidence.)

8. What, according to Collingwood, are the limitations of the ancient historical method? What analogy does he draw between Herodotus and Socrates as "great innovating geniuses"?

9. Looking back over the sections of this piece, make a considered comment, with "evidence," on the way in which Collingwood's definition of history controls, gives coherence to, and unifies the whole discussion.

10. Write a short paper defining what you would consider effective teaching, and support your definition by analysis of one or more examples of your experience under teachers (you could also use an example of poor teaching). You might, incidentally, take into consideration the "illusion of finality," or "dogmatism," Collingwood speaks of. Or you might include, as teachers, persons not in the formal profession of teaching—parents and others—for we are "taught" (for good or ill) by innumerable people other than our teachers in school.

Herodotus ✺ Concerning Egypt

✺ Cicero called Herodotus "the father of history," and nothing has ever happened to disturb that title. He was born about 484 B.C. at Halicarnassus in Caria, a province bordering the coast of Asia Minor. Gathering materials for his great *History,* he traveled extensively in Greece, Macedonia, what are now Bulgaria and Turkey, Israel, Iran, and Egypt. He died about 425 B.C. For Herodotus' historical method, see the preceding essay by R. G. Collingwood. ৡ

CONCERNING Egypt itself I shall extend my remarks to a great length, because there is no country that possesses so many wonders, nor any that has such a number of works which defy description. Not only is the climate different from that of the rest of the world, and the rivers unlike any other rivers, but the people also, in most of their manners and customs, exactly reverse the common practice of mankind. The women attend the markets and trade, while the men sit at home at the loom; and here, while the rest of the world works the woof up the warp, the Egyptians work it down; the women likewise carry burthens upon their shoulders, while the men carry them upon their heads. They eat their food out of doors in the streets, but retire for private purposes to their houses, giving as a reason that what is unseemly, but necessary, ought

From *History* (Vol. I) by Herodotus. Translated by George Rawlinson, Everyman's Library edition. Reprinted by permission of E. P. Dutton & Co., Inc.

to be done in secret, but what has nothing unseemly about it, should be done openly. A woman cannot serve the priestly office, either for god or goddess, but men are priests to both; sons need not support their parents unless they choose, but daughters must, whether they choose or no.

In other countries the priests have long hair, in Egypt their heads are shaven; elsewhere it is customary, in mourning, for near relations to cut their hair close: the Egyptians, who wear no hair at any other time, when they lose a relative, let their beards and the hair of their heads grow long. All other men pass their lives separate from animals, the Egyptians have animals always living with them; others make barley and wheat their food; it is a disgrace to do so in Egypt, where the grain they live on is spelt, which some call *zea*. Dough they knead with their feet; but they mix mud, and even take up dirt, with their hands. They are the only people in the world — they at least, and such as have learnt the practice from them — who use circumcision. Their men wear two garments apiece, their women but one. They put on the rings and fasten the ropes to sails inside; others put them outside. When they write or calculate, instead of going, like the Greeks, from left to right, they move their hand from right to left; and they insist, notwithstanding, that it is they who go to the right, and the Greeks who go to the left. They have two quite different kinds of writing, one of which is called sacred, the other common.

They are religious to excess, far beyond any other race of men, and use the following ceremonies: — They drink out of brazen cups, which they scour every day: there is no exception to this practice. They wear linen garments, which they are specially careful to have always fresh washed. They practise circumcision for the sake of cleanliness, considering it better to be cleanly than comely. The priests shave their whole body every other day, that no lice or other impure thing may adhere to them when they are engaged in the service of the gods. Their dress is entirely of linen, and their shoes of the papyrus plant: it is not lawful for them to wear either dress or shoes of any other material. They bathe twice every day in cold water, and twice each night; besides which they observe, so to speak, thousands of ceremonies. They enjoy, however, not a few advantages. They consume none of their own property, and are at no expense for anything; but every day bread is baked for them of the sacred corn, and a plentiful supply of beef and of goose's flesh is assigned to each, and also a portion of wine made from the grape. Fish they are not allowed to eat; and beans, — which none of the Egyptians ever sow, or eat, if they come up of their own accord, either raw or boiled — the priests will not even endure to look on, since they consider it an unclean kind of pulse. Instead of a single priest, each god has the attendance of a college, at the head of which is a chief priest, when one of these dies, his son is appointed in his room.

Male kine are reckoned to belong to Epaphus,[1] and are therefore tested in the following manner: — One of the priests appointed for the purpose searches to see if there is a single black hair on the whole body, since in that case the beast is unclean. He examines him all over, standing on his legs, and again laid upon his back; after which he takes the tongue out of his mouth, to see if it be clean in respect to the prescribed marks (what they are I will mention elsewhere); he also inspects the hairs of the tail, to observe if they grow naturally. If the animal is pronounced clean in all these various points, the priest marks him by twisting a piece of papyrus round his horns, and attaching thereto some sealing clay, which he then stamps with his own signet-ring. After this the beast is led away; and it is forbidden, under the penalty of death, to sacrifice an animal which has not been marked in this way.

The following is their manner of sacrifice: — They lead the victim, marked with their signet, to the altar where they are about to offer it, and setting the wood alight, pour a libation of wine upon the altar in front of the victim, and at the same time invoke the god. Then they slay the animal, and cutting off his head, proceed to flay the body. Next they take the head, and heaping imprecations on it, if there is a market-place and a body of Greek traders in the city, they carry it there and sell it instantly; if, however, there are no Greeks among them, they throw the head into the river. The imprecation is to this effect: — They pray that if any evil is impending either over those who sacrifice, or over universal Egypt, it may be made to fall upon that head. These practices, the imprecations upon the heads, and the libations of wine, prevail all over Egypt, and extend to victims of all sorts; and hence the Egyptians will never eat the head of any animal.

The disembowelling and burning are, however, different in differ-

---

[1] Son of Zeus by Io. In a jealous fit, the goddess Hera had changed Io into a cow, who wandered finally to Egypt, where Epaphus was born and where he became king and father of a famous line of heroes. The myth has interest in relation to the religious reverence for the cow in Egypt, sacred to the goddess Isis, as Herodotus says. A goddess perhaps older than Isis, Hathor, was represented as a cow in ancient Egyptian engravings, shown as standing over the earth and giving suck to mankind from her great udders.

ent sacrifices. I will mention the mode in use with respect to the goddess whom they regard as the greatest, and honour with the chiefest festival. When they have flayed their steer they pray, and when their prayer is ended they take the paunch of the animal out entire, leaving the intestines and the fat inside the body; they then cut off the legs, the ends of the loins, the shoulders, and the neck; and having so done, they fill the body of the steer with clean bread, honey, raisins, figs, frankincense, myrrh, and other aromatics. Thus filled, they burn the body, pouring over it great quantities of oil. Before offering the sacrifice they fast, and while the bodies of the victims are being consumed they beat themselves. Afterwards, when they have concluded this part of the ceremony, they have the other parts of the victim served up to them for a repast.

The male kine, therefore, if clean, and the male calves, are used for sacrifice by the Egyptians universally; but the females they are not allowed to sacrifice since they are sacred to Isis.[2] The statue of this goddess has the form of a woman but with horns like a cow, resembling thus the Greek representations of Io; and the Egyptians, one and all, venerate cows much more highly than any other animal. This is the reason why no native of Egypt, whether man or woman, will give a Greek a kiss, or use the knife of a Greek, or his spit, or his cauldron, or taste the flesh of an ox, known to be pure, if it has been cut with a Greek knife. When kine die, the following is the manner of their sepulture: — The females are thrown into the river; the males are buried in the suburbs of the towns, with one or both of their horns appearing above the surface of the ground to mark the place. When the bodies are decayed, a boat comes, at an appointed time, from the island called Prosôpitis — which is a portion of the Delta, nine schoenes[3] in circumference, — and calls at the several cities in turn to collect the bones of the oxen. Prosôpitis is a district containing several cities; the name of that from which the boats come is Atarbêchis. Venus has a temple there of much sanctity. Great numbers of men go forth from this city and proceed to the other towns, where they dig up the bones, which they take away with them and bury together in one place. The same practice prevails with

[2] Great nature-goddess, worshiped with Osiris as his sister and wife. (See Note 1, on Hathor the cow-goddess, whose worship blended into and became identified with that of Isis.) Later in this book there is an account of the initiation mysteries of Isis, from Apuleius' *Golden Ass* (see page 951).

[3] A land measurement of several miles.

respect to the interment of all other cattle — the law so determining; they do not slaughter any of them.

Such Egyptians as possess a temple of the Theban Jove, or live in the Thebaïc canton, offer no sheep in sacrifice, but only goats; for the Egyptians do not all worship the same gods, excepting Isis and Osiris,[4] the latter of whom they say is the Grecian Bacchus. Those, on the contrary, who possess a temple dedicated to Mendes, or belong to the Mendesian canton, abstain from offering goats, and sacrifice sheep instead. The Thebans, and such as imitate them in their practice, give the following account of the origin of the custom: — "Hercules," they say, "wished of all things to see Jove, but Jove did not choose to be seen of him. At length, when Hercules persisted, Jove hit on a device — to flay a ram, and, cutting off his head, hold the head before him, and cover himself with fleece. In this guise he showed himself to Hercules." Therefore the Egyptians give their statues of Jupiter the face of a ram: and from them the practice has passed to the Ammonians, who are a joint colony of Egyptians and Ethiopians, speaking a language between the two; hence also, in my opinion, the latter people took their name of Ammonians, since the Egyptian name for Jupiter is Amun. Such, then, is the reason why the Thebans do not sacrifice rams, but consider them sacred animals. Upon one day in the year, however, at the festival of Jupiter, they slay a single ram, and stripping off the fleece, cover with it the statue of that god, as he once covered himself, and then bring up to the statue of Jove an image of Hercules. When this has been done, the whole assembly beat their breasts in mourning for the ram, and afterwards bury him in a holy sepulchre. . . .

The pig is regarded among them as an unclean animal, so much so that if a man in passing accidentally touch a pig, he instantly hurries to the river, and plunges in with all his clothes on. Hence, too, the

---

[4] Osiris was a plant-god and fertility-god, actually a "Lord of Life" like Dionysus (Bacchus), Adonis, Atys (or Attis), Tammuz, and others. He was slain in youth by his brother Set, and the pieces of his body were scattered over the land. Isis, his sister-wife, wandered everywhere searching for him and grieving, until the fragments of his body were collected and put together. Then the god was resurrected into life. This fertility myth has many parallels (see "The Myth and Ritual of Adonis," from Frazer's *Golden Bough*, page 919), originally symbolizing the cycle of winter and summer, the death of vegetation and its annual renewal. Later the myth came to symbolize the more mystical belief in human resurrection and immortality (compare Question 1 on the selection from Jessica Mitford, page 323).

swineherds, notwithstanding that they are of pure Egyptian blood, are forbidden to enter into any of the temples, which are open to all other Egyptians; and further, no one will give his daughter in marriage to a swineherd, or take a wife from among them, so that the swineherds are forced to intermarry among themselves. They do not offer swine in sacrifice to any of their gods, excepting Bacchus and the Moon,[5] whom they honour in this way at the same time, sacrificing pigs to both of them at the same full moon, and afterwards eating of the flesh. There is a reason alleged by them for their detestation of swine at all other seasons, and their use of them at this festival, with which I am well acquainted, but which I do not think it proper to mention. The following is the mode in which they sacrifice the swine to the Moon: — As soon as the victim is slain, the tip of the tail, the spleen, and the caul are put together, and having been covered with all the fat that has been found in the animal's belly, are straightway burnt. The remainder of the flesh is eaten on the same day that the sacrifice is offered, which is the day of the full moon: at any other time they would not so much as taste it. The poorer sort, who cannot afford live pigs, form pigs of dough, which they bake and offer in sacrifice.

To Bacchus, on the eve of his feast, every Egyptian sacrifices a hog before the door of his house, which is then given back to the swineherd by whom it was furnished, and by him carried away. In other respects the festival is celebrated almost exactly as Bacchic festivals are in Greece, excepting that the Egyptians have no choral dances. They also use instead of phalli[6] another invention, consisting of images a cubit high, pulled by strings, which the women carry round to the villages.

[5] Osiris and Isis. Herodotus has previously suggested an identification between Osiris and the Greek Bacchus; and Isis was goddess of the moon as well as of the rest of nature (One of her emblems was the crescent moon). Pigs are one of the ancient animal symbols of reproductive fertility. In the custom Herodotus speaks of here, it is because of the fertility aspect of Osiris and Isis that pigs were sacrificed to them. The custom corresponds to that of the ancient Greeks, who threw slaughtered pigs into crevices of the earth as offerings to Persephone (daughter of Demeter, the corn-goddess). In Ireland, pigs carved out of bog oak are given as good-luck symbols. The normal Egyptian taboo on the eating of swine meat (except for the monthly sacrifice) was no doubt acquired by the Hebrews during their stay in Egypt, like the practice of circumcision.

[6] This religious fertility symbolism is universal. In the myth of the death and the scattering of the parts of Osiris' body, the phallus was the last to be found, and without it Osiris could not come back to life. It had fallen into the Nile, on which Egyptian agriculture depends.

A piper goes in front, and the women follow, singing hymns in honour of Bacchus. They give a religious reason for the peculiarities of the image.

Melampus,[7] the son of Amytheon, cannot (I think) have been ignorant of this ceremony — nay, he must, I should conceive, have been well acquainted with it. He it was who introduced into Greece the name of Bacchus, the ceremonial of his worship, and the procession of the phallus. He did not, however, so completely apprehend the whole doctrine as to be able to communicate it entirely, but various sages since his time have carried out his teaching to greater perfection. Still it is certain that Melampus introduced the phallus, and that the Greeks learnt from him the ceremonies which they now practise. I therefore maintain that Melampus, who was a wise man, and had acquired the art of divination, having become acquainted with the worship of Bacchus through knowledge derived from Egypt, introduced it into Greece, with a few slight changes, at the same time that he brought in various other practices. For I can by no means allow that it is by mere coincidence that the Bacchic ceremonies in Greece are so nearly the same as the Egyptian — they would then have been more Greek in their character, and less recent in their origin. Much less can I admit that the Egyptians borrowed these customs, or any other, from the Greeks. My belief is that Melampus got his knowledge of them from Cadmus the Tyrian, and the followers whom he brought from Phoenicia into the country which is now called Boeotia.[8]

Almost all the names of the gods came into Greece from Egypt. My inquiries prove that they were all derived from a foreign source, and my opinion is that Egypt furnished the greater number. For with the exception of Neptune and the Dioscûri, whom I mentioned above, and Juno, Vesta, Themis, the Graces, and the Nereids, the other gods have been known from time immemorial in Egypt. This I assert on the authority of the Egyptians themselves. The gods, with whose names they profess themselves unacquainted, the Greeks received, I believe, from the Pelasgi, except Neptune. Of him they got their knowledge from the

---

[7] Mythological seer who understood the speech of all creatures.

[8] Cadmus, legendary founder of Thebes, was said to have brought the alphabet from Tyre in Phoenicia (on the eastern Mediterranean coast) to Greece. Boeotia was the ancient name of the country north of the Gulf of Corinth, dominated by Thebes.

Libyans, by whom he has been always honoured, and who were anciently the only people that had a god of the name. The Egyptians differ from the Greeks also in paying no divine honours to heroes. . . .[9]

Whence the gods severally sprang, whether or no they had all existed from eternity, what forms they bore — these are questions of which the Greeks knew nothing until the other day, so to speak. For Homer and Hesiod were the first to compose Theogonies, and give the gods their epithets, to allot them their several offices and occupations, and describe their forms; and they lived but four hundred years before my time, as I believe. As for the poets who are thought by some to be earlier than these, they are, in my judgment, decidedly later writers. In these matters I have the authority of the priestesses of Dodôna for the former portion of my statements; what I have said of Homer and Hesiod is my own opinion. . . .[10]

The Egyptians first made it a point of religion to have no converse with women in the sacred places,[11] and not to enter them without washing, after such converse. Almost all other nations, except the Greeks and the Egyptians, act differently, regarding man as in this matter under no

---

[9] The Dioscuri (*dios-kuroi*, god's sons) were Castor and Pollux, sons of Zeus and Leda, conceived when Zeus met Leda in the form of a swan, and brothers of Helen and Clytemnestra. They were patrons of horsemanship, boxing, and all the athletic skills of the Olympic Games. At their death they became the constellation Gemini, the Twins. Vesta was an ancient earth-goddess who became, in the Olympian pantheon, goddess of the home and hearth. Themis was another very ancient earth-goddess, a Titaness (the Titans were nature-gods who preceded the Olympians), mother of Prometheus. The oracle at Delphi spoke through her priestesses. The Pelasgi were, so far as is known, aboriginal inhabitants of Greece, whose immense rough stonework is found in various parts of Greece. The Nereids were daughters of an ancient sea-god, Nereus, who were represented as attending the later sea-god, Poseidon, riding sea horses; they are the original "mermaids" from which come T. S. Eliot's lines at the end of *The Love Song of J. Alfred Prufrock* (from *Collected Poems 1909–1962*, Harcourt, Brace & World, Inc.)—

I have seen them riding seaward on the waves
Combing the white hair of the waves blown back
When the wind blows the water white and black.

The Graces were a late mythological concept of the attendants on Venus or Aphrodite, representing her charms.

[10] Modern scholars tend to accept Herodotus' date for Homer ("four hundred years before my time") as correct. Theogonies are genealogies of the gods. Dodona was a famous oracle of Zeus in northwestern Greece.

[11] Ritual prostitution in temple precincts, setting a symbolic example to the earth to renew its fertility, was common in ancient Greece (see Frazer, page 925). D. H. Lawrence's story, *The Man Who Died*, has as a principal character a priestess of those rituals.

other law than the brutes. Many animals, they say, and various kinds of birds, may be seen to couple in the temples and the sacred precincts, which would certainly not happen if the gods were displeased at it. Such are the arguments by which they defend their practice, but I never-theless can by no means approve of it. In these points the Egyptians are specially careful, as they are indeed in everything which concerns their sacred edifices.

Egypt, though it borders upon Libya, is not a region abounding in wild animals. The animals that do exist in the country, whether domes-ticated or otherwise, are all regarded as sacred. If I were to explain why they are consecrated to the several gods, I should be led to speak of religious matters, which I particularly shrink from mentioning;[12] the points whereon I have touched slightly hitherto have all been intro-duced from sheer necessity. Their custom with respect to animals is as follows: — For every kind there are appointed certain guardians, some male, some female, whose business it is to look after them; and this honour is made to descend from father to son. The inhabitants of the various cities, when they have made a vow to any god, pay it to his animals in the way which I will now explain. At the time of making the vow they shave the head of the child, cutting off all the hair, or else half, or sometimes a third part, which they then weigh in a balance against a sum of silver; and whatever sum the hair weighs is presented to the guardian of the animals, who thereupon cuts up some fish, and gives it to them for food — such being the stuff whereon they fed. When a man has killed one of the sacred animals, if he did it with malice prepense,[13] he is punished with death; if unwittingly, he has to pay such a fine as the priests choose to impose. When an ibis, however, or a hawk is killed, whether it was done by accident or on purpose, the man must needs die.

The number of domestic animals in Egypt is very great, and would be still greater were it not for what befalls the cats. As the females, when they have kittened, no longer seek the company of the males, these last, to obtain once more their companionship, practise a curious artifice. They seize the kittens, carry them off, and kill them, but do not eat them afterwards. Upon this the females, being deprived of their young, and

---

[12] The sacred mysteries were not to be lightly spoken of or gossiped about, even by a historian. The famous mysteries of Eleusis (a few miles from Athens), which apparently had much in common with those of Isis and Osiris in Egypt, were so sacrosanct that modern researchers have been able to discover little about them.

[13] Malice aforethought.

longing to supply their place, seek the males once more, since they are particularly fond of their offspring. On every occasion of a fire in Egypt the strangest prodigy occurs with the cats. The inhabitants allow the fire to rage as it pleases, while they stand about at intervals and watch these animals, which, slipping by the men or else leaping over them, rush headlong into the flames. When this happens, the Egyptians are in deep affliction. If a cat dies in a private house by a natural death, all the inmates of the house shave their eyebrows; on the death of a dog they shave the head and the whole of the body.

The cats on their decease are taken to the city of Bubastis, where they are embalmed, after which they are buried in certain sacred repositories. The dogs are interred in the cities to which they belong, also in sacred burial-places. The same practice obtains with respect to the ichneumons; the hawks and shrew-mice, on the contrary, are conveyed to the city of Buto for burial, and the ibises to Hermopolis. The bears, which are scarce in Egypt, and the wolves, which are not much bigger than foxes, they bury wherever they happen to find them lying. . . .

They have also another sacred bird called the phoenix, which I myself have never seen, except in pictures. Indeed it is a great rarity, even in Egypt, only coming there (according to the accounts of the people of Heliopolis) once in five hundred years, when the old phoenix dies. Its size and appearance, if it is like the pictures, are as follow: — The plumage is partly red, partly golden, while the general make and size are almost exactly that of the eagle. They tell a story of what this bird does, which does not seem to me to be credible: that he comes all the way from Arabia, and brings the parent bird, all plastered over with myrrh, to the temple of the Sun, and there buries the body. In order to bring him, they say, he first forms a ball of myrrh as big as he finds that he can carry; then he hollows out the ball, and puts his parent inside, after which he covers over the opening with fresh myrrh, and the ball is then of exactly the same weight as at first; so he brings it to Egypt, plastered over as I have said, and deposits it in the temple of the Sun. Such is the story they tell of the doings of this bird. . . .

With respect to the Egyptians themselves, it is to be remarked that those who live in the corn country, devoting themselves, as they do, far more than any other people in the world, to the preservation of the memory of past actions, are the best skilled in history of any men that I have ever met. The following is the mode of life habitual to them: —

For three successive days in each month they purge the body by means of emetics and clysters, which is done out of a regard for their health, since they have a persuasion that every disease to which men are liable is occasioned by the substances whereon they feed. Apart from any such precautions, they are, I believe, next to the Libyans, the healthiest people in the world — an effect of their climate, in my opinion, which has no sudden changes. Diseases almost always attack men when they are exposed to a change, and never more than during changes of the weather. They live on bread made of spelt, which they form into loaves called in their own tongue *cyllêstis.* Their drink is a wine which they obtain from barley, as they have no vines in their country. Many kinds of fish they eat raw, either salted or dried in the sun. Quails also, and ducks and small birds, they eat uncooked, merely first salting them. All other birds and fishes, excepting those which are set apart as sacred, are eaten either roasted or boiled.

In social meetings among the rich, when the banquet is ended, a servant carries round to the several guests a coffin, in which there is a wooden image of a corpse, carved and painted to resemble nature as nearly as possible, about a cubit or two cubits in length. As he shows it to each guest in turn, the servant says, "Gaze here, and drink and be merry; for when you die, such will you be.". . .

The Egyptian likewise discovered to which of the gods each month and day is sacred; and found out from the day of a man's birth, what he will meet with in the course of his life, and how he will end his days, and what sort of man he will be — discoveries whereof the Greeks engaged in poetry have made a use. The Egyptians have also discovered more prognostics than all the rest of mankind besides. Whenever a prodigy takes place, they watch and record the result; then, if anything similar ever happens again, they expect the same consequences. . . .

The following is the way in which they conduct their mournings and their funerals: — On the death in any house of a man of consequence, forthwith the women of the family beplaster their heads, and sometimes even their faces, with mud; and then, leaving the body indoors, sally forth and wander through the city, with their dress fastened by a band, and their bosoms bare, beating themselves as they walk. All the female relations join them and do the same. The men too, similarly begirt, beat their breasts separately. When these ceremonies are over, the body is carried away to be embalmed.

There are a set of men in Egypt who practice the art of embalming, and make it their proper business. These persons, when a body is brought to them, show the bearers various models of corpses, made in wood, and painted so as to resemble nature. The most perfect is said to be after the manner of him whom I do not think it religious to name[14] in connection with such a matter; the second sort is inferior to the first, and less costly; the third is the cheapest of all. All this the embalmers explain, and then ask in which way it is wished that the corpse should be prepared. The bearers tell them, and having concluded their bargain, take their departure, while the embalmers left to themselves, proceed to their task. The mode of embalming, according to the most perfect process, is the following: — They take first a crooked piece of iron, and with it draw out the brain through the nostrils, thus getting rid of a portion, while the skull is cleared of the rest by rinsing with drugs; next they make a cut along the flank with a sharp Ethiopian stone, and take out the whole contents of the abdomen, which they then cleanse, washing it thoroughly with palm wine, and again frequently with an infusion of pounded aromatics. After this they fill the cavity with purest bruised myrrh, with cassia, and every other sort of spicery except frankincense, and sew up the opening. Then the body is placed in natrum[15] for seventy days, and covered entirely over. After the expiration of that space of time, which must not be exceeded, the body is washed, and wrapped round, from head to foot, with bandages of fine linen cloth, smeared over with gum, which is used generally by the Egyptians in the place of glue, and in this state it is given back to the relations, who enclose it in a wooden case which they have had made for the purpose, shaped into the figure of a man. Then fastening the case, they place it in a sepulchral chamber, upright against the wall. Such is the most costly way of embalming the dead.

If persons wish to avoid expense, and choose the second process, the following is the method pursued: — Syringes are filled with oil made from the cedar-tree, which is then, without any incision or disembowelling, injected into the abdomen. The passage by which it might be likely to return is stopped, and the body laid in natrum the prescribed

[14] Undoubtedly Osiris. Though he might feel free to name Osiris in other contexts, Herodotus speaks again here as one who was under the seal of mysteries corresponding with those of Egypt.

[15] Sodium carbonate.

number of days. At the end of the time the cedar-oil is àllowed to make its escape; and such is its power that it brings with it the whole stomach and intestines in a liquid state. The natrum meanwhile has dissolved the flesh, and so nothing is left of the dead body but the skin and the bones. It is returned in this condition to the relatives, without any further trouble being bestowed upon it.

The third method of embalming, which is practised in the case of the poorer classes, is to clear out the intestines with a clyster, and let the body lie in natrum the seventy days, after which it is at once given to those who come to fetch it away.

The wives of men of rank are not given to be embalmed immediately after death, nor indeed are any of the more beautiful and valued women. It is not till they have been dead three or four days that they are carried to the embalmers. This is done to prevent indignities from being offered them. It is said that once a case of this kind occurred; the man was detected by the information of his fellow-workman. . . .

Thus far I have spoken of Egypt from my own observation, relating what I myself saw, the ideas that I formed, and the results of my own researches.

⤳§ FOR DISCUSSION AND WRITING

1. The expository principle which Herodotus uses in the first two paragraphs is that of comparison and contrast, between a representative number of strange Egyptian customs and the corresponding, but different, customs that would be familiar to his own countrymen. Why, considering the subject, is this principle, or method, a particularly good one for gaining immediate interest and also for introducing the unfamiliar?

2. Note how many different kinds of customs he illustrates (and always through concrete detail): market shopping, weaving, carrying parcels, the support of parents, hair styles, fashions in clothes, bathing, diet and cooking, etc., etc. If such a large accumulation of detailed observations were set down at random, just as they occurred or were remembered, the reader's attention and interest would be swamped and stultified. The mind can't take in so much detail if it isn't somehow organized or classified. Herodotus does, of course, organize his observations carefully. Point out

a half-dozen specific signposts which he sets up at the heads of paragraphs to organize the material that follows.

3. Collingwood, in the first essay in this section, says that Herodotus initiated the modern historical sense in at least three ways: a) he was "scientific," in that he began by asking questions about things of which there was little or no knowledge; b) he conceived history as "humanistic"—concerning things done by men at determinate times (rather than by legendary or mythological beings at indeterminate times); c) he "ministers to man's knowledge of man" by relating what man has done. One cannot judge very well about all these attributes from the relatively short selection given here, for the third one, especially, can be seen fairly only by reading the *History* as a whole, with its massive comparison of cultures. But, from this extract, how would you judge Herodotus on Collingwood's second point? (Don't be too quick; there may be reservations.) As to the first point, what particular kind of questions (thinking of how his mind would have been working, judging from the material here) did he evidently ask himself and go about asking others?

4. Collingwood makes qualifications on the Greek historian's use of "evidence." What is Herodotus' own observation, at the end of the piece, on the way he collected his material? Now look back carefully through the whole piece and note down (in the margin of your book, or in your own notebook) the places where Herodotus comments on the sources of his data: as, for instance, "This I assert on the authority of . . . ," or "in my opinion . . . ," or "which does not seem to me to be credible." How would you sum up, generally, Herodotus' use of source material and his attitude toward it? Is his attitude critical or uncritical? Incidentally, in your own writing, when you have to use data from other sources and need to add to them your own opinions or inferences, it would be well to follow Herodotus' simple and honest method of indicating where you got your data and what statements represent only your own deductions or opinions; this is just good manners.

5. Now to look specifically at some of those customs of the ancient Egyptians in which Herodotus was interested. He gives a lot of attention to religious customs, for one must remember that the Egypt he describes was a theocratic civilization, in which every act had religious significance. But the ritual observances he notices are not quite so odd, unfamilar, and unaccountable as they might seem at first glance. He speaks of various animal sacrifices—sacrifices of animals held sacred and taboo except on certain

ceremonial feast days, when they were offered to the gods and eaten. We, on Thanksgiving Day, prepare a special ceremonial sacrifice of the turkey, sharing out the honorific parts with our grandparents or godparents or parents, with a great to-do about the wishbone. On Christmas Day we have again the turkey or the suckling pig with an apple in his mouth (see note on pigs, page 480), and on Easter we arrange egg hunts for our children, going to great trouble to dye them the night before in magnificent colors and interesting designs. The religious rituals described by Herodotus have to do with the insurance of fertility, fertility of the soil, of plants and animals, of people. What is our Easter egg hunt for? Think for a little bit, and write a short paper on our fertility ceremonies.

6. Or write a paper presenting some of our strange customs (in dress, in barbershops, in shopping, in matrimonial habits, in education) to an Eskimo or to someone on Mars.

Arnold J. Toynbee ✺§ Challenge and Response

✺§ From 1925 to 1955, when he retired, Professor Toynbee held the chair of Research Professor of International History at the University of London, and was also Director of Studies at the Royal Institute of International Affairs. Since his retirement he has traveled and lectured widely, and has received, both in England and America, the highest honors awarded for scholarly distinction. His is undoubtedly the greatest name among living historians, as well as the most controversial. His distinction goes far outside his special field, for his multivolumed work *A Study of History* performs an intellectual synthesis—of the historical patterns of twenty-six civilizations —that presents a challenge in every area of modern thought concerned with human destiny and responsibility. At seventy-five, Professor Toynbee is still engaged in active field work and in writing challenging articles. ठ≫

THE PROBLEM STATED

WHAT is the essential difference between the primitive and the higher societies? It does not consist in the presence or absence of institutions for institutions are the vehicles of the impersonal relations between individuals in which all societies have their existence, because even the smallest of primitive societies is built on a wider basis than the narrow circle of an individual's direct personal ties. Institutions are attributes of the whole genus 'societies' and therefore common properties of both its species. Primitive societies have their institutions — the religion of the annual agricultural cycle; totemism and exogamy; tabus, initiations and age-classes; segregations of the sexes, at certain stages of life, in separate communal establishments — and some of these institutions are certainly as elaborate and perhaps as subtle as those which are characteristic of civilizations.

From *A Study of History* by Arnold J. Toynbee, abridged by D. C. Somervell (New York: Oxford University Press, 1947). Reprinted by permission of the publisher.

Nor are civilizations distinguished from primitive societies by the division of labour, for we can discern at least the rudiments of the division of labour in the lives of primitive societies also. Kings, magicians, smiths and minstrels are all 'specialists' — though the fact that Hephaestus,[1] the smith of Hellenic legend, is lame, and Homer, the poet of Hellenic legends, is blind, suggests that in primitive societies specialism is abnormal and apt to be confined to those who lack the capacity to be 'all-round men' or 'jacks of all trades.'

An essential difference between civilizations and primitive societies *as we know them* (the *caveat*[2] will be found to be important) is the direction taken by mimesis or imitation. Mimesis is a generic feature of all social life. Its operation can be observed both in primitive societies and in civilizations, in every social activity from the imitation of the style of film-stars by their humbler sisters upwards. It operates, however, in different directions in the two species of society. In primitive societies, as we know them, mimesis is directed towards the older generation and towards dead ancestors who stand, unseen but not unfelt, at the back of the living elders, reinforcing their prestige. In a society where mimesis is thus directed backward towards the past, custom rules and society remains static. On the other hand, in societies in process of civilization, mimesis is directed towards creative personalities who commanded a following because they are pioneers. In such societies, 'the cake of custom,' as Walter Bagehot[3] called it in his *Physics and Politics,* is broken and society is in dynamic motion along a course of change and growth.

But if we ask ourselves whether this difference between primitive and higher societies is permanent and fundamental, we must answer in the negative; for, if we only know primitive societies in a static condition, that is because we know them from direct observation only in the last phases of their histories. Yet, though direct observation fails us, a train of reasoning informs us that there must have been earlier phases in the histories of primitive societies in which these were moving more dynamically than any 'civilized' society has moved yet. We have said that primitive societies are as old as the human race, but we should more properly have said that they are older. Social and institutional life of a kind is found among some of the higher mammals other than man,

---

[1] God of fire and metalworking, hence of artisanship and mechanic skills; identified in Roman mythology with Vulcan (compare the words "volcano," "vulcanize").

[2] A warning or reservation.

[3] Nineteenth-century English economist and journalist.

and it is clear that mankind could not have become human except in a social environment. This mutation of sub-man into man, which was accomplished, in circumstances of which we have no record, under the aegis of primitive societies, was a more profound change, a greater step in growth, than any progress which man has yet achieved under the aegis of civilization.

Primitive societies, as we know them by direct observation, may be likened to people lying torpid upon a ledge on a mountain-side, with a precipice below and a precipice above; civilizations may be likened to companions of these sleepers who have just risen to their feet and have started to climb up the face of the cliff above; while we for our part may liken ourselves to observers whose field of vision is limited to the ledge and to the lower slopes of the upper precipice and who have come upon the scene at the moment when the different members of the party happen to be in these respective postures and positions. At first sight we may be inclined to draw an absolute distinction between the two groups, acclaiming the climbers as athletes and dismissing the recumbent figures as paralytics; but on second thoughts we shall find it more prudent to suspend judgement.

After all the recumbent figures cannot be paralytics in reality; for they cannot have been born on the ledge, and no human muscles except their own can have hoisted them to this halting-place up the face of the precipice below. On the other hand, their companions who are climbing at the moment have only just left this same ledge and started to climb the precipice above; and, since the next ledge is out of sight, we do not know how high or how arduous the next pitch may be. We only know that it is impossible to halt and rest before the next ledge, wherever that may lie, is reached. Thus, even if we could estimate each present climber's strength and skill and nerve, we could not judge whether any of them have any prospect of gaining the ledge above, which is the goal of their present endeavours. We can, however, be sure that some of them will never attain it. And we can observe that, for every single one now strenuously climbing, twice that number (our extinct civilization) have fallen back onto the ledge, defeated. . . .

This alternating rhythm of static and dynamic, of movement and pause and movement, has been regarded by many observers in many different ages as something fundamental in the nature of the Universe. In their pregnant imagery the sages of the Sinic[4] Society described these

4 Chinese.

alternations in terms of Yin and Yang — Yin the static and Yang the dynamic. The nucleus of the Sinic character which stands for Yin seems to represent dark coiling clouds overshadowing the Sun, while the nucleus of the character which stands for Yang seems to represent the unclouded sun-disk emitting its rays. In the Chinese formula Yin is always mentioned first, and, within our field of vision, we can see that our breed, having reached the 'ledge' of primitive human nature 300,000 years ago, has reposed there for ninety-eight per cent of that period before entering on the Yang-activity of civilization. We have now to seek for the positive factor, whatever it may be, which has set human life in motion again by its impetus. . . .

THE MYTHOLOGICAL CLUE

An encounter between two superhuman personalities is the plot of some of the greatest dramas that the human imagination has conceived. An encounter between Yahweh[5] and the Serpent is the plot of the story of the Fall of Man in the Book of Genesis; a second encounter between the same antagonists, transfigured by a progressive enlightenment of Syriac souls, is the plot of the New Testament which tells the story of the Redemption; an encounter between the Lord and Satan is the plot of the Book of Job; an encounter between the Lord and Mephistopheles is the plot of Goethe's *Faust;* an encounter between Gods and Demons is the plot of the Scandinavian *Voluspa;*[6] an encounter between Artemis and Aphrodite[7] is the plot of Euripides' *Hippolytus.*

We find another version of the same plot in that ubiquitous and ever-recurring myth — a 'primordial image'[8] if ever there was one —

[5] Jehovah.

[6] An Old Norse epic poem.

[7] See Note 11 on Collingwood, page 467. Hippolytus was a follower of Artemis (Diana) and therefore vowed to chastity. By this vow he incurred the enmity of Aphrodite, goddess of love, who took her revenge on him through the unnatural lust of his stepmother, Phaedra.

[8] A type of image or plot-pattern that has recurred immemorially in myths and legends all over the world. Compare C. G. Jung's explanation, page 859. Among the other references in this paragraph, Danaë, Europa, and Semele were mortal girls with whom Zeus fell in love; to Danaë he came as a shower of gold, and she bore Perseus (who slew the Gorgon Medusa); to Europa he came as a bull, and she bore Minos (king of Crete, whose wife Pasiphaë also coupled with a bull and bore the Minotaur); to Semele he came as lightning and thunder, and she gave premature birth to Dionysus. Creusa was the mother, by Apollo, of Ion, the eponymous ancestor of the Ionian Greeks, who settled parts of the coast of Asia Minor and the offshore islands.

of the encounter between the Virgin and the Father of her Child. The characters in this myth have played their allotted parts on a thousand different stages under an infinite variety of names: Danae and the Shower of Gold; Europa and the Bull; Semele the Stricken Earth and Zeus the Sky that launches the thunderbolt; Creusa and Apollo in Euripides' *Ion*; Psyche and Cupid; Gretchen and Faust. The theme recurs, transfigured, in the Annunciation.[9] In our own day in the West this protean myth has re-expressed itself as the last word of our astronomers on the genesis of the planetary system, as witness the following *credo*:

'We believe . . . that some two thousand million years ago . . . a second star, wandering blindly through space, happened to come within hailing distance of the Sun. Just as the Sun and Moon raise tides on the Earth, this second star must have raised tides on the surface of the Sun. But they would be very different from the puny tides which the small mass of the Moon raises in our oceans; a huge tidal wave must have travelled over the surface of the Sun, ultimately forming a mountain of prodigious height, which would rise ever higher and higher as the cause of the disturbance came nearer and nearer. And, before the second star began to recede, its tidal pull had become so powerful that this mountain was torn to pieces and threw off small fragments of itself, much as the crest of a wave throws off spray. These small fragments have been circulating round their parent sun ever since. They are the planets, great and small, of which our Earth is one.'[10]

Thus out of the mouth of the mathematical astronomer, when all his complex calculations are done, there comes forth, once again, the myth of the encounter between the Sun Goddess and her ravisher that is so familiar a tale in the mouths of the untutored children of nature.

The presence and potency of this duality in the causation of the civilizations whose geneses we are studying is admitted by a Modern Western archaeologist whose studies begin with a concentration on environment and end with an intuition of the mystery of life:

'Environment . . . is not the total causation in culture-shaping. . . . It is, beyond doubt, the most conspicuous single factor. . . . But there is still an indefinable factor which may best be designated quite frankly as *x*, the unknown quantity, apparently psychological in kind. . . . If *x* be not the most

[9] The annunciation, by an angel, to Mary that she would bear the son of God.

[10] Sir James Jeans, *The Mysterious Universe*.

conspicuous factor in the matter, it certainly is the most important, the most fate-laden.'[11]

In our present study of history this insistent theme of the super-human encounter has asserted itself already. At an early stage we observed that 'a society . . . is confronted in the course of its life by a succession of problems' and that 'the presentation of each problem is a challenge to undergo an ordeal.'

Let us try to analyse the plot of this story or drama which repeats itself in such different contexts and in such various forms.

We may begin with two general features: the encounter is conceived of as a rare and sometimes as a unique event; and it has consequences which are vast in proportion to the vastness of the breach which it makes in the customary course of nature.

Even in the easy-going world of Hellenic mythology, where the gods saw the daughters of men that they were fair, and had their way with so many of them that their victims could be marshalled and paraded in poetic catalogues, such incidents never ceased to be sensational affairs and invariably resulted in the births of heroes. In the versions of the plot in which both parties to the encounter are super-human, the rarity and momentousness of the event are thrown into stronger relief. In the Book of Job, 'the day when the Sons of God came to present themselves before the Lord, and Satan came also among them', is evidently conceived of as an unusual occasion; and so is the encounter between the Lord and Mephistopheles in the 'Prologue in Heaven' (suggested, of course, by the opening of the Book of Job) which starts the action of Goethe's *Faust*. In both these dramas the consequences on Earth of the encounter in Heaven are tremendous. The personal ordeals of Job and Faust represent, in the intuitive language of fiction, the infinitely multiple ordeal of mankind; and, in the language of theology, the same vast consequence is represented as following from the superhuman encounters that are portrayed in the Book of Genesis and in the New Testament. The expulsion of Adam and Eve from the Garden of Eden, which follows the encounter between Yahweh and the Serpent, is nothing less than the Fall of Man; the passion of Christ in the New Testament is nothing less than Man's Redemption. Even the birth of our planetary system from the encounter of two suns, as pictured by our modern astronomer, is declared by the same authority to be 'an event of almost unimaginable rarity'.

[11] P. A. Means, *Ancient Civilizations of the Andes.*

In every case the story opens with a perfect state of Yin. Faust is perfect in knowledge; Job is perfect in goodness and prosperity; Adam and Eve are perfect in innocence and ease; the Virgins — Gretchen, Danae and the rest — are perfect in purity and beauty. In the astronomer's universe the Sun, a perfect orb, travels on its course intact and whole. When Yin is thus complete, it is ready to pass over into Yang. But what is to make it pass? A change in a state which, by definition, is perfect after its kind can only be started by an impulse or motive which comes from outside. If we think of the state as one of physical equilibrium, we must bring in another star. If we think of it as one of psychic beatitude or *nirvana*,[12] we must bring another actor on to the stage: a critic to set the mind thinking again by suggesting doubts; an adversary to set the heart feeling again by instilling distress or discontent or fear or antipathy. This is the role of the Serpent in Genesis, of Satan in the Book of Job, of Mephistopheles in *Faust*, of Loki in the Scandinavian mythology, of the Divine Lovers in the Virgin myths.

In the language of science we may say that the function of the intruding factor is to supply that on which it intrudes with a stimulus of the kind best calculated to evoke the most potently creative variations. In the language of mythology and theology, the impulse or motive which makes a perfect Yin-state pass over into new Yang-activity comes from an intrusion of the Devil into the universe of God. The event can best be described in these mythological images because they are not embarrassed by the contradiction that arises when the statement is translated into logical terms. In logic, if God's universe is perfect, there cannot be a Devil outside it, while, if the Devil exists, the perfection which he comes to spoil must have been incomplete already through the very fact of his existence. This logical contradiction, which cannot be logically resolved, is intuitively transcended in the imagery of the poet and prophet, who give glory to an omnipotent God yet take it for granted that He is subject to two crucial limitations.

The first limitation is that, in the perfection of what He has created already, He cannot find an opportunity for further creative activity. If God is conceived of as transcendent, the works of creation are as glorious as ever they were but they cannot 'be changed from glory into glory'. The second limitation on God's power is that when the opportunity for fresh creation is offered to Him from outside He cannot but take it.

---

[12] In Buddhism, state of supreme enlightenment and bliss, through emancipation from the passions and from temporal illusion.

When the Devil challenges Him He cannot refuse to take the challenge up. God is bound to accept the predicament because He can refuse only at the price of denying His own nature and ceasing to be God.

If God is thus not omnipotent in logical terms, is He still mythologically invincible? If He is bound to take up the Devil's challenge, is He also bound to win the ensuing battle? In Euripides' *Hippolytus*, where God's part is played by Artemis and the Devil's by Aphrodite, Artemis is not only unable to decline the combat but is foredoomed to defeat. The relations between the Olympians[13] are anarchic and Artemis in the epilogue can console herself only by making up her mind that one day she will play the Devil's role herself at Aphrodite's expense. The result is not creation but destruction. In the Scandinavian version destruction is likewise the outcome in Ragnarök[14] — when 'Gods and Demons slay and are slain' — though the unique genius of the author of *Voluspa* makes his Sibyl's vision pierce the gloom to behold the light of a new dawn beyond it. On the other hand, in another version of the plot, the combat which follows the compulsory acceptance of the challenge takes the form, not of an exchange of fire in which the Devil has the first shot and cannot fail to kill his man, but of a wager which the Devil is apparently bound to lose. The classic works in which this wager *motif* is worked out are the Book of Job and Goethe's *Faust*.

It is in Goethe's drama that the point is most clearly made. After the Lord has accepted the wager with Mephistopheles in Heaven, the terms are agreed on Earth, between Mephistopheles and Faust, as follows:

> *Faust.* Comfort and quiet!—no, no! none of these
> For me—I ask them not—I seek them not.
> If ever I upon the bed of sloth
> Lie down and rest, then be the hour in which
> I so lie down and rest my last of life.
> Canst thou by falsehood or by flattery
> Delude me into self-complacent smiles,

---

[13] The gods who live on Mount Olympus.

[14] Old Norse equivalent of the German *Götterdämmerung*, the "twilight of the gods." In this part of the *Voluspa*, there is catastrophic slaughter on all sides between the gods and the powers of evil led by Loki, resulting in universal destruction. But at the end of the poem, the Sibyl, Voluspa, sees in vision the world regenerated through the efforts of the god Balder, resurrected from the nether regions of the dead, and through two remaining human beings called "Life" and "Desiring Life," who are to repeople the earth.

> Cheat me into tranquillity? Come then,
> And welcome, life's last day—be this our wager.
> *Meph.* Done.
> *Faust.*   Done, say I: clench we at once the bargain.
> If ever time should flow so calmly on,
> Soothing my spirits in such oblivion
> That in the pleasant trance I would arrest
> And hail the happy moment in its course,
> Bidding it linger with me . . . .
> Then willingly do I consent to perish.[15]

The bearing of this mythical compact upon our problem of the geneses of civilizations can be brought out by identifying Faust, at the moment when he makes his bet, with one of those 'awakened sleepers' who have risen from the ledge on which they had been lying torpid and have started to climb on up the face of the cliff. In the language of our simile, Faust is saying: 'I have made up my mind to leave this ledge and climb this precipice in search of the next ledge above. In attempting this I am aware that I am leaving safety behind me. Yet, for the sake of the possibility of achievement, I will take the risk of a fall and destruction.'

In the story as told by Goethe the intrepid climber, after an ordeal of mortal dangers and desperate reverses, succeeds in the end in scaling the cliff triumphantly. In the New Testament the same ending is given, through the revelation of a second encounter between the same pair of antagonists, to the combat between Yahweh and the Serpent which, in the original version in Genesis, had ended rather in the manner of the combat between Artemis and Aphrodite in the *Hippolytus*.[16]

In Job, *Faust* and the New Testament alike it is suggested, or even declared outright, that the wager cannot be won by the Devil; that the Devil, in meddling with God's work, cannot frustrate but can only serve the purpose of God, who remains master of the situation all the time and

---

[15] *Faust*, I, 1,692-1,706, in translation of John Anster.

[16] The syntax of this sentence is rather confusing. In the Old Testament story of the Fall of Man, the Serpent or Satan has an apparent victory, for by his temptation of the original parents, he succeeds in bringing upon the human race the evils of pain, suffering, and finally death. In the New Testament, Christ is tempted by Satan during the forty days in the wilderness ("a second encounter between the same pair of antagonists," as Toynbee says), and refuses the temptation; he is then attacked by the most appalling *human* evil, resulting in his crucifixion; but the end is the redemption of mankind.

gives the Devil rope for the Devil to hang himself. Then has the Devil
been created? Did God accept a wager which He knew He could not
lose? That would be a hard saying; for if it were true the whole transaction would have been a sham. An encounter which was no encounter
could not produce the consequences of an encounter — the vast cosmic
consequence of causing Yin to pass over into Yang. Perhaps the explanation is that the wager which the Devil offers and which God accepts
covers, and thereby puts in real jeopardy, a part of God's creation but
not the whole of it. The part really is at stake; and, though the whole is
not, the chances and changes to which the part is exposed cannot conceivably leave the whole unaffected. In the language of mythology,
when one of God's creatures is tempted by the Devil, God Himself is
thereby given the opportunity to re-create the World. The Devil's intervention, whether it succeeds or fails on the particular issue — and either
result is possible — has accomplished that transition from Yin to Yang
for which God has been yearning.

As for the human protagonist's part, suffering is the keynote of it
in every presentation of the drama, whether the player of the part is
Jesus or Job or Faust or Adam and Eve. The picture of Adam and Eve
in the Garden of Eden is a reminiscence of the Yin-state to which primitive man attained in the food-gathering phase of economy, after he had
established his ascendancy over the rest of the flora and fauna of the
Earth. The Fall, in response to the temptation to eat of the Tree of the
Knowledge of Good and Evil, symbolizes the acceptance of a challenge
to abandon this achieved integration and to venture upon a fresh differentiation out of which a fresh integration may — or may not — arise.
The expulsion from the Garden into an unfriendly world in which the
Woman must bring forth children in sorrow and the Man must eat
bread in the sweat of his face, is the ordeal which the acceptance of
the Serpent's challenge has entailed. The sexual intercourse between
Adam and Eve, which follows, is an act of social creation. It bears fruit in
the birth of two sons who impersonate two nascent civilizations: Abel the
keeper of sheep and Cain the tiller of the ground.

In our own generation, one of our most distinguished and original-
minded students of the physical environment of human life tells the
same story in his own way:

'Ages ago a band of naked, houseless, fireless savages started from their
warm home in the torrid zone and pushed steadily northward from the be-

ginning of spring to the end of summer. They never guessed that they had left the land of constant warmth until in September they began to feel an uncomfortable chill at night. Day by day it grew worse. Not knowing its cause, they travelled this way or that to escape. Some went southward, but only a handful returned to their former home. There they resumed the old life, and their descendants are untutored savages to this day. Of those who wandered in other directions, all perished except one small band. Finding that they could not escape the nipping air, the members of this band used the loftiest of human faculties, the power of conscious invention. Some tried to find shelter by digging in the ground, some gathered branches and leaves to make huts and warm beds, and some wrapped themselves in the skins of the beasts that they had slain. Soon these savages had taken some of the greatest steps towards civilization. The naked were clothed; the houseless sheltered; the improvident learnt to dry meat and store it, with nuts, for the winter; and at last the art of preparing fire was discovered as a means of keeping warm. Thus they subsisted where at first they thought that they were doomed. And in the process of adjusting themselves to a hard environment they advanced by enormous strides, leaving the tropical part of mankind far in the rear.' [17]

A classical scholar likewise translates the story into the scientific terminology of our age:

'It is . . . a paradox of advancement that, if Necessity be the mother of Invention, the other parent is Obstinacy, the determination that you will go on living under adverse conditions rather than cut your losses and go where life is easier. It was no accident, that is, that civilization, as we know it, began in that ebb and flow of climate, flora and fauna which characterizes the fourfold Ice Age. Those primates who just "got out" as arboreal conditions wilted retained their primacy among the servants of natural law, but they forewent the conquest of nature. Those others won through, and became men, who stood their ground when they were no more trees to sit in, who "made do" with meat when fruit did not ripen, who made fires and clothes rather than follow the sunshine; who fortified their lairs and trained their young and vindicated the reasonableness of a world that seemed so reasonless.' [18]

The first stage, then, of the human protagonist's ordeal is a transition from Yin to Yang through a dynamic act — performed by God's creature under temptation from the Adversary — which enables God Himself to resume His creative activity. But this progress has to be paid

[17] Ellsworth Huntington, *Civilization and Climate.*
[18] J. L. Myres, *Who Were the Greeks?*

for; and it is not God but God's servant, the human sower, who pays the price. Finally, after many vicissitudes, the sufferer triumphant serves as the pioneer. The human protagonist in the divine drama not only serves God by enabling Him to renew His creation but also serves his fellow men by pointing the way for others to follow. . . .

THE MYTH APPLIED TO THE PROBLEM

The Unpredictable Factor

By the light of mythology we have gained some insight into the nature of challenges and responses. We have come to see that creation is the outcome of an encounter, that genesis is a product of interaction. . . . We shall no longer be surprised if, in the production of civilizations, the same race or the same environment appears to be fruitful in one instance and sterile in another. . . . We shall be prepared now to recognize that, even if we were exactly acquainted with all the racial, environmental, and other data that are capable of being formulated scientifically, we should not be able to predict the outcome of the interaction between the forces which these data represent, any more than a military expert can predict the outcome of a battle or campaign from an 'inside knowledge' of the dispositions and resources of both the opposing general staffs, or a bridge expert the outcome of a game from a similar knowledge of all the cards in every hand.

In both these analogies 'inside knowledge' is not sufficient to enable its possessor to predict results with any exactness or assurance because it is not the same thing as complete knowledge. There is one thing which must remain an unknown quantity to the best-informed onlooker because it is beyond the knowledge of the combatants, or players, themselves; and it is the most important term in the equation which the would-be calculator has to solve. This unknown quantity is the reaction of the actors to the ordeal when it actually comes. These psychological momenta, which are inherently impossible to weigh and measure and therefore to estimate scientifically in advance, are the very forces which actually decide the issue when the encounter takes place. And that is why the very greatest military geniuses have admitted an incalculable element in their successes. If religious, they have attributed their victories to God, like Cromwell; if merely superstitious, to the ascendancy of their 'star', like Napoleon.

৺ৡ FOR DISCUSSION AND WRITING

1. The first section in this piece is headed "The Problem Stated." What is the "problem," and where is it stated? Why, according to the argument here, do not the presence of institutions and division of labor offer a valid differentiation between civilizations and primitive societies? (If you have read Ruth Benedict's description of Zuñi society earlier in this book, draw examples from it to illustrate the preceding point.) What does Toynbee mean by "mimesis"? In our own society how does the principle of mimesis work? Do we copy our parents? the "group" (what group)? "creative personalities" (which ones—artists, scientists, industrial tycoons, movie stars, statesmen)? Or can this question be handled only as an individual rather than as a social tendency?

2. All the way through this piece Toynbee uses analogy as his main principle of exposition. Write out in your own words (two or three sentences) your interpretation of his analogy of the cliff-climbers and the ledge-sitters. Why, according to the argument, is there no way of predicting whether people in certain situations will move forward—climb the cliff—or stay on the ledge? If you have read Ruth Benedict's article, where would you place the Zuñi? Where would you place the Egyptians under Nasser? South Africa? France under DeGaulle? the United States?

3. Explain, in two or three written sentences, Toynbee's analogy between the movements of history and the ancient Chinese symbol of *Yin* and *Yang*. Why does he say that "our breed" (and what does he mean by "our breed"?) has reposed for some 300,000 years in the *Yin* state before entering on *Yang*-activity? (If you have read the piece by Teilhard de Chardin, earlier in this book, how would you correlate the *Yin* and *Yang* phases with what Teilhard has to say about neolithic man? and with Western civilization in the nineteenth and twentieth centuries?)

4. In the section "The Mythological Clue," it is clear that Toynbee does not use the term "myth" in its common, journalistic meaning of "falsehood," illusion, or superstitious fantasy; but, rather, as a profoundly valid symbolic dramatization by which man has ever, intuitively, represented to himself the dynamisms of human life, the psychological forces that create the movements of human history. Put in your own words, in a carefully

considered paragraph, your understanding of three of the "mythological" references, including the reference to the genesis of the planetary system, as these illustrate analogically the dynamic movement from *Yin* to *Yang*. We tend to think of modern scientific theory (like that of the genesis of the universe represented here in the quotation from Sir James Jeans) as being in an altogether different category from "myth"; what justification is there, in terms of the context here, for treating it as myth, side by side with the encounters of Satan and Yahweh, Faust and Mephistopheles, etc.?

5. The greatest problem in human experience and in religious thought is the existence of evil. What is Toynbee's interpretation of the role of the "adversary" (evil in all its forms) in the world? (To answer this question thoughtfully, you would, of course, have to figure out what you yourself understand by the word "evil.") How does Toynbee's discussion at this point, of the concept of a benevolent and omnipotent God who yet allows evil to exist, bear on the movement from *Yin* to *Yang* phases in human history?

6. How does the "mythological clue" apply to human evolution? Why is the outcome, in any case, unpredictable? What is the "unknown quantity," the *x*-factor?

7. What single expository purpose (idea, or thought), whether implicit or explicit, unifies this whole piece, complex as the piece is? Appraise the effectiveness of Toynbee's "argument by analogy." Why is that method the only possible one for Toynbee's purpose here?

8. Write a short paper on the subject of "mimesis" in our society, as suggested by the latter part of Question 1, using mainly your own personal experience for illustration—for there is an enormous amount of "mimesis" in college life and personal life (for instance, what about hairdos, dress, speech idioms, mass media of various kinds, morals, ideals, the influence of advertising, etc., etc.?). Or write a paper on "challenge and response" in modern Russia, or China, or India, or one or other of the African nations, or the Southern states of the U.S.—or even in personal life.

Plutarch ✎§ Alexander, Conqueror

✎§ Greek biographer of Greek and Roman heroes, Plutarch was born in A.D. 42, seems to have lived contentedly—so far as is known—all his life in the small town of Chaeronea in Boeotia (a part of Greece that was the traditional equivalent for backwardness and boorishness), and died about 120. His famous *Lives*—of which there were some sixty-five originally, though only fifty have survived—are anything but boorish; even through translation they have enormous charm of style and the brilliantly sparkling interest of a mind that focused on all the small and most human expressions of character that history generally omits; yet they are kept firmly in a moral and philosophical perspective. All this reflects great wisdom and great sophistication. §∾

IN THIS chapter we shall give the life of Alexander the Great. And, as the quantity of materials is so great, we shall only premise that we hope for indulgence, though we do not give the actions in full detail and with scrupulous exactness, but rather a short summary since we are not writing histories but lives. Nor is it always in the most distinguished achievements that men's virtues or vices may be best discerned, but very often an action of small note, a short saying, or a jest, shall distinguish a person's real character more than the greatest sieges or the most important battles. Therefore, as painters in their portraits labor over the likeness in the face and particularly about the eyes, in which the peculiar turn of mind most appears, and run over the rest with a more careless hand,

Reprinted from *Life Stories of Men Who Shaped History*, from Plutarch's *Lives*. Mentor edition, 1950, edited by Eduard C. Lindeman, published by the New American World Library of Literature, Inc., New York. The life of Alexander is much abridged here.

so we may be permitted to strike off the features of the soul in order to give a real likeness of this great man and leave to others the circumstantial detail of his labors and achievements.

His father Philip is said to have been initiated, when very young, along with Olympias in the mysteries at Samothrace;[1] and having conceived an affection for her, he obtained her in marriage. . . . The night before the consummation of the marriage she dreamed that a thunderbolt fell upon her belly which kindled a great fire and that the flame extended itself far and wide before it disappeared. . . . A serpent was also seen lying by Olympias as she slept, which is said to have cooled Philip's passion for her more than anything, so that he seldom repaired to her bed afterwards. Either he feared her as an enchantress, or he abstained from her embraces because he thought she had commerce with the gods.

Some, indeed, relate the affair in another manner. They tell us that the women of this country were of old extremely fond of the ceremonies of Orpheus and the orgies of Bacchus. . . .[2] Olympias, being remarkably ambitious of these inspirations and desirous of giving the enthusiastic solemnities a more strange and horrid appearance, introduced a number of large tame serpents which, often creeping out of the ivy and entwining about the sacred spears and garlands of the women, struck the spectators with terror.

Philip upon his vision sent Chaeron of Megalopolis to consult the oracle at Delphi, and we are told Apollo commanded him to sacrifice to Jupiter Ammon and to pay his homage principally to that god.[3] It is also

[1] Aegean island where fertility mysteries of great antiquity and similar to those of Eleusis were celebrated.

[2] Orpheus, Thracian poet and musician of the magical lyre that could charm beasts and trees and stones, was said to have been a priest of Dionysus (Bacchus); the religion of Orphism, which he founded, was a mystical reinterpretation of the primitive orgiastic rites of Dionysus. Plutarch is writing at a time of religious confusion and eclecticism; actually, sacred snakes had played a part in the earliest forms of these cults. Their chthonic habits and their mysterious power to rejuvenate themselves by shedding their skins made them the symbolic associates of the great fertility goddess, the Earth-mother, about whom the cults centered, while they were also the emblematic type of the annually reborn god, her son. Hence the story of the serpent (the god himself) in Olympias' bed; as to her introducing snakes into the rites, they were there long before.

[3] Apollo's oracle at Delphi was the most famous oracle in the ancient world. Jupiter Ammon is another instance of eclecticism; Ammon was one of the names of the Egyptian sun-god, Ra, who was identified with Jupiter.

said he lost one of his eyes — the one which he applied to the chink of the door when he saw the god in his wife's embraces in the form of a serpent. According to Eratosthenes,[4] Olympias, when she conducted Alexander on his way in the first expedition, privately disclosed to him the secret of his birth and exhorted him to behave with a dignity suitable to his divine extraction. Others affirm that she absolutely rejected it as an impious fiction and used to say: "Will Alexander never leave off embroiling me with Juno?"

Alexander was born on the sixth of . . . July, . . . the same day that the temple of Diana at Ephesus was burned; upon which Hegesias the Magnesian has uttered a conceit frigid enough to have extinguished the flames. "It is no wonder," said he, "that the temple of Diana was burned, for the goddess was at a distance employed in bringing Alexander into the world." [5] . . .

The statues of Alexander which most resembled him were those of Lysippus, who alone had his permission to represent him in marble. The turn of his head, which leaned a little to one side, and the quickness of his eye, in which many of his friends and successors most affected to imitate him, were best hit off by that artist. Apelles painted him in the character of Jupiter armed with thunderbolts, but did not succeed as to his complexion. He overcharged the coloring and made his skin too brown, whereas Alexander was fair with a tinge of red in his face and upon his breast. We read in the memoirs of Aristoxenus that a most agreeable scent emanated from his skin and that his breath and whole body were so fragrant that they perfumed his undergarments. . . .[6]

His continence showed itself at an early period. For, though he was vigorous and rather violent in his other pursuits, he was not easily moved by the pleasures of the body, and if he tasted them it was with great moderation. But there was something superlatively great and sublime in his ambition, far beyond his years. It was not all sorts of honor that he

---

[4] Greek savant of the third century B.C.

[5] The Diana at Ephesus little resembles the chaste, girlish huntress of late Roman mythology. She was an earth-goddess of great antiquity, and her tremendous statue at Ephesus, in Asia Minor, showed her with several tiers of breasts like ostrich eggs, to represent her fecundity. One of her functions was to preside over childbirth; hence the "conceit" (extravagant notion) mentioned here, that she brought Alexander into the world. Alexander was born in 356 B.C.

[6] Lysippus, a Greek sculptor, and Apelles, a painter, were both of the fourth century B.C. Aristoxenus was, like Alexander, a pupil of Aristotle.

courted, nor did he seek it in every field like his father Philip, who was as proud of his eloquence as any sophist could be, and who had the vanity to record his victories in the Olympic chariot races on his coins. Alexander, on the other hand, when he was asked by some of the people about whether he would run in the Olympic race — for he was swift of foot — answered: "Yes, if I had kings for my antagonists." It appears that he had a strong aversion to the whole exercise of wrestling. Though he exhibited many other sorts of games and public diversions in which he proposed prizes for tragic poets, for musicians who practiced on the flute and lyre, and for rhapsodists too; though he entertained the people with the hunting of all manner of wild beasts and with fencing or fighting with the staff, yet he gave no encouragement to boxing or wrestling.

Ambassadors from Persia happened to arrive in the absence of his father Philip, and Alexander, receiving them in his stead, impressed them greatly by his politeness and solid sense. He asked them no childish or trifling questions but inquired the distances of places and the roads through the upper provinces of Asia. He desired to be informed of the character of their King, in what manner he behaved to his enemies, and in what the strength and power of Persia consisted. The ambassadors were struck with admiration and looked upon the celebrated shrewdness of Philip as nothing in comparison to the lofty and enterprising genius of his son.

Accordingly, whenever news was brought that Philip had taken some strong town or won some great battle, the young man, instead of appearing delighted with it, used to say to his companions: "My father will go on conquering until there will be nothing extraordinary left for you and me to do." . . .

When Philonicus the Thessalian offered the horse named Bucephalus for sale to Philip at the price of thirteen talents, the King with the prince and many others went into the field to see some trial made of him. The horse appeared extremely vicious and unmanageable and was so far from suffering himself to be mounted that he would not bear to be spoken to, but turned fiercely upon all the grooms. Philip was displeased at their bringing him so wild and ungovernable a horse and bade them take him away. But Alexander, who had observed him well, said: "What a horse they are losing for want of skill and spirit to manage him!" Philip at first took no notice of this, but upon the prince's often repeating the same expression and showing great vexation when the horse was led away, said: "Young man, you find fault with your elders, as if you knew more than they, or could manage the horse better." "And I certainly could," answered the prince. "If you should not be able to ride him, what forfeiture will you submit to for your rashness?" "I will pay the price of the horse."

Upon this all the company laughed, but, the King and prince agreeing as to the forfeiture, Alexander ran to the horse and laying hold on the bridle turned him to the sun, for he had apparently observed that the shadow which fell before the horse and continually moved as he moved, greatly disturbed him. While his fierceness and fury lasted he kept speaking to him softly and stroking him; after which he gently let fall his mantle, leaped lightly upon his back, and secured his seat. Then, without pulling the reins too hard or using either whip or spur, he set him going. As soon as he perceived that the horse's uneasiness abated and that he wanted only to run, he put him in a full gallop and pushed him on both with the voice and the spur.

Philip and all his court were in great distress for him at first and there was a profound silence. But when the prince had turned him and brought him straight back, they all received Alexander with loud acclamations, except his father, who wept with joy, and, kissing him, said: "Seek another kingdom, my son, that may be worthy of thy abilities, for Macedonia is too small for thee." Perceiving that Alexander did not easily submit to authority, because he would not be forced into anything, but that he might be led to his duty by the gentler hand of reason, Philip took the method of persuasion rather than of command. He saw that Alexander's education was a matter of too great importance to be entrusted to the ordinary masters in music and the common circle of sciences, and that his genius, to use the expression of Sophocles, required:

"The rudder's guidance, and the curb's restraint."

Philip therefore sent for Aristotle, the most celebrated and learned of all the philosophers, and the reward he gave him for forming his son was not only honorable, but remarkable for its propriety. Philip had formerly dismantled the city of Stagira where that philosopher was born, and now he rebuilt it and re-established the inhabitants who had either fled or been reduced to slavery. He also prepared a lawn, called

Mieza, for their studies and literary conversations, where they still show us Aristotle's stone seats and shady walks.

Alexander gained from Aristotle not only moral and political knowledge, but was also instructed in those more secret and profound branches of science which they call *acroamatic* and *epoptic*,[7] and which they did not communicate to every common scholar. . . .

It appears also to me that it was by Aristotle rather than any other person that Alexander was assisted in the study of medicine, for he not only loved the theory but the practice too, as is clear from his epistles, where we find that he prescribed to his friends medicines and a proper regimen.

He loved polite learning too, and his natural thirst of knowledge made him a man of extensive reading. The Iliad he thought as well as called a portable treasure of military knowledge and he had a copy corrected by Aristotle, called the casket copy. Onesicritus informs us that he used to place it under his pillow with his dagger. As he could not find many other books in the upper provinces of Asia, he wrote to Harpalus for a supply, who sent him . . . most of the tragedies of Euripides, Sophocles and Aeschylus. . . .

Aristotle was the man Alexander admired in his younger years and, as he said himself, he had no less affection for him than for his own father: from the one he derived the blessing of life, from the other the blessing of a good life. . . .

He was only twenty years old when he succeeded to the crown and found the kingdom torn in pieces by dangerous parties and implacable animosities. The barbarous nations, even those that bordered upon Macedonia, could not brook subjection and they longed for their native kings. Philip had subdued Greece by his victorious arms but, not having had time to accustom her to the yoke, he had thrown matters into confusion rather than produced any firm settlement, and he left the whole in a tumultuous state. The young King's Macedonian counselors, alarmed at the troubles which threatened him, advised him to give up Greece entirely or at least to make no attempts upon it with the sword, and to recall the wavering barbarians in a mild manner to their duty by applying healing measures to the beginning of the revolt. Alexander, on the

[7] Esoteric and mystical.

contrary, was of the opinion that the only way to security and a thorough establishment of his affairs was to proceed with spirit and magnanimity. For he was persuaded that if he appeared to abate of his dignity in the least, he would be universally insulted. He therefore quieted the commotions and put a stop to the rising wars among the barbarians by marching with the utmost speed as far as the Danube, where he fought a great battle with King Syrmus of the Triballians and defeated him.

Some time after this, having intelligence that the Thebans had revolted and that the Athenians had adopted the same sentiments, he resolved to show them he was no longer a boy and advanced immediately through the pass of Thermopylae. "Demosthenes,"[8] he said, "called me a boy while I was in Illyria and among the Triballians, and a stripling when in Thessaly, but I will show him before the walls of Athens that I am a man."

When he made his appearance before Thebes he was willing to give the inhabitants time to change their sentiments. He only demanded of them Phoenix and Prothytes, the first promoters of the revolt, and proclaimed an amnesty to all the rest. But the Thebans in their turn demanded that he should deliver up to them Philotas and Antipater and invited, by sound of trumpet, all men to join them who chose to assist in recovering the liberty of Greece. Alexander then gave the reins to the Macedonians and the war began with great fury. The Thebans, who had to combat against forces vastly superior in number, behaved with a courage and ardor far above their strength. But when the Macedonian garrison fell down from the citadel and charged them in the rear, they were surrounded on all sides and most of them cut to pieces. The city was taken, plundered and leveled to the ground. . . .

As for the Athenians, he forgave them, though they expressed great concern at the misfortune of Thebes. For though they were upon the point of celebrating the feasts of the great mysteries,[9] they omitted it on account of the mourning that took place and received such of the Thebans as escaped the general wreck with all imaginable kindness into their city. But whether his fury, like that of a lion, was satiated with blood, or whether he had a mind to efface a most cruel and barbarous action by an act of clemency, he not only overlooked the complaints he

---

[8] Famous Athenian orator and statesman of the fourth century B.C.

[9] Those of Eleusis, near Athens. The Eleusinian mysteries were part of the state religion of Athens.

had against them but desired them to look well to their affairs because if anything happened to him, Athens would give law to Greece. . . .

A general assembly of the Greeks being held at the Isthmus of Corinth, they came to a resolution to send their quota of troops with Alexander against the Persians, and he was unanimously elected captain-general. Many statesmen and philosophers came to congratulate him on the occasion and he hoped that Diogenes of Sinope,[10] who then lived at Corinth, would be among them. Finding, however, that he thought but little of Alexander and that he preferred the enjoyment of his leisure in a part of the suburbs called Cranium, he went to see him. Diogenes happened to be lying in the sun, and at the approach of so many people, he raised himself up a little, and fixed his eyes upon Alexander. The King addressed him in an obliging manner and asked him if there was anything he could serve him in. "Only stand a little out of my sunshine," said Diogenes. Alexander, we are told, was struck with such surprise at finding himself so little regarded and saw something so great in that carelessness that, while his courtiers were ridiculing the philosopher as a monster, he said: "If I were not Alexander, I should wish to be Diogenes." . . .

When he was on the point of setting out upon his expedition he had many signs from the divine powers. Among the rest, the statue of Orpheus in Libethra, which was of cypress wood, was in a profuse sweat for several days. The people apprehended this to be an ill presage, but Aristander bade them dismiss their fears. It signified, he said, that "Alexander would perform actions so worthy to be celebrated that they would cost the poets and musicians much labor and sweat."

As to the number of his troops, those that put it at the least say he carried over thirty thousand foot and five thousand horse; and they who put it at the most tell us his army consisted of thirty four thousand foot and four thousand horse. . . .

As soon as he landed[11] he went up to Troy where he sacrificed to Minerva and offered libations to the heroes buried there. He also anointed the pillar on Achilles' tomb with oil and ran around it with his friends, naked, according to the custom, after which he put a crown

---

[10] Cynic philosopher. The Cynics taught that virtue is the only good and that its essence lies in self-control and independence. The word "cynic" had not then its cruder modern meaning.

[11] That is, after crossing the Hellespont.

upon it, declaring he thought that hero extremely happy in having found a faithful friend while he lived, and after his death an excellent herald to set forth his praise. As he went about the city to look upon the antiquities he was asked whether he chose to see Paris' lyre. "I set but little value," he said, "upon the lyre of Paris, but it would give me pleasure to see that of Achilles, to which he sang the glorious actions of the brave."

In the meantime, Darius'[12] generals had assembled a great army and taken post upon the banks of the Granicus so that Alexander was under the necessity of fighting there to open the gates of Asia. Many of his officers were apprehensive of the depth of the river and the rough and uneven banks on the other side, . . . When Parmenio objected to his attempting a passage . . . , he said the Hellespont would blush if, after having passed it, he should be afraid of the Granicus.

At the same time he threw himself into the stream with thirteen troops of horse, and as he advanced in the face of the enemy's arrows — in spite of the steep banks which were lined with cavalry well armed, and in spite of the rapidity of the river which often bore him down or covered him with its waves — his motions seemed rather the effects of madness than sound sense. He held on, however, until by great and surprising efforts he gained the opposite banks, which the mud made extremely slippery and dangerous. When he was there he was forced to stand an engagement with the enemy, hand to hand, and with great confusion on his part because they attacked his men as fast as they came over, before he had time to form them. The Persian troops, charging with loud shouts and with horse against horse, made good use of their spears and when those were broken, of their swords.

Numbers pressed hard on Alexander because he was easily distinguished, both by his buckler and by his crest, on each side of which was a large and beautiful plume of white feathers. His cuirass was pierced by a javelin at the joint, but he escaped unhurt. After this, Rhoesaces and Spithridates, two officers of great distinction, attacked him at once. He avoided Spithridates with great address and received Rhoesaces with such a stroke of his spear upon his breastplate that it broke into pieces. Then he drew his sword to dispatch him, but his adversary still maintained the combat. Meanwhile, Spithridates came up on one side of him

[12] Persian king. Persia was the greatest power in the Near East and the traditional foe of Greece.

and raising himself on his horse, gave him a blow with his battle-ax which cut off his crest with one side of his plume. The force of it was such that the helmet could hardly resist it, and it even touched his hair. Spithridates was going to repeat his stroke when the celebrated Clitus prevented him by running his spear through his body. At the same time Alexander brought Rhoesaces to the ground with his sword.

While the cavalry were fighting with so much fury the Macedonian phalanx,[13] passed the river and then the infantry likewise engaged. The enemy made no great or long resistance but soon turned their backs and fled, all but the Grecian mercenaries who, making a stand on a hill, desired Alexander to give his word of honor that they should be spared. But Alexander, influenced rather by his passion than his reason, instead of giving them quarter advanced to attack them and was so warmly received that he had his horse killed under him. It was not, however, the famous Bucephalus. In this dispute he had more of his men killed and wounded than in all the rest of the battle, for here they had to do with experienced soldiers who fought with a courage heightened by despair.

The barbarians, we are told, lost in this battle twenty thousand foot and two thousand five hundred horse, whereas Alexander had no more than thirty four men killed, nine of which were infantry. To do honor to their memory he erected a statue to each of them in brass, the workmanship of Lysippus. And that the Greeks might have their share in the glory of the day, he sent them presents out of the spoils. To the Athenians, in particular, he sent three hundred bucklers. Upon the rest of the spoils he put this pompous inscription: *Won by Alexander the Son of Philip, and the Greeks (excepting the Lacedaemonians), of the Barbarians in Asia.*[14] The greatest part of the plate, the purple robes and other things of that kind which he took from the Persians, he sent to his mother.

This battle made a great and immediate change in the course of Alexander's affairs, so much that Sardis, the principal ornament of the Persian empire on the maritime side, made its submission. All the other

13 The Macedonian phalanx, formed by Philip, Alexander's father, was a body of heavy-armed infantry trained to fight in a close formation of from twelve to sixteen ranks, carrying lances eighteen feet long. Greek mercenaries (referred to in the next sentence), largely from the Greek settlements along the coast of Asia Minor and the islands, had long been employed by the Asiatic powers.

14 The Lacedaemonians were the people of Sparta, in the Peloponnesus. The "Barbarians" were any non-Greek people, no matter how civilized.

cities followed its example, except Halicarnassus and Miletus; these he took by storm and subdued all the adjacent country. . . .

Upon taking Gordium, which is said to have been the seat of the ancient Midas, he found the famed chariot fastened with cords, made of the bark of the corneltree, and was informed of a tradition firmly believed among the barbarians, that the Fates had decreed the empire of the world to the man who should untie the knot. Most historians say it was twisted so many intricate ways and the ends so artfully concealed within that Alexander, finding he could not untie it, cut it asunder with his sword and so made many ends instead of two. But Aristobulus affirms that he easily untied it by taking out the pin which fastened the yoke to the beam and then drawing out the yoke itself. . . .[15]

There was in the army of Darius a Macedonian fugitive named Amyntas, who knew perfectly well the disposition of Alexander. This man, perceiving that Darius prepared to march through the passes and defiles in quest of Alexander, begged him to remain where he was and take the advantage of receiving an enemy, so much inferior to him in number, upon large and spacious plains. Darius answered he was afraid in that case the enemy would fly without coming to an action and Alexander escape him. "If that is all you fear," replied the Macedonian, "let it give you no further uneasiness, for he will come to seek you and is already on his march." However, his counsel had no effect.

Darius set out for Cilicia and Alexander was making for Syria in quest of him. But happening to miss each other in the night, they both turned back, Alexander rejoicing in his good fortune and hastening to meet Darius in the defiles, while Darius endeavored to disengage himself and recover his former ground. For by this time he was aware of his error of throwing himself into a country hemmed in by the sea on one side and the mountains on the other and intersected by the river Pinarus, so that it was impracticable for cavalry and his infantry could only act in small and broken parties, while at the same time this situation was extremely convenient for the enemy's inferior numbers.

Thus, fortune befriended Alexander as to the scene of action, but the skillful disposition of his forces contributed still more to his gaining the victory. As his army was very small in comparison to that of Darius, he took care to draw it up so as to prevent its being surrounded by stretching out his right wing farther than the enemy's left. In that wing

[15] This is the proverbial occasion of "cutting the Gordian knot."

he acted in person and, fighting in the foremost ranks, put the barbarians to flight. . . .

The victory was a very signal one, for he killed more than a hundred and ten thousand of the enemy. Nothing was wanting to complete it but the capture of Darius, and that prince narrowly escaped, having got the start of his pursuer only by four or five furlongs. Alexander took his chariot and his bow and returned with them to his Macedonians. He found them loading themselves with the plunder of the enemy's camp, which was rich and various, though Darius, to make his troops fitter for action, had left most of the baggage in Damascus. The Macedonians had reserved for their master the tent of Darius in which he found officers of the household magnificently clothed, rich furniture, and great quantities of gold and silver.

As soon as he had put off his armor he went to the bath, saying to those about him: "Let us go and refresh ourselves after the fatigues of the field in the bath of Darius." "Nay," said one of his friends, "rather in the bath of Alexander, for the goods of the conquered are, and should be called, the conqueror's." When he had beheld the basins, vials, boxes and other vases, curiously wrought in gold, smelled the fragrant odors of essences and seen the splendid furniture of spacious apartments, he turned to his friends and said: "This, then, it seems, it was to be a King."

As Alexander was sitting down to table an account was brought him that among the prisoners were the mother and wife of Darius and two unmarried daughters, and that upon seeing his chariot and bow they broke into great lamentations, concluding that he was dead. Alexander, after some pause, during which he was rather commiserating with their misfortunes than rejoicing in his own success, sent Leonnatus to assure them that Darius was not dead, that they had nothing to fear from Alexander, for his dispute with Darius was only for empire, and that they should find themselves provided for in the same manner as when Darius was in his greatest prosperity. If this message to the captive princesses was gracious and humane, his actions were still more so. He allowed them to do funeral honors to what Persians they pleased and for that purpose furnished them, out of the spoils, with robes and all the other garments that were customary. They had as many domestics and were served in all respects in as honorable a manner as before; if anything, their appointments were greater. But there was another part of his behavior toward them which was still more noble and princely. Though they were now captives, he considered that they were ladies not only of high rank but of great modesty and virtue, and took care that they should not hear an indecent word nor have the least cause to suspect any danger to their honor. Nay, as if they had been in a holy temple of asylum of virgins rather than in an enemy's camp, they lived unseen and unapproached in the most sacred privacy.

It is said the wife of Darius was one of the most beautiful women, as Darius was one of the tallest and handsomest men in the world, and that their daughters resembled them. But Alexander no doubt thought it more glorious and worthy of a king to conquer himself than to subdue his enemies and, therefore, never approached one of them. Indeed, his continence was such that he knew not any woman before his marriage, except Barsine, who became a widow by the death of her husband, Memnon, and was taken prisoner near Damascus. She was well versed in the Greek literature, a woman of the most agreeable temperament and of royal extraction, for her father, Artabazus, was grandson to a king of Persia. According to Aristobulus, it was Parmenio who established Alexander's connection with so accomplished a woman, whose beauty was her least perfection. As for the other female captives, though they were tall and beautiful, Alexander took no further notice of them than to say by way of jest: "What eyesores these Persian women are!" He found a counter-charm in the beauty of self-government and sobriety and, thus strengthened, passed them by as so many statues. . . .

Being informed that two Macedonians named Damon and Timotheus had corrupted the wives of some of his mercenaries who served under Parmenio, he ordered that officer to inquire into the affair and if they were found guilty, to put them to death as no better than savages, bent on the destruction of human kind. In the same letter, speaking of his own conduct, he expressed himself in these terms: "For my part, I have neither seen nor desired to see the wife of Darius; far from that, I have not suffered any man to speak of her beauty before me." He used to say that sleep and the commerce with the sex were the things that made him most sensible of his mortality. For he considered both weariness and pleasure as the natural effects of our weakness.

He was also very temperate in eating. Of this there are many proofs and we have a remarkable one in his words to Ada, whom he called his mother and had made Queen of Caria. Ada, to express her affectionate regards, sent him every day a number of excellent dishes and a handsome dessert, and at last she sent him some of her best cooks and bakers. But he said he had no need of them, for he had been supplied with better things by his tutor Leonidas: a march before daybreak to dress his dinner and a light dinner to have an appetite for supper. He added that the same Leonidas used to examine the chests and wardrobes in which his bedding and clothes were put, lest something of luxury and superfluity should be introduced there by his mother.

Nor was he so much addicted to wine as he was thought to be. It was supposed so because he passed a great deal of time at table, but that time was spent rather in talking than drinking, every cup introducing some long discourse. Besides, he never made these long meals except when he had abundant leisure on his hands. When business called he was not to be detained by wine or sleep or pleasure or honorable love or the most entertaining spectacle, though the actions of other generals have been retarded by some of these things. His life sufficiently confirms this assertion, for, though very short, he performed in it innumerable great exploits. . . .

From [Tyre] he marched into Syria and laid siege to Gaza, the capital of that country. While he was engaged there, a bird as it flew by dropped a clod of earth upon his shoulder and then, going to perch on the cross-cords with which they turned the engines, was entangled and caught. Subsequent events answered Aristander's interpretation of this sign: Alexander was wounded in the shoulder but he took the city. He sent most of its spoils to Olympias and Cleopatra and others of his friends. His tutor Leonidas was not forgotten, and the present he made him had a special meaning. It consisted of five hundred talents' weight of frankincense and a hundred of myrrh and was sent in remembrance of the hopes he had conceived when a boy. It seems Leonidas one day had observed Alexander at a sacrifice throwing incense into the fire by handfuls, upon which he said: "Alexander, when you have conquered the country where spices grow you may be thus liberal with your incense, but, in the meantime, use what you have more sparingly." Alexander therefore wrote: "I have sent you frankincense and myrrh in abundance that you may be no longer a churl to the gods."

One day a casket was brought him which appeared to be one of the most curious and valuable things among the treasures and the whole equipage of Darius. He asked his friends what they thought most worthy to be put in it. Different things were proposed, but he said the Iliad most deserved such a case. This is mentioned by several writers of credit. And if what the Alexandrians say upon the faith of Heraclides be true, Homer was no bad auxiliary or useless counselor in the course of the war. They tell us that when Alexander had conquered Egypt and determined to build there a great city which was to be peopled with Greeks and called after his own name,[16] by the advice of his architects he had marked out a piece of ground and was preparing to lay the foundation, but a wonderful dream made him fix upon another location. He dreamed a grey-headed person of very venerable aspect approached him and repeated the following lines:

> "An island lies, where loud the billows roar,
> Pharos they call it, on the Egyptian shore."

Upon this, Alexander immediately left his bed and went to Pharos, which at that time was an island lying a little above the Canobic mouth of the Nile but now is joined to the continent by a causeway. He no sooner cast his eyes upon the place than he perceived the commodiousness of the site. It is a tongue of land, not unlike an isthmus, whose breadth is proportionate to its length. On one side it has a great lake and on the other the sea which forms a capacious harbor. This led him to declare that "Homer, among his many other admirable qualifications, was an excellent architect," and he ordered a city to be planned suitable to the ground and its appendant conveniences. For want of chalk, they made use of flour, which served the purpose well enough upon a black soil, and they drew a line with it about the semicircular bay. The arms of this semicircle were terminated by straight lines so that the whole was in the form of a Macedonian cloak.

While the King was enjoying the design, suddenly an infinite number of large birds of various kinds rose like a black cloud out of the river and the lake, and lighting upon the place, ate up all the flour that was used in marking out the lines. Alexander was disturbed at the omen, but the diviners encouraged him to proceed, assuring him it was a sign that the city he was going to build would be blessed with such plenty as to furnish a supply to all who should repair to it from other nations.

The execution of the plan he left to his architects, and then went to visit the temple of Jupiter Ammon. It was a long and laborious journey and besides the fatigue, there were two great dangers attending it. The

[16] The city of Alexandria.

one was that their water might fail in a desert of many days' travel which afforded no supply; and the other, that they might be surprised by a violent south wind amidst the wastes of sand as it happened long before to the army of Cambyses.[17] The wind had raised the sand and rolled in such waves that it devoured full fifty thousand men. These difficulties were considered and represented to Alexander, but it was not easy to divert him from any of his purposes. Fortune had supported him in such a manner that his resolutions had become invincibly strong and his courage inspired him with such a spirit of adventure that he thought it not enough to be victorious in the field but he must conquer both time and place.

The divine assistance which Alexander experienced in this march met with more credit than the oracles delivered at the end of it, though this extraordinary assistance in some measure confirmed the oracles. In the first place, Jupiter sent such copious and constant rain as not only delivered them from all fear of suffering by thirst but, by moistening the sand and making it firm under the foot, made the air clear and fit for respiration. In the next place, when they found the marks which were to serve as guides to travelers removed or defaced and in consequence wandered up and down without any certain route, a flock of crows made their appearance and directed them in the way. When they marched briskly on the crows flew with equal alacrity; when they lagged behind or halted the crows also stopped. What is still stranger, Callisthenes avers, is that at night when they happened to be going wrong these birds called them by their croaking and put them right again.

When he had crossed the desert and had arrived at the place, the high priest of Ammon received him with salutations from the god, as from a father. And when he inquired whether any of the assassins of his father had escaped him, the priest declared he would not express himself in that manner, for his father was not a mortal. Then he asked whether all the murderers of Philip were punished, and whether it was given the proponent to be the conqueror of the world. Jupiter answered that he granted him that high distinction and that the death of Philip was sufficiently avenged. Upon this, Alexander made his acknowledgments to the god by rich offerings and loaded the priests with presents of great value. This is the account most historians give us of the affair of the oracle, but Alexander himself, in the letter he wrote to his mother on

17 Sixth-century B.C. Persian king.

that occasion, only says he received certain private answers from the oracle, which he would communicate to her, and to her only, on his return.

Some say, Ammon's prophet being desirous to address him in an obliging manner in Greek, intended to say, O *Paidion*, which signifies *My Son*, but in his barbarous pronunciation made the word end with an *s* instead of an *n*, and so said, O *Pai Dios*, which signifies O *Son of Jupiter*. Alexander, they add, was delighted with the mistake in the pronunciation and from that error was circulated a report that Jupiter himself had called him his son.

He went to hear Psammon, an Egyptian philosopher, and the saying of his which pleased him most was: "All men are governed by God, for in everything that which rules and governs is divine." But Alexander's own maxim was more agreeable to sound philosophy. He said: "God is the common father of men, but more particularly of the good and virtuous."

When among the barbarians, he indeed affected a lofty mien, such as might suit a man perfectly convinced of his divine origin, but it was in a small degree and with great caution that he assumed anything of divinity among the Greeks. We must except, however, what he wrote to the Athenians concerning Samos: "It was not I who gave you that free and famous city, but your then lord, who was called my father," meaning Philip.

Yet, long after this, when he was wounded with an arrow and experienced great torture from it, he said: "My friends, this is blood, and not the ichor

"Such as immortal gods are wont to shed."

One day, it happened to thunder in such a dreadful manner that it astonished all who heard it, upon which Anaxarchus the sophist, being in company with him, said: "Son of Jupiter,[18] could you do so?" Alexander answered with a smile: "I do not choose to be so terrible to my friends as you would have me, who despise my entertainments, because you see fish served up and not the heads of Persian grandees." It seems the King had made Hephaestion a present of some small fish, and Anaxarchus observing it, said: "Why did he not rather send you the heads of princes?" — intimating how truly despicable those glittering

[18] The reference is to Jupiter the Thunderer, wielder of the lightning bolt.

things are which conquerors pursue with so much danger and fatigue, since, after all, their enjoyments are little or in no way superior to those of other men. It appears, then, from what has been said, that Alexander neither believed nor was elated with the notion of his divinity but that he only made use of it as a means of bringing others into subjection.

On his return from Egypt to Phoenicia he honored the gods with sacrifices and solemn processions, on which occasion the people were entertained with music and dancing, and tragedies were presented in the greatest perfection, not only in respect to the magnificence of the scenery, but the spirit of emulation in those who exhibited them. . . .

Alexander, having subdued all on this side the Euphrates, began his march against Darius, who had taken the field with a million men. . . .

In the month of September there happened an eclipse of the moon, about the beginning of the festival of the great mysteries in Athens. The eleventh night after that eclipse, the two armies being in view of each other, Darius kept his men under arms and took a general review of his troops by torchlight. Meantime, Alexander suffered his Macedonians to repose themselves and with his soothsayer Aristander performed some private ceremonies before his tent and offered sacrifices to the god of fear. The oldest of his friends, and Parmenio in particular, when they beheld the plain between Niphates and the Gordyaean mountains all illuminated with the torches of the barbarians and heard the tumultuous and appalling noise from their camp, like the bellowings of an immense sea, were astonished at their numbers and observed among themselves how arduous an enterprise it would be to meet such a torrent of war in open day. They waited upon the King, therefore, when he had finished the sacrifice, and advised him to attack the enemy in the night when darkness would hide what was most dreadful in the combat. Upon which he gave them that celebrated answer: *"I will not steal a victory."*

It is true this answer had been thought by some to savor of the vanity of a young man who derided the most obvious danger; yet others have thought it not only well calculated to encourage his troops at that time but politic enough in respect to the future. If Darius happened to be beaten, it left him no possibility to proceed to another trial, under pretence that night and darkness had been his adversaries, as he had previously paid the blame upon the mountains, the narrow passes and the sea. For in such a vast empire it could never be the lack of arms or men that would bring Darius to give up the strife but the ruin of his hopes and spirits following the loss of a battle where he had the advantages of numbers and of daylight. . . .

It was not, however, only before the battle but in the face of danger that Alexander showed his intrepidity and excellent judgment, for the outcome of the battle was for some time doubtful. The left wing, commanded by Parmenio, was almost broken by the impetuosity with which the Bactrian cavalry charged and Mazaeus had, moreover, detached a party of horse with orders to wheel around and attack the corps that was left to guard the Macedonian baggage. Parmenio, greatly disturbed at these circumstances, sent messengers to acquaint Alexander that his camp and baggage would be taken if he did not immediately dispatch a strong reinforcement from the front to the rear. The moment that account was brought him he was giving the right wing, which he commanded in person, the signal to charge. He stopped, however, to tell the messenger: "Parmenio must have lost his senses and in his disorder must have forgotten that the conquerors are always masters of all that belonged to the enemy, and the conquered need not give themselves any concern about their treasures or prisoners, nor have anything to think of but how to sell their lives dearly and die in the bed of honor."

As soon as he had given Parmenio this answer he put on his helmet, for in all other respects he stepped fully armed out of his tent. He wore a short, close-fitting coat of Sicilian fashion and over that a breast-plate of linen strongly quilted, which was found among the spoils at the battle of Issus. His helmet, the workmanship of Theophilus, was of iron but so well polished that it shone like the brightest silver. To this was fitted a gorget of the same metal set with precious stones. His sword, the weapon he generally used in battle, was a present from the King of the Citieans and could not be excelled for lightness or for temper. But the belt which he wore in all engagements was more superb than the rest of his armor. It was given him by the Rhodians as a mark of their respect, and old Helicon had exerted all his art in it. In drawing up his army and giving orders, as well as exercising and reviewing it, he spared Bucephalus on account of his age and rode another horse; but he constantly charged upon him and he had no sooner mounted him than the signal was always given.

The speech he made to the Thessalians and the other Greeks was of some length on this occasion. When he found that they in turn strove to heighten his confidence and called out to him to lead them against the barbarians, he shifted his javelin to his left hand and, stretching his right hand toward heaven, according to Callisthenes, he entreated the gods to defend and invigorate the Greeks, if he really was the son of Jupiter.

Aristander the soothsayer, who rode by his side in a white robe and with a crown of gold upon his head, then pointed out an eagle flying over him and directing his course against the enemy. The sight of this so animated the troops that, after mutual exhortations to bravery, the cavalry charged at full speed and the phalanx rushed on like a torrent. Before the first ranks were well engaged the barbarians gave way, and Alexander pressed hard upon the fugitives in order to penetrate into the midst of the host where Darius himself was, for he beheld him at a distance, over the foremost ranks, amidst his royal squadron. Besides being mounted upon a lofty chariot, Darius was easily distinguished by his size and beauty. A numerous body of select cavalry stood in close order about the chariot and seemed well prepared to receive the enemy. But Alexander's approach appeared so terrible, as he drove the fugitives upon those who still maintained their ground, that they were seized with consternation and the greatest part of them dispersed. A few of the best and bravest of them met their death before the King's chariot, and falling in heaps one upon another, strove to stop the pursuit, for in the very pangs of death they clung to the Macedonians and caught hold of their horses' legs as they lay upon the ground.

Darius now saw the most dreadful dangers before his eyes. His own forces, placed in the front to defend him, were driven back upon him; the wheels of his chariot were, moreover, entangled among the dead bodies so that it was almost impossible to turn it, and the horses plunging among heaps of the slain bounded up and down and no longer obeyed the hands of the charioteer. In this extremity he quitted the chariot and his arms and fled, as they tell us, upon a mare which had newly foaled. . . .

The battle having such an issue, the Persian empire appeared to be entirely destroyed and Alexander was acknowledged King of all Asia. The first thing he did was to make his acknowledgments to the gods by magnificent sacrifices, and then to his friends by rich gifts of houses, estates and governments. As he was particularly ambitious of recommending himself to the Greeks, he signified by letter that all tyrannies should be abolished and that they should be governed by their own laws, under the auspices of freedom. . . .

He found that his great officers set no bounds to their luxury and that they were most extravagantly delicate in their diet and prodigal in other respects. Hagnon of Teos wore silver nails in his shoes; Leonnatus had many camel-loads of earth brought from Egypt to rub himself with when he went to the wrestling ring; Philotas had hunting nets that would enclose the space of a hundred furlongs; more made use of rich essences than oil after bathing and had their grooms of the bath, as well as chamberlains who excelled in bedmaking. This degeneracy he reproved with all the temper of a philosopher. He told them it was very strange to him that, after having undergone so many glorious conflicts, they did not remember that those who come from labor and exercise always sleep more sweetly than the inactive and effeminate, and that in comparing the Persian manners with the Macedonian they did not perceive that nothing was more servile than the love of pleasure or more princely than a life of toil. "How will that man," he continued, "take care of his own horse or furbish his lance and helmet, whose hands are too delicate to wait on his own dear person? Know you not that the end of conquest is not to do what the conquered have done but something greatly superior?"

After this he constantly took the exercise of war or hunting and exposed himself to danger and fatigue with less precaution than ever, so that a Lacedaemonian ambassador who attended him one day when he killed a fierce lion said: "Alexander, you have disputed the prize of royalty gloriously with the lion." . . .

His next movement was into Hyrcania, which he entered with the flower of his army. There he saw the Caspian Sea, which appeared to him not much less than the Euxine, but its water was of a sweeter taste. He could get no definite information as to how it was formed, but he conjectured that it came from an outlet of the lake of Maeotis. Yet the ancient naturalists were not ignorant of its origin, for, many years before Alexander's expedition, they wrote that there are four seas which stretch from the main ocean into the continent, the farthest north of which is the Hyrcanian, or the Caspian.

The barbarians here fell suddenly upon a party who were leading his horse Bucephalus, and captured the steed. This provoked him so much that he sent a herald to threaten them, their wives and children with utter extermination if they did not restore him the horse. But when they brought him back and surrendered to him their cities, he treated them with great clemency and paid a considerable sum — so to speak, as ransom — to those who took the horse.

From there he marched into Parthia[19] where, finding no occasion to use his armed might, he first put on the robe of the barbarian kings. Perhaps he did this to conform a little to their customs, because he knew how much a similarity of manners tends to reconcile and gain men's hearts; or perhaps he did it by way of experiment to see if the Macedonians might be brought to pay him the greater deference, by accustoming them imperceptibly to the new barbaric attire which he assumed. However, he thought the Median habit was too stiff and exotic in appearance. Therefore, he did not wear the long breeches or the sweeping train or the tiara, but adopted something between the Median and Persian mode, contrived vestments less pompous than the former and more majestic than the latter. At first he used this dress only before the barbarians or his particular friends and while indoors, but in time he came to wear it when he sat in public attending to matters of business.

This was a mortifying sight to the Macedonians; yet as they admired his other virtues, they thought he might be allowed to please himself a little and enjoy his vanity. Some indulgence seemed due to a prince who, beside his other hardships, had lately been wounded in the leg with an arrow which shattered the bone in such a manner that splinters had to be taken out. Another time, he received such a violent blow from a stone upon the nape of his neck that an alarming darkness covered his eyes and continued for some time, and yet he went on exposing his person without the least precaution. To the contrary, when he had passed the Orexartes river, which he supposed to be the Tanais, he not only attacked the Scythians and routed them, but pursued them a hundred furlongs, in spite of suffering at the time from diarrhoea.

As he was afraid that many of the Macedonians might resent the fatigues of the expedition, he left the greater part of the army in quarters and entered Hyrcania with a select body of twenty thousand foot and three thousand horse. The purport of his speech upon the occasion was this: "Hitherto the barbarians have seen us only as in a dream. If you should think of returning after having given Asia the alarm only, they will fall upon you with contempt, as unenterprising and effeminate.

[19] Southeast of the Caspian.

Nevertheless, such as desire to depart have my consent to do so, but at the same time I call the gods to witness that they desert their King when he is conquering the world for the Macedonians and leave him to the kinder and more faithful attachment of those few friends who will follow his fortune." This is almost word for word what he wrote to Antipater and he added that he had no sooner done speaking than they cried he might lead them to what part of the world he pleased. Thus he tested the disposition of these brave men and there was no difficulty in uniting the whole body in their sentiments; they followed him unconditionally.

After this, he accommodated himself more than ever to the manners of the Asiatics and at the same time persuaded them to adopt some of the Macedonian fashions, for by a mixture of both he thought a union might be promoted much better than by force, and his authority maintained when he was at a distance. For the same reason he selected thirty thousand boys and gave them masters to instruct them in Grecian literature as well as to train them in the Macedonian manner of combat.

As for his marriage to Roxana, it was entirely a matter of love. He saw her at an entertainment and found her charms irresistible. Nor was the match unsuitable to the state of affairs. The barbarians placed greater confidence in him on account of that alliance and his chastity gained their affection; it delighted them to think he would not approach the only woman he ever passionately loved without the sanction of marriage. . . .

When Alexander was on the point of setting out for India he saw his troops were so laden with spoils that they were unfit to march. Therefore, early in the morning, when he was to take his departure, after the carriages were assembled, he first set fire to his own baggage and that of his friends and then gave orders that the rest should be served in the same manner. The resolution appeared more difficult to take than it was to execute. Few were displeased at it and numbers received it with acclamations of joy. They freely gave part of their equipage to such as were in need and burned and destroyed whatever was superfluous. This greatly encouraged and fortified Alexander in his plans. Besides, by this time he had become inflexibly severe in punishing offenses. Menander, though one of his friends, he put to death for refusing to stay in a fortress he had given him the charge of, and one of the barbarians, named Orsodates, he shot dead with an arrow for the crime of rebellion.

About this time a sheep yeaned a lamb with the perfect form and color of a tiara on its head, on each side of which were testicles. Looking upon the monstrosity with horror, he employed the Chaldeans,[20] who attended him for such purposes, to purify him with their expiations. He told his friends on this occasion that he was more troubled on their account than his own, for he was afraid that after his death fortune would throw the empire into the hands of some obscure and weak man. A better omen, however, soon dissipated his fears. A Macedonian named Proxenus, who had charge of the King's equipage, on spading the ground by the river Oxus in order to pitch his master's tent, discovered a spring of a gross oily liquid which, after the surface was taken off, came perfectly clear and neither in taste nor smell differed from real oil, nor was inferior to it in smoothness and brightness, though there are no olives in that country. It is said, indeed, that the water of the Oxus is of so unctuous a quality that it makes the skins of those who bathe in it smooth and shining.

It appears from a letter of Alexander's to Antipater that he was greatly delighted with this incident and reckoned it one of the happiest presages the gods had afforded him. The soothsayers said it betokened that the expedition would prove a glorious one, but at the same time laborious and difficult because heaven has given men oil to refresh them after their labors.[21] Accordingly, he met with great dangers in the battles that he fought and received very considerable wounds. But his army suffered most from want of necessities and by the climate. For Alexander's part, he was ambitious to show that courage can triumph over fortune and magnanimity over force. He thought nothing invincible to the brave nor impregnable to the bold. . . .

It is said the dominions of King Taxiles in India were as large as Egypt. They afforded excellent pasturage too and were the most fertile in all respects. As he was a man of great prudence, he waited on Alexander and after the first compliments thus addressed him: "What occasion

---

[20] Astrologers and soothsayers of Chaldean (Babylonian) stock.

[21] The practice of rubbing oil on the body after exercise and bathing was a protection against the intense and drying sunlight of Mediterranean and Eastern countries.

is there for wars between you and me, if you are not come to take from us our water and other necessities of life, the only things that reasonable men will take up arms for? As to gold and silver, and other possessions, if I am richer than you, I am willing to oblige you with a part; if I am poorer, I have no objection to sharing in your bounty." Charmed with his frankness, Alexander took his hand and answered: "Think you, then, with all this civility, to escape without a conflict? You are much deceived if you do. I will dispute it with you to the last, but it shall be in favors and benefits; for I will not have you exceed me in generosity." Therefore, after having received great presents from him and made greater he said to him one evening: "I drink to you, Taxiles, and as sure as you pledge me, you shall have a thousand talents." His friends were offended at his giving away such immense sums but it made many of the barbarians look upon him with a kinder eye.

The most warlike of the Indians used to fight for pay. On this invasion they defended the cities that hired them with great vigor and Alexander suffered by them not a little. To one of the cities he granted an honorable capitulation and yet seized the mercenaries as they were upon their march homewards and put them all to the sword. This is the only blot in his military conduct. All his other proceedings were agreeable to the laws of war and worthy of a king. . . .

Alexander, in his march from there, was eager to see the ocean,[22] for which purpose he caused a number of rowboats and rafts to be constructed and upon them floated down the rivers at his leisure. Nor was this navigation unattended with hostilities. He made several descents on the bank by the way and attacked adjacent cities, which were all forced to submit to his victorious arms. However, he was very near being cut to pieces by the Malli, who are called the most warlike people in India. He had driven some of them from a fortified wall with showers of arrows and was the first man that ascended it. But after he was up, the scaling-ladder broke. Finding himself and his small company much exposed to the darts of the barbarians from below, he poised himself and leaped down into the midst of the enemy. By good fortune he fell upon his feet and the barbarians were so astonished at the flashing of his arms as he came down that they thought they saw lightning or some supernatural splendor issuing from his body.

At first, therefore, they drew back and dispersed, but when they

[22] The Indian Ocean.

saw him attended only by two of his guards, they attacked him hand to hand and wounded him through his armor with their swords and spears, notwithstanding the valor with which he fought. One of them standing farther off drew an arrow with such strength that it made its way through his cuirass and entered the ribs under the breast. Its force was so great that he reeled back and was brought upon his knees, and the barbarian ran up with his drawn cimitar to dispatch him. Peucestes and Limnaeus placed themselves before him, but the one was wounded and the other killed. Peucestes, who survived, was still making some resistance when Alexander recovered himself and laid the barbarian at his feet. The King, however, received new wounds and at last had such a blow from a bludgeon upon his neck that he was forced to support himself against the wall and there stood with his face to the enemy. The Macedonians, who by this time had made their way in, gathered about him and carried him off to his tent.

His senses were gone and the current report in the army was he was dead. When they had with great difficulty sawed off the arrow shaft, which was of wood, and with equal trouble had taken off the cuirass they proceeded to extract the head, which was three fingers broad and four long, and stuck fast in the bone. Alexander fainted under the operation and was very near expiring, but when the head was got out he came to himself. Yet, after the danger was over he continued to be weak and for a long time confined himself to a regular diet, attending solely to the cure of his wound. The Macedonians could not bear to be so long deprived of the sight of their King; they assembled in a tumultuous manner about his tent. When he perceived this he put on his robe and made his appearance, but as soon as he had sacrificed to the gods he retired again.

Alexander spent seven months in coasting down the rivers to the ocean. When he arrived there he embarked and sailed to an island which he called Scillustis, but others call it Psiltucis. There he landed and sacrificed to the gods. He likewise considered the nature of the sea and of the coast, as far as it was accessible. And after having besought heaven that no man might ever go beyond the bounds of his expedition, he prepared to set out on his way back. He appointed Nearchus admiral and Onesicritus chief pilot and ordered his fleet to sail round, keeping India on the right hand. With the rest of his forces he returned by land through the country of the Orites, in which he was reduced to such extremities and lost such numbers of men that he did not bring back from

India above a fourth part of the army he entered it with, which was no less than a hundred and twenty thousand foot and fifteen thousand horse. Violent distempers, ill diet and excessive heats destroyed multitudes but famine made still greater ravages, for it was a barren and uncultivated country, the natives lived miserably, having nothing to subsist on but a few sheep which were fed on the fish thrown up by the sea; consequently they were poor and their flesh of a bad flavor.

With much difficulty he traversed this country in sixty days and then arrived at Gedrosia.[23] There he found provisions in abundance, for, besides the land being fertile, the neighboring princes and grandees supplied him. After he had given his army some time to refresh themselves he marched through Carmania for seven days in a kind of Bacchanalian procession. His chariot, which was very magnificent, was drawn by eight horses. Upon it was placed a lofty platform where he and his principal friends reveled day and night. This carriage was followed by many others, some covered with rich tapestry and purple hangings and others shaded with branches of trees, fresh gathered and flourishing. In these were the rest of the King's friends and generals, crowned with flowers and exhilarated with wine.

In this whole company there was not to be seen a buckler, a helmet or spear but, instead of them, cups, flagons and goblets. These the soldiers dipped in huge vessels of wine and drank to each other, some as they marched along and others seated at tables which were placed at proper distances on the way. The whole country resounded with flutes, clarinets and songs, and with the dances and riotous frolics of the women. . . .

When Alexander arrived at Susa[24] he married his friends to Persian ladies. He set them the example by taking Statira, the daughter of Darius, to wife and then distributed among his principal officers the virgins of highest quality. As for those Macedonians who had already married in Persia, he made a general entertainment in commemoration of their nuptials. It is said that no less than nine thousand guests sat down and yet he presented each with a golden cup for the libations. Everything else was conducted with the utmost magnificence. He even paid off all their debts; the whole expense amounted to nine thousand eight hundred and seventy talents. . . .

[23] In what is now southeast Iran.
[24] Ancient capital city north of Persian Gulf.

One day, after he had given Nearchus a sumptuous banquet, he went according to custom to refresh himself in the bath, in order to retire to rest. But in the meantime, Medius came and invited him to take part in a carousal, and he could not deny him. There he drank all that night and the next day until at last he found a fever coming upon him. It did not, however, seize him as he was drinking the cup of Hercules,[25] nor did he find a sudden pain in his back, as if it had been pierced with a spear. These are circumstances invented by writers who thought the catastrophe of so noble a tragedy should be something affecting and extraordinary. Aristobulus tells us that in the rage of his fever and the violence of thirst, he took a draught of wine which threw him into a frenzy, and that he died the thirtieth of the month Daesius, or June.

But in his journals the account of his sickness is as follows: "On the eighteenth of the month Daesius, finding the fever upon him, he lay in his bathroom. The next day, after he had bathed, he withdrew into his own chamber and played many hours at dice with Medius. In the evening he bathed again, and after having sacrificed to the gods he ate his supper. In the night the fever returned. The twentieth he also bathed and, after the customary sacrifice, sat in the bathroom and diverted himself with hearing Nearchus tell the story of his voyage and the observations he had made at sea. The twenty-first was spent in the same manner. The fever increased and he had a very bad night. The twenty-second, the fever was violent. He ordered his bed to be removed and placed by the great bath. There he talked to his generals about the vacancies in his army and desired they might be filled with experienced officers. The twenty-fourth he was much worse. He chose, however, to be carried to assist at the sacrifice. He likewise gave orders that the principal officers of the army should wait within the court and the officers keep watch all night without. The twenty-fifth, he was removed to his palace on the other side of the river, where he slept a little, but the fever did not abate and when his generals entered the room he was speechless. He continued so the day following. The Macedonians, by this time thinking he was dead, came to the gates with great clamor and threatened the great officers in such a manner that they were forced to admit them and suffer them all to pass unarmed by the bedside. The twenty-seventh, Python and Seleucus were sent to the temple of Serapis to inquire whether they

---

[25] The *rhyton* or "hero cup," actually a drinking horn of large capacity such as is seen in Greek vase paintings of feasting gods and heroes.

should carry Alexander thither, and the deity ordered that they should not remove him. The twenty-eighth, in the evening, he died."[26] These particulars are taken, almost word for word, from his diary.

✍ FOR DISCUSSION AND WRITING

1. What is Plutarch's attitude toward the stories he relates of Alexander's birth and youthful virtuosity? Is he critical of their validity or uncritical? How can you tell? For some obscure reason, in some obscure but comprehensive way, twentieth-century education has biased our minds against full-hearted appreciation of noble and heroic characters; we look for the Achilles' heel, the vulnerable part that gives us the privilege of contempt, of minimizing greatness. Can you explain this tendency? For many centuries, Plutarch's *Lives* have been essential reading for young people, not only as sources of historical information, but more particularly as a stimulus to the moral imagination, thrilling the mind with heroic vistas and noble possibilities; but few modern college students are familiar with the *Lives*. Judging from this biography of Alexander, what is your considered opinion of the modern tendency to reduce heroic achievement to "nothing but" some egotistic motive or Freudian infantilism, as against Plutarch's clearly appreciative and admiring presentation of Alexander?

2. Name five different branches of learning in which Alexander was educated before he was twenty, when he had to take on the responsibilities of kingship. How would you compare his education with your own? Has education advanced or receded since then? (In considering these questions, one should be aware of the fact that Alexander's Macedonia was actually a pretty backward and barbarous country—in comparison, certainly, with Athenian civilization, as well as with the ancient civilization of the Persian empire which he conquered.)

3. What does the incident with Diogenes show about Alexander? Is the story consistent with his character and background? When he crossed the Hellespont and came to the ancient site of Troy, he made libations for the Homeric heroes, showing particular reverence to Achilles; what was there in common between Achilles and Alexander? A number of the incidents Plutarch relates show acute psychology on Alexander's part in using acci-

---

[26] Alexander died in 323 B.C., at the age of thirty-three.

dental opportunities to invigorate the morale of his army (opportunities like the famous one seized by Julius Caesar, when he stumbled and fell on his face in getting off the boat that landed him in Africa—an ominous accident—and got up grasping two handfuls of dirt, saying, "Look! I have Africa in my grasp!"). Do you find this kind of psychology in the incident of the sweating of the statue? in that of the Gordian knot? the flight of birds that guided the army in Egypt? his reaction to the oracle of Ammon? and other incidents? Does his psychological exploitation of these incidents minimize his heroic character—his capacity for leadership—or illustrate it in a positive way?

4. How did Alexander show his political—as well as personal and moral— capacity in his treatment of subject peoples? One of the criticisms Plutarch mentions is against his adoption of Asiatic dress; do you find in the political context any justification for this?

5. If you have read Teilhard de Chardin's article in this book, illustrate from Alexander's biography the idea of creative "confluences" of cultures that act in human evolution like the confluence of genes at one's birth.

6. Earlier in this book we have suggested an essay problem on the idea of "leadership" (particularly in regard to Robert Falcon Scott and T. E. Lawrence): could you write a short paper on Alexander in comparison with these others? Or else do a bit of research for a paper on the geographical routes of Alexander's expeditions; or on Persian costume in his time; or on ancient armor.

Edward Gibbon ✑ Christianity under the Roman Empire

✑ English historian (1737-1794). Gibbon's vast, panoramic *Decline and Fall of the Roman Empire* is one of the great classics of literature as well as of history. Its scope and organization are architectonic, and its language is that of a master builder, building in contrapuntal phalanxes of words, sturdy as a cathedral, gargoyled with wit. The selection here is from the sixteenth chapter, one of the most famous chapters of the work—or infamous, as one may look upon it; for Gibbon's view of Christianity under the Roman Empire is typically that of an eighteenth-century rationalist and skeptic, who would, no doubt, have approved of the setting up of the Goddess of Reason in Notre Dame in place of the Virgin, a ceremony which he just missed. ଛ

IF WE seriously consider the purity of the Christian religion, the sanctity of its moral precepts, and the innocent as well as austere lives of the greater number of those who during the first ages embraced the faith of the Gospel, we should naturally suppose that so benevolent a doctrine would have been received with due reverence even by the unbelieving world; that the learned and the polite, however they might deride the miracles, would have esteemed the virtues of the new sect; and that the magistrates, instead of persecuting, would have protected an order of men who yielded the most passive obedience to the laws, though they declined the active cares of war and government. If, on the other hand, we recollect the universal toleration of Polytheism, as it was invariably

From *The History of the Decline and Fall of the Roman Empire* by Edward Gibbon (first published from 1776 to 1788), Chapter 16, abridged by the editors.

maintained by the faith of the people, the incredulity of philosophers, and the policy of the Roman senate and emperors, we are at a loss to discover what new offence the Christians had committed, what new provocation could exasperate the mild indifference of antiquity, and what new motives could urge the Roman princes, who beheld without concern a thousand forms of religion subsisting in peace under their gentle sway, to inflict a severe punishment on any part of their subjects who had chosen for themselves a singular but an inoffensive mode of faith and worship. . . .

To separate (if it be possible) a few authentic as well as interesting facts from an undigested mass of fiction and error, and to relate, in a clear and rational manner, the causes, the extent, the duration, and the most important circumstances of the persecutions to which the first Christians were exposed, is the design of the present chapter. . . .

Malice and prejudice concurred in representing the Christians as a society of atheists, who, by the most daring attack on the religious constitution of the empire, had merited the severest animadversion of the civil magistrate. They had separated themselves (they gloried in the confession) from every mode of superstition which was received in any part of the globe by the various temper of Polytheism: but it was not altogether so evident what deity, or what form of worship, they had substituted to the gods and temples of antiquity. The pure and sublime idea which they entertained of the Supreme Being escaped the gross conception of the Pagan multitude, who were at a loss to discover a spiritual and solitary God, that was neither represented under any corporeal figure or visible symbol, nor was adored with the accustomed pomp of libations and festivals, of altars and sacrifices. The sages of Greece and Rome, who had elevated their minds to the contemplation of the existence and attributes of the First Cause,[1] were induced by reason or by vanity to reserve for themselves and their chosen disciples the privilege of this philosophical devotion. They were far from admitting the prejudices of mankind as the standard of truth, but they considered them as flowing from the original disposition of human nature; and they sup-

---

[1] In Aristotelian metaphysics, for instance, the First Cause is the "unmoved mover" or unchanging cause of all change, determining the direction of all natural processes; but it is not the creator of the universe, like the Hebrew and Christian God, for matter is uncreated. The principle is rather one of dynamics than a religious principle.

posed that any popular mode of faith and worship which presumed to disclaim the assistance of the senses would, in proportion as it receded from superstition, find itself incapable of restraining the wanderings of the fancy and the visions of fanaticism. The careless glance which men of wit and learning condescended to cast on the Christian revelation served only to confirm their hasty opinion, and to persuade them that the principle, which they might have revered, of the Divine Unity, was defaced by the wild enthusiasm, and annihilated by the airy speculations, of the new sectaries. . . .

It might appear less surprising that the founder of Christianity should not only be revered by his disciples as a sage and a prophet, but that he should be adored as a God. The Polytheists were disposed to adopt every article of faith which seemed to offer any resemblance, however distant or imperfect, with the popular mythology; and the legends of Bacchus, of Hercules, and of Aesculapius,[2] had, in some measure, prepared their imagination for the appearance of the Son of God under a human form. But they were astonished that the Christians should abandon the temples of those ancient heroes who, in the infancy of the world, had invented arts, instituted laws, and vanquished the tyrants or monsters who infested the earth; in order to choose for the exclusive object of their religious worship an obscure teacher, who, in a recent age, and among a barbarous people, had fallen a sacrifice either to the malice of his own countrymen, or to the jealousy of the Roman government. . . .

The personal guilt which every Christian had contracted, in thus preferring his private sentiment to the national religion, was aggravated in a very high degree by the number and union of the criminals. It is well known, and has been already observed, the Roman policy viewed with the utmost jealousy and distrust any association among its subjects; and that the privileges of private corporations, though formed for the most harmless or beneficial purposes, were bestowed with a very sparing hand. The religious assemblies of the Christians, who had separated themselves from the public worship, appeared of a much less innocent nature: they were illegal in their principle, and in their consequences might become dangerous; nor were the emperors conscious that they

---

[2] Worshiped as gods, all these, according to popular mythology, were sons of mortal mothers by Zeus and had had historical existence; hence the parallel with Christ. For Aesculapius (or Asclepius), see note on the last words of Socrates, page 315.

violated the laws of justice, when, for the peace of society, they pro-hibited those secret and sometimes nocturnal meetings. . . .

We have already seen that the active and successful zeal of the Christians had insensibly diffused them through every province and almost every city of the empire. The new converts seemed to renounce their family and country, that they might connect themselves in an indissoluble band of union with a peculiar society, which everywhere assumed a different character from the rest of mankind. Their gloomy and austere aspect, their abhorrence of the common business and pleasures of life, and their frequent predictions of impending calamities, inspired the Pagans with the apprehension of some danger which would arise from the new sect, the more alarming as it was the more obscure. "Whatever," says Pliny,[3] "may be the principle of their conduct, their inflexible obstinacy appeared deserving of punishment."

The precautions with which the disciples of Christ performed the offices of religion were at first dictated by fear and necessity; but they were continued from choice. By imitating the awful secrecy which reigned in the Eleusinian mysteries,[4] the Christians had flattered them-selves that they should render their sacred institutions more respectable in the eyes of the Pagan world. But the event, as it often happens to the operations of subtle policy, deceived their wishes and their expectations. It was concluded that they only concealed what they would have blushed to disclose. Their mistaken prudence afforded an opportunity for malice to invent, and for suspicious credulity to believe, the horrid tales which describe the Christians as the most wicked of human kind, who practised in their dark recesses every abomination that a depraved fancy could suggest, and who solicited the favour of their unknown God by the sacrifice of every moral virtue. There were many who pretended

---

[3] Pliny the Younger (A.D. 62-113), learned Roman orator, writer, senator, consul, and under Trajan governor in Asia Minor, where Christian proselytization had been most vigorous.

[4] The Eleusinian mysteries, held at Eleusis, a few miles from Athens, were the most famous religious mysteries of the ancient world. They were incorporated in the state religion of Athens, but their origin is prehistoric, far antedating Athenian political power. The rites were so sacred and so secret that very little is known about them, except that they celebrated the earth-mother Demeter or Ceres (from whose name our word "cereal" comes), her daughter Persephone (actually an-other form of herself), and the annual rebirth of Dionysus, under the name of Iacchus.

to confess or to relate the ceremonies of this abhorred society. It was asserted, "that a new-born infant, entirely covered over with flour, was presented, like some mystic symbol of initiation, to the knife of the proselyte, who unknowingly inflicted many a secret and mortal wound on the innocent victim of his error; that as soon as the cruel deed was perpetrated, the sectaries drank up the blood, greedily tore asunder the quivering members, and pledged themselves to eternal secrecy, by a mutual consciousness of guilt. It was as confidently affirmed that this inhuman sacrifice was succeeded by a suitable entertainment, in which intemperance served as a provocative to brutal lust; till, at the appointed moment, the lights were suddenly extinguished, shame was banished, nature was forgotten; and, as accident might direct, the darkness of the night was polluted by the incestuous commerce of sisters and brothers, of sons and of mothers."

History, which undertakes to record the transactions of the past, for the instruction of future ages, would ill deserve that honourable office, if she condescended to plead the cause of tyrants, or to justify the maxims of persecution. It must, however, be acknowledged that the conduct of the emperors who appeared the least favourable to the primitive church is by no means so criminal as that of modern sovereigns who have employed the arm of violence and terror against the religious opinions of any part of their subjects. . . . As they were actuated, not by the furious zeal of bigots, but by the temperate policy of legislators, contempt must often have relaxed, and humanity must frequently have suspended, the execution of those laws which they enacted against the humble and obscure followers of Christ. From the general view of their character and motives we might naturally conclude: I. That a considerable time elapsed before they considered the new sectaries as an object deserving of the attention of government. II. That in the conviction of any of their subjects who were accused of so very singular a crime, they proceeded with caution and reluctance. III. That they were moderate in the use of punishments; and IV. That the afflicted church enjoyed many intervals of peace and tranquillity. Notwithstanding the careless indifference which the most copious and the most minute of the Pagan writers have shown to the affairs of the Christians, it may still be in our power to confirm each of these probable suppositions by the evidence of authentic facts.

By the wise dispensation of Providence a mysterious veil was cast over the infancy of the church, which, till the faith of the Christians was matured, and their numbers were multiplied, served to protect them not only from the malice but even from the knowledge of the Pagan world. The slow and gradual abolition of the Mosaic ceremonies[5] afforded a safe and innocent disguise to the more early proselytes of the Gospel. As they were for the greater part of the race of Abraham, they were distinguished by the peculiar mark of circumcision, offered up their devotions in the Temple of Jerusalem till its final destruction, and received both the Law and the Prophets as the genuine inspirations of the Deity. The Gentile converts who by a spiritual adoption had been associated to the hope of Israel, were likewise confounded under the garb and appearance of Jews; and as the Polytheists paid less regard to articles of faith than to the external worship, the new sect, which carefully concealed, or faintly announced, its future greatness and ambition, was permitted to shelter itself under the general toleration which was granted to an ancient and celebrated people in the Roman empire. It was not long, perhaps, before the Jews themselves, animated with a fiercer zeal and more jealous faith, perceived the gradual separation of their Nazarene brethren[6] from the doctrine of the synagogue: and they would gladly have extinguished the dangerous heresy in the blood of its adherents. But the decrees of Heaven had already disarmed their malice; and though they might sometimes exert the licentious privilege of sedition, they no longer possessed the administration of criminal justice; nor did they find it easy to infuse into the calm breast of a Roman magistrate the rancour of their own zeal and prejudice. The provincial governors declared themselves ready to listen to any accusation that might affect the public safety; but as soon as they were informed that it was a question not of facts but of words, a dispute relating only to the interpretation of the Jewish laws and prophecies, they deemed it unworthy of the majesty of Rome seriously to discuss the obscure differences which might arise among a barbarous and superstitious people. The innocence of the first Christians was protected by ignorance and contempt; and the tri-

---

[5] Laws and rites of the Hebrews which, according to Biblical history, had been instituted by Moses. The word "Gentile," in the following sentence, comes from the Latin *gens,* meaning tribe, race, nation (compare the words "genus," "generation," etc.), and was used by the Romans to refer to non-Roman (that is, "barbarous") peoples and by the Jews to non-Jewish peoples.

[6] Jesus began his preaching in Nazareth of Galilee (northwestern province of Palestine); hence his followers were called Nazarenes.

bunal of the Pagan magistrate often proved their most assured refuge against the fury of the synagogue. If, indeed, we were disposed to adopt the traditions of a too credulous antiquity, we might relate the distant peregrinations, the wonderful achievements, and the various deaths of the twelve apostles: but a more accurate inquiry will induce us to doubt whether any of those persons who had been witnesses to the miracles of Christ were permitted, beyond the limits of Palestine, to seal with their blood the truth of their testimony. From the ordinary term of human life, it may very naturally be presumed that most of them were deceased before the discontent of the Jews broke out into that furious war which was terminated only by the ruin of Jerusalem.[7] During a long period, from the death of Christ to that memorable rebellion, we cannot discover any traces of Roman intolerance, unless they are to be found in the sudden, the transient, but the cruel persecution, which was exercised by Nero against the Christians of the capital, thirty-five years after the former, and only two years before the latter, of those great events. The character of the philosophic historian,[8] to whom we are principally indebted for the knowledge of this singular transaction, would alone be sufficient to recommend it to our most attentive consideration.

In the tenth year of the reign of Nero[9] the capital of the empire was afflicted by a fire which raged beyond the memory or example of former ages. The monuments of Grecian art and of Roman virtue, the trophies of the Punic and Gallic wars, the most holy temples, and the most splendid palaces were involved in one common destruction. Of the fourteen regions or quarters into which Rome was divided, four only subsisted entire, three were levelled with the ground, and the remaining seven, which had experienced the fury of the flames, displayed a melancholy prospect of ruin and desolation. The vigilance of government appears not to have neglected any of the precautions which might alleviate the sense of so dreadful a calamity. The Imperial gardens were thrown open to the distressed multitude, temporary buildings were erected for their accommodation, and a plentiful supply of corn and provisions was distributed at a very moderate price. The most generous policy seemed to have dictated the edicts which regulated the disposition of the

[7] Jerusalem was leveled by Titus in A.D. 70, after the rebellion led by Judas the Gaulonite.

[8] Tacitus, greatest of the Roman historians (A.D. 55-117).

[9] Nero reigned from A.D. 54 to 68.

streets and the construction of private houses; and, as it usually happens in an age of prosperity, the conflagration of Rome, in the course of a few years, produced a new city, more regular and more beautiful than the former. But all the prudence and humanity affected by Nero on this occasion were insufficient to preserve him from the popular suspicion. Every crime might be imputed to the assassin of his wife and mother; nor could the prince who prostituted his person and dignity on the theatre be deemed incapable of the most extravagant folly. The voice of rumour accused the emperor as the incendiary of his own capital; and, as the most incredible stories are the best adapted to the genius of an enraged people, it was gravely reported, and firmly believed, that Nero, enjoying the calamity which he had occasioned, amused himself with singing to his lyre the destruction of ancient Troy. To divert a suspicion which the power of despotism was unable to suppress, the emperor resolved to substitute in his own place some fictitious criminals. "With this view (continues Tacitus) he inflicted the most exquisite tortures on those men who, under the vulgar appellation of Christians, were already branded with deserved infamy. They derived their name and origin from Christ, who, in the reign of Tiberius, had suffered death by the sentence of the procurator Pontius Pilate. For a while this dire superstition was checked, but it again burst forth; and not only spread itself over Judaea, the first seat of this mischievous sect, but was even introduced into Rome, the common asylum which receives and protects whatever is impure, whatever is atrocious. The confessions of those who were seized discovered a great multitude of their accomplices, and they were all convicted, not so much for the crime of setting fire to the city as for their hatred of human kind. They died in torments, and their torments were embittered by insult and derision. Some were nailed on crosses; others sewn up in the skins of wild beasts, and exposed to the fury of dogs; others again, smeared over with combustible materials, were used as torches to illuminate the darkness of the night. The gardens of Nero were destined for the melancholy spectacle, which was accompanied with a horse-race, and honoured with the presence of the emperor, who mingled with the populace in the dress and attitude of a charioteer. The guilt of the Christians deserved indeed the most exemplary punishment, but the public abhorrence was changed into commiseration, from the opinion that those unhappy wretches were sacrificed, not so much to the public welfare as to the cruelty of a jealous tyrant." Those who survey with a curious eye the revolutions of mankind may observe that the gardens and circus of Nero on the Vatican, which were polluted with the blood of the first Christians, have been rendered still more famous by the triumph and by the abuse of the persecuted religion. On the same spot a temple, which far surpasses the ancient glories of the Capitol, has been since erected by the Christian Pontiffs, who, deriving their claim of universal dominion from an humble fisherman of Galilee, have succeeded to the throne of the Caesars, given laws to the barbarian conquerors of Rome, and extended their spiritual jurisdiction from the coast of the Baltic to the shores of the Pacific Ocean.

But it would be improper to dismiss this account of Nero's persecution till we have made some observations that may serve to remove the difficulties with which it is perplexed, and to throw some light on the subsequent history of the church.

1. The most sceptical criticism is obliged to respect the truth of this extraordinary fact, and the integrity of this celebrated passage of Tacitus. The former is confirmed by the diligent and accurate Suetonius,[10] who mentions the punishment which Nero inflicted on the Christians, a sect of men who had embraced a new and criminal superstition. The latter may be proved by the consent of the most ancient manuscripts; by the inimitable character of the style of Tacitus; by his reputation, which guarded his text from the interpolations of pious fraud; and by the purport of his narration, which accused the first Christians of the most atrocious crimes, without insinuating that they possessed any miraculous or even magical powers above the rest of mankind. 2. Notwithstanding it is probable that Tacitus was born some years before the fire of Rome, he could derive only from reading and conversation the knowledge of an event which happened during his infancy. Before he gave himself to the public he calmly waited till his genius had attained its full maturity, and he was more than forty years of age when a grateful regard for the memory of the virtuous Agricola[11] extorted from him the most early of those historical compositions which will delight and instruct the most distant posterity. . . .

It was the duty of the annalist to adopt the narratives of contemporaries; but it was natural for the philosopher to indulge himself in

[10] Roman historian (A.D. 69-140), author of *The Lives of the Twelve Caesars*. He acted as secretary to the Emperor Hadrian.

[11] Roman general (A.D. 37-93) who reconquered Britain.

the description of the origin, the progress, and the character of the new sect, not so much according to the knowledge or prejudices of the age of Nero, as according to those of the time of Hadrian.[12] 3. Tacitus very frequently trusts to the curiosity or reflection of his readers to supply those intermediate circumstances and ideas which, in his extreme conciseness, he has thought proper to suppress. We may therefore presume to imagine some probable cause which could direct the cruelty of Nero against the Christians of Rome, whose obscurity, as well as innocence, should have shielded them from his indignation, and even from his notice. The Jews, who were numerous in the capital and oppressed in their own country, were a much fitter object for the suspicions of the emperor and of the people: nor did it seem unlikely that a vanquished nation, who already discovered their abhorrence of the Roman yoke, might have recourse to the most atrocious means of gratifying their implacable revenge.[13] But the Jews possessed very powerful advocates in the palace, and even in the heart of the tyrant; his wife and mistress, the beautiful Poppaea, and a favourite player of the race of Abraham, who had already employed their intercession on behalf of the obnoxious people. In their room it was necessary to offer some other victims, and it might easily be suggested that, although the genuine followers of Moses were innocent of the fire of Rome, there had arisen among them a new and pernicious sect of GALILAEANS,[14] which was capable of the most horrid crimes. Under the appellation of GALILAEANS two distinctions of men were confounded, the most opposite to each other in their manners and principles; the disciples who had embraced the faith of Jesus of Nazareth, and the zealots who had followed the standard of Judas the Gaulonite. The former were the friends, the latter were the enemies, of human kind; and the only resemblance between them consisted in the same inflexible constancy which, in the defence of their cause, rendered them insensible of death and tortures. The followers of Judas, who impelled their countrymen into rebellion, were soon buried under the ruins of Jerusalem; whilst those of Jesus, known by the more

[12] Emperor from A.D. 117 to 138. In the piece that follows, Eleanor Clark gives a subtle and fascinating portrait of Hadrian.

[13] Gibbon is not indulging here in egregious anti-Semitism, but referring to the historical reasons the Jews had for harboring resentment against Rome (see Note 7).

[14] See Note 6.

celebrated name of Christians, diffused themselves over the Roman empire. How natural was it for Tacitus, in the time of Hadrian, to appropriate to the Christians the guilt and the sufferings which he might, with far greater truth and justice, have attributed to a sect whose odious memory was almost extinguished! 4. Whatever opinion may be entertained of this conjecture (for it is no more than a conjecture), it is evident that the effect, as well as the cause, of Nero's persecution, were confined to the walls of Rome; that the religious tenets of the Galilaeans, or Christians, were never made a subject of punishment, or even of inquiry; and that, as the idea of their sufferings was, for a long time, connected with the idea of cruelty and injustice, the moderation of succeeding princes inclined them to spare a sect oppressed by a tyrant whose rage had been usually directed against virtue and innocence.

It is somewhat remarkable that the flames of war consumed almost at the same time the Temple of Jerusalem and the Capitol of Rome; and it appears no less singular that the tribute which devotion had destined to the former should have been converted by the power of an assaulting victor to restore and adorn the splendour of the latter.[15] The emperors levied a general capitation tax on the Jewish people; and although the sum assessed on the head of each individual was inconsiderable, the use for which it was designed, and the severity with which it was exacted, were considered as an intolerable grievance. Since the officers of the revenue extended their unjust claim to many persons who were strangers to the blood or religion of the Jews, it was impossible that the Christians, who had so often sheltered themselves under the shade of the synagogue, should now escape this rapacious persecution. Anxious as they were to avoid the slightest infection of idolatry, their conscience forbade them to contribute to the honour of that daemon who had assumed the character of the Capitoline Jupiter.[16] As a very numerous though declining party among the Christians still adhered to the law of Moses, their efforts to dissemble their Jewish origin were detected by the decisive test of circumcision; nor were the Roman magistrates at leisure to inquire into the difference of their religious

---

[15] The point may not be clear. The funds with which the Jews wanted to rebuild Jerusalem were exacted from them as a capitation tax to rebuild Rome after the fire.

[16] The Roman emperors were "deified" as reincarnations of Jupiter Optimus Maximus, whose shrine was on the Capitoline Hill in Rome.

tenets. Among the Christians who were brought before the tribunal of the emperor, or, as it seems more probable, before that of the procurator of Judaea, two persons are said to have appeared, distinguished by their extraction, which was more truly noble than that of the greatest monarchs. These were the grandsons of St. Jude the apostle, who himself was the brother of Jesus Christ. Their natural pretensions to the throne of David might perhaps attract the respect of the people, and excite the jealousy of the governor; but the meanness of their garb and the simplicity of their answers soon convinced him that they were neither desirous nor capable of disturbing the peace of the Roman empire. They frankly confessed their royal origin, and their near relation to the Messiah; but they disclaimed any temporal views, and professed that his kingdom, which they devoutly expected, was purely of a spiritual and angelic nature. When they were examined concerning their fortune and occupation, they showed their hands hardened with daily labour, and declared that they derived their whole subsistence from the cultivation of a farm near the village of Cocaba, of the extent of about twenty-four English acres, and of the value of nine thousand drachms, or three hundred pounds sterling. The grandsons of St. Jude were dismissed with compassion and contempt.

Under the reign of Trajan, the younger Pliny was intrusted by his friend and master with the government of Bithynia and Pontus.[17] He soon found himself at a loss to determine by what rule of justice or of law he should direct his conduct in the execution of an office the most repugnant to his humanity. Pliny had never assisted at any judicial proceedings against the Christians, with whose name alone he seems to be acquainted; and he was totally uninformed with regard to the nature of their guilt, the method of their conviction, and the degree of their punishment. In this perplexity he had recourse to his usual expedient, of submitting to the wisdom of Trajan an impartial, and, in some respects, a favourable account of the new superstition, requesting the emperor that he would condescend to resolve his doubts and to instruct his ignorance. The life of Pliny had been employed in the acquisition of learning, and in the business of the world. Since the age of nineteen he had pleaded with distinction in the tribunals of Rome, filled a place in the senate, had been invested with the honours of the consulship, and had formed very numerous connections with every order of men, both

[17] Roman provinces in Asia Minor. See also Note 3.

in Italy and in the provinces. From *his* ignorance therefore we may derive some useful information. We may assure ourselves that when he accepted the government of Bithynia there were no general laws or decrees of the senate in force against the Christians; that neither Trajan nor any of his virtuous predecessors, whose edicts were received into the civil and criminal jurisprudence, had publicly declared their intentions concerning the new sect; and that, whatever proceedings had been carried on against the Christians, there were none of sufficient weight and authority to establish a precedent for the conduct of a Roman magistrate.

The answer of Trajan, to which the Christians of the succeeding age have frequently appealed, discovers as much regard for justice and humanity as could be reconciled with his mistaken notions of religious policy. Instead of displaying the implacable zeal of an Inquisitor, anxious to discover the most minute particles of heresy, and exulting in the number of his victims, the emperor expresses much more solicitude to protect the security of the innocent than to prevent the escape of the guilty. He acknowledges the difficulty of fixing any general plan; but he lays down two salutary rules, which often afforded relief and support to the distressed Christians. Though he directs the magistrates to punish such persons as are legally convicted, he prohibits them, with a very humane inconsistency, from making any inquiries concerning the supposed criminals. Nor was the magistrate allowed to proceed on every kind of information. Anonymous charges the emperor rejects, as too repugnant to the equity of his government; and he strictly requires, for the conviction of those to whom the guilt of Christianity is imputed, the positive evidence of a fair and open accuser. It is likewise probable that the persons who assumed so invidious an office were obliged to declare the grounds of their suspicions, to specify (both in respect to time and place) the secret assemblies which their Christian adversary had frequented, and to disclose a great number of circumstances which were concealed with the most vigilant jealousy from the eye of the profane. If they succeeded in their prosecution, they were exposed to the resentment of a considerable and active party, to the censure of the more liberal portion of mankind, and to the ignominy which, in every age and country, has attended the character of an informer. If, on the contrary, they failed in their proofs, they incurred the severe and perhaps capital penalty, which, according to a law published by the emperor Hadrian, was inflicted on those who falsely attributed to their fellow-citizens the crime of Christianity. The violence of personal or superstitious animosity might sometimes prevail over the most natural apprehensions of disgrace and danger; but it cannot surely be imagined that accusations of so unpromising an appearance were either lightly or frequently undertaken by the Pagan subjects of the Roman empire.

The expedient which was employed to elude the prudence of the laws affords a sufficient proof how effectually they disappointed the mischievous designs of private malice or superstitious zeal. In a large and tumultuous assembly the restraints of fear and shame, so forcibly on the minds of individuals, are deprived of the greatest part of their influence. The pious Christian, as he was desirous to obtain, or to escape, the glory of martyrdom, expected, either with impatience or with terror, the stated returns of the public games and festivals. On those occasions the inhabitants of the great cities of the empire were collected in the circus or the theatre, where every circumstance of the place, as well as of the ceremony, contributed to kindle their devotion and to extinguish their humanity. Whilst the numerous spectators, crowned with garlands, perfumed with incense, purified with the blood of victims, and surrounded with the altars and statues of their tutelar deities, resigned themselves to the enjoyment of pleasures which they considered as an essential part of their religious worship, they recollected that the Christians alone abhorred the gods of mankind, and, by their absence and melancholy on these solemn festivals, seemed to insult or to lament the public felicity. If the empire had been afflicted by any recent calamity, by a plague, a famine, or an unsuccessful war; if the Tiber had, or if the Nile had not, risen beyond its banks; if the earth had shaken, or if the temperate order of the seasons had been interrupted, the superstitious Pagans were convinced that the crimes and the impiety of the Christians, who were spared by the excessive lenity of the government, had at length provoked the Divine justice. It was not among a licentious and exasperated populace that the forms of legal proceedings could be observed; it was not in an amphitheatre, stained with the blood of wild beasts and gladiators, that the voice of compassion could be heard. The impatient clamours of the multitude denounced the Christians as the enemies of gods and men, doomed them to the severest tortures, and, venturing to accuse by name some of the most distinguished of the new sectaries, required with irresistible vehemence that they should be instantly apprehended and cast to the lions. The provincial governors and magistrates who presided in the public spectacles were usually inclined to gratify the inclinations, and to appease the rage of the people, by the sacrifice of a few obnoxious victims. But the wisdom of the emperors protected the church from the danger of these tumultuous clamours and irregular accusations, which they justly censured as repugnant both to the firmness and to the equity of their administration. The edicts of Hadrian and of Antoninus Pius expressly declared that the voice of the multitude should never be admitted as legal evidence to convict or to punish those unfortunate persons who had embraced the enthusiasm of the Christians.

Punishment was not the inevitable consequence of conviction, and the Christians whose guilt was the most clearly proved by the testimony of witnesses, or even by their voluntary confession, still retained in their own power the alternative of life or death. It was not so much the past offence, as the actual resistance, which excited the indignation of the magistrate. He was persuaded that he offered them an easy pardon, since, if they consented to cast a few grains of incense upon the altar, they were dismissed from the tribunal in safety and with applause. It was esteemed the duty of a humane judge to endeavour to reclaim, rather than to punish, those deluded enthusiasts. Varying his tone according to age, the sex, or the situation of the prisoners, he frequently condescended to set before their eyes every circumstance which could render life more pleasing, or death more terrible; and to solicit, nay to entreat them, that they would show some compassion to themselves, to their families, and to their friends. If threats and persuasions proved ineffectual, he had often recourse to violence; the scourge and the rack were called in to supply the deficiency of argument, and every art of cruelty was employed to subdue such inflexible, and, as it appeared to the Pagans, such criminal obstinacy. The ancient apologists of Christianity have censured, with equal truth and severity, the irregular conduct of their persecutors, who, contrary to every principle of judicial proceeding, admitted the use of torture, in order to obtain, not a confession, but a denial, of the crime which was the object of their inquiry. The monks of succeeding ages, who, in their peaceful solitudes, entertained themselves with diversifying the deaths and sufferings of the primitive martyrs, have frequently invented torments of a much more refined and ingenious nature. In particular, it has pleased them to suppose that the zeal of the Roman magistrates, disdaining every consideration of

moral virtue or public decency, endeavoured to seduce those whom
they were unable to vanquish, and that by their orders the most brutal
violence was offered to those whom they found it impossible to seduce.
It is related that pious females, who were prepared to despise death,
were sometimes condemned to a more severe trial, and called upon to
determine whether they set a higher value on their religion or on their
chastity. The youths to whose licentious embraces they were abandoned
received a solemn exhortation from the judge to exert their most stren-
uous efforts to maintain the honour of Venus against the impious virgin
who refused to burn incense on her altars. Their violence, however, was
commonly disappointed, and the seasonable interposition of some miraculous power preserved the chaste spouses of Christ from the dishonour
even of an involuntary defeat. We should not indeed neglect to remark
that the more ancient as well as authentic memorials of the church are
seldom polluted with these extravagant and indecent fictions.*

The total disregard of truth and probability in the representation
of these primitive martyrdoms was occasioned by a very natural mistake. The ecclesiastical writers of the fourth or fifth centuries ascribed
to the magistrates of Rome the same degree of implacable and unrelenting zeal which filled their own breasts against the heretics or the idol-
aters of their own times. It is not improbable that some of those persons
who were raised to the dignities of the empire might have imbibed the
prejudices of the populace, and that the cruel disposition of others
might occasionally be stimulated by motives of avarice or of personal
resentment. But it is certain, and we may appeal to the grateful confessions of the first Christians, that the greatest part of those magistrates
who exercised in the provinces the authority of the emperor or of the
senate, and to whose hands alone the jurisdiction of life and death was
intrusted, behaved like men of polished manners and liberal educations,
who respected the rules of justice, and who were conversant with the
precepts of philosophy. They frequently declined the odious task of
persecution, dismissed the charge with contempt, or suggested to the
accused Christian some legal evasion by which he might elude the
severity of the laws. Whenever they were invested with a discretionary

---

* Jerome, in his Legend of Paul the Hermit, tells a strange story of a young man
who was chained naked on a bed of flowers, and assaulted by a beautiful and
wanton courtezan. He quelled the rising temptation by biting off his tongue.
[Author's note.]

power, they used it much less for the oppression than for the relief and benefit of the afflicted church. . . .

The learned Origen,[18] who, from his experience as well as reading, was intimately acquainted with the history of the Christians, declares, in the most express terms, that the number of martyrs was very inconsiderable. His authority would alone be sufficient to annihilate that formidable army of martyrs, whose relics, drawn for the most part from the catacombs of Rome, have replenished so many churches, and whose marvellous achievements have been the subject of so many volumes of holy romance. But the general assertion of Origen may be explained and confirmed by the particular testimony of his friend Dionysius, who, in the immense city of Alexandria, and under the rigorous persecution of Decius,[19] reckons only ten men and seven women who suffered for the profession of the Christian name.

⌘ FOR DISCUSSION AND WRITING

1. Analyze the syntax of the first two sentences—long sentences that between them make up the whole first paragraph. Where, in each, is the main clause? Students in first-year writing courses often write long sentences, but sentences that are like a grandmother's rag bag, with everything stuffed at random in them—that is, sentences without *logical structure*. Why is it that we can speak of these first two sentences of Gibbon's as having "structure" or logical "organization"? What is the grammatical parallelism between the two sentences? How does that parallelism serve to connect two large, complex groupings of ideas? What does the syntactical organization say, here, for the writer's command of his thoughts?

2. Where does Gibbon state his subject for this chapter?

3. Why did first-century polytheists (one's neighbors, like the grocery clerk across the street) find incomprehensible the Christian notion of God? Why did learned people, those educated in philosophy, look upon the Christians as fanatics addicted to a vulgar superstition not worth intelli-

---

[18] Christian theologian of Alexandria (A.D. 185-254), whose attempt to work out a complete neo-Platonic philosophy from the Gospels caused violent controversy.

[19] Emperor from A.D. 249 to 251.

gent consideration? Why does Gibbon say that the conception of Christ
as a god who had taken human form might well have appealed to popular habits of religious thought? Why, according to this account, did the
mean birth of the Nazarene carpenter and the fact that he was an "obscure teacher . . . among a barbarous people" seem insulting and outrageous both to the Roman masses and to the intelligentsia?

4. If you have been brought up in a Jewish family with European traditions
   behind it, what familiar idea do you find in the story of the Christians'
   bloody sacrifice and eating of a child, accompanied by unspeakably
   obscene procedures? Or, if you know Chaucer, where do you find a somewhat similar story in Chaucer's *Canterbury Tales*, only told of a Christian
   child ritually sacrificed by the Jews? Recalling Collingwood's fourth pre-
   scription for history—that it "ministers to man's self-knowledge"—how
   would you say these parallels of racial and religious prejudice so minister? Where are there other such parallels, perhaps more extensive, that
   you can point out in this piece?

5. Why, through their identification with the Jews, were the Christians at
   first relatively well protected under Roman law and custom?

6. Looking now at Gibbon's use of historical "evidence" (and recalling that
   the historian's use of "evidence" was one of Collingwood's chief points
   about the modern historical sense), where does Gibbon refer to sources
   of information for the period? Where does he take some pains to evaluate his source or sources? Why is this necessary?

7. What was Tacitus' view of the early Christians?

8. Consider the following sentence:

   On the same spot a temple, which far surpasses the ancient glories of the
   Capitol, has been since erected by the Christian Pontiffs, who, deriving
   their claim of universal dominion from an humble fisherman of Galilee,
   have succeeded to the throne of the Caesars, given laws to the barbarian
   conquerors of Rome, and extended their spiritual jurisdiction from the
   coast of the Baltic to the shores of the Pacific Ocean.

   Place the sentence in the context of the chapter. What "temple" is meant?
   What "humble fisherman"? What is the irony? Where is the main clause?
   Is it in the active or passive voice? What is the subject of the subordinate
   clause? How many syntactical parallelisms are there in the sentence?

What has the grammatical structure of the sentence to do with its ironic effectiveness? How do the geographical references support the irony?

9. In an historian's work, documentary "evidence" is one thing and the historian's personal attitude—his *reflection* upon the evidence—is another. Gibbon is much too sophisticated, learned, shrewd, elegant in manner, and ironic in intelligence, to wear his personal attitude on his sleeve; but it is nevertheless definitely evident. Where, for instance, do you find his attitude reflected in his evaluation of the positions of Tacitus and Pliny? of the writings of the monks of immediately succeeding centuries? or in what one may infer from the *tone* of such statements as the following:

In particular, it has pleased them [the monks] to suppose that the zeal of the Roman magistrates, disdaining every consideration of moral virtue or public decency, endeavoured to seduce those whom they were unable to vanquish. . . . Their violence, however, was commonly disappointed, and the seasonable interposition of some miraculous power preserved the chaste spouses of Christ from the dishonour even of an involuntary defeat.

What does an historian's attitude have to do with history? If he did *not* have an attitude, what would history be?

10. Write a short paper using Toynbee's idea of "challenge and response" in relation to the early Christians and the Roman Empire, as you see that idea reflected in the chapter from Gibbon; or write a paper on the "human self-knowledge" reflected here, particularly in respect to religious prejudice, with illustrations from your own experience.

Eleanor Clark ✑ Hadrian's Villa

✑ American novelist, short-story writer, and essayist. Though Miss Clark writes in prose, it is with the subtle sensibility of a poet—finding metaphor and meaning in all appearances, searchingly curious and acutely aware, constantly renewing the marvel of the world through language. Her description of Hadrian's villa is, unfortunately, much abridged here, through considerations of space. ✑

IT is the saddest place in the world, gaunt as an old abandoned graveyard, only what is buried there is the Roman Empire. There was a good deal more of it after that — the "noble" Antonines[1] and the rule of the soldiers and so on, before Constantine packed up for Byzantium, but one feels this, wandering there, as the end, the delicate ghastly moment of the turn; there was never such a fling again, thought and the arts fell fast from then on and power slowly after them. Jack and Jill had lost their pail of water.

[1] Antoninus Pius reigned from Hadrian's death, in A.D. 138, to 161; he was followed by his adopted son, Marcus Aurelius, who reigned until 180. Constantine, who reigned from 306 to 337, changed the seat of the empire to Byzantium, renaming it Constantinople.

And one wonders if at that point anyone really knew it: did Hadrian, of all people? The decay of morals, waning *virtus*[2] were an old, old story by then and not too interesting; morals in fact were about to have a fine new heyday, glum, smug and bourgeois; nobility of that kind had not been so hard to retrieve, and the empire, just then after Trajan's death, was at its grandest. No new conquests were planned. The Jews were making trouble again, for the last time, but on the whole in his thousands of miles of travel in Roman territory Hadrian the elegant, the sophist, met with no great unpleasantness, unless he should have minded all the scraping before himself. He could indulge the building craze peacefully everywhere. Something else was at the turn; for one thing there had been no poet worth speaking of for a long time, but that was only part of the subtlety of doom, of something else — you catch your breath thinking of it, wandering through the tragic heaps of masonry that loom still so huge over the olive trees, presenting a razor's edge of history and a character more complex than any in Proust.

Complex: but perhaps not, after all, so "enigmatic." The word got stuck to him some time ago, perhaps mainly because he was not wicked, at least not in the gross way of the century before; but one knows the face only too well, statues of the emperor amounted to a plague in this case, and there is the villa; it is his memoir, no matter how wrongly its courts and rooms and gardens came to be labeled. The idea was that Hadrian had re-created there the spots that had most attracted him on his Eastern travels, and so some very unlikely names were pinned on the ruins and scholars sweated over resemblances. It is not important. The fantasy is clear enough anyway, and so are the scale and the location; and how much too familiar one is with the brainless, incredible beauty of young Antinous,[3] dead in the Nile, the new Apollo for this

---

[2] The word derives from the Latin *vir*, a man, and is used here in its ancient sense, meaning strength, valor, and other characteristic manly excellencies (compare the word "virile").

[3] Shepherd boy whom Hadrian discovered in Bithynia (now part of Turkey) when Antinous was twelve or thirteen, and who accompanied the emperor on his journeys until he was drowned in the Nile at the age of nineteen or twenty. The accounts of his drowning are ambiguous, and there is a suggestion that it may have been suicide. Hadrian mourned him deeply, established the city of Antinopolis, in Egypt, in his name, ordered thousands of statues made of him and placed about the Roman Empire, had him officially deified and a cult organized about him.

time that one thinks of as a *fin-de-siècle*[4] of giants, a tremendous mauve convulsion that afterwards was immediately hushed up and patched up as if nothing had happened. He is the other character among the ruins, poignant enough, but not heartbreaking; grandeur is missing in that story. . . .

It took years to build, naturally, and Hadrian was not even there very much until nearly the end of his life, when his only desire was to die. He is supposed to have started it soon after the beginning of his reign in 117 and to have gone on until his death, but most of those twenty-one years he was traveling, seeking "into all curiosities" as somebody put it at the time, also looking after the empire. He was a public servant, trained under Trajan; he knew his duties; he had been a soldier and governor of a province. But something else was always driving him, not westward as people are driven in different times toward freshness and new lands, though he did his stint in Gaul and Germany, but east to the old and defeated ones, to art and symbols and the oldest mysteries; everything else was too easy, and in any case the thing was to keep moving, keep inquiring, otherwise every day would be a new boredom and life intolerable. Virtue and vice had stopped meaning anything, the oracles had gone dumb, the gods were part of the game to be played, he being one of them and for most purposes the chief one; he outdid all his predecessors in that, nobody had ever been worshiped in so many places, and he was not averse to it, which was perhaps another reason for going east: they did that sort of thing so well there. But worship does not fill up a crack in the soul.

So he came back to Rome now and then and would be off again before long, like a butterfly, really like a cargo of elephants, with all the world whispering about it every time. But it was not for him to feel weighted down by the thought of his baggage, or the thousand or ten thousand men who might be carrying it and making the arrangements. In that respect he was as free as a hobo, and could devote himself, among other things, to the serious profession of architecture. That was his passion, his true work, and it must have made up very often for the terrible absence, though not in the beginning, of love. One imagines him working late over the plans, furious at interruption, missing his meals like someone in a garret. Unfortunately Nero only fifty years before had done the same, to practice on his lyre, and had had the same

[4] End of an era.

appetite for the East, especially Greece but the rest of it too, where he had been adulated just as if he had not been a monster. But the times were not so simple now. Greece was everyone's Paris, that was inevitable, but Hadrian would never steal from it; the statues he could not buy he would have copied, there were plenty of artists for that, and he would make Greece more beautiful than ever. That was the compact: he, god, and Rome his instrument would glorify the spirit, which is beyond nationality.

The spirit was a little too subtle. The truth was the water was running out of the pail, there was not much time; pretty soon nobody would know how to do anything but copy. Meantime, however, the fine new temples were being strewn over Greece and Asia Minor, many dedicated to the emperor, and cities which he had beautified were being named for him all over the place. He flitted, with a sure hand however, with all his baggage trains from one place and project to another; it was Olympus on the move, shrewd and mobile as a newspaperman, subject to fits of melancholy. His taste ran to the ornate, and his sense of scale, rather naturally, was bizarre, though not peculiar to him: bigness was in the air and was expected of him. Even so, his temple of Venus and Rome over the Forum was really overbearing, and it seems the great architect Apollodorus fell out of favor for caviling at Hadrian's designs for it, one of his objections being that if the gods stood up they would lift the roof off. Another important project was his tomb, across the Tiber from the tomb of Augustus and more splendid, to be decked with statues like a Christmas tree. But the great toy, or piece of autobiography, the true private and desperate expression of the man, was in Tivoli.[5] It is there among the brambles that you get the only real glimpse of him, standing between the glory and the dark, like a colossal Des Esseintes[6] studding the back of some impossible tortoise, to be defeated in the end by what he must have hated most: smug virtue, and common sense. . . .

The whole sense of the place is individual, violently so; it is the expression of a single artist, straining away from the standard so far that with the least slip of taste it could fall into freakishness or vulgarity and that achieves greatness instead: a tour de force, certainly, like a

5 Resort near Rome where Hadrian built his villa.
6 Character in Huysmans' novel, À Rebours (English title, Against the Grain), who cultivated and experimented with the most exotic sensuous pleasures.

Turner or Tiepolo[7] sky, but convincing, through sheer personal brilliance.

That is the passion in these ruins: a creative one; and the application is not so startling, not necessarily. Hadrian is one of the richest as well as brightest men in the empire, which is how he happens inevitably to be at the head of it, whatever else his cousin Trajan might really have preferred; and one of the most cultivated: he has been to the best schools, entertained the best philosophers and probably subsidized quite a stable of them. There is no need to imagine him skulking around his marble labyrinth. He is as busy as the President of the United States to begin with, the hundred-year rampage in the wake of Augustus being finally up; he has all sorts of things to see to besides architecture: codifying laws, building the first wall across barbarous Britain, like patroling the Arctic now, pulling in the empire on the east to a tenable line, pushing reforms for slaves and prisoners past a grudging if more or less powerless senate, stamping out Christians and so on; in short delivering the new golden age, and in his leisure time exemplifying it. It was never more proper to do so: for the head of the state to stroll in brilliant company through the most magnificent of country houses, concerning himself with love, cooking and the things of the mind, while beyond the fountain at the edge of the cypress grove a favorite peacock pecks for grub. The obligations of the ruler in this age are not simple, when half Italy is studded with villas and Herodes Atticus,[8] a private citizen, can build cities as splendid as Hadrian's. And he has other passions too, especially for hunting: he can work off his conflicts in that.

Nevertheless there is a sound in the place that leads you past the forms of art, and like a mosquito in your ear drowns out the visceral struggle of centuries that came forward for a moment in the big baths. It is a very modern sound: the scream of the *I*; the geometry of these vast courts is all a dialogue with self; they are not public at all but private as a dream and whatever company moves in them will also be a projection of the dreamer's mind. What is shared with Versailles and the palaces of the Czars, the lavishness and the arrogance of the dimen-

---

[7] Both Turner (nineteenth-century English painter) and Tiepolo (eighteenth-century Venetian painter) were virtuosos in creating subtle and dazzling effects of light.

[8] Wealthy Greek rhetorician and patron of learning who expended his fortune in adorning Athens and other cities.

sions, becomes something more insidious here, not the simple effrontery of despotism. The thrust is obsessive. The rooms high as Grand Central Station, the maze of half-lit halls and those others where slaves must have hurried with torches at high noon — containing without knowing it the end of all the emperor's culture and mystical experiments — the feminine niche in the liplike fold of a garden court, the honeycomb guardhouse and more secretive cliffside burrow of the Hundred Room-lets, the playing with planes, pure abstraction, lined as with fur with every voluptuary fantasy, the tiny tight theatrical center of it all, the im-possibility of an end: all are the innermost statement of a mind, a true Folly, just the opposite of innocent Versailles. And when you are this far into it it is not sad, nor even particularly ironic; it is what they call entertainment; you want to know what is hidden in the Maritime The-atre, so valuable that it has to be protected with a moat.

It is at least clear that you will not find simplicity. This is the house of a man who will always seem false, and most when he is not; whose anger is less offensive than his kindnesses; from whom the simplest good-ness comes out as the worst ambiguity. Between him and shrewd, good-hearted, ambitious Trajan, his guardian and predecessor, who liked the company of honest soldiers, it must have been a more ticklish business than anyone now knows; there will have been a moat there too, and a wretched effort to cross it going on perhaps for years, until the issue could only be decided on the basis of rank power, perhaps even the rankest or almost, everything short of murder, while on both sides the heart was still crying out for confidence. The pattern will be repeated many times, when it is not broken off sooner with plain hatred. This is Hadrian's curse, and he will build it into his villa, along with the shiny, shifting dream-world in which for a moment at a time the self finds it comfort and revenge, never imagining the portrait it will have left. It is a clear one, however. No man who was loved, or who was easy in the lack of love, could have built such a house; among the gods and temples strewn about the place there is one real invisible altar, and that is to romantic sexual love, which is a version of the glorified Self.

It is in the neighborhood of the libraries that you think of Antinous, because they are the only places that look like bedrooms. There is more to the story than that, even an extraordinary perception of the future, no more perverse than most at the time. It is an age of anxiety. What

will roll into the dominating force of centuries is popping up in all kinds
of clownish, incongruous forms like a boxful of Punch-and-Judys whack-
ing each other over the head, and the beautiful boy from Bithynia,
Hadrian's love, has his place among them. But what his statues announce
and glorify is sex, and less a fulfillment than a long languorous exacer-
bation, a voluptuous delay such as Tivoli had never heard of before.
A new kind of experience has come in: the romantic obsession, and
wrapped in a sensuality the very opposite of Roman; this sultry shepherd child could only have come from the East.

Look at him in the little Sala Rotonda, that wonderful room with
its niches and cupola and the great porphyry cup, so much in Hadrian's
spirit it might almost have been arranged to commemorate the love
affair; you even enter it at either door between pairs of objects from
the villa, the Egyptian telamones at one and herms of Tragedy and
Comedy at the other.[9] Antinous is there twice: in the bust whose gaze
ironically crosses Hadrian's past the chunky primitive bronze Hercules,
so strangely solid and out of place between them; and as the full-length
Bacchus by the door, with the old sexual symbol of the pine cone, turned
now to what unfertile suggestion, on his head. It is a good place to see
him. The beautiful mosaic floor too could as well have been Hadrian's;
this was the grandeur that was left, of architecture and objects; it is in
such rooms as this, and some twenty times bigger, and among such fur-
nishings, statues, gods and all, that the boy, probably only twelve or
thirteen years old in the beginning, leads his short domestic life with
the most powerful man in the world.

The rest of the setting is there too, sketched in in a few strokes
around the walls, the whole lurid story from five hundred years back,
with its slow merciless progressions of power and belief, the whole
dynamic tangle of causalities in which for a moment there occurs this
particular twist; and who would dare to assign responsibility among
them? The great Jove from Otricoli is there, the deep-bearded bull-like
bust, five hundred years old in Hadrian's time, shown in all the raging
fullness of his power as Michelangelo would have done it, with his hair
like the sides of a cavern and the middle of his forehead thrust out so
far with the power he has over the world it is nearly bursting; no sculptor was turning out anything like that any more; divinity has dribbled

---

[9] Telamones are male figures used, like caryatids, as supporting columns or pilasters.
A herm is an image set on a stone column.

away — you can see it in the room — among the emperors, everywhere, and the emperor himself is the chief loser. Who will now be father to him? Certainly not the people; he has been turned loose among the horrors of infinite possibility, everything depends on a mere trick of disposition. And there is the terrible strength of Roman women, the good and the wicked, beginning with frigid Juno:[10] no romance there, nothing at any rate for the anguished mind of these times to look to. It seems that this sad ponderous image of Antinous was what had to be created; it has the same dead weight of inevitability about it as Augustus; and he is undoubtedly handsome, even if the statues are not.

It is a lush Middle Eastern handsomeness, even rather gross, and more than anything, empty; you could take him for a young Armenian rug salesman, or for King David, and this is curious because the shape of the face is new, and unique; you would know it anywhere. It is rounder than any classic face though the nose and forehead line is still nearly straight, with more cheek space and the eyes farther apart, so that it is at the same time softer and more angular, more the face of a specific person, although idealized; only blank, as though the artist had not quite known what was expected of him. But this is corrected by the pose, more or less the same in all the statues, at least all that one is likely to see; there must have been thousands once. There is no confusion there. His head seems nearly too heavy to hold, not with the physical weight of the skull but the vague burden of languor, conveyed in a nuance; it is just that the old divine self-sufficiency is gone, the picture is of indeterminate sorrow and a life that has meaning only in sensual rapport. The face, crowned with the richest ringlets yet seen in art, bends just a little downwards as in the resignation of the captive, nostalgic for a happiness he is no longer fit for and can scarcely remember; playing Bacchus, he holds up his grapes, or flowers or thyrsus,[11] in a mood that could not be farther from Bacchanalian: deadly serious. The spring and tension of the perfect body have vanished; this one would change its pose only to sink, to fall, though in build it suggests great strength, more than any Apollo; it is broad-shouldered but passive as a plum, close to fat, with untrained muscles and a succulence of flesh at the breasts and armpits; no little sleeping hermaphrodite, but a power

[10] Consort of Jupiter, sharing with him the dominant state cult.

[11] Staff surmounted by a pine cone or by a bunch of vine leaves and grape clusters, attribute of Bacchus.

to be shown on a scale with Hercules, a subtle and murderous triumph of the female principle.

It is the natural thing; it was to be expected, especially taken together with another of the busts in the room, his perfect antithesis: all strength and what Protestants call character, enough to have pushed the empire through a delicate moment, yet securely, even massively feminine too. This is no poor brittle Sabina.[12] It is Plotina, Trajan's wife and Hadrian's adoptive mother, the one person who can perhaps have given him, and for many years, the sober intimate sanction he needs, and he does need it. He is not a person who can easily stand alone, though in fact he does more and more; he would wish for the security of general love if that were possible, but it is not, except from people too simple or silly to see into him at all and with them he is at his most gracious. The rest he alienates when he needs them most; he exposes himself on all sides, he who cannot stand it on any: that is not his kind of courage. This powerful woman is his natural counterpart too, and it is only after her death that he has his revenge for the lifelong devotion; it could have been told beforehand.

You could tell it even from the official face, bearded but so unfatherly and not handsome at all, which could so easily have lent itself to caricature; and in fact the whole story was probably better drawn in the back alleys of Rome than in all the solemn nudes, as Mars or Jupiter, and the portrait busts that must have had all the sculptors in the empire working like script writers. The face asks for it, aside from anything else. Everything in it is a little exaggerated, including the conflicts and irritability; the look too of having a marvelous gamut of expressions if they could only be seen, though you would never guess the great charm of the man — it must have been one of the main points, it would all have been so much simpler without that — from these features. The eyes are much too narrow set, and have something a bit weaselish about them that jars with the noble, over-protuberant nose; the hair is combed down nearly to the eyebrows across a low forehead as though in a chronic urge to concealment but perhaps really more out of vanity, not to leave too exposed the long bellying ill-proportioned cheeks, which are not cushy like the boy's but more rankly sensuous, swollen and stuffed-looking; and in his expression too there is something of the captive, but only of his own mind. His preoccupation seems

12 Wife of Nero.

real, not the kind so shrewdly wrapped around the tricky, neurotic
features of Augustus; this is Hadrian himself, but the preoccupation is
not quite pure, though it creates threats as chimerical and aggravations
as real as if it were; and his majesty, which seems also entirely native, is
more of the man of wealth than of the thinker. Yet he thinks, continually;
that could have been made to look very funny too.

Especially as his vice is mental, not the mere physical indulgence
so easily tolerated among the Romans and by now such a worn-out
theme as connected with emperors. It is the mental trappings, the lack
of promiscuity in this case that will offend; the romantic agony is having
its first tryout; the individual soul is asserting itself in strange and dangerous fashion, in fact in a way that seems to make even power secondary, a most un-Roman business, particularly as so entwined with the
highest and rightest national aspirations. . . .

You have come to the Maritime Theatre, the jewel-like heart of
the villa and one of Hadrian's loveliest works, so drab now you could
walk through without thinking about it; six columns of the colonnade
around the moat are left, half of them minus their capitals, and a couple
of others and three clumps of masonry on the island. Probably it was
built much earlier, but it is now that you can understand it; it goes with
the image of Antinous, it comes from the same need. Ordinary love
does not build so tensely, it needs no protection, it can set up its cerebral
center like a tent anywhere; but then the whole drive and character of
the house, all the luxury and torment of it, come into their own at this
time. The ego that everything combined to swell and sicken has now
at one blow been nearly severed from the real world, which more and
more becomes only an intrusion and a threat; true communication is
with an image made flawless by death; the playboy side of the man has
come into its grandest justification, among the mysteries of afterlife.

The artist keeps up with it; the wonderful private poem goes on
growing, in marble and water and gold, but tight at the center of it
remains this little moat-bound shrine, one of the most splendid toys in
architecture, linked in all its substance to that sacrifice in the Nile.
The temple of Venus and Rome above the Roman Forum could have
existed without Antinous, but not this. But the colossal statue of him
as an Egyptian god would not have been here, there is no room for it,
and it is not necessary; perhaps it is in the apse of the structure called

the Vestibule, below the baths, or more likely among the fancier trappings and richer waterfalls of Canopus, to be approached by boat down the canal: it is that kind of game, as if nobody were looking, and the little round marble island far away in the palace is part of it. Hadrian is playing Robinson Crusoe, as everyone does in childhood and longs to do forever after; the island is the oldest, most necessary image, older than the Dying God;[13] that is the true romantic impossible, to be separated from the rubs and nudges and impurities of society by the primordial, deathly medium of water; the perfect assertion of self and the regions of the dead are alike surrounded by water. Of course it is a game; in reality Crusoe goes crazy; but the poetry is true, and the form in this case charming.

The touch has been kept light. The whole affair is in a tub: a high circular wall and portico held up by forty columns of Ionic order; then the moat, crossed by two playful wooden bridges that swing open or shut along a semicircle — every intelligent child's desire; and within, unassailable as a foot-high fortress in the sand, the tiny elegant palace, complete, at least for the purposes of the game, with the design of some diminutive four-petaled flower. It has nine more or less open roomlets, one a little bathing place, all scarcely big enough for an adult chaise longue; and an exquisite atrium,[14] decorated with marine figures in marble, the four sides curving inward, in a graceful scalloping edged with small columns, toward the centerpiece. That is not Antinous; it seems not to have been a statue at all, though there were surely some around in the niches; it is just a fountain. The whole beautiful fantasy, set like the soul's treasure at the center of acres of methodical flamboyance, brings you to nothing but that. A real toy; just a marble gazebo.

Archaeologists a long time ago hit on the idea, and have stuck to it, that this is where Hadrian came to "be alone"; they like the thought of him swinging the bridges to behind him and welcoming the muses, that is concerning himself somehow or other with music, painting and so on, while affairs of state wait across the moat. It won't do; he is not that kind

[13] The "primordial image" of the youthful god (like Osiris, Adonis, Attis, Tammuz), who suffers a violent death and is reborn. See Frazer's *Myth and Ritual of Adonis* later in this book.

[14] The atrium was the principal room in a Roman house. A gazebo (see end of paragraph) is a fanciful piece of architecture built rather for the amusement of the eyes than for any practical purpose.

of charlatan. It is more likely that he comes there to cut himself off from women if anything, there is that feeling about it, but that too is only part of the essential poetry of the place, in which it is hard enough to imagine anyone listening to the victrola, let alone drawing up plans for a temple. It is in the middle of everything, utterly exposed, in spite of the wall, and Italians were never quiet; it could hardly give him much peace to station guards at the entrance to shoo off the guests and servants, he is far too irritable not to notice, he registers everything, and not like Julius Caesar; besides, there are the threats, more and more, to be listened for. But the place in any case is too theatrical; its seriousness is only as a poem; in real life, since he is not actually mad, far from it, the first thing he will do is what anyone else does on an island, that is to ask someone over, even if he is not very fond of them. He will have his after-dinner coffee there, an apéritif perhaps, with an acquaintance or two, among a few favorite objects; he can treat it lightly, and must if he is to be there at all; it is not adapted to anything else. For work there will be the neutral place, nothing that involves the eye or spirit, and a serious, not this fake isolation.

What is not fake is the expression; the need is real; one symbol of purity, one fountain indistinguishable to the public eye from a thousand others must be conceived of as unapproachable, beyond the touch of the commonplace. Certainly the gesture is theatrical too: to have literally built the island, actually played out the game; but what in the villa is not? This staginess is of his deepest nature, the very stuff of his genius. Everything in him, the grand and the tawdry, the terror and the boredom, requires to be turned into a visible object; if he does not express his perceptions in architecture they will grow to madness, and the deepest and most private will be the most urgent; he has to build himself a plain of philosophy, a valley of the dead guarded by a stone Cerberus; if he is not on a stage he is nothing, he will lose all belief in himself.

But on this little stage, this island, he invokes his purest part. It is the other side of the shameless public bombast that goes on around the dead Antinous, by his orders and with his inspiration. It is not enough for him to glorify his private experience to himself, the whole world has to be brought into it. The resources of the empire must be lent to the apotheosis of his love. Slaves sweat, ships scurry about the seas getting stone for it, the priests have to be dealt with, threatened if necessary, the public initiated; the shrines pop up in a dozen countries; the city of

Antinopolis appears on the Nile, whose inhabitants will be scurrilously linked forever with those of the cities named for Hadrian; the statues for which gods are stripped of their symbols right and left roll out of the workshops by hundreds. You would think it would sicken him to have thrust at him from everywhere, wrapped in every atrocious hypocrisy, the face that he had known in ecstasy and sleep, to whose risky eyes he had entrusted all that is most secret and true in himself. No; he demands it. The world is his stage too, and on it through any loathsome obsequiousness, to be valued by volume, he is paying his most sacred debt, more sacred because of his guilt; such a man is always guilty toward those he loves, even if he has not killed them, it is the same; and so he calls for more and still more of the cringing adulation, refused only by Rome; he exposes himself more recklessly.

Especially after his last return; that is when the real outrage comes. But first he manages to linger on in the East for four more years, probably having one of his best creative periods as artists generally do after the tragic end of an impossible love affair; there is as much relief as grief, the dead and idealized love really suits him better than the rather embarrassing live one, and that will be part of the guilt too. He is perhaps in Athens, his true home, which he continues to beautify as though imperial handouts could restore the living spirit; it is Athens that he has wanted to give to the world, it will be the place for him now in his cruel detachment. There is the Jewish war now too, a nasty business, perhaps more than necessary; and why not: that single jealous god[15] could never have been so repugnant to him as at this moment. But the real enemy is waiting for him at home, and is deadly; it is virtue; a horrible pedantry of virtue, always the Roman forte, is slowly closing in on the creative imagination of the world. You will see it soon in Marcus Aurelius:[16] the fear of passion, the hatred of art, the scorn of life itself, that other, more hateful egotism of self-congratulation dressed as humility; and against that, Hadrian when he finally returns makes his last heroic, ridiculous gesture in defense of a world that is already in smithereens. There is perhaps some mysterious personal loyalty in it too, which would be like him, but it would not be only that. He appoints the worst of all the possible candidates, his friend Lucius Verus, as his successor; the perfect playboy, rich, dissipated and astonishingly beautiful

15 The God of the Jews.
16 See Note 1.

it seems — almost to be deified for nothing but that — an expert in sensuality, poetaster and inventor of a certain meat pie, probably a good talker; nothing else. It is not certain he was not the emperor's illegitimate son; he was at any rate all that his bright nervous world — of joy, of wanderlust, of the mind's daring — could offer by way of an heir.

It is Hadrian's last great insult to Rome, the final alienation of all those right-minded men he has never really been able to do without; and Plotina[17] is not by him now. That is when the madness sets in. He becomes a murderer. Not for the first time: he had always had his suspicions, his spies, had been too quick to look over his shoulder, though he had sometimes exaggerated in forgiveness too, but now it is different. He strikes out among his relatives, friends, anywhere, until nobody is safe near him, nobody is left who ever assumed a relation with him; if he refrains from poisoning his wife he will be accused of it anyway, it almost seems that she manages to die just then so that he will be. It is as though an ancient nightmare, a poetry of horror established long ago, waiting to spring forth in every scene and circumstance of his position, had finally found the crack in him to flood through and become reality, and he had no choice but to be its agent. Nero and his crazy Golden House are very close; there had perhaps not been so much difference after all. The real world is very dim. . . .

The land rises in one last green sweep south of the tower, the part farthest away from the entrance and the parking lot and the overtrodden cypress alleys, before sheering away to its precipitous end, that almost seems to curve in under you like the stern of some huge silent ship riding at anchor in a green cove. It is the Little Palace, not often visited and never owned by the state, so that it has a different quality from the rest, more what it all was for Count Fede.[18] You go back from Roccabruna or scramble up behind the Serapeum, through mud and nettles and barbed wire, and find yourself after a while in a court probably as rich and glittering once as most of the big palace, but so tangled and shady and still now, it is as though somewhere among the olives you had crossed a line beyond which the tremendous tensions of the villa have no more hold; they have snapped away from you, and you have moved on in a sudden lightness and peace to another kind of place. The ruins

17 Trajan's wife, Hadrian's adoptive mother.
18 Italian owner of the estate.

do not stick out here; a single dead pine towering over the grove, a shiny skeleton without a green twig or a stitch of bark left, that ought to have toppled years ago, has far more rage and drama. They have given in; their geometry is dominated by trees and innumerable birds, thrushes and all kinds of little field ones and nightingales, and over your head the roots of other trees push clutching and fearfully exposed, like the minds of sleepwalkers, down the ancient walls.

They are most beautiful in this state,[19] with all their insistence gone and their secrets taken back into the larger course of things; the sick screaming *I* was transcended ages ago, leaving only a suggestion as spacious as the rest but gentler — a charity of time, beyond tragedy, and beyond respect. They do not ask even for that, and though there must be a little or they will disappear, it is the violations of them, as in Rome, that are most moving: a tremendous speckled pig wallowing in a stubby relic of one of Hadrian's buildings, off by itself in the sun-speckled orchard beyond the farm that is a little farther on; the farm itself, more charmed and still-looking than the ones on the other edges of the land, being so far away and without any visible road leading to it; and in this first court, the most entranced of all, a high pointed tower of a thousand and some years later, already in the groaning stage, its wooden stairs inside too rotten to risk: it rests on, or seems more to have grown up in an inevitable, vegetable way from the three tall arches of the end building of the ancient court, but the splicing point has gone dim and the two epochs have become one substance, as if the thousand-year misery between were nothing at all.

It is misleading, though not entirely. Hadrian comes closest of all here if you let him; from beneath the thick protective bangs, sticky now with fever, the narrow eyes look out at you with a sick hatred that in a moment will have turned to some sharp gay disposal of life and his own state, some Parisian quip, before the dull intolerable load, which must still be tolerated, settles back on him again; the big muscular lips move as in a separate delirium of their own, like a mouth floating on the ocean, remembering their own sensuality. Everything is finished; virtue has won, he has bowed to it; now there is nothing but pain and more horror, until he manages to die, which will not be in Tivoli or Rome either; naturally; a haven or point of rest is what he could not bear, and he

[19] The ruins of the Little Palace.

happens to be in Baia[20] at that moment, the Bar Harbor of the time but richer and more insidious — he could get at least that far — where he dies in a last agony of silence, living out his curse to the end, in the arms of that noble stranger, his heir.

Virtue, or call it the genius of Rome, which was his own too; the enemy could not really strike except from within himself; and in the end there was nothing to believe in but that: the greatness of Rome. He has acknowledged it, has risen at the last to an act of simple moral splendor — one imagines it done with a sigh of exhaustion, but this is also when one sees him for a moment as most tremendous, not with all the baggage and scintillation of his state and the tonnage of his temples, but stripped to the moral bone: a lucid melancholy figure standing tall as Paul Bunyan against these mountains and against his century, with at his back the derelict shreds of the world that he has loved with such passionate extravagance, and that still shoots off its most brilliant rays behind his head, and far off under his gaze the dull seething movement of the barbarians. Or not so far; it all happens terribly fast; but he has delayed it, providing the empire with not one but two generations of everything that his deepest nature rejects: altogether some forty more years of commendable not to say unheard-of decency, dignity and security before the thugs and the military take over, and perhaps there were some who thought it would be four hundred, or eternity. And for this great gift to Rome,[21] which is also an act of self-condemnation, he will be more suspect than he had been as a murderer; he is surely used to it by now.

It can all be slurred over a little; there are ties, which perfect the irony. They go through the same forms, he and these Eskimos, these noble Stoics;[22] they meet at parties, invest in the same businesses, have the same views of statecraft and the same kind of country houses gen-

20 On the Bay of Naples, ancient bathing and boating resort. The reference that follows, to "that noble stranger," is to Antoninus Pius, Hadrian's successor.

21 His choice of the Antonines as his successors. See Note 1.

22 Antoninus and Marcus Aurelius were of the Stoic school of philosophy, founded by Zeno, about 308 B.C., in Athens. The Stoics were pessimists in that they believed that all reality is material and that the soul suffers dissolution with the body, but this belief gave nobility to their moral thought, for they held that man should submit intelligently to natural law and that his freedom lay in control of his passions, constant discipline over the senses and the emotions. One can see, taking Hadrian's point of view, why "these noble Stoics" would seem as alien as Eskimos.

erally speaking, it is a gentleman's world and they are the gentlemen; and Antoninus will be as great in loyalty as in wisdom. He, a man so unworldly he hadn't even wanted the job — you can tell the species from that; who in a reign longer than Hadrian's will not once travel farther from Rome than to his nearby country estate, will use all his power afterwards to rehabilitate the hated name of Hadrian, and will build to him the temple that is now the Stock Exchange and the tenderest monument in Rome. The Castel Sant'Angelo was only one of Hadrian's splashiest tributes to himself; the temple is one of the world's enduring tokens of respect, or it could be of love, from one species of man to another, raised over a bottomless hollow of non-communication.

There are ties with his further choice too, young Marcus Aurelius, intense and willowy at the time and probably with a certain adolescent leaning to the abstruse which he will outgrow shortly: his patrician mother had made part of her fortune selling bricks for the emperor's villa, and for his building in general. But this youth who also professes loyalty is a different kettle of fish from Antoninus; many hundreds of years later he turns up as the white-haired boy of a self-interested bourgeoisie very like the one that Hadrian despised, and every worthy maxim[23] he gets off will be a crack at his imperial grandfather; that great and various nature seems to taunt him so from the grave, he cannot leave any part of it unpilloried: boys, building, art. Yet there were statues of him in the villa, the count and the others found them, and so one imagines him stopping off now and then at the crazy old place, in the triumph of his survival and the safety of an unimpeachable character: uncomfortable, out of place, jealous as a Protestant minister, and with a worm of ecstasy in his heart from the contact with what he condemns. Still, he was a good ruler as opposed to a wicked one, very good indeed; Hadrian had chosen well.

There were other posthumous items too, before the Vandals came through; the place was not quite uninhabited. There are touches of restoration from later in that century and the next, and it can happen, though this is the rarest thing, that in one of the fields near the palace you will pick up a little fragment of pottery from a still later time, left by some caretaker or squatter on the land, or perhaps the retinue of the captive Queen Zenobia. Some of the soldier-emperors will no doubt have

[23] Referring to the *Meditations* of Marcus Aurelius.

used parts of it for a week-end camp — there was every facility for keeping fit, after all, and those who felt like it could amuse themselves in the evening knocking the noses off the statues. But really it had ceased to exist long before, and before Hadrian's death; he himself had condemned it. It had been many things, many kinds of expression noble and ignoble, but it was always, along with the rest, his private work of homage to a civilization founded, as on a rock, on the knowledge of the world's beauty and delight, and it ends, as if he had ordered its literal destruction, at that great moment of his defeat. There are no theatrics in that; he rises for once in all simplicity, and for that one last second you can see the whole villa strewn twinkling and absurd around his ankles, already old hat, the sense of it simply gone; then the nightmare closes over him again and he sinks back to wait to die.

Not patiently, he is still in character, irascible, scathing, spoiled; he longs for death with the same passionate appetite he has had for everything else, only he cannot bribe anyone to kill him and is evidently too weak or not quite willing to do it himself; there is a touch of the old game again in this, his passions have always bred their own negations. So he lingers on with his horrid disease, dropsy, in such suffering it will become a legend for generations and is thought to give him powers more miraculous than any he has as emperor; the physical pain alone is punishment enough, but the rest is worse — for him there can be no resolution — and it is just here on this last gentle hill that one imagines him then. It is the natural retreat, or seems so; the main palace will be too ironic now, though he is still adding patches here and there, and really this far place is neither so different nor separate from the rest; the torment if anything is only clearer. The most monstrous of his crypto-porticoes, the one called a little too literally his Underworld or Inferi,[24] is here, and the biggest of the theatres; none of it could stop; he spins down through the crack in the split world, in all his agony, with the whole show still raging.

There is a strong touch of comedy in it, of course. Those once famous Inferi, out in the big field beyond the farm, are as stagy as anything else in the place, and in fact seem to have been connected underground with the theatre; the thing is a splurge of gloom in the Max

[24] A portico is a covered passage or walking-place (like a cloister), usually open and colonnaded on one side; a crypto-portico would be secret or hidden; Inferi are the regions of the dead.

Reinhardt[25] manner, and could hardly have been made more serious by having a Cerberus[26] at the entrance, if it did; very likely it was a place for the emperor's well-dressed audiences to stroll in bad or hot weather, though it looks more like something made by some huge prehistoric mole. In any case the staging is brilliant, is and no doubt was; nothing else could be so shocking after the grace and restraint of the Academy, could so pitch you forth into still another emotional area, when it seemed no more was possible; it is the grandest effect of them all, the most violent and the funniest — and always missed. Nobody but an occasional archaeologist ever comes this far, and of those perhaps not more than one in two or three years; it is off the guidebook map, and if you do get there you are not sure to find it. The place is not even a hayfield; there are a few trees, scrub, a few figures of peasants near or far gathering brush: a proper setting for this hilariously macabre affair, so much more sophisticated than any niche or statue.

The wonder among others is that it is still not filled in, or not entirely; the round skylights are still open, and are marked, as you discover eventually, by the bushes growing out of them regularly all along like clumps of hairs from a nostril; the pines too follow the lines of the tunnel, which traces out an enormous trapezoid, so although you could hardly get in, or rather out, without a rope ladder, you can lie on your stomach among the bushes at various points and look down into a construction that brings you back not so much to the other underground passages in the place, however bizarre, as to the Golden Court. That is the scale; they are of the same stunning exorbitance, the dark and the brilliant making one entity; this is one man's alley, not the Saint Gothard,[27] though the effort must have been equivalent to a good piece of that. It is fifteen feet across and with its four sides nearly a mile long, cut deep out of bedrock, and for no practical purpose at all or none to warrant such an enormity. One of the smaller passageways leading off from it had opening on to it a series of small chambers taken to be wine cellars, but there could be no such reason for this, and besides it was decorated like a salon, with paintings and elaborate stuccos. It is a necessity of another kind, like the island, and as genuine: a fantasy of dread made literal and elegant, normal enough in the general poem of

25 Theatrical producer known for his spectacular effects.
26 The mythological three-headed dog who guarded the entrance to Hades.
27 Nine-mile tunnel through the Alps.

Rome but that shakes one nevertheless in this context, in spite of the comedy, like the sound of a splitting skull. Not that it was conceived of, it is what everyone conceives of: this too is one of the oldest images; but that it was built. It is the necessary complement to Antinous, the rest of the twin metaphor love and death, and the only other perfect denial of society. The bonds are broken; the individual soul lives with its own heaven and hell, staged in this case with all the impudence inherited from some of the world's leading criminals; which only gives it a greater charm of familiarity now. And this is the mind that has made its peace with the sober citizens; you can imagine it. . . .

Early or late, it is Hadrian, the part of him that one sees rising at the end through all the wreckage and pathos, a thin clear light, something like the upward jet of a single fountain, that somehow disengaged itself from the appalling mesh of pomp and personality, and hovers behind the grim jumble of the human mind a thousand years, waiting to be known again. Its sound is the simplest note of laughter; its spring you have seen; it was horror.

But that is not where you stop. From one corner of the field in which you trace out that mammoth tunnel, looking back toward the villa, you can see over to the mysterious little canal parallel to Canopus and ending in a grotto, which has been taken to be the main entrance to the Inferi though it is hard to see why. Whether it was or not, it stretches the fantasy out still farther. It is another shape, another meaning, so out of the way and suggestive and sad-looking as it lies there now, like a toy that has lain twenty years out in the rain, all the complex of feelings built up from the beginning suddenly resolves itself into a rush of sympathy — or call it love, for this imagination that could not repeat itself and that nothing could stop, and the whole wonderful joke of the place is there for you, as fresh and bright as if it had been scribbled across the fields that moment. You are in it, you understand it finally, and all you can express it with is a little echo of Hadrian's own laughter; which returns in a moment to silence. The joke was serious; and the great and sorrowful scene you glimpse briefly in the theatre — going back now toward the farm, and you must not be in a hurry — is of Hadrian the lover of the past, the playboy diver into every dread and flaunter of every glory, dividing, as he dies, with a successor he cannot speak to, a future they both despise. They contain each a part of it, he with his mysteries and his poet's anguish and Antoninus in the goodness of his heart, as much as any Christian martyr, and both are of such stature it seems the stage, though it has stood for two thousand years, will not be able to hold up under the spectacle, which all of Rome sits watching. But it is short, and very quiet. The body is carried off, to be hidden until the hatred of the Senate subsides, and the silent chorus and the other actors follow, leaving for a few seconds, until they are removed, those disembodied masks you saw before, with their refugees' eyes and their great open mouths that birds could nest in or that could be spigots for fountains. . . .

✑§ FOR DISCUSSION AND WRITING

1. This is an extremely original kind of writer, whose work tends to escape from under the ordinary classifications, except for that rag-bag, all-purpose genre of the "essay." What is *Hadrian's Villa?* Is it history? biography? architectural description? a scenic travelogue? Is its subject a man? a place? an epoch? a state of mind? Consider the first sentence: "It is the saddest place in the world, gaunt as an old abandoned graveyard, only what is buried there is the Roman Empire." Does this sentence contain Miss Clark's subject? and if so, what is it? Does it also contain an attitude toward the subject? and if so, what is the attitude? Where exactly does that attitude place us in time—in the past or in the present? Is there "irony" in this first sentence, in the sense of some kind of incongruity between what is said and the implications of what is said?

2. Whether or not you have read the preceding piece from Gibbon's *The Decline and Fall of the Roman Empire* (incidentally, could this have been an appropriate title for Miss Clark's piece?), make a comparison between Gibbon's first paragraph and the first paragraph here (the best way to start doing this is to copy both of them out—to give your fingers and elbow, as well as your eyes, an experience of the style). What conspicuous difference in syntactical construction do you find? in diction? Can you imagine Gibbon making an analogy between Hadrian's time and the nursery rhyme about Jack and Jill?

3. Turn back to R. G. Collingwood's "What Is History?" and reconsider his fourfold definition of history on page 461 (it doesn't matter whether or not you have read the whole piece—his points are clear enough). Which

parts of the definition apply to Miss Clark's work? What kind of "evidence" does she use? Is her "evidence" the usual documentary kind used by modern historians? Thinking of Collingwood's fourth point, as to what history is "for," that is, its value, do you feel that this piece has the value Collingwood speaks of—the value of teaching us "what man is" through what man has done, in a word, "self-knowledge"? Try writing a carefully considered paragraph on this question—and expand it into a theme assignment if it seems fruitful.

4. Let us look at some individual phrases and sentences, for the language of this piece is packed with suggestion and implication. For instance: "Something else was at the turn; for one thing there had been no poet worth speaking of for a long time, but that was only part of the subtlety of doom, of something else—you catch your breath thinking of it, wandering through the tragic heaps of masonry that loom still so huge over the olive trees, presenting a razor's edge of history and a character more complex than any in Proust." (You had better look first for the context of the sentence.) Why is it significant that "there had been no poet worth speaking of"? Where, in the sentence, are you yourself brought bodily into the scene, to share with quick immediacy the writer's experience of the place? By what phrases is history made *visible*? What is the meaning of the metaphor "a razor's edge of history"? Even if you know nothing about the complexity of Proust's characters, what telescoping of the past into the present is effected by the reference to Hadrian as "a character more complex than any in Proust"? Point out five other places where there is a similar kind of correspondence, either explicit or implicit, between Hadrian's personal problems and modern problems, or between Hadrian's age and our own. In what sense can you say that Hadrian, as presented here, is a symbolic character?

5. Now make the same kind of analysis of this: "Nevertheless there is a sound in the place that leads you past the forms of art, and like a mosquito in your ear drowns out the visceral struggle of centuries. . . . It is a very modern sound: the scream of the *I*; the geometry of these vast courts is all a dialogue with self; they are not public at all but private as a dream. . . ." What, in view of the whole subject, is the irony of the figure "like a mosquito in your ear"? What is the peculiar force and implication of the word "visceral," and how does it interact with the mosquito buzz? What is meant by "the scream of the *I*"? and by the rest, "a dialogue with self," "private as a dream"? Does this kind of comment *belittle* Hadrian? Does

it make him less significant or more significant, less symbolic or more symbolic, to the modern reader?

6. Remembering Jack and Jill in the first paragraph, analyze some of these minor ironies in Miss Clark's style: "the gods were part of the game to be played, he being one of them and for most purposes the chief one"; "he was free as a hobo"; "Greece was everyone's Paris"; "fine new temples were being strewn over Greece"; "Olympus on the move, shrewd and mobile as a newspaperman"; "Another important project was his tomb, . . . to be decked with statues like a Christmas tree"; "he has all sorts of things to see to . . . stamping out Christians and so on; in short delivering the new golden age." Find and write down a half-dozen other instances of this kind, being ready to point out the nature of the irony.

7. You have seen here a whole history interpreted from a sculptured face and the ruins of a place. Compose a paper doing something of the same kind —studying a face or a place and interpreting the history behind it, what it means. (Since we are doing this all the time, every day, the writing assignment should be a natural.) Or look up Hadrian in the encyclopedia and write up whatever qualifications or differences or additions seem to you significant, between that account and Miss Clark's. Or take a try at the *Meditations* of Marcus Aurelius—a book very much worthwhile in itself —and see if you can find any of those "cracks at his imperial grandfather" which Miss Clark mentions.

Francis Parkman ✑ The Death of Pontiac

✑ American historian (1823-1893). Parkman came from a prominent Boston family, graduated from Harvard in 1844, and two years later—both to improve his frail health and to study frontier life—set out upon the Oregon Trail, which gave the title to one of his first books. Under the handicap of near-blindness (he had to hire others to read to him, and invented a special device that permitted him to write without looking at the manuscript), he produced a series of volumes on the French and English struggle for Colonial America, combining accuracy of scholarship with a keen sense of setting, drama, and human values that gives his work importance as literature.

Pontiac was a chief of the Ottawa Indians, who had settled on the shores of Lake Superior and Lake Michigan. He headed the great rebellion of Indian tribes against the British, attacking them at Detroit in 1764 and laying siege to the fort. The siege lasted for a year and was almost successful, but was baffled by British reinforcements. A treaty was signed in 1766. Pontiac was pardoned and went west, to be murdered by an Indian assassin hired by the English. The final irony is, perhaps, that he became the eponymous ancestor of the Pontiac car. ৡ

THE WINTER passed quietly away. Already the Indians began to feel the blessings of returning peace in the partial reopening of the fur-trade; and the famine and nakedness, the misery and death, which through the previous season had been rife in their encampments, were exchanged for comparative comfort and abundance. With many precautions, and in meagre allowances, the traders had been permitted to throw their goods into the Indian markets; and the starving hunters were no longer left, as many of them had been, to gain precarious sustenance by the bow, the arrow, and the lance, — the half-forgotten weapons of their fathers. Some troubles arose along the frontiers of Pennsylvania and Virginia. The reckless borderers, in contempt of common humanity and prudence, murdered several straggling Indians, and enraged others by abuse and insult; but these outrages could not obliterate the remem-

From *The Conspiracy of Pontiac* by Francis Parkman (first published in 1851).

brance of recent chastisement, and, for the present at least, the injured warriors forbore to draw down the fresh vengeance of their destroyers.

Spring returned, and Pontiac remembered the promise he had made to visit Sir William Johnson at Oswego. He left his encampment on the Maumee, accompanied by his chiefs, and by an Englishman named Crawford, a man of vigor and resolution, who had been appointed, by the superintendent, to the troublesome office of attending the Indian deputation, and supplying their wants.

We may well imagine with what bitterness of mood the defeated war-chief urged his canoe along the margin of Lake Erie, and gazed upon the horizon-bounded waters, and the lofty shores, green with primeval verdure. Little could he have dreamed, and little could the wisest of that day have imagined, that, within the space of a single human life, that lonely lake would be studded with the sails of commerce; that cities and villages would rise upon the ruins of the forest; and that the poor mementoes of his lost race — the wampum beads, the rusty tomahawk, and the arrowhead of stone, turned up by the ploughshare — would become the wonder of school-boys, and the prized relics of the antiquary's cabinet. Yet it needed no prophetic eye to foresee that, sooner or later, the doom must come. The star of his people's destiny was fading from the sky; and, to a mind like his, the black and withering future must have stood revealed in all its desolation.

The birchen flotilla gained the outlet of Lake Erie, and, shooting downwards with the stream, landed beneath the palisades of Fort Schlosser. The chiefs passed the portage, and, once more embarking, pushed out upon Lake Ontario. Soon their goal was reached, and the cannon boomed hollow salutation from the batteries of Oswego.

Here they found Sir William Johnson waiting to receive them, attended by the chief sachems of the Iroquois, whom he had invited to the spot, that their presence might give additional weight and solemnity to the meeting. As there was no building large enough to receive so numerous a concourse, a canopy of green boughs was erected to shade the assembly from the sun; and thither, on the twenty-third of July, repaired the chiefs and warriors of the several nations. Here stood the tall figure of Sir William Johnson, surrounded by civil and military officers, clerks, and interpreters; while before him reclined the painted sachems of the Iroquois, and the great Ottawa war-chief, with his dejected followers.

Johnson opened the meeting with the usual formalities, presenting his auditors with a belt of wampum[1] to wipe the tears from their eyes, with another to cover the bones of their relatives, another to open their ears that they might hear, and another to clear their throats that they might speak with ease. Then, amid solemn silence, Pontiac's great peace-pipe was lighted and passed round the assembly, each man present inhaling a whiff of the sacred smoke. These tedious forms, together with a few speeches of compliment, consumed the whole morning; for this savage people, on whose supposed simplicity poets and rhetoricians have lavished their praises, may challenge the world to outmatch their bigoted adherence to usage and ceremonial.

On the following day, the council began in earnest, and Sir William Johnson addressed Pontiac and his attendant chiefs: —

"Children, I bid you heartily welcome to this place; and I trust that the Great Spirit will permit us often to meet together in friendship, for I have now opened the door and cleared the road, that all nations may come hither from the sunsetting. This belt of wampum confirms my words.

"Children, it gave me much pleasure to find that you who are present behaved so well last year, and treated in so friendly a manner Mr. Croghan, one of my deputies; and that you expressed such concern for the bad behavior of those, who, in order to obstruct the good work of peace, assaulted and wounded him, and killed some of his party, both whites and Indians; a thing before unknown, and contrary to the laws and customs of all nations. This would have drawn down our strongest resentment upon those who were guilty of so heinous a crime, were it not for the great lenity and kindness of your English father, who does not delight in punishing those who repent sincerely of their faults.

"Children, I have now, with the approbation of General Gage (your father's chief warrior in this country), invited you here in order to confirm and strengthen your proceedings with Mr. Croghan last year. I hope that you will remember all that then passed, and I desire that you will often repeat it to your young people, and keep it fresh in your minds.

"Children, you begin already to see the fruits of peace, from the number of traders and plenty of goods at all the garrisoned posts; and our enjoying the peaceable possession of the Illinois will be found of

[1] Strip of hide heavily sewn with colored beads, used as ceremonial pledges and as money.

great advantage to the Indians in that country. You likewise see that proper officers, men of honor and probity, are appointed to reside at the posts, to prevent abuses in trade, to hear your complaints, and to lay before me such of them as they cannot redress. Interpreters are likewise sent for the assistance of each of them; and smiths are sent to the posts to repair your arms and implements. All this, which is attended with a great expense, is now done by the great King, your father, as a proof of his regard; so that, casting from you all jealousy and apprehension, you should now strive with each other who should show the most gratitude to this best of princes. I do now, therefore, confirm the assurances which I give you of his Majesty's good will, and do insist on your casting away all evil thoughts, and shutting your ears against all flying idle reports of bad people."

The rest of Johnson's speech was occupied in explaining to his hearers the new arrangements for the regulation of the fur-trade; in exhorting them to forbear from retaliating the injuries they might receive from reckless white men, who would meet with due punishment from their own countrymen; and in urging them to deliver up to justice those of their people who might be guilty of crimes against the English. "Children," he concluded, "I now, by this belt, turn your eyes to the sun-rising, where you will always find me your sincere friend. From me you will always hear what is true and good; and I charge you never more to listen to those evil birds, who come, with lying tongues, to lead you astray, and to make you break the solemn engagements which you have entered into, in presence of the Great Spirit, with the King your father and the English people. Be strong, then, and keep fast hold of the chain of friendship, that your children, following your example, may live happy and prosperous lives."

Pontiac made a brief reply, and promised to return on the morrow an answer in full. The meeting then broke up.

The council of the next day was opened by the Wyandot chief, Teata, in a short and formal address; at the conclusion of which Pontiac himself arose, and addressed the superintendent in words, of which the following is a translation: —

"Father, we thank the Great Spirit for giving us so fine a day to meet upon such great affairs. I speak in the name of all the nations to the westward, of whom I am the master. It is the will of the Great Spirit that we should meet here to-day; and before him I now take you by the hand. I call him to witness that I speak from my heart; for since I took Colonel Croghan by the hand last year, I have never let go my hold, for I see that the Great Spirit will have us friends.

"Father, when our great father of France was in this country, I held him fast by the hand. Now that he is gone, I take you, my English father, by the hand, in the name of all the nations, and promise to keep this covenant as long as I shall live."

Here he delivered a large belt of wampum.

"Father, when you address me, it is the same as if you addressed all the nations of the west. Father, this belt is to cover and strengthen our chain of friendship, and to show you that, if any nation shall lift the hatchet against our English brethren, we shall be the first to feel it and resent it."

Pontiac next took up in succession the various points touched upon in the speech of the superintendent, expressing in all things a full compliance with his wishes. The succeeding days of the conference were occupied with matters of detail relating chiefly to the fur-trade, all of which were adjusted to the apparent satisfaction of the Indians, who, on their part, made reiterated professions of friendship. Pontiac promised to recall the war-belts[2] which had been sent to the north and west, though, as he alleged, many of them had proceeded from the Senecas, and not from him; adding that, when all were gathered together, they would be more than a man could carry. The Iroquois sachems then addressed the western nations, exhorting them to stand true to their engagements, and hold fast the chain of friendship; and the councils closed on the thirty-first, with a bountiful distribution of presents to Pontiac and his followers.

Thus ended this memorable meeting, in which Pontiac sealed his submission to the English, and renounced forever the bold design by which he had trusted to avert or retard the ruin of his race. His hope of seeing the empire of France restored in America was scattered to the winds, and with it vanished every rational scheme of resistance to English encroachment. Nothing now remained but to stand an idle spectator, while, in the north and in the south, the tide of British power rolled westward in resistless might; while the fragments of the rival empire, which he would fain have set up as a barrier against the flood, lay scattered a miserable wreck; and while the remnant of his people melted away or

[2] Wampum belts of special symbolism sent (like letters) to alert other tribes to war.

fled for refuge to remoter deserts. For them the prospects of the future were as clear as they were calamitous. Destruction or civilization — between these lay their choice; and few who knew them could doubt which alternative they would embrace.

Pontiac, his canoe laden with the gifts of his enemy, steered homeward for the Maumee; and in this vicinity he spent the following winter, pitching his lodge in the forest with his wives and children, and hunting like an ordinary warrior. With the succeeding spring, 1767, fresh murmurings of discontent arose among the Indian tribes, from the lakes to the Potomac, the first precursors of the disorders which, a few years later, ripened into a brief but bloody war along the borders of Virginia. These threatening symptoms might easily be traced to their source. The incorrigible frontiersmen had again let loose their murdering propensities; and a multitude of squatters had built their cabins on Indian lands beyond the limits of Pennsylvania, adding insult to aggression, and sparing neither oaths, curses, nor any form of abuse and maltreatment against the rightful owners of the soil. The new regulations of the fur-trade could not prevent disorders among the reckless men engaged in it. This was particularly the case in the region of the Illinois, where the evil was aggravated by the renewed intrigues of the French, and especially of those who had fled from the English side of the Mississippi, and made their abode around the new settlement of St. Louis. It is difficult to say how far Pontiac was involved in this agitation. It is certain that some of the English traders regarded him with jealousy and fear, as prime mover of the whole, and eagerly watched an opportunity to destroy him.

The discontent among the tribes did not diminish with the lapse of time; yet for many months we can discern no trace of Pontiac. Records and traditions are silent concerning him. It is not until April, 1769, that he appears once more distinctly on the scene. At about that time he came to the Illinois, with what design does not appear, though his movements excited much uneasiness among the few English in that quarter. Soon after his arrival, he repaired to St. Louis, to visit his former acquaintance, Saint-Ange, who was then in command at that post, having offered his services to the Spaniards after the cession of Louisiana. After leaving the fort, Pontiac proceeded to the house of which young Pierre Chouteau was an inmate; and to the last days of his protracted life, the latter could vividly recall the circumstances of the interview. The savage chief was arrayed in the full uniform of a French officer, which had been presented to him as a special mark of respect and favor by the Marquis of Montcalm, towards the close of the French war, and which Pontiac never had the bad taste to wear, except on occasions when he wished to appear with unusual dignity. Saint-Ange, Chouteau, and the other principal inhabitants of the infant settlement, whom he visited in turn, all received him cordially, and did their best to entertain him and his attendant chiefs. He remained at St. Louis for two or three days, when, hearing that a large number of Indians were assembled at Cahokia, on the opposite side of the river, and that some drinking bout or other social gathering was in progress, he told Saint-Ange that he would cross over to see what was going forward. Saint-Ange tried to dissuade him, and urged the risk to which he would expose himself; but Pontiac persisted, boasting that he was a match for the English, and had no fear for his life. He entered a canoe with some of his followers, and Chouteau never saw him again.

He who, at the present day, crosses from the city of St. Louis to the opposite shore of the Mississippi, and passes southward through a forest festooned with grapevines, and fragrant with the scent of flowers, will soon emerge upon the ancient hamlet of Cahokia. To one fresh from the busy suburbs of the American city, the small French houses, scattered in picturesque disorder, the light-hearted, thriftless look of their inmates, and the woods which form the background of the picture, seem like the remnants of an earlier and simpler world. Strange changes have passed around that spot. Forests have fallen, cities have sprung up, and the lonely wilderness is thronged with human life. Nature herself has taken part in the general transformation; and the Mississippi has made a fearful inroad, robbing from the luckless Creoles a mile of rich meadow and woodland. Yet, in the midst of all, this relic of the lost empire of France has preserved its essential features through the lapse of a century, and offers at this day an aspect not widely different from that which met the eye of Pontiac when he and his chiefs landed on its shore.

The place was full of Illinois Indians; such a scene as in our own time may often be met with in some squalid settlement of the border, where the vagabond guests, bedizened with dirty finery, tie their small horses in rows along the fences, and stroll idly among the houses, or lounge about the dram-shops. A chief so renowned as Pontiac could not

remain long among the friendly Creoles of Cahokia without being
summoned to a feast; and at such primitive entertainment the whiskey-
bottle would not fail to play its part. This was in truth the case. Pontiac
drank deeply, and, when the carousal was over, strode down the village
street to the adjacent woods, where he was heard to sing the medicine
songs,[3] in whose magic power he trusted as the warrant of success in all
his undertakings.

An English trader, named Williamson, was then in the village. He
had looked on the movements of Pontiac with a jealousy probably not
diminished by the visit of the chief to the French at St. Louis; and he
now resolved not to lose so favorable an opportunity to despatch him.
With this view, he gained the ear of a strolling Indian, belonging to the
Kaskaskia tribe of the Illinois, bribed him with a barrel of liquor, and
promised him a farther reward if he would kill the chief. The bargain
was quickly made. When Pontiac entered the forest, the assassin stole
close upon his track; and, watching his moment, glided behind him, and
buried a tomahawk in his brain.

The dead body was soon discovered, and startled cries and wild
howlings announced the event. The word was caught up from mouth to
mouth, and the place resounded with infernal yells. The warriors
snatched their weapons. The Illinois took part with the guilty countryman; and the few followers of Pontiac, driven from the village, fled to
spread the tidings and call the nations to revenge. Meanwhile the murdered chief lay on the spot where he had fallen, until Saint-Ange, mindful of former friendship, sent to claim the body, and buried it with warlike honors near his fort of St. Louis.

Thus basely perished this champion of a ruined race. But could his
shade have revisited the scene of murder, his savage spirit would have
exulted in the vengeance which overwhelmed the abettors of the crime.
Whole tribes were rooted out to expiate it. Chiefs and sachems, whose
veins had thrilled with his eloquence; young warriors, whose aspiring
hearts had caught the inspiration of his greatness, mustered to revenge
his fate; and, from the north and the east, their united bands descended
on the villages of the Illinois. Tradition has but faintly preserved the
memory of the event; and its only annalists, men who held the intestine
feuds of the savage tribes in no more account than the quarrels of
panthers or wildcats, have left but a meagre record. Yet enough remains

3 Magical formulas.

to tell us that over the grave of Pontiac more blood was poured out in atonement, than flowed from the veins of the slaughtered heroes on the corpse of Patroclus; and the remnant of the Illinois who survived the carnage remained forever after sunk in utter insignificance.

Neither mound nor tablet marked the burial-place of Pontiac. For a mausoleum, a city has risen above the forest hero; and the race whom he hated with such burning rancor trample with unceasing footsteps over his forgotten grave.

✑ FOR DISCUSSION AND WRITING

1. In the third paragraph, by what means does Parkman place before the reader a perspective stretching far beyond the historical episode itself?

2. In setting the scene of the meeting with Sir William Johnson, what techniques does Parkman use that we associate with the art of the dramatist or the fiction writer?

3. If, instead of giving Johnson's address to the Indians in the form of direct speech, Parkman had paraphrased or summarized, what would have been the difference in effect?

4. At this distance of time, we recognize certain ironies—even tragic ironies—in this episode. Does Johnson himself seem to be aware of the ironies he is uttering? Does it seem that Parkman is aware of them?

5. Analyze the ironic implications of the following: the fact that Johnson addresses the Indians as "Children"; that he speaks of the English king as "your father"; that he praises the chieftains present at the meeting for having "behaved so well" and for their disapproval of "the bad behavior" of other tribes; that he urges them to "repent sincerely" for their "faults"; that he speaks of the "great advantage" to the Indians of co-operation with the English; that he urges them to "strive with each other" to "show the most gratitude" to the "best of princes"; that he tells them they will always hear from him "what is true and good"; that he refers them to the "Great Spirit" as having sanctioned the authority of the British and their enterprises in America, inasmuch as the purpose of it all is that the Indians "may live happy . . . lives."

6. In the paragraph beginning "Thus ended this memorable meeting," Parkman's own attitude toward his subject becomes clearer. What do you infer about his attitude from this paragraph? Is it right, or not, for an historian to have an attitude (that is, an attitude of judgment) toward his material, instead of just giving "facts"? Are "facts" ever available except under the aspect of human judgment?

7. How does Parkman set the scene for, and put in perspective, the assassination of Pontiac? The American Indians are one of the most obscure races on earth, for they had no way to make themselves articulate in modern history. How, in the last two paragraphs, does Parkman manage to give significant and noble perspective to an obscure hero of this obscure people?

8. The subject suggests, for a theme, a small adventure in research, for which you might look at one or more of the following books:
   Oliver La Farge: *Laughing Boy*
   R. H. Lowie: *Indians of the Plains*
   P. I. Wellman: *Indian Wars of the West*
   A. M. Josephy: *The Patriot Chiefs*
   W. T. Hagan: *American Indians*
   R. H. Pearce: *The Savages of America*
   F. J. Rochstader: *Indian Art in America*

9. Or you might write a short paper comparing what happened to the American Indians with what happened to the American Negroes.

Edmund Wilson ⊷ Lenin at the Finland Station

⊷ Born in 1895 in Red Bank, New Jersey, and educated at Princeton, Mr. Wilson's distinction is such that he may be called the dean of contemporary American letters. He is most widely known for his works of criticism, among them *Axel's Castle*, *The Triple Thinkers*, *The Wound and the Bow*, and *The Shores of Light*, works that are seminal in thought, catholic in principle, illuminated by wide learning and by clarity and justice of mind. The same qualities inform his historical work, *To the Finland Station*, a study in the backgrounds of the 1917 Russian Revolution, of which the final chapter is printed here. The book takes its title from the symbolic moment of Lenin's arrival, after his long exile in Switzerland, at the railway terminal in Petrograd for trains from Finland—a moment which served as signal for the Bolsheviks' seizure of power. ⊱

ON January 22, 1917, Lenin said to an audience of young people in a lecture on the 1905 Revolution: "We of the older generation may not live to see the decisive battles of this coming revolution." On the 15th of February, he wrote his sister María, asking about certain sums of money which had been sent him without explanation from Russia, "Nádya," he told her, "is teasing me, says I'm beginning to draw my pension. Ha! ha! that's a good joke because living is infernally expensive, and my capacity for work is desperately low on account of my bad nerves."

They had been living on a small legacy which had been inherited by Krúpskaya's[1] mother. A broker in Vienna had taken half of it for transferring it to them in wartime, and there had not been very much

From *To the Finland Station* by Edmund Wilson. Copyright 1940 by Edmund Wilson. Reprinted by permission of Doubleday & Company, Inc.

[1] Lenin's wife, Nadézhda Konstantínova Krúpskaya.

more than the equivalent of a thousand dollars left. Their funds were so low in 1917 that Lenin tried to get his brother-in-law in Russia to arrange for the publication of a "pedagogical encyclopaedia," which he proposed to have Krúpskaya write.

They had lodged at first in Zürich at a boarding-house where "Ilyích[2] liked the simplicity of the service, the fact that the coffee was served in a cup with a broken handle, that we ate in the kitchen, that the conversation was simple." But it turned out to be an underworld hangout. There was a prostitute who "spoke quite openly of her profession," and a man who, though he "did not talk much," revealed "by the casual phrases he uttered that he was of an almost criminal type." They were interested in these people, but Krúpskaya insisted they should move, for fear they should get into trouble. So they transferred to a shoemaker's family, where they occupied a single room in an old and gloomy house that went back almost to the sixteenth century. They could have got a better room for the money: there was a sausage factory opposite their windows, and the stench was so overwhelming that they opened them only late at night and spent most of their time in the library. But Vladímir Ilyích would never consent to leave after he had heard his landlady declare that "the soldiers ought to turn their weapons against their governments." They often had only oatmeal for lunch, and when it got scorched, Lenin would say to the landlady: "We live in grand style, you see. We have roasts every day."

The years, as Vladímir had written his sister, had told pretty severely on their nerves. It had been hard, after 1905, to settle down to exile again, and that had been twelve years ago. Their comrades[3] had been cracking up even worse than after the arrests of the nineties. One of them went to pieces in Lenin's house and had delusions about seeing his sister, who had been hanged. Another had caught tuberculosis during a sentence in a penal regiment; they sent him to Davos, but he died. Another, a survivor of the Moscow insurrection, came to see them one day and "began talking excitedly and incoherently about chariots filled with sheaves of corn and beautiful girls standing in the chariots." Vladímir stayed with him while Nádya got a psychiatrist, who said the man was going crazy from starvation. Later, he tied stones to his feet and neck and drowned himself in the Seine. Another, a factory worker in Russia,

[2] Lenin's full name was Vladímir Ilyích Ulyanov.

[3] Bolsheviks, radicals of the Marxian Socialists.

who, due to his political activities, found it difficult to keep a job and was unable to support his wife and children, broke down and became an *agent provocateur*.[4] He took to drink, and one evening drove his family out of the house, stuffed up the chimney, lit the stove, and in the morning was found dead. Now they were plagued by a new kind of spies: not the old race of obvious dicks[5] who used to stand on the street-corners and wait for them and whom they could easily dodge, but plausible and exalted young men, who talked themselves into posts in the party.

They had gone to see the Lafargues in Paris, and Krúpskaya, a little excited at meeting the daughter of Marx, had babbled something rather inarticulately about the part that women were playing in the revolutionary movement; the conversation had lagged. Lenin had talked to Lafargue about the book, *Materialism and Empirio-Criticism,* that he was writing against the Marxist mystics, and Lafargue agreed about the hollowness of religion. Laura had glanced at her husband and said: "He will soon prove the sincerity of his convictions." Lenin had been deeply moved when he had heard of their double suicide. "If one cannot work for the Party any longer," he had said to Krúpskaya at the time, "one must be able to look truth in the face and die the way the Lafargues did."

Elizavéta Vasílevna, his mother-in-law, used to say to people: "He'll kill both Nadyúsha and himself with that life." She herself died in 1915. She had wanted that last year to go to Russia, but there was no one to look after her there, and just before her death she said to Nádya, "I'll wait till I can go with you two." She had worked hard for the comrades as they came and went, had sewed "armor" into skirts and waistcoats in which illegal literature was to be carried and composed endless bogus letters that were to have messages written between the lines. Vladímir used to buy her presents in order to make her life a little more cheerful; once when she had failed to lay in cigarettes for a holiday, had ransacked the town to find her some. She had always regarded herself as a believer, and would not talk to them about sacred subjects; but had said suddenly, just before her death: "I used to be religious when I was young, but as I lived on and learned about life, I saw that it was all nonsense." And she asked to be cremated after her death. She died after an outing on a warm day of March, when she and Nádya had sat out for half an hour on a bench in the Berne forest.

Krúpskaya herself became ill after her mother's death. It was a re-

---

[4] Espionage agent.
[5] Detectives.

crudescence of an ailment that had first appeared in 1913. Something had gone wrong with her heart then; her hands had begun to tremble. The doctor had said that she had a weak heart and that her nerves were giving way. The cobbler's wife, who did their shopping — they were in Cracow now — was indignant: "Who said you were nervous — big ladies are nervous and throw the dishes around!" But she found that she couldn't work, and Vladímir took her to the mountains. It turned out that she had exophthalmic goiter. It had been always a slightly sore point with Nádya that people thought she looked like a fish. She complains in one of her early letters that Vladímir's sister Anna had said she had the look of a herring, and her conspiratorial names had been "Lamprey" and "Fish"; I once heard her described as "an old codfish" by a lady who had visited her in the Kremlin. Now the goiter, by swelling her neck and causing her eyes to protrude, intensified this effect. Vladímir had her operated on in Berne: the operation turned out to be difficult; they were working over her three hours without giving her an anesthetic — to the usual effect on Lenin that was produced by the presence of suffering. Lenin's letters through all this period show the strain of Nádya's illness.

One day in the middle of March when they had just finished eating dinner and Nádya had done the dishes and Ilyích was about to go to the library, a Polish comrade came bursting in, crying: "Haven't you heard the news? There's been a revolution in Russia!"

This time the defeats of the World War were carrying the tide across the barriers that had curbed it in 1905. The coal mines and factories of Poland had been lost with the Russian defeats; and half the production of the country was being expended on the fighting forces. On January 22, the anniversary of Father Gapón's demonstration, there had been a strike of a hundred and fifty thousand in Petrograd; and on March 8 a new general strike had begun: the workers poured into the streets. Now the army, full of peasant conscripts, could no longer be mobilized against them. Even the Cossacks, even the Semyónovsky Regiment, which had put down the Moscow insurrection, came over to the side of the rebels. The people were disgusted with the war, and they had completely lost confidence in the Tsar; the royal family, under the dominion of Raspútin,[6] were secretly trying to make peace with the Germans; the big landlords and the bourgeoisie, who had an interest in

---

[6] Russian Orthodox priest who had complete influence over the Tsarina.

continuing the war, were also eager to get rid of the autocracy. The Tsar himself had gone to General Headquarters in order to get away from the trouble; and when he attempted to return to Petrograd, the railroad workers held up his train. The whole machinery of the monarchy had stopped: the Tsar was forced to send his abdication by telegram, and a few days later was put under arrest. He had tried to dissolve the Fourth Duma,[7] as he had done with its predecessors, but this time they refused to disband, and formed a Provisional Committee, which appointed a Provisional Government. A Workers' Soviet, with an Executive Committee that included both Mensheviks and Bolsheviks, sprang to life from its paralyzation of 1905, like one of the victims of Koshchéy, the deathless enchanter of the Russian folk-tale, who was finally slain by the breaking of an egg; and the Committee decided to bring in the army and make it a Soviet of Workers' and Soldiers' Deputies.

Lenin had to depend on foreign newspapers; but through their blurred and biased despatches he managed to grasp the fundamental factors. In the few articles he wrote for *Právda,* which was now being published again, before he was able to return to Russia, he laid down the general assumptions on which he was afterwards to act. The power hung between the two bodies, Provisional Government and Petrograd Soviet — which represented two groupings of interests, irreconcilable with one another. The Soviet was the spokesman of the people, who wanted peace, bread, liberty, land. The Provisional Government, whatever it might say, was recruited from a bourgeoisie whose tendencies toward liberalism were limited to the desire to get rid of the Románovs:[8] the Minister of War and Marine was Guchkóv, a big Moscow industrialist and real-estate owner; the Minister of Foreign Affairs was Milyukóv, a former professor of History and the founder of the Kadet Party — the principal leader of the Russian bourgeoisie; and the Minister of Justice was a young lawyer only a shade further to the left than the Kadets. This last was the son of old Kerénsky, the director of the *gimnáziya* at Simbírsk, who had given Vladímir Ulyánov a good character after the execution of his brother and had guaranteed that his mother would keep him out of trouble. Kerénsky[9] the younger had grown up to be a

[7] Russian Parliament.

[8] Russian royal family.

[9] Leader of the more moderate Socialist party, who became head of the Provisional Government, on the Tsar's abdication.

highly successful orator of the emotional and ornamental kind, badly spoiled by the ladies of Petrograd and cherishing an almost mystical conviction that he had been chosen for some illustrious role.

This government, Lenin said, could never give the people what they wanted. It could not give them peace, because it depended on the subsidy of France and England and was committed to carrying on their war: it had never yet said a word about repudiating the imperialistic policy of annexing Armenia, Galicia and Turkey and capturing Constantinople. It could not give them bread, because the only way to give them bread would be by violating the sanctities of both capital and landlordship, and the bourgeoisie by definition were bound to protect the principle of property. It would not give them freedom, because it was the government of those landlords and capitalists who had always shown themselves afraid of the people. The only potential allies of the Soviet were, first, the small peasants and the other impoverished groups in Russia, and second, the proletariat of the other warring nations.

The revolution was only as yet in its first and transitory phase, and it would still have to wrest the power away from the bourgeoisie. The workers, the peasants and the soldiers must organize all over Russia under the leadership of the Petrograd Soviet. They must do away with the old police and establish a "people's militia"; and this militia must take upon itself to distribute such food as there was, seeing to it "that every child should have a bottle of good milk and that no adult of a rich family should dare to take extra milk till the children had all been supplied," and "that the palaces and luxurious homes left by the Tsar and the aristocracy should not stand idle but should provide shelter for the homeless and destitute." The Soviet, once it was dominant, must declare itself not responsible for treaties concluded by the monarchy or by any bourgeois government, and it must publish all secret treaties; it must propose an immediate armistice to all the nations; it must insist on the liberation of all colonies and dependent peoples; it must propose to the workers of all countries that they overthrow their bourgeois governments and transfer power to workers' Soviets; it must declare that the billion-dollar debts contracted by the bourgeois governments for the purpose of carrying on the war should be paid by the capitalists themselves: for the workers and peasants to pay interest on these debts "would mean paying tribute to the capitalists over a period of many, many years for having generously permitted the workers to kill one another over the division of spoils by the capitalists." — And now we must answer the objections of Kautsky,[10] who, writing on the Russian situation, warns us that "two things are absolutely necessary to the proletariat: democracy and socialism." But precisely what does this mean? Milyukóv would say he wanted democracy; Kerénsky would say he wanted socialism —

But here the fifth letter breaks off. Lenin is on his way to Russia and will not now be obliged to finish it. — The first days he had lain awake nights trying to work out ways to get back. The French and British would not give him a passport for the same reason that the British were to take Trotsky[11] off his ship at Halifax — though Plekhánov and other nationalist socialists were to be sent home in a British ironclad with a guard of torpedo-boats. The truth was that Milyukóv himself had telegraphed the Russian consuls not to repatriate the internationalist socialists. Lenin thought seriously about going in an airplane, but in the morning he knew he couldn't manage it. Then he decided he would have to get a false passport — if possible, a Swedish one, because a Swede would be least suspect. Unfortunately he knew no Swedish, and he wondered whether he could get enough up to pass himself off at the frontier; then concluded he ought not to take chances, ought not to try to speak at all; and wrote to a comrade in Sweden asking him to find two Swedish deaf mutes who looked like Zinóvyev and him. "You'll fall asleep," Krúpskaya told him, "and see Mensheviks in your dreams, and you'll start swearing and shouting 'Scoundrels, scoundrels!' and give the whole plot away."

On March 19 there was a meeting of exiles to discuss getting back to Russia. Mártov had worked up a plan for persuading the German government to let them return through Germany in exchange for German and Austrian prisoners. Lenin leaped at the idea, which hadn't occurred to him; but nobody else wanted to risk it. Mártov himself got cold feet, and it was Lenin who put the scheme through. Appeals to the Swiss government came to nothing, and telegrams to Russia got no answers: the patriots of the Provisional Government did not want the internationalists back, and the socialists themselves were in doubt. "What torture it is for us all," Lenin wrote to the comrade in Stockholm,

[10] German Socialist who opposed Lenin.

[11] Leon Trotsky (1877-1940), principal leader, with Lenin, of the Russian Revolution; assassinated in Mexico by a Stalin agent.

"to be sitting here at such a time!" He was sitting himself in his low-ceilinged room writing his *Letters from Afar*. At last Lenin wired the comrade in Sweden to send somebody to Chkheídze, the Menshevik who was President of the Petrograd Soviet, to appeal to him on the ground that it was his duty to get the stranded Mensheviks back. Other pressure was brought to bear, and permission was finally wired in the form, "Ulyánov must come immediately." It was arranged with the German ambassador in Switzerland that a party was to be sent through Germany: the Germans were hoping that Lenin would further disorganize the Russian government. It was agreed that while they were passing through Germany, nobody should leave the train or communicate with anyone outside, and that nobody should be allowed to enter without the permission of the Swiss socialist who accompanied them. The German government insisted that Lenin should receive a representative of the trade unions. Lenin told them that if any boarded the train, he would refuse to have anything to do with him.

When Lenin got the news that they could go, he insisted on their taking the next train, which left in a couple of hours. Krúpskaya didn't think she could get packed, settle her accounts with the landlady and take the books back to the library in time, and suggested that she might follow later. But Vladímir insisted she must come with him. They left a lot of their things in a box in the event that they might have to return. Their landlord, who has written an account of their tenancy, had never paid any special attention to them. When Frau Lenin had first come about the room, his wife had not wanted to take her: "You could see that she was the Russian type," and "she wore a dress that was a little bit short"; but when Lenin appeared himself, he made a better impression. They could see that he had strength in his chest: "My God," their son used to say, "he's got a neck like a bull!" For the rest, they were punctual about paying, and Herr Lenin got along well with his wife. "I think the two of them never quarreled. With Frau Lenin it was easy to get along. She was allowed to cook in our kitchen with my wife. We had agreed to let her do that. The two women always got along well together, which is something to wonder at, if one considers that the kitchen was a narrow intestine of a room, and that they had to squeeze by each other to pass. Frau Lenin would have made a good Hausfrau,[12] but she always had her mind on other work." When Frau Lenin mentioned to

[12] Housewife.

Frau Kammerer that she wanted to get to Russia, Frau Kammerer ex-
expressed concern about her going into "that insecure country at such an
uncertain time." "You see, Frau Kammerer," Frau Lenin said, "that's
where I have work to do. Here I have nothing to do." Her husband said
to Herr Kammerer just before he left: "So, Herr Kammerer, now there's
going to be peace."

In the train that left the morning of April 8 there were thirty Russian exiles, including not a single Menshevik. They were accompanied
by the Swiss socialist Platten, who made himself responsible for the trip,
and the Polish socialist Radek. Some of the best of the comrades had
been horrified by the indiscretion of Lenin in resorting to the aid of the
Germans and making the trip through an enemy country. They came to
the station and besieged the travelers, begging them not to go. Lenin
got into the train without replying a word. In the carriage he found a
comrade, who had been suspected of being a stool-pigeon. "The man had
made a little too sure of his seat. Suddenly we saw Lenin seize him by the
collar and in an incomparably matter-of-fact manner pitch him out on
to the platform."

The Germans overpowered them with meals of a size to which
they were far from accustomed, in order to demonstrate to the Russians
the abundance of food in Germany. Lenin and Krúpskaya, who had
never up to now been in any of the belligerent countries during this later
period of the War, were surprised, as they passed through Germany, at
the absence of adult men: at the stations, in the fields and the city streets,
there were only a few women and children, and boys and girls in their
teens. Lenin believed they would be arrested as soon as they arrived in
Russia, and he discussed with his comrades a speech of defense which he
was preparing on the way. But on the whole he kept much to himself.
At Stuttgart, the trade union man got on with a cavalry captain and sat
down in a special compartment. He sent his compliments to the Russians
through Platten, in the name of the liberation of peoples, and requested
an interview. Platten answered that they did not want to talk to him
and could not return his greeting. The only person who spoke to the
Germans was the four-year-old son of one of the Russians, who stuck his
head into the compartment and said in French: "What does the conductor do?"

On the way to Stockholm, Lenin declared that the Central Committee of the Party must positively have an office in Sweden. When they got

in, they were met and feted by the Swedish socialist deputies. There was a red flag hung up in the waiting-room and a gigantic Swedish repast. Radek took Lenin to a shop and bought him a new pair of shoes, insisting that he was now a public man and must give some thought to the decency of his appearance; but Lenin drew the line at a new overcoat or extra underwear, declaring that he was not going to Russia to open a tailor's shop.

They crossed from Sweden to Finland in little Finnish sleighs. Platten and Radek were stopped at the Russian frontier. Lenin sent a telegram to his sisters, announcing that he was arriving Monday night at eleven. In Russianized Finland, Krúpskaya says, "everything was already familiar and dear to us: the wretched third-class cars, the Russian soldiers. It was terribly good." Here the soldiers were back in the streets again. The station platforms were crowded with soldiers. An elderly man picked the little boy up and fed him some Easter cheese. A comrade leaned out the window and shouted, "Long live the world revolution"; but the soldiers looked around at him puzzled. Lenin got hold of some copies of *Právda*, which Kámenev and Stalin were editing, and discovered that they were talking mildly of bringing pressure on the Provisional Government to make it open negotiations for peace, and loyally proclaiming that so long as the German army obeyed the Emperor, so long must the Russian soldier "firmly stand at his post, and answer bullet with bullet and shell with shell."

He was just expressing himself on the subject when the train whistle blew and some soldiers came in. A lieutenant with a pale face walked back and forth past Lenin and Krúpskaya, and when they had gone to sit in a car that was almost empty, he came and sat down beside them. It turned out that he, too, believed in a war for defense. Lenin told him that they should stop the war altogether, and he, too, grew very pale. Other soldiers came into the car and they crowded around Lenin, some standing up on the benches. They were jammed so tight you could hardly move. "And as the minutes passed," says Krúpskaya, "they became more attentive, and their faces became more tense." He cross-examined them about their lives and about the general state of mind in the army: "How? what? why? what proportion?" reports a non-commissioned officer who was there. — Who were their commanders? — Mostly officers with revolutionary views. — Didn't they have a junior staff? didn't these take any part in the command? . . . Why was there so little promotion? — They didn't have the knowledge of operations, so they stuck to their old staff. — It would be better to promote the non-commissioned officers. The rank and file can trust its own people more than it can the white-handed ones. — He suggested that they ask the conductor to let them into a car with more space so that they could hold something in the nature of a meeting, and he talked to them about his "theses" all night.

Early in the morning, at Beloóstrov, a delegation of Bolsheviks got in, Kámenev and Stalin among them. The moment Lenin laid eyes on Kámenev, whom he had not seen in several years, he burst out: "What's this you're writing in *Právda?* We've just seen some numbers, and we gave it to you good and proper!" Lenin's younger sister María was also there, and a delegation of women workers. The women wanted Krúpskaya to say something, but she found that words had left her. There was a demand for Lenin to speak, and the train-crew, who knew nothing about their passenger except that he was somebody special, picked him up and carried him into the buffet and stood him on a table. A crowd slowly gathered around; then the conductor came up and told the trainmen that it was time to start on. Lenin cut short his speech. The train pulled out of the station. Lenin asked the comrades whether they thought that the group would be arrested as soon as they arrived in Petrograd. The Bolsheviks only smiled.

Two hundred years before, Giambattista Vico, at his books in a far corner of Europe the whole width of the continent away, in asserting that "the social world" was "certainly the work of man," had refrained from going further and declaring, as Grotius had done, that the social institutions of men could be explained in terms of man alone. Grotius, though one of Vico's masters, had been a Protestant and a heretic, and his great book had been put on the *Index*, so that Vico was afraid even to edit it. In the Catholic city of Naples, in the shadow of the Inquisition, Vico had to keep God in his system.[13]

At the end of the eighteenth century, Babeuf, who not only believed that human society had been made by man but who wanted to remake that society, had said in explaining his failure: "We have but to

---

[13] Vico (1668-1744) was an Italian historian and philosopher of history, exponent of the cyclical idea of history, and considered to be the founder of modern historical methods. Hugo Grotius (1583-1645) was a Dutch jurist who initiated the study of international law. The *Index Librorum Prohibitorum* is a list of books drawn up by the Roman Catholic church, either prohibited or for restricted reading. Babeuf was a French revolutionist of the 18th century who expounded an early brand of Communism.

reflect for a moment on the multitude of passions in the ascendancy in this period of corruption we have come to, to convince ourselves that the chances against the possibility of realizing such a project are in the proportion of more than a hundred to one."

Lenin in 1917, with a remnant of Vico's God still disguised in the Dialectic, but with no fear of Roman Pope or Protestant Synod, not so sure of the controls of society as the engineer was of the engine that was taking him to Petrograd, yet in a position to calculate the chances with closer accuracy than a hundred to one, stood on the eve of the moment when for the first time in the human exploit the key of a philosophy of history was to fit an historical lock.

If the door that Lenin was to open did not give quite on the prospect he hoped, we must remember that of all the great Marxists he was least in love with prophetic visions, most readily readjusted his prospects. "Theoretical classification doesn't matter now," he had just written in *Letters from Afar*, apropos of whether the immediate measures he contemplated for feeding the Russian people should be regarded as constituting a "dictatorship of the proletariat" or a "revolutionary-democratic dictatorship of the proletariat and the poorest peasantry." . . . "It would be indeed a grave error if we tried now to fit the complex, urgent, rapidly-unfolding practical tasks of the revolution into the Procrustean bed of a narrowly conceived 'theory,' instead of regarding theory first of all and above all as a *guide to action*."

We have watched the attempts of Michelet[14] to relive the recorded events of the past as a coherent artistic creation, and we have seen how the material of history always broke out of the pattern of art. Lenin is now to attempt to impose on the events of the present a pattern of actual direction which will determine the history of the future. We must not wonder if later events are not always amenable to this pattern. The point is that western man at this moment can be seen to have made some definite progress in mastering the greeds and the fears, the bewilderments, in which he has lived.

The terminal where the trains get in from Finland is today a little shabby stucco station, rubber-gray and tarnished pink, with a long trainshed held up by slim columns that branch where they meet the roof. On one side the trains come in; on the other are the doors to the waiting-

[14] Nineteenth-century French historian.

rooms, the buffet and the baggage-room. It is a building of a size and design which in any more modern country of Europe would be considered appropriate to a provincial town rather than to the splendors of a capital; but, with its benches rubbed dull with waiting, its ticketed cakes and rolls in glass cases, it is the typical small station of Europe, the same with that sameness of all the useful institutions that have spread everywhere with middle-class enterprise. Today the peasant women with bundles and baskets and big handkerchiefs around their heads sit quietly on the benches.

But at the time of which I am writing there was a rest-room reserved for the Tsar, and there the comrades who met him took Lenin, when the train got in very late the night of April 16. On the platform he had been confronted by men come back from prison or exile, who greeted him with tears on their cheeks.

There is an account of Lenin's reception by N. Sukhánov, a non-party socialist, who was present. He came walking into the Tsar's room at a speed that was almost running. His coat was unbuttoned; his face looked chilled; he was carrying a great bouquet of roses, with which he had just been presented. When he ran into the Menshevik, Chkheídze, the President of the Petrograd Soviet, he suddenly stopped in his tracks, as if he had come up against an unexpected obstacle. Chkheídze, without dropping the morose expression which he had been wearing while waiting for Lenin, addressed him in the sententious accents of the conventional welcoming speech. "Comrade Lenin," he said, "in the name of the Petrograd Soviet and of the whole revolution, we welcome you to Russia . . . *but* we consider that at the present time the principal task of the revolutionary democracy is to defend our revolution against every kind of attack, both from within and from without. . . . We hope that you will join us in striving toward this goal." Lenin stood there, says Sukhánov, "looking as if all this that was happening only a few feet away did not concern him in the least; he glanced from one side to the other; looked the surrounding public over, and even examined the ceiling of the 'Tsar's Room,' while rearranging his bouquet (which harmonized rather badly with his whole figure)." At last, turning away from the committee and not replying directly to the speech, he addressed the crowd beyond them: "Dear comrades, soldiers, sailors and workers, I am happy to greet in you the victorious Russian revolution, to greet you as the advance guard of the international proletarian army. . . . The war

of imperialist brigandage is the beginning of civil war in Europe. . . . The
hour is not far when, at the summons of our Comrade Karl Liebknecht,
the people will turn their weapons against their capitalist exploiters. . . .
In Germany, everything is already in ferment! Not today, but tomorrow,
any day, may see the general collapse of European capitalism. The Russian revolution you have accomplished has dealt it the first blow and
has opened a new epoch. . . . Long live the International Social Revolution!"

He left the room. On the platform outside, an officer came up and
saluted. Lenin, surprised, returned the salute. The officer gave a command: a detachment of sailors with bayonets stood at attention. The
place was being spotted by searchlights and bands were playing the
Marseillaise. A great roar of a cheer went up from a crowd that was
pressing all around. "What's this?" Lenin said, stepping back. They told
him it was a welcome to Petrograd by the revolutionary workers and
sailors: they had been roaring one word — "Lenin." The sailors presented arms, and their commander reported to Lenin for duty. It was
whispered that they wanted him to speak. He walked a few paces and
took off his bowler hat. "Comrade sailors," he said, "I greet you without
knowing yet whether or not you have been believing in all the promises
of the Provisional Government. But I am convinced that when they talk
to you sweetly, when they promise you a lot, they are deceiving you and
the whole Russian people. The people needs peace; the people needs
bread; the people needs land. And they give you war, hunger, no bread
— leave the landlords still on the land. . . . We must fight for the social
revolution, fight to the end, till the complete victory of the proletariat.
Long live the world social revolution!"

"How extraordinary it was!" says Sukhánov. "To us, who had been
ceaselessly busy, who had been completely sunk in the ordinary vulgar
work of the revolution, the current needs, the immediately urgent things
that are inconspicuous 'in history,' " a sudden dazzling light seemed to
flash. "Lenin's voice, issuing straight from the railway carriage, was a
'voice from the outside.' Upon us, in the midst of the revolution, broke
— the truth, by no means dissonant, by no means violating its context,
but a *new* and brusque, a somewhat stunning note." They were pulled
up by the realization "that Lenin was undeniably right, not only in announcing to us that the world socialist revolution had begun, not only in
pointing out the indissoluble connection between the world war and the

collapse of the imperialist system, but in emphasizing and bringing to the fore the 'world revolution' itself, insisting that we must hold our course by it and evaluate in its light all the events of contemporary history." All this, they could now see, was unquestionable; but did he really understand, they wondered, how these ideas could be made practical use of in the politics of their own revolution? Did he really know the situation in Russia? Never mind for the present. The whole thing was very extraordinary!

The crowd carried Lenin on their shoulders to one of the armored cars that had been drawn up outside. The Provisional Government, who had done their best to bar the streets against the gathering throngs, had forbidden bringing out their cars, which could become formidable factors in a mass demonstration; but this had had no effect on the Bolsheviks. He had to make another speech, standing above the crowd on top of the car. The square in front of the station was jammed: there they were, the textile workers, the metal workers, the peasant soldiers and sailors. There was no electric light in the square, but the searchlights showed red banners with gold lettering.

The armored car started on, leading a procession from the station. The other cars dimmed their lights to bring out the brightness of Lenin's. In this light he could see the workers' guard stretching all along both sides of the road. "Those," says Krúpskaya, "who have not lived through the revolution cannot imagine its grand solemn beauty." The sailors had been the Kronstadt garrison; the searchlights were from the Peter-Paul Fortress. They were going to the Kshesínskaya Palace, the house of the prima ballerina who had been the Tsar's mistress, which the Bolsheviks, in a gesture deliberately symbolic and much to the indignation of its inmate, had taken over for Party headquarters.

Inside it was all big mirrors, crystal candelabra, frescoed ceilings, satin upholstery, wide staircases and broad white cupboards. A good many of the bronze statues and marble cupids had been broken by the invaders; but the furniture of the ballerina had been carefully put away and replaced by plain chairs, tables and benches, set about, rather sparsely, where they were needed. Only a few Chinese vases, left stranded among the newspapers and manifestoes, were still getting in people's way. They wanted to give Lenin tea and to treat him to speeches of welcome, but he made them talk about tactics. The palace was surrounded by a crowd who were shouting for him to speak. He went out on a balcony to meet them. It was as if all the stifled rebellion on which the great flat and heavy city had pressed with its pompous facades since the time of those artisans whom Peter the Great had sent to perish in building it in the swamp, had boiled up in a single night. And Lenin, who had talked only at party meetings, before audiences of Marxist students, who had hardly appeared in public in 1905, now spoke to them with a voice of authority that was to pick up all their undirected energy, to command their uncertain confidence, and to swell suddenly to a world-wide resonance.

Yet at first, as they heard him that night — says Sukhánov, who was standing outside — there were signs that they were shocked and frightened. As Lenin's hoarse accents crackled out over them, with his phrases about the "robber-capitalists . . . the destruction of the peoples of Europe for the profits of a gang of exploiters . . . what the defense of the fatherland means is the defense of the capitalists against everybody else" — as these phases broke over them like shells, the soldiers of the guard of honor itself muttered: "What's that? What's he saying? If he'd come down here, we'd show him!" They had, however, Sukhánov says, made no attempt to "show him" when he was talking to them face to face, and Sukhánov never heard of their doing so later.

He went in again, but had to return and make a second speech. When he came back, a meeting was called. In the great ballroom, the long speeches of welcome began to gush afresh. Trotsky says that Lenin endured their flood "like an impatient pedestrian in a doorway, waiting for the rain to stop." From time to time he glanced at his watch. When he spoke, he talked for two hours and filled his audience with turmoil and terror.

"On the journey here with my comrades," he said, "I was expecting that they would take us straight from the station to Peter and Paul.[15] We are far from that, it seems. But let us not give up the hope that we shall still not escape that experience." He swept aside agrarian reform and other legal measures proposed by the Soviet, and declared that the peasants themselves should organize and seize the land without the aid of governmental intervention. In the cities, the armed workers must take over the direction of the factories. He threw overboard the Soviet majority, and hauled the Bolsheviks themselves over the coals. The proletarian revolution was imminent: they must give no countenance to the

[15] The Peter and Paul Fortress, used as a prison.

Provisional Government. "We don't need any parliamentary republic. We don't need any bourgeois democracy. We don't need any government except the Soviet of Workers', Soldiers', and Peasants' Deputies!"

The speech, says Sukhánov, for all its "staggering content and its lucid and brilliant eloquence," conspicuously lacked "one thing: an analysis of the 'objective premises,' of the social-economic foundations for socialism in Russia." But he goes on to say that he "came out on the street feeling as if I had been flogged over the head with a flail. Only one thing was clear: there was no way for me, a non-party man, to go along with Lenin. In delight I drank in the air, freshening now with spring. The morning had all but dawned, the day was already there." A young Bolshevik naval officer who took part in the meeting writes: "The words of Ilyích laid down a Rubicon[16] between the tactics of yesterday and today."

But most of the leaders were stunned. There was no discussion of the speech that night; but indignation was to break out the next day when Lenin discharged another broadside at a general meeting of the Social Democrats. "Lenin," declared one of the Bolsheviks, "has just now presented his candidacy for one throne in Europe which has been vacant thirty years: I mean, the throne of Bakúnin.[17] Lenin in new words is telling the same old story: it is the old discarded notions of primitive anarchism all over again. Lenin the Social Democrat, Lenin the Marxist, Lenin the leader of our militant Social Democracy — this Lenin is no more!" And the Left-Wing Bogdánov, who sat just under the platform, furiously scolded the audience: "You ought to be ashamed to applaud this nonsense — you cover yourselves with shame! And you call yourselves Marxists!"

The purpose of Lenin's speech had been to prevent a proposed amalgamation of Bolsheviks and Mensheviks; but at that moment it looked as if he was to have the effect of driving the Bolsheviks in the other direction.[18] To many of the Bolsheviks themselves, it seemed, as it had done to his opponents after the rupture of 1903, that Lenin had simply succeeded in getting himself out on a limb.

[16] River crossed by Caesar in entering Gaul; proverbially, a decisive step committing one to a hazardous enterprise.

[17] Nineteenth-century Russian anarchist.

[18] The direction of anarchism.

The night of their arrival, Krúpskaya records, after the reception in the Kshesínskaya Palace, she and Lenin "went home to our people, to Anna Ilyínishna and Mark Timoféyevich." María Ilyínishna was living with her brother-in-law and sister. Vladímir Ilyích and Nádya were given a separate room; and there they found that Anna's foster son had hung up over their beds the last words of the *Communist Manifesto:* "Workers of the World, Unite!"

Krúpskaya says she hardly spoke to Ilyích. "Everything was understood without words."

ᐧᐧᐧᐧ§ FOR DISCUSSION AND WRITING

1. Wilson's subject is of the very greatest historical significance, yet he starts out with a number of homely personal references—a letter of Lenin's to his sister joking about being hard up and in need of cash, the state of the crockery in the boardinghouse, the scorched oatmeal for lunch, Krúpskaya's goiter and her resemblance to "an old codfish." These details obviously have nothing to do with the Russian Revolution; what purpose do they serve, then, and how do they contribute to Wilson's design? The beginning of any piece of writing is usually the hardest part to do, for one has to awaken the reader's interest (which requires imaginative psychology) and at the same time ease him into the heart of the subject. Suppose Wilson had started out this way: "The revolution was only as yet in its first and transitory phase, and it would still have to wrest the power away from the bourgeoisie. The workers, the peasants, and the soldiers must . . . etc., etc." As against that kind of beginning, what advantage does the actual beginning of the piece have? Why is one's interest more readily focused by the fact that "the coffee was served in a cup with a broken handle" than by the much more important fact that the revolution "would still have to wrest the power away from the bourgeoisie"?

2. How does the personal and anecdotal character of the beginning build up dramatic potential for this (actually world-shaking) announcement?— "One day in the middle of March when they had just finished eating dinner and Nádya had done the dishes and Ilyích was about to go to the library, a Polish comrade came bursting in, crying: 'Haven't you heard the news? There's been a revolution in Russia!' "

3. At what specific point does Wilson change from the anecdotal method to the method of summary? Glancing swiftly through the whole piece, mark in the page margin the other places where this kind of change of method occurs — from anecdote to summary, or summary to anecdote. On the whole, what would you say is the purpose of these switches from one kind of expository technique to another? (Could you compare them, for instance, to different photographic techniques used in films?)

4. What are the chief kinds of documentary evidence employed by Wilson? Does he use any "living witness" evidence? Point out five places where he tells you the sources of his information. (It is very important for college students to acquire some skill in handling source material and in giving proper credit, for a good deal of one's written work in college courses depends on that kind of skill. One should watch attentively the practice, in these matters, of professional writers who employ various types of source material.)

5. The subtitle to the book from which this piece was taken is "A Study in the Writing and Acting of History." This is a very dexterous description of the book, for what Wilson is studying here is not history *already written up by historians,* but the "writing and acting" *of the actors themselves* as they create an epochal event of contemporary history. In what way does this view of Wilson's purpose explain and justify his use of so much anecdotal material? Wilson has also written a number of short stories, a play, and a novel; how does his fictional and dramatic talent serve him in the present piece of historical writing?

6. Now consider his use of the method of summary, for instance in the paragraph (page 591) beginning: "This government, Lenin said, could never give the people what they wanted. It could not give them peace. . . ." The paragraph summarizes an article Lenin had written for the Russian newspaper *Pravda.* The technique of summary requires an eye for the main points (a sort of mental outline), an ability to *condense* the material succinctly, and a kind of sentence and paragraph structure which shows clearly the logical sequences and coherence of the material. What are the chief points in this paragraph? How many parallel syntactical constructions do you find? How do these constructions point up and hold together, as a logical unit, the chief sequences of thought?

7. Again, another observation of the method of summary: consider the five paragraphs of the section (page 596) beginning, "Two hundred years

before, Giambattista Vico, at his books in a far corner of Europe . . . ," and ending, "The point is that western man. . . ." These five short paragraphs really contain the core of Wilson's whole book (a book of nearly 500 pages), and they summarize two centuries of social-political philosophy. Put yourself to this exercise: write five brief, succinct sentences, one for each paragraph, containing the main point of each paragraph and showing a clear logical succession between the points (you don't need to know anything more about Vico or Babeuf or Michelet than what Wilson says here, in order to do this exercise). It is an excellent exercise to test your grasp of what you read and to give you practice in summarizing.

8. Turn back to page 363, where Sir Julian Huxley is quoted as saying that, in the modern period, "evolution has at last become conscious of itself," and read the rest of that editorial foreword. (You may already have read the piece by Teilhard de Chardin in this book, which would help with the present question.) Now look again at Wilson's statement at the end of the section just referred to: "The point is that western man at this moment can be seen to have made some definite progress in mastering . . . ," etc. (page 597). How, specifically, does Wilson's study of the making of history in this piece illustrate the fact that "evolution has at last become conscious of itself"?

9. Here are two suggestions for writing assignments. Do a bit of research in one or more of the following books:
   N. K. Krúpskaya (Lenin's wife): *Memories of Lenin*
   Louis Fischer: *The Life of Lenin*
   Robert Payne: *Lenin*
   Boris Pasternak: *Doctor Zhivago*
   Arthur Koestler: *Darkness at Noon*
   Alexander Solzhenitsyn: *One Day in the Life of Ivan Denisovich*
   With the piece by Wilson in mind, try out the techniques of direct quotation and summary in writing up your findings. Or an assignment of a different kind: read some fairly extensive article in *Time* or *Newsweek*, and condense it, using both quotation and summary.

John Hersey ◄◦§ A Noiseless Flash

◄◦§ John Hersey's foreign dispatches in *Time* and *The New Yorker* were among the best to come out of World War II. Born in 1914, the son of American missionaries in Tientsin, he was educated in China, in America (Hotchkiss and Yale), and in England (Cambridge). He was Sinclair Lewis's secretary before joining the London office of *Time*, for which he covered almost every major action and front of the war. His novel *A Bell for Adano* was awarded the 1945 Pulitzer Prize. §◦►

AT EXACTLY fifteen minutes past eight in the morning, on August 6, 1945, Japanese time, at the moment when the atomic bomb flashed above Hiroshima, Miss Toshiko Sasaki, a clerk in the personnel department of the East Asia Tin Works, had just sat down at her place in the plant office and was turning her head to speak to the girl at the next desk. At that same moment, Dr. Masakazu Fujii was settling down cross-legged to read the Osaka *Asahi* on the porch of his private hospital, overhanging one of the seven deltaic rivers which divide Hiroshima; Mrs. Hatsuyo Nakamura, a tailor's widow, stood by the window of her kitchen, watching a neighbor tearing down his house because it lay in the path of an air-raid-defense fire lane; Father Wilhelm Kleinsorge, a German priest of the Society of Jesus, reclined in his underwear on a cot on the top floor of his order's three-story mission house, reading a Jesuit magazine, *Stimmen der Zeit;* Dr. Terufumi Sasaki, a young member of the surgical staff of the city's large, modern Red Cross Hospital, walked along one of the hospital corridors with a blood specimen for a Wassermann test in his hand; and the Reverend Mr. Kiyoshi Tanimoto, pastor of the Hiroshima Methodist Church, paused at the door of a rich man's house in Koi, the city's western suburb, and prepared to unload a handcart full of things he had evacuated from town in fear of the massive B-29 raid which everyone expected Hiroshima to suffer. A hundred thousand people were killed by the atomic bomb, and these six were among the survivors. They still wonder why they lived when so many others died. Each of them counts many small items of chance or volition — a step taken in time, a decision to go indoors, catching one streetcar instead of the next — that spared him. And now each knows that in the act of survival he lived a dozen lives and saw more death than he ever thought he would see. At the time, none of them knew anything.

The Reverend Mr. Tanimoto got up at five o'clock that morning. He was alone in the parsonage, because for some time his wife had been commuting with their year-old baby to spend nights with a friend in Ushida, a suburb to the north. Of all the important cities of Japan, only two, Kyoto and Hiroshima, had not been visited in strength by *B-san*, or Mr. B, as the Japanese, with a mixture of respect and unhappy familiarity, called the B-29; and Mr. Tanimoto, like all his neighbors and friends, was almost sick with anxiety. He had heard uncomfortably detailed accounts of mass raids on Kure, Iwakuni, Tokuyama, and other nearby towns; he was sure Hiroshima's turn would come soon. He had slept badly the night before, because there had been several air-raid warnings. Hiroshima had been getting such warnings almost every night for weeks, for at that time the B-29s were using Lake Biwa, northeast of Hiroshima, as a rendezvous point, and no matter what city the Americans planned to hit, the Superfortresses streamed in over the coast near Hiroshima. The frequency of the warnings and the continued abstinence of Mr. B with respect to Hiroshima had made its citizens jittery; a rumor was going around that the Americans were saving something special for the city.

Mr. Tanimoto is a small man, quick to talk, laugh, and cry. He wears his black hair parted in the middle and rather long; the prominence of the frontal bones just above his eyebrows and the smallness of his mustache, mouth, and chin give him a strange, old-young look, boyish and yet wise, weak and yet fiery. He moves nervously and fast, but with a restraint which suggests that he is a cautious, thoughtful man. He showed, indeed, just those qualities in the uneasy days before the bomb fell. Besides having his wife spend the nights in Ushida, Mr. Tanimoto had been carrying all the portable things from his church, in the close-packed residential district called Nagaragawa, to a house that belonged to a rayon manufacturer in Koi, two miles from the center of town. The rayon man, a Mr. Matsui, had opened his then unoccupied estate to a large number of his friends and acquaintances, so that they might evacuate whatever they wished to a safe distance from the probable target area. Mr. Tanimoto had had no difficulty in moving chairs, hymnals, Bibles, altar gear, and church records by pushcart himself, but the organ console and an upright piano required some aid. A friend of his named Matsuo had, the day before, helped him get the piano out to Koi; in return, he had promised this day to assist Mr. Matsuo in hauling out a daughter's belongings. That is why he had risen so early.

Mr. Tanimoto cooked his own breakfast. He felt awfully tired. The effort of moving the piano the day before, a sleepless night, weeks of worry and unbalanced diet, the cares of his parish — all combined to make him feel hardly adequate to the new day's work. There was another thing, too: Mr. Tanimoto had studied theology at Emory College, in Atlanta, Georgia; he had graduated in 1940; he spoke excellent English; he dressed in American clothes; he had corresponded with many American friends right up to the time the war began; and among a people obsessed with a fear of being spied upon — perhaps almost obsessed himself — he found himself growing increasingly uneasy. The police had questioned him several times, and just a few days before, he had heard that an influential acquaintance, a Mr. Tanaka, a retired officer of the Toyo Kisen Kaisha steamship line, an anti-Christian, a man famous in Hiroshima for his showy philanthropies and notorious for his personal tyrannies, had been telling people that Tanimoto should not be trusted. In compensation, to show himself publicly a good Japanese, Mr. Tanimoto had taken on the chairmanship of his local *tonarigumi*, or Neighborhood Association, and to his other duties and concerns this position had added the business of organizing air-raid defense for about twenty families.

Before six o'clock that morning, Mr. Tanimoto started for Mr.

Matsuo's house. There he found that their burden was to be a *tansu*, a large Japanese cabinet, full of clothing and household goods. The two men set out. The morning was perfectly clear and so warm that the day promised to be uncomfortable. A few minutes after they started, the air-raid siren went off — a minute-long blast that warned of approaching planes but indicated to the people of Hiroshima only a slight degree of danger, since it sounded every morning at this time, when an American weather plane came over. The two men pulled and pushed the handcart through the city streets. Hiroshima was a fan-shaped city, lying mostly on the six islands formed by the seven estuarial rivers that branch out from the Ota River; its main commercial and residential districts, covering about four square miles in the center of the city, contained three-quarters of its population, which had been reduced by several evacuation programs from a wartime peak of 380,000 to about 245,000. Factories and other residential districts, or suburbs, lay compactly around the edges of the city. To the south were the docks, an airport, and the island-studded Inland Sea. A rim of mountains runs around the other three sides of the delta. Mr. Tanimoto and Mr. Matsuo took their way through the shopping center, already full of people, and across two of the rivers to the sloping streets of Koi, and up them to the outskirts and foothills. As they started up a valley away from the tight-ranked houses, the all-clear sounded. (The Japanese radar operators, detecting only three planes, supposed that they comprised a reconnaissance.) Pushing the handcart up to the rayon man's house was tiring, and the men, after they had maneuvered their load into the driveway and to the front steps, paused to rest awhile. They stood with a wing of the house between them and the city. Like most homes in this part of Japan, the house consisted of a wooden frame and wooden walls supporting a heavy tile roof. Its front hall, packed with rolls of bedding and clothing, looked like a cool cave full of fat cushions. Opposite the house, to the right of the front door, there was a large, finicky rock garden. There was no sound of planes. The morning was still; the place was cool and pleasant.

Then a tremendous flash of light cut across the sky. Mr. Tanimoto has a distinct recollection that it travelled from east to west, from the city toward the hills. It seemed a sheet of sun. Both he and Mr. Matsuo reacted in terror — and both had time to react (for they were 3,500 yards, or two miles, from the center of the explosion). Mr. Matsuo dashed up the front steps into the house and dived among the bedrolls and buried himself there. Mr. Tanimoto took four or five steps and threw himself between two big rocks in the garden. He bellied up very hard against one of them. As his face was against the stone, he did not see what happened. He felt a sudden pressure, and then splinters and pieces of board and fragments of tile fell on him. He heard no roar. (Almost no one in Hiroshima recalls hearing any noise of the bomb. But a fisherman in his sampan on the Inland Sea near Tsuzu, the man with whom Mr. Tanimoto's mother-in-law and sister-in-law were living, saw the flash and heard a tremendous explosion; he was nearly twenty miles from Hiroshima, but the thunder was greater than when the B-29s hit Iwakuni, only five miles away.)

When he dared, Mr. Tanimoto raised his head and saw that the rayon man's house had collapsed. He thought a bomb had fallen directly on it. Such clouds of dust had risen that there was a sort of twilight around. In panic, not thinking for the moment of Mr. Matsuo under the ruins, he dashed out into the street. He noticed as he ran that the concrete wall of the estate had fallen over — toward the house rather than away from it. In the street, the first thing he saw was a squad of soldiers who had been burrowing into the hillside opposite, making one of the thousands of dugouts in which the Japanese apparently intended to resist invasion, hill by hill, life for life; the soldiers were coming out of the hole, where they should have been safe, and blood was running from their heads, chests, and backs. They were silent and dazed.

Under what seemed to be a local dust cloud, the day grew darker and darker.

At nearly midnight, the night before the bomb was dropped, an announcer on the city's radio station said that about two hundred B-29s were approaching southern Honshu and advised the population of Hiroshima to evacuate to their designated "safe areas." Mrs. Hatsuyo Nakamura, the tailor's widow, who lived in the section called Noboricho and who had long had a habit of doing as she was told, got her three children — a ten-year-old boy, Toshio, an eight-year-old girl, Yaeko, and a five-year-old girl, Myeko — out of bed and dressed them and walked with them to the military area known as the East Parade Ground, on the northeast edge of the city. There she unrolled some mats and the children lay down on them. They slept until about two, when they were awakened by the roar of the planes going over Hiroshima.

As soon as the planes had passed, Mrs. Nakamura started back with her children. They reached home a little after two-thirty and she immediately turned on the radio, which, to her distress, was just then broadcasting a fresh warning. When she looked at the children and saw how tired they were, and when she thought of the number of trips they had made in past weeks, all to no purpose, to the East Parade Ground, she decided that in spite of the instructions on the radio, she simply could not face starting out all over again. She put the children in their bedrolls on the floor, lay down herself at three o'clock, and fell asleep at once, so soundly that when planes passed over later, she did not waken to their sound.

The siren jarred her awake at about seven. She arose, dressed quickly, and hurried to the house of Mr. Nakamoto, the head of her Neighborhood Association, and asked him what she should do. He said that she should remain at home unless an urgent warning — a series of intermittent blasts of the siren — was sounded. She returned home, lit the stove in the kitchen, set some rice to cook, and sat down to read the morning's Hiroshima *Chugoku*. To her relief, the all-clear sounded at eight o'clock. She heard the children stirring, so she went and gave each of them a handful of peanuts and told them to stay on their bedrolls, because they were tired from the night's walk. She had hoped that they would go back to sleep, but the man in the house directly to the south began to make a terrible hullabaloo of hammering, wedging, ripping, and splitting. The prefectural government, convinced, as everyone in Hiroshima was, that the city would be attacked soon, had begun to press with threats and warnings for the completion of wide fire lanes, which, it was hoped, might act in conjunction with the rivers to localize any fires started by an incendiary raid; and the neighbor was reluctantly sacrificing his home to the city's safety. Just the day before, the prefecture had ordered all able-bodied girls from the secondary schools to spend a few days helping to clear these lanes, and they started work soon after the all-clear sounded.

Mrs. Nakamura went back to the kitchen, looked at the rice, and began watching the man next door. At first, she was annoyed with him for making so much noise, but then she was moved almost to tears by pity. Her emotion was specifically directed toward her neighbor, tearing down his home, board by board, at a time when there was so much unavoidable destruction, but undoubtedly she also felt a generalized, community pity, to say nothing of self-pity. She had not had an easy time. Her husband, Isawa, had gone into the Army just after Myeko was born, and she had heard nothing from or of him for a long time, until, on March 5, 1942, she received a seven-word telegram: "Isawa died an honorable death at Singapore." She learned later that he had died on February 15th, the day Singapore fell, and that he had been a corporal. Isawa had been a not particularly prosperous tailor, and his only capital was a Sankoku sewing machine. After his death, when his allotments stopped coming, Mrs. Nakamura got out the machine and began to take in piecework herself, and since then had supported the children, but poorly, by sewing.

As Mrs. Nakamura stood watching her neighbor, everything flashed whiter than any white she had ever seen. She did not notice what happened to the man next door; the reflex of a mother set her in motion toward her children. She had taken a single step (the house was 1,350 yards, or three-quarters of a mile, from the center of the explosion) when something picked her up and she seemed to fly into the next room over the raised sleeping platform, pursued by parts of her house.

Timbers fell around her as she landed, and a shower of tiles pommelled her; everything became dark, for she was buried. The debris did not cover her deeply. She rose up and freed herself. She heard a child cry, "Mother, help me!" and saw her youngest — Myeko, the five-year-old — buried up to her breast and unable to move. As Mrs. Nakamura started frantically to claw her way toward the baby, she could see or hear nothing of her other children.

In the days right before the bombing, Dr. Masakazu Fujii, being prosperous, hedonistic, and at the time not too busy, had been allowing himself the luxury of sleeping until nine or nine-thirty, but fortunately he had to get up early the morning the bomb was dropped to see a house guest off on a train. He rose at six, and half an hour later walked with his friend to the station, not far away, across two of the rivers. He was back home by seven, just as the siren sounded its sustained warning. He ate breakfast and then, because the morning was already hot, undressed down to his underwear and went out on the porch to read the paper. This porch — in fact, the whole building — was curiously constructed. Dr. Fujii was the proprietor of a peculiarly Japanese institution: a private, single-doctor hospital. This building, perched beside and over the water of the Kyo River, and next to the bridge of the same name, contained thirty rooms for thirty patients and their kinfolk — for, according to Japanese custom, when a person falls sick and goes to a hospital, one or more members of his family go and live there with him, to cook for him, bathe, massage, and read to him, and to offer incessant familial sympathy, without which a Japanese patient would be miserable indeed. Dr. Fujii had no beds — only straw mats — for his patients. He did, however, have all sorts of modern equipment: an X-ray machine, diathermy apparatus, and a fine tiled laboratory. The structure rested two-thirds on the land, one-third on piles over the tidal waters of the Kyo. This overhang, the part of the building where Dr. Fujii lived, was queer-looking, but it was cool in summer and from the porch, which faced away from the center of the city, the prospect of the river, with pleasure boats drifting up and down it, was always refreshing. Dr. Fujii had occasionally had anxious moments when the Ota and its mouth branches rose to flood, but the piling was apparently firm enough and the house had always held.

Dr. Fujii had been relatively idle for about a month because in July, as the number of untouched cities in Japan dwindled and as Hiroshima seemed more and more inevitably a target, he began turning patients away, on the ground that in case of a fire raid he would not be able to evacuate them. Now he had only two patients left — a woman from Yano, injured in the shoulder, and a young man of twenty-five recovering from burns he had suffered when the steel factory near Hiroshima in which he worked had been hit. Dr. Fujii had six nurses to tend his patients. His wife and children were safe; his wife and one son were living outside Osaka, and another son and two daughters were in the country on Kyushu. A niece was living with him, and a maid and a man-servant. He had little to do and did not mind, for he had saved some money. At fifty, he was healthy, convivial, and calm, and he was pleased to pass the evenings drinking whiskey with friends, always sensibly and for the sake of conversation. Before the war, he had affected brands imported from Scotland and America; now he was perfectly satisfied with the best Japanese brand, Suntory.

Dr. Fujii sat down cross-legged in his underwear on the spotless matting of the porch, put on his glasses, and started reading the Osaka *Asahi.* He liked to read the Osaka news because his wife was there. He saw the flash. To him — faced away from the center and looking at his paper — it seemed a brilliant yellow. Startled, he began to rise to his feet. In that moment (he was 1,550 yards from the center), the hospital leaned behind him rising and, with a terrible ripping noise, toppled into the river. The Doctor, still in the act of getting to his feet, was thrown forward and around and over; he was buffeted and gripped; he lost track of everything, because things were so speeded up; he felt the water.

Dr. Fujii hardly had time to think that he was dying before he realized that he was alive, squeezed tightly by two long timbers in a V across his chest, like a morsel suspended between two huge chopsticks — held upright, so that he could not move, with his head miraculously above water and his torso and legs in it. The remains of his hospital were all around him in a mad assortment of splintered lumber and materials for the relief of pain. His left shoulder hurt terribly. His glasses were gone.

Father Wilhelm Kleinsorge, of the Society of Jesus, was, on the morning of the explosion, in rather frail condition. The Japanese war-time diet had not sustained him, and he felt the strain of being a foreigner in an increasingly xenophobic Japan; even a German, since the defeat of the Fatherland, was unpopular. Father Kleinsorge had, at thirty-eight, the look of a boy growing too fast — thin in the face, with a prominent Adam's apple, a hollow chest, dangling hands, big feet. He walked clumsily, leaning forward a little. He was tired all the time. To make matters worse, he had suffered for two days, along with Father Cieslik, a fellow-priest, from a rather painful and urgent diarrhea, which they blamed on the beans and black ration bread they were obliged to eat. Two other priests then living in the mission compound, which was in the Nobori-cho section — Father Superior LaSalle and Father Schiffer — had happily escaped this affliction.

Father Kleinsorge woke up about six the morning the bomb was dropped, and half an hour later — he was a bit tardy because of his sickness — he began to read Mass in the mission chapel, a small Japanese-style wooden building which was without pews, since its worshippers knelt on the usual Japanese matted floor, facing an altar graced with splendid silks, brass, silver, and heavy embroideries. This morning, a Monday, the only worshippers were Mr. Takemoto, a theological student living in the mission house; Mr. Fukai, the secretary of the diocese; Mrs.

Murata, the mission's devoutly Christian housekeeper; and his fellow-priests. After Mass, while Father Kleinsorge was reading the Prayers of Thanksgiving, the siren sounded. He stopped the service and the missionaries retired across the compound to the bigger building. There, in his room on the ground floor, to the right of the front door, Father Kleinsorge changed into a military uniform which he had acquired when he was teaching at the Rokko Middle School in Kobe and which he wore during air-raid alerts.

After an alarm, Father Kleinsorge always went out and scanned the sky, and in this instance, when he stepped outside, he was glad to see only the single weather plane that flew over Hiroshima each day about this time. Satisfied that nothing would happen, he went in and breakfasted with the other Fathers on substitute coffee and ration bread, which, under the circumstances, was especially repugnant to him. The Fathers sat and talked awhile, until, at eight, they heard the all-clear. They went then to various parts of the building. Father Schiffer retired to his room to do some writing. Father Cieslik sat in his room in a straight chair with a pillow over his stomach to ease his pain, and read. Father Superior LaSalle stood at the window of his room, thinking. Father Kleinsorge went up to a room on the third floor, took off all his clothes except his underwear, and stretched out on his right side on a cot and began reading his *Stimmen der Zeit.*

After the terrible flash — which, Father Kleinsorge later realized, reminded him of something he had read as a boy about a large meteor colliding with the earth — he had time (since he was 1,400 yards from the center) for one thought: A bomb has fallen directly on us. Then, for a few seconds or minutes, he went out of his mind.

Father Kleinsorge never knew how he got out of the house. The next things he was conscious of were that he was wandering around in the mission's vegetable garden in his underwear, bleeding slightly from small cuts along his left flank; that all the buildings round about had fallen down except the Jesuits' mission house, which had long before been braced and double-braced by a priest named Gropper, who was terrified of earthquakes; that the day had turned dark; and that Murata-san, the housekeeeper, was nearby, crying over and over, "*Shu Jesusu, awaremi tamai!* Our Lord Jesus, have pity on us!"

On the train on the way into Hiroshima from the country, where he lived with his mother, Dr. Terufumi Sasaki, the Red Cross Hospital surgeon, thought over an unpleasant nightmare he had had the night before. His mother's home was in Mukaihara, thirty miles from the city, and it took him two hours by train and tram to reach the hospital. He had slept uneasily all night and had wakened an hour earlier than usual, and, feeling sluggish and slightly feverish, had debated whether to go to the hospital at all; his sense of duty finally forced him to go, and he had started out on an earlier train than he took most mornings. The dream had particularly frightened him because it was so closely associated, on the surface at least, with a disturbing actuality. He was only twenty-five years old and had just completed his training at the Eastern Medical University, in Tsingtao, China. He was something of an idealist and was much distressed by the inadequacy of medical facilities in the country town where his mother lived. Quite on his own, and without a permit, he had begun visiting a few sick people out there in the evenings, after his eight hours at the hospital and four hours' commuting. He had recently learned that the penalty for practicing without a permit was severe; a fellow-doctor whom he had asked about it had given him a serious scolding. Nevertheless, he had continued to practice. In his dream, he had been at the bedside of a country patient when the police and the doctor he had consulted burst into the room, seized him, dragged him outside, and beat him up cruelly. On the train, he just about decided to give up the work in Mukaihara, since he felt it would be impossible to get a permit, because the authorities would hold that it would conflict with his duties at the Red Cross Hospital.

At the terminus, he caught a streetcar at once. (He later calculated that if he had taken his customary train that morning, and if he had had to wait a few minutes for the streetcar, as often happened, he would have been close to the center at the time of the explosion and would surely have perished.) He arrived at the hospital at seven-forty and reported to the chief surgeon. A few minutes later, he went to a room on the first floor and drew blood from the arm of a man in order to perform a Wassermann test. The laboratory containing the incubators for the test was on the third floor. With the blood specimen in his left hand, walking in a kind of distraction he had felt all morning, probably because of the dream and his restless night, he started along the main corridor on his way toward the stairs. He was one step beyond an open window when the light of the bomb was reflected, like a gigantic photographic flash, in the corridor. He ducked down on one knee and said to himself, as only a Japanese would, "Sasaki, *gambare!* Be brave!" Just then (the building was 1,650 yards from the center), the blast ripped through the hospital. The glasses he was wearing flew off his face; the bottle of blood crashed against one wall; his Japanese slippers zipped out from under his feet — but otherwise, thanks to where he stood, he was untouched.

Dr. Sasaki shouted the name of the chief surgeon and rushed around to the man's office and found him terribly cut by glass. The hospital was in horrible confusion: heavy partitions and ceilings had fallen on patients, beds had overturned, windows had blown in and cut people, blood was spattered on the walls and floors, instruments were everywhere, many of the patients were running about screaming, many more lay dead. (A colleague working in the laboratory to which Dr. Sasaki had been walking was dead; Dr. Sasaki's patient, whom he had just left and who a few moments before had been dreadfully afraid of syphilis, was also dead.) Dr. Sasaki found himself the only doctor in the hospital who was unhurt.

Dr. Sasaki, who believed that the enemy had hit only the building he was in, got bandages and began to bind the wounds of those inside the hospital; while outside, all over Hiroshima, maimed and dying citizens turned their unsteady steps toward the Red Cross Hospital to begin an invasion that was to make Dr. Sasaki forget his private nightmare for a long, long time.

Miss Toshiko Sasaki, the East Asia Tin Works clerk, who is not related to Dr. Sasaki, got up at three o'clock in the morning on the day the bomb fell. There was extra housework to do. Her eleven-month-old brother, Akio, had come down the day before with a serious stomach upset; her mother had taken him to the Tamura Pediatric Hospital and was staying there with him. Miss Sasaki, who was about twenty, had to cook breakfast for her father, a brother, a sister, and herself, and — since the hospital, because of the war, was unable to provide food — to prepare a whole day's meals for her mother and the baby, in time for her father, who worked in a factory making rubber earplugs for artillery crews, to take the food by on his way to the plant. When she had finished and had cleaned and put away the cooking things, it was nearly seven. The family lived in Koi, and she had a forty-five-minute trip to the tin works, in the section of town called Kannonmachi. She was in charge of the personnel records in the factory. She left Koi at seven, and as soon as she reached the plant, she went with some of the other girls from the personnel department to the factory auditorium. A prominent local Navy man, a former employee, had committed suicide the day before by throwing himself under a train — a death considered honorable enough to warrant a memorial service, which was to be held at the tin works at ten o'clock that morning. In the large hall, Miss Sasaki and the others made suitable preparations for the meeting. This work took about twenty minutes.

Miss Sasaki went back to her office and sat down at her desk. She was quite far from the windows, which were off to her left, and behind her were a couple of tall bookcases containing all the books of the factory library, which the personnel department had organized. She settled herself at her desk, put some things in a drawer, and shifted papers. She thought that before she began to make entries in her lists of new employees, discharges, and departures for the Army, she would chat for a moment with the girl at her right. Just as she turned her head away from the windows, the room was filled with a blinding light. She was paralyzed by fear, fixed still in her chair for a long moment (the plant was 1,600 yards from the center).

Everything fell, and Miss Sasaki lost consciousness. The ceiling dropped suddenly and the wooden floor above collapsed in splinters and the people up there came down and the roof above them gave way; but principally and first of all, the bookcases right behind her swooped forward and the contents threw her down, with her left leg horribly twisted and breaking underneath her. There, in the tin factory, in the first moment of the atomic age, a human being was crushed by books.

✑⸗ FOR DISCUSSION AND WRITING

1. The subject of John Hersey's book *Hiroshima* (of which this is the first chapter) is no less than the apocalypse of a new age in the history of mankind, the "atomic age." How would you justify his approach to that subject through a few moments of clock time in the lives of six very obscure and ordinary people? Who are those six, what makes them representative, and what do they represent? Consider Hersey's method at the beginning;

why does he start out, in the first paragraph, by naming all six and noting briefly what they were doing "at exactly fifteen minutes past eight in the morning, on August 6, 1945," before he goes on to describe at length the experience of each? Why, throughout, does he keep mentioning exact clock time?

2. What implicit irony (tragic irony) is there in the disparity or incongruity between the gigantic significance of the first atomic bomb and the small, homely, human concerns and occupations of the six people? Hersey says that a hundred thousand people were killed by the bomb; people in so large a number become altogether abstract, a nameless, meaningless horde like the ants in an anthill; one's mind is incapable of conceiving such destruction, any more than it can conceive what it may mean to ants to have creosote poured on the anthill. How does Hersey's account correct our perspective?

3. He describes the normal concerns and worries of the six people, but does he give any indication of pain, horror, or fear that they might have felt at the moment of the explosion? What is the significance of the omission of such feelings? What ominous implication is there in the word "noiseless" in the title of the chapter, "A Noiseless Flash"?

4. What is the purpose of recording such details as these?—"Mr. Tanimoto is a small man, quick to talk, laugh, and cry. He wears his black hair parted in the middle and rather long . . . ," etc. Mrs. Nakamura "heard the children stirring, so she went and gave each of them a handful of peanuts and told them to stay on their bedrolls, because they were tired from the night's walk." Dr. Fujii, "squeezed tightly by two long timbers . . . like a morsel suspended between two huge chopsticks," found that "his glasses were gone." Father Kleinsorge "was wandering around in the mission's vegetable garden in his underwear."

5. There might be any number of ways of describing the same catastrophe, signalizing its enormity, but what is the particular effect of Hersey's understated way of doing it in the last paragraph—"Everything fell. . . . The ceiling dropped suddenly . . . the people up there came down . . ."? From *whose* point of view are these impressions registered? Does Hersey anywhere in this chapter tell you what *he* thinks about the event? What is the advantage of his impersonal, camera-like, detail-recording objectivity? What is the irony of the final sentence: "There, in the tin factory, in the first moment of the atomic age, a human being was crushed by books"?

6. Hersey's technique, in this piece, is a special use of the expository method
   of illustration, or example. Prepare a short paper using the same technique,
   recording the reactions of three or four people to some event within the
   scope of your own daily life—like the announcement of an exam or term
   paper, a class lecture (exciting or boring), someone's engagement or marriage or death. Or write a paper bringing together, by quotation or description, the reactions of a number of people to the possibilities of atomic
   bombing.

Eugene Kinkead ✍ American P.O.W.'s in Korea

✍ Mr. Kinkead is a staff writer and editor on *The New Yorker*, where "The Study of Something New in History" (the final section of which is printed here) originally appeared. The study forms part of Mr. Kinkead's book *In Every War but One.* ✍

NEXT I called on the doctor — Major Clarence L. Anderson,[1] a tall, dark-haired thirty-two-year-old man, who was then on temporary duty in the Pentagon. (He is currently attached to the Letterman Army Hospital, in San Francisco.) Anderson himself was captured by the Chinese on November 3, 1950, at Unsan. After his repatriation, nearly three years later, he was awarded the Distinguished Service Cross for his heroism in rounding up the wounded there and administering first aid to them, and for his refusal to leave them when the unwounded members

[1] Earlier in the article, Mr. Kinkead had described the results of his interviews with various other Pentagon officials. This is the last part of the article, describing what he learned from Major Anderson, Army doctor, and Major Segal, Army psychiatrist.

of his battalion pulled out in retreat. In the weeks that followed his capture, he was marched along Korean roads with columns of other prisoners, pausing at temporary holding camps on the way. Then, in January,
1951, he was assigned to the first permanent prison camp, situated in an
evacuated portion of the Yalu River town of Pytok-tong. Later known
as Camp No. 5, this camp eventually became the headquarters of the
whole Chinese prison system, and it was notorious as a center of highly
intensive indoctrination. During the first months of his captivity, Major
Anderson was allowed by the Communists to move freely among the
camp compounds and give medical attention to prisoners. Consequently,
his knowledge of conditions among the prisoners was much wider than
that of most captives, who knew only the men in their own squads.

The death rate among American prisoners, I knew, was highest in
the early days of the war — of the 2,634 Army captives who died, ninety-
nine and two-thirds per cent died in the first year — and I had, of course,
heard that the Army felt the deaths to be the result less of Communist
maltreatment than of the shortcomings of our own men. After capture,
many of the men appeared to lose all sense of allegiance not only to their
country but to their fellow-prisoners — a lapse that psychologists have
accounted for, in part, by the fact that all prisoners are initially in a
state of shock. "While this may be an explanation, it is not an excuse, and
the Army does not consider it one," I had been told.

Now Major Anderson bore out what I had heard. "It is a sad fact,
but it is a fact, that the men who were captured in large groups early in
the war often became unmanageable," he said. "They refused to obey
orders, and they cursed and sometimes struck officers who tried to enforce orders. Naturally, the chaos was encouraged by the Communists,
who told the captives immediately after they were taken that rank no
longer existed among them — that they were all equal as simple prisoners of war released from capitalist bondage. At first, the badly
wounded suffered most. On the marches back from the line to the temporary holding camps, casualties on litters were often callously abandoned beside the road. Able-bodied prisoners refused to carry them,
even when their officers commanded them to do so. If a Communist
guard ordered a litter shouldered, our men obeyed; otherwise, the
wounded were left to die. On the march, in the temporary camps, and in
the permanent ones, the strong regularly took food from the weak.
There was no discipline to prevent it. Many men were sick, and these

men, instead of being helped and nursed by the others, were ignored, or worse. Dysentery was common, and it made some men too weak to walk. On winter nights, helpless men with dysentery were rolled outside the huts by their comrades, and left to die in the cold."

What struck Major Anderson most forcibly was the almost universal inability of the prisoners to adjust to a primitive situation. "They lacked the old Yankee resourcefulness," he said. "This was partly — but *only* partly, I believe — the result of the psychic shock of being captured. It was also, I think, the result of some new failure in the childhood and adolescent training of our young men — a new softness." For a matter of months — until about April of 1951, Anderson said — most prisoners displayed signs of shock, remaining within little shells they had created to protect them from reality. There was practically no communication among the men, and most of them withdrew into a life of inactivity. In fact, very few seemed to be interested even in providing themselves with the basic necessities of food, warmth, and shelter. The Chinese sometimes gave prisoners a chance to go up into the nearby hills and bring down firewood, but the men were too lethargic to do it. The whole routine of Army life collapsed. One prisoner could not challenge another to act like a soldier, because too often the other man would say he wasn't a soldier any more. As Anderson and another doctor made their daily rounds, the one way they could even begin to arouse a sense of responsibility in the men was by urging them to act not like soldiers but like human beings — to wash once in a while, to keep their clothes and their quarters moderately clean, and to lend each other a hand sometimes. This very weak plea, Anderson said, was the only one to which there was any response at all.

The prisoners' attitude was not "What can I do to help myself?" but "What can be done to help me?" The doctors saw it in practically every hut they visited. Although the Communists had segregated the officers, each compound still had a senior noncommissioned officer, who, if he had exercised control, could have improved the lot of the entire group. "Let me show you what I mean by a healthy prisoner organization," the Major said. "If things had been done right, the men in a squad or a platoon would have got up at a specified time in the morning at an order from their senior member, washed, and lined up for chow. They would have eaten indoors or out, depending on the temperature, and then cleaned up the area, gathered wood, and got water. Each man would have seen to keeping his body and his clothing free of lice by squeezing the insects between two fingernails — an important and time-consuming task. In a properly run unit, men would have been detailed to look after the sick — wash their clothes, give them water, prevent them from lying in one position too long and getting bedsores, and scrounge better food for them. In the Korean prison camps, a man's thigh muscles, apparently because of poor diet, would often contract so the knee was bent, and he sometimes could not rise after a night's sleep. A little massage would have corrected this, and it could have been done by the other men in the hut. It usually wasn't. Anything that keeps prisoners occupied, gets their minds off themselves, is good for them, so the leader of a well-run outfit would have organized calisthenics and sports, and got the men to make chess and checker sets. If this sort of disciplined program had been carried out, our prisoners would have maintained their identities as loyal American soldiers and would have functioned as such. Captivity is a miserable situation under the best of conditions, but in Korea it could have been much easier than it was. If we had had proper organization, many of those who returned would not be haunted, as they are, by nightmares of guilt. And, of course, more of us would have returned."

Major Anderson told me that the Army's daily combat ration is thirty-five hundred calories, and that early in the war the prisoners, by his estimate, were getting twelve hundred. This is an inadequate diet, he said, but not a starvation one. In the main, the North Koreans gave the prisoners corn or millet, which was boiled in the usual Korean manner — in an iron pot hung over a fire — and these cereals contained very few proteins, minerals, and vitamins. The lack was sometimes aggravated, as it happened, by the prisoners themselves. "During the worst early days," the Major said, "the enemy gave us a few soybeans. They contained more protein than anything else we had, but the men disliked them, and thought they caused diarrhea. When they did, it was only because they had been insufficiently cooked, as some of the more intelligent men tried to make plain. Nobody believed them, and the men complained so much about the beans that the Chinese stopped giving them to us. This left a big gap in our nutriment. If our organization had been better, we would have had regular cooks among the prisoners. The cooks we had were volunteers, and they made no effort to prepare the beans properly. If the men complained, those cooks just quit." Anderson said that in his opinion most of the deaths from malnutrition — and mal-

nutrition ranked right after pneumonia and dysentery as the chief cause
of death — were the result of a deficiency of proteins, minerals, or vitamins, rather than a calorie deficiency, and that almost all cases of
malnutrition were aggravated, if not actually caused, by the prisoners'
disinclination to eat unfamiliar foods. Not long after the Chinese put
the system of permanent camps into operation, the food improved in
both quality and quantity, eventually reaching a level of twenty-four
hundred calories, which was pretty well maintained till the end of the
war.

I asked Anderson about housing conditions in the camps, and about
clothing. He said that since most of the camps had formerly been villages,
the prisoners were housed in thatched huts. These had mud walls and
were usually divided into two rooms. Some of the windows had glass,
and some did not. The rooms were small, and prisoners slept on the floor
— sometimes in a space per man half as wide as an upper berth in a
Pullman. A single electric-light bulb in one of the rooms was the only
illumination, and heat came from a stove in the cellar that sent hot air
through flues beneath the floor — a simple version of the radiant heat
now fashionable with our architects, though in Korea it sometimes had
the disadvantage of making the floor too hot to lie on. That wasn't a
common complaint in winter, though, particularly when the temperature
fell to thirty or forty degrees below zero. At Camp No. 5, the huts were
in a valley that in winter got only three hours of sunshine a day. The
summers, however, were pleasant — rather like summers in the Adiron-
dacks, Anderson said — and prisoners were then allowed to swim in the
Yalu. Clothing, on the whole, was adequate, and the prisoners probably
suffered less from lack of it than from any other cause. There was an
issue of clothing two or three times a year, and generally the total issue
for the year consisted of three shirts, three pairs of shorts, three pairs
of socks, one quilted winter uniform, and two cotton summer uniforms.
Other winter clothes, issued somewhat irregularly, were quilted over-
coats, fur-lined leather-and-canvas boots, and hair-lined caps. In cold
weather, summer uniforms were often worn under the quilted clothing
for greater warmth. Socks wore out first, and until new ones were issued
the prisoners improvised foot wrappings from any cloth they had.

One of the worst problems in the camps, Anderson told me, was an
illness known, at least in Camp No. 5, as "give-up-itis." "You could
follow its progress all too easily," he said. "First, the sufferer became

despondent; then he lay down and covered his head with a blanket; then he wanted ice water to drink with his food; next, no food, only water; and eventually, if he was not got to and helped, he would die. You could actually predict how long it would take. If you didn't get to him within three weeks, he was a goner; if you got to him sooner, he could usually be saved. But in a camp of three thousand men, which was what we had at the start, and with only a few doctors, it was hard to locate all these cases." I asked Anderson whether it was the younger or the older men who tended to succumb to give-up-itis, and he said that as a rule it was the younger. The treatment was to force-feed the man and then drag him upright and compel him to move his limbs. Sometimes a man was choked till he consented to take food. If he spat it out, it was scooped up and put back in his mouth. Only if he agreed to sit up and eat something would the doctor take his hands off him. Thereafter, he was carefully watched, and if he continued to eat and to move about a little, he was usually all right in ten days. "One of the best ways to get a man on his feet to begin with," the Major said, "was to make him so mad by goading him, or even hitting him, that he tried to get up and beat you. If this happened, the man invariably got well."

Major Anderson said that after repatriation he and four other Army physicians who had been prisoners were called in to advise the Surgeon General's Office on methods by which Army personnel could in the future be better prepared to face internment in a Communist prison camp. The doctors all agreed that by far the greatest error of our troop-training program had been to teach the men that Americans are "the best-cared-for soldiers on the globe." "An American soldier goes into the field with comforts that the majority of the world's population doesn't have even at home," said Anderson. "What he was not told in the Korean War was that if he was captured the comforts would vanish into thin air. Why, during those early marches in Korea I saw sick prisoners lying down at the side of the road and waiting to be picked up by an ambulance. They thought that just because our Army had ambulances for picking up straggling prisoners, the Communists would have them, too. Well, they didn't. When you're a Communist prisoner, such comforts do not exist. It should be explained emphatically to our soldiers that people have always got sick, and through the centuries most of them subsequently got well without elaborate care or extensive medication." One of the first things that all five doctors noted in the camps was the reaction of the average prisoner to the lack of ordinary field and hospital comforts. He seemed lost without a bottle of pills and a toilet that flushed. In order to survive under prison conditions, a man must often consume things that would normally be repellent, such as wormy indigenous foods and dirty water; he needs to realize that he will die a lot sooner from starvation than he will from ailments that he might possibly get as a result of eating unpleasant things. "The prisoner in a camp has to be ready to live like an animal," Anderson said. "Plenty of people, including our enemies, live that way. If it means the difference between life and death for our men, the policy of teaching them to live like animals should be adopted without hesitation or apology." In essence, the doctors felt that the Army should maintain the high standard of living of its soldiers in the field but at the same time should make its trainees understand that upon capture their comforts may abruptly disappear, and teach them how to make do with practical, if disagreeable, substitutes.

The majority of the American prisoners in Korea yielded in some degree to Communist pressure. No matter how they rationalized this, they knew that it was wrong; they knew that they had betrayed their better natures, and violated the ideals under which they had been reared. Consciously or unconsciously, they were burdened, as Major Anderson had said, with guilt — perhaps the most corrosive emotion that the human spirit has to bear. I discussed this matter, and the psychology of prisoners in general, with Major Henry A. Segal, a psychiatrist in the Army Medical Corps who has since returned to private practice. The Army felt that Major Segal, as chief of the Neuropsychiatric Consultation Service at Walter Reed Army Hospital and, before that, chief of psychiatric personnel on the Joint Intelligence Processing Teams, knew more than anyone else about the psychological condition of the returned prisoners. He had personally conducted psychiatric interviews with eighty of them; he had later studied the files of eight hundred more, in an attempt to isolate emotional factors that might have produced collaborators or, on the other hand, resisters; and he had reviewed psychiatric reports on a total of fourteen hundred cases that were considered to be possibly in need of hospital treatment.

The Army psychiatrists had drawn certain general conclusions about the returned prisoners, Segal told me, and one was that the incidence among them of psychiatric disorders requiring hospitalization was no higher than that of the country as a whole. This is not to say that the men did not show the effects of their imprisonment. They did, and markedly. For one thing, they displayed much less than the average amount of interest in their environment; their outlook was a noticeably restricted one, and they expressed few, if any, demands or desires for the present, or plans and thoughts about the future. They discussed their lives in an extraordinarily flat and unemotional way, using stock phrases over and over. Their apathy was not like that seen in psychotics, who are often abject; the returned prisoners were capable of response, but their reaction time had been measurably slowed and they showed only a limited capacity for elaborating the ideas they expressed. Beneath this apathetic surface, however, they were turbulent, ready to be extremely aggressive, to tear into something in a rage. The Rorschach tests given the men during the repatriation processing clearly showed this latent aggressiveness. One description that repatriates frequently gave of a certain blot[2] was that it represented two men ripping something apart, perhaps another man's chest, from which they were removing his heart. Among the words that came out repeatedly in the sentence-completion tests were "blood," "fire," and "hand grenade."

The fantastic amount of fraternizing with the enemy in the Korean prison camps was in strong contrast to the hatred that American prisoners had felt toward the Japanese in the Second World War. The Japanese, who wanted no Americans in their Greater East Asia Co-Prosperity Sphere, treated captives with physical harshness, thus solidly banding the men together against them. The Chinese, on the other hand, subtly controlled the prisoners' resentment, transferring it from themselves to other objects. Often, in fact, a prisoner's resentment was ultimately turned against himself. Most returned prisoners expressed sincere gratitude for the way the Chinese treated them, although the conditions they had lived under were far worse than anything they had previously known. When they talked about politics, they often used the word "Socialism" rather than "Communism," thus showing a significant emotional identification with the enemy's point of view, and many of them said that while Socialism might not work in the United States, where the people are for the most part well off to begin with, it was a good thing

[2] The Rorschach test employs ink blots; the psychological information gained from the test depends on what one "sees" in the blots.

for China and other less advanced nations. As further evidence of the success of the Communist techniques, Segal told me that most of the repatriates came home thinking of themselves not as part of a group, bound by common loyalties, but as isolated individuals. This emerged in their response to questions about what their service outfit had been. Where the Turks, for example, said proudly, "Third Company, First Regiment, Turkish Volunteer Brigade," or whatever it may have been, the Americans were likely to respond with the number of their prison camp and the company or platoon they had belonged to there.

As Segal saw it, the prisoners fell into six categories. Three of these, together comprising about thirteen per cent of the total, came under the general heading of hard-core collaborators. The first of the three consisted of men with little capacity for enduring stress, who capitulated early in the game. Reaction to stress, Segal told me, was a highly individual matter. One of the collaborators, by his own admission, gave information to the Communists after thirty-five minutes of not very intensive questioning. "They said they had ways of making me talk, so I talked," he explained. Another man, who had said nothing throughout his three years of captivity, explained, "I was told not to communicate with the enemy, so I didn't." Prisoners in this first group lacked the moral stamina to resist even the minimum of emotional discomfort. They were, in ordinary language, cowards; there seems to be no other word for them.

The second group of collaborators might be labelled opportunists. They would inform, sign petitions, and make broadcasts for the sake of the tangible benefits they were told they would receive — freedom to walk outside the camp compound, an egg or two, cigarettes. "They were also given power over the other men, prestige, and the approval of their captors — very important rewards to such persons," said Segal. "During a psychiatric interview, one of them was talking of his ability to expound Communist doctrine. 'The Communists told me I was a young Lenin,' he said, and as he remembered this, his face lit up." Despite their acts of collaboration, these men appeared to have no deep-seated convictions about Communism and no real understanding of its techniques. Upon their release, interestingly enough, many tried to continue in the role of informer, approaching high-level officers in our own Army with offers to give information about other repatriates.

The third, and smallest, group of collaborators consisted of those who actually accepted Communism. In general, they seemed to be men who, for one reason or another, had been unable to form any strong attachments or loyalties in their past lives. "The simplest way to define this group," said Segal, "would be to say that they were the sort of men who say to themselves, 'I'm just a kid. I don't know where I'm going. I don't know whether people actually like me. Will I ever really be a success?' Because they were uncertain of themselves and unsatisfied with what they had been so far, they were willing to become part of a system as different as possible from the one that had produced them."

The fourth large category, and the one that included the overwhelming majority of the prisoners — three out of four, in fact — consisted of men who chose what seemed to them to be the line of least resistance. In the absence of group discipline, they tried to substitute a form of protection of their own making. They complied outwardly with the Communists' less extreme demands, and some of them signed petitions and made broadcasts, but these were relatively harmless. On the whole, this group refused to do anything obviously traitorous. Among the prisoners, outward compliance was known as "playing it cool." The men who played it cool believed that the Communists would be more lenient to them — a complete fallacy, as time proved. "The motive behind much of what the men did was their erroneous anticipation of what might happen to them if they didn't do it," Segal told me. "I must sign this or I will be tortured, they thought. If only it could have been pointed out to this group that their attitude was not realistic, and if they could then have based their behavior on reality, rather than on fantasy, the entire camp experience would have been easier for all of them. Playing it cool was what made the Communists' system operate. Without it, the Communists would have been powerless."

The reactionaries, who, like the collaborators, numbered about thirteen per cent, were divided by the psychiatrists into two groups. The first, and smaller, of these consisted of individuals with a long history of unwillingness to accept any kind of authority — men with bad behavior records in our own Army, who in prison camp simply followed their old patterns. As resisters, they were not effective; they might, for example, bullheadedly set fire to a barracks, even though it was they themselves who would suffer for it. The other group of reactionaries, numbering about ten per cent of all prisoners, was made up of the mature, well-integrated individuals who knew how to use their intelligence constructively, how to work with all types of men, and how to influence these men in order to attain a goal of importance to them all. "These were the true heroes of the prison camps," said Segal. "Men who were manly enough to refuse to submit to indoctrination, who refused to accept favors from the Communists, and who maintained their integrity and personal honor throughout their captivity."

From Major Segal I heard a bit more about why the Army is careful to make a distinction between brainwashing and indoctrination. Brainwashing, he said, is a process that produces obvious alteration of character, as in the case of Cardinal Mindszenty. Whether the change is accomplished by hypnosis, drugs, physical torture, extreme psychological pressure, or some combination of these is not known, but clearly the subject ceases to be the person he was before. The indoctrination used in the camps, Segal went on, was aimed at manipulating the character a man already had, taking advantage of its weakest points. If he seemed the type who would give in to harassments or threats, he was harassed or threatened. If he would respond to flattery or reward, he was flattered or rewarded. The rewards were small, Segal remarked, and the degree to which they were increased never matched the growing demands made upon the man who had yielded; the collaborator was never paid in full. "Unfortunately," he went on, "the distinction between brainwashing and indoctrination is not clear in the public mind. The general conception, I'm afraid, has been of Communist techniques so irresistible that no prisoner could keep his integrity in the face of them — indeed that no people could hold out against such an enemy. This is what distresses me so much about the popular use of a word like 'brainwashing.' When a phenomenon that we do not completely understand occurs in our society, we are apt to give it a name indicating that there is something magical about it, something beyond the reach of man's powers of comprehension. 'My goodness!' we say in effect. 'Look at this! You can remove a man's brain and wash out what's in it, and wash into it whatever you want, just as if it were a tape recorder!' The terrifying implications of the term undermine the will to resist. Actually, there is nothing even novel, let alone mysterious, about much of the Communist process of indoctrination. If only our men had understood indoctrination, they could have defeated it.

"Let me give you an illustration of how such knowledge can help. In the early days of the war, Chinese bugle calls often panicked our troops in the front line. What did a particular call mean — a flanking movement, a retreat, an attack? Sometimes a bugle was blown in the dead of night, around the time when attacks were generally launched, and then no attack came. Quite a few of these calls apparently meant nothing, but not understanding them put our men at a psychological disadvantage that was a real handicap to them in combat. One of our generals heard about this, and he got troops returning from the front lines to describe the various calls, even the ones that seemed to mean nothing. By correlating them with what had actually happened in the line each time a call was heard, he was able to decode them. They proved to be an easily recognizable set of signals, and once the information as to what each one stood for was disseminated among our troops, the calls completely lost their menace, and even became a help to us in combat. If we could do away with all the awe and mystery surrounding indoctrination, that, too, would lose its terror."

Segal believes, as the other officers do, that silence is the most effective countermeasure to indoctrination. "Talking is always the first step toward collaborating," he told me. "Once a man starts talking, there is no escape from more talking. And the more he talks, the greater his guilt and anxiety become, and the less able he is to cope with the normal stresses of prison life. His whole personality tends to disintegrate. He knows he has done something wrong, and his conscience will not let him rest. The 'mental torture' offered by certain collaborators as an excuse for their conduct was not necessarily inflicted by the Communists. In most cases, it could have more accurately been termed self-torture. On the voyage home, many men said, 'If I had known what yielding was going to mean eventually, I would never have done it in the first place.'

"If I knew a man was to become a prisoner," Segal went on, "I would like to say to him, 'First, your own best chance for survival lies in your not talking. And, second, your *buddies'* best chance for survival lies in your not talking.' I would see to it that the man was packed full of arguments as to why he must not talk. A good many of these would be examples from the case histories of men who had talked. If a man doesn't talk, he can't incriminate himself. Or anybody else. Or give information. Or be duped. The best way to maintain silence, and loyalty, I would tell a future prisoner, is by joining with other soldiers to preserve discipline and give and receive help. Survival is an absolute im-

possibility for one man without the support of the group, and the way a
man behaves is, to a large extent, dependent on how the group permits
him to behave. When *esprit de corps* and discipline are good, men are
brave and resistant, and the reverse is unalterably true. This is elementary. But in the Korean War, some Army men seemed to forget it. Once
a man starts talking, the picture is black. He has to keep asking himself
constantly, 'What did I say? Is my story still straight? Did I implicate
So-and-So? Should I confess to this false crime? If I do, will my buddies
understand? If I do, will I become a criminal?' And yet a man *can't* stop
talking. Having once yielded to pressure, he is psychologically more
vulnerable to future pressures. Invariably he goes on."

Segal reflected for a moment or two, and then said, "Let's look at
the talking from the other side of the fence — the Communist side. We
know from the returnees' accounts that once a man refused to talk he
was pretty much let alone. The Communist attitude seemed to be 'The
hell with him; he's not worth the trouble.' But those who yielded were
forced to yield more and more. The Communists never stopped pumping them, because their own system never stops pumping *them*. It demands and demands, and enlarges and reënlarges its demands, as if to
prove to itself every day that its followers are still faithful, and haven't
deviated an inch from the accepted line on which they were examined
the day before. The system itself is paranoid. It's so suspicious that it
demands checks and rechecks on what was said a month ago, a week
ago, even an hour ago. Communists are repressed and frightened people.
The captor in Korea was in exactly the same position as the captive,
except that he was farther along on the assembly line. He had his responsibilities to the system, and if his fulfillment of them was called
into question he was terrified. A ridiculous incident that took place in
one of the prison camps illustrates this. After an indoctrination session,
a G.I. was walking away from headquarters between two political instructors, one of whom was expounding some Marxist doctrine. When
he finished, the prisoner said, pointing to the other man, 'But your friend
here told me different.' For a moment, the two Communists stared at
each other. Then both started running back toward headquarters as fast
as they could, each, presumably, intent on preventing the other from
denouncing him as a deviationist. Such conduct is understandable only
when you realize that the basic psychological aim of Communism, the
aim that is at once its greatest strength and its greatest weakness, is the

utter isolation of the individual from his fellows — a really diabolical strategy. One of the big problems the Communists faced in the beginning, when they were organizing their government, was how to keep their people strictly loyal to the Party line. It was a police problem, but it would have required one policeman per person, and anyway who would have policed the policeman? The problem seemed insoluble. So what did the Communists do? They simply evolved a means of isolating every person emotionally from every other person, permitting each to turn only to the system for guidance and friendship. This was, in its way, a brilliant maneuver. It created a new kind of police force — a completely effective one that operates around the clock without a hitch and requires no salary. Some of the seemingly absurd demands of the Communists in the Korean camps make sense in the light of this psychological objective. Now and then, a Communist would bawl out a G.I. violently for some trivial offense, such as not brushing his teeth. The G.I. would be puzzled, and rise meekly before everybody and confess that he hadn't brushed his teeth. It seemed too foolish a thing to take a stand on. But once a man had humbled himself, even about something as meaningless as this, the Communists found it easier to get him to criticize himself and other prisoners on more important grounds. The men did not realize that acceding in these matters was subtly alienating them from each other and making them emotionally dependent on the system, until at length it became the only source of either praise or blame."

When I saw Mr. Milton[3] again, he said, "By now, you have a broad picture of the conditions that necessitated the setting up of the Code of Conduct, and you know something about what caused these conditions. As you can see, the picture isn't a pretty one. But it has its compensations. For one thing, the Army has met a Communist enemy for the first time, and that has given us a good insight into Communist methods of handling prisoners. We have learned that they play no favorites. What they did to us they do to their own people. Now that we know what they do, we've found that the Army's training and previous standards of conduct, while essentially right and proper, did not go far

[3] Hugh M. Milton II, Assistant Secretary of the Army for Manpower and Reserve Forces, who had been in charge of the Army study of Korean prisoner-of-war problems.

enough. We have therefore taken additional steps to prepare the men for the kind of thing they encountered in Korea, and we are confident these will be helpful. I also ought to say at this point that after we had learned more about the Communists' handling of prisoners and had begun to understand it, we were very pleased that so many of our men had stood up so well, when they had nothing to fall back on but their own staunch characters and our insufficient training."

Milton told me that while the Army is still concentrating, first and foremost, on producing a healthy, hardy, well-disciplined, and properly motivated soldier who will avoid capture — a captured soldier has naturally failed in his primary purpose, which is to destroy the enemy — it has changed its policy on telling men what to do in case of capture. In the past, there was strong resistance among the authorities to giving them such information; the argument against it was that if a man knew what to do he was more likely to surrender. The Korean experience and the changing nature of warfare in general have, the Army feels, made this argument an outmoded one. With greater mobility of troops in combat and with the increased use of paratroopers, the risk of capture has mounted. Reasoning in the old way, it is felt, is like arguing that a sailor should be forbidden to learn to swim because his superiors want him to stay with his ship until the last possible moment. Suppose an enemy torpedo dumps him into the water and he finds himself six feet from a life preserver? Figuratively speaking, this occurred too many times in the Korean prison camps.

"Experience has shown that the Communists will humiliate and debase anyone in their hands," Milton said. "The soldier's best defense against this treatment, of course, is his own raw courage. But the Army now realizes that a man's nerve can be greatly stiffened if he is taught exactly how his captors will go about trying to break that nerve. Their step-by-step undermining of loyalty will be made much more difficult if our troops are forewarned. Returned prisoners have agreed that one of the best possible defenses against Communist tactics would be mental preparation. That sounds elementary, yet it is a new concept, resulting from a new set of international conditions and from the new experiences we had in Korea. Our service men in prison camps must work together as disciplined units to resist the enemy's demands — mentally and morally. They may be deprived of sleep, food, and medical attention in a prison camp, and they should expect this and have the will to live while these things are lacking. If there's nothing else to support life, they must not balk at whatever food and drink — however unpleasant — the enemy offers them. They should have some familiarity with nutrition, first aid, and preventive medicine. On the spiritual side, *esprit de corps* and a feeling of comradeship are great aids to morale. So are faith in democracy and adherence to religious beliefs. Many of the men said that in prison camps these intangibles were of greater help to them than anything else. Now, much more than in the past, such things bulk large in Army training."

A number of measures have been taken as a result of the prisoner-of-war study. Perhaps the most important are based on the President's six-point code, and deal with the education of the whole Army in the proper conduct of troops after capture. "Many of the men who collaborated in Korean camps pleaded innocent of misconduct on the ground that they had acted on orders from their superiors," said Milton. "One of the hardest things to make clear, both legally and logically, is that a man has a loyalty to discipline but also an independent loyalty to his country. The two should be reconciled, and they must be reconciled if our men are to cope with a devious enemy like the Communists, who, naturally, try to see to it that orders favorable to their own ends will be issued by weak officers and that weak men will obey them. With our new program, the Army feels that this reconciliation between the two kinds of loyalty can be accomplished." In connection with this program, the Army has issued a basic pamphlet explaining Communist indoctrination and interrogation methods in detail and suggesting simple ways to render them ineffective, and has also prepared several training circulars and films presenting techniques that will help men trapped behind enemy lines to evade capture or, if they are captured, to escape. Tackling the problem from another direction, the Army has instituted a group replacement policy, known as Operation Gyroscope, whereby units, instead of individuals, are rotated in assignments at home and abroad. This, it is believed, enables a soldier to identify himself more strongly with his unit, and thus greatly increases his loyalty to it; the unit should consequently be more effective in combat, and also, if any of its members are captured, they should be more able to resist pressure in a prison camp.

The Army has decided to adhere to its policy of authorizing prisoners to give the enemy nothing more than their name, rank, serial number, and date of birth. This decision was reached after months of investigation and soul-searching as to the best course to follow, both practically and ethically. "You can argue about such things till dooms-day, but the Communist challenge has got to be met," said Milton. "And it's got to be met in an American way — no compromise with evil. If this means that our troops must withstand emotional pressure and psychological pain, then, for the good of the country, these must be borne. If the Communists alter their methods to include physical tor-ture, that, too, must be endured."

The Army, Milton went on, wants as many people as possible to think about these matters. "Overcoming Communism is not simply an Army problem," he said. "It's a truly national problem. And don't forget — the battle against Communism is waged largely at the level of the individual, and the earlier the preparation the better. The Army would like to see every American parent, teacher, and clergyman work to instill in every one of our children a specific understanding of the dif-ferences between our way of life and the Communist way of life, and, even more important, give every child, in the blunt, old-fashioned spirit, a firm regard for right and an abiding distaste for wrong. The Army's period of training is too brief to make changes in the habits of a life-time. By the time a young man enters the Army, he should possess a set of sound moral values and the strength of character to live by them. Then, with Army training, he may become something very close to military perfection — the ideal citizen soldier."

⇜§ FOR DISCUSSION AND WRITING

1. Mr. Kinkead entitled the article of which this is the last part "The Study of Something New in History." What is the "something new"? Why, in the study of this subject, is there need for very great care in weighing evidence and in ascertaining the background and reliability of witnesses?

2. Point out four or five examples given here of loss of allegiance not only to one's country but to one's fellow prisoners. Why is the latter the more shocking? What examples does Kinkead cite of the inability of American prisoners to adjust to primitive conditions of living? What reason is sug-gested for that inability? What explanation is given of the Amercans' re-

jection of the one protein-and-mineral food available, soybeans? In what sense was this rejection a form of suicide?

3. Where does Kinkead show that there was an actual sufficiency for living, in terms of food, shelter, and clothing (although, unfortunately, there were no hamburgers or flush toilets)? How is the disease "give-up-itis" illustrated? Is the situation Kinkead describes a case of actual *loss* of instinct (instinct to "live like an animal") or of some sort of special short-circuiting of instinct by a particular kind of background? What would you say for or against a deliberate training of young people in the exigencies of living "like an animal"?

4. How, according to this article, did the Chinese technique of indoctrination work on the prisoners' sense of guilt? on their stock ideas? on their apathy? Kinkead makes five classifications of those Americans who went over to the Communists; what are the five classifications? What was the technique used in exploiting them?

5. What distinction is made between "brainwashing" and "indoctrination"?

6. Why is the problem raised in this article more than an Army problem? At what level of education should it be encountered, and how?

7. Write a paper on one of the following subjects: the assumptions of perpetual ease and security in "the American way of life"; an incident, or incidents, which you have observed that illustrate the ageless question, "Am I my brother's keeper?"; a program of education that would counteract the phenomena observed in this article.

The Example of Perfection

THE IDEA *of a paradise island, where nature is untiringly bountiful and where man may experience his own perfection in untainted happiness, is a conception older than history, old as those oldest myths that had already, through oral transmission, become confused and fragmented by the time there were written records—like the Sumerian myth of Gilgamesh, who came upon an island Eden in the course of his search for a plant known to give eternal life to those who ate of its leaves. Such legends, incorporating what C. G. Jung would call the "primordial image" of an earthly paradise, are universal. Geographically, islands are preferred—like the Greek Isles of the Blest, or Fortunate Isles, lying in the western sea, peopled by those mortals on whom the gods had conferred immortality, and the Welsh Avalon, or Isle of Apples, an abode of heroes to which King Arthur was conveyed, and many others that have been the subject of sagas in all languages. One may speculate on the preference for islands: removal from the mainland by distances of water suggests a total moral and spiritual removal from old corrupt histories, habits, and harms—a "rebirth," a "new start." Also, imagination easily exploits the possibility that, in the vast oceans of the earth, there may really be such islands, known to ancient travelers and reported by legend,* but far, far away, the routes lost; therefore cartographers of the fourteenth and fifteenth centuries put them on maps and they became objects of search for voyages of discovery.

Plato, in the TIMAEUS, describes the legendary island of Atlantis (as a report made by the sixth-century Athenian sage and lawgiver Solon, of what he had been told by Egyptian priests). It was an island bigger than Asia Minor, lying just beyond the Pillars of Hercules (the straits of Gibraltar), with an archipelago of lesser islands behind it; it had been a powerful kingdom 9,000 years before the birth of Solon, until the sea overwhelmed it. In the CRITIAS, Plato starts to develop the history of Atlantis as an ideal commonwealth. In the REPUBLIC (from which the selection here is taken) he loosens the Utopian conception of Atlantis from its mythological moorings and develops the idea dialectically as a problem in practical politics. The REPUBLIC is the most comprehensively detailed and the most powerfully influential of all Utopian imaginings; it has acted as the original yeast of all modern socialist planning. Some of its chief principles were incorporated in the earlier stages of the Russian Revolution and are still dominant in revolutionary modern China. They are implicit in modern Israeli kibbutz culture—described, in the following section, by Melford Spiro, in pages from his KIBBUTZ: VENTURE IN UTOPIA. Even Paul Goodman's conception of "community" —represented here in his essay "Utopian Thinking"—was brought to birth by Plato.

In Gilgamesh's mythical adventure, the trees of the earthly paradise were hung with jewels, a notion that appears to be in somewhat debased taste; but there is always a chance for vulgarity in fantasies of perfect happiness, perfect satisfaction of human desires —as in the middle-aged Middle Westerner's idea of retirement in Florida or California, where oranges and figs and purple clusters of grapes fall effortlessly into the mouth as one lies supine in perpetual sunshine on the ocean strand. Corrective of that inanity, a snake wriggled into the Biblical Eden, and immediately interesting things

*began to happen; for though privileged places of outdoor nature
may bloom eternally, providing a warm bath of food and pleasant
sensations like a placenta, man carries within him his imperfections,
seeds of destruction, the dynamics of a possible adulthood. The way
in which the natural evils of the human condition—the
psychologically innate possibilities for evil—are encountered in
Utopian literature is one of its most interesting aspects. Voltaire,
at the end of his chapter on Eldorado in* CANDIDE, *puts the problem,
with witty simplicity, as a matter of choice: ". . . these two happy men
resolved to be so no longer" (an index of human precociousness
which Dostoievsky developed at length in his* NOTES FROM
UNDERGROUND). *Plato put rigorous educational controls on that kind
of perverse choice; Samuel Butler, in his* EREWHON, *treated it by family
"straighteners," or headshrinkers, general practitioners whose
profession is moral rather than physical science. Thomas Mann,
returning to the primordial image of an earthly paradise, in Hans
Castorp's vision in* THE MAGIC MOUNTAIN, *integrates with that
charming vision the most obscene evil, belonging to each other as
the palm and back of the hand.*

*The mind swirls and maintains substance and gravity on the axis
of its antipodes—its consciousness of imperfection and its idea of
perfection. That bipolarity has never been more naïvely visible than
today, when the hungry generations come into being faster than the
food to feed them, and when the best of human genius is used to
devise landings on a barren moon, a perverse Utopia. The word
"Utopia" means "nowhere." The literature of Utopia provides a
spectrum of human self-consciousness, consciousness of lack and ideals
of fulfillment, from the green world of the primordial paradisiacal
image to the breathless smallpoxed nowhere of a dead star.*

Plato ❧ The Guardians of the Republic

❧ See note on Plato, page 139. The persons in the dialogue are Socrates and Glaucon, and briefly Adeimantus. ❧

[*Socrates:*] What is the next point to be settled? Is it not the question, which of these Guardians are to be rulers and which are to obey?

[*Glaucon:*] No doubt.

Well, it is obvious that the elder must have authority over the young, and that the rulers must be the best.

Yes.

And as among farmers the best are those with a natural turn for farming, so, if we want the best among our Guardians, we must take those naturally fitted to watch over a commonwealth. They must have the right sort of intelligence and ability; and also they must look upon the commonwealth as their special concern — the sort of concern that is felt for something so closely bound up with oneself that its interests and fortunes, for good or ill, are held to be identical with one's own.

From the *Republic* by Plato, translated by F. M. Cornford. Oxford University Press, 1941.

Exactly.

So the kind of men we must choose from among the Guardians will be those who, when we look at the whole course of their lives, are found to be full of zeal to do whatever they believe is for the good of the commonwealth and never willing to act against its interest.

Yes, they will be the men we want.

We must watch them, I think, at every age and see whether they are capable of preserving this conviction that they must do what is best for the community, never forgetting it or allowing themselves to be either forced or bewitched into throwing it over.

How does this throwing over come about?

I will explain. When a belief passes out of the mind, a man may be willing to part with it, if it is false and he has learnt better, or unwilling, if it is true.

I see how he might be willing to let it go; but you must explain how he can be unwilling.

Where is your difficulty? Don't you agree that men are unwilling to be deprived of good, though ready enough to part with evil? Or that to be deceived about the truth is evil, to possess it good? Or don't you think that possessing truth means thinking of things as they really are?

You are right. I do agree that men are unwilling to be robbed of a true belief.

When that happens to them, then, it must be by theft, or violence, or bewitchment.

Again I do not understand.

Perhaps my metaphors are too high-flown. I call it theft when one is persuaded out of one's belief or forgets it. Argument in the one case, and time in the other, steal it away without one's knowing what is happening. You understand now?

Yes.

And by violence I mean being driven to change one's mind by pain or suffering.

That too I understand, and you are right.

And bewitchment, as I think you would agree, occurs when a man is beguiled out of his opinion by the allurements of pleasure or scared out of it under the spell of panic.

Yes, all delusions are like a sort of bewitchment.

As I said just now, then, we must find out who are the best guardians of this inward conviction that they must always do what they believe to be best for the commonwealth. We shall have to watch them from earliest childhood and set them tasks in which they would be most likely to forget or to be beguiled out of this duty. We shall then choose only those whose memory holds firm and who are proof against delusion.

Yes.

We must also subject them to ordeals of toil and pain and watch for the same qualities there. And we must observe them when exposed to the test of yet a third kind of bewitchment. As people lead colts up to alarming noises to see whether they are timid, so these young men must be brought into terrifying situations and then into scenes of pleasure, which will put them to severer proof than gold tried in the furnace. If we find one bearing himself well in all these trials and resisting every enchantment, a true guardian of himself, preserving always that perfect rhythm and harmony of being which he has acquired from his training in music and poetry, such a one will be of the greatest service to the commonwealth as well as to himself. Whenever we find one who has come unscathed through every test in childhood, youth, and manhood, we shall set him as a Ruler to watch over the commonwealth; he will be honoured in life, and after death receive the highest tribute of funeral rites and other memorials. All who do not reach this standard we must reject. And that, I think, my dear Glaucon, may be taken as an outline of the way in which we shall select Guardians to be set in authority as Rulers.

I am very much of your mind.

These, then, may properly be called Guardians in the fullest sense, who will ensure that neither foes without shall have the power, nor friends within the wish, to do harm. Those young men whom up to now we have been speaking of as Guardians, will be better described as Auxiliaries, who will enforce the decisions of the Rulers.

I agree.

Now, said I, can we devise something in the way of those convenient fictions we spoke of earlier, a single bold flight of invention, which we may induce the community in general, and if possible the Rulers themselves, to accept?

What kind of fiction?

Nothing new; something like an Eastern tale of what, according to the poets, has happened before now in more than one part of the world. The poets have been believed; but the thing has not happened in our day, and it would be hard to persuade anyone that it could ever happen again.

You seem rather shy of telling this story of yours.

With good reason, as you will see when I have told it.

Out with it; don't be afraid.

Well, here it is; though I hardly know how to find the courage or the words to express it. I shall try to convince, first the Rulers and the soldiers,* and then the whole community, that all that nurture and education which we gave them was only something they seemed to experience as it were in a dream. In reality they were the whole time down inside the earth, being moulded and fostered while their arms and all their equipment were being fashioned also; and at last, when they were complete, the earth sent them up from her womb into the light of day. So now they must think of the land they dwell in as a mother and nurse, whom they must take thought for and defend against any attack, and of their fellow citizens as brothers born of the same soil.

You might well be bashful about coming out with your fiction.

No doubt; but still you must hear the rest of the story. It is true, we shall tell our people in this fable, that all of you in this land are brothers; but the god who fashioned you mixed gold in the composition of those among you who are fit to rule, so that they are of the most precious quality; and he put silver in the Auxiliaries,[1] and iron and brass in the farmers and craftsmen. Now, since you are all of one stock, although your children will generally be like their parents, sometimes a golden parent may have a silver child or a silver parent a golden one, and so on with all the other combinations. So the first and chief injunction laid by heaven upon the Rulers is that, among all the things of which they must show themselves good guardians, there is none that needs to be so carefully watched as the mixture of metals in the souls of the children. If a child of their own is born with an alloy of iron or brass, they must, without the smallest pity, assign him the station proper to his nature and thrust him out among the craftsmen or the farmers. If, on the contrary,

---

* Note that the Guardians themselves are to accept this allegory, if possible. It is not 'propaganda' foisted on the masses by the Rulers. [Translator's note.]

[1] The militia, the citizen army.

these classes produce a child with gold or silver in his composition, they will promote him, according to his value, to be a Guardian or an Auxiliary. They will appeal to a prophecy that ruin will come upon the state when it passes into the keeping of a man of iron or brass. Such is the story; can you think of any device to make them believe it?

Not in the first generation; but their sons and descendants might believe it, and finally the rest of mankind.

Well, said I, even so it might have a good effect in making them care more for the commonwealth and for one another; for I think I see what you mean.

So, I continued, we will leave the success of our story to the care of popular tradition; and now let us arm these sons of Earth and lead them, under the command of their Rulers, to the site of our city. There let them look round for the best place to fix their camp, from which they will be able to control any rebellion against the laws from within and to beat off enemies who may come from without like wolves to attack the fold. When they have pitched their camp and offered sacrifice to the proper divinities, they must arrange their sleeping quarters; and these must be sufficient to shelter them from winter cold and summer heat.

Naturally. You mean they are going to live there?

Yes, said I; but live like soldiers, not like men of business.

What is the difference?

I will try to explain. It would be very strange if a shepherd were to disgrace himself by keeping, for the protection of his flock, dogs who were so ill-bred and badly trained that hunger or unruliness or some bad habit or other would set them worrying the sheep and behaving no better than wolves. We must take every precaution against our Auxiliaries treating the citizens in any such way and, because they are stronger, turning into savage tyrants instead of friendly allies; and they will have been furnished with the best of safeguards, if they have really been educated in the right way.

But surely there is nothing wrong with their education.

We must not be too positive about that, my dear Glaucon; but we can be sure of what we said not long ago, that if they are to have the best chance of being gentle and humane to one another and to their charges, they must have the right education, whatever that may be.

We were certainly right there.

Then besides that education, it is only common sense to say that the dwellings and other belongings provided for them must be such as will neither make them less perfect Guardians nor encourage them to maltreat their fellow citizens.

True.

With that end in view, let us consider how they should live and be housed. First, none of them must possess any private property beyond the barest necessaries. Next, no one is to have any dwelling or storehouse that is not open for all to enter at will. Their food, in the quantities required by men of temperance and courage who are in training for war, they will receive from the other citizens as the wages of their guardianship, fixed so that there shall be just enough for the year with nothing over; and they will have meals in common and all live together like soldiers in a camp. Gold and silver, we shall tell them, they will not need, having the divine counterparts of those metals always in their souls as a god-given possession, whose purity it is not lawful to sully by the acquisition of that mortal dross, current among mankind, which has been the occasion of so many unholy deeds. They alone of all the citizens are forbidden to touch and handle silver or gold, or to come under the same roof with them, or wear them as ornaments, or drink from vessels made of them. This manner of life will be their salvation and make them the saviours of the commonwealth. If ever they should come to possess land of their own and houses and money, they will give up their guardianship for the management of their farms and households and become tyrants at enmity with their fellow citizens instead of allies. And so they will pass all their lives in hating and being hated, plotting and being plotted against, in much greater fear of their enemies at home than of any foreign foe, and fast heading for the destruction that will soon overwhelm their country with themselves. For all these reasons let us say that this is how our Guardians are to be housed and otherwise provided for, and let us make laws accordingly.

By all means, said Glaucon.

Here Adeimantus interposed. Socrates, he said, how would you meet the objection that you are not making these people particularly happy? It is their own fault too, if they are not; for they are really masters of the state, and yet they get no good out of it as other rulers do, who own lands, build themselves fine houses with handsome furniture, offer private sacrifices to the gods, and entertain visitors from abroad; who possess, in fact, that gold and silver you spoke of, with everything else that is usually thought necessary for happiness. These people seem like nothing so much as a garrison of mercenaries posted in the city and perpetually mounting guard.

Yes, I said, and what is more they will serve for their food only without getting a mercenary's pay, so that they will not be able to travel on their own account or to make presents to a mistress or to spend as they please in other ways, like the people who are commonly thought happy. You have forgotten to include these counts in your indictment, and many more to the same effect.

Well, take them as included now.

And you want to hear the answer?

Yes.

We shall find one, I think, by keeping to the line we have followed so far. We shall say that, though it would not be surprising if even these people were perfectly happy under such conditions, our aim in founding the commonwealth was not to make any one class specially happy, but to secure the greatest possible happiness for the community as a whole. We thought we should have the best chance of finding justice in a state so constituted, just as we should find injustice where the constitution was of the worst possible type; we could then decide the question which has been before us all this time. For the moment, we are constructing, as we believe, the state which will be happy as a whole, not trying to secure the well-being of a select few; we shall study a state of the opposite kind presently. It is as if we were colouring a statue** and someone came up and blamed us for not putting the most beautiful colours on the noblest parts of the figure; the eyes, for instance, should be painted crimson, but we had made them black. We should think it a fair answer to say: Really, you must not expect us to paint eyes so handsome as not to look like eyes at all. This applies to all the parts: the question is whether, by giving each its proper colour, we make the whole beautiful. So too, in the present case, you must not press us to endow our Guardians with a happiness that will make them anything rather than guardians. We could quite easily clothe our farmers in gorgeous robes, crown them with gold, and invite them to till the soil at their pleasure; or we might set our potters to lie on couches by their fire,

** Greek statues were commonly tinted, wholly or in part. [Translator's note.]

passing round the wine and making merry, with their wheel at hand to work at whenever they felt so inclined. We could make all the rest happy in the same sort of way, and so spread this well-being through the whole community. But you must not put that idea into our heads; if we take your advice, the farmer will be no farmer, the potter no longer a potter; none of the elements that make up the community will keep its character. In many cases this does not matter so much: if a cobbler goes to the bad and pretends to be what he is not, he is not a danger to the state; but, as you must surely see, men who make only a vain show of being guardians of the laws and of the commonwealth bring the whole state to utter ruin, just as, on the other hand, its good government and well-being depend entirely on them. We, in fact, are making genuine Guardians who will be the last to bring harm upon the commonwealth; if our critic aims rather at producing a happiness like that of a party of peasants feasting at a fair, what he has in mind is something other than a civic community. So we must consider whether our aim in establishing Guardians is to secure the greatest possible happiness for them, or happiness is something of which we should watch the development in the whole commonwealth. If so, we must compel these Guardians and Auxiliaries of ours to second our efforts; and they, and all the rest with them, must be induced to make themselves perfect masters each of his own craft. In that way, as the community grows into a well-ordered whole, the several classes may be allowed such measure of happiness as their nature will compass.

I think that is an admirable reply. . . .[2]

[*The discussion above is from Chapter X of the* Republic. *What follows is from Chapter XVI, on community of women and children in the ideal commonwealth.*]

So far, then, in regulating the position of women, we may claim to have come safely through with one hazardous proposal, that male and female Guardians shall have all occupations in common. The consistency of the argument is an assurance that the plan is a good one and also feasible. We are like swimmers who have breasted the first wave without being swallowed up.

Not such a small wave either.

[2] Compare page 659, where Socrates says that the Guardians will be happier than any Olympic victor.

You will not call it large when you see the next.

Let me have a look at the next one, then.

Here it is: a law which follows from that principle and all that has gone before, namely that, of these Guardians, no one man and one woman are to set up house together privately: wives are to be held in common by all; so too are the children, and no parent is to know his own child, nor any child his parent.

It will be much harder to convince people that that is either a feasible plan or a good one.

As to its being a good plan, I imagine no one would deny the immense advantage of wives and children being held in common, provided it can be done. I should expect dispute to arise chiefly over the question whether it is possible.

There may well be a good deal of dispute over both points.

You mean, I must meet attacks on two fronts. I was hoping to escape one by running away: if you agreed it was a good plan, then I should only have had to inquire whether it was feasible.

No, we have seen through that manoeuvre. You will have to defend both positions.

Well, I must pay the penalty for my cowardice. But grant me one favour. Let me indulge my fancy, like one who entertains himself with idle day-dreams on a solitary walk. Before he has any notion how his desires can be realized, he will set aside that question, to save himself the trouble of reckoning what may or may not be possible. He will assume that his wish has come true, and amuse himself with settling all the details of what he means to do then. So a lazy mind encourages itself to be lazier than ever; and I am giving way to the same weakness myself. I want to put off till later that question, how the thing can be done. For the moment, with your leave, I shall assume it to be possible, and ask how the Rulers will work out the details in practice; and I shall argue that the plan, once carried into effect, would be the best thing in the world for our commonwealth and for its Guardians. This is what I shall now try to make out with your help, if you will allow me to postpone the other question.

Very good; I have no objection.

Well, if our Rulers are worthy of the name, and their Auxiliaries likewise, these latter will be ready to do what they are told, and the Rulers, in giving their commands, will themselves obey our laws and will be faithful to their spirit in any details we leave to their discretion.

No doubt.

It is for you, then, as their lawgiver, who have already selected the men, to select for association with them women who are so far as possible of the same natural capacity. Now since none of them will have any private home of his own, but they will share the same dwelling and eat at common tables, the two sexes will be together; and meeting without restriction for exercise and all through their upbringing, they will surely be drawn towards union with one another by a necessity of their nature — necessity is not too strong a word, I think?

Not too strong for the constraint of love, which for the mass of mankind is more persuasive and compelling than even the necessity of mathematical proof.

Exactly. But in the next place, Glaucon, anything like unregulated unions would be a profanation in a state whose citizens lead the good life. The Rulers will not allow such a thing.

No, it would not be right.

Clearly, then, we must have marriages, as sacred as we can make them; and this sanctity will attach to those which yield the best results.

Certainly.

How are we to get the best results? You must tell me, Glaucon, because I see you keep sporting dogs and a great many game birds at your house; and there is something about their mating and breeding that you must have noticed.

What is that?

In the first place, though they may be of good stock, are there not some that turn out to be better than the rest?

There are.

And do you breed from all indiscriminately? Are you not careful to breed from the best so far as you can?

Yes.

And from those in their prime, rather than the very young or the very old?

Yes.

Otherwise, the stock of your birds or dogs would deteriorate very much, wouldn't it?

It would.

And the same is true of horses or of any animal?

It would be very strange if it were not.

Dear me, said I; we shall need consummate skill in our Rulers, if it is also true of the human race.

Well, it is true. But why must they be so skilful?

Because they will have to administer a large dose of that medicine we spoke of earlier.[3] An ordinary doctor is thought good enough for a patient who will submit to be dieted and can do without medicine; but he must be much more of a man if drugs are required.

True, but how does that apply?

It applies to our Rulers: it seems they will have to give their subjects a considerable dose of imposition and deception for their good. We said, if you remember, that such expedients would be useful as a sort of medicine.

Yes, a very sound principle.

Well, it looks as if this sound principle will play no small part in this matter of marriage and child-bearing.

How so?

It follows from what we have just said that, if we are to keep our flock at the highest pitch of excellence, there should be as many unions of the best of both sexes, and as few of the inferior, as possible, and that only the offspring of the better unions should be kept. And again, no one but the Rulers must know how all this is being effected; otherwise our herd of Guardians may become rebellious.

Quite true.

We must, then, institute certain festivals at which we shall bring together the brides and the bridegrooms. There will be sacrifices, and our poets will write songs befitting the occasion. The number of marriages we shall leave to the Rulers' discretion. They will aim at keeping the number of the citizens as constant as possible, having regard to losses caused by war, epidemics, and so on; and they must do their best to see that our state does not become either great or small.

Very good.

I think they will have to invent some ingenious system of drawing lots, so that, at each pairing off, the inferior candidate may blame his luck rather than the Rulers.

Yes, certainly.

Moreover, young men who acquit themselves well in war and other

[3] A "convenient fiction." See page 645.

duties, should be given, among other rewards and privileges, more liberal opportunities to sleep with a wife, for the further purpose that, with good excuse, as many as possible of the children may be begotten of such fathers.

Yes.

As soon as children are born, they will be taken in charge by officers appointed for the purpose, who may be men or women or both, since offices are to be shared by both sexes. The children of the better parents they will carry to the crèche[4] to be reared in the care of nurses living apart in a certain quarter of the city. Those of the inferior parents and any children of the rest that are born defective will be hidden away, in some appropriate manner that must be kept secret.

They must be, if the breed of our Guardians is to be kept pure.

These officers will also superintend the nursing of the children. They will bring the mothers to the crèche when their breasts are full, while taking every precaution that no mother shall know her own child; and if the mothers have not enough milk, they will provide wet-nurses. They will limit the time during which the mothers will suckle their children, and hand over all the hard work and sitting up at night to nurses and attendants.

That will make child-bearing an easy business for the Guardians' wives.

So it should be. To go on with our scheme: we said that children should be born from parents in the prime of life. Do you agree that this lasts about twenty years for a woman, and thirty for a man? A woman should bear children for the commonwealth from her twentieth to her fortieth year; a man should begin to beget them when he has passed 'the racer's prime in swiftness,' and continue till he is fifty-five.

Those are certainly the years in which both the bodily and the mental powers of man and woman are at their best.

If a man either above or below this age meddles with the begetting of children for the commonwealth, we shall hold it an offence against divine and human law. He will be begetting for his country a child conceived in darkness and dire incontinence, whose birth, if it escape detection, will not have been sanctioned by the sacrifices and prayers offered at each marriage festival, when priests and priestesses join with the whole community in praying that the children to be born may be even better and more useful citizens than their parents.

4 Public nursery.

You are right.

The same law will apply to any man within the prescribed limits who touches a woman also of marriageable age when the Ruler has not paired them. We shall say that he is foisting on the commonwealth a bastard, unsanctioned by law or by religion.

Perfectly right.

As soon, however, as the men and the women have passed the age prescribed for producing children, we shall leave them free to form a connexion with whom they will, except that a man shall not take his daughter or daughter's daughter or mother or mother's mother, nor a woman her son or father or her son's son or father's father; and all this only after we have exhorted them to see that no child, if any be conceived, shall be brought to light, or, if they cannot prevent its birth, to dispose of it on the understanding that no such child can be reared.

That too is reasonable. But how are they to distinguish fathers and daughters and those other relations you mentioned?

They will not, said I. But, reckoning from the day when he becomes a bridegroom, a man will call all children born in the tenth or the seventh month sons and daughters, and they will call him father. Their children again he will call grandchildren, and they will call his group grandfathers and grandmothers; and all who are born within the period during which their mothers and fathers were having children will be called brothers and sisters. This will provide for those restrictions on unions that we mentioned; but the law will allow bothers and sisters to live together, if the lot so falls out and the Delphic oracle also approves.

Very good.

This, then, Glaucon, is the manner in which the Guardians of your commonwealth are to hold their wives and children in common. Must we not next find arguments to establish that it is consistent with our other institutions and also by far the best plan?

Yes, surely.

We had better begin by asking what is the greatest good at which the lawgiver should aim in laying down the constitution of a state, and what is the worst evil. We can then consider whether our proposals are in keeping with that good and irreconcilable with the evil.

By all means.

Does not the worst evil for a state arise from anything that tends to rend it asunder and destroy its unity, while nothing does it more good than whatever tends to bind it together and make it one?

That is true.

And are not citizens bound together by sharing in the same pleasures and pains, all feeling glad or grieved on the same occasions of gain or loss; whereas the bond is broken when such feelings are no longer universal, but any event of public or personal concern fills some with joy and others with distress?

Certainly.

And this disunion comes about when the words 'mine' and 'not mine,' 'another's' and 'not another's' are not applied to the same things throughout the community. The best ordered state will be the one in which the largest number of persons use these terms in the same sense, and which accordingly most nearly resembles a single person. When one of us hurts his finger, the whole extent of those bodily connexions which are gathered up in the soul and unified by its ruling element is made aware and it all shares as a whole in the pain of the suffering part; hence we say that the man has a pain in his finger. The same thing is true of the pain or pleasure felt when any other part of the person suffers or is relieved.

Yes; I agree that the best organized community comes nearest to that condition.

And so it will recognize as a part of itself the individual citizen to whom good or evil happens, and will share as a whole in his joy or sorrow.

It must, if the constitution is sound.

It is time now to go back to our own commonwealth and see whether these conclusions apply to it more than to any other type of state. In all alike there are rulers and common people, all of whom will call one another fellow citizens.

Yes.

But in other states the people have another name as well for their rulers, haven't they?

Yes; in most they call them masters; in democracies, simply the government.

And in ours?

The people will look upon their rulers as preservers and protectors.

And how will our rulers regard the people?

As those who maintain them and pay them wages.

And elsewhere?

As slaves.

And what do rulers elsewhere call one another?

Colleagues.

And ours?

Fellow Guardians.

And in other states may not a ruler regard one colleague as a friend in whom he has an interest, and another as a stranger with whom he has nothing in common?

Yes, that often happens.

But that could not be so with your Guardians? None of them could ever treat a fellow Guardian as a stranger.

Certainly not. He must regard everyone whom he meets as brother or sister, father or mother, son or daughter, grandchild or grandparent.

Very good; but here is a further point. Will you not require them, not merely to use these family terms, but to behave as a real family? Must they not show towards all whom they call 'father' the customary reverence, care, and obedience due to a parent, if they look for any favour from gods or men, since to act otherwise is contrary to divine and human law? Should not all the citizens constantly reiterate in the hearing of the children from their earliest years such traditional maxims of conduct towards those whom they are taught to call father and their other kindred?

They should. It would be absurd that terms of kinship should be on their lips without any action to correspond.

In our community, then, above all others, when things go well or ill with any individual everyone will use that word 'mine' in the same sense and say that all is going well or ill with him and his.

Quite true.

And, as we said, this way of speaking and thinking goes with fellow-feeling; so that our citizens, sharing as they do in a common interest which each will call his own, will have all their feelings of pleasure or pain in common.

Assuredly.

A result that will be due to our institutions, and in particular to our Guardians' holding their wives and children in common.

Very much so.

But you will remember how, when we compared a well-ordered community to the body which shares in the pleasures and pains of any member, we saw in this unity the greatest good that a state can enjoy. So the conclusion is that our commonwealth owes to this sharing of wives and children by its protectors its enjoyment of the greatest of all goods.

Yes, that follows.

Moreover, this agrees with our principle that they were not to have houses or lands or any property of their own, but to receive sustenance from the other citizens, as wages for their guardianship, and to consume it in common. Only so will they keep to their true character; and our present proposals will do still more to make them genuine Guardians. They will not rend the community asunder by each applying that word 'mine' to different things and dragging off whatever he can get for himself into a private home, where he will have his separate family, forming a centre of exclusive joys and sorrows. Rather they will all, so far as may be, feel together and aim at the same ends, because they are convinced that all their interests are identical.

Quite so.

Again, if a man's person is his only private possession, lawsuits and prosecutions will all but vanish, and they will be free of those quarrels that arise from ownership of property and from having family ties. Nor would they be justified even in bringing actions for assault and outrage; for we shall pronounce it right and honourable for a man to defend himself against an assailant of his own age, and in that way they will be compelled to keep themselves fit.

That would be a sound law.

And it would also have the advantage that, if a man's anger can be satisfied in this way, a fit of passion is less likely to grow into a serious quarrel.

True.

But an older man will be given authority over all younger persons and power to correct them; whereas the younger will, naturally, not dare to strike the elder or do him any violence, except by command of a Ruler. He will not show him any sort of disrespect. Two guardian spirits, fear and reverence, will be enough to restrain him — reverence forbidding him to lay hands on a parent, and fear of all those others who as sons or brothers or fathers would come to the rescue.

Yes, that will be the result.

So our laws will secure that these men will live in complete peace with one another; and if they never quarrel among themselves, there is no fear of the rest of the community being divided either against them or against itself.

No.

There are other evils they will escape, so mean and petty that I hardly like to mention them: the poor man's flattery of the rich, and all the embarrassments and vexations of rearing a family and earning just enough to maintain a household; now borrowing and now refusing to repay, and by any and every means scraping together money to be handed over to wife and servants to spend. These sordid troubles are familiar and not worth describing.

Only too familiar.

Rid of all these cares, they will live a more enviable life than the Olympic victor, who is counted happy on the strength of far fewer blessings than our Guardians will enjoy. Their victory is the nobler, since by their success the whole commonwealth is preserved; and their reward of maintenance at the public cost is more complete, since their prize is to have every need of life supplied for themselves and for their children; their country honours them while they live, and when they die they receive a worthy burial.

Yes, they will be nobly rewarded.

Do you remember, then, how someone who shall be nameless reproached us for not making our Guardians happy: they were to possess nothing, though all the wealth of their fellow citizens was within their grasp? We replied, I believe, that we would consider that objection later, if it came in our way: for the moment we were bent on making our Guardians real guardians, and moulding our commonwealth with a view to the greatest happiness, not of one section of it, but of the whole.

Yes, I remember.

Well, it appears now that these protectors of our state will have a life better and more honourable than that of any Olympic victor; and we can hardly rank it on a level with the life of a shoemaker or other artisan or of a farmer.

I should think not.

However, it is right to repeat what I said at the time: if ever a Guardian tries to make himself happy in such a way that he will be a guardian no longer; if, not content with the moderation and security of this way of living which we think the best, he becomes possessed with some silly and childish notion of happiness, impelling him to make his power a means to appropriate all the citizens' wealth, then he will learn the wisdom of Hesiod's saying that the half is more than the whole.

My advice would certainly be that he should keep to his own way of living.

You do agree, then, that women are to take their full share with men in education, in the care of children, and in the guardianship of the other citizens; whether they stay at home or go out to war, they will be like watch-dogs which take their part either in guarding the fold or in hunting and share in every task so far as their strength allows. Such conduct will not be unwomanly, but all for the best and in accordance with the natural partnership of the sexes.

Yes, I agree.

✑ FOR DISCUSSION AND WRITING

1. Try to imagine your own psychological reaction if the ideas presented in this part of the *Republic* had been put in a straight essay form as dogmatic principles of the "ideal" society. What difference does the dialogue form make in determining one's interest, attention, and what might be called "intellectual tolerance"? The dialogue form shows us a live thought-process—thinking on the hoof, so to speak—more or less as our own thought-processes occur under the stimulus of conversation; thus what we are presented with is speculation rather than dogma. Why do we tend to give more serious and sympathetic consideration to ideas presented this way? (We can't all write Platonic dialogues, but the point is a valuable one to remember in any argumentative situation.) Where, occasionally, do you find Socrates' own personal qualities—of charm or wit or the way he insinuates that he himself is an intellectual coward or lazy, implying that his interlocutors are more intelligent? How would you characterize him —as really "humble" and without intellectual confidence, or as immensely shrewd in the psychology of persuasion?

2. If you have read other excerpts from Plato in this book (pages 139 and 305), you will recognize Socrates' reference, early in this selection, to men's natural love of the "good." How is that assumption shown in the first part

of the argument, about how men can be deprived of "true belief"? What particular educational means are suggested for young children to discipline them in such a way that they will not, when they become Guardians, forget what is "best" or be beguiled from it by delusions? What relationship is suggested between being "a true guardian of oneself" and a Guardian of the commonwealth?

3. What are the purposes of the "convenient fictions" that all members of the society are born out of the same earth and that each person has certain "metals" prevailing in him? (It would be a mistake, at this point, to be snooty about the gullibility of the ancient Greeks, for Socrates is merely suggesting parables of social commonplaces—for instance, such commonplace beliefs as those prevalent in our own society that the people "on the other side of the tracks" are inferior, that "blue blood" is different from other kinds of blood, that race or skin-color or religion makes one a different kind of human being from others, etc., etc.) How many classes are there in the Republic? What should be done if a Guardian happens to have a child in whom "iron" or "brass" predominates? Do you find any parallel here with modern educational selection, particularly with regard to high "I.Q.'s" and scientific talent?

4. Why should the future Guardians be made to live like soldiers, "as if training for war," rather than like "men of business"? Why should they have no private property, no private dwellings, no money of their own?

5. Adeimantus interposes the objection that this way of living prohibits happiness. What principle does Socrates set up to counter the objection?

6. Describe carefully the program for community of wives and children. What is the provision against promiscuous sexual unions? What comparison is made between human breeding and the breeding of animals? By what means would the breeding of the best of the race be secured? What punishment would be used to inhibit illicit unions? How would marriage between close relations be prevented? Why would this be a problem in the Republic? What exception is made for "brothers" and "sisters"? Is there a possible eugenic factor in this exception?

7. What, according to the argument here, is the "greatest good" of the state and therefore of the people who make up the state? How do the various social principles set forth in the preceding argument contribute to that "greatest good"?

8. How, finally, does Socrates speak of the question of "happiness"?

9. These portions of the *Republic* suggest a large number of subjects for papers. For instance, one might put up acute arguments on either side of the proposition that it is better that the parent should not know his own child nor the child his parent (one should be careful here of arguing wholly in abstractions; individual examples would be enlightening); or one might compare the education and discipline of Plato's Guardians with the education and discipline (if one can use the word in this context) of our modern "guardians of the Republic"—politicians, legislators, governors, statesmen; or one might write a critical paper—critical point for point—on Plato's conception of the ideal commonwealth; or one might write up one's own conception of an ideal society.

Voltaire ᱬᱟ The Best of All Possible Worlds

ᱬᱟ Pseudonym of François-Marie Arouet, French philosopher and satirist (1694-1778). Voltaire died just eleven years before the outbreak of the French Revolution, which so largely owed its articulation of principles to his tireless pamphleteering. On his hearse these words appeared: "He gave wings to the human intelligence; he prepared us for freedom." His wit is still fresh and brilliant in his *Philosophical Letters on the English* and in the "philosophical tales," *Zadig* and *Candide*—where he was able to utter the most dangerous political heresies against the ancien régime under cover of outrageous fantasy. The selection here is from the description of the country of Eldorado in *Candide;* it is suggested that the piece be read in conjunction with James Agee's fantasy on Candide in Eldorado, which immediately follows. ᱬᱟ

THEY drifted for some leagues between banks which were sometimes flowery, sometimes bare, sometimes flat, sometimes steep. The river continually became wider; finally it disappeared under an arch of frightful rocks which towered up to the very sky. The two travellers[1] were bold enough to trust themselves to the current under this arch. The stream, narrowed between walls, carried them with horrible rapidity and noise. After twenty-four hours they saw daylight again; but their canoe was wrecked on reefs; they had to crawl from rock to rock for a whole league and at last they discovered an immense horizon, bordered by inaccessible mountains. The country was cultivated for pleasure as well as for neces-

From *Candide* by Voltaire, translated by Richard Aldington (Nonesuch Press, n. d.).

[1] Candide and his valet, Cacambo. Candide (whose name implies his youthful candor, guilelessness, and sincerity) is a prince of Westphalia, Germany; after the most hair-raising adventures, he has now arrived in South America—presumably somewhere in Peru.

sity; everywhere the useful was agreeable. The roads were covered or rather ornamented with carriages of brilliant material and shape, carrying men and women of singular beauty, who were rapidly drawn along by large red sheep whose swiftness surpassed that of the finest horses of Andalusia, Tetuan and Mequinez.

"This country," said Candide, "is better than Westphalia."

He landed with Cacambo near the first village he came to. Several children of the village, dressed in torn gold brocade, were playing coits[2] outside the village. Our two men from the other world amused themselves by looking on; their coits were large round pieces, yellow, red and green, which shone with peculiar lustre. The travellers were curious enough to pick up some of them; they were of gold, emeralds and rubies, the least of which would have been the greatest ornament in the Mogul's throne.

"No doubt," said Cacambo, "these children are the sons of the King of this country playing at coits."

At that moment the village schoolmaster appeared to call them into school.

"This," said Candide, "is the tutor of the Royal Family."

The little beggars immediately left their game, abandoning their coits and everything with which they had been playing. Candide picked them up, ran to the tutor, and presented them to him humbly, giving him to understand by signs that their Royal Highnesses had forgotten their gold and their precious stones. The village schoolmaster smiled, threw them on the ground, gazed for a moment at Candide's face with much surprise and continued on his way.

The travellers did not fail to pick up the gold, the rubies and the emeralds.

"Where are we?" cried Candide. "The children of the Kings must be well brought up, since they are taught to despise gold and precious stones."

Cacambo was as much surprised as Candide. At last they reached the first house in the village, which was built like a European palace. There were crowds of people round the door and still more inside; very pleasant music could be heard and there was a delicious smell of cooking. Cacambo went up to the door and heard them speaking Peruvian; it was his maternal tongue, for every one knows that Cacambo was born in a village of Tucuman where nothing else is spoken.

[2] Quoits, a game something like horseshoes.

"I will act as your interpreter," he said to Candide, "this is an inn, let us enter."

Immediately two boys and two girls of the inn, dressed in cloth of gold, whose hair was bound up with ribbons, invited them to sit down to the table d'hôte. They served four soups each garnished with two parrots, a boiled condor which weighed two hundred pounds, two roast monkeys of excellent flavour, three hundred colibris in one dish and six hundred hummingbirds in another, exquisite ragouts and delicious pastries, all in dishes of a sort of rock-crystal. The boys and girls brought several sorts of drinks made of sugar-cane. Most of the guests were merchants and coachmen, all extremely polite, who asked Cacambo a few questions with the most delicate discretion and answered his in a satisfactory manner.

When the meal was over, Cacambo, like Candide, thought he could pay the reckoning by throwing on the table two of the large pieces of gold he had picked up; the host and hostess laughed until they had to hold their sides. At last they recovered themselves.

"Gentlemen," said the host, "we perceive you are strangers; we are not accustomed to seeing them. Forgive us if we began to laugh when you offered us in payment the stones from our highways. No doubt you have none of the money of this country, but you do not need any to dine here. All the hotels established for the utility of commerce are paid for by the government. You have been ill-entertained here because this is a poor village; but everywhere else you will be received as you deserve to be."

Cacambo explained to Candide all that the host had said, and Candide listened in the same admiration and disorder with which his friend Cacambo interpreted.

"What can this country be," they said to each other, "which is unknown to the rest of the world and where all nature is so different from ours? Probably it is the country where everything is for the best; for there must be one country of that sort. And, in spite of what Dr. Pangloss[3] said, I often noticed that everything went very ill in Westphalia."

[3] Dr. Pangloss (whose name puns on his wordiness and the specious explanations he has for everything) is Candide's tutor, famous for his parody of Leibniz—"Everything is for the best in this best of all possible worlds." For the time being, Dr. Pangloss has been lost along the way, but will turn up again, after being hanged, drawn, quartered, and disemboweled, with a ready explanation of why these experiences have been all for the best in the best of all possible worlds. His name has become an equivalent for fatuous optimism.

Cacambo informed the host of his curiosity, and the host said:

"I am a very ignorant man and am all the better for it; but we have here an old man who has retired from the court and who is the most learned and most communicative man in the kingdom."

And he at once took Cacambo to the old man. Candide now played only the second part and accompanied his valet.

They entered a very simple house, for the door was only of silver and the panelling of the apartments in gold, but so tastefully carved that the richest decorations did not surpass it. The antechamber indeed was only encrusted with rubies and emeralds; but the order with which everything was arranged atoned for this extreme simplicity.

The old man received the two strangers on a sofa padded with colibri feathers,[4] and presented them with drinks in diamond cups; after which he satisfied their curiosity in these words:

"I am a hundred and seventy-two years old and I heard from my late father, the King's equerry, the astonishing revolutions of Peru of which he had been an eye-witness. The kingdom where we now are is the ancient country of the Incas, who most imprudently left it to conquer part of the world and were at last destroyed by the Spaniards.

"The princes of their family who remained in their native country had more wisdom; with the consent of the nation, they ordered that no inhabitants should ever leave our little kingdom, and this it is that has preserved our innocence and our felicity. The Spaniards had some vague knowledge of this country, which they called Eldorado, and about a hundred years ago an Englishman named Raleigh came very near to it; but, since we are surrounded by inaccessible rocks and precipices, we have hitherto been exempt from the rapacity of the nations of Europe who have an inconceivable lust for the pebbles and mud of our land and would kill us to the last man to get possession of them."

The conversation was long; it touched upon the form of the government, manners, women, public spectacles and the arts. Finally Candide, who was always interested in metaphysics, asked through Cacambo whether the country had a religion. The old man blushed a little.

"How can you doubt it?" said he. "Do you think we are ingrates?"

Cacambo humbly asked what was the religion of Eldorado. The old man blushed again.

"Can there be two religions?" said he. "We have, I think, the religion of every one else; we adore God from evening until morning."

4 Hummingbird feathers.

"Do you adore only one god?" said Cacambo, who continued to act as the interpreter of Candide's doubts.

"Manifestly," said the old man, "there are not two or three or four. I must confess that the people of your world ask very extraordinary questions."

Candide continued to press the old man with questions; he wished to know how they prayed to God in Eldorado.

"We do not pray," said the good and respectable sage, "we have nothing to ask from him; he has given us everything necessary and we continually give him thanks."

Candide was curious to see the priests; and asked where they were. The good old man smiled.

"My friends," said he, "we are all priests; the King and all the heads of families solemnly sing praises every morning, accompanied by five or six thousand musicians."

"What! Have you no monks to teach, to dispute, to govern, to intrigue and to burn people who do not agree with them?"

"For that, we should have to become fools," said the old man; "here we are all of the same opinion and do not understand what you mean with your monks."

At all this Candide was in an ecstasy and said to himself:

"This is very different from Westphalia and the castle of His Lordship the Baron; if our friend Pangloss had seen Eldorado, he would not have said that the castle of Thunder-ten-tronckh was the best of all that exists on the earth; certainly, a man should travel."

After this long conversation the good old man ordered a carriage to be harnessed with six sheep and gave the two travellers twelve of his servants to take them to court.

"You will excuse me," he said, "if my age deprives me of the honour of accompanying you. The King will receive you in a manner which will not displease you and doubtless you will pardon the customs of the country if any of them disconcert you."

Candide and Cacambo entered the carriage; the six sheep galloped off and in less than four hours they reached the King's palace, which was situated at one end of the capital. The portal was two hundred and twenty feet high and a hundred feet wide; it is impossible to describe its material. Anyone can see the prodigious superiority it must have over the pebbles and sand we call *gold* and *gems*.

Twenty beautiful maidens of the guard received Candide and

Cacambo as they alighted from the carriage, conducted them to the baths and dressed them in robes woven from the down of colibris; after which the principal male and female officers of the Crown led them to his Majesty's apartment through two files of a thousand musicians each, according to the usual custom. As they approached the throne-room, Cacambo asked one of the chief officers how they should behave in his Majesty's presence; whether they should fall on their knees or flat on their faces, whether they should put their hands on their heads or on their backsides; whether they should lick the dust of the throne-room; in a word, what was the ceremony?

"The custom," said the chief officer, "is to embrace the King and to kiss him on either cheek."

Candide and Cacambo threw their arms around his Majesty's neck; he received them with all imaginable favour and politely asked them to supper.

Meanwhile they were carried to see the town, the public buildings rising to the very skies, the market-places ornamented with thousands of columns, the fountains of pure water, the fountains of rose-water and of liquors distilled from sugar-cane, which played continually in the public squares paved with precious stones which emitted a perfume like that of cloves and cinnamon.

Candide asked to see the law-courts; he was told there were none, and that nobody ever went to law. He asked if there were prisons and was told there were none. He was still more surprised and pleased by the palace of sciences, where he saw a gallery two thousand feet long, filled with instruments of mathematics and physics.

After they had explored all the afternoon about a thousandth part of the town, they were taken back to the King. Candide sat down to table with his Majesty, his valet Cacambo and several ladies. Never was better cheer, and never was anyone wittier at supper than his Majesty. Cacambo explained the King's witty remarks to Candide and even when translated they still appeared witty. Among all the things which amazed Candide, this did not amaze him the least.

They enjoyed this hospitality for a month. Candide repeatedly said to Cacambo:

"Once again, my friend, it is quite true that the castle where I was born cannot be compared with this country; but then Miss Cunegonde[5] is not here and you probably have a mistress in Europe. If we remain

[5] Candide's sweetheart, now held captive by the governor of Buenos Aires.

here, we shall only be like everyone else; but if we return to our own world with only twelve sheep laden with Eldorado pebbles, we shall be richer than all the kings put together; we shall have no more Inquisitors to fear and we can easily regain Miss Cunegonde."

Cacambo agreed with this; it is so pleasant to be on the move, to show off before friends, to make a parade of the things seen on one's travels, that these two happy men resolved to be so no longer and to ask his Majesty's permission to depart.

"You are doing a very silly thing," said the King. "I know my country is small; but when we are comfortable anywhere we should stay there; I certainly have not the right to detain foreigners, that is a tyranny which does not exist either in our manners or our laws; all men are free, leave when you please, but the way out is very difficult. It is impossible to ascend the rapid river by which you miraculously came here and which flows under arches of rock. The mountains which surround the whole of my kingdom are ten thousand feet high and as perpendicular as rocks; they are more than ten leagues broad and you can only get down from them by way of precipices. However, since you must go, I will give orders to the directors of machinery to make a machine which will carry you comfortably. When you have been taken to the other side of the mountains, nobody can proceed any farther with you; for my subjects have sworn never to pass this boundary and they are too wise to break their oath. Ask anything else of me you wish."

"We ask nothing of your Majesty," said Cacambo, "except a few sheep laden with provisions, pebbles, and the mud of this country."

The King laughed.

"I cannot understand," said he, "the taste you people of Europe have for our yellow mud; but take as much as you wish, and much good may it do you."

He immediately ordered his engineers to make a machine to hoist these two extraordinary men out of his kingdom.

Three thousand learned scientists worked at it; it was ready in a fortnight and only cost about twenty million pounds sterling in the money of that country. Candide and Cacambo were placed on the machine; there were two large red sheep saddled and bridled for them to ride on when they had passed the mountains, twenty sumpter sheep[6] laden with provisions, thirty carrying presents of the most curious pro-

6 Baggage animals.

ductions of the country and fifty laden with gold, precious stones and diamonds. The King embraced the two vagabonds tenderly.

Their departure was a splendid sight and so was the ingenious manner in which they and their sheep were hoisted onto the top of the mountains.

The scientists took leave of them after having landed them safely, and Candide's only desire and object was to go and present Miss Cunegonde with his sheep.

"We have sufficient to pay the governor of Buenos Ayres," said he, "if Miss Cunegonde can be bought. Let us go to Cayenne, and take ship, and then we will see what kingdom we will buy."

ᴇᴈ FOR DISCUSSION AND WRITING

1. What foundation of truth or legend has Voltaire for locating his fabulous Eldorado somewhere in the Andean wilderness of Peru?

2. At what moment in the first paragraph do you become aware of the element of fantasy? At what point do we first see that Candide and Cacambo have imported with them and are acting on assumptions and values that are ridiculous in this country? (If you have ever been a tourist in Europe, or have observed tourists, can you cite instances of similar false assumptions?)

3. The technique of satire used here is that of a "transvaluation," or reversal of values; and to be effective as social criticism, the values which are reversed must be real ones. Does this hold true of the "lust [of Europeans] for the pebbles and mud," as against the indifference of the Eldoradans toward their precious metals and gems? Does it hold true of the courtesy shown the two foreigners and their entertainment at the inn? Of what aspects of the religion practiced in Eldorado does it hold true? What reversal of values occurs when Candide and Cacambo meet the king? Why is Candide so amazed to find that the king is witty?

4. What is the satirical point in Candide's reasons for wanting to leave Eldorado? Is any psychological truth implicit in the statement that "these two happy men resolved to be so no longer"?

5. It is suggested that you read James Agee's fantasy on Eldorado that immediately follows, so that you will have both of these short, related pieces on which to base a writing assignment.

James Agee ✎§ Candide in Eldorado

✎§ The tender and moving novel *A Death in the Family* describes James Agee's own boyhood background in Tennessee (he was born in 1909), and is perhaps the one work in which his fine creative gift came to full realization. He was on the writing staff of *Time* and *Life* magazines for a number of years—years of increasing frustration—and then began free-lancing in Hollywood as a script writer, meanwhile writing film criticism for *The Nation*. With photographer Walker Evans he prepared the book *Let Us Now Praise Famous Men*. He died of a heart attack in 1955. The following letter is taken from the collection of his *Letters to Father Flye*, published since his death. It is suggested that the student read this short piece in conjunction with the preceding selection from Voltaire's *Candide*. ☙

[New York City]
Dec. 4, '54

DEAR FATHER:[1]

I am very thankful for your letter for my birthday. What you say in the several first lines of it expresses, more clearly than I am generally able to realize it, what I wish I could realize at all times about the obligations between being alive, and what — including life itself — is given one. I've been finding more and more constant awareness of death, and the shortness of time, and of time wasted. Also, these seem to grow "organically", rather than through any special effort or taking of thought,

[1] When James Agee was nine, his own father died, and Father Flye, an Episcopal priest, took the boy into his home and became something of a second father to him. The correspondence between them was kept up while Agee was at Exeter and at Harvard and continued until Agee's death. The letters are a sensitive and important reflection of the development of a gifted mind.

and that — except for the relative lack of effort — I am glad of. But of itself, it isn't by a great deal enough. Too much of the senses of wonder and of gratitude are lacking. And there are still only the beginnings of self-discipline I need, at least until I learn much better than I ever have, to regard much in myself as the enemy of all I most owe to God, and most want. I was reading yesterday in Gorki's memoirs about Andreyev,[2] that he handles his talent the way an unskilful rider handles a superb horse — racing it, beating it, neglecting it, never caressing it, or feeding it carefully. If I could begin to apply this I could begin to do better: but only through two steps: 1) continual awareness: 2) continual effort to practice according to that awareness. When I see how seldom I am aware, and how little, — above all in practice — the awareness comes strongly through to me — I'm surprised I have gotten done even the little that I have.

I'm currently, in that direction, trying to take on two jobs at once. This feels dangerous to me: I'm not yet sure how it will work out, but I feel it's a good idea to try. One is going on with the Tanglewood story, trying to get to the heart of it; if I can't within a few more weeks, I will not take on the writing of the screenplay. . . . The other is to write a scene in *Candide* which Lillian Hellman and Leonard Bernstein[3] are turning into a musical play. I will write of Eldorado, the Earthly Paradise, and this scene should be entirely in verse, entirely sung, and most of it, probably, danced. I think of centering it around three events in court, in which "the people" bring before their mild, saintlike king, not pleas, but three events or statements of intention, for his hearing, and his blessing: the celebration of a birth; the intent for divorce and re-marriage; and the intent to die. The first is self-evident, as among people who need fear no evil, and only sorrow which is to be accepted in gratitude and reverence. The second: the husband, in the presence of the community and of his wife and her lover, declares that he yields her to her lover. Candide: "But don't you *love* her?" Husband: "How, otherwise, could I yield her up and wish her so well?" Candide (after trying to describe the agonies of jealousy): "Don't you *desire* her?" Husband: "How could a true man, or woman, desire one whose desire is for another?" The third: A very fine old man, surrounded by 4 generations of his magnificent family, appears before the king. The old man is a farmer:

[2] See note on Gorky, page 5. Andreyev was a contemporary Russian author.

[3] Lillian Hellman's and Leonard Bernstein's *Candide* was produced, but unsuccessfully.

"I have loved God; and the poets; and my wives; and their children; and theirs; and I have loved the soil, and have dealt with it reverently. Now, I declare my wish to die." He briefly describes two main things: that he has, of late, after being ever more grateful for life, decade after decade, begun in every way to tire: to long for the unknown, whatever it may be; and to tire in his faculties. He can foresee an ever saddening decline, which he does not wish to inflict either on those who love him, or upon himself. And so: The king nods, and signals; a draught is brought; he sings an extempore farewell to his loved ones and to the world and to life, drinks, and dies quickly and without pain, surrounded by his family. Instantly a sublime and serene celebration of his death begins — all white, silver, gold, and peaceful joy. Candide is much moved and perplexed: "So, you all believe in a life after death?" The king gently shrugs: "It is one of the few questions on which we differ among ourselves." Candide: "But you adore God." King: "Indeed yes. Too deeply to enquire into matters He prefers to keep secret from us." Then, comfortingly and politely, "Surely you will understand: we trust His Will and His Wisdom. The old man has passed out of our hands, into God's. How can we be troubled for him?" Or even, "His Will is our Peace."

And at the end, when Candide decides to leave and return to Europe — I must back-track. Earlier in the scene, Candide asks about kings. Hereditary, he supposes. No, they are neither hereditary nor by election. It is, simply, that (as with the Dalai Lama) in every generation one child is born who is unmistakable to everyone as the new receptacle and mirror of Divinity; there is never any quarreling about it. "Would Candide like to see the next King?" He is shown him: the most beautiful imaginable child. Candide: "Before him, dear Sir, how can you keep your throne?" King: "Don't be deceived: he is only a child still. Here too, sorrow ripens, sex ripens, wisdom ripens; he and I will know, when we are ready, won't we?" he asks the child. The child nods and smiles, and stands by the King's knee. Candide: "But — suppose he should die?" King: "He won't: all others may, but not he. He has been struck by a fer-de-lance,[4] he has been taken by a condor. He will live out his time." (Or other examples of the invulnerability of genius which approaches divinity.)

When Candide leaves, we begin with the ceremonial, farewell embrace with the King. Then in exchanges, songs of farewell between

[4] Venomous South American snake, allied to the rattlesnake.

Candide and the King, and big choral blocks from the people. Finally, the Royal Child runs forward, weeping, and embraces Candide, saying or singing, "dear son." And Candide, after a deep sigh of wondering and reverent tenderness: "Our Father . . ." And all others, courteous and silent, glance towards each other: They have never heard of the prayer or the religion.

I am so much interested, and so glad, of all you write me about the people you have been seeing, — especially the two children.* I fully have the sense of miracle you speak of. I also suspect that you are an agent of the miraculous. I wouldn't mention this if I thought it would embarrass or disconcert you — let alone corrupt in you the power of which you may be the conductive. For one thing, no such imaginable miracle does more than postpone death, short or long. For another, if my rather wild conjecture of conceivability is right, you are well beyond vanity in it: you have simply an exceptional capacity for love, especially for the young, and through that, you may well be a particularly pure conductive metal for God's healing love. If this is so, or even if it isn't, I feel you are beyond any imaginable danger in having it mentioned as possible, by another. . . .

I hope you like the rough sketch of Eldorado. In some ways I think you won't, but on the whole I think you may. The scene should be a lyrical sketch of the best that is humanly conceivable and the keys to that, I am supposing to be: all physical needs are well enough supplied that gold, etc. — all our symbols of wealth — are used only for personal and religious decoration. The other parts of the key are: the absence of Theory; the careful use of Common Sense ("Reason") and of the Applied Sciences; Love and Consent among human beings; the Love of God, which expresses itself not in propitiation or begging prayer, but in thankfulness and adoration. (From Voltaire: there are no priests; we are all priests; and we praise and thank God in every moment of our lives.) They live in such wealth that their habit is a kind of rich frugality — of

---

* One of the things I had begun at once in Wichita was daily hospital visiting, and I had written something about this to Jim. In a letter in November I had told of two children with leukemia. One, Terry Neukomm, a very winsome boy of seven, had had what seemed an almost miraculous recovery from cancer the previous spring. Now leukemia had developed, but I hoped that maybe this time, too, even if it meant a miracle, he might be saved. (He lived till March.) It is he who is referred to here and again in a later letter. [Father Flye's note.]

which the King is the model. Envy is virtually impossible: for every man can have what he wishes; he becomes gently laughable if he wishes too much, and envy is swallowed up in this tenderness towards eccentricity. I think of having an older European beachcomber, who describes it to Candide in terms of the seven deadly sins. Gluttony (for instance:) where liquors flow from half the fountains — (rose-water from the others) — everyone gets drunk, from time to time; but who could possibly become a drunkard? There are no laws, for the laws of love preclude that possibility, as Christianity precludes the possibility of a State. There are no poisons: what need of any, where the infinitely strong restraint is the despair one foresees, through causing injury or disadvantage to another?

I must quit.

I think I will tell you, my dearest friend; last night I had a dream, during which, in context of general dying (Mia was going to have to die) your wife and my beloved friend,[5] as I arrived at St. Andrew's for her burial, stepped out of her coffin (without stepping back into life) and came towards me up a crowded aisle in the Chapel, and we embraced and kissed as we always have, after a long time apart, — as if it were only a few days since we had seen each other. She is among the Saints, and I think she always was.

Jim

✌❦ FOR DISCUSSION AND WRITING

1. One usually doesn't "plan" a letter so personal as this the way one would plan an essay, for the essence of personal letters is their spontaneity of feeling; nevertheless, when the feeling and thought are spontaneous, the letter will tend to have a certain implicit unity, inasmuch as the writer's mind is moving "all in one piece," under one stimulus to expression. Do you find in the first paragraph any underlying continuity of thought or feeling connecting it with the *Candide* sketches?

2. It has been suggested that you read the piece preceding this one, from Voltaire's *Candide*, for Agee's fantasy stems directly from Voltaire's. What chief difference do you find between the two, in the main bias or slant of

---

[5] Mrs. Flye had recently died. Mia was Agee's wife.

the writer's interests? What chief parallels do you find between them, showing where Agee took his cues from Voltaire?

3. What are the three "events" around which Agee plans his scenes? Explain the statement: "The first is self-evident, as among people who need fear no evil, and only sorrow which is to be accepted in gratitude and reverence." We have noticed, in the selection from Voltaire, that Candide imports with him into Eldorado certain assumptions that are entirely foreign there. What two assumptions, about "love" and "desire," are implied here in Candide's questions about the divorce case? Is it implied that Candide has been badly educated *intellectually* (according to Eldoradan standards) or badly educated *emotionally*? How would you define the difference between intellectual education and emotional education? How can people's emotions be "educated"? How important is this kind of education?

4. In the questions on Voltaire, we have spoken of a "transvaluation of values" as forming the basis of this kind of "Utopian" writing. In the case of Agee's old man, do you find anything resembling a transvaluation of ordinary American values in his statement that he has "loved God; and the poets," as well as his wives and children and grandchildren, "and I have loved the soil, and have dealt with it reverently"? A fairly widespread vulgarization of Freudian psychology has made us very suspicious of what is called "the death-wish," and we wouldn't be caught dead having one; in the old man's desire to die, what transvaluation of values is there? Perhaps you have read the excerpt from Jessica Mitford's *The American Way of Death* earlier in this book (see page 318); in what way does the old man's wish to die, and his reason for wishing to die, undermine the undertakers' expensive illusionism?

5. What is the attitude toward immortality in Agee's Eldorado?

6. How is the next king chosen in this country? Is what is said about the kingly child merely a kind of superstitious blather, or does it have some psychological basis? What paradoxical significance is there in the fact that the child says to Candide, "dear son," and Candide replies with "Our Father . . ."? What are some of the "keys" Agee says he wants to use in developing the scenes in *Candide*?

7. Write, in any form, one scene of your conception of what might take place in an "Eldorado" of your own envisaging—using, if you like, the convenient character of the youthful, ignorant, but sincere and ardent Candide himself.

Samuel Butler *Erewhonian Customs*

English novelist (1835-1902). Son of a famous headmaster and bishop, Butler tells—in the autobiographical novel, *The Way of All Flesh*—of his own narrow escape from clerical orders, for which he was wholly unsuited, and of other harrowing penalties of a Victorian education designed to make the susceptible young unfit for life. The book, reflecting a wryly humanistic temperament, is one of the wittiest novels of the turn of the century. He made a success of sheep breeding in New Zealand, translated the *Iliad* and the *Odyssey* in vigorous, homely prose, supplemented the translations with *The Authoress of the Odyssey*, where he maintained that Homer was a woman, and wrote the satirical Utopian fiction *Erewhon*, from which the selection here is taken.

WE were now nearing the metropolis and I could see great towers and fortifications, and lofty buildings that looked like palaces. I began to be nervous as to my reception; but I had got on very well so far, and resolved to continue upon the same plan as hitherto — namely, to behave just as though I were in England until I saw that I was making a blunder, and then to say nothing till I could gather how the land lay. We drew nearer and nearer. The news of my approach had got abroad, and there was a great crowd collected on either side the road, who greeted me with marks of most respectful curiosity, keeping me bowing constantly in acknowledgment from side to side.

When we were about a mile off, we were met by the Mayor and several Councilors, among whom was a venerable old man, who was

From *Erewhon* by Samuel Butler (first published in 1872; New York: Random House, 1927).

introduced to me by the Mayor (for so I suppose I should call him) as the gentleman who had invited me to his house. I bowed deeply and told him how grateful I felt to him, and how gladly I would accept his hospitality. He forbade me to say more, and pointing to his carriage, which was close at hand, he motioned me to a seat therein. I again bowed profoundly to the Mayor and Councilors, and drove off with my entertainer, whose name was Senoj Nosnibor. After about half a mile the carriage turned off the main road, and we drove under the walls of the town till we reached a *palazzo* on a slight eminence, and just on the outskirts of the city. This was Senoj Nosnibor's house, and nothing can be imagined finer. It was situated near the magnificent and venerable ruins of the old railway station, which formed an imposing feature from the gardens of the house. The grounds, some ten or a dozen acres in extent, were laid out in terraced gardens, one above the other, with flights of broad steps ascending and descending the declivity of the garden. On these steps there were statues of most exquisite workmanship. Besides the statues there were vases filled with various shrubs that were new to me; and on either side the flights of steps there were rows of old cypresses and cedars, with grassy alleys between them. Then came choice vineyards and orchards of fruit-trees in full bearing.

The house itself was approached by a court-yard, and round it was a corridor on to which rooms opened, as at Pompeii. In the middle of the court there was a bath and a fountain. Having passed the court we came to the main body of the house, which was two stories in height. The rooms were large and lofty; perhaps at first they looked rather bare of furniture, but in hot climates people generally keep their rooms more bare than they do in colder ones. I missed also the sight of a grand piano or some similar instrument, there being no means of producing music in any of the rooms save the large drawing-room, where there were half a dozen large bronze gongs, which the ladies used occasionally to beat about at random. It was not pleasant to hear them, but I have heard quite as unpleasant music both before and since.

Mr. Nosnibor took me through several spacious rooms till we reached a boudoir where were his wife and daughters, of whom I had heard from the interpreter. Mrs. Nosnibor was about forty years old, and still handsome, but she had grown very stout: her daughters were in the prime of youth and exquisitely beautiful. I gave the preference almost at once to the younger, whose name was Arowhena; for the elder sister was haughty, while the younger had a very winning manner. Mrs. Nosnibor received me with the perfection of courtesy, so that I must have indeed been shy and nervous if I had not at once felt welcome. Scarcely was the ceremony of my introduction well completed before a servant announced that dinner was ready in the next room. I was exceedingly hungry, and the dinner was beyond all praise. Can the reader wonder that I began to consider myself in excellent quarters? "That man embezzle money?" thought I to myself; "impossible."

But I noticed that my host was uneasy during the whole meal, and that he ate nothing but a little bread and milk; towards the end of dinner there came a tall, lean man with a black beard, to whom Mr. Nosnibor and the whole family paid great attention: he was the family straightener. With this gentleman Mr. Nosnibor retired into another room, from which there presently proceeded a sound of weeping and wailing. I could hardly believe my ears, but in a few minutes I got to know for a certainty that they came from Mr. Nosnibor himself.

"Poor papa," said Arowhena, as she helped herself composedly to the salt, "how terribly he has suffered."

"Yes," answered her mother; "but I think he is quite out of danger now."

Then they went on to explain to me the circumstances of the case, and the treatment which the straightener had prescribed, and how successful he had been — all which I will reserve for another chapter, and put rather in the form of a general summary of the opinions current upon these subjects than in the exact words in which the facts were delivered to me; the reader, however, is earnestly requested to believe that both in this next chapter and in those that follow it I have endeavored to adhere most conscientiously to the strictest accuracy, and that I have never willingly misrepresented, though I may have sometimes failed to understand all the bearings of an opinion or custom.

This is what I gathered. That in that country if a man falls into ill health, or catches any disorder, or fails bodily in any way before he is seventy years old, he is tried before a jury of his countrymen, and if convicted is held up to public scorn and sentenced more or less severely as the case may be. There are subdivisions of illnesses into crimes and misdemeanors as with offenses amongst ourselves — a man being punished very heavily for serious illness, while failure of eyes or hearing in one over sixty-five, who has had good health hitherto, is dealt with by fine only, or imprisonment in default of payment. But if a man forges a check, or sets his house on fire, or robs with violence from the person, or does any other such things as are criminal in our own country, he is either taken to a hospital and most carefully tended at the public expense, or if he is in good circumstances, he lets it be known to all his friends that he is suffering from a severe fit of immorality, just as we do when we are ill, and they come and visit him with great solicitude, and inquire with interest how it all came about, what symptoms first showed themselves, and so forth, — questions which he will answer with perfect unreserve; for bad conduct, though considered no less deplorable than illness with ourselves, and as unquestionably indicating something seriously wrong with the individual who misbehaves, is nevertheless held to be the result of either pre-natal or post-natal misfortune.

The strange part of the story, however, is that though they ascribe moral defects to the effect of misfortune either in character or surroundings, they will not listen to the plea of misfortune in cases that in England meet with sympathy and commiseration only. Ill luck of any kind, or even ill treatment at the hands of others, is considered an offense against society, inasmuch as it makes people uncomfortable to hear of it. Loss of fortune, therefore, or loss of some dear friend on whom another was much dependent, is punished hardly less severely than physical delinquency.

Foreign, indeed, as such ideas are to our own, traces of somewhat similar opinions can be found even in nineteenth-century England. If a person has an abscess, the medical man will say that it contains "peccant" matter, and people say that they have a "bad" arm or finger, or that they are very "bad" all over, when they only mean "diseased." Among foreign nations Erewhonian opinions may be still more clearly noted. The Mahommedans, for example, to this day, send their female prisoners to hospitals, and the New Zealand Maories visit any misfortune with forcible entry into the house of the offender, and the breaking up and burning of all his goods. The Italians, again, use the same word for "disgrace" and "misfortune." I once heard an Italian lady speak of a young friend whom she described as endowed with every virtue under heaven, "ma," she exclaimed, "povero disgraziato, ha ammazzato suo zio." ("Poor unfortunate fellow, he has murdered his uncle.")

On mentioning this, which I heard when taken to Italy as a boy by my father, the person to whom I told it showed no surprise. He said that he had been driven for two or three years in a certain city by a young Sicilian cabdriver of prepossessing manners and appearance, but then lost sight of him. On asking what had become of him, he was told that he was in prison for having shot at his father with intent to kill him — happily without serious results. Some years later my informant again found himself warmly accosted by the prepossessing young cabdriver. "Ah, caro signore," he exclaimed, "sono cinque anni che non lo vedo — tre anni di militare, e due anni di disgrazia," &c. ("My dear sir, it is five years since I saw you — three years of military service, and two of misfortune") — during which last the poor fellow had been in prison. Of moral sense he showed not so much as a trace. He and his father were now on excellent terms, and were likely to remain so unless either of them should again have the misfortune mortally to offend the other.

In the following chapter I will give a few examples of the way in which what we should call misfortune, hardship, or disease are dealt with by the Erewhonians, but for the moment will return to their treatment of cases that with us are criminal. As I have already said, these, though not judicially punishable, are recognized as requiring correction. Accordingly, there exists a class of men trained in soul-craft, whom they call straighteners, as nearly as I can translate a word which literally means "one who bends back the crooked." These men practice much as medical men in England, and receive a quasi-surreptitious fee on every visit. They are treated with the same unreserve, and obeyed as readily, as our own doctors — that is to say, on the whole sufficiently — because people know that it is their interest to get well as soon as they can, and that they will not be scouted[1] as they would be if their bodies were out of order, even though they may have to undergo a very painful course of treatment.

When I say that they will not be scouted, I do not mean that an Erewhonian will suffer no social inconvenience in consequence, we will say, of having committed fraud. Friends will fall away from him because of his being less pleasant company, just as we ourselves are disinclined to make companions of those who are either poor or poorly. No one with any sense of self-respect will place himself on an equality in the matter of affection with those who are less lucky than himself in birth, health, money, good looks, capacity, or anything else. Indeed, that dislike and

1 Rejected, or treated with contempt.

even disgust should be felt by the fortunate for the unfortunate, or at any rate for those who have been discovered to have met with any of the more serious and less familiar misfortunes, is not only natural, but desirable for any society, whether of man or brute.

The fact, therefore, that the Erewhonians attach none of that guilt to crime which they do to physical ailments, does not prevent the more selfish among them from neglecting a friend who has robbed a bank, for instance, till he has fully recovered; but it does prevent them from even thinking of treating criminals with that contemptuous tone which would seem to say, "I, if I were you, should be a better man than you are," a tone which is held quite reasonable in regard to physical ailment. Hence, though they conceal ill health by every cunning and hypocrisy and artifice which they can devise, they are quite open about the most flagrant mental diseases, should they happen to exist, which to do the people justice is not often. Indeed, there are some who are, so to speak, spiritual valetudinarians, and who make themselves exceedingly ridiculous by their nervous supposition that they are wicked, while they are very tolerable people all the time. This however is exceptional; and on the whole they use much the same reserve or unreserve about the state of their moral welfare as we do about our health.

Hence all the ordinary greetings among ourselves, such as, How do you do? and the like, are considered signs of gross ill-breeding; nor do the politer classes tolerate even such a common complimentary remark as telling a man that he is looking well. They salute each other with, "I hope you are good this morning;" or "I hope you have recovered from the snappishness from which you were suffering when I last saw you"; and if the person saluted has not been good, or is still snappish, he says so at once and is condoled with accordingly. Indeed, the straighteners have gone so far as to give names from the hypothetical language (as taught at the Colleges of Unreason), to all known forms of mental indisposition, and to classify them according to a system of their own, which, though I could not understand it, seemed to work well in practice; for they are always able to tell a man what is the matter with him as soon as they have heard his story, and their familiarity with the long names assures him that they thoroughly understand his case.

The reader will have no difficulty in believing that the laws regarding ill health were frequently evaded by the help of recognized fictions, which every one understood, but which it would be considered gross ill-

breeding to even seem to understand. Thus, a day or two after my arrival
at the Nosnibors', one of the many ladies who called on me made excuses for her husband's only sending his card, on the ground that when
going through the public market-place that morning he had stolen a pair
of socks. I had already been warned that I should never show surprise,
so I merely expressed my sympathy, and said that though I had only been
in the capital so short a time, I had already had a very narrow escape
from stealing a clothes-brush, and that though I had resisted temptation
so far, I was sadly afraid that if I saw any object of special interest that
was neither too hot nor too heavy, I should have to put myself in the
straightener's hands.

Mrs. Nosnibor, who had been keeping an ear on all that I had been
saying, praised me when the lady had gone. Nothing, she said, could
have been more polite according to Erewhonian etiquette. She then
explained that to have stolen a pair of socks, or "to have the socks" (in
more colloquial language), was a recognized way of saying that the
person in question was slightly indisposed.

In spite of all this they have a keen sense of the enjoyment consequent upon what they call being "well." They admire mental health and
love it in other people, and take all the pains they can (consistently with
their other duties) to secure it for themselves. They have an extreme
dislike to marrying into what they consider unhealthy families. They
send for the straightener at once whenever they have been guilty of
anything seriously flagitious — often even if they think that they are on
the point of committing it; and though his remedies are sometimes
exceedingly painful, involving close confinement for weeks, and in some
cases the most cruel physical tortures, I never heard of a reasonable
Erewhonian refusing to do what his straightener told him, any more than
of a reasonable Englishman refusing to undergo even the most frightful
operation, if his doctors told him it was necessary.

We in England never shrink from telling our doctor what is the
matter with us merely through the fear that he will hurt us. We let him
do his worst upon us, and stand it without a murmur, because we are
not scouted for being ill, and because we know that the doctor is doing
his best to cure us, and that he can judge of our case better than we can;
but we should conceal all illness if we were treated as the Erewhonians
are when they have anything the matter with them; we should do the
same as with moral and intellectual diseases, — we should feign health

with the most consummate art, till we were found out, and should hate a single flogging given in the way of mere punishment more than the amputation of a limb, if it were kindly and courteously performed from a wish to help us out of our difficulty, and with the full consciousness on the part of the doctor that it was only by an accident of constitution that he was not in the like plight himself. So the Erewhonians take a flogging once a week, and a diet of bread and water for two or three months together, whenever their straightener recommends it.

I do not suppose that even my host, on having swindled a confiding widow out of the whole of her property, was put to more actual suffering than a man will readily undergo at the hands of an English doctor. And yet he must have had a very bad time of it. The sounds I heard were sufficient to show that his pain was exquisite, but he never shrank from undergoing it. He was quite sure that it did him good; and I think he was right. I cannot believe that that man will ever embezzle money again. He may — but it will be a long time before he does so.

✣ FOR DISCUSSION AND WRITING

1. We have spoken before of the technique of a "transvaluation of values" in this kind of fantasy, and of the fact that, if the social satire is to be effective, it must have a solid foundation in actuality; in other words, we must be made aware of a certain set of *actual* "values," or assumptions, in our society, which the fantasy shows us reversed (as in *Alice Through the Looking Glass*). In the customs of Erewhon described here, what actual social assumptions are shown us in a transvalued or reversed form? Incidentally, how does the name of Mr. Senoj Nosnibor carry out that technique of reversal?

2. Anciently, what we know as "satire" originated in the no-holds-barred, often scurrilous, pratfalling, pie-throwing comedy (like that of Aristophanes) that followed on the tragic trilogies performed in the theater of Dionysus in Athens. Comedy and free-tongued wit are natural aspects of satire (aspects which we sometimes forget in looking for serious, long-nosed social criticism). Where do you find these elements in Butler? Social criticism, when it noses out our unconscious assumptions and the automatism of most of our behavior, is not pleasant to take, and our instinct is to

be angrily self-righteous; how does the comic element in satire like that of Butler or Voltaire contribute to the effectiveness of the implicit social criticism?

3. What is the treatment of illness and disease in Erewhon? What is the treatment of crime? What "transvaluation of values" is represented in these instances? One of the chief varieties of Utopian writing is that which shows us an ideal society, a "perfect" society, organized in such a way that only the best in human nature is brought out, so that everyone in the society is an ideal or "perfect" human being, whatever his role or job. How does Butler's Erewhon differ from that kind of Utopia? Does his less-than-perfect conception of human nature strengthen his social criticism or weaken it?

4. What is the modern equivalent of the "family straightener"? What is meant by the straightener's training in "soul-craft"? Is there any contemporary tendency to treat crime the way it is treated in Erewhon? What is the therapeutic effect on the Erewhonian criminal of having his "illness" openly discussed and sympathized with? Why is it that he makes no attempt to conceal his awkward condition, but, instead, is ready to answer all questions and discuss all his "symptoms"?

5. What is the rationale for treating physical illness as a crime? Why does such treatment tend to keep the people of Erewhon healthy?

6. What suggestion is there in this piece that most of us are not so moral, such "good guys," as we pretend to be? What would happen to our notions of ourselves if we adopted the psychology of Erewhon?

7. Write your own satirical fantasy "transvaluing" certain modern assumptions and pretensions. Or put your mind, for a couple of days, to watching and listening to people around you as they show, quite unconsciously in their ordinary remarks and behavior, their unexamined moral and other values; and write up your findings.

Melford E. Spiro ✑ Kibbutz: Venture in Utopia

✑ American anthropologist, educated at the University of Minnesota and Northwestern University, now Professor of Anthropology at the University of Washington, Seattle, Washington. Mr. Spiro has done anthropological field work among the Ojibwa Indians of Wisconsin, and in Ifaluk, an atoll in the South Seas. He spent eleven months in Kiryat Yedidim, the kibbutz described in his book *Kibbutz: Venture in Utopia*.

The student should have no difficulty with the Hebrew and Yiddish words used in this article, for their meaning is immediately made clear by the text. ✑

To have begun this monograph in the usual fashion, with a description of the natural environment or of the subsistence economy of Kiryat Yedidim,[1] would do violence to the inner meaning of its culture. . . . Kiryat Yedidim, to be sure, is an agricultural village consisting of men and women who inhabit a common geographic area and who make their living by tilling the soil in a cooperative fashion. But Kiryat Yedidim is also — and primarily — a fellowship of those who share a common faith and who have banded together to implement that faith. To live *in* Kiryat Yedidim means to become a member *of* a kibbutz, and member-

Reprinted by permission of the publishers from Melford E. Spiro, *Kibbutz: Venture in Utopia*. Cambridge, Mass.: Harvard University Press. Copyright, 1956, by the President and Fellows of Harvard College. The selection given here appeared as the second chapter ("The Moral Postulates of Kibbutz Culture") of the book.

[1] Mr. Spiro has given this fictitious name to the kibbutz where he did his research.

ship in a kibbutz[2] entails more than voting at town meetings, or driving a
tractor in the wheat fields, or living in a lovely village. It means, primarily, becoming a *chaver kibbutz* (a comrade of the kibbutz), that is,
a person who is dedicated to the social, economic, and national ideals for
which the kibbutz stands. These ideals were formulated before Kiryat
Yedidim came into being and, indeed, it was founded with the purpose
of bringing these ideals into being. Hence, these ideals must be understood, if Kiryat Yedidim is to be understood.

Probably the single most important ideal upon which the entire
kibbutz culture is based is what might be termed the moral value of
labor. It is no accident, for example, that today, when the entire kibbutz
movement is experiencing a profound crisis, it is this principle of *avodah
atzmit*, or self-labor, which has become the measure of the devotion of a
kibbutz to its original ideals. The founders of Kiryat Yedidim, in many
instances, were intellectuals for whom labor was a "calling" rather than
a habit. For them, labor was not merely a means for the satisfaction of
human needs; rather, labor itself was reviewed as a need — probably
man's most important need — the satisfaction of which became an end
in itself. *Ki ha-avodah hi chayenu* is the way the kibbutz expresses it.
"For labor is (the essence of) our life"; and this phrase may be said to
be the *leitmotif*[3] of kibbutz living.

This attitude toward labor did not, of course, originate with the
vattikim, the founders, of Kiryat Yedidim. Emphasis on labor has long
been integral to the *chalutz*, or pioneering, tradition in Zionism. As early
as 1882, when one of the first contingents of Russian Jews migrated to
Palestine, the ideal of labor on the land was already in process of formulation. As one pioneer put it:

> Farmer! Be a free man among men, but a slave to the soil . . . Kneel and
> bow down to it every day. Nurse its furrows — and then even its stony clods
> will yield a blessing! And in this "slavery" remember that you are a tiller of
> the soil! A tiller of the soil in Palestine! This must become a badge of honor
> among our people.

This attitude to labor is particularly significant and, in a profoundly
psychological sense, explicable only in view of the *petit bourgeois*[4] back-

---

[2] Commune, collective settlement.
[3] Recurring theme.
[4] Lower middle class.

grounds of the vattikim. Before their immigration to Israel, they had not engaged in physical labor; moreover, they were reared in a culture that demeaned labor, as well as the laborer. The persons who were looked down upon in the *shtetl*, the Eastern European villages in which the vattikim were born, were the *proste. Prost* is the Yiddish equivalent of "crude" or "vulgar," and the attitude towards unskilled workers on the part of the shtetl is revealed most clearly in its appellation of these workers as the proste. In the shtetl,

> It is better . . . to be a salesman than to be an artisan. A salesman works with his brain, an artisan merely with his brawn.
> For a man who "comes from yikhus" (a respected family) to engage in manual labor, even under stress of economic necessity, is a calamity for manual labor has come to symbolize the antithesis of the social ideal — a life devoted entirely to study.

Hence, the ideal of work as an ultimate value — the dat ha-avodah — represents, in the case of the vattikim, a cultural revolution; to achieve it they had to overcome the resistance of both their trained values and their untrained muscles. It is little wonder that one of their first goals was *kibbush ha-avodah,* "the conquest of labor."

Kiryat Yedidim, then, is not a worker's community in the same sense that many of the utopian societies of nineteenth-century America were. This is a community which was founded, for the most part, by middle-class intellectuals who deliberately chose to be workers; by so choosing, they reversed both the traditional prestige hierarchy and the historical aspiration of upward mobility. Instead of aspiring to "rise" in the social ladder, they aspired to "descend." For the chaverim,[5] then, it is not business (as in European bourgeois culture) or scholarship (as in the shtetl culture), but labor which is the highest vocational goal. This goal, it must be stressed, is primarily a spiritual goal — it is a means to self-realization. As the chalutz folk-song has it: "To Palestine we have come, to build and to be built in it (the land)." This Tolstoyan attitude toward work could be evolved, it is not hazardous to say, only by romantic, urban intellectuals.

The "moral value of labor" stresses not only the latter aspect of the principle of avodah atzmit, self-*labor;* the former aspect, which empha-

---

[5] Plural of *chaver,* "comrade," member of the kibbutz. The feminine form, occurring later, is *chavera.*

sizes *self*-labor, is equally important. This general principle of the labor movement, when applied to the kibbutz, means that no one may be employed from the outside to work in the kibbutz, and that all work must be performed by the members of the kibbutz. Exceptions might be made in certain kinds of labor for which chaverim may have had no training, such as house construction or language instruction in the high school, but no exception may be made in the case of other kinds of labor, no matter how difficult or repulsive they might be. The opposition to hired labor is based on three ethical considerations. First, there is the *mystique*[6] of labor — already hinted at — which stresses the dignity and creativeness of labor and the need to strike roots in the soil. Then, there is the fear, which first arose when the Arabs were the majority group in Palestine, that the introduction of hired labor would open the way to the employment of cheap Arab *fellah* labor. If this happened, it was thought, the kibbutz would eventually become a plantation, worked by Arab labor for the benefit of (what would then become) the leisure class kibbutz owners. The socialist ideology of Kiryat Yedidim, with its abhorrence of "surplus value"[7] and its notion that all wage labor entails exploitation, is the third ethical opposition to hired labor and the insistence on self-labor.

The chaverim, in short, constitute a class conscious proletariat, *par excellence;* and it is not surprising that one's prestige in Kiryat Yedidim is determined primarily by excellence in and devotion to one's work.

Not all work, however, is equally valued. Physical labor enjoys the greatest prestige. The further removed it is from physical labor, the less prestige a job confers. This means, of course, that pure intellectual work does not confer great prestige, despite the fact that Kiryat Yedidim is a highly cultured community, one which is devoted to intellectual and artistic experience. Of the various categories of physical labor, agricultural labor is valued the most. Even among the agricultural branches, however, differential stereotypes have arisen. Those who work in the orchards and vineyards are thought to be intellectual, easygoing people, who are not particularly energetic. Shepherds are supposedly romantic, and inclined to be a bit lazy. On the other hand, the *falachim*, those who work in the grain fields, are presumably hard, energetic workers. They enjoy a national reputation, moreover, for the stereotype has it that the falachim of the past have become the country's leaders, and have built

[6] Cultism.

[7] Differential between actual value of labor performed and the wages paid.

the important labor institutions. It is difficult to assess the relative physical difficulty of these various occupations. It is probably true that, in many respects, the falach has the hardest job, and there are certain periods — such as the harvest, when the combines work almost twenty-four hours a day — which demand almost superhuman effort. But there is another, and probably more cogent, reason for his prestige which has little to do with the difficulty of his work. The kibbutz, as will be noted in the discussion of economic organization, distinguishes between "productive" work and "services." The former enjoys the greater prestige, and (or, perhaps, because) it yields a cash income. Hence, *falcha* — cereal crops — is the most important agricultural branch in the kibbutz economy, for it normally yields the highest economic return. The economic importance of the branch has been generalized to the social importance of the person who works in that branch.

The importance attached to work is in constant evidence in Kiryat Yedidim and almost everyone responds to it. Work has become almost a compulsive habit, so that absence from work, even for good cause, elicits feelings of guilt. For three months, for example, the author had been working in the fields with a chavera whose work was characterized by drive and great energy, and who seldom took a break. He was amazed to discover somewhat later that this labor was torturous to her; she could not tolerate the heat, and she suffered constant pains in her arms and hands. Again, a chavera of the kibbutz donated one day a week to work in an immigrants' camp. She became quite ill, and was ordered to bed by the doctor. She complained, however, that she must return to her work, and when she heard that there was no one to take her place in the camp, she insisted on rising from her sickbed and returning to the camp. It is interesting to note in this connection that, according to the kibbutz nurse, there are no cases of malingering or of "goldbricking." How compelling this drive for work can become, even for an outsider, is illustrated by an experience of the author. It was mutually decided that he would pay for his expenses by working half a day and by paying the kibbutz for the other half-day. Toward the end of the study, it became apparent that it would be impossible to complete his projected research aims, unless he had more free time for his research. He obtained permission from the Secretariat to work only one-quarter time for two months and to make up the difference in cash payment. As soon as he started his quarter-time schedule, however, the author realized that he would accomplish little work. His own guilt feelings were too great. No one mentioned the fact that he was not working regular hours, and probably few knew of it; nevertheless, he felt that he was shirking his responsibility. He stayed away from public places during the day, trying to avoid the chaverim. The influence of this dominant attitude is so great, that a complete stranger becomes acculturated to it within a few months.

Since labor is of such great importance, it follows that the individual who shirks his work responsibilities, or who is inefficient in his work, does not enjoy the respect of his fellows. Regardless of his other talents, the *batlan*, or the lazy person, occupies the position of lowest prestige in the prestige hierarchy of Kiryat Yedidim.

A second moral principle of kibbutz culture is that the property used and produced by the entire community rightfully belongs to the entire community. Hence, the economy rests on the public ownership of property. The land inhabited and worked by the kibbutz is not owned by any individual or by any family, nor even by the kibbutz itself. It is owned, rather, by the entire nation, having been acquired by a national agency, the *Keren Kayemet* (Jewish National Fund), by funds raised through voluntary contributions. The Keren Kayemet rents the land to the kibbutz on a ninety-nine year renewable lease, for which the latter pays an annual rent (starting only after its fifth year) of 2 percent of the original cost of the land, plus improvements. National ownership of land is an ethical imperative, it is believed, because it precludes such "evils" as land speculation, absentee ownership, and "unearned" income through rent. Moreover, it prevents the rise of a society composed of a landed gentry and a disinherited peasantry.

Although its land is owned by the nation, all other property in Kiryat Yedidim is owned collectively by the members of the kibbutz. Ideally, the individual owns nothing with the exception of small personal gifts and those personal effects which he may buy with his annual "vacation allowance" of nine Israeli pounds (approximately nine dollars). Hence, the house in which he lives, the trucks and tractors he operates, the cattle he cares for, the clothes he wears, and the food he eats are owned by the kibbutz. Since private property has been abolished, the individual receives no wages for his work; since he lives in a house owned by the kibbutz, he pays no rent; and since he eats in the kibbutz dining room, he has no food bills. Moreover, he receives his clothes, like everyone else, from the kibbutz clothing room; smaller articles, like combs, toothbrushes, etc., he obtains at the kibbutz "store." Should he be ill, his medical and hospital bills are taken care of by the kibbutz. In short, the individual has no money, nor does he need any, because his economic needs are satisfied by the kibbutz.

The principle of public ownership derives, of course, from the emphasis placed on the moral value of equality. Private property, it is felt, together with the profit motive and the competitiveness that accompany it, destroy the bonds of brotherhood. The kibbutz insists that only in the absence of private property is it possible to establish an economic system in which economic classes and economic inequalities are abolished and, consequently, in which greater brotherhood can be achieved.

Communal ownership, then, is related to another moral principle underlying kibbutz culture: the principle of social and economic *equality*. In the event that Kiryat Yedidim does not have enough goods or services to supply all its members equally, distribution is regulated according to seniority of arrival in the country. For example, the new housing development, consisting of two-room, instead of the usual one-room apartments, is open only to those persons who have been in the country for at least thirty years. Except for such special cases, however, economic distribution is formally equal. In the distribution of clothes, for example, all women receive one good dress every two years, and a plain dress on alternate years. Men receive three pairs of *shabbat* (sabbath) pants and four shirts every year.

In the past the emphasis on formal economic equality was taken much more literally than it is today. Clothes, for example, were not marked in the laundry, on the principle that all clothes were publicly owned. Hence, a person did not receive from the laundry the same clean clothes that he had previously worn. Instead, he was given the first pair of pants, dress, or socks that happened to be on top of the laundry pile. This, of course, created highly ludicrous situations, such as tall persons having to wear short pants, or slender persons being forced to wear large dresses. This system, known as *kommuna alef* (first commune), was soon modified at the insistence of the women, who demanded that they be fitted for dresses. The sizes of the clothes were marked, so that a chaver, when he came for his weekly laundry, would not necessarily receive the some clothes he had worn the week before, but he would, at least, receive his own size.

In the middle 1930's *kommuna bet* (second commune) was instituted. It was becoming apparent that the chaverim were not entirely careful with the clothes they wore, and there was a high percentage of torn and soiled clothes. It was felt that if the clothes were marked, and if each chaver were to receive the same clothes from the laundry, he could then be held responsible for their care. This is the system that is still in operation. All clothing, like everything else, is technically owned by the kibbutz. But each chaver receives his clothing allowance for the year, and the clothes he receives are "his," in the sense that they are marked with his name, he wears them, and he is responsible for them.

Despite this formal equality in the basic necessities, certain inequalities in luxuries have arisen due to conditions not provided for in the formal structure of the kibbutz. Some people receive presents of food, clothing, furniture, etc., from relatives who do not reside in Kiryat Yedidim, while others do not. Some individuals, moreover, work outside the kibbutz during their vacations, and purchase what they please with the money they earn. Some have relatives or friends outside the kibbutz with whom they can stay when they go to the cities, which enables them to save from their annual "vacation money" what others must pay in hotel and restaurant bills. This saving enables them to purchase small personal objects. As a result of all these factors, the complete economic equality that once characterized the kibbutz has been slightly qualified.

It may be stated as a general rule, however, that all individuals receive the same clothing allotment, eat the same food in the communal dining room, and enjoy the same (approximately) housing conditions, regardless of their economic skill, their economic importance to the kibbutz, their prestige, or their power. For, despite its awareness that persons differ greatly in ability or in skill — though it seems that it denied it, or at least ignored it, in its early history — the kibbutz insists that such differences should not be used as a basis for differences in privileges. All individuals have an equal right to the good things of the community, although they do not contribute to it equally.

This observation serves to remind us that the equality principle of kibbutz culture is qualified by another ethical consideration — that of need. The kibbutz believes in the principle of "from each according to his ability, to each according to his need," a principle which conflicts at times with its principle of equality. In resolving this conflict, it is usually the "need," rather than the equality, that prevails. A field hand, whose relative productivity is great, eats the common austerity fare of the dining room, though he has worked strenuously in the hot Israeli sun; but an office worker (of low prestige in the kibbutz value hierarchy), whose productivity is low, may receive a special diet, comparatively sumptuous, because of some physical condition. A man with children works no harder than a man without children; but the kibbutz provides not only for his wants, but also for the care of his children. In effect, those with no children, or with few children, subsidize those who do have children.

Not so obvious upon first arrival in Kiryat Yedidim, but just as important for an understanding of kibbutz culture, is the social equality which exists, and of which one becomes acutely aware whenever he leaves the kibbutz for even a short time. There is no class structure in Kiryat Yedidim, and there is no differential reward system for different kinds of labor based on some ranking technique. Some kinds of work, as has already been observed, are valued more highly than others; but those who occupy the more highly valued jobs receive no greater reward than the others. The important psychological fact about kibbutz culture is that everyone, regardless of his work, is viewed as a worker, with the same privileges and responsibilities as anyone else. Menial work, which in capitalist society might mark one as a social inferior, does not carry that stigma in Kiryat Yedidim. The general manager — the highest elective officer in the kibbutz — is not the social superior of the cleaner of the latrines. Hence, there is no work which a person is ashamed to accept because it would demean him socially. There is, thus, little if any subordination of one group of individuals to another; there is no polarization of society into those who command and those who obey, those who are respected and those who respect. There is no need for some to be subservient before others, or to be "nice" to them, for fear of losing their jobs. In short, many of the social inequalities existing in a stratified society do not exist in Kiryat Yedidim.

This achievement can be illustrated by two examples. The recently arrived European physician, not a member of the kibbutz, asked one of the women for the name of the "maid" in the clinic. She did not understand to whom he was referring until he explained that he meant the woman who regularly cleaned the clinic. The woman then explained to him that there were no "maids" in Kiryat Yedidim, that this woman would probably be sitting next to him at dinner that evening, and, moreover, that this "maid'" was an important official in the kibbutz. While making a survey of the various types of kibbutzim, we arrived at a certain kibbutz in order to interview a member of the Israeli Parliament. We were told, on our arrival, that he was to be found in the cemetery — for his job, when Parliament was not in session, consisted in caring for the graveyard. He came to greet us in his work clothes and kindly consented to grant us an interview in the meadow, for his wife, who worked nights in the dairy, was sleeping in their room.

It should be emphasized that the absence of social classes as conventionally conceived, does not imply the absence of either some type of ranking system in Kiryat Yedidim or of "horizontal" social groupings. The kibbutz is *not* a homogeneous concentration of persons, all of whom enjoy equal prestige and power, and each of whom interacts with all others with equal frequency. On the contrary, differential prestige and power as well as social cliques are to be found in Kiryat Yedidim; and it may be well to delineate their broad outlines at the very beginning.

Although the various kibbutz offices are held on a temporary and a rotation basis, those who happen to hold these offices do enjoy considerable power. Moreover, as is noted below, though the tenure of office is limited to two or three years, only a small number of chaverim possess the necessary skills required to cope with the complexities of such offices as general manager, secretary, treasurer, etc., so that in effect these offices rotate among a small core of twelve to fifteen persons. Hence, power within the kibbutz is not equally distributed; it is, rather, concentrated within this small core. It should nevertheless be emphasized that those who occupy these offices enjoy no special privileges and receive no material rewards. Their power, moreover, is limited by the fact that major decisions are made, not by them, but by the town meeting; and that they are under the constant surveillance of the town meeting, and subject to its power of recall. At the same time this core is not a united group, but is comprised of individuals and of sub-groups who disagree, and are often in conflict, with each other. Finally, this is neither a closed nor a self-appointed group. Rather, it is a group whose members are elected by the kibbutz on the basis of ability and demonstrated performance, and one which is always open to recruits chosen by the town meeting should it deem them capable of holding office.

Many of these same considerations apply to those who enjoy prestige. With one possible exception, prestige in Kiryat Yedidim is a function of achieved, rather than of ascribed, status; and the persons of prestige constitute a social category rather than a social group. Prestige is achieved by being a productive and devoted worker, by implementing kibbutz ideals in one's daily life, by being a "synthetic personality," and by being a vattik, a founder of the kibbutz. The first three qualifications are, of course, attained only through achievement and they are open to all. The fourth, though not open to present achievement, was attained through past achievement. Moreover, it is not sufficient merely to *be* a vattik; to merit prestige, the vattik must constantly validate his status by his daily behavior rather than by resting on the glories of his past. Nor, it should be noted, is the prestige of the vattikim inherited by their children. The latter must achieve their own prestige through the same avenues that are open to children of other chaverim, and the status of their parents confers upon them no competitive advantage. . . .

Another principle underlying the culture of Kiryat Yedidim is that of individual liberty; indeed, the kibbutz prides itself on being the freest society in the world. In the early history of Kiryat Yedidim, emphasis on freedom meant primarily freedom from the "artificial conventions" of an urban civilization. Once it was settled on its own land, however, and the necessity for some kind of social organization and authority arose, this earlier notion of freedom was expanded to include opposition to any system of authority. The kibbutz, it was assumed, was an "organic community," and its work would somehow get accomplished without the necessity of investing any individual or individuals with power over their fellows. Hence, Kiryat Yedidim had no officers, and all decisions were made in informal group discussions that included neither a chairman nor an agenda. As it grew larger, however, and as its economy expanded, it became evident that some kind of formal organization was required and that it was necessary to delegate power. But in order to prevent any individual from acquiring personal power and/or to prevent the rise of an entrenched bureaucracy, it was decided that all offices — from the most menial to that of the general manager — should be held for a maximum of two or three years. This tenure limitation, it was hoped, would lead to a rotation of individuals in the various power positions, and would, therefore, ensure the maximum liberty of the kibbutz members.

This emphasis on freedom, it should be noted, is manifested not only in its formal structure, but in its freedom of expression as well. Any curtailment of freedom of speech or of reading is abhorrent to its members, and no censorship of any kind exists.

Finally, a discussion of the moral postulates of this culture must include the principle which might be termed the moral value of the group. The group, in kibbutz culture, is not only a means to the happiness of the individual; the group and group processes are moral ends in their own right. This has three aspects. It means, first, that the interests of the individual must be subordinate to the interests of the group. When the needs of the individual and those of the group come into conflict, the individual is expected to abdicate his needs in favor of the group's. This applies to vocational interests, as well as to ideological convictions. A person's vocational preferences are usually considered in deciding his work assignment; but if the kibbutz requires his labor or skill in some special branch, he is expected to recognize the paramount needs of the group. The same logic applies to ideological matters. An individual is permitted complete freedom in the process of arriving at political decisions and in attempting to convince others of his point of view. But once a formal decision is reached by the kibbutz, he is expected to acquiesce in its decision and to support it, however much it conflicts with his personal views.

A second aspect of the emphasis on the ethical value of the group involves the assumption that the individual's motivations will always be directed to the promotion of the group's interests, as well as of his own. Behavior is expected to be characterized by *ezra hadadit*, or mutual aid. This means that every member of the kibbutz is responsible for the welfare of every other member and for the welfare of the kibbutz as a whole, just as the kibbutz is responsible for the welfare of each individual. The consequence of this principle is that no one is to suffer for lack of medical care, education for his children, food, shelter, clothing, or any other need, as long as the kibbutz can provide him with these requirements.

The emphasis on the moral value of the group means, finally, that group living and group experiences are valued more highly than their individual counterparts. Indeed, so important is the value of group experience that those chaverim who seek a great degree of privacy are viewed as "queer." The kibbutz is interested in creating a *chevra*. The ultimate criterion of either a good kibbutz, a good high school, or a good kindergarten, is whether or not it has become a chevra. The term, chevra, literally, denotes a society; but its connotation — and its meaning for Kiryat Yedidim — is a group which is characterized by the intimacy of interaction, and by mutual concern, if not by love. A chevra, in short, is a *gemeinschaft* or, to use their term, an "organic community." It is apparent, therefore, that the individualist, the person who cherishes his own privacy more than a group experience, constitutes a threat to the group. His desire for privacy either prevents the group from becoming a chevra, or symbolizes the fact that it is not a chevra, for if it were, he would prefer to be with the group than to be alone.*

In this respect, the kibbutz shows its kinship with the shtetl. The following description of the shtetl applies, without qualification, to Kiryat Yedidim.

To insist on privacy if you are not sinning is a serious misdemeanor . . . One of the worst things you can say of a man is, "he keeps it for himself" or

---

* The belief in the primacy of the group has many ramifications. In the realm of art, for example, a teacher criticized *Tobacco Road* because it is "pornographic," and because it represents the feeling of the author alone, and not of the group. A chaver criticized the novel, *Young Hearts*, because it is "not true." When the writer protested that the author may have presented the "truth" as he saw it, he retorted, "Literature must express the feeling of the entire group, and not of one individual, or it is not literature." A kibbutz intellectual criticized Chagall as being "unrealistic," in the sense that he evades the important *social* problems and becomes absorbed in his *private* fantasies.

Moreover, this emphasis on the group explains why The Federation is entirely opposed to what it calls, "careerism." In speeches and articles attempting to encourage the city youth to join the kibbutz movement, opposition to the pursuit of a personal career is a constant theme. In the present world, with its oppressions and inequities, it is argued it is indecent to pursue a personal career, to seek one's personal pleasure, or to satisfy selfish ambition. The morally sensitive person eschews personal ambition and a desire for a better personal life in order to work for a better world.

This emphasis on the group and its welfare, moreover, probably accounts for the almost complete absence of concern with psychiatric values in the kibbutz. At no time during this study did the writer hear any conversation dealing with such topics as "peace of mind," "personality adjustment," "freedom from anxiety," and the host of other psychological concerns that are endemic in contemporary American culture. At times, one hears talk concerning an individual's lack of integration into the kibbutz, a problem which is of serious concern to the chaverim; but one seldom hears discussions of intra-personal adjustment. The elimination of *social* conflicts and of *international* tensions, and the achievement of *world* peace — these are the goals to be achieved, not their individual counterparts. [Author's note.]

"he hides it from others" whether "it" is money or wisdom, clothes or news.

Locked doors, isolation, avoidance of community control, arouse suspicion . . . "Home people," *heymisheh mentschen* . . . are free to come in whenever they like at any time of the day . . .

Withdrawal is felt as attack, whether physical or psychological, and isolation is intolerable. "Life is with people". . .

Everywhere people cluster to talk, at home, in the market place, on the street. Everyone wants to pick up the latest news, the newest gossip . . .

The freedom to observe and to pass judgment on one's fellows, the need to communicate and share events and emotions is inseparable from a strong feeling that individuals are responsible to and for each other.

These moral postulates constitute the social ethics of Kiryat Yedidim and represent, for them, the basic tenets of socialism. But socialism is only one of the twin principles on which kibbutz culture rests; the other principle is Zionism. For Kiryat Yedidim, the kibbutz is not only a means to social and personal liberation, it is a means to national liberation, as well. Socialism, as defined by the tenets described in this chapter, represents the universalistic principle of kibbutz culture; Zionism represents its particularistic, Jewish principle. It is no accident, therefore, that Kiryat Yedidim was founded in Palestine rather than in Eastern Europe, the birthplace of the founders.

The Zionist convictions of Kiryat Yedidim which, for the most part, they share with the entire Zionist movement, may be simply stated. The Jews constitute a Nation, however dispersed they may have been in the last 1900 years of their history, and however lacking they may have been in the external *accoutrement*[8] of nationhood. Every Nation has not only a right, but a duty to survive and to perpetuate its national culture. The physical survival of the Jewish Nation is under a constant threat as long as the Jews remain a national minority living among other political Nations. Only in their own "historical homeland" is it possible for them to escape antisemitism and to escape their anomalous minority status. But this minority status has not only made the Jews an easy target for antisemitism, it has distorted their psychological and cultural complexion. Being deprived of numerous channels for economic activity, the Jews have been forced into a narrow range of economic outlets — they have

[8] Outfit, equipment, appearance.

become "middlemen." Middlemen are not only economic parasites, but they become distorted by the very nature of their work. They have no appreciation for nature and, hence, strike no roots in the soil; they have no understanding of the essential dignity and creativity of physical labor; they develop a sterile intellectualism, a scholasticism which has no basis in real life.

Zionism can change all these characteristics. By living in their own "homeland," Jews are no longer economic parasites, for they are not only middlemen, but they also work the land and run the factories. Having "normalized," that is, broadened, their economic base to include the entire range of economic activities, the cultural and intellectual life of the Jews will become "normalized" as well, since it will have its roots in the creative life of the people. And this economic and cultural normalization, in conjunction with its national normalization — escape from a minority status and, hence, from antisemitism — will enable the Jews to take their rightful and normal place among the nations of the world. In short, Zionism, for Kiryat Yedidim, although a particularistic movement, has as its ultimate aim a universalistic and humanistic goal. This goal is not the geographic segregation of Jews, with the intention of developing specific Jewish characteristics that will separate the Jews from the non-Jewish world. Its aim, rather, is the concentration of Jews in their homeland so that they may develop a "normal" national life which, in turn, will enable them to interact with the rest of the world as normal human beings, rather than as members of a dependent, parasitic, fearful minority. For Kiryat Yedidim, then, national liberation is not only as important as social and personal liberation, it is a necessary condition for their existence. . . .

The Zionist philosophy of Kiryat Yedidim serves to explain some of its important characteristics and behavior. Its emphasis on physical labor and its choice of rural, rather than urban living, stems not only from its general social philosophy, but from its Zionist convictions: the "normalization" of Jewish national life requires that Jews return to physical labor and that they strike roots in the soil. Moreover, the very geographic location of the kibbutz was dictated by its Zionist conviction. Kiryat Yedidim was founded on what was then swampland, in an area which was remote from Jewish settlement. This was part of deliberate Zionist settlement policy, whose aim was to drain the Palestinian swampland so that more acreage could be brought under cultivation, and to continuously extend the frontiers of Jewish colonization so that all of mandated Palestine would be dotted with Jewish settlements.

It is this same Zionist philosophy that today motivates Kiryat Yedidim, together with other kibbutzim, to devote so much of its manpower and energies to non-kibbutz, nationalist goals. During, and immediately following, World War II kibbutz members were to be found in Europe in the vanguard of those who risked their lives in order to smuggle Jewish refugees out of Europe and into Palestine. Since the war, the kibbutzim have lent some of their members for work in the refugee camps that are scattered throughout Israel. Finally, since Kiryat Yedidim views itself as a Zionist agency, it has opened its doors for the settlement and rehabilitation of refugee youth. When children from Hitler's Europe and, more recently, from Moslem countries arrived in Israel, the country was faced with the problem of how to provide for their care. The kibbutzim, in an agreement with the Jewish Agency, agreed to accept groups of adolescents who would live and be educated in a kibbutz until they were prepared to take their place in the life of the country. And when one group leaves, another takes its place. The kibbutzim provide them with food, shelter, and their entire education. This is not to say that their motivations were entirely altruistic. Kiryat Yedidim, for example, derives some benefit from this arrangement in the stipend it receives from the Agency for each child it accepts and in the work performed by the youths in the kibbutz economy. The fact is, however, that the financial gain is small, and is more than offset by the great inconveniences which this arrangement causes the kibbutz, all of whose facilities are already strained.

These, then, are the moral postulates of Kiryat Yedidim and, indeed, of all kibbutzim. They are important, not only because they constitute the basis for the social structure of the kibbutz, but because they provide a clue to an important premise of its living: the premise that life is serious. It is serious because the realization of these values, rather than immediate pleasure or self-seeking, is taken to be the purpose of living.

The feeling that life's primary meaning is to be sought in the realization of values that transcend one's own personal importance was best expressed by a chavera who had recently returned from a visit to the United States. When asked by the author how long it had taken her to become lonesome for Israel, she replied that she missed it almost at once. In America, she said,

. . . they have no values. Of course, in Israel we have austerity, but we have values: we are absorbing immigrants, building a new society. Hence, you feel that your life has meaning. But what meaning does it have in America?

ᏹ FOR DISCUSSION AND WRITING

1. What, according to Mr. Spiro's analysis, is the most important principle on which kibbutz culture is founded? In what sense is it a principle of "moral value" or an "ideal"? Is it a principle universally accepted? For instance, do you accept it yourself? Is it, do you think, accepted by the workingmen you know—truck driver, plumber, brakeman, etc.? In what sense is it called a "spiritual" goal in kibbutz culture? How is it linked with the bourgeois backgrounds of the Israeli pioneers? Why does Mr. Spiro say that "this Tolstoyan attitude" could be evolved "only by romantic, urban intellectuals"?

2. What accounts for the devaluation of intellectual work? What kind of labor has the most prestige, and why?

3. What is the second moral principle of kibbutz culture? Why is it called a "moral" principle, whereas an economist would be more likely to call it an "economic" principle? Incidentally, what is the meaning of the word "culture" as it is used throughout the article?

4. What is the third moral principle Mr. Spiro speaks of? How completely or incompletely is this principle carried out in the kibbutz? Why did it have to be modified in the case of clothing? Are differences of ability or skill recognized by increased privileges? What significance have the examples of the physician's "maid" and the member of the Israeli Parliament?

5. Are there any differentials of social prestige or power? Any "class" stratifications? How is power limited and kept fluid?

6. What are the fourth and fifth moral principles of the culture? How is individual liberty interpreted in this society? What is the relationship between the liberty of the individual and the value ascribed to the group? How, for instance, are personal vocational preferences affected by the primacy of group interests? What happens to personal "privacy"? How does group primacy operate in the realms of art, literature, and personal psychology?

7. How are the socialistic tenets of this society related to Zionism? How is the value placed upon agricultural labor related to the past history of the Jews? Whereas Zionism might be thought to be a separative principle, why does Mr. Spiro say that it "has as its ultimate aim a universalistic and humanistic goal"?

8. What is the meaning (at the end of the article) of "the premise that life is serious"? What "values" are referred to in the last paragraph?

9. Take as a writing assignment what is said in the last paragraph about "values" and "meaning" in American life. If you feel explosive about the criticism here, control your explosiveness enough to arrange your ideas under three or four clearly articulated principles, illustrating each principle with concrete examples, following the admirable model of exposition which Mr. Spiro sets.

Paul Goodman *Utopian Thinking*

Mr. Goodman, born in 1911, is a maverick among contemporary writers and teachers, escaping any particular "school" of thought and constantly creating a new one, but he is best described as a sociologist. He has written many books and taught in many institutions. Most recently he has been a government consultant in Washington.

LET me use ideas of mine as an example, since I am notoriously a "utopian thinker." That is, on problems great and small, I try to think up direct expedients that do not follow the usual procedures, and they are always called "impractical" and an "imposition on people by an intellectual." The question is — and I shall try to pose it fairly — in what sense are such expedients really practical, and in what sense are they really *not* practical? Consider half a dozen little thumbnail ideas:

The ceremony at my boy's public school commencement is poor. We ought to commission the neighborhood writers and musicians to design it. There is talk about aiding the arts, and this is the way to advance them, for, as Goethe said, "The poetry of public occasions is the highest kind." It gives a real subject to the poet, and ennobles the occasion.

Similarly, we do not adequately use our best talents. We ought to get our best designers to improve some of the thousands of ugly small towns and make them unique places to be proud of, rather than delegate such matters to professionals in bureaucratic agencies, when we attend to them at all. A few beautiful models would be a great incentive to others.

In our educational system, too much is spent for plant and not enough for teachers. Why not try, as a pilot project, doing without the school building altogether for a few hundred kids for most of the day? Conceive of a teacher in charge of a band of ten, using the city itself as the material for the curriculum and the background for the teaching. Since we are teaching *for* life, try to get a little closer to it. My guess is that one could considerably diminish the use of present classrooms and so not have to increase their number.

The problem with the old ladies in a Home is to keep them from degenerating, so we must provide geriatric "occupational therapy." The problem with the orphans in their Home is that, for want of individual attention, they may grow up as cold or "psychopathic personalities." But the old ladies could serve as grandmothers for the orphans, to their mutual advantage. The meaning of community is people using one another as resources.

It is false to say that community is not possible in a great city, for 6,000,000 can be regarded as 2,000 neighborhoods of 3,000. These make up one metropolis and enjoy its central advantages, yet they can have a variety of particular conditions of life and have different complexes of community functions locally controlled. E.g., many neighborhoods might have local control of their small grade-schools, with the city enforcing minimum standards and somewhat equalizing the funds. Political initiative is the means of political education.

In any city, we can appreciably diminish commutation by arranging mutually satisfactory exchanges of residence to be near work. The aim of planning is to diminish in-between services that are neither production nor consumption. More generally, if this wasted time of commutation were considered *economically* as part of the time of labor, there would soon be better planning and more decentralization.

In New York City, the automobile traffic is not worth the nuisance it causes. It would be advantageous simply to ban all private cars. Nearly everyone would have faster transportation. Besides, we could then close off about three-quarters of the streets and use them as a fund of land for neighborhood planning.

Now, apart from the particular merits or demerits of any of these ideas, what is wrong with this *style* of thinking, which aims at far-reaching social and cultural advantages by direct and rather dumb-bunny expedients? I think that we can see very simply why it is "utopian."

It is risky. The writers and musicians designing the commencement ceremony would offend the parents, and the scandal would be politically ruinous to the principal, the school board, and the mayor. Nobody expects the ceremonial to be anything but boring, so let sleeping dogs lie. Artists are conceited anyway and would disdain the commissions. So with the small towns: the "best designers" would make the local hair stand on end. As for the thought of children being educated by roaming the streets and blocking traffic, it is a lulu and the less said the better.

Further, such thinking confuses administrative divisions. Community arrangements are always awkwardly multipurpose. What department is responsible? Who budgets? It is inefficient not to have specialized equipment, special buildings, and specialists.

Further, community creates conflict, for incompatibles are thrown together. And there is definitely an imposition of values. "Community" is an imposed value, for many people want to be alone instead of sharing responsibilities or satisfactions; that is why they came to the big city. The notion of living near work, or of a work-residence community, implies that people like their work; but most people today don't.

Further, most such proposals are probably illegal; there would never be an end to litigation. They override the usual procedures, so there is no experience of the problems that might arise; one cannot assess consequences or refer to standard criteria.

Further, they are impracticable. To effect a change in the usual procedures generally requires the pressure of some firm that will profit by it; such things do not happen just because they would be "advantageous"; one can hardly get the most trivial zoning regulation passed.

Finally, such proposals are impractical if only because they assume that the mass of people have more sense and energy than they in fact have. In emergencies, people show remarkable fortitude and choose sensible values and agree to practical expedients because it is inevitable; but not ordinarily. The quotation from Goethe is typical; it is "true," but not for us.

This is a fair picture of our dilemma. A direct solution of social problems disturbs too many fixed arrangements. Society either does not want such solutions, or society is not up to them — it comes to the same thing. The possibility of a higher quality of experience arouses distrust rather than enthusiasm. People must be educated slowly. On the other hand, the only way *to* educate them, to change the present tone, is to cut through habits, especially the character-defense of saying "nothing can be done" and withdrawing into conformity and privacy. We must prove by experiment that direct solutions are feasible. To "educate" in the accustomed style only worsens the disease. And if we do *not* improve the standard of our present experience, it will utterly degenerate.

Therefore we must confront the dilemma as our problem. Our present "organized" procedures are simply not good enough to cope with our technological changes. They debase the users of science, they discourage inventive solutions, they complicate rather than simplify, they drive away some of the best minds. Yet other procedures rouse anxiety and seem unrealistic and irresponsible — whether or not they actually are. The question is, what kind of social science can solve a dilemma of this kind? Let us approach this question by deviating to a more philosophical consideration.

Let us attempt a list of postulates for a pragmatic social science:

(1) The fact that the problem is being studied is a factor in the situation. The experimenter is one of the participants and this already alters the locus of the problem, usefully objectifying it.

(2) The experimenter cannot know definitely what he is after, he has no fixed hypothesis to demonstrate, for he hopes that an unthought-of-solution will emerge in the process of coping with the problem. It is an "open" experiment.

(3) The experimenter, like the other participants, is "engaged"; he has a moral need to come to a solution, and is therefore willing to change his own conceptions, and even his own character. As Biddle has said: "A hopeful attitude toward man's improvability may become a necessary precondition to further research," for otherwise one cannot morally engage oneself.

(4) Since he does not know the outcome, the experimenter must risk confusion and conflict, and try out untested expedients. The safeguard is to stay in close contact with the concrete situation and to be objective and accurate in observation and reporting, and rigorous in analysis.

In the context of a pragmatic social science, utopian thinking at once falls into place. Utopian ideas may be practical hypotheses, that is, expedients for pilot experimentation. Or they may be stimuli for response, so that people get to know what they themselves mean. The fact that such ideas go against the grain of usual thinking is an advantage, for they thereby help to change the locus of the problem, which could not be solved in the usual terms. For instance, they may raise the target of conceivable advantages to a point where certain disadvantages, which were formerly prohibitive, now seem less important. (The assurance of help for an underprivileged child to go to college may make it worth while for him not to become delinquent. This has been the point of the "utopian" Higher Horizons program in the New York City schools.) Further, if a utopian expedient seems *prima facie*[1] sensible, directly feasible, and technically practical, and is nevertheless unacceptable, there is a presumption that we are dealing with an "inner conflict," prejudice, the need to believe that nothing can be done, and the need to maintain the status quo.

As an illustration of the several points of this essay, consider utopian planning for increased face-to-face community, people using one another as resources and sharing more functions of life and society. In a recent discussion I had with Herbert Gans of the University of Pennsylvania and other sociologists, it was agreed by all that our present social fragmentation, individual isolation, and family privacy are undesirable. Yet it was also agreed that to throw people together *as they are* — and how else do we have them? — causes inevitable conflicts. Here is our dilemma.

Gans argued that the attempt at community often leads to nothing at all being done, instead of, at least, some useful accommodation. In Levittown, for example, a project in the community school fell through because the middle-class parents wanted a more intensive program to assure their children's "careers" (preparation for "prestige" colleges), whereas the lower-middle-class parents, who had lower status aims, preferred a more "progressive" program. "In such a case," said Gans, "a utopian will give up the program altogether and say that people are stupid."

My view is very different. It is that such a conflict is not an obstacle to community but a golden opportunity, *if the give-and-take can continue, if contact can be maintained.* The continuing conflict cuts through

[1] On the face of it; in appearance.

the character-defense of people and *defeats* their stupidity, for stupidity is a character-defense. And the heat of the conflict results in better mutual understanding and fraternity. In Levittown, the job of the sociologist should have been not merely to infer the class conflict, but to bring it out into the open, to risk intensifying it by moving also into concealed snobbery and resentment (and racial feeling?), and to confront these people with the *ad hominem* problem: are such things indeed more important to you than, as neighbors, educating your children together?

In our era, to combat the emptiness of technological life, we have to think of a new form, the conflictful community. Historically, close community has provided warmth and security, but it has been tyrannical, anti-liberal, and static (conformist small towns). We, however, have to do with already thoroughly urbanized individuals with a national culture and a scientific technology. The Israeli kibbutzim[2] offer the closest approximation. Some of them have been fanatically dogmatic according to various ideologies, and often tyrannical; nevertheless, their urban Jewish members, rather well educated on the average, have inevitably run into fundamental conflict. Their atmosphere has therefore been sometimes unhappy but never deadening, and they have produced basic social inventions and new character-types. Is such a model improvable and adaptable to cities and industrial complexes? Can widely differing communities be accommodated in a larger federation? How can they be encouraged in modern societies? These are utopian questions.

⊷ FOR DISCUSSION AND WRITING

1. In view of the usual cliché attitude toward "utopian thinking" (equating "utopian" with "fantastically idealistic and impractical"), what is the effectiveness of Paul Goodman's personal, off-beat approach? He makes seven thumbnail criticisms and suggestions; what do you think of them?

2. What would be the risks in adopting these suggestions?

3. Why is the idea of "community" said to be an "imposed value"? What are the main resistances to it?

---

[2] See the immediately preceding article.

4. What are Goodman's four postulates for "a pragmatic social science"?

5. Explain the inferences in the statement that "it was agreed by all that our present social fragmentation, individual isolation, and family privacy are undesirable."

6. What does Goodman mean, in the first sentence of the last paragraph, by "the emptiness of technological life"?

7. What, on the whole, do you gather as Goodman's idea of "community"? Are advantages indicated, or only criticisms of present conditions?

8. Write up your own thumbnail criticisms of community mores and your propositions for changing them. Or write a paper on collisions between your own personal desires, needs, or preferences and community rule. Or a paper criticizing, from the personal point of view, the whole idea of "community" as Goodman sees it—or a paper doing exactly the reverse, supporting Goodman's ideas.

Thomas Mann ◄§ The Earthly Paradise

◄§ German novelist and tale-teller, one of the great creative figures of the twentieth century (1875-1955). As Tolstoy and Dostoievsky had done for the Russian novel in the nineteenth century, Mann remade the modern European novel into a form that could express dramatically, with all the density, subtlety, and vitality of actual life, the fullest burden of ideas; in other words, he gave "intellectual physiognomy" to the modern novel. Aside from his magnificent and haunting *novelle* (such as *Death in Venice*), he is best known for his longer works, *Buddenbrooks*, *The Magic Mountain*, *Joseph and His Brothers* (a tetralogy), and *Doctor Faustus*. The excerpt here is from *The Magic Mountain*, that most radiant drama of spiritual dialectic since Plato. §◄

It was a park.[1] It lay beneath the terrace on which he seemed to stand — a spreading park of luxuriant green shade-trees, elms, planes, beeches, birches, oaks, all in the dappled light and shade of their fresh, full, shimmering foliage, and gently rustling tips. They breathed a deliciously moist, balsamic breath into the air. A warm shower passed over them, but the rain was sunlit. One could see high up in the sky the whole air filled with the bright ripple of raindrops. How lovely it was! Oh, breath

Reprinted by permission of Alfred A. Knopf, Inc., from *The Magic Mountain* by Thomas Mann, translated by H. T. Lowe-Porter. Copyright 1927 by Alfred A. Knopf, Inc. Renewed 1955 by Alfred A. Knopf, Inc.

[1] This is the beginning of a dream. The dreamer, Hans Castorp, has been skiing far beyond his base—the Berghof sanitarium in the Swiss Alps—and has been caught by a blizzard. He has found a bit of shelter at the side of a hut, and has sunk down in the snow, at the point of giving up altogether to numbness and unconsciousness.

of the homeland, oh, fragrance and abundance of the plain, so long fore-gone![2] The air was full of bird song — dainty, sweet, blithe fluting, pip-ing, twittering, cooing, trilling, warbling, though not a single little creature could be seen. Hans Castorp smiled, breathing gratitude. But still more beauties were preparing. A rainbow flung its arc slanting across the scene, most bright and perfect, a sheer delight, all its rich glossy, banded colours moistly shimmering down into the thick, lustrous green. It was like music, like the sound of harps commingled with flutes and violins. The blue and the violet were transcendent. And they descended and magically blended, were transmuted and re-unfolded more lovely than before. Once, some years earlier, our young Hans Castorp had been privileged to hear a world-famous Italian tenor, from whose throat had gushed a glorious stream to witch the world with gracious art. The singer took a high note, exquisitely; then held it, while the passionate harmony swelled, unfolded, glowed from moment to moment with new radiance. Unsuspected veils dropped from before it one by one; the last one sank away, revealing what must surely be the ultimate tonal purity — yet no, for still another fell, and then a well-nigh incredible third and last, shak-ing into the air such an extravagance of tear-glistening splendour, that confused murmurs of protest rose from the audience, as though it could bear no more; and our young friend found that he was sobbing. — So now with the scene before him, constantly transformed and transfigured as it was before his eyes. The bright, rainy veil fell away; behind it stretched the sea, a southern sea of deep, deepest blue shot with silver lights, and a beautiful bay, on one side mistily open, on the other enclosed by moun-tains whose outline paled away into blue space. In the middle distance lay islands, where palms rose tall and small white houses gleamed among cypress groves. Ah, it was all too much, too blest for sinful mortals, that glory of light, that deep purity of the sky, that sunny freshness on the water! Such a scene Hans Castorp had never beheld, nor anything like it. On his holidays he had barely sipped at the south, the sea for him meant the colourless, tempestuous northern tides, to which he clung with in-articulate, childish love. Of the Mediterranean, Naples, Sicily, he knew nothing. And yet — he *remembered*. Yes, strangely enough, that was recognition which so moved him. "Yes, yes, its very image," he was cry-ing out, as though in his heart he had always cherished a picture of this

---

[2] Hans's home was in Hamburg, the "flatland," as it is called in the novel; he has been for months now among the Alpine snows.

spacious, sunny bliss. Always — and that always went far, far, unthinkably far back, as far as the open sea there on the left where it ran out to the violet sky bent down to meet it.

The sky-line was high, the distance seemed to mount to Hans Castorp's view, looking down as he did from his elevation onto the spreading gulf beneath. The mountains held it embraced, their tree-clad foothills running down to the sea; they reached in half-circle from the middle distance to the point where he sat, and beyond. This was a mountainous littoral, at one point of which he was crouching upon a sun-warmed stone terrace, while before him the ground, descending among undergrowth, by moss-covered rocky steps, ran down to a level shore, where the reedy shingle formed little blue-dyed bays, minute archipelagoes and harbours. And all the sunny region, these open coastal heights and laughing rocky basins, even the sea itself out to the islands, where boats plied to and fro, was peopled far and wide. On every hand human beings, children of sun and sea, were stirring or sitting. Beautiful young human creatures, so blithe, so good and gay, so pleasing to see — at sight of them Hans Castorp's whole heart opened in a responsive love, keen almost to pain.

Youths were at work with horses, running hand on halter alongside their whinnying, head-tossing charges; pulling the refractory ones on a long rein, or else, seated bareback, striking the flanks of their mounts with naked heels, to drive them into the sea. The muscles of the riders' backs played beneath the sun-bronzed skin, and their voices were enchanting beyond words as they shouted to each other or to their steeds. A little bay ran deep into the coast line, mirroring the shore as does a mountain lake; about it girls were dancing. One of them sat with her back toward him, so that her neck, and the hair drawn to a knot above it smote him with loveliness. She sat with her feet in a depression of the rock, and played on a shepherd's pipe, her eyes roving above the stops to her companions, as in long, wide garments, smiling, with outstretched arms, alone, or in pairs swaying gently toward each other, they moved in the paces of the dance. Behind the flute-player — she too was white-clad, and her back was long and slender, laterally rounded by the movement of her arms — other maidens were sitting, or standing entwined to watch the dance, and quietly talking. Beyond them still, young men were practising archery. Lovely and pleasant it was to see the older ones show the younger, curly-locked novices, how to span the bow and take aim; draw with them, and laughing support them staggering back from the push of the arrow as it leaped from the bow. Others were fishing, lying prone on a jut of rock, waggling one leg in the air, holding the line out over the water, approaching their heads in talk. Others sat straining forward to fling the bait far out. A ship, with mast and yards, lying high out of the tide, was being eased, shoved, and steadied into the sea. Children played and exulted among the breaking waves. A young female, lying outstretched, drawing with one hand her flowered robe high between her breasts, reached with the other in the air after a twig bearing fruit and leaves, which a second, a slender-hipped creature, erect at her head, was playfully withholding. Young folk were sitting in nooks of the rocks, or hesitating at the water's edge, with crossed arms clutching either shoulder, as they tested the chill with their toes. Pairs strolled along the beach, close and confiding, at the maiden's ear the lips of the youth. Shaggy-haired goats leaped from ledge to ledge of the rocks, while the young goatherd, wearing perched on his brown curls a little hat with the brim turned up behind, stood watching them from a height, one hand on his hip, the other holding the long staff on which he leaned.

"Oh, lovely, lovely," Hans Castorp breathed. "How joyous and winning they are, how fresh and healthy, happy and clever they look! It is not alone the outward form, they seem to be wise and gentle through and through. That is what makes me in love with them, the spirit that speaks out of them, the sense, I might almost say, in which they live and play together." By which he meant the friendliness, the mutual courteous regard these children of the sun showed to each other, a calm, reciprocal reverence veiled in smiles, manifested almost imperceptibly, and yet possessing them all by the power of sense association and ingrained idea. A dignity, even a gravity, was held, as it were, in solution in their lightest mood, perceptible only as an ineffable spiritual influence, a high seriousness without austerity, a reasoned goodness conditioning every act. All this, indeed, was not without its ceremonial side. A young mother, in a brown robe loose at the shoulder, sat on a rounded mossy stone and suckled her child, saluted by all who passed with a characteristic gesture which seemed to comprehend all that lay implicit in their general bearing. The young men, as they approached, lightly and formally crossed their arms on their breasts, and smilingly bowed; the maidens shaped the suggestion of a curtsy, as the worshipper does when he passes the high altar, at the same time nodding repeatedly, blithely and heartily. This mixture of formal homage with lively friendliness, and the slow, mild mien of the mother as well, where she sat pressing her breast with her forefinger to ease the flow of milk to her babe, glancing up from it to acknowledge with a smile the reverence paid her — this sight thrilled Hans Castorp's heart with something very close akin to ecstasy. He could not get his fill of looking, yet asked himself in concern whether he had a right, whether it was not perhaps punishable, for him, an outsider, to be a party to the sunshine and gracious loveliness of all these happy folk. He felt common, clumsy-booted. It seemed unscrupulous.

A lovely boy, with full hair drawn sideways across his brow and falling on his temples, sat directly beneath him, apart from his companions, with arms folded on his breast — not sadly, not ill-naturedly, quite tranquilly on one side. This lad looked up, turned his gaze upward and looked at him, Hans Castorp, and his eyes went between the watcher and the scenes upon the strand, watching his watching, to and fro. But suddenly he looked past Hans Castorp into space, and that smile, common to them all, of polite and brotherly regard, disappeared in a moment from his lovely, purely cut, half-childish face. His brows did not darken, but in his gaze there came a solemnity that looked as though carven out of stone, inexpressive, unfathomable, a deathlike reserve, which gave the scarcely reassured Hans Castorp a thorough fright, not unaccompanied by a vague apprehension of its meaning.

He too looked in the same direction. Behind him rose towering columns, built of cylindrical blocks without bases, in the joinings of which moss had grown. They formed the façade of a temple gate, on whose foundations he was sitting, at the top of a double flight of steps with space between. Heavy of heart he rose, and, descending the stair on one side, passed through the high gate below, and along a flagged street, which soon brought him before other propylaea.[3] He passed through these as well, and now stood facing the temple that lay before him, mossy, weathered to a grey-green tone, on a foundation reached by a steep flight of steps. The broad brow of the temple rested on the capitals of powerful, almost stunted columns, tapering toward the top — sometimes a fluted block had been shoved out of line and projected a little in profile. Painfully, helping himself on with his hands, and sighing for the growing oppression of his heart, Hans Castorp mounted the high

[3] Colonnaded porches to a temple.

steps and gained the grove of columns. It was very deep, he moved in it as among the trunks in a forest of beeches by the pale northern sea. He purposely avoided the centre, yet for all that slanted back again, and presently stood before a group of statuary, two female figures carved in stone, on a high base: mother and daughter, it seemed; one of them sitting, older than the other, more dignified, right goddesslike and mild, yet with mourning brows above the lightless empty eye-sockets; clad in a flowing tunic and a mantle of many folds, her matronly brow with its waves of hair covered with a veil. The other figure stood in the protecting embrace of the first, with round, youthful face, and arms and hands wound and hidden in the folds of the mantle.

Hans Castorp stood looking at the group, and from some dark cause his laden heart grew heavier still, and more oppressed with its weight of dread and anguish. Scarcely daring to venture, but following an inner compulsion, he passed behind the statuary, and through the double row of columns beyond. The bronze door of the sanctuary stood open, and the poor soul's knees all but gave way beneath him at the sight within. Two grey old women, witchlike, with hanging breasts and dugs of finger-length, were busy there, between flaming braziers, most horribly. They were dismembering a child. In dreadful silence they tore it apart with their bare hands — Hans Castorp saw the bright hair blood-smeared — and cracked the tender bones between their jaws, their dreadful lips dripped blood. An icy coldness held him. He would have covered his eyes and fled, but could not. They at their gory business had already seen him, they shook their reeking fists and uttered curses — soundlessly, most vilely, with the last obscenity, and in the dialect of Hans Castorp's native Hamburg. It made him sick, sick as never before. He tried desperately to escape; knocked into a column with his shoulder — and found himself, with the sound of that dreadful whispered brawling still in his ears, still wrapped in the cold horror of it, lying by his hut, in the snow, leaning against one arm, with his head upon it, his legs in their skis stretched out before him.

It was no true awakening. He blinked his relief at being free from those execrable hags, but was not very clear, nor even greatly concerned, whether this was a hay-hut, or the column of a temple, against which he lay; and after a fashion continued to dream, no longer in pictures, but in thoughts hardly less involved and fantastic.

"I felt it was a dream, all along," he rambled. "A lovely and horrible

dream. I knew all the time that I was making it myself — the park with
the trees, the delicious moisture in the air, and all the rest, both dreadful
and dear. In a way, I knew it all beforehand. But how is it a man can
know all that and call it up to bring him bliss and terror both at once?
Where did I get the beautiful bay with the islands, where the temple
precincts, whither the eyes of that charming boy pointed me, as he stood
there alone? Now I know that it is not out of our single souls we dream.
We dream anonymously and communally, if each after his fashion. The
great soul of which we are a part may dream through us, in our manner
of dreaming, its own secret dreams, of its youth, its hope, its joy and
peace — and its blood-sacrifice. Here I lie at my column and still feel
in my body the actual remnant of my dream — the icy horror of the
human sacrifice, but also the joy that had filled my heart to its very
depths, born of the happiness and brave bearing of those human creatures in white. It is meet and proper, I hereby declare that I have a
prescriptive right to lie here and dream these dreams. . . .

"The recklessness of death is in life, it would not be life without it —
and in the centre is the position of the *Homo Dei*,[4] between recklessness
and reason, as his state is between mystic community and windy individualism. I, from my column, perceive all this. In this state he must live
gallantly, associate in friendly reverence with himself, for only he is
aristocratic, and the counter-positions are not at all. Man is the lord of
counter-positions, they can be only through him, and thus he is more
aristocratic than they. More so than death, too aristocratic for death —
that is the freedom of his mind. More aristocratic than life, too aristocratic for life, and that is the piety in his heart. There is both rhyme and
reason in what I say, I have made a dream poem of humanity. I will cling
to it. I will be good. I will let death have no mastery over my thoughts.
For therein lies goodness and love of humankind, and in nothing else.
Death is a great power. One takes off one's hat before him, and goes
weavingly on tiptoe. He wears the stately ruff of the departed and we do
him honour in solemn black. Reason stands simple before him, for
reason is only virtue, while death is release, immensity, abandon, desire.
Desire, says my dream. Lust, not love. Death and love — no, I cannot
make a poem of them, they don't go together. Love stands opposed to
death. It is love, not reason, that is stronger than death. Only love, not
reason, gives sweet thoughts. And from love and sweetness alone can

[4] The man of God.

form come: form and civilization, friendly, enlightened, beautiful human intercourse — always in silent recognition of the blood-sacrifice. Ah, yes, it is well and truly dreamed. I have taken stock. I will remember. I will keep faith with death in my heart, yet well remember that faith with death and the dead is evil, is hostile to humankind, so soon as we give it power over thought and action. *For the sake of goodness and love, man shall let death have no sovereignty over his thoughts.* — And with this — I awake. For I have dreamed it out to the end, I have come to my goal....

"I have dreamed of man's state, of his courteous and enlightened social state; behind which, in the temple, the horrible blood-sacrifice was consummated. Were they, those children of the sun, so sweetly courteous to each other, in silent recognition of that horror? It would be a fine and right conclusion they drew. I will hold to them, in my soul, I will hold with them....

"Deep into the snow mountains my search has led me. Now I have it fast. My dream has given it me, in utter clearness, that I may know it for ever. Yes, I am in simple raptures, my body is warm, my heart beats high and knows why. It beats not solely on physical grounds, as finger-nails grow on a corpse; but humanly, on grounds of my joyful spirits. My dream world was a draught, better than port or ale, it streams through my veins like love and life, I tear myself from my dream and sleep, knowing as I do, perfectly well, that they are highly dangerous to my young life.[5] Up, up! Open your eyes! These are your limbs, your legs here in the snow! Pull yourself together, and up! Look — fair weather!"

The bonds held fast that kept his limbs involved. He had a hard struggle to free himself — but the inner compulsion proved stronger. With a jerk he raised himself on his elbows, briskly drew up his knees, shoved, rolled, wrestled to his feet; stamped with his skis in the snow, flung his arms about his ribs and worked his shoulders violently, all the while casting strained, alert glances about him and above, where now a pale blue sky showed itself between grey-bluish clouds, and these presently drew away to discover a thin sickle of a moon. Early twilight reigned: no snowfall, no storm. The wall of the opposite mountain with its shaggy, tree-clad ridge stretched out before him plain and peaceful. Shadow lay on half its height, but the upper half was bathed in palest rosy light. How were things in the world? Was it morning? Had he, des-

[5] Dream and sleep are highly dangerous right now because he is nearly freezing to death.

pite what the books said, lain all night in the snow and not frozen? Not a member was frost-bitten, nothing snapped when he stamped, shook and struck himself, as he did vigorously, all the time seeking to establish the facts of his situation. Ears, toes, finger-tips, were of course numb, but not more so than they had often been at night in his loggia. He could take his watch from his pocket — it was still going, it had not stopped, as it did if he forgot to wind it. It said not yet five — it was in fact considerably earlier, twelve, thirteen minutes. Preposterous! Could it be he had lain here in the snow only ten minutes or so, while all these scenes of horror and delight and those presumptuous thoughts had spun themselves in his brain . . . ?

Be all that as it might, and whether it was morning or afternoon — there could in fact be no doubt that it was still late afternoon — in any case, there was nothing in the circumstances or in his own condition to prevent his going home, which he accordingly did: descending in a fine sweep, as the crow flies, to the valley, where, as he reached it, lights were showing, though his way had been well enough lighted by reflection from the snow. . . .

He left his skis at the grocer's, rested a little in Herr Settembrini's attic cell, and told him how the storm had overtaken him in the mountains. The horrified humanist scolded him roundly, and straightway lighted his spirit-kettle to brew coffee for the exhausted one — the strength of which did not prevent Hans Castorp from falling asleep as he sat.

An hour later the highly civilized atmosphere of the Berghof[6] caressed him. He ate enormously at dinner. What he had dreamed was already fading from his mind. What he had thought — even that self-same evening it was no longer so clear as it had been at first.

 FOR DISCUSSION AND WRITING

1. Since Hans is freezing to death in a glacial blizzard, it is natural enough that he should dream of a lovely warm green world. Through the first long paragraph, his impressions are only of nature (without any people). By how many elements does Mann make the natural scene seem happy and alive and heart-warming? (If you have read the piece from Voltaire, what is the

[6] The sanitarium for tubercular patients.

contrast between what Voltaire first has his characters take notice of and
the first impressions of the dreamer here?) By what stylistic means does
Mann identify the reader's feelings and emotions with those of Hans?

2. Why, though Hans has never been on the Mediterranean coast, does he
   feel that this sunny southern scene of archipelagoes and islands is something "remembered," "recognized," from "far, far, unthinkably far back"?
   (For this question, you don't have to know the book at all; all you have to
   know is yourself.)

3. What are all the young people doing? How do their occupations differ
   from your own? How are their "friendliness," their "mutual courteous regard," and their "calm, reciprocal reverence" shown? How is the "ceremonial" quality of their life shown in their attitude toward the mother
   suckling her child, and why is it shown in this particular instance? What
   is the meaning of the word "ceremonial" here?

4. Technically, how does Mann manage the radical change of view from the
   sunny coast, with all the happy young people, to the temple on the mountainside behind where Hans is sitting? What is the significance of the
   statuary group of the mother and daughter, and why does it fill Hans with
   anguish and dread? (Again, you don't need to know anything about the
   book; all you need to know about is yourself.) What is the significance of
   the hideous old hags, dismembering a child and eating it, with obscene
   words and gestures? Why is this scene placed in a *temple?*

5. By what means is Hans's waking-up managed, and how does it resemble
   one's own waking from a nightmare? When he first wakes from the dream,
   his mind works in a pretty confused way, half in and half out of the
   dreaming state, but he knows that his dream has been an important one.
   He says to himself: "I have dreamed of man's state, of his courteous and
   enlightened social state; behind which, in the temple, the horrid blood-
   sacrifice was consummated. Were they, those children of the sun, so
   sweetly courteous to each other, in silent recognition of that horror? It
   would be a fine and right conclusion they drew." What does all this mean?

6. When Hans gets back to the Berghof and has a good dinner, his dream
   fades, he cannot hold it clearly in his thought. Does this mean that it
   wasn't "true"?

7. Write your own dream, no matter how mysterious. Or write a paper comparing the main elements of the various "Utopian" pieces in this section,
   giving them your own evaluation.

THREE ◌ THE ORDERS OF KNOWLEDGE

The Order of Nature

ONE OF *Teilhard de Chardin's books has the dedication: "For those who love the world." The phrase might be used as epigraph to the following pages on the physical universe and its creatures. For though the concerns of the writers represented here range from a fragile green bug, almost transparent on a grass stem and crushable between the finger tips, to the galaxies rushing through black infinities, this they have in common: love of the world in its sheer phenomenality, the kind of love that is both delight and reverence.*

Lucretius was for his time, the first century before the Christian era, what we would call a philosopher of science; a modern editor of the classics speaks of him as "the finest thinker the Romans produced." He is also a great poet—though none of the modern verse translations of his work into English approaches the distinction of the prose translation by W. H. D. Rouse used here. His subject, the atomic theory of the universe, seems to him so marvelous that poetry alone commands a language noble enough to represent it. After 2,000 years his scientific position seems astonishingly modern, while his exposition of it brings to life the whole Roman world in its immense complexity. Something of the same sense of the marvelous gives magnificence to the PENSEÉS *of the seventeenth-century mathematician and physicist Pascal, who, after probing the vastnesses of sidereal space, asks us to look into "the womb of this abridged atom" and "see therein an infinity of universes, each of which has its firmament, its planets, its earth, in the same proportion as in the visible world; . . . wonders as amazing in their littleness as the others in their vastness." Probably neither Lucretius nor Pascal would find difficulty in discussing with the modern astrophysicist Fred Hoyle the discoveries made through the Palomar telescope, the expanding universe, and Hoyle's conception of continuous creation. In this kind of contemplation, poet, philosopher, and scientist meet in an act of praise.*

A similar passion informs that classic of entomology which is also a literary classic, Henri Fabre's study of the praying mantis—the cannibal queen clothed with the chic of a Dior model, striking awe with her attitudes of a Delphic priestess delivering oracles, launching her fearful sails and her great saw-tooth guillotine arms as nicely and horribly engineered for execution as the machine described by Kafka in his story "In the Penal Colony." And it informs the chapter from Konrad Lorenz's KING SOLOMON'S RING, describing the battle of the doves in which the victor executes the vanquished with the fastidious and deliberate blood lust of an accomplished sadist, and the battle of the wolves in which the victor's bite of kill is withheld through a mysterious instinct of respect for his adversary's vulnerability, an instinct one might call "humane" if it were as characteristic of the human species as of wolves. Love of the phenomenal world gives the scientist his patience in observation and his objectivity; it also gives him insight into marvels and miracles. Commonly we think of miracles as contrary to natural law, but Loren Eiseley, in "The Judgment of the Birds," finds miracles in the habits of New York pigeons observed at dawn from the window of a hotel room, in a flight of warblers over the dreary western Badlands, in the bumbling of a frantic crow through a fog, in a spider's web spun on a lamppost on the edge of winter. The chapter from Rachel Carson's SILENT SPRING places the order of nature in a violently different perspective, that of our chemical rampage against the ecology of living things. What Albert Schweitzer calls "reverence for life" is clearly more than an ethical principle—it is a principle of biological survival. A line from one of W. H. Auden's poems might be adapted as rubric to Miss Carson's study of planned destruction: "We must love each other or die."

Jean Henri Fabre ❦ *The Praying Mantis*

❦ French entomologist (1823-1915). Fabre's parents were illiterate, poverty-stricken peasants; he learned to read by a fluke of chance, and educated himself enough to get a teaching job in primary school and later in the Lycée of Avignon. With a large family, he was dogged by poverty all his life, as well as by the jealousy and hatred of his colleagues—for he taught and wrote about natural science in such an attractive way that he was thought to be academically "unsound." It was not until he was seventy-four and "retired" from his professorship (actually fired) that he was able to devote himself to the laboratory study of insects. In those last eighteen years before his death, at ninety-two, he accomplished the great and loving studies that compose the ten-volume *Souvenirs entomologiques.* ❧

ANOTHER creature of the south is at least as interesting as the Cicada, but much less famous, because it makes no noise. Had Heaven granted it a pair of cymbals, the one thing needed, its renown would eclipse the great musician's, for it is most unusual in both shape and habits. Folk hereabouts call it *lou Prègo-Diéu,* the animal that prays to God. Its official name is the Praying Mantis. . . .

The language of science and the peasant's artless vocabulary agree in this case and represent the queer creature as a pythoness[1] delivering

Reprinted by permission of Dodd, Mead & Company from *The Insect World of J. Henri Fabre,* edited by Edwin Way Teale. Copyright 1949 by Edwin Way Teale. The translation is by Alexander Teixeira de Mattos.

[1] The priestess who uttered the oracles of Apollo at Delphi. The name is related to the myth of Apollo's slaying a monstrous serpent that inhabited the caves of Mount Parnassus. Actually, a sacred snake was kept in the underground chamber from which the priestess delivered the oracle.

her oracles or an ascetic rapt in pious ecstasy. The comparison dates a long way back. Even in the time of the Greeks the insect was called Μάντις, the divine, the prophet. The tiller of the soil is not particular about analogies: where points of resemblance are not too clear, he will make up for their deficiencies. He saw on the sun-scorched herbage an insect of imposing appearance, drawn up majestically in a half-erect posture. He noticed its gossamer wings, broad and green, trailing like long veils of finest lawn; he saw its fore-legs, its arms so to speak, raised to the sky in a gesture of invocation. That was enough; popular imagination did the rest; and behold the bushes from ancient times stocked with Delphic priestesses, with nuns in orison.

Good people, with your childish simplicity, how great was your mistake! Those sanctimonious airs are a mask for Satanic habits; those arms folded in prayer are cut-throat weapons: they tell no beads, they slay whatever passes within range. Forming an exception which one would never have suspected in the herbivorous order of the Orthoptera, the Mantis feeds exclusively on living prey. She is the tigress of the peaceable entomological tribes, the ogress in ambush who levies a tribute of fresh meat. Picture her with sufficient strength; and her carnivorous appetites, combined with her traps of horrible perfection, would make her the terror of the country-side. The *Prègo-Diéu* would become a devilish vampire.

Apart from her lethal implement, the Mantis has nothing to inspire dread. She is not without a certain beauty, in fact, with her slender figure, her elegant bust, her pale-green colouring and her long gauze wings. No ferocious mandibles, opening like shears; on the contrary, a dainty pointed muzzle that seems made for billing and cooing. Thanks to a flexible neck, quite independent of the thorax, the head is able to move freely, to turn to right or left, to bend, to lift itself. Alone among insects, the Mantis directs her gaze; she inspects and examines; she almost has a physiognomy.

Great indeed is the contrast between the body as a whole, with its very pacific aspect, and the murderous mechanism of the forelegs, which are correctly described as raptorial.[2] The haunch is uncommonly long and powerful. Its function is to throw forward the rat-trap, which does not await its victim but goes in search of it. The snare is decked out with some show of finery. The base of the haunch is adorned on the inner

2 Adapted to seize prey.

surface with a pretty, black mark, having a white spot in the middle; and a few rows of bead-like dots complete the ornamentation.

The thigh, longer still, a sort of flattened spindle, carries on the front half of its lower surface two rows of sharp spikes. In the inner row there are a dozen, alternately black and green, the green being shorter than the black. This alternation of unequal lengths increases the number of cogs and improves the effectiveness of the weapon. The outer row is simpler and has only four teeth. Lastly, three spurs, the longest of all, stand out behind the two rows. In short, the thigh is a saw with two parallel blades, separated by a groove in which the leg lies when folded back.

The leg, which moves very easily on its joint with the thigh, is likewise a double-edged saw. The teeth are smaller, more numerous and closer together than those on the thigh. It ends in a strong hook whose point vies with the finest needle for sharpness, a hook fluted underneath and having a double blade like a curved pruning-knife.

This hook, a most perfect instrument for piercing and tearing, has left me many a painful memory. How often, when Mantis-hunting, clawed by the insect which I had just caught and not having both hands at liberty, have I been obliged to ask somebody else to release me from my tenacious captive! To try to free yourself by force, without first disengaging the claws implanted in your flesh, would expose you to scratches similar to those produced by the thorns of a rose-tree. None of our insects is so troublesome to handle. The Mantis claws you with her pruning-hooks, pricks you with her spikes, seizes you in her vice and makes self-defence almost impossible if, wishing to keep your prize alive, you refrain from giving the pinch of the thumb that would put an end to the struggle by crushing the creature.

When at rest, the trap is folded and pressed back against the chest and looks quite harmless. There you have the insect praying. But, should a victim pass, the attitude of prayer is dropped abruptly. Suddenly unfolded, the three long sections of the machine throw to a distance their terminal grapnel, which harpoons the prey and, in returning, draws it back between the two saws. The vice closes with a movement like that of the fore-arm and the upper arm; and all is over: Locusts, Grasshoppers and others even more powerful, once caught in the mechanism with its four rows of teeth, are irretrievably lost. Neither their desperate fluttering nor their kicking will make the terrible engine release its hold.

An uninterrupted study of the Mantis' habits is not practicable in the open fields; we must rear her at home. There is no difficulty about this: she does not mind being interned under glass, on condition that she be well fed. Offer her choice viands, served up fresh daily, and she will hardly feel her absence from the bushes.

As cages for my captives I have some ten large wire-gauze dish-covers, the same that are used to protect meat from the Flies. Each stands in a pan filled with sand. A dry tuft of thyme and a flat stone on which the laying may be done later constitute all the furniture. These huts are placed in a row on the large table in my insect laboratory, where the sun shines on them for the best part of the day. I instal my captives in them, some singly, some in groups.

It is in the second fortnight of August that I begin to come upon the adult Mantis in the withered grass and on the brambles by the road-side. The females, already notably corpulent, are more frequent from day to day. Their slender companions, on the other hand, are rather scarce; and I sometimes have a good deal of difficulty in making up my couples, for there is an appalling consumption of these dwarfs in the cages. Let us keep these atrocities for later and speak first of the females.

They are great eaters, whose maintenance, when it has to last for some months, is none too easy. The provisions, which are nibbled at disdainfully and nearly all wasted, have to be renewed almost every day. I trust that the Mantis is more economical on her native bushes. When game is not plentiful, no doubt she devours every atom of her catch; in my cages she is extravagant, often dropping and abandoning the rich morsel after a few mouthfuls, without deriving any further benefit from it. This appears to be her particular method of beguiling the tedium of captivity.

To cope with these extravagant ways I have to employ assistants. Two or three small local idlers, bribed by the promise of a slice of melon or bread-and-butter, go morning and evening to the grass-plots in the neighbourhood and fill their game-bags — cases made of reed-stumps — with live Locusts and Grasshoppers. I on my side, net in hand, make a daily circuit of my enclosure, in the hope of obtaining some choice morsel for my boarders.

These tit-bits are intended to show me to what lengths the Mantis' strength and daring can go. They include the big Grey Locust . . . , who is larger than the insect that will consume him; the White-faced Decticus, armed with a vigorous pair of mandibles whereof our fingers would do well to fight shy; the quaint Tryxalis, who wears a pyramid-shaped mitre on her head; the Vine Ephippiger, who clashes cymbals and sports a sword at the bottom of her pot-belly. To this assortment of game that is not any too easy to tackle, let us add two monsters, two of the largest Spiders of the district: the Silky Epeira, whose flat, festooned abdomen is the size of a franc piece; and the Cross Spider, or Diadem Epeira, who is hideously hairy and obese.

I cannot doubt that the Mantis attacks such adversaries in the open, when I see her, under my covers, boldly giving battle to whatever comes in sight. Lying in wait among the bushes, she must profit by the fat prizes offered by chance even as, in the wire cage, she profits by the treasures due to my generosity. Those big hunts, full of danger, are no new thing; they form part of her normal existence. Nevertheless they appear to be rare, for want of opportunity, perhaps to the Mantis' deep regret.

Locusts of all kinds, Butterflies, Dragon-flies, large Flies, Bees and other moderate-sized captures are what we usually find in the lethal limbs. Still the fact remains that, in my cages, the daring huntress recoils before nothing. Sooner or later, Grey Locust and Decticus, Epeira and Tryxalis are harpooned, held tight between the saws and crunched with gusto. The facts are worth describing.

At the sight of the Grey Locust who has heedlessly approached along the trelliswork of the cover, the Mantis gives a convulsive shiver and suddenly adopts a terrifying posture. An electric shock would not produce a more rapid effect. The transition is so abrupt, the attitude so threatening that the observer beholding it for the first time at once hesitates and draws back his fingers, apprehensive of some unknown danger. Old hand as I am, I cannot even now help being startled, should I happen to be thinking of something else.

You see before you, most unexpectedly, a sort of bogey-man or Jack-in-the-box. The wing-covers open and are turned back on either side, slantingly; the wings spread to their full extent and stand erect like parallel sails or like a huge heraldic crest towering over the back; the tip of the abdomen curls upwards like a crosier, rises and falls, relaxing with short jerks and a sort of sough, a "Whoof! Whoof!" like that of a Turkeycock spreading his tail. It reminds one of the puffing of a startled Adder.

Planted defiantly on its four hind-legs, the insect holds its long bust almost upright. The murderous legs, originally folded and pressed together upon the chest, open wide, forming a cross with the body and revealing the arm-pits decorated with rows of beads and a black spot with a white dot in the centre. These two faint imitations of the eyes in a Peacock's tail, together with the dainty ivory beads, are warlike ornaments kept hidden at ordinary times. They are taken from the jewel-case only at the moment when we have to make ourselves brave and terrible for battle.

Motionless in her strange posture, the Mantis watches the Locust, with her eyes fixed in his direction and her head turning as on a pivot whenever the other changes his place. The object of this attitudinizing is evident: the Mantis wants to strike terror into her dangerous quarry, to paralyze it with fright, for, unless demoralized by fear, it would prove too formidable.

Does she succeed in this? Under the shiny head of the Decticus, behind the long face of the Locust, who can tell what passes? No sign of excitement betrays itself to our eyes on those impassive masks. Nevertheless it is certain that the threatened one is aware of the danger. He sees standing before him a spectre, with uplifted claws, ready to fall upon him; he feels that he is face to face with death; and he fails to escape while there is yet time. He who excels in leaping and could so easily hop out of reach of those talons, he, the big-thighed jumper, remains stupidly where he is, or even draws nearer with a leisurely step.

They say that little birds, paralysed with terror before the open jaws of the Snake, spell-bound by the reptile's gaze, lose their power of flight and allow themselves to be snapped up. The Locust often behaves in much the same way. See him within reach of the enchantress. The two grapnels fall, the claws strike, the double saws close and clutch. In vain the poor wretch protests: he chews space with his mandibles and, kicking desperately, strikes nothing but the air. His fate is sealed. The Mantis furls her wings, her battle-standard; she resumes her normal posture; and the meal begins.

In attacking the Tryxalis and the Ephippiger, less dangerous game than the Grey Locust and the Decticus, the spectral attitude is less imposing and of shorter duration. Often the throw of the grapnels is sufficient. This is likewise so in the case of the Epeira, who is grasped round the body with not a thought of her poison-fangs. With the smaller

Locusts, the usual fare in my cages as in the open fields, the Mantis seldom employs her intimidation-methods and contents herself with seizing the reckless one that passes within her reach.

When the prey to be captured is able to offer serious resistance, the Mantis has at her service a pose that terrorizes and fascinates her quarry and gives her claws a means of hitting with certainty. Her rat-traps close on a demoralized victim incapable of defence. She frightens her victim into immobility by suddenly striking a spectral attitude.

The wings play a great part in this fantastic pose. They are very wide, green on the outer edge, colourless and transparent every elsewhere. They are crossed lengthwise by numerous veins, which spread in the shape of a fan. Other veins, transversal and finer, intersect the first at right angles and with them form a multitude of meshes. In the spectral attitude, the wings are displayed and stand upright in two parallel planes that almost touch each other, like the wings of a Butterfly at rest. Between them the curled tip of the abdomen moves with sudden starts. The sort of breath which I have compared with the puffing of an Adder in a posture of defence comes from this rubbing of the abdomen against the nerves of the wings. To imitate the strange sound, all that you need do is to pass your nail quickly over the upper surface of an unfurled wing.

Wings are essential to the male, a slender pigmy who has to wander from thicket to thicket at mating-time. He has a well-developed pair, more than sufficient for his flight, the greatest range of which hardly amounts to four or five of our paces. The little fellow is exceedingly sober in his appetites. On rare occasions, in my cages, I catch him eating a lean Locust, an insignificant, perfectly harmless creature. This means that he knows nothing of the spectral attitude, which is of no use to an unambitious hunter of his kind.

On the other hand, the advantage of the wings to the female is not very obvious, for she is inordinately stout at the time when her eggs ripen. She climbs, she runs; but, weighed down by her corpulence, she never flies. Then what is the object of wings, of wings, too, which are seldom matched for breadth?

The question becomes more significant if we consider the Grey Mantis . . . , who is closely akin to the Praying Mantis. The male is winged and is even pretty quick at flying. The female, who drags a great belly full of eggs, reduces her wings to stumps and, like the cheese-makers of Auvergne and Savoy, wears a short-tailed jacket. For one who is not meant to leave the dry grass and the stones, this abbreviated costume is more suitable than superfluous gauze furbelows. The Grey Mantis is right to retain but a mere vestige of the cumbrous sails.

Is the other wrong to keep her wings, to exaggerate them, even though she never flies? Not at all. The Praying Mantis hunts big game. Sometimes a formidable prey appears in her hiding-place. A direct attack might be fatal. The thing to do is first to intimidate the new-comer, to conquer his resistance by terror. With this object she suddenly unfurls her wings into a ghost's winding-sheet. The huge sails incapable of flight are hunting-implements. This stratagem is not needed by the little Grey Mantis, who captures feeble prey, such as Gnats and new-born Locusts. The two huntresses, who have similar habits and, because of their stoutness, are neither of them able to fly, are dressed to suit the difficulties of the ambuscade. The first, an impetuous amazon, puffs her wings into a threatening standard; the second, a modest fowler, reduces them to a pair of scanty coat-tails.

In a fit of hunger, after a fast of some days' duration, the Praying Mantis will gobble up a Grey Locust whole, except for the wings, which are too dry; and yet the victim of her voracity is as big as herself, or even bigger. Two hours are enough for consuming this monstrous head of game. An orgy of the sort is rare. I have witnessed it once or twice and have always wondered how the gluttonous creature found room for so much food and how it reversed in its favour the axiom that the cask must be greater than its contents. I can but admire the lofty privileges of a stomach through which matter merely passes, being at once digested, dissolved and done away with.

The usual bill of fare in my cages consists of Locusts of greatly varied species and sizes. It is interesting to watch the Mantis nibbling her Acridian, firmly held in the grip of her two murderous fore-legs. Notwithstanding the fine, pointed muzzle, which seems scarcely made for this gorging, the whole dish disappears, with the exception of the wings, of which only the slightly fleshy base is consumed. The legs, the tough skin, everything goes down. Sometimes the Mantis seizes one of the big hinder thighs by the knuckle-end, lifts it to her mouth, tastes it and crunches it with a little air of satisfaction. The Locust's fat and juicy thigh may well be a choice morsel for her, even as a leg of mutton is for us.

The prey is first attacked in the neck. While one of the two lethal legs holds the victim transfixed through the middle of the body, the other presses the head and makes the neck open upwards. The Mantis' muzzle roots and nibbles at this weak point in the armour with some persistency. A large wound appears in the head. The Locust gradually ceases kicking and becomes a lifeless corpse; and, from this moment, freer in its movements, the carnivorous insect picks and chooses its morsel.

The Mantis naturally wants to devour the victuals in peace, without being troubled by the plunges of a victim who absolutely refuses to be devoured. A meal liable to interruptions lacks savour. Now the principal means of defence in this case are the hind-legs, those vigorous levers which can kick out so brutally and which moreover are armed with toothed saws that would rip open the Mantis' bulky paunch if by ill-luck they happen to graze it. What shall we do to reduce them to helplessness, together with the others, which are not dangerous but troublesome all the same, with their desperate gesticulations?

Strictly speaking, it would be practicable to cut them off one by one. But that is a long process and attended with a certain risk. The Mantis has hit upon something better. She has an intimate knowledge of the anatomy of the spine. By first attacking her prize at the back of the half-opened neck and munching the cervical ganglia, she destroys the muscular energy at its main seat; and inertia supervenes, not suddenly and completely, for the clumsily-constructed Locust has not the Bee's exquisite and frail vitality, but still sufficiently, after the first mouthfuls. Soon the kicking and the gesticulating die down, all movement ceases and the game, however big it be, is consumed in perfect quiet.

The little that we have seen of the Mantis' habits hardly tallies with what we might have expected from her popular name. To judge by the term *Prègo-Diéu*, we should look to see a placid insect, deep in pious contemplation; and we find ourselves in the presence of a cannibal, of a ferocious spectre munching the brain of a panic-stricken victim. Nor is even this the most tragic part. The Mantis has in store for us, in her relations with her own kith and kin, manners even more atrocious than those prevailing among the Spiders, who have an evil reputation in this respect.

To reduce the number of cages on my big table and give myself a little more space while still retaining a fair-sized menagerie, I install several females, sometimes as many as a dozen, under one cover. So far as accommodation is concerned, no fault can be found with the common lodging. There is room and to spare for the evolutions of my captives, who naturally do not want to move about much with their unwieldy bellies. Hanging to the trelliswork of the dome, motionless they digest their food or else await an unwary passer-by. Even so do they act when at liberty in the thickets.

Cohabitation has its dangers. I know that even Donkeys, those peace-loving animals, quarrel when hay is scarce in the manger. My boarders, who are less complaisant, might well, in a moment of dearth, become sour-tempered and fight among themselves. I guard against this by keeping the cages well supplied with Locusts, renewed twice a day. Should civil war break out, famine cannot be pleaded as the excuse.

At first, things go pretty well. The community lives in peace, each Mantis grabbing and eating whatever comes near her, without seeking strife with her neighbours. But this harmonious period does not last long. The bellies swell, the eggs are ripening in the ovaries, marriage and laying-time are at hand. Then a sort of jealous fury bursts out, though there is an entire absence of males who might be held responsible for feminine rivalry. The working of the ovaries seems to pervert the flock, inspiring its members with a mania for devouring one another. There are threats, personal encounters, cannibal feasts. Once more the spectral pose appears, the hissing of the wings, the fearsome gesture of the grapnels outstretched and uplifted in the air. No hostile demonstration in front of a Grey Locust or White-faced Decticus could be more menacing.

For no reason that I can gather, two neighbours suddenly assume their attitude of war. They turn their heads to right and left, provoking each other, exchanging insulting glances. The "Puff! Puff!" of the wings rubbed by the abdomen sounds the charge. When the duel is to be limited to the first scratch received, without more serious consequences, the lethal fore-arms, which are usually kept folded, open like the leaves of a book and fall back sideways, encircling the long bust. It is a superb pose, but less terrible than that adopted in a fight to the death.

Then one of the grapnels, with a sudden spring, shoots out to its full length and strikes the rival; it is no less abruptly withdrawn and resumes the defensive. The adversary hits back. The fencing is rather like that of two Cats boxing each other's ears. At the first blood drawn from her flabby paunch, or even before receiving the last wound, one of the duellists confesses herself beaten and retires. The other furls her battle-standard and goes off elsewhither to meditate the capture of a Locust, keeping apparently calm, but ever ready to repeat the quarrel.

Very often, events take a more tragic turn. At such times, the full posture of the duels to the death is assumed. The murderous fore-arms are unfolded and raised in the air. Woe to the vanquished! The other seizes her in her vice and then and there proceeds to eat her, beginning at the neck, of course. The loathsome feast takes place as calmly as though it were a matter of crunching up a Grasshopper. The diner enjoys her sister as she would a lawful dish; and those around do not protest, being quite willing to do as much on the first occasion.

Oh, what savagery! Why, even Wolves are said not to eat one another. The Mantis has no such scruples; she banquets off her fellows when there is plenty of her favourite game, the Locust, around her. She practises the equivalent of cannibalism, that hideous peculiarity of man.

These aberrations, these child-bed cravings can reach an even more revolting stage. Let us watch the pairing and, to avoid the disorder of a crowd, let us isolate the couples under different covers. Each pair shall have its own home, where none will come to disturb the wedding. And let us not forget the provisions, with which we will keep them well supplied, so that there may be no excuse of hunger.

It is near the end of August. The male, that slender swain, thinks the moment propitious. He makes eyes at his strapping companion; he turns his head in her direction; he bends his neck and throws out his chest. His little pointed face wears an almost impassioned expression. Motionless, in this posture, for a long time he contemplates the object of his desire. She does not stir, is as though indifferent. The lover, however, has caught a sign of acquiescence, a sign of which I do not know the secret. He goes nearer; suddenly he spreads his wings, which quiver with a convulsive tremor. That is his declaration. He rushes, small as he is, upon the back of his corpulent companion, clings on as best he can, steadies his hold. As a rule, the preliminaries last a long time. At last, coupling takes place and is also long drawn out, lasting sometimes for five or six hours.

Nothing worthy of attention happens between the two motionless partners. They end by separating, but only to unite again in a more intimate fashion. If the poor fellow is loved by his lady as the vivifier of her ovaries, he is also loved as a piece of highly-flavoured game. And, that same day, or at latest on the morrow, he is seized by his spouse, who first gnaws his neck, in accordance with precedent, and then eats him deliberately, by little mouthfuls, leaving only the wings. Here we have no longer a case of jealousy in the harem, but simply a depraved appetite.

I was curious to know what sort of reception a second male might expect from a recently fertilized female. The result of my enquiry was shocking. The Mantis, in many cases, is never sated with conjugal raptures and banquets. After a rest that varies in length, whether the eggs be laid or not, a second male is accepted and then devoured like the first. A third succeeds him, performs his function in life, is eaten and disappears. A fourth undergoes a like fate. In the course of two weeks I thus see one and the same Mantis use up seven males. She takes them all to her bosom and makes them all pay for the nuptial ecstasy with their lives.

Orgies such as this are frequent, in varying degrees, though there are exceptions. On very hot days, highly charged with electricity, they are almost the general rule. At such times the Mantes are in a very irritable mood. In the cages containing a large colony, the females devour one another more than ever; in the cages containing separate pairs, the males, after coupling, are more than ever treated as an ordinary prey.

I should like to be able to say, in mitigation of these conjugal atrocities, that the Mantis does not behave like this in a state of liberty; that the male, after doing his duty, has time to get out of the way, to make off, to escape from his terrible mistress, for in my cages he is given a respite, lasting sometimes until next day. What really occurs in the thickets I do not know, chance, a poor resource, having never instructed me concerning the love-affairs of the Mantis when at large. I can only go by what happens in the cages, when the captives, enjoying plenty of sunshine and food and spacious quarters, do not seem to suffer from homesickness in any way. What they do here they must also do under normal conditions.

Well, what happens there utterly refutes the idea that the males are given time to escape. I find, by themselves, a horrible couple engaged as follows. The male, absorbed in the performance of his vital functions, holds the female in a tight embrace. But the wretch has no head; he has no neck; he has hardly a body. The other, with her muzzle turned over her shoulder continues very placidly to gnaw what remains of the gentle swain. And, all the time, that masculine stump, holding on firmly, goes on with the business!

Love is stronger than death, men say. Taken literally, the aphorism has never received a more brilliant confirmation. A headless creature, an insect amputated down to the middle of the chest, a very corpse persists in endeavouring to give life. It will not let go until the abdomen, the seat of the procreative organs, is attacked.

Eating the lover after consummation of marriage, making a meal of the exhausted dwarf, henceforth good for nothing, can be understood, to some extent, in the insect world, which has no great scruples in matters of sentiment; but gobbling him up during the act goes beyond the wildest dreams of the most horrible imagination. I have seen it done with my own eyes and have not yet recovered from my astonishment.

ᴥᏕ FOR DISCUSSION AND WRITING

1. The writing assignment obviously suggested by this piece is a descriptive exercise modeled upon it, taking as subject either an insect or some other living creature you can observe closely—anything from a cockroach to a horse. You should expect to spend several hours of time, and all your patience, on the "research," if necessary making a field trip (perhaps to the zoo) in search of your subject. Keep this assignment in mind as you analyze Fabre's essay, watching what methods he uses to give his subject high visibility and dramatic interest, at the same time preserving absolute accuracy of observation.

2. The mantis is actually a very slender and fragile insect, so delicate that it is almost invisible on a green stem or leaf. Point out several places in the essay where Fabre manages to place it before the eye of your imagination in such strong outline and precise detail that it might be as big as a dragon—and as terrifying. Is this illusionary enhancement of size "unscientific" (that is, does it diminish Fabre's reliability as an observer), or does it serve a purpose of scientific communication? (After all, what do protozoa look like under a microscope?)

3. Fabre's chief descriptive method is analogy. "Analogy" means simply a likeness or resemblance, and may be anything from a general comparison to a
simile or metaphor, or one of those "buried metaphors" hidden in verbs
and adjectives. Point out all the analogies you find in the first four paragraphs. Where do you find the mantis compared (not directly, but by
indirect means) to a chic and dainty woman? How does this implicit
analogy sharpen the significance of the mantis's actual behavior? Why does
Fabre constantly refer to the bug as a "she" (though we learn later that
there *are* males)? Why does the feminine pronoun increase the horror of
the description? Fabre says that "alone among insects, the Mantis directs
her gaze; she inspects and examines; she almost has a physiognomy." In
what way do these abilities suggest the human, and why is the suggestion
horrible?

4. Point out the chief analogies used in the sixth to ninth paragraphs. How
many of these comparisons, either implicit or explicit, are with tools or machinery? Considering the fact that the mantis is a fragile creature, as fragile
as the petal of a flower, how do these machinery-analogies increase one's
understanding of nature? Do they also increase one's understanding of man
as an inventor of machinery, and of his uses of it?

5. What analogies appear in the description of the great warlike killer-attitude
of the mantis? What is her purpose in putting on this guise? What is the
effect on the locust? If you were "strictly scientific," would you say that
Fabre anthropomorphizes these insects too much—as, for instance, when
he speaks of the locust as "demoralized"?

6. What does the mantis do to her food when it insists on kicking? What are
the peculiar satisfactions of the egg-heavy mantis's pregnancy cravings?
By what means does Fabre put the courtship and wedding of the mantis
into the perspective of human behavior? What are the romantic implications in the statement that, after conjugation, the mantis unites with her
husband "in a more intimate fashion," and that she takes all subsequent
suitors "to her bosom"? Do you find any resemblance between the love
life of the mantis and that of human beings?

Konrad Lorenz ✒ The Dove and the Wolf

✒ Austrian naturalist, born in 1903. Lorenz is an outstanding authority on the basic principles and theories of animal mind and behavior. He has been called "the modern Fabre," although his subject matter is mainly birds and fishes rather than insects. Like Fabre, he has given the devotion of a lifetime to the study of his subjects in their natural state of freedom, and has written about them with unusual charm. ﻉ

IT IS EARLY one Sunday morning at the beginning of March, when Easter is already in the air, and we are taking a walk in the Vienna forest whose wooded slopes of tall beeches can be equalled in beauty by few and surpassed by none. We approach a forest glade. The tall smooth trunks of the beeches soon give place to the Hornbeam which are clothed from top to bottom with pale green foliage. We now tread slowly and more carefully. Before we break through the last bushes and out of cover on to the free expanse of the meadow, we do what all wild animals and all good naturalists, wild boars, leopards, hunters and zoologists would do under similar circumstances: we reconnoitre, seeking, before

From *King Solomon's Ring*, by Konrad Z. Lorenz. Copyright 1952 by Thomas Y. Crowell Company, New York, publishers. The translation is by Marjorie Kerr Wilson.

we leave our cover, to gain from it the advantage which it can offer alike to hunter and hunted, namely, to see without being seen.

Here, too, this age-old strategy proves beneficial. We do actually see someone who is not yet aware of our presence, as the wind is blowing away from him in our direction: in the middle of the clearing sits a large fat hare. He is sitting with his back to us, making a big V with his ears, and is watching intently something on the opposite edge of the meadow. From this point, a second and equally large hare emerges and with slow, dignified hops, makes his way towards the first one. There follows a measured encounter, not unlike the meeting of two strange dogs. This cautious mutual taking stock soon develops into sparring. The two hares chase each other round, head to tail, in minute circles. This giddy rotating continues for quite a long time. Then suddenly, their pent-up energies burst forth into a battle royal. It is just like the outbreak of war, and happens at the very moment when the long mutual threatening of the hostile parties has forced one to the conclusion that neither dares to make a definite move. Facing each other, the hares rear up on their hind legs and, straining to their full height, drum furiously at each other with their fore pads. Now they clash in flying leaps and, at last, to the accompaniment of squeals and grunts, they discharge a volley of lightning kicks, so rapidly that only a slow motion camera could help us to discern the mechanism of these hostilities. Now, for the time being, they have had enough, and they recommence their circling, this time much faster than before; then follows a fresh, more embittered bout. So engrossed are the two champions, that there is nothing to prevent myself and my little daughter from tiptoeing nearer, although that venture cannot be accomplished in silence. Any normal and sensible hare would have heard us long ago, but this is March and March Hares are mad! The whole boxing match looks so comical that my little daughter, in spite of her iron upbringing in the matter of silence when watching animals, cannot restrain a chuckle. That is too much even for March Hares — two flashes in two different directions and the meadow is empty, while over the battlefield floats a fistful of fluff, light as a thistledown.

It is not only funny, it is almost touching, this duel of the unarmed, this raging fury of the meek in heart. But are these creatures really so meek? Have they really got softer hearts than those of the fierce beasts of prey? If, in a zoo, you ever watched two lions, wolves or eagles in conflict, then, in all probability, you did not feel like laughing. And yet, these sovereigns come off no worse than the harmless hares. Most people have the habit of judging carnivorous and herbivorous animals by quite inapplicable moral criteria. Even in fairy-tales, animals are portrayed as being a community comparable to that of mankind, as though all species of animals were beings of one and the same family, as human beings are. For this reason, the average person tends to regard the animal that kills animals in the same light as he would the man that kills his own kind. He does not judge the fox that kills a hare by the same standard as the hunter who shoots one for precisely the same reason, but with that severe censure that he would apply to the gamekeeper who made a practice of shooting farmers and frying them for supper! The "wicked" beast of prey is branded as a murderer, although the fox's hunting is quite as legitimate and a great deal more necessary to his existence than is that of the gamekeeper, yet nobody regards the latter's "bag" as his prey, and only one author, whose own standards were indicted by the severest moral criticism, has dared to dub the fox-hunter "the unspeakable in pursuit of the uneatable"! In their dealing with members of their own species, the beasts and birds of prey are far more restrained than many of the "harmless" vegetarians.

Still more harmless than a battle of hares appears the fight between turtle- or ring-doves. The gentle pecking of the frail bill, the light flick of the fragile wing seems, to the uninitiated, more like a caress than an attack. Some time ago I decided to breed a cross between the African blond ring-dove and our own indigenous somewhat frailer turtle-dove, and, with this object, I put a tame, home-reared male turtle-dove and a female ring-dove together in a roomy cage. I did not take their original scrapping seriously. How could these paragons of love and virtue dream of harming one another? I left them in their cage and went to Vienna. When I returned, the next day, a horrible sight met my eyes. The turtle-dove lay on the floor of the cage; the top of his head and neck, as also the whole length of his back, were not only plucked bare of feathers, but so flayed as to form a single wound dripping with blood. In the middle of this gory surface, like an eagle on his prey, stood the second harbinger of peace. Wearing that dreamy facial expression that so appeals to our sentimental observer, this charming lady pecked mercilessly with her silver bill in the wounds of her prostrated mate. When the latter gathered his last resources in a final effort to escape, she set on him again, struck him to the floor with a light clap of her wing and continued with her slow pitiless work of destruction. Without my interference she would undoubtedly have finished him off, in spite of the fact that she was already so tired that she could hardly keep her eyes open. Only in two other instances have I seen similar horrible lacerations inflicted on their own kind by vertebrates: once, as an observer of the embittered fights of cichlid fishes who sometimes actually skin each other, and again as a field surgeon, in the late war, where the highest of all vertebrates perpetrated mass mutilations on members of his own species. But to return to our "harmless" vegetarians. The battle of the hares which we witnessed in the forest clearing would have ended in quite as horrible a carnage as that of the doves, had it taken place in the confines of a cage where the vanquished could not flee the victor.

If this is the extent of the injuries meted out to their own kind by our gentle doves and hares, how much greater must be the havoc wrought amongst themselves by those beasts to whom nature has relegated the strongest weapons with which to kill their prey? One would certainly think so, were it not that a good naturalist should always check by observation even the most obvious-seeming inferences before he accepts them as truth. Let us examine that symbol of cruelty and voraciousness, the wolf. How do these creatures conduct themselves in their dealings with members of their own species? At Whipsnade, that zoological country paradise, there lives a pack of timber wolves. From the fence of a pine-wood of enviable dimensions we can watch their daily round in an environment not so very far removed from conditions of real freedom. To begin with, we wonder why the antics of the many woolly, fat-pawed whelps have not led them to destruction long ago. The efforts of one ungainly little chap to break into a gallop have landed him in a very different situation from that which he intended. He stumbles and bumps heavily into a wicked-looking old sinner. Strangely enough, the latter does not seem to notice it, he does not even growl. But now we hear the rumble of battle sounds! They are low, but more ominous than those of a dog-fight. We were watching the whelps and have therefore only become aware of this adult fight now that it is already in full swing.

An enormous old timber wolf and a rather weaker, obviously younger one are the opposing champions and they are moving in circles round each other, exhibiting admirable "footwork". At the same time, the bared fangs flash in such a rapid exchange of snaps that the eye can scarcely follow them. So far, nothing has really happened. The jaws of one wolf close on the gleaming white teeth of the other who is on the alert and wards off the attack. Only the lips have received one or two minor injuries. The younger wolf is gradually being forced backwards. It dawns upon us that the older one is purposely manoeuvring him towards the fence. We wait with breathless anticipation what will happen when he "goes to the wall". Now he strikes the wire netting, stumbles . . . and the old one is upon him. And now the incredible happens, just the opposite of what you would expect. The furious whirling of the grey bodies has come to a sudden standstill. Shoulder to shoulder they stand, pressed against each other in a stiff and strained attitude, both heads now facing in the same direction. Both wolves are growling angrily, the elder in a deep bass, the younger in higher tones, suggestive of the fear that underlies his threat. But notice carefully the position of the two opponents; the older wolf has his muzzle close, very close against the neck of the younger, and the latter holds away his head, offering unprotected to his enemy the bend of his neck, the most vulnerable part of his whole body! Less than an inch from the tensed neck-muscles, where the jugular vein lies immediately beneath the skin, gleam the fangs of his antagonist from beneath the wickedly retracted lips. Whereas, during the thick of the fight, both wolves were intent on keeping only their teeth, the one invulnerable part of the body, in opposition to each other, it now appears that the discomfited fighter proffers intentionally that part of his anatomy to which a bite must assuredly prove fatal. Appearances are notoriously deceptive, but in his case, surprisingly, they are not!

This same scene can be watched any time wherever street-mongrels are to be found. I cited wolves as my first example because they illustrate my point more impressively than the all-too familiar domestic dog. Two adult male dogs meet in the street. Stiff-legged, with tails erect and hair on end, they pace towards each other. The nearer they approach, the stiffer, higher and more ruffled they appear, their advance becomes slower and slower. Unlike fighting cocks they do not make their encounter head to head, front against front, but make as though to pass each other, only stopping when they stand at last flank to flank, head to tail, in close juxtaposition. Then a strict ceremonial demands that each should sniff the hind regions of the other. Should one of the dogs be overcome with fear at this juncture, down goes his tail between his legs and he jumps with a quick, flexible twist, wheeling at an angle of 180 degrees thus modestly retracting his former offer to be smelt. Should the two

dogs remain in an attitude of self-display, carrying their tails as rigid
as standards, then the sniffing process may be of a long protracted nature.
All may be solved amicably and there is still the chance that first one
tail and then the other may begin to wag with small but rapidly increasing beats and then this nerve-racking situation may develop into nothing
worse than a cheerful canine romp. Failing this solution the situation becomes more and more tense, noses begin to wrinkle and to turn up with
a vile, brutal expression, lips begin to curl, exposing the fangs on the
side nearer the opponent. Then the animals scratch the earth angrily
with their hind feet, deep growls rise from their chests, and, in the next
moment, they fall upon each other with loud piercing yells.

But to return to our wolves, whom we left in a situation of acute
tension. This was not a piece of inartistic narrative on my part, since the
strained situation may continue for a great length of time which is minutes to the observer, but very probably seems hours to the losing wolf.
Every second you expect violence and await with bated breath the moment when the winner's teeth will rip the jugular vein of the loser. But
your fears are groundless, for it will not happen. In this particular situation, the victor will definitely not close on his less fortunate rival. You
can see that he would like to, but he just cannot! A dog or wolf that offers
its neck to its adversary in this way will never be bitten seriously. The
other growls and grumbles, snaps with his teeth in the empty air and
even carries out, without delivering so much as a bite, the movement of
shaking something to death in the empty air. However, this strange
inhibition from biting persists only so long as the defeated dog or wolf
maintains his attitude of humility. Since the fight is stopped so suddenly by this action, the victor frequently finds himself straddling his
vanquished foe in anything but a comfortable position. So to remain,
with his muzzle applied to the neck of the "under-dog" soon becomes
tedious for the champion, and, seeing that he cannot bite anyway, he
soon withdraws. Upon this, the under-dog may hastily attempt to put distance between himself and his superior. But he is not usually successful
in this, for, as soon as he abandons his rigid attitude of submission, the
other again falls upon him like a thunderbolt and the victim must again
freeze into his former posture. It seems as if the victor is only waiting
for the moment when the other will relinquish his submissive attitude,
thereby enabling him to give vent to his urgent desire to bite. But, luckily

for the "under-dog", the top-dog at the close of the fight is overcome by the pressing need to leave his trade-mark on the battlefield, to designate it as his personal property — in other words, he must lift his leg against the nearest upright object. This right-of-possession ceremony is usually taken advantage of by the under-dog to make himself scarce.

By this commonplace observation, we are here, as so often, made conscious of a problem which is actual in our daily life and which confronts us on all sides in the most various forms. Social inhibitions of this kind are not rare, but so frequent that we take them for granted and do not stop to think about them. An old German proverb says that one crow will not peck out the eye of another and for once the proverb is right. A tame crow or raven will no more think of pecking at your eye than he will at that of one of his own kind. Often when Roah, my tame raven, was sitting on my arm, I purposely put my face so near to his bill that my open eye came close to its wickedly curved point. Then Roah did something positively touching. With a nervous, worried movement he withdrew his beak from my eye, just as a father who is shaving will hold back his razor blade from the inquisitive fingers of his tiny daughter. Only in one particular connection did Roah ever approach my eye with his bill during this facial grooming. Many of the higher, social birds and mammals, above all monkeys, will groom the skin of a fellow-member of their species in those parts of his body to which he himself cannot obtain access. In birds, it is particularly the head and the region of the eyes which are dependent on the attentions of a fellow. In my description of the jackdaw, I have already spoken of the gestures with which these birds invite one another to preen their head feathers. When, with half-shut eyes. I held my head sideways towards Roah, just as corvine birds do to each other, he understood this movement in spite of the fact that I have no head feathers to ruffle, and at once began to groom me. While doing so, he never pinched my skin, for the epidermis of birds is delicate and would not stand such rough treatment. With wonderful precision, he submitted every attainable hair to a dry-cleaning process by drawing it separately through his bill. He worked with the same intensive concentration that distinguishes the "lousing" monkey and the operating surgeon. This is not meant as a joke: the social grooming of monkeys, and particularly of anthropoid apes has not the object of catching vermin — these animals usually have none — and is not limited to the cleaning of the skin, but serves also more remarkable operations, for instance the dexterous removal of thorns and even the squeezing-out of small carbuncles.

The manipulations of the dangerous-looking corvine beak round the open eye of a man naturally appear ominous and, of course, I was always receiving warnings from onlookers at this procedure. "You never know — a raven is a raven — " and similar words of wisdom. I used to respond with the paradoxical observation that the warner was for me potentially more dangerous than the raven. It has often happened that people have been shot dead by madmen who have masked their condition with the cunning and pretence typical of such cases. There was always a possibility, though admittedly a very small one, that our kind adviser might be afflicted with such a disease. But a sudden and unpredictable loss of the eye-pecking inhibition in a healthy, mature raven is more unlikely by far than an attack by a well-meaning friend.

Why has the dog the inhibition against biting his fellow's neck? Why has the raven an inhibition against pecking the eye of his friend? Why has the ring-dove no such "insurance" against murder? A really comprehensive answer to these questions is almost impossible. It would certainly involve a *historical* explanation of the process by which these inhibitions have been developed in the course of evolution. There is no doubt that they have arisen side by side with the development of the dangerous weapons of the beast of prey. However, it is perfectly obvious why these inhibitions are necessary to all weapon-bearing animals. Should the raven peck, without compunction, at the eye of his nest-mate, his wife or his young, in the same way as he pecks at any other moving and glittering object, there would, by now, be no more ravens in the world. Should a dog or wolf unrestrainedly and unaccountably bite the neck of his packmates and actually execute the movement of shaking them to death, then his species also would certainly be exterminated within a short space of time.

The ring-dove does not require such an inhibition since it can only inflict injury to a much lesser degree, while its ability to flee is so well developed that it suffices to protect the bird even against enemies equipped with vastly better weapons. Only under the unnatural conditions of close confinement which deprive the losing dove of the possibility of flight does it become apparent that the ring-dove has no inhibitions which prevent it from injuring or even torturing its own kind. Many other "harmless" herbivores prove themselves just as unscrupulous when they are kept in narrow captivity. One of the most disgusting, ruthless and blood-thirsty murderers is an animal which is generally considered as being second only to the dove in the proverbial gentleness of its nature, namely the roe-deer. The roe-buck is about the most malevolent beast I know and is possessed, into the bargain, of a weapon, its antlers, which it shows mighty little restraint in putting into use. The species can "afford" this lack of control since the fleeing capacity even of the weakest doe is enough to deliver it from the strongest buck. Only in very large paddocks can the roe-buck be kept with females of his own kind. In smaller enclosures, sooner or later he will drive his fellows, females and young ones included, into a corner and gore them to death. The only "insurance against murder" which the roe-deer possesses, is based on the fact that the onslaught of the attacking buck proceeds relatively slowly. He does not rush with lowered head at his adversary as, for example, a ram would do, but he approaches quite slowly, cautiously feeling with his antlers for those of his opponent. Only when the antlers are interlocked and the buck feels firm resistance does he thrust with deadly earnest. According to the statistics given by W. T. Hornaday, the former director of the New York Zoo, tame deer cause yearly more serious accidents than captive lions and tigers, chiefly because an uninitiated person does not recognize the slow approach of the buck as an earnest attack, even when the animal's antlers have come dangerously near. Suddenly there follows, thrust upon thrust, the amazingly strong stabbing movement of the sharp weapon, and you will be lucky if you have time enough to get a good grip on the aggressor's antlers. Now there follows a wrestling-match in which the sweat pours and the hands drip blood, and in which even a very strong man can hardly obtain mastery over the roe-buck unless he succeeds in getting to the side of the beast and bending his neck backwards. Of course, one is ashamed to call for help — until one has the point of an antler in one's body! So take my advice and if a charming, tame roe-buck comes playfully towards you, with a characteristic prancing step and flourishing his antlers gracefully, hit him, with your walking stick, a stone or the bare fist, as hard as you can, on the side of his nose, before he can apply his antlers to your person.

And now, honestly judged: who is really a "good" animal, my friend Roah to whose social inhibitions I could trust the light of my eyes, or the gentle ring-dove that in hours of hard work nearly succeeded in tortur-

ing its mate to death? Who is a "wicked" animal, the roe-buck who will
slit the bellies even of females and young of his own kind if they are
unable to escape him, or the wolf who cannot bite his hated enemy if
the latter appeals to his mercy?

Now let us turn our mind to another question. Wherein consists the
essence of all the gestures of submission by which a bird or animal of a
social species can appeal to the inhibitions of its superior? We have just
seen, in the wolf, that the defeated animal actually facilitates his own
destruction by offering to the victor those very parts of his body which he
was most anxious to shield as long as the battle was raging. All submissive attitudes with which we are so far familiar, in social animals, are
based on the same principle: The supplicant always offers to his adversary the most vulnerable part of his body, or, to be more exact, that part
against which every killing attack is inevitably directed! In most birds,
this area is the base of the skull. If one jackdaw wants to show submission to another, he squats back on his hocks, turns away his head, at the
same time drawing in his bill to make the nape of his neck bulge, and,
leaning towards his superior, seems to invite him to peck at the fatal spot.
Seagulls and herons present to their superior the top of their head,
stretching their neck forward horizontally, low over the ground, also a
position which makes the supplicant particularly defenceless.

With many gallinaceous birds, the fights of the males commonly end
by one of the combatants being thrown to the ground, held down and
then scalped as in the manner described in the ring-dove. Only one
species shows mercy in this case, namely the turkey: and this one only
does so in response to a specific submissive gesture which serves to fore-
stall the intent of the attack. If a turkey-cock has had more than his share
of the wild and grotesque wrestling-match in which these birds indulge,
he lays himself with outstretched neck upon the ground. Whereupon the
victor behaves exactly as a wolf or dog in the same situation, that is to
say, he evidently *wants* to peck and kick at the prostrated enemy, but
simply cannot: he would if he could but he can't! So, still in threatening
attitude, he walks round and round his prostrated rival, making tentative
passes at him, but leaving him untouched.

This reaction — though certainly propitious for the turkey species
— can cause a tragedy if a turkey comes to blows with a peacock, a thing
which not infrequently happens in captivity, since these species are
closely enough related to "appreciate" respectively their mutual mani-

festations of virility. In spite of greater strength and weight the turkey
nearly always loses the match, for the peacock flies better and has a
different fighting technique. While the red-brown American is muscling
himself up for the wrestling-match, the blue East-Indian has already
flown above him and struck at him with his sharply pointed spurs. The
turkey justifiably considers this infringement of his fighting code as unfair and, although he is still in possession of his full strength, he throws
in the sponge and lays himself down in the above depicted manner now.
And a ghastly thing happens: the peacock does not "understand" this submissive gesture of the turkey, that is to say, it elicits no inhibition of his
fighting drives. He pecks and kicks further at the helpless turkey, who, if
nobody comes to his rescue, is doomed, for the more pecks and blows he
receives, the more certainly are his escape reactions blocked by the
psycho-physiological mechanism of the submissive attitude. It does not
and cannot occur to him to jump up and run away.

The fact that many birds have developed special "signal organs" for
eliciting this type of social inhibition, shows convincingly the blind instinctive nature and the great evolutionary age of these submissive gestures. The young of the water-rail, for example, have a bare red patch at
the back of their head which, as they present it meaningly to an older
and stronger fellow, takes on a deep red colour. Whether, in higher animals and man, social inhibitions of this kind are equally mechanical,
need not for the moment enter into our consideration. Whatever may be
the reasons that prevent the dominant individual from injuring the submissive one, whether he is prevented from doing so by a simple and
purely mechanical reflex process or by a highly philosophical moral standard, is immaterial to the practical issue. The essential behaviour of the
submissive as well as of the dominant partner remains the same: the
humbled creature suddenly seems to lose his objections to being injured
and removes all obstacles from the path of the killer, and it would seem
that the very removal of these outer obstacles raises an insurmountable
inner obstruction in the central nervous system of the aggressor.

And what is a human appeal for mercy after all? Is it so very different from what we have just described? The Homeric warrior who wishes
to yield and plead mercy, discards helmet and shield, falls on his knees
and inclines his head, a set of actions which should make it easier for the
enemy to kill, but, in reality, hinders him from doing so. As Shakespeare
makes Nestor say to Hector:

> "Thou hast hung thy advanced sword i' the air,
> Not letting it decline on the declined."

Even to-day, we have retained many symbols of such submissive attitudes in a number of our gestures of courtesy: bowing, removal of the hat, and presenting arms in military ceremonial. If we are to believe the ancient epics, an appeal to mercy does not seem to have raised an "inner obstruction" which was entirely insurmountable. Homer's heroes were certainly not as soft-hearted as the wolves of Whipsnade! In any case, the poet cites numerous instances where the supplicant was slaughtered with or without compunction. The Norse heroic sagas bring us many examples of similar failures of the submissive gesture and it was not till the era of knight-errantry that it was no longer considered "sporting" to kill a man who begged for mercy. The Christian knight is the first who, for reasons of traditional and religious morals, is as chivalrous as is the wolf from the depth of his natural impulses and inhibitions. What a strange paradox!

Of course, the innate, instinctive, fixed inhibitions that prevent an animal from using his weapons indiscriminately against his own kind are only a functional analogy, at the most a slight foreshadowing, a genealogical predecessor of the social morals of man. The worker in comparative ethology does well to be very careful in applying moral criteria to animal behaviour. But here, I must myself own to harbouring sentimental feelings: I think it a truly magnificent thing that one wolf finds himself unable to bite the proffered neck of the other, but still more so that the other relies upon him for his amazing restraint. Mankind can learn a lesson from this, from the animal that Dante calls "la bestia senza pace".[1] I at least have extracted from it a new and deeper understanding of a wonderful and often misunderstood saying from the Gospel which hitherto had only awakened in me feelings of strong opposition: "And unto him that smiteth thee on the one cheek offer also the other." (St Luke vi, 26). A wolf has enlightened me: not so that your enemy may strike you again do you turn the other cheek toward him, but to make him unable to do it.

When, in the course of its evolution, a species of animals develops a weapon which may destroy a fellow-member at one blow, then, in order to survive, it must develop, along with the weapon, a social inhibition to

---

[1] "The implacable beast"—the she-wolf that appears in the first canto of Dante's *Inferno*.

prevent a usage which could endanger the existence of the species. Among the predatory animals, there are only a few which lead so solitary a life that they can, in general, forego such restraint. They come together only at the mating season when the sexual impulse outweighs all others, including that of aggression. Such unsociable hermits are the polar bear and the jaguar and, owing to the absence of these social inhibitions, animals of these species, when kept together in Zoos, hold a sorry record for murdering their own kind. The system of special inherited impulses and inhibitions, together with the weapons with which a social species is provided by nature, form a complex which is carefully computed and self-regulating. All living beings have received their weapons through the same process of evolution that moulded their impulses and inhibitions; for the structural plan of the body and the system of behaviour of a species are parts of the same whole.

> "If such be Nature's holy plan,
> Have I not reason to lament
> What man has made of man?"

Wordsworth is right: there is only one being in possession of weapons which do not grow on his body and of whose working plan, therefore, the instincts of his species know nothing and in the usage of which he has no correspondingly adequate inhibition. That being is man. With unarrested growth his weapons increase in monstrousness, multiplying horribly within a few decades. But innate impulses and inhibitions, like bodily structures, need time for their development, time on a scale in which geologists and astronomers are accustomed to calculate, and not historians. We did not receive our weapons from nature. We made them ourselves, of our own free will. Which is going to be easier for us in the future, the production of the weapons or the engendering of the feeling of responsibility that should go along with them, the inhibitions without which our race must perish by virtue of its own creations? We must build up these inhibitions purposefully for we cannot rely upon our instincts. Fourteen years ago, in November 1935, I concluded an article on "Morals and Weapons of Animals" which appeared in a Viennese journal, with the words, "The day will come when two warring factions will be faced with the possibility of each wiping the other out completely. The day may come when the whole of mankind is divided into two such opposing camps. Shall we then behave like doves or like wolves? The fate of mankind will be settled by the answer to this question." We may well be apprehensive.

✍️ FOR DISCUSSION AND WRITING

1. In his descriptions of animal combats here, Lorenz uses mainly the present tense. This tense is not frequently used in description or narration of any length, for it tends to become awkward—for the good reason that we don't usually have a chance to describe events at the moment of their happening, but only afterwards, when they have fallen into the past tense. Why is the present tense especially suitable for Lorenz's purpose? Could you compare the technique of tense here to that of a movie, for instance, or to a "live" television showing of a prize fight or football game? What is the common element?

2. What is the implication about rabbits in the phrases, "this duel of the unarmed, this raging fury of the meek in heart"? What cliché symbolisms are discredited by Lorenz's description of the battle of the hares and the battle of the doves? Explain the statement that "Most people have the habit of judging carnivorous and herbivorous animals by quite inapplicable moral criteria." What implicit comparison is contained in Lorenz's reference to his experience as a field surgeon in the last war, "where the highest of all vertebrates perpetrated mass mutilations on members of his own species"?

3. What traditional symbolism is discredited by Lorenz's description of the battle of the wolves? Why does the younger wolf, when he is cornered, intentionally proffer his most vulnerable part to his enemy? Why does the stronger wolf not take advantage of this submission?

4. For what purpose of illustration does Lorenz use the description of his tame raven's grooming services?

5. What general explanation, in terms of evolution, is given for the instinctive restraints of "weapon-bearing" birds and animals?

6. What parallels or contrasts does Lorenz draw between the animal instincts he has illustrated and human morals and mores? In what way did "a wolf enlighten him" as to the meaning of the Biblical injunction to "turn the

other cheek"? Why does not the human race have an inherited "self-regulating" principle to inhibit the destructive use of weapons against its own
species? Since it does not have such a built-in restraint, what kind of substitute is enjoined upon it by the peculiar nature of human evolution?

7. For a short descriptive and analytical paper on human behavior in occasions
of hostility it is not at all difficult to find live "research" material—the normal scrapping in one's own family, for instance. Observe one of these occasions (not excepting one's own behavior) as objectively and in as careful
detail as Lorenz observes his animal subjects, and write up your findings.
(After all, there should be as much interest for a "naturalist" in human
combats as in those of birds and animals.) Or observe and describe certain
symbolic "ceremonials" of either animals or people, or both.

Loren Eiseley ✑ The Judgment of the Birds

✑ Dr. Eiseley was born in 1907 in Lincoln, Nebraska, of a family that had homesteaded that territory as pioneers. He did his undergraduate work at the University of Nebraska and his graduate work in anthropology at the University of Pennsylvania. He taught first at the University of Kansas, then at Oberlin College as head of the Department of Sociology and Anthropology, and finally at the University of Pennsylvania as head of the Department of Anthropology. ৡ

IT IS a commonplace of all religious thought, even the most primitive, that the man seeking visions and insight must go apart from his fellows and live for a time in the wilderness. If he is of the proper sort, he will return with a message. It may not be a message from the god he set out to seek, but even if he has failed in that particular, he will have had a vision or seen a marvel, and these are always worth listening to and thinking about.

The world, I have come to believe, is a very queer place, but we have been part of this queerness for so long that we tend to take it for granted. We rush to and fro like Mad Hatters upon our peculiar errands, all the time imagining our surroundings to be dull and ourselves quite ordinary creatures. Actually, there is nothing in the world to encourage

this idea, but such is the mind of man, and this is why he finds it necessary from time to time to send emissaries into the wilderness in the hope
of learning of great events, or plans in store for him, that will resuscitate
his waning taste for life. His great news services, his world-wide radio
network, he knows with a last remnant of healthy distrust will be of no
use to him in this matter. No miracle can withstand a radio broadcast,
and it is certain that it would be no miracle if it could. One must seek,
then, what only the solitary approach can give — a natural revelation.

Let it be understood that I am not the sort of man to whom is entrusted direct knowledge of great events or prophecies. A naturalist, however, spends much of his life alone, and my life is no exception. Even in
New York City there are patches of wilderness, and a man by himself is
bound to undergo certain experiences falling into the class of which I
speak. I set mine down, therefore: a matter of pigeons, a flight of chemicals, and a judgment of birds, in the hope that they will come to the eye
of those who have retained a true taste for the marvelous, and who are
capable of discerning in the flow of ordinary events the point at which
the mundane world gives way to quite another dimension.

New York is not, on the whole, the best place to enjoy the downright
miraculous nature of the planet. There are, I do not doubt, many remarkable stories to be heard there and many strange sights to be seen, but to
grasp a marvel fully it must be savored from all aspects. This cannot be
done while one is being jostled and hustled along a crowded street.
Nevertheless, in any city there are true wildernesses where a man can be
alone. It can happen in a hotel room, or on the high roofs at dawn.

One night on the twentieth floor of a midtown hotel I awoke in the
dark and grew restless. On an impulse I climbed upon the broad old-
fashioned window sill, opened the curtains and peered out. It was the
hour just before dawn, the hour when men sigh in their sleep, or, if
awake, strive to focus their wavering eyesight upon a world emerging
from the shadows. I leaned out sleepily through the open window. I had
expected depths, but not the sight I saw.

I found I was looking down from that great height into a series of
curious cupolas or lofts that I could just barely make out in the darkness.
As I looked, the outlines of these lofts became more distinct because the
light was being reflected from the wings of pigeons who, in utter silence,
were beginning to float outward upon the city. In and out through the
open slits in the cupolas passed the white-winged birds on their mysteri-

ous errands. At this hour the city was theirs, and quietly, without the
brush of a single wing tip against stone in that high, eerie place, they
were taking over the spires of Manhattan. They were pouring upward in
a light that was not yet perceptible to human eyes, while far down in the
blackness of the alleys it was still midnight.

As I crouched half asleep across the sill, I had a moment's illusion
that the world had changed in the night, as in some immense snowfall,
and that if I were to leave, it would have to be as these other inhabitants
were doing, by the window. I should have to launch out into that great
bottomless void with the simple confidence of young birds reared high
up there among the familiar chimney pots and interposed horrors of the
abyss.

I leaned farther out. To and fro went the white wings, to and fro.
There were no sounds from any of them. They knew man was asleep and
this light for a little while was theirs. Or perhaps I had only dreamed
about man in this city of wings — which he could surely never have
built. Perhaps I, myself, was one of these birds dreaming unpleasantly
a moment of old dangers far below as I teetered on a window ledge.

Around and around went the wings. It needed only a little courage,
only a little shove from the window ledge to enter that city of light. The
muscles of my hands were already making little premonitory lunges. I
wanted to enter that city and go away over the roofs in the first dawn. I
wanted to enter it so badly that I drew back carefully into the room and
opened the hall door. I found my coat on the chair, and it slowly became
clear to me that there was a way down through the floors, that I was,
after all, only a man.

I dressed then and went back to my own kind, and I have been
rather more than usually careful ever since not to look into the city of
light. I had seen, just once, man's greatest creation from a strange inverted angle, and it was not really his at all. I will never forget how those
wings went round and round, and how, by the merest pressure of the
fingers and a feeling for air, one might go away over the roofs. It is a
knowledge, however, that is better kept to oneself. I think of it sometimes in such a way that the wings, beginning far down in the black
depths of the mind, begin to rise and whirl till all the mind is lit by their
spinning, and there is a sense of things passing away, but lightly, as a
wing might veer over an obstacle.

To see from an inverted angle, however, is not a gift allotted merely

to the human imagination. I have come to suspect that within their degree it is sensed by animals, though perhaps as rarely as among men.
The time has to be right; one has to be, by chance or intention, upon the
border of two worlds. And sometimes these two borders may shift or
interpenetrate and one sees the miraculous.

I once saw this happen to a crow.

This crow lives near my house, and though I have never injured him,
he takes good care to stay up in the very highest trees and, in general, to
avoid humanity. His world begins at about the limit of my eyesight.

On the particular morning when this episode occurred, the whole
countryside was buried in one of the thickest fogs in years. The ceiling
was absolutely zero. All planes were grounded, and even a pedestrian
could hardly see his outstretched hand before him.

I was groping across a field in the general direction of the railroad
station, following a dimly outlined path. Suddenly out of the fog, at
about the level of my eyes, and so closely that I flinched, there flashed a
pair of immense black wings and a huge beak. The whole bird rushed
over my head with a frantic cawing outcry of such hideous terror as I
have never heard in a crow's voice before, and never expect to hear
again.

He was lost and startled, I thought, as I recovered my poise. He
ought not to have flown out in this fog. He'd knock his silly brains out.

All afternoon that great awkward cry rang in my head. Merely being
lost in a fog seemed scarcely to account for it — especially in a tough, intelligent old bandit such as I knew that particular crow to be. I even
looked once in the mirror to see what it might be about me that had so
revolted him that he had cried out in protest to the very stones.

Finally, as I worked my way homeward along the path, the solution
came to me. It should have been clear before. The borders of our worlds
had shifted. It was the fog that had done it. That crow, and I knew him
well, never under normal circumstances flew low near men. He had been
lost all right, but it was more than that. He had thought he was high up,
and when he encountered me looming gigantically through the fog, he
had perceived a ghastly and, to the crow mind, unnatural sight. He had
seen a man walking on air, desecrating the very heart of the crow kingdom, a harbinger of the most profound evil a crow mind could conceive
of — air-walking men. The encounter, he must have thought, had taken
place a hundred feet over the roofs.

He caws now when he sees me leaving for the station in the morning, and I fancy that in that note I catch the uncertainty of a mind that has come to know things are not always what they seem. He has seen a marvel in his heights of air and is no longer as other crows. He has experienced the human world from an unlikely perspective. He and I share a viewpoint in common: our worlds have interpenetrated, and we both have faith in the miraculous.

It is a faith that in my own case has been augmented by two remarkable sights. As I have hinted previously, I once saw some very odd chemicals fly across a waste so dead it might have been upon the moon, and once, by an even more fantastic piece of luck, I was present when a group of birds passed a judgment upon life.

On the maps of the old voyageurs·it is called *Mauvaises Terres*, the evil lands, and, slurred a little with the passage through many minds, it has come down to us anglicized as the Badlands. The soft shuffle of moccasins has passed through its canyons on the grim business of war and flight, but the last of those slight disturbances of immemorial silences died out almost a century ago. The land, if one can call it a land, is a waste as lifeless as that valley in which lie the kings of Egypt. Like the Valley of the Kings, it is a mausoleum, a place of dry bones in what once was a place of life. Now it has silences as deep as those in the moon's airless chasms.

Nothing grows among its pinnacles; there is no shade except under great toadstools of sandstone whose bases have been eaten to the shape of wine glasses by the wind. Everything is flaking, cracking, disintegrating, wearing away in the long, imperceptible weather of time. The ash of ancient volcanic outbursts still sterilizes its soil, and its colors in that waste are the colors that flame in the lonely sunsets on dead planets. Men come there but rarely, and for one purpose only, the collection of bones.

It was a late hour on a cold, wind-bitten autumn day when I climbed a great hill spined like a dinosaur's back and tried to take my bearings. The tumbled waste fell away in waves in all directions. Blue air was darkening into purple along the bases of the hills. I shifted my knapsack, heavy with the petrified bones of long-vanished creatures, and studied my compass. I wanted to be out of there by nightfall, and already the sun was going sullenly down in the west.

It was then that I saw the flight coming on. It was moving like a little close-knit body of black specks that danced and darted and closed again. It was pouring from the north and heading toward me with the undeviating relentlessness of a compass needle. It streamed through the shadows rising out of monstrous gorges. It rushed over towering pinnacles in the red light of the sun, or momentarily sank from sight within their shade. Across that desert of eroding clay and wind-worn stone they came with a faint wild twittering that filled all the air about me as those tiny living bullets hurtled past into the night.

It may not strike you as a marvel. It would not, perhaps, unless you stood in the middle of a dead world at sunset, but that was where I stood. Fifty million years lay under my feet, fifty million years of bellowing monsters moving in a green world now gone so utterly that its very light was travelling on the farther edge of space. The chemicals of all that vanished age lay about me in the ground. Around me still lay the shearing molars of dead titanotheres, the delicate sabers of soft-stepping cats, the hollow sockets that had held the eyes of many a strange, outmoded beast. Those eyes had looked out upon a world as real as ours; dark, savage brains had roamed and roared their challenges into the steaming night.

Now they were still here, or, put it as you will, the chemicals that made them were here about me in the ground. The carbon that had driven them ran blackly in the eroding stone. The stain of iron was in the clays. The iron did not remember the blood it had once moved within, the phosphorus had forgot the savage brain. The little individual moment had ebbed from all those strange combinations of chemicals as it would ebb from our living bodies into the sinks and runnels of oncoming time.

I had lifted up a fistful of that ground. I held it while that wild flight of south-bound warblers hurtled over me into the oncoming dark. There went phosphorus, there went iron, there went carbon, there beat the calcium in those hurrying wings. Alone on a dead planet I watched that incredible miracle speeding past. It ran by some true compass over field and waste land. It cried its individual ecstasies into the air until the gullies rang. It swerved like a single body, it knew itself and, lonely, it bunched close in the racing darkness, its individual entities feeling about them the rising night. And so, crying to each other their identity, they passed away out of my view.

I dropped my fistful of earth. I heard it roll inanimate back into the gully at the base of the hill: iron, carbon, the chemicals of life. Like men from those wild tribes who had haunted these hills before me seeking visions, I made my sign to the great darkness. It was not a mocking sign, and I was not mocked. As I walked into my camp late that night, one man, rousing from his blankets beside the fire, asked sleepily, "What did you see?"

"I think, a miracle," I said softly, but I said it to myself. Behind me that vast waste began to glow under the rising moon.

I have said that I saw a judgment upon life, and that it was not passed by men. Those who stare at birds in cages or who test minds by their closeness to our own may not care for it. It comes from far away out of my past, in a place of pouring waters and green leaves. I shall never see an episode like it again if I live to be a hundred, nor do I think that one man in a million has ever seen it, because man is an intruder into such silences. The light must be right, and the observer must remain unseen. No man sets up such an experiment. What he sees, he sees by chance.

You may put it that I had come over a mountain, that I had slogged through fern and pine needles for half a long day, and that on the edge of a little glade with one long, crooked branch extending across it, I had sat down to rest with my back against a stump. Through accident I was concealed from the glade, although I could see into it perfectly.

The sun was warm there, and the murmurs of forest life blurred softly away into my sleep. When I awoke, dimly aware of some commotion and outcry in the clearing, the light was slanting down through the pines in such a way that the glade was lit like some vast cathedral. I could see the dust motes of wood pollen in the long shaft of light, and there on the extended branch sat an enormous raven with a red and squirming nestling in his beak.

The sound that awoke me was the outraged cries of the nestling's parents, who flew helplessly in circles about the clearing. The sleek black monster was indifferent to them. He gulped, whetted his beak on the dead branch a moment and sat still. Up to that point the little tragedy had followed the usual pattern. But suddenly, out of all that area of woodland, a soft sound of complaint began to rise. Into the glade fluttered small birds of half a dozen varieties drawn by the anguished outcries of the tiny parents.

No one dared to attack the raven. But they cried there in some instinctive common misery, the bereaved and the unbereaved. The glade filled with their soft rustling and their cries. They fluttered as though to point their wings at the murderer. There was a dim intangible ethic he had violated, that they knew. He was a bird of death.

And he, the murderer, the black bird at the heart of life, sat on there, glistening in the common light, formidable, unmoving, unperturbed, untouchable.

The sighing died. It was then I saw the judgment. It was the judgment of life against death. I will never see it again so forcefully presented. I will never hear it again in notes so tragically prolonged. For in the midst of protest, they forgot the violence. There, in that clearing, the crystal note of a song sparrow lifted hesitantly in the hush. And finally, after painful fluttering, another took the song, and then another, the song passing from one bird to another, doubtfully at first, as though some evil thing were being slowly forgotten. Till suddenly they took heart and sang from many throats joyously together as birds are known to sing. They sang because life is sweet and sunlight beautiful. They sang under the brooding shadow of the raven. In simple truth they had forgotten the raven, for they were the singers of life, and not of death.

I was not of that airy company. My limbs were the heavy limbs of an earthbound creature who could climb mountains, even the mountains of the mind, only by a great effort of will. I knew I had seen a marvel and observed a judgment, but the mind which was my human endowment was sure to question it and to be at me day by day with its heresies until I grew to doubt the meaning of what I had seen. Eventually darkness and subtleties would ring me round once more.

And so it proved until, on the top of a stepladder, I made one more observation upon life. It was cold that autumn evening, and, standing under a suburban street light in a spate of leaves and beginning snow, I was suddenly conscious of some huge and hairy shadows dancing over the pavement. They seemed attached to an odd, globular shape that was magnified above me. There was no mistaking it. I was standing under the shadow of an orb-weaving spider. Gigantically projected against the street, she was about her spinning when everything was going underground. Even her cables were magnified upon the sidewalk and already I was half-entangled in their shadows.

"Good Lord," I thought, "she has found herself a kind of minor sun and is going to upset the course of nature."

I procured a ladder from my yard and climbed up to inspect the situation. There she was, the universe running down around her, warmly arranged among her guy ropes attached to the lamp supports — a great black and yellow embodiment of the life force, not giving up to either frost or stepladders. She ignored me and went on tightening and improving her web.

I stood over her on the ladder, a faint snow touching my cheeks, and surveyed her universe. There were a couple of iridescent green beetle cases turning slowly on a loose strand of web, a fragment of luminescent eye from a moth's wing and a large indeterminable object, perhaps a cicada, that had struggled and been wrapped in silk. There were also little bits and slivers, little red and blue flashes from the scales of anonymous wings that had crashed there.

Some days, I thought, they will be dull and gray and the shine will be out of them; then the dew will polish them again and drops hang on the silk until everything is gleaming and turning in the light. It is like a mind, really, where everything changes but remains, and in the end you have these eaten-out bits of experience like beetle wings.

I stood over her a moment longer, comprehending somewhat reluctantly that her adventure against the great blind forces of winter, her seizure of this warming globe of light, would come to nothing and was hopeless. Nevertheless it brought the birds back into my mind, and that faraway song which had traveled with growing strength around a forest clearing years ago — a kind of heroism, a world where even a spider refuses to lie down and die if a rope can still be spun on to a star. Maybe man himself will fight like this in the end, I thought, slowly realizing that the web and its threatening yellow occupant had been added to some luminous store of experience, shining for a moment in the fogbound reaches of my brain.

The mind, it came to me as I slowly descended the ladder, is a very remarkable thing; it has gotten itself a kind of courage by looking at a spider in a street lamp. Here was something that ought to be passed on to those who will fight our final freezing battle with the void. I thought of setting it down carefully as a message to the future: *In the days of the frost seek a minor sun.*

But as I hesitated, it became plain that something was wrong. The marvel was escaping — a sense of bigness beyond man's power to grasp, the essence of life in its great dealings with the universe. It was better,

I decided, for the emissaries returning from the wilderness, even if they were merely descending from a stepladder, to record their marvel, not to define its meaning. In that way it would go echoing on through the minds of men, each grasping at that beyond out of which the miracles emerge, and which, once defined, ceases to satisfy the human need for symbols.

In the end I merely made a mental note: One specimen of Epeira observed building a web in a street light. Late autumn and cold for spiders. Cold for men, too. I shivered and left the lamp glowing there in my mind. The last I saw of Epeira she was hauling steadily on a cable. I stepped carefully over her shadow as I walked away.

ᴥᏋ FOR DISCUSSION AND WRITING

1. Eiseley's writing has an appearance of great simplicity, but his thought is not at all simple. If you feel, for instance, that you understand quite clearly what the second paragraph is about, try putting the gist of it into a paragraph of your own. (For a paraphrasing exercise of this kind, close the book so that you won't be tempted to use the author's words or even the exact sequence of his thought; the words as well as the thinking should come out of your own head.) After writing the paraphrase, do you find that you have clarified these questions: Why does Eiseley find the modern world "a very queer place"? Why is it queer that we imagine "our surroundings to be dull and ourselves quite ordinary creatures," and do we? What is the justification for saying that "there is nothing in the world to encourage this idea"? What is meant by the need "to send emissaries into the wilderness"? What wilderness? What justification is there for speaking of man's "waning taste for life"? Why is the world-wide radio network "of no use to him in this matter"? What is meant by "miracle"? What is meant by "a natural revelation"? Why is solitude necessary for such a revelation?

2. What is the revelation effected by the incident of the pigeons seen just before dawn from the window of a New York hotel room? Read over again very carefully the paragraphs relating this incident. Is there anything in any of them that suggests anything more than the purely natural—a man of good sense, who hasn't been able to sleep, looking out of a hotel window at those New York pigeons (a city nuisance, scattering disease germs from their feathers, plastering window sills with guano)? Why, then, does

Eiseley imply that the experience was "miraculous"? What is meant by this statement: "I had seen, just once, man's greatest creation from a strange inverted angle, and it was not really his at all"? Looking back to the second paragraph, where it is said that we imagine "our surroundings to be dull and ourselves quite ordinary creatures," could you say that the incident of the pigeons (the dullest and most ordinary creatures in New York) afforded some sort of release or liberation from the assumption that our surroundings are dull and ourselves ordinary? How is that release or liberation connected with the assertion that "man's greatest creation" is "not really his at all"?

3. How does the incident of the crow in the fog almost exactly reverse what happened in the incident of the pigeons? Describing the pigeons, Eiseley was speaking from his own human point of view—from his hotel window, he had "seen a marvel"; describing the crow in the fog, what point of view does he take? He says of the crow: "he has seen a marvel"; what does he mean? Do you think that he anthropomorphizes the crow too much— attributes to it too much of the intelligence we think of as specifically human? How does the incident widen the boundaries of existence for both crow and man?

4. The Badlands that are spoken of in the next incident are probably the desert country of western North Dakota and eastern Montana, where the soft rock has been eroded into shapes like those of a miniature Grand Canyon, a bleak country of sparse grass and sagebrush. Through how many paragraphs, and by what specific means, does Eiseley prepare the landscape—the backdrop, the dramatic scenery—for the "miracle" of the flight of warblers? What is the "miracle"? What, in relation to the flight of the birds, is the significance of the fact that "fifty million years lay under my feet"? Why does he speak of being "alone on a dead planet"? Why does he say of the birds, "There went phosphorus, there went iron, there went carbon, there beat the calcium in those hurrying wings"?

5. In the incident of "the judgment of the birds," what is meant by the "dim intangible ethic" that has been violated? Is it justifiable to speak of an "ethic" among birds? If you have read the piece by Thomas Mann in this book (see page 711), do you find, between Eiseley and Mann, any common recognition of the dynamism of opposites in nature? What is the "judgment" of the birds?

6. What is the significance of the fact that the spider spins its elaborate web

on a lamppost in late autumn when snow is falling? What is implied by
Eiseley's notation that he "was half-entangled" in the shadows of the
spider's cables, and later, that he "stepped carefully" over the spider's
shadow as he walked away? Why, after trying to explain to himself the
spider's symbolism, does he say that it is better simply to record the "marvel, not to define its meaning"?

7. Eiseley's essay is so thought-provoking that it should be an occasion for a
   paper that simply turns over, thoughtfully, the ideas presented here. Or one
   might have been witness to a "miracle" such as those Eiseley describes
   (they occur all over, even among flowers and vegetables, even among human beings) and want to write about it.

Rachel Carson ❦ The Obligation to Endure

❦ American marine biologist (1907-1964), born in Pennsylvania, M.A. of Johns Hopkins University. Miss Carson wrote several books on sea life, of which the best known is *The Sea Around Us*. Reprinted here are the first two chapters of *Silent Spring*, a book that became a highly controversial best seller. ❧

THERE WAS ONCE a town in the heart of America where all life seemed to live in harmony with its surroundings. The town lay in the midst of a checkerboard of prosperous farms, with fields of grain and hillsides of orchards where, in spring, white clouds of bloom drifted above the green fields. In autumn, oak and maple and birch set up a blaze of color that flamed and flickered across a backdrop of pines. Then foxes barked in the hills and deer silently crossed the fields, half hidden in the mists of the fall mornings.

Along the roads, laurel, viburnum and alder, great ferns and wildflowers delighted the traveler's eye through much of the year. Even in winter the roadsides were places of beauty, where countless birds came to feed on the berries and on the seed heads of the dried weeds rising above the snow. The countryside was, in fact, famous for the abundance and variety of its bird life, and when the flood of migrants was pouring through in spring and fall people traveled from great distances to observe them. Others came to fish the streams, which flowed clear and cold out of the hills and contained shady pools where trout lay. So it had been from the days many years ago when the first settlers raised their houses, sank their wells, and built their barns.

Then a strange blight crept over the area and everything began to change. Some evil spell had settled on the community: mysterious maladies swept the flocks of chickens; the cattle and sheep sickened and died. Everywhere was a shadow of death. The farmers spoke of much illness among their families. In the town the doctors had become more and more puzzled by new kinds of sickness appearing among their patients. There had been several sudden and unexplained deaths, not only among adults but even among children, who would be stricken suddenly while at play and die within a few hours.

There was a strange stillness. The birds, for example — where had they gone? Many people spoke of them, puzzled and disturbed. The feeding stations in the backyards were deserted. The few birds seen anywhere were moribund; they trembled violently and could not fly. It was a spring without voices. On the mornings that had once throbbed with the dawn chorus of robins, catbirds, doves, jays, wrens, and scores of other bird voices there was now no sound; only silence lay over the fields and woods and marsh.

On the farms the hens brooded, but no chicks hatched. The farmers complained that they were unable to raise any pigs — the litters were small and the young survived only a few days. The apple trees were coming into bloom but no bees droned among the blossoms, so there was no pollination and there would be no fruit.

The roadsides, once so attractive, were now lined with browned and withered vegetation as though swept by fire. These, too, were silent, deserted by all living things. Even the streams were now lifeless. Anglers no longer visited them, for all the fish had died.

In the gutters under the eaves and between the shingles of the roofs, a white granular powder still showed a few patches; some weeks before it had fallen like snow upon the roofs and the lawns, the fields and streams.

No witchcraft, no enemy action had silenced the rebirth of new life in this stricken world. The people had done it themselves.

This town does not actually exist, but it might easily have a thousand counterparts in America or elsewhere in the world. I know of no community that has experienced all the misfortunes I describe. Yet every one of these disasters has actually happened somewhere, and many real communities have already suffered a substantial number of them. A grim specter has crept upon us almost unnoticed, and this imagined tragedy may easily become a stark reality we all shall know.

What has already silenced the voices of spring in countless towns in America? This book is an attempt to explain.

The history of life on earth has been a history of interaction between living things and their surroundings. To a large extent, the physical form and the habits of the earth's vegetation and its animal life have been molded by the environment. Considering the whole span of earthly time, the opposite effect, in which life actually modifies its surroundings, has been relatively slight. Only within the moment of time represented by the present century has one species — man — acquired significant power to alter the nature of his world.

During the past quarter century this power has not only increased to one of disturbing magnitude but it has changed in character. The most alarming of all man's assaults upon the environment is the contamination of air, earth, rivers, and sea with dangerous and even lethal materials. This pollution is for the most part irrevocable; the chain of evil it initiates not only in the world that must support life but in living tissues is for the most part irreversible. In this now universal contamination of the environment, chemicals are the sinister and little-recognized partners of radiation in changing the very nature of the world — the very nature of its life. Strontium 90, released through nuclear explosions into the air, comes to earth in rain or drifts down as fallout, lodges in soil, enters into the grass or corn or wheat grown there, and in time takes up its abode in the bones of a human being, there to remain until his death. Similarly, chemicals sprayed on croplands or forests or gardens lie long in soil, entering into living organisms, passing from one to another in a chain of poisoning and death. Or they pass mysteriously by underground streams until they emerge and, through the alchemy of air and sunlight, combine into new forms that kill vegetation, sicken cattle, and work unknown harm on those who drink from once pure wells. As Albert Schweitzer has said, "Man can hardly even recognize the devils of his own creation."

It took hundreds of millions of years to produce the life that now inhabits the earth — eons of time in which that developing and evolving and diversifying life reached a state of adjustment and balance with its surroundings. The environment, rigorously shaping and directing the life it supported, contained elements that were hostile as well as supporting. Certain rocks gave out dangerous radiation; even within the light of the sun, from which all life draws its energy, there were short-wave radiations with power to injure. Given time — time not in years but in millennia — life adjusts, and a balance has been reached. For time is the essential ingredient; but in the modern world there is no time.

The rapidity of change and the speed with which new situations are created follow the impetuous and heedless pace of man rather than the deliberate pace of nature. Radiation is no longer merely the background radiation of rocks, the bombardment of cosmic rays, the ultraviolet of the sun that have existed before there was any life on earth; radiation is now the unnatural creation of man's tampering with the atom. The chemicals to which life is asked to make its adjustment are no longer merely the calcium and silica and copper and all the rest of the minerals washed out of the rocks and carried in rivers to the sea; they are the synthetic creations of man's inventive mind, brewed in his laboratories, and having no counterparts in nature.

To adjust to these chemicals would require time on the scale that is nature's; it would require not merely the years of a man's life but the life of generations. And even this, were it by some miracle possible, would be futile, for the new chemicals come from our laboratories in an endless stream; almost five hundred annually find their way into actual use in the United States alone. The figure is staggering and its implications are not easily grasped — 500 new chemicals to which the bodies of men and animals are required somehow to adapt each year, chemicals totally outside the limits of biologic experience.

Among them are many that are used in man's war against nature. Since the mid-1940's over 200 basic chemicals have been created for use in killing insects, weeds, rodents, and other organisms described in the modern vernacular as "pests"; and they are sold under several thousand different brand names.

These sprays, dusts, and aerosols are now applied almost universally to farms, gardens, forests, and homes — nonselective chemicals that have the power to kill every insect, the "good" and the "bad," to still the song of birds and the leaping of fish in the streams, to coat the leaves with a deadly film, and to linger on in soil — all this though the intended target may be only a few weeds or insects. Can anyone believe it is possible to lay down such a barrage of poisons on the surface of the earth without making it unfit for all life? They should not be called "insecticides," but "biocides."

The whole process of spraying seems caught up in an endless spiral. Since DDT was released for civilian use, a process of escalation has been going on in which ever more toxic materials must be found. This has happened because insects, in a triumphant vindication of Darwin's principle of the survival of the fittest, have evolved super races immune to the particular insecticide used, hence a deadlier one has always to be developed — and then a deadlier one than that. It has happened also because, for reasons to be described later, destructive insects often undergo a "flareback," or resurgence, after spraying, in numbers greater than before. Thus the chemical war is never won, and all life is caught in its violent crossfire.

Along with the possibility of the extinction of mankind by nuclear war, the central problem of our age has therefore become the contamination of man's total environment with such substances of incredible potential for harm — substances that accumulate in the tissues of plants and animals and even penetrate the germ cells to shatter or alter the very material of heredity upon which the shape of the future depends.

Some would-be architects of our future look toward a time when it will be possible to alter the human germ plasm by design. But we may easily be doing so now by inadvertence, for many chemicals, like radiation, bring about gene mutations. It is ironic to think that man might determine his own future by something so seemingly trivial as the choice of an insect spray.

All this has been risked — for what? Future historians may well be amazed by our distorted sense of proportion. How could intelligent beings seek to control a few unwanted species by a method that contaminated the entire environment and brought the threat of disease and death even to their own kind? Yet this is precisely what we have done. We have done it, moreover, for reasons that collapse the moment we examine them. We are told that the enormous and expanding use of pesticides is necessary to maintain farm production. Yet is our real problem not one of *overproduction?* Our farms, despite measures to remove acreages from production and to pay farmers *not* to produce, have yielded such a staggering excess of crops that the American taxpayer in 1962 is paying out more than one billion dollars a year as the total carrying cost of the surplus-food storage program. And is the situation helped when one branch of the Agriculture Department tries to reduce production while another states, as it did in 1958, "It is believed generally that reduction of crop acreages under provisions of the Soil Bank will stimulate interest in use of chemicals to obtain maximum production on the land retained in crops."

All this is not to say there is no insect problem and no need of control. I am saying, rather, that control must be geared to realities, not to mythical situations, and that the methods employed must be such that they do not destroy us along with the insects.

The problem whose attempted solution has brought such a train of disaster in its wake is an accompaniment of our modern way of life. Long before the age of man, insects inhabited the earth — a group of extraordinarily varied and adaptable beings. Over the course of time since man's advent, a small percentage of the more than half a million species of insects have come into conflict with human welfare in two principal ways: as competitors for the food supply and as carriers of human disease.

Disease-carrying insects become important where human beings are crowded together, especially under conditions where sanitation is poor, as in time of natural disaster or war or in situations of extreme poverty and deprivation. Then control of some sort becomes necessary. It is a sobering fact, however, as we shall presently see, that the method of massive chemical control has had only limited success, and also threatens to worsen the very conditions it is intended to curb.

Under primitive agricultural conditions the farmer had few insect problems. These arose with the intensification of agriculture — the devotion of immense acreages to a single crop. Such a system set the stage for explosive increases in specific insect populations. Single-crop farming does not take advantage of the principles by which nature works; it is agriculture as an engineer might conceive it to be. Nature has introduced great variety into the landscape, but man has displayed a passion for simplifying it. Thus he undoes the built-in checks and balances by which nature holds the species within bounds. One important natural check is a limit on the amount of suitable habitat for each species. Obviously then, an insect that lives on wheat can build up its population to much higher levels on a farm devoted to wheat than on one in which wheat is intermingled with other crops to which the insect is not adapted.

The same thing happens in other situations. A generation or more ago, the towns of large areas of the United States lined their streets with the noble elm tree. Now the beauty they hopefully created is threatened with complete destruction as disease sweeps through the elms, carried by a beetle that would have only limited chance to build up large populations and to spread from tree to tree if the elms were only occasional trees in a richly diversified planting.

Another factor in the modern insect problem is one that must be viewed against a background of geologic and human history: the spreading of thousands of different kinds of organisms from their native homes to invade new territories. This worldwide migration has been studied and graphically decribed by the British ecologist Charles Elton in his recent book *The Ecology of Invasions*. During the Cretaceous Period, some hundred million years ago, flooding seas cut many land bridges between continents and living things found themselves confined in what Elton calls "colossal separate nature reserves." There, isolated from others of their kind, they developed many new species. When some of the land masses were joined again, about 15 million years ago, these species began to move out into new territories — a movement that is not only still in progress but is now receiving considerable assistance from man.

The importation of plants is the primary agent in the modern spread of species, for animals have almost invariably gone along with the plants, quarantine being a comparatively recent and not completely effective innovation. The United States Office of Plant Introduction alone has introduced almost 200,000 species and varieties of plants from all over the world. Nearly half of the 180 or so major insect enemies of plants in the United States are accidental imports from abroad, and most of them have come as hitchhikers on plants.

In new territory, out of reach of the restraining hand of the natural enemies that kept down its numbers in its native land, an invading plant or animal is able to become enormously abundant. Thus it is no accident that our most troublesome insects are introduced species.

These invasions, both the naturally occurring and those dependent on human assistance, are likely to continue indefinitely. Quarantine and massive chemical campaigns are only extremely expensive ways of buying time. We are faced, according to Dr. Elton, "with a life-and-death need not just to find new technological means of suppressing this plant or that animal"; instead we need the basic knowledge of animal populations and their relations to their surroundings that will "promote an even balance and damp down the explosive power of outbreaks and new invasions."

Much of the necessary knowledge is now available but we do not use it. We train ecologists in our universities and even employ them in our governmental agencies but we seldom take their advice. We allow the chemical death rain to fall as though there were no alternative, whereas in fact there are many, and our ingenuity could soon discover many more if given opportunity.

Have we fallen into a mesmerized state that makes us accept as inevitable that which is inferior or detrimental, as though having lost the will or the vision to demand that which is good? Such thinking, in the words of the ecologist Paul Shepard, "idealizes life with only its head out of water, inches above the limits of toleration of the corruption of its own environment. . . . Why should we tolerate a diet of weak poisons, a home in insipid surroundings, a circle of acquaintances who are not quite our enemies, the noise of motors with just enough relief to prevent insanity? Who would want to live in a world which is just not quite fatal?"

Yet such a world is pressed upon us. The crusade to create a chemically sterile, insect-free world seems to have engendered a fanatic zeal on the part of many specialists and most of the so-called control agencies. On every hand there is evidence that those engaged in spraying operations exercise a ruthless power. "The regulatory entomologists . . . function as prosecutor, judge and jury, tax assessor and collector and sheriff to enforce their own orders," said Connecticut entomologist Neely Turner. The most flagrant abuses go unchecked in both state and federal agencies.

It is not my contention that chemical insecticides must never be used. I do contend that we have put poisonous and biologically potent chemicals indiscriminately into the hands of persons largely or wholly ignorant of their potentials for harm. We have subjected enormous numbers of people to contact with these poisons, without their consent, and often without their knowledge. If the Bill of Rights contains no guarantee that a citizen shall be secure against lethal poisons distributed either by private individuals or by public officials, it is surely only because our forefathers, despite their considerable wisdom and foresight, could conceive of no such problem.

I contend, furthermore, that we have allowed these chemicals to be used with little or no advance investigation of their effect on soil, water, wildlife, and man himself. Future generations are unlikely to condone our lack of prudent concern for the integrity of the natural world that supports all life.

There is still very limited awareness of the nature of the threat. This is an era of specialists, each of whom sees his own problem and is unaware of or intolerant of the larger frame into which it fits. It is also an era dominated by industry, in which the right to make a dollar at whatever cost is seldom challenged. When the public protests, confronted with some obvious evidence of damaging results of pesticide applications, it is fed little tranquilizing pills of half truth. We urgently need an end to these false assurances, to the sugar coating of unpalatable facts. It is the public that is being asked to assume the risks that the insect controllers calculate. The public must decide whether it wishes to continue on the present road, and it can do so only when in full possession of the facts. In the words of Jean Rostand,[1] "The obligation to endure gives us the right to know."

ﻬﻰ FOR DISCUSSION AND WRITING

1. The title of the book from which this excerpt is taken is *Silent Spring*, and the book is prefaced by Keats's lines:

> The sedge is wither'd from the lake
> And no birds sing.

---

[1] French biologist.

What symbolism (significance) is there in bird song that accounts for the peculiar ominousness of the idea of a *silent* spring, when "no birds sing"? How is that symbolism woven into Miss Carson's thesis?

2. She starts with a fable about a land mysteriously stricken with sterility and disease. There are many fairy tales, of all lands and all ages, in which the same situation occurs—a general blight caused by the malice of a witch or a magician, who may send a plague of mice to eat up all the corn, or who may go so far as to make the land disappear (become "invisible") altogether. Instead of a witch or magician, what is the more horrifying cause of the blight in Miss Carson's fable? Why is it more horrifying than some supernatural infliction? In a more sophisticated form than fairy tale —in, for instance, Sophocles' plays *Oedipus Rex* and *Antigone*—plagues ravage both people and land because of some deep moral ailment at the very source of power, in the kingship itself (T. S. Eliot uses a similar parable in his *The Waste Land*). Is there in Miss Carson's fable, and not only in the introductory fable but in the actual situation she deals with, any element of *moral* irresponsibility? If so, what is it?

3. In the first paragraph of the section following the fable, the paragraph beginning "The history of life on earth. . . , " Miss Carson says that only in the present century "has one species—man—acquired significant power to alter the nature of his world." From time to time in these studies (see pages 363, 605) we have had occasion to use Julian Huxley's characterization of the modern scientific period as "evolution become conscious of itself." What ironic comment is made on our conscious conduct of evolution, our power to alter the nature of our world, by the employment of chemistry with which Miss Carson is concerned? What point does she make about the long periods of time needed for the adjustment of biological life to its environment ("time is the essential ingredient; . . . in the modern world there is no time")?

4. We have, in America, a fetish of cleanliness (for whatever historical reasons), which often causes us a great deal of compulsive discomfort when we visit older countries whose civilization is immensely more ancient and complex than our own, but which affront us with animal smells to which our nostrils are unaccustomed and which we tend to think of as disgustingly primitive, dirty, and even immoral. Does that fetish play any part in the irrational, irresponsible use of chemicals discussed here? Could you give any instances? An axiom of our immediate forefathers was that "cleanliness is next to godliness"; but if the glass of water you draw from the kitchen

faucet has a rich detergent foam on it, like the head on a glass of beer, how godly do we become through the cleansing properties of detergents?

5. What important point, relating to natural evolutionary adjustment, does Miss Carson make in the paragraph beginning "The rapidity of change and the speed with which new situations are created . . ." and in the paragraph immediately following, ending with ". . . chemicals totally outside the limits of biologic experience"?

6. Why does she suggest that "insecticides" should be called "biocides"? What is the "endless spiral" she speaks of, and why is "the chemical war never won"? What is the irony in altering human genes by an insect spray? Why do we have such difficulty in conceiving that a bug poison may leave our children a sterile and crippled inheritance?

7. What point does Miss Carson make about the planting of single crops, as against natural diversification? What does she mean by "built-in checks and balances" in natural diversity? What does she say has been the effect on natural ecology of the importation of plants?

8. The problem, she suggests, is not to be solved by new technological means of suppressing this or that plant or animal, but how? She asks, "Have we fallen into a mesmerized state . . . ?" Well, have we? Where does she lay the blame? Is she against ecological control? or against the controllers? which controllers, and why?

9. There are many theme suggestions in all these questions. Whichever one you tackle, try at some point to bring it home through personal experience.

THE ATOM AND THE UNIVERSE

Lucretius ✑§ The Seeds of Things

✑§ Roman poet and philosopher (*ca.* 96-55 B.C.), of whom almost nothing is known and whose only book was *De Rerum Natura* (On the Nature of Things).

Robert Lind, head of the Classics Department of the University of Kansas, says: "Lucretius wrote in this glowing, magnificent poem the most complete analysis of the atomic composition of matter ever made until modern science revived atomism and led the way through nuclear physics to the atom bomb." And further:

"The purpose of Lucretius in writing on materialistic theories was to dispel fear of Nature, of the gods, and of death; hence his description of the causes of natural phenomena leads to the loftiest ethical conclusions. The principles of conservation of matter and energy, the constitution of the universe from atoms and void, the postulation of infinite worlds, the emphasis on the mortality of the soul, and the evidence of the senses as the sole guide to certain knowledge are fundamental to Lucretius' treatment of physics, cosmology, psychology, sociology, optics, mechanics, anthropology, linguistics, meteorology, and theology. . . .

"The purpose of his thought was a social reform that was to begin in the heart of the individual. . . . His intense faith in life, in love as the generative force of the universe, and in the physical foundations of existence makes him a modern among moderns. In addition he is the finest thinker the Romans produced." (L. R. Lind, *Latin Poetry in Verse Translation*, Houghton Mifflin, 1957.) ੩➳

COME now, mark and learn what remains, and hear it more clearly. Not that I am unaware how obscure these matters are; but the high hope of

Listen to my doctrine, which I commend to you by the charm of poesy.

From Lucretius' *De Rerum Natura*, translated by W. H. D. Rouse, The Loeb Classical Library edition (Cambridge, Mass.: Harvard University Press, 1924). Reprinted by permission of the publishers.

779

renown has struck my mind sharply with holy
wand, and at the same time has struck into my
heart sweet love of the Muses, thrilled by which
now in lively thought I traverse pathless tracts of
the Pierides[1] never yet trodden by any foot. I love
to approach virgin springs and there to drink; I love
to pluck fresh flowers, and to seek an illustrious
chaplet for my head from fields whence ere this the
Muses have crowned the brows of none: first because my teaching is of high matters, and I proceed
to unloose the mind from the close knots of religion; next because the subject is so dark[2] and the
lines I write so clear, as I touch all with the Muses'
grace. For even this seems not to be out of place;
but as with children, when physicians try to administer rank wormwood, they first touch the rims
about the cups with the sweet yellow fluid of honey,
that unthinking childhood be deluded as far as the
lips, and meanwhile that they may drink up the
bitter juice of wormwood, and though beguiled be
not betrayed, but rather by such means be restored
and regain health, so now do I: since this doctrine
commonly seems somewhat harsh to those who have
not used it, and the people shrink back from it, I
have chosen to set forth my doctrine to you in
sweet-speaking Pierian song, and as it were to touch
it with the Muses' delicious honey, if perchance by
such means I might engage your mind in my verses,
while you are learning to see in what shape is
framed the whole nature of things.

Are matter and space   But since I have taught that the bodies of mat-
infinite?   ter[3] are perfectly solid, and that they fly about con-

---

[1] Another name for the Muses, goddesses of the arts and sciences, to whom Mount
Pierus in Thessaly was sacred. Hence also Lucretius' reference to "sweet-speaking
Pierian song," below.

[2] So little understood and so difficult.

[3] The atoms, which he also calls "the generative bodies of matter," and the "first-
beginnings." "The void," mentioned below, is infinite space.

tinually unimpaired for ever, come now, let us unfold whether there be any limit to their sum or not:
likewise as regards the void which has been found
to exist, or place and space for all things to be done,
let us see clearly whether it be limited in its essence
or spread to breadth immeasurable and vasty depth.

The universe then is not limited along any of
its paths; for if so it ought to have an extremity. *(1) The universe is infi-*
Again, clearly nothing can have an extremity unless *nite since it has no*
there be something beyond to bound it, so that *boundary.*
something can be seen, beyond which this our sense
can follow no further. Now since we must confess
that there is nothing beyond the sum of things, it has
no extremity, and therefore it is without end or
limit. Nor does it matter in which of its quarters you
stand: so true is it, that whatever place anyone occupies, he leaves the whole equally infinite in every
direction. . . .

Besides, if all the space in the universe stood *(2) Space is infinite,*
contained within fixed boundaries on all sides and *or all matter would*
were limited, by this time the store of matter would *have collected*
by its solid weight have run together from all sides *at the bottom.*
to the bottom, nor could anything be done under
the canopy of heaven, nor would heaven exist at all
or the sun's light, because assuredly all matter
would have been lying already in a heap from sinking down through infinite ages past. But as it is, sure
enough no rest is given to the bodies of the first-beginnings, because there is no bottom whatsoever,
for them to run together as it were into it and fix
their abode there. Always the business of the universe is going on with incessant motion in every
part, and the elements of matter are being supplied
from beneath rushing from infinite space. Therefore
the nature of space and the extent of the deep is so
great, that neither bright lightnings can traverse it
in their course, though they glide onwards through
endless tracts of time; nor can they by all their

travelling make their journey any the less to go: so
widely spreads the great store of space in the universe all around without limit in every direction.

*(3) Matter is infinite,
or nothing would
ever have been made:*

Furthermore, nature withholds the sum of existing things from providing a limit for itself, because she compels body to be bounded by void and
that again which is void to be bounded by body, so
that by this alternation she renders the universe infinite, or else, either one of these two, if the other
did not bound it, would yet by itself spread abroad
without limit. [But I have laid down above that
space is infinite; if therefore the sum of matter were
finite], neither sea nor land nor the gleaming regions of the sky nor the race of men nor the holy
bodies of gods could stand fast for the fraction of an
hour; for the store of matter driven abroad from its
union would be rushing dissolved through the great
void, or rather would never have been compacted to
form anything, since when scattered abroad it could
never have been brought together. For certainly

*for it was not made
by any intention
of the atoms,*

neither did the first-beginnings[4] place themselves
by design each in its own order with keen intelligence, nor assuredly did they make agreement what
motions each should produce; but because being
many and shifted in many ways, they are harried
and set in motion with blows throughout the universe from infinity, thus by trying every kind of motion and combination, at length they fall into such
arrangements as this sum of things consists of; and
this being also preserved through many great cycles
of years, when once it has been cast together into
convenient motions, brings it about that rivers refill
the greedy sea with generous flow, and earth cherished by the sun's heat renews its offspring, and the
generation of living things springs up and flourishes,
and the gliding fires of heaven do live: which they
would by no means do, unless a store of matter

[4] See Note 3.

could arise up out of the infinite, from which they *and chance movements*
are wont to replace in season all that has been *could make nothing out of finite matter.*
lost. . . .

Come now, and I will set forth by what motion *I. Motion.*
the generative bodies of matter beget the various *Atoms are in constant motion,*
things and once begotten dissolve them, and by what
force they are compelled to do it, and what swiftness has been given them to travel through the great
void: do you remember to give heed to my words.
For certainly matter is not one packed and coherent
mass, since we see each thing decreasing, and we
perceive all things as it were ebbing through length
of time, and age withdrawing them from our eyes;
although nevertheless the sum is seen to remain un- *increasing this,*
impaired for this reason, that whenever bodies pass *diminishing that, while the sum*
away from a thing, they diminish that from which *remains unchanged.*
they pass and increase that to which they have
come, they compel the first to fade and the second
on the contrary to bloom, yet do not linger there.
Thus the sum of things is ever being renewed, and
mortal creatures live dependent one upon another.
Some nations increase, others diminish, and in a
short space the generations of living creatures are
changed and like runners pass on the torch of life.

If you think the first-beginnings of things can *Some move free*
stand still, and by standing still can beget new mo- *through the void;*
tions amongst things, you are astray and travel far
from true reasoning. For since the first-beginnings
of things travel through the void, they must needs
all be carried on either by their own weight or by a
chance blow from one or other. For when in quick
motion they have often met and collided, it follows
that they leap apart suddenly in different directions;
and no wonder, since they are perfectly hard in
their solid weight and nothing obstructs them from
behind. And to show you more clearly that all the
bodies of matter are constantly being tossed about,
remember that there is no bottom in the sum of

things and the first bodies have nowhere to rest, since space is without end or limit, and I have shown at large and proved by irrefragable reasoning that it extends immeasurable from all sides in all directions. Since this stands firm, beyond doubt no rest is granted to the first bodies throughout the profound void, but rather driven by incessant and varied motions, some after being pressed together then leap back with wide intervals, some again after the blow are tossed about within a narrow compass. *those which are combined into groups move also,* And those which being held in combination more closely condensed collide and leap back through tiny intervals, caught fast in the complexity of their own shapes, these constitute the strong roots of stone and the bodies of fierce iron and the others of their kind. Those are few, moreover, which travel through the great void. The rest leap far apart and pass far back with long intervals between: these supply thin air for us and the gleaming light of the sun. And many besides travel through the great void which have been rejected from combination with things, and have nowhere been able to conjoin their motions even when received. Of this as I now describe it there is an image and similitude always *like motes in a sunbeam.* moving and present before our eyes. Do but apply your scrutiny when the sun's light and his rays penetrate and spread through a dark room: you will see many minute specks mingling in many ways throughout the void in the light itself of the rays, and as it were in everlasting conflict struggling, fighting, battling in troops without any pause, driven about with frequent meetings and partings; so that you may conjecture from this what it is for the first-beginnings of things to be ever tossed about in the great void. So far as it goes, a small thing may give an analogy of great things, and show the tracks of knowledge. Even more for another reason, it is proper that you give attention to these bodies which

are seen to be in turmoil within the sun's rays, because such turmoil indicates that there are secret
and blind motions also hidden in matter. For there
you will see how many things set in motion by blind
blows change their course and beaten back return
back again, now this way now that way, in all directions. You may be sure that all take their restlessness
from the first-beginnings. For first the first-beginnings of things move of themselves; then the bodies
that form a small combination and as one may say
are nearest to the powers of the beginnings, are set
moving, driven by the blind blows of these, while
they in their turn attack those that are a little larger.
Thus the movement ascends from the beginnings
and by successive degrees emerges upon our senses,
so that those bodies also are moved which we are
able to perceive in the sun's light, yet it does not
openly appear by what blows they are made to do
so.

Their unseen motions cause all other motions.

   Now Memmius,[5] what swiftness is granted to
the bodies of matter you may understand from what
follows in a few words. First, when the dawn diffuses new light over the earth, and the many-coloured birds flitting about through pathless woods
fill the spaces of soft air with their liquid notes, how
suddenly at such time the sun arising is wont to en-
velop and flood the whole world with his light, we
see to be plain and manifest to all. But that heat and
that light serene which the sun sends, does not pass
through empty void; wherefore it is forced to go
more slowly, while it beats its way so to speak
through waves of air. Nor do the particles of heat
move alone and singly, but linked together and
massed together; wherefore they are at the same
time retarded from within and obstructed from
without, so that they are forced to go more slowly.
But the first-beginnings, which are of solid single-

The speed of the atoms is greater than that of light,

which is combined in molecules,

whereas the atoms are unchecked.

5 A friend of Lucretius, to whom the poem is addressed.

ness, when they pass through the empty void, are not delayed by anything from without, and being units although composed of their own parts, when they are carried each to that one point to which their first efforts tend, most certainly they must be of exceeding swiftness and must be carried far more quickly than the light of the sun, and traverse a space many times as wide, in the same time that the sun's lightnings take to pervade the heavens. . . .

But some believe that the gods made the world for man;

But some in opposition to this, knowing nothing of matter, think that without the gods' power nature cannot with so exact conformity to the plans of mankind change the seasons of the year, and produce crops, and in a word all else which divine pleasure, the guide of life, persuades men to approach, herself leading them and coaxing them, through the ways of Venus,[6] to beget their generations, that the human race may not come to an end. But when they imagine the gods to have arranged all for the sake of men, they seem to have departed widely from true reasoning in every way. For although I might not know what first-beginnings are, this nevertheless I would make bold to maintain from the ways of heaven itself, and to demonstrate from many another source, that the nature of the universe has by no means been made through

now it is too faulty for that.

divine power, seeing how great are the faults it stands endowed with. All this, Memmius, I will make clear to you later. . . .

Although everything is in motion the whole seems at rest.

One point in these matters need cause no wonder, why, since all the first-beginnings of things are in motion, the sum total seems nevertheless to abide in supreme quietude, except for anything that may

---

[6] The poem begins with an invocation to Venus, the creative force in nature. Lucretius was a follower of the philosopher Epicurus (*ca.* 342-270 B.C.), who taught that pleasure is the only good, the cause and aim of all morality ("the guide of life," as Lucretius says here)—not in the sense of an irresponsible hedonism, for true pleasure is attained only through a life of prudence, honor, justice, and temperance.

show movement with its own body. For the nature
of the first things lies all hidden far beneath our
senses; wherefore since you cannot get so far as to
see the things themselves, they must necessarily
steal their motions from your sight, especially when
things that we can perceive do yet often conceal
their motions if they be withdrawn at a great dis-
stance. For often on a hill, cropping the rich pasture,   *Analogies.*
woolly sheep go creeping whither the grass all
sparkling with fresh dew tempts and invites each,
and full-fed the lambkins play and butt heads in
sport; all which things are seen by us blurred together in the distance, as a kind of whiteness resting
on a green hill. Besides, when great armies cover
the outspread plains in their manoeuvres waging
the mimicry of war, on the spot the sheen rises to the
sky and all the country around flashes back the bril-
liancy of bronze, and beneath, the ground quakes,
resounding with the mighty tramp of men's feet, the
mountains, stricken by the clamour, throw back the
sounds to the stars of heaven, horsemen gallop
around and suddenly course through the midst of
the plains, shaking them with their mighty rush:
and yet there is a place on the high mountains, from
which they seem to stand, and to be a brightness
resting upon a plain.

Mark now in the next place of what kinds are   *II. Shape.*
the beginnings of all things, and learn how far they   *There are many*
differ in shape, how varied they are in their mani-   *varieties of shape*
fold figures: not that there are only a few endowed   *in the atoms,*
with similar shape, but because commonly they are
not all like all. And no wonder: for since there is
so great a store that there is no end to them, as I
have taught, and no sum, they must assuredly not
be all of like frame with all and marked by the same
shape. Marshal before you the race of men, and the   *as there are in the units*
dumb swimming tribes of scaly fish, happy cattle,   *of any species which*
and wild beasts, the many kinds of birds which   *are superficially alike.*

throng the joyous regions of water around bank
and spring and lake, crowding the pathless woods
through and through as they flit about: and then go
on to take any one in any kind, you will find nevertheless that each differs from each in shape. Nor is

Examples from animals,

there any other way by which the young could
recognize the mother or the mother her young; and
this we see they can do, and that they are known
clearly to each other no less than men are. For often
in front of the noble shrines of the gods a calf falls
slain beside the incense-burning altars, breathing
up a hot stream of blood from his breast; but the
mother bereaved wanders through the green glens,
and knows the prints marked on the ground by the
cloven hooves, as she surveys all the regions if she
may espy somewhere her lost offspring, and coming
to a stand fills the leafy woods with her moaning,
and often revisits the stall pierced with yearning for
her young calf; nor can tender willow-growths, and
grass growing rich in the dew, and those rivers
flowing level with their banks, give delight to her
mind and rebuff that care which has entered there,
nor can the sight of other calves in the happy pastures divert her mind and lighten her load of care:
so persistently she seeks for something of her own
that she knows well. Besides, tender kids with trembling voices know their horned mothers, and mischievous lambkins the flocks of bleating sheep: so,
as nature demands, they run down each to its own

grains of corn,

udder of milk. Lastly, take any kind of corn, you
will see that the grains are nevertheless not all so
alike by their common species, but that there is a
certain difference of shape between them. And in

shells.

the same way we see the multitude of shells painting the lap of the earth, where with soft waves the
sea beats on the thirsty sand of the curving shore.
Wherefore again and again I say that the first-beginnings of things in the same way, since they exist

by nature and are not made by hand after the fixed
model of one single atom, must necessarily have
some of them different shapes as they fly about.

It is very easy in such a way for us to explain
why the fire of lightning is far more penetrating
than ours is that arises from terrestrial torches; for
you could say that lightning, the heavenly fire, is
finer and made of smaller shapes, and therefore
passes through openings through which this fire of
ours, sprung from wood and made from a torch,
cannot pass. Besides, light passes through horn, but
rain is rejected: why? unless those bodies of light
are smaller than those which make up the nourishing liquid of water. And we see wine, as quickly as
you will, strain through a colander; but contrariwise
olive oil lags and lingers, either to be sure because
its elements are larger, or because they are more
hooked and entangled more closely, and therefore
it happens that the separate first-beginnings cannot
be so suddenly detached and ooze one by one each
through its own opening.

This explains why some things can pass where others cannot;

Moreover, the liquids of honey and of milk
have a pleasant taste as they are moved about in
the mouth; but contrariwise the loathsome nature
of wormwood and of harsh centaury twists up the
mouth with a noisome flavour; so that you may
readily recognize that those bodies which can touch
our senses pleasantly are made of smooth and round
atoms, but contrariwise all that seem to be bitter
and rough are held in connexion by atoms more
hooked, and are therefore wont to tear open their
way into our senses and to break the texture by their
intrusion. . . .

why some please the taste, others displease.

This also herewith you would do well to guard
sealed and treasured in memory, that there is none
of those things which are in plain view before us
which consists only of one kind of element, nothing
which does not consist of various seeds commin-

Nothing consists of only one kind of element.

gled; and the more powers and faculties a thing has in itself, the more kinds of elements and varied shapes does it show to be within it. First, the earth contains the first bodies from which the springs, rolling coolness along, industriously renew the illimitable sea, earth contains the source of fires. For in many places the crust of the earth burns aflame, while from the depths come the fiery eruptions of Etna.[7] Then further, she contains the means to raise up bright corn and fruitful trees for the races of mankind, the means to produce rivers and leaves and fruitful pastures for the mountain-ranging brood of wild beasts. Wherefore she is called great Mother of the gods, and Mother of the wild beasts,[8] and maker of our bodies, even she alone.

Earth contains all kinds,

wherefore she is rightly called Mother.

She it is of whom the ancient and learned poets of the Greeks have sung, [how that from her sanctuary she rides in state] on a chariot driving a pair of lions, thus teaching that the great world is poised in the spacious air, and that earth cannot rest on earth. They have yoked in wild beasts, because any offspring however wild ought to be softened and vanquished by the kindly acts of the parents. And they have surrounded the top of her head with a mural crown, because embattled in excellent positions she sustains cities; which emblem now adorns the divine mother's image as she is carried over the great earth in awful state. She it is whom different nations in their ancient ritual acclaim as the Idaean mother,[9] and give her troops of Phrygians to escort her, because men declare that first from that realm came the corn, which then spread over the round

Mother Earth as Cybele:

her attributes explained;

wild beasts,

crown,

Phrygian guards,

[7] Live volcano in Sicily.

[8] Under her many names in many lands and under different forms of worship, the great mother-goddess kept the title she had been given by hunter tribes, "Mother of the wild beasts."

[9] Mount Ida in Crete and Mount Ida in Asia Minor (ancient Phrygia) were both connected with the worship of the Great Goddess—hence "Idaean mother."

world. They give her eunuchs, as wishing to indicate that those who have violated the majesty of the   *eunuchs,*
Mother, and have been found ungrateful to their
parents, should be thought unworthy to bring living
offspring into the regions of light. The taut tom-
toms thunder under the open palm, the hollow cym-   *music,*
bals sound around, horns with hoarse-echoing blare
affright, tootling flutes prick up the spirits with
their Phrygian cadences, martial arms show a front   *weapons,*
of violent fury, that they may amaze the ungrateful
minds and impious hearts of the vulgar with fear of
the goddess's majesty. Therefore so soon as she rides
through mighty cities, silently blessing mankind
with unspoken benediction, they bestrew the whole
path of her progress with silver and copper, enrich-
ing it with bounteous largess, and snow down rose-
flowers in a shower, over-shadowing the Mother
and her escorting troops. Here an armed group,
whom the Greeks name the Phrygian Curetes,[10] —   *the Curetes*
because haply they sport with arms and leap up
streaming with blood, in measured tread shaking
their awful crests with the movement of their heads,
— recalls the Dictaean Curetes who are said once
upon a time to have concealed that infant wailing
of Jupiter in Crete; when, boys round a boy in rapid
dance, clad in armour, they clashed bronze upon
bronze to a measure, that Saturn might not catch
him and cast him into his jaws and plant an everlasting wound in the mother's heart. For this reason
they escort the great Mother armed; or else because   *the armed*
they indicate the command of the goddess that with   *escort.*
arms and valour they be ready to defend their native land, and to be both protection and pride to

[10] The Curetes were the priests of the Great Goddess, who engaged in armed dances
in her rituals. Mythologically, they were said to be earthborn daemons (Titans)
who protected the child Zeus, in the cave (Dicte—hence the adjective "Dictaean" used just below) on Mount Ida where his mother had hidden him from the
cannibalism of his father Cronus.

their parents. But well and excellently as all this is set forth and told, yet it is rejected far from true reasoning. For the very nature of divinity must

But the gods dwell apart in eternal peace,

necessarily enjoy immortal life in the deepest peace, far removed and separated from our troubles; for without any pain, without danger, itself mighty by its own resources, needing us not at all, it is neither propitiated with services nor touched by wrath. Here if anyone decides to call the sea Neptune, and corn Ceres, and to misapply the name of Bacchus rather than to use the title that is proper to that liquor, let us grant him to dub the round world Mother of the Gods, while he forbears in reality himself to infect his mind with base superstition.

and earth has no feeling, but contains many elements. . . .

The earth indeed lacks true sensation at all times, and only because it receives into itself the first-beginnings of many things does it bring forth many in many ways into the sun's light. . . .

The spectacle of the heavens: what does it mean?

Now I beg, apply your mind to true reasoning. For a mightily new thing is labouring to fall upon your ears, a new aspect of creation to show itself. But nothing is there so easy that at first it is not more difficult to believe, nothing again so great or so wonderful but all men by degrees abate their wonder. Look up to the clear and pure colour of the sky, and all the travelling constellations that it contains, the moon, and the bright light of the dazzling sun; if all these were now revealed for the first time to mortals, if they were thrown before them suddenly without preparation, what more wonderful than these things could be named, or such as the nations would not have dared to believe beforehand? Nothing, as I think: so wondrous this spectacle would have been, which now, look you, all are so wearied with often seeing, that no one thinks it worth while to look up towards the bright vault of heaven! Forbear then to be dismayed by mere novelty and to spew out reason from your mind, but

rather ponder it with keen judgment; and if it seems
to be true, own yourself vanquished, or if it is false,
gird up your loins to fight. For since the sum of
space is infinite abroad beyond the walls of the
heavens, the mind seeks to understand what is
there in the distance whither the intelligence continually desires to look forth, and whither the mind's
projection flies free of itself.

In the first place, all around us in every direc- *There are other*
tion and on both sides and above and below through *worlds than*
this of ours.
the universe there is no limit: even as I have shown,
and truth of itself crieth aloud, and the nature of the
unfathomable deep giveth forth light. Now since
there is illimitable space empty in every direction,
and since seeds innumerable in number and unfathomable in sum are flying about in many ways
driven in everlasting movement, it cannot by any
means be thought likely that this is the only round
earth and sky that has been made, that all those *For the infinite*
bodies of matter without have nothing to do: espe- *number of atoms*
must combine elsewhere
cially since this world was made by nature, even as *in some way,*
the seeds themselves of their own accord knocking
together and collected in all sorts of ways, heedless,
without aim, without intention, have allowed some
to filter through which suddenly thrown together
could become in each case the beginnings of mighty
things, of earth and sea and sky and the generation
of living creatures. Wherefore again and again I
say you must confess that there are other assem-
blages of matter in other places, such as this is
which the air holds in greedy embrace.

Besides, when abundant matter is ready, when *and since matter,*
space is to hand, and no thing and no cause hinders, *space, and nature*
are the same,
things must assuredly be done and completed. And *in the same way:*
if there is at this moment both so great store of seeds
as all the time of living existence could not suffice to
tell, and if the same power and the same nature
abides, able to throw the seeds of things together

in any place in the same way as they have been
thrown together into this place, then you are bound
to confess that there are other worlds in other regions and different races of men and generations of
wild beasts.

indeed,
nothing is
unique.

Moreover, there is no one thing in the whole
sum which is produced unique, and grows up
unique and alone, so as not to belong to some kind
and to be one of many like it. To begin with, cast
your mind to the animals: you will find that this is so
with the mountain-ranging generation of wild
beasts, this is so with the double breed of men,[11]
so also with the dumb scaly fish and all creatures
that fly. Wherefore you must in like manner confess
for sky and earth, for sun, moon, sea and all else that
exists, that they are not unique, but rather of number innumerable; since there is a deepset limit of life
equally awaiting them, and they are as much made
of a perishable body as any kind here on earth
which has so many specimens of its kind.

✌͡ɕ FOR DISCUSSION AND WRITING

1. The reading of Lucretius may seem difficult at first, because the form of
   expression—the "idiom" of the thought—is not one to which you are
   habituated; but the thought itself is not at all difficult to follow, for you
   have been familiar with the atomic principle probably since grade school.
   Once you understand what Lucretius means by "the bodies of matter," or
   "the generative bodies of matter," or "the first-beginnings"—his various
   expressions for what we call "atoms"—and that by "void" he means
   "space," there is no real difficulty: except, perhaps, that you must use your
   imagination to go 2,000 years backward in time and to place yourself in the
   position of Lucretius, to whom the atomic principle was not tired old hat
   but a thundering marvel—so marvelous that only poetry was a sufficiently
   noble way of talking about it. Where in the first paragraph does he give his
   reasons for writing about it in poetry? Reading Lucretius in a prose trans-

---

[11] The two sexes.

lation we are, of course, at an obvious disadvantage, but could you nevertheless point to certain characteristics of the writing and to certain particular passages which make one aware of the fact that it is a poet who is talking to us? Today, "science" and "poetry" seem to belong to altogether different orders of intelligence, and to have altogether different purposes. Do you find yourself sharing in that notion? and if so, try to explain it. To test the careful and sustained logic of Lucretius' argument, make a brief outline of his main points (the marginal glosses will help somewhat, and the following questions will also help).

2. What are the first two questions Lucretius considers? By what kind of reasoning does he conclude that the universe is unlimited, that is, infinite? Is his conclusion supported by modern theory or not? By what reasoning does he conclude that space (the "void") is infinite? (You may find his argument—that otherwise everything would fall to the "bottom"—a bit naïve here, but if you read Hoyle's essay on continuous creation in the universe, a few pages ahead, you will find that Hoyle uses a similar kind of argument to show that, in an expanding universe, everything would shortly disappear—fly out into sightless infinity—if creation were not continuous.) In the fourth paragraph, where Lucretius gives his argument about there being no "bottom," where do you find his poet's eye—the poet's ability to visualize?

3. What is the third question he considers? What reasoning does he use as to the infinitude of matter? In Hoyle's essay, mentioned above, one of the problems discussed is the question of how galaxies could form at all— since they are formed by condensation of gases—if the universe is flying apart (condensation and expansion being contradictory principles). Lucretius puts the same problem in only slightly different terms: How could things be formed—you, me, stones, trees, anything—if space is infinite but the atoms making up matter are limited in quantity? What is his conclusion? How does he deal with the possibility that the atoms may *want* to make you, me, stones, trees, etc.? Lucretius had none of the observational instruments of modern science; in view of that lack, how would you judge the conclusions he makes?

4. The principle of motion is Lucretius' next concern; we need to supply, for this discussion, our own terms—change, or "process." (If you have read R. G. Collingwood's essay earlier in this book, you will have a better understanding of the importance of the problem of motion—change—to the ancient philosopher-scientists who initiated modern scientific thinking.)

How does Lucretius explain the constant changes in all things? Though you may find the idiom a little strange, a little naïve, what astonishing perception does he have about the constitution of solids such as stone and iron? For what purpose does he use the analogy of dust motes in the rays of the sun? How does he illustrate the inconceivable speed of the atoms? Do you find any intuition here of what modern physicists and astronomers—flabbergasted, like Lucretius, by an inhuman wonder—call "light years"?

5. At the beginning he said that he wished to "unloose the mind from the close knots of religion"; does this purpose contradict his discussion of the great mother-goddess, the Earth? His description of the ancient festival processions for Cybele is done with the eye of the poet and dramatist. Is it irreverent? Why does he find the sky more wonderful than the mother of the gods? Although Lucretius was a poet, and although he lived 2,000 years ago, in what way would a modern scientist find in him a completely understanding colleague?

6. To read Lucretius gives us intellectual humility. Why? And what is the value of intellectual humility?

7. Projects for a short paper: Write up your opinion of Lucretius; take a section from the science textbook that, at present, gives you the worst headache or the most intellectual excitement, and rewrite it for laymen who know absolutely nothing about the subject (this, after all, is what Lucretius did); or do a small job of research on Democritus—the first philosopher to propose the atomic principle—and Epicurus—the philosopher whom Lucretius takes as his teacher.

Blaise Pascal ⚜ The Two Infinites

⚜ French mathematician, physicist, and religious philosopher (1623-1662). Before he was sixteen, Pascal had written a paper on conic sections that attracted the attention of leading mathematicians; at nineteen he invented a calculating machine; he is credited with founding the modern theory of probability; he created what is known in mathematics as "Pascal's triangle," and contributed to the development of differential calculus; his experiments in physics increased knowledge of atmospheric pressure through barometric measurements, and established what is known as "Pascal's law" on the equilibrium of fluids. But this astonishingly gifted genius is known best through his notes and memoranda in a personal journal called *Pensées* (Thoughts), where his chief concern is with the inadequacy of pure reason to solve human difficulties or to realize human hopes, and the consequent necessity of religious faith. ⚜

LET MAN contemplate the whole of nature in her full and grand majesty, and turn his vision from the low objects which surround him. Let him gaze on that brilliant light, set like an eternal lamp to illumine the universe; let the earth appear to him a point in comparison with the vast circle described by the sun; and let him wonder at the fact that this vast circle is itself but a very fine point in comparison with that described by the stars in their revolution round the firmament. But if our view be arrested there, let our imagination pass beyond; it will sooner exhaust the power of conception than nature that of supplying material for conception. The whole visible world is only an imperceptible atom in the ample bosom of nature. No idea approaches it. We may enlarge our conceptions beyond all imaginable space; we only produce atoms in comparison

From *Pensées* by Blaise Pascal. Translated by W. F. Trotter. Dutton Paperback Series. Reprinted by permission of E. P. Dutton & Co., Inc.

with the reality of things. It is an infinite sphere, the centre of which is everywhere, the circumference nowhere. In short it is the greatest sensible mark of the almighty power of God, that imagination loses itself in that thought.

Returning to himself, let man consider what he is in comparison with all existence; let him regard himself as lost in this remote corner of nature; and from the little cell in which he finds himself lodged, I mean the universe, let him estimate at their true value the earth, kingdoms, cities, and himself. What is a man in the Infinite?

But to show him another prodigy equally astonishing, let him examine the most delicate things he knows. Let a mite be given him, with its minute body and parts incomparably more minute, limbs with their joints, veins in the limbs, blood in the veins, humours in the blood, drops in the humours,[1] vapours in the drops. Dividing these last things again, let him exhaust his powers of conception, and let the last object at which he can arrive be now that of our discourse. Perhaps he will think that here is the smallest point in nature. I will let him see therein a new abyss. I will paint for him not only the visible universe, but all that he can conceive of nature's immensity in the womb of this abridged atom. Let him see therein an infinity of universes, each of which has its firmament, its planets, its earth, in the same proportion as in the visible world; in each earth animals, and in the last mites, in which he will find again all that the first had, finding still in these others the same thing without end and without cessation. Let him lose himself in wonders as amazing in their littleness as the others in their vastness. For who will not be astounded at the fact that our body, which a little while ago was imperceptible in the universe, itself imperceptible in the bosom of the whole, is now a colossus, a world, or rather a whole, in respect of the nothingness which we cannot reach? He who regards himself in this light will be afraid of himself, and observing himself sustained in the body given him by nature between those two abysses of the Infinite and Nothing, will tremble at the sight of these marvels; and I think that, as his curiosity changes into admiration, he will be more disposed to contemplate them in silence than to examine them with presumption.

For in fact what is man in nature? A Nothing in comparison with the Infinite, an All in comparison with the Nothing, a mean between nothing and everything. Since he is infinitely removed from compre-

[1] Corresponding, in the older physiology, with glandular secretions.

hending the extremes, the end of things and their beginning are hopelessly hidden from him in an impenetrable secret; he is equally incapable of seeing the Nothing from which he was made, and the Infinite in which he is swallowed up.

What will he do then, but perceive the appearance of the middle of things, in an eternal despair of knowing either their beginning or their end. All things proceed from the Nothing, and are borne towards the Infinite. Who will follow these marvellous processes? The Author of these wonders understands them. None other can do so.

Through failure to contemplate these Infinites, men have rashly rushed into the examination of nature, as though they bore some proportion to her. It is strange that they have wished to understand the beginnings of things, and thence to arrive at the knowledge of the whole, with a presumption as infinite as their object. For surely this design cannot be formed without presumption or without a capacity infinite like nature.

If we are well informed, we understand that, as nature has graven her image and that of her Author on all things, they almost all partake of her double infinity. Thus we see that all the sciences are infinite in the extent of their researches. For who doubts that geometry, for instance, has an infinite infinity of problems to solve? They are also infinite in the multitude and fineness of their premises; for it is clear that those which are put forward as ultimate are not self-supporting, but are based on others which, again having others for their support, do not permit of finality. But we represent some as ultimate for reason, in the same way as in regard to material objects we call that an indivisible point beyond which our senses can no longer perceive anything, although by its nature it is infinitely divisible.

Of these two Infinites of science, that of greatness is the most palpable, and hence a few persons have pretended to know all things. "I will speak of the whole," said Democritus.[2]

But the infinitely little is the least obvious. Philosophers have much oftener claimed to have reached it, and it is here they have all stumbled. This has given rise to such common titles as *First Principles, Principles of Philosophy*, and the like, as ostentatious in fact, though not in appearance, as that one which blinds us, *De omni scibili*.[3]

[2] One of the earliest Greek philosophers (born about 460 B.C.), founder of the atomic theory of nature.

[3] Concerning all knowable things.

We naturally believe ourselves far more capable of reaching the centre of things than of embracing their circumference. The visible extent of the world visibly exceeds us; but as we exceed little things, we think ourselves more capable of knowing them. And yet we need no less capacity for attaining the Nothing than the All. Infinite capacity is required for both, and it seems to me that whoever shall have understood the ultimate principles of being might also attain to the knowledge of the Infinite. The one depends on the other, and one leads to the other. These extremes meet and reunite by force of distance, and find each other in God, and in God alone.

Let us then take our compass; we are something, and we are not everything. The nature of our existence hides from us the knowledge of first beginnings which are born of the Nothing; and the littleness of our being conceals from us the sight of the Infinite.

Our intellect holds the same position in the world of thought as our body occupies in the expanse of nature.

Limited as we are in every way, this state which holds the mean between two extremes is present in all our impotence. Our senses perceive no extreme. Too much sound deafens us; too much light dazzles us; too great distance or proximity hinders our view. Too great length and too great brevity of discourse tend to obscurity; too much truth is paralysing (I know some who cannot understand that to take four from nothing leaves nothing). First principles are too self-evident for us; too much pleasure disagrees with us. Too many concords are annoying in music; too many benefits irritate us. . . .

. . . We feel neither extreme heat nor extreme cold. Excessive qualities are prejudicial to us and not perceptible by the senses; we do not feel but suffer them. Extreme youth and extreme age hinder the mind, as also too much and too little education. In short, extremes are for us as though they were not, and we are not within their notice. They escape us, or we them.

This is our true state; this is what makes us incapable of certain knowledge and of absolute ignorance. We sail within a vast sphere, ever drifting in uncertainty, driven from end to end. When we think to attach ourselves to any point and to fasten to it, it wavers and leaves us; and if we follow it, it eludes our grasp, slips past us, and vanishes for ever. Nothing stays for us. This is our natural condition, and yet most contrary to our inclination; we burn with desire to find solid ground and an ultimate sure foundation whereon to build a tower reaching to the Infinite. But our whole groundwork cracks, and the earth opens to abysses.

Let us therefore not look for certainty and stability. Our reason is always deceived by fickle shadows; nothing can fix the finite between the two Infinites, which both enclose and fly from it.

If this be well understood, I think that we shall remain at rest, each in the state wherein nature has placed him. As this sphere which has fallen to us as our lot is always distant from either extreme, what matters it that man should have a little more knowledge of the universe? If he has it, he but gets a little higher. Is he not always infinitely removed from the end, and is not the duration of our life equally removed from eternity, even if it lasts ten years longer?

In comparison with these Infinites all finites are equal, and I see no reason for fixing our imagination on one more than on another. The only comparison which we make of ourselves to the finite is painful to us.

If man made himself the first object of study, he would see how incapable he is of going further. How can a part know the whole? But he may perhaps aspire to know at least the parts to which he bears some proportion. But the parts of the world are all so related and linked to one another, that I believe it impossible to know one without the other and without the whole.

Man, for instance, is related to all he knows. He needs a place wherein to abide, time through which to live, motion in order to live, elements to compose him, warmth and food to nourish him, air to breathe. He sees light; he feels bodies; in short, he is in a dependent alliance with everything. To know man, then, it is necessary to know how it happens that he needs air to live, and, to know the air, we must know how it is thus related to the life of man, etc. Flame cannot exist without air; therefore to understand the one, we must understand the other.

Since everything then is cause and effect, dependent and supporting, mediate and immediate, and all is held together by a natural though imperceptible chain, which binds together things most distant and most different, I hold it equally impossible to know the parts without knowing the whole, and to know the whole without knowing the parts in detail. . . .

And what completes our incapability of knowing things, is the fact that they are simple, and that we are composed of two opposite natures, different in kind, soul and body. For it is impossible that our rational part should be other than spiritual; and if any one maintain that we are simply corporeal, this would far more exclude us from the knowledge of things, there being nothing so inconceivable as to say that matter knows itself. It is impossible to imagine how it should know itself.

So if we are simply material, we can know nothing at all; and if we are composed of mind and matter, we cannot know perfectly things which are simple, whether spiritual or corporeal. Hence it comes that almost all philosophers have confused ideas of things, and speak of material things in spiritual terms, and of spiritual things in material terms. For they say boldly that bodies have a tendency to fall, that they seek after their centre, that they fly from destruction, that they fear the void, that they have inclinations, sympathies, antipathies, all of which attributes pertain only to mind. And in speaking of minds, they consider them as in a place, and attribute to them movement from one place to another; and these are qualities which belong only to bodies.

Instead of receiving the ideas of these things in their purity, we colour them with our own qualities, and stamp with our composite being all the simple things which we contemplate.

Who would not think, seeing us compose all things of mind and body, but that this mixture would be quite intelligible to us? Yet it is the very thing we least understand. Man is to himself the most wonderful object in nature; for he cannot conceive what the body is, still less what the mind is, and least of all how a body should be united to a mind. This is the consummation of his difficulties, and yet it is his very being.

✒ः FOR DISCUSSION AND WRITING

1. Look up the word "paradox" to make sure of its meaning, and then interpret the following paradoxical statements: that nature "is an infinite sphere, the centre of which is everywhere, the circumference nowhere"; that in "the smallest point in nature" one may see an "abyss"; that "in the womb of this abridged atom" lies "not only the visible universe" but all that one can conceive "of nature's immensity." What is Pascal's purpose in presenting us with these paradoxes? Why does his purpose necessitate paradox? Pascal was engaged in these reflections more than 300 years ago; has modern physics negated or affirmed his speculations? If one did not know of his importance as a mathematician and physicist, one might think that he

was a poet, indulging in "poetic" flights of imagination. What is there in the way he presents his conceptions that suggests the imagination of a poet?

2. What are the *two* "abysses" that he brings before the imagination, and why does he say that anyone who contemplates these "will be afraid"? Why does he suggest that, before these perspectives, one may suffer despair? What presumption does he find in the idea that nature is ultimately comprehensible?

3. What arguments does he give as to the limitation of our knowledge through the senses? We are accustomed to look upon science as giving us certainties (although modern physics has moved to a position where uncertainty seems to be the ruling principle, rather than certainty); where does Pascal stand on the certainty or uncertainty of scientific truth?

4. What does he mean by saying, "In comparison with these Infinites all finites are equal"? How does he justify the statement that man "is in a dependent alliance with everything"? What has that dependent state of man to do with Pascal's argument that we cannot arrive at complete understanding of nature?

5. Summarize in a sentence the last four paragraphs of the piece. What does Pascal mean here by the division of human nature into the "spiritual" and the "corporeal"? Why does he say that we wouldn't be able to know anything about ourselves if there weren't these two parts to our nature? What bearing do these last four paragraphs have on the main argument of the piece?

6. One of the strangest things in our civilization—unprecedented in other civilizations—is the wall we have built between science and poetry. In recent years the best brains in our country have been trying to make a break in that wall, so that the imagination of the poet and the imagination of the scientist could work together on common ground. Looking back on the last part of the first question here, do you find a suggestion for a short paper on this problem? If you have read the preceding piece, by Lucretius, you may have more material for the paper. Or, for a different kind of paper, you might take up Pascal's question as to the validity of knowledge through the senses. For instance, how dependent on the sense-reactions of the human observer are scientific tabulations made by means of microscope or telescope; or how dependent on a priori assumptions and on the personsonality of the observer are scientific tabulations of the behavior of rats?

Fred Hoyle ⋖ᔉ The Continuous Creation of the Universe

⋖ᔉ English mathematician, astronomer, and astrophysicist, born in 1915 in Yorkshire. Hoyle worked for many years at the California Institute of Technology and at the Mount Wilson and Palomar Observatories. He is Professor of Astronomy and Experimental Philosophy at Cambridge University. He has written a number of books on astronomy and solar physics. ᔐ⋗

AT THE RISK of seeming a little repetitive I should like to begin this chapter by recalling some of our previous results. One of the things I have been trying to do is to break up our survey of the Universe into distinct parts. We started with the Sun and our system of planets. To get an idea of the size of this system we took a model with the Sun represented by a ball about six inches in diameter. In spite of this enormous reduction of scale we found that our model would still cover the area of a small town. On the same scale the Earth has to be represented by a speck of dust, and the nearest stars are 2,000 miles away. So it is quite unwieldy to use this model to describe the positions of even the closest stars.

Some other means had to be found to get to grips with the distances of the stars in the Milky Way. Choosing light as our measure of distance, we saw that light takes several years to travel to us from near-by stars, and that many of the stars in the Milky Way are at a distance of as much as 1,000 light years. But the Milky Way is only a small bit of a great disk-shaped system of gas and stars that is turning in space like a great wheel. The diameter of the disk is about 60,000 light years. This distance is so colossal that there has only been time for the disk to turn round about twenty times since the oldest stars were born — about 4,000,000,000 years ago. And this is in spite of the tremendous speed of nearly 1,000,000 miles an hour at which the outer parts of the disk are moving. We also saw that the Sun and our planets lie together near the edge of our Galaxy, as this huge disk is called.

Now we shall go out into the depths of space far beyond the confines of our own Galaxy. Look out at the heavens on a clear night; if you want a really impressive sight do so from a steep mountainside or from a ship at sea. As I have said before, by looking at any part of the sky that is distant from the Milky Way you can see right out of the disk that forms our Galaxy. What lies out there? Not just scattered stars by themselves, but in every direction space is strewn with whole galaxies, each one like our own. Most of these other galaxies — or extra-galactic nebulae as astronomers often call them — are too faint to be seen with the naked eye, but vast numbers of them can be observed with a powerful telescope. When I say that these other galaxies are similar to our Galaxy, I do not mean that they are exactly alike. Some are much smaller than ours, others are not disk-shaped but nearly spherical in form. The basic similarity is that they are all enormous clouds of gas and stars, each one with anything from 100,000,000 to 10,000,000,000 or so members.

Although most of the other galaxies are somewhat different from ours, it is important to realize that some of them are indeed very like our Galaxy even so far as details are concerned. By good fortune one of the nearest of them, only about 700,000 light years away, seems to be practically a twin of our Galaxy. You can see it for yourself by looking in the constellation of Andromeda. With the naked eye it appears as a vague blur, but with a powerful telescope it shows up as one of the most impressive of all astronomical objects. On a good photograph of it you can easily pick out places where there are great clouds of dust. These clouds are just the sort of thing that in our own Galaxy produces the troublesome fog I mentioned in earlier talks. It is this fog that stops us seeing more than a small bit of our own Galaxy. If you want to get an idea of what our Galaxy would look like if it were seen from outside, the best way is to study this other one in Andromeda. If the truth be known I expect that in many places there living creatures are looking out across space at our Galaxy. They must be seeing much the same spectacle as we see when we look at their galaxy.

It would be possible to say a great deal about all these other galaxies: how they are spinning round like our own; how their brightest stars are supergiants, just like those of our Galaxy; and how in those where supergiants are common, wonderful spiral patterns are found. . . . We can also find exploding stars in these other galaxies. In particular, super-novae[1] are so brilliant that they show up even though they are very far off. Now the existence of supernovae in other galaxies has implications for our cosmology. You will remember that in a previous chapter I described the way in which planetary systems like our own come into being; the basic requirement of the process was the supernova explosion. So we can conclude, since supernovae occur in the other galaxies, planetary systems must exist there just as in our own. Moreover, by observing the other galaxies we get a far better idea of the rate at which supernovae occur than we could ever get from our Galaxy alone. A general survey by the American observers Baade and Zwicky has shown that on the average there is a supernova explosion every four or five hundred years in each galaxy. So, remembering our previous argument, you will see that on the average each galaxy must contain more than 1,000,000 planetary systems.

How many of these gigantic galaxies are there? Well, they are strewn through space as far as we can see with the most powerful telescopes. Spaced apart at an average distance of rather more than 1,000,000 light years, they certainly continue out to the fantastic distance of 1,000,000,000 light years. Our telescopes fail to penetrate further than that, so we cannot be certain that the galaxies extend still deeper into space, but we feel pretty sure that they do. One of the questions we shall have to consider later is what lies beyond the range of our most powerful instruments. But even within the range of observation there are about 100,000,000 galaxies. With upward of 1,000,000 planetary systems per galaxy the combined total for the parts of the Universe that we can see

[1] The word *nova* (plural *novae*) means "new." A supernova is a star whose light and energy output is extraordinarily accelerated.

comes out at more than a hundred million million. I find myself wondering whether somewhere among them there is a cricket team that could beat the Australians.

We now come to the important question of where this great swarm of galaxies has come from. Perhaps I should first remind you of what was said when we were discussing the origin of the stars. We saw that in the space between the stars of our Galaxy there is a tenuous gas, the interstellar gas. At one time our Galaxy was a whirling disk of gas with no stars in it. Out of the gas, clouds condensed, and then in each cloud further condensations were formed. This went on until finally stars were born. Stars were formed in the other galaxies in exactly the same way. But we can go further than this and extend the condensation idea to include the origin of the galaxies themselves. Just as the basic step in explaining the origin of the stars is the recognition that a tenuous gas pervades the space within a galaxy, so the basic step in explaining the origin of the galaxies is the recognition that a still more tenuous gas fills the whole of space. It is out of this general background material, as I shall call it, that the galaxies have condensed.

Here now is a question that is important for our cosmology. What is the present density of the background material? The average density is so low that a pint measure would contain only about one atom. But small as this is, the total amount of the background material exceeds about a thousandfold the combined quantity of material in all the galaxies put together. This may seem surprising but it is a consequence of the fact that the galaxies occupy only a very small fraction of the whole of space. You see here the characteristic signature of the New Cosmology. We have seen that inside our Galaxy the interstellar gas outweighs the material in all the stars put together. Now we see that the background material outweighs by a large margin all the galaxies put together. And just as it is the interstellar gas that controls the situation inside our Galaxy, so it is the background material that controls the Universe as a whole. This will become increasingly clear as we go on.

The degree to which the background material has to be compressed to form a galaxy is not at all comparable with the tremendous compression necessary to produce a star. This you can see by thinking of a model in which our Galaxy is represented by a fifty-cent piece. Then the blob of background material out of which our Galaxy condensed would be only about a foot in diameter. This incidentally is the right way to think about the Universe as a whole. If in your mind's eye you take the average galaxy to be about the size of a bee — a small bee, a honeybee, not a bumblebee — our Galaxy, which is a good deal larger than the average, would be roughly represented in shape and size by the fifty-cent piece, and the average spacing of the galaxies would be about three yards, and the range of telescopic vision about a mile. So sit back and imagine a swarm of bees spaced about three yards apart and stretching away from you in all directions for a distance of about a mile. Now for each honeybee substitute the vast bulk of a galaxy and you have an idea of the Universe that has been revealed by the large American telescopes.

Next I must introduce the idea that this colossal swarm is not static: it is expanding. There are some people who seem to think that it would be a good idea if it was static. I disagree with this idea, if only because a static universe would be very dull. To show you what I mean by this I should like to point out that the Universe is wound up in two ways — that is to say, energy can be got out of the background material in two ways. Whenever a new galaxy is formed, gravitation supplies energy. For instance, gravitation supplies the energy of the rotation that develops when a galaxy condenses out of the background material. And gravitation again supplies energy during every subsequent condensation of the interstellar gas inside a galaxy. It is because of this energy that a star becomes hot when it is born. The second source of energy lies in the atomic nature of the background material. It seems likely that this was originally pure hydrogen. This does not mean that the background material is now entirely pure hydrogen, because it gets slightly adulterated by some of the material expelled by the exploding supernovae. As a source of energy hydrogen does not come into operation until high temperatures develop — and this only arises when stars condense. It is this second source of energy that is more familiar and important to us on the Earth.

Now, why would a Universe that was static on a large scale, that was not expanding in fact, be uninteresting? Because of the following sequence of events. Even if the Universe were static on a large scale it would not be locally static: that is to say, the background material would condense into galaxies, and after a few thousand million years this process would be completed — no background would be left. Furthermore, the gas out of which the galaxies were initially composed would condense into stars. When this stage was reached hydrogen would be steadily converted into helium. After several hundreds of thousands of millions of years this process would be everywhere completed and all the stars would evolve toward the black dwarfs[2] I mentioned in a previous chapter. So finally the whole Universe would become entirely dead. This would be the running down of the Universe that was described so graphically by Jeans.[3]

One of my main aims will be to explain why we get a different answer to this when we take account of the dynamic nature of the Universe. You might like to know something about the observational evidence that the Universe is indeed in a dynamic state of expansion. Perhaps you've noticed that a whistle from an approaching train has a higher pitch, and from a receding train a lower pitch, than a similar whistle from a stationary train. Light emitted by a moving source has the same property. The pitch of the light is lowered, or as we usually say reddened, if the source is moving away from us. Now we observe that the light from the galaxies is reddened, and the degree of reddening increases proportionately with the distance of a galaxy. The natural explanation of this is that the galaxies are rushing away from each other at enormous speeds, which for the most distant galaxies that we can see with the biggest telescopes become comparable with the speed of light itself.

My nonmathematical friends often tell me that they find it difficult to picture this expansion. Short of using a lot of mathematics I cannot do better than use the analogy of a balloon with a large number of dots marked on its surface. If the balloon is blown up the distances between the dots increase in the same way as the distances between the galaxies. Here I should give a warning that this analogy must not be taken too strictly. There are several important respects in which it is definitely misleading. For example, the dots on the surface of a balloon would themselves increase in size as the balloon was being blown up. This is not the case for the galaxies, for their internal gravitational fields are sufficiently strong to prevent any such expansion. A further weakness of our analogy is that the surface of an ordinary balloon is two dimensional — that is to say, the points of its surface can be described by two co-ordinates; for example, by latitude and longitude. In the case of the Universe we must

[2] Dead stars.

[3] Sir James Jeans (1877-1946), celebrated English mathematician, physicist, and astronomer.

think of the surface as possessing a third dimension. This is not as difficult as it may sound. We are all familiar with pictures in perspective —
pictures in which artists have represented three-dimensional scenes on
two-dimensional canvases. So it is not really a difficult conception to
imagine the three dimensions of space as being confined to the surface
of a balloon. But then what does the radius of the balloon represent, and
what does it mean to say that the balloon is being blown up? The answer to this is that the radius of the balloon is a measure of time, and
the passage of time has the effect of blowing up the balloon. This will
give you a very rough, but useful, idea of the sort of theory investigated
by the mathematician.

The balloon analogy brings out a very important point. It shows we
must not imagine that we are situated at the center of the Universe, just
because we see all the galaxies to be moving away from us. For, whichever dot you care to choose on the surface of the balloon, you will find
that the other dots all move away from it. In other words, whichever
galaxy you happen to be in, the other galaxies will appear to be receding from you.

Now let us consider the recession of the galaxies in a little more
detail. The greater the distance of a galaxy the faster it is receding. Every
time you double the distance you double the speed of recession. The
speeds come out as vast beyond all precedent. Near-by galaxies are
moving outward at several million miles an hour, whereas the most distant ones that can be seen with our biggest telescopes are receding at
over 200,000,000 miles an hour. This leads us to the obvious question:
If we could see galaxies lying at even greater distances, would their
speeds be still vaster? Nobody seriously doubts that this would be so,
which gives rise to a very curious situation that I will now describe.

Galaxies lying at only about twice the distance of the furthest ones
that actually can be observed with the new telescope at Mount Palomar
would be moving away from us at a speed that equalled light itself.
Those at still greater distances would have speeds of recession exceeding that of light. Many people find this extremely puzzling because they
have learned from Einstein's special theory of relativity that no material
body can have a speed greater than light. This is true enough in the
special theory of relativity which refers to a particularly simple system
of space and time. But it is not true in Einstein's general theory of relativity, and it is in terms of the general theory that the Universe has to be

discussed. The point is rather difficult, but I can do something toward making it a little clearer. The further a galaxy is away from us the more its distance will increase during the time required by its light to reach us. Indeed, if it is far enough away the light never reaches us at all because its path stretches faster than the light can make progress. This is what is meant by saying that the speed of recession exceeds the velocity of light. Events occurring in a galaxy at such a distance can never be observed at all by anyone inside our Galaxy, no matter how patient the observer and no matter how powerful his telescope. All the galaxies that we actually see are ones that lie close enough for their light to reach us in spite of the expansion of space that's going on. But the struggle of the light against the expansion of space does show itself, as I said before, in the reddening of the light.

As you will easily guess, there must be intermediate cases where a galaxy is at such a distance that, so to speak, the light it emits neither gains ground nor loses it. In this case the path between us and the galaxy stretches at just such a rate as exactly compensates for the velocity of the light. The light gets lost on the way. It is a case, as the Red Queen remarked to Alice, of "taking all the running you can do to keep in the same place." We know fairly accurately how far away a galaxy has to be for this special case to occur. The answer is about 2,000,000,000 light years, which is only about twice as far as the distances that we expect the giant telescope at Mount Palomar to penetrate. This means that we are already observing about half as far into space as we can ever hope to do. If we built a telescope a million times as big as the one at Mount Palomar we could scarcely double our present range of vision. So what it amounts to is that owing to the expansion of the Universe we can never observe events that happen outside a certain quite definite finite region of space. We refer to this finite region as the observable Universe. The word "observable" here does not mean that we actually observe, but what we could observe if we were equipped with perfect telescopes.

So far we have been entirely concerned with the rich fruits of twentieth century observational astronomy and in particular with the results achieved by Hubble[4] and his colleagues. We have seen that all space is strewn with galaxies, and we have seen that space itself is continually expanding. Further questions come crowding in: What causes

---

[4] E. P. Hubble (1889-1953), American astronomer and director of Mt. Wilson Observatory.

the expansion? Does the expansion mean that as time goes on the observable Universe is becoming less and less occupied by matter? Is space finite or infinite? How old is the Universe? To settle these questions we shall now have to consider new trains of thought. These will lead us to strange conclusions.

First I will consider the older ideas — that is to say, the ideas of the nineteen-twenties and the nineteen-thirties — and then I will go on to offer my own opinion. Broadly speaking, the older ideas fall into two groups. One of them is distinguished by the assumption that the Universe started its life a finite time ago in a single huge explosion. On this supposition the present expansion is a relic of the violence of this explosion. This big bang idea seemed to me to be unsatisfactory even before detailed examination showed that it leads to serious difficulties. For when we look at our own Galaxy there is not the smallest sign that such an explosion ever occurred. This might not be such a cogent argument against the explosion school of thought if our Galaxy had turned out to be much younger than the whole Universe. But this is not so. On the contrary, in some of these theories the Universe comes out to be younger than our astrophysical estimates of the age of our own Galaxy. Another really serious difficulty arises when we try to reconcile the idea of an explosion with the requirement that the galaxies have condensed out of diffuse background material. The two concepts of explosion and condensation are obviously contradictory, and it is easy to show, if you postulate an explosion of sufficient violence to explain the expansion of the Universe, that condensations looking at all like the galaxies could never have been formed.

And so we come to the second group of theories that attempt to explain the expansion of the Universe. These all work by monkeying with the law of gravitation. The conventional idea that two particles attract each other is only accepted if their distance apart is not too great. At really large distances, so the argument goes, the two particles repel each other instead. On this basis it can be shown that if the density of the background material is sufficiently small, expansion must occur. But once again there is a difficulty in reconciling all this with the requirement that the background material must condense to form the galaxies. For once the law of gravitation has been modified in this way the tendency is for the background material to be torn apart rather than for it to condense into galaxies. Actually there is just one way in which a theory along these lines can be built so as to get round this difficulty. This is a theory worked out by Lemaître[5] which was often discussed by Eddington in his popular books. But we now know that on this theory the galaxies would have to be vastly older than our astrophysical studies show them actually to be. So even this has to be rejected.

I should like now to approach more recent ideas by describing what would be the fate of our observable universe if any of these older theories had turned out to be correct. According to them every receding galaxy will eventually increase its distance from us until it passes beyond the limit of the observable universe — that is to say, they will move to a distance beyond the critical limit of about 2,000,000,000 light years that I have already mentioned. When this happens they will disappear — nothing that then occurs within them can ever be observed from our Galaxy. So if any of the older theories were right we should end in a seemingly empty universe, or at any rate in a universe that was empty apart perhaps from one or two very close galaxies that became attached to our Galaxy as satellites. Nor would this situation take very long to develop. Only about 10,000,000,000 years — that is to say, about a fifth of the lifetime of the Sun — would be needed to empty the sky of the 100,000,000 or so galaxies that we can now observe there.

My own view is very different. Although I think there is no doubt that every galaxy we observe to be receding from us will in about 10,-000,000,000 years have passed entirely beyond the limit of vision of an observer in our Galaxy, yet I think that such an observer would still be able to see about the same number of galaxies as we do now. By this I mean that new galaxies will have condensed out of the background material at just about the rate necessary to compensate for those that are being lost as a consequence of their passing beyond our observable universe. At first sight it might be thought that this could not go on indefinitely because the material forming the background would ultimately become exhausted. The reason why this is not so, is that new material appears to compensate for the background material that is constantly being condensed into galaxies. This is perhaps the most surprising of all the conceptions of the New Cosmology. For I find myself forced

[5] Georges Lemaître, Belgian astrophysicist who postulated the theory that the universe originated in an explosion, producing the force by which it continues to expand. Sir Arthur Stanley Eddington (1882–1944) was an English astronomer, astrophysicist, mathematician, and author of books on these sciences.

to assume that the nature of the Universe requires continuous creation — the perpetual bringing into being of new background material.

The idea that matter is created continuously represents our ultimate goal in this book. It would be wrong to suppose that the idea itself is a new one. I know of references to the continuous creation of matter that go back more than twenty years, and I have no doubt that a close inquiry would show that the idea, in its vaguest form, goes back very much further than that. What is new about it is this: it has now been found possible to put a hitherto vague idea in a precise mathematical form. It is only when this has been done that the consequences of any physical idea can be worked out and its scientific value assessed. I should perhaps explain that besides my personal views, which I shall now be putting forward, there are two other lines of thought on this matter. One comes from the German scientist P. Jordan, whose views differ from my own by so wide a gulf that it would be too wide a digression to discuss them. The other line of attack has come from the Cambridge scientists H. Bondi and T. Gold, who, although using quite a different form of argument from the one I adopted, have reached conclusions almost identical with those I am now going to discuss.

The most obvious question to ask about continuous creation is this: Where does the created material come from? It does not come from anywhere. Material simply appears — it is created. At one time the various atoms composing the material do not exist, and at a later time they do. This may seem a very strange idea and I agree that it is, but in science it does not matter how strange an idea may seem so long as it works — that is to say, so long as the idea can be expressed in a precise form and so long as its consequences are found to be in agreement with observation. Some people have argued that continuous creation introduces a new assumption into science — and a very startling assumption at that. Now I do not agree that continuous creation is an additional assumption. It is certainly a new hypothesis, but it only replaces a hypothesis that lies concealed in the older theories, which assume, as I have said before, that the whole of the matter in the Universe was created in one big bang at a particular time in the remote past. On scientific grounds this big bang assumption is much the less palatable of the two. For it is an irrational process that cannot be described in scientific terms. Continuous creation, on the other hand, can be represented by precise mathematical equations whose consequences can be worked out and compared with observation. On philosophical grounds too I cannot see any good reason for preferring the big bang idea. Indeed it seems to me in the philosophical sense to be a distinctly unsatisfactory notion, since it puts the basic assumption out of sight where it can never be challenged by a direct appeal to observation.

Perhaps you may think that the whole question of the creation of the Universe could be avoided in some way. But this is not so. To avoid the issue of creation it would be necessary for all the material of the Universe to be infinitely old, and this it cannot be for a very practical reason. For if this were so, there could be no hydrogen left in the Universe. As I think I demonstrated when I talked about the insides of the stars, hydrogen is being steadily converted into helium throughout the Universe and this conversion is a one-way process — that is to say, hydrogen cannot be produced in any appreciable quantity through the breakdown of the other elements. How comes it then that the Universe consists almost entirely of hydrogen? If matter were infinitely old this would be quite impossible. So we see that the Universe being what it is, the creation issue simply cannot be dodged. And I think that of all the various possibilities that have been suggested, continuous creation is easily the most satisfactory.

Now what are the consequences of continuous creation? Perhaps the most surprising result of the mathematical theory is that the average density of the background material must stay constant. The new material does not appear in a concentrated form in small localized regions but is spread throughout the whole of space. The average rate of appearance of matter amounts to no more than the creation of one atom in the course of about a year in a volume equal to that of a moderate-sized skyscraper. As you will realize, it would be quite impossible to detect such a rate of creation by direct experiment. But although this seems such a slow rate when judged by ordinary ideas, it is not small when you consider that it is happening everywhere in space. The total rate for the observable universe alone is about a hundred million, million, million, million, million tons per second. Do not let this surprise you because, as I have said, the volume of the observable universe is very large. Indeed I must now make it quite clear that here we have the answer to our question. Why does the Universe expand? For it is this creation that drives the Universe. The new material produces an outward pressure that leads to the steady expansion. But it does much more than that. With continuous creation the apparent contradiction between the expansion of the Universe and the requirement that the background material shall be able to condense into galaxies is completely overcome. For it can be shown that once an irregularity occurs in the background material a galaxy must eventually be formed. Such irregularities are constantly being produced by the gravitational effect of the galaxies themselves. For the gravitational field of the galaxies disturbs the background material and causes irregularities to form within it. So the background material must give a steady supply of new galaxies. Moreover, the created material also supplies unending quantities of atomic energy, since by arranging that newly created material should be composed of hydrogen we explain why in spite of the fact that hydrogen is being consumed in huge quantities in the stars, the Universe is nevertheless observed to be overwhelmingly composed of it.

We must now leave this extraordinary business of continuous creation for a moment to consider the question of what lies beyond the observable part of the Universe. In the first place you must let me ask, Does this question have any meaning? According to the theory it does. Theory requires the galaxies to go on forever, even though we cannot see them. That is to say, the galaxies are expanding out into an infinite space. There is no end to it all. And what is more, apart from the possibility of there being a few freak galaxies, one bit of this infinite space will behave in the same way as any other bit.

The same thing applies to time. You will have noticed that I have used the concepts of space and time as if they could be treated separately. According to the relativity theory this is a dangerous thing to do. But it so happens that it can be done with impunity in our Universe, although it is easy to imagine other universes where it could not be done. What I mean by this is that a division between space and time can be made and this division can be used throughout the whole of our Universe. This is a very important and special property of our Universe, which I think it is important to take into account in forming the equations that decide the way in which matter is created.

Perhaps you will allow me a short diversion here to answer the question: How does the idea of infinite space fit in with the balloon analogy that I mentioned earlier? Suppose you were blowing up a balloon that could never burst. Then it is clear that if you went on blowing long enough you could make its size greater than anything I cared to specify, greater for instance than a billion billion miles or a billion billion billion miles and so on. This is what is meant by saying that the radius of the balloon tends to infinity. If you are used to thinking in terms of the balloon analogy, this is the case that gives you what we call an infinite space.

Now let us suppose that a film is made from any space position in the Universe. To make the film, let a still picture be taken at each instant of time. This, by the way, is what we are doing in our astronomical observations. We are actually taking the picture of the Universe at one instant of time — the present. Next, let all the stills be run together so as to form a continuous film. What would the film look like? Galaxies would be observed to be continually condensing out of the background material. The general expansion of the whole system would be clear, but though the galaxies seemed to be moving away from us there would be a curious sameness about the film. It would be only in the details of each galaxy that changes would be seen. The overall picture would stay the same because of the compensation whereby the galaxies that were constantly disappearing through the expansion of the Universe were replaced by newly forming galaxies. A casual observer who went to sleep during the showing of the film would find it difficult to see much change when he awoke. How long would our film show go on? It would go on forever.

There is a complement to this result that we can see by running our film backward. Then new galaxies would appear at the outer fringes of our picture as faint objects that come gradually closer to us. For if the film were run backward the Universe would appear to contract. The galaxies would come closer and closer to us until they evaporated before our eyes. First the stars of a galaxy would evaporate back into the gas from which they were formed. Then the gas in the galaxy would evaporate back into the general background from which it had condensed. The background material itself would stay of constant density, not through matter being created, but through matter disappearing. How far could we run our hypothetical film back into the past? Again according to the theory, forever. After we had run backward for about 5,000,000,000 years our own Galaxy itself would disappear before our eyes. But although important details like this would no doubt be of great interest to us there would again be a general sameness about the whole proceeding. Whether we run the film backward or forward the large-scale features of the Universe remain unchanged.

It is a simple consequence of all this that the total amount of energy that can be observed at any one time must be equal to the amount observed at any other time. This means that energy is conserved. So continuous creation does not lead to nonconservation of energy as one or two critics have suggested. The reverse is the case for without continuous creation the total energy observed must decrease with time.

We see, therefore, that no large-scale changes in the Universe can be expected to take place in the future. But individual galaxies will change and you may well want to know what is likely to happen to our Galaxy. This issue cannot be decided by observation because none of the galaxies that we observe can be much more than 10,000,000,000 years old as yet, and we need to observe much older ones to find out anything about the ultimate fate of a galaxy. The reason why no observable galaxy is appreciably older than this is that a new galaxy condensing close by our own would move away from us and pass out of the observable region of space in only about 10,000,000,000 years. So we have to decide the ultimate fate of our Galaxy again from theory, and this is what theory predicts. It will become steadily more massive as more and more background material gets pulled into it. After about 10,000,000,000 years it is likely that our Galaxy will have succeeded in gathering quite a cloud of gas and satellite bodies. Where this will ultimately lead is difficult to say with any precision. The distant future of the Galaxy is to some extent bound up with an investigation made about thirty years ago by Schwarzschild, who found that very strange things happen when a body grows particularly massive. It becomes difficult, for instance, for light emitted by the body ever to get out into surrounding space. When this stage is reached, further growth is likely to be strongly inhibited. Just what it would then be like to live in our Galaxy I should very much like to know.

To conclude, I should like to stress that so far as the Universe as a whole is concerned the essential difference made by the idea of continuous creation of matter is this: Without continuous creation the Universe must evolve toward a dead state in which all the matter is condensed into a vast number of dead stars. The details of the way this happens are different in the different theories that have been put forward, but the outcome is always the same. With continuous creation, on the other hand, the Universe has an infinite future in which all its present very large-scale features will be preserved.

1. Since this piece deals with some of the most spectacular and revolutionary conceptions of modern astrophysics, conceptions that are bound to be a bit difficult to follow if one has not done special reading in this field, it is advisable that the student attempt to outline briefly the main points of the argument. (Hoyle's references to earlier chapters of the book should give no trouble, for he explains each reference.) Having made your outline— which presumably shows Hoyle's conclusion about "continuous creation" and the steps leading up to the conclusion—look back now over the first five or six paragraphs of the piece. Why, in these first paragraphs, does Hoyle try to illustrate, by various means, the immensity of the universe? Or, to put the question in another way, why do we need to have before us that vision of immensity in order to follow Hoyle's argument up to its conclusion about "continuous creation"?

2. One of the first steps in the argument is: Where does the great swarm of galaxies come from? Well, where does it come from? By what kind of reasoning does Hoyle postulate that a "tenuous gas fills the whole of space"? What is the density of that "background material"? (If you have read the excerpts from Lucretius, a few pages earlier, do you find any similarity between Hoyle's "tenuous gas" and Lucretius' "generative bodies of matter" or "first-beginnings" whirling about in the "void"?)

3. The next step is that the universe is not static, but "expanding." Hoyle says that there are two supplies of energy for that expansion; what are those two sources of energy? What would happen to all the stars if the universe were "static," running down to a dead end? What evidence is there in the degree of redness in the light of the galaxies that the universe is expanding—that is, dynamic rather than static?

4. Point out each of the analogies Hoyle uses in this piece. Why is it particularly necessary to use analogies with common experiences or with things easy to visualize when one is attempting to explain to the layman the kind of conceptions with which Hoyle is dealing?

5. When the recession of the galaxies goes beyond the speed of light, why would not telescopes bigger than that of Palomar allow us to see them?

What does Hoyle find wrong with the "big bang" idea? Why is the idea of
the creation of the universe by an explosion that took place "a finite time
ago" (and what does that phrase mean?) contradicted by the fact that
condensation of the galaxies is still going on?

6. At what precise point does Hoyle give his own explanation of why "condensation" and "expansion" are going on and are not contradictory to each
other? Why does he say that "the nature of the universe requires continuous
creation . . ."? When he puts the question, "Where does the created material come from?" and answers, "It does not come from anywhere," what
is his explanation for this anomaly? In what way does "continuous creation" explain the expansion of the universe? In what way does it also explain the condensation taking place in the galaxies?

7. Note how briefly and comprehensively Hoyle is able to round up in three
sentences, in the last paragraph, the extremely complex ideas of the chapter; and try, in your own expository writing, to keep in mind this example
of a firmly conclusive ending. For a paper assignment, you might (if you
have done reading in this field) criticize and evaluate Hoyle's argument.
Or, if you have read the selection from Lucretius, you might compare the
cosmology of Lucretius with that of Hoyle. Or, having in mind the "scientific" argument against the divine creation of the universe, you might write
on the religious implications of Hoyle's hypothesis of "continuous creation."
Or, if you have read the immediately preceding excerpts from both Lucretius and Pascal, as well as the Hoyle, you might write a comparison of the
three.

The Order of the Mind

THE MORE *scientific and technological knowledge we acquire, and the
more this knowledge is translated into power over the external
world—so that we can excite nature into producing phenomena it
never dreamed of, including the phenomenon of its own destruction—
the more important it becomes to acquire knowledge about the
knower and the instrument by which he does his knowing. But in
the area of knowledge about the human mind we are under the
disadvantage that here the knower and the object of knowledge are
the same thing—or, as William James put it, the thinker is the
thoughts. It is as if one should try to get out of the woods by climbing
trees. So far in our civilization, the great poets and novelists have
given us much more useful information about the mind than the
scientists have. Even today, analytical psychology has an uneasy status
in the scientific establishment and is almost disreputable in
comparison, say, with the study of the psychology of rats. Laurens
van der Post gives a striking instance of this tragicomic discrepancy.
While he was organizing his expedition into the Kalahari Desert
in search of the Bushmen, he was approached by two scientists who
wished to accompany the expedition in order to make cranial
measurements of Bushman heads; when he asked them if they were*

concerned with what went on inside the heads, they showed
no interest at all.

The pieces in the following section are roughly divided under the
headings "The Older Psyche" and "Theories of Knowledge."
In his epoch-making INTERPRETATION OF DREAMS, published in the
first year of the twentieth century, Sigmund Freud illuminated and
brought within our vision the suppressed and rejected world of the
night, where we exist for half our lives, and which surrounds, supports,
and nourishes our waking consciousness as the sea does an island.
In a noble elegy written at the time of Freud's death in 1939,
W. H. Auden compares the dark and dangerous and difficult mission
of the Viennese psychiatrist to that of Dante: "He went his way / Down
among the Lost People, like Dante," while, with the pathos of the
shades of the dead in Dante's INFERNO, the mentally ill, the helpless
neurotics and psychotics, "waited to enter / The bright circle of his
recognition." And Auden sums up in few words the enormous
change Freud wrought in our understanding of ourselves:

> To us he is no more a person
> Now, but a whole climate of opinion.[1]

Like Freud's piece on "Typical Dreams," C. G. Jung's discussion
of "The Personal and the Collective Unconscious" is a classic of the
literature of analytical psychology. The first few paragraphs of the
piece give a brief and useful summary of Freud's conception of
the unconscious mind, and Jung's critique of it. Although Jung revered
Freud as maestro in his field, the difference between the two men
is radical: while Freud's psychology sends us back to find the motives
of our behavior in infancy and childhood, and is as fatefully
determinative as Greek tragedy, Jung opens up resources of the mind
immensely older than personal experience and infinitely creative.

Laurens van der Post, in his "Love, the Aboriginal Tracker,"
presents his own characteristic image of the older psyche, in the person

[1] From "In Memory of Sigmund Freud," in *The Collected Poetry of W. H. Auden.*
Copyright 1940 by W. H. Auden. Reprinted by permission of Random House, Inc.

*of the little Bushman, the oldest man in Africa, a fabulous hunter
and artist who derives all his skills and lore from the "first people"—
the stars and the animals. Described by van der Post with the
eloquence of deep affection, the Bushman becomes a symbol of the
instinctive, intuitive part of ourselves that relates us to all other
creatures and gives us our only security in the universe—a part of
ourselves that our culture has neglected and disvalued, and that has
been pushed back into the hinterland of the unconscious as the
Bushman (despised by both Blacks and Whites in Africa as scarcely
human) has been pushed back into the Kalahari desert.*

*A key principle in the psychology of both Freud and Jung is that
of "integration"—deliberate integration of more and more of the
contents of the unconscious into consciousness. The whole of
Marcel Proust's great novel* REMEMBRANCE OF THINGS PAST *might be
looked upon as a study in psychological integration, between all the old
and buried, lost, rejected, and dismembered "selves" that make up
the self. The brief episode from the novel given here is a famous
illustration of that process, its immense difficulty and the deep joy
of self-recovery that attends it.*

*The short selections from the seventeenth- and eighteenth-century
philosophers, grouped under "Theories of Knowledge," have a much
more abstract character and view the mind in a very different way.
The primary question is: How do we know what we know?
To put the question in a rougher way: How does the idea of a
mountain or a goat or a freight train or an "I" get into our heads,
how can we be sure that it represents something "real," and how
trustworthy are the mental operations that link together the mountain
and the goat and the freight train and the "I"? These considerations
are not everybody's cup of tea, and if one has no taste for them
one may pass them by with a cold eye. But there are also those students
who have a natural affinity for philosophical abstraction, and who
may find intellectual excitement in the dialectic of Locke, Berkeley,
and Hume, the dialectic that has issued in the reigning modern*

philosophy of Positivism. And there, behind it all, sits Descartes in his shabby dressing gown before the hearth, fumbling with that piece of melting beeswax, deciding what is to become the ultimate basis of the modern sense of reality with his axiom "I think, therefore I am," thus projecting upon the twentieth century the Existentialist trauma, the scission of man as a "thinking thing" from all the rest of the universe.

THE OLDER PSYCHE

Laurens van der Post ⋅⋅⋅§ Love, the Aboriginal Tracker

⋅§ See biographical note on page 429. The selection is from *The Heart of the Hunter*. This book is a sequel to Colonel van der Post's *The Lost World of the Kalahari*, which describes his search for remnants of the aboriginal race of Bushmen in the Kalahari desert of South Africa. ᒃ⋅

I RECALLED something written many years ago: "Love is the aboriginal tracker, the Bushman on the faded desert spoor of our lost selves."[1] There was a great lost world to be rediscovered and rebuilt, not in the

[1] The Bushmen are regarded by ethnologists as the aborigines of central and southern Africa, related to the Pygmies. The few who remain of this ancient race live nomadically in remote wastes of the Kalahari desert, where Colonel van der Post discovered them and lived with them for several weeks, recording their rich folklore. They are extraordinarily skilled trackers and hunters, their only weapon the bow and arrow.

Kalahari but in the wasteland of our spirit where we had driven the first things of life, as we had driven the little Bushman into the desert of Southern Africa. There was indeed a cruelly denied and neglected first child of life, a Bushman in each of us. I remembered how audiences all over the world reacted when I spoke about the Bushman. Without exception their imaginations were, at the first description of his person, immediately alert. They were audiences of such different histories, cultures and races as Spanish, Swiss, Italian, Indian, French, Japanese, Finnish, German, Scandinavian, American and assorted British. I felt the Bushman could not have excited the interest of them all unless he represented some elemental common denominator in such diversity of spirit. Most significant, perhaps, was the large number of people who wrote to me saying they had dreamt about the Bushman after first hearing me talk about him. Many letters would begin in the same way: "I must tell you: it is so strange. I hardly ever dream, but the night after your talk I had a dream about a Bushman."

One dream moved me so much that I have remembered it in some detail. It was that of a Spaniard, who told me: "I have not had a dream for years, but last night after the talk I dreamt I was in a great dilapidated building rather like a neglected castle I once knew. Somewhere inside it a woman was weeping as if her heart would break. I rushed from room to room along corridor after corridor and down stair after stair, trying to find her so that I could comfort her. Everywhere I went was empty; the dust thick on the floor and cobwebs on the wall. I was in despair of ever finding her, though the sound of her weeping grew louder and more pitiful in my ears. Suddenly one of your little Bushmen appeared in a window. He beckoned to me urgently with his bow, indicating that he would lead me to the woman. I started out to follow him, but immediately there was a growl behind me. To my horror one of the fiercest of the wolfhounds, which I let loose in the grounds of my own house as watchdogs every night, leapt forward and dashed straight at the Bushman. I tried to call the hound back but I could not find my voice. In the struggle to find it, I woke up in great distress and could not sleep again. In fact I have felt out of sorts with myself the whole of today. Now what do you say to that?"

What indeed could one say about it, even now, except that although these great plains and mountains of South Africa through which I travelled on my way to the sea may know the Bushman no more, "the prophetic soul of the wide world dreaming on things to come," as Shakespeare put it, knew him still and was glad to meet him again on the lips of living men? Anything that set a dreamless heart dreaming again was not to be despised. For the dream is the keeper of the wonder of which I have spoken. It is there that we must go to "take upon ourselves the mystery of things as if we were God's spies."[2] The first time I came across this great cry which would deliver Lear from imprisonment in his own anguish, not by removing his suffering, but by giving it a meaning, the word spies troubled me greatly. After the trumpet call of the opening phrase it sounded oddly pejorative to me. Now I realized it could not have been more apt. Intimation of the new meaning to be lived never comes by battalions but by single spies. It comes as an improbable summons in some lonely, seemingly ill-equipped and often suffering individual heart, operating far ahead of the armies of new life, like a spy behind the lines of the totalitarian spirit of its day. The mystery we must take upon ourselves in order to free our arrested being is that of the first things of life, which our twentieth-century civilization puts last, but of which the Bushman gives us so consummate an image, representing the child before whom we are commanded to humble ourselves and to become like if we are to enter the Kingdom.

I thought, therefore, I would begin by trying to serve the first things in myself, to turn to the point of origin in myself, to my own moment of innocence when the first things of Africa came over the rim of imagination like starlight out of the night so dearly beloved by my native continent. I realized that earliest and latest, old and new, primitive and

[2] From *King Lear,* Act V, scene 3, where Lear and Cordelia are brought in as prisoners. The old king says:

> Come, let's away to prison;
> We two alone will sing like birds i' th' cage.
> When thou dost ask me blessing, I'll kneel down
> And ask of thee forgiveness. So we'll live,
> And pray, and sing, and tell old tales, and laugh
> At gilded butterflies, and hear poor rogues
> Talk of court news; and we'll talk with them too,
> Who loses and who wins; who's in, who's out;
> And take upon 's the mystery of things
> As if we were God's spies; and we'll wear out,
> In a wall'd prison, packs and sects of great ones,
> That ebb and flow by the moon.

The word "spies" here has the meaning of "scouts," sent ahead to spy out "the mystery of things." (Also below, not "by battalions but by single spies.")

civilized had met in my life in a way which was perhaps unique. I had experienced primitive Africa, the first life of the land. If I succeeded in rediscovering my own first experience of the first things of Africa, if I honoured them in myself, I might help others to rediscover and honour the same things in themselves. It would not matter that I possessed no expert training or special knowledge. Consciously or unconsciously, one lives not only one's own life but also the life of one's time. What was valid in my own experience would be valid in a measure also for my own day. I could let my experience of the primitive pattern of creation speak for me, since I have taken part in the most ancient working of the human spirit as it had been transmitted from the lives of the first people of Africa. I would merely be the bridge between the first pattern of things and my own time. I would use what knowledge I had of the first Africa, in particular the little I had now learnt of the Bushman, his mind and way of life in the desert, merely to interpret the experience into a contemporary idiom and so try to make it accessible to the modern imagination. That, however amateurish or small, could be the beginning of better things, because what the world lacks today is not so much knowledge of these first things as experience of them.

We know so much intellectually, indeed, that we are in danger of becoming the prisoners of our knowledge. We suffer from a hubris[3] of the mind. We have abolished superstition of the heart only to install a superstition of the intellect in its place. We behave as if there were some magic in mere thought, and we use thinking for purposes for which it was never designed. As a result we are no longer sufficiently aware of the importance of what we cannot know intellectually, what we must know in other ways, of the living experience before and beyond our transitory knowledge. The passion of the spirit, which would inspire man to live his finest hour dangerously on the exposed frontier of his knowledge, seemed to me to have declined into a vague and arid restlessness hiding behind an arrogant intellectualism, as a child of arrested development behind the skirts of its mother.

Intellectually, modern man knows almost all there is to know about the pattern of creation in himself, the forms it takes, the surface designs

[3] Arrogance leading to wanton disregard of natural and moral law. The term is often used of the heroes of classical tragedy, as that kind of "pride" which blinds them to the consequences of their acts.

it describes. He has measured the pitch of its rhythms and carefully recorded all the mechanics. From the outside he sees the desirable first object of life more clearly perhaps than man has ever seen it before. But less and less does he experience the process within. Less and less is he capable of committing himself body and soul to the creative experiment that is continually seeking to fire him and to charge his little life with great objective meaning. Cut off by accumulated knowledge from the heart of his own living experience, he moves among a comfortable rubble of material possession, alone and unbelonging, sick, poor, starved of meaning. How different the naked little Bushman, who could carry all he possessed in one hand! Whatever his life lacked, I never felt it was meaning. Meaning for him died only when we bent him to our bright twentieth-century will. Otherwise, he was rich where we were poor; he walked clear-cut through my mind, clothed in his own vivid experience of the dream of life within him. By comparison most of the people I saw on my way to the sea were blurred, and like the knight at arms in Keats' frightening allegory,[4] "palely loitering" through life.

The essence of all this was put to me once by a great hunter, who was born in Africa, and who died thereafter having wandered all over it for seventy years, from the trembling Bushveld of the Transvaal to where the baroque mountains of Abyssinia dwindle down in dead hills to the Red Sea. Africa, he told me, was truly God's country — the last in the world perhaps with a soul of its own; and the difference between those born of its great earth and those who invaded it from Europe and Asia was simply the difference between *being* and *having*. He said the natural child of Africa *is;* the European or Asian *has*. He was not alone in this assessment of the conflict: the primitive keepers of the soul of Africa were keenly aware of its dangers to the being of man. I could give many instances of this awareness manifesting itself tragically in the history of Africa, from the time my ancestors landed at the Cape of Good Hope three hundred years ago, to Mau Mau in Kenya and the latest series of ritual murders; but I prefer to give an illustration from my own life.

Soon after leaving school I heard that a new prophet had arisen among the great Zulu nation of South Africa. I was greatly excited by the news. Africa was still profoundly an Old Testament country, and the appearance of a prophet seemed not only natural and right but also an

[4] "La Belle Dame sans Merci," quoted on page 188.

event that might always be of some cosmic importance. I went to see
him as soon as I could. He lived in a round kraal,[5] grass beehive huts on
a hill standing among the complex of chasms and gorges of a deep and
intricate valley in Natal. It was early summer; one of those days that
come over the edge of time charged with a meaning of their own. The
valley was overflowing with light, sensitive and trembling like a heart
with its first apprehension of love. On the slope of the hill a long line of
women were hoeing the magenta earth. They were naked to the waist;
their strong bodies and full breasts were aubergine-coloured in the sun.
As they worked they sang together in soft voices a song of the earth, with
rhythm so in accord with the pulse of the light and the water-wheel-turn
of the day in the blue sky that it made one great round of summer music.
From the slopes beyond came the clear bright voices of the young boys
herding the cattle and talking easily to one another, often a mile apart.
Sometimes, too, one heard a cow calling for her calf, a goat's bright bleat
or a donkey's shattering plea for compassion, but the sound of the singing set to the rhythm of the day dominated the valley.

The first indication I had that the prophet was coming to meet us
was when the singing stopped abruptly. The women ceased hoeing and
turned to look down the hill behind them. From the bed of the stream
below, a man emerged. He was tall, dressed in a white gown that fell
to his feet, and with a long staff in his hand he slowly climbed the hill
towards us, as if deep in thought. The women watched him with such
close attention that one felt every step he took was fateful. At one moment I thought the women were going to break off working altogether
and form up in a body behind him to escort him back to his kraal: but he
made a gesture with his long arm, dignified and imperative, which immediately set them to work again, hoeing with such a will that the dust
flickered like fire around their feet. Noticing this my guide, a Zulu chief
himself, smiled with a dark satisfaction and remarked, "Not by the men,
but by the women who flock to him and their obedience, shall you first
know the true prophet."

When the seer stood before us at last, raising his hand palm-out-
wards in the ancient Zulu greeting, I thought I had never seen a more
beautiful person. His head was round and shapely, his forehead broad,
his features sensitive; the face as a whole naturally ascetic without being

[5] Enclosure of an African village. The word corresponds to the Spanish "corral,"
which we have taken over into English.

either austere or fanatic. His eyes were big and well-spaced, having the look of a personality in whom nothing was hidden. His hands were those of an artist, and he used them delicately to point his words. On his head he wore the round ring which among his people is a sign that the man is complete. He wore his ring so naturally that it did not seem to be imposed from without, but rather to emanate from him like a halo from a saint.

Outside his kraal there was a large wild fig tree whose dark green leaves were wet with light. We sat down in its shade and talked until the sun went down red behind the blue rim of the valley filled with evening smoke. The more we talked, the more I felt that I was not in the twentieth century but some early Biblical hour. We talked about a great many things of immense interest — I shall refer to them later — yet about the subject that mattered most to me I was disappointed. When I begged him to speak of the first spirit of the Zulu nation, Umkulunkulu, the Great One, he shook his beautiful old head and said with infinite sadness, "We do not speak of Umkulunkulu any longer. His praise-names are forgotten. People now talk only of things that are useful to them."

Recalling this conversation, which took place nearly thirty-five years ago, I realized that the situation which I believe we are all facing in the world today was one which the primitive world, the past life of Africa, knew only too well. It is a loss of first spirit, or to put it in the old-fashioned way, a loss of soul. Before my day with the Zulu prophet was over, I knew that he regarded this as the greatest calamity that could come to human beings. Other examples flooded my mind of how the keepers of man's first spirit in Africa constantly warned him against this peril. Indeed, the primitive world regarded the preservation of first spirit as the greatest, most urgent of all its tasks. It designed elaborate ritual, ceaselessly fashioned myths, legends, stories and music, to contain the meaning and feed the fire of the creative soul.

Here, from far back in my childhood, the memory of one of the servants in our large patriarchal household joined the Zulu seer. She was the lowest in the long hierarchy of black and coloured servants; yet, when we were hurt or distressed, she was the one we used to go to for comfort. One cold winter's evening when I could not sleep, she told me this story.

There was once, she said, a man of the early race who possessed a wonderful herd of cattle: every beast in the herd matched the others in coats of black and white stipples. She stressed the colour of the cattle repeatedly. Even then, young as I was, I had an idea how important the matter of colour was. Cattle were never mere cattle to primitive men, but creatures full of rare and ancient spirit. As he listened to them lowing in his kraal after the lion's roar or the leopard's cough, he heard again the accents of his ancestors. When they were born he regarded the colour of their coats closely because it showed some meaning, some degree of favour or disfavour on the part of the great spirit over all. He had single adjectives for describing each combination of colour, and was never compelled to use a phrase like "a sort of strawberry roan" to designate an animal: there was one exact word to do it for him. As a child I knew eight such adjectives for which we had no single equivalent in any European tongue.

This combination of black and white in cattle was the greatest and most significant colour scheme of all, and the word for it had profound mystical associations. For instance, I was once with our black herdsmen when a cow was safely delivered of a black and white stippled calf: the cry of joy, reverence and gratitude to creation for so great a favour which broke from their deep throats, was one of the most wonderful sounds I have ever heard. I knew too a tribe who, when a man among them died, brought the finest white and black stippled cow in his possession to the side of the open grave. There they made it lower its head so that it would look its dead master in the face for the last time. Thereafter it belonged utterly to the spirits, and no one in the dead man's family would ever dream of killing or selling it.

There was meaning in everything for the first people — from the birth of a calf to the death of a man and beyond; and enclosing all, there was an overwhelming sense that every living thing shared in the process of creation. When our servant told me how this man of the early race possessed cattle with such numenous[6] hides, my child imagination anticipated a story of more than usual significance, and I could not keep still in bed for excitement.

This man of the early race, therefore, she told me, dearly loved his black and white cattle. He always took them out into the veld[7] himself, chose the best possible grazing for them, and watched over them like a

---

[6] Having "numen," a divine force or potency or significance. The adjective is usually spelled "numinous." A rough equivalent would be "magic."

[7] Grassland of South Africa.

mother over her children, seeing that no wild animals came near to hurt or disturb them. In the evening he would bring them back to his kraal, seal the entrance carefully with branches of the toughest thorn, and watching them contentedly chewing the cud, think, "In the morning I shall have a wonderful lot of milk to draw from them." One morning, however, when he went into his kraal expecting to find the udders of the cows full and sleek with milk, he was amazed to see they were slack, wrinkled and empty. He thought with immediate self-reproach he had chosen their grazing badly, and took them to better grass. He brought them home in the evening and again thought, "Tomorrow for a certainty I shall get more milk than ever before." But again in the morning the udders were slack and dry. For the second time he changed their grazing, and yet again the cows had no milk. Disturbed and suspicious, he decided to keep a watch on the cattle throughout the dark.

In the middle of the night he was astonished to see a cord of finely-woven fibre descending from the stars; and down this cord, hand over hand, one after another came some young women of the people of the sky. He saw them, beautiful and gay, whispering and laughing softly among themselves, steal into the kraal and milk his cattle dry with calabashes.[8] Indignant, he jumped out to catch them but they scattered cleverly so that he did not know which way to run. In the end he did manage to catch one; but while he was chasing her the rest, calabashes and all, fled up the sky, withdrawing the cord after the last of them so that he could not follow. However, he was content because the young woman he had caught was the loveliest of them all. He made her his wife and from that moment he had no more trouble from the women of the people of the sky.

His new wife now went daily to work in the fields for him while he tended his cattle. They were happy and they prospered. There was only one thing that worried him. When he caught his wife she had a basket with her. It was skilfully woven, so tight that he could not see through it, and was always closed firmly on top with a lid that fitted exactly into the opening. Before she would marry him, his wife had made him promise that he would never lift the lid of the basket and look inside until she gave him permission to do so. If he did a great disaster might overtake them both. But as the months went by, the man began to forget his promise. He became steadily more curious, seeing the basket so near day

8 Gourds.

after day, with the lid always firmly shut. One day when he was alone he went into his wife's hut, saw the basket standing there in the shadows, and could bear it no longer. Snatching off the lid, he looked inside. For a moment he stood there unbelieving, then burst out laughing.

When his wife came back in the evening she knew at once what had happened. She put her hand to her heart, and looking at him with tears in her eyes, she said, "You've looked in the basket."

He admitted it with a laugh, saying, "You silly woman. You silly, silly creature. Why have you made such a fuss about this basket? There's nothing in it at all."

"Nothing?" she said, hardly finding the strength to speak.

"Yes, nothing," he answered emphatically.

At that she turned her back on him, walked away straight into the sunset and vanished. She was never seen on earth again.

To this day I can hear the old black servant woman saying to me, "And do you know why she went away, my little master? Not because he had broken his promise but because, looking into the basket, he had found it empty. She went because the basket was not empty: it was full of beautiful things of the sky she stored there for them both, and because he could not see them and just laughed, there was no use for her on earth any more and she vanished."

That story seems to me an accurate image of our predicament in the World now, both as individuals and as nations. The primitive spirit stands in rags and tatters, rejected by the contemporary mind, offering us such warnings. Laughing, unaware of peril, we lift the lids of our own particular baskets and, blindly declaring them to be empty, we lose our soul, of which woman is the immemorial image.

It is true there is no resolution, only tragedy and a warning, in this African tale. But the woman who walked into the bloodred sunset of Africa to vanish, the servant in rags and tatters still haunting the corridors of my own mind, the woman abandoned and weeping in the ruined castle in the dream of the Spaniard, and indeed the naked, demented Bushman woman[9] whimpering in the summer sunlight of the desert, each in her own way seemed to serve a single meaning. They

---

[9] A reference to an earlier incident in the book. Van der Post had seen this woman at a truck stop in the desert, and learned her history. She had been captured and raped by a white man and thenceforth, in a demented condition, was similarly treated by others.

all drew attention to the denial of something vital in the human spirit. The denial might be caused, as in the African tale, by the unawareness of man whose vision is so tied to the world *without* that he is incapable of seeing the spiritual content of his own inner world. It might be caused by the cruelty of man, who trespasses against his own humanity in doing violence to earth's children; or by mere inability to control that fierce watchdog of our daylight selves — the mind narrowed to an aggressive materialistic rationalism, as in the dream of the Spaniard who could not call back the wolfhound he kept to guard his home and treasured possessions.

The general state of neglect can be symbolized by a ruined castle, a desert in Southern Africa, or a despised basket in the shadows of an African hut. But they all conveyed only one thing to me — the peril of man when divorced from the first things in himself. Cut off from them for long, he loses his meaning just as that man of the early race, blind to the contents of the basket, lost his lovely lady of the starry sky. Only those who have seen the stars of Africa can know how terrible such a loss must have been. This peril appeared so active in the world around me that I felt I could say of it, as Dabé[10] said of the Bushman woman at Gemsbok Pan, "The Time of the Hyaena is upon us."

However, once I had discovered the kinship of these images, so far apart in their origins yet so closely related in their meaning, I began to consider more carefully the rest of the pattern of the first things of Africa. In particular, I examined the pattern of the Bushman as experienced through my own life and imagination. It was so much older than even the earliest known pattern of the most primitive of black races in Africa. It was, as far as I knew, the purest manifestation of life lived in the beginning according to life's own design rather than man's wilful and one-sided plan for it. It is true, I was not without prejudice in the matter, for I had a private hope of the utmost importance to me. The Bushman's physical shape combined those of a child and a man: I surmised that examination of his inner life might reveal a pattern which reconciled the spiritual opposites in the human being and made him whole.

More immediately, his tragedy was the only one I knew in Africa

---

10 Dabé was van der Post's Bushman guide on the expedition into the Kalahari. Among all the numinous animals in Bushman folklore, the hyena is the only one with an absolutely evil role.

for which White and Black shared an equal guilt. In the long and terrible history of Africa it was the one mirror wherein both White and
Black could clearly view not the unreal and conflicting abstractions they
have made of one another, but what is so tragically hidden from them
— their common, fallible and bewildered human faces. If that could
be done, it might start the first movement towards a reconciliation, first
in their imagination and then in their lives. But apart from these private
rationalizations, I was compelled toward the Bushman like someone
who walks in his sleep, obedient to a dream of finding in the dark what
the day has denied him.

So I collected all I could discover of what has been written about
the Bushman. I had read it all many times before in my life. It had become part of my imaginative experience: but, knowing how different
just one of the Bushman legends had appeared to me after my journey
into the desert, I was determined to take nothing for granted. I would
pool all I had learnt in the past with what I had brought back with me
from the desert, and see what came out of it at leisure on the long
voyage back to England by sea.

⋖§ FOR DISCUSSION AND WRITING

1. You may find this piece a bit hard to get into, until you adjust to Colonel
   van der Post's idiom and way of thought—as many things that are valuable seem difficult at first; but if you have trust and patience, you will come
   to his wonderful stories in the latter half of the piece, and the first part will
   be illuminated and become simple. (If you have already read the earlier
   piece by van der Post in this book, you will have no trouble with this one.)
   It is perhaps helpful to understand at the beginning that van der Post is
   an Afrikaner, of one of the first Dutch families to emigrate to South Africa
   some 300 years ago. In *The Lost World of the Kalahari*, he tells something
   of his childhood, nurtured by Zulu and Bushman folklore and mythology, in
   which the parts played by the "fairies" and "elves" of European folklore
   were taken, in his imagination, by the Bushmen, the "little people" who
   were conversant with the supernatural and had all sorts of magic skills, but
   who, wistfully, no longer existed; and he says that those childhood impressions impelled him, late in life, to undertake an expedition in search of the
   Bushmen, in the "lost world" of the Kalahari desert. This background to

some extent explains the movement of his thought in the present piece, where the Bushman becomes a symbol of a "lost world" within ourselves, a part of ourselves that it is worthwhile to rediscover. If you have read the whole piece carefully, how would you interpret what he means by "the first things of life"? (Be careful here that you don't fall into some facile irrelevancy.) How does van der Post alter our ordinary attitude toward, and evaluation of, what is called "primitive" (in both the ethnological and the psychological sense)?

2. What is his apology for offering his own experience as representative? Do you feel that your own experience is representative of your time? If one didn't feel that one's own psychological experience was representative, how could one make any generalizations at all?

3. The criticism that van der Post makes of the modern mind is a pretty radical and explosive one. What is it? Consider particularly the fifth paragraph. Explain what he means by "superstition of the intellect," "hubris of the mind," "a vague and arid restlessness hiding behind an arrogant intellectualism." (Be careful to distinguish between what van der Post means and your own attitude toward his meaning, for one can't argue intelligently about anything until one has distinguished precisely what it is one is arguing about.) Can you find, in your own experience of college courses, any illustrations of the "arrogant intellectualism" van der Post mentions?

4. Explain in your own words what van der Post means in the sixth paragraph as to modern man's intellectual knowledge "from the outside" of life, as against his ignorance of "the process within." Give some examples, from your own experience, of this discrepancy. (You might write up this question as a theme topic.) What is the significance of the comparison between modern man, with his "comfortable rubble of material possession," and the Bushman carrying all his possessions in one hand? Do you agree or disagree with the assertion that modern man, in the affluent society, is "alone and unbelonging, sick, poor, starved of meaning"? Cite some examples in evidence of your agreement or disagreement.

5. In terms of van der Post's thesis, what point is made in the interview with the Zulu prophet? How does the interview illustrate, or offer a parable of, "loss of soul"? What does van der Post mean here by "man's first spirit," and why is the loss of it a calamity? Does he mean we should all have Zulu gods, worship fetishes, and practice magic?

6. What is the significance — in terms of the piece as a whole — of the story of the man who had brindled cattle and who took one of the sky-women to wife? (Incidentally, you might be interested in a comparison of this story with that of Jacob in the Bible, who got his hardfisted uncle Laban to agree to give him all the "straked [streaked] and spotted" animals, then set up streaked poles before the animals as they coupled, so that, by prenatal influence, the young would be "straked and spotted." Both stories incorporate the same magical principle of the value of the brindled animal.) When van der Post says, "There was meaning in everything for the first people," what contrast is implied with modern life? Why was the sky-woman's basket empty? (It may be noted that to the indigenous African the stars are people, the "first people," who guide one in every operation, while to us—unless one is an astronomer—they are virtually nonexistent.)

7. How does van der Post bring back and tie in the Spaniard's dream? Why should *dreams* have significance in this kind of discussion?

8. Why does he say that both White and Black share the guilt for the tragic disappearance of the Bushman? (It would help here to do a little research of your own on Africa, perhaps in the way of a paper. Alan Moorehead's *The Blue Nile* and *The White Nile* are exciting books to start with.) What is his implication in saying that the Bushman's tragic history is "the one mirror wherein both White and Black could clearly view not the unreal and conflicting abstractions they have made of one another, but . . . their common, fallible and bewildered human faces"?

9. If you have not found a writing topic already in these questions, there is another one more important than them all: Who, and where, is that "first child of life," the Bushman in yourself, and how has he got manhandled, exploited, and squashed?

Sigmund Freud ✌§ Typical Dreams

✌§ Founder of psychoanalysis and one of the great seminal geniuses of modern times, whose analysis of subconscious processes and their relation to human behavior fundamentally altered man's conception of himself and provided a new perspective of self-knowledge. Freud was born in 1856 in a part of Austria that is now Czechoslovakia, of Jewish parents; he was brought up, from the age of four, in Vienna, and lived there until the last year of his long life, teaching at the University; he died in London in 1939, a refugee from the Nazi holocaust. In the large corpus of his writings, *The Interpretation of Dreams*, from which the selection here is taken, is a revolutionary classic; it was first published in 1900—an appropriately symbolic date, for it marked a profound change between nineteenth-century thinking and twentieth-century thinking. §❧

THE EMBARRASSMENT-DREAM OF NAKEDNESS

IN A DREAM in which one is naked or scantily clad in the presence of strangers, it sometimes happens that one is not in the least ashamed of one's condition. But the dream of nakedness demands our attention only when shame and embarrassment are felt in it, when one wishes to escape or to hide, and when one feels the strange inhibition of being unable to stir from the spot, and of being utterly powerless to alter the painful situation. It is only in this connection that the dream is typical; otherwise the nucleus of its content may be involved in all sorts of other connections, or may be replaced by individual amplifications. The essential point is that one has a painful feeling of shame, and is anxious to hide one's nakedness, usually by means of locomotion, but is absolutely unable to do so. I believe that the great majority of my readers will at some time have found themselves in this situation in a dream.

From *The Basic Writings of Sigmund Freud,* translated and edited by Dr. A. A. Brill. Copyright 1938 by Random House, Inc. Reprinted by permission.

839

The nature and manner of the exposure is usually rather vague. The dreamer will say, perhaps, "I was in my chemise," but this is rarely a clear image; in most cases the lack of clothing is so indeterminate that it is described in narrating the dream by an alternative: "I was in my chemise or my petticoat." As a rule the deficiency in clothing is not serious enough to justify the feeling of shame attached to it. For a man who has served in the army, nakedness is often replaced by a manner of dressing that is contrary to regulations. "I was in the street without my sabre, and I saw some officers approaching," or "I had no collar," or "I was wearing checked civilian trousers," etc.

The persons before whom one is ashamed are almost always strangers, whose faces remain indeterminate. It never happens, in the typical dream, that one is reproved or even noticed on account of the lack of clothing which causes one such embarrassment. On the contrary, the people in the dream appear to be quite indifferent; or, as I was able to note in one particularly vivid dream, they have stiff and solemn expressions. This gives us food for thought.

The dreamer's embarrassment and the spectator's indifference constitute a contradiction such as often occurs in dreams. It would be more in keeping with the dreamer's feelings if the strangers were to look at him in astonishment, or were to laugh at him, or be outraged. I think, however, that this obnoxious feature has been displaced by wish-fulfilment, while the embarrassment is for some reason retained, so that the two components are not in agreement. We have an interesting proof that the dream which is partially distorted by wish-fulfilment has not been properly understood; for it has been made the basis of a fairy-tale familiar to us all in Andersen's version of *The Emperor's New Clothes*, and it has more recently received poetical treatment by Fulda in *The Talisman*. In Andersen's fairly-tale we are told of two imposters who weave a costly garment for the Emperor, which shall, however, be visible only to the good and true. The Emperor goes forth clad in this invisible garment, and since the imaginary fabric serves as a sort of touchstone, the people are frightened into behaving as though they did not notice the Emperor's nakedness.

But this is really the situation in our dream. . . . The imposter is the dream, the Emperor is the dreamer himself, and the moralizing tendency betrays a hazy knowledge of the fact that there is a question, in the latent dream-content, of forbidden wishes, victims of repression. The connection in which such dreams appear during my analyses of neurotics proves beyond a doubt that a memory of the dreamer's earliest childhood lies at the foundation of the dream. Only in our childhood was there a time when we were seen by our relatives, as well as by strange nurses, servants and visitors, in a state of insufficient clothing, and at that time we were not ashamed of our nakedness. In the case of many rather older children it may be observed that being undressed has an exciting effect upon them, instead of making them feel ashamed. They laugh, leap about, slap or thump their own bodies; the mother, or whoever is present, scolds them, saying: "Fie, that is shameful — you mustn't do that!" Children often show a desire to display themselves; it is hardly possible to pass through a village in country districts without meeting a two- or three-year-old child who lifts up his or her blouse or frock before the traveller, possibly in his honour. One of my patients has retained in his conscious memory a scene from his eighth year, in which, after undressing for bed, he wanted to dance into his little sister's room in his shirt, but was prevented by the servant. In the history of the childhood of neurotics exposure before children of the opposite sex plays a prominent part; in paranoia the delusion of being observed while dressing and undressing may be directly traced to these experiences; and among those who have remained perverse there is a class in whom the childish impulse is accentuated into a symptom: the class of *exhibitionists*.

This age of childhood, in which the sense of shame is unknown, seems a paradise when we look back upon it later, and paradise itself is nothing but the mass-phantasy of the childhood of the individual. This is why in paradise men are naked and unashamed, until the moment arrives when shame and fear awaken; expulsion follows, and sexual life and cultural development begin. Into this paradise dreams can take us back every night; we have already ventured the conjecture that the impressions of our earliest childhood (from the prehistoric period[1] until about the end of the third year) crave reproduction for their own sake, perhaps without further reference to their content, so that their repetition is a wish-fulfilment. Dreams of nakedness, then, are *exhibition-dreams*.

The nucleus of an exhibition-dream is furnished by one's own person, which is seen not as that of a child, but as it exists in the present,

[1] The period of infancy before the child begins to have a conscious memory.

and by the idea of scanty clothing which emerges indistinctly, owing
to the superimposition of so many later situations of being partially
clothed, or out of consideration for the censorship;[2] to these elements
are added the persons in whose presence one is ashamed. I know of no
example in which the actual spectators of these infantile exhibitions reappear in a dream; for a dream is hardly ever a simple recollection.
Strangely enough, those persons who are the objects of our sexual interest in childhood are omitted from all reproductions, in dreams, in hys-
teria or in obsessional neurosis; paranoia alone restores the spectators,
and is fanatically convinced of their presence, although they remain
unseen. The substitute for these persons offered by the dream, the "number of strangers" who take no notice of the spectacle offered them, is
precisely the *counter-wish* to that single intimately-known person for
whom the exposure was intended. "A number of strangers," moreover,
often occur in dreams in all sorts of other connections; as a *counter-wish*
they always signify "a secret." It will be seen that even that restitution
of the old state of affairs that occurs in paranoia complies with this
counter-tendency. One is no longer alone; one is quite positively being
watched; but the spectators are "a number of strange, curiously indeterminate people."

Furthermore, repression finds a place in the exhibition-dream. For
the disagreeable sensation of the dream is, of course, the reaction . . .
to the fact that the exhibitionistic scene which has been condemned by
the censorship has nevertheless succeeded in presenting itself. The only
way to avoid this sensation would be to refrain from reviving the scene.

In a later chapter we shall deal once again with the feeling of inhibition. In our dreams it represents to perfection *a conflict of the will, a
denial.* According to our unconscious purpose, the exhibition is to proceed; according to the demands of the censorship, it is to come to an
end.

The relation of our typical dreams to fairy-tales and other fiction
and poetry is neither sporadic nor accidental. Sometimes the penetrating insight of the poet has analytically recognized the process of transformation of which the poet is otherwise the instrument, and has followed it up in the reverse direction; that is to say, has traced a poem

---

[2] The inhibiting function or agency of the mind, which acts like a censor in preventing the open emergence of unconscious materials into consciousness, or admits them
only under disguises so that they are unrecognizable.

to a dream. A friend has called my attention to the following passage in G. Keller's *Der Grüne Heinrich:* "I do not wish, dear Lee, that you should ever come to realize from experience the exquisite and piquant truth in the situation of Odysseus, when he appears, naked and covered with mud, before Nausicaä and her playmates![3] Would you like to know what it means? Let us for a moment consider the incident closely. If you are ever parted from your home, and from all that is dear to you, and wander about in a strange country; if you have seen much and experienced much; if you have cares and sorrows, and are, perhaps, utterly wretched and forlorn, you will some night inevitably dream that you are approaching your home; you will see it shining and glittering in the loveliest colours; lovely and gracious figures will come to meet you; and then you will suddenly discover that you are ragged, naked, and covered with dust. An indescribable feeling of shame and fear overcomes you; you try to cover yourself, to hide, and you wake up bathed in sweat. As long as humanity exists, this will be the dream of the care-laden, tempest-tossed man, and thus Homer has drawn this situation from the profoundest depths of the eternal nature of humanity."

What are the profoundest depths of the eternal nature of humanity, which the poet commonly hopes to awaken in his listeners, but these stirrings of the psychic life which are rooted in that age of childhood, which subsequently becomes prehistoric? Childish wishes, now suppressed and forbidden, break into the dream behind the unobjectionable and permissibly conscious wishes of the homeless man, and it is for this reason that the dream which is objectified in the legend of Nausicaä regularly develops into an anxiety-dream.

DREAMS OF THE DEATH OF BELOVED PERSONS

Another series of dreams which may be called typical are those whose content is that a beloved relative, a parent, brother, sister, child, or the like, has died. We must at once distinguish two classes of such dreams: those in which the dreamer remains unmoved, and those in which he feels profoundly grieved by the death of the beloved person, even expressing this grief by shedding tears in his sleep.

[3] In the sixth book of the *Odyssey,* Odysseus, who has been thrown by shipwreck on the shore of the land of the Phaeacians, is discovered in his nakedness and wretchedness by Nausicaä, the young princess of the Phaeacians, who devises means to escort him to her father, the king.

We may ignore the dreams of the first group; they have no claim to be reckoned as typical. If they are analysed, it is found that they signify something that is not contained in them, that they are intended to mask another wish of some kind. . . .

It is otherwise with those dreams in which the death of a beloved relative is imagined, and in which a painful affect is felt. These signify, as their content tells us, the wish that the person in question might die; and since I may here expect that the feelings of all my readers and of all who have had such dreams will lead them to reject my explanation, I must endeavour to rest my proof on the broadest possible basis.

We have already cited a dream from which we could see that the wishes represented as fulfilled in dreams are not always current wishes. They may also be bygone, discarded, buried and repressed wishes, which we must nevertheless credit with a sort of continued existence, merely on account of their reappearance in a dream. They are not dead, like persons who have died, in the sense that we know death, but are rather like the shades in the Odyssey which awaken to a certain degree of life so soon as they have drunk blood. . . .[4]

If anyone dreams that his father or mother, his brother or sister, has died, and his dream expresses grief, I should never adduce this as proof that he wishes any of them dead *now*. The theory of dreams does not go as far as to require this; it is satisfied with concluding that the dreamer has wished them dead at some time or other during his childhood. I fear, however, that this limitation will not go far to appease my critics; probably they will just as energetically deny the possibility that they ever had such thoughts, as they protest that they do not harbour them now. I must, therefore, reconstruct a portion of the submerged infantile psychology on the basis of the evidence of the present.

Let us first of all consider the relation of children to their brothers and sisters. I do not know why we presuppose that it must be a loving one, since examples of enmity among adult brothers and sisters are frequent in everyone's experience, and since we are so often able to verify the fact that this estrangement originated during childhood, or has always existed. Moreover, many adults who to-day are devoted to

[4] The reference is to the eleventh book of the *Odyssey*, which describes Odysseus' experience in the land of the dead. The thronging souls of the dead are unable to think or speak rationally, but gibber like bats, until they drink of the warm blood of a sheep which Odysseus kills; then they are able to communicate with him.

their brothers and sisters, and support them in adversity, lived with them in almost continuous enmity during their childhood. The elder child ill-treated the younger, slandered him, and robbed him of his toys; the younger was consumed with helpless fury against the elder, envied and feared him, or his earliest impulse toward liberty and his first revolt against injustice were directed against his oppressor. The parents say that the children do not agree, and cannot find the reason for it. It is not difficult to see that the character even of a well-behaved child is not the character we should wish to find in an adult. A child is absolutely egoistical; he feels his wants acutely, and strives remorselessly to satisfy them, especially against his competitors, other children, and first of all against his brothers and sisters. And yet we do not on that account call a child "wicked" — we call him "naughty"; he is not responsible for his misdeeds, either in our own judgment or in the eyes of the law. And this is as it should be; for we may expect that within the very period of life which we reckon as childhood, altruistic impulses and morality will awake in the little egoist. . . .

Many persons, then, who now love their brothers and sisters, and who would feel bereaved by their death, harbour in their unconscious hostile wishes, survivals from an earlier period, wishes which are able to realize themselves in dreams. It is, however, quite especially interesting to observe the behaviour of little children up to their third and fourth year towards their younger brothers or sisters. So far the child has been the only one; now he is informed that the stork has brought a new baby. The child inspects the new arrival, and expresses his opinion with decision: "The stork had better take it back again!"

I seriously declare it as my opinion that a child is able to estimate the disadvantages which he has to expect on account of a new-comer. A connection of mine, who now gets on very well with a sister, who is four years her junior, responded to the news of this sister's arrival with the reservation: "But I shan't give her my red cap, anyhow." If the child should come to realize only at a later stage that its happiness may be prejudiced by a younger brother or sister, its enmity will be aroused at this period. I know of a case where a girl, not three years of age, tried to strangle an infant in its cradle, because she suspected that its continued presence boded her no good. Children at this time of life are capable of a jealousy that is perfectly evident and extremely intense. . . .

Feelings of hostility towards brothers and sisters must occur far more frequently in children than is observed by their obtuse elders.

In the case of my own children, who followed one another rapidly, I missed the opportunity of making such observations, I am now retrieving it, thanks to my little nephew, whose undisputed domination was disturbed after fifteen months by the arrival of a feminine rival. I hear, it is true, that the young man behaves very chivalrously toward his little sister, that he kisses her hand and strokes her; but in spite of this I have convinced myself that even before the completion of his second year he is using his new command of language to criticize this person, who, to him, after all, seems superfluous. Whenever the conversation turns upon her he chimes in, and cries angrily: "Too (1)ittle, too (1)ittle!" During the last few months, since the child has outgrown this disparagement, owing to her splendid development, he has found another reason for his insistence that she does not deserve so much attention. He reminds us, on every suitable pretext: "She hasn't any teeth.". . .

I have never failed to come across this dream of the death of brothers or sisters, denoting an intense hostility, e.g. I have met it in all my female patients. I have met with only one exception, which could easily be interpreted into a confirmation of the rule. Once, in the course of a sitting, when I was explaining this state of affairs to a female patient, since it seemed to have some bearing on the symptoms under consideration that day, she answered, to my astonishment, that she had never had such dreams. But another dream occurred to her, which presumably had nothing to do with the case — a dream which she had first dreamed at the age of *four*, when she was the youngest child, and had since then dreamed repeatedly. "*A number of children, all her brothers and sisters with her boy and girl cousins, were romping about in a meadow. Suddenly they all grew wings, flew up, and were gone.*" She had no idea of the significance of this dream; but we can hardly fail to recognize it as a dream of the death of all the brothers and sisters, in its original form, and but little influenced by the censorship. I will venture to add the following analysis of it: on the death of one out of this large number of children — in this case the children of two brothers were brought up together as brothers and sisters — would not our dreamer, at that time not yet four years of age, have asked some wise, grown-up person: "What becomes of children when they are dead?" The answer would probably have been: "They grow wings and become angels." After this explanation, all the brothers and sisters and cousins in the dream now have wings, like angels and — this is the important point — they fly away. Our little angel-maker is left alone: just think, the only one out of such a crowd! That the children romp about a meadow, from which they fly away, points almost certainly to butterflies — it is as though the child had been influenced by the same association of ideas which led the ancients to imagine Psyche, the soul, with the wings of a butterfly.

Perhaps some readers will now object that the inimical impulses of children toward their brothers and sisters may perhaps be admitted, but how does the childish character arrive at such heights of wickedness as to desire the death of a rival or a stronger playmate, as though all misdeeds could be atoned for only by death? Those who speak in this fashion forget that the child's idea of "being dead" has little but the word in common with our own. The child knows nothing of the horrors of decay, of shivering in the cold grave, of the terror of the infinite Nothing, the thought of which the adult, as all the myths of the hereafter testify, finds so intolerable. The fear of death is alien to the child; and so he plays with the horrid word, and threatens another child: "If you do that again, you will die, just like Francis died;" at which the poor mother shudders, unable perhaps to forget that the greater proportion of mortals do not survive beyond the years of childhood. Even at the age of eight, a child returning from a visit to a natural history museum may say to her mother: "Mamma, I do love you so; if you ever die, I am going to have you stuffed and set you up here in the room, so that I can always, always see you!" So different from our own is the childish conception of being dead.

Being dead means, for the child, who has been spared the sight of the suffering that precedes death, much the same as "being gone," and ceasing to annoy the survivors. The child does not distinguish the means by which this absence is brought about, whether by distance, or estrangement, or death. If, during the child's prehistoric years, a nurse has been dismissed, and if his mother dies a little while later, the two experiences, as we discover by analysis, form links of a chain in his memory. The fact that the child does not very intensely miss those who are absent has been realized, to her sorrow, by many a mother, when she has returned home from an absence of several weeks, and has been told, upon inquiry: "The children have not asked for their mother once." But if she really departs to "that undiscovered country from whose bourne no traveller returns," the children seem at first to have forgotten her, and only *subsequently* do they begin to remember their dead mother.

While, therefore, the child has its motives for desiring the absence of another child, it is lacking in all those restraints which would prevent it from clothing this wish in the form of a death-wish; and the psychic reaction to dreams of a death-wish proves that, in spite of all the differences of content, the wish in the case of the child is after all identical with the corresponding wish in an adult.

If, then, the death-wish of a child in respect of his brothers and sisters is explained by his childish egoism, which makes him regard his brothers and sisters as rivals, how are we to account for the same wish in respect of his parents, who bestow their love on him, and satisfy his needs, and whose preservation he ought to desire for these very egoistical reasons?

Towards a solution of this difficulty we may be guided by our knowledge that the very great majority of dreams of the death of a parent refer to the parent of the same sex as the dreamer, so that a man generally dreams of the death of his father, and a woman of the death of her mother. I do not claim that this happens constantly; but that it happens in a great majority of cases is so evident that it requires explanation by some factor of general significance. Broadly speaking, it is as though a sexual preference made itself felt at an early age, as though the boy regarded his father, and the girl her mother, as a rival in love — by whose removal he or she could but profit.

Before rejecting this idea as monstrous, let the reader again consider the actual relations between parents and children. We must distinguish between the traditional standard of conduct, the filial piety expected in this relation, and what daily observation shows us to be the fact. More than one occasion for enmity lies hidden amidst the relations of parents and children; conditions are present in the greatest abundance under which wishes which cannot pass the censorship are bound to arise. Let us first consider the relation between father and son. In my opinion the sanctity with which we have endorsed the injunctions of the Decalogue[5] dulls our perception of the reality. Perhaps we hardly dare permit ourselves to perceive that the greater part of humanity

---

[5] The Ten Commandments, communicated to Moses on Mount Sinai (Exodus XX, 1-17). The fifth commandment is: "Honor thy father and thy mother."

neglects to obey the fifth commandment. In the lowest as well as in the highest strata of human society, filial piety towards parents is wont to recede before other interests. The obscure legends which have been handed down to us from the primeval ages of human society in mythology and folklore give a deplorable idea of the despotic power of the father, and the ruthlessness with which it was exercised. Kronos devours his children,[6] as the wild boar devours the litter of the sow; Zeus emasculates his father and takes his place as ruler. The more tyrannically the father ruled in the ancient family, the more surely must the son, as his appointed successor, have assumed the position of an enemy, and the greater must have been his impatience to attain to supremacy through the death of his father. Even in our own middle-class families the father commonly fosters the growth of the germ of hatred which is naturally inherent in the paternal relation, by refusing to allow the son to be a free agent or by denying him the means of becoming so. A physician often has occasion to remark that a son's grief at the loss of his father cannot quench his gratification that he has at last obtained his freedom. Fathers, as a rule, cling desperately to as much of the sadly antiquated *potestas patris familias*[7] as still survives in our modern society, and the poet who, like Ibsen, puts the immemorial strife between father and son in the foreground of his drama is sure of his effect. The causes of conflict between mother and daughter arise when the daughter grows up and finds herself watched by her mother when she longs for real sexual freedom, while the mother is reminded by the budding beauty of her daughter that for her the time has come to renounce sexual claims.

All these circumstances are obvious to everyone, but they do not help us to explain dreams of the death of their parents in persons for whom filial piety has long since come to be unquestionable. We are, however, prepared by the foregoing discussion to look for the origin of a death-wish in the earliest years of childhood.

In the case of psychoneurotics, analysis confirms this conjecture beyond all doubt. For analysis tells us that the sexual wishes of the child — in so far as they deserve this designation in their nascent state —

---

[6] Kronos (Cronus), the father of Zeus, devoured each of his sons at birth, for fear they might become his rivals and usurp the kingship. When Zeus was born, his mother, Rhea, hid him in a cave on Mount Ida and gave Kronos a stone to swallow instead of the child.

[7] Paternal authority. The play by Ibsen referred to here is probably *Ghosts*.

awaken at a very early age, and that the earliest affection of the girl-child is lavished on the father, while the earliest infantile desires of the boy are directed upon the mother. For the boy the father, and for the girl the mother, becomes an obnoxious rival, and we have already shown, in the case of brothers and sisters, how readily in children this feeling leads to the death-wish. As a general rule, sexual selection soon makes its appearance in the parents; it is a natural tendency for the father to spoil his little daughters, and for the mother to take the part of the sons, while both, so long as the glamour of sex does not prejudice their judgment, are strict in training the children. The child is perfectly conscious of this partiality, and offers resistance to the parent who opposes it. To find love in an adult is for the child not merely the satisfaction of a special need; it means also that the child's will is indulged in all other respects. Thus the child is obeying its own sexual instinct, and at the same time reinforcing the stimulus proceeding from the parents, when its choice between the parents corresponds with their own.

The signs of these infantile tendencies are for the most part overlooked; and yet some of them may be observed even after the early years of childhood. An eight-year-old girl of my acquaintance, whenever her mother is called away from the table, takes advantage of her absence to proclaim herself her successor. "Now I shall be Mamma; Karl, do you want some more vegetables? Have some more, do," etc. A particularly clever and lively little girl, not yet four years of age, in whom this trait of child psychology is unusually transparent, says frankly: "Now mummy can go away; then daddy must marry me, and I will be his wife." Nor does this wish by any means exclude the possibility that the child may most tenderly love its mother. If the little boy is allowed to sleep at his mother's side whenever his father goes on a journey, and if after his father's return he has to go back to the nursery, to a person whom he likes far less, the wish may readily arise that his father might always be absent, so that he might keep his place beside his dear, beautiful mamma; and the father's death is obviously a means for the attainment of this wish; for the child's experience has taught him that "dead" folks, like grandpapa, for example, are always absent; they never come back. . . .

According to my already extensive experience, parents play a leading part in the infantile psychology of all persons who subsequently become psychoneurotics. Falling in love with one parent and hating the other forms part of the permanent stock of the psychic impulses which arise in early childhood, and are of such importance as the material of the subsequent neurosis. But I do not believe that psychoneurotics are to be sharply distinguished in this respect from other persons who remain normal — that is, I do not believe that they are capable of creating something absolutely new and peculiar to themselves. It is far more probable — and this is confirmed by incidental observations of normal children — that in their amorous or hostile attitude toward their parents, psychoneurotics do no more than reveal to us, by magnification, something that occurs less markedly and intensively in the minds of the majority of children. Antiquity has furnished us with legendary matter which corroborates this belief, and the profound and universal validity of the old legends is explicable only by an equally universal validity of the above-mentioned hypothesis of infantile psychology.

I am referring to the legend of King Oedipus and the *Oedipus Rex* of Sophocles. Oedipus, the son of Laius, king of Thebes, and Jocasta, is exposed as a suckling, because an oracle had informed the father that his son, who was still unborn, would be his murderer. He is rescued, and grows up as a king's son at a foreign court, until, being uncertain of his origin, he, too, consults the oracle, and is warned to avoid his native place, for he is destined to become the murderer of his father and the husband of his mother. On the road leading away from his supposed home he meets King Laius, and in a sudden quarrel strikes him dead. He comes to Thebes, where he solves the riddle of the Sphinx, who is barring the way to the city, whereupon he is elected king by the grateful Thebans, and is rewarded with the hand of Jocasta. He reigns for many years in peace and honour, and begets two sons and two daughters upon his unknown mother, until at last a plague breaks out — which causes the Thebans to consult the oracle anew. Here Sophocles' tragedy begins. The messengers bring the reply that the plague will stop as soon as the murderer of Laius is driven from the country. But where is he?

> "Where shall be found,
> Faint, and hard to be known, the trace of the ancient guilt?"

The action of the play consists simply in the disclosure, approached step by step and artistically delayed (and comparable to the work of a psychoanalysis) that Oedipus himself is the murderer of Laius, and that he is the son of the murdered man and Jocasta. Shocked by the abominable crime which he has unwittingly committed, Oedipus blinds himself, and departs from his native city. The prophecy of the oracle has been fulfilled. . . .

If the *Oedipus Rex* is capable of moving a modern reader or play-goer no less powerfully than it moved the contemporary Greeks, the only possible explanation is that the effect of the Greek tragedy does not depend upon the conflict between fate and human will, but upon the peculiar nature of the material by which this conflict is revealed. There must be a voice within us which is prepared to acknowledge the compelling power of fate in the *Oedipus*. . . . And there actually is a motive in the story of King Oedipus which explains the verdict of this inner voice. His fate moves us only because it might have been our own, because the oracle laid upon us before our birth the very curse which rested upon him. It may be that we were all destined to direct our first sexual impulses toward our mothers, and our first impulses of hatred and violence toward our fathers; our dreams convince us that we were. King Oedipus, who slew his father Laius and wedded his mother Jocasta, is nothing more or less than a wish-fulfilment — the fulfilment of the wish of our childhood. But we, more fortunate than he, in so far as we have not become psychoneurotics, have since our childhood suc-ceeded in withdrawing our sexual impulses from our mothers, and in forgetting our jealousy of our fathers. We recoil from the person for whom this primitive wish of our childhood has been fulfilled with all the force of the repression which these wishes have undergone in our minds since childhood. As the poet brings the guilt of Oedipus to light by his investigation, he forces us to become aware of our own inner selves, in which the same impulses are still extant, even though they are sup-pressed. The antithesis with which the chorus departs: —

> ". . . Behold, this is Oedipus,
> Who unravelled the great riddle, and was first in power,
> Whose fortune all the townsmen praised and envied;
> See in what dread adversity he sank!"

— this admonition touches us and our own pride, us who since the years of our childhood have grown so wise and so powerful in our own estimation. Like Oedipus, we live in ignorance of the desires that offend morality, the desires that nature has forced upon us and after their unveiling we may well prefer to avert our gaze from the scenes of our childhood.

In the very text of Sophocles' tragedy there is an unmistakable reference to the fact that the Oedipus legend had its source in dream-material of immemorial antiquity, the content of which was the painful disturbance of the child's relations to its parents caused by the first impulses of sexuality. Jocasta comforts Oedipus — who is not yet enlightened, but is troubled by the recollection of the oracle — by an allusion to a dream which is often dreamed, though it cannot, in her opinion, mean anything: —

> "For many a man hath seen himself in dreams
> His mother's mate, but he who gives no heed
> To suchlike matters bears the easier life." . . .

Another of the great poetic tragedies, Shakespeare's *Hamlet,* is rooted in the same soil as *Oedipus Rex.* But the whole difference in the psychic life of the two widely separated periods of civilization, and the progress, during the course of time, of repression in the emotional life of humanity, is manifested in the differing treatment of the same material. In *Oedipus Rex* the basic wish-phantasy of the child is brought to light and realized as it is in dreams; in *Hamlet* it remains repressed, and we learn of its existence — as we discover the relevant facts in a neurosis — only through the inhibitory effects which proceed from it. In the more modern drama, the curious fact that it is possible to remain in complete uncertainty as to the character of the hero has proved to be quite consistent with the overpowering effect of the tragedy. The play is based upon Hamlet's hesitation in accomplishing the task of revenge assigned to him; the text does not give the cause or the motive of this hesitation, nor have the manifold attempts at interpretation succeeded in doing so. According to the still prevailing conception, a conception for which Goethe was first responsible, Hamlet represents the type of man whose active energy is paralysed by excessive intellectual activity: "Sicklied o'er with the pale cast of thought." According to another conception, the poet has endeavoured to portray a morbid, irresolute character, on the verge of neurasthenia. The plot of the drama, however, shows us that Hamlet is by no means intended to appear as a character wholly incapable of action. On two separate occasions we see him assert himself: once in a sudden outburst of rage, when he stabs the eaves-

dropper behind the arras, and on the other occasion when he deliberately, and even craftily, with the complete unscrupulousness of a prince
of the Renaissance, sends the two courtiers to the death which was intended for himself. What is it, then, that inhibits him in accomplishing
the task which his father's ghost has laid upon him? Here the explanation offers itself that it is the peculiar nature of this task. Hamlet is able
to do anything but take vengeance upon the man who did away with
his father and has taken his father's place with his mother — the man
who shows him in realization the repressed desires of his own childhood.
The loathing which should have driven him to revenge is thus replaced
by self-reproach, by conscientious scruples, which tell him that he himself is no better than the murderer whom he is required to punish.
I have here translated into consciousness what had to remain unconscious in the mind of the hero; if anyone wishes to call Hamlet an hysterical subject I cannot but admit that this is the deduction to be drawn
from my interpretation. The sexual aversion which Hamlet expresses in
conversation with Ophelia is perfectly consistent with this deduction
— the same sexual aversion which during the next few years was increasingly to take possession of the poet's soul, until it found its supreme
utterance in *Timon of Athens*. It can, of course, be only the poet's own
psychology with which we are confronted in *Hamlet;* and in a work
on Shakespeare by Georg Brandes (1896) I find the statement that the
drama was composed immediately after the death of Shakespeare's
father (1601) — that is to say, when he was still mourning his loss, and
during a revival, as we may fairly assume, of his own childish feelings
in respect of his father. It is known, too, that Shakespeare's son, who died
in childhood, bore the name of Hamnet (identical with Hamlet). . . . .
I have here attempted to interpret only the deepest stratum of impulses
in the mind of the creative poet.

◄§ FOR DISCUSSION AND WRITING

1. How does Freud define and qualify the type of dream in the first three
   paragraphs? What contradiction is there between the attitude of the
   "strangers" in the dream and the dreamer's sense of shame? Assuming
   that everyone knows Andersen's fairy tale *The Emperor's New Clothes*

(if not, Freud gives a clear synopsis of it here), what are the correspondences between the typical dream of nakedness and the story? What is the connection between this typical dream and early childhood? What "wish-fulfilment" is involved in the dream? If the dream satisfies a wish, and if there was no shame about nakedness in early childhood, why does the dreamer nevertheless feel anxiety, shame, or embarrassment?

2. In regard to "exhibitionism" in young children, does Freud set up any clear-cut distinction between what is "normal" and what is "neurotic"? What analogy does he draw between early childhood and "paradise" (that is, the Garden of Eden)? In the paragraph beginning "This age of childhood, in which the sense of shame is unknown . . . ," consider the sentence: "This is why in paradise men are naked and unashamed, until the moment arrives when shame and fear awaken; expulsion follows, and sexual life and cultural development begin." What comment does this sentence make on the "sin" committed by Adam and Eve (a comment which a fundamentalist interpreter of the Bible would not look upon very favorably), and on the connection between "cultural development" and the awakening of sexual life, together with "shame and fear"? (As a matter of fact, Freud's comment is firmly based in the Biblical story, for as soon as Adam and Eve were expelled from the Garden, they had to start hoeing the earth—"earning their bread in the sweat of their brows" —and thus initiated agriculture; while one of their sons, Cain, established the first city.)

3. If you understand what is meant by the "censorship" (see Note 2), what do you make of what Freud says about the "counter-wish" in connection with the indifferent "strangers" in the typical nakedness dream? What accounts for the disagreeable sensation of the dream? How does the dream show "a conflict of the will"?

4. Why does Freud say that the relation between the dream and fairy tale or poetry is not "accidental"? In the paragraph about the shipwrecked Odysseus and his discovery by Nausicaä (see Note 3), why is it said that "As long as humanity exists, this will be the dream of the care-laden, tempest-tossed man . . . ," and what connection has the passage from Homer with Freud's subject matter?

5. How is the typical dream of "the death of a beloved person" defined and qualified? Why does Freud say that all his readers will probably reject his explanation? Does such a dream necessarily express a *current* wish?

In what sense do the wishes of childhood have "a sort of continued existence"? He says that most people would deny having such a wish even in
childhood. Why? What cliché about childhood does his argument upset?

6. What accounts for sibling hostility among young children? Is it confined
   to young children? What is Freud's interpretation of the patient's dream
   of her cousins romping in a meadow, sprouting wings, and flying away?
   Why do the angelic prettiness and apparent innocence of the image stand
   in the way of recognition of the underlying wish? How do you find here a
   sample of the work of "the censorship"? How does the child's idea of
   death differ from the adult's, and how does that difference qualify the
   meaning of the death-dream?

7. How does Freud explain the dream of the death of a parent? He says that
   there are abundant conditions in the relationship between parents and
   young children for hostile wishes. Without flat-footedly acquiescing in
   Freud's argument, could you cite a few situations, perhaps from personal
   experience, in which actions of the parent may incite extreme hostility—
   even homicidal hostility—in the child?

8. Do you consider Freud's point about modern observance of the fifth
   commandment well taken or otherwise? Have you found, even in "normal"
   or "ordinary" families, indications of buried or not-so-buried hostility and
   rivalry between father and son, mother and daughter? How do such observations increase self-knowledge and possibly help us to avoid having
   our behavior controlled or overwhelmed by unconscious impulses?

9. How does Freud use the analogies from *Oedipus Rex* and *Hamlet?*

10. For a theme, write up your reactions to this piece. (There is certainly no
    necessity for agreement with Freud's argument, but you should have
    cogent reasons for disagreement.) Or if you have been stimulated by the
    piece to remember some of your own dreams of the same types, describe
    them and attempt to analyze them.

Carl Gustav Jung ⊷§ The Personal and the Collective Unconscious

⊷§ Born in 1875 in Switzerland, educated in Basel and Zurich, Jung received his medical degree in 1900 and began his career as psychiatrist in the same year at the University of Zurich. He met Sigmund Freud in 1907; he had long recognized Freud as a master in the psychiatric field, and Freud fairly soon made it clear that Jung was the heir apparent; but the master-disciple relationship broke over Freud's sexual theory of the unconscious, and the split widened as Jung developed his own theory of the "collective unconscious." The selections from Freud and Jung given here reflect fairly clearly their major differences. In the judgment of time, it may be Jung who is the greater, the more prophetic, genius. The best way for the student to approach Jung on his own is through Jung's last wonderful book, a kind of psychological autobiography that he started when he was eighty-three, called *Memories, Dreams, Reflections.* ३∾

I N FREUD'S view, as most people know, the contents of the unconscious are limited to infantile tendencies which are repressed because of their incompatible character. Repression is a process that begins in early childhood under the moral influence of the environment and lasts throughout life. Through analysis the repressions are removed and the repressed wishes made conscious.

According to this theory, the unconscious contains only those parts of the personality which could just as well be conscious and are in fact suppressed only through upbringing. Although from one point of view the infantile tendencies of the unconscious are the most conspicuous, it would nonetheless be incorrect to define or evaluate the unconscious

From *Two Essays on Analytical Psychology* by C. G. Jung, Volume 7 of the Collected Works, Bollingen Series XX, Pantheon. The translation is by R. F. C. Hull.

entirely in these terms. The unconscious has still another side to it: it includes not only repressed contents, but also all psychic material that lies below the threshold of consciousness. It is impossible to explain the subliminal[1] nature of all this material on the principle of repression; otherwise, through the removal of repressions, a man would acquire a phenomenal memory which would thenceforth forget nothing.

We therefore emphatically say that in addition to the repressed material the unconscious contains all those psychic components that have fallen below the threshold, including subliminal sense-perceptions. Moreover we know, from abundant experience as well as for theoretical reasons, that the unconscious also contains components that have *not yet* reached the threshold of consciousness. These are the seeds of future conscious contents. Equally we have reason to suppose that the unconscious is never at rest in the sense of being inactive, but is continually engaged in grouping and regrouping its contents. Only in pathological cases can this activity be regarded as completely autonomous; normally it is co-ordinated with the conscious mind in a compensatory relationship.[2]

It is to be assumed that all these contents are personal in so far as they are acquired during the individual's life. Since this life is limited, the number of acquired contents in the unconscious must also be limited. This being so, it might be thought possible to empty the unconscious either by analysis or by making a complete inventory of unconscious contents, on the ground that the unconscious cannot produce anything more than is already known and accepted in the conscious mind. We should also have to infer, as already indicated, that if one could stop the descent of conscious contents into the unconscious by doing away with repression, unconscious productivity would be paralysed. This is possible only to a very limited extent, as we know from experience. We urge our patients to hold fast to repressed contents that have been reassociated with consciousness, and to assimilate them into their plan of life. But this procedure, as we may daily convince ourselves, makes no impression on the unconscious, since it calmly continues to produce dreams and fantasies which, according to Freud's original

---

[1] From *limen*, meaning threshold; "subliminal" means below the threshold of consciousness, i.e., unconscious.

[2] Later in this piece Jung explains fully the "compensatory" or "complementary" relationship between the unconscious and the conscious mind.

theory, must arise from personal repressions. If in such cases we pursue our observations systematically and without prejudice, we shall find material which, although similar in form to the previous personal contents, yet seems to contain allusions that go far beyond the personal sphere. . . .

There are present in every individual, besides his personal memories, the great "primordial" images, as Jacob Burckhardt once aptly called them, the inherited powers of human imagination as it was from time immemorial. The fact of this inheritance explains the truly amazing phenomenon that certain motifs from myths and legends repeat themselves the world over in identical forms. It also explains why it is that our mental patients can reproduce exactly the same images and associations that are known to us from the old texts. I give some examples of this in my book *Symbols of Transformation*. In so doing I do not by any means assert the inheritance of ideas, but only of the possibility of such ideas, which is something very different.

In this further stage of treatment, then, when fantasies are produced which no longer rest on personal memories, we have to do with the manifestations of a deeper layer of the unconscious where the primordial images common to humanity lie sleeping. I have called these images or motifs "archetypes," also "dominants" of the unconscious. For a further elucidation of the idea I must refer the reader to the relevant literature.

This discovery means another step forward in our understanding: the recognition, that is, of two layers in the unconscious. We have to distinguish between a personal unconscious and an impersonal or transpersonal unconscious. We speak of the latter also as the collective unconscious, because it is detached from anything personal and is entirely universal, and because its contents can be found everywhere, which is naturally not the case with the personal contents. The personal unconscious contains lost memories, painful ideas that are repressed (i.e., forgotten on purpose), subliminal perceptions, by which are meant sense-perceptions that were not strong enough to reach consciousness, and finally, contents that are not yet ripe for consciousness. It corresponds to the figure of the shadow so frequently met with in dreams.

The primordial images are the most ancient and the most universal "thought-forms" of humanity. They are as much feelings as thoughts; indeed, they lead their own independent life rather in the manner of part-souls, as can easily be seen in those philosophical or Gnostic systems which rely on awareness of the unconscious as the source of knowledge. The idea of angels, archangels, "principalities and powers" in St. Paul, the archons of the Gnostics, the heavenly hierarchy of Dionysius the Areopagite,[3] all come from the perception of the relative autonomy of the archetypes. . . .

The greatest and best thoughts of man shape themselves upon these primordial images as upon a blueprint. I have often been asked where the archetypes or primordial images come from. It seems to me that their origin can only be explained by assuming them to be deposits of the constantly repeated experiences of humanity. One of the commonest and at the same time most impressive experiences is the apparent movement of the sun every day. We certainly cannot discover anything of the kind in the unconscious, so far as the known physical process is concerned. What we do find, on the other hand, is the myth of the sun-hero in all its countless modifications. It is this myth, and not the physical process, that forms the sun archetype. The same can be said of the phases of the moon. The archetype is a kind of readiness to produce over and over again the same or similar mythical ideas. Hence it seems as though what is impressed upon the unconscious were exclusively the subjective fantasy-ideas aroused by the physical process. Therefore we may take it that archetypes are recurrent impressions made by subjective reactions. Naturally this assumption only pushes the problem further back without solving it. There is nothing to prevent us from assuming that certain archetypes exist even in animals, that they are grounded in the peculiarities of the living organism itself and are therefore direct expressions of life whose nature cannot be further explained. Not only

---

[3] Gnosticism (from Greek *gnosis*, knowledge; cf. our word "know") was a syncretistic philosophical-religious movement which, in pre-Christian times, fused elements of Babylonian astral mythology, cabalistic Judaism, Persian Zoroastrianism, and Greek philosophy; at its first contact with Christianity, Gnosticism absorbed the doctrine of Christ as the Redeemer; it came down through the Middle Ages in the beliefs and mystical symbolism of alchemy; and continued into modern times in the occultism of such persons as Madame Blavatsky and the great Irish poet, William Butler Yeats. Dionysius the Areopagite was a first-century Athenian converted by the apostle Paul; in the Middle Ages certain writings of the late fifth or early sixth century were erroneously attributed to him; as author of these, he is now known as the "pseudo-Dionysius." These treatises, on such subjects as "The Celestial Hierarchies" and "The Divine Names," brought to medieval scholasticism —particularly through Thomas Aquinas—the concepts of neo-Platonism and the theology of angels. Jung's point of comparison here is that the "primordial" or "archetypal" contents of the unconscious act with the same independence (autonomy) as that attributed to angels, archangels, etc.

are the archetypes, apparently, impressions of ever-repeated typical experiences, but, at the same time, they behave empirically like agents that tend towards the repetition of these same experiences. For when an archetype appears in a dream, in a fantasy, or in life, it always brings with it a certain influence or power by virtue of which it either exercises a numinous[4] or a fascinating effect, or impels to action.

"No mortal mind can plumb the depths of nature" — nor even the depths of the unconscious. We do know, however, that the unconscious never rests. It seems to be always at work, for even when asleep we dream. There are many people who declare that they never dream, but the probability is that they simply do not remember their dreams. It is significant that people who talk in their sleep mostly have no recollection either of the dream which started them talking, or even of the fact that they dreamed at all. Not a day passes but we make some slip of the tongue, or something slips our memory which at other times we know perfectly well, or we are seized by a mood whose cause we cannot trace, etc. These things are all symptoms of some consistent unconscious activity which becomes directly visible at night in dreams, but only occasionally breaks through the inhibitions imposed by our daytime consciousness.

So far as our present experience goes, we can lay it down that the unconscious processes stand in a compensatory relation to the conscious mind. I expressly use the word "compensatory" and not the word "opposed," because conscious and unconscious are not necessarily in opposition to one another, but complement one another to form a totality, which is the *self*. According to this definition the self is a quantity that is superordinate to the conscious ego. It embraces not only the conscious but also the unconscious psyche, and is therefore, so to speak, a personality which we *also* are. It is easy enough to think of ourselves as possessing part-souls. Thus we can, for instance, see ourselves as a persona without too much difficulty.[5] But it transcends our powers of imagination to form a clear picture of what we are as a self, for in this operation the part

---

[4] See Note 6, page 832.

[5] The term "part-souls" refers here simply to that frequent experience we have of not being just one single, consistent personality, but several different personalities ("part-souls") depending on what different occasions bring to the surface. A "persona" anciently meant a character-mask worn by actors, or the character-type represented by the mask; in Jung's psychology, a "persona" is the character we adopt in public, the appearance we present to other people, the personality we have formed to deal with all our public behavior.

would have to comprehend the whole. There is little hope of our ever being able to reach even approximate consciousness of the self, since however much we may make conscious there will always exist an indeterminate and indeterminable amount of unconscious material which belongs to the totality of the self. Hence the self will always remain a superordinate quantity.

The unconscious processes that compensate the conscious ego contain all those elements that are necessary for the self-regulation of the psyche as a whole. On the personal level, these are the not consciously recognized personal motives which appear in dreams, or the meanings of daily situations which we have overlooked, or conclusions we have failed to draw, or affects we have not permitted, or criticisms we have spared ourselves. But the more we become conscious of ourselves through self-knowledge, and act accordingly, the more the layer of the personal unconscious that is superimposed on the collective unconscious will be diminished. In this way there arises a consciousness which is no longer imprisoned in the petty, oversensitive, personal world of the ego, but participates freely in the wider world of objective interests. This widened consciousness is no longer that touchy, egotistical bundle of personal wishes, fears, hopes, and ambitions which always has to be compensated or corrected by unconscious counter-tendencies; instead, it is a function of relationship to the world of objects, bringing the individual into absolute, binding, and indissoluble communion with the world at large. The complications arising at this stage are no longer egotistic wish-conflicts, but difficulties that concern others as much as oneself. At this stage it is fundamentally a question of collective problems, which have activated the collective unconscious because they require collective rather than personal compensation. We can now see that the unconscious produces contents which are valid not only for the person concerned, but for others as well, in fact for a great many people and possibly for all.

The Elgonyi, natives of the Elgon forests, of central Africa, explained to me that there are two kinds of dreams: the ordinary dream of the little man, and the "big vision" that only the great man has, e.g., the medicine-man or chief. Little dreams are of no account, but if a man has a "big dream" he summons the whole tribe in order to tell it to everybody.

How is a man to know whether his dream is a "big" or a "little" one? He knows it by an instinctive feeling of significance. He feels so overwhelmed by the impression it makes that he would never think of keeping the dream to himself. He *has* to tell it, on the psychologically correct assumption that it is of general significance. Even with us the collective dream has a feeling of importance about it that impels communication. It springs from a conflict of relationship and must therefore be built into our conscious relations, because it compensates these and not just some inner personal quirk.

The processes of the collective unconscious are concerned not only with the more or less personal relations of an individual to his family or to a wider social group, but with his relations to society and to the human community in general. The more general and impersonal the condition that releases the unconscious reaction, the more significant, bizarre, and overwhelming will be the compensatory manifestation. It impels not just private communication, but drives people to revelations and confessions, and even to a dramatic representation of their fantasies.

I will explain by an example how the unconscious manages to compensate relationships. A somewhat arrogant gentleman once came to me for treatment. He ran a business in partnership with his younger brother. Relations between the two brothers were very strained, and this was one of the essential causes of my patient's neurosis. From the information he gave me, the real reason for the tension was not altogether clear. He had all kinds of criticisms to make of his brother, whose gifts he certainly did not show in a very favourable light. The brother frequently came into his dreams, always in the role of a Bismarck, Napoleon, or Julius Caesar. His house looked like the Vatican or Yildiz Kiosk. My patient's unconscious evidently had the need to exalt the rank of the younger brother. From this I concluded that he was setting himself too high and his brother too low. The further course of analysis entirely justified this inference.

Another patient, a young woman who clung to her mother in an extremely sentimental way, always had very sinister dreams about her. She appeared in the dreams as a witch, as a ghost, as a pursuing demon. The mother had spoilt her beyond all reason and had so blinded her by tenderness that the daughter had no conscious idea of her mother's harmful influence. Hence the compensatory criticism exercised by the unconscious.

I myself once happened to put too low a value on a patient, both intellectually and morally. In a dream I saw a castle perched on a high cliff, and on the topmost tower was a balcony, and there sat my patient.

I did not hesitate to tell her this dream at once, naturally with the best results.

We all know how apt we are to make fools of ourselves in front of the very people we have unjustly underrated. Naturally the case can also be reversed, as once happened to a friend of mine. While still a callow student he had written to Virchow, the pathologist, craving an audience with "His Excellency." When, quaking with fear, he presented himself and tried to give his name, he blurted out, "My name is Virchow." Whereupon His Excellency, smiling mischievously, said, "Ah! So your name is Virchow too?" The feeling of his own nullity was evidently too much for the unconscious of my friend, and in consequence it instantly prompted him to present himself as equal to Virchow in grandeur.

In these more personal relations there is of course no need for any very collective compensations. On the other hand, the figures employed by the unconscious in our first case are of a definitely collective nature: they are universally recognized heroes. Here there are two possible interpretations: either my patient's younger brother is a man of acknowledged and far-reaching collective importance, or my patient is overestimating his own importance not merely in relation to his brother but in relation to everybody else as well. For the first assumption there was no support at all, while for the second there was the evidence of one's own eyes. Since the man's extreme arrogance affected not only himself, but a far wider social group, the compensation availed itself of a collective image.

The same is true of the second case. The "witch" is a collective image; hence we must conclude that the blind dependence of the young woman applied as much to the wider social group as it did to her mother personally. This was indeed the case, in so far as she was still living in an exclusively infantile world, where the world was identical with her parents. These examples deal with relations within the personal orbit. There are, however, impersonal relations which occasionally need unconscious compensation. In such cases collective images appear with a more or less mythological character. Moral, philosophical, and religious problems are, on account of their universal validity, the most likely to call for mythological compensation. In the aforementioned[6] novel by H. G. Wells we find a classical type of compensation: Mr. Preemby, a midget personality, discovers that he is really a reincarnation of Sargon, King of

[6] In an earlier part of the essay, not included here.

Kings. Happily, the genius of the author rescues poor old Sargon from pathological absurdity, and even gives the reader a chance to appreciate the tragic and eternal meaning in this lamentable affray. Mr. Preemby, a complete nonentity, recognizes himself as the point of intersection of all ages past and future. This knowledge is not too dearly bought at the cost of a little madness, provided that Preemby is not in the end devoured by that monster of a primordial image — which is in fact what nearly happens to him.

The universal problem of evil and sin is another aspect to our impersonal relations to the world. Almost more than any other, therefore, this problem produces collective compensations. One of my patients, aged sixteen, had as the initial symptom of a severe compulsion neurosis the following dream: *He is walking along an unfamiliar street. It is dark, and he hears steps coming behind him. With a feeling of fear he quickens his pace. The footsteps come nearer, and his fear increases. He begins to run. But the footsteps seem to be overtaking him. Finally he turns round, and there he sees the devil. In deathly terror he leaps into the air and hangs there suspended.* This dream was repeated twice, a sign of its special urgency.

It is a notorious fact that the compulsion neuroses, by reason of their meticulousness and ceremonial punctilio, not only have the surface appearance of a moral problem but are indeed brim-full of inhuman beastliness and ruthless evil, against whose integration[7] the otherwise very delicately organized personality puts up a desperate struggle. This explains why so many things have to be performed in ceremonially "correct" style, as though to counteract the evil hovering in the background. After this dream the neurosis started, and its essential feature was that the patient had, as he put it, to keep himself in a "provisional" or "uncontaminated" state of purity. For this purpose he either severed or made "invalid" all contact with the world and with everything that reminded him of the transitoriness of human existence, by means of lunatic formalities, scrupulous cleansing ceremonies, and the anxious observance of innumerable rules and regulations of an unbelievable complexity. Even before the patient had any suspicion of the hellish existence that lay before him, the dream showed him that if he wanted to come down to earth again there would have to be a pact with evil.

---

[7] Assimilation of the unconscious elements (here "beastliness" and "evil") to one's conscious understanding.

Elsewhere I have described a dream that illustrates the compensation of a religious problem in a young theological student. He was involved in all sorts of difficulties of belief, a not uncommon occurrence in the man of today. In his dream he was the pupil of the "white magician," who, however, was dressed in black. After having instructed him up to a certain point, the white magician told him that they now needed the "black magician." The black magician appeared, but clad in a white robe. He declared that he had found the keys of paradise, but needed the wisdom of the white magician in order to understand how to use them. This dream obviously contains the problem of opposites which, as we know, has found in Taoist philosophy a solution very different from the views prevailing in the West. The figures employed by the dream are impersonal collective images corresponding to the nature of the impersonal religious problem. In contrast to the Christian view, the dream stresses the relativity of good and evil in a way that immediately calls to mind the Taoist symbol of Yin and Yang.[8]

We should certainly not conclude from these compensations that, as the conscious mind becomes more deeply engrossed in universal problems, the unconscious will bring forth correspondingly far-reaching compensations. There is what one might call a legitimate and an illegitimate interest in impersonal problems. Excursions of this kind are legitimate only when they arise from the deepest and truest needs of the individual; illegitimate when they are either mere intellectual curiosity or a flight from unpleasant reality. In the latter case the unconscious produces all too human and purely personal compensations, whose manifest aim is to bring the conscious mind back to ordinary reality. People who go illegitimately mooning after the infinite often have absurdly banal dreams which endeavour to damp down their ebullience. Thus, from the nature of the compensation, we can at once draw conclusions as to the seriousness and rightness of the conscious strivings.

There are certainly not a few people who are afraid to admit that the unconscious could ever have "big" ideas. They will object, "But do you really believe that the unconscious is capable of offering anything

[8] Taoism is the traditional philosophy and religion of China, founded, according to legend, by Lao-tse (or Lao-tzu) in the sixth century B.C. While the opposites of "good" and "evil" are pitted against each other in Christianity, in Taoism both are integral to the whole of nature and experience. On the symbol of Yin and Yang, see page 493. The attitude of Taoism toward good and evil is related to that of Zen, described in Alan Watts' article on Zen later in this book.

like a constructive crticism of our Western mentality?" Of course, if we take the problem intellectually and impute rational intentions to the unconscious, the thing becomes absurd. But it would never do to foist our conscious psychology upon the unconscious. Its mentality is an instinctive one; it has no differentiated functions, and it does not "think" as we understand "thinking." It simply creates an image that answers to the conscious situation. This image contains as much thought as feeling, and is anything rather than a product of rationalistic reflection. Such an image would be better described as an artistic vision. We tend to forget that a problem like the one which underlies the dream last mentioned cannot, even to the conscious mind of the dreamer, be an intellectual problem, but is profoundly emotional. For a moral man the ethical problem is a passionate question which has its roots in the deepest instinctual processes as well as in his most idealistic aspirations. The problem for him is devastatingly real. It is not surprising, therefore, that the answer likewise springs from the depths of his nature. The fact that everyone thinks his psychology is the measure of all things, and, if he also happens to be a fool, will inevitably think that such a problem is beneath his notice, should not trouble the psychologist in the least, for he has to take things objectively, as he finds them, without twisting them to fit his subjective suppositions. The richer and more capacious natures may legitimately be gripped by an impersonal problem, and to the extent that this is so, their unconscious can answer in the same style. And just as the conscious mind can put the question, "Why is there this frightful conflict between good and evil?," so the unconscious can reply, "Look closer! Each needs the other. The best, just because it is the best, holds the seed of evil, and there is nothing so bad but good can come of it."

It might then dawn on the dreamer that the apparently insoluble conflict is, perhaps, a prejudice, a frame of mind conditioned by time and place. The seemingly complex dream-image might easily reveal itself as plain, instinctive common sense, as the tiny germ of a rational idea, which a maturer mind could just as well have thought consciously. At all events Chinese philosophy thought of it ages ago. The singularly apt, plastic configuration of thought is the prerogative of that primitive, natural spirit which is alive in all of us and is only obscured by a one-sided conscious development. If we consider the unconscious compensations from this angle, we might justifiably be accused of judging the unconscious too much from the conscious standpoint. And indeed, in pursuing these reflections, I have always started from the view that the unconscious simply reacts to the conscious contents, albeit in a very significant way, but that it lacks initiative. It is, however, far from my intention to give the impression that the unconscious is merely reactive in all cases. On the contrary, there is a host of experiences which seem to prove that the unconscious is not only spontaneous but can actually take the lead. There are innumerable cases of people who lingered on in a pettifogging unconsciousness, only to become neurotic in the end. Thanks to the neurosis contrived by the unconscious, they are shaken out of their apathy, and this in spite of their own laziness and often desperate resistance.

Yet it would, in my view, be wrong to suppose that in such cases the unconscious is working to a deliberate and concerted plan and is striving to realize certain definite ends. I have found nothing to support this assumption. The driving force, so far as it is possible for us to grasp it, seems to be in essence only an urge towards self-realization. If it were a matter of some general teleological plan, then all individuals who enjoy a surplus of unconsciousness would necessarily be driven towards higher consciousness by an irresistible urge. That is plainly not the case. There are vast masses of the population who, despite their notorious unconsciousness, never get anywhere near a neurosis. The few who are smitten by such a fate are really persons of the "higher" type who, for one reason or another, have remained too long on a primitive level. Their nature does not in the long run tolerate persistence in what is for them an unnatural torpor. As a result of their narrow conscious outlook and their cramped existence they save energy; bit by bit it accumulates in the unconscious and finally explodes in the form of a more or less acute neurosis. This simple mechanism does not necessarily conceal a "plan." A perfectly understandable urge towards self-realization would provide a quite satisfactory explanation. We could also speak of a retarded maturation of the personality.

Since it is highly probable that we are still a long way from the summit of absolute consciousness, presumably everyone is capable of wider consciousness, and we may assume accordingly that the unconscious processes are constantly supplying us with contents which, if consciously recognized, would extend the range of consciousness. Looked at in this way, the unconscious appears as a field of experience of unlimited extent. If it were merely reactive to the conscious mind, we might aptly call it a psychic mirror-world. In that case, the real source of all contents and activities would lie in the conscious mind, and there would be absolutely nothing in the unconscious except the distorted reflections of conscious contents. The creative process would be shut up in the conscious mind, and anything new would be nothing but conscious invention or cleverness. The empirical facts give the lie to this. Every creative man knows that spontaneity is the very essence of creative thought. Because the unconscious is not just a reactive mirror-reflection, but an independent, productive activity, its realm of experience is a self-contained world, having its own reality, of which we can only say that it affects us as we affect it— precisely what we say about our experience of the outer world. And just as material objects are the constituent elements of this world, so psychic factors constitute the objects of that other world.

The idea of psychic objectivity is by no means a new discovery. It is in fact one of the earliest and most universal achievements of humanity: it is nothing less than the conviction as to the concrete existence of a spirit-world. The spirit-world was certainly never an invention in the sense that fire-boring was an invention; it was far rather the experience, the conscious acceptance of a reality in no way inferior to that of the material world. I doubt whether primitives exist anywhere who are not acquainted with magical influence or a magical substance. ("Magical" is simply another word for "psychic.") It would also appear that practically all primitives are aware of the existence of spirits. "Spirit" is a psychic fact. Just as we distinguish our own bodiliness from bodies that are strange to us, so primitives—if they have any notion of "souls" at all — distinguish between their own souls and the spirits, which are felt as strange and as "not belonging." They are objects of outward perception, whereas their own soul (or one of several souls where a plurality is assumed), though believed to be essentially akin to the spirits, is not usually an object of so-called sensible perception. After death the soul (or one of the plurality of souls) becomes a spirit which survives the dead man, and often it shows a marked deterioration of character that partly contradicts the notion of personal immortality. The Bataks, of Sumatra, go so far as to assert that the people who were good in this life turn into malign and dangerous spirits. Nearly everything that the primitives say about the tricks which the spirits play on the living, and the general picture they give of the *revenants*,[9] corresponds down to the last detail with the phenomena established by spiritualistic experience. And

[9] From the French verb *revenir*, to come back: the spirits of the dead who come back to the realm of the living.

just as the communications from the "Beyond" can be seen to be the activities of broken-off bits of the psyche, so these primitive spirits are manifestations of unconscious complexes. The importance that modern psychology attaches to the "parental complex" is a direct continuation of primitive man's experience of the dangerous power of the ancestral spirits. Even the error of judgment which leads him unthinkingly to assume that the spirits are realities of the external world is carried on in our assumption (which is only partially correct) that the real parents are responsible for the parental complex. In the old trauma theory of Freudian psychoanalysis, and in other quarters as well, this assumption even passed for a scientific explanation. (It was in order to avoid this confusion that I advocated the term "parental imago."[10])

The simple soul is of course quite unaware of the fact that his nearest relations, who exercise immediate influence over him, create in him an image which is only partly a replica of themselves, while its other part is compounded of elements derived from himself. The imago is built up of parental influences plus the specific reactions of the child; it is therefore an image that reflects the object with very considerable qualifications. Naturally, the simple soul believes that his parents are as he sees them. The image is unconsciously projected, and when the parents die, the projected image goes on working as though it were a spirit existing on its own. The primitive then speaks of parental spirits who return by night (*revenants*), while the modern man calls it a father or mother complex.

The more limited a man's field of consciousness is, the more numerous the psychic contents (imagos) which meet him as quasi-external apparitions, either in the form of spirits, or as magical potencies projected upon living people (magicians, witches, etc.). At a rather higher stage of development, where the idea of the soul already exists, not all the imagos continue to be projected (where this happens, even trees and stones talk), but one or the other complex has come near enough to consciousness to be felt as no longer strange, but as somehow "belonging." Nevertheless, the feeling that it "belongs" is not at first sufficiently

[10] In its derivation from the Latin, "imago" means simply "image," copy, or reflection; but as used in modern psychology, an "imago"—for instance, the term "parental imago" used here—is not the same thing as an exact image or reflection of something external, such as the actual parent, but is a conception built up by the unconscious mind, a conception which may not have any exact resemblance to, for instance, the actual parent.

strong for the complex to be sensed as a subjective content of conscious-ness. It remains in a sort of no man's land between conscious and un-conscious, in the half-shadow, in part belonging or akin to the conscious subject, in part an autonomous being, and meeting consciousness as such. At all events it is not necessarily obedient to subjective intentions, it may even be of a higher order, more often than not a source of inspiration or warning, or of "supernatural" information. Psychologically such a con-tent could be explained as a partly autonomous complex that is not yet fully integrated. The archaic souls, the *ba* and *ka* of the Egyptians, are complexes of this kind.[11] At a still higher level, and particularly among the civilized peoples of the West, this complex is invariably of the femi-nine gender. . . . a fact for which deeper and cogent reasons are not lacking.

⌁ FOR DISCUSSION AND WRITING

1. In the first paragraph, where Jung describes briefly the Freudian theory of the unconscious, what three points does he make—namely, (a) about the contents of the unconscious, according to Freud, (b) about the pro-cess of "repression," and (c) about the removal of repressions through psychoanalysis? Study the second, third, and fourth paragraphs carefully, and then write down Jung's chief arguments against the Freudian view, using a sentence for each. If, through analysis, all those contents of the unconscious which have been acquired in one's personal life, and "re-pressed," could be brought into consciousness, would the unconscious then be entirely empty—that is, would one cease to have an uncon-scious?

2. What does Jung mean by "primordial" images or "archetypes"? Are these acquired through personal experience? How do they get into the uncon-scious? What are the "two layers" of the unconscious, according to Jung? Which of these "layers" corresponds to the unconscious as described by

---

[11] The *ba* and *ka* of the Egyptians were names for different spiritual entities sup-posed, in a very complex theory of human nature, to compose or partake in the human personality and to be separable from the body. In Western civilizations and languages, the "soul" has always been thought of as feminine, as in the Greek word *psyche* (from which our word "psychology" derives) and the Latin *anima*, meaning the "soul" as the principle of life or "animation."

Freud? (Note: Jung's term "the collective unconscious" means simply those contents of the unconscious that are *common* to everybody.)

3. How does Jung answer the question of where the archetypes or primordial images come from? How does he distinguish them from "ideas"?

4. What signs does he cite of the fact that the unconscious is ceaselessly active? In speaking of the relationship between the unconscious and the conscious mind, what term does he use for that relationship (instead, for instance, of the term "opposed")? What, in Jung's terminology, is the *self*? Is the "self" wholly conscious? Can it ever be wholly conscious? What does Jung mean by saying that the "self" is "superordinate to the conscious ego"? What do *you* mean by your "self"?

5. In the paragraph beginning "The unconscious processes that compensate the conscious ego contain all those elements that are necessary for the self-regulation of the psyche . . . ," what does Jung say is the effect of our becoming more and more aware of the content of our *personal* unconscious? Though he doesn't say anything explicitly here as to how that increased awareness can be achieved, can you make any inference as to how it is to be achieved? Why does a heavily burdened and active *personal* unconscious (busy with ego compensations, guilt feelings, etc.) prevent our engaging objectively in the wider human interests and thus realizing more completely our own potentialities? When the *personal* unconscious is diminished more and more by assimilation to consciousness (this, incidentally, is really a definition of "self-knowledge"), there is still the *common* or "collective" unconscious left in us; how does this deeper and immensely older part of the psyche interact with our wider and more objective human interests—once one is freed from the crippling repressions of the personal unconscious?

6. What analogy does Jung draw between the "big" and "little" dreams of more primitive peoples (he could have cited the American Plains Indians here, as well as the Elgonyi of central Africa) and the two "layers" of the unconscious? How does one know whether one's dream is a "big" one or a "little" one? (If the distinction doesn't ring any bell for you, you might go to the library and glance at the first page of Bunyan's *Pilgrim's Progress* and the first page of Keats's *The Fall of Hyperion: A Dream*. In these two instances, what signs of the "big" dream do you see?—that is, what signs that the "dream" has collective rather than narrowly personal implications?)

7. Jung has been using the terms "compensatory" and "compensation" for the relationship of the unconscious to the conscious mind, but has so far left the terms undefined; however, he begins to explain that relationship in the paragraph that starts with the sentence "I will explain by an example how the unconscious manages to compensate relationships." How is "compensation" illustrated in the case of the "somewhat arrogant gentleman" who frequently dreamed of his brother as a Bismarck, Napoleon, or Julius Caesar? How is it illustrated in the young woman's dreams of her mother as a witch or demon? How is it illustrated in the student's slip of the tongue in introducing himself as "Virchow"?

8. All those examples illustrate the compensatory activity of the *personal* unconscious (why of the *personal* unconscious?), but the first two also use "collective images"; explain why Jung calls the images in the first two dreams "collective images." Why does Jung conclude, therefore, that the problems of the arrogant gentleman and the young woman involve more than the brother of the one and the mother of the other—involve their general attitudes toward and relationships with their whole social environment?

9. What is the "collective image" (or, in other words, the "archetypal image" deriving from the "collective unconscious") in the sixteen-year-old's dream of being pursued by the devil? What is the "collective" character of the young theology student's dream of the white and black magicians? (If you have read or seen Genet's play *The Blacks*, you might be able to cite some similar "collective images" there.) Why should the problem of "evil and sin" produce "collective" or "archetypal" images in dreams and fantasies (as in both the dreams mentioned above)? If you have read Dickens' *Great Expectations*, do you find in Lawyer Jaggers' constant washing of his hands and manipulation of his big white handkerchief any parallel with the punctilious exorcism of evil in the "compulsion neuroses" described by Jung? Is there any aspect of "compulsion neurosis," and its occupation with "sin and evil," in our Puritan inheritance? Is there any similar aspect in our extreme concern with "germs," germicides, disinfectants, smell-killers, "cleanliness" as being next to "godliness"? (If you have read Rachel Carson's piece, earlier in this book, you may have noticed a "collective" parallel to "compulsion neurosis.")

10. According to Jung, has the unconscious any teleological plan or purpose? (If you don't know what "teleological" means, this is a good time to look it up.) Given the fact that "we are still a long way from the summit of

absolute consciousness," what *is* the use or value of coming to some understanding of the working of the unconscious mind? Why not just ignore
it, as inferior to the conscious mind? *Is* it inferior to the conscious mind?
Jung says, "it affects us as we affect it"; what does this mean as to the relationship between the conscious and the unconscious mind? Could one
infer here that one might *talk to* one's unconscious, telling it what one
would like it to do and what one would like it not to do — just as the unconscious mind talks to us in remembered dreams or in daytime fantasies?
(We are used to thinking of these parts of the mind as divided from each
other by floors or ceilings, like two apartments in an apartment building,
one above the other, with no door or intercourse between the two. A better
image is of the two hands clasped together, fingers interlaced.)

11. In the last three paragraphs of this piece, how does Jung account for the
universal belief in "spirits" and a "spirit-world"? Does his account of the
"spiritual" realm make it any less objective, and less real? What does
Jung have to say, at the end of the piece, about Freud's identification of
the "parental imago" with the real parents? What, according to Jung,
comprises the "parental imago"? What does he mean by the "projection"
of this imago upon the real parents? How do the beliefs of primitive people about the "ancestors" illustrate the kind of "projection" we all make
of our feelings about our parents?

12. For a writing assignment, you might make a considered comparison between Jung's and Freud's ideas of the unconscious, as shown in this and
the preceding piece. Or, if you have had "big" and "little" dreams, you
might describe and discuss them in relation to the two "layers" of the
unconscious. Or you might undertake the theme that "we are still a long
way from the summit of absolute consciousness," or its reverse.

Marcel Proust ◆§ The Bodily Memory

◆§ See note on page 125. Reprinted here are the last pages of the "Overture" to *Remembrance of Things Past*. The passage is the most famous in Proust, containing that unforgettable image of the relationship between the conscious and the unconscious mind—the "madeleine" cupcake dipped in the lime-flower tea. It is much later in Proust's great book that he uses, for the kind of recall illustrated here, the term "bodily memory." ℥

I FEEL that there is much to be said for the Celtic belief that the souls of those whom we have lost are held captive in some inferior being, in an animal, in a plant, in some inanimate object, and so effectively lost to us until the day (which to many never comes) when we happen to pass by the tree or to obtain possession of the object which forms their prison. Then they start and tremble, they call us by our name, and as soon as we have recognised their voice the spell is broken. We have delivered them: they have overcome death and return to share our life.

And so it is with our own past. It is a labour in vain to attempt to recapture it: all the efforts of our intellect must prove futile. The past is hidden somewhere outside the realm, beyond the reach of intellect, in

From "Swann's Way," Volume I in *Remembrance of Things Past* by Marcel Proust, translated by C. K. Scott Moncrieff. Copyright 1928 and renewed 1956 by The Modern Library. Reprinted by permission of Random House, Inc. Acknowledgment is also made to Mr. George Scott Moncrieff and, for the French edition, © Editions Gallimard.

some material object (in the sensation which that material object will give us) which we do not suspect. And as for that object, it depends on chance whether we come upon it or not before we ourselves must die.

Many years had elapsed during which nothing of Combray,[1] save what was comprised in the theatre and the drama of my going to bed there, had any existence for me, when one day in winter, as I came home, my mother, seeing that I was cold, offered me some tea, a thing I did not ordinarily take. I declined at first, and then, for no particular reason, changed my mind. She sent out for one of those short, plump little cakes called 'petites madeleines,' which look as though they had been moulded in the fluted scallop of a pilgrim's shell. And soon, mechanically, weary after a dull day with the prospect of a depressing morrow, I raised to my lips a spoonful of the tea in which I had soaked a morsel of the cake. No sooner had the warm liquid, and the crumbs with it, touched my palate than a shudder ran through my whole body, and I stopped, intent upon the extraordinary changes that were taking place. An exquisite pleasure had invaded my senses, but individual, detached, with no suggestion of its origin. And at once the vicissitudes of life had become indifferent to me, its disasters innocuous, its brevity illusory — this new sensation having had on me the effect which love has of filling me with a precious essence; or rather this essence was not in me, it was myself. I had ceased now to feel mediocre, accidental, mortal. Whence could it have come to me, this all-powerful joy? I was conscious that it was connected with the taste of tea and cake, but that it infinitely transcended those savours, could not, indeed, be of the same nature as theirs. Whence did it come? What did it signify? How could I seize upon and define it?

I drink a second mouthful, in which I find nothing more than in the first, a third, which gives me rather less than the second. It is time to stop; the potion is losing its magic. It is plain that the object of my quest, the truth, lies not in the cup but in myself. The tea has called up in me, but does not itself understand, and can only repeat indefinitely with a gradual loss of strength, the same testimony; which I, too, cannot interpret, though I hope at least to be able to call upon the tea for it again and to find it there presently, intact and at my disposal, for my final enlightenment. I put down my cup and examine my own mind. It is for it to discover the truth. But how? What an abyss of uncertainty whenever the

---

[1] The village where the hero of *Remembrance of Things Past* spent much of his childhood.

mind feels that some part of it has strayed beyond its own borders; when it, the seeker, is at once the dark region through which it must go seeking, where all its equipment will avail it nothing. Seek? More than that: create. It is face to face with something which does not so far exist, to which it alone can give reality and substance, which it alone can bring into the light of day.

And I begin again to ask myself what it could have been, this unremembered state which brought with it no logical proof of its existence, but only the sense that it was a happy, that it was a real state in whose presence other states of consciousness melted and vanished. I decide to attempt to make it reappear. I retrace my thoughts to the moment at which I drank the first spoonful of tea. I find again the same state, illumined by no fresh light. I compel my mind to make one further effort, to allow and recapture once again the fleeting sensation. And that nothing may interrupt it in its course I shut out every obstacle, every extraneous idea, I stop my ears and inhibit all attention to the sounds which come from the next room. And then, feeling that my mind is growing fatigued without having any success to report, I compel it for a change to enjoy that distraction which I have just denied it, to think of other things, to rest and refresh itself before the supreme attempt. And then for the second time I clear an empty space in front of it. I place in position before my mind's eye the still recent taste of that first mouthful, and I feel something start within me, something that leaves its resting-place and attempts to rise, something that has been embedded like an anchor at a great depth; I do not know yet what it is, but I can feel it mounting slowly; I can measure the resistance, I can hear the echo of great spaces traversed.

Undoubtedly what is thus palpitating in the depths of my being must be the image, the visual memory which, being linked to that taste, has tried to follow it into my conscious mind. But its struggles are too far off, too much confused; scarcely can I perceive the colourless reflection in which are blended the uncapturable whirling medley of radiant hues, and I cannot distinguish its form, cannot invite it, as the one possible interpreter, to translate to me the evidence of its contemporary, its inseparable paramour, the taste of cake soaked in tea; cannot ask it to inform me what special circumstance is in question, of what period in my past life.

Will it ultimately reach the clear surface of my consciousness, this memory, this old, dead moment which the magnetism of an identical moment has travelled so far to importune, to disturb, to raise up out of the very depths of my being? I cannot tell. Now that I feel nothing, it has stopped, has perhaps gone down again into its darkness, from which who can say whether it will ever rise? Ten times over I must essay the task, must lean down over the abyss. And each time the natural laziness which deters us from every difficult enterprise, every work of importance, has urged me to leave the thing alone, to drink my tea and to think merely of the worries of to-day and of my hopes for to-morrow, which let themselves be pondered over without effort or distress of mind.

And suddenly the memory returns. The taste was that of the little crumb of madeleine which on Sunday mornings at Combray (because on those mornings I did not go out before church-time), when I went to say good day to her in her bedroom, my aunt Léonie used to give me, dipping it first in her own cup of real or of lime-flower tea. The sight of the little madeleine had recalled nothing to my mind before I tasted it; perhaps because I had so often seen such things in the interval, without tasting them, on the trays in pastry-cooks' windows, that their image had dissociated itself from those Combray days to take its place among others more recent; perhaps because of those memories, so long abandoned and put out of mind, nothing now survived, everything was scattered; the forms of things, including that of the little scallop-shell of pastry, so richly sensual under its severe, religious folds, were either obliterated or had been so long dormant as to have lost the power of expansion which would have allowed them to resume their place in my consciousness. But when from a long-distant past nothing subsists, after the people are dead, after the things are broken and scattered, still, alone, more fragile, but with more vitality, more unsubstantial, more persistent, more faithful, the smell and taste of things remain poised a long time, like souls, ready to remind us, waiting and hoping for their moment, amid the ruins of all the rest; and bear unfaltering, in the tiny and almost impalpable drop of their essence, the vast structure of recollection.

And once I had recognized the taste of the crumb of madeleine soaked in her decoction of lime-flowers which my aunt used to give me (although I did not yet know and must long postpone the discovery of why this memory made me so happy) immediately the old grey house upon the street, where her room was, rose up like the scenery of a theatre to attach itself to the little pavilion, opening on to the garden, which had been built out behind it for my parents (the isolated panel which until that moment had been all that I could see); and with the house the town, from morning to night and in all weathers, the Square where I was sent before luncheon, the streets along which I used to run errands, the country roads we took when it was fine. And just as the Japanese amuse themselves by filling a porcelain bowl with water and steeping in it little crumbs of paper which until then are without character or form, but, the moment they become wet, stretch themselves and bend, take on colour and distinctive shape, become flowers or houses or people, permanent and recognisable, so in that moment all the flowers in our garden and in M. Swann's park, and the water-lilies on the Vivonne and the good folk of the village and their little dwellings and the parish church and the whole of Combray and of its surroundings, taking their proper shapes and growing solid, sprang into being, town and gardens alike, from my cup of tea.

✍ FOR DISCUSSION AND WRITING

1. What is the relation between the "Celtic belief" mentioned in the first paragraph and the episode of the madeleine and tea? (Incidentally, what does the word "Celtic" mean?) Explain Proust's statement in the second paragraph that one's personal past is "beyond the reach of intellect" and is hidden "in some material object." A good deal later on in Proust's huge novel, the protagonist (he is called "Marcel"), who wants to be a writer, tries to write a descriptive piece about his memories of Venice and finds that all the memories he can bring back by conscious intellectual effort have a thin, two-dimensional, abstract character like the lines on a blueprint or like the cliché writing of travel-bureau pamphlets; then one evening he happens to stumble over a cobblestone in the courtyard of a house in Paris, and suddenly, just through that sensation of stumbling on the cobblestone, all of Venice as he had known it in youth rushes back into him, three-dimensional, concrete, tangible through all the senses. Proust calls the first kind of memory "intellectual memory," and the second kind of memory "bodily memory." How is the term "*bodily* memory" illustrated in the episode here, and how does Proust show the resistance of this kind of memory to intellectual effort?

2. In the third paragraph, Proust switches to the present tense; try to explain in a "functional" way why he does so—why the present tense is more ef-

fective here than the past tense would be, although the incident occurred in the past. (The more perceptive you can become about the expressive, communicative functions of that horrid thing called "grammar," the more adept you will be in all your efforts to communicate, whether in prose or poetry. Even the most subtle poet learns that grammar—far from being the ugly old hag, repulsively arbitrary, domineering Freshman English courses—is a Muse, beautiful in power and grace, yielding unsuspected secrets of skill in communication, if one learns her ways and obeys her.)

3. Write down in your own words a condensed paraphrase of the last part of the fourth paragraph, beginning "What an abyss of uncertainty . . ." and ending ". . . which it alone can bring into the light of day," paying particular attention to these words and phrases: "the mind," "beyond its own borders," "the dark region," "create," "something which does not so far exist," "which it alone can bring into the light of day." If you have read the preceding pieces from Freud and Jung, you may find some of their concepts helpful. Explain the image of the anchor coming from a great depth. Can you think of any justification for Proust's obvious feeling that the effort of this kind of recall is important and worth the difficulty?

4. Scott Moncrieff's translation of Proust, which is the one we read here, ranks with the greatest achievements of translation; a hoary academic joke is about the person who enunciated a preference for Elizabeth Barrett Browning's sonnets in the original Portuguese and for Proust in French. The high quality of the translation justifies an analysis of style. Consider, for instance, the sentence that ends the next to the last paragraph, beginning "But when from a long-distant past nothing subsists, after the people are dead, after the things are broken and scattered. . . ." What, precisely, is the main clause of this sentence? How many predicates does the subject of the sentence have? What kind of grammatical construction begins the sentence? What kind of grammatical constructions are these: "alone, more fragile, but with more vitality, more unsubstantial, more persistent, more faithful . . ."? And what do these phrases modify: "like souls, ready to remind us, waiting and hoping . . ."? Grammar handbooks usually say that the proper use of the semicolon is between two independent clauses; is the part after the semicolon here an independent clause? What justifies its use? Now, with all that grammar under your hat, make a considered comment on the *function* of the grammar in that long sentence—a comment on how the grammar communicates *sensuously* or *kinetically* to the reader the meaning of the sentence.

5. Explain the analogy with Japanese paper flowers (if you have ever amused yourself with those pretty things). What is the relationship between this analogy and the "Celtic belief" mentioned at the beginning?

6. The experience described in this piece is of the kind called "*déjà vu,*" which everybody has had at one time or another, though we rarely make any attempt to trace it back to its source as Proust does. If you have had this kind of experience, try to write about it in a short paper, making the effort to trace it back, also attempting to explain why the experience is accompanied by a sense of a strange, new dimension in life and sometimes by the euphoria Proust describes in the third paragraph.

THEORIES OF KNOWLEDGE

Plato ⋙ The Allegory of the Cave

⋙ See note on Plato, page 139. The persons of the dialogue are Socrates and Glaucon. ⋘

The den, the prisoners: the light at a distance;

Socrates: And now, I said, let me show in a figure[1] how far our nature is enlightened or unenlightened: — Behold! human beings living in an underground den, which has a mouth open towards the light and reaching all along the den; here they have been from their childhood, and have their legs and necks chained so that they cannot move, and can

From Book VII of the *Republic* by Plato, translated by Benjamin Jowett (Random House, 1937).

[1] A semblance or image (as in "a figure of speech").

only see before them, being prevented by the chains from turning round their heads. Above and behind them a fire is blazing at a distance, and between the fire and the prisoners there is a raised way; and you will see, if you look, a low wall built along the way, like the screen which marionette players have in front of them, over which they show the puppets.

Glaucon: I see.

And do you see, I said, men passing along the wall carrying all sorts of vessels, and statues and figures of animals made of wood and stone and various materials, which appear over the wall? Some of them are talking, others silent.

You have shown me a strange image, and they are strange prisoners.

Like ourselves, I replied; and they see only their own shadows, or the shadows of one another, which the fire throws on the opposite wall of the cave?

the low wall, and the moving figures of which the shadows are seen on the opposite wall of the den.

True, he said; how could they see anything but the shadows if they were never allowed to move their heads?

And of the objects which are being carried in like manner they would only see the shadows?

Yes, he said.

And if they were able to converse with one another, would they not suppose that they were naming what was actually before them?

Very true.

And suppose further that the prison had an echo which came from the other side, would they not be sure to fancy when one of the passers-by spoke that the voice which they heard came from the passing shadow?

The prisoners would mistake the shadows for realities.

No question, he replied.

To them, I said, the truth would be literally nothing but the shadows of the images.

That is certain.

And now look again, and see what will naturally follow if the prisoners are released and disabused of their error. At first, when any of them is liberated and compelled suddenly to stand up and turn his neck round and walk and look towards the light, he will suffer sharp pains; the glare will distress him, and he will be unable to see the realities of which in his former state he had seen the shadows; and then conceive some one saying to him, that what he saw before was an illusion, but that now, when he is approaching nearer to being and his eye is turned towards more real existence, he has a clearer vision, — what will be his reply? And you may further imagine that his instructor is pointing to the objects as they pass and requiring him to name them, — will he not be perplexed? Will he not fancy that the shadows which he formerly saw are truer than the objects which are now shown to him?

And when released, they would still persist in maintaining the superior truth of the shadows.

Far truer.

And if he is compelled to look straight at the light, will he not have a pain in his eyes which will make him turn away to take refuge in the objects of vision which he can see, and which he will conceive to be in reality clearer than the things which are now being shown to him?

True, he said.

When dragged upwards, they would be dazzled by excess of light.

And suppose once more, that he is reluctantly dragged up a steep and rugged ascent, and held fast until he is forced into the presence of the sun himself, is he not likely to be pained and irritated? When he approaches the light his eyes will be dazzled, and he will not be able to see anything at all of what are now called realities.

Not all in a moment, he said.

He will require to grow accustomed to the sight of the upper world. And first he will see the shadows best, next the reflections of men and other objects in

the water, and then the objects themselves; then he
will gaze upon the light of the moon and the stars
and the spangled heaven; and he will see the sky
and the stars by night better than the sun or the
light of the sun by day?

Certainly.

Last of all he will be able to see the sun, and *At length they will see the sun and understand his nature.*
not mere reflections of him in the water, but he will
see him in his own proper place, and not in another;
and he will contemplate him as he is.

Certainly.

He will then proceed to argue that this is he
who gives the season and the years, and is the
guardian of all that is in the visible world, and in a
certain way the cause of all things which he and his
fellows have been accustomed to behold?

Clearly, he said, he would first see the sun and
then reason about him.

And when he remembered his old habitation, *They would then pity their old companions of the den,*
and the wisdom of the den and his fellow-prisoners,
do you not suppose that he would felicitate himself
on the change, and pity them?

Certainly, he would.

And if they were in the habit of conferring honours among themselves on those who were quickest
to observe the passing shadows and to remark which
of them went before, and which followed after, and
which were together; and who were therefore best
able to draw conclusions as to the future, do you
think that he would care for such honours and
glories, or envy the possessors of them? Would he
not say with Homer,

'Better to be the poor servant of a poor master,'

and to endure anything, rather than think as they
do and live after their manner?

Yes, he said, I think that he would rather suffer
anything than entertain those false notions and live
in this miserable manner.

Imagine once more, I said, such an one coming suddenly out of the sun to be replaced in his old situation; would he not be certain to have his eyes full of darkness?

To be sure, he said.

But when they returned to the den they would see much worse than those who had never left it.

And if there were a contest, and he had to compete in measuring the shadows with the prisoners who had never moved out of the den, while his sight was still weak, and before his eyes had become steady (and the time which would be needed to acquire this new habit of sight might be very considerable), would he not be ridiculous? Men would say of him that up he went and down he came without his eyes; and that it was better not even to think of ascending; and if any one tried to loose another and lead him up to the light, let them only catch the offender, and they would put him to death.

No question, he said.

The prison is the world of sight, the light of the fire is the sun.

This entire allegory, I said, you may now append, dear Glaucon, to the previous argument; the prison-house is the world of sight, the light of the fire is the sun, and you will not misapprehend me if you interpret the journey upwards to be the ascent of the soul into the intellectual world according to my poor belief, which, at your desire, I have expressed — whether rightly or wrongly God knows. But, whether true or false, my opinion is that in the world of knowledge the idea of good appears last of all, and is seen only with an effort; and when seen, is also inferred to be the universal author of all things beautiful and right, parent of light and of the lord of light in this visible world, and the immediate source of reason and truth in the intellectual; and that this is the power upon which he who would act rationally either in public or private life must have his eye fixed.

I agree, he said, as far as I am able to understand you.

↩§ FOR DISCUSSION AND WRITING

1. Look up the word "allegory" in the dictionary and state, in a single sentence, the application of the term to this piece. What is the relationship between an allegory and a metaphor? and between allegory and symbolism?

2. What, *in a single word*, is the subject of the piece?

3. This famous allegory is so neatly formed, with such precise visualization, that it should offer no difficulty at all to the student, but—just to be sure we understand it—let us follow each of the steps. Why do the prisoners in the cave think the shadows on the wall in front of them are "real"? When a prisoner is released and allowed to go outside the cave, what are his first sensations? Why does he refuse to believe in the reality of what he now sees? If he is pushed up the bank so that he looks straight at the sun, why can he at first see nothing at all? When his vision is a bit better adjusted, and he starts to reason about what he sees, what will he think is the cause of everything? What will be his appraisal of his former life and its values? If he returns then to the cave, will he be able to see as well as the other prisoners? Why will he be thought ridiculous? Why will the people in the cave put him to death and refuse to let anyone else go outside? Now go through this whole sequence again, this time giving the allegorical equivalent or *meaning* of the cave, the prisoners, the shadows, and so on.

4. Without falling into the anachronism of making Socrates into a kind of fifth-century B.C. Christian, explicate in your own words, in from one to three sentences, Socrates' last statement in this dialogue, beginning "But, whether true or false, my opinion is that in the world of knowledge. . . ." If you have read the selection from Plato's *Symposium* earlier in this book, what correspondences do you find between the allegory of the cave and the teachings of Diotima? (This question also might provide the subject for a short paper, giving you a good exercise in objective analysis and in firming up your understanding of Plato.)

5. In the history of philosophy, Plato's philosophy is what is known as "philosophical realism." The term "realism" has a number of other meanings, and in its common modern use it means something almost completely opposite

to what it means as applied to Plato. What meaning, or meanings, do you ordinarily give to the word? In the allegory of the cave, the terms "real" and "reality" are used several times; what is meant here by them? In view of their use here, how would you interpret the term "realism" in connection with Plato's philosophy?

6. A very interesting writing assignment for a short paper would be an application of the allegory of the cave to the experience of people living in an authoritarian state where the press and other media were state-controlled and young people were educated in a sealed system of propaganda, so that when they were allowed outside their country what they could "see" would be like what the prisoner of the cave saw when he first entered the outside world. One could turn this topic around in a number of ways.

René Descartes ✑ A Thinking Thing

✑ French mathematician and philosopher (1596-1650). Descartes was schooled in a Jesuit college, served as soldier in Holland, traveled and studied in France, Germany, and Italy, becoming learned not only in mathematics but also in chemistry, anatomy, physiology, and astronomy; in 1628 he settled in Holland as the country where he would be least disturbed in his studies and writing. He discovered and developed analytic geometry, formulated the Cartesian method of doubt as a scientific discipline, sought a foundation for all scientific truth in principles as "clear and distinct" as those of mathematics; though a devout Catholic, he showed how the world might have come into being according to physical laws and proposed a mechanical explanation of the human body (the body "as a machine made by the hands of God"). Descartes is looked upon as the founder of modern philosophy and of the philosophical bases of the sciences. His most famous works are his *Geometry*, his *Discourse on Method*, and his *Meditations*. ✑

THE MEDITATION[1] of yesterday has filled my mind with so many doubts, that it is no longer in my power to forget them. Nor do I see, meanwhile, any principle on which they can be resolved; and, just as if

From the *Meditations* of René Descartes, as published in *A Discourse on Method and Selected Writings*. Translated by John Veitch. Everyman's Library. Reprinted by permission of E. P. Dutton & Co., Inc. The selection here is from the second and sixth Meditations.

[1] In his *Meditations*, Descartes set himself the problem of finding some principle of absolute certainty on which all true knowledge could be founded. In his Meditation of the previous day, he had started out by submitting to radical skepticism every primary assumption about reality — the reality of both the self and the external world — in order, by a process of elimination, to find something that would resist all doubt. The first Meditation had ended in purely negative results. The external world could be an illusion like that of dreams, and so could one's own body (for in dreams we see semblances of external things, and we seem to have bodies). As for the reality of the mind, what if our minds were only an illusion created by some "great enchanter"?

I had fallen all of a sudden into very deep water, I am so greatly disconcerted as to be made unable either to plant my feet firmly on the bottom or sustain myself by swimming on the surface. I will, nevertheless, make an effort, and try anew the same path on which I had entered yesterday, that is, proceed by casting aside all that admits of the slightest doubt, not less than if I had discovered it to be absolutely false; and I will continue always in this track until I shall find something that is certain, or at least, if I can do nothing more, until I shall know with certainty that there is nothing certain. . . .

I suppose, accordingly, that all the things which I see are false; I believe that none of those objects which my fallacious memory represents ever existed; I suppose that I possess no senses; I believe that body, figure, extension, motion, and place are merely fictions of my mind. What is there, then, that can be esteemed true? Perhaps this only, that there is absolutely nothing certain. . . .

Am I, then, at least not something? But I before denied[2] that I possessed senses or a body; I hesitate, however, for what follows from that? Am I so dependent on the body and the senses that without these I cannot exist? But I had the persuasion that there was absolutely nothing in the world, that there was no sky and no earth, neither minds nor bodies; was I not, therefore, at the same time, persuaded that I did not exist? Far from it; I assuredly existed, since I was persuaded. But there is I know not what being, who is possessed at once of the highest power and the deepest cunning, who is constantly employing all his ingenuity in deceiving me. Doubtless, then, I exist, since I am deceived; and, let him deceive me as he may, he can never bring it about that I am nothing, so long as I shall be conscious that I am something. So that it must, in fine, be maintained, all things being maturely and carefully considered, that this proposition I am, I exist, is necessarily true each time it is expressed by me, or conceived in my mind.

But I do not yet know with sufficient clearness what I am, though assured that I am. . . . Can I affirm that I possess any one of all those attributes of which I have lately spoken as belonging to the nature of body? After attentively considering them in my own mind, I find none of them that can properly be said to belong to myself. To recount them were idle and tedious. Let us pass, then, to the attributes of the soul. The first mentioned were the powers of nutrition and walking; but, if it be

[2] Referring to the Meditation of the day before; as also, just below, "But there is I know not what being. . . ." See Note 1.

true that I have no body, it is true likewise that I am capable neither of walking nor of being nourished. Perception is another attribute of the soul; but perception too is impossible without the body: besides, I have frequently, during sleep, believed that I perceived objects which I after- wards observed I did not in reality perceive. Thinking is another attri- bute of the soul; and here I discover what properly belongs to myself. This alone is inseparable from me. I am — I exist: this is certain; but how often? As often as I think; for perhaps it would even happen, if I should wholly cease to think, that I should at the same time altogether cease to be. I now admit nothing that is not necessarily true: I am therefore, precisely speaking, only a thinking thing, that is, a mind, understanding, or reason,— terms whose signification was before unknown to me. I am, however, a real thing, and really existent; but what thing? The answer was, a thinking thing. . . .

But what, then, am I? A thinking thing, it has been said. But what is a thinking thing? It is a thing that doubts, understands, affirms, denies, wills, refuses, that imagines also, and perceives. Assuredly it is not little, if all these properties belong to my nature. But why should they not be- long to it? Am I not that very being who now doubts of almost every- thing; who, for all that, understands and conceives certain things, who affirms one alone as true, and denies the others; who desires to know more of them, and does not wish to be deceived; who imagines many things, sometimes even despite his will; and is likewise percipient of many, as if through the medium of the senses. . . .

For it is of itself so evident that it is I who doubt, I who understand, and I who desire, that it is here unnecessary to add anything by way of rendering it more clear. And I am as certainly the same being who imagines; for, although it may be (as I before supposed) that nothing I imagine is true, still the power of imagination does not cease really to exist in me and to form part of my thoughts. In fine, I am the same being who perceives, that is, who apprehends certain objects as by the organs of sense, since, in truth, I see light, hear a noise, and feel heat. But it will be said that these presentations are false, and that I am dreaming. Let it be so. At all events it is certain that I seem to see light, hear a noise, and feel heat; this cannot be false, and this is what in me is properly called perceiving, which is nothing else than thinking. From this I begin to know what I am with somewhat greater clearness and distinctness than heretofore. . . .

Let us now accordingly consider the objects that are commonly thought to be the most distinctly known, viz., the bodies we touch and see; not, indeed, bodies in general, for these general notions are usually somewhat more confused, but one body in particular. Take, for example, this piece of wax; it is quite fresh, having been but recently taken from the beehive; it has not yet lost the sweetness of the honey it contained; it still retains somewhat of the odour of the flowers from which it was gathered; its colour, figure, size, are apparent; it is hard, cold, easily handled; and sounds when struck upon with the finger. In fine, all that contributes to make a body as distinctly known as possible, is found in the one before us. But, while I am speaking, let it be placed near the fire — what remained of the taste exhales, the smell evaporates, the colour changes, its figure is destroyed, its size increases, it becomes liquid, it grows hot, it can hardly be handled, and, although struck upon, it emits no sound. Does the same wax still remain after this change? It must be admitted that it does remain; no one doubts it, or judges otherwise. What, then, was it I knew with so much distinctness in the piece of wax? Assuredly, it could be nothing of all that I observed by means of the senses, since all the things that fell under taste, smell, sight, touch, and hearing are changed, and yet the same wax remains. It was perhaps what I now think, viz., that this wax was neither the sweetness of honey, the pleasant odour of flowers, the whiteness, the figure, nor the sound, but only a body that a little before appeared to me conspicuous under these forms, and which is now perceived under others. But, to speak precisely, what is it that I imagine when I think of it in this way? Let it be attentively considered, and, retrenching all that does not belong to the wax, let us see what remains. There certainly remains nothing, except something extended, flexible, and movable. But what is meant by flexible and movable? Is it not that I imagine that the piece of wax, being round, is capable of becoming square, or of passing from a square into a triangular figure? Assuredly such is not the case, because I conceive that it admits of an infinity of similar changes; and I am, moreover, unable to compass this infinity by imagination, and consequently this conception which I have of the wax is not the product of the faculty of imagination. But what now is this extension? Is it not also unknown? for it becomes greater when the wax is melted, greater when it is boiled, and greater still when the heat increases; and I should not conceive clearly and according to truth, the wax as it is, if I did not suppose that the piece we are considering admitted even of a wider variety of extension than I ever imagined. I must, therefore, admit that I cannot even comprehend by imagination what the piece of wax is, and that it is the mind alone which perceives it. I speak of one piece in particular; for, as to wax in general, this is still more evident. But what is the piece of wax that can be perceived only by the mind? It is certainly the same which I see, touch, imagine; and, in fine, it is the same which, from the beginning, I believed it to be. But (and this it is of moment to observe) the perception of it is neither an act of sight, of touch, nor of imagination, and never was either of these, though it might formerly seem so, but is simply an intuition of the mind, which may be imperfect and confused, as it formerly was, or very clear and distinct, as it is at present, according as the attention is more or less directed to the elements which it contains, and of which it is composed.

But, meanwhile, I feel greatly astonished when I observe the weakness of my mind, and its proneness to error. For although, without at all giving expression to what I think, I consider all this in my own mind, words yet occasionally impede my progress, and I am almost led into error by the terms of ordinary language. We say, for example, that we see the same wax when it is before us, and not that we judge it to be the same from its retaining the same colour and figure: whence I should forthwith be disposed to conclude that the wax is known by the act of sight, and not by the intuition of the mind alone, were it not for the analogous instance of human beings passing on in the street below, as observed from a window. In this case I do not fail to say that I see the men themselves, just as I say that I see the wax; and yet what do I see from the window beyond hats and cloaks that might cover artificial machines, whose motions might be determined by springs? But I judge that there are human beings from these appearances, and thus I comprehend, by the faculty of judgment alone which is in the mind, what I believed I saw with my eyes. . . .

But, finally, what shall I say of the mind itself, that is, of myself? for as yet I do not admit that I am anything but mind. What, then! I who seem to possess so distinct an apprehension of the piece of wax, — do I not know myself, both with greater truth and certitude, and also much more distinctly and clearly? For if I judge that the wax exists because I see it, it assuredly follows, much more evidently, that I myself am or exist, for the same reason: for it is possible that what I see may not in truth be wax, and that I do not even possess eyes with which to see anything; but it cannot be that when I see, or, which comes to the same thing, when I think I see, I myself who think am nothing. So likewise, if I judge that the wax exists because I touch it, it will still also follow that I am; and if I determine that my imagination, or any other cause, whatever it be, persuades me of the existence of the wax, I will still draw the same conclusion. And what is here remarked of the piece of wax is applicable to all the other things that are external to me. And further, if the notion or perception of wax appeared to me more precise and distinct, after that not only sight and touch, but many other causes besides, rendered it manifest to my apprehension, with how much greater distinctness must I now know myself, since all the reasons that contribute to the knowledge of the nature of wax, or of any body whatever, manifest still better the nature of my mind? And there are besides so many other things in the mind itself that contribute to the illustration of its nature, and those dependent on the body, to which I have here referred, scarcely merit to be taken into account. . . .

Because I know with certitude that I exist, and because, in the meantime, I do not observe that aught necessarily belongs to my nature or essence beyond my being a thinking thing, I rightly conclude that my essence consists only in my being a thinking thing or a substance whose whole essence or nature is merely thinking. And although I may, or rather, as I will shortly say, although I certainly do possess a body with which I am very closely conjoined; nevertheless, because, on the one hand, I have a clear and distinct idea of myself, in as far as I am only a thinking and unextended thing, and as, on the other hand, I possess a distinct idea of body, in as far as it is only an extended and unthinking thing,[3] it is certain that I that is, my mind, by which I am what I am is entirely and truly distinct from my body, and may exist without it. . . .

I here remark, in the first place, that there is a vast difference between mind and body, in respect that body, from its nature, is always divisible, and that mind is entirely indivisible. For in truth, when I consider the mind, that is, when I consider myself in so far only as I am a thinking thing, I can distinguish in myself no parts, but I very clearly discern that I am . . . absolutely one and entire; and although the whole mind seems to be united to the whole body, yet, when a foot, an arm, or any other part is cut off, I am conscious that nothing has been taken from

[3] Extension here means simply occupying space. The thinking "I" does not occupy space (is an "unextended" thing), inasmuch as *thought* is not an object in space; the body, on the other hand, occupies space (is an "extended" thing).

my mind. . . . But quite the opposite holds in corporeal or extended things; for I cannot imagine any one of them . . . which I cannot easily sunder in thought, and which, therefore, I do not know to be divisible. This would be sufficient to teach me that the mind or soul of man is entirely different from the body, if I had not already been apprised of it on other grounds.

༄ FOR DISCUSSION AND WRITING

1. Abstract as this piece seems, it is not essentially difficult to follow at all. It is only a kind of thinking that any intelligent schoolboy might do if he faced—as many adolescents do face—the alarming questions: "What is real? Am I real? How does one know what is real?" Yet by asking these questions and answering them the way he did, Descartes set the main route (for good or ill) of modern scientific and philosophic thought. Let us follow the very simple course of the argument—and you would do well to outline the main steps, for the effort of making a written outline gives one a much more assured command of this kind of abstract thinking than a once-over reading can do. The first paragraph offers only a situation of wholesale doubt, where nothing is certain except that "there is nothing certain." Where, in the second paragraph, does Descartes say what he is searching for? In the third paragraph he arrives at his first certainty; what is that certainty? How does the fact that he can be "persuaded" and can be "deceived" establish that certainty?

2. In the fourth paragraph he takes up the problem of *what* he is (in this kind of inquiry, obviously one has to ascertain first *whether or not* one is, before undertaking the question of *what* one is). How does he discredit nutrition and walking as proofs of what kind of being one is? How does he use the word "soul" here? What does he decide at last is something "that properly belongs to myself"? How does he define the ultimate, unquestionable reality—the self?

3. If the self is "a thinking thing," the question that follows is: What *is* a "thinking thing"? How is this question answered in the fifth paragraph?

4. Now he turns to what are generally assumed to be the most distinct, solid, and incontrovertible "realities"—namely, the external physical objects

that one can touch and see—and he uses the piece of wax as an example. What is the problem the piece of wax offers, by changing its shape when held toward the fire, changing color and smell and size as it melts? By what argument, in the long seventh paragraph, does Descartes show that the senses are untrustworthy in establishing the existence of external objects and that "it is the mind alone" which perceives them? How, in the eighth paragraph, does he extend the argument to the existence of human beings?

5. By what reasoning, in the last two paragraphs, does he arrive at the assertion that "mind" and "body" are entirely different from each other?

6. It would be unfair to ask you to write at any length on problems suggested by this very slight selection from Descartes, but if you find yourself interested in this kind of discourse you might consider writing a *very* short paper (a couple of paragraphs perhaps) using one of the following as your topic: a) a free-wheeling criticism of the axiom "I think, therefore I am"; b) a criticism of the absolute dualism of "mind" and "body" that Descartes sets up; c) the implications of Descartes' ideas as to the superiority of the *rational* faculty of the mind over the senses and over the imagination; d) the isolation and loneliness of the self in a world where the only ultimate truth is "I think, therefore I am."

John Locke ⋖§ The Sources of Ideas

⋖§ English philosopher, founder of British empiricism (1632-1704). Locke was educated at Oxford and became a lecturer there in Greek, rhetoric, and philosophy; at the same time he studied medicine and became a qualified physician. His acquaintance with science had a strong influence on his philosophic thought and method. After 1667 he held minor diplomatic and civil posts, and lived for a time in France, where he associated with French scientists and philosophers. On his return to England he was suspected of radicalism because of his French associations, and, as Descartes had done, he settled in Holland in order to work without disturbance, completing there his famous *Essay Concerning Human Understanding*. Through his *Two Treatises on Civil Government*, he also became known as a champion of freedom. §⋗

IT IS an established opinion amongst some men, that there are in the understanding certain *innate principles;* some primary notions, . . . as it were stamped upon the mind of man; which the soul receives in its very first being, and brings into the world with it. It would be sufficient to convince unprejudiced readers of the falseness of this supposition, if I should only show (as I hope I shall in the following parts of this Discourse) how men, barely by the use of their natural faculties, may attain to all the knowledge they have, without the help of any innate impressions; and may arrive at certainty, without any such original notions or principles. . . .

All ideas come from sensation or reflection. Let us then suppose the mind to be, as we say, white paper, void of all characters, without any

From *Essay Concerning Human Understanding* by John Locke (first published in 1690).

ideas: — How comes it to be furnished? Whence comes it by that vast
store which the busy and boundless fancy of man has painted on it with
an almost endless variety? Whence has it all the *materials* of reason and
knowledge? To this I answer, in one word, from EXPERIENCE. In that all
our knowledge is founded; and from that it ultimately derives itself. Our
observation employed either, about external sensible objects, or about
the internal operations of our minds perceived and reflected on by ourselves, is that which supplies our understandings with all the *materials*
of thinking. These two are the fountains of knowledge, from whence all
the ideas we have, or can naturally have, do spring.

The objects of sensation one source of ideas. First, our Senses, conversant about particular sensible objects, do convey into the mind
several distinct perceptions of things, according to those various ways
wherein those objects do affect them. And thus we come by those *ideas*
we have of *yellow, white, heat, cold, soft, hard, bitter, sweet,* and all
those which we call sensible qualities; which when I say the senses convey into the mind, I mean, they from external objects convey into the
mind what produces there those perceptions. This great source of most of
the ideas we have, depending wholly upon our senses, and derived by
them to the understanding, I call SENSATION.

The operations of our minds, the other source of them. Secondly, the
other fountain from which experience furnisheth the understanding with
ideas is, — the perception of the operations of our own mind within us,
as it is employed about the ideas it has got; — which operations, when
the soul comes to reflect on and consider, do furnish the understanding
with another set of ideas, which could not be had from things without.
And such are *perception, thinking, doubting, believing, reasoning, knowing, willing,* and all the different actings of our own minds; — which we
being conscious of, and observing in ourselves, do from these receive
into our understandings as distinct ideas as we do from bodies affecting
our senses. This source of ideas every man has wholly in himself; and
though it be not sense, as having nothing to do with external objects, yet
it is very like it, and might properly enough be called *internal sense.* But
as I call the other SENSATION, so I call this REFLECTION, the ideas it affords
being such only as the mind gets by reflecting on its own operations
within itself. By reflection then, in the following part of this discourse, I
would be understood to mean, that notice which the mind takes of its
own operations, and the manner of them, by reason whereof there come

to be ideas of these operations in the understanding. These two, I say, viz. external material things, as the objects of SENSATION, and the operations of our own minds within, as the objects of REFLECTION, are to me the only originals from whence all our ideas take their beginnings. The term *operations* here I use in a large sense, as comprehending not barely the actions of the mind about its ideas, but some sort of passions arising sometimes from them, such as is the satisfaction or uneasiness arising from any thought.

All our ideas are of the one or the other of these. The understanding seems to me not to have the least glimmering of any ideas which it doth not receive from one of these two. *External objects* furnish the mind with the ideas of sensible qualities, which are all those different perceptions they produce in us; and *the mind* furnishes the understanding with ideas of its own operations.

These, when we have taken a full survey of them, and their several modes, combinations, and relations, we shall find to contain all our whole stock of ideas; and that we have nothing in our minds which did not come in one of these two ways. Let any one examine his own thoughts, and thoroughly search into his understanding; and then let him tell me, whether all the original ideas he has there, are any other than of the objects of his senses, or of the operations of his mind, considered as objects of his reflection. And how great a mass of knowledge soever he imagines to be lodged there, he will, upon taking a strict view, see that he has not any idea in his mind but what one of these two have imprinted; — though perhaps, with infinite variety compounded and enlarged by the understanding, as we shall see hereafter. . . .

A man begins to have ideas when he first has sensation. What sensation is. If it shall be demanded then, *when* a man *begins* to have any ideas, I think the true answer is,— *when he first has any sensation.* For, since there appear not to be any ideas in the mind before the senses have conveyed any in, I conceive that ideas in the understanding are coeval with *sensation; which is such an impression or motion made in some part of the body, as produces some perception in the understanding.* It is about these impressions made on our senses by outward objects that the mind seems *first* to employ itself, in such operations as we call perception, remembering, consideration, reasoning, &c.

The original of all our knowledge. In time the mind comes to reflect on its own operations about the ideas got by sensation, and thereby

stores itself with a new set of ideas, which I call ideas of reflection. These
are the impressions that are made on our senses by outward objects that
are extrinsical to the mind; and its own operations, proceeding from
powers intrinsical and proper to itself, which, when reflected on by itself,
become also objects of its contemplation — are, as I have said, the
original of all knowledge. Thus the first capacity of human intellect is,
— that the mind is fitted to receive the impressions made on it; either
through the senses by outward objects, or by its own operations when it
reflects on them. This is the first step a man makes towards the discovery
of anything, and the groundwork whereon to build all those notions
which ever he shall have naturally in this world. All those sublime
thoughts which tower above the clouds, and reach as high as heaven itself, take their rise and footing here: in all that great extent wherein the
mind wanders, in those remote speculations it may seem to be elevated
with, it stirs not one jot beyond those ideas which *sense* or *reflection*
have offered for its contemplation.

ᵴ FOR DISCUSSION AND WRITING

1. What doctrine concerning human psychology (as stated in the first paragraph) is Locke concerned to undermine and invalidate?

2. In the second paragraph Locke suggests that the mind at birth may be
   compared to a piece of paper without any writing on it (you may be familiar
   with the expression *"tabula rasa"*—an "erased tablet"—which Locke
   made famous as a metaphor of the mind's initial emptiness). If, then, there
   are no "innate (inborn) ideas" and the mind is completely empty at birth,
   how, he asks, "comes it to be furnished?" What answer does he give? What
   are the two sources of ideas?

3. How does he define "sensation"? How does he define "reflection"? Write a
   well-considered paragraph in which—without looking at the book—
   you make very clear, in your own words, what Locke means by these two
   terms and his theory of how the contents of the mind are built up. Is
   Locke's theory consonant with modern psychology? with modern scientific
   assumptions? Look up the word "empiricism" in the dictionary and state
   in a sentence its application to Locke's point of view.

4. If you are going to read the next two pieces too—from Berkeley and
Hume (very short, like this one)—the most interesting and useful kind
of writing assignment would be a wrap-around one, comparing the three.
But for a brief piece of writing of just two or three paragraphs based on
Locke, you might consider these questions: What limitations does Locke's
psychology place on human understanding? What limitations does it place
on "originality"? If you have read Plato's allegory of the cave, a few pages
earlier, what application could you make of Locke's theory to the people in
the cave, and what would Plato think of Locke's argument? If you have
read the piece from Jung, also earlier in this book, can you find any parallel
between the "innate ideas" that Locke sets out to discredit and Jung's
"archetypes" or "primordial images"? Given Locke's theory of the *tabula
rasa* and the way in which the mind becomes "furnished," what would you
say would be the condition—as to "furniture"—of the mind of the freshman college student, and how does the theory apply to the whole principle
of formal education?

George Berkeley ᴁ Ideas and Spirits

ᴁ Irish philosopher and Bishop of Cloyne (1685-1753). Berkeley was educated at Trinity College, Dublin; he came to England in 1713 and associated there with the intellectuals and wits of the period, including Addison, Steele, and Swift; he spent three years in America, in Rhode Island, on an abortive plan for a college; his appointment to the Irish bishopric came in 1734. His chief philosophical works are the *Dialogues*, the *New Theory of Vision*, and the *Treatise Concerning the Principles of Human Knowledge*. ᴁ

IT IS EVIDENT to any one who takes a survey of the *objects* of human knowledge, that they are either ideas actually imprinted on the senses; or else such as are perceived by attending to the passions and operations of the mind; or lastly, ideas formed by help of memory and imagination — either compounding, dividing, or barely representing those originally perceived in the aforesaid ways. . . .

But, besides all that endless variety of ideas or objects of knowledge, there is likewise something which knows or perceives them, and exercises divers operations, as willing, imagining, remembering, about them. This perceiving, active being is what I call *mind, spirit, soul,* or *myself.* By which words I do not denote any one of my ideas, but a thing entirely distinct from them, wherein, they exist, or, which is the same thing,

From *A Treatise Concerning the Principles of Human Knowledge* by George Berkeley (first published in 1710 and 1734).

902

whereby they are perceived — for the existence of an idea consists in being perceived. . . .

Light and colours, heat and cold, extension and figures—in a word the things we see and feel—what are they but so many sensations, notions, ideas, or impressions on the sense? and is it possible to separate, even in thought, any of these from perception? . . .

Some truths there are so near and obvious to the mind that a man need only open his eyes to see them. Such I take this important one to be, viz., that all the choir of heaven and furniture of the earth, in a word all those bodies which compose the mighty frame of the world, have not any subsistence without a mind, that their *being* is to be perceived or known; that consequently so long as they are not actually perceived by me, or do not exist in my mind or that of any other created spirit, they must either have no existence at all, or else subsist in the mind of some Eternal Spirit—it being perfectly unintelligible, and involving all the absurdity of abstraction, to attribute to any single part of them an existence independent of a spirit. To be convinced of which, the reader need only reflect, and try to separate in his own thoughts the *being* of a sensible thing from its *being perceived.*

From what has been said it follows there is not any other Substance than *Spirit,* or that which perceives. . . .

But, say you, surely there is nothing easier than for me to imagine trees, for instance, in a park, or books existing in a closet, and nobody by to perceive them. I answer, you may so, there is no difficulty in it; but what is all this, I beseech you, more than framing in your mind certain ideas which you call books and trees, and the same time omitting to frame the idea of any one that may perceive them? But do not you yourself perceive or think of them all the while? This therefore is nothing to the purpose; it only shews you have the power of imagining or forming ideas in your mind: but it does not shew that you can conceive it possible the objects of your thought may exist without the mind. To make out this, it is necessary that you conceive them existing unconceived or unthought of, which is a manifest repugnancy. When we do our utmost to conceive the existence of external bodies, we are all the while only contemplating our own ideas. But the mind taking no notice of itself, is deluded to think it can and does conceive bodies existing unthought of or without the mind, though at the same time they are apprehended by or exist in itself. A little attention will discover to any one the truth and evidence of what is here said, and make it unnecessary to insist on any other proofs against the existence of *material substance*. . . .

Before we proceed any farther it is necessary we spend some time in answering objections which may probably be made against the principles we have hitherto laid down. . . .

First, then, it will be objected that by the foregoing principles all that is real and substantial in nature is banished out of the world, and instead thereof a chimerical scheme of *ideas* takes place. All things that exist, exist only in the mind, that is, they are purely notional. What therefore becomes of the sun, moon and stars? What must we think of houses, rivers, mountains, trees, stones; nay, even of our own bodies? Are all these but so many chimeras and illusions on the fancy? To all which, and whatever else of the same sort may be objected, I answer, that by the principles premised we are not deprived of any one thing in nature. Whatever we see, feel, hear, or anywise conceive or understand remains as secure as ever, and is as real as ever. . . .

I do not argue against the existence of any one thing that we can apprehend either by sense or reflexion. That the things I see with my eyes and touch with my hands do exist, really exist, I make not the least question. The only thing whose existence we deny is that which *philosophers* call Matter or corporeal substance. And in doing of this there is no damage done to the rest of mankind, who, I dare say, will never miss it. . . .

If any man thinks this detracts from the existence or reality of things, he is very far from understanding what hath been premised in the plainest terms I could think of. Take here an abstract of what has been said: — There are spiritual substances, minds, or human souls, which will or excite ideas in themselves at pleasure; but these are faint, weak, and unsteady in respect of others they perceive by sense — which, being impressed upon them according to certain rules or laws of nature, speak themselves the effects of a mind more powerful and wise than human spirits. These latter[1] are said to have more *reality* in them than the former: — by which is meant that they are more affecting, orderly, and distinct, and that they are not fictions of the mind perceiving them. And in this sense the sun that I see by day is the real sun, and that which I imagine by night is the idea of the former. In the sense here given of *reality* it is evident that every vegetable, star, mineral, and in general

[1] Impressions of the senses, sensations, as contrasted with abstract reflection.

each part of the mundane system, is as much a *real being* by our principles as by any other. Whether others mean anything by the term *reality*
different from what I do, I entreat them to look into their own thoughts
and see. . . .

From the principles we have laid down it follows human knowledge
may naturally be reduced to two heads — that of *ideas* and that of *spirits*.
Of each of these I shall treat in order.

And *first* as to ideas or unthinking things.[2] Our knowledge of these
hath been very much obscured and confounded, and we have been led
into very dangerous errors, by supposing a twofold existence of the objects of sense — the one *intelligible* or in the mind, the other *real* and
without the mind; whereby unthinking things are thought to have a
natural subsistence of their own distinct from being perceived by spirits.
This, which, if I mistake not, hath been shewn to be a most groundless
and absurd notion, is the very root of Scepticism; for, so long as men
thought that real things subsisted without the mind, and that their knowledge was only so far forth *real* as it was conformable to *real things*, it
follows they could not be certain they had any real knowledge at all. For
how can it be known that the things which are perceived are conformable to those which are not perceived, or exist without the mind? . . .

So long as we attribute a real existence to unthinking things, distinct from their being perceived, it is not only impossible for us to know
with evidence the nature of any real unthinking being, but even that it
exists. Hence it is that we see philosophers distrust their senses, and
doubt of the existence of heaven and earth, of everything they see or feel,
even of their own bodies. And, after all their labour and struggle of
thought, they are forced to own we cannot attain to any self-evident or
demonstrative knowledge of the existence of sensible things. But, all
this doubtfulness, which so bewilders and confounds the mind and makes
philosophy ridiculous in the eyes of the world, vanishes if we annex a
meaning to our words, and not amuse ourselves with the terms "absolute," "external," "exist," and suchlike, signifying we know not what. I
can as well doubt of my own being as of the being of those things which
I actually perceive by sense; it being a manifest contradiction that any
sensible object should be immediately perceived by sight or touch, and

___

[2] The distinction here is between the perceiving and thinking mind (which Berkeley
calls "spirit") and the perceptions or thoughts of the mind, between the mind as
the "thinking thing" and its thoughts as "unthinking things."

at the same time have no existence in nature, since the very *existence* of an unthinking being consists in *being perceived*. . . .

Ideas imprinted on the senses are real things, or do really exist; this we do not deny, but we deny they can subsist without the minds which perceive them. . . . Again, the things perceived by sense may be termed *external*, with regard to their origin — in that they are not generated from within by the mind itself, but imprinted by a Spirit distinct from that which perceives them. . . .

Having despatched what we intended to say concerning the knowledge of IDEAS, the method we proposed leads us in the next place to treat of SPIRITS — with regard to which, perhaps, human knowledge is not so deficient as is vulgarly imagined. The great reason that is assigned for our being thought ignorant of the nature of spirits is our not having an *idea* of it. But, surely it ought not to be looked on as a defect in a human understanding that it does not perceive the idea of spirit, if it is manifestly impossible there should be any such idea. . . . A spirit has been shewn to be the only substance or support wherein unthinking beings or ideas can exist; but that this *substance* which supports or perceives ideas should itself be an idea or like an idea is evidently absurd. . . .

For, by the word *spirit* we mean only that which thinks, wills, and perceives; this, and this alone, constitutes the signification of the term. If therefore it is impossible that any degree of those powers should be represented in an idea, it is evident there can be no idea of a spirit. . . .

But it will be objected that, if there is no idea signified by the terms *soul, spirit, and substance*, they are wholly insignificant, or have no meaning in them. I answer, those words do mean or signify a real thing, which is neither an idea nor like an idea, but that which perceives ideas, and wills, and reasons about them. What I am myself, that which I denote by the term *I*, is the same with what is meant by *soul* or *spiritual substance*. . . .

It is evident to every one that those things which are called the Works of Nature, that is, the far greater part of the ideas or sensations perceived by us, are not produced by, or dependent on, the wills of men. There is therefore some other Spirit that causes them. . . .

But, if we attentively consider the constant regularity, order, and concatenation of natural things, the surprising magnificence, beauty, and perfection of the larger, and the exquisite contrivance of the smaller parts of creation, together with the exact harmony and correspondence of the whole, but above all the never-enough-admired laws of pain and pleasure, and the instincts or natural inclinations, appetites, and passions of animals; I say if we consider all these things, and at the same time attend to the meaning and import of the attributes One, Eternal, Infinitely Wise, Good, and Perfect, we shall clearly perceive that they belong to the aforesaid Spirit, "who works all in all," and "by whom all things consist.". . .

Hence, it is evident that God is known as certainly and immediately as any other mind or spirit whatsoever distinct from ourselves. . . . He alone it is who, "upholding all things by the word of His power," maintains that intercourse between spirits whereby they are able to perceive the existence of each other. And yet this pure and clear light which enlightens every one is itself invisible.

ﾠ FOR DISCUSSION AND WRITING

1. In the first two paragraphs Berkeley accepts Locke's psychology of the origin of ideas in sensation and reflection, and Descartes' distinction between the *thinking self* and the objects of thought; then in the third paragraph he puts a question with which you may be familiar in some such form as this: If a volcano explodes in the middle of a desert where there is no one to see it or hear it, does it really explode and does it really exist? How does Berkeley phrase the question? How does he answer it in the fourth paragraph? The second sentence in this paragraph is a mighty one, in which we see something of that power of expression which makes Berkeley one of the great stylists of English prose. Analyze the syntax of the sentence—the structure of the clause beginning "that all the choir of heaven . . . ," the structure of the clause beginning "that consequently . . . ," and the grammatical rationale of the phrase beginning "it being perfectly unintelligible. . . ." What images give resonance and comprehensiveness to the thought of the sentence? Take up the problem in the last sentence of the fourth paragraph; *can* you separate external things from your ideas of them?

2. How does the single sentence of the fifth paragraph logically "follow" from what has been said before?

3. How does Berkeley strengthen his argument in the sixth paragraph? In the

eighth paragraph, how does he counter the objection that "all that is real
and substantial in nature is banished out of the world" by the principles he
has set forth? How can he assert, as in the ninth paragraph, that "the things
I see with my eyes and touch with my hands do exist, really exist," and yet
deny the existence of "matter or corporeal substance"?

4. What two divisions of inquiry does he set up in the eleventh paragraph?
Why, according to the argument in the twelfth paragraph, should the belief in "a twofold existence of the objects of sense—the one *intelligible* or
in the mind, the other *real* and without the mind," lead to complete skepticism as to the possibility of "any real knowledge at all"?

5. What is Berkeley's argument in the thirteenth and fourteenth paragraphs
as to the "reality" of external objects?

6. How does he define "spirit" in the fifteenth paragraph? and in the sixteenth? Why can we have no idea of "spirit," by virtue of the very definition of "idea" and "spirit"? Why, since Nature and the objects of sensation
are not produced by men, must they be the products of "some other Spirit"?
Why does it follow, from Berkeley's argument, that God is known "certainly and immediately," and yet is invisible?

7. If you have read the preceding piece from Locke, and intend to read the
next one, from Hume, the best suggestion for a writing assignment would
be a comparison of the three; but for an extremely short paper (of two or
three paragraphs), you might be interested in working up either a corroboration or a criticism of Berkeley's point of view.

David Hume ✑ Sceptical Doubts Concerning the Operations of the Understanding

✑ Scottish philosopher, historian, and political economist (1711-1776). Hume was born in Edinburgh and educated at the University of Edinburgh. After engaging in several diplomatic missions, he went to Paris in 1763 as Secretary of the British Embassy; there he became a friend of Rousseau, to whom he later gave refuge in England. In 1767 he was appointed Undersecretary of State. The last years of his life were spent in Edinburgh. Hume was popularly known for his voluminous *History of England,* which went into many editions and was the standard history for many years; despite factual errors, it remains a prose classic. In his *Essays, Moral and Political* he attacked the mercantile system and anticipated the views of later economists such as Adam Smith. But his fame rests mainly on *An Enquiry Concerning Human Understanding* and *An Enquiry Concerning the Principles of Morals.* He is the greatest of the British empiricists, and his influence upon modern philosophy has been incalculable. ❧

ALL the objects of human reason or enquiry may naturally be divided into two kinds, to wit, *Relations of Ideas,* and *Matters of Fact.* Of the first kind are the sciences of Geometry, Algebra, and Arithmetic; and in short, every affirmation which is either intuitively or demonstratively certain. *That the square of the hypothenuse is equal to the square of the two sides,* is a proposition which expresses a relation between these figures. *That three times five is equal to the half of thirty,* expresses a relation between these numbers. Propositions of this kind are discoverable by the mere operation of thought, without dependence on what is anywhere existent in the universe. Though there never were a circle or triangle in nature, the truths demonstrated by Euclid would for ever retain their certainty and evidence.

From *An Enquiry Concerning Human Understanding* by David Hume, first published (1748) as *Philosophical Essays Concerning Human Understanding.*

Matters of fact, which are the second objects of human reason, are not ascertained in the same manner; nor is our evidence of their truth, however great, of a like nature with the foregoing. . . . *That the sun will not rise tomorrow* is no less intelligible a proposition, and implies no more contradiction than the affirmation, *that it will rise*. We should in vain, therefore, attempt to demonstrate its falsehood. . . .

It may, therefore, be a subject worthy of curiosity, to enquire what is the nature of that evidence which assures us of any real existence and matter of fact, beyond the present testimony of our senses, or the records of our memory. This part of philosophy, it is observable, has been little cultivated, either by the ancients or moderns; and therefore our doubts and errors, in the prosecution of so important an enquiry, may be the more excusable; while we march through such difficult paths without any guide or direction. They may even prove useful, by exciting curiosity, and destroying that implicit faith and security, which is the bane of all reasoning and free enquiry. . . .

All reasonings concerning matter of fact seem to be founded on the relation of *Cause and Effect*. By means of that relation alone we can go beyond the evidence of our memory and senses. If you were to ask a man, why he believes any matter of fact, which is absent; for instance, that his friend is in the country, or in France; he would give you a reason; and this reason would be some other fact; as a letter received from him, or the knowledge of his former resolutions and promises. A man finding a watch or any other machine in a desert island, would conclude that there had once been men in that island. All our reasonings concerning fact are of the same nature. And here it is constantly supposed that there is a connexion between the present fact and that which is inferred from it. Were there nothing to bind them together, the inference would be entirely precarious. The hearing of an articulate voice and rational discourse in the dark assures us of the presence of some person: Why? because these are the effects of the human make and fabric, and closely connected with it. If we anatomize all the other reasonings of this nature, we shall find that they are founded on the relation of cause and effect, and that this relation is either near or remote, direct or collateral. Heat and light are collateral effects of fire, and the one effect may justly be inferred from the other.

If we would satisfy ourselves, therefore, concerning the nature of that evidence, which assures us of matters of fact, we must enquire how we arrive at the knowledge of cause and effect.

I shall venture to affirm, as a general proposition, which admits of no exception, that the knowledge of this relation is not, in any instance, attained by reasonings *a priori*;[1] but arises entirely from experience, when we find that any particular objects are constantly conjoined with each other. Let an object be presented to a man of ever so strong natural reason and abilities; if that object be entirely new to him, he will not be able, by the most accurate examination of its sensible qualities, to discover any of its causes or effects. Adam, though his rational faculties be supposed, at the very first, entirely perfect, could not have inferred from the fluidity and transparency of water that it would suffocate him, or from the light and warmth of fire that it would consume him. No object ever discovers, by the qualities which appear to the senses, either the causes which produced it, or the effects which will arise from it; nor can our reason, unassisted by experience, ever draw any inference concerning real existence and matter of fact. . . .

We fancy, that were we brought on a sudden into this world, we could at first have inferred that one billiard-ball would communicate motion to another upon impulse; and that we needed not to have waited for the event, in order to pronounce with certainty concerning it. Such is the influence of custom, that, where it is strongest, it not only covers our natural ignorance, but even conceals itself. . . .

But to convince us that all the laws of nature, and all the operations of bodies without exception, are known only by experience, the following reflections may, perhaps, suffice. Were any object presented to us, and were we required to pronounce concerning the effect, which will result from it, without consulting past observation; after what manner, I beseech you, must the mind proceed in this operation? It must invent or imagine some event, which it ascribes to the object as its effect; and it is plain that this invention must be entirely arbitrary. The mind can never possibly find the effect in the supposed cause, by the most accurate scrutiny and examination. For the effect is totally different from the cause, and consequently can never be discovered in it. Motion in the second billiard-ball is a quite distinct event from motion in the first; nor is there anything in the one to suggest the smallest hint of the other. A

[1] Reasoning from prior assumptions, i.e., from the examination of ideas alone.

stone or piece of metal raised into the air, and left without any support, immediately falls: but to consider the matter *a priori,* is there anything we discover in this situation which can beget the idea of a downward, rather than an upward, or any other motion, in the stone or metal? . . .

In a word, then, every effect is a distinct event from its cause. It could not, therefore, be discovered in the cause, and the first invention or conception of it, *a priori,* must be entirely arbitrary. And even after it is suggested, the conjunction of it with the cause must appear equally arbitrary; since there are always many other effects, which, to reason, must seem fully as consistent and natural. In vain, therefore, should we pretend to determine any single event, or infer any cause or effect, without the assistance of observation and experience. . . .

The most perfect philosophy of the natural kind[2] only staves off our ignorance a little longer: as perhaps the most perfect philosophy of the moral or metaphysical kind serves only to discover larger portions of it. Thus the observation of human blindness and weakness is the result of all philosophy, and meets us at every turn, in spite of our endeavours to elude or avoid it. . . .

Suppose a person, though endowed with the strongest faculties of reason and reflection, to be brought on a sudden into this world; he would, indeed, immediately observe a continual succession of objects, and one event following another; but he would not be able to discover anything farther. He would not, at first, by any reasoning, be able to reach the idea of cause and effect; since the particular powers, by which all natural operations are performed, never appear to the senses; nor is it reasonable to conclude, merely because one event, in one instance, precedes another, that therefore the one is the cause, the other the effect. Their conjunction may be arbitrary and casual. There may be no reason to infer the existence of one from the appearance of the other. . . .

Suppose, again, that he has acquired more experience, and has lived so long in the world as to have observed familiar objects or events to be constantly conjoined together; what is the consequence of this experience? He immediately infers the existence of one object from the appearance of the other. Yet he has not, by all his experience, acquired any idea or knowledge of the secret power by which the one object produces the other; nor is it, by any process of reasoning, he is engaged to draw this

[2] Philosophy concerned with the operations and laws of the physical universe, or what Hume calls "matter of fact."

inference. But still he finds himself determined to draw it: And though he should be convinced that his understanding has no part in the operation, he would nevertheless continue in the same course of thinking. There is some other principle which determines him to form such a conclusion. . . .

This principle is Custom or Habit. For wherever the repetition of any particular act or operation produces a propensity to renew the same act or operation, without being impelled by any reasoning or process of the understanding, we always say, that this propensity is the effect of *Custom*. By employing that word, we pretend not to have given the ultimate reason of such a propensity. We only point out a principle of human nature, which is universally acknowledged, and which is well known by its effects. Perhaps we can push our enquiries no farther, or pretend to give the cause of this cause; but must rest contented with it as the ultimate principle, which we can assign, of all our conclusions from experience. It is sufficient satisfaction, that we can go so far, without repining at the narrowness of our faculties because they will carry us no farther. And it is certain we here advance a very intelligible proposition at least, if not a true one, when we assert that, after the constant conjunction of two objects — heat and flame, for instance, weight and solidity — we are determined by custom alone to expect the one from the appearance of the other. . . .

Custom, then, is the great guide of human life. It is that principle alone which renders our experience useful to us, and makes us expect, for the future, a similar train of events with those which have appeared in the past. Without the influence of custom, we should be entirely ignorant of every matter of fact beyond what is immediately present to the memory and senses. We should never know how to adjust means to ends, or to employ our natural powers in the production of any effect. There would be an end at once of all action, as well as of the chief part of speculation. . . .

What, then, is the conclusion of the whole matter? A simple one; though, it must be confessed, pretty remote from the common theories of philosophy. All belief of matter of fact or real existence is derived merely from some object, present to the memory or senses, and a customary conjunction between that and some other object. Or in other words; having found, in many instances, that any two kinds of objects — flame and heat, snow and cold — have always been conjoined together; if flame or snow be presented anew to the senses, the mind is carried by custom to expect heat or cold, and to *believe* that such a quality does exist, and will discover itself upon a nearer approach. This belief is the necessary result of placing the mind in such circumstances. It is an operation of the soul, when we are so situated, as unavoidable as to feel the passion of love, when we receive benefits; or hatred, when we meet with injuries. All these operations are a species of natural instincts, which no reasoning or process of the thought and understanding is able either to produce or to prevent. . . .

◄§ FOR DISCUSSION AND WRITING

1. What are the two classifications of the objects of human reason or inquiry stated in the first paragraph? What illustrations are given of the first kind? Why are propositions of this kind discoverable by thought alone, quite independently of anything existing in nature? How are "matters of fact" differentiated from "relations of ideas"? While one can, by reasoning, demonstrate the truth or falsehood of the relations of ideas, why is it impossible to do so with matters of fact? or, to put the question in another way, why are matters of fact independent of reason? Think of two more illustrations for each of these classifications.

2. Where does Hume state the subject of his present inquiry? Why does he say that "implicit faith and security" should be destroyed?

3. Why does he say that all reasoning about matters of fact is founded on the relation of cause and effect? What examples does he give in illustration of this statement? Why, according to Hume's argument, is it impossible to arrive at any knowledge about cause and effect by *a priori* reasoning? How *do* we acquire a conception of cause and effect? Explain this statement at the end of the sixth paragraph: "No object ever discovers, by the qualities which appear to the senses, either the causes which produced it, or the effects which will arise from it; nor can our reason, unassisted by experience, ever draw any inference concerning real existence and matter of fact." (Note: The word "discovers" is used here in an older sense, meaning "shows.")

4. In what way does the example of the billiard balls illustrate Hume's argu-

ment? In what way does the dropping of a stone or some metal object illustrate it?

5. How does the statement of philosophical skepticism in the tenth paragraph follow from the previous argument? What *is* philosophical skepticism? (If you have read the piece from Descartes a little earlier in this book, do you find in Hume's method any development of the Cartesian method of doubt?)

6. At the end of the twelfth paragraph Hume says that "there is some other principle" that determines all inferences about cause and effect. What is that principle? What is Hume's conclusion about all belief concerning "matter of fact or real existence"? Where does this conclusion leave us as to true knowledge about the world?

7. If you have a real aptitude for philosophical thought, and if you have read all or several of the philosophers represented here (starting with Plato's allegory of the cave, then jumping to Descartes, and going on through Locke, Berkeley, and Hume), the most rewarding writing assignment, to clarify your own thinking, would be a careful comparison of their theories of knowledge and their methods. (A professor of philosophy would probably be rather scornful of such an attempt, based only on these brief pieces; but fortunately no professor of philosophy is around at the moment to discourage us, and there is no law preventing nonphilosophy majors from exercising their minds in philosophical analysis, if they find it pleasurable.)

The Spiritual Order

IN C. G. JUNG's *last book*, MEMORIES, DREAMS, REFLECTIONS, *there are a few pages describing his experiences among the Pueblo Indians of New Mexico. The following is an account of a conversation with an Indian called Mountain Lake.* " 'Why,' Mountain Lake said, 'do the Americans not let us alone? Why do they want to forbid our dances? Why do they make difficulties when we want to take our young people from school in order to lead them to the* kiva *(site of the rituals), and instruct them in our religion? We do nothing to harm the Americans!' After a prolonged silence he continued, 'The Americans want to stamp out our religion. Why can they not let us alone? What we do, we do not only for ourselves but for the Americans also. Yes, we do it for the whole world. Everyone benefits by it.'*

"*I could observe from his excitement that he was alluding to some extremely important element of his religion. I therefore asked him: 'You think, then, that what you do in your religion benefits the whole world?' He replied with great animation, 'Of course. If we did not do it, what would become of the world?' And with a significant gesture he pointed to the sun.*

"*I felt that we were approaching extremely delicate ground here, verging on the mysteries of the tribe. 'After all,' he said, 'we are a* people who live on the roof of the world; we are the sons of Father Sun, and with our religion we daily help our father go across the sky. We do this not only for ourselves, but for the whole world. If we were to cease practicing our religion, in ten years the sun would no longer rise. Then it would be night forever.' "

And Dr. Jung says that he then realized on what the dignity, the tranquil composure of these Indians was founded: it sprang from the fact that their lives were "cosmologically meaningful," for by their actions they helped the sun, the father and preserver of all life, in his daily rise and descent. "If we set against this our own self-justifications," Jung continues, "the meaning of our own lives as it is formulated by our reason, we cannot help but see our poverty. Out of sheer envy we are obliged to smile at the Indians' naïvete and to plume ourselves on our cleverness; for otherwise we would discover how impoverished and down at heels we are. Knowledge does not enrich us; it removes us more and more from the mythic world in which we were once at home by right of birth."[1] This is not a counsel of retreat but a counsel of recovery of something valuable that we have lost along the way.

In the pieces that follow, we come at the spiritual order of knowledge through the back door, so to speak—through the door of paganism and comparative religion, the rites of Adonis and Isis, of Haitian "Voodoo" and the Pueblo Indians' corn dance—rather than through the front door of moralism and guilt which leads to the modern religious establishment. C. S. Lewis tells of a poll he took among his Oxford students on their notions of God, and one of the most definitive opinions he came up with was that God is "a kind of force, a kind of substance, lying over everything, sort of like tapioca pudding." If we can't do any better than that, let's acknowledge that as novices in the spiritual realm we might learn something from voodoo and corn dances.

[1] C. G. Jung, *Memories, Dreams, Reflections* (Random House, 1963), pp. 251-52.

Sir James George Frazer ◆§ The Myth and Ritual of Adonis

◆§ Scottish classicist and anthropologist (1854-1941). Frazer was born in Glasgow, son of a Presbyterian minister, was educated at Glasgow and Cambridge, became a Fellow of Trinity College, Cambridge, and in a life devoted to scholarship was awarded the most distinguished honors by learned societies and the great European universities. He was knighted in 1914. The publication of each of the successive volumes of his encyclopedic, thirteen-volume study in comparative folklore, magic, and religion, *The Golden Bough*, was an international intellectual event of the first magnitude. From Frazer's work stem the investigations of such scholars as Jane Ellen Harrison, Gilbert Murray, Jessie Weston, F. M. Cornford, Bronislaw Malinowsky; both Freud and Jung used his work liberally as authority; T. S. Eliot's *The Waste Land* derives its chief motif from him (via Jessie Weston's *From Ritual to Romance*); and his influence on modern thought has been profound in many directions. ठ✦

THE MYTH OF ADONIS

THE SPECTACLE of the great changes which annually pass over the face of the earth has powerfully impressed the minds of men in all ages, and stirred them to meditate on the causes of transformations so vast and wonderful. Their curiosity has not been purely disinterested; for even the savage cannot fail to perceive how intimately his own life is bound up with the life of nature, and how the same processes which freeze the stream and strip the earth of vegetation menace him with extinction. At a certain stage of development men seem to have imagined that the means of averting the threatened calamity were in their own hands, and that they could hasten or retard the flight of the seasons by magic art. Accordingly they performed ceremonies and recited spells to make the rain to fall, the sun to shine, animals to multiply, and the fruits of the earth to grow. In course of time the slow advance of knowledge, which has dispelled so many cherished illusions, convinced at least the more thoughtful portion of mankind that the alternations of summer and winter, of spring and autumn, were not merely the result of their own magical rites, but that some deeper cause, some mightier power, was at work behind the shifting scenes of nature. They now pictured to themselves the growth and decay of vegetation, the birth and death of living creatures, as effects of the waxing or waning strength of divine beings, of gods and goddesses, who were born and died, who married and begot children, on the pattern of human life.

Thus the old magical theory of the seasons was displaced, or rather supplemented, by a religious theory. For although men now attributed the annual cycle of change primarily to corresponding changes in their deities, they still thought that by performing certain magical rites they could aid the god who was the principle of life, in his struggle with the opposing principle of death. They imagined that they could recruit his failing energies and even raise him from the dead. The ceremonies which they observed for this purpose were in substance a dramatic representation of the natural processes which they wished to facilitate; for it is a familiar tenet of magic that you can produce any desired effect by merely imitating it. And as they now explained the fluctuations of growth and decay, of reproduction and dissolution by the marriage, the death, and the rebirth or revival of the gods, their religious or rather magical dramas turned in great measure on these themes. They set forth the fruitful union of the powers of fertility, the sad death of one at least of the divine partners, and his joyful resurrection. Thus a religious theory was blended with a magical practice. . . .

Of the changes which the seasons bring with them, the most striking within the temperate zone are those which affect vegetation. The influence of the seasons on animals, though great, is not nearly so manifest. Hence it is natural that in the magical dramas designed to dispel winter and bring back spring the emphasis should be laid on vegetation, and that trees and plants should figure in them more prominently than beasts and birds. Yet the two sides of life, the vegetable and the animal, were not dissociated in the minds of those who observed the ceremonies. Indeed they commonly believed that the tie between the animal and the vegetable world was even closer than it really is; hence they often combined the dramatic representation of reviving plants with a real or a dramatic union of the sexes for the purpose of furthering at the same time and by the same act the multiplication of fruits, of animals, and of men. To them the principle of life and fertility, whether animal or vegetable, was one and indivisible. To live and to cause to live, to eat food and to beget children, these were the primary wants of men in the past, and they will be the primary wants of men in the future so long as the world lasts. Other things may be added to enrich and beautify human life, but unless these wants are first satisfied, humanity itself must cease to exist. These two things, therefore, food and children, were what men chiefly sought to procure by the performance of magical rites for the regulation of the seasons.

Nowhere, apparently, have these rites been more widely and solemnly celebrated than in the lands which border the Eastern Mediterranean. Under the names of Osiris, Tammuz, Adonis, and Attis, the peoples of Egypt and Western Asia represented the yearly decay and revival of life, especially of vegetable life, which they personified as a god who annually died and rose again from the dead. In name and detail the rites varied from place to place: in substance they were the same. The supposed death and resurrection of this oriental deity, a god of many names but of essentially one nature, is now to be examined. We begin with Tammuz or Adonis.

The worship of Adonis was practised by the Semitic peoples of Babylonia and Syria, and the Greeks borrowed it from them as early as the seventh century before Christ. The true name of the deity was Tammuz: the appellation of Adonis is merely the Semitic *Adon*, "lord," a title of honour by which his worshippers addressed him. But the Greeks through a misunderstanding converted the title of honour into a proper name. In the religious literature of Babylonia Tammuz appears as the youthful spouse or lover of Ishtar, the great mother goddess, the embodiment of the reproductive energies of nature. The references to their connexion with each other in myth and ritual are both fragmentary and obscure, but we gather from them that every year Tammuz was believed to die, passing away from the cheerful earth to the gloomy subterranean world, and that every year his divine mistress journeyed in quest of him "to the land from which there is no returning, to the house of darkness, where dust lies on door and bolt." During her ab-

sence the passion of love ceased to operate: men and beasts alike forgot
to reproduce their kinds: all life was threatened with extinction. So
intimately bound up with the goddess were the sexual functions of the
whole animal kingdom that without her presence they could not be discharged. . . .

Laments for the departed Tammuz are contained in several Babylonian hymns, which liken him to plants that quickly fade. He is

> A tamarisk that in the garden has drunk no water,
> Whose crown in the field has brought forth no blossom.
> A willow that rejoiced not by the watercourse,
> A willow whose roots were torn up. . . .

His death appears to have been annually mourned, to the shrill music
of flutes, by men and women about midsummer in the month named
after him, the month of Tammuz. The dirges were seemingly chanted
over an effigy of the dead god, which was washed with pure water,
anointed with oil, and clad in a red robe, while the fumes of incense
rose into the air, as if to stir his dormant senses by their pungent fragrance and wake him from the sleep of death. In one of these dirges,
inscribed *Lament of the Flutes for Tammuz,* we seem still to hear the
voices of the singers chanting the sad refrain and to catch, like far-away
music, the wailing notes of the flutes:

> At his vanishing away she lifts up a lament,
> "Oh my child!" at his vanishing away she lifts up a lament;
> "My Damu!" at his vanishing away she lifts up a lament.
> "My enchanter and priest!" at his vanishing away she lifts up a lament.
> At the shining cedar, rooted in a spacious place. . . .
> Like the lament that a house lifts up for its master, lifts she up a lament,
> Like the lament that a city lifts up for its lord, lifts she up a lament.
> Her lament is the lament for a herb that grows not in the bed,
> Her lament is the lament for the corn that grows not in the ear.
> Her chamber is a possession that brings not forth a possession,
> A weary woman, a weary child, forspent.
> Her lament is for a great river, where no willows grow,
> Her lament is for a field, where corn and herbs grow not. . . .
> Her lament is for a thicket of reeds, where no reeds grow. . . .
> Her lament is for the depth of a garden of trees, where honey and wine
>   grow not.
> Her lament is for meadows, where no plants grow. . . .

The tragical story and the melancholy rites of Adonis are better known to us from the descriptions of Greek writers than from the fragments of Babylonian literature or the brief reference of the prophet Ezekiel, who saw the women of Jerusalem weeping for Tammuz at the north gate of the temple. Mirrored in the glass of Greek mythology, the oriental deity appears as a comely youth beloved by Aphrodite. In his infancy the goddess hid him in a chest, which she gave in charge to Persephone, queen of the nether world. But when Persephone opened the chest and beheld the beauty of the babe, she refused to give him back to Aphrodite, though the goddess of love went down herself to hell to ransom her dear one from the power of the grave. The dispute between the two goddesses of love and death was settled by Zeus, who decreed that Adonis should abide with Persephone in the under world for one part of the year, and with Aphrodite in the upper world for another part. At last the fair youth was killed in hunting by a wild boar, or by the jealous Ares, who turned himself into the likeness of a boar in order to compass the death of his rival. Bitterly did Aphrodite lament her loved and lost Adonis. . . .

ADONIS IN SYRIA

The myth of Adonis was localised and his rites celebrated with much solemnity at two places in Western Asia. One of these was Byblus on the coast of Syria, the other was Paphos in Cyprus. Both were great seats of the worship of Aphrodite, or rather of her Semitic counterpart, Astarte. . . . In historical times it [Byblus] ranked as a holy place, the religious capital of the country, the Mecca or Jerusalem of the Phoenicians. The city stood on a height beside the sea, and contained a great sanctuary of Astarte, where in the midst of a spacious open court, surrounded by cloisters and approached from below by staircases, rose a tall cone or obelisk, the holy image of the goddess. In this sanctuary the rites of Adonis were celebrated. Indeed the whole city was sacred to him, and the river Nahr Ibrahim, which falls into the sea a little to the south of Byblus, bore in antiquity the name of Adonis. . . .

The temple, of which some massive hewn blocks and a fine column of Syenite granite still mark the site, occupied a terrace facing the source of the river and commanding a magnificent prospect. Across the foam and the roar of the waterfalls you look up to the cavern and away to the top of the sublime precipices above. So lofty is the cliff that the goats which creep along its ledges to browse on the bushes appear like

ants to the spectator hundreds of feet below. Seaward the view is especially impressive when the sun floods the profound gorge with golden
light, revealing all the fantastic buttresses and rounded towers of its
mountain rampart, and falling softly on the varied green of the woods
which clothe its depths. It was here that, according to the legend, Adonis
met Aphrodite for the first or the last time, and here his mangled body
was buried. A fairer scene could hardly be imagined for a story of tragic
love and death. . . .

In antiquity the whole of the lovely vale appears to have been
dedicated to Adonis, and to this day it is haunted by his memory; for
the heights which shut it in are crested at various points by ruined
monuments of his worship, some of them overhanging dreadful abysses,
down which it turns the head dizzy to look and see the eagles wheeling
about their nests far below. One such monument exists at Ghineh. The
face of a great rock, above a roughly hewn recess, is here carved with
figures of Adonis and Aphrodite. He is portrayed with spear in rest,
awaiting the attack of a bear, while she is seated in an attitude of sorrow. . . . Every year, in the belief of his worshippers, Adonis was
wounded to death on the mountains, and every year the face of nature
itself was dyed with his sacred blood. So year by year the Syrian dam-
sels lamented his untimely fate, while the red anemone, his flower,
bloomed among the cedars of Lebanon, and the river ran red to the
sea, fringing the winding shores of the blue Mediterranean, whenever
the wind set inshore, with a sinuous band of crimson.

ADONIS IN CYPRUS

The island of Cyprus lies but one day's sail from the coast of Syria.
Indeed, on fine summer evenings its mountains may be descried looming low and dark against the red fires of sunset. With its rich mines of
copper and its forests of firs and stately cedars, the island naturally
attracted a commercial and maritime people like the Phoenicians; while
the abundance of its corn, its wine, and its oil must have rendered it in
their eyes a Land of Promise by comparison with the niggardly nature
of their own rugged coast, hemmed in between the mountains and the
sea. Accordingly they settled in Cyprus at a very early date and remained there long after the Greeks had also established themselves on
its shores. . . .

The sanctuary of Aphrodite at Old Paphos (the modern Kuklia) was one of the most celebrated shrines in the ancient world. According to Herodotus, it was founded by Phoenician colonists from Ascalon; but it is possible that a native goddess of fertility was worshipped on the spot before the arrival of the Phoenicians, and that the newcomers identified her with their own Baalath or Astarte, whom she may have closely resembled. If two deities were thus fused in one, we may suppose that they were both varieties of that great goddess of motherhood and fertility whose worship appears to have been spread all over Western Asia from a very early time. The supposition is confirmed as well by the archaic shape of her image as by the licentious character of her rites; for both that shape and those rites were shared by her with other Asiatic deities. Her image was simply a white cone or pyramid. . . .

In Cyprus it appears that before marriage all women were formerly obliged by custom to prostitute themselves to strangers at the sanctuary of the goddess, whether she went by the name of Aphrodite, Astarte, or what not. Similar customs prevailed in many parts of Western Asia. Whatever its motive, the practice was clearly regarded, not as an orgy of lust, but as a solemn religious duty performed in the service of that great Mother Goddess of Western Asia whose name varied, while her type remained constant, from place to place. Thus at Babylon every woman, whether rich or poor, had once in her life to submit to the embraces of a stranger at the temple of Mylitta, that is, of Ishtar or Astarte, and to dedicate to the goddess the wages earned by this sanctified harlotry. The sacred precinct was crowded with women waiting to observe the custom. Some of them had to wait there for years. At Heliopolis or Baalbec in Syria, famous for the imposing grandeur of its ruined temples, the custom of the country required that every maiden should prostitute herself to a stranger at the temple of Astarte, and matrons as well as maids testified their devotion to the goddess in the same manner. The emperor Constantine abolished the custom, destroyed the temple, and built a church in its stead. In Phoenician temples women prostituted themselves for hire in the service of religion, believing that by this conduct they propitiated the goddess and won her favour. "It was a law of the Amorites, that she who was about to marry should sit in fornication seven days by the gate." At Byblus the people shaved their heads in the annual mourning for Adonis. Women who refused to sacrifice their hair had to give themselves up to strangers on a certain day of the festival, and the money which they thus earned was devoted to the goddess. A Greek inscription found at Tralles in Lydia proves that the practice of religious prostitution survived in that country as late as the second century of our era. . . .

We may conclude that a great Mother Goddess, the personification of all the reproductive energies of nature, was worshipped under different names but with a substantial similarity of myth and ritual by many peoples of Western Asia; that associated with her was a lover, or rather series of lovers, divine yet mortal, with whom she mated year by year, their commerce being deemed essential to the propagation of animals and plants, each in their several kind; and further, that the fabulous union of the divine pair was simulated and, as it were, multiplied on earth by the real, though temporary, union of the human sexes at the sanctuary of the goddess for the sake of thereby ensuring the fruitfulness of the ground and the increase of man and beast.

Among the stories which were told of Cinyras, the ancestor of the priestly kings of Paphos and the father of Adonis, there are some that deserve our attention. In the first place, he is said to have begotten his son Adonis in incestuous intercourse with his daughter Myrrha at a festival of the corn-goddess, at which women robed in white were wont to offer corn-wreaths as first-fruits of the harvest and to observe strict chastity for nine days. Similar cases of incest with a daughter are reported of many ancient kings. It seems unlikely that such reports are without foundation, and perhaps equally improbable that they refer to mere fortuitous outbursts of unnatural lust. We may suspect that they are based on a practice actually observed for a definite reason in certain special circumstances. Now in countries where the royal blood was traced through women only, and where consequently the king held office merely in virtue of his marriage with an hereditary princess, who was the real sovereign, it appears to have often happened that a prince married his own sister, the princess royal, in order to obtain with her hand the crown which otherwise would have gone to another man, perhaps to a stranger. May not the same rule of descent have furnished a motive for incest with a daughter? For it seems a natural corollary from such a rule that the king was bound to vacate the throne on the death of his wife, the queen, since he occupied it only by virtue of his marriage with her. When that marriage terminated, his right to the throne terminated with it and passed at once to his daughter's husband.

Hence if the king desired to reign after his wife's death, the only way in which he could legitimately continue to do so was by marrying his daughter, and thus prolonging through her the title which had formerly been his through her mother.

Cinyras is said to have been famed for his exquisite beauty and to have been wooed by Aphrodite herself. Thus it would appear, as scholars have already observed, that Cinyras was in a sense a duplicate of his handsome son Adonis, to whom the inflammable goddess also lost her heart. Further, these stories of the love of Aphrodite for two members of the royal house of Paphos can hardly be dissociated from the corresponding legend told of Pygmalion, a Phoenician king of Cyprus, who is said to have fallen in love with an image of Aphrodite and taken it to his bed. When we consider that Pygmalion was the father-in-law of Cinyras, that the son of Cinyras was Adonis, and that all three, in successive generations, are said to have been concerned in a love-intrigue with Aphrodite, we can hardly help concluding that the early Phoenician kings of Paphos, or their sons, regularly claimed to be not merely priests of the goddess but also her lovers, in other words, that in their official capacity they personated Adonis. At all events Adonis is said to have reigned in Cyprus, and it appears to be certain that the title of Adonis was regularly borne by the sons of all the Phoenician kings of the island. It is true that the title strictly signified no more than "lord"; yet the legends which connect these Cyprian princes with the goddess of love make it probable that they claimed the divine nature as well as the human dignity of Adonis. The story of Pygmalion points to a ceremony of a sacred marriage in which the king wedded the image of Aphrodite, or rather of Astarte. If that was so, the tale was in a sense true, not of a single man only, but of a whole series of men. . . .

As the custom of religious prostitution at Paphos is said to have been founded by king Cinyras and observed by his daughters, we may surmise that the kings of Paphos played the part of the divine bridegroom in a less innocent rite than the form of marriage with a statue; in fact, that at certain festivals each of them had to mate with one or more of the sacred harlots of the temple, who played Astarte to his Adonis. . . . The fruit of their union would rank as sons and daughters of the deity, and would in time become the parents of gods and goddesses, like their fathers and mothers before them. . . .

THE RITUAL OF ADONIS

At the festivals of Adonis, which were held in Western Asia and in Greek lands, the death of the god was annually mourned, with a bitter wailing, chiefly by women; images of him, dressed to resemble corpses, were carried out as to burial and then thrown into the sea or into springs; and in some places his revival was celebrated on the following day. But at different places the ceremonies varied somewhat in the manner and apparently also in the season of their celebration. At Alexandria images of Aphrodite and Adonis were displayed on two couches; beside them were set ripe fruits of all kinds, cakes, plants growing in flower-pots, and green bowers twined with anise. The marriage of the lovers was celebrated one day, and on the morrow women attired as mourners, with streaming hair and bared breasts, bore the image of the dead Adonis to the sea-shore and committed it to the waves. Yet they sorrowed not without hope, for they sang that the lost one would come back again. The date at which this Alexandrian ceremony was observed is not expressly stated; but from the mention of the ripe fruits it has been inferred that it took place in late summer. In the great Phoenician sanctuary of Astarte at Byblus the death of Adonis was annually mourned, to the shrill wailing notes of the flute, with weeping, lamentation, and beating of the breast; but next day he was believed to come to life again and ascend up to heaven in the presence of his worshippers. The disconsolate believers, left behind on earth, shaved their heads as the Egyptians did on the death of the divine bull Apis; women who could not bring themselves to sacrifice their beautiful tresses had to give themselves up to strangers on a certain day of the festival, and to dedicate to Astarte the wages of their shame.

This Phoenician festival appears to have been a vernal one, for its date was determined by the discoloration of the river Adonis, and this has been observed by modern travellers to occur in spring. At that season the red earth washed down from the mountains by the rain tinges the water of the river, and even the sea, for a great way with a blood-red hue, and the crimson stain was believed to be the blood of Adonis, annually wounded to death by the boar on Mount Lebanon. Again, the scarlet anemone is said to have sprung from the blood of Adonis, or to have been stained by it; and as the anemone blooms in Syria about Easter, this may be thought to show that the festival of Adonis, or at least one of his festivals, was held in spring. The name of the flower is probably derived from Naaman ("darling"), which seems to have been an epithet of Adonis. The Arabs still call the anemone "wounds of the Naaman.". . .

In Attica, certainly, the festival fell at the height of summer. For the fleet which Athens fitted out against Syracuse, and by the destruction of which her power was permanently crippled, sailed at midsummer, and by an ominous coincidence the sombre rites of Adonis were being celebrated at the very time. As the troops marched down to the harbour to embark, the streets through which they passed were lined with coffins and corpse-like effigies, and the air was rent with the noise of women wailing for the dead Adonis. The circumstance cast a gloom over the sailing of the most splendid armament that Athens ever sent to sea. Many ages afterwards, when the Emperor Julian made his first entry into Antioch, he found in like manner the gay, the luxurious capital of the East plunged in mimic grief for the annual death of Adonis; and if he had any presentiment of coming evil, the voices of lamentation which struck upon his ear must have seemed to sound his knell.

The resemblance of these ceremonies to the Indian and European ceremonies which I have described elsewhere is obvious. In particular, apart from the somewhat doubtful date of its celebration, the Alexandrian ceremony is almost identical with the Indian. In both of them the marriage of two divine beings, whose affinity with vegetation seems indicated by the fresh plants with which they are surrounded, is celebrated in effigy, and the effigies are afterwards mourned over and thrown into the water. From the similarity of these customs to each other and to the spring and midsummer customs of modern Europe we should naturally expect that they all admit of a common explanation. Hence, if the explanation which I have adopted of the latter is correct, the ceremony of the death and resurrection of Adonis must also have been a dramatic representation of the decay and revival of plant life. The inference thus based on the resemblance of the customs is confirmed by the following features in the legend and ritual of Adonis. His affinity with vegetation comes out at once in the common story of his birth. He was said to have been born from a myrrh-tree, the bark of which bursting, after a ten months' gestation, allowed the lovely infant to come forth. According to some, a boar rent the bark with his tusk and so opened a passage for the babe. A faint rationalistic colour was given to the legend by saying that his mother was a woman named Myrrh, who had been turned into a myrrh-tree soon after she had conceived the child. The use of myrrh as incense at the festival of Adonis may have given rise to the fable. We have seen that incense was burnt at the corresponding Babylonian rites, just as it was burnt by the idolatrous Hebrews in honour of the Queen of Heaven, who was no other than Astarte. Again, the story that Adonis spent half, or according to others a third, of the year in the lower world and the rest of it in the upper world, is explained most simply and naturally by supposing that he represented vegetation, especially the corn, which lies buried in the earth half the year and reappears above ground the other half. Certainly of the annual phenomena of nature there is none which suggests so obviously the idea of death and resurrection as the disappearance and reappearance of vegetation in autumn and spring. . . .

The annual death and revival of vegetation is a conception which readily presents itself to men in every stage of savagery and civilisation; and the vastness of the scale on which this ever-recurring decay and regeneration takes place, together with man's intimate dependence on it for subsistence, combine to render it the most impressive annual occurrence in nature, at least within the temperate zones. It is no wonder that a phenomenon so important, so striking, and so universal should, by suggesting similar ideas, have given rise to similar rites in many lands. We may, therefore, accept as probable an explanation of the Adonis worship which accords so well with the facts of nature and with the analogy of similar rites in other lands. Moreover, the explanation is countenanced by a considerable body of opinion amongst the ancients themselves, who again and again interpreted the dying and reviving god as the reaped and sprouting grain.

The character of Tammuz or Adonis as a corn-spirit comes out plainly in an account of his festival given by an Arabic writer of the tenth century. In describing the rites and sacrifices observed at the different seasons of the year by the heathen Syrians of Harran, he says: "Tammuz (July). In the middle of this month is the festival of el-Bûgât, that is, of the weeping women, and this is the Tâ-uz festival, which is celebrated in honour of the god Tâ-uz. The women bewail him, because his lord slew him so cruelly, ground his bones in a mill, and then scattered them to the wind. The women (during this festival) eat nothing which has been ground in a mill, but limit their diet to steeped wheat,

sweet vetches, dates, raisins, and the like." Tâ-uz, who is no other than
Tammuz, is here like Burns's John Barleycorn:

> They wasted o'er a scorching flame
> The marrow of his bones;
> But a miller us'd him worst of all—
> For he crush'd him between two stones.

This concentration, so to say, of the nature of Adonis upon the
cereal crops is characteristic of the stage of culture reached by his worshippers in historical times. They had left the nomadic life of the wandering hunter and herdsman far behind them; for ages they had been
settled on the land, and had depended for their subsistence mainly on
the products of tillage. The berries and roots of the wilderness, the grass
of the pastures, which had been matters of vital importance to their
ruder forefathers, were now of little moment to them: more and more
their thoughts and energies were engrossed by the staple of their life,
the corn; more and more accordingly the propitiation of the deities of
fertility in general and of the corn-spirit in particular tended to become
the central feature of their religion. The aim they set before themselves
in celebrating the rites was thoroughly practical. It was no vague poetical
sentiment which prompted them to hail with joy the rebirth of vegetation and to mourn its decline. Hunger, felt or feared, was the main-
spring of the worship of Adonis.

It has been suggested by Father Lagrange that the mourning for
Adonis was essentially a harvest rite designed to propitiate the corn-god,
who was then either perishing under the sickles of the reapers or being
trodden to death under the hoofs of the oxen on the threshing-floor.
While the men slew him, the women wept crocodile tears at home to
appease his natural indignation by a show of grief for his death. The
theory fits in well with the dates of the festivals, which fell in spring
or summer; for spring and summer, not autumn, are the seasons of the
barley and wheat harvests in the lands which worshipped Adonis. Further, the hypothesis is confirmed by the practice of the Egyptian reapers, who lamented, calling upon Isis, when they cut the first corn; and
it is recommended by the analogous customs of many hunting tribes,
who testify great respect for the animals which they kill and eat.

Thus interpreted, the death of Adonis is not the natural decay of vegetation in general under the summer heat or the winter cold; it is the violent destruction of the corn by man, who cuts it down on the field, stamps it to pieces on the threshing-floor, and grinds it to powder in the mill. That this was indeed the principal aspect in which Adonis presented himself in later times to the agricultural peoples of the Levant may be admitted; but whether from the beginning he had been the corn and nothing but the corn, may be doubted. At an earlier period he may have been to the herdsman, above all, the tender herbage which sprouts after rain, offering rich pasture to the lean and hungry cattle. Earlier still he may have embodied the spirit of the nuts and berries which the autumn woods yield to the savage hunter and his squaw. . . .

THE GARDENS OF ADONIS

Perhaps the best proof that Adonis was a deity of vegetation, and especially of the corn, is furnished by the gardens of Adonis, as they were called. These were baskets or pots filled with earth, in which wheat, barley, lettuces, fennel, and various kinds of flowers were sown and tended for eight days, chiefly or exclusively by women. Fostered by the sun's heat, the plants shot up rapidly, but having no root they withered as rapidly away, and at the end of eight days were carried out with the images of the dead Adonis, and flung with them into the sea or into springs.

These gardens of Adonis are most naturally interpreted as representatives of Adonis or manifestations of his power; they represented him, true to his original nature, in vegetable form, while the images of him, with which they were carried out and cast into the water, portrayed him in his later human shape. All these Adonis ceremonies, if I am right, were originally intended as charms to promote the growth or revival of vegetation; and the principle by which they were supposed to produce this effect was homoeopathic or imitative magic. For ignorant people suppose that by mimicking the effect which they desire to produce they actually help to produce it; thus by sprinkling water they make rain, by lighting a fire they make sunshine, and so on. Similarly, by mimicking the growth of the crops they hope to ensure a good harvest. The rapid growth of the wheat and barley in the gardens of Adonis was intended to make the corn shoot up; and the throwing of the gardens and of the images into the water was a charm to secure a due supply of fertilising rain. The same, I take it, was the object of throwing the

effigies of Death and the Carnival into water in the corresponding ceremonies of modern Europe. Certainly the custom of drenching with water
a leaf-clad person, who undoubtedly personifies vegetation, is still resorted to in Europe for the express purpose of producing rain. Similarly
the custom of throwing water on the last corn cut at harvest, or on the
person who brings it home (a custom observed in Germany and France,
and till lately in England and Scotland), is in some places practised
with the avowed intent to procure rain for the next year's crops. Thus
in Wallachia and amongst the Roumanians in Transylvania, when a girl
is bringing home a crown made of the last ears of corn cut at harvest,
all who meet her hasten to throw water on her, and two farm-servants
are placed at the door for the purpose; for they believe that if this were
not done, the crops next year would perish from drought. At the spring
ploughing in Prussia, when the ploughmen and sowers returned in the
evening from their work in the fields, the farmer's wife and the servants
used to splash water over them. The ploughmen and sowers retorted
by seizing every one, throwing them into the pond, and ducking them
under the water. The farmer's wife might claim exemption on payment
of a forfeit, but every one else had to be ducked. By observing this custom they hoped to ensure a due supply of rain for the seed. . . .

In Sardinia the gardens of Adonis are still planted in connexion
with the great midsummer festival which bears the name of St. John.
At the end of March or on the first of April a young man of the village
presents himself to a girl, and asks her to be his *comare* (gossip or
sweetheart), offering to be her *compare*. The invitation is considered
as an honour by the girl's family, and is gladly accepted. At the end of
May the girl makes a pot of the bark of the cork-tree, fills it with earth,
and sows a handful of wheat and barley in it. The pot being placed in
the sun and often watered, the corn sprouts rapidly and has a good
head by Midsummer Eve (St. John's Eve, the twenty-third of June).
The pot is then called *Erme* or *Nenneri*. On St. John's Day the young
man and the girl, dressed in their best, accompanied by a long retinue
and preceded by children gambolling and frolicking, move in procession to a church outside the village. Here they break the pot by throwing it against the door of the church. Then they sit down in a ring on the
grass and eat eggs and herbs to the music of flutes. Wine is mixed in a
cup and passed round, each one drinking as it passes. Then they join
hands and sing "Sweethearts of St. John" (*Compare e comare di San*

Giovanni) over and over again, the flutes playing the while. When they
tire of singing they stand up and dance gaily in a ring till evening. This
is the general Sardinian custom. As practised at Ozieri it has some special features. In May the pots are made of cork-bark and planted with
corn, as already described. Then on the Eve of St. John the window-
sills are draped with rich cloths, on which the pots are placed, adorned
with crimson and blue silk and ribbons of various colours. On each of
the pots they used formerly to place a statuette or cloth doll dressed as
a woman, or a Priapus-like figure made of paste; but this custom, rigorously forbidden by the Church, has fallen into disuse. The village
swains go about in a troop to look at the pots and their decorations and
to wait for the girls, who assemble on the public square to celebrate the
festival. Here a great bonfire is kindled, round which they dance and
make merry. Those who wish to be "Sweethearts of St. John" act as
follows. The young man stands on one side of the bonfire and the girl on
the other, and they, in a manner, join hands by each grasping one end
of a long stick, which they pass three times backwards and forwards
across the fire, thus thrusting their hands thrice rapidly into the flames.
This seals their relationship to each other. Dancing and music go on
till late at night. The correspondence of these Sardinian pots of grain
to the gardens of Adonis seems complete, and the images formerly
placed in them answer to the images of Adonis which accompanied his
gardens. . . .

In some parts of Sicily the gossips[1] of St. John present each other
with plates of sprouting corn, lentils, and canary seed, which have been
planted forty days before the festival. The one who receives the plate
pulls a stalk of the young plants, binds it with a ribbon, and preserves
it among his or her greatest treasures, restoring the platter to the giver.
At Catania the gossips exchange pots of basil and great cucumbers; the
girls tend the basil, and the thicker it grows the more it is prized.

In these midsummer customs of Sardinia and Sicily it is possible
that St. John has replaced Adonis. . . .

At the approach of Easter, Sicilian women sow wheat, lentils, and
canary-seed in plates, which they keep in the dark and water every
two days. The plants soon shoot up; the stalks are tied together with

---

[1] This word has run through many shades of meaning, from the Anglo-Saxon *godsibb*
("God-sibling," such as a godfather or godson) to its common modern meaning.
As used here it means comrades or companions.

red ribbons, and the plates containing them are placed on the sepulchres which, with the effigies of the dead Christ, are made up in Catholic and Greek churches on Good Friday, just as the gardens of Adonis
were placed on the grave of the dead Adonis. The practice is not confined to Sicily, for it is observed also at Cosenza in Calabria, and perhaps
in other places. The whole custom — sepulchres as well as plates of
sprouting grain — may be nothing but a continuation, under a different
name, of the worship of Adonis.

Nor are these Sicilian and Calabrian customs the only Easter ceremonies which resemble the rites of Adonis. "During the whole of Good
Friday a waxen effigy of the dead Christ is exposed to view in the
middle of the Greek churches and is covered with fervent kisses by the
thronging crowd, while the whole church rings with melancholy, monotonous dirges. Late in the evening, when it has grown quite dark, this
waxen image is carried by the priests into the street on a bier adorned
with lemons, roses, jessamine, and other flowers, and there begins a
grand procession of the multitude, who move in serried ranks, with
slow and solemn step, through the whole town. Every man carries his
taper and breaks out into doleful lamentation. At all the houses which
the procession passes there are seated women with censers to fumigate
the marching host. Thus the community solemnly buries its Christ as if
he had just died. At last the waxen image is again deposited in the
church, and the same lugubrious chants echo anew. These lamentations, accompanied by a strict fast, continue till midnight on Saturday.
As the clock strikes twelve, the bishop appears and announces the glad
tidings that 'Christ is risen,' to which the crowd replies, 'He is risen indeed,' and at once the whole city bursts into an uproar of joy, which
finds vent in shrieks and shouts, in the endless discharge of carronades
and muskets, and the explosion of fire-works of every sort. In the very
same hour people plunge from the extremity of the fast into the enjoyment of the Easter lamb and neat wine.". . .

When we reflect how often the Church has skilfully contrived to
plant the seeds of the new faith on the old stock of paganism, we may
surmise that the Easter celebration of the dead and risen Christ was
grafted upon a similar celebration of the dead and risen Adonis, which,
as we have seen reason to believe, was celebrated in Syria at the same
season. The type, created by Greek artists, of the sorrowful goddess
with her dying lover in her arms, resembles and may have been the

model of the *Pietà* of Christian art, the Virgin with the dead body of her divine Son in her lap, of which the most celebrated example is the one by Michael Angelo in St. Peters. That noble group, in which the living sorrow of the mother contrasts so wonderfully with the languor of death in the son, is one of the finest compositions in marble. Ancient Greek art has bequeathed to us few works so beautiful, and none so pathetic.

In this connexion a well-known statement of Jerome[2] may not be without significance. He tells us that Bethlehem, the traditionary birth-place of the Lord, was shaded by a grove of that still older Syrian Lord, Adonis, and that where the infant Jesus had wept, the lover of Venus was bewailed. Though he does not expressly say so, Jerome seems to have thought that the grove of Adonis had been planted by the heathen after the birth of Christ for the purpose of defiling the sacred spot. In this he may have been mistaken. If Adonis was indeed, as I have argued, the spirit of the corn, a more suitable name for his dwelling-place could hardly be found than Bethlehem, "the House of Bread," and he may well have been worshipped there at his House of Bread long ages before the birth of Him who said, "I am the bread of life."

✌ৡ FOR DISCUSSION AND WRITING

1. What is Frazer's theory of the origin of the belief in gods? How, according to Frazer, is that belief related to the vegetational cycle? Explain the last sentence of the second paragraph: "Thus a religious theory was blended with a magical practice." What distinction does he make between magic and religion?

2. What does he say were the "primary wants" of our primitive ancestors? Are our own "primary wants" different? and if so, what is the main difference? Consider the statement in the third paragraph: "To them the principle of life and fertility, whether animal or vegetable, was one and indivisible." What does this mean? Do we have the same or a different attitude toward "the principle of life and fertility," or do we have any attitude at all?

---

[2] Saint Jerome, one of the early Christian scholars and fathers of the church.

3. What is the relationship between the Greek Adonis and the Babylonian Tammuz? Because the earth is universally thought of as female, being the producer of the food on which all men depend, and probably also because man is born of woman, goddesses came before gods. With what Great Goddess was Tammuz associated? and Adonis? What was the origin of the name "Adonis"? (As you perhaps know, "Adonai" was also an ancient Hebrew form of address to God, and is used in the Bible and in Christian liturgy, meaning "Lord.") What was the effect on the earth of the annual disappearance or "death" of Tammuz? Where did he go? Point out various ways in which he is connected with vegetation in the "Lament of the Flutes for Tammuz."

4. Interpret as a vegetation myth the rivalry of Aphrodite and Persephone for Adonis.

5. What visual and sensuous aids of imagery does Frazer bring to the understanding of ancient myth? Point out several examples.

6. What was the purpose of "sacred prostitution" in the temples of Ishtar, Astarte, and Aphrodite? What symbolic relationship did it have to the growth of crops and the fertility of animals and men? We tend to look on such ancient practices with moralistic eyes, judging them from the point of view of our own moral tradition; and it is true that these practices degenerated as the ancient cities grew more wealthy and luxurious (one of the famous temples of Aphrodite, with its sacred prostitutes, was in the very rich city of Corinth, and the apostle Paul thundered there in the marketplace against the licentiousness practiced by the Corinthians in the name of religion); but why is moralistic judgment irrelevant to the archaic significance of such rites?

7. What is Frazer's explanation of the incestuous character of royal marriages in ancient Cyprus and elsewhere? One doesn't need to become "Freudian" about this; what did matrilineal descent have to do with it? (If you know Sophocles' *Oedipus Rex*, could you support the view that, since the king was dead, the young hero acclaimed king by the people of Thebes naturally had to marry the queen, Jocasta, in order to validate his kingship?)

8. How does Frazer explain the annual redness of the river Adonis as, swollen by spring freshets from the mountains, it flows into the Mediterranean? (Incidentally, this still happens.) What was the ancient myth-

ological explanation? What connection has the anemone with Adonis?
What relationship does Frazer point out between Adonis and "John
Barleycorn"?

9. Explain what the "gardens of Adonis" are and their relationship with the
myth and ritual of Adonis. (Herodotus describes a similar custom in ancient Egypt, associated with the god Osiris.) If you live or have lived in
a rural part of America where old customs are still practiced, do you find
any connection between May-day baskets and the "gardens of Adonis"?

10. How does Frazer connect the ancient symbolism of the religion of Adonis
with that of Christianity?

11. The study of comparative religion may act in two opposite ways on one's
religious belief. It may destroy that belief by reducing it to a "nothing but"
—nothing but some sort of primitive superstition or "projection"; or it
may deepen, strengthen, and educate one's belief, by showing a marvelous
continuity going back unfathomably into past ages and into prehistory. If
this subject interests you, you might use it as a writing assignment, bas-
ing your paper on Frazer. Or you might write a short paper with no particular relationship to the religious question, just giving your reactions to
this piece. If you know Shelley's poem *Adonais*, you might reread it and
write about it, showing how Shelley used the myth and ritual of Adonis
in the poem.

Apuleius ✑ The Mysteries of Isis

✑ Of Roman citizenship, Greek stock, and North African birth, Apuleius lived and wrote in the second century A.D. His description of the mysteries of Isis is from that remarkable novel *The Golden Ass*, which holds in its savorous mixture a bit of everything from picaresque adventure and gross ribaldry to the most sensitive and poetic retelling of myth (the story of Psyche and Eros is told in its most complete form here) and to one of the fullest and most reliable records we have of ancient religious initiation. Apuleius uses his own first name, Lucius, as the name of the hero of the book, who, at an early point in his career, was turned into an ass (not a "golden" one; the epithet "golden" was a cliché for popular entertainments in Apuleius' time). ✑

CENCHREAE[1] has a safe harbour and is always crowded with visitors, but I wanted to keep away from people. I went to a secluded beach and stretched my tired body in a hollow of the sand, close to where the waves were breaking in spray. It was evening. The chariot of the sun was at the point of ending its day's course across the sky; so I too resigned myself to rest, and was presently overcome by a sweet, sound sleep.

Not long afterwards I awoke in sudden terror. A dazzling full moon was rising from the sea. It is at this secret hour that the Moon-goddess, sole sovereign of mankind, is possessed of her greatest power and maj-

Reprinted by permission of Willis Kingsley Wing. Copyright © 1951 by International Authors N.V. From *The Golden Ass* published by Penguin Books Ltd. & Farrar, Straus & Co., Inc. The translation is by Robert Graves.

[1] Ancient port near Corinth.

esty. She is the shining deity by whose divine influence not only all beasts, wild and tame, but all inanimate things as well, are invigorated; whose ebbs and flows control the rhythm of all bodies whatsoever, whether in the air, on earth, or below the sea. Of this I was well aware, and therefore resolved to address the visible image of the goddess, imploring her help; for Fortune seemed at last to have made up her mind that I had suffered enough and to be offering me a hope of release.

Jumping up and shaking off my drowsiness, I went down to the sea to purify myself by bathing in it. Seven times I dipped my head under the waves — seven, according to the divine philosopher Pythagoras,[2] is a number that suits all religious occasions — and with joyful eagerness, though tears were running down my hairy face,[3] I offered this soundless prayer to the supreme Goddess:

'Blessed Queen of Heaven, whether you are pleased to be known as Ceres, the original harvest mother who in joy at the finding of your lost daughter Proserpine abolished the rude acorn diet of our forefathers and gave them bread raised from the fertile soil of Eleusis;[4] or whether as celestial Venus, now adored at sea-girt Paphos, who at the time of the first Creation coupled the sexes in mutual love and so contrived that man should continue to propagate his kind for ever; or whether as Artemis, the physician sister of Phoebus Apollo, reliever of the birth pangs of women, and now adored in the ancient shrine at Ephesus;[5] or whether as dread Proserpine to whom the owl cries at night, whose triple face[6] is potent against the malice of ghosts, keeping them imprisoned below earth; you who wander through many sacred groves and are propitiated with many different rites — you whose womanly light

---

[2] Greek philosopher of the sixth century B.C., whose followers, in the Greek cities of southern Italy, held number as a supreme metaphysical principle and made considerable advances in mathematics and astronomy. Pythagoras himself was said to have taught the doctrine of metempsychosis and that earthly life served as a purification of the soul (hence he is called here "divine philosopher").

[3] It must be remembered that he has been transformed into an ass.

[4] Small town near Athens, where the most famous of the ancient mysteries were performed, for Demeter or Ceres.

[5] Ancient city in what is now Turkey, about thirty-five miles from Smyrna (Izmir), where the stupendous sculptured figure of Artemis (or Diana) may still be seen as it appeared to her worshipers.

[6] The Great Goddess who had all these names was represented sometimes as having three faces, symbolizing the three realms of her power—the heavens, the earth, and the underworld.

illuminates the walls of every city, whose misty radiance nurses the happy seeds under the soil, you who control the wandering course of the sun and the very power of his rays — I beseech you, by whatever name, in whatever aspect, with whatever ceremonies you deign to be invoked, have mercy on me in my extreme distress, restore my shattered fortune, grant me repose and peace after this long sequence of miseries. End my sufferings and perils, rid me of this hateful four-footed disguise, return me to my family, make me Lucius once more. But if I have offended some god of unappeasable cruelty who is bent on making life impossible for me, at least grant me one sure gift, the gift of death.'

When I had finished my prayer and poured out the full bitterness of my oppressed heart, I returned to my sandy hollow, where once more sleep overcame me. I had scarcely closed my eyes before the apparition of a woman began to rise from the middle of the sea with so lovely a face that the gods themselves would have fallen down in adoration of it. First the head, then the whole shining body gradually emerged and stood before me poised on the surface of the waves. Yes, I will try to describe this transcendent vision, for though human speech is poor and limited, the Goddess herself will perhaps inspire me with poetic imagery sufficient to convey some slight inkling of what I saw.

Her long thick hair fell in tapering ringlets on her lovely neck, and was crowned with an intricate chaplet in which was woven every kind of flower. Just above her brow shone a round disc, like a mirror, or like the bright face of the moon, which told me who she was. Vipers rising from the left-hand and right-hand partings of her hair supported this disc, with ears of corn bristling beside them.[7] Her many-coloured robe was of finest linen; part was glistening white, part crocus-yellow, part glowing red and along the entire hem a woven bordure of flowers and fruit clung swaying in the breeze. But what caught and held my eye more than anything else was the deep black lustre of her mantle. She wore it slung across her body from the right hip to the left shoulder, where it was caught in a knot resembling the boss of a shield; but part of it hung in innumerable folds, the tasselled fringe quivering. It was embroidered with glittering stars on the hem and everywhere else, and in the middle beamed a full and fiery moon.

[7] Snakes were characteristic emblems of the Great Goddess, her chthonic attribute (see Note 2, page 505). The ears of corn are, of course, emblematic of her agricultural functions.

In her right hand she held a bronze rattle, of the sort used to frighten away the God of the Sirocco;[8] its narrow rim was curved like a sword-belt and three little rods, which sang shrilly when she shook the handle, passed horizontally through it. A boat-shaped gold dish hung from her left hand, and along the upper surface of the handle writhed an asp with puffed throat and head raised ready to strike. On her divine feet were slippers of palm leaves, the emblem of victory.

All the perfumes of Arabia floated into my nostrils as the Goddess deigned to address me: 'You see me here, Lucius, in answer to your prayer. I am Nature, the universal Mother, mistress of all the elements, primordial child of time, sovereign of all things spiritual, queen of the dead, queen also of the immortals, the single manifestation of all gods and goddesses that are. My nod governs the shining heights of Heaven, the wholesome sea-breezes, the lamentable silences of the world below. Though I am worshipped in many aspects, known by countless names, and propitiated with all manner of different rites, yet the whole round earth venerates me. The primeval Phrygians call me Pessinuntica, Mother of the gods; the Athenians, sprung from their own soil, call me Cecropian Artemis; for the islanders of Cyprus I am Paphian Aphrodite; for the archers of Crete I am Dictynna; for the trilingual Sicilians, Stygian Proserpine; and for the Eleusinians their ancient Mother of the Corn.

'Some know me as Juno, some as Bellona of the Battles; others as Hecate, others again as Rhamnubia, but both races of Aethiopians, whose lands the morning sun first shines upon, and the Egyptians who excel in ancient learning and worship me with ceremonies proper to my godhead, call me by my true name, namely, Queen Isis. I have come in pity of your plight, I have come to favour and aid you. Weep no more, lament no longer; the hour of deliverance, shone over by my watchful light, is at hand.

'Listen attentively to my orders.

'The eternal laws of religion devote to my worship the day born from this night. Tomorrow my priests offer me the first-fruits of the new

---

[8] The "rattle" was a sacred instrument of prehistoric antiquity (the Australian aborigines still use it in religious rites); in the Roman syncretistic religion of the Great Goddess, the priestly emblem of the rattle derived from the Asiatic cult of Cybele. It was a kind of bull-roarer, and a much more alarming and resounding instrument than the word "rattle" implies. Apuleius compares it here with some sort of rattle used superstitiously to drive off the hot, dusty wind of the sirocco.

sailing season by dedicating a ship to me: for at this season the storms of winter lose their force, the leaping waves subside and the sea becomes navigable once more. You must wait for this sacred ceremony, with a mind that is neither anxious for the future nor clouded with profane thoughts; and I shall order the High Priest to carry a garland of roses in my procession, tied to the rattle which he carries in his right hand. Do not hesitate, push the crowd aside, join the procession with confidence in my grace. Then come close up to the High Priest as if you wished to kiss his hand, gently pluck the roses with your mouth and you will immediately slough off the hide of what has always been for me the most hateful beast in the universe.

'Above all, have faith: do not think that my commands are hard to obey. For at this very moment, while I am speaking to you here, I am also giving complementary instructions to my sleeping High Priest; and tomorrow, at my commandment, the dense crowds of people will make way for you. I promise you that in the joy and laughter of the festival nobody will either view your ugly shape with abhorrence or dare to put a sinister interpretation on your sudden return to human shape. Only remember, and keep these words of mine locked tight in your heart, that from now onwards until the last day of your life you are dedicated to my service. It is only right that you should devote your whole life to the Goddess who makes you a man again. Under my protection you will be happy and famous, and when at the destined end of your life you descend to the land of ghosts, there too in the subterrene hemisphere you shall have frequent occasion to adore me. From the Elysian fields you will see me as queen of the profound Stygian realm, shining through the darkness of Acheron[9] with a light as kindly and tender as I show you now. Further, if you are found to deserve my divine protection by careful obedience to the ordinances of my religion and by perfect chastity, you will become aware that I, and I alone, have power to prolong your life beyond the limits appointed by destiny.'

With this, the vision of the invincible Goddess faded and dissolved.

I rose at once, wide awake, bathed in a sweat of joy and fear.

---

[9] The Elysian fields, or "Happy Isles," or "Isles of the West," were the place of eternity for the most blessed of the dead, the great heroes and philosophers. The Stygian realm was that of the river Styx, which flowed in the shadowy underworld of the dead; and Acheron was another river in the dark world of Hades.

Astonished beyond words at this clear manifestation of her godhead,
I splashed myself with sea water and carefully memorized her orders,
intent on obeying them to the letter. Soon a golden sun arose to rout the
dark shadows of night, and at once the streets were filled with people
walking along as if in a religious triumph. Not only I, but the whole
world, seemed filled with delight. The animals, the houses, even the
weather itself reflected the universal joy and serenity, for a calm sunny
morning had succeeded yesterday's frost, and the song-birds, assured
that spring had come, were chirping their welcome to the queen of the
stars, the Mother of the seasons, the mistress of the universe. The trees,
too, not only the orchard trees but those grown for their shade, roused
from their winter sleep by the warm breezes of the south and tasselled
with green leaves, waved their branches with a pleasant rustling noise;
and the crash and thunder of the surf was stilled, for the gales had
blown themselves out, the dark clouds were gone and the calm sky
shone with its own deep blue light.

Presently the vanguard of the grand procession came in view. It
was composed of a number of people in fancy dress of their own choosing; a man wearing a soldier's sword-belt; another dressed as a hunts-
man, a thick cloak caught up to his waist with hunting knife and javelin;
another who wore gilt sandals, a wig, a silk dress and expensive jewellery
and pretended to be a woman. Then a man with heavy boots, shield,
helmet and sword, looking as though he had walked straight out of the
gladiators' school; a pretended magistrate with purple robe and rods
of office; a philosopher with cloak, staff, clogs and billy-goat beard; a
bird-catcher, carrying lime and a long reed; a fisherman with another
long reed and a fish-hook. Oh, yes, and a tame she-bear dressed like a
woman, carried in a sedan chair; and an ape in a straw hat and a saffron-
coloured Phrygian cloak with a gold cup grasped in its paws — a caricature of Jupiter's beautiful cup-bearer Ganymede. Finally an ass with
wings glued to its shoulders and a doddering old man seated on its rump;
you would have laughed like anything at that pair, supposed to be
Pegasus and Bellerophon.[10] These fancy-dress comedians kept running
in and out of the crowd, and behind them came the procession proper.

[10] Pegasus was a winged horse sacred to the Muses; with a stamp of his hoof he
was said to have opened the spring from which the Muses drank their inspiration.
Bellerophon was a Corinthian hero who was sent by a sly and cruel king to kill
the Chimera, a nightmare beast, and who succeeded in doing so by the help of the
winged horse Pegasus.

At the head walked women crowned with flowers, who pulled more flowers out of the folds of their beautiful white dresses and scattered them along the road; their joy in the Saviouress appeared in every gesture. Next came women with polished mirrors tied to the backs of their heads, which gave all who followed them the illusion of coming to meet the Goddess, rather than marching before her. Next, a party of women with ivory combs in their hands who made a pantomime of combing the Goddess's royal hair, and another party with bottles of perfume who sprinkled the road with balsam and other precious perfumes; and behind these a mixed company of women and men who addressed the Goddess as 'Daughter of the Stars' and propitiated her by carrying every sort of light — lamps, torches, wax-candles and so forth.

Next came musicians with pipes and flutes, followed by a party of carefully chosen choir-boys singing a hymn in which an inspired poet had explained the origin of the procession. The temple pipers of the great god Serapis[11] were there, too, playing their religious anthem on pipes with slanting mouth-pieces and tubes curving around their right ears; also a number of beadles and whifflers crying: 'Make way there, way for the Goddess!' Then followed a great crowd of the Goddess's initiates, men and women of all classes and every age, their pure white linen clothes shining brightly. The women wore their hair tied up in glossy coils under gauze head-dresses; the men's heads were completely shaven, representing the Goddess's bright earthly stars, and they carried rattles of brass, silver and even gold, which kept up a shrill and ceaseless tinkling.

The leading priests, also clothed in white linen drawn tight across their breasts and hanging down to their feet, carried the oracular emblems of the deity. The High Priest held a bright lamp, which was not at all like the lamps we use at night banquets; it was a golden boat-shaped affair with a tall tongue of flame mounting from a hole in the centre. The second priest held an *auxiliaria,* or sacrificial pot, in each of his hands — the name refers to the Goddess's providence in helping her devotees. The third priest carried a miniature palm-tree with gold leaves, also the serpent wand of Mercury.[12] The fourth carried the model of a

---

[11] The Egyptian fertility god Osiris in his bull form (corresponding with the bull forms of Dionysus and Zeus).

[12] Mercury was the Roman equivalent of Hermes, who had many functions, including that of sponsorship of science; his snake-entwined staff has survived as the emblem of physicians.

left hand with the fingers stretched out, which is an emblem of justice because the left hand, with its natural slowness and lack of any craft or subtlety, seems more impartial than the right. He also held a golden vessel, rounded in the shape of a woman's breast, from the nipple of which a thin stream of milk fell to the ground. The fifth carried a winnowing fan woven with golden rods, not osiers.[13] Then came a man, not one of the five, carrying a wine-jar.

Next in the procession followed those deities that deigned to walk on human feet. Here was the frightening messenger of the gods of Heaven, and of the gods of the dead: Anubis with a face black on one side, golden on the other, walking erect and holding his herald's wand in one hand, and in the other a green palm-branch. Behind, danced a man carrying on his shoulders, seated upright, the statue of a cow,[14] representing the Goddess as the fruitful Mother of us all. Then along came a priest with a box containing the secret implements of her wonderful cult. Another fortunate priest had an ancient emblem of her godhead hidden in the lap of his robe: this was not made in the shape of any beast, wild or tame, or any bird or human being, but the exquisite beauty of its workmanship no less than the originality of its design called for admiration and awe. It was a symbol of the sublime and ineffable mysteries of the Goddess, which are never to be divulged: a small vessel of burnished gold, upon which Egyptian hieroglyphics were thickly crowded, with a rounded bottom, a long spout, and a generously curving handle along which sprawled an asp, raising its head and displaying its scaly, wrinkled, puffed-out throat.

At last the moment had come when the blessing promised by the almighty Goddess was to fall upon me. The High Priest in whom lay my hope of salvation approached, and I saw that he carried the rattle

[13] Osiers are pliable willow twigs, used in the making of a kind of flat basket called a "winnowing fan," which has for many ages been used in the winnowing of grain; when the basket is shaken, the chaff is carried off by the wind. Later in this piece winnowing fans are put on board a consecrated ship, for they had a natural, primary, agricultural symbolism. In the cult of Dionysus, the annually newborn god was symbolized, in a great ceremony held at midnight, by the showing forth of one of these winnowing baskets as the cradle of the infant god. (The corresponding symbolism of the birth of the holy child in the straw of the stable in Bethlehem is clear.)

[14] Another example of syncretism. The Egyptian goddess Hathor had the form of a cow, represented as standing over the earth and nourishing the human race from her udders. Here the cow has become the emblem of Isis.

and the garland in his right hand just as I had been promised — but, oh, it was more than a garland to me, it was a crown of victory over cruel Fortune, bestowed on me by the Goddess after I had endured so many hardships and run through so many dangers! Though overcome with sudden joy, I refrained from galloping forward at once and disturbing the calm progress of the pageant by a brutal charge, but gently and politely wriggled my way through the crowd which gave way before me, clearly by the Goddess's intervention, until at last I emerged at the other side. I saw at once that the priest had been warned what to expect in his vision of the previous night but was none the less astounded that the fulfilment came so pat. He stood still and held out the rose garland to the level of my mouth. I trembled and my heart pounded as I ate those roses with loving relish; and no sooner had I swallowed them than I found that the promise had been no deceit. My bestial features faded away, the rough hair fell from my body, my sagging paunch tightened, my hind hooves separated into feet and toes, my fore hooves now no longer served only for walking upon, but were restored, as hands, to my human uses. Then my neck shrank, my face and head rounded, my great hard teeth shrank to their proper size, my long ears shortened, and my tail which had been my worst shame vanished altogether.

A gasp of wonder went up and the priests, aware that the miracle corresponded with the High Priest's vision of the Great Goddess, lifted their hands to Heaven and with one voice applauded the blessing which she had vouchsafed me: this swift restoration to my proper shape.

When I saw what had happened to me I stood rooted to the ground with astonishment and could not speak for a long while, my mind unable to cope with so great and sudden a joy. I could find no words good enough to thank the Goddess for her extraordinary loving-kindness. But the High Priest, who had been informed by her of all my miseries, though himself taken aback by the weird sight, gave orders in dumb-show that I should be lent a linen garment to cover me; for as soon as I regained my human shape, I had naturally done what any naked man would do — pressed my knees closely together and put both my hands down to screen my private parts. Someone quickly took off his upper robe and covered me with it, after which the High Priest gazed benignly at me, still wondering at my perfectly human appearance.

'Lucius, my friend,' he said, 'you have endured and performed many labours and withstood the buffetings of all the winds of ill luck. Now at

last you have put into the harbour of peace and stand before the altar
of loving-kindness. Neither your noble blood and rank nor your education sufficed to keep you from falling a slave to pleasure; youthful follies
ran away with you. Your luckless curiosity earned you a sinister punishment. But blind Fortune, after tossing you maliciously about from peril
to peril has somehow, without thinking what she was doing, landed you
here in religious felicity. Let her begone now and fume furiously where-
ever she pleases, let her find some other plaything for her cruel hands.
She has no power to hurt those who devote their lives to the honour and
service of our Goddess's majesty. The jade! What use was served by
making you over to bandits, wild dogs and cruel masters, by setting your
feet on dangerous stony paths, by holding you in daily terror of death?
Rest assured that you are now safe under the protection of the true
Fortune, all-seeing Providence, whose clear light shines for all the gods
that are. Rejoice now, as becomes a wearer of white linen. Follow triumphantly in the train of the Goddess who has delivered you. Let the
irreligious see you and, seeing, let them acknowledge the error of their
ways. Let them cry: "Look, there goes Lucius, rescued from a dreadful
fate by the intervention of the Goddess Isis; watch him glory in the
defeat of his ill luck!" But to secure today's gains, you must enrol yourself in this holy Order as last night you pledged yourself to do, voluntarily undertaking the duties to which your oath binds you; for her
service is perfect freedom.'

When the High Priest had ended his inspired speech, I joined the
throng of devotees and went forward with the procession, an object of
curiosity to all Corinth. People pointed or jerked their heads at me and
said: 'Look, there goes Lucius, restored to human shape by the power
of the Almighty Goddess! Lucky, lucky man to have earned her compassion on account of his former innocence and good behaviour, and
now to be reborn as it were, and immediately accepted into her most
sacred service!' Their congratulations were long and loud.

Meanwhile the pageant moved slowly on and we approached the
sea shore, at last reaching the very place where on the previous night
I had lain down as an ass. There the divine emblems were arranged in
due order and there with solemn prayers the chaste-lipped priest consecrated and dedicated to the Goddess a beautifully built ship, with
Egyptian hieroglyphics painted over the entire hull; but first he carefully purified it with a lighted torch, an egg and sulphur. The sail was

shining white linen, inscribed in large letters with the prayer for the Goddess's protection of shipping during the new sailing season. The long fir mast with its shining head was now stepped, and we admired the gilded prow shaped like the neck of Isis's sacred goose, and the long, highly-polished keel cut from a solid trunk of citrus-wood. Then all present, both priesthood and laity, began zealously stowing aboard winnowing-fans heaped with aromatics and other votive offerings and poured an abundant stream of milk into the sea as a libation. When the ship was loaded with generous gifts and prayers for good fortune, they cut the anchor cables and she slipped across the bay with a serene breeze behind her that seemed to have sprung up for her sake alone. When she stood so far out to sea that we could no longer keep her in view, the priests took up the sacred emblems again and started happily back towards the temple, in the same orderly procession as before.

On our arrival the High Priest and the priests who carried the oracular emblems were admitted into the Goddess's sanctuary with other initiates and restored them to their proper places. Then one of them, known as the Doctor of Divinity, presided at the gate of the sanctuary over a meeting of the Shrine-bearers, as the highest order of the priests of Isis are called. He went up into a high pulpit with a book and read out a Latin blessing upon 'our liege lord, the Emperor, and upon the Senate, and upon the Order of Knights, and upon the Commons of Rome, and upon all sailors and all ships who owe obedience to the aforesaid powers.' Then he uttered the traditional Greek formula, 'Ploea-phesia', meaning that vessels were now permitted to sail, to which the people responded with a great cheer and dispersed happily to their homes, taking all kinds of decorations with them: such as olive boughs, scent shrubs and garlands of flowers, but first kissing the feet of a silver statue of the Goddess that stood on the temple steps. I did not feel like moving a nail's breadth from the place, but stood with my eyes intently fixed on the statue and relived in memory all my past misfortunes. . . .

Thereafter I devoted my whole time to attendance on the Goddess, encouraged by these tokens to hope for even greater marks of her favour, and my desire for taking holy orders increased. I frequently spoke of it to the High Priest, begging him to initiate me into the mysteries of the holy night. He was a grave man, remarkable for the strict observance of his religious duties, and checked my restlessness, as parents calm down children who are making unreasonable demands, but so gently and kindly that I was not in the least discouraged. He explained that the day on which a postulant might be initiated was always indicated by signs from the Goddess herself, and that it was she who chose the officiating priest and announced how the incidental expenses of the ceremony were to be paid. In his view I ought to wait with attentive patience and avoid the two extremes of over-eagerness and obstinacy; being neither unresponsive when called nor importunate while awaiting my call. 'No single member of the brotherhood,' he said, 'has ever been so wrong-minded and sacrilegious, in fact so bent on his own destruction, as to partake of the mystery without direct orders from the Goddess, and so fall into deadly sin. The gates of the Underworld and the guardianship of life are in her hands, and the rites of initiation approximate to a voluntary death from which there is only a precarious hope of resurrection. So she usually chooses old men who feel that their end is fast approaching yet are not too senile to be capable of keeping a secret; by her grace they are, in a sense, born again and restored to new and healthy life.'

He said, in fact, that I must be content to await definite orders, but agreed that I had been foreordained for the service of the Goddess by clear marks of her favour. Meanwhile I must abstain from forbidden food, as the priests did, so that when the time came for me to partake of their most holy mysteries I could enter the sanctuary with unswerving steps.

I accepted his advice and learned to be patient, taking part in the daily services of the temple as calmly and quietly as I knew how, intent on pleasing the Goddess. Nor did I have a troublesome and disappointing probation. Soon after this she gave me proof of her grace by a midnight vision in which I was plainly told that the day for which I longed, the day on which my greatest wish would be granted, had come at last. I learned that she had ordered the High Priest Mithras, whose destiny was linked with mine by planetary sympathy, to officiate at my initiation.

These orders and certain others given me at the same time so exhilarated me that I rose before dawn to tell the High Priest about them, and reached his door just as he was coming out. I greeted him and was about to beg him more earnestly than ever to allow me to be initiated, as a privilege that was now mine by right, when he spoke first. 'Dear Lucius,' he said, 'how lucky, how blessed you are that the Great Goddess has graciously deigned to honour you in this way. There is no time to waste.

The day for which you prayed so earnestly has dawned. The many-named Goddess orders me to initiate you into her most holy mysteries.'

He took me by the hand and led me courteously to the doors of the vast temple, and when he had opened them in the usual solemn way and performed the morning sacrifice he went to the sanctuary and took out two or three books written in characters unknown to me: some of them animal hieroglyphics, some of them ordinary letters protected against profane prying by having their tops and tails wreathed in knots or rounded like wheels or tangled together in spirals like vine tendrils. From these books he read me out instructions for providing the necessary clothes and accessories for my initiation.

I at once went to my friends the priests and asked them to buy part of what I needed, sparing no expense: the rest I went to buy myself.

In due time the High Priest summoned me and took me to the nearest public baths, attended by a crowd of priests. There, when I had enjoyed my ordinary bath, he himself washed and sprinkled me with holy water, offering up prayers for divine mercy. After this he brought me back to the temple and placed me at the very feet of the Goddess.

It was now early afternoon. He gave me certain orders too holy to be spoken above a whisper, and then commanded me in everyone's hearing to abstain from all but the plainest food for the ten succeeding days, to eat no meat and drink no wine.

I obeyed his instructions in all reverence and at last the day came for taking my vows. As evening approached a crowd of priests came flocking to me from all directions, each one giving me congratulatory gifts, as the ancient custom is. Then the High Priest ordered all uninitiated persons to depart, invested me in a new linen garment and led me by the hand into the inner recesses of the sanctuary itself. I have no doubt, curious reader, that you are eager to know what happened when I entered. If I were allowed to tell you, and you were allowed to be told, you would soon hear everything; but, as it is, my tongue would suffer for its indiscretion and your ears for their inquisitiveness.[15]

However, not wishing to leave you, if you are religiously inclined, in a state of tortured suspense, I will record as much as I may lawfully record for the uninitiated, but only on condition that you believe it. *I approached the very gates of death and set one foot on Proserpine's thresh-*

---

[15] This taboo of silence is observed with amazing consistency by the initiates of the mysteries; hence our little knowledge of the ancient ritual.

old, yet was permitted to return, rapt through all the elements. At mid-night I saw the sun shining as if it were noon; I entered the presence of the gods of the underworld and the gods of the upper-world, stood near and worshipped them.

Well, now you have heard what happened, but I fear you are still none the wiser.

The solemn rites ended at dawn and I emerged from the sanctuary wearing twelve different stoles, certainly a most sacred costume but one that there can be no harm in my mentioning. Many uninitiated people saw me wearing it when the High Priest ordered me to mount into the wooden pulpit which stood in the centre of the temple, immediately in front of the Goddess's image. I was wearing an outer garment of fine linen embroidered with flowers, and a precious scarf hung down from my shoulders to my ankles with sacred animals worked in colour on every part of it; for instance Indian serpents and Hyperborean griffins, which are winged lions generated in the more distant parts of the world. The priests call this scarf an Olympian stole. I held a lighted torch in my right hand and wore a white palm-tree chaplet with its leaves sticking out all round like rays of light.

The curtains were pulled aside and I was suddenly exposed to the gaze of the crowd, as when a statue is unveiled, dressed like the sun. That day was the happiest of my initiation, and I celebrated it as my birthday with a cheerful banquet at which all my friends were present. Further rites and ceremonies were performed on the third day, includ-ing a sacred breakfast, and these ended the proceedings. However, I remained for some days longer in the temple, enjoying the ineffable pleasure of contemplating the Goddess's statue, because I was bound to her by a debt of gratitude so large that I could never hope to pay it.

✆§ FOR DISCUSSION AND WRITING

1. What are some of the many names of the goddess who appears in Lucius' vision? What is she called, for instance, as goddess of agriculture and of the harvest? as goddess of fertility and procreation? as goddess of child-birth? as goddess of the underworld of death? (This invocation to the "god-dess of many names" gives you an expressive example of religious syncre-tism in the Roman empire of Apuleius' time.)

2. Robert Graves, the translator, is one of the finest modern poets, is an old hand at translation, and writes a prose that has its own characteristic distinction; so it is fair enough that we should consider an example of style here. Look over the sentence starting at the beginning of the fourth paragraph: Where is the main clause? the subject? the predicate? and what kind of constructions are those divided by semicolons? and how many appositional phrases do you find? Grammatically speaking, what keeps the sentence, long as it is, perfectly clear and at the same time gives it swing and power?

3. One of the most interesting things about this dreamside and roadside view of ancient religious belief and ritual is the experience of emblematic symbolism it offers—not merely fanciful or personal or highfalutin "literary" symbolism, but symbolism that is, for the most part, grounded in age-old, universal perception. Let's look at some of the emblems of the goddess (she is too overloaded with symbolic accessories to be really chic, but her beauty and grace are of another kind). Consider, for instance, her association with the moon—her appearance to Lucius first in her planetary form, as the moon rising over the sea, and then the moonlike disk she wears on her head when she appears in his dream as a queenly goddess. How is moon symbolism grounded in human experience—in the hidden or night-part of our lives, in our associations with love-making (one has only to think of the constancy of the word "moon" in the rhymes of popular sentimental lyrics), in the rhythms of ovarian functions, in the tidal rhythms of the sea, in the rhythms of agricultural functions (as one can see by a look at Farmers' Almanacs), in the construction of the calendar, and in innumerable other ways? The moon disk is held on the goddess's head by a sort of crown composed of ears of corn and vipers; the symbolism of the ears of corn is easy—what is it? and is this symbolism merely archaic and primitive, or is it still fundamental in the organization of life? What about the snakes? Most people have intense associations about snakes, and so did primitive people; what are your own associations, and can you explain them? The fact that snakes slough their old skins each year and appear in bright and shining new ones is one of their most impressive attributes; what kind of symbolism does this attribute suggest, and why does it account in part for the association of snakes with the Great Goddess of birth and death and rebirth? How does the fact that they live so secretly under the earth afford a symbolism consonant with the mystery of the goddess by whom all things are brought forth from the earth and through whom they return to the earth? As corn-goddess, goddess of the harvest, goddess of love and procreation, the Great Goddess appears in a wholly beneficent

aspect, but all things sacred are also dangerous—they must be treated carefully and with reverence, and if people get to feeling too intelligent and too smart, and thus become irreverent toward what is holy, nature strikes back and consumes them (thus God appeared to Moses on Mount Sinai not as a cooing dove but as volcanic fire and lava, striking terror into the patriarch); furthermore, life is not all beer and skittles, it is also suffering and destruction; how do the vipers guarding the goddess's crown symbolize these aspects? What is the symbolism of her many-colored robes —the white, yellow, and red, and the black mantle? (For this color symbolism, you need only consult your own simplest associations with colors.) Her "rattle" is explained in the footnote. She carries a sort of dish (the significance of the asp curling around it is clear enough from the discussion of snakes); in view of what dishes are ordinarily used for, what is the symbolism of the dish? If you know anything about the Grail stories in the cycle of legends associated with King Arthur, what continuity do you find between the goddess's symbolic dish and the symbolic dish of the Grail? What continuity is there between this ancient dish symbolism and the symbolism of the Last Supper celebrated in the Eucharist of the Mass?

4. If you have read the piece from Jung, earlier in this book, do you find in Lucius' vision what Jung calls a "primordial image" or "archetype"? Explain your answer.

5. In the description of the procession, we have an excellent close-up view of the public part of the ancient mysteries of the Great Goddess (later, Lucius goes through the esoteric, secret part of the mysteries). Can you explain the presence of the fancy-dress comics and the animal masquerade in a religious procession? Is there anything similar today in pre-Lenten carnival celebrations? From a dour puritanical point of view, the comic masquerade would seem the very antithesis of religion; but in the medieval morality plays, based on Biblical themes, the devil played the comedian, sticking his pitchfork into the buttocks of the rich and great, producing pratfalls, and so on; in a familiar medieval tale, a poor circus clown, who had nothing to offer the Virgin but his stunts, won her smile by turning comic somersaults before her; and in Spain and Mexico today, the animal-masked clown, with a furry tail on his behind, is an essential performer in Easter processions, tripping up the solemn dignitaries with his rambunctious antics. Can you find, by seeking simply through your own mind and feelings, any reason for the traditional connection between ribald comedy and religious faith?

6. What connection with the ideas suggested above has the fact that Lucius is a man in the form of that most ridiculous and pathetic animal, the ass, an animal whose very name has become a synonym for a fool and for the human backside? (One might recall here that Sancho Panza, the fat-bellied, earthy-minded companion of Don Quixote, rode on an ass; also that Christ rode on an ass in entering Jerusalem.)

7. For his spiritual rebirth, Lucius goes through an initiation that he is forbidden to describe, except to say that it was a kind of "death" (from the little that is known of the ancient mysteries, it seems that the initiate really had to go through terrors of labyrinthine darkness where he was exposed to experiences such as one might imagine as those of death, experiences so shocking that he went into a kind of trance, from which he awoke with a sense of being "reborn," rescued from infinite danger, and with a new personality able to face everything with serenity). Can you find here any parallel with modern psychoanalysis—including the terrifying difficulties of the process? How is the symbolism of Lucius' bath connected with that of baptism? and how is the symbolism of baptism connected with the effect of ordinary baths in a porcelain tub in a tiled bathroom?

8. Write a short paper on the symbolism of this piece, being careful that you don't interpret the symbolism in an arbitrary intellectual way; try to keep it to common, natural modes of perception.

Leo Tolstoy ✑§ Harvest Miracle

✑§ Tolstoy's splendor as a novelist is so great that it is best not to try to say anything about him in a note, except to give the dates of his birth and death, 1828-1910, and to send the student to his work. §✑

W HEN Levin[1] thought what he was and what he was living for, he could find no answer to the questions and was reduced to despair. . . .

So he lived, not knowing and not seeing any chance of knowing what he was and what he was living for, and harassed at this lack of

From the last chapters of *Anna Karenina*, translated by Constance Garnett (Random House, Inc.). The novel was first published in 1875–77.

[1] Levin is one of the two principal characters in the novel *Anna Karenina*, the other being Anna herself. Levin and Anna meet only once and very briefly, but their lives are counterpointed throughout the book: Anna, the woman in love, one of the most vibrant characters in fiction, who ends under the wheels of a railway engine; and Levin, the blundering intellectual farmer (like Pierre Bezukhov in *War and Peace*, a fictional projection of Tolstoy himself), who has sought through all the scientific, philosophical, and sociological literature of his time for a way of life and a reason for being, and whom we see here, near the end of the book, in his middle thirties, happily married, proficient and successful in his farming, and yet at the suicidal point of despair.

knowledge to such a point that he was afraid of suicide, and yet firmly laying down his own individual definite path in life. . . .

It was the very busiest working-time, when all the peasantry show an extraordinary intensity of self-sacrifice in labor, such as is esteemed in any other conditions of life, and would be highly esteemed if the men who showed these qualities themselves thought highly of them, and if it were not repeated every year, and if the results of this intense labor were not so simple.

To reap and bind the rye and oats and to carry it, to mow the meadows, turn over the fallows, thrash the seed and sow the winter corn — all this seems so simple and ordinary; but to succeed in getting through it all everyone in the village, from the old man to the young child, must toil incessantly for three or four weeks, three times as hard as usual, living on rye-beer, onions, and black bread, thrashing and carrying the sheaves at night, and not giving more than two or three hours in the twenty-four to sleep. And every year this is done all over Russia.

Having lived the greater part of his life in the country and in the closest relations with the peasants, Levin always felt in this busy time that he was infected by this general quickening of energy in the people.

In the early morning he rode over to the first sowing of the rye, and to the oats, which were being carried to the stacks, and returning home at the time his wife and sister-in-law were getting up, he drank coffee with them and walked to the farm, where a new thrashing-machine was to be set working to get ready the seed-corn.

He was standing in the cool granary, still fragrant with the leaves of the hazel branches interlaced on the freshly peeled aspen beams of the new thatch roof. He gazed through the open door in which the dry bitter dust of the thrashing whirled and played, at the grass of the thrashing-floor in the sunlight and the fresh straw that had been brought in from the barn, then at the speckly-headed, white-breasted swallows that flew chirping in under the roof and, fluttering their wings, settled in the crevices of the doorway, then at the peasants bustling in the dark, dusty barn, and he thought strange thoughts.

"Why is it all being done?" he thought. "Why am I standing here, making them work? What are they all so busy for, trying to show their zeal before me? What is that old Matrona, my old friend, toiling for? (I doctored her, when the beam fell on her in the fire)" he thought, looking at a thin old woman who was raking up the grain, moving painfully with her bare, sun-blackened feet over the uneven, rough floor. "Then she recovered, but to-day or to-morrow or in ten years she won't; they'll bury her, and nothing will be left either of her or of that smart girl in the red jacket, who with that skilful, soft action shakes the ears out of their husks. They'll bury her and this piebald horse, and very soon too," he thought, gazing at the heavily moving, panting horse that kept walking up the wheel that turned under him. "And they will bury her and Fyodor the thrasher with his curly beard full of chaff and his shirt torn on his white shoulders — they will bury him. He's untying the sheaves, and giving orders, and shouting to the women, and quickly setting straight the strap on the moving wheel. And what's more, it's not them alone — me they'll bury too, and nothing will be left. What for?"

He thought this, and at the same time looked at his watch to reckon how much they thrashed in an hour. He wanted to know this so as to judge by it the task to set for the day.

"It'll soon be one, and they're only beginning the third sheaf," thought Levin. He went up to the man that was feeding the machine, and shouting over the roar of the machine he told him to put it in more slowly. "You put in too much at a time, Fyodor. Do you see — it gets choked, that's why it isn't getting on. Do it evenly."

Fyodor, black with the dust that clung to his moist face, shouted something in response, but still went on doing it as Levin did not want him to.

Levin, going up to the machine, moved Fyodor aside, and began feeding the corn in himself. Working on till the peasants' dinner-hour, which was not long in coming, he went out of the barn with Fyodor and fell into talk with him, stopping beside a neat yellow sheaf of rye laid on the thrashing-floor for seed.

Fyodor came from a village at some distance from the one in which Levin had once allotted land to his cooperative association. Now it had been let to a former house-porter.

Levin talked to Fyodor about this land and asked whether Platon, a well-to-do peasant of good character belonging to the same village, would not take the land for the coming year.

"It's a high rent; it wouldn't pay Platon, Konstantin Dmitrievitch,"[2] answered the peasant, picking the ears off his sweat-drenched shirt.

[2] Levin's name in the Russian form of address: Konstantin, the first name, and Dmitrievitch, "son of Dmitri."

"But how does Kirillov make it pay?"

"Mituh!" (so the peasant called the house-porter, in a tone of contempt), "you may be sure he'll make it pay, Konstantin Dmitrievitch! He'll get his share, however he has to squeeze to get it! He's no mercy on a Christian. But Uncle Fokanitch" (so he called the old peasant Platon), "do you suppose he'd flay the skin off a man? Where there's debt, he'll let any one off. And he'll not wring the last penny out. He's a man too."

"But why will he let any one off?"

"Oh, well, of course, folks are different. One man lives for his own wants and nothing else, like Mituh, he only thinks of filling his belly, but Fokanitch, is a righteous man. He lives for his soul. He does not forget God."

"How thinks of God? How does he live for his soul?" Levin almost shouted.

"Why, to be sure, in truth, in God's way. Folks are different. Take you now, you wouldn't wrong a man. . . ."

"Yes, yes, good-bye!" said Levin, breathless with excitement, and turning round he took his stick and walked quickly away towards home. At the peasant's words that Fokanitch lived for his soul, in truth, in God's way, undefined but significant ideas seemed to burst out as though they had been locked up, and all striving towards one goal, they thronged whirling through his head, blinding him with their light.

Levin strode along the highroad, absorbed not so much in his thoughts (he could not yet disentangle them) as in his spiritual condition, unlike anything he had experienced before.

The words uttered by the peasant had acted on his soul like an electric shock, suddenly transforming and combining into a single whole the whole swarm of disjointed, impotent, separate thoughts that incessantly occupied his mind. These thoughts had unconsciously been in his mind even when he was talking about the land.

He was aware of something new in his soul, and joyfully tested this new thing, not yet knowing what it was.

"Not living for his own wants, but for God? For what God? And could one say anything more senseless than what he said? He said that one must not live for one's own wants, that is, that one must not live for what we understand, what we are attracted by, what we desire, but must live for something incomprehensible, for God, whom no one can understand nor even define. What of it? Didn't I understand those senseless words of Fyodor's? And understanding them, did I doubt of their truth? Did I think them stupid, obscure, inexact? No, I understood him, and exactly as he understands the words. I understood them more fully and clearly than I understand anything in life, and never in my life have I doubted nor can I doubt about it. And not only I, but every one, the whole world understands nothing fully but this, and about this only they have no doubt and are always agreed.

"And I looked out for miracles, complained that I did not see a miracle which would convince me. A material miracle would have persuaded me. And here is a miracle, the sole miracle possible, continually existing, surrounding me on all sides, and I never noticed it!

"Fyodor says that Kirillov lives for his belly. That's comprehensible and rational. All of us as rational beings can't do anything else but live for our belly. And all of a sudden the same Fyodor says that one mustn't live for one's belly, but must live for truth, for God, and at a hint I understand him! And I and millions of men, men who lived ages ago and men living now — peasants, the poor in spirit and the learned, who have thought and written about it, in their obscure words saying the same thing — we are all agreed about this one thing: what we must live for and what is good. I and all men have only one firm, incontestable, clear knowledge, and that knowledge cannot be explained by the reason — it is outside it, and has no causes and can have no effects.

"If goodness has causes, it is not goodness; if it has effects, a reward, it is not goodness either. So goodness is outside the chain of cause and effect.

"And yet I know it, and we all know it.

"What could be a greater miracle than that?

"Can I have found the solution of it all? can my sufferings be over?" thought Levin, striding along the dusty road, not noticing the heat nor his weariness, and experiencing a sense of relief from prolonged suffering. This feeling was so delicious that it seemed to him incredible. He was breathless with emotion and incapable of going farther; he turned off the road into the forest and lay down in the shade of an aspen on the uncut grass. He took his hat off his hot head and lay propped on his elbow in the lush, feathery, woodland grass.

"Yes, I must make it clear to myself and understand," he thought, looking intently at the untrampled grass before him, and following the movements of a green beetle, advancing along a blade of couch-grass and lifting up in its progress a leaf of goat-weed. "What have I discovered?" he asked himself, bending aside the leaf of goat-weed out of the beetle's way and twisting another blade of grass above for the beetle to cross over onto it. "What is it makes me glad? What have I discovered?

"I have discovered nothing. I have only found out what I knew. I understand the force that in the past gave me life, and now too gives me life. I have been set free from falsity, I have found the Master.

"Of old I used to say that in my body, that in the body of this grass and of this beetle (there, she didn't care for the grass, she's opened her wings and flown away), there was going on a transformation of matter in accordance with physical, chemical, and physiological laws. And in all of us, as well as in the aspens and the clouds and the misty patches, there was a process of evolution. Evolution from what? into what? — Eternal evolution and struggle. . . . As though there could be any sort of tendency and struggle in the eternal! And I was astonished that in spite of the utmost effort of thought along that road I could not discover the meaning of life, the meaning of my impulses and yearnings. Now I say that I know the meaning of my life: 'To live for God, for my soul.' And this meaning, in spite of its clearness, is mysterious and marvelous. Such, indeed, is the meaning of everything existing. Yes, pride," he said to himself, turning over on his stomach and beginning to tie a noose of blades of grass, trying not to break them.

"And not merely pride of intellect, but dulness of intellect. And most of all, the deceitfulness; yes, the deceitfulness of intellect. The cheating knavishness of intellect, that's it," he said to himself.

And he briefly went through, mentally, the whole course of his ideas during the last two years, the beginning of which was the clear confronting of death at the sight of his dear brother hopelessly ill.

Then, for the first time, grasping that for every man, and himself too, there was nothing in store but suffering, death, and forgetfulness, he had made up his mind that life was impossible like that, and that he must either interpret life so that it would not present itself to him as the evil jest of some devil, or shoot himself.

But he had not done either, but had gone on living, thinking, and feeling, and had even at that very time married, and had had many joys and had been happy, when he was not thinking of the meaning of his life.

What did this mean? It meant that he had been living rightly, but thinking wrongly.

He had lived (without being aware of it) on those spiritual truths that he had sucked in with his mother's milk, but he had thought, not merely without recognition of these truths, but studiously ignoring them.

Now it was clear to him that he could only live by virtue of the beliefs in which he had been brought up.

"What should I have been, and how should I have spent my life, if I had not had these beliefs, if I had not known that I must live for God and not for my own desires? I should have robbed and lied and killed. Nothing of what makes the chief happiness of my life would have existed for me." And with the utmost stretch of imagination he could not conceive the brutal creature he would have been himself, if he had not known what he was living for.

"I looked for an answer to my question. And thought could not give an answer to my question — it is incommensurable with my question. The answer has been given me by life itself, in my knowledge of what is right and what is wrong. And that knowledge I did not arrive at in any way, it was given to me as to all men, *given*, because I could not have got it from anywhere.

"Where could I have got it? By reason could I have arrived at knowing that I must love my neighbor and not oppress him? I was told that in my childhood, and I believed it gladly, for they told me what was already in my soul. But who discovered it? Not reason. Reason discovered the struggle for existence, and the law that requires us to oppress all who hinder the satisfaction of our desires. That is the deduction of reason. But loving one's neighbor reason could never discover, because it's irrational."

☙ FOR DISCUSSION AND WRITING

1. What, specifically, is Levin's problem? Is it a common problem or not?

2. Point out several instances of sensitively evocative physical detail in the description of the granary where the threshing is going on, and of the peasants. What significant correlation do you find between Levin's problem (which might be described as "metaphysical despair") and the scene and purpose of the threshing? Explain the state of mind, and the references to old Matrona and the girl in the red jacket and the piebald horse and Fyodor, in the paragraph starting " 'Why is it all being done?' " What is the

significance of the fact that, in spite of the despairing question occupying his mind, Levin looks at his watch in order to reckon how much the peasants are able to thresh in an hour, gives orders on feeding the threshing machine more slowly, and is so concerned with the work that he takes over Fyodor's job and starts feeding the machine himself? (To put the same question in other words, how do his actions show an assent and a commitment that his thoughts deny?)

3. What catalytic effect on Levin do old Fyodor's words have? Does he learn something new from them, or do they merely reorganize elements already present in his mind? What is meant by "a material miracle"? Is what Levin has just experienced a "material miracle" or some other kind? Why does he call it "the sole miracle possible, continually existing, surrounding me on all sides"?

4. Why is to "live for the belly" a "comprehensible and rational" motive? Why is the motive of living "for truth, for God," and why is "goodness" outside the "chain of cause and effect"?

5. Gorky said, after a visit to Tolstoy, that when Tolstoy was handling a horse, he seemed to be part horse, and when he was sitting alone and brooding on a big rock, he seemed part of the rock. In reading Tolstoy, one frequently has a similar sense of implicit relationship between human existence and the processes of the external natural world. In the second question we commented on the relationship between Levin's problem and the harvest work going on around him; and now, as he tries to make firm and clear to himself exactly what it is he has found, he is lying in the grass and watching a beetle crawl up a grass stem. What relationship is there between this setting and his state of mind now? (Don't get intellectual and allegorical about this question; it's merely a matter of natural suitability.)

6. What insufficiency does Levin find now in his former intellectual complacencies about evolution? What does he mean by "pride of intellect" as the "cheating" of the intellect? (One should keep in mind here that Levin, as the novel depicts him, is a person of powerful, learned, and deeply concerned "intellect.")

7. Explain this at the end of the piece: "Reason discovered the struggle for existence, and the law that requires us to oppress all who hinder the satisfaction of our desires. That is the deduction of reason. But loving one's neighbor reason could never discover, because it's irrational."

8. Write a short paper on your reactions to Levin's "miracle"; or a paper on
   whether or not it is necessary or advisable to occupy one's mind with the
   kind of questions Levin puts to himself; or, if you are familiar with Existentialist writings, a paper on the "existential" character of the problem set in
   this piece; or a paper examining and questioning what is said in the next
   to the last paragraph of the piece—particularly in relation to the origin
   of the knowledge of right and wrong, and to its being "given" to "all men."

Simone Weil *Spiritual Autobiography*

*"Since her death, Simone Weil has come to seem more and more a special exemplar of sanctity for our time—the Outsider as Saint in an age of alienation, our kind of saint," says Leslie Fiedler in his introduction to *Waiting for God*, the collection of Simone Weil's letters and essays from which the piece here is taken. She was born in Paris of Jewish parentage in 1909, received her baccalaureate degree with honors at fifteen, qualified as teacher of philosophy at twenty-two. All those who knew the thin, homely girl, who suffered constantly from ill health, recognized in her a prodigious intellectual and spiritual gift. For three or four years she taught in secondary schools, spending interim periods in farm work and factory work, voluntarily living on the wages and sharing the life of the worst-paid workers in France, meanwhile continuing her studies in philosophy, the Hindu scriptures, Greek, and Sanskrit. In 1936 she went to Spain, where she experienced, with the Republican army on the Catalonian front, the extreme sufferings and outrages of war. In Marseilles in 1941 she met Father Perrin, to whom the letter here is addressed; he was then at the Dominican Convent in Marseilles; two years later he was arrested by the Gestapo. Very ill, she was taken to England by her parents and died there in 1943, as a result of voluntary starvation, for she refused any food beyond the rations allowed to the French in the occupied zone.*

P.S. to be read first.

This letter is fearfully long — but as there is no question of an answer — especially as I shall doubtless have gone before it reaches you — you have years ahead of you in which to read it if you care to. Read it all the same, one day or another.

From Marseilles, about May 15[1]

Father,

Before leaving I want to speak to you again, it may be the last time perhaps, for over there I shall probably send you only my news from time to time just so as to have yours.

I told you that I owed you an enormous debt. I want to try to tell you exactly what it consists of. I think that if you could really understand what my spiritual state is you would not be at all sorry that you did not lead me to baptism. But I do not know if it is possible for you to understand this.

You neither brought me the Christian inspiration nor did you bring me to Christ; for when I met you there was no longer any need; it had been done without the intervention of any human being. If it had been otherwise, if I had not already been won, not only implicitly but consciously, you would have given me nothing, because I should have received nothing from you. My friendship for you would have been a reason for me to refuse your message, for I should have been afraid of the possibilities of error and illusion which human influence in the divine order is likely to involve.

I may say that never at any moment in my life have I 'sought for God.' For this reason, which is probably too subjective, I do not like this expression and it strikes me as false. As soon as I reached adolescence, I saw the problem of God as a problem the data of which could not be obtained here below, and I decided that the only way of being sure not to reach a wrong solution, which seemed to me the greatest possible evil, was to leave it alone. So I left it alone. I neither affirmed nor denied anything. It seemed to me useless to solve the problem, for I thought that, being in this world, our business was to adopt the best attitude with regard to the problems of this world, and that such an attitude did not depend upon the solution of the problem of God.

This held good as far as I was concerned at any rate, for I never hesitated in my choice of an attitude; I always adopted the Christian attitude as the only possible one. I might say that I was born, I grew up, and I always remained within the Christian inspiration. While the very name of God had no part in my thoughts, with regard to the problems of this world and this life I shared the Christian conception in an explicit and rigorous manner, with the most specific notions it involves. Some of

[1] May 15, 1942. Father Perrin was at that time away on a journey, and Simone Weil was on the point of leaving France.

these notions have been part of my outlook for as far back as I can remember. With others I know the time and manner of their coming and the form under which they imposed themselves upon me. . . .

At fourteen I fell into one of those fits of bottomless despair that come with adolescence, and I seriously thought of dying because of the mediocrity of my natural faculties. The exceptional gifts of my brother, who had a childhood and youth comparable to those of Pascal, brought my own inferiority home to me. I did not mind having no visible successes, but what did grieve me was the idea of being excluded from that transcendent kingdom to which only the truly great have access and wherein truth abides. I preferred to die rather than live without that truth. After months of inward darkness, I suddenly had the everlasting conviction that any human being, even though practically devoid of natural faculties, can penetrate to the kingdom of truth reserved for genius, if only he longs for truth and perpetually concentrates all his attention upon its attainment. He thus becomes a genius too, even though for lack of talent his genius cannot be visible from outside. Later on, when the strain of headaches caused the feeble faculties I possess to be invaded by a paralysis, which I was quick to imagine as probably incurable, the same conviction led me to persevere for ten years in an effort of concentrated attention that was practically unsupported by any hope of results.

Under the name of truth I also included beauty, virtue, and every kind of goodness, so that for me it was a question of a conception of the relationship between grace and desire.[2] The conviction that had come to me was that when one hungers for bread one does not receive stones. But at that time I had not read the Gospel. . . .

As for the spirit of poverty, I do not remember any moment when it was not in me, although only to that unhappily small extent compatible with my imperfection. I fell in love with Saint Francis of Assisi as soon as I came to know about him. I always believed and hoped that one day Fate would force upon me the condition of a vagabond and a beggar which he embraced freely. Actually I felt the same way about prison.

[2] Grace is a gift of whatever it is that one needs (desires)—mercy or enlightenment —that comes from God alone. What is said here—"for me it was a question of a conception of the relationship between grace and desire"—is a summary restatement of what was said in the preceding paragraph: the conviction that if one desires patiently enough and with concentrated attention, the enlightenment or "grace" will come. The same thought is repeated in the metaphor of the next sentence: "when one hungers for bread one does not receive stones."

From my earliest childhood I always had also the Christian idea of love for one's neighbor, to which I gave the name of justice — a name it bears in many passages of the Gospel and which is so beautiful. You know that on this point I have failed seriously several times.

The duty of acceptance in all that concerns the will of God, whatever it may be, was impressed upon my mind as the first and most necessary of all duties from the time when I found it set down in Marcus Aurelius under the form of the *amor fati*[3] of the Stoics. I saw it as a duty we cannot fail in without dishonoring ourselves.

The idea of purity, with all that this word can imply for a Christian, took possession of me at the age of sixteen, after a period of several months during which I had been going through the emotional unrest natural in adolescence. This idea came to me when I was contemplating a mountain landscape and little by little it was imposed upon me in an irresistible manner.

Of course I knew quite well that my conception of life was Christian. That is why it never occurred to me that I could enter the Christian community. I had the idea that I was born inside. But to add dogma to this conception of life, without being forced to do so by indisputable evidence, would have seemed to me like a lack of honesty. I should even have thought I was lacking in honesty had I considered the question of the truth of dogma as a problem for myself or even had I simply desired to reach a conclusion on this subject. I have an extremely severe standard for intellectual honesty, so severe that I never met anyone who did not seem to fall short of it in more than one respect; and I am always afraid of failing in it myself.

Keeping away from dogma in this way, I was prevented by a sort of shame from going into churches, though all the same I like being in them. Nevertheless, I had three contacts with Catholicism that really counted.

After my year in the factory,[4] before going back to teaching, I had been taken by my parents to Portugal, and while there I left them to go alone to a little village. I was, as it were, in pieces, soul and body. That contact with affliction had killed my youth. Until then I had not had any experience of affliction. . . .

I knew quite well that there was a great deal of affliction in the world, I was obsessed with the idea, but I had not had prolonged and

[3] Serene acceptance of destiny (literally, love of what is ordained).
[4] The Renault automobile factory.

first-hand experience of it. As I worked in the factory, indistinguishable
to all eyes, including my own, from the anonymous mass, the affliction
of others entered into my flesh and my soul. Nothing separated me from
it, for I had really forgotten my past and I looked forward to no future,
finding it difficult to imagine the possibility of surviving all the fatigue.
What I went through there marked me in so lasting a manner that still
today when any human being, whoever he may be and in whatever circumstances, speaks to me without brutality, I cannot help having the
impression that there must be a mistake and that unfortunately the mistake will in all probability disappear. There I received forever the mark
of a slave, like the branding of the red-hot iron the Romans put on the
foreheads of their most despised slaves. Since then I have always regarded myself as a slave.

In this state of mind then, and in a wretched condition physically, I
entered the little Portuguese village, which, alas, was very wretched too,
on the very day of the festival of its patron saint. I was alone. It was the
evening and there was a full moon over the sea. The wives of the fisher-
men were, in procession, making a tour of all the ships, carrying candles
and singing what must certainly be very ancient hymns of a heart-rending sadness. Nothing can give any idea of it. I have never heard anything so poignant unless it were the song of the boatmen on the Volga.
There the conviction was suddenly borne in upon me that Christianity
is pre-eminently the religion of slaves, that slaves cannot help belonging
to it, and I among others.

In 1937 I had two marvelous days at Assisi. There, alone in the little
twelfth-century Romanesque chapel of Santa Maria degli Angeli, an
incomparable marvel of purity where Saint Francis often used to pray,
something stronger than I was compelled me for the first time in my
life to go down on my knees.

In 1938 I spent ten days at Solesmes,[5] from Palm Sunday to Easter
Tuesday, following all the liturgical services, I was suffering from splitting headaches; each sound hurt me like a blow; by an extreme effort of
concentration I was able to rise above this wretched flesh, to leave it to
suffer by itself, heaped up in a corner, and to find a pure and perfect joy
in the unimaginable beauty of the chanting and the words. This experience enabled me by analogy to get a better understanding of the pos-

[5] French village with a famous Benedictine abbey, founded in 1010, which was responsible for the revival of Gregorian chants.

sibility of loving divine love in the midst of affliction. It goes without saying that in the course of these services the thought of the Passion of Christ entered into my being once and for all.

There was a young English Catholic there from whom I gained my first idea of the supernatural power of the sacraments because of the truly angelic radiance with which he seemed to be clothed after going to communion. Chance — for I always prefer saying chance rather than Providence — made of him a messenger to me. For he told me of the existence of those English poets of the seventeenth century who are named metaphysical. In reading them later on, I discovered the poem of which I read you what is unfortunately a very inadequate translation. It is called "Love".[6] I learned it by heart. Often, at the culminating point of a violent headache, I make myself say it over, concentrating all my attention upon it and clinging with all my soul to the tenderness it enshrines. I used to think I was merely reciting it as a beautiful poem, but without my knowing it the recitation had the virtue of a prayer. It was during one of these recitations that, as I told you, Christ himself came down and took possession of me.

In my arguments about the insolubility of the problem of God I had never foreseen the possibility of that, of a real contact, person to person, here below, between a human being and God. I had vaguely heard tell of things of this kind, but I had never believed in them. In the *Fioretti*[7] the accounts of apparitions rather put me off if anything, like the miracles in the Gospel. Moreover, in this sudden possession of me by Christ, neither my senses nor my imagination had any part; I only felt in the midst of my suffering the presence of a love, like that which one can read in the smile on a beloved face.

I had never read any mystical works because I had never felt any call to read them. In reading as in other things I have always striven to practice obedience. There is nothing more favorable to intellectual progress, for as far as possible I only read what I am hungry for at the moment when I have an appetite for it, and then I do not read, I *eat*. God in his mercy had prevented me from reading the mystics, so that it should be evident to me that I had not invented this absolutely unexpected contact.

Yet I still half refused, not my love but my intelligence. For it

[6] By George Herbert.

[7] Legends of Saint Francis of Assisi.

seemed to me certain, and I still think so, today, that one can never wrestle enough with God if one does so out of pure regard for the truth. Christ likes us to prefer truth to him because, before being Christ, he is truth. If one turns aside from him to go toward the truth, one will not go far before falling into his arms.

After this I came to feel that Plato was a mystic, that all the *Iliad* is ba*hed in Christian light, and that Dionysus and Osiris are in a certain sense Christ himself; and my love was thereby redoubled.

I never wondered whether Jesus was or was not the Incarnation of God; but in fact I was incapable of thinking of him without thinking of him as God.

In the spring of 1940 I read the *Bhagavad-Gita.*[8] Strange to say it was in reading those marvelous words, words with such a Christian sound, put into the mouth of an incarnation of God, that I came to feel strongly that we owe an allegiance to religious truth which is quite different from the admiration we accord to a beautiful poem; it is something far more categorical.

Yet I did not believe it to be possible for me to consider the question of baptism. I felt that I could not honestly give up my opinions concerning the non-Christian religions and concerning Israel — and as a matter of fact time and meditation have only served to strengthen them — and I thought that this constituted an absolute obstacle. I did not imagine it as possible that a priest could even dream of granting me baptism. If I had not met you, I should never have considered the problem of baptism as a practical problem.

During all this time of spiritual progress I had never prayed. I was afraid of the power of suggestion that is in prayer — the very power for which Pascal recommends it. Pascal's method seems to me one of the worst for attaining faith.

Contact with you was not able to persuade me to pray. On the contrary I thought the danger was all the greater, since I also had to beware of the power of suggestion in my friendship with you. At the same time I found it very difficult not to pray and not to tell you so. Moreover I knew I could not tell you without completely misleading you about myself. At that time I should not have been able to make you understand.

Until last September I had never once prayed in all my life, at least

[8] Sacred Hindu scripture of the first or second century A.D.

not in the literal sense of the word. I had never said any words to God, either out loud or mentally. I had never pronounced a liturgical prayer. I had occasionally recited the *Salve Regina,* but only as a beautiful poem.

Last summer, doing Greek with T——, I went through the Our Father word for word in Greek. We promised each other to learn it by heart. I do not think he ever did so, but some weeks later, as I was turning over the pages of the Gospel, I said to myself that since I had promised to do this thing and it was good, I ought to do it. I did it. The infinite sweetness of this Greek text so took hold of me that for several days I could not stop myself from saying it over all the time. A week afterward I began the vine harvest. I recited the Our Father in Greek every day before work, and I repeated it very often in the vineyard.

Since that time I have made a practice of saying it through once each morning with absolute attention. If during the recitation my attention wanders or goes to sleep, in the minutest degree, I begin again until I have once succeeded in going through it with absolutely pure attention. Sometimes it comes about that I say it again out of sheer pleasure, but I only do it if I really feel the impulse.

The effect of this practice is extraordinary and surprises me every time, for, although I experience it each day, it exceeds my expectation at each repetition.

At times the very first words tear my thoughts from my body and transport it to a place outside space where there is neither perspective nor point of view. The infinity of the ordinary expanses of perception is replaced by an infinity to the second or sometimes the third degree. At the same time, filling every part of this infinity of infinity, there is silence, a silence which is not an absence of sound but which is the object of a positive sensation, more positive than that of sound. Noises, if there are any, only reach me after crossing this silence.

Sometimes, also, during this recitation or at other moments, Christ is present with me in person, but his presence is infinitely more real, more moving, more clear than on that first occasion when he took possession of me.

I should never have been able to take it upon myself to tell you all this had it not been for the fact that I am going away. And as I am going more or less with the idea of probable death,[9] I do not believe that I have

---

[9] She had been ill all her life and was extremely weak at this time; she was evidently aware here that she would die soon.

the right to keep it to myself. For after all, the whole of this matter is not a question concerning me myself. It concerns God. I am really nothing in it all. If one could imagine any possibility of error in God, I should think that it had all happened to me by mistake. But perhaps God likes to use castaway objects, waste, rejects. After all, should the bread of the host[10] be moldy, it would become the Body of Christ just the same after the priest had consecrated it. Only it cannot refuse, while we can disobey. It sometimes seems to me that when I am treated in so merciful a way, every sin on my part must be a mortal sin. And I am constantly committing them.

I have told you that you are like a father and brother at the same time to me. But these words only express an analogy. Perhaps at bottom they only correspond to a feeling of affection, of gratitude and admiration. For as to the spiritual direction of my soul, I think that God himself has taken it in hand from the start and still looks after it.

That does not prevent me from owing you the greatest debt of gratitude that I could ever have incurred toward any human being. This is exactly what it consists of.

First you once said to me at the beginning of our relationship some words that went to the bottom of my soul. You said: "Be very careful, because if you should pass over something important through your own fault it would be a pity."

That made me see intellectual honesty in a new light. Till then I had only thought of it as opposed to faith; your words made me think that perhaps, without my knowing it, there were in me obstacles to the faith, impure obstacles, such as prejudices, habits. I felt that after having said to myself for so many years simply: "Perhaps all that is not true," I ought, without ceasing to say it — I still take care to say it very often now — to join it to the opposite formula, namely: "Perhaps all that is true," and to make them alternate.

At the same time, in making the problem of baptism a practical problem for me, you have forced me to face the whole question of the faith, dogma, and the sacraments, obliging me to consider them closely

---

10 The consecrated wafer of the Eucharist. The word "host" in this sense has a long and curious history, but there is a clear relationship between the modern meaning of "host"—the one who provides hospitality and especially food—and the Eucharistic meaning of the word: Christ as the host at the celebration of the Last Supper, who provides the bread and is the bread.

and at length with the fullest possible attention, making me see them as things toward which I have obligations that I have to discern and perform. I should never have done this otherwise and it is indispensable for me to do it.

But the greatest blessing you have brought me is of another order. In gaining my friendship by your charity (which I have never met anything to equal), you have provided me with a source of the most compelling and pure inspiration that is to be found among human things. For nothing among human things has such power to keep our gaze fixed ever more intensely upon God, than friendship for the friends of God. . . .

I have not been able to avoid causing you the greatest disappointment it was in my power to cause you. But up to now, although I have often asked myself the question during prayer, during Mass, or in the light of the radiancy that remains in the soul after Mass, I have never once had, even for a moment, the feeling that God wants me to be in the Church. I have never even once had a feeling of uncertainty. I think that at the present time we can finally conclude that he does not want me in the Church. Do not have any regrets about it.

He does not want it so far at least. But unless I am mistaken I should say that it is his will that I should stay outside for the future too, except perhaps at the moment of death. Yet I am always ready to obey any order, whatever it may be. I should joyfully obey the order to go to the very center of hell and to remain there eternally. I do not mean, of course, that I have a preference for orders of this nature. I am not perverse like that.

Christianity should contain all vocations without exception since it is catholic.[11] In consequence the Church should also. But in my eyes Christianity is catholic by right but not in fact. So many things are outside it, so many things that I love and do not want to give up, so many things that God loves, otherwise they would not be in existence. All the immense stretches of past centuries, except the last twenty are among them; all the countries inhabited by colored races; all secular life in the white peoples' countries; in the history of these countries, all the traditions banned as heretical, those of the Manicheans and Albigenses for instance; all those things resulting from the Renaissance, too often degraded but not quite without value.

---

[11] Look up the word "catholic," without a capital letter, in the dictionary, and apply it to the statement that "Christianity is catholic by right [by its guarantees or beliefs] but not in fact."

Christianity being catholic by right but not in fact, I regard it as legitimate on my part to be a member of the Church by right but not in fact, not only for a time, but for my whole life if need be.

But it is not merely legitimate. So long as God does not give me the certainty that he is ordering me to do anything else, I think it is my duty.

I think, and so do you, that our obligation for the next two or three years, an obligation so strict that we can scarcely fail in it without treason, is to show the public the possibility of a truly incarnated Christianity.[12] In all the history now known there has never been a period in which souls have been in such peril as they are today in every part of the globe. . . .

But everything is so closely bound up together that Christianity cannot be really incarnated unless it is catholic in the sense that I have just defined. How could it circulate through the flesh of all the nations of Europe if it did not contain absolutely everything in itself? Except of course falsehood. But in everything that exists there is most of the time more truth than falsehood.

Having so intense and so painful a sense of this urgency, I should betray the truth, that is to say the aspect of truth that I see, if I left the point, where I have been since my birth, at the intersection of Christianity and everything that is not Christianity. . . .

I think that you should understand why I have always resisted you, if in spite of being a priest you can admit that a genuine vocation[13] might prevent anyone from entering the Church.

Otherwise a barrier of incomprehension will remain between us, whether the error is on my part or on yours. This would grieve me from the point of view of my friendship for you, because in that case the result of all these efforts and desires, called forth by your charity toward me, would be a disappointment for you. Moreover, although it is not my fault, I should not be able to help feeling guilty of ingratitude. For, I repeat, my debt to you is beyond all measure.

12 "Incarnated" is a powerful word deriving from the Latin word for meat or flesh (as in *chili con carne*, chili peppers with meat). An "incarnated Christianity" would be a Christianity made blood and bones and flesh, a Christianity completely realized in the behavior of people. The word is particularly powerful here because of its relation to the doctrine of the Incarnation—the doctrine that God was "incarnated" as man in the person of Christ—which is the basis of Christianity.

13 Literally, a calling, in the sense of a summons, used here with reference to a religious profession undertaken in the service of God—but notice what a startling turn Simone Weil gives to the word.

✍§ FOR DISCUSSION AND WRITING

1. What does she say was her reason, even in adolescence, for refusing to attempt any solution, either positive or negative, of "the problem of God"? What was her early attitude (at fourteen) as to the possibility that a person of no gifts and of poor mental endowment might "penetrate to the kingdom of truth"? (In view of her profound humility, one should remember that her intellectual gifts—which she denied having—were actually those of genius.) What does she say she included under the name of "truth"? Explain the statement "The conviction that had come to me was that when one hungers for bread one does not receive stones."

2. What was her attitude toward "the spirit of poverty"? What significance does that term have? How is Saint Francis of Assisi associated with "the spirit of poverty"? (If you don't know, look up Saint Francis in the encyclopedia.) What was her attitude toward the idea of love for one's neighbor? What was her attitude toward acceptance of the will of God, and through what pagan means did she come to that attitude? What was her attitude toward "the idea of purity," and what does that term mean? What is her purpose here in describing these attitudes of her adolescence? If you don't know the use of the word "dogma" in reference to religion, look it up in the big dictionary; then try to explain the statement "But to add dogma to this conception of life, without being forced to do so by indisputable evidence, would have seemed to me like a lack of honesty."

3. What was the effect of her "experience of affliction" when she was working in the factory? (It should be remembered that she undertook this work not through necessity but by choice, as also the work in the vineyards which she mentions later.) What conviction came to her in the little Portuguese village, and why?

4. What was the effect of the Easter week at Solesmes? How did Herbert's poem affect her? (Since this poem is a fine one, it might be a good idea to look it up, in a volume of George Herbert's work or in an anthology of seventeenth-century poetry.) Why did she not read mystical works?

5. Why did she avoid prayer? How do the attitudes so far described reflect her intellectual integrity?

6. Where does she speak of a deliberate practice of intellectual doubt, and of a discipline of doubt with regard to possible prejudices and habits of thought?

7. Why did she refuse baptism?

8. Carefully explain her reasoning in the whole paragraph beginning "Christianity should contain all vocations without exception since it is catholic." (But make sure you understand the use of the word "catholic" here.)

9. Make sure of the meaning of the term "incarnated" as it is used in the last few paragraphs, and then explain why the principle of "catholicism" and the principle of "a truly incarnated Christianity" prevented Simone Weil from entering the Church.

10. Possibilities for papers: a paper simply showing your reactions to this piece, if you have been interested in it and moved by it; or a paper taking up a particular aspect, such as Simone Weil's resistance to joining the Church, or her saintliness (for whatever one means by the term, she was undoubtedly "saintly"—but if you took this topic it would be well to look up, in the encyclopedia or elsewhere, some general information about "saints" and "saintliness"); or, if you have read the piece about Joan of Arc, early in this book, an interesting paper could be written comparing Joan's experience with that of Simone Weil; or you might like to follow up Simone Weil further, doing a bit of research on her life and perhaps reading something more of her work.

Alan W. Watts ❧ Beat Zen, Square Zen, and Zen

❧ Born in England in 1914, Alan Watts came to the United States in 1938, and now lives in California. He had been an ordained Anglican minister, but left the church to devote himself to the study of Eastern religions, religious symbolism, and psychology. He has published a number of brilliantly written books on these subjects, including *The Way of Zen* and *Psychotherapy East and West,* has lectured at universities and medical and psychiatric institutions on both sides of the Atlantic, and conducted a National Education television program called "Eastern Wisdom and Modern Life." ❧

IT IS as difficult for Anglo-Saxons as for the Japanese to absorb anything quite so Chinese as Zen. For though the word "Zen" is Japanese and though Japan is now its home, Zen Buddhism is the creation of T'ang dynasty[1] China. I do not say this as a prelude to harping upon the incommunicable subtleties of alien cultures. The point is simply that people who feel a profound need to justify themselves have difficulty in understanding the viewpoints of those who do not, and the Chinese who

This essay first appeared in the *Chicago Review,* Summer, 1958, and is reprinted here (in abridged form) from its publication by City Lights Books (1959) by permission of the publisher. Copyright © 1959 by Alan W. Watts. Assistance in annotation for the selection reprinted here has been provided by the author.

[1] The T'ang dynasty lasted from about A.D. 618 to 906. It was distinguished by wide territorial expansion, great wealth, the invention of printing, and the flourishing of art and poetry.

created Zen were the same kind of people as Lao-tzu,[2] who, centuries before, had said, "Those who justify themselves do not convince." For the urge to make or prove oneself right has always jiggled the Chinese sense of the ludicrous, since as both Confucians and Taoists — however different these philosophies in other ways — they have invariably appreciated the man who can "come off it." To Confucius it seemed much better to be human-hearted than righteous, and to the great Taoists, Lao-tzu and Chuang-tzu,[3] it was obvious that one could not be right without also being wrong, because the two were as inseparable as back and front. As Chuang-tzu said, "Those who would have good government without its correlative misrule, and right without its correlative wrong, do not understand the principle of the universe."

To Western ears such words may sound cynical, and the Confucian admiration of "reasonableness" and compromise may appear to be a weak-kneed lack of commitment to principle. Actually they reflect a marvelous understanding and respect for what we call the balance of nature, human and otherwise — a universal vision of life is the Tao or way of nature in which the good and the evil, the creative and the destructive, the wise and the foolish are the inseparable polarities of existence. "Tao," said the *Chung-Yung*,[4] "is that from which one cannot depart. That from which one can depart is not the Tao." Therefore wisdom did not consist in trying to wrest the good from the evil but in learning to "ride" them as a cork adapts itself to the crests and troughs of the waves. At the roots of Chinese life there is a trust in the good-and-evil of one's own nature which is peculiarly foreign to those brought up with the chronic uneasy conscience of the Hebrew-Christian cultures. Yet it was always obvious to the Chinese that a man who mistrusts himself cannot even trust his mistrust, and must therefore be hopelessly confused.

For rather different reasons, Japanese people tend to be as uneasy in themselves as Westerners, having a sense of social shame quite as acute as our more metaphysical sense of sin. This was especially true of

---

[2] Lao-tzu (*ca.* 604-531 B.C.) was the legendary founder of Taoism.

[3] Chuang-tzu, or Chuang-chou, was a Taoist philosopher in China *ca.* 290 B.C. See Lin Yutang, *The Wisdom of Lao-tse* (New York: Modern Library, 1948).

[4] The *Chung-yung* or *The Book of the Unwobbling Pivot* is one of the principal Confucian classics, dating from the fourth century B.C.

the class most attracted to Zen, the *samurai*.[5] Ruth Benedict, in that very uneven work *Chrysanthemum and Sword*, was, I think, perfectly correct in saying that the attraction of Zen to the *samurai* class was its power to get rid of an extremely awkward self-consciousness induced in the education of the young. Part-and-parcel of this self-consciousness is the Japanese compulsion to compete with oneself — a compulsion which turns every craft and skill into a marathon of self-discipline. Although the attraction of Zen lay in the possibility of liberation from self-consciousness, the Japanese version of Zen fought fire with fire, overcoming the "self observing the self" by bringing it to an intensity in which it exploded. How remote from the regimen of the Japanese Zen monastery are the words of the great T'ang master Lin-chi:

> In Buddhism there is no place for using effort. Just be ordinary and nothing special. Eat your food, move your bowels, pass water, and when you're tired go and lie down. The ignorant will laugh at me, but the wise will understand.

. . . The Buddha or awakened man of Chinese Zen is "ordinary and nothing special"; he is humorously human like the Zen tramps portrayed by Mu-chi and Liang-k'ai.[6] We like this because here, for the first time, is a conception of the holy man and sage who is not impossibly remote, not superhuman but fully human, and, above all, not a solemn and sexless ascetic. Furthermore, in Zen the *satori* experience of awakening to our "original inseparability" with the universe seems, however elusive, always just round the corner. One has even met people to whom it has happened, and they are no longer mysterious occultists in the Himalayas nor skinny *yogis* in cloistered *ashrams*.[7] They are just like us, and yet much more at home in the world, floating much more easily upon the ocean of transience and insecurity.

Above all, I believe that Zen appeals to many in the post-Christian West because it does not preach, moralize, and scold in the style of Hebrew-Christian prophetism. Buddhism does not deny that there is a relatively limited sphere in which human life may be improved by art and science, reason and good-will. However, it regards this sphere of

---

[5] Warrior class of feudal Japan.

[6] Outstanding Chinese painters in the Zen tradition of black-ink brushwork. They flourished in the thirteenth century.

[7] Ascetic practitioners of yoga, living in hermitages.

activity as important but nonetheless subordinate to the comparatively limitless sphere in which things are as they are, always have been, and always will be — a sphere entirely beyond the categories of good and evil, success and failure, and individual health and sickness. On the one hand, this is the sphere of the great universe. Looking out into it at night, we make no comparisons between right and wrong stars, nor between well and badly arranged constellations. Stars are by nature big and little, bright and dim. Yet the whole thing is a splendor and a marvel which sometimes makes our flesh creep with awe. On the other hand, this is also the sphere of human, everyday life which we might call existential.

For there is a standpoint from which human affairs are as much beyond right and wrong as the stars, and from which our deeds, experiences, and feelings can no more be judged than the ups and downs of a range of mountains. Though beyond moral and social valuation, this level of human life may also be seen to be just as marvelous and uncanny as the great universe itself. This feeling may become particularly acute when the individual ego tries to fathom its own nature, to plumb the inner sources of its own actions and consciousness. For here it discovers a part of itself — the inmost and greatest part — which is strange to itself and beyond its understanding and control. Odd as it may sound, the ego finds that its own center and nature is beyond itself. The more deeply I go into myself, the more I am not myself, and yet this is the very heart of me. Here I find my own inner workings functioning of themselves, spontaneously, like the rotation of the heavenly bodies and the drifting of the clouds. Strange and foreign as this aspect of myself at first seems to be, I soon realize that it *is* me, and much more me than my superficial ego. This is not fatalism or determinism, because there is no longer anyone being pushed around or determined; there is nothing that this deep "I" is not doing. The configuration of my nervous-system, like the configuration of the stars, happens of itself, and this "itself" is the real "myself."

From this standpoint — and here language reveals its limitations with a vengeance — I find that I cannot help doing and experiencing, quite freely, what is always "right," in the sense that the stars are always in their "right" places. As Hsiang-yen[8] put it,

---

[8] A Chinese Zen master of the ninth to tenth centuries A.D., disciple of the great master Lin-chi, who originated the Rinzai school of Zen, the form of Zen most widely known in the West.

> There's no use for artificial discipline,
> For, move as I will, I manifest the ancient Tao.

At this level, human life is beyond anxiety, for it can never make a mistake. If we live, we live; if we die, we die; if we suffer, we suffer; if we are terrified, we are terrified. There is no problem about it. A Zen "master" was once asked, "It is terribly hot, and how shall we escape the heat?" "Why not," he answered, "go to the place where it is neither hot or cold?" "Where is that place?" "In summer we sweat; in winter we shiver." In Zen one does not feel guilty about dying, or being afraid, or disliking the heat. At the same time, Zen does not insist upon this point of view as something which one *ought* to adopt; it does not preach it as an ideal. For if you don't understand it, your very not understanding is also IT. There would be no bright stars without dim stars, and, without the surrounding darkness, no stars at all.

The Hebrew-Christian universe is one in which moral urgency, the anxiety to be right, embraces and penetrates everything. God, the Absolute itself, is good as against bad, and thus to be immoral or in the wrong is to feel oneself an outcast not merely from human society but also from existence itself, from the root and ground of life. To be in the wrong therefore arouses a metaphysical anxiety and sense of guilt — a state of eternal damnation — utterly disproportionate to the crime. This metaphysical guilt is so insupportable that it must eventually issue in the rejection of God and of his laws — which is just what has happened in the whole movement of modern secularism, materialism, and naturalism. Absolute morality is profoundly destructive of morality, for the sanctions which it invokes against evil are far, far too heavy. One does not cure the headache by cutting off the head. The appeal of Zen, as of other forms of Eastern philosophy, is that it unveils behind the urgent realm of good and evil a vast region of oneself about which there need be no guilt or recrimination, where at last the self is indistinguishable from God.

But the Westerner who is attracted by Zen and who would understand it deeply must have one indispensable qualification: he must understand his own culture so thoroughly that he is no longer swayed by its premises unconsciously. He must really have come to terms with the Lord God Jehovah and with his Hebrew-Christian conscience so that he can take it or leave it without fear or rebellion. He must be free of the itch to justify himself. Lacking this, his Zen will be either "beat" or "square," either a revolt from the culture and social order or a new form of stuffiness and respectability. For Zen is above all the liberation of the mind from conventional thought, and this is something utterly different from rebellion against convention, on the one hand, or adapting foreign conventions, on the other. . . .

The "beat" mentality as I am thinking of it is something much more extensive and vague than the hipster life of New York and San Francisco. It is a younger generation's nonparticipation in "the American Way of Life," a revolt which does not seek to change the existing order but simply turns away from it to find the significance of life in subjective experience rather than objective achievement. . . .

Beat Zen is a complex phenomenon. It ranges from a use of Zen for justifying sheer caprice in art, literature, and life to a very forceful social criticism and "digging of the universe" such as one may find in the poetry of Ginsberg, Whalen and Snyder, and, rather unevenly, in Kerouac, who is always a shade too self-conscious, too subjective, and too strident to have the flavor of Zen.

When Kerouac gives his philosophical final statement, "I don't know. I don't care. And it doesn't make any difference" — that cat is out of the bag, for there is a hostility in these words which clangs with self-defense. But just because Zen truly surpasses convention and its values, it has no need to say "To hell with it," nor to underline with violence the fact that anything goes.

It is indeed the basic intuition of Zen that there is an ultimate standpoint from which "anything goes." In the celebrated words of the master Yun-men, "Every day is a good day." Or as is said in the *Hsin-hsin Ming:*

> If you want to get the plain truth,
> Be not concerned with right and wrong.
> The conflict between right and wrong
> Is the sickness of the mind.[9]

But this standpoint does not exclude and is not hostile towards the distinction between right and wrong at other levels and in more limited frames of reference. The world is seen to be beyond right and wrong

---

[9] *Hsin-hsin Ming,* the *Treatise on Faith in Mind,* by the Chinese Zen master Seng-ts'an (d. A.D. 606). Translated by D. T. Suzuki, in *Manual of Zen Buddhism.* (There is an American paperback.)

when it is not framed: that is to say, when we are not looking at a particular situation by itself — out of relation to the rest of the universe. Within this room there is a clear difference between up and down; out in interstellar space there is not. Within the conventional limits of a human community there are clear distinctions between good and evil. But these disappear when human affairs are seen as part and parcel of the whole realm of nature. Every framework sets up a restricted field of relationships, and restriction is law or rule.

Now a skilled photographer can point his camera at almost any scene or object and create a marvelous composition by the way in which he frames and lights it. An unskilled photographer attempting the same thing creates only messes, for he does not know how to place the frame, the border of the picture, where it will be in relation to the contents. How eloquently this demonstrates that as soon as we introduce a frame anything does *not* go. But every work of art involves a frame. A frame of some kind is precisely what distinguishes a painting, a poem, a musical composition, a play, a dance, or a piece of sculpture from the rest of the world. Some artists may argue that they do not want their works to be distinguishable from the total universe, but if this be so they should not frame them in galleries and concert halls. Above all they should not sign them nor sell them. This is as immoral as selling the moon or signing one's name to a mountain. (Such an artist may perhaps be forgiven if he knows what he is doing, and prides himself inwardly, not on being a poet or painter, but a competent crook.) Only destructive little boys and vulgar excursionists go around initialling the trees.

Today there are Western artists avowedly using Zen to justify the indiscriminate framing of simply anything — blank canvases, totally silent music, torn up bits of paper dropped on a board and stuck where they fall, or dense masses of mangled wire. The work of the composer John Cage[10] is rather typical of this tendency. In the name of Zen, he has forsaken his earlier and promising work with the "prepared piano," to confront audiences with eight Ampex tape-recorders simultaneously bellowing forth random noises. There is, indeed, a considerable therapeutic value in allowing oneself to be deeply aware of any sight or sound that may arise. For one thing, it brings to mind the marvel of seeing and hearing as such. For another, the profound willingness to listen to or gaze upon anything at all frees the mind from fixed preconceptions of beauty,

[10] See the article by John Cage, page 1107.

creating, as it were, a free space in which altogether new forms and relationships may emerge. But this is therapy; it is not yet art. It is on the level of the random ramblings of a patient on the analyst's couch: very important indeed as therapy, though it is by no means the aim of psychoanalysis to substitute such ramblings for conversation and literature. Cage's work would be redeemed if he framed and presented it as a kind of group session in audio-therapy, but as a concert it is simply absurd. One may hope, however, that *after* Cage has, by such listening, set his own mind free from the composer's almost inevitable plagiarism of the forms of the past, he will present us with the new musical patterns and relationships which he has not yet uttered.

Just as the skilled photographer often amazes us with his lighting and framing of the most unlikely subjects, so there are painters and writers in the West, as well as in modern Japan, who have mastered the authentically Zen art of controlling accidents. Historically this first arose in the Far-East in the appreciation of the rough texture of brush-strokes in calligraphy and painting, and in the accidental running of the glaze on bowls made for the tea-ceremony. One of the classical instances of this kind of thing came about through the shattering of a fine ceramic tea-caddy, belonging to one of the old Japanese tea-masters. The fragments were cemented together with gold, and its owner was amazed at the way in which the random network of thin gold lines enhanced its beauty. It must be remembered, however, that this was an *objet trouvé*[11] — an accidental effect *selected* by a man of exquisite taste, and treasured as one might treasure and exhibit a marvelous rock or a piece of driftwood. For in the Zen-inspired art of *bonseki* or rock-gardening, the stones are selected with infinite care, and though the hand of man may never have changed them it is far from true that any old stone will do. Furthermore, in calligraphy, painting, and ceramics, the accidental effects of running glaze or of flying hair-lines of the brush were only accepted and presented by the artist when he felt them to be fortuitous and unexpected marvels within the context of the work as a whole.

What governed his judgment? What gives *certain* accidental effects in painting the same beauty as the accidental outlines of clouds? According to Zen feeling there is no precise rule, no rule, that is to say, which can be formulated in words and taught systematically. On the

[11] An object discovered to have artistic merit even though not deliberately designed for that effect; literally, a "found" object.

other hand, there is in all these things a principle of order which in Chinese philosophy is termed *li*, and which Joseph Needham has translated "organic pattern."[12] *Li* originally meant the markings in jade, the grain in wood, and the fiber in muscle. It designates a type of order which is too multi-dimensional, too subtly interrelated, and too squirmingly vital to be represented in words or mechanical images. The artist has to know it as he knows how to grow his hair. He can do it again and again, but can never explain how. In Taoist philosophy this power is called *te*, or "magical virtue." It is the element of the miraculous which we feel both at the stars in heaven and at our own ability to be conscious.

It is the possession of *te*, then, which makes all the difference between mere scrawls and the "white writing" of Mark Tobey[13] which admittedly derived its inspiration from Chinese calligraphy. It was by no means a purely haphazard drooling of paint or uncontrolled wandering of the brush, for the character and taste of such an artist is visible in the grace (a possible equivalent of *te*) with which his strokes are formed even when he is not trying to represent anything except strokes. . . .

The real genius of Chinese and Japanese Zen artists in their use of controlled accidents goes beyond the discovery of fortuitous beauty. It lies in being able to express, at the level of artistry, the realization of that ultimate standpoint from which "anything goes" and at which "all things are of one suchness." The mere selection of any random shape to stick in a frame simply confuses the metaphysical and the artistic domains; it does not express the one in terms of the other. Set in a frame, any old mess is at once cut off from the totality of its natural context, and for this very reason its manifestation of the Tao is concealed. The formless murmer of night noises in a great city has an enchantment which immediately disappears when formally presented as music in a concert hall. A frame outlines a universe, a microcosm, and if the contents of the frame are to rank as art they must have the same quality of relationship to the whole and to each other as events in the great universe, the macrocosm of nature. In nature the accidental is always recognized in relation to what is ordered and controlled. The dark *yin* is never without the bright

---

12 See Joseph Needham, *Science and Civilization in China*, Vol. 2 (Cambridge University Press, 1956).

13 Distinguished modern American painter. Calligraphy is handwriting developed as an art in itself.

yang.[14] Thus the painting of Sesshu,[15] the calligraphy of Ryokwan,[16] and the ceramic bowls of the Hagi or Karatsu schools[17] reveal the wonder of accidents in nature through accidents in a context of highly disciplined art.

The realization of the unswerving "rightness" of whatever happens is no more manifested by utter lawlessness in social conduct than by sheer caprice in art. As Zen has been used as a pretext for the latter in our times, its use as a pretext for the former is ancient history. Many a rogue has justified himself with the Buddhist formula, "Birth-and-death (*samsara*) is Nirvana; worldly passions are Enlightenment." This danger is implicit in Zen because it is implicit in freedom. Power and freedom can never be safe. They are dangerous in the same way that fire and electricity are dangerous. But it is quite pitiful to see Zen used as a pretext for license when the Zen in question is no more than an idea in the head, a simple rationalization. To some extent "Zen" is so used in the underworld which often attaches itself to artistic and intellectual communities. After all, the Bohemian way of life is primarily the natural consequence of artists and writers being so absorbed in their work that they have no interest in keeping up with the Joneses. It is also a symptom of creative changes in manners and morals which at first seem as reprehensible to conservatives as new forms in art. But every such community attracts a number of weak imitators and hangers-on, especially in the great cities, and it is mostly in this class that one now finds the stereotype of the "beatnik" with his phony Zen. . . .

One of the most problematic characteristics of beat Zen, shared to some extent both by the creative artists and their imitators, is the fascination for marijuana and peyote, and the notion that the states of consciousness produced by these substances have some affinity with *satori*. That many of these people "take drugs" naturally lays them wide open to the most extreme forms of righteous indignation, despite the fact that marijuana and peyote (or its derivative, mescaline) are far less harmful and habit-forming than whiskey or tobacco. But while it is true that these

[14] See page 493.

[15] Fifteenth-century Japanese master of black-ink (*sumi*) painting who was also a Zen priest.

[16] Japanese Zen priest and calligrapher (1758-1831).

[17] Schools of Japanese pottery celebrated for their "rough" naturalistic style.

drugs induce states of great aesthetic insight and, perhaps, therapeutic value, the *satori*-experience is so startlingly different from anything of this kind that no one who had shared both could possibly confuse them. Both states of consciousness require an apparently paradoxical type of language to describe them, for which reason one might easily confuse the drug-induced states with written accounts of *satori*. But *satori* is always marked by a kind of intense clarity and simplicity from which complex imagery, jazzed-up sense perceptions, and the strange "turned-on" feeling invariably produced by these drugs are absent. It is not by chance that *satori* is called *fu-sho* or "unproduced," which means among other things, that there is no gimmick whether psychological or chemical for bringing it about. *Satori* always remains inaccessible to the mind preoccupied with its own states or with the search for ecstasy.

Now the underlying protestant lawlessness of beat Zen disturbs the square Zennists very seriously. For square Zen is the Zen of established tradition in Japan with its clearly defined hierarchy, its rigid discipline, and its specific tests of *satori*. More particularly, it is the kind of Zen adopted by Westerners studying in Japan, who will before long be bringing it back home. But there is an obvious difference between square Zen and the common-or-garden squareness of the Rotary Club or the Presbyterian Church. It is infinitely more imaginative, sensitive and interesting. But it is still square because it is a quest for the *right* spiritual experience, for a *satori* which will receive the stamp (*inka*) of approval and established authority. There will even be certificates to hang on the wall.

If square Zen falls into any serious excess it is in the direction of spiritual snobbism and artistic preciousness, though I have never known an orthodox Zen teacher who could be accused of either. These gentlemen seem to take their exalted office rather lightly, respecting its dignity without standing on it. The faults of square Zen are the faults of any spiritual in-group with an esoteric discipline and degrees of initiation. Students in the lower ranks can get unpleasantly uppity about inside knowledge which they are not at liberty to divulge — "and you wouldn't understand even if I could tell you"— and are apt to dwell rather sickeningly on the immense difficulties and iron disciplines of their task. There are times, however, when this is understandable, especially when someone who is just goofing-off claims that he is following the Zen ideal of "naturalness."

The student of square Zen is also inclined at times to be niggling in his recognition of parallels to Zen in other spiritual traditions. Because the essentials of Zen can never be accurately and fully formulated, being an experience and not a set of ideas, it is always possible to be critical of anything anyone says about it, neither putting up nor shutting up. Any statement about Zen, or about spiritual experience of any kind, will always leave some aspect, some subtlety, unexpressed. No one's mouth is big enough to utter the whole thing. . . .

There was never a spiritual movement without its excesses and distortions. The experience of awakening which truly constitutes Zen is too timeless and universal to be injured. The extremes of beat Zen need alarm no one since, as Blake said, "the fool who persists in his folly will become wise." As for square Zen, "authoritative" spiritual experiences have always had a way of wearing thin, and thus of generating the demand for something genuine and unique which needs no stamp.

I have known followers of both extremes to come up with perfectly clear *satori* experiences, for since there is no real "way" to *satori* the way you are following makes very little difference. . . .

The old Chinese Zen masters were steeped in Taoism. They saw nature in its total interrelatedness, and saw that every creature and every experience is in accord with the Tao of nature just as it is. This enabled them to accept themselves as they were, moment by moment, without the least need to justify anything. They didn't do it to defend themselves or to find an excuse for getting away with murder. They didn't brag about it and set themselves apart as rather special. On the contrary, their Zen was *wu-shih*, which means approximately "nothing special" or "no fuss." But Zen is "fuss" when it is mixed up with Bohemian affectations, and "fuss" when it is imagined that the only proper way to find it is to run off to a monastery in Japan or to do special exercises in the lotus posture for five hours a day. And I will admit that the very hullabaloo about Zen, even in such an essay as this, is also fuss — but a little less so.

Having said that, I would like to say something for all Zen fussers, beat or square. Fuss is all right, too. If you are hung on Zen, there's no need to try to pretend that you are not. If you really want to spend some years in a Japanese monastery, there is no earthly reason why you shouldn't. Or if you want to spend your time hopping freight cars and digging Charlie Parker, it's a free country.

> In the landscape of Spring there is neither better
>   nor worse;
> The flowering branches grow naturally, some long,
>   some short.

❧ FOR DISCUSSION AND WRITING

1. Why is Zen difficult for people "who feel a profound need to justify themselves"? Why should Watts classify Anglo-Saxons and Japanese in this
   category? He says that, according to the great Taoist teachers, "one could
   not be right without also being wrong," and that "those who would
   have good government [which could mean "self-government" as well as
   civic government] without its correlative misrule, and right without its
   correlative wrong, do not understand the principles of the universe."
   Explain these statements.

2. How does Watts define "Tao" in the second paragraph? What is meant by
   "inseparable polarities of existence"? What, according to Watts, is the
   distinguishing difference between the Taoist attitude and "the chronic
   uneasy conscience of the Hebrew-Christian cultures"? So that these
   phrases won't remain mere abstractions, can you give any substance,
   from your own experience, to what Watts speaks of as "the chronic uneasy
   conscience of the Hebrew-Christian cultures"? Do you know of any contemporary cultures to which this phrase would not apply? What is meant
   by the Japanese "sense of social shame" and "our more metaphysical sense
   of sin"?

3. How is the "awakened man" of Chinese Zen described? The experience of
   satori, a word which is used frequently in the later part of the essay, is
   implicitly defined in the fourth paragraph; what does it seem to mean?
   How does Zen differ from "Hebrew-Christian" moralism? What is the
   significance of Watts's analogy between the constellations of the night sky
   and the Zen attitude toward good and evil, success and failure?

4. Explain the paragraph beginning "For there is a standpoint from which
   human affairs are as much beyond right and wrong as the stars. . . ." Explain, in its context, the statement in the next paragraph that "I cannot
   help doing and experiencing, quite freely; what is always 'right.' . . ."

5. Evaluate the statements in the paragraph beginning "The Hebrew-Christian universe is one in which moral urgency . . ." and ending "where at last the self is indistinguishable from God." It's a pretty big mouthful to say that the self can become indistinguishable from God; what are your reactions to the notion?

6. How is the "beat" mentality defined? What criticism does Watts make of the "beat" interpretation of Zen?

7. Explain his analogy of the "frame" in photography, painting, and music. What does he mean by "controlled accidents" in art?

8. How does he define "square" Zen?

9. What is meant by "no fuss" at the end of the piece? What is the relevance of the bit of verse at the end?

10. For a writing assignment, you might consider the relevance of Zen to modern history and the "cold war"—to the rightness of our causes and the wrongness of the adversary's causes. What would happen if both sides adopted Zen, and what would happen if only one side adopted it? Or you might write a paper, as personal as you like, on Zen and accepted morality. Watts is a brilliant man and has written a number of brilliant books, but he is also a very fallible writer whose personal assumptions often warp his "facts." You might write a paper criticizing his assumptions in this piece.

Maya Deren ⋐ Voudoun in Haiti

⋐ American film-maker and anthropologist (1917-1961). Educated at Smith College, where she majored in English literature and wrote her Master of Arts dissertation on symbolist poetry, Maya Deren later became interested in photography and the film, and achieved distinction with her experimental films. She went to Haiti to make a film on the rites of Voudoun ("Voodoo") and became involved in extensive research, which resulted in her *Divine Horsemen: The Living Gods of Haiti;* she also made recordings of native Haitian music, which are available on long-playing records. ⋑

Sunday, September 28, 1947

I DO NOT know whether I shall manage to set it all down on paper. The mood is strange. I am both tense and exhausted, balanced on a razor's edge between sleep and violent action and the tension between them so utterly consumes my energy that a kind of balance of paralysis is achieved. I neither sleep nor move. I say to myself: you must write down everything now, today, before it is forgotten or becomes unreal. Yet so much would I rather dream on it that to arrange sentences, to formulate precisions, seems an impossible effort of the will. My mind flows like a thick, slow-moving liquid in and out of all the crevices of last night. How can I ever record all the sounds, smells, movements, relationships, memories, desires, and those flashes of "seeing" in that ancient sense — that totality of any moment which completely involves one and thus involves all history.

From "The Artist as God in Haiti" by Maya Deren, in *The Tiger's Eye*, No. 6 (December 15, 1948). Reprinted by permission.

How reluctant my mind is to face its task! How it loiters about the edges and finds, suddenly, urgent interest in some tangential preoccupation. There are times when one must lash and leash it and lead it, as one would a reluctant beast, grasping first at one firm real object, and then another until there is no other way for it to go and one mounts the beast and rides it, perhaps fearfully.

Yesterday evening S. came to have a drink with me at the hotel. He is very nice, but, as does C., he imagines that progress (with which these city Haitians are so obsessed) consists in an increasing intellectualization. This, aggravated by his anxiety to please, made for what was almost a parody of an intellectual conversation. It was incredible to sit there on the verandah, politely passing back and forth the proper ideas, while, in the distance, the sound of drums, growing with the dusk as if this luminous blackness which is the Haitian night was indeed its color, vibrated like the murmur of blood in the pulse of a body which was living through something.

It is not morbidity which draws crowds to scenes of disaster or unusual joy. It is the desire to participate in a moment when life breaks through to some higher level of intensity so that one's own life might take fire from that sudden spurted flame. A great heart pounds as if the body could not catch its breath in the hills above us. The cutlets, the rice and beans, are meaningless. Abruptly I announce that I am off to hunt down the drums. C. and S. may accompany me if they would like. Partly they are themselves curious, having caught fire from my urgent interest. Partly they imagine their role protective.

We cross the great park, full of girls in fluttery summer dresses, the men all in white, and start up a street which soon is no longer paved. The direction of the drums seems suddenly to reverse itself and we feel lost until we realize that it is the echo, bouncing off a tall wall which we are passing, that makes it seem so. This is the first mischief, and the sound seems to gradually begin a deliberate game of confoundment. It fades and grows for no reason at all. Often we imagine the drums just around the next crossways, and then, suddenly, hopelessly distant in the hills. The steep, rutted paths are almost deserted. We pass the roofless shell of a house — either the remains after a fire or an abandoned effort at construction — its doors and windows leading from nowhere to nowhere and the moon, shining inside on the grass of the rectangle that was to have been the floor, is like a triumph over it altogether.

And then, suddenly, the voices, singing with the drums, come through and we know we are nearer. The pursuit creates its own compulsion and we accelerate. We begin to ask our way and a man who says he is going himself, undertakes to lead us. We pass through a narrow alley between two houses and around the corner of another and, suddenly, there it is, a kind of patio with a roof, and a fence-like construction around its four sides, and a pole up the center, the three drummers at one end, the oil lamp hanging from a rafter. It is the peristyle of the hounfor.[1]

In the center there are girls and some men dancing and they sing as they dance and suddenly it is clear singing and dancing are not separate forms of expression. They dance as if they were marionettes tied to the drums by invisible strings of sound. They are not dancing with one another, nor are they dancing to the drums, nor do the drums accompany them. Their movements are sound made visible and their voices are, in turn, the transfiguration of their movements back into human sound. Or is it that the drums emanate a vibration which plays on all that it touches, the muscles of the body, the chords of the throat, the trees beyond the peristyle, the sensitive fibres of a mind in the hotel — fingers of sound jangling all that is tuned tight for them.

I would linger on the outskirts of this peristyle, standing with the other watchers in the shadows. I would circle timidly about its edges in a gently decreasing spiral of precious desire as the child, new come to the neighborhood, insinuates itself delicately into the group. I sense that this slow embrace is right. It is a little crowded here on the edges and all bodies brush casually by each other. A shoulder rubs by mine. Someone else presses by. I feel that if I stayed so, the strangeness would be rubbed from me, that my body would be moulded into the shape of this reality as the sea grinds the new fallen stone gradually into the form of its movements.

But it is not possible. S., feeling that I should be able to "observe" everything, has gone forward and now returns to fetch me forward, also, to where some chairs have been placed for us right almost in the center, directly near the drums, where the "action" may be going on. The light is bright here and I feel conspicuous. I am isolated on my chair. The contact which I had is lost and I can only look, now.

I notice, emerging from the house to which this patio-like arrange-

1 The entrance to the sacred dancing compound.

ment is attached, a very tall, thin man. There is a fragility in his movement which is curious, particularly in the manner in which he sets his
feet down in their worn leather scuffs — as if they were delicate, even
precious. As he achieves the lighted center spot in front of the drums he
begins singing, not loudly, and shaking a small gourd around which a
mesh of brightly colored beads has been woven. Attached to it is a small
silver bell and now the clacking of the beads and the ringing of the bell
seem to infuse the dancers with a new life. He looks finally in our direction and nods to us in greeting and the dignity of his salutation makes us
feel honored. "Who is that man?" S. asks of a bystander. "It is the priest,
the houngan," I answer, and he who was to have answered looks at me
with a surprise which melts into a smile of comradely conspiracy with
me against those who do not know, who cannot recognize. "Houngan
Champagne," the man says, and I smile and nod with an old knowledge,
newly discovered. It is the first of these knowledges which are direct between me and the thing, having no source in information.

It was somewhere in my legs that the muscles first understood that
fragility and conveyed to my heart and mind the shock of knowledge. He
had carried himself as one might carry a precious vessel filled to overflowing with a potent magic potion which must not be spilled nor wasted
until the moment of sacred use, when all is ready to receive it. So I have
carried the line of a poem or the image for a film, so I have carried myself
carrying it, gently, floating almost, careful against jarrings, protective
against jostlings, and the tensions of caution becoming almost unbear-
able until that moment, when, finally, all else was ready and fitting.

S. is talking in my ear. He is "analyzing" the scene. I am trying to
experience it. His analysis interrupts and obstructs my experience of it.
I try to make myself deaf to him, and I wish desperately that he would
stop talking. I feel that the people do not like to be talked about. I pretend not to hear him and I smile at them instead to indicate there is a
difference between S. and me, and that I am on their side against him.
They smile back. The lamp goes out in a gust of wind. There is, for a
moment, only the moonlight shooting in sideways into the peristyle. The
lamp is relit. It blows out again and is again relit.

And now the houngan has a bottle in his hand and he pours some of
the liquid in front of each of the three drums and lights it and it flames
up in a blue flame which seems alive for it travels as the liquid runs over
the ground. S. is talking in my ear with the desperate insistence of a com-

mentator. It is his protection against feeling but I need none. On the pretext of seeing better, I leave my chair and move forward. The dancers
have run forward towards the flame too and, as I approach, the warm,
intoxicating aroma of burning rum floods my face. They pass their hands
through the flames, their fingers cupped and, as if it were a liquid, they
pass the warmth of the aroma over their faces and arms as if bathing in
it. It is smothered, finally, by their hands.

Behind me I hear suddenly a scream as if of great agony and protest.
I turn and see a woman violently swinging back and forth, her eyes wide
with terror, the pupils dilated, the scream starting from her very belly.
Two others are trying to still her violence but she breaks away and rico-
chets with a violence from one side to the other of the circle which has
formed to give her room. At times she spins on one leg as if it were rooted
to the earth; then she frees the leg and shuffles backwards rapidly as if
she were fending off something. In her ricochet she seems about to lose
her balance, but the others sustain her on her feet, and she re-enters the
circle. She is being pitched forward and back, buffeted without mercy
by a war within her. Her body is no more than a glove over which two
hands struggle for possession and that thin frame seems about to be
broken by the savage battle. She runs into the houngan and clings to
him. He supports her with all his strength, helping to hold that ravaged
body together but the buffetings are strong and he is thrown off balance
too. Clasped together, he struggling to sustain her, she hanging frantically on to him, they ricochet together about the circle which has tightened. Everyone is ready to help, to hold them up should they fall in their
direction. With a supreme effort the houngan gains his balance. His legs
braced, his face abstract with strength and tenderness, he sustains and
holds her wide movements together until they are compressed into a
tremor. The pitch of her screaming drops. When she seems reasonably
still, he pushes her slightly away, she finds her own balance, and turning
once to the left, once to the right and once more to the left, each turn
concluded by a sort of curtsy, salutes him. Her face is dazed and she can
hardly keep her balance. She falls, rather than kneels before him, and
kisses the ground. He takes her hand and helps her to her feet. And
suddenly the struggle threatens to start again. He shakes his rattle in her
face determinedly and little by little she recognizes it. She makes the
salute again, and rises from the ground this time with new born eyes. She
looks about as one awakened from sleep, re-establishes the world about

her, and walks quietly to the edge of the peristyle. I watch her, careful not to seem to be watching as no one else is doing so. I see her reaffirm the world . . . the reality of the faces about her, the bench upon which she is sitting and which she strokes once with her hand. This done, a fatigue inundates her face and she slumps sideways into a deep sleep.

The drums have ceased, and now again they have recommenced. I will not go back to sit with S. How shall I say to these people that I am not an outsider, that I, too, am of the race of those whose bodies are ravaged by invisibles, by Gods, which are ideas too large for the human frame? That I, too, with the other artists, have known such agony, such loss of balance, such sense of the skin bursting with not being able to contain something more than human. *And to whom could we cling until the last tremor had ceased* and we were returned to ourselves again?

Even if I could speak their language I could not say this. Let me at least dance with them. I move shyly and inconspicuously to the shadowed outskirts of the dancing and begin some timid movements. I am glad, glad that I have always been able to dance. It seems to go well, and they are pleased that I am able to do their movements. They dance towards me and smile and, imperceptibly, a path opens towards the center. I am timid to go forward, but I sense at the same time, that this timidity might be understood as a shame of being seen. That I can dance is a triumph for their form.

I sense, across the distance of the peristyle, that the houngan near the drums knows that the stranger is dancing their dances. I sense that one demands that I salute him in this, and there is nothing for it but to dance slowly down the small aisle that has been opened for me towards him. He is authority, here, for this form. I who partake of it must salute him. The form has disciplines which even he and I must observe. The masters are more dedicated, are less themselves, than the others. I arrive before him, saying mutely, "I, myself, with my own dedication, salute you, with yours." We dance facing each other, recognizing each other strangely, honoring in each other the knowledge of dedications.

My eyes are locked with his, but around the edges, the iris of my vision, there is a circle of dancing movement. There is, encircling us, also, a cylinder of song and deep beats. And there is a third unseen, unheard circle about us, too . . . a tension, a watching . . . the band of a barrel being vised with an expectancy no one would dare disappoint. And we two, dancing in the center. I dance as I have never danced before. It is not more violent, nor more expertly, cleverly achieved. It is simply correct in a very final sense, in the fact that there is neither decision nor triumph, but only the immaculate execution of an inevitability. Yet, I feel as if a transparent level of consciousness were super-imposed upon this reality; that there is something about these movements which is still my own; in the shorter length of my limbs, in the longer drop of my hair, in some attitude of fingers which articulates my own singular history of ecstasy and pain. This is not sound making of an anonymous and willing chaos some first definition of form. This is a greater triumph: that I—personal, individual, singular — return, bringing the loot of all my forays, back to the collective, the racial, the parent body.

I do not follow him, nor he, me. But so inevitable is each movement according to the logic to which we both are committed, that we are united in it . . . as the distended legs of a triangle find, in the point of apex, some timeless, spaceless, singleness. Nothing is difficult; neither to know or to do. Face to face, we mirror each other's movements. Is it each other we mirror? Or are we but the double reflections, perpetuated infinitely on both sides, of some dancing figure who knows reality only in such mirrors?

My eyes sting suddenly with the salt of my own water. It is the sting of the ocean. I sense the sweat dripping from my chin, spattered to right and to left with the turns of my head. I am glad of it. There is a sense in it of being cleansed of all oldness from within.

I do not know how long we dance but we cross some invisible threshold, which advanced toward us, and on the other side of it he removes the black handkerchief around his neck. He wipes his face with it — it has been flowing with his labor — and then wipes mine with it, and still dancing, knots it about my neck. With this act something is accomplished. The vise is relaxed, the sound and the moving cease. One stands about a moment, and then I move back to my chair. I can even smile gently, now, at S. Who, now could sever the labored waters mingled on the handkerchief around my neck, or the invisible leash by which I and the houngan are bound in a common service?

The drums start up again, and the singing, but now there is a curious ease between that and myself. We know each other and need not hurry. "In a moment," I say to myself, "In a moment." I lean back in the chair and, feeling sorry now for their isolation, I say to C. and S., "It is hot, very hot." This is not quite true, for the sweat which runs down my face comes from within. Still, I use my pretty fan, am gracious as a hostess. He says, "Here, this will make you cooler," and he reaches for the knot of the handkerchief around my neck. I start up with a kind of terror. "Oh, no, who has placed it there . . . only he can remove it," and, finding myself on my feet, I start dancing.

I dance opposite one woman, then a man, then a girl, then another. They seem to wish to mirror with me, and there is a curious graciousness in my accepting and permitting this with one then another, for these are the preliminaries in some act which, in its accomplishment, will bless all those who have partaken of it. And now, turning towards center, I find myself facing, once more, the houngan. "Let us move now, to the removal of the handkerchief," I say mutely. And suddenly our mirroring movements slip into the accord of complete unity. Meaning takes flight from mile post to mile post. The cadence of singing is sharper and sharper. I swear there is only *his* singing now and the drums. My left foot seems rooted and I try not to fall but when I do it is without fear. People hold me up. I feel my shoes being removed. Then I am stood up again like a doll set on its own feet. The trampled earth is warm and soft. The left leg sinks roots again and up those roots and up that leg flows a kind of paralysis which strikes terror into me. I try to rip the leg loose. I cannot. I start to fall. My reaching arms meet a voice and cling to it and that which has been travelling up my leg, reaches the mind and obliterates it.

And then I find myself held up by three or four people. A bottle rests heavily on the corner of my mouth and I taste the sharp bite of rum. I push it away and stand up by myself and everything . . . the drums, the dancing, the people are sharp and clear but terribly distant, as if through the wrong end of opera glasses. In this distinct, remote world I take my bearings and go to my chair. C. and S. hover about with a solicitude which irritates me. I am quite all right. The others look at me but only casually. An older woman comes forward with my shoes and puts them on. "Gagne loa: Loa na tête ou," she says, smiling at me. "What is she saying," I ask S. "Oh, nothing," he answers. I become imperious, "Translate what she said," I demand. "She says, you have gods in your head." I smile at her. "Of course," I say to her, "I always have had." She has understood the sense of my French.

And then I am tired. I feel suddenly as if I must have walked miles, climbed mountains, fallen, been bruised, battled. I have been a long way and I have returned and now I am tired from my travels. I rise to leave, and my hand goes to my throat even before I have thought, and discovers the handkerchief gone. That is as it should be. Half way out I remember the houngan, and I return to bid him goodnight. We shake hands and smile tiredly at each other, and with the casualness as between those who have no need to protest their kinship, say goodnight.

The moon has set. I stumble along the ruts in a daze of fatigue, remarking that we cross a bridge, and a fountain, before the descent becomes steep. A feeling of aloneness becomes more and more acute. I have nothing to say or do with the men who walk on either side. The hotel is only a place to lie my body down. I have left the scene of the evening's events. All the reality which encompassed all this vanishes, and only the beauty of it is real . . . an odor, a sense spreading into the air until I feel I cannot breathe. I begin weeping, and running and the two men run after me, frightened at this outburst.

The way back is always shorter.

Monday, September 29

It has finally cooled enough in this room so that I can pull myself up to jot down the day. Except for my short visit to M. I have stayed in my room all day because of this mark which runs down from the corner of my mouth to my chin. I saw it this morning when I looked in the mirror and since it didn't hurt, but seemed rather a stain on the skin, I used everything from soap and water to alcohol to get it off, and, failing, became a little worried. I had breakfast and lunch sent up, having the curious feeling that this mark, this seal should be protected — that it was part of a completely integrated system: that its dilemmas are resolved in its own terms and one must not go outside the form for its resolutions. I could not go to Champagne to ask, for he might understand such questions as a reproach. But M. is supposed to be a houngan, and I went to see him.

He listened quietly while I described to him, as accurately as I could, the whole Saturday night business. I surprised myself by saying things I had not thought I thought. At some indiscernible moment the idea of death had entered my sense of the evening, and now I found myself saying the paralysis which inundated my brain was like a death, that the moment of coming to, was a resurrection and that, on the way home I had wept as if for something dead, or perhaps the idea of death. M. smiled and asked me several questions; the color of the handkerchief?

Black. The movements of the dance? It was a hip dance. Had I asked what the drums were playing? I remember S. saying something about Nago. It was Ghede, M. says. Ghede is the god of the dead, the god of the cemetery. It is extremely unusual, M. says, for a houngan to work so hard. He had been strong. I too must have somehow inspired it.

After this we did not talk much longer. How was I to say to this man whom I hardly knew that, indeed, leaving the States had been a death in many ways. That this was right, all of it. In the taxi, on the way home, I remember that he had said nothing about the mark on my face except that it would go away.

I have just ordered a rum and as I tasted it I remembered suddenly that moment Saturday when I pushed it away from my mouth. Experimenting with the Seven-up bottle which has come with the rum, I see quite clearly that the bruise does follow the direction that a bottle, pressed too hard against the corner of my mouth, would take. A bruise, then. I am terribly glad that I had not had that anxiety which would have driven me to inquire of the people outside.

Courlander writes, in *Haiti Singing*, "Ghede is not simply the loa of the cemetery, he is a personification of Death. With the Haitian, death is not a man dying, or a used-up unliving body; it is an entity, a positive power in nature." Of course, of course.

He describes a possession by Ghede which involves even lascivious movements, and also of Ghede as the protector of children.

And could this be, and is it really, that here, in that hounfor, the idea of life out of death . . . that whole vibrant dynamic . . . can be realized with such accuracy. And if art consists in the *realization* — that word in its original sense: to give real form to, to make real — of imaginary concepts, of abstract ideas, then what was it all except the immaculate, accurate realization of the idea of death and life out of death? The gods as the personification of ideas.

Suppose, then, one thinks of the collective mind creating over centuries this realization of an idea; of the priest as mentor, director, teacher, perhaps, of the person possessed by the god as the work of art accomplished. But then, what of myself who had known nothing of the form which this collective had created and taught? Could it be that, believing intensely in the idea, determined to realize it in the terms set before me, tuned tight to the integrities, the logics of that form, I had arrived at the same concept of its reality in physical terms? Had I created Ghede as I might create a film, searching for the form of the idea which is achieved out of the instrument by which it is realized? And I try to make the film the form emergent of the camera, so this, the form emergent of the totality of the hounfor . . . its sounds, its moments, its people, myself? My mind refuses to push forward further. The hotel is still. In the distance the cocks crow suddenly, in the middle of the night. The mosquito net is a lovely white veil behind which I shall sleep.

Tuesday, September 30

There is something terribly important in all this and I have determined to push it through. By late afternoon I had decided to go and visit Champagne. I went alone because I wanted that going alone to be a statement of my feeling, by myself, of being at home there. I wore my becoming blue dress and my best perfume. I did not go casually, and why then should I dress casually?

It did not occur to me that I might not find the way, and indeed, with very few hesitations, I arrived quite easily. I had not realized, in the night, how far on the outskirts of town this is . . . almost the country. From the hill one can see the sea.

In a way I was a little disappointed. He received me in a little booth where he sells soft drinks and candy, and although neither he nor the others seemed too surprised to see me, the contact between Champagne and myself seemed almost nonexistent. I used very very simple French, which is near enough to Creole, but he seemed not to understand me at all, and called a young boy to act as translator. I thanked him for working so hard for me. He acknowledged it and that brought us to silent impasse which made me feel desperate. It was hot. I had the fleeting notion that this was all very foolish of me. I asked whether there was to be another dance next Saturday. Laboriously straining back and forth through the boy, who hardly spoke better French than Champagne, he explained that a poor hounfor like his could not afford to have dances every week. Once a month perhaps. I wish to communicate that I am more than curious, that it is all important to me, and since conversation is impossible I can communicate this only by offering to contribute the four dollars that is necessary. He accepts this with quiet poise and I promise to return the next day with the money.

He walks out onto the road with me, and the fragile walk is like an echo of Saturday. As a last minute thought, he leads me through the peristyle, and unlocks the door through which I had first seen him come. The peristyle, deserted, except for an old woman who drowses on one of the benches, is, and is not, the same place as Saturday night. The drums hang in a mute cluster from a rafter. Inside, the room is tiny and very neat. There is a kind of altar running its width, the walls decorated with symbols. There are pictures of saints. He lights a wick which floats in oil and brings two chairs from the adjoining room. We sit awhile; I sense that this is an honor and bear myself accordingly. I sense, too, that everything in this room is precious, important. But we still cannot manage to talk together, and, pleading an appointment in town, I leave soon.

I am certain that somehow the contact depends on me . . . that there are some requirements which I must perceive and answer, and that is the difficulty, for I do not know what they are. . . . There is some image that I am supposed to fulfill, realize, with the same perfection that I danced on Saturday. But I am not certain, at all, what it is.

Thursday, October 2

My tenderness towards these last two visits, yesterday and today, with Champagne almost prohibits the hardness of definition. How to speak of that little room, with the wick floating in the oil, while through the rectangle of door, the blue deepens into the black of night. Inside we sit and we enact, *we are,* an idea.

I tell him of Lilith. I tell him of the Book of the Dead of Egypt. He tells me of Erzulie,[2] for whom he has a special altar. She is the Virgin Mary. Her colors are white. Her sense is purity. And yet she wears perfumes and loves flowers and all the men like her and she likes all the men. And here is the promiscuous virgin. For is this not the idea of woman . . . of the perfect woman, or, let us say, the idea of love — available to all men?

So we exchange gossip about the gods. In the tiny room, with singing beginning outside. "It is the Protestants singing against me," Cham-

---

2 Lilith, whose name comes from an Assyrian-Babylonian word meaning "belonging to the night," was, in Semitic myth, the first wife of Adam. The Egyptian Book of the Dead is composed of ritual instructions, of immense antiquity, showing what should be said and done in order that the dead person might safely pass through the terrors of the underworld and emerge as an immortal among the gods. Erzulie is the queen-goddess of Voudoun, corresponding, as is said here, with the Virgin.

pagne says, and we both laugh uproariously at the futile foolishness of that effort. There is neither time nor space. Sitting together we chatter idly about all gods, finding them named differently in different countries — ideas with aliases.

We speak personally, too. Water is my element. I ask him what of a ceremony for Aguet, god of the waters, and he says yes, sometimes. And that he is afraid of water. I tell him I swim very well, that I have saved two persons from drowning. He says, yes, he knows I swim well for Aguet is the consort of Erzulie. I accept this. I say he need not be afraid, next time, that I would save him. He smiles happily and says he will never be afraid, and it is this which will save him. This is the only magic possible, the only purposiveness present in myth — that the miracle is interior.

Today, because Erzulie loves flowers, there were fresh flowers on the altar. I find the fan which I left him as a gift yesterday among the precious objects arranged there. It is not my fan. It is one of the proper properties of Erzulie. The image to which I must measure up grows clearer each minute. It is an idea which I am to become, which is expected of me. Just as he is being an idea, gloriously so — prompter and protector, vis-à-vis the people, of all the splendid ideas which are Voudoun[3] — realizer of them, laboring meticulously for each detail.

These last two days we have done without a translator. Language is not the means of communication. It is the symptom of a communication. We understand each other and it follows that we would understand each other's words, as we understand each other's movements, or as I understand that, smoking together, we must alternate on the lighting of cigarettes: that I first give him fire, and that on the next round, he light mine with a bit of paper from the floating wick.

Nothing is difficult — neither to know or to do.

The form is complete. In the tiny room neither of us are ourselves. He, knowing, and I, learning through a tuning stretched tight to the most subtle expectation, realize in collaboration a complete, a perfect mythology. To achieve the impersonal perfectly is a personal triumph.

But how demanding it is, to be tuned to this highest pitch of perception. How demanding upon oneself to be a myth, to recreate in oneself, to grasp out of oneself, the original abstraction, the integrity of that realization which is being, and to create out of oneself the disciplines of

[3] A religion of the West Indies, particularly Haiti, with complex ritual and symbolism incorporating primitive African elements. Commonly known as "Voodoo."

a god. The tension — to perceive the immutable inevitability, the moral premises.

The black handkerchief hangs on the wall. Today as I left it had begun raining and he had placed it ceremoniously over my head, saying it would protect me. I believe, indeed, that the sight of it will protect me, being material evidence, as it were, of the resurrection which is each awakening. The idea of love is protected not by men but by love. The fatigue is, today, just and sweet, I shall sleep well.

ᴥᔥ FOR DISCUSSION AND WRITING

1. One should read this piece with an awareness of the form in which it is written, that of a personal journal, a kind of day-by-day consultation with oneself in which one attempts to understand one's experience. Could you give a psychological reason for Maya Deren's use of the present tense through most of the piece?

2. What significant difference is there between her own attitude and that of her companion, S., who wishes to "observe" and to "analyze"? She says that he keeps talking, commenting on what is happening, as a "protection against feeling": is this an idiosyncratic attitude or a fairly common one? How widespread is it, what other forms does it take, and can you explain it? If you have read either of Laurens van der Post's pieces in this book, can you draw a parallel between what van der Post says of the lost instinctive or "natural" self and S.'s attitude?

3. What meaning (symbolism) do you find in the spilling of the rum and setting it afire in front of the drums, and the dancers' actions in passing their cupped hands through the fire and seeming to bathe their faces in it? For this kind of question, intellectualizing or "literary" symbolism won't do, since people don't stick their hands in fire in order to provide allegorical guessing games; you have to consult your own instincts and intuitions. For instance, what natural associations do you have with fire? and how could those associations lead to a ritual use of fire? (One might remember that lighted candles are a constant part of both Judaic and Christian ritual.) Instead of rum, gasoline could have been used to make the symbolic fire: why rum? (A parallel question would be: why is wine used in both Judaic and Christian sacraments—why not grape juice?)

4. Try to explain the paragraph beginning "The drums have ceased, and now again they have recommenced. . . ." What special meaning is given to the word "Gods" in this paragraph, and what do "Gods" have to do with the experience of artists? Later Maya Deren is told by one of the Haitians that she has "gods in the head"; what does that mean? (You might find some help here in the piece by C. G. Jung earlier in this book.)

5. Maya Deren is remembered by those who knew her as a dancer of extraordinary beauty and vitality, although she did not think of herself as a dancer. Why does she dance here? Can you speculate on why dancing is the oldest and most universal expression of religious feeling? (The piece by D. H. Lawrence that follows may give you some suggestions.) Explain the meaning of this: "I—personal, individual, singular—return, bringing the loot of all my forays, back to the collective, the racial, the parent body." Why is the experience felt as a blessing? Why is it felt as a kind of "death" and resurrection?—death of what? resurrection of what?

6. The journal entries for Tuesday and Thursday come back to the commonplace. The houngan (priest) makes his living in a little booth selling candy and soft drinks; it seems impossible, in this commonplace setting, to reestablish the spiritual significance of the dance or even to talk about it. Is this because the psychic state induced by the dance was mere illusionism? If you feel that it was, you should base your opinion on a strong argument that can be examined for *a priori* assumptions. Or is the descent to the commonplaces of everyday life a necessary part of "religious" or "spiritual" experience?

7. In the paragraph toward the end, beginning "We speak personally, too. . . ," what is the meaning of the last sentence: "This is the only magic possible, the only purposiveness present in myth—that the miracle is interior"? If you have read the piece by Tolstoy, a little earlier, what correspondence do you find between the meaning of "miracle" here and Tolstoy's use of the word?

8. For a writing assignment, you might find a subject in Question 2, above. Or you might consider this question: What do you yourself mean by the word "spiritual," and in terms of that meaning is the experience described by Maya Deren a spiritual one, or not? Or, if you find the word "spiritual" meaningless, you might discuss the piece in whatever terms you find more suitable.

D. H. Lawrence ᴈ The Dance of the Sprouting Corn

ᴈ See note on Lawrence, page 211. Ruth Benedict, in her description of Pueblo Indian culture in *Patterns of Culture*, says that no one has represented the feeling and meaning of the corn dance as well as Lawrence has done here. ॐ

PALE, dry, baked earth, that blows into dust of fine sand. Low hills of baked pale earth, sinking heavily, and speckled sparsely with dark dots of cedar bushes. A river on the plain of drought, just a cleft of dark, reddish-brown water, almost a flood. And over all, the blue, uneasy, alkaline sky.

A pale, uneven, parched world, where a motor-car rocks and lurches and churns in sand. A world pallid with dryness, inhuman with a faint taste of alkali. Like driving in the bed of a great sea that dried up unthinkable ages ago, and now is drier than any other dryness, yet still reminiscent of the bottom of the sea, sand-hills sinking, and straight, cracked mesas, like cracks in the dry-mud bottom of the sea.

So, the mud church standing discreetly outside, just outside the

Reprinted by permission of Alfred A. Knopf, Inc., from *The Later D. H. Lawrence,* edited by William York Tindall. Copyright 1927 by Alfred A. Knopf, Inc. Renewed 1955 by Frieda Lawrence Ravagli.

pueblo, not to see too much. And on its façade of mud, under the tim-
bered mud-eaves, two speckled horses rampant, painted by the Indians,
a red piebald and a black one.

Swish! Over the logs of the ditch-bridge, where brown water is
flowing full. There below is the pueblo, dried mud like mud-pie houses,
all squatting in a jumble, prepared to crumble into dust and be invisible,
dust to dust returning, earth to earth.

That they don't crumble is the mystery. That these little squarish
mud-heaps endure for centuries after centuries, while Greek marble
tumbles asunder, and cathedrals totter, is the wonder. But then, the
naked human hand with a bit of new soft mud is quicker than time, and
defies the centuries.

Roughly the low, square, mud-pie houses make a wide street where
all is naked earth save a doorway or a window with a pale-blue sash. At
the end of the street, turn again into a parallel wide, dry street. And
there, in the dry, oblong aridity, there tosses a small forest that is alive;
and thud — thud — thud goes the drum, and the deep sound of men
singing is like the deep soughing of the wind, in the depths of a wood.

You realize that you had heard the drum from the distance, also the
deep, distant roar and boom of the singing, but that you had not heeded,
as you don't heed the wind.

It all tosses like young, agile trees in a wind. This is the dance of
the sprouting corn, and everybody holds a little, beating branch of green
pine. Thud — thud — thud — thud — thud! goes the drum, heavily the
men hop and hop and hop, sway, sway, sway, sway go the little branches
of green pine. It tosses like a little forest, and the deep sound of men's
singing is like the booming and tearing of a wind deep inside a forest.
They are dancing the spring corn dance.

This is the Wednesday after Easter, after Christ Risen and the corn
germinated. They danced on Monday and on Tuesday. Wednesday is
the third and last dance of this green resurrection.

You realize the long lines of dancers, and a solid cluster of men singing near the drum. You realize the intermittent black-and-white fantasy
of the hopping Koshare, the jesters, the Delight-Makers. You become
aware of the ripple of bells on the knee-garters of the dancers, a continual pulsing ripple of little bells; and of the sudden wild, whooping
yells from near the drum. Then you become aware of the seed-like shudder of the gourd rattles, as the dance changes, and the swaying of the

tufts of green pine-twigs stuck behind the arms of all the dancing men, in the broad green arm-bands.

Gradually comes through to you the black, stable solidity of the dancing women, who poise like solid shadow, one woman behind each rippling, leaping male. The long, silky black hair of the women, streaming down their backs, and the equally long, streaming, gleaming hair of the males, loose over broad, naked, orange-brown shoulders.

Then the faces, the impassive, rather fat, golden-brown faces of the women, with eyes cast down, crowned above with the green tableta, like a flat tiara. Something strange and noble about the impassive, barefoot women in the short black cassocks, as they subtly tread the dance, scarcely moving, and yet edging rhythmically along, swaying from each hand the green spray of pine-twig out — out — out — out, to the thud of the drum, immediately behind the leaping fox-skin of the men dancers. And all the emerald-green, painted tabletas, the flat wooden tiaras shaped like a castle gateway, rise steady and noble from the soft, slightly bowed heads of the women, held by a band under the chin. All the tabletas down the line, emerald green, almost steady, while the bright black heads of the men leap softly up and down, between.

Bit by bit you take it in. You cannot get a whole impression, save of some sort of wood tossing, a little forest of trees in motion, with gleaming black hair and gold-ruddy breasts that somehow do not destroy the illusion of forest.

When you look at the women, you forget the men. The bare-armed, bare-legged, barefoot women with streaming hair and lofty green tiaras, impassive, downward-looking faces, twigs swaying outwards from subtle, rhythmic wrists; women clad in the black, prehistoric short gown fastened over one shoulder, leaving the other shoulder bare, and showing at the arm-place a bit of pink or white undershirt; belted also round the waist with a woven woollen sash, scarlet and green on the hand-woven black cassock. The noble, slightly submissive bending of the tiara-ed head. The subtle measure of the bare, breathing, bird-like feet, that are flat, and seem to cleave to earth softly, and softly lift away. The continuous outward swaying of the pine-sprays.

But when you look at the men, you forget the women. The men are naked to the waist, and ruddy-golden, and in the rhythmic, hopping leap of the dance their breasts shake downwards, as the strong, heavy body comes down, down, down, down, in the downward plunge of the dance.

The black hair streams loose and living down their backs, the black brows are level, the black eyes look out unchanging from under the silky lashes. They are handsome, and absorbed with a deep rhythmic absorption, which still leaves them awake and aware. Down, down, down they drop, on the heavy, ceaseless leap of the dance, and the great necklaces of shell-cores spring on the naked breasts, the neck-shell flaps up and down, the short white kilt of woven stuff, with the heavy woollen embroidery, green and red and black, opens and shuts slightly to the strong lifting of the knees: the heavy whitish cords that hang from the kilt-band at the side sway and coil forever down the side of the right leg, down to the ankle, the bells on the red-woven garters under the knees ripple without end, and the feet, in buckskin boots furred round the ankle with a beautiful band of skunk fur, black with a white tip, come down with a lovely, heavy, soft precision, first one, then the other, dropping always plumb to earth. Slightly bending forward, a black gourd rattle in the right hand, a small green bough in the left, the dancer dances the eternal drooping leap, that brings his life down, down, down, down from the mind, down from the broad, beautiful, shaking breast, down to the powerful pivot of the knees, then to the ankles, and plunges deep from the ball of the foot into the earth, towards the earth's red centre, where these men belong, as is signified by the red earth with which they are smeared.

And meanwhile, the shell-cores from the Pacific sway up and down, ceaselessly, on their breasts.

Mindless, without effort, under the hot sun, unceasing, yet never perspiring nor even breathing heavily, they dance on and on. Mindless, yet still listening, observing. They hear the deep, surging singing of the bunch of old men, like a great wind soughing. They hear the cries and yells of the man waving his bough by the drum. They catch the word of the song, and at a moment, shudder the black rattles, wheel, and the line breaks, women from men, they thread across to a new formation. And as the men wheel round, their black hair gleams and shakes, and the long fox-skin sways, like a tail.

And always, when they form into line again, it is a beautiful long straight line, flexible as life, but straight as rain.

The men round the drum are old, or elderly. They are all in a bunch, and they wear day dress, loose cotton drawers, pink or white cotton shirt, hair tied up behind with the red cords, and banded round the head with a strip of pink rag, or white rag, or blue. There they are, solid like a cluster of bees, their black heads with the pink rag circles all close together, swaying their pine-twigs with rhythmic, wind-swept hands, dancing slightly, mostly on the right foot, ceaselessly, and singing, their black bright eyes absorbed, their dark lips pushed out, while the deep strong sound rushes like wind, and the unknown words form themselves in the dark.

Suddenly the solitary man pounding the drum swings his drum round, and begins to pound on the other end, on a higher note, pang — pang — pang! instead of the previous brumm! brumm! brumm! of the bass note. The watchful man next the drummer yells and waves lightly, dancing on birdfeet. The Koshare make strange, eloquent gestures to the sky.

And again the gleaming bronze-and-dark men dancing in the rows shudder their rattles, break the rhythm, change into a queer, beautiful two-step, the long lines suddenly curl into rings, four rings of dancers, the leaping, gleaming-seeming men between the solid, subtle, submissive blackness of the women who are crowned with emerald-green tiaras, all going subtly round in rings. Then slowly they change again, and form a star. Then again, unmingling, they come back into rows.

And all the while, all the while the naked Koshare are threading about. Of bronze-and-dark men dancers there are some forty-two, each with a dark, crowned woman attending him like a shadow. The old men, the bunch of singers in shirts and tied-up black hair, are about sixty in number, or sixty-four. The Koshare are about twenty-four.

They are slim and naked, daubed with black-and-white earth, their hair daubed white and gathered upwards to a great knot on top of the head, whence springs a tuft of cornhusks, dry corn leaves. Though they wear nothing but a little black square cloth, front and back, at their middle, they do not seem naked, for some are white with black spots, like a leopard, and some have broad black lines or zigzags on their smeared bodies, and all their faces are blackened with triangles or lines till they look like weird masks. Meanwhile their hair, gathered straight up and daubed white and sticking up from the top of the head with corn-husks, completes the fantasy. They are anything but natural. Like blackened ghosts of a dead corn-cob, tufted at the top.

And all the time, running like queer spotted dogs, they weave nakedly through the unheeding dance, comical, weird, dancing the dance-step naked and fine, prancing through the lines, up and down the lines, and making fine gestures with their flexible hands, calling something down from the sky, calling something up from the earth, and dancing forward all the time. Suddenly as they catch a word from the singers, name of a star, of a wind, a name for the sun, for a cloud, their hands soar up and gather in the air, soar down with a slow motion. And again, as they catch a word that means earth, earth deeps, water within the earth, or red-earth-quickening, the hands flutter softly down, and draw up the water, draw up the earth-quickening, earth to sky, sky to earth, influences above to influences below, to meet in the germ-quick of corn, where life is.

And as they dance, the Koshare watch the dancing men. And if a fox-skin is coming loose at the belt, they fasten it as the man dances, or they stoop and tie another man's shoe. For the dancer must not hesitate to the end.

And then, after some forty minutes, the drum stops. Slowly the dancers file into one line, woman behind man, and move away, threading towards their kiva,[1] with no sound but the tinkle of knee-bells in the silence.

But at the same moment the thud of an unseen drum, from beyond, the soughing of deep song approaching from the unseen. It is the other half, the other half of the tribe coming to continue the dance. They appear round the kiva — one Koshare and one dancer leading the rows, the old men all abreast, singing already in a great strong burst.

So, from ten o'clock in the morning till about four in the afternoon, first one-half then the other. Till at last, as the day wanes, the two halves meet, and the two singings like two great winds surge one past the other, and the thicket of the dance becomes a real forest. It is the close of the third day.

Afterwards, the men and women crowd on the roofs of the two low round towers, the kivas, while the Koshare run round jesting and miming, and taking big offerings from the women, loaves of bread and cakes of blue-maize meal. Women come carrying big baskets of bread and guayaba, on two hands, an offering.

And the mystery of germination, not procreation, but *putting forth*, resurrection, life springing within the seed, is accomplished. The sky has its fire, its waters, its stars, its wandering electricity, its winds, its fingers

[1] Ceremonial chamber of Pueblo Indians.

of cold. The earth has its reddened body, its invisible hot heart, its inner waters and many juices and unaccountable stuffs. Between them all, the little seed: and also man, like a seed that is busy and aware. And from the heights and from the depths man, the caller, calls: a man, the knower, brings down the influences and brings up the influences, with his knowledge: man, so vulnerable, so subject, and yet even in his vulnerability and subjection, a master, commands the invisible influences and is obeyed. Commands in that song, in that rhythmic energy of dance, in that still-submissive mockery of the Koshare. And he accomplishes his end, as master. He partakes in the springing of the corn, in the rising and budding and earing of the corn. And when he eats his bread, at last, he recovers all he once sent forth, and partakes again of the energies he called to the corn, from out of the wide universe.

⨕ FOR DISCUSSION AND WRITING

1. This is a wonderful piece for study of the evocative effect of language, of imagery, and especially of prose rhythms. To educate our language sense, let's try this experiment: rewrite the first five paragraphs, condensing them into a single paragraph in which you state only their *factual* meaning, and in which you use only complete sentences having the grammatically prescribed form of subject and predicate. Now compare your paragraph—what it has accomplished in the way of communication—and Lawrence's five. What does Lawrence communicate that your paragraph does not? Don't let the comparison give you an inferiority trauma; we all know we aren't likely to write as brilliantly as Lawrence, but we can learn from this exercise something about the potentialities of language that mere reading, however appreciative, would not teach. Is there some single main effect on the reader's visual imagination, his thermal imagination, and his sense of time, that Lawrence makes here and that your transcription of the factual sense does not make? Reconsider his use of the adjective-noun combination, as in "Pale, dry, baked earth," then immediately "baked pale earth," then "the blue, uneasy, alkaline sky," then "A pale, uneven, parched world," then "a world pallid with dryness," then "sand-hills sinking, and straight, cracked mesas," and so on. As to factual sense, there is a good deal of repetition here (it's a dry country—why insist on the point?); well, what *does* the insistence accomplish? Now listen to these phrases with the

ear of your imagination. Can you hear them as having certain rhythms, never exactly alike, but carrying over from phrase to phrase just as some of the words are carried over? (You might try using some simple scansion method to mark long and short syllables and to show the relative length of the phrases.) You may have noticed that throughout the piece Lawrence uses the combination of three-adjectives-and-noun with unusual frequency, a combination that could become exceedingly boring and bad style if the rhythms were not so varied and, of course, if the imagery were not so sensitive and concrete. Glance through the pages again and write down some of the three-adjectives-and-noun combinations, and prepare a comment on the variety of rhythms as well as on the imagery. We seldom have an opportunity, in classes in prose composition, to study prose with our *ears* (which is rather strange, since our ears are such sensitive instruments in picking up nuances of meaning in oral communication). From the exercise here, have you learned anything definite about the relationship between *hearing* and *writing*? If you have, you might try testing your own written work by reading it aloud to yourself and really *listening* to it. One last query here: where, in the first five paragraphs, does Lawrence first pick up the subject-predicate form of the sentence, and what reason (in terms of purpose and effectiveness of communication) can you give for his avoidance of the complete sentence form up to that point?

2. Now explore the rest of the piece for some illustrations of style similar to those suggested above, and also, if you can, find some that are not suggested here but that your own eye and ear discover, and be prepared to comment on them.

3. Effective description requires a good deal of intelligent awareness of how the senses and the mind work in taking in a scene. Lawrence starts with landscape—the desert setting—then goes to the "mud-pie houses" (no people yet), then to the sound of drums and singing heard at a distance like the sound of wind rather than people, then . . . now finish this up with your own analysis of the changing focus of observation. What, implicitly, is the psychology behind the narrowing of focus?

4. The dance of the sprouting corn takes place in the three days following Easter. The magical dance is far older, of course, than the reception of Christianity among the Indians of the Southwest; nevertheless, what congruence is there between the meaning of the dance and the meaning of Easter? Explain the double reference—to the symbolism of the dance and the symbolism of Easter—of Lawrence's phrase, "this green resurrection."

What is the significance of the cornhusks on the heads of the male dancers?
(If you have read the piece from Apuleius, a few pages earlier, do you find
any common symbolism between the two pieces?) In describing the paint
and headdress of the dancers, Lawrence says, "They are anything but
natural." What reason can you find for the *un*naturalness of the appearance
of the dancers, in view of the purpose of the dance? In modern Christian
ritual, is there any corresponding reason for the special dress of the minister or priest?

5. Reread the final paragraph very carefully. Explain the distinction Lawrence
   makes between "germination" and "procreation." Explain what this means:
   "The sky has its fire, its waters. . . ." And this: "The earth has its reddened
   body, . . . its inner waters and many juices. . . ." And this: "and also man,
   like a seed. . . ." And this: "man, the caller. . . ." Ignoring the subject of the
   piece, how can it be said that man "partakes in the springing of the corn,
   in the rising and budding and earing of the corn"? Without being a member of a farm club, do you?

6. For a short writing assignment, you might consider the purpose (or purposes) and the form (or forms) of modern dance, either social dancing or
   the dance as an art, perhaps (not necessarily) making a comparison with
   the "dance of the sprouting corn."

The Order of Art

IN THAT *stimulating newspaper of the "socially conscious" thirties
called* P.M., *a cartoon appeared showing a fat, well-heeled, and
well-minked bourgeois couple of the type George Grosz used to draw,
standing before an abstract painting in an art gallery, one sneering
to the other, "What does it* mean?" *A hand shoots out of the painting
at them with the terrifying question, "What do* you *mean?"*

*The oldest and most durable critical theory of art is the theory
of mimesis, or "imitation"—found in the following pages in the*
POETICS *of Aristotle, in Susanne Langer's chapter on "The Tragic
Rhythm," in Vasari's "Life of Leonardo," in John Cage's discussion
of "Experimental Music"—for it is a theory that accommodates both
the ancient and the modern intelligence and all ranges of simplicity
and subtlety. What does art "imitate"? Obviously there is nothing else
for it to imitate but ourselves and the modes of our existence on this
planet. If our mode of existence has only so much "meaning" as the
label on a can of Campbell's soup, then the label on a can of
Campbell's soup is what art will imitate.*

*The imitative function of art has much in common with the
imitative function of magic—magic not in any metaphorical sense
but in the practical sense, magic used to bring about some practical*

result; as when a rain maker imitates the noise of thunder with a rattle
and the falling of the rain by sprinkling water on the earth from a can
with holes in the bottom, to give the sky an object lesson as to
what it should do; or as when Aurignacian men painted those fabulous
bison in the caves of France, so that the bison would be brought
under the power of the hunter as their imitated forms were produced
by the power of the painter; or as when an ancient Irish augur
chanted the following charm for a fertile season—

> Good tidings: sea fruitful, wave-washed strand,
> smiling woods; witchcraft flees, orchards blossom,
> cornfields ripen, bees swarm, a cheerful world,
> peace and plenty, happy summer . . .

the words of the spell "imitating" the desired magical result; or as
when Sappho, in what is perhaps the oldest European lyric, calls upon
Aphrodite to help her win the favor of her beloved, and describes
the goddess as actually standing beside her with smiling help; or as
when Keats, obeying the same instinct as the old Irish auspex
quoted above, wrote in his ode TO AUTUMN:

> Season of mists and mellow fruitfulness,
>   Close bosom-friend of the maturing sun;
> Conspiring with him how to load and bless
>   With fruit the vines that round the thatch-eves run;
> To bend with apples the moss'd cottage-trees,
>   And fill all fruit with ripeness to the core. . . .

The arts of music and the dance, of painting and sculpture and
poetry, even of architecture, all developed as forms of imitative magic,
and it is a mistake to think that the modern arts have lost their
practical magical effect, replacing it with some lean and ghostly
"aesthetic emotion"; for their function is still, like the function of the
magical spell, to "raise spirits" (what W. H. Auden, in his piece
in this section, calls "sacred beings") by calling their names and

imitating their forms. This is the tremendous importance of the arts,
their power to call up spirits—spirits that may be good or bad or,
what is perhaps worse, indifferent. The spirits that are called up come,
of course, not from outside but from ourselves. As an ancient Zen
poem says, "If you do not get it from yourself, / Where
will you go for it?"

Aristotle ✎ Poetics

✎ Fifteen hundred years after his death, Dante spoke of him as "the master of those who know." Aristotle's influence on Western thought has operated in two strangely different directions. Through the medieval Scholastics, and particularly through Aquinas, he shaped the logical foundations of Catholic theology, psychology, and ethics; on the other hand, his empirical approach to knowledge in every field, and his systematic classification of the data of knowledge, provided the basis of modern science. He was born in 384 B.C. in the village of Stagira, studied philosophy in Athens under Plato, tutored Alexander of Macedon from 343 to 336 (see Plutarch's life of Alexander in this book), wrote or left lecture notes for a *Logic*, a *Physics*, a *Metaphysics*, an *Ethics*, a *Politics*, and a *Poetics*. He established his own school in Athens, but left the city when Alexander died, in 323, and political dissension and insurrection broke out—saying that he did not wish the Athenians to sin against philosophy twice (alluding to the trial and death of Socrates). He died in the following year. The *Poetics* is a set of notes rather than a deliberately formulated exposition; nevertheless, it is the most important piece of criticism ever written. It is abridged here to the sections bearing on tragedy. ϙ

POETRY in general[1] seems to have sprung from two causes, each of them lying deep in our nature. First, the instinct of imitation is implanted in man from childhood, one difference between him and other animals being that he is the most imitative of living creatures, and through imitation learns his earliest lessons; and no less universal is the pleasure felt in things imitated. We have evidence of this in the facts of experience. Objects which in themselves we view with pain, we delight to contemplate when reproduced with minute fidelity: such as the forms of the most ignoble animals and of dead bodies. The cause of this again is, that

The translation is that of S. H. Butcher, in his *Aristotle's Theory of Poetry and Fine Art.*

[1] "Poetry" has wider reference here than it has to us. Aristotle is going to talk chiefly about drama, and one must remember that classical Greek dramas, both tragedy and comedy, were in the form of poetry.

to learn gives the liveliest pleasure, not only to philosophers but to men in general; whose capacity, however, of learning is more limited. Thus the reason why men enjoy seeing a likeness is, that in contemplating it they find themselves learning or inferring, and saying perhaps, "Ah, that is he." For if you happen not to have seen the original, the pleasure will be due not to the imitation as such, but to the execution, the colouring, or some such other cause.

Imitation, then, is one instinct of our nature. Next, there is the instinct for "harmony" and rhythm, metres being manifestly sections of rhythm. Persons, therefore, starting with this natural gift developed by degrees their special aptitudes, till their rude improvisations gave birth to Poetry.

Poetry now diverged in two directions, according to the individual character of the writers. The graver spirits imitated noble actions, and the actions of good men. The more trivial sort imitated the actions of meaner persons, at first composing satires, as the former did hymns to the gods and the praises of famous men. . . .

But when Tragedy and Comedy came to light, the two classes of poets still followed their natural bent: the lampooners became writers of Comedy, and the Epic poets were succeeded by Tragedians, since the drama was a larger and higher form of art. . . .

Tragedy — as also Comedy—was at first mere improvisation. The one originated with the authors of the Dithyramb, the other with those of the phallic songs,[2] which are still in use in many of our cities. Tragedy advanced by slow degrees; each new element that showed itself was in turn developed. Having passed through many changes, it found its natural form, and there it stopped. . . .

Comedy is, as we have said, an imitation of characters of a lower type — not, however, in the full sense of the word bad, the Ludicrous being merely a subdivision of the ugly. It consists in some defect or ugliness which is not painful or destructive. To take an obvious example, the comic mask is ugly and distorted, but does not imply pain.

Epic poetry agrees with Tragedy in so far as it is an imitation in verse of characters of a higher type. They differ, in that Epic poetry

[2] Both dithyramb and phallic songs originated in the religious ritual of Dionysus. The former was a choric hymn; the latter were boisterous choruses and dialogues performed by players in phallic costumes and animal masks.

admits but one kind of metre, and is narrative in form. They differ, again, in their length: for Tragedy endeavours, as far as possible, to confine itself to a single revolution of the sun, or but slightly to exceed this limit; whereas the Epic action has no limits of time. . . .

Of their constituent parts some are common to both, some peculiar to Tragedy: whoever, therefore, knows what is good or bad Tragedy, knows also about Epic poetry. All the elements of an Epic poem are found in Tragedy, but the elements of a Tragedy are not all found in the Epic poem. . . .

Let us now discuss Tragedy, resuming its formal definition, as resulting from what has been already said.

Tragedy then, is an imitation of an action that is serious, complete, and of a certain magnitude; in language embellished with each kind of artistic ornament, the several kinds being found in separate parts of the play; in the form of action, not of narrative; through pity and fear effecting the proper purgation[3] of these emotions. By "language embellished," I mean language into which rhythm, "harmony," and song enter. By "the several kinds in separate parts," I mean, that some parts are rendered through the medium of verse alone, others again with the aid of song.

Now as tragic imitation implies persons acting, it necessarily follows, in the first place, that Spectacular equipment[4] will be a part of Tragedy. Next, Song and Diction, for these are the medium of imitation. By "Diction" I mean the mere metrical arrangement of the words: as for "Song," it is a term whose sense every one understands.

Again, Tragedy is the imitation of an action; and an action implies personal agents, who necessarily possess certain distinctive qualities both of character and thought; for it is by these that we qualify actions themselves, and these — thought and character — are the two natural causes from which actions spring, and on actions again all success or failure depends. Hence, the Plot is the imitation of the action: — for by plot I here mean the arrangement of the incidents. By Character I mean that in virtue of which we ascribe certain qualities to the agents. Thought is required wherever a statement is proved, or, it may be, a general truth enunciated. Every Tragedy, therefore, must have six parts, which parts determine its quality — namely, Plot, Character, Diction, Thought, Spec-

[3] The idea of "purgation," or catharsis, is taken up in Question 12, page 1033.
[4] See Question 8, page 1033.

tacle, Song. Two of the parts constitute the medium of imitation, one the manner, and three the objects of imitation. And these complete the list. These elements have been employed, we may say, by the poets to a man; in fact, every play contains Spectacular elements as well as Character, Plot, Diction, Song, and Thought. . . .

But most important of all is the structure of the incidents. For Tragedy is an imitation, not of men, but of an action and of life, and life consists in action, and its end is a mode of action, not a quality. Now character determines men's qualities, but it is by their actions that they are happy or the reverse. Dramatic action, therefore, is not with a view to the representation of character: character comes in as subsidiary to the actions. Hence the incidents and the plot are the end of a tragedy; and the end is the chief thing of all. Again, without action there cannot be a tragedy; there may be without character. . . .

Again, if you string together a set of speeches expressive of character, and well finished in point of diction and thought, you will not produce the essential tragic effect nearly so well as with a play which, however deficient in these respects, yet has a plot and artistically constructed incidents. Besides which, the most powerful elements of emotional interest in Tragedy — Peripeteia or Reversal of the Situation, and Recognition scenes — are parts of the plot. A further proof is, that novices in the art attain to finish of diction and precision of portraiture before they can construct the plot. It is the same with almost all the early poets.

The Plot, then, is the first principle, and, as it were, the soul of a tragedy: Character holds the second place. . . .

Thus Tragedy is the imitation of an action, and of the agents, mainly with a view to the action.

Third in order is Thought — that is, the faculty of saying what is possible and pertinent in given circumstances. In the case of oratory, this is the function of the political art and of the art of rhetoric: and so indeed the older poets make their characters speak the language of civic life; the poets of our time, the language of the rhetoricians.

Character is that which reveals moral purpose, showing what kind of things a man chooses or avoids. Speeches, therefore, which do not make this manifest, or in which the speaker does not choose or avoid anything whatever, are not expressive of character. Thought, on the other hand, is found where something is proved to be or not to be, or a general maxim is enunciated.

Fourth among the elements enumerated comes Diction; by which

I mean, as has been already said, the expression of the meaning in words; and its essence is the same both in verse and prose.

Of the remaining elements Song holds the chief place among the embellishments.

The Spectacle has, indeed, an emotional attraction of its own, but, of all the parts, it is the least artistic, and connected least with the art of poetry. For the power of Tragedy, we may be sure, is felt even apart from representation and actors. Besides, the production of spectacular effects depends more on the art of the stage machinist than on that of the poet.

These principles being established, let us now discuss the proper structure of the Plot, since this is the first and most important part of Tragedy.

Now, according to our definition, Tragedy is an imitation of an action that is complete, and whole, and of a certain magnitude; for there may be a whole that is wanting in magnitude. A whole is that which has a beginning, a middle, and an end. A beginning is that which does not itself follow anything by causal necessity, but after which something naturally is or comes to be. An end, on the contrary, is that which itself naturally follows some other thing, either by necessity, or as a rule, but has nothing following it. A middle is that which follows something as some other thing follows it. A well constructed plot, therefore, must neither begin nor end at haphazard, but conform to these principles.

Again, a beautiful object, whether it be a living organism or any whole composed of parts, must not only have an orderly arrangement of parts, but must also be of a certain magnitude; for beauty depends on magnitude and order. Hence an exceedingly small picture cannot be beautiful; for the view of it is confused, the object being seen in an almost imperceptible moment of time. Nor, again, can one of vast size be beautiful; for as the eye cannot take it all in at once, the unity and sense of the whole is lost for the spectator; as for instance if there were a picture a thousand miles long. As, therefore, in the case of animate bodies and pictures a certain magnitude is necessary, and a magnitude which may be easily embraced in one view; so in the plot, a certain length is necessary, and a length which can be easily embraced by the memory. The limit of length in relation to dramatic competition and sensuous presentment, is no part of artistic theory. For had it been the rule for a hundred tragedies to compete together, the performance would have been regulated by the water-clock — as indeed we are told was formerly done. But the limit as fixed by the nature of the drama itself is this: — the greater the length, the more beautiful will the piece be by reason of its size, provided that the whole be perspicuous. And to define the matter roughly, we may say that the proper magnitude is comprised within such limits, that the sequence of events, according to the law of probability or necessity, will admit of a change from bad fortune to good, or from good fortune to bad.

Unity of plot does not, as some persons think, consist in the unity of the hero. For infinitely various are the incidents in one man's life, which cannot be reduced to unity; and so, too, there are many actions of one man out of which we cannot make one action. Hence the error, as it appears, of all poets who have composed a *Heracleid*, a *Theseid*,[5] or other poems of the kind. They imagine that as Heracles was one man, the story of Heracles must also be a unity. But Homer, as in all else he is of surpassing merit, here too — whether from art or natural genius — seems to have happily discerned the truth. In composing the *Odyssey* he did not include all the adventures of Odysseus — such as his wound on Parnassus, or his feigned madness at the mustering of the host — incidents between which there was no necessary or probable connexion: but he made the *Odyssey*, and likewise the *Iliad*, to centre round an action that in our sense of the word is one.[6] As therefore, in the other imitative arts, the imitation is one when the object imitated is one, so the plot, being an imitation of an action, must imitate one action and that a whole, the structural union of the parts being such that, if any one of them is displaced or removed, the whole will be disjointed and disturbed. For a thing whose presence or absence makes no visible difference, is not an organic part of the whole.

It is, moreover, evident from what has been said, that it is not the function of the poet to relate what has happened, but what may happen — what is possible according to the law of probability or necessity. The

---

[5] Poems about the adventures of Hercules and Theseus.

[6] In Aristotle's sense of "an action that is one," the action of the *Odyssey* may be said to center on the efforts of Odysseus to get back home to Ithaca and resume his kingship there; while the action of the *Iliad* is centered on the problem of getting Achilles into the fight after his quarrel with Agamemnon.

poet and the historian differ not by writing in verse or in prose. The work
of Herodotus might be put into verse, and it would still be a species of
history, with metre no less than without it. The true difference is that one
relates what has happened, the other what may happen. Poetry, therefore, is a more philosophical and a higher thing than history: for poetry
tends to express the universal, history the particular. . . .

It clearly follows that the poet or "maker"[7] should be the maker of
plots rather than of verses; since he is a poet because he imitates, and
what he imitates are actions. And even if he chances to take an historical
subject, he is none the less a poet; for there is no reason why some events
that have actually happened should not conform to the law of the probable and possible, and in virtue of that quality in them he is their poet or
maker.

Of all plots and actions the episodic are the worst. I call a plot
"episodic" in which the episodes or acts succeed one another without
probable or necessary sequence. Bad poets compose such pieces by their
own fault, good poets, to please the players; for, as they write show
pieces for competition, they stretch the plot beyond its capacity, and
are often forced to break the natural continuity.

But again, Tragedy is an imitation not only of a complete action, but
of events terrible and pitiful. Such an effect is best produced when the
events come on us by surprise; and the effect is heightened when, at the
same time, they follow as cause and effect. The tragic wonder will then
be greater than if they happened of themselves or by accident; for even
coincidences are most striking when they have an air of design. We may
instance the statue of Mitys at Argos, which fell upon his murderer while
he was a spectator at a festival, and killed him. Such events seem not to
be due to mere chance. Plots, therefore, constructed on these principles
are necessarily the best.

Plots are either Simple or Complex, for the actions in real life, of
which the plots are an imitation, obviously show a similar distinction.
An action which is one and continuous in the sense above defined, I call
Simple, when the change of fortune takes place without Reversal of the
Situation and without Recognition.

A Complex action is one in which the change is accompanied by

---

[7] The words "poet" and "poetry" come from the Greek verb *poiein*, "to make" (in the
sense of "create").

such Reversal, or by Recognition, or by both. These last should arise from the internal structure of the plot, so that what follows should be the necessary or probable result of the preceding action. . . .

Reversal of the Situation is a change by which the action veers round to its opposite, subject always to our rule of probability or necessity. Thus in the *Oedipus*, the messenger comes to cheer Oedipus and free him from his alarms about his mother, but by revealing who he is, he produces the opposite effect. . . .

Recognition, as the name indicates, is a change from ignorance to knowledge, producing love or hate between the persons destined by the poet for good or bad fortune. The best form of recognition is coincident with a Reversal of the Situation as in the *Oedipus*. There are indeed other forms. Even inanimate things of the most trivial kind may sometimes be objects of recognition. Again, we may recognise or discover whether a person has done a thing or not. But the recognition which is most intimately connected with the plot and action is, as we have said, the recognition of persons. This recognition, combined with Reversal, will produce either pity or fear; and actions producing these effects are those which, by our definition, Tragedy represents. Moreover, it is upon such situations that the issues of good or bad fortune will depend. Recognition, then, being between persons, it may happen that one person only is recognised by the other — when the latter is already known — or it may be necessary that the recognition should be on both sides. Thus Iphigenia is revealed to Orestes by the sending of the letter; but another act of recognition is required to make Orestes known to Iphigenia.

Two parts, then, of the Plot — Reversal of the Situation and Recognition — turn upon surprises. A third part is the Tragic Incident. The Tragic Incident is a destructive or painful action, such as death on the stage, bodily agony, wounds, and the like. . . .

As the sequel to what has already been said, we must proceed to consider what the poet should aim at, and what he should avoid, in constructing his plots; and by what means the specific effect of Tragedy will be produced.

A perfect Tragedy should, as we have seen, be arranged not on the simple but on the complex plan. It should, moreover, imitate actions which excite pity and fear, this being the distinctive mark of tragic imitation. It follows plainly, in the first place, that the change of fortune presented must not be the spectacle of a virtuous man brought from prosperity to adversity: for this moves neither pity nor fear; it merely shocks us. Nor, again, that of a bad man passing from adversity to prosperity: for nothing can be more alien to the spirit of Tragedy; it possesses no single tragic quality; it neither satisfies the moral sense, nor calls forth pity or fear. Nor, again, should the downfall of the utter villain be exhibited. A plot of this kind would, doubtless, satisfy the moral sense, but it would inspire neither pity nor fear; for pity is aroused by unmerited misfortune, fear by the misfortune of a man like ourselves. Such an event, therefore, will be neither pitiful nor terrible. There remains, then, the character between these two extremes — that of a man who is not eminently good and just, yet whose misfortune is brought about not by vice or depravity, but by some error or frailty. He must be one who is highly renowned and prosperous — a personage like Oedipus, Thyestes, or other illustrious men of such families.

A well constructed plot should, therefore, be single in its issue, rather than double as some maintain. The change of fortune should be not from bad to good, but, reversely, from good to bad. It should come about as the result not of vice, but of some great error or frailty, in a character either such as we have described, or better rather than worse. The practice of the stage bears out our view. At first the poets recounted any legend that came in their way. Now, the best Tragedies are founded on the story of a few houses — on the fortunes of Alcmaeon, Oedipus, Orestes, Meleager, Thyestes, Telephus, and those others who have done or suffered something terrible. A Tragedy, then, to be perfect according to the rules of art should be of this construction. Hence they are in error who censure Euripides just because he follows this principle in his plays, many of which end unhappily. It is, as we have said, the right ending. The best proof is that on the stage and in dramatic competition, such plays, if well worked out, are the most tragic in effect; and Euripides, faulty though he may be in the general management of his subject, yet is felt to be the most tragic of the poets.

In the second rank comes the kind of Tragedy which some place first. Like the *Odyssey,* it has a double thread of plot, and also an opposite catastrophe for the good and for the bad. It is accounted the best because of the weakness of the spectators; for the poet is guided in what he writes by the wishes of his audience. The pleasure, however, thence derived is not the true tragic pleasure. It is proper rather to Comedy, where those who, in the piece, are the deadliest enemies — like Orestes and Aegisthus — quit the stage as friends at the close, and no one slays or is slain.

Fear and pity may be aroused by spectacular means; but they may also result from the inner structure of the piece, which is the better way, and indicates a superior poet. For the plot ought to be so constructed that, even without the aid of the eye, he who hears the tale told will thrill with horror and melt to pity at what takes place. This is the impression we should receive from hearing the story of the *Oedipus*. But to produce this effect by the mere spectacle is a less artistic method, and dependent on extraneous aids. Those who employ spectacular means to create a sense not of the terrible but only of the monstrous, are strangers to the purpose of Tragedy; for we must not demand of Tragedy any and every kind of pleasure, but only that which is proper to it. And since the pleasure which the poet should afford is that which comes from pity and fear through imitation, it is evident that this quality must be impressed upon the incidents.

Let us then determine what are the circumstances which strike us as terrible or pitiful.

Actions capable of this effect must happen between persons who are either friends or enemies or indifferent to one another. If an enemy kills an enemy, there is nothing to excite pity either in the act or the intention — except so far as the suffering in itself is pitiful. So again with indifferent persons. But when the tragic incident occurs between those who are near or dear to one another — if, for example, a brother kills, or intends to kill, a brother, a son his father, a mother her son, a son his mother, or any other deed of the kind is done — these are the situations to be looked for by the poet. . . .

In respect of Character there are four things to be aimed at. First, and most important, it must be good. Now any speech or action that manifests moral purpose of any kind will be expressive of character: the character will be good if the purpose is good. This rule is relative to each class. Even a woman may be good, and also a slave; though the woman may be said to be an inferior being, and the slave quite worthless. The second thing to aim at is propriety. There is a type of manly valour; but valour in a woman, or unscrupulous cleverness, is inappropriate. Thirdly, character must be true to life: for this is a distinct thing from goodness and propriety, as here described. The fourth point is consistency: for though the subject of the imitation, who suggested the type, be inconsistent, still he must be consistently inconsistent. . . .

As in the structure of the plot, so too in the portraiture of character, the poet should always aim either at the necessary or the probable. Thus a person of a given character should speak or act in a given way, by the rule either of necessity or of probability; just as this event should follow that by necessary or probable sequence. It is therefore evident that the unravelling of the plot, no less than the complication, must arise out of the plot itself, it must not be brought about by the *Deus ex Machina*[8] — as in the *Medea*. . . . The *Deus ex Machina* should be employed only for events external to the drama — for antecedent or subsequent events, which lie beyond the range of human knowledge, and which require to be reported or foretold; for to the gods we ascribe the power of seeing all things. Within the action there must be nothing irrational. If the irrational cannot be excluded, it should be outside the scope of the tragedy. Such is the irrational element in the *Oedipus* of Sophocles. . . .

⌘ FOR DISCUSSION AND WRITING

1. According to Aristotle, from what two causes "lying deep in our nature" does poetry spring? Can you give any support to the assertion that we have an "instinct" for harmony and rhythm? (In relation to this question, you might consider the organic rhythms of our bodies, heartbeat, breathing, even walking.) Mimesis, or "imitation," is the oldest and most constant explanation of the function of the arts, and this idea should be worked out thoroughly in any discussion of the *Poetics*. Its application to representational art (for instance, painting that aims at photographic realism, "program" music, "documentary" films) is clear enough; but what about more sophisticated forms of art? What does Martha Graham "imitate"? Stravinsky? Picasso? Joyce? Virginia Woolf? Frank Lloyd Wright? What do Shakespeare's *Hamlet, King Lear,* and *Macbeth* imi-

---

[8] Literally, the god from the machine—the "machine" being any stage contraption, such as pulleys, by which supernatural beings are brought on the scene. The term has come to be used for artificial or makeshift means of resolving a plot.

tate? Obviously the idea of mimesis in the arts is a fertile one and not at all simple.

2. What distinction does Aristotle make between the type of character "imitated" by comedy, and the type of character imitated by epic poetry and tragedy? Try to apply this distinction to examples within your own experience: for instance, to the pie-throwing, pratfall kind of comedy, or the Mickey Mouse type of animated cartoon, or Chaplin's little tramp, or the Noel Coward kind of comedy; and as to epic poetry and tragedy, do you find Aristotle's distinction carried out in the characters "imitated" in Milton's *Paradise Lost,* in Shakespeare's tragedies, in Eugene O'Neill's, in Arthur Miller's *Death of a Salesman?* Questions such as these are bound to land one in difficulties, but that is one of the chief values of the *Poetics* —that the principles Aristotle lays down make one think, creating problems of application, and stimulating one to formulate one's own critical discriminations.

3. What is Aristotle's definition of tragedy?

4. Now let us take up the "parts" of tragedy as he sees them (keeping in mind the fact that classical Greek tragedy was in poetic form and that the scenes of the main action were separated by choral interludes with instrumental accompaniment). There are six of these "parts," and it would be a good idea to write them down in an outline, with your own explanatory notations. First is "plot." How is plot defined? Why does Aristotle consider it the most important part—the "soul"—of tragedy? Explain the statement that "Tragedy is an imitation, not of men, but of an action and of life, and life consists in action, and its end is a mode of action, not a quality." It is clear enough how there can be description of character without any action—as in the "My Favorite Character" kind of sketch you have no doubt been asked to do with monotonous frequency as a theme assignment; but, of course, that kind of description does not make a drama—does not even make a "story," as you may have found out if you have tried to write a short story. Clearly, anything of a dramatic nature, including the short story and the novel, demands first of all some kind of action.

5. Character, then, is the second part. How does Aristotle define character? (The Greek word *ethos* may come in handy here—character conceived ethically, as "that which reveals moral purpose.")

6. The third part is thought. Why does Aristotle place thought after character? (Can you conceive of thoughts without characters to think them?)

7. Then comes diction. Define diction. Why, in this analysis, does diction come after thought?

8. The last two parts are spectacle and music. Spectacle is simply that part of a play which strikes the eye—what we would call setting, costuming, and properties. In plays or films with which you are familiar, can you cite examples of the importance of spectacle? (Feel free to disagree with Aristotle on this point or any other.) The musical part of drama was much more important in Aristotle's time, when the chorus was an integral part of the play, than it is now. Does music still have a function in drama? How is the order of importance of all six of these parts reversed in opera and musical comedy?

9. Now let us reconsider the nature of the action or plot. What does Aristotle mean by saying that the action must be "one," rather than several? Can you illustrate that "one-ness" or unity of action from plays or films that you know—or, if you can extend Aristotle a little further, from short stories or novels that you know? What is "episodic" action, and why does he say this is the worst kind? Suppose you should write your autobiography, jotting down everything that had happened to you; the events would be tied together by the fact that they all concern one person—yourself; but would your own "unity," as a person, give to your account of your life the kind of unity Aristotle is talking about?

10. What is meant by the "reversal" (*peripeteia,* or peripety) of the plot? Illustrate this moment of the plot from some play or story that you know. What is meant by "recognition"? Illustrate "recognition" from your own experience of plays or stories. Aristotle says that the most effective drama is that in which "reversal" and "recognition" coincide; can you support this point with your own examples? What does he mean by the "tragic incident" (*pathos,* literally "suffering")?

11. Why does he say that poetry is "more philosophic" than history?

12. Earlier, in his formal definition of tragedy, he has said that the action of tragedy is that kind which, through pity and fear, effects the purgation of these emotions. This is the famous doctrine of "catharsis," which Aristotle

borrowed from the medical practice of his time. Each year, on a day of early spring, the Athenians were accustomed to holding a "spring house-cleaning" ceremony that had both a spiritual and a physical intent; houses were thoroughly cleansed, streets swept, all the trashy accumulations of the year got rid of; the lids of the great burial *pithoi* (huge jars, sunk in the earth, holding the bones and ash of the dead) were lifted off, so that the spirits of the dead could fly around for that day; and everyone chewed a certain herb which had a purgative effect and which they also fastened on the doors of their houses. Thus, when Aristotle used the metaphor of catharsis in reference to the effect of tragedy, his students knew what he was talking about, for they had had experience of the ceremonial purgation of those things which cause disease and chaos, pity and terror, in the life of a community; furthermore, capping the "spring housecleaning," came the presentation of the year's winning plays in the theater of Dionysus, which all citizens had to attend as part of the state-controlled religious program, and which had developed out of the ritual of Dionysus as an essential part of the ceremonies necessary for the insurance of civic health. But the idea of dramatic catharsis has given a great deal of trouble to modern commentators, and almost every interpreter has his own notion of it. The student will find, in the big Webster's, a couple of interpretations that are useful as grounds for discussion. Given these grounds, try to apply the idea of tragic catharsis to one older play and one modern play—for instance, to *Hamlet* and *Death of a Salesman*, or to *Macbeth* and *A Streetcar Named Desire*.

13. Explain Aristotle's argument as to why the protagonist of tragedy must not be a perfectly virtuous man, nor a thoroughly evil one. What kind of man must he be? How does this discussion hinge directly on the idea of the cathartic function of tragedy?

14. What is meant by the rule of necessity or probability? What is meant by the *Deus ex Machina?*

15. Perhaps the most useful writing assignment here would be a paper briefly recapitulating what seem to you the most important points of Aristotle's argument, for this would require that you work out in your own language, with your own illustrations, your understanding of the *Poetics*. Otherwise, there are many topics for papers in the application of the principles of the *Poetics* (any one principle or several) to plays or films or novels or stories with which you are familiar.

Susanne K. Langer ✑ The Tragic Rhythm

✑ Distinguished American philosopher, born in 1895 in New York City, educated at Radcliffe and the University of Vienna. Mrs. Langer has held numerous university posts and has lectured and written extensively. Her most widely known books are *Philosophy in a New Key*, a study in symbolic modes, and *Feeling and Form*, the most important work in aesthetics that has appeared in the century. ✑

As COMEDY presents the vital rhythm of self-preservation, tragedy exhibits that of self-consummation.

The lilting advance of the eternal life process, indefinitely maintained or temporarily lost and restored, is the great general vital pattern that we exemplify from day to day.[1] But creatures that are destined, sooner or later, to die — that is, all individuals that do not pass alive into new generations, like jellyfish and algae — hold the balance of life only precariously, in the frame of a total movement that is quite different; the

Reprinted with the permission of Charles Scribner's Sons from *Feeling and Form*, pages 351-366, by Susanne Langer. Copyright 1953 by Charles Scribner's Sons.

[1] In an earlier chapter, Mrs. Langer has discussed the plot-rhythm of comedy, with its ups and downs, always ending in an "up," as the general rhythm of organic life, of the species, of society.

movement from birth to death. Unlike the simple metabolic process, the deathward advance of their individual lives has a series of stations that are not repeated; growth, maturity, decline. That is the tragic rhythm.

Tragedy is a cadential form. Its crisis is always the turn toward an absolute close. This form reflects the basic structure of personal life, and therewith of feeling when life is viewed as a whole. It is that attitude — "the tragic sense of life," as Unamuno[2] called it — that is objectified and brought before our eyes in tragedy. . . .

Tragedy dramatizes human life as potentiality and fulfillment. Its virtual future, or Destiny, is therefore quite different from that created in comedy. Comic Destiny is Fortune — what the world will bring, and the man will take or miss, encounter or escape; tragic Destiny is what the man brings, and the world will demand of him. That is his Fate.

What he brings is his potentiality: his mental, moral and even physical powers, his powers to act and suffer. Tragic action is the realization of all his possibilities, which he unfolds and exhausts in the course of the drama. His human nature is his Fate. Destiny conceived as Fate is, therefore, not capricious, like Fortune, but is predetermined. Outward events are merely the occasions for its realization. . . .

I do not mean to say that a tragic hero is to be regarded as primarily a symbol for mankind. What the poet creates is a personality; and the more individual and powerful that personality is, the more extraordinary and overwhelming will be the action. Since the protagonist is the chief agent, his relation to the action is obvious; and since the course of the action is the "fable" or "plot" of the play, it is also obvious that creating the characters is not something apart from building the plot, but is an integral portion of it. The agents are prime elements in the action; but the action is the play itself, and artistic elements are always for the sake of the whole. That was, I think, what prompted Aristotle to say: "Tragedy is essentially an imitation not of persons but of action and life, of happiness and misery. All human happiness or misery takes the form of action; the end for which we live is a certain kind of activity, not a quality. Character gives us qualities, but it is in our actions — what we do — that we are happy or the reverse. In a play accordingly they do not act in order to portray the Characters; they include the Characters for the sake of the action. So that it is the action in it, i.e. its Fable or

---

[2] Miguel de Unamuno, Spanish philosopher who died in 1936.

Plot, that is the end and purpose of the tragedy; and the end is everywhere the chief thing." This "end" is the work as such. The protagonist and all characters that support him are introduced that we may see the fulfillment of his Fate, which is simply the complete realization of his individual "human nature."

The idea of personal Fate was mythically conceived long before the relation of life history to character was discursively understood. The mythical tradition of Greece treated the fate of its "heroes" — the personalities springing from certain great, highly individualized families — as a mysterious power inherent in the world rather than in the man and his ancestry; it was conceived as a private incubus bestowed on him at birth by a vengeful deity, or even through a curse pronounced by a human being. Sometimes no such specific cause of his peculiar destiny is given at all; but an oracle foretells what he is bound to do. It is interesting to note that this conception of Fate usually centers in the mysterious predictability of *acts* someone is to perform. The occasions of the acts are not foretold; the world will provide them.

For the development of tragedy, such determination of the overt acts without circumstances and motives furnished an ideal starting point, for it constrained the poets to invent characters whose actions would issue naturally in the required fateful deeds. The oracular prophecy, then, became an intensifying symbol of the necessity that was really given with the agent's personality; the "fable"[3] being just one possible way the world might elicit his complete self-realization in endeavor and error and discovery, passion and punishment, to the limit of his powers. The prime example of this passage from the mythical idea of Fate to the dramatic creation of Fate as the protagonist's natural, personal destiny is, of course, the *Oedipus Tyrannus* of Sophocles. With that tremendous piece of self-assertion, self-divination and self-exhaustion, the "Great Tradition" of tragedy was born in Europe.

There is another mythical conception of Fate that is not a forerunner of tragedy, but possibly of some kinds of comedy: that is the idea of Fate as the will of supernatural powers, perhaps long decreed, perhaps spontaneous and arbitrary. It is the "Fate" of the true fatalist, who takes no great care of his life because he deems it entirely in the hand of Allah (or some other God), who will slay or spare at his pleasure no matter

---

[3] The plot—from the Latin *fabula,* meaning fiction or narrative.

what one does. That is quite a different notion from the "oracular" Fate[4] of Greek mythology; the will of a god who gives and takes away, casts down or raises up, for inscrutable reasons of his own, is Kismet, and that is really a myth of Fortune.[*] Kismet is what a person encounters, not what he is. Both conceptions often exist side by side. The Scotsman who has to "dree his weird"[5] believes nonetheless that his fortunes from moment to moment are in the hands of Providence. Macbeth's Weird Sisters were perfectly acceptable to a Christian audience. Even in the ancient lore of our fairy tales, the Sleeping Beauty is destined to prick herself — that is, she has a personal destiny. In Greek tradition, on the other hand, where the notion of "oracular Fate" was so generally entertained that the Oracle was a public institution, Fate as the momentary decree of a ruling Power is represented in the myth of the Norns, who spin the threads of human lives and cut them where they list; the Three Fates are as despotic and capricious as Allah, and what they spin is, really, Kismet.

Tragedy can arise and flourish only where people are aware of individual life as an end in itself, and as a measure of other things. In tribal cultures where the individual is still so closely linked with his family that not only society but even he himself regards his existence as a communal value, which may be sacrificed at any time for communal ends, the development of personality is not a consciously appreciated life pattern. Similarly, where men believe that Karma,[6] or the tally of their deeds, may be held over for recompense or expiation in another earthly life, their current incarnation cannot be seen as a self-sufficient whole in which their entire potentialities are to be realized. Therefore genuine tragedy — drama exhibiting "the tragic rhythm of action," as Professor Fergusson has called it[**] — is a specialized form of art, with problems and devices of its own. . . .

A dramatic act is a commitment. It creates a situation in which the agent or agents must necessarily make a further move; that is, it moti-

[4] Predictions of future events as delivered by oracles, conceived as supernaturally sanctioned.

[*] Cf. N. N. Martinovitch, *The Turkish Theatre*, p. 36: "According to Islamic speculation, man has almost no influence on the development of his own fate. Allah is sovereign, doing as he likes and accounting to no one." [Author's note.]

[5] To suffer or endure his fate.

[6] In Hinduism and Buddhism, *Karma* is the continuous consequence of every thought and deed throughout eternity.

[**] In *The Idea of a Theater*, especially p. 18. [Author's note.]

vates a subsequent act (or acts). The situation, which is the completion of a given act, is already the impetus to another — as, in running, the footfall that catches our weight at the end of one bound already sends us forward to land on the other foot. The bounds need not be alike, but proportional, which means that the impetus of any specially great leap must have been prepared and gathered somewhere, and any sudden diminution be balanced by some motion that carries off the driving force. Dramatic acts are analogously connected with each other so that each one directly or indirectly motivates what follows it. In this way a genuine rhythm of action is set up, which is not simple like that of a physical repetitive process (e.g. running, breathing), but more often intricate. . . . That rhythm is the "commanding form" of the play; it springs from the poet's original conception of the "fable," and dictates the major divisions of the work, the light or heavy style of its presentation, the intensity of the highest feeling and most violent act, the great or small number of characters, and the degrees of their development. The total action is a cumulative form; and because it is constructed by a rhythmic treatment of its elements, it appears to *grow* from its beginnings. That is the playwright's creation of "organic form."

The tragic rhythm, which is the pattern of a life that grows, flourishes, and declines, is abstracted by being transferred from that natural activity to the sphere of a characteristically human action, where it is exemplified in mental and emotional growth, maturation, and the final relinquishment of power. In that relinquishment lies the hero's true "heroism" — the vision of life as accomplished, that is, life in its entirety, the sense of fulfillment that lifts him above his defeat.

A remarkable expression of this idea of tragedy may be found in the same book from which I borrowed, a few paragraphs above, the phrase, "the tragic rhythm of action." Speaking of Hamlet, Professor Fergusson observes: "In Act V . . . he feels that his role, all but the very last episode, has been played. . . . He is content, now, to let the fated end come as it will. . . . One could say that he feels the poetic rightness of his own death. . . .

"However one may interpret it, when his death comes it 'feels right,' the only possible end for the play. . . . We are certainly intended to feel that Hamlet, however darkly and uncertainly he worked, had discerned the way to be obedient to his deepest values, and accomplished some sort of purgatorial progress for himself and Denmark." . . .

Tragic drama is so designed that the protagonist grows mentally, emotionally, or morally, by the demand of the action, which he himself initiated, to the complete exhaustion of his powers, the limit of his possible development. He spends himself in the course of the one dramatic action. This is, of course, a tremendous foreshortening of life; instead of undergoing the physical and psychical, many-sided, long process of an actual biography, the tragic hero lives and matures in some particular respect; his entire being is concentrated in one aim, one passion, one conflict and ultimate defeat. For this reason the prime agent of tragedy is heroic; his character, the unfolding situation, the scene, even though ostensibly familiar and humble, are all exaggerated, charged with more feeling than comparable actualities would possess. . . .***

Drama is not psychology, nor (though the critical literature tends to make it seem so) is it moral philosophy. It offers no discourse on the hero's or heroine's native endowments, to let us estimate at any stage in the action how near they must be to exhaustion. The action itself must reveal the limit of the protagonist's powers and mark the end of his self-realization. And so, indeed, it does: the turning point of the play is the situation he cannot resolve, where he makes his "tragic error" or exhibits his "tragic weakness." He is led by his own action and its repercussions in the world to respond with more and more competence, more and more daring to a constantly gathering challenge; so his character "grows," i.e. he unfolds his will and knowledge and passion, as the situation grows. His career is not change of personality, but maturation. When he reaches his limit of mental and emotional development, the crisis occurs; then comes the defeat, either by death or, as in many modern tragedies, by hopelessness that is the equivalent of death, a "death of the soul," that ends the career.

It has been reiterated so often that the hero of tragedy is a strong man with one weakness, a good man with one fault, that a whole ethics of tragedy has grown up around the significance of this single flaw. Chapters upon chapters — even books — have been written on the required mixture of good and evil in his character, to make him command pity and yet make his downfall not repugnant to "our moral sense." Critics and

*** As Robert Edmond Jones has put it: "Great drama does not deal with cautious people. Its heroes are tyrants, outcasts, wanderers. From Prometheus, the first of them all, the thief who stole the divine fire from heaven, these protagonists are all passionate, excessive, violent, terrible. 'Doom eager,' the Icelandic saga calls them." *The Dramatic Imagination*, p. 42. [Author's note.]

philosophers, from Aristotle to Croce, have written about the spectator's acceptance of the hero's fate as a recognition of the moral order he has defied or ignored, the triumph of justice the hero himself is supposed to accept in his final "conciliation" or "epiphany." The restoration of the great moral order through suffering is looked upon as the Fate he has to fulfill. He must be imperfect to break the moral law, but fundamentally good, i.e. striving for perfection, in order to achieve his moral salvation in sacrifice, renunciation, death.

All this concern with the philosophical and ethical significance of the hero's sufferings, however, leads away from the *artistic* significance of the play, to discursive ideas about life, character, and the world. . . .

The kind of art theory that measures the value of drama by the way it represents life, or by the poet's implied beliefs about life, not only leads criticism away from poetry into philosophy, religion, or social science, but also causes people to think of the protagonist as an ordinary fellow man whom they are to approve or condemn and, in either case, pity. This attitude, which is undoubtedly derived — whether rightly or mistakenly — from Aristotle, has given rise to the many moral demands on the hero's character: he must be admirable but not perfect, must command the spectators' sympathy even if he incurs their censure; they must feel his fate as their own, etc.

In truth, I believe, the hero of tragedy must *interest* us all the time, but not as a person of our own acquaintance. His tragic error, crime, or other flaw is not introduced for moral reasons, but for structural purposes: it marks his limit of power. His potentialities appear on stage only as successful acts; as soon as his avowed or otherwise obvious intentions fail, or his acts recoil on him and bring him pain, his power has reached its height, he is at the end of his career. In this, of course, drama is utterly different from life. The moral failure in drama is not a normal incident, something to be lived down, presumably neither the doer's first transgression nor his last; the act that constitutes the protagonist's tragic error or guilt is the high-water mark of his life, and now the tide recedes. His "imperfection" is an artistic element: that is why a single flaw will do.

All persistent practices in art have a creative function. They may serve several ends, but the chief one is the shaping of the work. This holds not only for character traits which make a dramatic personage credible or sympathetic, but also for another much-discussed device in drama — so-called "comic relief," the introduction of trivial or humorous interludes in midst of serious, ominous, tragic action. The term "comic

relief" indicates the supposed purpose of that practice: to give the audience a respite from too much emotional tension, let them have entertainment as well as "pity and fear." Here again traditional criticism rests too
confidently, I think, on Aristotle's observations, which — after all —
were not the insights of a playwright, but the reflections of a scientifically
inclined man interested in psychology. Aristotle considered the comic
interlude as a concession to human weakness; and "comic relief" has
been its name ever since.

The humorous interludes in tragedy are merely moments when the
comic spirit rises to the point of hilarity. Such moments may result from
all sorts of poetic exigencies; the famous drunken porter in *Macbeth*
makes a macabre contrast to the situation behind the door he beats upon,
and is obviously introduced to heighten rather than relieve the tense
secrecy of the murder.

But the most important fact about these famous touches of "comic
relief" is that they always occur in plays which have a vein of comedy
throughout, kept for the most part below the level of laughter. This vein
may be tapped for special effects, even for a whole scene, to slow and
subdue the action or to heighten it with grotesque reflection. . . .

In *Macbeth* (and, indeed, all Shakespearean plays) there is a large,
social, everyday life of soldiers, grooms, gossips, courtiers and com-
moners, that provides an essentially comic substructure for the heroic
action. Most of the time this lower stratum is subdued, giving an impression of realism without any obvious byplay; but this realism carries the
fundamental comic rhythm from which grotesque interludes may arise
with perfect dramatic logic.

The fact that the two great rhythms, comic and tragic, are radically
distinct does not mean that they are each other's opposites, or even incompatible forms. Tragedy can rest squarely on a comic substructure,
and yet be pure tragedy. This is natural enough, for life — from which
all felt rhythms spring — contains both, in every mortal organism. Society is continuous though its members, even the strongest and fairest,
live out their lives and die; and even while each individual fulfills the
tragic pattern it participates also in the comic continuity. The poet's task
is, of course, not to copy life, but to organize and articulate a symbol for
the "sense of life"; and in the symbol one rhythm always governs the
dynamic form, though another may go through the whole piece in a contrapuntal fashion. The master of this practice is Shakespeare.

Did the stark individual Fate of the purest Greek tragedy rule out, by its intense deathward movement, the comic feeling of the eternally full and undulating stream of life? Or was the richness that the comic-tragic counterpoint creates in other poetic traditions supplied to Aeschylus and Sophocles by the choric dance which framed and embellished the play? The satyr play[7] at the end of the long, tragic presentation may well have been necessary, to assure its truth to the structure of subjective reality by an exuberant celebration of life. . . .

The element of pure show has an important function in dramatic art, for it tends to raise feeling, whatever the feeling is. It does this even in actual life: a splendid hall, an ornate table arrangement, a company in full dress, make a feast seem bigger and the gathering more illustrious than a plain table in a cafeteria, refectory, or gymnasium, with the guests in street dress. A splendid funeral, passing in procession behind chanting priests, is more solemn than a drab one, though perhaps no one at the spectacular service feels more sad than at the colorless one. In the theater, the element of show is a means of heightening the atmosphere, whether of gaiety or terror or woe; so it is, first of all, a ready auxiliary.

But in tragedy it has a more specialized and essential function, too. Tragedy, which expresses the consciousness of life and death, must make life seem worth while, rich, beautiful, to make death awesome. The splendid exaggerations of the stage serve tragic feeling by heightening the lure of the world. The beautiful world, as well as the emotional tone of the action, is magnified by the element of spectacle — by lighting and color, setting and grouping, music, dance, "excursions and alarums." Some playwrights avail themselves freely of this help; others dispense with it almost entirely (never quite; the theater is spectacular at any time), because they have other poetic means of giving virtual life the glory that death takes away, or despair — the "death of the soul" — corrupts. . . .

Drama is a great form, which not only invites expression of elemental human feeling, but also permits a degree of articulation, complexity, detail within detail, in short: organic development, that smaller poetic forms cannot exhibit without confusion. To say that such works express "a concept of feeling" is misleading unless one bears in mind that it is the whole life of feeling — call it "felt life," "subjectivity," "direct experience," or what you will — which finds its articulate expression in art, and, I believe, only in art. So great and fully elaborated a form as (say) a Shakespearean tragedy may formulate the characteristic mode

[7] The comedy that came after the performance of the tragic trilogy.

of perception and response, sensibility and emotion and their sympathetic overtones, that constitutes a whole personality. Here we see the process of art expression "writ large," as Plato would say; for the smallest work does the same thing as the greatest, on its own scale: it reveals the patterns of possible sentience, vitality, and mentality, objectifying our subjective being — the most intimate "Reality" that we know. This function, and not the recording of contemporary scenes, politics, or even moral attitudes, is what relates art to life; and the big unfolding of feeling in the organic, personal pattern of a human life, rising, growing, accomplishing destiny and meeting doom — that is tragedy.

ᴇᴈ FOR DISCUSSION AND WRITING

1. What is the "tragic rhythm"? How is it related to the "basic structure of personal life"? What is the distinction between comic destiny and tragic destiny? Can you relate what Mrs. Langer says in the fifth paragraph, about tragic destiny, with the famous statement of Heraclitus that "destiny is character"? How does she interpret what Aristotle says in the *Poetics* about the primacy of plot? A good exercise in clarification and in keeping your ideas straight would be to write a paragraph carefully summing up what Mrs. Langer says in the first six paragraphs of this piece.

2. What was the ancient mythical conception of fate? Explain why that conception provided a starting point for the tragic poets' creation of "character" as we understand the word today. What is the distinctive contrast between the mythical conception of fate and the conception of tragic destiny? Do we have any notion of "fate" today, as represented in common popular thought and expression, and if so, what is it?

3. Explain this statement, at the beginning of the tenth paragraph: "Tragedy can arise and flourish only where people are aware of individual life as an end in itself, and as a measure of other things." Why is it impossible for tribal cultures to conceive such a form? (If you have read Ruth Benedict's description of Zuñi culture, earlier in this book, you might use it in support of your answer to this question.)

4. What is the meaning of "A dramatic act is a commitment"? How does the "commitment" implied by a dramatic act lead to a "rhythm of action," or

"commanding form," or "organic form"? (If you have read Aristotle's *Poetics*, how are these terms related to what he calls "unity of action," and to the rule of "probability or necessity"?)

5. How, in the twelfth paragraph, is the term "heroism" interpreted? How, in the next two paragraphs, is this interpretation applied to *Hamlet*? And in the paragraph that follows, what distinction is made between actual biography and the life of the tragic hero?

6. Why does Mrs. Langer say that "drama is not psychology, nor . . . moral philosophy"? Does this statement conflict with your own ideas of what drama is or is for, and if so, what are the grounds of disagreement? (You might use some well-known play, such as *Hamlet,* as a case in point. Is it important chiefly as a psychological case history? or as an essay in moral philosophy? or what else? Since great drama is many things to many people, there may be no final, dogmatic answer to such questions, but to think about them and formulate one's own answers may be very helpful in clarifying one's attitudes.) In most classroom discussions of tragedy, what Aristotle speaks of as an "error or frailty" in the principal character (*hamartia,* or "tragic flaw") assumes a good deal of importance, more importance than it is actually given in the *Poetics*—probably because it is so easy for us to think of moral flaws as bringing about automatic retributive punishment (on our neighbors, of course—whereas we ourselves expect to live to a ripe old age, quite pleasantly, with our moral flaws). Explain Mrs. Langer's argument that the "tragic flaw" is an element of tragic art rather than of doctrinary morals or psychology.

7. How does she account, in terms of the "tragic rhythm" and "comic rhythm," for the presence of comic elements in tragedy—like the joshing of the gravediggers in *Hamlet,* or the scene in *Macbeth* where the drunken porter is aroused by the knocking at the gate? Explain this statement: "Tragedy can rest squarely on a comic substructure."

8. Why does she say that "the element of pure show" (what Aristotle calls "spectacle") has an important function in dramatic art and a special function in tragedy?

9. Write a short paper (two pages) showing your own understanding of Mrs. Langer's chapter on "The Tragic Rhythm," or comparing it with the *Poetics*, or interpreting either a Shakespearean or a modern tragedy in the terms set up here.

Giorgio Vasari ≈§ The Life of Leonardo da Vinci

≈§ Italian painter, architect, and art historian (1511-1574). Vasari studied under Michelangelo, but he is best known for his *Lives of the Painters, Sculptors, and Architects*. He was a child of eight when Leonardo died, in 1519, so that he had first-hand sources of information about that fabulous painter and inventive genius. (The translation below uses the variant spelling "Lionardo," but in common usage, both Italian and English, the spelling is "Leonardo.") ᶜᵉ

THE HEAVENS often rain down the richest gifts on human beings, naturally, but sometimes with lavish abundance bestow upon a single individual beauty, grace and ability, so that, whatever he does, every action is so divine that he distances all other men, and clearly displays how his genius is the gift of God and not an acquirement of human art. Men saw this in Lionardo da Vinci, whose personal beauty could not be exaggerated, whose every movement was grace itself and whose abilities were so extraordinary that he could readily solve every difficulty. He possessed great personal strength, combined with dexterity, and a spirit and courage invariably royal and magnanimous, and the fame of his name so spread abroad that, not only was he valued in his own day, but his renown has greatly increased since his death.

From *Lives of the Painters, Sculptors and Architects* by Giorgio Vasari. Translated by A. B. Hinds. Everyman's Library. Reprinted by permission of E. P. Dutton & Co., Inc.

This marvellous and divine Lionardo was the son of Piero da Vinci. He would have made great profit in learning had he not been so capricious and fickle, for he began to learn many things and then gave them up. Thus in arithmetic, during the few months that he studied it, he made such progress that he frequently confounded his master by continually raising doubts and difficulties. He devoted some time to music, and soon learned to play the lyre, and, being filled with a lofty and delicate spirit, he could sing and improvise divinely with it. Yet though he studied so many different things, he never neglected design and working in relief, those being the things which appealed to his fancy more than any other. When Ser Piero perceived this, and knowing the boy's soaring spirit, he one day took some of his drawings to Andrea del Verrocchio, who was his close friend, and asked his opinion whether Lionardo would do anything by studying design. Andrea was so amazed at these early efforts that he advised Ser Piero to have the boy taught. So it was decided that Lionardo should go to Andrea's workshop.* The boy was greatly delighted, and not only practised his profession, but all those in which design has a part. Possessed of a divine and marvellous intellect, and being an excellent geometrician, he not only worked in sculpture, doing some heads of women smiling, which were casts, and children's heads also, executed like a master, but also prepared many architectural plans and elevations, and he was the first, though so young, to propose to canalise the Arno from Pisa to Florence. He made designs for mills, fulling machines, and other engines to go by water, and as painting was to be his profession he studied drawing from life. He would make clay models of figures, draping them with soft rags dipped in plaster, and would then draw them patiently on thin sheets of cambric or linen, in black and white, with the point of the brush. He did these admirably, as may be seen by specimens in my book of designs. He also drew upon paper so carefully and well that no one has ever equalled him. I have a head in grisaille[1] which is divine. The grace of God so possessed his mind, his memory and intellect formed such a mighty union, and he could so clearly express his ideas in discourse, that he was able to confound the boldest opponents. Every day he made models and designs for the removal of mountains with ease and to pierce them to pass from one place to another, and by means of levers, cranes and winches to raise and draw

* About 1468.

[1] Gray monochrome painting.

heavy weights; he devised a method for cleansing ports, and to raise water from great depths, schemes which his brain never ceased to evolve. Many designs for these notions are scattered about, and I have seen numbers of them. He spent much time in making a regular design of a series of knots so that the cord may be traced from one end to the other, the whole filling a round space. There is a fine engraving of this most difficult design, and in the middle are the words: *Leonardus Vinci Academia.* Among these models and designs there was one which he several times showed to many able citizens who then ruled Florence, of a method of raising the church of S. Giovanni and putting steps under it without it falling down. He argued with so much eloquence that it was not until after his departure that they recognised the impossibility of such a feat.

His charming conversation won all hearts, and although he possessed nothing and worked little, he kept servants and horses of which he was very fond, and indeed he loved all animals, and trained them with great kindness and patience. Often, when passing places where birds were sold, he would let them out of their cages and pay the vendor the price asked. Nature had favoured him so greatly that in whatever his brain or mind took up he displayed unrivalled divinity, vigour, vivacity, excellence, beauty and grace. His knowledge of art, indeed, prevented him from finishing many things which he had begun, for he felt that his hand would be unable to realise the perfect creations of his imagination, as his mind formed such difficult, subtle and marvellous conceptions that his hands, skilful as they were, could never have expressed them. His interests were so numerous that his inquiries into natural phenomena led him to study the properties of herbs and to observe the movements of the heavens, the moon's orbit and the progress of the sun.

Lionardo was placed, as I have said, with Andrea del Verrocchio in his childhood by Ser Piero, and his master happened to be painting a picture of St. John baptising Christ.** For this Lionardo did an angel holding some clothes, and, although quite young, he made it far better than the figures of Andrea. The latter would never afterwards touch colours, chagrined that a child should know more than he. Lionardo was next employed to draw a cartoon of the Fall[2] for a portière in tapestry, to be made in Flanders of gold and silk, to send to the King of Portugal.

** About 1470.

[2] A "cartoon" is a sketch or preliminary drawing. The "Fall" refers to the Biblical story of the temptation of Adam and Eve — the "Fall of Man."

Here he did a meadow in grisaille, with the lights in white lead, containing much vegetation and some animals, unsurpassed for finish and naturalness. There is a fig-tree, the leaves and branches beautifully foreshortened and executed with such care that the mind is amazed at the amount of patience displayed. There is also a palm-tree, the rotundity of the dates being executed with great and marvellous art, due to the patience and ingenuity of Lionardo. This work was not carried farther, and the cartoon is now in Florence in the fortunate house of Ottaviano de' Medici the Magnificent, to whom it was given not long ago by Lionardo's uncle.

It is said that when Ser Piero was at his country-seat he was requested by a peasant of his estate to get a round piece of wood painted for him at Florence, which he had cut from a fig-tree on his farm. Piero readily consented, as the man was very skilful in catching birds and fishing, and was very useful to him in such matters. Accordingly Piero brought the wood to Florence and asked Lionardo to paint something upon it, without telling him its history. Lionardo, on taking it up to examine it one day, found it warped, badly prepared and rude, but with the help of fire he made it straight, and giving it to a turner, had it rendered soft and smooth instead of being rough and rude. Then, after preparing the surface in his own way, he began to cast about what he should paint on it, and resolved to do the Medusa head[3] to terrify all beholders. To a room, to which he alone had access, Lionardo took lizards, newts, maggots, snakes, butterflies, locusts, bats, and other animals of the kind, out of which he composed a horrible and terrible monster, of poisonous breath, issuing from a dark and broken rock, belching poison from its open throat, fire from its eyes, and smoke from its nostrils, of truly terrible and horrible aspect. He was so engrossed with the work that he did not notice the terrible stench of the dead animals, being absorbed in his love for art. His father and the peasant no longer asked for the work, and when it was finished Lionardo told his father to send for it when he pleased, as he had done his part. Accordingly Ser Piero went to his rooms one morning to fetch it. When he knocked at the door Lionardo opened it and told him to wait a little, and, returning to his room, put the round panel in the light on his easel, and having arranged the window to make the light dim, he called his father in. Ser Piero, taken unaware, started back, not thinking of the round piece of wood, or that the face which he

[3] The Medusa was one of the snake-haired Gorgons, whose look turned men to stone.

saw was painted, and was beating a retreat when Lionardo detained him and said, "This work has served its purpose; take it away, then, as it has produced the effect intended." Ser Piero indeed thought it more than miraculous, and he warmly praised Lionardo's idea. He then quietly went and bought another round wheel with a heart transfixed by a dart painted upon it, and gave it to the peasant, who was grateful to Piero all his life. Piero took Lionardo's work secretly to Florence and sold it to some merchants for 100 ducats, and in a short time it came into the hands of the Duke of Milan, who bought it of them for 300 ducats.

Lionardo next did a very excellent Madonna, which afterwards belonged to Pope Clement VII. Among other things it contained a bowl of water with some marvellous flowers, the dew upon them seeming actually to be there, so that they looked more real than reality itself. For his good friend Antonio Segni he drew a Neptune on paper, with so much design and care that he seemed alive. The sea is troubled and his car is drawn by sea-horses, with the sprites, monsters, and south winds and other fine marine creatures. . . .

Lionardo was so delighted when he saw curious heads, whether bearded or hairy, that he would follow about anyone who had thus attracted his attention for a whole day, acquiring such a clear idea of him that when he went home he would draw the head as well as if the man had been present. In this way many heads of men and women came to be drawn, and I have several such pen-and-ink drawings in my book, so often referred to. Among them is the head of Amerigo Vespucci, a fine old man, drawn in carbon, and that of Scaramuccia, the gipsy captain. . . .

On the death of Giovan. Galeazzo, Duke of Milan, and the accession of Ludovico Sforza in the same year, 1493, Lionardo was invited to Milan with great ceremony by the duke to play the lyre, in which that prince greatly delighted. Lionardo took his own instrument, made by himself in silver, and shaped like a horse's head, a curious and novel idea to render the harmonies more loud and sonorous, so that he surpassed all the musicians who had assembled there. Besides this he was the best reciter of improvised rhymes of his time. The duke, captivated by Lionardo's conversation and genius, conceived an extraordinary affection for him. He begged him to paint an altar-picture of the Nativity, which was sent by the duke to the emperor. Lionardo then did a Last Supper for the Dominicans at S. Maria delle Grazie in Milan, endowing the heads of the

Apostles with such majesty and beauty that he left that of Christ unfinished, feeling that he could not give it that celestial divinity which it demanded. This work left in such a condition has always been held in the greatest veneration by the Milanese and by other foreigners, as Lionardo has seized the moment when the Apostles are anxious to discover who would betray their Master. All their faces are expressive of love, fear, wrath or grief at not being able to grasp the meaning of Christ, in contrast to the obstinacy, hatred and treason of Judas, while the whole work, down to the smallest details, displays incredible diligence, even the texture of the tablecloth being clearly visible so that actual cambric would not look more real. It is said that the prior incessantly importuned Lionardo to finish the work, thinking it strange that the artist should pass half a day at a time lost in thought. He would have desired him never to lay down the brush, as if he were digging a garden. Seeing that his importunity produced no effect, he had recourse to the duke, who felt compelled to send for Lionardo to inquire about the work, showing tactfully that he was driven to act by the importunity of the prior. Lionardo, aware of the acuteness and discretion of the duke, talked with him fully about the picture, a thing which he had never done with the prior. He spoke freely of his art, and explained how men of genius really are doing most when they work least, as they are thinking out ideas and perfecting the conceptions, which they subsequently carry out with their hands. He added that there were still two heads to be done, that of Christ, which he would not look for on the earth, and felt unable to conceive the beauty of the celestial grace that must have been incarnate in the divinity. The other head was that of Judas, which also caused him thought, as he did not think he could express the face of a man who could resolve to betray his Master, the Creator of the world, after having received so many benefits. But he was willing in this case to seek no farther, and for lack of a better he would do the head of the importunate and tactless prior. The duke was wonderfully amused, and laughingly declared that he was quite right. Then the poor prior, covered with confusion, went back to his garden and left Lionardo in peace, while the artist indeed finished his Judas, making him a veritable likeness of treason and cruelty. The head of Christ was left unfinished, as I have said. The nobility of this painting, in its composition and the care with which it was finished, induced the King of France to wish to take it home with him. Accordingly he employed architects to frame it in wood and iron, so that it might be transported in safety, without any regard for the cost, so great was his desire. But the king was thwarted by its being done on the wall, and it remained with the Milanese. . . .

He afterwards devoted even greater care to the study of the anatomy of men, aiding and being aided by M. Marcantonio della Torre, a profound philosopher, who then professed at Padua and wrote upon the subject.[4] I have heard it said that he was one of the first who began to illustrate the science of medicine, by the learning of Galen, and to throw true light upon anatomy, up to that time involved in the thick darkness of ignorance. In this he was marvellously served by the genius, work and hands of Lionardo, who made a book about it with red crayon drawings[***] outlined with the pen, in which he foreshortened and portrayed with the utmost diligence. He did the skeleton, adding all the nerves and muscles, the first attached to the bone, the others keeping it firm and the third moving, and in the various parts he wrote notes in curious characters, using his left hand, and writing from right to left, so that it cannot be read without practice, and only at a mirror. . . .

When Lionardo was at Milan the King of France came there and desired him to do something curious; accordingly he made a lion whose chest opened after he had walked a few steps, discovering himself to be full of lilies. At Milan Lionardo took Salai of that city as his pupil. This was a graceful and beautiful youth with fine curly hair, in which Lionardo greatly delighted. He taught him many things in art, and some works which are attributed in Milan to Salai were retouched by Lionardo. He returned to Florence, where he found that the Servite friars had allotted to Filippino[5] the picture of the high altar of the Nunziata. At this Lionardo declared that he should like to have done a similar thing. Filippino heard this, and being very courteous, he withdrew. The friars, wishing Lionardo to paint it, brought him to their house, paying all his expenses and those of his household. He kept them like this for a long time, but never began anything. At length he drew a cartoon of the Virgin and St. Anne with a Christ, which not only filled every artist with wonder, but, when it was finished and set up in the room, men and

---

[4] The word "professed" is used here in the sense of "taught" (compare the word "professor"). Galen, mentioned below, was a Greek physician of the second century A.D.

[***] Between 1495 and 1498.

[5] Filippino Lippi, fifteenth-century painter.

women, young and old, flocked to see it for two days, as if it had been a
festival, and they marvelled exceedingly. The face of the Virgin displays
all the simplicity and beauty which can shed grace on the Mother of God,
showing the modesty and humility of a Virgin contentedly happy, in
seeing the beauty of her Son, whom she tenderly holds in her lap. As she
regards it the little St. John at her feet is caressing a lamb, while St. Anne
smiles in her great joy at seeing her earthly progeny become divine, a
conception worthy of the great intellect and genius of Lionardo. . . .

   For Francesco del Giocondo Lionardo undertook the portrait of
Mona Lisa, his wife, and left it incomplete after working at it for four
years. This work is now in the possession of Francis, King of France, at
Fontainebleau. This head is an extraordinary example of how art can
imitate Nature, because here we have all the details painted with great
subtlety. The eyes possess that moist lustre which is constantly seen in
life, and about them are those livid reds and hair which cannot be rendered without the utmost delicacy. The lids could not be more natural,
for the way in which the hairs issue from the skin, here thick and there
scanty, and following the pores of the skin. The nose possesses the fine
delicate reddish apertures seen in life. The opening of the mouth, with
its red ends, and the scarlet cheeks seem not colour but living flesh. To
look closely at her throat you might imagine that the pulse was beating.
Indeed, we may say that this was painted in a manner to cause the
boldest artists to despair. Mona Lisa was very beautiful, and while Lionardo was drawing her portrait he engaged people to play and sing, and
jesters to keep her merry, and remove that melancholy which painting
usually gives to portraits. This figure of Lionardo's has such a pleasant
smile that it seemed rather divine than human, and was considered
marvellous, an exact copy of Nature.

   The fame of this divine artist grew to such a pitch by the excellence
of his works that all who delighted in the arts and the whole city wished
him to leave some memorial, and they endeavoured to think of some
noteworthy decorative work through which the state might be adorned
and honoured by the genius, grace and judgment characteristic of his
work. The great hall of the council was being rebuilt . . . , and being
finished with great speed, it was ordained by public decree that Lionardo
should be employed to paint some fine work. . . . He designed a group of
horsemen fighting for a standard, a masterly work on account of his
treatment of the fight, displaying the wrath, anger and vindictiveness of

men and horses; two of the latter, with their front legs involved, are waging war with their teeth no less fiercely than their riders are fighting for the standard. One soldier, putting his horse to the gallop, has turned round and, grasping the staff of the standard, is endeavouring by main force to wrench it from the hands of four others, while two are defending it, trying to cut the staff with their swords; an old soldier in a red cap has a hand on the staff, as he cries out, and holds a scimetar in the other and threatens to cut off both hands of the two, who are grinding their teeth and making every effort to defend their banner. On the ground, between the legs of the horses, are two foreshortened figures who are fighting together, while a soldier lying prone has another over him who is raising his arm as high as he can to run his dagger with his utmost strength into his adversary's throat; the latter, whose legs and arms are helpless, does what he can to escape death. The manifold designs Lionardo made for the costumes of his soldiers defy description, not to speak of the scimetars and other ornaments, and his incredible mastery of form and line in dealing with horses, which he made better than any other master, with their powerful muscles and graceful beauty. It is said that for designing the cartoon he made an ingenious scaffolding which rose higher when pressed together and broadened out when lowered. Thinking that he could paint on the wall in oils, he made a composition so thick for laying on the wall that when he continued his painting it began to run and spoil what had been begun, so that in a short time he was forced to abandon it. . . .

He went to Rome with Duke Giuliano de' Medici on the election of Leo X,[6] who studied philosophy and especially alchemy. On the way he made a paste with wax and constructed hollow animals which flew in the air when blown up, but fell when the wind ceased. On a curious lizard found by the vine-dresser of Belvedere he fastened scales taken from other lizards, dipped in quicksilver, which trembled as it moved, and after giving it eyes, a horn and a beard, he tamed it and kept it in a box. All the friends to whom he showed it ran away terrified. He would often dry and purge the guts of a wether and make them so small that they might be held in the palm of the hand. In another room he kept a pair of smith's bellows, and with these he would blow out one of the guts until it filled the room, which was a large one, forcing anyone there to

[6] Giovanni de' Medici, elected Pope in 1513.

take refuge in a corner. The fact that it had occupied such a little space at first only added to the wonder. He perpetrated many such follies, studied mirrors and made curious experiments to find oil for painting and varnish to preserve the work done. . . . It is said that, on being commissioned by the Pope to do a work, he straightway began to distil oil and herbs to make the varnish, which induced Pope Leo to say: "This man will never do anything, for he begins to think of the end before the beginning!"

There was no love lost between him and Michelagnolo Buonarroti, so that the latter left Florence owing to their rivalry, Duke Giuliano excusing him by saying that he was summoned by the Pope to do the façade of S. Lorenzo. When Lionardo heard this, he left for France, where the king had heard of his works and wanted him to do the cartoon of St. Anne in colours. But Lionardo, as was his wont, gave him nothing but words for a long time. At length, having become old, he lay sick for many months, and seeing himself near death, he desired to occupy himself with the truths of the Catholic Faith and the holy Christian religion. Then, having confessed and shown his penitence with much lamentation, he devoutly took the Sacrament out of his bed, supported by his friends and servants, as he could not stand. The king arriving, for he would often pay him friendly visits, he sat up in bed from respect, and related the circumstances of his sickness, showing how greatly he had offended God and man in not having worked in his art as he ought. He was then seized with a paroxysm, the harbinger of death, so that the king rose and took his head to assist him and show him favour as well as to alleviate the pain. Lionardo's divine spirit, then recognising that he could not enjoy a greater honour, expired in the king's arms, at the age of seventy-five. The loss of Lionardo caused exceptional grief to those who had known him, because there never was a man who did so much honour to painting. By the splendour of his magnificent mien he comforted every sad soul, and his eloquence could turn men to either side of a question. His personal strength was prodigious, and with his right hand he could bend the clapper of a knocker or a horseshoe as if they had been of lead. His liberality warmed the hearts of all his friends, both rich and poor, if they possessed talent and ability. His presence adorned and honoured the most wretched and bare apartment. Thus Florence received a great gift in the birth of Lionardo, and its loss in his death was immeasurable.

◄§ FOR DISCUSSION AND WRITING

1. Vasari's life of Leonardo gives us an invaluable view of the great painter, because Vasari was a countryman and near contemporary of Leonardo and himself a painter. What is Vasari's general attitude toward Leonardo? Point out four or five sentences that clearly express his attitude. Our century often seems flat, drab, and cinderish for lack of heroes and lack of the temperament for admiration and praise; even in college classrooms we tend to feel that we enhance our personal intellectual status if we can tear down or do damage to heroic images and submit them to the test of the dust. Can you explain this tendency? You might find here a subject for a short paper, using Vasari's life of Leonardo as example of an opposite attitude.

2. What explanation does Vasari offer of Leonardo's capriciousness in beginning projects and not finishing them? What examples does he give of Leonardo's gift for mechanics and engineering? Point out two or three places where Vasari praises Leonardo's painting for its "imitation of nature." Vasari's interpretation of mimesis or "imitation" is fairly typical of Renaissance thought about the function of the arts, which was to "hold the mirror up to nature," as Hamlet put it. If you have read the *Poetics*, do you feel that Vasari's idea of "imitation" agrees with that of Aristotle? (You might consider his remarks on the "Mona Lisa" in this connection.)

3. Suggestions for writing: look up, in the Fine Arts section of the library, some good reproductions of Leonardo's paintings, and write a paper simply describing them (this simple kind of descriptive paper can turn out to be a real joy, holding more challenge and excitement than one may have imagined); or look up Leonardo's famous Notebooks (which he wrote in "mirror-writing"), where you will find all sorts of curious ideas coming hot off the brainpan, and write a paper describing them; or, if you have an interest in psychology, you might want to read Freud's essay on Leonardo —which is fairly short but full of challenging ideas—and write a paper on it.

The Genius of Michelangelo ⇜ An Interview with Henry Moore

⇜ The following interview with the celebrated English sculptor Henry Moore is conducted by David Sylvester, British critic and lecturer; it marks the four-hundredth year since the death of Michelangelo. Moore was born in 1898 and studied at the Royal College of Art. His early work was angular and rough, inspired by pre-Columbian art. From about 1928 he began to develop a more personal style, working in wood, stone, and cement without clay models. During the Second World War, when materials for carving were scarce, he concentrated on drawing, and in 1940 was commissioned by the government to do a series of studies in the underground bomb shelters. His monumental sculptures, characterized by organic form, often with holes in the solid mass that open up the form to the space around it, are found in almost every leading museum in the world and have made him one of the very few great sculptors of our time. (See Frontispiece.)

Michelangelo Buonarroti (1475-1564), one of the most powerful sculptors of the Italian Renaissance, was also a brilliant painter and architect and a prolific poet. Most of his important work was done in Florence and Rome; sponsored early in his life (1489-1492) by Lorenzo de' Medici, he later executed numerous commissions for members of the Medici family. The "Moses" discussed in this selection was part of the tomb of Pope Julius II; the "Night" and "Day" are reclining figures on the sarcophagi of Giuliano and Lorenzo de' Medici. The Rondanini Pietà is in the Castello Sforza in Milan. ⇝

SYLVESTER: Your generation of *avant-garde* artists tended to react against Renaissance art. I know that you yourself as a student were especially interested in things like pre-Columbian and African art. Where did you see Michelangelo in relation to this?

MOORE: I still knew that as an individual he was an absolute superman. Even before I became a student, I'd taken a peculiar obsessive

This interview appeared in the *New York Times Magazine* for March 8, 1964. © 1964 by The New York Times Company. Reprinted by permission. Acknowledgment is also made to Sir Henry Moore and Mr. David Sylvester.

interest in him, though I didn't know what his work was like until I won a traveling scholarship and went to Italy. And then I saw he had such ability that beside him any sculptor must feel as a miler would knowing someone had once run a three-minute mile.

Take the "Moses." The way he builds up a mass of detail yet keeps the same vision and dignity throughout it — it really is staggering that anyone should do that out of such an intractable material as marble. There's an ability to realize his conception completely in the material and to find no restrictions or difficulties in doing it. You look at any of the parts and it's absolutely perfect: there's no hesitation — it's by someone who can do just what he wants to do. But later his technical achievement became less important to him, when he knew that the technical thing was something he could do without worrying.

I do dislike in some of his sculptures, like the figures of "Night" and "Day," the kind of leathery thickness of the skin. You feel that the bodies are covered with a skin that is half an inch thick rather than a skin such as you see in the Ilissus of the Parthenon. The skin there is exactly skin thick, whereas in some of Michelangelo's middle-period sculptures there's a thick leatheriness that looks to me a little bit repellent. Nevertheless in a work like the "Night," there's a grandeur of gesture and scale that for me is what great sculpture is. The reason I can't look at Bernini, or even Donatello,[1] beside him is his tremendous monumentality, his over-life-size vision. What sculpture should have for me is this monumentality rather than details that are sensitive.

SYLVESTER: Do you ever find yourself put off by that high polish on his marble?

MOORE: Sometimes. But in the "Night" or the "Moses" you'd lose something without that high polish. In some of his works he used contrast between a highly finished part and a part that is not so finished, and this is something one likes.

I would say that all young sculptors would be better if they were made to finish their early works to the very utmost. It's like a singer learning to sing higher than he can readily go, so that he can then sing within his own range. In the same way, if you can finish a sculpture, later you can afford to leave some parts unfinished. And for me Michel-

[1] Bernini was an Italian sculptor of the seventeenth century, Donatello of the fifteenth.

angelo's greatest work is one that was in his studio partly finished, partly unfinished, when he died — the Rondanini "Pietà."[2] I don't know of any other single work of art by anyone that is more poignant, more moving. It isn't the most powerful of Michelangelo's works — it's a mixture, in fact, of two styles.

It must have been started at least 10 years before his death and at some stage was probably nearly finished throughout, in the style that the legs are in still. Then Michelangelo must have decided that he was dissatisfied with it or wanted to change it. And the changing became so drastic that I think he knocked the head off the sculpture. Because, if you look at that arm, which hangs there detached from the body of Christ, you see that it ends less than halfway up the biceps, yet this brings it nearly level to the shoulder of the existing figure. So the figure must originally have been a good deal taller. And if we also see the proportion of the length of the body of Christ compared with the length of the legs, there's no doubt that the whole top of the original sculpture has been cut away.

Now this to me is a great question. Why should I and other sculptors I know, my contemporaries — I think that Giacometti feels this, I know Marino Marini feels it — find this work one of the most moving and greatest works we know of when it's a work which has such disunity in it? There's a fragment — the arm — of the sculpture in a previous stage still left there; here are the legs finished as they were perhaps 10 years previously, but the top recarved so that the hand of the Madonna on the chest of Christ is only a paper-thin ribbon.

But that's so moving, so touching; the position of the heads, the whole tenderness of the top part of the sculpture, is in my opinion more what it is by being in contrast with the rather finished, tough, leathery, typical Michelangelo legs. The top part is Gothic and the lower part is sort of Renaissance. So it's a work of art that for me means more because it doesn't fit in with all the theories of critics and estheticians who say that one of the great things about a work of art must be its unity of style.

SYLVESTER: It has been called by some historians a wreck — which seems obtuse.

MOORE: It does to me, because it's like finding the altered work of all old men a wreck. I think the explanation is perhaps that by this time

[2] See Question 2, page 1062.

Michelangelo knew he was near death and his values were more spiritual than they had been. I think also he came to know that, in a work of art, the expression of the spirit of the person — the expression of the artist's outlook on life — is what matters more than a finished or a beautiful or a perfect work of art.

I'm sure that had he taken away the nearly detached arm we should find it less moving because that part is near the new part. And undoubtedly, in my opinion, had he recarved the legs to have the same quality as the top, the whole work would have lost its point. This contrast, this disunity of style, brings together two of the Ages of Man, as it were.

SYLVESTER: It's not great in spite of its disunity but because of it?

MOORE: For me it's great because the very things that a lot of art writers would find wrong in it are what give it its greatness. There's something of the same principle in his unfinished "Slaves"— so-called unfinished: I don't think they're unfinished, because though Michelangelo might have gone on a bit more, I can't conceive that he would ever have wanted to finish them in the high way he finished other works.

Here again it's that same contrast — a contrast between two opposites, like the rough and the smooth, the old and the new, the spiritual and the anatomic. Here in this "Pietà" is the thin expressionist work set against the realistic style of the arm. Why should that hand, which scarcely exists, be so expressive? Why should Michelangelo, out of nothing, achieve that feeling of somebody touching another body with such tenderness? I just don't know. But it comes, I think, from the spirit. And it seems to me to have something of the same quality as the late "Crucifixion" drawings.

SYLVESTER: They are certainly the other works by Michelangelo to which the Rondanini "Pietà" relates. For one thing, they have the same stark up-and-down movement.

MOORE: Yes, I think that toward the end of his life he was someone who knew that a lot of the swagger didn't count. His values had changed to more deeply fundamental human values.

SYLVESTER: By the way, the arm that remains from the earlier state echoes the vertical movement of the group.

MOORE: Yes, that's maybe why he left it and didn't want to lose it. He wasn't dissatisfied. But I think there was no such conscious kind of design. I think that the parts he disliked he would alter and the parts he didn't dislike he'd leave.

And this is how artists work. It isn't that they work out — at least

I don't — a theory, like saying, "This is upright and I'm going to leave it because it fits in with my new thing." It's because you *see* it fits in that you leave it — you're satisfied with it. It's that you work from satisfaction and dissatisfaction. You alter the things that don't seem right and you leave the things that are more right to go on with sometime later.

SYLVESTER: But why does this kind of simplicity in Michelangelo produce such a different effect from the kind you get in archaic forms of sculpture?

MOORE: Well, I think that if you do the opposite of something which you have a full experience of doing, the seeds of the previous thing will still be there. That is, nothing is ever lost, nothing is ever missing. The "Crucifixion" drawings are very simplified, without the twisting and turning of the earlier Michelangelo, yet they have a slight movement, a slight hang and turn that give a sense of agonized weight. All his past experience is in them.

This is the kind of quality you get in the work of old men who are really great. They can simplify; they can leave out. Even someone like Matisse can just sit in his bed, ill and sick, nearly dying, and with a pair of scissors and so on he can cut out things — and why they're so good is because of the past history of Matisse. There's this little difference that he makes which some young man trying to imitate him would never make.

SYLVESTER: But what is it that makes you like the unfinished "Slaves" better than the finished ones?

MOORE: I prefer them because they have more power in them, to me, much more power than the finished ones. That one in the Louvre is much too weary and sleepy and lackadaisical.

SYLVESTER: Well, it's meant to be dying.

MOORE: I know, but I mean you can have a thing that's dying and yet it has the vitality of the sculptor in it.

SYLVESTER: Maybe the more finished works are often less sympathetic just because they express Michelangelo's fantasy more clearly and we find certain things in his fantasy repellent. For instance, that leathery skin in the figure of "Night." With the unfinished "Slaves," you don't refer them back in a literal way to life in the same way as you do the "Night."

MOORE: No. And when one compares her breasts to a real woman's breasts, one finds them unpleasant. And I think in some of Michelangelo there can be a kind of melancholic, lazy slowness. I admire that, but I don't like it, and that's perhaps why, when he hasn't arrived at that, like in the unfinished "Slaves"— where that can't come in because he hasn't had the time to put it in — they appeal to one more.

But one still admires "Night." I mean, this is still an unbelievable pose. The whole attitude of the figure, the grandeur, the magnificence of the conception is still a wonderful thing. In all his work — early, middle, late — there's no sculptor of more ability. He could do anything he wanted.

✑ FOR DISCUSSION AND WRITING

1. As a part of this assignment you should look up some reproductions of Moore's own work as well as Michelangelo's; you should be able to find these in the Fine Arts section of your college library. With several of Michelangelo's sculptures before you either in photographic reproduction or in your mind's eye, do you find any examples of the contrast Moore speaks of, between highly finished parts and parts left fairly rough? He says, "This is something one likes"; could you go farther and attempt to explain why it is "something one likes"? (Since we aren't pretending to be art critics or connoisseurs here, one needn't be timid about expressing one's own reaction.) What point does Moore make about an artist's learning to give high finish to his early work, before experimenting with unfinished parts? Does this point apply to other arts than sculpture? Does it apply to writing? (Instead of answering such questions with an "Ummm-hmmm" and a bright look on your face signifying comprehension, try to illustrate your answers with concrete examples.)

2. A good part of Moore's discussion concerns the Rondanini *Pietà*. "*Pietà*" is a term used for representations of the Virgin Mary holding or supporting the dead body of Christ just after he was taken down from the cross. Since there is another famous *Pietà* by Michelangelo, in which the Virgin holds the dead Christ across her knees, you want to make sure—in looking for reproductions—that you have the *Pietà* Moore is talking about, called the Rondanini, where both figures are upright and the whole sculpture is on vertical lines. From Moore's description you will not mistake it, but you must see a reproduction, or his discussion of it will have little meaning. Where in this sculpture do you find "finished" and "unfinished" parts, the "mixture of two styles" Moore speaks of? (The story, presumably true, is that Michelangelo—then a crippled and ailing old man—got out of bed one night, took a hammer, and ruthlessly knocked off the whole top part of

the finished work: an incident that is one of the most heroic and deeply moving examples of the integrity of the artist.) We are all acquainted, in one relationship or another, with the critical dictum about the necessity of unity in a work of art; if you have read the *Poetics*, you will have found it in Aristotle's discussion of unity of action; and your English professor has undoubtedly called your attention to the dismal effect, on your grade, of lack of unity in your written compositions. What is Moore's attitude about the "disunity" of the Rondanini *Pietà?* (This does not mean, of course, that we can all become Michelangelesque by flouting the principle of unity.)

3. What does Moore mean when he attempts to explain the Rondanini *Pietà* by saying that Michelangelo's "values" became "more spiritual" in his old age, and how does the statement apply to the sculpture in an artistic sense—aside from the religious subject matter? What does he mean by the following: "I think also he came to know that, in a work of art, the expression of the spirit of the person . . . is what matters more than a finished or a beautiful or a perfect work of art"? What does Moore have to say about "conscious design" in a work such as the *Pietà?*

4. In an oral interview one does not look for exactly the same qualities one may expect to find in a considered piece of writing; the occasion is quite different, more than one person is involved, and there is no time for polishing up one's statements as one might do in writing. But there are qualities in an oral situation that can be transferred very helpfully to writing situations, particularly when one's writing tends to become overcomplicated, floundering about in a lot of words, or when one is paralyzed by the prospect of filling up a sheet of blank paper, with one's mind empty as an old barn. *Talking* about the topic, either to someone else or to oneself, and then putting down immediately on paper what one has said orally, just the way it was said, may solve the problem, giving naturalness and spontaneity to one's writing, releasing ideas that have become strangled, even curing deficiencies of grammar and of coherence. As a writing assignment you might try out this method by deliberately arranging an "interview" with someone, preferably someone who has excellence in his job—whether the job is cooking, or repairing automobiles, or selling insurance or vacuum cleaners or Fuller brushes, or digging postholes, or managing a bank, or painting, or dancing, or acting, or even teaching. Write up the interview following as closely as possible the actual words said, both your own and the other person's.

5. Another writing assignment might be on Michelangelo's life, which would involve a bit of research.

John Ruskin ⤐ The Stones of St. Mark's

⤐ English art critic and social theorist (1819-1900). Ruskin was educated at Oxford; when he was twenty-one he suffered a breakdown in health and thereafter traveled widely in the attempt to recover. From boyhood he had been an ardent student of art, and in 1843, when he was twenty-four, published the first volume of *Modern Painters*, a work that went on for five volumes. *The Seven Lamps of Architecture* and *The Stones of Venice* followed, and then works in which art criticism became social and political criticism— *Sesame and Lilies, The Crown of Wild Olive, Fors Clavigera*. He held the first Professorship of Art in England, as Slade Professor at Oxford. ⤏

AND NOW I wish that the reader, before I bring him into St. Mark's Place,[1] would imagine himself for a little time in a quiet English cathedral town, and walk with me to the west front of its cathedral. Let us go together up the more retired street, at the end of which we can see the pinnacles of one of the towers, and then through the low grey gateway, with its battlemented top and small latticed window in the centre, into the inner private-looking road or close, where nothing goes in but the carts of the tradesmen who supply the bishop and the chapter,[2] and where there are little shaven grass-plots, fenced in by neat rails, before

From *The Stones of Venice* by John Ruskin, edited by J. G. Links (London: Collins, 1960).

[1] The great square in Venice before the cathedral.

[2] The clergy associated with the cathedral.

old-fashioned groups of somewhat diminutive and excessively trim houses, with little oriel and bay windows, jutting out here and there, and deep wooden cornices and eaves painted cream colour and white, and small porches to their doors in the shape of cockle-shells, or little, crooked, thick, indescribable wooden gables warped a little on one side; and so forward till we come to larger houses, also old-fashioned, but of red brick, and with garden behind them, and fruit walls, which show here and there, among the nectarines, the vestiges of an old cloister arch or shaft, and looking in front on the cathedral square itself, laid out in rigid divisions of smooth grass and gravel walk, yet not un-cheerful, especially on the sunny side, where the canons'[3] children are walking with their nurserymaids. And so, taking care not to tread on the grass, we will go along the straight walk to the west front, and there stand for a time, looking up at its deep-pointed porches and the dark places between their pillars where there were statues once, and where the fragments, here and there, of a stately figure are still left, which has in it the likeness of a king, perhaps indeed a king on earth, perhaps a saintly king long ago in heaven; and so higher and higher up to the great mouldering wall of rugged sculpture and confused arcades, shat-tered, and grey, and grisly with heads of dragons and mocking fiends, worn by the rain and swirling winds into yet unseemlier shape, and coloured on their stony scales by the deep russet-orange lichen, melan-choly gold; and so, higher still, to the bleak towers, so far above that the eye loses itself among the bosses[4] of their traceries, though they are rude and strong, and only sees like a drift of eddying black points, now closing, now scattering, and now settling suddenly into invisible places among the bosses and flowers, the crowd of restless birds that fill the whole square with that strange clangour of theirs, so harsh and yet so soothing, like the cries of birds on a solitary coast between the cliffs and sea.

Think for a little while of that scene, and the meaning of all its small formalisms, mixed with its serene sublimity. Estimate its secluded, continuous, drowsy felicities, and its evidence of the sense and steady performance of such kind of duties as can be regulated by the cathedral clock; and weigh the influence of those dark towers on all who have passed through the lonely square at their feet for centuries, and on all

[3] Chapter members (see preceding note).

[4] Protuberant ornamental carvings marking centers of architectural design.

who have seen them rising far away over the wooded plain, or catching on their square masses the last rays of the sunset, when the city at their feet was indicated only by the mist at the bend of the river. And then let us quickly recollect that we are in Venice, and land at the extremity of the Calle Lunga San Moisè, which may be considered as there answering to the secluded street that led us to our English cathedral gateway.

We find ourselves in a paved alley, some seven feet wide where it is widest, full of people, and resonant with cries of itinerant salesmen, — a shriek in their beginning, and dying away into a kind of brazen ringing, all the worse for its confinement between the high houses of the passage along which we have to make our way. Overhead an inextricable confusion of rugged shutters, and iron balconies and chimney flues pushed out on brackets to save room, and arched windows with projecting sills of Istrian stone, and gleams of green leaves here and there where a fig-tree branch escapes over a lower wall from some inner cortile,[5] leading the eye up to the narrow stream of blue sky high over all. On each side, a row of shops, as densely set as may be, occupying, in fact, intervals between the square stone shafts, about eight feet high, which carry the first floors: intervals of which one is narrow and serves as a door; the other is, in the more respectable shops, wainscotted to the height of the counter and glazed above, but in those of the poorer tradesmen left open to the ground, and the wares laid on benches and tables in the open air, the light in all cases entering at the front only, and fading away in a few feet from the threshold into a gloom which the eye from without cannot penetrate, but which is generally broken by a ray or two from a feeble lamp at the back of the shop, suspended before a print of the Virgin.

A yard or two farther, we pass the hostelry of the Black Eagle, and glancing as we pass through the square door of marble, deeply moulded, in the outer wall, we see the shadows of its pergola of vines resting on an ancient well, with a pointed shield carved on its side; and so presently emerge on the bridge and Campo San Moisè, whence to the entrance into St. Mark's Place, called the Bocca di Piazza (mouth of the square), the Venetian character is nearly destroyed, first by the frightful façade of San Moisè and then by the modernising of the shops as they near the piazza, and the mingling with the lower Venetian populace of

[5] Small patio or courtyard.

lounging groups of English and Austrians. We will push fast through them into the shadow of the pillars at the end of the "Bocca di Piazza," and then we forget them all; for between those pillars there opens a great light, and, in the midst of it, as we advance slowly, the vast tower of St. Mark seems to lift itself visibly forth from the level field of chequered stones; and, on each side, the countless arches prolong themselves into ranged symmetry, as if the rugged and irregular houses that pressed together above us in the dark alley had been struck back into sudden obedience and lovely order, and all their rude casements and broken walls had been transformed into arches charged with goodly sculpture, and fluted shafts of delicate stone.

And well may they fall back, for beyond those troops of ordered arches there rises a vision out of the earth, and all the great square seems to have opened from it in a kind of awe, that we may see it far away; — a multitude of pillars and white domes, clustered into a long low pyramid of coloured light; a treasure-heap, it seems, partly of gold, and partly of opal and mother-of-pearl, hollowed beneath into five great vaulted porches, ceiled with fair mosaic, and beset with sculpture of alabaster, clear as amber and delicate as ivory, — sculpture fantastic and involved, of palm leaves and lilies, and grapes and pomegranates, and birds clinging and fluttering among the branches, all twined together into an endless network of buds and plumes; and in the midst of it, the solemn forms of angels, sceptred, and robed to the feet, and leaning to each other across the gates, their figures indistinct among the gleaming of the golden ground through the leaves beside them, interrupted and dim, like the morning light as it faded back among the branches of Eden, when first its gates were angel-guarded long ago. And round the walls of the porches there are set pillars of variegated stones, jasper and porphyry, and deep-green serpentine spotted with flakes of snow, and marbles, that half refuse and half yield to the sunshine, Cleopatra-like, "their bluest veins to kiss" — the shadow, as it steals back from them, revealing line after line of azure undulation, as a receding tide leaves the waved sand; their capitals rich with interwoven tracery, rooted knots of herbage, and drifting leaves of acanthus and vine, and mystical signs, all beginning and ending in the Cross; and above them, in the broad archivolts,[6] a continuous chain of language and of life — angels, and the signs of heaven, and the labours of men, each in its

6 Parts of the masonry making up an arch.

appointed season upon the earth; and above these, another range of glittering pinnacles, mixed with white arches edged with scarlet flowers, — a confusion of delight, amidst which the breasts of the Greek horses are seen blazing in their breadth of golden strength, and the St. Mark's lion, lifted on a blue field covered with stars, until at last, as if in ecstasy, the crests of the arches break into a marble foam, and toss themselves far into the blue sky in flashes and wreaths of sculptured spray, as if the breakers on the Lido shore had been frost-bound before they fell, and the sea-nymphs had inlaid them with coral and amethyst.

Between that grim cathedral of England and this, what an interval! There is a type of it in the very birds that haunt them; for, instead of the restless crowd, hoarse-voiced and sable-winged, drifting on the bleak upper air, the St. Mark's porches are full of doves, that nestle among the marble foliage, and mingle the soft iridescence of their living plumes, changing at every motion, with the tints, hardly less lovely, that have stood unchanged for seven hundred years.

And what effect has this splendour on those who pass beneath it? You may walk from sunrise to sunset, to and fro, before the gateway of St. Mark's, and you will not see an eye lifted to it, nor a countenance brightened by it. Priest and layman, soldier and civilian, rich and poor, pass by it alike regardlessly. Up to the very recesses of the porches, the meanest tradesmen of the city push their counters; nay, the foundations of its pillars are themselves the seats — not "of them that sell doves" for sacrifice, but of the vendors of toys and caricatures. Round the whole square in front of the church there is almost a continuous line of cafés, where the idle Venetians of the middle classes lounge, and read empty journals; in its centre the Austrian bands play during the time of vespers, their martial music jarring with the organ notes, — the march drowning the miserere,[7] and the sullen crowd thickening round them, — a crowd, which, if it had its will, would stiletto every soldier that pipes to it. And in the recesses of the porches, all day long, knots of men of the lowest classes, unemployed and listless, lie basking in the sun like lizards; and unregarded children, — every heavy glance of their young eyes full of desperation and stony depravity, and their throats hoarse with cursing, — gamble, and fight, and snarl, and sleep, hour after hour, clashing their bruised centesimi[8] upon the marble ledges of the church

[7] The 50th psalm in the Vulgate, named for its first word.

[8] Very small coins, like pennies.

porch. And the images of Christ and His angels look down upon it continually.

Let us enter the church. It is lost in still deeper twilight, to which the eye must be accustomed for some moments before the form of the building can be traced; and then there opens before us a vast cave, hewn out into the form of a Cross, and divided into shadowy aisles by many pillars. Round the domes of its roof the light enters only through narrow apertures like large stars; and here and there a ray or two from some far-away casement wanders into the darkness, and casts a narrow phosphoric stream upon the waves of marble that heave and fall in a thousand colours along the floor. What else there is of light is from torches, or silver lamps, burning ceaselessly in the recesses of the chapels; the roof sheeted with gold, and the polished walls covered with alabaster, give back at every curve and angle some feeble gleaming to the flames; and the glories round the heads of the sculptured saints flash out upon us as we pass them, and sink again into the gloom. Under foot and over head, a continual succession of crowded imagery, one picture passing into another, as in a dream; forms beautiful and terrible mixed together; dragons and serpents, and ravening beasts of prey, and graceful birds that in the midst of them drink from running fountains and feed from vases of crystal; the passions and the pleasures of human life symbolised together, and the mystery of its redemption; for the mazes of interwoven lines and changeful pictures lead always at last to the Cross, lifted and carved in every place and upon every stone; sometimes with the serpent of eternity wrapt round it, sometimes with doves beneath its arms, and sweet herbage growing forth from its feet; but conspicuous most of all on the great rood that crosses the church before the altar, raised in bright blazonry against the shadow of the apse.[9]

Now the first broad characteristic of the building, and the root nearly of every other important peculiarity in it, is its confessed *incrustation*. It is the purest example in Italy of the great school of architecture in which the ruling principle is the incrustation of brick with more precious materials; and it is necessary, before we proceed to criticise any one of its arrangements, that the reader should carefully consider the

---

[9] "Rood" is an ancient Anglo-Saxon word for the cross or crucifix, which was often placed on a large ornamental screen (the rood screen). The apse is the termination of the nave, traditionally the east end, beyond the altar, semicircular or polygonal in plan and with a vaulted or domed roof.

principles which are likely to have influenced, or might legitimately influence the architects of such a school, as distinguished from those whose designs are to be executed in massive materials. This incrusted school appears *insincere* at first to a Northern builder, because, accustomed to build with solid blocks of freestone, he is in the habit of supposing the external superficies of a piece of masonry to be some criterion of its thickness. But, as soon as he gets acquainted with the incrusted style, he will find that the Southern builders had no intention to deceive him. He will see that every slab of facial marble is fastened to the next by a confessed *rivet,* and that the joints of the armour are so visibly and openly accommodated to the contours of the substance within that he has no more right to complain of treachery than a savage would have, who, for the first time in his life seeing a man in armour, had supposed him to be made of solid steel. Acquaint him with the customs of chivalry, and with the uses of the coat of mail, and he ceases to accuse of dishonesty either the panoply or the knight.

These laws and customs of the St. Mark's architectural chivalry it must be our business to develop.

First, consider the natural circumstances which give rise to such a style. Suppose a nation of builders, placed far from any quarries of available stone, and having precarious access to the mainland where they exist; compelled therefore either to build entirely with brick, or to import whatever stone they use from great distances, in ships of small tonnage, and, for the most part, dependent for speed on the oar rather than the sail. The labour and cost of carriage are just as great, whether they import common or precious stone, and therefore the natural tendency would always be to make each shipload as valuable as possible. But in proportion to the preciousness of the stone, is the limitation of its possible supply; limitation not determined merely by cost, but by the physical conditions of the material, for of many marbles pieces above a certain size are not to be had for money. There would also be a tendency in such circumstances to import as much stone as possible ready sculptured, in order to save weight; and therefore, if the traffic of their merchants led them to places where there were ruins of ancient edifices, to ship the available fragments of them home. Out of this supply of marble, partly composed of pieces of so precious a quality that only a few tons of them could be on any terms obtained, and partly of shafts, capitals, and other portions of foreign buildings, the island architect has to fashion, as best he may, the anatomy of his edifice. It is at his choice either to lodge his few blocks of precious marble here and there among his masses of brick, and to cut out of the sculptured fragments such new forms as may be necessary for the observance of fixed proportions in the new building; or else to cut the coloured stones into thin pieces, of extent sufficient to face the whole surface of the walls, and to adopt a method of construction irregular enough to admit the insertion of fragmentary sculptures; rather with a view of displaying their intrinsic beauty, than of setting them to any regular service in the support of the building.

An architect who cared only to display his own skill, and had no respect for the works of others, would assuredly have chosen the former alternative, and would have sawn the old marbles into fragments in order to prevent all interference with his own designs. But an architect who cared for the preservation of noble work, whether his own or others', and more regarded the beauty of his building than his own fame, would have done what those old builders of St. Mark's did for us, and saved every relic with which he was entrusted.

But these were not the only motives which influenced the Venetians in the adoption of their method of architecture. It might, under all the circumstances above stated, have been a question with other builders, whether to import one shipload of costly jaspers, or twenty of chalk flints; and whether to build a small church faced with porphyry and paved with agate, or to raise a vast cathedral in freestone. But with the Venetians it could not be a question for an instant; they were exiles from ancient and beautiful cities, and had been accustomed to build with their ruins, not less in affection than in admiration; they had thus not only grown familiar with the practice of inserting older fragments in modern buildings, but they owed to that practice a great part of the splendour of their city, and whatever charm of association might aid its change from a Refuge into a Home. The practice which began in the affections of a fugitive nation, was prolonged in the pride of a conquering one; and besides the memorials of departed happiness, were elevated the trophies of returning victory. The ship of war brought home more marble in triumph than the merchant vessel in speculation; and the front of St. Mark's became rather a shrine at which to dedicate the splendour of miscellaneous spoil, than the organized expression of any fixed architectural law or religious emotion.

It is on its value as a piece of perfect and unchangeable colouring, that the claims of this edifice to our respect are finally rested; and a deaf man might as well pretend to pronounce judgment on the merits of a full orchestra, as an architect trained in the composition of form only, to discern the beauty of St. Mark's. It possesses the charm of colour in common with the greater part of the architecture, as well as of the manufactures, of the East; but the Venetians deserve especial note as the only European people who appear to have sympathized to the full with the great instinct of the Eastern races. They indeed were compelled to bring artists from Constantinople to design the mosaics of the vaults of St. Mark's, and to group the colours of its porches; but they rapidly took up and developed, under more masculine conditions, the system of which the Greeks had shown them the example: while the burghers and barons of the North were building their dark streets and grisly castles of oak and sandstone, the merchants of Venice were covering their palaces with porphyry and gold; and at last, when her mighty painters had created for her a colour more priceless than gold or porphyry, even this, the richest of her treasures, she lavished upon walls whose foundations were beaten by the sea; and the strong tide, as it runs beneath the Rialto, is reddened to this day by the reflection of the frescoes of Giorgione.[10]

If, therefore, the reader does not care for colour, I must protest against his endeavour to form any judgment whatever of this church of St. Mark's. But, if he both cares for and loves it let him remember that the school of incrusted architecture is *the only one in which perfect and permanent chromatic decoration is possible;* and let him look upon every piece of jasper and alabaster given to the architect as a cake of very hard colour, of which a certain portion is to be ground down or cut off, to paint the walls with. Once understand this thoroughly, and accept the condition that the body and availing strength of the edifice are to be in brick, and that this under muscular power of brickwork is to be clothed with the defence and the brightness of the marble, as the body of an animal is protected and adorned by its scales or its skin, and all the consequent fitnesses and laws of the structure will be easily discernible.

There are those who suppose the mosaics of St. Mark's, and others of the period, to be utterly barbarous as representations of religious history. Let it be granted that they are so; we are not for that reason to suppose they were ineffective in religious teaching. The whole church may be seen as a great Book of Common Prayer; the mosaics were its illumi-

[10] Venetian painter of the fifteenth century.

nations, and the common people of the time were taught their Scripture history by means of them, more impressively perhaps, though far less fully, than ours are now by Scripture reading. They had no other Bible, and — Protestants do not often enough consider this — *could* have no other. We find it somewhat difficult to furnish our poor with printed Bibles; consider what the difficulty must have been when they could be given only in manuscript. The walls of the church necessarily became the poor man's Bible, and a picture was more easily read upon the walls than a chapter. Under this view, and considering them merely as the Bible pictures of a great nation in its youth, I have to deprecate the idea of their execution being in any sense barbarous. I have conceded too much to modern prejudice, in permitting them to be rated as mere childish efforts at coloured portraiture: they have characters in them of a very noble kind; nor are they by any means devoid of the remains of the science of the later Roman empire. The character of the features is almost always fine, the expression stern and quiet, and very solemn, the attitudes and draperies always majestic in the single figures, and in those of the groups which are not in violent action; while the bright colouring and disregard of chiaroscuro[11] cannot be regarded as imperfections, since they are the only means by which the figures could be rendered clearly intelligible in the distance and darkness of the vaulting. So far am I from considering them barbarous, that I believe of all works of religious art whatsoever, these, and such as these, have been the most effective.

Missal-painting[12] could not, from its minuteness, produce the same sublime impressions, and frequently merged itself in mere ornamentation of the page. Modern book illustration has been so little skilful as hardly to be worth naming. Sculpture, though in some positions it becomes of great importance, has always a tendency to lose itself in architectural effect; and was probably seldom deciphered, in all its parts, by the common people, still less the traditions annealed in the purple burning of the painted window. Finally, tempera pictures and frescoes were often of limited size or of feeble colour. But the great mosaics of the twelfth and thirteenth centuries covered the walls and roofs of the churches with inevitable lustre; they could not be ignored or escaped

[11] From the Italian words for "clear" and "dark," referring to the perspective or sense of dimension in depth achieved by the light and dark areas in drawing.

[12] Medieval decoration of books of the Mass.

from; their size rendered them majestic, their distance mysterious, their colour attractive. They did not pass into confused or inferior decorations; neither were they adorned with any evidences of skill or science, such as might withdraw the attention from their subjects. They were before the eyes of the devotee at every interval of his worship; vast shadowings forth of scenes to whose realization he looked forward, or of spirits whose presence he invoked. And the man must be little capable of receiving a religious impression of any kind, who, to this day, does not acknowledge some feeling of awe, as he looks up to the pale countenances and ghastly forms which haunt the dark roofs of the Baptisteries of Parma and Florence, or remains altogether untouched by the majesty of the colossal images of apostles, and of Him who sent apostles, that look down from the darkening gold of the domes of Venice and Pisa.

⊷ᴣ FOR DISCUSSION AND WRITING

1. Why does Ruskin start this piece on St. Mark's with a description of an English cathedral? The first paragraph affords a good example of what is perhaps the most important principle of descriptive writing, a principle that might be called "control of the changing focus of attention." At what points in the paragraph do you find Ruskin deliberately guiding visual attention in correspondence with what would be the actual changes of visual focus as one approached so large an object as a cathedral?

2. Since Ruskin is one of the great English stylists, let us do a little stylistic analysis—for instance, of the third sentence in the first paragraph. It is a long one (he runs to long sentences), but the syntactical organization is fairly simple. In analyzing syntax, the first thing to do always is to find the subject and verb or verbs of the main clause; with this settled, what is the grammatical form of the rest of the sentence structure up to the first semicolon? from the first to the second semicolon? and from the second semicolon to the end? Does the syntax of the sentence—the articulation and movement of the parts—have any *kinetic* relationship with the changing view as the eye mounts higher and higher? Syntax alone does not constitute "style," for syntax is only an arrangement of the basic units of writing—words; but syntax has the relation to words that breathing has to breath, or that the pulsation of the heart has to the blood that is pumped —the one is the muscular action, the other is what is acted upon. Cast

your eye again over the sentence we have been considering. What words
or combinations of words (they don't have to be exotic—they may be very
simple) seem to you distinctive of a definite kind of perception, an individual "style" of the mind? (For instance, how about this?—"coloured on
their stony scales by the deep russet-orange lichen, melancholy gold.")

3. How does Ruskin make his transition from the English cathedral town to
   Venice? What major contrast does he draw between them? Point out
   specific places where he uses, in the approach to St. Mark's (before we get
   into the church), the same psychological technique of changing visual
   focus that he used in the first paragraph. Analyze the syntax of the first
   sentence in the fifth paragraph. What is the main clause and what is the
   chief subordinate clause? and what is the grammatical relationship between these and the patterns of syntax beginning: "a multitude of pillars . . . ," "a treasure-heap . . . ," "sculpture fantastic . . . ," "and in the midst
   of it, the solemn forms . . ."? The words of the sentence refer to a multitude
   of things, but how does the *syntax* itself control and at the same time
   build up one's sense of luxurious profusion? What images or what combinations of adjective and noun or simply what choice of words do you find
   particularly effective in this paragraph?

4. Where, in the paragraph beginning "Let us enter the church," do you find
   Ruskin deliberately changing visual focus in accordance with the natural
   psychology of attention? We can't see anything without light, and the
   quality of light—artificial or natural, through dirty windows or clear ones
   or colored ones, at high noon or evening—and the angles at which light
   falls, have a great deal to do with the appearances of objects; hence painters
   and sculptors and architects study the effects of light very closely and incorporate them in their work (one has only to think of Rembrandt, Vermeer,
   Cézanne); and the skilled descriptive writer does so also. How many times
   and in how many ways—in adjective or noun or verb—does Ruskin note
   effects of light (including, of course, gloom and shadow) in this paragraph?

5. What is meant by "incrustation"? Why might the incrusted style appear
   "insincere," and what is Ruskin's argument against that attitude? What
   historical explanation does he give of the incrusted style of St. Mark's?
   Why does he say that St. Mark's should not be judged by the criterion of
   "composition of form only"? and what other criterion does he use?

6. Why does he call the church "a great Book of Common Prayer"—and what
   is the Book of Common Prayer? What is his argument against the opinion

that the mosaics of St. Mark's are aesthetically "childish" or "barbarous"? What criterion of *function* does he bring us back to at the end?

7. The obvious writing assignment here is a descriptive piece about some sizable object in your neighborhood, a church or a house or some other building, or you could take some natural view that offered sufficiently interesting perspective and detail, a stretch of country seen from higher ground and with or without human things in it, or you could describe an interior, or both exterior and interior as Ruskin does; the point would be to exercise some of the technique you have learned from Ruskin—for instance, control of the focus of attention in accordance with the natural psychology of attention, and observation of the effects of light as these single out certain objects and parts of objects, determining what one sees and how one sees it.

Mary McCarthy ⋙ The Paradox of St. Mark's

⋙ American novelist, short-story writer, essayist, and critic; born in 1912 in Seattle, Washington; educated at a convent, an Episcopal school, and Vassar; now living in Paris. Miss McCarthy's intellectual virtuosity, stylistic brilliance, and mordant wit have given her a place of high distinction in contemporary American letters. Among her better-known works are *The Company She Keeps*, a volume of short stories, and the novels *The Groves of Academe*, *A Charmed Life*, and *The Group*.

I T WAS from Byzantium that the taste for refinement and sensuous luxury came to Venice. *"Artificiosa voluptate se mulcebat,"*[1] a chronicler wrote of the Greek wife of an early doge. Her scents and perfumes, her baths of dew, her sweet-smelling gloves and dresses, the fork she used at table scandalized her subjects, plain Italian pioneer folk. The husband of this effeminate woman had Greek tastes also. He began, says the chronicler, "to work in mosaic," importing mosaic workers — and marbles and precious stones — to adorn his private chapel, St. Mark's, in the Eastern style that soon became second nature to the Venetians.

The Byzantine mode, in Venice, lost something of its theological

[1] "She indulged herself in artificial desire." The doge was the chief magistrate of the republic of Venice.

awesomeness. The stern, solemn figure of the Pantocrator[2] who dominates the Greek churches with his frowning brows and upraised hand does not appear in St. Mark's in His arresting majesty. In a Greek church, you feel that the Eye of God is on you from the moment you step in the door; you are utterly encompassed by this all-embracing gaze, which in peasant chapels is often represented by an eye over the door. The fixity of this divine gaze is not punitive; it merely calls you to attention and reminds you of the eternal, the Law of the universe arching over time and circumstance. The Pantocrator of the Greeks has traits of the old Nemesis,[3] sweetened and purified by the Redemption. He is also a Platonic idea, the End of the chain of speculation.

The Venetians were not speculators or philosophers, and the theological assertion is absent from St. Mark's mosaics, which seek rather to tell a Biblical story than to convey an abstraction. The *clothing* of the story assumes, in Venice, an adventitious interest, as in the fluffy furs worn by Salome in the Baptistery mosaic. . . .

St. Mark's, in the Ravenna style, was begun in 829, but it was twice destroyed, burned down once by the people in rebellion against a tyrannous doge, restored, and torn down again by an eleventh-century doge who wanted his chapel in the fashionable Byzantine style. (It was his successor, Doge Selvo, that married the Greek wife.) The present St. Mark's in the shape of a Greek cross with five domes and modeled, some think, on the church of the Twelve Apostles in Constantinople, is the result of his initiative. . . .

From the outside, as is often observed, St. Mark's looks like an Oriental pavilion — half pleasure-house, half war-tent, belonging to some great satrap. Inside, glittering with jewels and gold, faced with precious Eastern marbles, jasper and alabastar, porphyry and verd-antique, sustained by Byzantine columns in the same materials, of varying sizes and epochs, scarcely a pair alike, this dark cruciform cave has the look of a robber's den. In the chapel of the Crucifix, with a pyramidal marble roof topped by a huge piece of Oriental agate and supported by six Byzantine columns in black and white African marble, stands a painted crucifix, of special holiness, taken from Constantinople. In the atrium, flanking St. Clement's door, are two pairs of black and white marble columns, with wonderful lion's and eagle's heads in yellowish

[2] Christ as "Ruler of All."

[3] An ancient goddess who dealt out retributive justice.

ivory; tradition says they came from the Temple of Solomon in Jerusalem. From Tyre came the huge block of Mountain Tabor granite on the altar in the Baptistery — said to be the stone on which Christ was wont to pray. In the Zen chapel, the wall is lined with onion marbles and verdantique, reputedly the gravestones of the Byzantine Emperors.

In the chapel of St. Isidore sleeps the saint stolen from Chios; he was hidden for two centuries for fear of confiscation. St. Theodore, stolen from Byzantium, was moved to San Salvatore. St. Mark himself was lost for a considerable period, after the fire in 976, which destroyed most of the early church; he revealed his presence by thrusting forth his arm. He was not the original saint of Venice, but, so to speak, a usurper, displacing St. Theodore. Thus, he himself, the patron, was a kind of thieving cuckoo bird, and his church, which was only the Doge's private chapel, imitated him by usurping the functions of San Pietro in Castello, the seat of the Patriarch and the real Cathedral (until very recent times) of Venice. In the same style, the early doges had themselves buried, in St. Mark's porch, in sarcophagi that did not belong to them, displacing the bones of old pagans and paleo-Christians.

Venice, unlike Rome or Ravenna or nearby Verona, had nothing of its own to start with. Venice, as a city, was a foundling, floating upon the waters like Moses in his basket among the bulrushes. It was therefore obliged to be inventive, to steal and improvise. Cleverness and adaptivity were imposed by the original situation, and the get-up-and-go of the early Venetian business men was typical of a self-made society. St. Mark's church is a (literally) shining example of this spirit of initiative, this gift for improvisation, for turning everything to account. It is made of bricks, like most Venetian churches, since brick was the easiest material to come by. Its external beauty comes from the thin marble veneers with which the brick surface is coated, just as though it were a piece of furniture. These marbles, for the most part, like the columns and facing inside, were the spoils of war, and they were put on almost haphazardly, green against gray, against red or rose or white with red veining, without any general principle of design beyond the immediate pleasure of the eye. On the Piazzetta side, this gives the effect of a gay abstract painting. Parvenu art, more like painting than architecture . . . , and yet it "worked." The marble veneers of St. Mark's sides, especially when washed by the rain so that they look like oiled silk, are among the most beautiful things in Venice. And it is their very thinness, the sense they give of being a mere lustrous coating, a film, that makes them beautiful. A palace of solid marble, rainwashed, simply looks bedraggled.

St. Mark's as a whole, unless seen from a distance or at twilight, is not beautiful. The modern mosaics (seventeenth century) are generally admitted to be extremely ugly, and I myself do not care for most of the Gothic statuary of the pinnacles. The horses, the colored marble veneers, the Byzantine Madonna of the front, the old mosaic on the left, the marble columns of the portal, the gold encrustations of the top, the five grey domes with their strange ornaments, like children's jacks — these are the details that captivate. As for the rest, it is better not to look too closely, or the whole will begin to seem tawdry, a hodge-podge, as so many critics have said. The whole is not beautiful, and yet again it is. It depends on the light and the time of day or on whether you narrow your eyes, to make it look flat, a painted surface. And it can take you unawares, looking beautiful or horribly ugly, at a time you least expect. Venice, Henry James said, is as changeable as a nervous woman, and this is particularly true of St. Mark's façade.

But why should it be beautiful at all? Why should Venice, aside from its situation, be a place of enchantment? One appears to be confronted with a paradox. A commercial people who lived solely for gain — how could they create a city of fantasy, lovely as a dream or a fairy-tale? This is the central puzzle of Venice, the stumbling-block that one keeps coming up against if one tries to *think* about her history, to put the facts of her history together with the visual fact that is there before one's eyes. It cannot be that Venice is a happy accident or a trick of light. I have thought about this a long time, but now it occurs to me that, as with most puzzles, the clue to the answer lies in the way the question is framed. "Lovely as a dream or a fairy tale. . . ." There is no contradiction, once you stop to think what images of beauty arise from fairy tales. They are images of money. Gold, caskets of gold, caskets of silver, the miller's daughter spinning gold all night long, thanks to Rumplestiltskin, the cave of Ali Baba stored with stolen gold and silver, the underground garden in which Aladdin found jewels growing on trees, so that he could gather them in his hands, rubies and diamonds and emeralds, the Queen's lovely daughter whose hair is black as ebony and lips are red as rubies, treasure buried in the forest, treasure guarded by dogs with eyes as big as carbuncles, treasure guarded by a Beast — this is the spirit of the enchantment under which Venice lies, pearly and roseate, like the

Sleeping Beauty, changeless throughout the centuries, arrested, while the concrete forest of the modern world grows up around her.

A wholly materialist city is nothing but a dream incarnate. Venice is the world's unconscious: a miser's glittering hoard, guarded by a Beast whose eyes are made of white agate, and by a saint who is really a prince who has just slain a dragon.

A list of the goods in which the early Venetian merchants trafficked arouses a sense of pure wonder: wine and grain from Apulia, gems and drugs from Asia, metal-work, silk, and cloth of gold from Byzantium and Greece. These are the gifts of the Magi, in the words of the English hymn: "Pearls from the ocean and gems from the mountain; myrrh from the forest and gold from the mine." During the Middle Ages, as a part of his rightful revenue, the doge had his share in the apples of Lombardy and the crayfish and cherries of Treviso — the Venetian mind, interested only in the immediate and the solid, leaves behind it, for our minds, clear, dawn-fresh images out of fairy tales.

✑ FOR DISCUSSION AND WRITING

1. To what extent does the first paragraph, about the doge's wife, "condition" one's attitude toward St. Mark's in the description that follows? Explain what is meant in the third paragraph by the comment: "The *clothing* of the story assumes, in Venice, an adventitious interest. . . ."

2. Particularly in description of something extremely large and complex, a simile or metaphor or analogy may be very useful for giving an over-all impression before attention is guided to details. What general, governing comparisons, aimed at giving a sense of the whole, do you find in the fifth paragraph? Analyze the second sentence of the paragraph: where is the main clause? and what is the structure of the parallelisms in "glittering with jewels . . . ," "faced with precious Eastern marbles . . . ," and "sustained by Byzantine columns . . ."? How does the *syntax* of the sentence (the way the parts are organized) contribute to the impression the sentence is trying to give—of an *Arabian Nights* kind of robber's den?

3. In the fifth paragraph (starting with "robber's den"), and the sixth and the seventh, how many references are there to some kind of stealing or usurpa-

tion? If you have read the preceding piece by Ruskin on St. Mark's, what major difference do you find between Mary McCarthy's attitude toward the style of the church and Ruskin's? Do you find that they also have some perceptions in common?

4. What does she say is "the central puzzle of Venice"? What analogy does she draw between fairy tales and Venice? Explain what is meant by the following: "A wholly materialist city is nothing but a dream incarnate. Venice is the world's unconscious. . . ." What is the point of the list of objects of commerce in the last paragraph, and what connection is there between these commercial matters and "the gifts of the Magi" and "dawn-fresh images out of fairy tales"?

5. If you have read the piece by Ruskin, you might write a short paper comparing his description of St. Mark's with Mary McCarthy's—two writers divided by nearly a century and very different in attitude and tone. Or, since Mary McCarthy's piece emphasizes the commercial, materialistic aspects of the history of Venice, you might be interested in describing the visual features of your own town as products of American commercialism and materialism (not necessarily pejorative words in themselves—although you might find yourself coming out with something less than Venice).

Gustave Flaubert ❧ Letters to Louise Colet

❧ French novelist (1821-1880), whose work has been perhaps the single most important influence on the technique of the modern novel. Each of his works is a masterpiece, but the most famous is *Madame Bovary*. The poet Louise Colet was, for a time, his mistress. ❧

Tuesday, [Croisset, July 6, 1852]

MUSSET[1] has never separated poetry from the sensations of which it is the consummate expression. Music, according to him, was made for serenades, painting for portraits, and poetry for consoling the heart. But if you put the sun inside your trousers, all you do is burn your trousers and wet the sun. That is what has happened to him. Nerves, magnetism: for him poetry is those things. Actually, it is something less turbulent. If sensitive nerves were the only requirement of a poet, I should be superior to Shakespeare and to Homer, whom I picture as a not very nervous individual. Such confusion is blasphemy. I know whereof I speak: I used to be able to hear what people were saying in low voices behind closed

From *The Selected Letters of Gustave Flaubert*. Translated and edited by Francis Steegmuller. Farrar, Straus and Giroux, Inc. Copyright 1953 by Francis Steegmuller. Reprinted by permission of Brandt & Brandt.

[1] Alfred de Musset, French writer contemporary with Flaubert.

doors thirty paces away; all my viscera could be seen quivering under my skin; and sometimes I experienced in the space of a single second a million thoughts, images, associations of all kinds which exploded in my mind like a grand display of fireworks. But all this, closely related though it is to the emotions, is mere parlor talk.

Poetry is by no means an infirmity of the mind; whereas these nervous susceptibilities are. Extreme sensitivity is a weakness. Let me explain:

If my mind had been stronger, I shouldn't have fallen ill as a result of studying law and being bored. I'd have turned those circumstances to good account instead of being worsted by them. My unhappiness, instead of confining itself to my brain, affected the rest of my body and threw me into convulsions. It was a "deviation." One often sees children whom music hurts physically: they have great talent, retain melodies after but one hearing, become over-excited when they play the piano; their hearts pound, they grow thin and pale and fall ill, and their poor nerves writhe in pain at the sound of notes — like dogs. These are never the future Mozarts. Their vocation has been misplaced: the idea has passed into the flesh, and there it remains sterile and causes the flesh to perish; neither genius nor health results.

It is the same with art. Passion does not make poetry, and the more personal you are, the weaker. I have always sinned in that direction myself, because I have always put myself into what I was doing. Instead of Saint Anthony,[2] for example, *I* am in my book; and I, rather than the reader, underwent the temptation. *The less you feel a thing, the fitter you are to express it as it is* (as it *always* is, in itself, in its essence, freed of all ephemeral contingencies). But you must have the capacity to *make yourself feel it*. This capacity is what we call genius: the ability to *see*, to have your model constantly posing in front of you.

That is why I detest so-called poetic language. When there are no words, a glance is enough. Soulful effusions, lyricism, descriptions — I want all these embodied in Style. To put them elsewhere is to prostitute art and feeling itself.

Thursday, 4 A.M., [Croisset, July 22, 1852]
I am in the process of copying and correcting the entire first part of

[2] The reference is to Flaubert's *Temptations of Saint Anthony*, a magnificent fantasy about the trials of the famous anchorite.

Bovary. My eyes are smarting. I should like to be able to read these 158 pages at a single glance and grasp them with all their details in a single thought. A week from Sunday I shall read the whole thing to Bouilhet, and a day or two later you will see me. What a bitch of a thing prose is! It is never finished; there is always something to be done over. Still, I think it is possible to give it the consistency of verse. A good prose sentence should be like a good line of poetry — *unchangeable*, just as rhythmic, just as sonorous. Such, at least, is my ambition (I am sure of one thing: no one has ever conceived a more perfect type of prose than I; but as to the execution, how weak, how weak, oh God!). Nor does it seem to me impossible to give psychological analysis[3] the swiftness, clarity, and impetus of a strictly dramatic narrative. That has never been attempted, and it would be beautiful. Have I succeeded a little in this? I have no idea. At this moment I have no definite opinion about my work.

Monday, 1 A.M., [Croisset, July 27, 1852]
Yes, it is a strange thing, the relation between one's writing and one's personality. Is there anyone more in love with antiquity than I, anyone more haunted by it, anyone who has made a greater effort to understand it? And yet in my books I am as far from antiquity as possible. From my appearance one would think me a writer of epic, drama, brutally factual narrative; whereas actually I feel at home only in analysis — in anatomy, if I may call it such. By natural disposition I love what is vague and misty; and it is only patience and study that have rid me of all the white fat that clogged my muscles. The books I most long to write are precisely those for which I am least endowed. *Bovary*, in this sense, is an unprecedented tour de force (a fact of which I alone shall ever be aware): its subject, characters, effects, etc. — all are alien to me. It should make it possible for me to take a great step forward later. Writing this book I am like a man playing the piano with leaden balls attached to his fingers. But once I have mastered my technique, and find a piece that's to my taste and that I can play at sight, the result will perhaps be good. In my case, I think I am doing the right thing. What one does is not for one's self, but for others. Art is not interested in the personality of the artist. So much the worse for him if he doesn't like red or green or yellow: all colors are beautiful, and his task is to use them. . . .

[3] Flaubert refers here to his *Madame Bovary*.

Sunday, 11 P.M., [Croisset, September 19, 1852]

What trouble my *Bovary* is giving me! Still, I am beginning to see my way a little. Never in my life have I written anything more difficult than what I am doing now — trivial dialogue. . . . I have to portray, simultaneously and in the same conversation, five or six characters who speak, several others who are spoken about, the scene, and the whole town, giving physical descriptions of people and objects; and in the midst of all that I have to show a man and a woman who are beginning (through a similarity in tastes) to fall in love with each other.[4] If only I had space! But the whole thing has to be swift without being dry, and well worked out without taking up too much room; and many details which would be more striking here I have to keep in reserve for use elsewhere. I am going to put the whole thing down quickly, and then proceed by a series of increasingly drastic revisions; by going over and over it I can perhaps pull it together. The language itself is a great stumbling-block. My characters are completely commonplace, but they have to speak in a literary style, and politeness of language takes away so much picturesqueness from any speech!

Night of Friday-Saturday, 2 A.M., [Croisset, October 1-2, 1852]

The other day I learned that a young man I knew at school had been interned at Saint-Yon (the Rouen insane asylum). A year ago I read a book of stupid poems by him; but I was moved by the sincerity, enthusiasm, and faith expressed in the preface. I was told that like me he lived in the country, secluded and working as hard as he could. The bourgeois had the greatest contempt for him. He complained of being constantly slandered and insulted; he suffered the common ordeal of unrecognized geniuses. Eventually he lost his mind, and now he is raving and screaming and treated with cold baths. Who can assure me that I am not on the same path? What is the line of demarcation between inspiration and madness, between stupidity and ecstasy? To be an artist is it not necessary to *see everything* differently from other men? Art is no mere game of the intellect; it is a special atmosphere that we breathe. But if in search of more and more potent air we descend ever deeper into art's subterranean recesses, who knows that we may not end by breathing deadly miasmas? It would make a nice book — the story of a man whose mind is sound (quite possibly my young friend is sane) locked up as insane and treated by stupid doctors.

4 The reference is to the scene of the Agricultural Fair in *Madame Bovary*.

Sunday, 4 o'clock, Easter Day [Croisset, March 27, 1853]

As for me, the more I realize the difficulties of writing, the more daring I become; this is what keeps me from pedantry, into which I should otherwise doubtless fall. I have plans for writing that will keep me busy till the end of my life, and though I sometimes have moments of bitterness that make me almost scream with rage (so acutely do I feel my own impotence and weakness) I have others when I can scarcely contain myself for joy. Something deep and extra-voluptuous gushes out of me, like an ejaculation of the soul. I feel transported, drunk with my own thought, as though a hot gust of perfume were being wafted to me through some inner conduit. I shall never go very far; I know my limitations. But the goal I have set for myself will be achieved by others: thanks to me someone more talented, more instinctive, will be set on the right path. It is perhaps absurd to want to give prose the rhythm of verse (keeping it distinctly prose, however) and to write of ordinary life as one writes history or epic (but without falsifying the subject). I often wonder about this. But on the other hand it is perhaps a great experiment, and very original too. I know where I fail. (Ah, if only I were fifteen!) No matter: I shall always be given some credit for my stubbornness. And then, who can tell? Some day I may find a good motif, an air completely suited to my voice, neither too high nor too low. In any case I shall have lived nobly and often delightfully.

There is a saying by La Bruyère that serves me as a guide: "A good author likes to think that he writes sensibly."[5] That is what I ask—to write sensibly; and it is asking a good deal. Still, one thing is depressing, and that is to see how easily the great men achieve their effects by means extraneous to Art. What is more badly put together than much of Rabelais, Cervantes, Molière, and Hugo? But such quick punches! Such power in a single word! We have to pile up a lot of little pebbles to build our pyramids; theirs, a hundred times greater, are made with a single block. But to seek to imitate the method of these geniuses would be fatal. They are great for the very reason that they have no method.

Friday night, 1 A.M., [Croisset, July 15, 1853]

What artists we should be if we had never read, seen, or loved anything that was not beautiful; if from the outset some guardian angel of the purity of our pens had kept us from all contamination; if we had never known fools or read newspapers! The Greeks were like that. . . .

[5] Seventeenth-century French author and moralist.

But classic form is insufficient for our needs, and our voices are not made to sing such simple tunes. Let us be as dedicated to art as they were, if we can, but differently. The human mind has broadened since Homer. Sancho Panza's belly has burst the seams of Venus' girdle. Rather than persisting in copying old modes we should exert ourselves to invent new ones. I think Leconte de Lisle[6] is unaware of all this. He has no instinct for modern life; he lacks heart. By this I do not mean personal or even humanitarian feelings, no — but *heart*, almost in the medical sense of the word. His ink is pale; his muse suffers from lack of fresh air. Thoroughbred horses and thoroughbred styles have plenty of blood in their veins, and it can be seen pulsing everywhere beneath the skin and the words. Life! Life! . . . That is the only thing that counts! That is why I love lyricism so much. It seems to me the most natural form of poetry — poetry in all its nakedness and freedom. All the power of a work of art lies in this mystery, and it is this primordial quality, this *motus animi continuus* (vibration, continual movement of the mind — Cicero's definition of eloquence), which gives conciseness, distinctness, form, energy, rhythm, diversity. It doesn't require much brains to be a critic: you can judge the excellence of a book by the strength of its punches and the time it takes you to recover from them. And then the excesses of the great masters! They pursue an idea to its furthermost limits. In Molière's *Monsieur de Pourceaugnac* there is a question of giving a man an enema, and a whole troop of actors carrying syringes pour down the aisles of the theatre. Michelangelo's figures have cables rather than muscles; in Rubens' bacchanalian scenes men piss on the ground; and think of everything in Shakespeare, etc., etc., and the most recent representative of the family, old Hugo. What a beautiful thing *Notre-Dame* is! I lately reread three chapters in it, including the sack of the church by the vagabonds. That's the sort of thing that's strong! I think that the greatest characteristic of genius is, above all, *energy*. Hence, what I detest most of all in the arts, what sets me on edge, is the *ingenious*, the clever. This is not at all the same as bad taste, which is a good quality gone wrong. In order to have what is called bad taste, you must have a sense for poetry; whereas cleverness, on the contrary, is incompatible with genuine poetry. Who was cleverer than Voltaire, and who less a poet? In our darling France, the public will accept poetry only if it is disguised. If it is given to them raw they protest. They have to be treated like the horses

6 French poet, contemporary with Flaubert.

of Abbas-Pasha, who are fed a tonic of meat balls covered with flour. That's what Art is: knowing how to make the covering! But have no fear: if you offer this kind of flour to lions, they will recognize the smell twenty paces away and spring at it.

꜀꜆ FOR DISCUSSION AND WRITING

1. In the first paragraph, what is the conception of poetry and the poetic temperament that Flaubert objects to, and why does he object to it? To your knowledge, do many people share this conception of poetry? Do you? How would you explain the statement in the fourth paragraph, that "the less you feel a thing, the fitter you are to express it"? What do you think he means by the "poetic language" he says he detests? From the occasions in this book when we have talked about style, you should have a fairly clear idea of the significance of the word. What would you say Flaubert means by it in the next to last sentence of the first letter?—"Soulful effusions, lyricism, description—I want all these embodied in Style." Could you apply the same statement to other arts, to the disciplines of acting and dancing for instance?

2. In the second letter, what does Flaubert mean by saying that it should be be possible to give prose "the consistency of verse"? Glance back over some of the pieces you have liked best in this book and see if you can find half a dozen sentences to which the following criterion might be applied: "A good prose sentence should be like a good line of poetry—*unchangeable*, just as rhythmic, just as sonorous."

3. In the third letter, what attitude does he say he has toward his great novel *Madame Bovary?* What division in his temperament does he describe here? What does he mean by saying that "Art is not interested in the personality of the artist"? Do you find any relationship between this statement and what he says in the first letter about poetry? In the fourth letter, what does he say of his method of writing? How does your own practice of revision compare with Flaubert's?

4. In the fifth letter, what analogy does he draw between the madman and the artist? Can you find any grounds of relationship between that analogy and what he says toward the end of the sixth letter about wanting "to write

sensibly"? Can you relate the ideal of "writing sensibly" to the attitudes shown in the previous letters? At the end of the sixth letter, what implicit comparison does he make between his own writing and the work of "geniuses"? Why does he say that to imitate genius would be fatal? (It is well to bear in mind that later generations have placed Flaubert in the rank of "geniuses.")

5. Do you find any consistency between what he has said earlier about writing and what he says in the last letter about the necessity of "*heart*"? What does he mean by "heart"? Explain his distinction between "energy" and "the ingenious, the clever."

6. You could do an extremely valuable written exercise if you were to search through this book, or others, for examples of the qualities Flaubert speaks of in the last letter, "conciseness, distinctness, form, energy, rhythm, diversity," copying them down and analyzing each of them in terms of the qualities you find. Or you could make up a sort of notebook of key statements about writing that you have found here or elsewhere in this book, with your own comments on them, bringing them into relationship with your personal writing problems. (Simply to be able to select such passages intelligently deserves credit.) Or you could do a bit of biographical research on Flaubert and write it up.

Rainer Maria Rilke ✑ Letter to a Young Poet

✑ See biographical note on page 205. ✑

Paris, February 17th, 1903

My Dear Sir,

Your letter only reached me a few days ago. I want to thank you for its great and kind confidence. I can hardly do more. I cannot go into the nature of your verses; for all critical intention is too far from me. With nothing can one touch a work of art so little as with critical words: they always come down to more or less lucky misunderstandings. Things are not all so comprehensible and expressible as one would mostly have us believe; most events are inexpressible, take place in a realm which no word has ever entered, and more inexpressible than all else are works of art, mysterious existences, the life of which, while ours passes away, endures.

After these prefatory remarks, let me only tell you further that your verses have no individual style, although they do show a quiet and hidden incipience of the personal. I feel this most clearly in the last poem "My Soul." There something of your own wants to come through to expression. And in the lovely poem "To Leopardi" there does perhaps grow up a sort of kinship with that great solitary man. Nevertheless the poems are not yet anything on their own account, nothing independent, even the last and the one to Leopardi. Your kind letter, which accompanied them, does not fail to make clear to me various shortcomings which I felt in reading your verses without at the time being able particularly to name them.

You ask whether your verses are good. You ask me. You have asked others before. You send them to magazines. You compare them with other poems, and you are disturbed when certain editors reject your efforts. Now (since you have allowed me to advise you) I beg you to give up all that. You are looking outward, and that above all you should not now do. Nobody can counsel and help you, nobody. There is only one single way. Go into yourself. Investigate the reason that bids you write; find out whether it is spreading out its roots in the deepest places of your heart, acknowledge to yourself whether you would have to die if it were denied you to write. This above all: ask yourself in the stillest hour of your night: *must* I write? Delve into yourself for a deep answer. And if this should be affirmative, if you may meet this earnest question with a strong and simple "I must," then build your life according to this necessity; your life even into its most indifferent and slightest hour must be a sign of this urge and a testimony to it. Then draw near to Nature. Then try, as a first human being, to say what you see and experience and love and lose. Do not write love-poems; avoid at first those forms that are too hackneyed and commonplace: they are the most difficult, for it takes a great, fully matured power to give something of your own where good and even excellent traditions come to mind in quantity. Therefore save yourself from these general themes and seek those which your own everyday life offers you; describe your sorrows and desires, passing thoughts and the belief in some sort of beauty — describe all these with loving, quiet, humble sincerity and use, to express yourself, the things in your environment, the pictures from your dreams, and the subjects of your memory. If your daily life seems poor, do not blame it; blame yourself, tell yourself that you are not poet enough to call forth its riches;

for to the creator there is no poverty and no poor indifferent place. And even if you were in some prison the walls of which let none of the sounds of the world come to your senses — would you not then still have your childhood, that precious, kingly possession, that treasure-house of memories? Turn your attention thither. Try to bring up the sunken sensations of that far past; your personality will grow more firm, your solitude will widen and will become a dusky dwelling by which the noise of others passes far away. — And if out of this turning inward, out of this sinking into your own world verses come, then it will not occur to you to ask any one whether they are good verses. Nor will you try to interest magazines in your poems: for you will see in them your fond natural possession, a fragment and a voice of your life. A work of art is good if it has sprung from necessity. In this nature of its origin lies its judgment: there is no other. Therefore, my dear sir, I have known no advice for you save this: to go into yourself and test the deeps in which your life takes rise; at its source you will find the answer to the question whether you *must* create. Accept it, just as it sounds, without trying to interpret it. Perhaps it will turn out that you are called to be an artist. Then take that destiny upon yourself and bear it, its burden and its greatness, without ever asking what recompense might come from outside. For the creator must be a world for himself and find everything in himself and in Nature with whom he has allied himself.

But perhaps after this descent into yourself and into your inner solitude you will have to give up becoming a poet; (it is enough, as I have said, to feel that one could live without writing: then one should not be allowed to do it at all). But even then this inward searching which I ask of you will not have been in vain. Your life will in any case find its own ways thence, and that they may be good, rich and wide I wish you more than I can say.

What more shall I say to you? Everything seems to me to have its just emphasis; and after all I do only want to advise you to keep growing quietly and seriously throughout your development; you cannot disturb it more rudely than by looking outward and expecting from outside replies to questions that only your inmost feeling in your quietest hours can perhaps answer.

It was a pleasure to me to find in your letter the name of Professor Horáček; I keep for that lovable and learned man a great veneration and a gratitude that endures through the years. Will you, please, tell him how

I feel; it is very good of him still to think of me, and I know how to appreciate it.

The verses which you kindly entrusted to me I am returning at the same time. And I thank you once more for your great and sincere confidence, of which I have tried, through this honest answer given to the best of my knowledge, to make myself a little worthier than, as a stranger, I really am.

Yours faithfully and with all sympathy:

RAINER MARIA RILKE

ᴥᶘ FOR DISCUSSION AND WRITING

1. What is Rilke's attitude toward criticism? How is that attitude related to his conception of art? Explain this statement: "most events are inexpressible, take place in a realm which no word has ever entered, and more inexpressible than all else are works of art, mysterious existences. . . ." Since poetry is made of words that presumably "express" (or "mean" or "communicate") something, and if poetry has its source in a realm of "inexpressible" events, could you make any suggestion as to how there can be any poetry at all? (It's of no use to say that Rilke is talking nonsense, for he was a man of extraordinary intelligence and integrity.) If you have read the piece by W. H. Auden, which follows, do you find any relationship between the "inexpressible" realm of "mysterious existences" that Rilke speaks of, and what Auden calls the realm of Primary Imagination, inhabited by "sacred beings"? or, if you have read the piece by Carl Jung, do you find any relationship with the realm of the "collective unconscious," inhabited by "primordial images" or "archetypes"? As a matter of fact, Rilke's own greatest poems are full of "sacred beings" and "primordial images." If you are interested in poetry and have not read Rilke's, you can have an exciting experience by looking up his *Sonnets to Orpheus* or the *Duino Elegies*, which have had excellent translations in English. You might take as a subject for a paper the "sacred beings" of Rilke's poems.

2. In the second paragraph of the letter, Rilke speaks of the lack of an "individual style" in the verses of his young correspondent; in the context of the whole letter, what do you think Rilke means by an "individual style"? If you have read the immediately preceding letters by Flaubert, would you say that Flaubert and Rilke mean the same things by the word "style" or

not? Why is it impossible for anyone to "counsel and help" one in finding an "individual style"? Instead of seeking criticism, what does Rilke say the young poet must do? The word "nature" has many meanings; what do you think Rilke means by "draw near to Nature"? Why do you think he advises the young poet not to write love poems? Why does he advise him to avoid "general themes"? What does he suggest as a source of subject matter? Even though you may not be a poet, is there any way you could use this advice in your own themes? Do you find any corroborating testimony in yourself to what Rilke says of childhood—"that precious, kingly possession, that treasure-house"? If you have read, earlier in this book, the piece by Proust called here "The Bodily Memory," do you find any relationship between Proust's and Rilke's attitudes toward the "sunken sensations" of childhood? What does Rilke mean by "test the deeps in which your life takes rise"? Does this advice seem to you to have larger relevance than to the writing of poetry?

3. If you have read the pieces by Auden and Flaubert, you might write a paper comparing their ideas with those of Rilke. Or you might draw up a sort of notebook of what you consider to be the most significant statements in these pieces—if you can get your teacher to agree that the discrimination needed for such notes deserves credit. Or you might do a bit of research on Rilke's life and write a paper on whether or not he followed his own advice that the poet must build his life, "its most indifferent and slightest hour," according to the psychological imperatives of poetry.

W. H. Auden ❧ Poetry Must Praise

❧ Anglo-American poet, critic, essayist, librettist, born in England in 1907, educated at Oxford, became an American citizen in 1946. After the generation of T. S. Eliot and Ezra Pound, Auden became the most articulate, skillful, and influential poet writing in English. Some of his better-known books are *Look, Stranger, New Year Letter, For the Time Being: A Christmas Oratorio,* and *The Age of Anxiety.* He has taught and lectured widely in the United States, received the Pulitzer Prize for Poetry in 1948, returned to England in 1956 to take the Chair of Poetry at Oxford. ❧

AWAY back[1] we left a young poet who had just written his first real poem and was wondering if it would be his last. We must assume that it was not, that he has arrived on the literary scene in the sense that now people pass judgment on his work without having read it. Twenty years have gone by. The table of his Mad Hatter's Tea-Party has gotten much longer and there are thousands of new faces, some charming, some quite horrid. Down at the far end, some of those who used to be so amusing have turned into crashing bores or fallen asleep, a sad change which has often come over later guests after holding forth for a few years. Boredom does not necessarily imply disapproval; I still think Rilke a great poet though I cannot read him any more.

From W. H. Auden's inaugural lecture at Oxford, called "Making, Knowing, and Judging," as published in *The Dyer's Hand* (New York: Random House, Inc., 1962). Reprinted by permission of Random House, Inc.

[1] The reference is to the earlier part of this lecture.

Many of the books which have been most important to him have not been works of poetry or criticism but books which have altered his way of looking at the world and himself, and a lot of these, probably, are what an expert in their field would call "unsound." The expert, no doubt, is right, but it is not for a poet to judge; his duty is to be grateful.

And among the experiences which have influenced his writing, a number may have been experiences of other arts. I know, for example, that through listening to music I have learned much about how to organize a poem, how to obtain variety and contrast through change of tone, tempo and rhythm, though I could not say just how. Man is an analogy-drawing animal; that is his great good fortune. His danger is of treating analogies as identities, of saying, for instance, "Poetry should be as much like music as possible." I suspect that the people who are most likely to say this are the tone-deaf. The more one loves another art, the less likely it is that one will wish to trespass upon its domain.

During these twenty years, one thing has never changed since he wrote his first poem. Every time he writes a new one, the same question occurs to him: "Will it ever happen again," but now he begins to hear his Censor[2] saying: "It must never happen again." Having spent twenty years learning to be himself, he finds that he must now start learning not to be himself. At first he may think this means no more than keeping a sharper look out for obsessive rhythms, tics of expression, privately numinous words, but presently he discovers that the command not to imitate himself can mean something harder than that. It can mean that he should refrain from writing a poem which might turn out to be a good one, and even an admired one. He learns that, if on finishing a poem he is convinced that it is good, the chances are that the poem is a self-imitation. The most hopeful sign that it is not is the feeling of complete uncertainty: "Either this is quite good or it is quite bad, I can't tell." And, of course, it may very well be quite bad. Discovering oneself is a passive process because the self is already there. Time and attention are all that it takes. But changing oneself means changing in one direction rather than another, and towards one goal rather than another. The goal may be unknown but movement is impossible without a hypothesis as to where it lies. It is at this point, therefore, that a poet often begins to take an interest in theories of poetry and even to develop one of his own.

I am always interested in hearing what a poet has to say about the

[2] Auden uses the word "censor" here in its Freudian sense (see page 842).

nature of poetry, though I do not take it too seriously. As objective statements his definitions are never accurate, never complete and always one-sided. Not one would stand up under a rigorous analysis. In unkind moments one is almost tempted to think that all they are really saying is: "Read me. Don't read the other fellows." But, taken as critical admonitions addressed by his Censor to the poet himself, there is generally something to be learned from them.

Baudelaire[3] has given us an excellent account of their origin and purpose.

> I pity the poets who are guided solely by instinct; they seem to me incomplete. In the spiritual life of the former there must come a crisis when they would think out their art, discover the obscure laws in consequence of which they have produced, and draw from this study a series of precepts whose divine purpose is infallibility in poetic production.

The evidence, that is to say, upon which the poet bases his conclusions consists of his own experiences in writing and his private judgments upon his own works. Looking back, he sees many occasions on which he took a wrong turning or walked up a blind alley, mistakes which, it seems to him now, he could have avoided, had he been more conscious at the time of the choice he was making. Looking over the poems he has written, he finds that, irrespective of their merits, there are some which he particularly dislikes and some which are his favorites. Of one he may think: "This is full of faults, but it is the kind of poem I ought to write more of"; of another: "This may be all right in itself but it's exactly the sort of thing I must never do again." The principles he formulates, therefore, are intended to guard himself against making unnecessary mistakes and provide him with a guesswork map of the future. They are fallible, of course — like all guesses — the word *infallibility* in Baudelaire's description is typical poet's fib. But there is a difference between a project which may fail and one which must.

In trying to formulate principles, a poet may have another motive which Baudelaire does not mention, a desire to justify his writing poetry at all, and in recent years this motive seems to have grown stronger. The Rimbaud Myth[4] — the tale of a great poet who ceases writing, not because, like Coleridge, he has nothing more to say, but because he chooses

---

[3] One of the greatest French poets (1821–1867).

[4] This prodigiously talented French poet (1854-1891) stopped writing at the age of nineteen and went to Africa to become a nomad trader.

to stop — may not be true, I am pretty sure it is not, but as a myth it haunts the artistic conscience of this century.

Knowing all this, and knowing that you know it, I shall now proceed to make some general statements of my own. I hope they are not non-sense, but I cannot be sure. At least, even as emotive noises, I find them useful to me. The only verifiable facts I can offer in evidence are these.

Some cultures make a social distinction between the sacred and the profane, certain human beings are publicly regarded as numinous, and a clear division is made between certain actions which are regarded as sacred rites of great importance to the well-being of society, and every-day profane behavior. In such cultures, if they are advanced enough to recognize poetry as an art, the poet has a public — even a professional status — and his poetry is either public or esoteric.

There are other cultures, like our own, in which the distinction be-tween the sacred and the profane is not socially recognized. Either the distinction is denied or it is regarded as an individual matter of taste with which society is not and should not be concerned. In such cultures, the poet has an amateur status and his poetry is neither public nor esoteric but intimate. That is to say, he writes neither as a citizen nor as a member of a group of professional adepts, but as a single person to be read by other single persons. Intimate poetry is not necessarily obscure; for someone not in the know, ancient esoteric poetry can be more obscure than the wildest modern. Nor, needless to say, is intimate poetry neces-sarily inferior to other kinds.

In what follows, the terms Primary and Secondary Imagination are taken, of course, from the thirteenth chapter of *Biographia Literaria*.[5]

[5] Auden refers to the following passage from Coleridge's *Biographia Literaria*: "The imagination then I consider either as primary, or secondary. The primary imagina-tion I hold to be the living power and prime agent of all human perception, and as a repetition in the finite mind of the eternal act of creation in the infinite I AM. The secondary I consider as an echo of the former, co-existing with the conscious will, yet still as identical with the primary in the kind of its agency, and differing only in degree, and in the mode of its operation. It dissolves, diffuses, dissipates, in order to re-create; or where this process is rendered impossible, yet still, at all events, it struggles to idealize and to unify. It is essentially *vital*, even as all objects (as objects) are essentially fixed and dead."

Coleridge then goes on to differentiate "fancy" from imagination: "Fancy, on the contrary, has no other counters to play with but fixities and definites. The fancy is indeed no other than a mode of memory emancipated from the order of time and space; and blended with, and modified by that empirical phaenomenon of the will which we express by the word *choice*. But equally with the ordinary memory it must receive all its materials ready made from the law of association."

I have adopted them because, though my description may differ from Coleridge's, I believe we are both trying to describe the same phenomena.

Herewith, then, what I might describe as a literary dogmatic psalm. . . .

The concern of the Primary Imagination, its only concern, is with sacred beings and sacred events. The sacred is that to which it is obliged to respond; the profane is that to which it cannot respond and therefore does not know. The profane is known to other faculties of the mind, but not to the Primary Imagination. A sacred being cannot be anticipated; it must be encountered. On encounter the imagination has no option but to respond. All imaginations do not recognize the same sacred beings or events, but every imagination responds to those it recognizes in the same way. The impression made upon the imagination by any sacred being is of an overwhelming but undefinable importance — an unchangeable quality, an Identity, as Keats said:[6] I-am-that-I-am is what every sacred being seems to say. The impression made by a sacred event is of an overwhelming but undefinable significance. In his book *Witchcraft,* Mr. Charles Williams has described it thus:

> One is aware that a phenomenon, being wholly itself, is laden with universal meaning. A hand lighting a cigarette is the explanation of everything; a foot stepping from the train is the rock of all existence. . . . Two light dancing steps by a girl appear to be what all the Schoolmen were trying to express . . . but two quiet steps by an old man seem like the very speech of hell. Or the other way round.

The response of the imagination to such a presence or significance is a passion of awe. This awe may vary greatly in intensity and range in tone from joyous wonder to panic dread. A sacred being may be attractive or repulsive — a swan or an octopus — beautiful or ugly — a toothless hag or a fair young child — good or evil — a Beatrice or a Belle Dame Sans Merci[7] — historical fact or fiction — a person met on the road or an image encountered in a story or a dream — it may be noble or something unmentionable in a drawing room, it may be anything it likes

---

[6] See Note 8.

[7] The references are to the Beatrice of *The Divine Comedy,* by whose influence Dante was led from the borders of Hell to a celestial vision of Paradise, and to the Belle Dame of Keats's ballad (see page 188), who led the knight-at-arms to a frightful vision of death.

on condition, but this condition is absolute, that it arouse awe. The realm of the Primary Imagination is without freedom, sense of time or humor. Whatever determines this response or lack of response lies below consciousness and is of concern to psychology, not art.

Some sacred beings seem to be sacred to all imaginations at all times. The Moon, for example, Fire, Snakes and those four important beings which can only be defined in terms of nonbeing: Darkness, Silence, Nothing, Death. Some, like kings, are only sacred to all within a certain culture; some only to members of a social group — the Latin language among humanists — and some are only sacred to a single imagination. Many of us have sacred landscapes which probably all have much in common, but there will almost certainly be details which are peculiar to each. An imagination can acquire new sacred beings and it can lose old ones to the profane. Sacred beings can be acquired by social contagion but not consciously. One cannot be taught to recognize a sacred being, one has to be converted. As a rule, perhaps, with advancing age sacred events gain in importance over sacred beings.

A sacred being may also be an object of desire but the imagination does not desire it. A desire can be a sacred being but the imagination is without desire. In the presence of the sacred, it is self-forgetful; in its absence the very type of the profane, "The most unpoetical of all God's creatures."[8] A sacred being may also demand to be loved or obeyed, it

---

[8] Auden refers here (as also, a little earlier, when he speaks of Keats's use of the word "Identity" for what Auden means by a "sacred being") to Keats's famous description of the "poetical character" in a letter to Richard Woodhouse, written in October, 1818:

"As to the poetical Character itself (I mean that sort of which, if I am any thing, I am a Member; that sort distinguished from the wordsworthian or egotistical sublime; which is a thing per se and stands alone) it is not itself — it has no self — it is every thing and nothing — It has no character — it enjoys light and shade; it lives in gusto, be it foul or fair, high or low, rich or poor, mean or elevated — It has as much delight in conceiving an Iago as an Imogen. What shocks the virtuous philosopher, delights the camelion Poet. It does no harm from its relish of the dark side of things any more than from its taste for the bright one; because they both end in speculation. A Poet is the most unpoetical of any thing in existence; because he has no Identity — he is continually in for — and filling some other Body — The Sun, the Moon, the Sea and Men and Women who are creatures of impulse are poetical and have about them an unchangeable attribute — the poet has none; no identity — he is certainly the most unpoetical of all God's Creatures. If then he has no self, and if I am a Poet, where is the Wonder that I should say I would . . . write no more? Might I not at that very instant have been cogitating on the Characters of Saturn and Ops? It is a wretched thing to confess; but is a very fact that not one

may reward or punish, but the imagination is unconcerned: a law can be a sacred being, but the imagination does not obey. To the imagination a sacred being is self-sufficient, and like Aristotle's God can have no need of friends.

The Secondary Imagination is of another character and at another mental level. It is active not passive, and its categories are not the sacred and the profane, but the beautiful and ugly. Our dreams are full of sacred beings and events — indeed, they may well contain nothing else, but we cannot distinguish in dreams — or so it seems to me, though I may be wrong — between the beautiful and the ugly. Beauty and ugliness pertain to Form not to Being. The Primary Imagination only recognizes one kind of being, the sacred, but the Secondary Imagination recognizes both beautiful and ugly forms. To the Primary Imagination a sacred being is that which it is. To the Secondary Imagination a beautiful form is as it ought to be, an ugly form as it ought not to be. Observing the beautiful, it has the feeling of satisfaction, pleasure, absence of conflict; observing the ugly, the contrary feelings. It does not desire the beautiful, but an ugly form arouses in it a desire that its ugliness be corrected and made beautiful. It does not worship the beautiful; it approves of it and can give reasons for its approval. The Secondary Imagination has, one might say, a bourgeois nature. It approves of regularity, of spatial symmetry and temporal repetition, of law and order: it disapproves of loose ends, irrelevance and mess.

Lastly, the Secondary Imagination is social and craves agreement with other minds. If I think a form beautiful and you think it ugly, we cannot both help agreeing that one of us must be wrong, whereas if I think something is sacred and you think it is profane, neither of us will dream of arguing the matter.

Both kinds of imagination are essential to the health of the mind. Without the inspiration of sacred awe, its beautiful forms would soon become banal, its rhythms mechanical; without the activity of the Sec-

---

word I ever utter can be taken for granted as an opinion growing out of my identical nature — how can it, when I have no nature? When I am in a room with People if I ever am free from speculating on creations of my own brain, then not myself goes home to myself: but the identity of every one in the room begins to press upon me that I am in a very little time an⟨ni⟩hilated — not only among Men; it would be the same in a Nursery of children: I know not whether I make myself wholly understood: I hope enough so to let you see that no dependence is to be placed on what I said that day."

ondary Imagination the passivity of the Primary would be the mind's undoing; sooner or later its sacred beings would possess it, it would come
to think of itself as sacred, exclude the outer world as profane and so go
mad.

The impulse to create a work of art is felt when, in certain persons,
the passive awe provoked by sacred beings or events is transformed into
a desire to express that awe in a rite of worship or homage, and to be fit
homage, this rite must be beautiful. This rite has no magical or idolatrous
intention; nothing is expected in return. Nor is it, in a Christian sense, an
act of devotion. If it praises the Creator, it does so indirectly by praising
His creatures — among which may be human notions of the Divine
Nature. With God as Redeemer, it has, so far as I can see, little if anything to do.

In poetry the rite is verbal; it pays homage by naming. I suspect that
the predisposition of a mind towards the poetic medium may have its
origin in an error. A nurse, let us suppose, says to a child, "Look at the
moon!" The child looks and for him this is a sacred encounter. In his mind
the word "moon" is not a name of a sacred object but one of its most important properties and, therefore, numinous. The notion of writing
poetry cannot occur to him, of course, until he has realized that names
and things are not identical and that there cannot be an intelligible
sacred language, but I wonder if, when he has discovered the social
nature of language, he would attach such importance to one of its uses,
that of naming, if he had not previously made this false identification.

The pure poem, in the French sense of *la poésie pure* would be, I
suppose, a celebration of the numinous-in-itself in abstraction from all
cases and devoid of any profane reference whatsoever — a sort of *sanctus, sanctus, sanctus*. If it could be written, which is doubtful, it would
not necessarily be the best poem.

A poem is a rite; hence its formal and ritualistic character. Its use
of language is deliberately and ostentatiously different from talk. Even
when it employs the diction and rhythms of conversation, it employs
them as a deliberate informality, presupposing the norm with which they
are intended to contrast.

The form of a rite must be beautiful, exhibiting, for example, balance, closure and aptness to that which it is the form of. It is over this
last quality of aptness that most of our aesthetic quarrels arise, and must
arise, whenever our sacred and profane worlds differ.

> To the Eyes of a Miser, a Guinea is far more beautiful than the Sun &
> a bag worn with the use of Money has more beautiful proportions than a
> Vine filled with Grapes.

Blake, it will be noticed, does not accuse the Miser of lacking imagination.

The value of a profane thing lies in what it usefully does, the value of a sacred thing lies in what it *is:* a sacred thing may also have a function but it does not have to. The apt name for a profane being, therefore, is the word or words that accurately describe his function — a Mr. Smith, a Mr. Weaver. The apt name for a sacred being is the word or words which worthily express his importance — Son of Thunder, The Well-Wishing One.

Great changes in artistic style always reflect some alteration in the frontier between the sacred and profane in the imagination of a society. Thus, to take an architectural example, a seventeenth-century monarch had the same function as that of a modern State official — he had to govern. But in designing his palace, the Baroque architect did not aim, as a modern architect aims when designing a government building, at making an office in which the king could govern as easily and efficiently as possible; he was trying to make a home fit for God's earthly representative to inhabit; in so far as he thought at all about what the king would do in it as a ruler, he thought of his ceremonial not his practical actions.

Even today few people find a functionally furnished living room beautiful because, to most of us, a sitting room is not merely a place to sit in; it is also a shrine for father's chair.

Thanks to the social nature of language, a poet can relate any one sacred being or event to any other. The relation may be harmonious, an ironic contrast or a tragic contradiction like the great man, or the beloved, and death; he can relate them to every other concern of the mind, the demands of desire, reason and conscience, and he can bring them into contact and contrast with the profane. Again the consequences can be happy, ironic, tragic and, in relation to the profane, comic. How many poems have been written, for example, upon one of these three themes:

> This was sacred but now it is profane. Alas, or thank goodness!
> This is sacred but ought it to be?
> This is sacred but is that so important?

But it is from the sacred encounters of his imagination that a poet's impulse to write a poem arises. Thanks to the language, he need not name them directly unless he wishes; he can describe one in terms of another and translate those that are private or irrational or socially unacceptable into such as are acceptable to reason and society. Some poems are directly *about* the sacred beings they were written *for:* others are not, and in that case no reader can tell what was the original encounter which provided the impulse for the poem. Nor, probably, can the poet himself. Every poem he writes involves his whole past. Every love poem, for instance, is hung with trophies of lovers gone, and among these may be some very peculiar objects indeed. The lovely lady of the present may number among her predecessors an overshot waterwheel. But the encounter, be it novel or renewed by recollection from the past, must be suffered by a poet before he can write a genuine poem.

Whatever its actual content and overt interest, every poem is rooted in imaginative awe. Poetry can do a hundred and one things, delight, sadden, disturb, amuse, instruct — it may express every possible shade of emotion, and describe every conceivable kind of event, but there is only one thing that all poetry must do; it must praise all it can for being and for happening.

⌇§ FOR DISCUSSION AND WRITING

1. Explain the following statement, in the fourth paragraph: "Having spent twenty years learning to be himself, he finds that he must now start learning not to be himself." If you have read the interview with Henry Moore, a few pages earlier, on Michelangelo, do you find any correspondence between Auden's point here and what Moore says about the Rondanini *Pietà?*

2. Explain Auden's distinction between cultures that make a clear division between the "sacred" and the "profane," and those that do not. If you can, give examples. In which category does he place our own culture? Is he justified in doing so, or not? What has the distinction to do with poets and poetry? What does Auden mean by the words "sacred" and "profane"?

3. Footnote 5 gives Coleridge's famous definition of the "primary" and "secondary" imagination, of which there are almost as many interpretations

as there are scholars of Coleridge. What is Auden's interpretation of the Primary Imagination? What examples does he give of "sacred beings"? If you have read the selection from Jung, earlier in this book, do you find any correspondence between what Auden calls "sacred beings" and what Jung calls "primordial images" or "archetypes"? Do you find any correspondence between the Primary Imagination, as Auden interprets it, and what Jung calls the "collective unconscious"? One must be careful here to avoid having one's judgment swamped by arbitrary terminology. According to Jung, the archetypes of the collective unconscious are common to everybody. Which of the "sacred beings" mentioned by Auden are common to everybody? Which are not? Can you explain why Auden says that the imagination (that is, the Primary Imagination) does not have attitudes of desire or choice about "sacred beings"? You might test this question on your own experience of "sacred beings" (indeed, the whole discussion here will be meaningless unless you can correlate it with "sacred beings" of your own). For instance, he mentions the Moon, Fire, Darkness, and Death as common "sacred beings"; are your reactions toward these a matter of your own decision and control or not? Auden says that our dreams are full of "sacred beings"; can you corroborate this from your own dreams?

4. What is Auden's interpretation of what Coleridge calls the Secondary Imagination? What distinction does he make between the attitudes of the Primary and the Secondary Imagination toward the "beautiful" and the "ugly," and how do they differ with regard to social agreement? Can you find personal illustrations?

5. Explain Auden's description of a work of art as a "rite of worship or homage." How does he distinguish the language of poetry from ordinary language? Explain this statement, in the next to the last paragraph: "The lovely lady of the present may number among her predecessors an overshot waterwheel." (It would be advisable here, of course, to find out what an overshot waterwheel is.)

6. What connection with the rest of the essay does the final statement have, that poetry "must praise all it can for being and for happening"?

7. Write a paper on a topic suggested by the second or third question—on your own "sacred beings," or on the "sacred" and "profane" in our culture.

John Cage ◄§ Experimental Music

◄§ American composer, born in 1912. Cage is the best-known and most articulate of avant-garde composers. His compositions have made use of the prepared piano, magnetic tape, sleigh bells, oxen bells, Turkish and Chinese
cymbals, wind glass, tin cans, and teponaztli (two-tone wooden gongs). ξ➤

FORMERLY, whenever anyone said the music I presented was experimental, I objected. It seemed to me that composers knew what they
were doing, and that the experiments that had been made had taken
place prior to the finished works, just as sketches are made before paintings and rehearsals precede performances. But, giving the matter further
thought, I realized that there is ordinarily an essential difference between making a piece of music and hearing one. A composer knows his
work as a woodsman knows a path he has traced and retraced, while a
listener is confronted by the same work as one is in the woods by a plant
he has never seen before.

Now, on the other hand, times have changed; music has changed;
and I no longer object to the word "experimental." I use it in fact to

describe all the music that especially interests me and to which I am devoted, whether someone else wrote it or I myself did. What has happened is that I have become a listener and the music has become something to hear. Many people, of course, have given up saying "experimental" about this new music. Instead, they either move to a halfway point and say "controversial" or depart to a greater distance and question whether this "music" is music at all.

For in this new music nothing takes place but sounds: those that are notated and those that are not. Those that are not notated appear in the written music as silences, opening the doors of the music to the sounds that happen to be in the environment. This openness exists in the fields of modern sculpture and architecture. The glass houses of Mies van der Rohe reflect their environment, presenting to the eye images of clouds, trees, or grass, according to the situation. And while looking at the constructions in wire of the sculptor Richard Lippold, it is inevitable that one will see other things, and people too, if they happen to be there at the same time, through the network of wires. There is no such thing as an empty space or an empty time. There is always something to see, something to hear. In fact, try as we may to make a silence, we cannot. For certain engineering purposes, it is desirable to have as silent a situation as possible. Such a room is called an anechoic chamber, its six walls made of special material, a room without echoes. I entered one at Harvard University several years ago and heard two sounds, one high and one low. When I described them to the engineer in charge, he informed me that the high one was my nervous system in operation, the low one my blood in circulation. Until I die there will be sounds. And they will continue following my death. One need not fear about the future of music.

But this fearlessness only follows if, at the parting of the ways, where it is realized that sounds occur whether intended or not, one turns in the direction of those he does not intend. This turning is psychological and seems at first to be a giving up of everything that belongs to humanity — for a musician, the giving up of music. This psychological turning leads to the world of nature, where, gradually or suddenly, one sees that humanity and nature, not separate, are in this world together; that nothing was lost when everything was given away. In fact, everything is gained. In musical terms, any sounds may occur in any combination and in any continuity.

And it is a striking coincidence that just now the technical means to produce such a free-ranging music are available. When the Allies entered Germany towards the end of World War II, it was discovered that improvements had been made in recording sounds magnetically such that tape had become suitable for the high-fidelity recording of music. First in France with the work of Pierre Schaeffer, later here, in Germany, in Italy, in Japan, and perhaps, without my knowing it, in other places, magnetic tape was used not simply to record performances of music but to make a new music that was possible only because of it. Given a minimum of two tape recorders and a disk recorder, the following processes are possible: 1) a single recording of any sound may be made; 2) a rerecording may be made, in the course of which, by means of filters and circuits, any or all of the physical characteristics of a given recorded sound may be altered; 3) electronic mixing (combining on a third machine sounds issuing from two others) permits the presentation of any number of sounds in combination; 4) ordinary splicing permits the juxtaposition of any sounds, and when it includes unconventional cuts, it, like rerecording, brings about alterations of any or all of the original physical characteristics. The situation made available by these means is essentially a total sound-space, the limits of which are ear-determined only, the position of a particular sound in this space being the result of five determinants: frequency or pitch, amplitude or loudness, overtone structure or timbre, duration, and morphology (how the sound begins, goes on, and dies away). By the alteration of any one of these determinants, the position of the sound in sound-space changes. Any sound at any point in this total sound-space can move to become a sound at any other point. But advantage can be taken of these possibilities only if one is willing to change one's musical habits radically. That is, one may take advantage of the appearance of images without visible transition in distant places, which is a way of saying "television," if one is willing to stay at home instead of going to a theatre. Or one may fly if one is willing to give up walking.

Musical habits include scales, modes, theories of counterpoint and harmony, and the study of the timbres, singly and in combination of a limited number of sound-producing mechanisms. In mathematical terms these all concern discrete steps. They resemble walking — in the case of pitches, on steppingstones twelve in number. This cautious stepping is not characteristic of the possibilities of magnetic tape, which is revealing to us that musical action or existence can occur at any point or along any line or curve or what have you in total sound-space; that we are, in fact, technically equipped to transform our contemporary awareness of nature's manner of operation into art.

Again there is a parting of the ways. One has a choice. If he does not wish to give up his attempts to control sound, he may complicate his musical technique towards an approximation of the new possibilities and awareness. (I use the word "approximation" because a measuring mind can never finally measure nature.) Or, as before, one may give up the desire to control sound, clear his mind of music, and set about discovering means to let sounds be themselves rather than vehicles for man-made theories or expressions of human sentiments.

This project will seem fearsome to many, but on examination it gives no cause for alarm. Hearing sounds which are just sounds immediately sets the theorizing mind to theorizing, and the emotions of human beings are continually aroused by encounters with nature. Does not a mountain unintentionally evoke in us a sense of wonder? otters along a stream a sense of mirth? night in the woods a sense of fear? Do not rain falling and mists rising up suggest the love binding heaven and earth? Is not decaying flesh loathsome? Does not the death of someone we love bring sorrow? And is there a greater hero than the least plant that grows? What is more angry than the flash of lightning and the sound of thunder? These responses to nature are mine and will not necessarily correspond with another's. Emotion takes place in the person who has it. And sounds, when allowed to be themselves, do not require that those who hear them do so unfeelingly. The opposite is what is meant by response ability.

New music: new listening. Not an attempt to understand something that is being said, for, if something were being said, the sounds would be given the shapes of words. Just an attention to the activity of sounds.

Those involved with the composition of experimental music find ways and means to remove themselves from the activities of the sounds they make. Some employ chance operations, derived from sources as ancient as the Chinese *Book of Changes,* or as modern as the tables of random numbers used also by physicists in research. Or, analogous to the Rorschach tests of psychology, the interpretation of imperfections in the paper upon which one is writing may provide a music free from one's memory and imagination. Geometrical means employing spatial superimpositions at variance with the ultimate performance in time may be used. The total field of possibilities may be roughly divided and the actual sounds within these divisions may be indicated as to number but left to the performer or to the splicer to choose. In this latter case, the composer resembles the maker of a camera who allows someone else to take the picture.

Whether one uses tape or writes for conventional instruments, the present musical situation has changed from what it was before tape came into being. This also need not arouse alarm, for the coming into being of something new does not by that fact deprive what was of its proper place. Each thing has its own place, never takes the place of something else; and the more things there are, as is said, the merrier.

But several effects of tape on experimental music may be mentioned. Since so many inches of tape equal so many seconds of time, it has become more and more usual that notation is in space rather than in symbols of quarter, half, and sixteenth notes and so on. Thus where on a page a note appears will correspond to when in a time it is to occur. A stop watch is used to facilitate a performance; and a rhythm results which is a far cry from horse's hoofs and other regular beats.

Also it has been impossible with the playing of several separate tapes at once to achieve perfect synchronization. This fact has led some towards the manufacture of multiple-tracked tapes and machines with a corresponding number of heads; while others — those who have accepted the sounds they do not intend — now realize that the score, the requiring that many parts be played in a particular togetherness, is not an accurate representation of how things are. These now compose parts but not scores, and the parts may be combined in any unthought ways. This means that each performance of such a piece of music is unique, as interesting to its composer as to others listening. It is easy to see again the parallel with nature, for even with leaves of the same tree, no two are exactly alike. The parallel in art is the sculpture with moving parts, the mobile.

It goes without saying that dissonances and noises are welcome in this new music. But so is the dominant seventh chord if it happens to put in an appearance.

Rehearsals have shown that this new music, whether for tape or for instruments, is more clearly heard when the several loud-speakers or performers are separated in space rather than grouped closely together.

For this music is not concerned with harmoniousness as generally under-stood, where the quality of harmony results from a blending of several elements. Here we are concerned with the coexistence of dissimilars, and the central points where fusion occurs are many: the ears of the listeners wherever they are. This disharmony, to paraphrase Bergson's statement about disorder, is simply a harmony to which many are unaccustomed.

Where do we go from here? Towards theatre. That art more than music resembles nature. We have eyes as well as ears, and it is our busi-ness while we are alive to use them.

And what is the purpose of writing music? One is, of course, not dealing with purposes but dealing with sounds. Or the answer must take the form of paradox: a purposeful purposelessness or a purposeless play. This play, however, is an affirmation of life — not an attempt to bring order out of chaos nor to suggest improvements in creation, but simply a way of waking up to the very life we're living, which is so excellent once one gets one's mind and one's desires out of its way and lets it act of its own accord.

⇜ FOR DISCUSSION AND WRITING

1. What change in his own attitude toward music does Cage speak of in the first two paragraphs?

2. In the third paragraph he speaks of the "silences" notated in written music; does he consider these as absolute silences? In relation to his subject, what does he mean by saying that "there is no such thing as an empty space or an empty time"? The title of the book from which this chapter is taken is *Silence;* in view of the content of the chapter, what would you say is the implication of that title? What is the relationship he suggests between the "silences" of music and the "openness" of modern architecture and sculp-ture? He cites the work of Mies van der Rohe and Richard Lippold as ex-amples of "openness"; can you suggest other examples?

3. In the fourth paragraph, what particular relationship between music and "the world of nature" does he refer to? If you have read Aristotle's *Poetics,* earlier in this book, do you find any grounds of comparison between Cage's idea of music and the Aristotelian concept of "imitation"?

4. What does Cage mean, in the fifth paragraph, by "a total sound-space"? Given the fact that, by definition, art is not nature and nature is not art, do you find in the various tape-recording processes mentioned here any implicit or explicit differentiation between natural sounds as such and the musician's manipulation of them (that is, between "nature" and "art")?

5. How would you interpret, in terms both of the context of this piece and your own conception of music, the last sentence of the seventh paragraph, about letting "sounds be themselves rather than vehicles for man-made theories or expressions of human sentiments"? Music, as an art, is a creation of human beings; why should it not embody "man-made theories" and "human sentiments"? The epithet "man-made" is frequently used in a derogatory way; it is quite likely that you have used it that way yourself. Can you explain the derogatory assumption that lurks in the epithet? Are man-made things less worthy than ant-made things or bird-made things? In the recording processes Cage speaks of in the fifth paragraph and in the possibilities of technical manipulation he suggests, is there nothing "man-made"? and are sounds actually allowed to "be themselves"?

6. Point out several effects, mentioned by Cage, of the invention and use of magnetic tape on the composing, notation, performance, and qualities of experimental music. Can you offer any suggestion as to why, in the next to the last paragraph, his answer to his own question, "Where do we go from here?" is "Towards theatre"? Can you explain why he says that the art of the theater "more than music resembles nature"?

7. What is your interpretation of the paradox in the last paragraph—that the purpose of writing music is "a purposeful purposelessness or a purposeless play"? Why is such "play" an "affirmation of life"?

8. If you have read Alan Watts' piece on Zen earlier in this book, you might find a very interesting subject for a writing assignment in a comparison of Cage's philosophy of music (for it is, of course, a philosophy, as the last two paragraphs clearly show) with what Watts has to say as to the meaning, purpose, and discipline of Zen, and of Zen art. In Question 5, we picked some holes in Cage's logic, but picking holes is far easier than thinking creatively and constructively; in his ideas about "new music, new listening" he is obviously getting at something important and renovating in our relationship to sounds; as a written assignment, you might review the piece from that point of view. Or you might write a paper, entirely from your own point of view, on modern music.

Sergei Eisenstein ✥ The Cinematographic Principle and the Ideogram

✥ Russian film director and writer on the aesthetics of the film (1898-1948). Eisenstein was one of the earliest and greatest of those who made an art of the film, as in his *Potemkin, Alexander Nevsky, Ivan the Terrible,* and *Thunder over Mexico.* He was an ardent supporter of the Communist revolution in its earlier stages, but was apparently a victim of the later "purges." ✥

IT IS a weird and wonderful feat to have written a pamphlet on something that in reality does not exist. There is, for example, no such thing as a cinema without cinematography. And yet the author of the pamphlet preceding this essay* has contrived to write a book about the *cinema* of a country that has no *cinematography.* About the cinema of a country that has, in its culture, an infinite number of cinematographic traits, strewn everywhere with the sole exception of — its cinema.

This essay is on the cinematographic traits of Japanese culture that lie outside the Japanese cinema. . . .

From *Film Form* by Sergei Eisenstein, edited and translated by Jay Leyda. Copyright, 1949, by Harcourt, Brace & World, Inc., and reprinted with their permission.

* Eisenstein's essay was originally published as an "afterword" to N. Kaufman's pamphlet, *Japanese Cinema* (Moscow, 1929).

Cinema is: so many corporations, such and such turnovers of capital, so and so many stars, such and such dramas.

Cinematography is, first and foremost, montage.[1]

The Japanese cinema is excellently equipped with corporations, actors, and stories. But the Japanese cinema is completely unaware of montage. Nevertheless the principle of montage can be identified as the basic element of Japanese representational culture.

Writing — for their writing is primarily representational.

The hieroglyph.

The naturalistic image of an object, as portrayed by the skilful Chinese hand of Ts'ang Chieh 2650 years before our era, becomes slightly formalized and, with its 539 fellows, forms the first "contingent" of hieroglyphs. Scratched out with a stylus on a slip of bamboo, the portrait of an object maintained a resemblance to its original in every respect.

But then, by the end of the third century, the brush is invented. In the first century after the "joyous event" (A.D.) — paper. And, lastly, in the year 220 — India ink.

A complete upheaval. A revolution in draughtsmanship. And, after having undergone in the course of history no fewer than fourteen different styles of handwriting, the hieroglyph crystallized in its present form. The means of production (brush and India ink) determined the form.

The fourteen reforms had their way. As a result:

In the fierily cavorting hieroglyph *ma* (a horse) it is already impossible to recognize the features of the dear little horse sagging pathetically in its hindquarters, in the writing style of Ts'ang Chieh, so well-known from ancient Chinese bronzes.

[1] This term is explained fully in the essay.

But let it rest in the Lord, this dear little horse, together with the other 607 remaining *hsiang cheng* symbols — the earliest extant category of hieroglyphs.

The real interest begins with the second category of hieroglyphs — the *huei-i*, i.e., "copulative."

The point is that the copulation (perhaps we had better say, the combination) of two hieroglyphs of the simplest series is to be regarded not as their sum, but as their product, i.e., as a value of another dimension, another degree; each, separately, corresponds to an *object*, to a fact, but their combination corresponds to a *concept*. From separate hieroglyphs has been fused — the ideogram. By the combination of two "depictables" is achieved the representation of something that is graphically undepictable.

For example: the picture for water and the picture of an eye signifies "to weep"; the picture of an ear near the drawing of a door = "to listen";

a dog + a mouth = "to bark";

a mouth + a child = "to scream";

a mouth + a bird = "to sing";

a knife + a heart = "sorrow," and so on.

But this is — montage!

Yes. It is exactly what we do in the cinema, combining shots that are *depictive*, single in meaning, neutral in content — into *intellectual* contexts and series.

This is a means and method inevitable in any cinematographic exposition. And, in a condensed and purified form, the starting point for the "intellectual cinema."

For a cinema seeking a maximum laconism[2] for the visual representation of abstract concepts.

And we hail the method of the long-lamented Ts'ang Chieh as a first step along these paths.

We have mentioned laconism. Laconism furnishes us a transition to another point. Japan possesses the most laconic form of poetry: the *haikai* (appearing at the beginning of the thirteenth century and known today as "haiku" or "hokku") and the even earlier *tanka* (mythologically assumed to have been created along with heaven and earth).

[2] Originally referring to the speech of the ancient Laconians (Spartans), the word means a short, concise, condensed form of utterance; it is more familiar in its adjectival form, "laconic."

Both are little more than hieroglyphs transposed into phrases. . . .

As the ideogram provides a means for the laconic imprinting of an abstract concept, the same method, when transposed into literary exposition, gives rise to an identical laconism of pointed imagery. . . .

But let us turn to examples.

The *haiku* is a concentrated impressionist sketch:

> A lonely crow
> On leafless bough,
> One autumn eve.
>
> BASHŌ[3]

> What a resplendent moon!
> It casts the shadow of pine boughs
> Upon the mats.
>
> KIKAKU

> An evening breeze blows.
> The water ripples
> Against the blue heron's legs.
>
> BUSON

> It is early dawn.
> The castle is surrounded
> By the cries of wild ducks.
>
> KYOROKU

The earlier *tanka* is slightly longer (by two lines):

> O mountain pheasant
> long are the feathers trail'st thou
> on the wooded hill-side —
> as long the nights seem to me
> on lonely couch sleep seeking.
>
> HITOMARO[?]

From our point of view, these are montage phrases. Shot lists.[4] The simple combination of two or three details of a material kind yields a perfectly finished representation of another kind — psychological. . . .

---

[3] Bashō, Kikaku, etc., are the names of the poets who composed these *haiku*.

[4] The word "shot" is used in the photographic sense.

We should observe that the emotion is directed towards the reader, for, as Yone Noguchi has said, "it is the readers who make the *haiku*'s imperfection a perfection of art."

Exactly the same method (in its depictive aspect) operates also in the most perfect examples of Japanese pictorial art.

Sharaku — creator of the finest prints of the eighteenth century, and especially of an immortal gallery of actors' portraits. The Japanese Daumier.[5] Despite this, almost unknown to us. The characteristic traits of his work have been analyzed only in our century. One of these critics, Julius Kurth, in discussing the question of the influence on Sharaku of sculpture, draws a parallel between his wood-cut portrait of the actor Nakayama Tomisaburō and an antique mask of the semi-religious Nō theater, the mask of a Rozo.

The faces of both the print and the mask wear an *identical expression.* . . . Features and masses are similarly arranged although the mask represents an old priest, and the print a young woman. This relationship is striking, yet these two works are otherwise totally dissimilar; this in itself is a demonstration of Sharaku's originality. While the carved mask was constructed according to fairly accurate anatomical proportions, the proportions of the portrait print are simply impossible. The space between the eyes comprises a width that makes mock of all good sense. The nose is almost twice as long in relation to the eyes as any normal nose would dare to be, and the chin stands in no sort of relation to the mouth; the brows, the mouth, and every feature — is hopelessly misrelated. *This observation may be made in all the large heads by Sharaku.* That the artist was unaware that all these proportions are false is, of course, out of

[5] Nineteenth-century French caricaturist.

the question. It was with a full awareness that he repudiated normalcy, and, while the drawing of the separate features depends on severely concentrated naturalism, their proportions have been subordinated to purely intellectual considerations. *He set up the essence of the psychic expression as the norm for the proportions of the single features.*

Is not this process that of the ideogram, combining the independent "mouth" and the dissociated symbol of "child" to form the significance of "scream"?

Is this not exactly what we of the cinema do temporally, just as Sharaku in simultaneity, when we cause a monstrous disproportion of the parts of a normally flowing event, and suddenly dismember the event into "close-up of clutching hands," "medium shots of the struggle," and "extreme close-up of bulging eyes," in making a montage disintegration of the event in various planes? In making an eye twice as large as a man's full figure?! By combining these monstrous incongruities we newly collect the disintegrated event into one whole, but in *our* aspect. According to the treatment of our relation to the event.

The disproportionate depiction of an event is organically natural to us from the beginning. Professor Luriya, of the Psychological Institute in Moscow, has shown me a drawing by a child of "lighting a stove." Everything is represented in passably accurate relationship and with great care. Firewood. Stove. Chimney. But what are those zigzags in that huge central rectangle? They turn out to be — matches. Taking into account the crucial importance of these matches for the depicted process, the child provides a proper scale for them. . . .**

** It is possible to trace this particular tendency from its ancient, almost pre-historical source (". . . in all ideational art, objects are given size according to their importance, the king being twice as large as his subjects, or a tree half the size of a man when it merely informs us that the scene is out-of-doors. Something of this principle of size according to significance persisted in the Chinese tradition. The favorite disciple of Confucius looked like a little boy beside him and the most important figure in any group was usually the largest.") through the highest development of Chinese art, parent of Japanese graphic arts: ". . . natural scale always had to bow to pictorial scale . . . size according to distance never followed the laws of geometric perspective but the needs of the design. Foreground features might be diminished to avoid obstruction and overemphasis, and far distant objects, which were too minute to count pictorially, might be enlarged to act as a counterpoint to the middle distance or foreground." [Author's note.]

Both in painting and sculpture there is a periodic and invariable return to periods of the establishment of absolutism. Displacing the expressiveness of archaic disproportion for regulated "stone tables" of officially decreed harmony.

Absolute realism is by no means the correct form of perception. It is simply the function of a certain form of social structure. Following a state monarchy, a state uniformity of thought is implanted. Ideological uniformity of a sort that can be developed pictorially in the ranks of colors and designs of the Guards regiments. . . .

A shot. A single piece of celluloid. A tiny rectangular frame in which there is, organized in some way, a piece of an event. . . .

The shot is a montage *cell.*

Just as cells in their division form a phenomenon of another order, the organism or embryo, so, on the other side of the dialectical leap from the shot, there is montage.

By what, then, is montage characterized and, consequently, its cell — the shot?

By collision. By the conflict of two pieces in opposition to each other. By conflict. By collision. . . .

As the basis of every art is conflict (an "imagist" transformation of the dialectical principle). The shot appears as the *cell* of montage. Therefore it also must be considered from the viewpoint of *conflict.*

Conflict within the shot is potential montage, in the development of its intensity shattering the quadrilateral cage of the shot and exploding its conflict into montage impulses *between* the montage pieces. . . .

If montage is to be compared with something, then a phalanx of montage pieces, of shots, should be compared to the series of explosions of an internal combustion engine, driving forward its automobile or tractor: for similarly, the dynamics of montage serve as impulses driving forward the total film.

Conflict within the frame. . . .

Conflict of graphic directions.

　　　　　　　　　　　　　　(*Lines — either static or dynamic*)

Conflict of scales.

Conflict of volumes.

Conflict of masses.

　　　　　　　(*Volumes filled with various intensities of light*)

Conflict of depths.

Close shots and long shots.

Pieces of darkness and pieces of lightness.

And, lastly, there are such unexpected conflicts as:

Conflicts between an object and its dimension — and conflicts between an event and its duration.

These may sound strange, but both are familiar to us. The first is accomplished by an optically distorted lens, and the second by stop-motion or slow-motion. . . .

Whereas we know a good deal about montage, in the theory of the shot we are still floundering about amidst the most academic attitudes, some vague tentatives, and the sort of harsh radicalism that sets one's teeth on edge.

To regard the frame as a particular, as it were, molecular case of montage makes possible the direct application of montage practice to the theory of the shot.

And similarly with the theory of lighting. To sense this as a collision between a stream of light and an obstacle, like the impact of a stream from a fire-hose striking a concrete object, or of the wind buffeting a human figure, must result in a usage of light entirely different in comprehension from that employed in playing with various combinations of "gauzes" and "spots."

Thus far we have one such significant principle of conflict: *the principle of optical counterpoint.*

And let us not now forget that soon we shall face another and less simple problem in counterpoint: *the conflict in the sound film of acoustics and optics.*

Let us return to one of the most fascinating of optical conflicts: the conflict between the frame of the shot and the object! . . .

And once again we are in Japan! For the cinematographic method is used in teaching drawing in Japanese schools.

What is our method of teaching drawing? Take any piece of white paper with four corners to it. Then cram onto it, usually even without using the edges (mostly greasy from the long drudgery!), some bored caryatid, some conceited Corinthian capital, or a plaster Dante.

The Japanese approach this from a quite different direction: Here's the branch of a cherry-tree. And the pupil cuts out from this whole, with a square, and a circle, and a rectangle — compositional units:

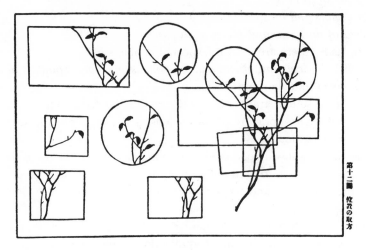

He frames a shot!

These two ways of teaching drawing can characterize the two basic tendencies struggling within the cinema of today. One — the expiring method of artificial spatial organization of an event in front of the lens. . . .

The other — a "picking-out" by the camera: organization by means of the camera. Hewing out a piece of actuality with the ax of the lens. . . .

Let us turn back to the question of methods of montage in the Japanese theater, particularly in acting.

The first and most striking example, of course, is the purely cinematographic method of "acting without transitions." Along with mimic transitions carried to a limit of refinement, the Japanese actor uses an exactly contrary method as well. At a certain moment of his performance he halts; the black-shrouded *kurogo* obligingly conceals him from the spectators. And lo! — he is resurrected in a new make-up. And in a new wig. Now characterizing another stage (degree) of his emotional state.

Thus, for example, in the Kabuki play *Narukami,* the actor Sadanji must change from drunkenness to madness. This transition is solved by a mechanical cut. And a change in the arsenal of grease-paint colors on his face, emphasizing those streaks whose duty it is to fulfill the expression of a higher intensity than those used in his previous make-up.

This method is organic to the film. The forced introduction into the film, by European acting traditions, of pieces of "emotional transitions" is yet another influence forcing the cinema to mark time. Whereas the method of "cut" acting makes possible the construction of entirely new methods. Replacing one changing face with a whole scale of facial types of varying moods affords a far more acutely expressive result than does the changing surface, too receptive and devoid of organic resistance, of any single professional actor's face.

In our new film [*Old and New*] I have eliminated the intervals between the sharply contrasting polar stages of a face's expression. . . . Here the psychological process of mingled faith and doubt is broken up into its two extreme states of joy (confidence) and gloom (disillusionment). Furthermore, this is sharply emphasized by light — illumination in no wise conforming to actual light conditions. This brings a distinct strengthening of the tension.

Another remarkable characteristic of the Kabuki theater is the principle of "disintegrated" acting. Shocho, who played the leading female rôles in the Kabuki theater that visited Moscow, in depicting the dying daughter in *Yashaō* (*The Mask-Maker*), performed his rôle in pieces of acting completely detached from each other: Acting with only the right arm. Acting with one leg. Acting with the neck and head only. (The whole process of the death agony was disintegrated into solo performances of each member playing its own rôle: the rôle of the leg, the rôle of the arms, the rôle of the head.) A breaking-up into shots. With a gradual shortening of these separate, successive pieces of acting as the tragic end approached. . . .

So, it has been possible to establish (cursorily) the permeation of the most varied branches of Japanese culture by a pure cinematographic element — its basic nerve, montage. . . .

Instead of learning how to extract the principles and technique of their remarkable acting from the traditional feudal forms of their materials, the most progressive leaders of the Japanese theater throw their energies into an adaptation of the spongy shapelessness of our own "inner" naturalism. The results are tearful and saddening. In its cinema Japan similarly pursues imitations of the most revolting examples of American and European entries in the international commercial film race.

To understand and apply her cultural peculiarities to the cinema, this is the task of Japan! Colleagues of Japan, are you really going to leave this for us to do?

~§ FOR DISCUSSION AND WRITING

1. Eisenstein's notebook-jotting style is not one that your English professor is likely to recommend for your use (you would probably find "sentence frag-ment" written in red all over your paper), but it does convey the impatient energy and swift movement of a brilliant, innovating mind. In reading the piece, one must remember the date of writing—1929—for Japanese cinema has changed a good deal since then; actually, Eisenstein's own pioneer work in cinematic montage was in large measure responsible for the international development of the film as an art form. If you are a film addict and know some of the great Japanese films of recent years, could you comment on the changes that have occurred since Eisenstein wrote this piece?

2. What is the distinction between cinema and cinematography? What is the meaning of the words "naturalistic," "formalized," and "hieroglyph," in the sentence: "The naturalistic image of an object . . . becomes slightly form-alized . . . ," etc.? What was the effect on writing of the invention of the brush and India ink? Explain the statement that "the copulation . . . of two hieroglyphs . . . is to be regarded not as their sum, but as their product. . . ." Explain the word "ideogram" as used here in relation to hieroglyphic depiction of objects and ideogrammatic expression of concepts. Eisenstein gives a few examples of the coupling of "depictables" to form ideograms representing concepts; he then says, "But this is—montage!" Could you put in your own words the meaning of "montage" as he illustrates it here? How does he relate the same process to the cinema? He goes on to speak of "intellectual cinema," a term that may give a bit of trouble since the word "intellectual" has acquired odd connotations in American usage. In terms of the exposition so far, what does he mean by "intellectual cinema"? Can you give your own examples, from films, of what you understand him to mean?

3. What do you understand by his use of the word "laconism" in reference to the Japanese poetic forms of the *haiku* and *tanka*, and what relationship is

there between that "laconism" and cinematic montage? Why does he say that both poetic forms are "little more than hieroglyphs transposed into phrases"? Using one or two of the quoted *haiku* for illustration, explain why he calls them "montage phrases," "shot lists." Explain the statement: "The simple combination of two or three details of a material kind yields a perfectly finished representation of another kind—psychological."

4. What relationship does Eisenstein point out between the antique mask and the eighteenth-century woodcut portrait? What analogy does he draw between the ideogram, the *haiku*, and the portrait? and between these and the cinema? What relationship with these has the child's drawing of "lighting a stove"? Explain the statement that "absolute realism is by no means the correct form of perception." Eisenstein shared the Marxist ideology of the early stages of the Russian Revolution, but he seems also to have been a victim of the Stalinist purges; hence one finds an unwitting irony in what he says here about "realism" in art as being a function of an absolutist social structure requiring ideological uniformity; modern Soviet "realism" quite confirms his perception. Can you offer any suggestion as to why an absolutist state finds genuine creativity and innovation in the arts dangerous?

5. In his discussion of the "shot"—the "montage cell"—Eisenstein uses the Hegelian idiom of the Marxist: "the dialectical leap," "the dialectical principle." If you understand this idiom, would you explain to the class what these phrases mean in their context? Do you agree that "the basis of every art is conflict"? What relationship has montage to conflict? Consider the list Eisenstein gives of kinds of cinematic conflict; from your own experience of films (or of other arts), attempt to explain each of these types of conflict. How does the use of lighting exemplify "collision" or "conflict"? What is meant by "the principle of optical counterpoint"?

6. Explain the analogy between the Japanese method of teaching drawing and "the conflict between the frame of the shot and the object." Explain the analogy between acting methods in the Japanese Kabuki theater and cinematography. Can you find any examples of your own to substantiate these analogies?

7. This piece sprouts with possible writing topics. The film (including television) has become the most important of mass media. Write a paper on this subject, using illustrations from your own experience and observation. Or write on the film as an art form, with specific illustration. Or look up

some more about *haiku* in the library (there are four volumes on the subject by R. H. Blyth, rather dated now in their commentary, but containing a wealth of examples), and write a paper about *haiku* as montage. Or, after studying the principle of *haiku*, write some of your own and persuade your teacher to accept them in place of prose. Or, if you are interested in graphic art, write about children's drawing or about the teaching of drawing, following up the suggestions in this piece. Or, if you are conversant with the works of Joyce or Proust or Virginia Woolf or T. S. Eliot or Ezra Pound or Wallace Stevens, you might write about the principle of "montage" as it appears there—for instance, in Stevens' "Thirteen Ways of Looking at a Blackbird." Or you might write about montage as it is exhibited in dreams.

The Process of Learning

FROM THE *first article in this section it would appear that flatworms are much superior to ourselves in their ability to absorb education from head to tail. When an educated flatworm is cut in two, the tail regenerates a head with just as much learning in it as the head that regenerates a tail. Although a great many learned human heads have been cut off in the course of history there has never been a human tail-end separated from a head that showed that proclivity. Furthermore, the primitive, uncouth flatworm that eats an educated member of his species immediately acquires, in the course of digestion, the learning of the educated worm he has eaten. If our own metabolism were as talented, and if dedicated professors would, on retirement, commend themselves thus to our diet, we might all be born with Ph.D.'s.*

The experience of the flatworm is not without symbolic relevance to the pieces that follow—the famous chapters from the autobiographies of John Stuart Mill and Henry Adams, Ezra Pound's scorching essay HOW TO READ, *and T. S. Eliot's essay* TRADITION AND THE INDIVIDUAL TALENT. *The flatworm finds himself in no difficulty about what Mill calls "the internal culture of the individual," for he evidently takes all his culture internally in every cell of his body. But Mill, who had received a superbly rational education, suffered, at the moment when he should have been most creative, a deadly apathy of the mind,* a "dark night of the soul," which robbed him of all energy and desire for putting into action what he had learned. Mill found his way laboriously back to action by a series of blind discoveries—among them, the poetry of Wordsworth—which taught him that education as preparation for life must train not only the rational faculties but also the feelings and emotions.

Henry Adams' ice-edged account of his term at Harvard has something of the same implication. The school, he says, turned out a type of mind that was "an autobiographical blank." To be without "autobiography," in Adams' sense, is to be without internal, individual, individuating life. Both Mill's and Adams' criticism of their education was more prophetic than they knew, for our education today is geared to cold-war competition in science and technology, and to economic competition for jobs, while "autobiography"—an "internal" life—becomes scarcer and scarcer.

The essays of Pound and Eliot are concerned with literature as education of the feelings and emotions, the intuitions and instincts, and especially with literature as language—that bank account we have in the experience of our forebears, a deposit made at the beginning of history and built up through all the civilized ages, which gives us our most valuable insurance of life, our most negotiable property. As against the specialization and fragmentation of modern education, both Pound's and Eliot's essays, like those of Mill and Adams, recommend to us the holistic and indivisible character of culture— for which, in the last piece of the book, Buckminster Fuller's image of a "Minni-Earth," hung out over New York's East River harbor as an educational facility for the engineers and architects of the twenty-first century, offers a fabulous technological symbol.

Jay Boyd Best ❧ The Education of Flatworms

❧ After serving as combat intelligence officer with a heavy bomber squadron in the Pacific and Far Eastern theaters during World War II, Mr. Best received his A.B. in physics from the University of Texas and his doctorate in physiology from the University of Chicago. Until recently he held the position of associate professor of physiology at the University of Illinois College of Medicine, and at present has the chair of Distinguished Professor of Biophysics at Colorado State University. ❧

IT IS generally accepted that the behavior exhibited by an animal, from the most primitive to the most advanced, arises from its brain. But how highly evolved a brain does it take to manifest those psychological attributes that we have come to associate with sentient behavior, as opposed to "mindless" or "automatic" behavior? The main structures found in the brains of men and monkeys are present in all vertebrate brains. The basic plan of this brain may have been laid down as long as 400 million years ago with the appearance of sharks in the Devonian period. Is this plan a prerequisite for anthropomorphic, or even "vertebramorphic," behavior? Is the hypothalamus necessary for hunger? Is the region of the midbrain known as the limbic system needed for fear and pleasure? Is the cerebral cortex required for pattern recognition and "complex" behavior?

When a group of us at the University of Chicago were considering such problems in 1954, it seemed to us that planarian worms might provide clues to these related riddles. The fresh-water planarian is a primitive animal that has bilateral symmetry, a rudimentary central nervous system and a distinct head end that exerts control over the rest of its body. A member of the phylum of flatworms, it has a blind-ended gut and no circulatory system. Planarians are the contemporary representatives of what must have been a very ancient form of animal, from which many higher forms of invertebrates and also the vertebrates presumably evolved.

We were aware that fresh-water planarian worms can grow a new brain, if the original one is removed, and that they will accept tissue transplants from other planarians. It seemed to us that an animal with a brain that could be regenerated and transplanted might lend itself — if it could also learn something — to experiments not possible with higher animals such as rats. What, if anything, planarians could learn was not clear. This in itself was a question of some importance.

About 40 years ago, when many workers were studying the "conditioned reflexes" first described by the Russian physiologist I. P. Pavlov, a number of conditioning experiments were performed with planarians and other kinds of worms. These early investigators were largely unaware, however, of the unlearned modifications in behavior, called pseudo-conditioning, that can be produced simply by barraging the nervous system of an animal with nonspecific stimuli. Many of their results were therefore difficult to interpret and not up to the standards of rigor currently demanded of studies of this sort. As the concepts of experimental psychology became more sophisticated and its experimentation more refined, attention was largely focused on such animals as pigeons, rats and monkeys. Between 1956 and 1959 fewer than 3 per cent of all animal-behavior experiments were performed on invertebrates, although invertebrates constitute 12 of the 13 animal phyla.

Just prior to that period Robert Thompson and James V. McConnell, working at the University of Texas, performed a classical conditioning experiment with planarians that was better controlled than any up to that time. Classical conditioning experiments are learning experiments similar to those undertaken by Pavlov. In these experiments some stimulus, such as food, acts as the "unconditioned stimulus." This is a stimulus that normally, and without training, evokes a response from the animal. For example, in a dog the normal response to food is salivation. Shortly before the unconditioned stimulus is presented, the animal is exposed to a "conditioned stimulus," such as the sound of a buzzer. The conditioned stimulus normally produces no response, or a response different from that evoked by the unconditioned stimulus. After a number of trials the conditioned stimulus evokes a response resembling that normally evoked by the unconditioned stimulus. Thus the dog will begin to salivate on hearing a buzzer that alerts him to the fact that food is coming.

In the Thompson and McConnell experiment a conditioning trial consisted of suddenly shining a strong light on a planarian. Several seconds after the light was turned on, the planarian received a mild electric shock. The planarian's normal response to the light alone was to stretch itself. When it received the shock, it contracted or turned its head. After 100 or so conditioning trials, in which shock followed light, the normal response to the onset of light became modified into a response resembling that originally evoked by the shock.

These conditioning trials were repeated until a certain training criterion was attained; for instance, a worm was considered trained when the modified response was evoked in 23 out of 25 successive trials. If a trained animal is not exposed periodically to the experimental conditions, it tends to forget what it has learned. If it can be retrained with fewer trials than were originally required to reach a certain criterion, however, one can assume that the animal has not completely forgotten what it once knew. The amount of retention, as measured by the reduction in training trials, is referred to as a savings.

Later McConnell, Allan L. Jacobson and Daniel P. Kimble, working at the University of Michigan, carried the planarian conditioning experiment one step further. Worms were trained to criterion, cut in two and the two halves were allowed to regenerate. On retraining to criterion a savings was found in the worms derived from tail pieces as well as in those derived from head pieces. It appeared from this that both the tail portion and the head portion were capable of memory storage.

How is this memory stored? It is known that genetic information is stored in deoxyribonucleic acid (DNA). Conceivably information about experienced events is stored in nerve cells in a closely related giant molecule: ribonucleic acid (RNA). This hypothesis is supported by recent experiments with rabbits, performed by Holger Hydén of the University of Göteborg in Sweden [see "Satellite Cells in the Nervous System," by Holger Hydén; SCIENTIFIC AMERICAN, December, 1961]. Following this lead William C. Corning, working in E. R. John's laboratory at the University of Rochester, undertook the following experiment. Planarians were trained and cut in the same way as they had been in the Michigan experiment except that the pieces were allowed to regenerate in a solution of ribonuclease instead of the usual spring water. Ribonuclease is an enzyme that specifically destroys RNA. Corning found a savings for those derived from head pieces but not for those from tail pieces.

What do these interesting results mean? Failure of ribonuclease to obliterate the memory of the head piece may mean that the memory storage in the head is not coded into RNA or, more likely, that the large protein molecule of ribonuclease cannot get into the head to attack the RNA and attacks only the RNA of regenerated tissue. Since the head controls the worm, a worm whose head contained the memory would show savings. One whose head did not contain the memory — even though its tail did — would not show savings. It does not seem likely that the ribonuclease specifically obliterates memory-containing RNA in the tail piece. Since RNA is known to be involved in protein synthesis, ribonuclease may nonspecifically disrupt an entire complex of processes involved in transmitting the memory from the tail to the regenerated head. In support of this idea is the observation by Corning and John that ribonuclease concentrations only slightly higher than those employed in the basic experiment produced many deformities in the regenerated heads. Weighing against the notion of nonspecific damage, however, is the fact that worms derived from ribonuclease-treated tails could be retrained in approximately the same number of trials as the original worms.

Meanwhile, back at the Michigan laboratory, a simple experiment was done that yielded an incredible result. McConnell, Jacobson and Barbara Humphries trained planarians to criterion using the same classical conditioning procedure described above. The trained planarians were chopped into pieces and fed to a group of untrained planarians. A second group of untrained planarians was fed pieces of other untrained planarians. The cannibals that had eaten the trained planarians yielded a higher proportion of conditioned responses than those that had eaten untrained ones!

Does this perhaps mean that human cannibals were right in believing they would acquire the personality traits of some respected person if they ate him? Probably not. The planarian digestive tract, unlike the human, does not seem to carry out digestion by extracellular enzymes that break down the large molecules of protein, nucleic acid and polysaccharide. Instead it contains amoebalike cells that engulf food particles by a process resembling the ingestion of a bacterium by a white blood cell. It is quite likely that in the planarian large molecular units, and perhaps whole cells, are taken up undegraded.

Two other features of planarians point toward yet another possibility. First, planarians do not show the exacting immunological specificity found in humans or other mammals, since transplants of tissue from one planarian to another are readily accepted. Second, the cells inside the planarian seem to be rather loosely packed; this allows unspecialized cells to migrate the length of the worm. It is therefore not improbable that many cells of the eaten planarian, escaping detection because of their similarity to the cannibal's cells, infiltrate the cannibal and migrate to appropriate sites in its tissues.

All the experiments performed by the Michigan and Rochester groups rest on the classical conditioning regime of Thompson and McConnell. Is this learning in the conventional sense one applies to higher animals? Or is it, in spite of the controls, a complex trick of nature like pseudo-conditioning or the speech of a parrot, which yields only a mimicry of intelligence?

In 1958 Irvin Rubinstein and I, working at the Walter Reed Army Institute of Research in Washington and unaware of the Michigan experiments, set out to ascertain if planarians were capable of "instrumental" learning. Instrumental learning differs from classical conditioning in that the animal is trained to do something in order to get or avoid something. Thus whether the animal gets reinforced, by punishment or reward, depends on its response.

Maze learning, in which the animal is punished for making a wrong choice of alternative paths or rewarded for making the correct choice, is an example of instrumental learning. Rubinstein and I wanted a situation that would eliminate the disturbing effect produced by handling the worm between trials and provide unequivocal evidence of learning. To achieve these objectives we built a simple maze consisting of three identical cylindrical wells connected by a symmetrical Y-shaped tunnel. The entire maze was made from a block of clear acrylic plastic and was equipped with lights so that the wells could be illuminated individually. Each well could be made to appear bright, dimly lighted or dark. The maze was filled with water and a worm was placed in it.

For a training trial the water was withdrawn from the maze. Thereupon the worm would enter one of the wells and crawl into the Y-shaped tunnel looking for water. When the worm was securely in the tunnel, the well connecting to one fork of the Y directly ahead of the worm was brightly lighted and that connecting to the other fork was totally darkened. If the worm chose the lighted well, the maze was flooded with water. If it chose the darkened one, water was withheld and the lights were switched around so that it again had to make a choice between the branches leading to the darkened and the brightly lighted well. Following a correct choice, all the wells were switched to dim illumination and the worm was allowed to remain in the water-filled maze undisturbed for 15 minutes. It would then be put through another trial in the same way.

To eliminate any systematic coincidence of right-left choice between worm and experimenter, the well to be darkened and the well to be illuminated in each trial were determined by lottery. Moreover, about half of the worms in the experiment were trained to go to darkened rather than lighted wells. After 10 to 15 trials the worm was put back into a finger bowl filled with spring water, which served as its home during the period of the experiment. It was put through a training session every two days.

In the first session of trials the worms would pick the lighted well about as often as the darkened one. By the second session they would show a marked preference for the reinforced alternative. That is, the worms that received water for choosing the lighted well chose the lighted well more often, and those that received water for choosing the darkened well chose the darkened well more often. Some of our worms continued to increase their preference for the rewarded alternative still further into the third session and a few still more in the fourth session. But an odd thing eventually happened with all of them.

In the session following the one in which a worm showed its most marked preference for the rewarded alternative, it rejected the rewarded alternative and chose the other instead. This happened whether the worm had been trained to choose the lighted well or the darkened one. A session or two following the one in which the worm rejected the rewarded alternative it acted lethargic when placed in the maze and refused to play the game at all.

Rubinstein and I were appalled at this complex turn of events in our seemingly simple experiment. It was clear from the structure of the experiment that the switch in preference from the rewarded to the unrewarded alternative was not mere forgetting; in that session the worms did worse than they would have on a random basis and worse than they had done in their first session, when they had had no previous training. The only way a worm could perform worse than randomly in this particular experiment was to know what the correct choice was and choose the opposite. But why would it do that?

The lethargy too was baffling. If the incentive had been something to which the worms might have adapted, we would have seized on this explanation, but the worms cannot live for long without water. At first we speculated that we had driven the worms to exhaustion. Then we noticed that most of the lethargic worms exhibited normal activity in their home bowl both immediately before and immediately after the session in the maze during which they refused to perform. The lethargy thus seemed — from its context, speed of onset and speed of recovery — to be a kind of psychological state rather than exhaustion.

Higher animals, particularly cats, frequently exhibit behavior that appears to be "rebellious" or negativistic when one is attempting to train them to an avoidance task. Some investigators have reported instances in which cats would simply lie down on an electric grid and take a shock rather than try to avoid it. Increasing the shock intensity will not force some recalcitrants to perform and may ruin them as subjects for future experiments. Because neither Rubinstein nor I had had any experience in avoidance conditioning of higher animals, and because there are few published accounts of such perverse behavior, we were unaware of its existence when we first encountered the lethargic state in planarians. Only later, when we were discussing our findings with workers who were familiar with the psychological behavior of rats, cats and monkeys, did we become aware of this prevalent but poorly understood phenomenon in higher animals. Most workers agreed that it was usually evoked by overpunishment and that it represented some kind of emotional response toward the entire test situation.

Aside from the trials themselves we could see nothing very punishing about our maze situation. We thought, however, that by linking some positive association such as feeding with the maze we might be able to offset whatever it was the worm found unpleasant about the situation. We put planarians that had fasted and had not been through any trials into water-filled maze wells that contained a small piece of raw beef liver. Ordinarily a hungry planarian will eat beef liver without much hesitation; in the maze wells they would not eat at all. It occurred to us that their loss of appetite might be due to some chemical property of the acrylic plastic of which the maze was built, but when planarians were placed in large trays made of the same plastic, they ate readily.

At a loss for an explanation, I was glumly watching my cat trying to get into a closet past the closet door, which was slightly ajar. Only the day before, when I needed her out of the way briefly, I had put her into the closet with a plate of food. Instead of quietly eating, she had thrown a terrible feline tantrum, ignoring the food, yowling and scratching the door. Yet this same closet, a dungeon yesterday when escape was blocked, now, with the door ajar, became attractive. Why?

I decided to present the planarians with a situation analogous to the cat and the closet. A small piece of liver was placed in the flooded maze well as before. The entire maze block was put into the home bowl of the planarian and the water level adjusted until it was just slightly higher than the top of the maze block. The planarian could now, remaining in water, pass between the well and its home bowl at its own discretion. The "open door" stratagem succeeded. Under these circumstances the planarians climbed into the well and ate.

In higher animals such as cats and rats inhibition of the feeding response in a hungry animal is frequently used as a behavioral indicator of an emotional state akin to "anxiety." It is probably premature to refer to the cat-and-the-closet effect as claustrophobia, but it does suggest that confinement in the close quarters of the maze well-and-tunnel system was unpleasant to planarians. Moreover, one can conceive how this particular form of behavior might be of value to planarians in their natural habitat. One species of planarian used in our investigation lives in fresh-water streams. The other inhabits the bayous of southern Louisiana and the Mississippi delta country. Fresh-water streams become swollen and overflow their banks in times of heavy rainfall and may diminish to mere rivulets in dry weather. Bayous not only become flooded but also rise and fall with the tide. As either flood or tidal waters recede they leave small pools that may dry up and kill a planarian trapped in them. A small pool with an escape route to a larger pool is not so dangerous as a small pool with no such escape. Natural selection is apt to be hard on animals that do not manifest the appropriate anxiety in the face of frequently encountered dangerous situations.

With this in mind we built a maze of the same kind and dimensions as before but with a rim extending above the maze block. When filled with water, this produced a larger chamber into which the worm could crawl from the maze wells. A trial was the same as before except that between trials the worm could now crawl out of the cramped quarters of the maze wells and use the more spacious quarters provided by the upper chamber. The worms did in fact use the upper chamber nearly every time it was made available to them. The choice point and the geometry of the tunnels in which the decision was actually made were the same as before.

In this rim maze the planarians never perversely rejected the choice (light or dark) that was rewarded with water, nor did they refuse to run through the tunnel. These results seemed consistent with the idea that the rejection of the reinforced choice and the lethargy were produced by unpleasant aspects of the over-all situation in the maze.

Closely associated with this behavior pattern is one that seems to occur widely throughout the animal kingdom. A good example of such behavior is exhibited by a single-celled trumpet-shaped aquatic animal, the stentor. The stentor ordinarily lives with the mouthpiece of its trumpet anchored to a water plant or some other stable object. If it is disturbed by some stimulus such as a jet of water, the stentor will twist or bend on its anchor to avoid the jet. If, however, this is repeated a number of times, the stentor will detach its grip and seek a new location. In shifting to this new response the stentor is reacting to the entire sequence in which the irritating stimulus keeps recurring.

When we reconsidered the planarian's behavior, we conjectured that perhaps it included a counterpart to the behavioral program of the stentor: "If the situation continues to be unpleasant, try something different." We had found in our original maze experiments that, when only two choices are available to the planarian, it first responds at random, then it learns to respond correctly, then it responds incorrectly and finally it does not respond at all. We wondered what would happen if the planarian were given a situation allowing a greater range of response within the basic framework of the same learning situation.

By way of a test a planarian was trained in the original Y maze to choose the lighted alternative whether it occurred on the right or on the left. When we reached the stage of the experiment at which the worm began to reject the lighted alternative, we switched it into a second Y maze. The second maze was identical with the first except that the walls of its wells were scored with a gridwork of scratches in the plastic; the well walls of the first maze were smooth. From this point on, in each day's session, half of the trials were conducted in the smooth maze and half in the scratched maze. In the smooth maze the planarian now had to pick the darkened alternative, in the scratched maze the lighted alternative. Clearly this was a more complex situation than the one we had set up earlier. Only one out of every three worms tested in the dual-maze situation was able to learn it; this one, however, after having rejected the correct alternative in the initial single-maze stage, began to respond correctly in the dual-maze situation. Nor did it ever show the lethargy observed in all the worms tested in the single-maze task.

When a higher animal is confronted with an experimental situation in which it must choose between alternative doors or alleyways, it tends at first to choose one without much hesitation. After a few trials in which it has been punished (or rewarded) for its choice, but before it has learned which choice to make, it behaves quite differently at the point of decision. It may now hesitate at the choice point, turning its head first toward one door, then toward the other, looking as though it were trying to make up its mind which to take. Animal psychologists refer to this as "vicarious trial-and-error" behavior.

We have seen planarians exhibit similar behavior under comparable circumstances. In the initial trials a planarian in the Y maze just chooses one of the tunnels. After 10 to 15 trials in which it has received water or had it withheld, depending on its choice, it will now hesitate at the choice point, turning its head first one way and then the other. Sometimes it seems unable to decide at all and may crawl back to the starting well and begin over again. Although there has been much speculation about the nerve mechanisms responsible for decision making, no one really knows what goes on in the head of a planarian or any other animal trying to make up its "mind" between alternative courses of action. What is striking, we think, is that vicarious trial-and-error behavior — common enough in higher animals — has its counterpart in the primitive planarian worm.

I shall give one more example in which planarian behavior parallels that found in much higher animals. When an animal such as a rat is offered food in a strange environment, it refuses to eat at first, even though it may be hungry. But if the environment is familiar, the animal will usually eat with little hesitation, even though it has never received food there before.

An animal's reluctance to eat in a strange environment provides a simple means of demonstrating whether or not the animal "recognizes" an environment to which it may have been previously exposed. Such recognition does not necessarily imply that the animal possesses cognitive memory of the environment itself. Animals often leave a mark or spoor of some kind, which they detect on revisiting the locale. To demonstrate that an animal has cognitive memory, one must devise an experiment in which spoors play no role. If this is done, one can use feeding delay as behavioral evidence of the strangeness of an environment. Without markers or memory all environments must be alien.

Rubinstein and I devised the following experiment to test the delayed feeding effect on planarians. Worms that had fasted varying lengths of time were divided into two groups. Members of one group were given a familiarization period in a small plastic receptacle. After they had been taken from the receptacle it was washed to remove any marker spoors they might have left. After an interval of 25 minutes the familiarized worms were returned to the receptacle and given a small piece of liver. The length of time until they began to eat was measured. Worms that had never been in the receptacle before were similarly tested. The familiarized worms ate sooner than the controls, indicating that planarians do show the delayed feeding effect.

Does the feeding delay mean that planarians are exhibiting some sort of "anxiety" or "caution" in the strange environment, as this behavior is usually interpreted when it is observed in higher animals? The question is difficult to answer. One can, however, devise further experiments to see if the feeding delay regularly appears in situations comparable to those that produce "anxiety" in rats and humans.

If the delay in feeding is a manifestation of a primitive anxiety pattern, one would expect an even longer delay in feeding for planarians in an environment that had proved to be dangerous in the past. A preliminary study suggests that this is true. Planarians that had fasted were placed in a plastic receptacle and given brief electric shocks. Tested later in the same receptacle with a piece of liver and without being shocked, they delayed feeding much longer than those that had not been shocked.

In doing studies of the sort described here one must be constantly on the watch for covert behavior patterns that could invalidate one's observations. For example, I discovered quite by accident that at least one species of planarian has a strong time sense. Very late one night I placed a planarian of the species *Dugesia tigrina* in a bowl with several *Cura foremani*. The *tigrina* quickly attacked the *foremani*. When I tried to repeat the experiment the next afternoon, I found that the two species completely ignored each other. Subsequently I learned that the *tigrina* would attack the *foremani* only at night. Moreover, the behavior remained on a fixed daily schedule even when the two species were maintained under constant illumination for an extended period.

Many questions are raised by these investigations. If one finds that planarian behavior resembles behavior that in higher animals one calls boredom, interest, conflict, decision, frustration, rebellion, anxiety, learning and cognitive awareness, is it permissible to say that planarians also display these attributes? The question can only be answered obliquely. All one knows of the "mind" of another organism is inferred from its behavior and its similarity to one's own. To indicate that these behavioral programs of primitive animals may be precursors of the psychological patterns of rats and men, one perhaps should speak of protoboredom, protointerest, protorebellion and protoanxiety.

Planarian worms are very primitive. Their nervous system is so rudimentary that its nerve cells can scarcely be distinguished from the surrounding tissue. Completely absent is the intricate meshwork of nerve circuitry that is found in the vertebrate brain and that is considered necessary for the behavior ordinarily identified with higher psychologies. Suppose the apparent similarity between the protopsychological patterns of planarians and the psychological patterns of rats and men turns out to be more than superficial. This would indicate that psychological characteristics are more ancient and widespread than the neurophysiological structures from which they are thought to have arisen. Perhaps it is time to recognize, in any case, that there is only limited evidence for the common belief that complex psychological behavior has its origin in the particular anatomy and physiology of the vertebrate brain. A probable reason for this belief is that more investigations of animal behavior have been conducted with birds and mammals. Quite possibly the world of lower animal life is a psychological wasteland only because it has not been studied.

Another reason for this belief is that investigators have become accustomed to thinking that invertebrate behavior must be primitive and therefore have tended to look only for relatively simple responses to simple stimuli. For example, if one of the eyes of a honeybee is blinded, the bee will travel in a circle. Similarly, an intact bee will orient with respect to an artificial light source. From such studies one might conclude that the bee is a simple automaton, the behavior of which is governed largely by asymmetric stimulation to a pair of photoelectric cells in its head. Yet the amazing work of Karl von Frisch of Austria has shown that bees possess a language for communicating precise navigational information [see "Dialects in the Language of Bees," by Karl von Frisch; SCIENTIFIC AMERICAN, August, 1962].

If the major psychological patterns are not unique to the vertebrate brain but can be produced even by such primitive animals as planarians, two possibilities suggest themselves. Such patterns may stem from some primordial properties of living matter, arising from some cellular or subcellular level of organization rather than nerve circuitry. These protopsychological properties may in turn serve as the building blocks of vertebrate psychology in the way electronic computer subroutines enter as parts of a larger program.

An alternative possibility is that the behavioral programs may have arisen independently in various species by a kind of convergent evolution. In other words, the psychology of animals may evolve in response to compelling considerations of optimal design in the same way that whales and other cetacean mammals have evolved a fishlike shape. Both possibilities seem likely and do not exclude each other.

There are great difficulties in working with a truly alien species.

Nearly any experiment in learning is simultaneously an experiment in perception; conversely, almost all experiments on the perception of another animal are done by teaching it some kind of discrimination. When one does not know how an animal perceives the world, it is difficult to know whether an animal's failure to learn a task set by the experimenter arises from incapacity or communication failure.

We are encouraged to believe as a result of our experiments with planarians that the strange, little-explored domain of protopsychology will shed new light on the ultimate nature of the human brain.

✑§ FOR DISCUSSION AND WRITING

1. What general assumption about animal behavior is spoken of in the first paragraph? The paragraph goes on to ask a number of questions. Put all these questions into a single question of your own wording and write it down—the question that seems to you to be basic to all the experiments described in the article. What reason is given for the use of the planarian in these experiments? In an article involving specialized scientific background and research, it is natural—and to an extent, necessary—that the vocabulary also should be specialized; but the vocabulary in this piece does not put extraordinary demands on the lay reader who is accustomed to keeping his dictionary within easy reach (and certainly the student should have been using his dictionary all through this book with the same frequency as pencil, pen, or typewriter). What is meant by the Devonian period? Explain the coined word "vertebramorphic" in terms of analogy with "anthropomorphic." What is the hypothalamus? What is meant by "limbic system"? What is the cerebral cortex? What is meant by "bilateral symmetry"? What is a "phylum," and to what phylum does the planarian belong? Through all the rest of the article, keep your dictionary at your elbow and make sure that you know the meaning of every word. What is your own feeling about the relative ease or difficulty of the specialized vocabulary of this piece?

2. Explain the second sentence in the fourth paragraph, beginning "These early investigators. . . ." What is the chief point of this paragraph? Why does the author review some of the history of experiments in "conditioning" before he talks about his own experiments? What is meant, in the fifth paragraph, by the term "classical conditioning"? What is meant by

"unconditioned stimulus" and by "conditioned stimulus"? Does the experiment spoken of in the sixth paragraph involve a "conditioned" or an "unconditioned" stimulus? What is the relationship between Pavlov's experiments on dogs and the question with which the author is concerned (which you were asked to formulate at the beginning)? What is the author's use of the word "criterion"?

3. What was learned from the experiment of cutting the educated worm in two (see the eighth paragraph)? What relation has this result to the controlling question which you have formulated for the whole article? What is meant by "savings"? What does "genetic information" mean?

4. What was the result of the experiment (see the eleventh paragraph) of chopping up educated worms and feeding them to uneducated worms? What relationship does the author suggest between this experiment and the savage custom of eating that part of the enemy—human or animal— in which his special strength is supposed to reside? How does the author answer the query? (Incidentally, is there much difference between a savage's eating the tiger's heart to gain his strength, courage, and skill, and our eating the hearts, livers, and kidneys of various animals to replenish our own metabolism?)

5. In the fourteenth paragraph, what is the distinction between "learning" and "pseudo-conditioning," and what relation did this question have to the experiments started by Best and Rubinstein? In the fifteenth paragraph, what is meant by "instrumental learning"? What connection has the maze, described in the sixteenth paragraph, with "instrumental learning"? Describe this first experiment of Best and Rubinstein in your own words, explaining its purpose.

6. What were the results of the first, second, third, and fourth trials? What unexpected behavior did the educated worms then show? What experiment did Best's own cat suggest to him? How is the word "anxiety" used in relation to the planarian's behavior? How does the author relate that exhibition of "anxiety" to what happens in the planarian's natural environment? What role does that "anxiety" have in the preservation and adaptation of the species?

7. Describe the next experiment that was devised to test the worm's reaction to environment. What did this experiment show as to the worm's capacity for "decision" and its "cognitive memory"? What does "cognitive mem-

ory" mean? Note the use of words like "decide," "decision," "mind," "cognitive," and "caution" (as well as "anxiety"), words we think of as applying only to human behavior, but applied here to the behavior of a worm. What does Best seem to feel about the propriety of such words in relation to the worm's behavior?

8. Put into your own words (preferably in a written sentence) the gist of the sixth-to-last paragraph. What reason does the author suggest as to why science has neglected to study the "psychology" of invertebrates? What difference is there between "psychological" behavior and automatic behavior—and how is the point illustrated by the honeybee?

9. What are the conclusions of the author, and how are they related to the questions set in the first paragraph?

10. If you are majoring in a science and doing laboratory work in it, you might write a short paper describing an experiment in a way that would interest the lay reader, as Best does in this piece. If you have a funny bone—a bent for the comic or for parody—you might write up a comparison between the learning capacities of flatworms and college students. If you are interested in scientific subjects and have not yet made the acquaintance of that admirable magazine for both specialists and laymen, the *Scientific American,* you might look over a few issues in the library and write up a short report on an article that interested you particularly, being careful to give proper credit and, when you quote, to quote accurately.

John Stuart Mill ❧ A Crisis in My Mental History

❧ English philosopher and economist (1806-1873), associated with his
father, James Mill, and Jeremy Bentham in the Utilitarian school of ethical
thought—the doctrine (as defined in Webster's) that the useful is the good,
that the determining consideration of right conduct is the usefulness of its
consequences, and that the aim of moral action is the largest possible balance
of pleasure over pain, or the greatest happiness of the greatest number.
Mill's education was conducted largely by his father, and began virtually in
babyhood with a rigorous training in the classics. One of the effects of that
precociously accelerated discipline was the mental crisis described here in
the fifth chapter of his *Autobiography*. Besides the *Autobiography*, the best
known of Mill's works are his *Principles of Political Economy*, his *Utilitarian-
ism*, and his famous *Essay on Liberty*. ❧

FROM the winter of 1821, when I first read Bentham, and especially
from the commencement of the Westminster Review,[1] I had what might
truly be called an object in life: to be a reformer of the world. My conception of my own happiness was entirely identified with this object.
The personal sympathies I wished for were those of fellow labourers
in this enterprise. I endeavoured to pick up as many flowers as I could
by the way; but as a serious and permanent personal satisfaction to rest
upon, my whole reliance was placed on this; and I was accustomed to
felicitate myself on the certainty of a happy life which I enjoyed,
through placing my happiness in something durable and distant, in

From John Stuart Mill's *Autobiography*, in Volume 25 of the Harvard Classics (New
York: P. F. Collier & Son, 1909). The *Autobiography* first appeared in 1873.

[1] The *Westminster Review* was founded by Jeremy Bentham and James Mill as an
organ of Utilitarian doctrine and philosophic radicalism. (Later—in 1855—George
Eliot became an assistant editor of the magazine.)

which some progress might be always making, while it could never be exhausted by complete attainment. This did very well for several years, during which the general improvement going on in the world and the idea of myself as engaged with others in struggling to promote it, seemed enough to fill up an interesting and animated existence. But the time came when I awakened from this as from a dream. It was in the autumn of 1826. I was in a dull state of nerves, such as everybody is occasionally liable to; unsusceptible to enjoyment or pleasureable excitement; one of those moods when what is pleasure at other times, becomes insipid or indifferent; the state, I should think, in which converts to Methodism[2] usually are, when smitten by their first "conviction of sin." In this frame of mind it occurred to me to put the question directly to myself: "Suppose that all your objects in life were realized; that all the changes in institutions and opinions which you are looking forward to, could be completely effected at this very instant: would this be a great joy and happiness to you?" And an irrepressible self-consciousness distinctly answered, "No!" At this my heart sank within me: the whole foundation on which my life was constructed fell down. All my happiness was to have been found in the continual pursuit of this end. The end had ceased to charm, and how could there ever again be any interest in the means? I seemed to have nothing left to live for.

At first I hoped that the cloud would pass away of itself; but it did not. A night's sleep, the sovereign remedy for the smaller vexations of life, had no effect on it. I awoke to a renewed consciousness of the woeful fact. I carried it with me into all companies, into all occupations. Hardly anything had power to cause me even a few minutes' oblivion of it. For some months the cloud seemed to grow thicker and thicker. The lines in Coleridge's "Dejection" — I was not then acquainted with them — exactly describe my case:

> "A grief without a pang, void, dark and drear,
> A drowsy, stifled, unimpassioned grief,
> Which finds no natural outlet or relief
> In word, or sigh, or tear."

[2] Methodism started at Oxford in 1829; under John and Charles Wesley and others, it became a powerful evangelical movement preaching the sinful state of man and redemption through faith.

In vain I sought relief from my favourite books; those memorials of past nobleness and greatness from which I had always hitherto drawn strength and animation. I read them now without feeling, or with the accustomed feeling *minus* all its charm; and I became persuaded, that my love of mankind, and of excellence for its own sake, had worn itself out. I sought no comfort by speaking to others of what I felt. If I had loved any one sufficiently to make confiding my griefs a necessity, I should not have been in the condition I was. I felt, too, that mine was not an interesting, or in any way respectable distress. There was nothing in it to attract sympathy. Advice, if I had known where to seek it, would have been most precious. The words of Macbeth to the physician often occurred to my thoughts.[3] But there was no one on whom I could build the faintest hope of such assistance. My father, to whom it would have been natural to me to have recourse in any practical difficulties, was the last person to whom, in such a case as this, I looked for help. Everything convinced me that he had no knowledge of any such mental state as I was suffering from, and that even if he could be made to understand it, he was not the physician who could heal it. My education, which was wholly his work, had been conducted without any regard to the possibility of its ending in this result; and I saw no use in giving him the pain of thinking that his plans had failed, when the failure was probably irremediable, and, at all events, beyond the power of *his* remedies. Of other friends, I had at that time none to whom I had any hope of making my condition intelligible. It was however abundantly intelligible to myself; and the more I dwelt upon it, the more hopeless it appeared.

My course of study had led me to believe, that all mental and moral feelings and qualities, whether of a good or of a bad kind, were the results of association; that we love one thing, and hate another, take pleasure in one sort of action or contemplation, and pain in another sort, through the clinging of pleasurable or painful ideas to those things,

---

[3] Act IV, scene iii of *Macbeth:*

> Canst thou not minister to a mind diseas'd,
> Pluck from the memory a rooted sorrow,
> Raze out the written troubles of the brain,
> And with some sweet oblivious antidote
> Cleanse the stuff'd bosom of that perilous stuff
> Which weighs upon the heart?

from the effect of education or of experience.[4] As a corollary from this, I had always heard it maintained by my father, and was myself convinced, that the object of education should be to form the strongest possible associations of the salutary class; associations of pleasure with all things beneficial to the great whole, and of pain with all things hurtful to it. This doctrine appeared inexpugnable; but it now seemed to me, on retrospect, that my teachers had occupied themselves but superficially with the means of forming and keeping up these salutary associations. They seemed to have trusted altogether to the old familiar instruments, praise and blame, reward and punishment. Now, I did not doubt that by these means, begun early, and applied unremittingly, intense associations of pain and pleasure, especially of pain, might be created, and might produce desires and aversions capable of lasting undiminished to the end of life. But there must always be something artificial and casual in associations thus produced. The pains and pleasures thus forcibly associated with things, are not connected with them by any natural tie; and it is therefore, I thought, essential to the durability of these associations, that they should have become so intense and inveterate as to be practically indissoluble, before the habitual exercise of the power of analysis had commenced. For I now saw, or thought I saw, what I had always before received with incredulity — that the habit of analysis has a tendency to wear away the feelings: as indeed it has, when no other mental habit is cultivated, and the analysing spirit remains without its natural complements and correctives. The very excellence of analysis (I argued) is that it tends to weaken and undermine whatever is the result of prejudice; that it enables us mentally to separate ideas which have only casually clung together: and no associations whatever could ultimately resist this dissolving force, were it not that we owe to analysis our clearest knowledge of the permanent sequences in nature; the real connexions between Things, not dependent on our will and feelings; natural laws, by virtue of which, in many cases, one thing is inseparable from another in fact; which laws, in proportion as they are clearly perceived and imaginatively realized, cause our ideas of things which are always joined together in Nature, to cohere more and more closely in our thoughts. Analytic habits may thus even

[4] This is the "association psychology" linked with the name of David Hartley (1732-1813), English philosopher, and stemming, ultimately, from John Locke's theory of the understanding.

strengthen the associations between causes and effects, means and ends, but tend altogether to weaken those which are, to speak familiarly, a *mere* matter of feeling. They are therefore (I thought) favourable to prudence and clear-sightedness, but a perpetual worm at the root both of the passions and of the virtues; and, above all, fearfully undermine all desires, and all pleasures, which are the effects of association, that is, according to the theory I held, all except the purely physical and organic; of the entire insufficiency of which to make life desirable, no one had a stronger conviction than I had. These were the laws of human nature, by which, as it seemed to me, I had been brought to my present state. All those to whom I looked up were of opinion that the pleasure of sympathy with human beings, and the feelings which made the good of others, and especially of mankind on a large scale, the object of existence, were the greatest and surest sources of happiness. Of the truth of this I was convinced, but to know that a feeling would make me happy if I had it, did not give me the feeling. My education, I thought, had failed to create these feelings in sufficient strength to resist the dissolving influence of analysis, while the whole course of my intellectual cultivation had made precocious and premature analysis the inveterate habit of my mind. I was thus, as I said to myself, left stranded at the commencement of my voyage, with a well-equipped ship and a rudder, but no sail; without any real desire for the ends which I had been so carefully fitted out to work for: no delight in virtue, or the general good, but also just as little in anything else. The fountains of vanity and ambition seemed to have dried up within me, as completely as those of benevolence. I had had (as I reflected) some gratification of vanity at too early an age: I had obtained some distinction, and felt myself of some importance, before the desire of distinction and of importance had grown into a passion: and little as it was which I had attained, yet having been attained too early, like all pleasures enjoyed too soon, it had made me *blasé* and indifferent to the pursuit. Thus neither selfish nor unselfish pleasures were pleasures to me. And there seemed no power in nature sufficient to begin the formation of my character anew, and create in a mind now irretrievably analytic, fresh associations of pleasure with any objects of human desire.

These were the thoughts which mingled with the dry heavy dejection of the melancholy winter of 1826-7. During this time I was not incapable of my usual occupations. I went on with them mechanically, by the mere force of habit. I had been so drilled in a certain sort of mental exercise, that I could still carry it on when all the spirit had gone out of it. I even composed and spoke several speeches at the debating society, how, or with what degree of success, I know not. Of four years continual speaking at that society, this is the only year of which I remember next to nothing. Two lines of Coleridge, in whom alone of all writers I have found a true description of what I felt, were often in my thoughts, not at this time (for I had never read them), but in a later period of the same mental malady:

> "Work without hope draws nectar in a sieve,
> And hope without an object cannot live."

In all probability my case was by no means so peculiar as I fancied it, and I doubt not that many others have passed through a similar state; but the idiosyncrasies of my education had given to the general phenomenon a special character, which made it seem the natural effect of causes that it was hardly possible for time to remove. I frequently asked myself, if I could, or if I was bound to go on living, when life must be passed in this manner. I generally answered to myself, that I did not think I could possibly bear it beyond a year. When, however, not more than half that duration of time had elapsed, a small ray of light broke in upon my gloom. I was reading, accidentally, Marmontel's "Memoires,"[5] and came to the passage which relates his father's death, the distressed position of the family, and the sudden inspiration by which he, then a mere boy, felt and made them feel that he would be everything to them — would supply the place of all that they had lost. A vivid conception of the scene and its feelings came over me, and I was moved to tears. From this moment my burden grew lighter. The oppression of the thought that all feeling was dead within me, was gone. I was no longer hopeless: I was not a stock or a stone. I had still, it seemed, some of the material out of which all worth of character, and all capacity for happiness, are made. Relieved from my ever present sense of irremedial wretchedness, I gradually found that the ordinary incidents of life could again give me some pleasure; that I could again find enjoyment, not intense, but sufficient for cheerfulness, in sunshine and sky, in books, in conversation, in public affairs; and that there was, once more, excitement, though of a moderate kind, in exerting myself for my opinions,

[5] Jean François Marmontel was an eighteenth-century French author.

and for the public good. Thus the cloud gradually drew off, and I again enjoyed life: and though I had several relapses, some of which lasted many months, I never again was as miserable as I had been.

The experiences of this period had two very marked effects on my opinions and character. In the first place, they led me to adopt a theory of life, very unlike that on which I had before acted, and having much in common with what at that time I certainly had never heard of, the anti-self-consciousness theory of Carlyle.[6] I never, indeed, wavered in the conviction that happiness is the test of all rules of conduct, and the end of life. But I now thought that this end was only to be attained by not making it the direct end. Those only are happy (I thought) who have their minds fixed on some object other than their own happiness; on the happiness of others, on the improvement of mankind, even on some art or pursuit, followed not as a means, but as itself an ideal end. Aiming thus at something else, they find happiness by the way. The enjoyments of life (such was now my theory) are sufficient to make it a pleasant thing, when they are taken *en passant*,[7] without being made a principal object. Once make them so, and they are immediately felt to be insufficient. They will not bear a scrutinizing examination. Ask yourself whether you are happy, and you cease to be so. The only chance is to treat, not happiness, but some end external to it, as the purpose of life. Let your self-consciousness, your scrutiny, your self-interrogation, exhaust themselves on that; and if otherwise fortunately circumstanced you will inhale happiness with the air you breathe, without dwelling on it or thinking about it, without either forestalling it in imagination, or puttng it to flight by fatal questioning. This theory now became the basis of my philosophy of life. And I still hold to it as the best theory for all those who have but a moderate degree of sensibility and of capacity for enjoyment, that is, for the great majority of mankind.

The other important change which my opinions at this time underwent, was that I, for the first time, gave its proper place, among the prime necessities of human well-being, to the internal culture of the individual. I ceased to attach almost exclusive importance to the ordering of outward circumstances, and the training of the human being for speculation and for action.

[6] Thomas Carlyle, distinguished Scottish essayist and historian contemporary with Mill.

[7] In passing.

I had now learnt by experience that the passive susceptibilities needed to be cultivated as well as the active capacities, and required to be nourished and enriched as well as guided. I did not, for an instant, lose sight of, or undervalue, that part of the truth which I had seen before; I never turned recreant to intellectual culture, or ceased to consider the power and practice of analysis as an essential condition both of individual and of social improvement. But I thought that it had consequences which required to be corrected, by joining other kinds of cultivation with it. The maintenance of a due balance among the faculties, now seemed to me of primary importance. The cultivation of the feelings became one of the cardinal points in my ethical and philosophical creed. And my thoughts and inclinations turned in an increasing degree towards whatever seemed capable of being instrumental to that object.

I now began to find meaning in the things which I had read or heard about the importance of poetry and art as instruments of human culture. But it was some time longer before I began to know this by personal experience. The only one of the imaginative arts in which I had from childhood taken great pleasure, was music; the best effect of which (and in this it surpasses perhaps every other art) consists in exciting enthusiasm; in winding up to a high pitch those feelings of an elevated kind which are already in the character, but to which this excitement gives a glow and a fervor, which, though transitory at its utmost height, is precious for sustaining them at other times. This effect of music I had often experienced; but like all my pleasurable susceptibilities it was suspended during the gloomy period. I had sought relief again and again from this quarter, but found none. After the tide had turned, and I was in process of recovery, I had been helped forward by music, but in a much less elevated manner. I at this time first became acquainted with Weber's[8] Oberon, and the extreme pleasure which I drew from its delicious melodies did me good, by showing me a source of pleasure to which I was as susceptible as ever. The good, however, was much impaired by the thought, that the pleasure of music (as is quite true of such pleasure as this was, that of mere tune) fades with familiarity, and requires either to be revived by intermittence, or fed by continual novelty. And it is very characteristic both of my then state, and of the general tone of my mind at this period of my life, that I was seriously

[8] German composer of the early nineteenth century.

tormented by the thought of the exhaustibility of musical combinations. The octave consists only of five tones and two semitones, which can be put together in only a limited number of ways, of which but a small proportion are beautiful: most of these, it seemed to me, must have been already discovered, and there could not be room for a long succession of Mozarts and Webers, to strike out, as these had done, entirely new and surpassingly rich veins of musical beauty. This source of anxiety may, perhaps, be thought to resemble that of the philosophers of La-puta,[9] who feared lest the sun should be burnt out. It was, however, connected with the best feature in my character, and the only good point to be found in my very unromantic and in no way honourable distress. For though my dejection, honestly looked at, could not be called other than egotistical, produced by the ruin, as I thought, of my fabric of happiness, yet the destiny of mankind in general was ever in my thoughts, and could not be separated from my own. I felt that the flaw in my life, must be a flaw in life itself; that the question was, whether, if the reformers of society and government could succeed in their objects, and every person in the community were free and in a state of physical comfort, the pleasures of life, being no longer kept up by struggle and privation, would cease to be pleasures. And I felt that unless I could see my way to some better hope than this for human happiness in general, my dejection must continue; but that if I could see such an outlet, I should then look on the world with pleasure; content as far as I was myself concerned, with any fair share of the general lot.

This state of my thoughts and feelings made the fact of my reading Wordsworth for the first time (in the autumn of 1828), an important event in my life. I took up the collection of his poems from curiosity, with no expectation of mental relief from it, though I had before resorted to poetry with that hope. In the worst period of my depression, I had read through the whole of Byron (then new to me), to try whether a poet, whose peculiar department was supposed to be that of the intenser feelings, could rouse any feeling in me. As might be expected, I got no good from this reading, but the reverse. The poet's state of mind was too like my own. His was the lament of a man who had worn out all pleasures, and who seemed to think that life, to all who possess the good things of it, must necessarily be the vapid, uninteresting thing

[9] Science-fiction characters in the third book of Swift's *Gulliver's Travels.*

which I found it. His Harold and Manfred had the same burden on them which I had; and I was not in a frame of mind to desire any comfort from the vehement sensual passion of his Giaours, or the sullenness of his Laras.[10] But while Byron was exactly what did not suit my condition, Wordsworth was exactly what did. I had looked into the Excursion two or three years before, and found little in it; and I should probably have found as little, had I read it at this time. But the miscellaneous poems, in the two-volume edition of 1815 (to which little of value was added in the latter part of the author's life) proved to be the precise thing for my mental wants at that particular juncture.

In the first place, these poems addressed themselves powerfully to one of the strongest of my pleasurable susceptibilities, the love for rural objects and natural scenery; to which I had been indebted not only for much of the pleasure of my life, but quite recently for relief from one of my longest relapses into depression. In this power of rural beauty over me, there was a foundation laid for taking pleasure in Wordsworth's poetry; the more so, as his scenery lies mostly among mountains, which, owing to my early Pyrenean excursion, were my ideal of natural beauty. But Wordsworth would never have had any great effect on me, if he had merely placed before me beautiful pictures of natural scenery. Scott does this still better than Wordsworth, and a very second-rate landscape does it more effectually than any poet. What made Wordsworth's poems a medicine for my state of mind, was that they expressed, not mere outward beauty, but states of feeling, and of thought coloured by feeling, under the excitement of beauty. They seemed to be the very culture of the feelings, which I was in quest of. In them I seemed to draw from a source of inward joy, of sympathetic and imaginative pleasure, which could be shared in by all human beings; which had no connexion with struggle or imperfection, but would be made richer by every improvement in the physical or social condition of mankind. From them I seemed to learn what would be the perennial sources of happiness, when all the greater evils of life shall have been removed. And I felt myself at once better and happier as I came under their influence. There have certainly been, even in our own age, greater poets than Wordsworth; but poetry of deeper and loftier feeling could not have done for me at that time what his did. I needed to be made to feel that there was real, permanent happiness in tranquil contemplation. Wordsworth

[10] The references in this sentence are to characters in Byron's poems.

taught me this, not only without turning away from, but with a greatly increased interest in the common feelings and common destiny of human beings. And the delight which these poems gave me, proved that with culture of this sort, there was nothing to dread from the most confirmed habit of analysis. At the conclusion of the Poems came the famous Ode, falsely called Platonic, "Intimations of Immortality": in which, along with more than his usual sweetness of melody and rhythm, and along with the two passages of grand imagery but bad philosophy so often quoted, I found that he too had had similar experience to mine; that he also had felt that the first freshness of youthful enjoyment of life was not lasting; but that he had sought for compensation, and found it, in the way in which he was now teaching me to find it. The result was that I gradually, but completely, emerged from my habitual depression, and was never again subject to it. I long continued to value Wordsworth less according to his intrinsic merits, than by the measure of what he had done for me. Compared with the greatest poets, he may be said to be a poet of unpoetical natures, possessed of quiet and contemplative tastes. But unpoetical natures are precisely those which require poetic cultivation. This cultivation Wordsworth is much more fitted to give, than poets who are intrinsically far more poets than he.

⤳ FOR DISCUSSION AND WRITING

1. In reading this piece, one needs to be aware of the rather special nature of Mill's educational background, for it is in the context of that background that the mental crisis described here acquires significance; hence, if you have not read the biographical note on page 1145, do so now. How old was Mill in 1821, when, as he says in the first sentence, he decided definitely on his object in life? What was that object? Is it a rare or common ideal at that age? While such an ideal may, under the stresses of a competitive society, fade fairly quickly in other young people, what was there in Mill's background, in his relationship with his father, and in the very acceleration of his education, that gave to that early decision a psychological depth, maturity, and permanence that it might not have in others? Why does this fact give greater significance to the mental crisis he describes? How old was he at the onset of the crisis? Psychological patter has become so common (every student nowadays is a "lay analyst") that the first reaction

to this piece may be the facile one which would make of Mill's experience a neurotic "case history," involving only Mill as an individual and having nothing to do with the rest of us "normal" people; but in that case the inclusion of the piece in this book would be utterly pointless. The most general and the most important questions that the piece brings up are: What deficiencies in our own education parallel those in Mill's? How does the help he blindly found suggest needs we may realize, in our own lives, too desperately and too late? What reorganization of college curriculums (specifically in your own major field) is implied by these parallels? And finally, are you aware of a "philosophy of education" that is common and integrative to all the courses you are pursuing, and if so, is it designed for the exigency Mill faced? Any combination of these questions could provide a highly important subject for a paper.

2. Having got rid of these general questions first, let us go back to specific aspects of the piece. What, exactly, was the nature of Mill's mental crisis? Why did he not confide his distress to others? Why not to his father?

3. In the fourth paragraph, what does he mean by "mental and moral feelings and qualities"? What does he say as to how these come into existence and as to their part in education? What do you think of this psychological theory? Do "mental and moral feelings and qualities" play any part in your present education? What is Mill's criticism of the educational system of rewards and punishments? What is the meaning of the word "analysis" as he uses it in this paragraph ("the power of analysis," "the habit of analysis," etc.)? What does he say is the "excellence of analysis"—its virtue, what it is useful for, why it should be cultivated? And what is it that he finds wrong with the rigorous inculcation of the analytical habit of mind? How does it work against the "association" psychology of education—the pain-and-pleasure, punishment-and-reward principle? Explain, with great care for the meaning of each term and statement, the following sentence in the middle of the fourth paragraph: "They [analytic habits] are therefore (I thought) favourable to prudence and clear-sightedness, but a perpetual worm at the root both of the passions and of the virtues; and, above all, fearfully undermine all desires, and all pleasures, which are the effects of association, that is, according to the theory I held, all except the purely physical and organic; of the entire insufficiency of which to make life desirable, no one had a stronger conviction than I had."

4. Still in the fourth paragraph, consider the following: "All those to whom I looked up were of opinion that the pleasure of sympathy with human

beings, and the feelings which made the good of others, and especially of mankind on a large scale, the object of existence, were the greatest and surest sources of happiness. Of the truth of this I was convinced, but to know that a feeling would make me happy if I had it, did not give me the feeling." Do you agree, or disagree, with the premise made in the first sentence? If you feel that the statement in the first sentence is ethically logical, how do you explain the failure of "logical" result that the second sentence speaks of? Is there something wrong with the ethical premise? What would be its opposite? Would the opposite objective be a sounder psychological basis of happiness? There is a Biblical injunction, "Love thy neighbor as thyself," which implies that love of one's self (interest in purely personal happiness) should serve as a model for love of others— concern with the "good of mankind"; how does this ancient advice apply to Mill's problem?

5. What was the effect of his reading of Marmontel? Why should this reaction have assumed such importance as a first "breakthrough" in his psychological problem? In the seventh paragraph, what does he mean by "the internal culture of the individual," and in the eighth paragraph what does he mean by the need to cultivate "the passive susceptibilities"?

6. What necessary reorientation did Mill find in Wordsworth, and why in poetry rather than in music, and why in Wordsworth rather than in Byron? Does Mill suggest that his particular solution to his problem is one that would fit all other people's problems of a similar kind? What qualifications does he make? Despite the personal qualifications, what general significance—in our own world, in our own educational environment—does Mill's experience of Wordsworth have?

Henry Adams ৶ Harvard College

৶ Henry Adams (1838-1918) came from one of the most distinguished families in the United States, a family of presidents, statesmen, and educators. His autobiography, *The Education of Henry Adams,* from which the selection here is taken, and his *Mont-Saint-Michel and Chartres* are two of the most exciting, penetratingly thoughtful, and magnificently written classics of American literature. ৶

ONE day in June, 1854, young Adams walked for the last time down the steps of Mr. Dixwell's school in Boylston Place, and felt no sensation but one of unqualified joy that this experience was ended. Never before or afterwards in his life did he close a period so long as four years without some sensation of loss — some sentiment of habit — but school was what in after life he commonly heard his friends denounce as an intolerable bore. He was born too old for it. The same thing could be said of most New England boys. Mentally they never were boys. Their education as men should have begun at ten years old. They were fully five years more mature than the English or European boy for whom schools were made. For the purposes of future advancement, as afterwards appeared, these first six years of a possible education were wasted in doing imperfectly what might have been done perfectly in one, and

From *The Education of Henry Adams* by Henry Adams (Boston: Houghton Mifflin Company, 1927). Reprinted by permission of the publisher.

in any case would have had small value. The next regular step was Harvard College. He was more than glad to go. For generation after generation, Adamses and Brookses and Boylstons and Gorhams had gone to Harvard College, and although none of them, as far as known, had ever done any good there, or thought himself the better for it, custom, social ties, convenience, and, above all, economy, kept each generation in the track. Any other education would have required a serious effort, but no one took Harvard College seriously. All went there because their friends went there, and the College was their ideal of social self-respect.

Harvard College, as far as it educated at all, was a mild and liberal school, which sent young men into the world with all they needed to make respectable citizens, and something of what they wanted to make useful ones. Leaders of men it never tried to make. Its ideals were altogether different. The Unitarian clergy had given to the College a character of moderation, balance, judgment, restraint, what the French called *mesure;* excellent traits, which the College attained with singular success, so that its graduates could commonly be recognized by the stamp, but such a type of character rarely lent itself to autobiography. In effect, the school created a type but not a will. Four years of Harvard College, if successful, resulted in an autobiographical blank, a mind on which only a water-mark had been stamped.

The stamp, as such things went, was a good one. The chief wonder of education is that it does not ruin everybody concerned in it, teachers and taught. Sometimes in after life, Adams debated whether in fact it had not ruined him and most of his companions, but, disappointment apart, Harvard College was probably less hurtful than any other university then in existence. It taught little, and that little ill, but it left the mind open, free from bias, ignorant of facts, but docile. The graduate had few strong prejudices. He knew little, but his mind remained supple, ready to receive knowledge.

What caused the boy most disappointment was the little he got from his mates. Speaking exactly, he got less than nothing, a result common enough in education. Yet the College Catalogue for the years 1854 to 1861 shows a list of names rather distinguished in their time. Alexander Agassiz and Phillips Brooks led it; H. H. Richardson and O. W. Holmes helped to close it. As a rule the most promising of all die early, and never get their names into a Dictionary of Contemporaries, which seems to be the only popular standard of success. Many died in the war.

Adams knew them all, more or less; he felt as much regard, and quite as much respect for them then, as he did after they won great names and were objects of a vastly wider respect; but, as help towards education, he got nothing whatever from them or they from him until long after they had left college. Possibly the fault was his, but one would like to know how many others shared it. Accident counts for much in companionship as in marriage. Life offers perhaps only a score of possible companions, and it is mere chance whether they meet as early as school or college, but it is more than a chance that boys brought up together under like conditions have nothing to give each other. The Class of 1858, to which Henry Adams belonged, was a typical collection of young New Englanders, quietly penetrating and aggressively commonplace; free from meannesses, jealousies, intrigues, enthusiasms, and passions; not exceptionally quick; not consciously sceptical; singularly indifferent to display, artifice, florid expression, but not hostile to it when it amused them; distrustful of themselves, but little disposed to trust any one else; with not much humor of their own, but full of readiness to enjoy the humor of others; negative to a degree that in the long run became positive and triumphant. Not harsh in manners or judgment, rather liberal and open-minded, they were still as a body the most formidable critics one would care to meet, in a long life exposed to criticism. They never flattered, seldom praised; free from vanity, they were not intolerant of it; but they were objectiveness itself; their attitude was a law of nature; their judgment beyond appeal, not an act either of intellect or emotion or of will, but a sort of gravitation.

This was Harvard College incarnate, but even for Harvard College, the Class of 1858 was somewhat extreme. Of unity this band of nearly one hundred young men had no keen sense, but they had equally little energy of repulsion. They were pleasant to live with, and above the average of students — German, French, English, or what not — but chiefly because each individual appeared satisfied to stand alone. It seemed a sign of force; yet to stand alone is quite natural when one has no passions; still easier when one has no pains.

Into this unusually dissolvent medium, chance insisted on enlarging Henry Adams's education by tossing a trio of Virginians as little fitted for it as Sioux Indians to a treadmill. By some further affinity, these three outsiders fell into relation with the Bostonians among whom Adams as a schoolboy belonged, and in the end with Adams himself, although they and he knew well how thin an edge of friendship separated them in 1856 from mortal enmity. One of the Virginians was the son of Colonel Robert E. Lee, of the Second United States Cavalry; and two others who seemed instinctively to form a staff for Lee, were town-Virginians from Peters-burg. A fourth outsider came from Cincinnati and was half Kentuckian, N. L. Anderson, Longworth on the mother's side. For the first time Adams's education brought him in contact with new types and taught him their values. He saw the New England type measure itself with an-other, and he was part of the process.

Lee, known through life as "Roony," was a Virginian of the eigh-teenth century, much as Henry Adams was a Bostonian of the same age. Roony Lee had changed little from the type of his grandfather, Light Horse Harry. Tall, largely built, handsome, genial, with liberal Virginian openness towards all he liked, he had also the Virginian habit of com-mand and took leadership as his natural habit. No one cared to contest it. None of the New Englanders wanted command. For a year, at least, Lee was the most popular and prominent young man in his class, but then seemed slowly to drop into the background. The habit of com-mand was not enough, and the Virginian had little else. He was simple beyond analysis; so simple that even the simple New England student could not realize him. No one knew enough to know how ignorant he was; how childlike; how helpless before the relative complexity of a school. As an animal, the Southerner seemed to have every advantage, but even as an animal he steadily lost ground.

The lesson in education was vital to these young men, who, within ten years, killed each other by scores in the act of testing their college conclusions. Strictly, the Southerner had no mind; he had temperament. He was not a scholar; he had no intellectual training; he could not analyze an idea, and he could not even conceive of admitting two; but in life one could get along very well without ideas, if one had only the social instinct. Dozens of eminent statesmen were men of Lee's type, and main-tained themselves well enough in the legislature, but college was a sharper test. The Virginian was weak in vice itself, though the Bostonian was hardly a master of crime. The habits of neither were good; both were apt to drink hard and to live low lives; but the Bostonian suffered less than the Virginian. Commonly the Bostonian would take some care of himself even in his worst stages, while the Virginian became quarrel-some and dangerous. When a Virginian had brooded a few days over an imaginary grief and substantial whiskey, none of his Northern friends could be sure that he might not be waiting, round the corner, with a knife or pistol, to revenge insult by the day light of *delirium tremens;* and when things reached this condition, Lee had to exhaust his authority over his own staff. Lee was a gentleman of the old school, and, as every one knows, gentlemen of the old school drank almost as much as gentlemen of the new school; but this was not his trouble. He was sober even in the excessive violence of political feeling in those years; he kept his temper and his friends under control.

Adams liked the Virginians. No one was more obnoxious to them, by name and prejudice; yet their friendship was unbroken and even warm. At a moment when the immediate future posed no problem in education so vital as the relative energy and endurance of North and South, this momentary contact with Southern character was a sort of education for its own sake; but this was not all. No doubt the self-esteem of the Yankee, which tended naturally to self-distrust, was flattered by gaining the slow conviction that the Southerner, with his slave-owning limitations, was as little fit to succeed in the struggle of modern life as though he were still a maker of stone axes, living in caves, and hunting the *bos primigenius,*[1] and that every quality in which he was strong, made him weaker; but Adams had begun to fear that even in this respect one eighteenth-century type might not differ deeply from another. Roony Lee had changed little from the Virginian of a century before; but Adams was himself a good deal nearer the type of his great-grandfather than to that of a railway superintendent. He was little more fit than the Virginians to deal with a future America which showed no fancy for the past. Already Northern society betrayed a preference for economists over diplomats or soldiers — one might even call it a jealousy — against which two eighteenth-century types had little chance to live, and which they had in common to fear.

Nothing short of this curious sympathy could have brought into close relations two young men so hostile as Roony Lee and Henry Adams, but the chief difference between them as collegians consisted only in their difference of scholarship: Lee was a total failure; Adams a partial one. Both failed, but Lee felt his failure more sensibly, so that he gladly seized the chance of escape by accepting a commission offered him by General Winfield Scott in the force then being organized against

[1] The aurochs, a wild ox of prehistoric times.

the Mormons. He asked Adams to write his letter of acceptance, which flattered Adams's vanity more than any Northern compliment could do, because, in days of violent political bitterness, it showed a certain amount of good temper. The diplomat felt his profession.

If the student got little from his mates, he got little more from his masters. The four years passed at college were, for his purposes, wasted. Harvard College was a good school, but at bottom what the boy disliked most was any school at all. He did not want to be one in a hundred — one per cent of an education. He regarded himself as the only person for whom his education had value, and he wanted the whole of it. He got barely half of an average. Long afterwards, when the devious path of life led him back to teach in his turn what no student naturally cared or needed to know, he diverted some dreary hours of faculty-meetings by looking up his record in the class-lists, and found himself graded precisely in the middle. In the one branch he most needed — mathematics — barring the few first scholars, failure was so nearly universal that no attempt at grading could have had value, and whether he stood fortieth or ninetieth must have been an accident or the personal favor of the professor. Here his education failed lamentably. At best he could never have been a mathematician; at worst he would never have cared to be one; but he needed to read mathematics, like any other universal language, and he never reached the alphabet.

Beyond two or three Greek plays, the student got nothing from the ancient languages. Beyond some incoherent theories of free-trade and protection, he got little from Political Economy. He could not afterwards remember to have heard the name of Karl Marx mentioned, or the title of "Capital." He was equally ignorant of Auguste Comte. These were the two writers of his time who most influenced its thought. The bit of practical teaching he afterwards reviewed with much curiosity was the course in Chemistry, which taught him a number of theories that befogged his mind for a lifetime. The only teaching that appealed to his imagination was a course of lectures by Louis Agassiz on the Glacial Period and Palaeontology, which had more influence on his curiosity than the rest of the college instruction altogether. The entire work of the four years could have been easily put into the work of any four months in after life.

Harvard College was a negative force, and negative forces have value. Slowly it weakened the violent political bias of childhood, not by putting interests in its place, but by mental habits which had no bias at all. It would also have weakened the literary bias, if Adams had been capable of finding other amusement, but the climate kept him steady to desultory and useless reading, till he had run through libraries of volumes which he forgot even to their title-pages. Rather by instinct than by guidance, he turned to writing, and his professors or tutors occasionally gave his English composition a hesitating approval; but in that branch, as in all the rest, even when he made a long struggle for recognition, he never convinced his teachers that his abilities, at their best, warranted placing him on the rank-list, among the first third of his class. Instructors generally reach a fairly accurate gauge of their scholars' powers. Henry Adams himself held the opinion that his instructors were very nearly right, and when he became a professor in his turn, and made mortifying mistakes in ranking his scholars, he still obstinately insisted that on the whole, he was not far wrong. Student or professor, he accepted the negative standard because it was the standard of the school.

He never knew what other students thought of it, or what they thought they gained from it; nor would their opinion have much affected his. From the first, he wanted to be done with it, and stood watching vaguely for a path and a direction. The world outside seemed large, but the paths that led into it were not many and lay mostly through Boston, where he did not want to go. As it happened, by pure chance, the first door of escape that seemed to offer a hope led into Germany, and James Russell Lowell opened it.

Lowell, on succeeding Longfellow as Professor of Belles-Lettres, had duly gone to Germany, and had brought back whatever he found to bring. The literary world then agreed that truth survived in Germany alone, and Carlyle, Matthew Arnold, Renan, Emerson, with scores of popular followers, taught the German faith. The literary world had revolted against the yoke of coming capitalism — its money-lenders, its bank directors, and its railway magnates. Thackeray and Dickens followed Balzac in scratching and biting the unfortunate middle class with savage ill-temper, much as the middle class had scratched and bitten the Church and Court for a hundred years before. The middle class had the power, and held its coal and iron well in hand, but the satirists and idealists seized the press, and as they were agreed that the Second Empire[2] was a disgrace to France and a danger to England, they turned to Germany because at that moment Germany was neither economical nor

2 The reign of Napoleon III, 1852-1870.

military, and a hundred years behind western Europe in the simplicity of
its standard. German thought, method, honesty, and even taste, became
the standards of scholarship. Goethe was raised to the rank of Shakespeare — Kant ranked as a law-giver above Plato. All serious scholars
were obliged to become German, for German thought was revolutioniz-
ing criticism. Lowell had followed the rest, not very enthusiastically, but
with sufficient conviction, and invited his scholars to join him. Adams
was glad to accept the invitation, rather for the sake of cultivating Lowell
than Germany, but still in perfect good faith. It was the first serious attempt he had made to direct his own education, and he was sure of getting some education out of it; not perhaps anything that he expected,
but at least a path.

Singularly circuitous and excessively wasteful of energy the path
proved to be, but the student could never see what other was open to
him. He could have done no better had he foreseen every stage of his
coming life, and he would probably have done worse. The preliminary
step was pure gain. James Russell Lowell had brought back from Germany the only new and valuable part of its universities, the habit of
allowing students to read with him privately in his study. Adams asked
the privilege, and used it to read a little, and to talk a great deal, for the
personal contact pleased and flattered him, as that of older men ought
to flatter and please the young even when they altogether exaggerate
its value. Lowell was a new element in the boy's life. As practical a New
Englander as any, he leaned towards the Concord faith rather than towards Boston where he properly belonged; for Concord, in the dark days
of 1856, glowed with pure light.[3] Adams approached it in much the same
spirit as he would have entered a Gothic Cathedral, for he well knew
that the priests regarded him as only a worm. To the Concord Church
all Adamses were minds of dust and emptiness, devoid of feeling, poetry
or imagination; little higher than the common scourings of State Street;[4]
politicians of doubtful honesty; natures of narrow scope; and already, at

[3] Emerson's home was in Concord, Massachusetts, and the references here are to the
"transcendentalist" philosophy of Emerson and his circle. American transcenden-
talism began as a dissenting movement in the Unitarian Church (of which Emerson
was a minister), against what was felt as the sterile rationalism of Unitarian belief;
it developed the emphasis of post-Kantian idealism on the unknowable character of
ultimate reality, as transcending sense experience, on the primacy of the intuitional
and spiritual forms of experience as against the materialistic and empirical, and on
the immanence of God in nature.

[4] State Street is the financial district of Boston—an obvious symbol of the "materialism" abhorred by the Emersonian transcendentalists.

eighteen years old, Henry had begun to feel uncertainty about so many matters more important than Adamses that his mind rebelled against no discipline merely personal, and he was ready to admit his unworthiness if only he might penetrate the shrine. The influence of Harvard College was beginning to have its effect. He was slipping away from fixed principles; from Mount Vernon Street; from Quincy; from the eighteenth century; and his first steps led toward Concord.[5]

He never reached Concord, and to Concord Church he, like the rest of mankind who accepted a material universe, remained always an insect, or something much lower — a man. It was surely no fault of his that the universe seemed to him real; perhaps — as Mr. Emerson justly said — it was so; in spite of the long-continued effort of a lifetime, he perpetually fell back into the heresy that if anything universal was unreal, it was himself and not the appearances; it was the poet and not the banker; it was his own thought, not the thing that moved it. He did not lack the wish to be transcendental. Concord seemed to him, at one time, more real than Quincy; yet in truth Russell Lowell was as little transcendental as Beacon Street. From him the boy got no revolutionary thought whatever — objective or subjective as they used to call it — but he got good-humored encouragement to do what amused him, which consisted in passing two years in Europe after finishing the four years of Cambridge.

The result seemed small in proportion to the effort, but it was the only positive result he could ever trace to the influence of Harvard College, and he had grave doubts whether Harvard College influenced even that. Negative results in plenty he could trace, but he tended towards negation on his own account, as one side of the New England mind had always done, and even there he could never feel sure that Harvard College had more than reflected a weakness. In his opinion the education was not serious, but in truth hardly any Boston student took it seriously, and none of them seemed sure that President Walker himself, or President Felton after him, took it more seriously than the students. For them all, the college offered chiefly advantages vulgarly called social, rather than mental.

Unluckily for this particular boy, social advantages were his only capital in life. Of money he had not much, of mind not more, but he

[5] Mount Vernon Street, Quincy, and Beacon Street (below) were the precincts of the blue-blood aristocracy and the Adams family.

could be quite certain that, barring his own faults, his social position would never be questioned. . . .

Socially or intellectually, the college was for him negative and in some ways mischievous. The most tolerant man of the world could not see good in the lower habits of the students, but the vices were less harmful than the virtues. The habit of drinking — though the mere recollection of it made him doubt his own veracity, so fantastic it seemed in later life — may have done no great or permanent harm; but the habit of looking at life as a social relation — an affair of society — did no good. It cultivated a weakness which needed no cultivation. If it had helped to make men of the world, or give the manners and instincts of any profession — such as temper, patience, courtesy, or a faculty of profiting by the social defects of opponents — it would have been education better worth having than mathematics or languages; but so far as it helped to make anything, it helped only to make the college standard permanent through life. The Bostonian educated at Harvard College remained a collegian, if he stuck only to what the college gave him. If parents went on, generation after generation, sending their children to Harvard College for the sake of its social advantages, they perpetuated an inferior social type, quite as ill-fitted as the Oxford type for success in the next generation.

Luckily the old social standard of the college, as President Walker or James Russell Lowell still showed it, was admirable, and if it had little practical value or personal influence on the mass of students, at least it preserved the tradition for those who liked it. The Harvard graduate was neither American nor European, nor even wholly Yankee; his admirers were few, and his critics many; perhaps his worst weakness was his self-criticism and self-consciousness; but his ambitions, social or intellectual, were not necessarily cheap even though they might be negative. Afraid of serious risks, and still more afraid of personal ridicule, he seldom made a great failure of life, and nearly always led a life more or less worth living. So Henry Adams, well aware that he could not succeed as a scholar, and finding his social position beyond improvement or need of effort, betook himself to the single ambition which otherwise would scarcely have seemed a true outcome of the college, though it was the last remnant of the old Unitarian supremacy. He took to the pen. He wrote.

The College Magazine printed his work, and the College Societies

listened to his addresses. Lavish of praise the readers were not; the audiences, too, listened in silence; but this was all the encouragement any
Harvard collegian had a reasonable hope to receive; grave silence was a
form of patience that meant possible future acceptance; and Henry
Adams went on writing. No one cared enough to criticise, except himself
who soon began to suffer from reaching his own limits. He found that he
could not be this — or that — or the other; always precisely the things
he wanted to be. He had not wit or scope or force. Judges always ranked
him beneath a rival, if he had any; and he believed the judges were
right. His work seemed to him thin, commonplace, feeble. At times he
felt his own weakness so fatally that he could not go on; when he had
nothing to say, he could not say it, and he found that he had very little
to say at best. Much that he then wrote must be still in existence in
print or manuscript, though he never cared to see it again, for he felt no
doubt that it was in reality just what he thought it. At best it showed
only a feeling for form; an instinct of exclusion. Nothing shocked — not
even its weakness.

Inevitably an effort leads to an ambition — creates it — and at that
time the ambition of the literary student, which almost took place of
the regular prizes of scholarship, was that of being chosen as the representative of his class — the Class Orator — at the close of their
course. This was political as well as literary success, and precisely the sort
of eighteenth-century combination that fascinated an eighteenth-century boy. The idea lurked in his mind, at first as a dream, in no way serious or even possible, for he stood outside the number of what were
known as popular men. Year by year, his position seemed to improve, or
perhaps his rivals disappeared, until at last, to his own great astonishment, he found himself a candidate. The habits of the college permitted
no active candidacy; he and his rivals had not a word to say for or against
themselves, and he was never even consulted on the subject; he was not
present at any of the proceedings, and how it happened he never could
quite divine, but it did happen, that one evening on returning from Boston he received notice of his election, after a very close contest, as Class
Orator over the head of the first scholar, who was undoubtedly a better
orator and a more popular man. In politics the success of the poorer candidate is common enough, and Henry Adams was a fairly trained poli-
tician, but he never understood how he managed to defeat not only a
more capable but a more popular rival. . . .

Henry Adams never professed the smallest faith in universities of any kind, either as boy or man, nor had he the faintest admiration for the university graduate, either in Europe or in America; as a collegian he was only known apart from his fellows by his habit of standing outside the college; and yet the singular fact remained that this commonplace body of young men chose him repeatedly to express his and their commonplaces. Secretly, of course, the successful candidate flattered himself — and them — with the hope that they might perhaps not be so commonplace as they thought themselves; but this was only another proof that all were identical. . . .

All the same, the choice was flattering; so flattering that it actually shocked his vanity; and would have shocked it more, if possible, had he known that it was to be the only flattery of the sort he was ever to receive. The function of Class Day was, in the eyes of nine-tenths of the students, altogether the most important of the college, and the figure of the Orator was the most conspicuous in the function. Unlike the Orators at regular Commencements, the Class Day Orator stood alone, or had only the Poet for rival. Crowded into the large church, the students, their families, friends, aunts, uncles and chaperones, attended all the girls of sixteen or twenty who wanted to show their summer dresses or fresh complexions, and there, for an hour or two, in a heat that might have melted bronze, they listened to an Orator and a Poet in clergyman's gowns, reciting such platitudes as their own experience and their mild censors permitted them to utter. What Henry Adams said in his Class Oration of 1858 he soon forgot to the last word, nor had it the least value for education; but he naturally remembered what was said of it. He remembered especially one of his eminent uncles or relations remarking that, as the work of so young a man, the oration was singularly wanting in enthusiasm. The young man — always in search of education — asked himself whether, setting rhetoric aside, this absence of enthusiasm was a defect or a merit, since, in either case, it was all that Harvard College taught, and all that the hundred young men, whom he was trying to represent, expressed. Another comment threw more light on the effect of the college education. One of the elderly gentlemen noticed the orator's "perfect self-possession." Self-possession indeed! If Harvard College gave nothing else, it gave calm. For four years each student had been obliged to figure daily before dozens of young men who knew each other to the last fibre. One had done little but read papers to Societies, or act comedy in the Hasty Pudding,[6] not to speak of all sorts of regular exercises, and no audience in future life would ever be so intimately and terribly intelligent as these. Three-fourths of the graduates would rather have addressed the Council of Trent or the British Parliament than have acted Sir Anthony Absolute or Dr. Ollapod before a gala audience of the Hasty Pudding. Self-possession was the strongest part of Harvard College, which certainly taught men to stand alone, so that nothing seemed stranger to its graduates than the paroxysms of terror before the public which often overcame the graduates of European universities. Whether this was, or was not, education, Henry Adams never knew. He was ready to stand up before any audience in America or Europe, with nerves rather steadier for the excitement, but whether he should ever have anything to say, remained to be proved. As yet he knew nothing. Education had not begun.

⤳ FOR DISCUSSION AND WRITING

1. Adams writes his autobiography in the third person rather than the first. Judging from this chapter, can you see any specific advantage he gains by objectifying himself in the grammatical third person (as if he were writing a novel about a character named "Adams")? Does the chapter reflect any particular quality of temperament which might make the third-person technique more suitable to him? (You may have read, in the first section of this book, one or more of the selections from the autobiographies of Gorky, Yeats, and Emlyn Williams, all of them written in the first person; these might give you some basis of comparison for the questions here.) Does the present chapter on Adams' experience at Harvard seem to you to have some more general and objective purpose—a purpose lying in the realm of ideas and criticism—than the autobiographical impulse simply as such (again, here, comparison with Gorky, Yeats, or Williams might help)? If you find such a purpose in the chapter, would that, too, explain to some extent the choice of the third-person technique?

2. In the second paragraph Adams says that Harvard turned out a "type of character" that "rarely lent itself to autobiography"; explain the implication. What does he mean when he says that the school "created a type but

---

[6] The dramatic society of Harvard.

not a will"? Explain the metaphor in the last sentence of the paragraph. (You may have read the piece by the philosopher John Locke earlier in this book; if so, you are acquainted with the expression *tabula rasa* describing the mind at birth—a blank sheet of paper, as our translator puts it. Since Adams was, of course, familiar with the famous expression, do you find any ironic wit in his metaphor of the Harvard-educated mind as "an autobiographical blank . . . on which only a water-mark had been stamped"?)

3. Can you gather, from the chapter as a whole, any specific evidence for Adams' statement in the third paragraph that the College "taught little, and that little ill"? In the fourth paragraph he says that what caused him most disappointment "was the little he got from his mates"; and then, "Speaking exactly, he got less than nothing, a result common enough in education." What specific social circumstance caused this dearth in Adams' case? Could you use the quoted statement as basis for a paper of your own, on the gain or non-gain, stimulus or absence of stimulus, in your relationship with classmates (remembering that Adams is talking about mental stimulus and not about "fun and games")?

4. What picture does he give of the Virginians, and particularly of Roony Lee? What implicit irony is there in the combination of childlike simpleness in Lee's character with the "habit of command"? What greater and tragic irony is there in Adams' description of both these groups of young men, the New Englanders and the Southerners, in view of the conflict they were to face a few years later and in view of what their education at Harvard was doing—or not doing—for them in the way of preparation? What is meant in the eighth paragraph by the statement, "Strictly, the Southerner had no mind; he had temperament"? In the context, is it merely a pejorative statement? In the fourth sentence of the ninth paragraph, what is the meaning of this: "every quality in which he was strong, made him weaker"? Do you find in Adams' characterization of the Southerner anything applicable to the Southerner today?

5. Again and again he uses the word "negative" in relation to his experience at Harvard; point out a half-dozen places where he uses this word and explain its use in each case. When, years later, he looked up his scholastic record, he "found himself graded precisely in the middle." In view of that fact, explain what he says in the eleventh paragraph about the four years of college having been wasted because, while "he wanted the whole" of his education (since he was the only person to whom it had value), he got

only "one per cent of an education"—or, as he puts it a couple of sentences later, "He got barely half of an average." In all probability, a great many of the students who are reading this book are also receiving grades more or less "in the middle"—just this side or that side of a "C." If you are one of those in the middle, do you find your feelings about your grades in agreement or disagreement with those of Adams?

6. Why were the "social advantages" of Harvard merely negative for Adams? Why were the collegiate vices "less harmful than the virtues"? What irony is there in the reason he gives for starting to write? What critical help did he receive in his writing? What ironic reason does he give for being chosen to represent his graduating class as Class Orator? In connection with the remark of one of his uncles that his valedictory oration "was singularly wanting in enthusiasm," he says that absence of enthusiasm was "all that Harvard College taught," and that he asked himself if this were a defect or a merit. In considering your own attitudes toward your college courses, do you find enthusiasm or indifference or possibly even repugnance? To what causes would you trace these attitudes? The subject might be recommended for a paper, if you can attempt to emulate the clarity, patience, and objectivity that Adams shows.

7. We have mentioned Adams' irony several times. His whole subject in this chapter is, of course, an ironic one—four years of college education at the end of which "education had not begun." But his style also is imbued with irony, giving to his turns of phrase a quality of paradox and of highly condensed implication. Starting with the more obvious kind of irony of his comment in the eighth paragraph about the Virginian who might be waiting with knife or pistol around the corner "to revenge insult by the dry light of *delirium tremens*," find a half-dozen other instances of ironic effects of style, and explain why you call them "ironic."

8. If you have not already found a topic for a paper in these questions, try this one (from the third paragraph of the piece): "The chief wonder of education is that it does not ruin everybody concerned in it, teachers and taught." Or imagine yourself a modern Henry Adams and think over your whole education so far, attempting to make a coherent and clear-eyed judgment of it.

Ezra Pound ✑§ How to Read

✑§ American poet, critic, translator, born in 1885. T. S. Eliot dedicated his poem *The Waste Land* to Pound, calling him *il miglior fabbro,* "the best maker," in the ancient sense of the word for "poet"—a creator, an inventor —but also carrying something of the rough Italian sense of "workman." They were the words Dante used, in the twenty-sixth canto of the *Purgatorio,* for Arnaut Daniel, the Provençal poet from whose work Dante had learned much of his own style, the *dolce stil nuovo.* The value of Pound's work will probably not be assessed accurately for years to come, since so much of it lay in living influence on other poets (William Butler Yeats among them); meanwhile, some of his poems are among the best in modern anthologies. §✑

Part one: Introduction

LITERARY instruction in our "institutions of learning" was, at the beginning of this century, cumbrous and inefficient. I dare say it still is. Certain more or less mildly exceptional professors were affected by the 'beauties' of various authors (usually deceased), but the system, as a whole, lacked sense and co-ordination. I dare say it still does. When studying physics we are not asked to investigate the biographies of all the disciples of Newton who showed interest in science, but who failed to make any discovery. Neither are their unrewarded gropings, hopes, passions, laundry bills, or erotic experiences thrust on the hurried student or considered germane to the subject.

The general contempt of 'scholarship', especially any part of it connected with subjects included in university 'Arts' courses; the shrinking
of people in general from any book supposed to be 'good'; and, in another
mode, the flamboyant advertisements telling 'how to seem to know it
when you don't,' might long since have indicated to the sensitive that
there is something defective in the contemporary methods of purveying
letters.

As the general reader has but a vague idea of what these methods
are at the 'centre', i.e. for the specialist who is expected to serve the general reader, I shall lapse or plunge into autobiography.

In my university I found various men interested (or uninterested)
in their subjects, but, I think, no man with a view of literature as a whole,
or with any idea whatsoever of the relation of the part he himself taught
to any other part.

Those professors who regarded their 'subject' as a drill manual rose
most rapidly to positions of executive responsibility (one case is now a
provost). Those professors who had some natural aptitude for comprehending their authors and for communicating a general sense of comfort in the presence of literary masterwork remained obscurely in their
less exalted positions.

A professor of Romanics admitted that the *Chanson de Roland*[1] was
inferior to the *Odyssey*, but then the Middle Ages were expected to present themselves with apologies, and this was, if I remember rightly, an
isolated exception. English novelists were not compared with the French.
'Sources' were discussed; forthy versions of a Chaucerian anecdote were
'compared', but not on points of respective literary merit. The whole field
was full of redundance. I mean that what one had learned in one class,
in the study of one literature, one was told again in some other.

One was asked to remember what some critic (deceased) had said,
scarcely to consider whether his views were still valid, or ever had been
very intelligent.

In defence of this dead and uncorrelated system, it may be urged
that authors like Spengler,[2] who attempt a synthesis, often do so before

---

[1] The earliest extant poem of substantial length in Old French, concerning the knight
Roland's heroic rear-guard action and death in defense of Charlemagne's army
against the Saracens.

[2] Oswald Spengler (1880-1936), German philosopher of history, whose *Decline of
the West* is an encyclopedic, cyclical view of the rise and fall of civilizations.

they have attained sufficient knowledge of detail: that they stuff expand-able and compressible objects into rubber-bag categories, and that they limit their reference and interest by supposing that the pedagogic follies which they have themselves encountered, constitute an error universally distributed, and encountered by every one else. In extenuation of their miscalculations we may admit that any error or clumsiness of method that has sunk into, or been hammered into one man, over a period of years, probably continues as an error — not merely passively, but as an error still being propagated, consciously or unconsciously, by a number of educators, from laziness, from habits, or from natural cussedness.

'Comparative literature' sometimes figures in university curricula, but very few people know what they mean by the term, or approach it with a considered conscious method.

To tranquillize the low-brow reader, let me say at once that I do not wish to muddle him by making him read more books, but to allow him to read fewer with greater result. (I am willing to discuss this pri-vately with the book trade.) I have been accused of wanting to make people read all the classics; which is not so. I have been accused of wish-ing to provide a 'portable substitute for the British Museum', which I would do, like a shot, were it possible. It isn't. . . .

FOR A METHOD
. . . People regard literature as something vastly more flabby and floating and complicated and indefinite than, let us say, mathematics. Its subject-matter, the human consciousness, is more complicated than are number and space. It is not, however, more complicated than biology, and no one ever supposed that it was. We apply a loose-leaf system to book-keeping so as to have the live items separated from the dead ones. In the study of physics we begin with simple mechanisms, wedge, lever and fulcrum, pulley and inclined plane, all of them still as useful as when they were first invented. We proceed by a study of discoveries. We are not asked to memorize a list of the parts of a side-wheeler engine.

And we could, presumably, apply to the study of literature a little of the common sense that we currently apply to physics or to biology. In poetry there are simple procedures, and there are known discoveries, clearly marked. As I have said in various places in my unorganized and fragmentary volumes: in each age one or two men of genius find some-thing, and express it. It may be in only a line or in two lines, or in some quality of a cadence; and thereafter two dozen, or two hundred, or two or more thousand followers repeat and dilute and modify.

And if the instructor would select his specimens from works that contain these discoveries and solely on the basis of discovery — which may lie in the dimension of depth, not merely of some novelty on the surface — he would aid his student far more than by presenting his authors at random, and talking about them *in toto.*

Needless to say, this presentation would be entirely independent of consideration as to whether the given passages tended to make the student a better republican, monarchist, monist, dualist, rotarian, or other sectarian. To avoid confusion, one should state at once that such method has nothing to do with those allegedly scientific methods which approach literature as if it were something *not literature,* or with scientists' attempts to sub-divide the elements in literature according to some non-literary categoric division.

You do not divide physics or chemistry according to racial or religious categories. You do not put discoveries by Methodists and Germans into one category, and discoveries by Episcopalians or Americans or Italians into another. . . .

WHY BOOKS?

Has literature a function in the state, in the aggregation of humans, in the republic, in the *res publica,*[3] which ought to mean the public convenience (despite the slime of bureaucracy, and the execrable taste of the populace in selecting its rulers)? It has.

And this function is *not* the coercing or emotionally persuading, or bullying or suppressing people into the acceptance of any one set or any six sets of opinions as opposed to any other one set or half-dozen sets of opinions.

It has to do with the clarity and vigour of 'any and every' thought and opinion. It has to do with maintaining the very cleanliness of the tools, the health of the very matter of thought itself. Save in the rare and limited instances of invention in the plastic arts, or in mathematics, the individual cannot think and communicate his thought, the governor and legislator cannot act effectively or frame his laws, without words, and the solidity and validity of these words is in the care of the damned and

[3] The Latin phrase from which the word "republic" derives: literally, a thing pertaining to the people.

despised *litterati*.[4] When this work goes rotten — by that I do not mean when they express indecorous thoughts — but when their very medium, the very essence of their work, the application of word to thing goes rotten, i.e. becomes slushy and inexact, or excessive or bloated, the whole machinery of social and of individual thought and order goes to pot. This is a lesson of history, and a lesson not yet half learned. . . .

It is not only a question of rhetoric, of loose expression, but also of the loose use of individual words. What the renaissance gained in direct examination of natural phenomena, it in part lost in losing the feel and desire for exact descriptive terms. I mean that the medieval mind had little but words to deal with, and it was more careful in its definitions and verbiage. It did not define a gun in terms that would just as well define an explosion, nor explosions in terms that would define triggers.

Misquoting Confucius, one might say: It does not matter whether the author desire the good of the race or acts merely from personal vanity. The thing is mechanical in action. In proportion as his work is exact, i.e., true to human consciousness and to the nature of man, as it is exact in formulation of desire, so is it durable and so is it 'useful'; I mean it maintains the precision and clarity of thought, not merely for the benefit of a few dilettantes and 'lovers of literature', but maintains the health of thought outside literary circles and in non-literary existence, in general individual and communal life.

. . . One 'moves' the reader only by clarity. In depicting the motions of the 'human heart' the durability of the writing depends on the exactitude. It is the thing that is true and stays true that keeps fresh for the new reader. . . .

Part two: or what may be an introduction to method

It is as important for the purpose of thought to keep language efficient as it is in surgery to keep tetanus bacilli out of one's bandages.

In introducing a person to literature one would do well to have him examine works where language is efficiently used; to devise a system for getting directly and expeditiously at such works, despite the smoke-screens erected by half-knowing and half-thinking critics. To get at them, despite the mass of dead matter that those people have heaped up

---

[4] "Lettered" people, scholars, writers.

and conserved round about them in the proportion: one barrel of saw-dust to each half-bunch of grapes.

Great literature is simply language charged with meaning to the utmost possible degree.

When we set about examining it we find that this charging has been done by several clearly definable sorts of people, and by a periphery of less determinate sorts.

(*a*) *The inventors,* discoverers of a particular process or of more than one mode and process. Sometimes these people are known, or dis-coverable; for example, we know, with reasonable certitude, that Arnaut Daniel introduced certain methods of rhyming, and we know that certain finenesses of perception appeared first in such a troubadour or in G. Cavalcanti.[5] We do not know, and are not likely to know, anything defi-nite about the precursors of Homer.

(*b*) *The masters.* This is a very small class, and there are very few real ones. The term is properly applied to inventors who, apart from their own inventions, are able to assimilate and co-ordinate a large number of preceding inventions. I mean to say they either start with a core of their own and accumulate adjuncts, or they digest a vast mass of subject-matter, apply a number of known modes of expression, and succeed in pervading the whole with some special quality or some special character of their own, and bring the whole to a state of homogeneous fullness.

(*c*) *The diluters,* these who follow either the inventors or the 'great writers', and who produce something of lower intensity, some flabbier variant, some diffuseness or tumidity in the wake of the valid.

(*d*) (And this class produces the great bulk of all writing.) The men who do more or less good work in the more or less good style of a period. Of these the delightful anthologies, the song books, are full, and choice among them is the matter of taste, for you prefer Wyatt to Donne, Donne to Herrick, Drummond of Hawthornden to Browne,[6] in response

---

[5] Arnaut Daniel was a Provençal troubadour of the twelfth century, whom Dante regarded as one of the most important inventors and masters of the vernacular style in poetry, the *dolce stil nuovo* ("sweet new style"), and to whom he gave some poignantly dramatic lines at the end of the twenty-sixth canto of the *Purgatorio.* Guido Cavalcanti was a Florentine poet and friend of Dante; the two young men used to exchange sonnets on their love affairs and their dreams; Dante dedicated his first book of poems, the *Vita Nuova,* to him.

[6] These are sixteenth- and seventeenth-century poets whose work you will find in any good anthology of the period.

to some purely personal sympathy, these people add but some slight personal flavour, some minor variant of a mode, without affecting the main course of the story.

(*e*) *Belles Lettres*. Longus, Prévost, Benjamin Constant,[7] who are not exactly 'great masters', who can hardly be said to have originated a form, but who have nevertheless brought some mode to a very high development.

(*f*) And there is a supplementary or sixth class of writers, the starters of crazes, the Ossianic McPhersons, the Gongoras[8] whose wave of fashion flows over writing for a few centuries or a few decades, and then subsides, leaving things as they were.

It will be seen that the first two classes are the more sharply defined: that the difficulty of classification for particular lesser authors increases as one descends the list, save for the last class, which is again fairly clear.

The point is, that if a man knows the facts about the first two categories, he can evaluate almost any unfamiliar book at first sight. I mean he can form a just estimate of its worth, and see how and where it belongs in this schema. . . .

The fact that six different critics will each have a different view concerning what author belongs in which of the categories here given, does not in the least invalidate the categories. When a man knows the facts about the first two categories, the reading of work in the other categories will not greatly change his opinion about those in the first two.

LANGUAGE

Obviously this knowledge cannot be acquired without knowledge of various tongues. The same discoveries have served a number of races. If a man has not time to learn different languages he can at least, and with

---

[7] *Belles lettres* (of which an approximate translation would be "fine writing") is a traditional rag-bag term for all the kinds of writing that have aesthetic value— as against merely informational writing. Longus was an Alexandrian Greek of the third or fourth century who wrote a pastoral romance called *Daphnis and Chloë*, which has considerable charm in itself and which set a fashion for fiction writers, poets, and playwrights (including Shakespeare) in the sixteenth and seventeenth centuries. Prévost and Constant were French novelists of the eighteenth century.

[8] James Macpherson was an eighteenth-century Scot whose *Poems of Ossian*, which he presented as translations from an ancient Irish bard, created a literary furor and had a good deal of influence on the burgeoning "Romantic" movement. Gongora was a Spanish poet contemporary with Shakespeare, whose poems are highly elaborate in style.

very little delay, be told what the discoveries were. If he wish to be a good critic he will have to look for himself.

Bad critics have prolonged the use of demoded terminology, usually a terminology originally invented to describe what had been done before 300 B.C., and to describe it in a rather exterior fashion. Writers of second order have often tried to produce works to fit some category or term not yet occupied in their own local literature. If we chuck out the classifications which apply to the outer shape of the work, or to its occasion, and if we look at what actually happens, in, let us say, poetry, we will find that the language is charged or energized in various manners.

That is to say, there are three 'kinds of poetry':

MELOPOEIA, wherein the words are charged, over and above their plain meaning, with some musical property, which directs the bearing or trend of that meaning.

PHANOPOEIA, which is a casting of images upon the visual imagination.

LOGOPOEIA, 'the dance of the intellect among words', that is to say, it employs words not only for their direct meaning, but it takes count in a special way of habits of usage, of the context we *expect* to find with the word, its usual concomitants, of its known acceptances, and of ironical play. It holds the aesthetic content which is peculiarly the domain of verbal manifestation, and cannot possibly be contained in plastic or in music. It is the latest come, and perhaps most tricky and undependable mode.

The *melopoeia* can be appreciated by a foreigner with a sensitive ear, even though he be ignorant of the language in which the poem is written. It is practically impossible to transfer or translate it from one language to another, save perhaps by divine accident, and for half a line at a time.

Phanopoeia can, on the other hand, be translated almost, or wholly, intact. When it is good enough, it is practically impossible for the translator to destroy it save by very crass bungling, and the neglect of perfectly well-known and formulative rules.

Logopoeia does not translate; though the attitude of mind it expresses may pass through a paraphrase. Or one might say, you can *not* translate it 'locally', but having determined the original author's state of mind, you may or may not be able to find a derivative or an equivalent.

PROSE

The language of prose is much less highly charged, that is perhaps the only availing distinction between prose and poesy. Prose permits greater factual presentation, explicitness, but a much greater amount of language is needed. During the last century or century and a half, prose has, perhaps for the first time, perhaps for the second or third time, arisen to challenge the poetic pre-eminence. . . .

The total charge in certain nineteenth-century prose works possibly surpasses the total charge found in individual poems of that period; but that merely indicates that the author has been able to get his effect cumulatively, by a greater heaping up of factual data; imagined fact, if you will, but nevertheless expressed in factual manner.

By using several hundred pages of prose, Flaubert, by force of architectonics, manages to attain an intensity comparable to that in Villon's *Heaulmière*,[9] or his prayer for his mother. This does not invalidate my dissociation of the two terms: poetry, prose.

In *Phanopoeia* we find the greatest drive toward utter precision of word; this art exists almost exclusively by it.

In *melopoeia* we find a contrary current, a force tending often to lull, or to distract the reader from the exact sense of the language. It is poetry on the borders of music and music is perhaps the bridge between consciousness and the unthinking sentient or even insentient universe.

All writing is built up of these three elements, plus 'architectonics' or 'the form of the whole', and to know anything about the relative efficiency of various works one must have some knowledge of the maximum already attained by various authors, irrespective of where and when. . . .

But the books that a man needs to know in order to 'get his bearings', in order to have a sound judgement of any bit of writing that may come before him, are very few. The list is so short, indeed, that one wonders that people, professional writers in particular, are willing to leave them ignored and to continue dangling in mid-chaos emitting the most imbecile estimates, and often vitiating their whole lifetime's production. . . .

9 François Villon is one of the earliest and greatest of French poets. He was born in 1431, and lived as a vagabond, beggar, and thief in a plague-stricken Paris. His poems have never been adequately translated in English. Two of his poems concern *la belle heaulmière*—the helmet-maker's beautiful wife; now an old woman, she urges young girls to make the most of their opportunities for love.

Part three: Conclusions, exceptions, curricula

ENGLAND[10]

We speak a language that was English. When Richard Cœur de Lion first heard Turkish he said: 'He spik lak a fole Britain.' From which orthography one judges that Richard himself probably spoke like a French-Canadian.

It is a magnificent language, and there is no need of, or advantage in, minimizing the debt we owe to Englishmen who died before 1620. Neither is there any point in studying the 'History of English Literature' as taught. Curiously enough, the histories of Spanish and Italian literature always take count of translators. Histories of English literature always slide over translation — I suppose it is inferiority complex — yet some of the best books in English are translations. This is important for two reasons. First, the reader who has been appalled by the preceding parts and said, 'Oh, but I can't learn all these languages', may in some measure be comforted. He can learn the art of writing precisely where so many great local lights learned it. . . .

We may count the *Seafarer*, the *Beowulf*, and the remaining Anglo-Saxon fragments as indigenous art; at least, they dealt with a native subject, and by an art not newly borrowed. . . .

After this period English literature lives on translation, it is fed by translation; every new exuberance, every new heave is stimulated by translation, every allegedly great age is an age of translations, beginning with Geoffrey Chaucer, Le Grand Translateur, translator of the *Romaunt of the Rose*, paraphraser of Virgil and Ovid, condenser of old stories he had found in Latin, French, and Italian.

After him even the ballads that tell a local tale tell it in art indebted to Europe. It is the natural spreading ripple that moves from the civilized Mediterranean centre out through the half-civilized and into the barbarous peoples.

The Britons never have shed barbarism; they are proud to tell you that Tacitus[11] said the last word about Germans. When Mary Queen of

[10] An extensive part of the essay, dealing with literature in other languages, has been omitted here.

[11] Roman historian (A.D. 55–*ca.* 117), who described the customs of the German tribes in his time.

Scots went to Edinburgh she bewailed going out among savages, and she
herself went from a sixteenth-century court that held but a barbarous, or
rather a drivelling and idiotic and superficial travesty of the Italian culture as it had been before the débâcle of 1527. The men who tried to
civilize these shaggy and uncouth marginalians by bringing them news
of civilization have left a certain number of translations that are better
reading today than are the works of the ignorant islanders who were too
proud to translate. After Chaucer we have Gavin Douglas's *Eneados*,
better than the original, as Douglas had heard the sea. Golding's
Metamorphoses, from which Shakespeare learned so much of his trade.
Marlowe's translation of Ovid's *Amores*. We have no satisfactory translation of any Greek author. Chapman and Pope have left Iliads that are
of interest to specialists; so far as I know, the only translation of Homer
that one can read with continued pleasure is in early French by Hugues
Salel; he, at least, was intent on telling the story, and not wholly muddled
with accessories. I have discussed the merits of these translators[12] elsewhere. I am now trying to tell the reader what he can learn of comparative literature through translations that are in themselves better
reading than the 'original verse' of their periods. . . .

Apart from these early translations, a man may enlarge his view of
international poetry by looking at Swinburne's Greek adaptations. The
Greeks stimulated Swinburne; if he had defects, let us remember that,
apart from Homer, the Greeks often were rather Swinburnian. Catullus
wasn't, or was but seldom. From which one may learn the nature of the
Latin, non-Greek contribution to the art of expression.[13]

Swinburne's Villon is not Villon very exactly, but it is perhaps the
best Swinburne we have. Rossetti's translations were perhaps better than
Rossetti, and his *Vita Nuova* and early Italian poets guide one to originals, which he has now and again improved. Our contact with Oriental
poetry begins with FitzGerald's Rubáiyát. Fenollosa's essay on the Chi-

---

[12] Gavin Douglas was a Scottish poet of the early sixteenth century who translated
Virgil's *Aeneid*. Golding translated Ovid's *Metamorphoses* in the late sixteenth
century. Chapman was a playwright contemporary with Shakespeare; one of the
best of Keats's sonnets is written on his translation of Homer. Hugues Salel was a
sixteenth-century French poet and translator.

[13] Swinburne was a late nineteenth-century English poet whose translations of the
Greek poets are among the best that we have. Catullus, who died about 54 B.C.,
was one of the finest Roman lyric poets.

nese written character opens a door that the earlier students had, if not 'howled without', at least been unable to open.[14]

In mentioning these translations, I don't in the least admit or imply that any man in our time can think with only one language. He may be able to invent a new carburettor, or even work effectively in a biological laboratory, but he probably won't even try to do the latter without study of at least one foreign tongue. Modern science has always been multilingual. A good scientist simply would not be bothered to limit himself to one language and be held up for news of discoveries. The writer or reader who is content with such ignorance simply admits that his particular mind is of less importance than his kidneys or his automobile. The French who know no English are as fragmentary as the Americans who know no French. One simply leaves half of one's thought untouched in their company.

Different languages — I mean the actual vocabularies, the idioms — have worked out certain mechanisms of communication and registration. No one language is complete. A master may be continually expanding his own tongue, rendering it fit to bear some charge hitherto borne only by some other alien tongue, but the process does not stop with any one man. While Proust is learning Henry James, preparatory to breaking through certain French paste-board partitions, the whole American speech is churning and chugging, and every other tongue doing likewise.

To be 'possible' in mentally active company the American has to learn French, the Frenchman has to learn English or American. The Italian has for some time learned French. The man who does not know the Italian of the duocento and trecento[15] has in him a painful lacuna, not necessarily painful to himself, but there are simply certain things he don't know,[16] and can't; it is as if he were blind to some part of the spectrum. Because of the determined attempt of the patriotic Latinists of

---

[14] Dante Gabriel Rossetti was an English painter and poet of the later nineteenth century. Ernest Fenollosa was an American scholar in Oriental studies who lived much of his life in Japan and who died in 1908. Some sense of the reason for Pound's interest in the Chinese ideogram may be gained from the essay by Sergei Eisenstein, earlier in this book, on "The Cinematographic Principle and the Ideogram."

[15] The centuries beginning with the twelve hundreds and thirteen hundreds.

[16] This is one of Pound's rather painful exploitations of American solecism—a defiance of grammar that seems to be made for its own sake.

Italy in the renaissance to 'conquer' Greek by putting every Greek author effectively into Latin it is now possible to get a good deal of Greek through Latin cribs. The disuse of Latin cribs in Greek study, beginning, I suppose, about 1820, has caused no end of damage to the general distribution of 'classic culture'.

Another point miscomprehended by people who are clumsy at languages is that one does not need to learn a whole language in order to understand some one or some dozen poems. It is often enough to understand thoroughly the poem, and every one of the few dozen or few hundred words that compose it.

This is what we start to do as small children when we memorize some lyric of Goethe or Heine. Incidentally, this process leaves us for life with a measuring rod (*a*) for a certain type of lyric, (*b*) for the German language, so that . . . we never wholly forget the feel of the language.

VACCINE

Do I suggest a remedy? I do. I suggest several remedies. I suggest that we throw out all critics who use vague general terms. Not merely those who use vague terms because they are too ignorant to have a meaning; but the critics who use vague terms to *conceal* their meaning, and all critics who use terms so vaguely that the reader can think he agrees with them or assents to their statements when he doesn't.

The first credential we should demand of a critic is *his* ideograph[17] of the good; of what he considers valid writing, and indeed of all his general terms. Then we know where he is. He cannot simply stay in London writing of French pictures that his readers have not seen. He must begin by stating that such and such *particular* works seem to him 'good', 'best', 'indifferent', 'valid', 'non-valid'. I suggest a definite curriculum in place of the present *émiettements*,[18] of breaking the subject up into crumbs quickly dryable. A curriculum for instructors, for obstreperous students who wish to annoy dull instructors, for men who haven't

---

[17] Ideogram (see Note 14, above, and Eisenstein's essay in this book). Pound uses the word "ideograph" here in an interesting metaphoric way, on which the student might exercise his mind.

[18] Crumbs, fragments.

had time for systematized college courses. Call it the minimum basis for a sound and liberal education in letters (with French and English 'aids' in parenthesis).

CONFUCIUS — In full (there being no complete and intelligent English version, one would have either to learn Chinese or make use of the French version by Pauthier).

HOMER — in full (Latin cribs, Hugues Salel in French, no satisfactory English, though Chapman can be used as reference).

OVID — And the Latin 'personal' poets, Catullus and Propertius. (Golding's *Metamorphoses*, Marlowe's *Amores*. There is no useful English version of Catullus.)

A PROVENÇAL SONG BOOK — With cross reference to Minnesingers, and to Bion, perhaps thirty poems in all.

DANTE — 'And his circle'; that is to say Dante, and thirty poems by his contemporaries, mostly by Guido Cavalcanti.

VILLON —

PARENTHETICALLY — Some other medieval matter might be added, and some general outline of history of thought through the Renaissance.

VOLTAIRE — That is to say, some incursion into his critical writings, not into his attempts at fiction and drama, and some dip into his contemporaries (prose).

STENDHAL — (At least a book and half).

FLAUBERT (omitting *Salambô* and the *Tentation*) — And the Goncourts.

GAUTIER, CORBIÈRE, RIMBAUD.[19]

This would not overburden the three- or four-year student. After this inoculation he could be 'with safety exposed' to modernity or anything else in literature. I mean he wouldn't lose his head or ascribe ridiculous values to works of secondary intensity. He would have axes of reference and, would I think, find them dependable.

For the purposes of general education we could omit all study of monistic totemism and voodoo for at least fifty years and study of Shakespeare for thirty on the ground that acquaintance with these subjects is already very widely diffused, and that one absorbs quite enough knowledge of them from boring circumjacent conversation.

[19] For Stendhal and Flaubert, see the table of contents of this book. Théophile Gautier was a nineteenth-century French poet, novelist, and critic; Tristan Corbière was a French poet of the same period; for Rimbaud, see page 1098.

This list does not, obviously, contain the names of every author who has ever written a good poem or a good octave or sestet.[20] It is the result of twenty-seven years' thought on the subject and a resumé of conclusions. That may be a reason for giving it some consideration. It is not a reason for accepting it as a finality. Swallowed whole it is useless. For practical class work the instructor should try, and incite his students to try, to pry out some element that I have included and to substitute for it something more valid. The intelligent lay reader will instinctively try to do this for himself.

I merely insist that *without* this minimum the critic has almost no chance of sound judgment. Judgment will gain one more chance of soundness if he can be persuaded to consider Fenollosa's essay or some other, and to me unknown but equally effective, elucidation of the Chinese written character.

Before I die I hope to see at least a few of the best Chinese works printed bilingually, in the form that Mori and Ariga prepared certain texts for Fenollosa, a 'crib', the picture of each letter accompanied by a full explanation.

For practical contact with all past poetry that was actually *sung* in its own day I suggest that each dozen universities combine in employing a couple of singers who understand the meaning of words. Men like Yves Tinayre and Robert Maitland are available. A half-dozen hours spent in listening to the lyrics actually performed would give the student more knowledge of that sort of *melopoeia* than a year's work in philology. The Kennedy-Frasers have dug up music that fits the *Beowulf*. It was being used for heroic song in the Hebrides. There is other available music, plenty of it, from at least the time of Faidit (A.D. 1190).

I cannot repeat too often or too forcibly my caution against so-called critics who talk 'all around the matter', and who do not define their terms, and who won't say frankly that certain authors are demnition bores. Make a man tell you *first* and specially what writers he thinks are good writers, after that you can listen to his explanation.

Naturally, certain professors who have invested all their intellectual capital, i.e., spent a lot of time on some perfectly dead period, don't like to admit they've been sold, and they haven't often the courage to cut a loss. There is no use in following them into the shadows. . . .

[20] The chief divisions of a sonnet: the octave—the first eight lines; the sestet—the last six lines.

◄§ FOR DISCUSSION AND WRITING

1. Pound starts out with a reference to literary instruction in the early part
   of the century, but it would be a mistake to assume that his criticism is
   antiquated, applying only to the dark ages before the student reading this
   was born; for the fragmentation in literary scholarship of which Pound
   speaks has been an inheritance of graduate schools right down through
   the century, one generation of professors handing it on to the next, with
   yourself as the most recent pedagogic inheritor. What, precisely, are the
   chief criticisms Pound makes in the first section of the piece? (The best
   way to handle the question is to write down the chief points in a rough
   outline.) Which of the pedagogical situations he mentions have you encountered in your own schooling? For instance, have you had teachers of
   English who taught their subject as a "drill manual"? What English courses
   have you had in which the subject matter seemed trivial and unrelated
   to your general mental development? What English courses have you had
   in which you felt you had learned genuine criteria of excellence? What
   English courses have you had in which the teacher seemed really to *like*
   literature, or seemed *not* to like it (for it's a sad fact that a great many
   don't), and what effect had the teacher's attitude on the student's? In this
   clutch of questions there is a theme topic you might wish to pursue.

2. Pound's personality and opinions, as reflected in his writings, have a
   crotchetiness that alienates many people (one can readily understand how
   the present piece might alienate a good many English professors); but
   both personality and opinions are certainly highly defined—*somebody
   is really there* behind the impersonal lines of type, an original, acute, deeply
   instructed and deeply concerned, impatient, combative, totally committed
   person. Where do you find that distinct personal "voice" in the style of the
   piece? Point out places where you find it in figures of speech—analogies
   or metaphors; in the verve or animation of tempo (are the ideas developed
   in an involved and leisurely way, or do they hit you fast?); in choice of
   words (is the vocabulary oversophisticated, obscure, recherché, polysyl-
   labic, monosyllabic, simple, ordinary, "lowbrow," "highbrow," slangy, elegant, eccentric?—use your own terms).

3. A typical instance of Pound's use of analogy occurs in the first paragraph
   of the second section ("For a Method"). Explain the analogical point of his
   reference to loose-leaf bookkeeping, to physics, to a "side-wheeler engine."

What is his point in the fourth and fifth paragraphs of this section, about "non-literary" ways of going about the study of literature? If you have had courses in "American literature" or "English literature," can you make an application of his criticism?

4. In the third section ("Why Books?") Pound asks, "Has literature a function in the state?" What would be your own unbiased answer to this question? How does Pound answer it? In the fifth and sixth paragraphs of this section, he speaks of "precision and clarity of thought," or "exactitude," as the qualities by which the usefulness of literature should be judged. Why? Although these may be criteria of "literature," are they fair criteria of your own writing? (This question really calls for a judgment of the usefulness of the course in composition you are now taking.)

5. Do you agree or disagree with the first statement in Part II of the essay, and on what grounds? What is Pound's definition of "great literature"? Can you give examples of your own of "language charged with meaning" (perhaps from this book)? In the last paragraph of the first section of Part II Pound acknowledges that different scholars and critics would place different authors in the six categories he makes here, but what is his main point (as he puts it in the next-to-last paragraph of the section) in suggesting these categories?

6. What three kinds of poetry does Pound speak of in the section called "Language"? Can you find examples for them in your own experience of poetry?—for instance, for *melopoeia* in Poe, for *phanopoeia* in Keats, for *logopoeia* in Shakespeare? In the section headed "Prose," Pound says that "all writing is built up of these three elements, plus 'architectonics.'" Select some piece of writing, poetry or prose, that you consider excellent (perhaps in this book) and show how it exhibits—or does not exhibit—the elements Pound speaks of. What does he mean by "architectonics"?

7. In the third section of the essay, what point does Pound make about the relationship of the English language, in its development, to other languages? What point does he make about the relationship of English literature to translations from other literatures? Do you agree or disagree with his notion of the use of learning foreign languages? In the last section of the piece, what is the "first credential" Pound asks of the critic?

8. Write a short paper on the relationship of Pound's ideas of literary education to the political concept of the United Nations. Or write a paper comparing Pound's program to your own experience of courses in literature.

T. S. Eliot ᴥᵹ Tradition and the Individual Talent

ᴥᵹ Born in St. Louis in 1888, educated at Harvard, the Sorbonne, and Merton College, Oxford, Mr. Eliot became a British citizen in 1927 and made his home in England until his death in 1965. The publication of his *Prufrock* in 1917, and *The Waste Land* in 1922, brought into being—more than any other single influence—what is known as "modern" poetry. Similarly, his critical essays, particularly those on the seventeenth-century dramatists and poets, created a new way of looking at literature that has since developed into what is called the "new criticism." Harvard, Princeton, and Yale are among the many universities that have conferred honorary degrees upon him, and in 1948 he was awarded the Nobel Prize for Literature, as well as one of England's highest awards, the Order of Merit. ᶘᴥ

IN English writing we seldom speak of tradition, though we occasionally apply its name in deploring its absence. We cannot refer to "the tradition" or to "a tradition"; at most, we employ the adjective in saying that the poetry of So-and-so is "traditional" or even "too traditional." Seldom, perhaps, does the word appear except in a phrase of censure. If otherwise, it is vaguely approbative, with the implication, as to the work approved, of some pleasing archaeological reconstruction. You can hardly make the word agreeable to English ears without this comfortable reference to the reassuring science of archaeology.

Certainly the word is not likely to appear in our appreciations of living or dead writers. Every nation, every race, has not only its own creative, but its own critical turn of mind; and is even more oblivious of

the shortcomings and limitations of its critical habits than of those of its
creative genius. We know, or think we know, from the enormous mass of
critical writing that has appeared in the French language the critical
method or habit of the French; we only conclude (we are such unconscious people) that the French are "more critical" than we, and sometimes even plume ourselves a little with the fact, as if the French were
the less spontaneous. Perhaps they are; but we might remind ourselves
that criticism is as inevitable as breathing, and that we should be none
the worse for articulating what passes in our minds when we read a book
and feel an emotion about it, for criticizing our own minds in their work
of criticism. One of the facts that might come to light in this process is
our tendency to insist, when we praise a poet, upon those aspects of his
work in which he least resembles any one else. In these aspects or parts
of his work we pretend to find what is individual, what is the peculiar
essence of the man. We dwell with satisfaction upon the poet's difference
from his predecessors, especially his immediate predecessors; we endeavour to find something that can be isolated in order to be enjoyed.
Whereas if we approach a poet without this prejudice we shall often
find that not only the best, but the most individual parts of his work may
be those in which the dead poets, his ancestors, assert their immortality
most vigorously. And I do not mean the impressionable period of adolescence, but the period of full maturity.

Yet if the only form of tradition, of handing down, consisted in following the ways of the immediate generation before us in a blind or timid
adherence to its successes, "tradition" should positively be discouraged.
We have seen many such simple currents soon lost in the sand; and
novelty is better than repetition. Tradition is a matter of much wider
significance. It cannot be inherited, and if you want it you must obtain it
by great labour. It involves, in the first place, the historical sense, which
we may call nearly indispensable to any one who would continue to be a
poet beyond his twenty-fifth year; and the historical sense involves a
perception, not only of the pastness of the past, but of its presence; the
historical sense compels a man to write not merely with his own generation in his bones, but with a feeling that the whole of the literature of
Europe from Homer and within it the whole of the literature of his own
country has a simultaneous existence and composes a simultaneous order.
This historical sense, which is a sense of the timeless as well as of the
temporal and of the timeless and of the temporal together, is what makes

a writer traditional. And it is at the same time what makes a writer most acutely conscious of his place in time, of his own contemporaneity.

No poet, no artist of any art, has his complete meaning alone. His significance, his appreciation is the appreciation of his relation to the dead poets and artists. You cannot value him alone; you must set him, for contrast and comparison, among the dead. I mean this as a principle of aesthetic, not merely historical, criticism. The necessity that he shall conform, that he shall cohere, is not onesided; what happens when a new work of art is created is something that happens simultaneously to all the works of art which preceded it. The existing monuments form an ideal order among themselves, which is modified by the introduction of the new (the really new) work of art among them. The existing order is complete before the new work arrives; for order to persist after the supervention of novelty, the *whole* existing order must be, if ever so slightly, altered; and so the relations, proportions, values of each work of art toward the whole are readjusted; and this is conformity between the old and the new. Whoever has approved this idea of order, of the form of European, of English literature will not find it preposterous that the past should be altered by the present as much as the present is directed by the past. And the poet who is aware of this will be aware of great difficulties and responsibilities.

In a peculiar sense he will be aware also that he must inevitably be judged by the standards of the past. I say judged, not amputated, by them; not judged to be as good as, or worse or better than, the dead; and certainly not judged by the canons of dead critics. It is a judgment, a comparison, in which two things are measured by each other. To conform merely would be for the new work not really to conform at all; it would not be new, and would therefore not be a work of art. And we do not quite say that the new is more valuable because it fits in; but its fitting in is a test of its value — a test, it is true, which can only be slowly and cautiously applied, for we are none of us infallible judges of conformity. We say: it appears to conform, and is perhaps individual, or it appears individual, and many conform; but we are hardly likely to find that it is one and not the other.

To proceed to a more intelligible exposition of the relation of the poet to the past: he can neither take the past as a lump, an indiscriminate bolus, nor can he form himself wholly on one or two private admirations, nor can he form himself wholly upon one preferred period. The first course is inadmissible, the second is an important experience of youth, and the third is a pleasant and highly desirable supplement. The poet must be very conscious of the main current, which does not at all flow invariably through the most distinguished reputations. He must be quite aware of the obvious fact that art never improves, but that the material of art is never quite the same. He must be aware that the mind of Europe — the mind of his own country — a mind which he learns in time to be much more important than his own private mind — is a mind which changes, and that this change is a development which abandons nothing *en route*, which does not superannuate either Shakespeare, or Homer, or the rock drawing of the Magdalenian draughtsmen. That this development, refinement perhaps, complication certainly, is not, from the point of view of the artist, any improvement. Perhaps not even an improvement from the point of view of the psychologist or not to the extent which we imagine; perhaps only in the end based upon a complication in economics and machinery. But the difference between the present and the past is that the conscious present is an awareness of the past in a way and to an extent which the past's awareness of itself cannot show.

Some one said: "The dead writers are remote from us because we *know* so much more than they did." Precisely, and they are that which we know.

I am alive to a usual objection to what is clearly part of my programme for the *métier* of poetry.[1] The objection is that the doctrine requires a ridiculous amount of erudition (pedantry), a claim which can be rejected by appeal to the lives of poets in any pantheon. It will even be affirmed that much learning deadens or perverts poetic sensibility. While, however, we persist in believing that a poet ought to know as much as will not encroach upon his necessary receptivity and necessary laziness, it is not desirable to confine knowledge to whatever can be put into a useful shape for examinations, drawing-rooms, or the still more pretentious modes of publicity. Some can absorb knowledge, the more tardy must sweat for it. Shakespeare acquired more essential history from Plutarch than most men could from the whole British Museum. What is to be insisted upon is that the poet must develop or procure the consciousness of the past and that he should continue to develop this consciousness throughout his career.

What happens is a continual surrender of himself as he is at the

[1] Poetry considered as a trade or craft, as well as a profession or calling.

moment to something which is more valuable. The progress of an artist is a continual self-sacrifice, a continual extinction of personality.

There remains to define this process of depersonalization and its relation to the sense of tradition. It is in this depersonalization that art may be said to approach the condition of science. I, therefore, invite you to consider, as a suggestive analogy, the action which takes place when a bit of finely filiated platinum is introduced into a chamber containing oxygen and sulphur dioxide.

II

Honest criticism and sensitive appreciation are directed not upon the poet but upon the poetry. If we attend to the confused cries of the newspaper critics and the *susurrus*[2] of popular repetition that follows, we shall hear the names of poets in great numbers; if we seek not Blue-book knowledge but the enjoyment of poetry, and ask for a poem, we shall seldom find it. I have tried to point out the importance of the relation of the poem to other poems by other authors, and suggested the conception of poetry as a living whole of all the poetry that has ever been written. The other aspect of this Impersonal theory of poetry is the relation of the poem to its author. And I hinted, by an analogy, that the mind of the mature poet differs from that of the immature one not precisely in any valuation of "personality," not being necessarily more interesting, or having "more to say," but rather by being a more finely perfected medium in which special, or very varied, feelings are at liberty to enter into new combinations.

The analogy was that of the catalyst. When the two gases previously mentioned are mixed in the presence of a filament of platinum, they form sulphurous acid. This combination takes place only if the platinum is present; nevertheless the newly formed acid contains no trace of platinum, and the platinum itself is apparently unaffected; has remained inert, neutral, and unchanged. The mind of the poet is the shred of platinum. It may partly or exclusively operate upon the experience of the man himself; but, the more perfect the artist, the more completely separate in him will be the man who suffers and the mind which creates; the more perfectly will the mind digest and transmute the passions which are its material.

The experience, you will notice, the elements which enter the presence of the transforming catalyst, are of two kinds: emotions and feel-

2 A whispering or muttering sound.

ings. The effect of a work of art upon the person who enjoys it is an experience different in kind from any experience not of art. It may be formed out of one emotion, or may be a combination of several; and various feelings, inhering for the writer in particular words or phrases or images, may be added to compose the final result. Or great poetry may be made without the direct use of any emotion whatever: composed out of feelings solely. Canto XV of the *Inferno* (Brunetto Latini)[3] is a work-

[3] Brunetto Latini was an illustrious citizen of Florence, both in its political life and as an author. Dante regarded him with the reverence of a pupil for a teacher from whom he had learned much. In the *Commedia* he finds him in the circle of Hell where the sodomites run forever on burning sands. Dante's discovery of his old teacher under these circumstances is deeply moving:

> ... we met a troop of spirits, who were coming alongside the bank; and
> each looked at us, as in the evening men are wont
> to look at one another under a new moon; and towards us sharpened
> their vision, as an aged tailor does at the eye of his needle.
> Thus eyed by that family, I was recognized by one who took me by the
> skirt, and said: "What a wonder!"
> And I, when he stretched out his arm to me, fixed my eyes on his baked
> aspect, so that the scorching of his visage hindered not
> my mind from knowing him; and bending my face to his, I answered:
> "Are you here, Ser Brunetto?"

After that shocked, incredulous question, Dante wants to stop and talk, but the old man says that is impossible because of the flames striking up from the sands. They walk along together for a few minutes, while Brunetto speaks of the political corruption in Florence. Dante tells him:

> "Were my desire all fulfilled, ... you had not yet been banished from
> human nature:
> for in my memory is fixed, and now goes to my heart, the dear and kind,
> paternal image of you, when in the world, hour by hour
> you taught me how man makes himself eternal; and whilst I live, be-
> seems my tongue should show what gratitude I have for it."

Brunetto has to start running again then on the fiery sands, for that is his eternal doom, and Dante compares him to one of the racers in the annual race that was run at Verona on the first Sunday of Lent, for which the prize was a piece of green cloth: he

> ... seemed like one of those who run for the green cloth at Verona
> through the open field; and of them seemed he who gains, not he who
> loses.

This is the last quatrain of which Eliot speaks. The image of the race echoes almost verbatim the words of Paul to the early Christian converts, urging them to be like runners who strive to win the race—an echo that has exquisite irony in Brunetto's situation. The irony is further compounded by the impossibility of "winning" in hell, no matter how hard one runs. (Quotations are taken from Dante's *The Divine Comedy* in Italian and English. English translation by J. A. Carlyle, Thomas Okey, and P. H. Wicksteed. Temple Classics Edition published by E. P. Dutton & Co., Inc. and reprinted with their permission.)

ing up of the emotion evident in the situation; but the effect, though single as that of any work of art, is obtained by considerable complexity of detail. The last quatrain gives an image, a feeling attaching to an image, which "came," which did not develop simply out of what precedes, but which was probably in suspension in the poet's mind until the proper combination arrived for it to add itself to. The poet's mind is in fact a receptacle for seizing and storing up numberless feelings, phrases, images, which remain there until all the particles which can unite to form a new compound are present together.

If you compare several representative passages of the greatest poetry you see how great is the variety of types of combination, and also how completely any semi-ethical criterion of "sublimity" misses the mark. For it is not the "greatness," the intensity, of the emotions, the components, but the intensity of the artistic process, the pressure, so to speak, under which the fusion takes place, that counts. The episode of Paolo and Francesca employs a definite emotion, but the intensity of the poetry is something quite different from whatever intensity in the supposed experience it may give the impression of. It is no more intense, furthermore, than Canto XXVI, the voyage of Ulysses, which has not the direct dependence upon an emotion.[4] Great variety is possible in the process of transmutation of emotion: the murder of Agamemnon, or the agony of Othello, gives an artistic effect apparently closer to a possible original than the scenes from Dante. In the *Agamemnon*,[5] the artistic emotion approximates to the emotion of an actual spectator; in *Othello* to the emotion of the protagonist himself. But the difference between art and the event is always absolute; the combination which is the murder of Agamemnon is probably as complex as that which is the voyage of Ulysses. In either case there has been a fusion of elements. The ode of Keats contains a number of feelings which have nothing particular to do with the nightingale, but which the nightingale, partly, perhaps, because of its attractive name, and partly because of its reputation, served to bring together.

The point of view which I am struggling to attack is perhaps related

---

[4] To understand Eliot's meaning here, the student should look up these episodes, which are too complex to represent in a footnote—the episode of Paolo and Francesca in the fifth canto of the *Inferno*, and that of Ulysses in the twenty-sixth.

[5] The tragedy by Aeschylus.

to the metaphysical theory of the substantial unity of the soul:[6] for my
meaning is, that the poet has, not a "personality" to express, but a
particular medium, which is only a medium and not a personality, in
which impressions and experiences combine in peculiar and unexpected
ways. Impressions and experiences which are important for the man
may take no place in the poetry and those which become important in
the poetry may play quite a negligible part in the man, the personality.

I will quote a passage which is unfamiliar enough to be regarded
with fresh attention in the light — or darkness — of these observations:

> And now methinks I could e'en chide myself
> For doating on her beauty, though her death
> Shall be revenged after no common action.
> Does the silkworm expend her yellow labours
> For thee? For thee does she undo herself?
> Are lordships sold to maintain ladyships
> For the poor benefit of a bewildering minute?
> Why does yon fellow falsify highways,
> And put his life between the judge's lips,
> To refine such a thing—keeps horse and men
> To beat their valours for her? . . .[7]

In this passage (as is evident if it is taken in its context) there is a combination of positive and negative emotions: an intensely strong attraction
toward beauty and an equally intense fascination by the ugliness which
is contrasted with it and which destroys it. This balance of contrasted
emotion is in the dramatic situation to which the speech is pertinent, but
that situation alone is inadequate to it. This is, so to speak, the structural
emotion, provided by the drama. But the whole effect, the dominant
tone, is due to the fact that a number of floating feelings, having an
affinity to this emotion by no means superficially evident, have combined with it to give us a new art emotion.

It is not in his personal emotions, the emotions provoked by particular events in his life, that the poet is in any way remarkable or interesting.
His particular emotions may be simple, or crude, or flat. The emotion in

[6] Probably a reference to the Aristotelian conception of man as all one, body and
soul; whereas Eliot is speaking here of man suffering (or "feeling") and man creating as separate aspects.

[7] From Cyril Tourneur's *The Revenger's Tragedy*.

his poetry will be a very complex thing, but not with the complexity of the emotions of people who have very complex or unusual emotions in life. One error, in fact, of eccentricity in poetry is to seek for new human emotions to express; and in this search for novelty in the wrong place it discovers the perverse. The business of the poet is not to find new emotions, but to use the ordinary ones and, in working them up into poetry, to express feelings which are not in actual emotions at all. And emotions which he has never experienced will serve his turn as well as those familiar to him. Consequently, we must believe that "emotion recollected in tranquillity"[8] is an inexact formula. For it is neither emotion, nor recollection, nor, without distortion of meaning, tranquillity. It is a concentration, and a new thing resulting from the concentration, of a very great number of experiences which to the practical and active person would not seem to be experiences at all; it is a concentration which does not happen consciously or of deliberation. These experiences are not "recollected," and they finally unite in an atmosphere which is "tranquil" only in that it is a passive attending upon the event. Of course this is not quite the whole story. There is a great deal, in the writing of poetry, which must be conscious and deliberate. In fact, the bad poet is usually unconscious where he ought to be conscious, and conscious where he ought to be unconscious. Both errors tend to make him "personal." Poetry is not a turning loose of emotion, but an escape from emotion; it is not the expression of personality, but an escape from personality. But, of course, only those who have personality and emotions know what it means to want to escape from these things.

III

This essay proposes to halt at the frontier of metaphysics or mysticism, and confine itself to such practical conclusions as can be applied by the responsible person interested in poetry. To divert interest from the poet to the poetry is a laudable aim: for it would conduce to a juster estimation of actual poetry, good and bad. There are many people who appreciate the expression of sincere emotion in verse, and there is a smaller number of people who can appreciate technical excellence. But very few know when there is an expression of *significant* emotion, emotion which has its life in the poem and not in the history of the poet. The emotion of art is impersonal. And the poet cannot reach this impersonality without surrendering himself wholly to the work to be done. And he is

[8] Wordsworth's definition of poetry.

not likely to know what is to be done unless he lives in what is not merely the present, but the present moment of the past, unless he is conscious, not of what is dead, but of what is already living.

✑ FOR DISCUSSION AND WRITING

1. This essay by Eliot is most directly concerned with poetry and the education of the poet, but indirectly it is concerned also with the development of the civilized mind and thus with general education. Since "tradition" is a key word in the essay, the first thing to do is to examine what you yourself mean by "tradition," so that you can sort out the meanings you bring to the word and the meanings it has in Eliot's essay. In your own understanding of the word, what is its denotative meaning and what connotative meanings does it have (including attitudes such as approval or disapproval)? To what extent does your understanding of the word coincide or not coincide with Eliot's?

2. Take up in the same way the word "criticism" in the second paragraph. What denotation does it have for you and what connotations? Does Eliot extend or make more exact your understanding of "criticism"? Explain his statement that "criticism is as inevitable as breathing." In what sense could you say that you yourself are constantly engaged in criticism while you are studying, and that your teacher is constantly engaged in criticism while he is teaching? What implicit relationship between "tradition" and "criticism" do you find in the first two paragraphs of the essay?

3. In the third paragraph he says that tradition "involves, in the first place, the historical sense." What does "the historical sense" mean? Do you have it? If so, where and how did you get it? Do high schools teach the historical sense? Have you found it in your college courses? Do you feel that the historical sense is valuable or not valuable? If valuable, what is its value? What does Eliot mean by saying that "the historical sense involves a perception, not only of the pastness of the past, but of its presence"?

4. How does what Eliot says in the fifth and preceding paragraphs apply to "originality"? Do you find justification, or not, for his statement in the sixth paragraph that "art never improves"? To what extent does the very short seventh paragraph imply a theory of education? Do you approve of the educational theory implied? if so, why? if not, why not?

5. What is meant in the ninth paragraph by "a continual surrender . . . to something which is more valuable"? If you have read Flaubert's letters in the preceding section of this book, what comparison would you make between Flaubert's attitude toward his art and Eliot's idea of the "depersonalization" of the artist?

6. There follows, in the second section of the essay, Eliot's famous comparison of the poet's mind with a chemical catalyst. Explain the comparison fully. What part, according to Eliot, do the artist's emotions and feelings have in the work of art? With the help of footnotes 3 and 4, can you explain Eliot's theory of poetry in reference to the cited passages from Dante? In the fourth paragraph of the second section, Eliot says that "the difference between art and the event is always absolute"; what does he mean? At the end of the same paragraph he refers to Keats's *Ode to a Nightingale;* you probably know the poem very well, but look it up again and try to explain Eliot's comment on it.

7. In his reference to the passage quoted from Tourneur's *The Revenger's Tragedy,* what does he mean by "a combination of positive and negative emotions"? How does the rest of his comment on this passage carry out the analogy of the catalyst? (If you are a student of literature, or even if you are not a student of literature but a person interested in getting as much stimulation out of this course as possible, you might read *The Revenger's Tragedy*—as well as the *Agamemnon* of Aeschylus, which Eliot mentions a little earlier.)

8. Explain as fully as you can this statement in the last paragraph of the second section: "Poetry is not a turning loose of emotion, but an escape from emotion; it is not the expression of personality, but an escape from personality." Does Eliot mean the same thing here as is meant in the common cliché about art and poetry and, indeed, all literature as "escape from reality"? Explain the paradoxes in the final sentence of the essay.

9. If you have had strong reactions in reading this essay, either *pro* or *contra,* write them up. If you have read Auden's essay in the preceding section of this book, you might write a short paper comparing Auden's and Eliot's views. If you have a genuine interest in poetry, you might look up Yeats's sonnet *Leda and the Swan* or his *Two Songs from a Play* and write about one or the other, incorporating Eliot's ideas about tradition (you could do this kind of paper on one of Eliot's poems, but it would seem a fairer test to exercise the ideas on someone else's work).

Richard Buckminster Fuller ᴥ§ World Planning

ᴥ§ American architect and engineer, born in 1895. Largely self-taught, except for a brief spell at Harvard, Buckminster Fuller has devoted his life to the invention of revolutionary technological designs to solve the problems of modern living. His developments include the "dymaxion house" and the "dymaxion auto"—the word "dymaxion" standing for Fuller's principle of deriving maximum output from minimum input of material and energy. This principle is best realized in his geodesic structures, spherical domes made of extremely light members, which acquire enormous strength through the structuring of triangular parts. These are widely used by the military and in industry. The student might be interested in looking up the leading article on Buckminster Fuller in *Time*, January 10, 1964. ᶝᴥ

THE entire world's industrial resources are now preoccupied in serving only forty-four per cent of humanity with the advancing standards of living exclusively provided by the world's progressively enlarging and integrating industrial networks. Making the world's totally available resources serve one hundred per cent of an exploding population may only be accomplished by a boldly accelerated design evolution which adequately increases the present over-all performance per units of invested resources. This is a task of radical technical innovation rather than political rationalization. It is a task which can only be accomplished by the world's architects, inventors and scientist-artists. The engineer has been deliberately trained by society to be an unquestionable authority: an engineer must not invent, for his authority is thus violated.

From the book, *Ideas and Integrities*, by Buckminster Fuller. © 1963 by Richard Buckminster Fuller. Published by Prentice-Hall, Inc., Englewood Cliffs, New Jersey.

Since aircraft and space technology is already operating at high levels of performance per units of invested resources, the recent decade's realization that space can be enclosed for environment-controlling purposes with approximately one per cent of the weight of resources at present employed by the conventional building arts for a given task, indicates that the conversion of the world resources from their present service of only forty-four per cent to service of one hundred per cent of humanity is to be uniquely effected within the livingry arts in contradistinction to the weaponry arts. The latter alone up to this moment in history has been benefited directly by the highest science and technology. Any and all improvements in the home front's peace extending livingry advantage have been post-weaponry byproducts.

This brings the solution of the forward livingry design problems into direct focus as the responsibility of the architect (as the only technical profession concerned with "putting things together" in an era of the increased fractionation by intensive specialization). Since the practicing architect may operate only when funded by a client and there is no apparent client to retain the architect to solve this world problem, it may only be solved by the world architects taking the initiative, as have the medical scientists, in the development of a comprehensive anticipatory design science dedicating at least its next ten years to making the total world's resources serve one hundred per cent of humanity at higher standards of living than hitherto experienced by any men through competent industrially produceable design — rather than leaving the evolutionary advance to political reforms catalyzed by accelerating frequency of world political crises. Because the economics of the architectural profession, at present, precludes the devotion of adequate time and resources to the solution of this task by the graduate practicing architects, it is in evidence that the architectural profession may activate this comprehensive anticipatory design initiative through encouragement of its professional university schools of architecture to invest the extraordinary intellectual resources and available student time within the universities to the establishment of the design science and its application to world-planning. This could be inaugurated with a ten-year sequence of joined world architectural schools' annual programs organized for the progressive discovery and design solution of the comprehensive family of economic, technical and scientific factors governing such a world-planning program.

Several dramatically communicated solutions come immediately to mind, such as the use of the total facade of a skyscraper or a mountain cliff. The following is an example of a satisfactory solution: the design of a two-hundred-foot diameter Miniature Earth. This Minni-Earth could be fabricated of a light metal trussing. Its interior and exterior surfaces could be symmetrically dotted with ten million small variable intensity light bulbs and the lights controllably connected up with an electronic computer. The whole Minni-Earth array could be suspended by fine high strength alloy wires from masts surrounding Minni-Earth and at some distance from it. If the sphere were suspended two hundred feet above the ground, the wires would become invisible and it would seem to hover above the earth as an independent asteroid. At a two-hundred-foot distance away from the viewer, the light bulbs' sizes and distance apart would become indistinguishable, as do the size and distances between the points in a fine half tone print. Patterns introduced into the bulb matrix at various light intensities, through the computer, would create an omni-directional spherical picture analogous to that of a premium television tube, but a television tube whose picture could be seen all over its surface both from inside and outside not as a "framed" picture.

Information could be programmed into the computer, and "remembered" by the computer, regarding all the geographical features of the earth, or all those geographical features under a great variety of weather conditions. How exquisite the geographical data may be is appreciated when we realize that if we use the 35 millimeter contact prints of the photographs taken by the aerial surveyors at their lowest altitude of operation, in which individual houses, as homes of men, may be discerned by the naked eye, and paste them together edge-to-edge on a sphere large enough to accommodate them in their respective geographical positions, that sphere would be two hundred feet in diameter — the size of our hypothetical Minni-Earth. Man on earth, invisible to man even from the height of two thousand feet, would be able to see the whole earth and at true scale in respect to the works and habitat of man. He could pick out his own home. Thus Minni-Earth becomes a potent symbol of man visible in universe.

Man recognizes a very limited range of motions in the spectrum of motion. He cannot see the motions of atoms, molecules, cell growth, hair or toenail growth; he cannot see the motion of planets, stars and galaxies; he cannot see the motions of the hands of the clock. Most of the important trends and surprise events in the life of man are invisible, inexorable motion patterns creeping up surprisingly upon him. Historical patterns too slow for the human eye and mind to comprehend, such as changing geology, population growths and resource transpositions, may be comprehensively introduced into the computer's memory and acceleratingly pictured around the surface of the earth.

The total history of world population's progressive positionings, waxings and wanings, individual and popular migrations and redeployments could be presented and run off acceleratingly in minutes, disclosing powerful eastward, westward, northward and southward swirlings, thickenings and thinnings, with a center of gravity momentum of such trendings permitting the computer to surge ten or one hundred years ahead providing reasonable probability for the planner-designer's anticipatory advantage. So could all the patterns of man's removal from the earth's crust of the various minerals, their progressive forwardings and temporary lodgings in various design occupations — such as in buildings, ships, railway systems and factories and their progressive meltings-out and scrapped drifting into new design formulations in other tasks and other geographies.

Our hypothetical Minni-Earth, which the world architectural students may if they wish employ as their design facility, should be located as a major world city's focal design structure, analogous to the Eiffel Tower in Paris, as a continuing feature of World Olympic Games, to be reinstalled at each successive world site. Or Minni-Earth might be suspended from masts mounted on the ring of rocks in midstream of New York City's East River, one quarter mile distant from the great east face of the United Nations building, to serve as a constant confronter of all nations' representatives of the integrating patterns, both expected and unexpected, occurring around the face of man's constantly shrinking "one-town world."

Designs should provide for computer housing remote from the sphere, and for ferries, bridges, tunnels or other approaching means to a position two hundred feet below the Minni-Earth's surface from which point mechanical means, such as elevators, will transport large numbers of people upward and into the sphere to a platform at the Minni-Earth's center from which, at night, individuals would be able to view stars in the heavens seen through the lacy openings of the Minni-Earth, giving them the same orientation that they would obtain if they could go to the center of the real earth and could look out with X-ray vision to see those very same stars seemingly fixed above specific geographical points of the earth. (A star seen in zenith over Budapest from the center of Minni-Earth could be checked by telephone with real Budapest as in zenith over that city at that very moment.) A press of a button would show the Minni-Earth central observer the position of all the satellites which men have now sent aloft and, though their circling of the earth is as slow as the circling of the hands of the clock and is therefore invisible, the touch of another button could accelerate their motions so that their total interactions and coursings for a period of years to come could be witnessed in a minute. (A bank of cloud lying apparently motionless in America's vast Grand Canyon was photographed over a long period of time by a cinecamera and the resultant picture accelerated into a one-minute sequence. To the surprise of the original viewers of the seemingly still scene a very regular pattern of waves such as those on the surface of a coffee cup in a railway dining car was seen to occur in the cloud surface between the Canyon walls.)

If the students choose to employ Minni-Earth as their facility, they will find the United Nations rich in economic, demographic and sociologic data. They will find the latest publications on the International Geophysical Year rich in data that may be dramatically displayed on Minni-Earth — for instance, an accelerated historical sequence of all the world's earthquakes would give startling indications of further recurrences. The world's electromagnetic field patterns, the varying astrophysical patterns would each provide spectacular Minni-Earth displays.

The students should consider their Minni-Earth as a twenty-four-hour visual phenomenon, in contradistinction to the conceiving of buildings as visible only in the daylight, a viewpoint which has recently been compromisingly altered by secondary lighting at night. The Minni-Earth should disclose the world news and events on a twenty-four-hour basis, its patterns being altered periodically for the disclosure of the long-time weather history integrated with the present forecasting.

The students will be greatly advantaged by the development of models of Minni-Earth at their own schools which could range from ten millimeters to thirty meters in diameter. Photographs of data arrays on their models would be appropriate for their final project forwarding to the U.I.A. Congress exhibition.

In the development of the research for and design solution of this world pattern inventorying facility, the usual procedure in respect to architectural problems may, with the approval of the schools' professors, be altered so that the students will coordinate their activities as a team, meeting daily to consider the whole progress of the undertaking, but deploying to perform their complementary missions in economic, technical, etc., data-procurement and information-gathering, processing and design realizations.

In the same way, within any one country, the schools might profitably divide up the many tasks in a manner appropriate to the special kinds of information most available in their respective localities or universities. If the students are willing, the advantages of team coordination might be instituted between countries. The expansion of the rate at which the team coordination advantage might enter into the ten successive years of the world-planning and design phases may develop its own logical pace, and students or universities electing to research and design the entire programs themselves would undoubtedly demonstrate unique advantages accruing to concentrated effort and would also serve as experimental controls for comparison with the results accruing to widely distributed coordinate team functioning.

The first year's design program of all individuals, university teams, continental or intercontinental teams should all include prominent citation of the second and *sequitur* years looming high priority design problems most evidently essential to the accelerated adaptation of man to his evolutionary trendings through comprehensive anticipatory design science.

The professors of universities or schools will establish the detailed programs themselves which will be proposed to their students. The time dedicated to the study of the project will be fixed by the program. It depends upon the organization of each school's teamwork.

The international program does not prescribe any particular drawing to provide; the choice is left to the professors. It is the same thing for the scale of these designs. The projects may be presented either in original drawing, or in any other way, under the condition that the sizes are kept (panels or shoots of 100 c.m. x 100 c.m.) — totalling two square meters rather than separate panels. The documents (drawings, photos, etc.) will be stuck on rigid panels (Isorel, light metal, or any other light material). The respective schools or students would be permitted to divide their total two square meters of surface into microfilm increments totalling that amount, and would consequently have to plan to install an automatic sequence-operating microfilm projector at the next U.I.A. Congress exhibition of the students' work.

In the advanced technology which this world-planning program is meant to employ in direct benefit to livingry, the parts production tolerances are held to sub-visible dimensions ranging from one-thousandth to one ten-millionth of an inch. Unlike present architectural practices, wherein prints of detailed drawings are translated by masons and carpenters into components with one-fourth inch errors tolerated, the advanced technology makes conceptually schematic drawings with schedules only of dimensions between theoretical points. The dimensioning is subsequently scheduled into the production work by instruments and indexing machines, controlling dimensions far below man's direct discernment. For the bold new design evolution to win the initiative in employment of the world's prime resources on behalf of livingry from its preoccupation in weaponry, will require the architectural students not only to employ the most advanced scientific designing techniques, but also to adopt a progressive, comprehensive education in mathematics, physics, chemistry, economics, sociology and general history.

The ten-year world-planning and design programming should at all times be considered in the light of its regenerative potentials. As with the calculus, we cannot ascertain the second derivative's challenging prospect until we have differentiated our way through the first phases. It may be assumed that the first year's work when finally presented at the U.I.A. Congress will not only be of interest to world architects and students but that the results of their work will, for the first time, catalyze world attention and recognition of the significance and potentials of their enterprise. The regenerative consequences will probably be of surprising magnitude.

⇜§ FOR DISCUSSION AND WRITING

1. For nearly a half century Buckminster Fuller was considered as little more than a bohemian crackpot, while he continued to pour out brilliantly in-

ventive technological ideas in prodigious number; it is only fairly recently that he has begun to be recognized as one of the very great geniuses who prepare the world of the twenty-first century. In all that long time of neglect, and of contempt as well as neglect, it is very natural that he should have developed a style of communication resembling nobody else's, horny with polysyllables and strange coinages, a style which most English professors might—rightfully—call barbarous; for when nobody will listen to what one has to say, when one's intellectual peers refuse to take one seriously, when all the movements of one's mind are made in loneliness, one's mode of expression is bound to become eccentric, idiosyncratic, "difficult." (One of the greatest advantages of a college education lies not so much in the content of courses as in the opportunity for oral and written discussion under conditions that insure genuine two-way communication, the dialectic that civilizes the mind by criticism and that tests both one's own comprehension and the clarity and cogency of what one has to say. We can't all be Buckminster Fullers.) Point out two or three passages in this article in which the meaning seems hard to get at through the bristle of words; when you have decided what the meaning is in these passages, does it seem to you that the difficulty lies in the concept—the "meaning" —itself, or in the way it is expressed, and if the latter, what particular traits of the mode of expression seem to cause the difficulty? Point out a few of Buckminster Fuller's coinages; do the coinages seem necessary to understanding or could you put the same concepts in ordinary words? (Often, in elementary college courses in composition one is asked to read and analyze pieces of "bad writing," writing that may be objectionable for sinister semantic traits or for incoherence of reasoning or jargon or solecisms of grammar: the assumption being that if one can recognize the fault one will avoid it in one's own writing. Here we are doing something slightly different; instead of studying the shoddy writing of shoddy minds, for what we can learn to avoid, we are looking critically at the somewhat-less-than-transparent exposition of a brilliant idea by a genius, in the hope of accomplishing the same pedagogical purpose. Life is too short to spend any of it in the study of the poor products of poor minds.)

2. What is the problem announced in the first paragraph? Why does the author say that the task can be accomplished only by architects, inventors, and "scientist-artists"? What *are* "scientist-artists"? Explain, with specific examples, what is meant by "livingry arts." Why (in the third paragraph) is the problem made the special responsibility of the architect, and what is meant here by the architect's concern with "putting things together"? Do you know of any architects who are concerned with "putting things

together" in Buckminster Fuller's sense? What hinders practicing architects from solving the problem, and why must it become the problem of professional university schools of architecture?

3. Still staying with the third paragraph, which actually presents no real difficulty of comprehension, but which is only sort of bumpy in the esophagus with all those polysyllables, try condensing the gist of the paragraph in your own words, making the words as simple as possible.

4. Write a paragraph describing and explaining the functions of the Minni-Earth in such a way that an intelligent ten-year-old would understand you.

5. Explain this sentence at the end of the fifth paragraph: "Thus Minni-Earth becomes a potent symbol of man visible in universe."

6. Explain the first sentence in the sixth paragraph: "Man recognizes a very limited range of motions in the spectrum of motion." Point out in this and the following paragraphs the specific ways in which the hypothetical Minni-Earth could rectify that limitation: for instance, in regard to geological movements, population movements, etc., etc. What could the Minni-Earth contribute to knowledge of earthquakes, electromagnetic fields, astrophysics? Can you figure out, from the description, where the observer would be placed?

7. How could the idea of the Minni-Earth be adapted to elementary schools, in small models? What group procedure and "team coordination" is suggested? What is suggested as to the effect of Minni-Earth educational projects on all the rest of the educational curriculum?

8. Write a paper on your own reactions to the idea of a Minni-Earth as an educational facility, on whether or not it is feasible, on what you would do with it if you were the engineer, on what effect it might have on the future of mankind.

Index

This index is comprised of the following categories: (1) authors and titles of selections; (2) rhetorical principles and devices mentioned in the comments and questions following each selection; and (3) subject categories mentioned in introductions, comments, and questions.

Major rhetorical and subject entries are followed by a list of the selections best illustrating these entries. The lists are not intended to be exhaustive but should serve as an aid for study and comparison.

Page numbers referring to comments, questions, and introductory notes are in italic type, and those referring to selections are in roman. Suggestions for student writing assignments, which have been made for every selection, are indicated by a *w* following an italic page number.